INTRODUCTION TO
SOCIOLOGY
FOURTH EDITION

225 — 250   Total
                   To Dul

7
10
10
8
10.
10'
7
10
9
9
6   10
58   58
           60
10   170
9   179
7   196
10   9
9   205

17
6

1
205
95
30   8
      16
      316

      60
      37 6

INTRODUCTION TO
SOCIOLOGY

FOURTH EDITION

Henry L. Tischler
Framingham State College

Built-in Study Guide and Practice Tests
by Patrick J. Ashton
Indiana University – Purdue University Fort Wayne

THE HARCOURT PRESS

Harcourt Brace College Publishers

Fort Worth   Philadelphia   San Diego   New York   Orlando   Austin   San Antonio
Toronto   Montreal   London   Sydney   Tokyo

Editor-in-chief Ted Buchholz
Acquisitions editor Chris Klein
Developmental editor Karee Galloway
Project editor Steve Norder
Production manager Mandy Manzano
Book designer Pat Bracken
Permissions editor Van E. Strength
Photo permissions editor Annette Coolidge
Cover: Peter Till/The Image Bank.

Literary and illustration credits appear on p. 455.

Library of Congress Catalog Card Number: 92-74724

Address for Editorial Correspondence:
Harcourt Brace & Company, 301 Commerce Street, Suite 3700, Fort Worth, TX 76102.

Address for Orders:
Harcourt Brace, 6277 Sea Harbor Drive, Orlando, FL 32887. 1-800-782-4479, or 1-800-433-0001 (in Florida).

ISBN: 0-03-076681-8

Printed in the United States of America

3 4 5 6 7 8 9 0 1 2 062 9 8 7 6 5 4 3 2

*Dedicated to
Linda Tischler
and the
research assistance
from
1 Wingo Way*

▪ ABOUT THE AUTHOR ▪

Henry L. Tischler grew up in Philadelphia and received his bachelor's degree from Temple University and his master's and doctorate degrees from Northeastern University. He pursued post-doctoral studies at Harvard University.

His first venture into textbook publishing took place while he was still a graduate student in sociology when he wrote the 4th edition of *Race and Ethnic Relations* with Brewton Berry. The success of that book led to his authorship of the four editions of *Introduction to Sociology*.

Tischler has been a professor at Framingham State College in Framingham, Massachusetts, since 1969. He continues to teach introductory sociology every semester and has been instrumental in encouraging many students to major in the field. His other areas of interest are race and ethnicity, urban sociology, and organizational behavior.

Professor Tischler has also been active in making sociology accessible to the general population and is currently the host of a radio show on sociological issues on National Public Radio. He has also written a weekly newspaper column, called "Society Today," which dealt with a wide variety of sociological topics.

Tischler lives in Sudbury, Massachusetts, with his wife Linda, a journalist; a teenage daughter, Melissa; and a preteen son, Ben.

▪ PREFACE ▪

As a new freshman at Temple University in the 1960s, my first experience with a college textbook was in my sociology course. I dutifully read the assigned chapter during my first week of class hoping to become familiar with the subject matter of this required course. The only problem was that I had no idea what the author was saying. The writing level was advanced, the style dense, and the book downright threatening, without photos or illustrations. After several hours of reading I felt frustrated and stupid, and I knew no more about sociology than when I started. If this was what college was going to be like, I was not going to make it, I thought. I remember thinking to myself that I was probably not what guidance counselors in that day referred to as "college material." I could already picture myself dropping out after the first semester and looking for a job selling furniture or driving a cab. My family would be disappointed, but my father was a factory worker and there was no family history of college attendance to live up to. I continued to struggle with the book and earned a D on the mid-term exam. After much effort, I managed to finish the course with a C, and a burning disinterest in the field of sociology. I did not take another sociology course for two years, and when I did it was "Marriage and the Family," the easiest course on campus.

I often wonder how I came from this inauspicious beginning to be a sociology professor, let alone the author of an introductory sociology textbook. Then again, maybe it is not all that unusual, because that experience continues to have an effect on me each day. Those first fifteen weeks helped develop my view that little is to be gained by presenting information in an incomprehensible or unnecessarily complicated way or by making yourself unapproachable. Pompous professors and intimidating books are doing a disservice to education. Learning should be an exciting, challenging, eye-opening experience, not a threatening one. I have taught my courses with this in mind, and I hope it comes through in this book.

One of the real benefits from writing four editions of this textbook is that I have been forced periodically to reexamine every concept and theory presented in an introductory course. In doing so I have approached the subject matter through a new set of eyes, and I have tried to find better ways of presenting the material. Teachers rarely venture into each others' classrooms and hardly ever receive honest, detailed, constructive criticism of how well they are transmitting the subject matter. As authors of textbooks, we do receive this type of information and can radically restructure or fine tune our presentation.

Student-Oriented Edition

Prior to revising this edition of *Introduction to Sociology* we surveyed dozens of instructors to find out what material in a textbook would assist them in the teaching of sociology as well as satisfy student needs. Among other things, we learned that both students and professors are concerned about the cost of books. Introductory textbooks have become very attractive and very expensive during the last decade, as publishers have added hundreds of color photos. This trend has caused the price of textbooks to outpace inflation, making them a substantial purchase for the typical student. In response to this concern we are breaking ranks with textbooks with which we have typically competed and are going back to basics. A textbook after all is meant to be comprehensive and up-to-date and to serve as an important supplement to a course. It makes no sense to make a book so colorful, and therefore expensive, that students often forgo purchasing it. In order to give students the best value possible we are using only black and white photos and a paper cover.

We are not however content to merely provide better value. We also want to provide a better book. Our survey also showed us that professors and students wanted a study guide and practice exams to assist with teaching and learning. We have therefore included a study guide in this book that is as long or longer than those typically sold separately. Students will be able to purchase the combined textbook/study guide for considerably less than the price of a typical textbook. In fact, the price for our textbook/study guide combination will probably be lower than the *used* copy price of most introductory sociology textbooks.

We are very proud of the interactive, workbook-like study guide. It contains detailed chapter summaries and, it outlines all the major learning objectives of the text. All key terms and key sociologists are discussed, and matching exercises are included. Critical thinking questions and suggested readings provide depth to the material and are useful in preparing for essay exams and research papers. Practice tests, which appear at the end of the study guide, provide ample opportunity for review. The book also includes an important introductory section, "How to Get the Most Out of Sociology," which discusses general study techniques and provides specific recommendations on how to use the textbook, study guide, practice tests, and lecture material in preparing for exams and getting the most out of an introductory sociology course.

Presentation

My goal is to demonstrate the vitality, interest, and utility associated with the study of sociology. Examining society and its institutions and processes is an exciting and absorbing undertaking. I have not set out to make sociologists of the readers (although if that is an outcome I will be delighted), but rather to show how sociology applies to many areas of life and how it is used in day-to-day activities. In meeting this objective I focused on two basic ideas: that sociology is a rigorous scientific discipline and that a basic knowledge of sociology is essential for understanding social interactions in many different settings, work or social. In order to understand society, we need to understand how it shapes people and how people in turn shape society. We need to develop a new way of understanding the world we have been experiencing for so many years.

Each chapter progresses from a specific to a general analysis of society, with each part introducing increasingly more comprehensive factors necessary for a broad-based understanding of social organization. Great care has been taken to structure the book in such a way as to permit flexibility in the presentation of the material. All chapters are self-contained and, therefore, may be taught in any order.

New in this Edition

It has taken nearly two years to produce this revision. Every aspect of this book has been updated, and a great deal has been changed. The information is as current and up-to-date as possible.

A new chapter, "Health and Health Care," has been added in response to the growing interest among students and faculty in the field of medical sociology and related issues. Not only do I focus on health care issues in the United States, but also world health trends, with particular emphasis on issues affecting infants and children. The chapter also includes a section on AIDS, which has had an enormous impact on health care throughout the world. Additionally, a section on issues related to aging has been added to the Gender chapter to reflect increased interest in the field of gerontology.

Comparative and Cross-cultural Perspective

Sociology is a highly organized discipline shaped by several theoretical perspectives or schools of thought. It is not merely the study of social problems or the random voicing of opinions. No single perspective is given excessive emphasis; a balanced presentation of both functionalist theory and conflict theory is supplemented whenever possible by the symbolic interactionist viewpoint.

The book has received a great deal of praise for embodying a cross-cultural approach and for using examples from a wide variety of cultures. Sociology is concerned with the interactions of people wherever and whenever they occur. It would be shortsighted, therefore, to concentrate on only our own society. Often, in fact, the best way to appreciate our own situation is through comparison with other societies. We use a cross-cultural focus as a basis for comparison and contrast with U.S. society.

Features

Opening Vignettes
Each chapter begins with a lively vignette that introduces the student to the subject matter of the chapter. Many of these are from real life events to which students can relate—a discussion of missing and abducted children (Chapter 1) or of education in inner-city schools (Chapter 13). Other vignettes refer to current situations that have received media attention—*The Kinsey Institute New Report on Sex* (Chapter 2) and the Los Angeles Riots (Chapter 18). Still others deal with unusual circumstances that will help students appreciate the wide range of events that sociology applies to—whites who claim to be black (Chapter 9), the Chinese one-child population control policy (Chapter 15), giving birth in rural India (Chapter 17), and William McKibben's attempt to understand society by watching one day's worth of television on ninety-three stations (Chapter 19).

Controversies in Sociology
Appearing at the end of each chapter this boxed feature is designed to show students two opposing sides to an issue. Sociological controversies help students realize that most social events require close analysis and that hastily drawn conclusions are often wrong. Students will see that a good sociologist must be knowledgeable about disparate positions and willing to question the validity of any statements made by interested parties.

Included in this section are such controversies as "Is Daycare Harmful to Children?" (Chapter

4), "Does Capital Punishment Deter Murderers?" (Chapter 6), "Why is the Black Underclass Growing?" (Chapter 7), "Should English Be the Official Language of the United States?" (Chapter 9), "Euthanasia—What is the Good Death?" (Chapter 10), "Should Unmarried Partners Receive Married Benefits?" (Chapter 11), "Are Religious Cults Dangerous? (Chapter 12), "Do the Media Have Too Powerful a Role in Elections?" (Chapter 14), "What Causes the High U.S. Infant Mortality Rate? (Chapter 15), and "Is Disease Caused by Our State of Mind?" (Chapter 17).

Taking the Sociological Perspective

This feature expands on a concept, theory, or issue discussed in the chapter, allowing both teacher and student to examine a specific situation in depth and see its application to sociology. A few examples of the issues explored include "Are Geniuses Born or Created?" (Chapter 4), "Language and Social Interaction in the Courtroom" (Chapter 5), "The Elderly—Rich or Poor?" (Chapter 8), and "How Did the AIDS Epidemic Begin?" (Chapter 17).

Sociology at Work

Special interviews with researchers working with the topic of discussion allow students to experience the vibrant nature of the field of sociology. This section includes interviews with Jack Levin on Serial Murderers and Mass Murderers (Chapter 6), Orlando Patterson on Slavery and Freedom, (Chapter 9), Arlie Hochschild on Working Parents (Chapter 11), Deborah Tannen on Communication between Men and Women (Chapter 10), Jonathan Kozol on Unequal Schooling (Chapter 13), Paul Ehrlich on the Population Explosion (Chapter 15), William H. Whyte on the Role of the City Center (Chapter 16), and George Ritzer on the McDonaldization of Society (Chapter 19).

The Ancillary Package

The primary objective of a textbook is to provide clear information in a format that promotes learning. In order to assist the instructor in using *Introduction to Sociology* an extensive ancillary package has been developed.

Instructor's Manual and Test Bank

Patrick J. Ashton of Indiana University–Purdue University prepared the Instructor's Manual, Test Bank, and the "built-in" study guide. This provides for unusual consistency and integration among all elements of the teaching and learning package. Both the new and experienced instructor will find plenty

of useful ideas in the Instructor's Manual, which is correlated to both the text and the student study guide. Each chapter of the manual includes teaching objectives, key terms, lecture outlines, activities, discussion questions, and a section on computer exercises. The Test Bank contains multiple-choice, true/false, matching, and essay questions. All test items are page referenced to the textbook.

Computerized Test Bank

A computerized version of the Test Bank available for IBM, Macintosh, and Apple computers allows the instructor to modify and add questions and to create, scramble, and print tests and answer keys. A telephone hotline is available for anyone who experiences difficulty with the program or its interface with a particular printer.

Interactive Computer Program

Users of this book will also be able to obtain *The Social Scene,* an interactive computer program specifically designed for sociology students. This program familiarizes students with the basic procedures of survey data analysis by allowing them to manipulate data sets drawn from the General Social Survey (GSS). *The Social Scene* moves the learning of sociology into the twenty-first century.

Overhead Transparencies

A package of overhead transparencies has been developed to illustrate a variety of subjects in the sociology curriculum. These transparencies are based on the latest available data.

Sociology Videos

Harcourt Brace Jovanovich offers five "Currents" videos to accompany this edition of *Introduction to Sociology.* Currents is the highly acclaimed series produced by the PBS affiliate in New York City (WNET). The aim of this series is to provide a forum in which important changes in our society can be evaluated.

Acknowledgments

Anyone who has written an introductory textbook realizes that at various points a project of such magnitude becomes a team effort, with many people devoting enormous amounts of time to ensure that the final product is as good as it can possibly be.

This revision was based on an extensive survey of faculty and students at a wide variety of institutions. Although there are too many to list, I would like to thank those who participated for their comments and suggestions.

Many people at Harcourt Brace Jovanovich provided valuable assistance to this project. Chris Klein, the acquisitions editor, ushered this project through many difficult stages. Karee Galloway, the developmental editor, managed to keep the book on schedule despite a variety of obstacles. It was a privilege to have the support and assistance of these two very capable people. I would also like to thank Ted Buchholz, editor-in-chief, for his involvement and concern with this book.

I am also grateful to all those students and professors who have shared their thoughts about this book with me over the years.

Henry L. Tischler

■ A WORD TO THE STUDENT ■

HOW TO GET THE MOST OUT OF SOCIOLOGY

Effective Study: An Introduction

Why should you read this preface? Well, if you think you have an "A" in your back pocket, perhaps you shouldn't. Or maybe you are just not interested in sociology or in becoming a really successful student. Maybe you're just here because an advisor told you that you need a social science course. Maybe you feel, "Hey, a "C" is good. I'll never need this stuff." If so, you can stop reading now.

BUT if you want to ace sociology and learn some techniques to help you in other classes too, this preface is for you. It's filled with the little things no one ever tells you that improve grades, make for better understanding of classes—and may even make classes enjoyable for you. The **CHOICE** is yours: **To read, or not to read.** Be forwarned. The contents of this preface may challenge the habits of a lifetime—habits that have gotten you this far, but ones that may endanger your future success.

This preface contains ways to help you locate major ideas in your text. It contains many techniques which will be of help in reading your other course textbooks. If you learn these techniques early in your college career, you will have a head start on most other students. You will be able to locate important information, understand lectures better, and probably do better on tests. By understanding the material better, you will not only gain a better understanding of sociology, but might well find that you are able to enjoy your class more.

The Problem: Passive Reading

Do you believe reading is one-way communication? Do you expect the author's intent will become apparent if you read hard enough or long enough? (Many students feel this way.) Do you believe critical material is buried somewhere in the text, and that you need only find and highlight it to get all that's important? Do you believe that if you can memorize these highlighted details, you will do well on tests? If so, you are probably a passive reader.

The problem with passive reading is that it makes even potentially interesting writing boring. Passive reading reduces a chapter to individual, frequently unrelated facts instead of providing understanding of importrant concepts. It seldom digs beneath the surface, relying on literal meaning rather than potential implications. Since most college testing relies on the understanding of key concepts

rather than simple factual recall, passive reading fails to significantly help students to do well in courses.

The Solution: Active Reading

Active reading is recognizing that a textbook should provide two-way communication. It involves knowing what aids are available to help understand the text and then using them to find meaning. It involves pre-reading and questioning. It includes recording questions, learning vocabulary, and summarizing. Still, with all these techniques, active reading frequently takes less time and produces significantly better results than passive reading.

UNIQUE FEATURES OF THE STUDY GUIDE

For each chapter you will find a
- **Detailed chapter summary**
    contains all the main points of the chapter separated by major headings
- **Complete outline**
    includes every bold-faced heading in the text
    each heading is turned into a relevant question, with space to write in your answer.
- **Comprehensive set of learning objectives**
    objectives cover all major issues raised in the text
    comprehension/application exercises for each one, with space to write in your answer
- **Key concepts matching exercise**
    includes every term defined in the text
    also contains additional important concepts
    correct answers are provided
- **Key thinkers/researchers matching exercises (where relevant)**
    includes every theorist or researcher actually discussed in the text
    correct answers are provided
- **Critical thinking/application questions**
    promotes depth in reflecting on the material
    useful in preparing for essay exams and papers
- **Suggested readings**
    annotated to help you fine-tune your search for further information
    grouped by major text heading

This textbook—especially the Study Guide—is designed to help you become an active reader. In the Study Guide, you will find a variety of learning aids based on the latest research on study skills. If you get into the habit of using the aids presented here, you can apply similar techniques to your other textbooks and become a more successful learner.

Effective Reading: Your Textbook

As an active reader, how should you approach your textbook? Here are some techniques for reading text chapters that you should consider.

1. Think first about what you know. Read the title of your chapter; then ask yourself what experiences you have had that relate to that title. For example, if the title is "Social Interaction and Social Groups," ask yourself, "In what ways have I interacted with others in social situations? Have I ever been part of a social group? If so, what do I remember about the experience?" Answers to these questions personalize the chapter by making it relate to your experiences. They provide a background for the chapter, which experts say improves your chances of understanding the reading. They show that you do know something about the chapter so that its content won't be so alien.

2. Read your Study Guide summary as an index to important ideas *before* **reading the textbook chapter.** To make your reading easier and more effective, use the aids provided by the book for doing so. Turn to the appropriate chapter of the Study Guide at the back of your textbook. The Study Guide contains comprehensive, detailed summaries for all chapters in your book. This is a great benefit since it includes all the points you need to understand. You may find items in the summary you know already. You may be able to read more quickly through textbook sections covering these items. You may not know anything about other items in the summary. This tells you where to spend your textbook reading time. **A good rule:** Study most what you know least.

In most other textbooks, the summary will be found at the end of the chapter. Wherever it is, the summary is often your best guide to important material.

3. Pay attention to your Study Guide chapter outline. This textbook, as most other college textbooks, has an outline at the beginning of each chapter. If you do nothing else besides reading the summary and going through this outline before reading the textbook chapter, you will be far ahead of most students. (You will be clued in on what is important.) But you will gain even more help from using the outline in your Study Guide.

In addition to giving you a complete list of the main topics to be covered in the chapter, the study guide outline turns each one into a question. Most experts say that turning chapter headings into questions is a *most valuable* step in focusing reading on important information. The Study Guide has done this for you. Reading these questions gives you a solid idea before you even start reading of what kind of information you need under each heading.

4. Check the learning objectives in your Study Guide. Many textbooks list learning objectives in the text or in study guides. Your Study Guide includes learning objective questions and fill-in-the-blanks exercises to help you locate and understand key information. Read through these objectives. You may not be able to answer any learning objectives questions now, but these questions will help you focus on the kind of information you need to find and on how items relate to one another. For example, the Learning Objectives section of Study Guide Chapter 1 sets up the differences between sociology and the other social sciences and gives space to write in needed information. Not only does this tell you that you will need to know how psychology, economics, history, and so on differ from sociology, but it gives you space to write down these differences as you read.

5. Question as you read. Turn your chapter title into a question, then read up to the first heading to find your answer. The answer to your question will be the main idea for the entire chapter. In forming your question make sure it contains the chapter title. For example, if the chapter title is "Doing Sociology: Research Methods," your question might be "What research methods does sociol-

---

GUIDELINES FOR EFFECTIVE READING OF YOUR TEXTBOOK

1. Think first about what you know.
2. Read your Study Guide summary as a guide to important ideas *before* reading the textbook chapter.
3. Pay attention to your Study Guide chapter outline.
4. Check learning objectives in your Study Guide.
5. Question as you read.
6. Pay attention to graphic aids.
7. When in doubt, use clues to find main ideas.
8. Review right after reading.

ogy use?" or "Why does sociology use research methods?"

As you go through the chapter, either make up your own questions for each heading, or use those provided in the Study Guide. The Study Guide questions will point you toward the most important material in a section. However, it is also a good idea to form your own questions to get into practice for books not containing this helpful aid. A good technique might be to make your own question and then check it against the Study Guide question before reading. In any case, use a question, and highlight your answer in the text. This will be the most important information under each heading. Don't read as if every word is important; focus on finding answers.

6. **Pay attention to graphic aids.** As you read, note those important vocabulary words appearing in bold type. Find the definitions for these words (in this book, definitions will appear in italics right next to key words) and highlight them. These terms will be important to remember. Your Study Guide lists all of these terms in the sections headed "Key Concepts."

Pay attention to photos and photo captions. They make reading easier because they provide a visualization of important points in the textbook. If you can visualize what you read, you will ordinarily retain information better than people who don't use this technique. Special boxed sections usually give detailed research information about one or more studies related to a chapter heading. For in-depth knowledge, read these sections, but only after completing the section to which they refer. The main text will provide the background for a better understanding of the research, and the visualization provided by the boxed information will help illuminate the text discussion.

7. **When in doubt, use clues to find main ideas.** It is possible that, even using the questioning technique, there could be places where you are uncertain if you're getting the important information. Being sensitive to clues both in the text and in the Study Guide will help you through such places. In the text, it helps to know that main ideas in paragraphs occur more frequently at the beginning and end. Watch for repeated words or ideas—these are clues to important information. Check examples; any point that your author uses examples to document is important. Be alert for indicator words (such as *first, second, clearly, however, although,* and so on); these also point to important information. Names of researchers (except for those named only within parentheses) will almost always be important.

For those chapters in which important social scientists are discussed, you will find a "Key Thinkers/ Researchers" section in your Study Guide. This section asks you to match these people with their accomplishments.

Your Study Guide Learning Objectives section contains other clues too. For example, if material is mentioned under learning objectives, it is probably important to remember.

8. **Review right after reading.** Most forgetting takes place in the first day after reading. A review right after reading is your best way to hold text material in your memory. A strong aid in doing this review is your Study Guide. If a brief review is all you have time for, return to the Study Guide chapter outline and/or the Learning Objectives section. Reread the questions in the outline; see if you can answer them. If so, you probably know the material. If not, check the question, and reread that chapter section to get a better understanding.

An even better review technique is to write in the answers to the questions in the outline and to fill in the exercises in the learning objectives section. Writing makes for a more active review, and activity is the key to successful reading. If you can answer the outline questions and fill in the learning objectives exercises, you will have the information you need from the chapter. If there are blanks in your knowledge, you can return to the appropriate section of the textbook and write the information you find in your Study Guide. This technique is especially valuable in classes requiring essay exams or papers because it gives you a comprehensive understanding of the material as well as a sense of how it can be applied to real-world situations.

For a slightly longer, but more complete, review do the Key Concepts and Key Thinkers/Researchers matching tests. These will assure you that you have mastered the vocabulary and know the contributions of the most important researchers mentioned in the chapter. Since a majority of test questions are based on understanding the vocabulary, research findings, and major theories, you will be assuring yourself of a testing benefit during your review.

It is also a good idea to review the Critical Thinking/Application in the Study Guide. One key objective of Sociology—and indeed of most college courses—is to help you develop critical thinking skills. Though basic information may change from year to year as new scientific discoveries are made, the ability to think critically in any field is important. If you get in the habit of going beyond surface knowledge in sociology, you can transfer these skills to other areas. This can be a great benefit not only while you're in school but afterwards as well. As with the Learning Objectives section, the questions provide the kind of background that is extremely useful for essay exams.

Finally, if possible, you should turn to the Practice Tests section located after the last chapter of the Study Guide and complete the appropriate test for the chapter read. The Practice Tests offer double benefit. First, if you get a good score on this test, you know that you understand the material. If you get a low score, on the other hand, you know what material to review again. Second, the format of this test is very similar to what you will see when you take real tests. For this reason, you should develop some confidence in your ability to succeed in course tests from doing well on the practice test.

What other methods would an active student use to improve understanding and test scores in sociology? One might be to read selected materials from the annotated Suggested Readings sections of your Study Guide. This would help deepen your knowledge of important areas of sociology. Another is using the techniques discussed below.

Functioning in Class

There are two ways of participating in your sociology class: actively and passively. Passive participation involves sitting there, not contributing, waiting for the instructor to tell you what is important. Passive participation takes little effort, but it is unlikely to result in much learning. Unless you are actively looking for what is significant, the likelihood of finding the important material or of separating it effectively from what is less meaningful is not great. The passive student runs the risk of taking several pages of unneeded notes, or of missing key details altogether.

Active students **begin** each lecture **with a question.** "What is this lecture going to cover today?" They find an answer to that question, usually in the first minute, and use this as the key to important material throughout the lecture. When there is a point they don't understand, they *ask* questions. Active students know that information not understood in lectures has a way of turning up on tests. If classroom discussion is called for, they are quick to join in. And the funny thing is, they frequently wind up enjoying their sociology class as they learn.

Effective Studying

As you study your sociology text and notes, both the method you use and the time picked for study will have effects on comprehension. Establishing an effective study routine is important. Without a routine, it is easy to put off study—and put it off, and put it off . . . until it is too late. To be most effective, follow the few simple steps listed below.

1. When possible, **study at the same time and place each day.** Doing this makes use of psychological conditioning to improve study results. "Because it is 7:00 p.m. and I am sitting at my desk, I realize it is time to begin studying sociology."

2. **Study in half-hour blocks with five minute breaks.** Long periods of study without breaks frequently reduce comprehension to the 40 percent level. This is most inefficient. By using short periods (about 30 minutes) followed by short breaks, you can move that comprehension rate into the 70 percent range. *Note* that if 30 minutes end while you are still in the middle of a text section, you should go on to the end of that section before quitting.

3. For even more efficient study, **review frequently.** Take one or two minutes at the end of each study session to mentally review what you've studied so far. When you start the next study session, spend the first minute or two rehearsing in your mind what you studied in the previous session. This weaves a tight webbing in which to catch new associations.

4. **Don't mix study.** Do all of your sociology work before moving on to another course. Otherwise, your study can result in a confusion of ideas and relationships within the subjects studied.

5. Finally, **reward yourself** for a study task well done. Think of something you like to do, and do it when you finish studying for the day. This provides positive reinforcement, which makes for continued good study.

Successfully Taking Tests

Of course, tests are a payoff for you as a student. Tests are where you can demonstrate to yourself and to the teacher that you really know the material. The trouble is, few prople know how to take tests effectively. And knowing how to take tests effectively makes a serious difference in exam scores. Here are a few tips to improve your test-taking skills.

Studying for Tests

1. **Think before you study.** All material is not equal. What did the instructor emphasize in class? What was covered in a week? A day? A few minutes? Were any chapters emphasized more than others? Use these clues to decide where to spend *most of* your study time. Use the Practice Tests section to prepare for multiple choice questions. Review the

Key Thinkers/Researchers and Key Concepts sections in the Study Guide for important people and terms. Use the Learning Objectives and Critical Thinking/Application Questions sections to prepare for essay questions.

2. Begin study a week early. If you find material you don't know, you have time to find answers. If you see that you know blocks of material already, you have saved yourself time in future study sessions. You also avoid much of the forgetting which occurs with last-minute cramming.

3. Put notes and related chapters together for study. As you study, don't stop for unknown material. Study what you know. Once you know it, go back and look at what you don't know yet. There is no need to study what you already know again. Put it aside, and concentrate on the unknown.

Taking Tests

1. Don't come early; don't come late. Early people tend to develop anxieties; late people lose test time. Studies show that people who discuss test material with others just before a test may forget that material on the test. This is another reason that arriving too early puts students in jeopardy. Get there about two or three minutes early. Repeat to yourself as you get ready for the test, "I can do it! I will do it." This will set a positive mental tone for the test.

2. Be sure you understand all the directions before you start answering. Not following directions is the *biggest cause* for lost points on tests. Ask about whatever you don't understand.

3. Read through the test, carefully answering only items you know. Be sure you read every word and every answer choice as you go. Use a piece of paper or a card to cover the text below the line you are reading. This can help you focus on each line individually—and increase your test score.

Speed creates a serious problem in testing. The mind is moving so fast that it is easy to overlook important words such as except, but, best example, and so on. Frequently, questions will contain two close options, one of which is entirely correct, and the other only partially correct. Moving too fast without carefully reading items causes people to make wrong choices in these situations. Slowing reading speed makes for higher test scores.

The mind tends to work subconsciously on questions you've read but left unanswered. As you're doing questions later in the test, you may suddenly have the answer for an earlier question. In such cases, answer the question right away. These sudden insights quickly disappear and may never come again.

GUIDELINES FOR SUCCESSFULLY TAKING TESTS

Studying
1. Think before you study.
2. Begin study a week early.
3. Put notes and related chapters together for study.

Taking the Test
1. Don't come early; don't come late.
2. Be sure you understand all test directions before you start answering.
3. Read through the test carefully answering only items you know.
4. Now that you've answered what you know, look carefully at the other questions.
5. If you finish early, stay to check answers.
6. When you get your test back, use it as a learning experience.

---

4. Now that you've answered what you know, look carefully at the other questions. Eliminate alternatives you know are wrong and then *guess*. Never leave a blank on a test. Any chance is better than *no* chance.

5. If you finish early, stay to check answers. Speed causes many people to make answers that a moment's hesitation would show to be wrong. Read over your choices, especially those for questions that caused you trouble. Don't change answers because you suddenly feel one choice is better than others. However, if you see a mistake, change your answer.

6. When you get your test back, use it as a learning experience. Where did the material come from: book, lecture, or both? What kind of material was on the test: theories, problems, straight facts? The same kind of material taken from the same source(s) will be on future tests.

Look at each item you got wrong. Why is it wrong? If you know why you made mistakes, you are unlikely to make the same ones in future. Following this formula can make for more efficient use of textbooks, better note-taking, and higher test scores.

A Final Word

As you can see, the key to student success lies in becoming an active student. Managing time, questioning at the start of lectures, planning effective measures to increase test scores, and using all aids available to make reading and study easier are all elements in becoming an active student. The Study Guide and Practice Tests for this textbook have been specially designed to help you be that active student. Being passive may seem easier, but it is not. Passive students spend relatively similar amounts of time studying, but learn less. Their review time is likely to be inefficient. Their test scores are more frequently lower—and they usually have less fun in their classes.

The danger in becoming an active student is that activity is contagious; if you become an active student in sociology, it is hard not to practice the same active learning techniques in English and math as well. Once you start asking questions in your text and using your Study Guide, you may find that you start asking questions in class as well. As you acquire a greater understanding of your subject, you may find that you enjoy your class more—as well as learn more and do better on tests. That is the real danger in becoming an active learner.

Michael F. O'Hear is Assistant Dean of Arts and Sciences and Director of Transitional Studies at Indiana University–Purdue University Fort Wayne.

Patrick J. Ashton is an Associate Professor of Sociology at Indiana University–Purdue University Fort Wayne.

▪ CONTENTS IN BRIEF ▪

PART I: *The Study of Society*
Chapter 1   The Sociological Perspective
Chapter 2   Doing Sociology: Research Methods

PART II: *The Individual in Society*
Chapter 3   Culture
Chapter 4   Socialization and Development
Chapter 5   Social Interaction and Social Groups
Chapter 6   Deviant Behavior and Social Control

PART III: *Social Inequality*
Chapter 7   Social Stratification
Chapter 8   Social Class in the United States
Chapter 9   Racial and Ethnic Minorities
Chapter 10   Gender and Age Stratification

PART IV: *Institutions*
Chapter 11   Marriage and Alternative Family Lifestyles
Chapter 12   Religion
Chapter 13   Education
Chapter 14   Political and Economic Systems

PART V: *Social Change and Social Issues*
Chapter 15   Population and Demography
Chapter 16   Urban Society
Chapter 17   Health and Health Care
Chapter 18   Collective Behavior and Social Movements
Chapter 19   Social Change

STUDY GUIDE
PRACTICE TESTS

▪ CONTENTS ▪

PART I:
THE STUDY OF SOCIETY 1

CHAPTER 1 *The Sociological Perspective* 3
Sociology as a Point of View 4
  The Sociological Imagination 5
  Is Sociology Common Sense? 7
  Sociology and Science 8
  Sociology as a Social Science 8
The Development of Sociology 10
  Auguste Comte 11
  Classical Theorists 11
  The Development of Sociology in the United States 16
Theoretical Perspectives 17
  Functionalism 18
  Conflict Theory 18
  The Interactionist Perspective 18
  Contemporary Sociology 21
  Theory and Practice 23

CHAPTER 2 *Doing Sociology: Research Methods* 25
The Research Process 26
  Define the Problem 26
  Review Previous Research 28
  Develop One or More Hypotheses 28
  Determine the Research Design 29
  Define the Sample and Collect Data 32
  Analyze the Data and Draw Conclusions 34
  Prepare the Research Report 35
Objectivity in Sociological Research 36
Ethical Issues in Sociological Research 37
  Research Fraud 40

PART II:
THE INDIVIDUAL IN SOCIETY 42

CHAPTER 3 *Culture* 45
The Concept of Culture 46
  Culture and Biology 46
  Culture Shock 47
  Ethnocentrism and Cultural Relativism 47
Components of Culture 49
  Material Culture 50
  Normative Culture 51

Cognitive Culture 53
  Language and Culture 53
The Symbolic Nature of Culture 54
  Signs, Symbols, and Culture 55
Culture and Adaptation 56
  Human Evolution: Biological and Cultural 56
  Culture as an Adaptive Mechanism 57
  Mechanisms of Cultural Change 58
  Cultural Lag 59
Animals and Culture 60
Subcultures 61
  Types of Subcultures 61
Universals of Culture 62
  The Division of Labor 62
  The Incest Taboo, Marriage, and the Family 62
  Rites of Passage 63
  Ideology 64
Culture and Individual Choice 65

CHAPTER 4 *Socialization and Development* 69
Becoming a Person: Biology and Culture 70
  Nature versus Nurture: A False Debate 70
  Deprivation and Development 72
The Concept of Self 74
  Dimensions of Human Development 75
Theories of Development 76
  Charles Horton Cooley (1864–1929) 77
  George Herbert Mead (1863–1931) 77
  Sigmund Freud (1856–1939) 78
  Erik H. Erikson (1902–) 79
  Daniel Levinson (1920–) 79
Early Socialization in American Society 81
  The Family 82
  The School 84
  Peer Groups 84
  The Mass Media 85
Adult Socialization 87
  Marriage and Responsibility 88
  Parenthood 89
  Career Development: Vocation and Identity 90
  Aging and Society 90

CHAPTER 5 *Social Interaction and Social Groups* 93
Understanding Social Interaction 94
  Contexts 94
  Norms 95

Types of Social Interaction   96
    Nonverbal Behavior   96
    Exchange   98
    Cooperation   98
    Conflict   99
    Competition   99
Elements of Social Interaction   100
    Statuses   100
    Roles   100
    Role Sets   102
    Role Strain   102
    Role Conflict   102
    Role Playing   103
The Nature of Groups   104
    Primary and Secondary Groups   105
    Characteristics of Groups   106
    Reference Groups   109
Small Groups   109
Large Groups: Associations   110
    The Formal Structure   110
    The Informal Structure   111
Bureaucracy   111
    Weber's Model of Bureaucracy   112
    Bureaucracy Today: The Reality   114
    The Iron Law of Oligarchy   114
Institutions and Social Organization   116
    Social Institutions   116
    Social Organization   116

CHAPTER 6   *Deviant Behavior and Social Control*   119
Defining Normal and Deviant Behavior   120
    Making Moral Judgments   120
    The Functions of Deviance   121
    The Dysfunctions of Deviance   122
Mechanisms of Social Control   122
    Internal Means of Control   122
    External Means of Control: Sanctions   122
Theories of Crime and Deviance   124
    Biological Theories of Deviance   124
    Psychological Theories of Deviance   126
    Sociological Theories of Deviance   127
The Importance of Law   132
    The Emergence of Laws   133
Crime in the United States   133
    Crime Statistics   134
Kinds of Crime in the United States   135
    Juvenile Crime   135
    Violent Crime   136
    Property Crime   138
    White-Collar Crime   138
    Organized Crime   139
    Victimless Crime   140

Criminal Justice in the United States   140
    The Police   140
    The Courts   141
    Prisons   142

PART III:
SOCIAL INEQUALITY   148

CHAPTER 7   *Social Stratification*   151
The Nature of Social Stratification   151
    Social Mobility   152
Stratification Systems   154
    The Caste System   154
    The Estate System   155
    The Class System   155
The Dimensions of Social Stratification   156
    Economics   156
    Power   156
    Prestige   158
Theories of Stratification   161
    The Functionalist Theory   161
    Conflict Theory   162
    Modern Conflict Theory   166
    The Need for Synthesis   167

CHAPTER 8   *Social Class in the United States*   169
Studying Social Stratification   170
    Objective Approach   170
    Reputational Approach   170
    Subjective Approach   170
Social Class in the United States   171
    The Upper Class   171
    The Upper-Middle Class   172
    The Lower-Middle Class   172
    The Working Class   173
    The Lower Class   173
Income Distribution   174
Poverty   175
    The Feminization of Poverty   175
    How Do We Count the Poor?   176
    Myths about the Poor   178
Government Assistance Programs   179
Worldwide Comparisons   180
Consequences of Social Stratification   182

CHAPTER 9   *Racial and Ethnic Minorities*   187
The Concept of Race   188
    Genetic Definitions   188
    Legal Definitions   189
    Social Definitions   189

The Concept of Ethnic Group 190
The Concept of Minorities 190
Problems in Race and Ethnic Relations 191
Prejudice 191
Discrimination 192
Institutionalized Prejudice and
Discrimination 193
Patterns in Racial and Ethnic Relations 194
Assimilation 194
Pluralism 195
Subjugation 196
Segregation 196
Expulsion 196
Annihilation 198
Racial and Ethnic Immigration to the United
States 199
Illegal Immigration 201
Racial and Ethnic Groups in the United
States 202
White Anglo-Saxon Protestants 202
African Americans 204
Hispanics 205
Jews 208
Asian Americans 208
Native Americans (Indians) 210
Prospects for the Future 212

CHAPTER 10 *Gender and Age
Stratification 215*
Are the Sexes Separate and Unequal? 216
Historical Views 216
Religious Views 217
Biological Views 218
Sociological Views: Cross-Cultural
Evidence 220
What Produces Gender Inequality? 221
The Functionalist Viewpoint 221
The Conflict Theory Viewpoint 222
Gender-Role Socialization 223
Childhood Socialization 223
Adolescent Socialization 224
Adult Socialization 224
Gender Differences in Social
Interaction 226
Gender Inequality and Work 227
Job Discrimination 227
Gender Roles and the Future 230
Changes in Attitudes 230
Age Stratification 231
Composition of the Older Population 231
Aging by Sex Ratio 232
Aging by Race 232
Aging by Marital Status 232

Theories of Aging 233
Disengagement Theory 233
Activity Theory 233
Modernization Theory 234
Future Trends in Age Stratification 234

PART IV:
INSTITUTIONS 238

CHAPTER 11 *Marriage and Alternative
Family Lifestyles 241*
The Nature of Family Life 242
Functions of the Family 243
Family Structures 244
Defining Marriage 244
Romantic Love 246
Marriage Rules 247
Marital Residence 247
Mate Selection 248
The Transformation of the Family 250
Changes in the Marriage Rate 252
Childless Couples 253
Changes in Household Size 254
Premarital Sex 255
Working Women 255
Family Violence 255
Divorce 258
Alternative Lifestyles 262
The Growing Single Population 262
Single-Parent Families 263
Stepfamilies 263
Cohabitation 264
Homosexual and Lesbian Couples 265
The Future: Bright or Dismal? 265

CHAPTER 12 *Religion 269*
The Nature of Religion 270
The Elements of Religion 270
Magic 272
Major Types of Religion 272
Supernaturalism 272
Animism 273
Theism 273
Monotheism 273
Abstract Ideals 274
A Sociological Approach to Religion 275
The Functionalist Perspective 275
The Conflict Theory Perspective 279
Organization of Religious Life 279
The Universal Church 279
The Ecclesia 280
The Denomination 280

The Sect   280
Millenarian Movements   280
Aspects of American Religion   281
Widespread Belief   281
Secularism   282
Ecumenism   282
Television Evangelism   282
Major Religions in the United States   283
Protestantism   284
Catholicism   284
Judaism   285
Islam   286
Social Correlates of Religious Affiliation   287

CHAPTER 13   *Education   291*
Education: A Functionalist View   292
Socialization   292
Cultural Transmission   293
Academic Skills   294
Innovation   295
Child Care   296
Postponing Job Hunting   296
The Conflict Theory View   297
Social Control   297
Screening and Allocation: Tracking   298
The Credentialized Society   299
Issues in American Education   299
Unequal Access to Education   299
High School Dropouts   302
Violence in the Schools   304
Standardized Testing   304
The Gifted   305

CHAPTER 14   *Political and Economic*
Systems   309
Politics, Power, and Authority   309
Power   310
Political Authority   310
Government and the State   311
Functions of the State   312
The Economy and the State   313
Capitalism   313
The Marxist Response to Capitalism   315
Command Economies   315
Socialism   316
The Capitalist View of Socialism   316
Types of States   316
Autocracy   316
Totalitarianism   316
Democracy   317
Democracy and Socialism   318
Democratic Socialism   319

Functionalist and Conflict Theory Views of the
State   320
Political Change   321
Institutionalized Political Change   321
Rebellions   321
Revolutions   322
The American Political System   322
The Two-Party System   322
Voting Behavior   323
Special-Interest Groups   326

PART V:
SOCIAL CHANGE AND SOCIAL
ISSUES   330

CHAPTER 15   *Population and*
Demography   333
Population Dynamics   334
Fertility   336
Mortality   337
Migration   338
Theories of Population   339
Malthus's Theory of Population
Growth   339
Marx's Theory of Population Growth   340
Demographic Transition Theory   340
A Second Demographic Transition   341
Current Population Trends: A Ticking
Bomb?   342
Determinants of Fertility   344
Problems of Overpopulation   348
Predictions of Ecological Disaster   348
Sources of Optimism   351

CHAPTER 16   *Urban Society   353*
The Development of Cities   354
The Earliest Cities   354
Preindustrial Cities   355
Industrial Cities   356
Urbanization   357
Classification of Urban Environments   358
The Structure of Cities   359
The Nature of Urban Life   362
Gemeinschaft to *Gesellschaft*   362
Mechanical and Organic Solidarity   363
Social Interaction in Urban Areas   365
Urban Neighborhoods   366
Urban Decline   367
Homelessness   367
Future Urban Growth in the United States   369
Suburban Living   370
The Exurbs   373

CHAPTER 17 *Health and Health Care 377*

The Experience of Illness 378
Health Care in the United States 378
    Gender and Health 379
    Race and Health 380
    Social Class and Health 381
    Age and Health 382
Contemporary Health Care Issues in the United States 383
    Acquired Immunodeficiency Syndrome (AIDS) 383
    Health Insurance 386
    Preventing Illness 388
World Health Trends 389
    The Health of Infants and Children in Developing Countries 389

CHAPTER 18 *Collective Behavior and Social Movements 393*

Theories of Collective Behavior 394
    Contagion (Mentalist) Theory 395
    Emergent Norm Theory 395
    Convergence Theory 396
    Value-Added Theory 396
Crowds: Concentrated Collectivities 397
    Attributes of Crowds 397
    Types of Crowds 397
    The Changeable Nature of Crowds 398
Dispersed Collective Behavior 399
    Fads and Fashions 399
    Rumors 400
    Public Opinion 401

    Mass Hysterias and Panics 401
Social Movements 402
    Relative Deprivation Theory 402
    Resource-Mobilization Theory 403
    Types of Social Movements 404
    The Life Cycle of Social Movements 406

CHAPTER 19 *Social Change 411*

Society and Social Change 412
Sources of Social Change 412
    Internal Sources of Social Change 412
    External Sources of Social Change 413
Theories of Social Change 414
    Evolutionary Theory 415
    Conflict Theory 416
    Functionalist Theory 416
    Cyclical (Rise and Fall) Theory 417
Modernization: Global Social Change 419
    Modernization: An Overview 419
    Modernization in the Third World 420
    Modernization and the Individual 420
Social Change in the United States 421
    Technological Change 421
    The Workforce of the Future 422

GLOSSARY 427
REFERENCES 439
CREDITS 455
NAME INDEX 459
SUBJECT INDEX 465
STUDY GUIDE SG-1
PRACTICE TESTS PT-1

INTRODUCTION TO
SOCIOLOGY
FOURTH EDITION

PART I

THE STUDY OF SOCIETY

CHAPTER 1   *The Sociological Perspective*

CHAPTER 2   *Doing Sociology: Research Methods*

Congratulations. You are about to embark on an exciting voyage of discovery—one in which you will lay claim to a sociological understanding of society and social interaction. But, you may ask, why should you want to go on this expedition at all? Why should you want to study sociology? What does it have to offer—that is, what can sociologists tell you about your life that you don't already know?

The first section of this book is designed to answer these questions and more. In Chapter 1 you will encounter the sociological perspective and discover that the sociological point of view leads us to look at the world in a different way. That is, sociology compels us to go beyond our own personal experiences to see the world through the eyes of others and to look for recurring patterns in the behavior of many individuals. This, you will discover, is what makes sociology a social science. There are a number of social sciences, and, of course, all of them deal with people. In Chapter 1 you will learn how sociology is both different from and similar to these other disciplines. You will also discover how the sociological perspective was developed and employed by early sociologists, first in Europe, and then later in the United States. Like

other social scientists, however, sociologists do not agree on the best way to organize their understanding of the social world. Thus you will encounter the major theoretical perspectives used by sociologists.

If people and their social behaviors vary widely, and sociologists can't always agree on the best way to understand and interpret those behaviors, how do you know that sociologists really know anything at all? How can you trust what they tell you about how the social world works? The answer is to be found in a consideration of research methods, which is the subject of Chapter 2. In this chapter you will explore the research process in order to develop criteria for assessing sociological research as well as to understand where researchers can go wrong. You will see how bias creeps into social research, and what steps sociologists take to try and avoid it. You will also examine important ethical issues in the collection and use of sociological data.

When you have finished this section, you should have a basic understanding of what sociology is and is not, and how sociologists go about studying the social world. You will now be ready to move on to using sociology to understand social behavior.

The Sociological Perspective

Sociology as a Point of View
  The Sociological Imagination
  Is Sociology Common Sense?
  Sociology and Science
  Sociology as a Social Science

The Development of Sociology
  Auguste Comte
  Classical Theorists
  The Development of Sociology in the
    United States

Theoretical Perspectives
  Functionalism
  Conflict Theory
  The Interactionist Perspective
  Contemporary Sociology
  Theory and Practice

This morning while eating my bowl of breakfast cereal I looked at the milk carton and noticed a picture of a five-year-old girl with the accompanying headline asking, "Have You Seen Me?" This program is all part of an effort to help find abducted children. How big is this problem? U. S. Senator Paul Simon believes it is enormous and offers the number of 50,000 children abducted by strangers each year as "the most conservative estimate you will get anywhere." Child Find, a well-known child-search organization, believes that parents recover only 10 percent of these children, while another 10 percent are found dead, and the remaining 40,000 remain missing.

But wait. Let us step back a bit. No doubt we are talking about a social problem with very serious consequences. Is this sociology? Or for that matter is this what sociologists do when they study society? The answer would have to be no. A sociologist would want to know how this estimate of 50,000 abducted children was arrived at and the intent of the person presenting the information. A sociologist would also note that there is no proof whatsoever for the 50,000 figure and that other counts of children missing for more than 24 hours number just 550 (Best, 1990). A sociologist might also point to another study, this time of New York State in 1990, that found in 25,325 cases of reported missing children, only one was found to be a stranger abduction after examining all the data (Cohen and Vigars, 1991).

Far too infrequently do we realize that people use data to persuade and that statistics can be used as part of a social problems promotion strategy. Much of the information we read everyday and mistake for sociology is actually an attempt by one group or another to influence social policy. Other information mistaken for sociology is really an attempt to sell a book, or the result of efforts of television producers to present entertaining programs.

With the constant bombardment of information about social issues, we could come to believe that nearly everyone is engaged in the study of sociology to some extent and that everyone has not only the right but the ability to put forth "valid" information about society. This is not the case. Some people have no interest in putting forth objective information and are instead interested in getting us to support their position or point of view. Others do not have the ability or training to disseminate accurate information about drug abuse, homelessness, welfare, high school dropout rates, white-collar crime, or a host of other sociological topics.

Sociologists have very different goals in mind when they investigate a problem than do journalists or talk show hosts. A television talk show host needs to make the program entertaining and maintain high ratings or the show may be canceled. A journalist is writing for a specific readership. This will certainly limit the choice of topics as well as the manner in which an issue is investigated. On the other hand, a sociologist must answer to the scientific community as she or he tries to further our understanding of a topic. This means that the goal is not high ratings, but an accurate and scientific approach to the study of society.

In this book we will ask you to go beyond pop sociology and investigate society more scientifically than you did before. We will ask you to look at major events as well as everyday occurrences a little differently and start to notice patterns you may have never seen before. After you are equipped with the tools of study you should be able to critically evaluate popular presentations of sociology. You will see that sociology represents both a body of knowledge as well as a scientific approach to the study of social issues.

SOCIOLOGY AS A POINT OF VIEW

Sociology *is the scientific study of human society and social interactions.* As sociologists our main goal is to *understand* social situations and look for repeating patterns in society. We do not use facts selectively to make for a lively talk show, sell newspapers, or support one particular point of view. Instead we are engaged in a rigorous scientific endeavor which requires objectivity and detachment.

The main focus of sociology is the group, not the individual. Sociologists attempt to understand the forces that operate throughout society—forces that mold individuals, shape their behavior, and thus determine social events.

When you walk into an introductory physics class you may know very little about the subject, and hold very few opinions about the various topics within the field. On the other hand, when you enter your introductory sociology class for the first time you will feel quite familiar with the subject matter. You have the advantage of coming to sociology with a substantial amount of information which you have gained simply by being a member of society. Ironically, this knowledge also can leave you at a disadvantage because these views have not been gathered in a scientific fashion and may not be accurate.

Over the years and through a variety of experiences we develop a set of ideas about the world and how it operates. This point of view influences how we look at the world and guides our attempts to understand the actions and reactions of others. Even though we accept the premise that individuals are unique, we tend to categorize or even stereotype people in order to interpret and predict behavior and events.

Is this personalized approach adequate for bringing about an understanding of ourselves and society? Even though it may serve us quite well in our day-to-day lives, as a sociologist I would have to answer that it does not give us enough accurate information to develop an understanding of the broader social picture. This picture only becomes clear when we know something about the society in which we live, the social processes that affect us, and the patterns of interaction that characterize our lives.

If we rely only on our own experiences, we are like the blind men of Hindu legend trying to describe an elephant: The first man, feeling its trunk, asserted, "It is like a snake"; the second, trying to reach around the beast's massive leg, argued, "No, it is like a tree"; and the third, feeling its powerful side, disagreed, saying, "It is more like a wall." In a small way, each man was right, but not one of them was able to understand or describe the whole elephant.

Let us take a major-league baseball game as an example. If you were asked to go to a game and prepare a report on your observations of the spectators, your notes might contain comments about the woman next to you who carefully recorded each play on her scorecard, or the man behind you who seemed more interested in the offerings of the various food vendors than in the game, or the seven-year-old boy clutching his mitt in the hope of catching a foul ball. Sociologists, on the other hand, would more likely be interested in the age,

Vast differences often exist within the same society. In this scene from the Hong Kong harbor, the merchants who ply their trade on the water have very little contact with the people who live in the high-rise buildings in the background.

socioeconomic level, and ethnic background of the crowd, and perhaps of the ball players as well. They might want to compare the background and behavior of spectators at a baseball game with the characteristics of spectators at a tennis match and ask such questions as: Are there differences? If so, what kinds and why?

While studying sociology you will be asked to look at the world a little differently than you usually do. Because you will be looking through other people's eyes—using new points of view—you will start to notice things you may never have noticed before. When you look at life in a middle-class suburb, for instance, what do you see? How does your view differ from that of a poor slum resident? How does the suburb appear to a recent immigrant from Russia or Cuba or Haiti? How does it appear to a burglar? Finally, what does the sociologist see?

Sociology asks you to broaden your perspective on the world. You will start to see that the reason people act in markedly different ways is not because one person is "sane" and another is "crazy." Rather it is because they all have different ways of making sense out of what is going on in the world around them. These unique perceptions of reality produce varying lifestyles, which in turn produce different perceptions of reality. In order to understand other people, we must stop looking at the world from a perspective based solely on our own individual experiences.

The Sociological Imagination

While most people interpret social events on the basis of their individual experiences, sociologists step back and view society more as an outsider than as a personally involved and possibly biased participant. For example, while we assume that most people in the United States marry because of love, sociologists remind us that the decision to marry—or not to marry—is influenced by a variety of social values taught to us since early childhood. That is, we select our mates based on the social values we internalize from family, peers, neighbors, community leaders, and even our television heroes. As a result we are less likely to marry someone from a different socio-economic class, from a different race or religion, or from a markedly different educational background. Thus, as we pair off, we follow somewhat predictable patterns: In most cases the man is older, earns more money, and has a higher occupational status than the woman. These patterns may not be evident to the two people who are in love with each other; indeed, they may not be aware that anything other than romance played a role in their choice of a mate.

As sociologists we begin to discern marriage patterns. We may note that marriage rates are different in different parts of the country, that the average age of marriage is related to educational level, and that social class is related to marital stability. These patterns (discussed in Chapter 11) show us that there are forces at work which influence marriage that may not be evident to the individuals who fall in love and marry.

C. Wright Mills (1959) pointed out different levels on which social events can be perceived and interpreted. He used the term "the sociological imagination" to refer to this relationship between individual experiences and forces in the larger society which shape our actions.

If You Are Thinking About Sociology As a Career, Read This

Speaking from this side of the career-decision hurdle, I can say that being a sociologist has opened many doors for me. It gave me the credentials to teach at the college level and to become an author of a widely used sociology text. It also enabled me to be a newspaper columnist and a talk-show host. Would I recommend this field to anyone else? I would, but not blindly. Realize before you begin that sociology can be an extremely demanding discipline and, at times, an extremely frustrating one.

As in many other fields, the competition for jobs in sociology can be fierce. If you really want this work, do not let the herd stop you. Anyone with motivation, talent, and a determined approach to finding a job will do well. But be prepared for the long haul: To get ahead in many areas you will

need to spend more than four years in college. Consider your bachelor's degree as just the beginning. Fields like teaching at the college level and advanced research often *require* a Ph.D., which means at least four to six years of school beyond the B.A.

Now for the job possibilities. As you read through these careers, remember that right now your exposure to sociology is limited (you are only on Chapter 1 in your first college sociology text), so do not eliminate any possibilities right at the start. Spend some time thinking about each one as the semester progresses and you learn more about this fascinating discipline.

Most people who go into sociology become teachers. You will need a Ph.D. to teach in college, but you can get away with less if you teach on the high-school level.

Second in popularity to teaching are nonacademic research jobs in government agencies, private research institutions, and the research departments of private corporations. Researchers carry on many different functions, including conducting market research, public opinion surveys, and impact assessments. Evaluation research, as the latter field is known, has become more popular in recent years because the federal government now requires environmental impact studies on all large-scale federal projects. For example, before a new interstate highway is built, evaluation researchers attempt to determine the effect the highway will have on communities along the proposed route.

This is only one of many opportunities available in government work. Sociologists are also

The sociological imagination is the process of looking at all types of human behavior patterns and discerning previously unseen connections among them, noting similarities in the actions of individuals with no direct knowledge of one another, and finding subtle forces that mold people's actions. Like a museum-goer who draws back from a painting in order to see how the separate strokes and colors form subtly shaded images, sociologists stand back from individual events in order to see why and how they occurred. In so doing, they discover patterns that govern our social existence.

The sociological imagination focuses on every aspect of society and every relationship among individuals. It studies the behavior of crowds at ball games and racetracks; shifts in styles of dress and popular music; changing patterns of courtship and marriage; the emergence and fading of different lifestyles, political movements, and religious sects; the distribution of income and access to resources

and services; decisions made by the Supreme Court, by congressional committees, and by local zoning boards; and so on. Every detail of social existence is food for sociological thought and relevant to sociological analysis.

The potential for sociology to be put to use—applied to the solution of "real-world" problems—is very great. Proponents of the idea of applied sociology believe the work of sociologists can and should be used to help bring about an understanding of, and perhaps even guidelines for changing, the complexities of modern society.

The demand for applied sociology is growing, and many sociologists work directly with government agencies or private businesses in an effort to apply sociological knowledge to real-world problems. For example, they might investigate such questions as how the building of a dam will affect the residents of the area, how busing to integrate schools affects the children involved, why voters hired by federal, state, and local governments in policymaking and administrative functions. For example, a sociologist employed by a community hospital provides needed data on the population groups being served and on the health-care needs of the community. Another example: Sociologists working in a prison system can devise plans to deal with the social problems that are inevitable when people are put behind bars. Here are a few additional opportunities in government work: community planner, correction officer, environmental analyst, equal opportunity specialist, probation officer, rehabilitation counselor, resident director, and social worker.

A growing number of opportunities also exist in corporate America, including market researchers, pollsters, human resource managers, affirmative action coordinators, employee assistance program counselors, labor relations specialists, and pub-

lic information officers, just to name a few. These jobs are available in nearly every field from advertising to banking, from insurance to publishing. Although your corporate title will not be "sociologist," your educational background will give you the tools you need to do the job—and do it well, which, to corporations, is the bottom line.

Whether you choose government or corporate work, you will have the best chance of finding the job you want by specializing in a particular field of sociology while you are still in school. You can become an urban or family specialist or knowledgeable in organizational behavior before you enter the job market. For example, many demographers, who compile and analyze population data, have specialized in this aspect of sociology. Similarly, human ecologists, who investigate the structure and organization of a community in relation to its environment, have specialized ed-

ucational backgrounds as well. Keep in mind that many positions require a minor or some course work in other fields such as political science, psychology, ecology, law, or business. By combining sociology with these fields, you will be well prepared for the job market.

What next? Be optimistic and start planning. As the American Sociological Association observed, few fields are as relevant to today and as broadly based as sociology. Yet, ironically, its career potential is just beginning to be tapped. Start planning by reading the *Occupational Outlook Quarterly*, published by the U.S. Bureau of Labor Statistics, as well as academic journals to keep abreast of career trends. Then study hard and choose your specialty. With this preparation, when the time comes to find a job, you will be well prepared.

select one candidate over another, how a company can boost employee morale, and how relationships among administrators, doctors, nurses, and patients affect hospital care. The answers to these questions have practical applications. The growing demand for sociological information provides many new career choices for sociologists (see the box on careers in Sociology).

Is Sociology Common Sense?

Common sense is what people develop through everyday life. In a very real sense, it is the set of expectations about society and people's behavior that guides our own behavior. Unfortunately, these expectations are not always reliable or accurate because without further investigation, we tend to believe what we want to believe, to see what we want to see, and to accept as fact whatever appears to be logical. The "common sense" approach to

sociology is one of the major dangers the new student encounters.

While common sense is often vague, oversimplified, and frequently contradictory, sociology as a science attempts to be specific, to qualify its statements, and to prove its assertions. Upon closer inspection, we find that the proverbial words of wisdom rooted in common sense are often illogical. Why, for example, should you "look before you leap" if "he who hesitates is lost"? How can "absence make the heart grow fonder" when "out of sight, out of mind"? Why should "opposites attract" when "birds of a feather flock together"? Sociologists as scientists would attempt to qualify these statements by specifying, for example, under what conditions "opposites tend to attract" or "birds of a feather flock together."

While common sense gleaned from personal experience may help us in certain types of interactions, it will not help us understand why and under what conditions these interactions are taking place. Sociology as a science is oriented toward gaining knowledge about why and under what conditions they do take place, thus to understand human interactions better (Vernon, 1965).

Sociology and Science

Sociology is commonly described as one of the social sciences. **Science** *refers to a body of systematically arranged knowledge that shows the operation of general laws.*

Sociology also employs the same general methods of investigation that are used in the natural sciences. Like the natural scientists, sociologists use the **scientific method,** *a process by which a body of scientific knowledge is built through observation, experimentation, generalization, and verification.* The collection of data is an important aspect of the scientific method, but facts alone do not constitute a science. To have any meaning, facts must be ordered in some way, analyzed, generalized, and related to other facts. This is known as theory construction. Theories help us organize and interpret facts and relate them to previous findings of other researchers.

Science is only one of the ways in which human beings study the world around them. Unlike other means of inquiry that depend on a logical discussion of abstract concepts such as religion or philosophy, science for the most part limits its investigations to empirical entities, things that can be observed directly or that produce directly observable events. Therefore, one of the basic features of science is **empiricism,** *the view that generalizations are valid only if they rely on evidence that can be observed directly or verified through our senses.* For example, theologians might discuss the role of faith in producing "true happiness"; philosophers might deliberate over what happiness actually encompasses; but sociologists would note, analyze, and predict the consequences of such measurable items as job satisfaction, the relationship between income and stated contentment, and the role of social class in the incidence of depression.

Sociology as a Social Science

The **social sciences** *consist of all those disciplines that apply scientific methods to the study of human behavior.* Although there is some overlap, each of the social sciences has its own area of investigation. It is helpful to understand each of the social sciences and to examine sociology's relationship to them.

CULTURAL ANTHROPOLOGY The social science most closely related to sociology is *cultural anthropology.* The two have many theories and concepts in common and often overlap. The main difference is in the groups they study and the research methods they use. Sociologists tend to study groups and institutions within large, modern, industrial societies, using research methods that enable them rather quickly to gather specific information about large numbers of people. In contrast, cultural anthropologists often immerse themselves in another society for a long period of time, trying to learn as much as possible about that society and the relationships among its people. Thus, anthropologists tend to focus on the culture of small, preindustrial societies because they are less complex and more manageable using this method of study.

PSYCHOLOGY The study of individual behavior and mental processes is part of *psychology*; the

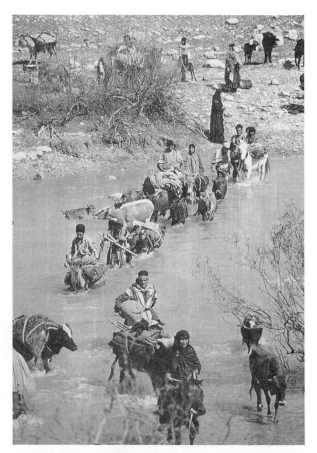

Sociologists and anthropologists share many theories and concepts. Whereas sociologists tend to study groups and institutions within large, modern, industrial societies, anthropologists tend to focus on the culture of small, preindustrial societies.

field is concerned with such issues as motivation, perception, cognition, creativity, mental disorders, and personality. More than any other social science, psychology uses laboratory experiments. Psychology and sociology overlap in a subdivision of each field known as *social psychology*—the study of how human behavior is influenced and shaped by various social situations. Social psychologists study such issues as how individuals in a group solve problems and reach a consensus, or what factors might produce nonconformity in a group situation. For the most part, however, psychology studies the individual, and sociology studies groups of individuals, as well as society's institutions.

The sociologist's perspective on social issues is broader than that of the psychologist. Take the case of alcoholism for example. The psychologist might view alcoholism as a personal problem that has the potential to destroy an individual's physical and emotional health, as well as marriage, career, and friendships. The sociologist, on the other hand, would look for patterns in alcoholism. Although each alcoholic makes the decision to take each drink—and each suffers the pain of addiction—the sociologist would remind us that to think of alcoholism as merely a personal problem is to misunderstand the issue. Sociologists encourage us to look at the social causes of alcoholism. They want to know who drinks excessively, when they drink, where they drink, and under what conditions they drink. Sociologists also want to know the social costs of chronic drinking—costs in terms of families torn apart, jobs lost, children severely abused and neglected, costs in terms of highway accidents and deaths, costs in terms of drunken quarrels leading to violence and to murder. Noting the startling increase in heavy alcohol use by adolescents over the last 10 years and the rapid rise of chronic alcoholism among women, sociologists ask: What forces are at work to account for these patterns?

ECONOMICS Economists have developed techniques for measuring such things as prices, supply and demand, money supplies, rates of inflation, and employment. It is this study of the creation, distribution, and consumption of goods and services that is known as *economics*. The economy, however, is just one part of society. It is each individual in society who decides whether to buy an American car or a Japanese import, whether she or he is able to handle the mortgage payment on a dream house, and so on. Whereas economists study price and availability factors, sociologists are interested in the social factors that influence the resulting economic behavior. Is it peer pressure that results in the buying

of the large flashy car, or is it concern about gas mileage that leads to the purchase of a small, fuel-efficient, modest vehicle? What social and cultural factors contribute to the differences in the portion of income saved by the average wage earner in different societies? What effect does the unequal allocation of resources have on social interaction? These are examples of the questions sociologists seek to answer.

HISTORY The study of *history* involves looking at the past in an attempt to learn what happened, when it happened, and why it happened. Sociology also looks at historical events within their social contexts to discover why things happened and, more importantly, to assess what their social significance was and is. Historians provide a narrative of the sequence of events during a certain period and may use sociological research methods to try to learn how social forces have shaped historical events. Sociologists, on the other hand, examine historical events to see how they influenced later social situations. Historians focus on individual events—the American Revolution or slavery—and sociologists generally focus on phenomena such as revolutions or the patterns of dominance and subordination that exist in slavery. They try to understand the common conditions that contribute to revolution or slavery wherever they occur.

Let us consider the subject of slavery in the United States. Traditionally, historians might focus on when the first slaves arrived, or how many slaves existed in 1700 or 1850 and the conditions under which they lived. Sociologists and modern social historians would use these data to ask many questions: What were the social and economic forces that shaped the institution of slavery in the United States? How did the Industrial Revolution affect slavery? How has the experience of slavery affected the black family? Although history and sociology have been moving toward each other over the last 20 years, each discipline still retains a somewhat different focus: sociology on the present, history on the past.

POLITICAL SCIENCE Concentrating on three major areas, *political science* is the study of political theory, the actual operation of government, and, in recent years, political behavior. This emphasis on political behavior overlaps with sociology. The primary distinction between the two disciplines is that sociology focuses on how the political system affects other institutions in society, while political science devotes more attention to the forces that shape political systems and the theories for understanding these forces. However, both disciplines share an interest in why people vote the way they do, why they join political movements, how the mass media are changing political parties and processes, and so on.

SOCIAL WORK   Much of the theory and research methods of social work are drawn from sociology and psychology, but social work focuses to a much greater degree on application and problem solving. The disciplines of sociology and social work are often confused with each other. The main goal of *social work* is to help people solve their problems, while the aim of sociology is to understand why the problems exist. Social workers provide help for individuals and families who have emotional and psychological problems or who experience difficulties that stem from poverty or other ongoing problems rooted in the structure of society. Social workers also organize community groups to tackle local issues such as housing problems and try to influence policy-making bodies and legislation. Sociologists provide many of the theories and ideas used to help

others. Although sociology is not social work, it is a useful area of academic concentration for those interested in entering the helping professions.

THE DEVELOPMENT OF SOCIOLOGY

It is hardly an accident that sociology emerged as a separate field of study in Europe during the nineteenth century. That was a time of turmoil, a period in which the existing social order was being shaken by the growing Industrial Revolution and by violent uprisings against established rulers (the American and French revolutions). People were also affected by the impact of discovering, through world exploration and colonialization, how others lived. At the same time, a void was left by the declining power of the church to impose its views of right and wrong. New social classes of industrialists and business people emerged to challenge the rule of the feudal aristocracies. Tightly knit communities, held to-

The changes that grew out of the French Revolution contributed to an environment in which the systematic study of society could emerge.

gether by centuries of tradition and well-defined social relationships, were strained by dramatic changes in the social environment. Factory cities began to replace the rural estates of nobles as a center for society at large. People with different backgrounds were brought together under the same factory roof to work for wages instead of exchanging their services for land and protection. Families now had to protect themselves, to buy food rather than grow it, and to pay rent for their homes. These new living and working conditions led to the development of an industrial, urban lifestyle, which, in turn, produced new social problems.

Many people were frightened by what was going on and wanted to find some way of understanding and dealing with the changes taking place. The need for a systematic analysis of society coupled with acceptance of the scientific method resulted in the emergence of sociology. Henri Saint-Simon (1760–1825) and Auguste Comte (1798–1857) were among the pioneers in the science of sociology.

Auguste Comte

Born in the French city of Montpellier on January 19, 1798, Auguste Comte grew up in the period of great political turmoil that followed the French Revolution of 1789–1799.

In August 1817, Comte met Henri Saint-Simon and became his secretary and eventually his close collaborator. Under Saint-Simon's influence, Comte converted from an ardent advocate of liberty and equality to a supporter of an elitist conception of society.

Saint-Simon and Comte rejected the lack of empiricism in the social philosophy of the day. Instead they turned for inspiration to the methods and intellectual framework of the natural sciences, which they perceived as having led to the spectacular successes of industrial progress. They set out to develop a "science of man" that would reveal the underlying principles of society much as the sciences of physics and chemistry explained nature and guided industrial progress. During their association the two men collaborated on a number of essays, most of which contained the seeds of Comte's major ideas. Their alliance came to a bitter end in 1824, when Comte broke with Saint-Simon for both financial and intellectual reasons.

Financial problems, lack of academic recognition, and marital difficulties combined to force Comte into a shell. Eventually, for reasons of "cerebral hygiene," he no longer read any scientific work related to the fields about which he was writing. Living in isolation at the periphery of the

August Comte coined the term sociology. He wanted to develop a "science of man" that would reveal the underlying principles of society much as the sciences of physics and chemistry explained nature and guided industrial progress.

academic world, Comte concentrated his efforts between 1830 and 1842 on writing his major work, *Cours de Philosophie Positive,* in which he coined the term *sociology.*

Auguste Comte devoted a great deal of his writing to describing the contributions he expected sociology would make in the future. He was much less concerned with defining sociology's subject matter than with showing how it would improve society. Although Comte was reluctant to specify subdivisions of sociology, he identified two major areas that sociology should concentrate on. These were social statics, the study of how various institutions of society are interrelated, focusing on order, stability, and harmony; and social dynamics, the study of complete societies and how they develop and change over time. Comte believed all societies move through certain fixed stages of development, eventually reaching perfection (as exemplified in his mind by industrial Europe). The idea of a perfect society, however, is no longer accepted by sociologists.

Classical Theorists

During the nineteenth century, sociology developed rapidly under the influence of four scholars of highly divergent temperaments and orientations. Despite their differences in aims and theories, however, these men—Karl Marx, Herbert Spencer, Émile Durkheim, and Max Weber—were responsible for shaping sociology into a relatively coherent discipline.

KARL MARX (1818–1883) Those who are unfamiliar with his writings often think of Karl Marx as a revolutionary proponent of the political and social system we see in countries today labeled communist.

Marx lived during the early period of industrialization when the overwhelming majority of people in such societies were poor. The rural poor moved to cities where employment was available in factories and workshops of the new industrial economies. Those who owned and controlled the factories exploited the masses who worked for them. Even children as young as five or six years old worked 12 hour days, six and seven days a week (Lipsey and Steiner, 1975), and received only a subsistence wage. "The iron law of wages"—the philosophy

Karl Marx's views on class conflict were shaped by the Industrial Revolution. He believed that capitalist societies produce greater conflict because of the deep divisions between the social classes.

that justified paying workers only enough money to keep them alive—prevailed during the early period of industrialization. In this way the rural poor were converted into an urban poor. Meanwhile, those who owned the means of production possessed great wealth, power, and prestige.

Karl Marx tried to understand the societal forces that produced such inequities and looked for a means to change them in order to improve the human condition. Marx believed the entire history of human societies could be seen as the history of class conflict: the struggle between those who own and control the means of production (capitalists) and the workers—the exploiters and the exploited. He believed the capitalists determined the distribution of wealth, power, and even ideas in that society. The wealthy get their power not just from their control of the economy, but from their control of the political, educational, and religious institutions in their society as well. According to Marx, capitalists make and enforce laws that serve their interests and act against the interests of workers. Their control over all institutions enables them to create common beliefs that make the workers accept their status. These economic, political, and religious ideologies make the masses loyal to the very institutions that are the source of their exploitation and that also are the source of the wealth, power, and prestige of the ruling class. Thus, the prevailing beliefs of any society are those of its dominant group.

Marx predicted that a capitalist society eventually would polarize into two broad classes—the capitalists and the increasingly impoverished workers. Intellectuals like himself would show the workers that the capitalist institutions were the source of exploitation and poverty. Gradually, the workers would become unified and organized, and then, through revolution, they would seize control of the economy. The means of production would then be owned and controlled by the workers' socialist state. Once the capitalist elements of the society had been eliminated, the government would wither away. Pure communism would evolve—a society in which people may work according to their ability and take according to their need. The seeds of societal conflict and social change would come to an end as the means of production were no longer privately owned.

In many of the capitalist societies of today, regulatory mechanisms have been introduced to prevent some of the excesses of capitalism. Unions have been integrated into the capitalist economy and the political system, giving workers a legal, legitimate means through which they can benefit from the capitalist system. Contrary to Marx's predictions, most revolutions have not taken place in the industrialized Western nations but rather in agrarian nations—the former Soviet Union, China, Cuba, and Vietnam, for example.

Karl Marx was not a sociologist, but his considerable influence on the field can be traced to his contributions to the development of *conflict theory,* which will be discussed more fully later in this chapter. Marx's conflict theory is thought to be as applicable to communist nations as it is to capitalist nations. In communist nations, it is the Communist party that is the source of control over the economy and other institutions.

HERBERT SPENCER (1820–1903) A largely self-educated Briton, Herbert Spencer had a talent for synthesizing information. In 1860 he started work toward the goal of organizing human knowledge into one system. The result was his *Principles of Sociology* (1876, 1882), the first sociology textbook. Unlike Comte, Spencer was precise in defining the subject matter of sociology. He noted the field of sociology included the study of the family, politics, religion, social control, work, and stratification.

Spencer believed society was similar to a living organism. Just as the individual organs of the body are interdependent and make their specialized contributions to the living whole, so, too, are the various segments of society interdependent. Every part of society serves a specialized function necessary to ensure society's survival as a whole.

Spencer became a proponent of a doctrine known as Social Darwinism. **Social Darwinism** *applied to society Darwin's notion of "survival of the fittest," in which those species of animals best adapted to the environment survived and prospered, while those poorly adapted died out.* Spencer reasoned that people who could not successfully compete in modern society were poorly adapted to their environment and therefore inferior. Lack of success was viewed as an individual failing, and that failure was in no way related to barriers (such as prejudice or racism) created by society. In this view, to help the poor and needy was to intervene vainly in a natural evolutionary process.

Social Darwinism had a significant effect on those who believed in the inequality of races. They now claimed that those who had difficulty succeeding in the white world were really members of inferior races. The fact that they lost out in the competition for status was proof of their poor adaptability to the environment. The survivors were clearly of superior stock (Berry and Tischler, 1978).

White society accepted Social Darwinism because it served as a justification for their control over institutions. It enabled them to oppose reforms

Herbert Spencer helped to define the subject matter of sociology. Spencer also became a proponent of a doctrine known as Social Darwinism.

or social welfare programs, which they viewed as interfering with nature's plan to do away with the unfit. Social Darwinism thus became a justification for the repression and neglect of U.S. blacks following the Civil War. It also justified policies that resulted in the decimation of North American Indian populations and the complete eradication of the native people of Tasmania (near Australia) by white settlers (Fredrickson, 1971).

Spencer's ties to Social Darwinism have led many scholars to disregard his original contributions to the discipline of sociology. However, many of the standard concepts and terms still current in sociology were originally formulated by Spencer, and their use derives directly from his works.

ÉMILE DURKHEIM (1858–1917) A student of law, philosophy, and social science, Émile Durkheim was the first professor of sociology at the University of Bordeaux, France. Whereas Spencer wrote the first textbook of sociology, it was Durkheim who produced the first true sociological study. Durkheim's work moved sociology fully out of the realm

Émile Durkheim produced the first true sociological study. Durkheim's work moved sociology fully out of the realm of social philosophy and charted the discipline's course as a social science.

of social philosophy and helped chart the discipline's course as a social science.

Durkheim believed individuals were exclusively the products of their social environment and that society shapes people in every possible way. In order to prove his point, Durkheim studied suicide. He believed that if he could take what was perceived to be a totally personal act and show that it is patterned by social factors rather than exclusively by individual mental disturbances, he would provide support for his point of view.

Durkheim began with the theory that the industrialization of Western society was undermining the social control and support that communities had historically provided for individuals. Industrialization forced or induced individuals to leave rural communities for urban areas, where there were usually greater economic opportunities. The anonymity and impersonality that they encountered in

these urban areas, however, caused many people to become isolated from both family and friends. In addition, in industrial societies people are frequently encouraged to aspire to goals that are difficult to attain. Suspecting this trend would have an impact on the suicide rate, Durkheim set out to prove that what was believed to be a totally personal act, namely suicide, was in fact a product of social forces. Durkheim refined his theory to state that suicide rates are influenced by group solidarity and societal stability. He believed that low levels of solidarity—which involve more individual choice, more reliance on oneself, and less adherence to group standards—would mean high rates of suicide.

In order to test his idea Durkheim decided to study the suicide rates of Catholic versus Protestant countries. He assumed the suicide rate in Catholic countries would be lower than in Protestant countries because Protestantism emphasized the individual's relationship to God over community ties. The comparison of suicide records in Catholic and Protestant countries in Europe supported his theory by showing the probability of suicide was indeed higher in Protestant countries.

Recognizing the fact that lower suicide rates among Catholics could be based on factors other than group solidarity, Durkheim proceeded to test other groups. Reasoning that married people would be more integrated into a group than single people, or people with children more than people without children, or noncollege-educated people more than college-educated people (because college tends to break group ties and encourage individualism), or Jews more than non-Jews, Durkheim tested each of these groups, and in each case his theory held.

Then, characteristic of the scientist that he was, Durkheim extended his theory by identifying three types of suicide—egoistic, altruistic, and anomic—that take place under different types of conditions.

Egoistic suicide comes from low group solidarity, an underinvolvement with others. Durkheim argued that loneliness and a commitment to personal beliefs rather than group values can lead to egoistic suicide. He found that single and divorced people had higher suicide rates than did married people and that Protestants, who tend to stress individualism, had higher rates of suicide than did Catholics.

Altruistic suicide derives from a very high level of group solidarity, an overinvolvement with others. The individual is so tied to a certain set of goals that he or she is willing to die for the sake of the community. This type of suicide, Durkheim noted, still exists in the military as well as in societies based on ancient codes of honor and obedience. Perhaps the best-known examples of altruistic suicide come

TABLE 1.1

Facts About Suicide Among College Students

1. Official records of college student suicides underestimate the incidence by about 30 percent.
2. College students commit suicide significantly less often than non-students.
3. Institutional prestige, college size, or class standing are not related to suicide rates.
4. Those students who have had contact with the college mental health service are six times more likely to commit suicide than those who have not.
5. Male college students are half as likely as males in general to use the most common means of suicide, namely firearms.
6. Suicides occur more frequently during September, January, and March.

Source: Allan J. Schwartz, "The Epidemiology of Suicide Among Students at Colleges and Universities in the United States," in Leighton C. Whitaker and Richard E. Slimak, eds. *College Student Suicide,* New York: The Haworth Press, 1990, pp. 25–44.

from Japan: the ceremonial rite of *segguku,* in which a disgraced person rips open his own belly, and the *kamikaze* attacks by Japanese pilots toward the end of World War II. Today we often see examples of altruistic suicide with terrorists. These individuals are willing to sacrifice their lives for their cause as they blow up a plane, restaurant, or military installation.

Anomic suicide results from a sense of feeling disconnected from society's values. A person may know what goals to strive for but not have the means of attaining them, or a person may not know what goals to pursue. Durkheim found that times of rapid social change or economic crisis are associated with high rates of anomic suicide.

Durkheim's study was noteworthy not only because it proved that the most personal of all acts, suicide, is in fact a product of social forces, but also because it was one of the first examples of a scientifically conducted sociological study. Durkheim systematically posed theories, tested them, and drew conclusions that led to further theories. He also published his results for everyone to see and criticize.

Durkheim's interests were not limited to suicide. His mind ranged over the entire spectrum of social activities. He published studies on *The Division of Labor in Society* (1893) and *The Elementary Forms of the Religious Life* (1917). In both works he drew on what was known about nonliterate societies,

following the lead of Comte and Spencer in viewing them as evolutionary precursors of the contemporary industrial societies of Europe.

Durkheim focused on the forces that hold society together—that is, on the functions of various social structures. This point of view, often called the *functionalist theory* or *functionalist perspective* remains one of the dominant approaches to the modern study of society.

MAX WEBER (1864–1920) Much of Weber's work attempted to clarify, criticize, and modify the works of Marx. For that reason we shall discuss Weber's ideas as they relate to and contrast with those of Marx. Unlike Marx, who was not only an intellectual striving to understand society but a revolutionary conspiring to overturn the capitalist social system, Weber was essentially a German academic attempting to understand human behavior. Weber believed the role of intellectuals should simply describe and explain truth, whereas Marx believed the scholar should also tell people what to do.

Marx believed that ownership of the means of production resulted in control of wealth, power, and ideas. Weber showed that economic control does not necessarily result in prestige and power. For example, the wealthy president of a chemical company whose toxic wastes have been responsible for the pollution of a local water supply might have little prestige in the community. Moreover, the company's board of directors may deprive the president of any real power.

Much of the work of Max Weber was an attempt to clarify, criticize, and modify the works of Karl Marx. He also showed how religion contributed to the creation of new economic conditions and institutions.

Although Marx maintained that control of production inevitably results in control of ideologies, Weber stated that the opposite may happen: Ideologies sometimes influence the economic system. When Marx called religion an "opiate to the people," he was referring to the ability of those in control to create an ideology that would justify the exploitation of the masses. Weber, however, showed that religion could be a belief system that contributed to the creation of new economic conditions and institutions. In *The Protestant Ethic and the Spirit of Capitalism* (1904–1905), Weber tried to demonstrate how the Protestant Reformation of the seventeenth century provided an ideology that gave religious justification to the pursuit of economic success through rational, disciplined, hard work. This ideology, called the Protestant Ethic, ultimately helped transform northern European societies from feudal agricultural communities to industrial capitalist societies.

On the other hand, Weber also predicted that science—the systematic, rational description, explanation, and manipulation of the observable world—would lead to a gradual turning away from religion. The apparent decline in the influence of organized religion in the highly industrialized societies seems to support Weber's prediction.

Understanding the development of bureaucracy interested Weber. Whereas Marx saw capitalism as the source of control, exploitation, and alienation of human beings and believed that socialism and communism would ultimately bring an end to this exploitation, Weber believed bureaucracy would characterize both socialist and capitalist societies. He anticipated and feared the domination of individuals by large bureaucratic structures. As he foresaw, our modern industrial world, both capitalist and socialist, is now ruled by bureaucracies—economic, political, military, educational, and religious. Given the existing situation, it is easy to appreciate Weber's anxiety. As he put it:

> . . . each man becomes a little cog in the machine and, aware of this, his one preoccupation is whether he can become a bigger cog . . . The problem which besets us now is not: how can this evolution be changed?—for that is impossible, but what will become of it. (Quoted in Coser, 1977)

The Development of Sociology in the United States

Sociology did not become recognized in the United States until the twentieth-century. The early growth

Max Weber was interested in understanding the means by which people and material resources could be organized for the pursuit of specific goals. Advances in space travel could not take place without bureaucracies.

of American sociology took place at the University of Chicago which provided a setting in which a large number of scholars and their students could work closely to refine their views of the discipline. The first graduate department of sociology in America was founded there in the 1890s. From the 1920s to the 1940s the so-called Chicago school of sociologists led American sociology in the study of communities, with particular emphasis on urban neighborhoods and ethnic areas. Many of America's leading sociologists from this period were members of the Chicago school, including Robert E. Park, W. I. Thomas, and Ernest W. Burgess. Most of these men were Protestant ministers or sons of ministers, and as a group were deeply concerned with social reform.

Perhaps the single most influential American sociologist was Talcott Parsons (1902–1979). He presided over the Department of Social Relations at Harvard University from the 1930s until he retired in 1973. Parsons' early research was quite empirical, but he later turned to the philosophical and theoretical side of sociology. In *The Structure of Social Action* (1937), Parsons presented English translations of the writings of European thinkers, most notably Weber and Durkheim. In his best-known work, *The Social System* (1951), Parsons portrayed society as a stable system of well-ordered, interrelated parts. His viewpoint elaborated on Durkheim's functionalist perspective.

Contemporary sociologist Robert K. Merton also has been an influential proponent of functionalist theory. In his classic work, *Social Theory and Social Structure* (1968), first published in 1949, Merton spelled out the functionalist view of society. One of his main contributions to sociology was to distinguish between two forms of social functions—manifest functions and latent functions. *By* **social functions** *Merton meant those social processes that contribute to the ongoing operation or maintenance of society.* **Manifest functions** *are the intended and recognized consequences of those processes.* For example, one of the manifest functions of going to college is to obtain knowledge, training, and a degree in a specific area. **Latent functions** *are the unintended or not readily recognized consequences of such processes.* Therefore, college may also offer the opportunity of making lasting friendships and finding potential marriage partners.

Under the leadership of Parsons and Merton, sociology in America moved away from a concern with social reform and adopted a so-called value-free perspective. This perspective, which Max Weber advocated, requires description and explanation

Talcott Parsons portrayed society as a stable system of well-ordered, interrelated parts.

rather than prescription; people should be told what is, not what should be. As critics of Parsons and Merton point out, however, interpretations of what exists may differ depending on the perspective from which reality is viewed and on the values of the viewer (Gouldner, 1970; Lee, 1978; Mills, 1959).

THEORETICAL PERSPECTIVES

Scientists need a set of working assumptions to guide them in their work. These assumptions suggest which problems are worth investigating and offer a framework for interpreting the results of studies. Such sets of assumptions are known as paradigms. **Paradigms** *are models or frameworks for questions that generate and guide research.* Of course, not all paradigms are equally valid, even though at first they seem to be. Sooner or later, some will be found rooted in fact, whereas others will remain abstract and unusable, finally to be discarded. We shall examine those paradigms that have withstood the scrutiny of major sociologists.

Functionalism

Functionalism—or structural functionalism, as it is often called—is rooted in the writings of Spencer and Durkheim and the work of such scholars as Parsons and Merton. **Functionalism** *views society as a system of highly interrelated structures or parts that function or operate together harmoniously.* Functionalists analyze society by asking what each different part contributes to the smooth functioning of the whole. For example, we may assume the education system serves to teach students specific subject matter. However, functionalists might note that it acts as a system for the socialization of the young and as a means for producing conformity. The education system serves as a gatekeeper to the rewards society offers to those who follow its rules.

From the functionalist perspective, society appears quite stable and self-regulating. Much like a biological organism, society is normally in a state of equilibrium or balance. Most members of a society share a value system and know what to expect from one another.

The best-known proponent of the structural-functionalist perspective was Talcott Parsons. His theory centered on the view that interrelated social systems consisted of major areas of social life, such as the family, religion, education, politics, and economics. These systems were analyzed according to functions they performed for society both as a whole and for one another.

Functionalism is a very broad theory in that it attempts to account for the complicated interrelationships of all the elements that make up human societies, including the complex societies of the industrialized (and industrializing) world. In a way it is impossible to be a sociologist and not be a functionalist, because most parts of society serve some stated or unstated purpose. Functionalism is limited in one regard, however: The preconception that societies are normally in balance or harmony makes it difficult for proponents of this view to account for how social change comes about.

A major criticism of functionalist theory is its conservative bias. That is, if all the parts of society fit together smoothly, we can assume that the social system is working well. Conflict is then seen as something that disrupts the essential orderliness of the social structure and produces imbalance between the parts and the whole.

Conflict Theory

Conflict theory is rooted in the work of Marx and other social critics of the nineteenth century. **Conflict theory** *sees society as constantly changing in response to social inequality and social conflict.* For the conflict theorists, social change pushed forward by social conflict is the normal state of affairs. Static periods are merely temporary way stations along the road.

Conflict theorists believe social order results from dominant groups making sure that subordinate groups are loyal to the institutions that are the dominant groups' sources of wealth, power, and prestige. The dominant groups will use coercion, constraint, and even force to help control those people who are not voluntarily loyal to the laws and rules they have made. When this order cannot be maintained and the subordinant groups rebel, change comes about.

Conflict theorists are concerned with the issue of who benefits from particular social arrangements and how those in power maintain their positions and continue to reap benefits from them. In this sense Randall Collins (1975) sees the conflict perspective as an attempt to study how those in power maintain and enlarge their sphere of influence over many aspects of a society, including its values and beliefs. The ruling class is seen as a group that spreads certain values, beliefs, and social arrangements in order to enhance its power and wealth. The social order then reflects the outcome of a struggle among those with unequal power and resources.

Conflict perspectives are often criticized for concentrating too much on conflict and change and too little on what produces stability in society. They are also criticized for being too ideologically based and making little use of research methods or objective statistical evidence. The conflict theorists counter that the complexities of modern social life cannot be reduced to statistical analysis, and that doing so has caused sociologists to become detached from their object of study and removed from the real causes of human problems.

Both functionalist and conflict theories are descriptive and predictive of social life. Each has its strengths and weaknesses, and each emphasizes an important aspect of society and social life. Table 1.2 compares the approaches of functionalist and conflict theory.

The Interactionist Perspective

Functionalism and conflict theory can be thought of as the opposite sides of the same coin. Although quite different from one another, they share certain similarities. Both approaches focus on major structural features of entire societies and attempt to give

TABLE 1.2

Comparison of Functionalist and Conflict Theory

Functionalist Theory	Conflict Theory
1. The various parts of society are interdependent and functionally related.	1. Society is a system of accommodations among competing interest groups.
2. Each part of the social system contributes positively to the continued operation of the system.	2. The social system may at any time become unbalanced because of shifts in power.
3. The various parts of the social system fit together harmoniously.	3. The various parts of the social system do not fit together harmoniously.
4. Social systems are highly stable.	4. Social systems are unstable and are likely to change rapidly.
5. Social life is governed by consensus and cooperation.	5. Social life involves conflict because of differing goals.
6. Functionalist sociologists are concerned with the role each part of society contributes to the smooth functioning of the whole.	6. Conflict sociologists are concerned with who benefits from particular social arrangements.
7. Social order is achieved through cooperation.	7. Social order is achieved through coercion and even force.

us an understanding of how societies survive and change. Social life, however, also occurs on an intimate scale between individuals. *The* **interactionist perspective** *focuses on how individuals make* ⟵

Interactionists recognize that there are symbolic meanings attached to many social events.

sense of—or interpret—the social world in which they participate. As such, this approach is primarily concerned with human behavior on a person-to-person level. Interactionists criticize functionalists and conflict theorists for implicitly assuming that social processes and social institutions somehow have a life of their own apart from the participants. Interactionists remind us that the educational system, the family, the political system, and indeed all of society's institutions are ultimately created, maintained, and changed by people interacting with one another.

The interactionist perspective includes a number of loosely linked approaches. George Herbert Mead devised a *symbolic interactionist* approach which focuses on signs, gestures, shared rules, and written and spoken language. Harold Garfinkel used *ethnomethodology* to show how people create and share their understandings of social life. Erving Goffman took a *dramaturgical* approach in which he saw social life as a form of theater. Of these three approaches the symbolic interactionist approach has received the widest attention and presents us with a well-formulated theory.

SYMBOLIC INTERACTIONISM As developed by George Herbert Mead (1863–1931), **symbolic interactionism** *is concerned with the meanings that people place on their own and one another's behavior.* Human beings are unique in that most of what they do with one another has meaning beyond the concrete act. According to Mead, people do not act or react automatically, but carefully consider and even rehearse what they are going to do. They take into account the other people involved and the situation in which they find themselves. The expectations and reactions of other people greatly affect each individual's actions. In addition, people give things meaning and act or react on the basis of these meanings. For example, when the flag of the United States is raised, people stand because they see the flag as representing their country.

Because most human activity takes place in social situations—in the presence of other people—we must fit what we as individuals do with what other people in the same situation are doing. We go about our lives with the assumption that most people share our definitions of basic social situations. This agreement on definitions and meanings is the key to human interactions in general, according to symbolic interactionists. For example, a staff nurse in a mental hospital unlocking a door for an inpatient is doing more than simply enabling the patient to pass from one ward to another. He or she also is communicating a position of social dominance over the patient (within the hospital) and is carrying a powerful symbol of that dominance—the key. The same holds true for a professor writing on a blackboard or a company vice-president dictating to a secretary. Such interactions, therefore, although they appear to be simple social actions, also are laden with highly symbolic social meanings. These symbolic meanings are intimately connected with our understanding of what it is to be and to behave as a human being. This includes our sense of self; how we experience others and their views of us; the joys and pains we feel at home, at school, at work, and among friends and colleagues; and so on.

ETHNOMETHODOLOGY Many of the social actions we engage in on a day-to-day basis are commonplace events. They tend to be taken for granted and rarely are examined or considered. Harold Garfinkel (1967) has proposed that it is important to study the commonplace. Those things we take for granted have a tremendous hold over us because we accept their demands without question or conscious consideration. **Ethnomethodology** *is the study of the sets of rules or guidelines that individuals use to initiate behavior, respond to behavior, and modify behavior in social settings.* For ethnomethodologists, all social interactions are equally important because they provide information about a society's unwritten rules for social behavior—the shared knowledge of which is basic to social life.

Garfinkel asked his students to participate in a number of experiments in which the researcher would violate some of the basic understandings among people. For example, when a conversation is held between two people, each assumes that certain things are perfectly clear and obvious and do not need further elaboration. Examine the following conversation and notice what happens when one individual violates some of these expectations:

BOB: That was a very interesting sociology class we had yesterday.
JOHN: How was it interesting?
BOB: Well, we had a lively discussion about deviant behavior, and everyone seemed to get involved.
JOHN: I'm not certain I know what you mean. How was the discussion lively? How were people involved?
BOB: You know, they really participated and seemed to get caught up in the discussion.
JOHN: Yes, you said that before, but I want to know what you mean by lively and interesting.
BOB: What's wrong with you? You know what I mean. The class was interesting. I'll see you later.

Bob's response is quite revealing. He is puzzled and does not know whether John is being serious. The normal expectations and understandings around which day-to-day forms of expression take place have been challenged. Still, is it not reasonable to ask for further elaboration of certain statements? Obviously not when it goes beyond a certain point.

Another example of the confusion brought on by the violation of basic understandings was shown when Garfinkel asked his students to act like boarders in their own homes. They were to ask whether they could use the phone, take a drink of water, have a snack, and so on. The results were quite dramatic:

Family members were stupefied. They vigorously sought to make the strange actions intelligible and to restore the situation to normal appearances. Reports were filled with accounts of astonishment, shock, anxiety, embarrassment and anger, and with charges by various family members that the student was mean, inconsiderate, selfish, nasty, or impolite. Family members demanded explanations: What's the matter? What's gotten into you? Did you get fired? Are you sick? What are you being so superior about? Why are you mad? Are you out of your mind? Are you stupid? One student acutely embarrassed his mother in front of her friends by asking if she minded if he had a little snack from the refrigerator. "Mind if you have a little snack? You've been eating little snacks around here for years without asking me. What's gotten into you?" (Garfinkel, 1972)

Ethnomethodology seeks to make us more aware of the subtle devices we use in creating the realities to which we respond. These realities are often intrinsic in human nature, rather than imposed from outside influences. Ethnomethodology addresses questions about the nature of social reality and how we participate in its construction.

DRAMATURGY People create impressions, and others respond with their own impressions. Erving Goffman (1959, 1963, 1971) concluded that a central feature of human interaction is impression formation—the attempt to present oneself to others in a particular way. Goffman believed that much human interaction can be studied and analyzed on the basis of principles derived from the theater. This approach, known as **dramaturgy,** *states that in order to create an impression, people play roles, and their performance is judged by others who are alert to any slips that might reveal the actor's true character.* For example, a job applicant at an interview tries to appear composed, self-confident, and capable of handling the position's responsibilities. The interviewer is seeking to find out whether the applicant is really able to work under pressure and perform the necessary functions of the job.

Most interactions require some type of play-acting in order to present an image that will bring about the desired behavior from others. Dramaturgy sees these interactions as governed by planned behavior designed to enable an individual to present a particular image to others.

Symbolic interaction and its various offshoots have been criticized for paying too little attention to the larger elements of society. Interactionists respond that societies and institutions are made up of individuals who interact with one another and do not exist apart from these basic units. They believe that an understanding of the process of social interaction will lead to an understanding of larger social structures. In actual fact interactionists still must bridge the gap between their studies of social interaction and those of the broader social structures. Nevertheless, symbolic interactionism does complement functionalism and conflict theory in important ways and gives us important insights into how people interact.

Contemporary Sociology

Contemporary sociological theory continues to build on the original ideas proposed in the interactionist perspective, functionalism, and conflict the-

Sociology helps us to understand the highly complex world in which we live.

Should Sociology Aim to Improve Society?

Shortly after the French Revolution, Auguste Comte dreamed of a harmonious society run by social scientists according to principles evolved from a science of society. He named this science *sociology*. The social scientists would solve social problems and determine the proper balance between the interests of the many competing groups. Comte believed the people would accept the judgment of the social scientists as authoritative in much the same way as the teachings of the church were accepted in the Middle Ages. The end result would be peace, prosperity, and solidarity.

More than 150 years have passed since Comte's utopian vision. Will Comte's dream of a scientifically managed society come true? It hardly seems likely. How much does sociology have to contribute to make society a better place to live in? For that matter, should sociology, in fact, attempt to improve society? Whose vision of that perfect society should we adopt? Sociologist Jack D. Douglas and writer Richard P. Appelbaum have conflicting opinions on this question.

Douglas challenges the notion that the goal of sociology is simply to understand society. He believes that the rapid increase in the complexity of American society and the rate of social change have meant that most people are ignorant of what is going on in those segments of society beyond their own immediate ex-

perience. The insight of the sociologist is essential. Casual observation by the outsider will not reveal the truth of events in urban ghettos or in corporate boardrooms. Policymakers are bound to be ever more dependent on the objective and specialized knowledge of social scientists. Sociologists must provide policymakers with reliable predictions based on information about social trends. In fact, sociologists have an obligation, Douglas believes, to not leave the field of policy advising to self-appointed specialists whose ignorance of the complexity of the problems leads them to promise certain superficial solutions.

Richard Appelbaum disagrees with this view and believes there has been a mystification of expert scientific knowledge that is not justified. He notes that there is a marked lack of theories in the social sciences in general, particularly as they are employed for the purposes of social planning. In the physical sciences the researcher knows what to look for and how to measure it. This situation is not true in sociology. In the absence of adequate theories, we must pick and choose the important explanatory variables. This is often done according to subjective criteria determined by the political or personal predispositions of the sociologist. The resulting solutions may or may not reflect the ways things really are. Important factors may be omitted or not considered important. Yet this uncertainty does not deter the sociol-

ogist from confidently putting all the facts into the hopper, processing them, and presenting the results as scientifically correct.

Given the underdeveloped state of sociology, Appelbaum believes that any attempt to provide information to policymakers should acknowledge that condition and proceed accordingly. This means that sociologists should make it clear that their information represents an informed, but by no means accurate, guess about the situation. Any other guess is almost as good as that of the sociologist. Appelbaum believes the role of the expert needs to be deprofessionalized, and ordinary people must be given the confidence and skills required to understand the forces that mold their lives.

In Appelbaum's view, the sociologist is another expert who serves influential groups by turning political issues into technical problems and removing them from public debate. He sees the only role for the sociologist as one in which he or she informs the citizenry in order to aid the democratic process. Instead of solving social problems, the sociologist should merely provide people with information they need in their quest for a democratic and just society.

Sources: Jack D. Douglas, *The Relevance of Sociology.* New York: Appleton-Century Crofts, 1970. Richard P. Appelbaum, "The Future is Made, Not Predicted: Technocratic Planners versus Public Interests." *Society,* May/June 1977.

ory. It would be difficult to call contemporary sociological theory as either conflict theory or functionalism in the original sense. Much of it has been modified to include important aspects of each theory. Even symbolic interactionism has not been whole-heartedly embraced and aspects of it have instead been absorbed into general sociological writing.

Very little contemporary sociological theory can still be identified as true functionalism. Part of this is due to the fact sociologists today have abandoned trying to develop all-inclusive theories and instead opt for what Merton (1968) referred to as middle-range theories. **Middle-range theories** *are concerned with explaining specific issues or aspects of society instead of trying to explain how all of society operates.* A middle-range theory might be one that explains why divorce rates rise and fall with certain economic conditions, or how crime rates are related to residential patterns.

Modern conflict theory was initially refined by such sociologists as C. Wright Mills (1959), Ralf Dahrendorf (1958), Randall Collins (1975, 1979), and Lewis Coser (1956) to reflect the realities of contemporary society. Mills and Dahrendorf did not see conflict as confined to class struggle. Rather, they viewed it as applicable to the inevitable tensions that arise between groups: parents and children, producers and consumers, professionals and their clients, unions and employers, the poor and the materially comfortable, and minority and majority ethnic groups. Members of these groups have both overlapping and competing interests, and their shared needs keep all parties locked together within one society. At the same time the groups actively pursue their own ends, thus constantly pushing the society to change in order to accommodate them.

Lewis Coser incorporated aspects of both functionalism and conflict theory, seeing conflict as an inevitable element of all societies and as both functional and dysfunctional for society. Conflict between two groups tends to increase their internal cohesion. For example, competition between two divisions of two computer companies to be the first to produce a new product may draw the members closer to each other as they strive to reach the desired goal. This feeling might not have occurred had it not been for the sense of competition, as the conflict itself becomes a form of social interaction. Conflict could also lead to cohesion by causing two or more groups to form alliances against a common enemy. For example, a political contest may cause several groups to unite in order to defeat a common opponent.

During the last twenty-five years, conflict theory has been influenced by a generation of neo-Marxists. These people have helped produce a more complex and sophisticated version of conflict theory that goes beyond the original emphasis on class conflict and instead shows that conflict exists within almost every aspect of society (Gouldner, 1970, 1980; Skocpol, 1979; Starr, 1982; Tilly, 1978, 1981; Wallerstein, 1974, 1979, 1980).

Theory and Practice

Sociological theory gives meaning to sociological practice. Merely assembling countless descriptions of social facts is inadequate for understanding society as a whole. Only when data are collected within the conceptual framework of a theory—in order to answer the specific questions growing out of that theory—is it possible to draw conclusions and make valid generalizations. This pursuit is the ultimate purpose of all science.

Theory without practice (research to test it) is at best poor philosophy and at worst unscientific, and practice uninformed by theory is at best trivial and at worst a tremendous waste of time and resources. Therefore, in the next chapter we shall move from theory to practice—to the methods and techniques of social research.

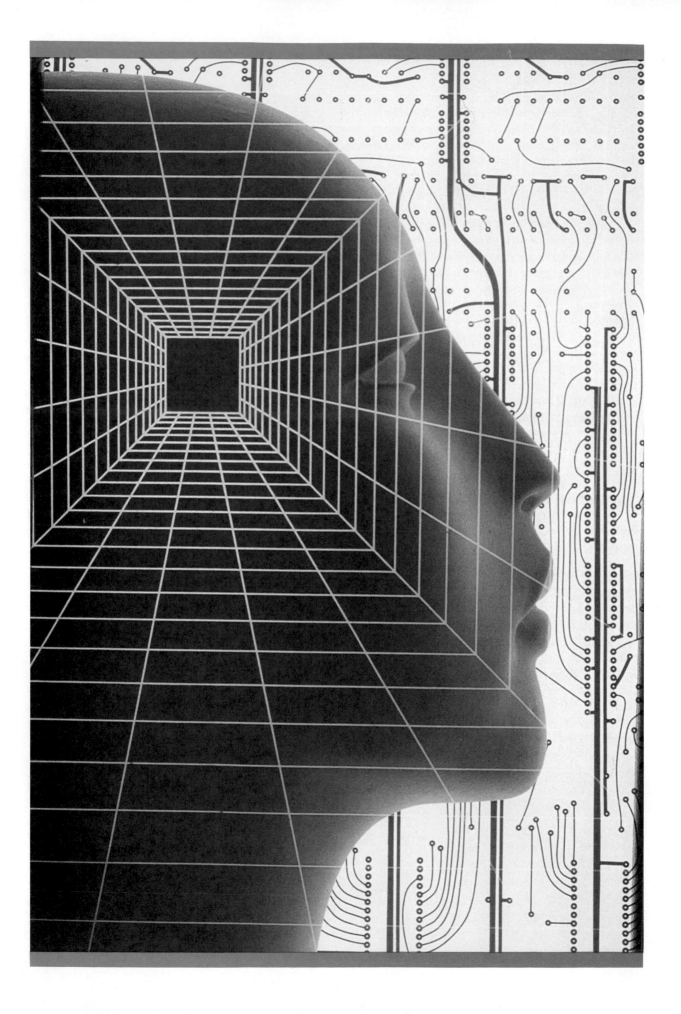

Doing Sociology: Research Methods

The Research Process
  Define the Problem
  Review Previous Research
  Develop One or More Hypotheses
  Determine the Research Design
  Define the Sample and Collect Data
  Analyze the Data and Draw
    Conclusions
  Prepare the Research Report

Objectivity in Sociological Research

Ethical Issues in Sociological Research
  Research Fraud

The Kinsey Institute for Sex Research has been investigating sexual behavior for over fifty years. The first two books published by this institute, *Sexual Behavior in the Human Male* (1948) and *Sexual Behavior in the Human Female* (1953) became nationwide best-sellers. Over the years the name Kinsey has become synonymous with sex research. So it came as little surprise when in 1990 *The Kinsey Institute New Report on Sex* was greeted with an avalanche of media attention.

The section of the book that received the most notice was a survey given to 1,974 Americans consisting of twenty questions about sexual facts and practices. In the survey, 55 percent of the respondents got at least half of the questions wrong, leading the current institute director Judith Reinisch to conclude that the public was woefully uninformed about sexual matters. However, while Alfred C. Kinsey was a Harvard trained zoology professor known for his exhaustive research on wasps who applied the same dedication to his initial research on sexual behavior, this could not be said for this survey. The way the questions were selected has raised some question as to the scientific rigor of the enterprise. Reinisch chose questions "most often asked by people who write to the Institute." Some people have suggested, however, that many of these questions were in the realm of trivia rather than essential information. For example, respondents were given twelve choices as to what percentage of American men have had extramarital affairs. Unless they answered either 30 percent or 40 percent their answer was wrong.

The "correct" answers were also the subject of debate. Reinisch compiled the information on which the answers were based from a variety of surveys, some dating back half a century and others taken by popular magazines (which rely on a self-selected sample that does not necessarily represent the population as a whole). To summarize the data, Reinisch set up a scale of the number of correct answers required to receive a grade of A, B, C, D, or F. On her scale only four percent of the people received an A or B, 14 percent received a C, 27 percent a D, and 55 percent an F. Reinisch used these results to announce that Americans were woefully misinformed about sex.

Finally, no attempt was made to submit the work for scientific review by peers before the book was published. It is only through the careful review of research methods and results by panels of experts that findings achieve validity in the scientific community.

The book contained two other sections rarely seen in any report of scientific research. The first requested people to send their names in and volunteer to be part of a future study. The other requested donations to keep the institute going.

Yet none of this stopped *Time, Newsweek, The New York Times, USA Today,* and various television talk shows from giving Reinisch and her study national attention.

What calls into question the validity of the study, and many other studies we hear about, is the failure to conduct research properly—to devise a research study that adheres to strict standards and follows those standards precisely.

As you will see in this chapter, the research process involves a number of specific steps that must be followed in order to produce a valid study. Only when this is done faithfully can we have any confidence in the results of the study. In this chapter we shall examine some of the methods used by scientists in general—and sociologists in particular—to collect data in order to test their ideas.

THE RESEARCH PROCESS

How should you conduct a research study? After reading Chapter 1, you know that you should not approach a study and draw conclusions on the basis of your personal experience and perceptions; rather, you should approach the study scientifically.

In order to approach a study scientifically, you should keep in mind that science has two main goals: (1) to describe in detail particular things or events and (2) to propose and test theories that help us understand these things or events.

There is a great deal of similarity between what a detective does in attempting to solve a crime and what a sociologist does in answering a research problem. In the course of their work, both detectives and sociologists must gather and analyze information. For detectives, the object is to identify and locate criminals and collect enough evidence to ensure their identification is correct. Sociologists, on the other hand, develop hypotheses, collect data, and develop theories to help them understand social behavior. Although their specific goals differ, both sociologists and detectives try to answer two general questions: "Why did it happen?" and "Under what circumstances is it likely to happen again?"—that is, to explain and predict.

All research problems require their own special emphasis and approach. The research procedure is usually custom tailored to the research problem. Nonetheless, there is a sequence of steps called the *research process* that is followed when designing a research project. *In short,* **the research process** *involves defining the problem, reviewing previous research on the topic, developing one or more hypotheses, determining the research design, defining the sample and collecting data, analyzing and interpreting the data, and finally preparing the research report.* The sequence of steps in this process and the typical questions asked at each step are illustrated in Table 2.1. If there are any terms in this table that you are not familiar with, do not become concerned. We will define them as we examine each of the various steps.

Define the Problem

"Love leads to marriage." Suppose you were given this statement as a subject for sociological research. How would you proceed to gather data to prove or disprove it? You must begin by defining love. This in itself would pose a serious problem, as to this day people are still grappling with the question "How do you know when you are in love?"

You could begin by defining love as "an intense emotional state in which positive feelings for another person are present." You would then have to find some way of determining whether this condition exists. You must also decide whether both people have to be in love in order for marriage to take place. You may already notice that it may be difficult to achieve the level of precision necessary for a useful research project. Once you accurately define your terms and provide details to clarify your descriptions, you can begin to test the statement we proposed.

Even after arriving at a careful definition of your terms and a detailed description of love, you may still have trouble answering the question empirically.

An **empirical question** *can be answered by observing and analyzing the world as it is known.* Examples: How many students in this class have an A average? How many millionaires are there in the

TABLE 2.1

The Research Process

Steps in the Process	Typical Questions
Define the problem	What is the purpose of the study?
	What information is needed?
	How can we operationalize the terms?
	How will the information be used?
Review previous research	What studies have already been done on this topic?
	Is additional information necessary before we begin?
	From what perspective should this issue be approached?
Develop one or more hypotheses	What are the independent and dependent variables?
	What is the relationship among the variables?
	What types of questions need to be answered?
Determine the research design	Can existing data be used?
	What is to be measured or observed?
	What research methods should be used?
Define the sample and collect data	Is there a specific population we are interested in?
	How large should the sample be?
	Who will gather the data?
	How long will it take?
Analyze the data and draw conclusions	What statistical techniques will be used?
	Have our hypotheses been proven or disproven?
	Is our information valid and reliable?
	What are the implications of our study?
Prepare the research report	Who will read the report?
	What is their level of familiarity with the subject?
	How should the report be structured?

United States? Scientists pose empirical questions in order to collect information, to add to what is already known, and to test hypotheses. To turn the statement about love into an empirical question, you must ask: How do we measure the existence of love?

In trying to define and measure love, one researcher (Rubin, 1970) used an interesting approach. He prepared a large number of self-descriptive statements that considered various aspects of loving relationships as mentioned by writers, philosophers, and social scientists. After administering these statements to a variety of subjects he was able to isolate nine items that best reflected feelings of love for another. Three of these items are cited in the following paragraph. In each sentence, the person is to fill in the blank with the name of a particular person, and indicate the degree to which the item describes the relationship.

The following statements reflect three components of love. The first is attachment-dependency: "If I were lonely, my first thought would be to seek (blank) out." The second component is caring: "If (blank) were feeling badly, my first duty would be to cheer him (her) up." The final component is intimacy: "I feel that I can confide in (blank) about

If you were doing a study of whether love leads to marriage, you would find that it would be quite difficult to define what is meant by "love."

virtually everything." These three statements show the strong aspect of mutuality in love relationships.

Using Rubin's scale you can begin to make some headway toward clarifying an important component of your research problem. In the language of science you have operationalized your definition of love. *An* **operational definition** *is a definition of an abstract concept in terms of the observable features that describe the thing being investigated.* Attachment-dependency, caring, and intimacy can be three features of an operational definition of love, and can indicate the presence of love in a research study.

Review Previous Research

Which questions are the "right" questions? Although there are no inherently correct questions, some are better suited to investigation than are others. To decide what to ask, researchers must first learn as much as possible about the subject. We would want to familiarize ourselves with as many of the previous studies on the topic as possible, particularly those closely related to what we want to do. By knowing as much as possible about previous research, we avoid duplicating a previous study and are able to build on contributions others have made to our understanding of the topic.

Develop One or More Hypotheses

Our original statement "love leads to marriage" is presented in the form of a hypothesis. *A* **hypothesis** *is a testable statement about the relationships between two or more empirical variables. A* **variable** *is anything that can change (vary).* The number of

Sociological research today often makes use of computer technology.

highway deaths on Labor Day weekends, the number of divorces that occur each year in the United States, the amount of energy the average American family consumes in the course of a year, the daily temperature in Dallas, the number of marathoners in Boston or in Knoxville, Tennessee—all these are variables. The following are not variables: the distance from Los Angeles to Las Vegas, the altitude of Denver, or the number of children who were abused in Ohio in 1991. These are fixed, unchangeable facts.

As we review the previous research on the topic of love, we find we can develop additional hypotheses which help us investigate the issue further. For example, our reading might show that a common stereotype people hold is the notion that women are more romantic than men. After all, it appears that women enjoy movies about love and romantic novels more than men.

But wait a minute. We may begin to suspect that common stereotypes may be all wrong, that they are related to traditional gender-role models. We note that in most traditional societies, the male is the breadwinner, while the female is dependent on him for economic support, status, and financial security. Therefore it would seem that when a man marries, he chooses a companion and perhaps a helpmate, while a woman chooses a companion as well as a standard of living. This leads us to hypothesize that in traditional societies men are more likely to marry for love, while women marry for economic security.

There is support for this hypothesis. One study designed a scale to measure belief in a romantic ideal in marriage. Males were more likely than females to agree with such statements as: "A person should marry whomever he loves regardless of social position," and "As long as they love one another, two people should have no difficulty getting along together in marriage." Men were more likely to disagree than women with the statement "Economic security should be carefully considered before selecting a marriage partner" (Rubin, 1973).

Additional cross-cultural research shows that romantic love is likely to be strong in societies where one member of the couple has primary responsibility for the economic well-being of the family (Rosenblatt, 1974). This evidence could lead us to hypothesize that as gender-role stereotyping declines in the United States and as more and more families come to depend on the income of both spouses, one of two things could happen. Either the importance of romantic love as a basis for marriage will begin to fade, or it will become stronger as the couple now comes together on the basis of mutual attraction, as opposed to economic considerations.

Hypotheses involve statements of causality or association. *A* **statement of causality** *says that something brings about, influences, or changes something else.* "Love between a man and a woman always produces marriage" is a statement of causality.

A **statement of association,** on the other hand, *says that changes in one thing are related to changes in another but that one does not necessarily cause the other.* Therefore, if we propose that "the greater the love relationship between a man and a woman, then the more likely it is they will marry," we are making a statement of association. We are noting a connection between love and marriage, but also that one does not necessarily cause the other.

Often hypotheses propose relationships between two different kinds of variables—a dependent variable and an independent variable. *A* **dependent variable** *changes in response to changes in the independent variable. An* **independent variable** *changes for reasons that have nothing to do with the dependent variable.* For example, we might propose the following hypothesis: Men who live in cities are more likely to marry young than are men who live in the country. In this hypothesis the independent variable is the location: Some men live in the city, some live in the country, but presumably their choice of where to live is not influenced by whether they marry young. The age of marriage is the dependent variable because it is possible that the age of marriage depends on where the men live. If research shows that the age of marriage (a dependent variable) is indeed younger among urban men than among rural men, the hypothesis probably is correct. If there is no difference in the age of marriage among urban and rural men—or if it is earlier among rural men—then the hypothesis is not supported by the data. Keep in mind that proving a hypothesis false can be scientifically useful: It eliminates unproductive avenues of thought and suggests other, more productive approaches to understanding a problem.

Even if research shows that a hypothesis is correct, it does not mean the independent variable necessarily produces or causes the dependent variable. For example, if it turns out that we can show that love leads to marriage, we still may not know why. In principle, at least, it is possible to be in love without getting married. However, we still do not know what causes people to take the next step.

Determine the Research Design

Once we have developed our hypotheses, we must design a project in which they can be tested. This is a difficult task which frequently causes researchers a great deal of trouble. If a research design is faulty,

it may be impossible to conclude whether the hypotheses are true or false, and the whole project will have been a waste of time, resources, and effort.

A research design must provide for the collection of all necessary and sufficient data to test the stated hypotheses. The important word here is "test." The researcher must not try to prove a point; rather, the goal is to test the validity of the hypotheses.

Although it is important to gather as much information as needed, research designs must guard against the collection of unnecessary information, which can lead to a waste of time and money.

When we design our research project we must also decide which of several research approaches to use. There are three main methods of research used by sociologists: surveys, participant observation, and experiments. Each has advantages and limitations. Therefore, the choice of methods depends on the questions the researcher hopes to answer.

SURVEYS   *A* **survey** *is a research method in which a population, or a portion thereof, is questioned in order to reveal specific facts about itself.* Surveys are used to discover the distribution and interrelationship of certain variables among large numbers of people.

The largest survey in the United States takes place every 10 years when the government takes its census. The U.S. Constitution requires this census in order to determine the apportionment of members

In an open-ended interview the investigator asks a list of questions, but is free to vary them or even to make up new questions on topics that take on importance during the course of the interview.

to the House of Representatives. In theory, at least, a representative of every family and every unmarried adult responds to a series of questions about his or her circumstances.

From these answers it is possible to construct a picture of the social and economic facts that characterize the American public at one point in time. *Such a study, which cuts across a population at a given time, is called a* **cross-sectional study.** Surveys, by their nature, usually are cross-sectional. If the same population is surveyed two or more times at certain intervals, a comparison of cross-sectional research can give a picture of changes in variables over time. *Research that investigates a population over a period of time is called* **longitudinal research.**

Survey research usually deals with large numbers of subjects in a relatively short time. One of the shortcomings resulting from this method is that investigators are not able to capture the full richness of feelings, attitudes, and motives underlying people's responses. Some surveys are designed to gather this kind of information through interviewing. *An* **interview** *consists of a conversation between two (or occasionally more) individuals in which one party attempts to gain information from the other(s) by asking a series of questions.*

It would, of course, be ideal to gather exactly the same kinds of information from each research subject. One way researchers attempt to achieve this is through interviews in which all questions are carefully worked out to get at precisely the information wanted (What is your income? How many years of schooling have you had?). Sometimes subjects are forced to choose among a limited number of responses to the questions (as in multiple-choice tests). This process results in very uniform data easily subjected to statistical analysis.

A research interview entirely predetermined by a questionnaire (or so-called interview schedule) that is followed rigidly is called a **structured interview.** Structured interviews tend to produce uniform or replicable data that can be elicited time after time by different interviewers.

The use of this method, however, may also allow useful information to slip into "cracks" between the predetermined questions. For example, a questionnaire being administered to married individuals might ask about their age, family background, and what role love played in their reasons for getting married. If, however, we do not ask about social class or ethnicity we may not find out that these characteristics are very important for our study. If such questions were not built into the questionnaire from the beginning, it is impossible to recover this "lost" information later in the process when its importance may become apparent.

One technique that can prevent this kind of information loss is the **semistructured,** *or* **open-ended interview** *in which the investigator asks a list of questions but is free to vary them or even to make up new questions on topics that take on importance in the course of the interview.* This means that each interview will cover those topics important to the research project but, in addition, will yield additional data somewhat different for each subject. Analyzing such diverse and complex data is difficult, but the results are often rewarding.

Interviewing, although it may produce valuable information, is a complex, time-consuming art. Some research studies try to get similar information by distributing questionnaires directly to the subjects and asking them to complete and return them. This is the way the federal government obtains much of its census data. Although it is perhaps the least expensive way of doing social research, it is often difficult to assess the quality of data obtained in this manner. For example, people may not answer honestly or seriously for a variety of reasons: They may not understand the questions, they may fear the information will be used against them, and so on. But even data gained from personal interviews may be unreliable. In one study, student interviewers were embarrassed to ask preassigned questions on sexual habits, so they left these questions out of the interviews and filled the answers in themselves afterward. In another study, follow-up research found subjects had consistently lied to interviewers.

PARTICIPANT OBSERVATION Researchers entering into a group's activities and observing the group members are engaged in **participant observation.** Unlike the usual practice in survey research, participant observers do not try to make sure they are studying a carefully chosen sample. Rather, they attempt to get to know all members of the group being studied to whatever degree possible.

This research method is generally used to study relatively small groups over an extended period of time. The goal is to obtain a detailed portrait of the group's day-to-day activities, to observe individual and group behavior, and to interview selected informants. Participant observation depends for its success on the relationship that develops between the researchers and research subjects. The closer and more trusting the relationship, the more information will be revealed to the researcher—especially the kind of personal information often crucial for successful research.

One of the first and most famous studies em-

In participant observation the researcher tries to personally know as many members of the group in question as possible.

ploying the technique of participant observation was a study of Cornerville, a lower-class Italian neighborhood in Boston. William Foote Whyte moved into the neighborhood and lived for three years with an Italian family. He published his results in a book called *Street Corner Society* (1943). All the information for the book came from his field notes, which described the behavior and attitudes of the people whom he came to know.

Several years after Whyte's study, Herbert Gans conducted a participant observation study, published as *The Urban Villagers* (1962), of another Italian neighborhood in Boston. The picture Gans drew of the West End was broader than Whyte's study of Cornerville. Gans included descriptions of the family, work experience, education, medical care, relationships with social workers, and other aspects of life in the West End. Although he covered a wider range of activities than Whyte, his observations were not as detailed.

On rare occasions, participant observers hide their identities while doing research and join groups under false pretenses. Leon Festinger and his students hid their identities when they studied a religious group preaching the end of the world and the arrival of flying saucers to save the righteous (Festinger, Riecken, and Schacter, 1956). However, most sociologists consider this deception unethical. They believe it is better for participant observers to be honest about their intentions and work together

with their subjects to create a mutually satisfactory situation. By declaring their positions at the outset, sociologists can then ask appropriate questions, take notes, and carry out research tasks without fear of detection.

Participant observation is a highly subjective research approach. In fact, some scholars reject it outright because the results often cannot be duplicated by another researcher. This method, however, has the benefit of revealing the social life of a group in far more depth and detail than surveys or interviews alone. The participant observer who is able to establish good rapport with the subjects is likely to uncover information that would never be revealed to a survey taker.

The participant observer is in a difficult position, however. He or she will be torn between the need to become trusted (therefore emotionally involved in the group's life), and the need to remain a somewhat detached observer striving for scientific objectivity.

EXPERIMENTS The most precise research method available to sociologists is the controlled **experiment**, *an investigation in which the variables being studied are controlled and the researcher obtains the results through precise observation and measurement.*

Because of their precision, experiments are an attractive means of doing research. Experiments have been used to study patterns of interaction in small groups under a variety of conditions such as stress, fatigue, or limited access to information.

Although experimentation is appropriate for small-group research, most of the issues that interest sociologists cannot be investigated in totally controlled situations. Social events usually cannot be studied in controlled experiments because they simply cannot be controlled. For these reasons experiments remain the least used research method in sociology.

Define the Sample and Collect Data

After determining how the needed information will be collected, the researchers must decide what group will be observed or questioned. Depending on the study, this group might be college students, Texans, or baseball players. *The particular subset of the population chosen for study is known as a* **sample.**

Sampling *is a research technique through which investigators study a manageable number of people, known as the sample, selected from a larger population or group.* If the procedures are carried out correctly, the sample can be called a **representative sample,** or *one that shows, in equivalent proportion, the significant variables that characterize the population as a whole.* In other words, the sample will be representative of the larger population, and the findings from the research will tell us something about the larger group. *The failure to achieve a representative sample is called* **sampling error.**

Suppose you wanted to sample the attitudes of the American public on some issue such as military spending or federal aid for abortions. You could not limit your sample to only New Yorkers or Republicans or Catholics or blacks or home owners. These groups do not represent the nation as a whole, and any findings you came up with would contain a sampling error.

How do researchers make sure their samples are representative? The basic technique is to use a **random sample**—*to select subjects so that each individual in the population has an equal chance of being chosen.* For example, if we wanted a random sample of all college students in the United States, we might choose every fifth or tenth or hundredth person from a comprehensive list of all college students registered in this country. Or we might assign each student a number and have a computer pick a sample randomly. However, there is a possibility that simply by chance, a small segment of the total college student population would fail to be represented adequately. This might happen with Native American students, for instance, who make

These elderly people are enjoying themselves in Florida. Would they be considered representative of the elderly in the United States as a whole? Why or why not?

up less than one percent of college students in America. For some research purposes this might not matter, but if ethnicity is an important aspect of the research, it would be important to make sure Native American students were included.

The method used to prevent certain groups from being under- or over-represented in a sample is to choose a **stratified random sample.** With this technique the population being studied is first divided into two or more groups (or strata) such as age, sex, or ethnicity. A simple random sample is then taken within each group. Finally, the subsamples are combined (in proportion to their numbers in the population) to form a total sample. In our example of college students, the researcher would identify all ethnic groups represented among college students in America. Then the researchers would calculate the proportion of the total number of college students represented by each group and draw a random sample separately from each ethnic group. The number chosen from each group should be proportional to its representation in the entire college student population. The sample would still be random, but it would be stratified for ethnicity.

In order for a study to be accurate it is crucial that a sample be chosen with care. The most famous example of sampling error occurred in 1936, when *Literary Digest* magazine incorrectly predicted that Alfred E. Landon would win the presidential election. Using telephone directories and automobile registration lists to recruit subjects, *Literary Digest* pollsters sent out more than 10 million straw vote ballots and received 2.3 million completed responses. The survey gave the Republican candidate Landon 55 percent of the vote and Roosevelt only 41 percent (the remaining four percent went to a third candidate). Based on this poll the *Digest* confidently predicted Landon's victory. Instead Alfred E. Landon has become known as the candidate who was buried in a landslide vote for Franklin D. Roosevelt (Squire, 1988).

How could this happen? Two major flaws in the sample accounted for the mistake. First, although the *Literary Digest* sample was large, it was not representative of the nation's voting population because it contained a major sampling error. During the Depression years, only the well-to-do could afford telephones and automobiles, and these people were likely to vote Republican.

The second problem with the study was the response rate. Interestingly, of those who claimed to have received a *Literary Digest* ballot, 55 percent claimed they would have voted for Roosevelt and 44 percent for Landon. If these people had actually voted in the poll, the *Digest* would have predicted the correct winner. As it turned out there was a low response rate, and those who did respond were generally better-educated, wealthier people who tended to be Landon supporters (Squire, 1988).

The outcome of the election was not entirely a surprise to everyone. A young pollster named George Gallup forecasted the results accurately. He realized that the majority of Americans supported the New Deal policies proposed by the Democrats. Gallup's

sample was much smaller, but far more representative of the American public than that of the *Literary Digest*. This points out that the representativeness of the sample is more important than its size.

There are many other more recent examples of surveys using unrepresentative samples. *USA Today* published the results of a survey that reported that 39 percent of women with a college degree were earning more than $30,000 a year. This information was obtained from a subscriber survey done by *Working Woman* magazine. This subscriber survey is not representative of American women, however, and the information is incorrect. According to the Census Bureau only 7 percent of women with college degrees earn over $30,000 a year (American Demographics, February, 1986).

Just as misleading was a survey that columnist Ann Landers conducted. She asked her readers if their sex lives had gone downhill after marriage. "The verdict was clear," noted Landers. "Eighty-two percent said sex after marriage was less exciting."

Lending the illusion of accuracy to this survey was the fact that 141,000 readers from all 50 states, including every Canadian province, Asia, and Europe responded to the survey. Yet despite this large response, the fact that no attempt was made to make the sample representative, or to ask the questions in an unbiased fashion, makes the information useless and irrelevant for providing any real understanding of sex after marriage.

Landers noted: "I found the results of the survey disturbing. These people are saying more than they

Harry Truman is enjoying the 1948 election headline that erroneously announced his defeat.

realize . . . They are talking about the state of their marriage." (Editor and Publisher, February 4, 1989). What is really disturbing, however, is that Ann Landers is presenting herself as a researcher and interpreter of information about the family, and that this survey which has little, if any, real value is taken seriously by large numbers of people.

RESEARCHER BIAS One of the most serious problems in data collection is **researcher bias,** *the tendency for researchers to select data that support, and to ignore data that seem to go against, their hypotheses.* We see this quite often in mass media publications. They may structure their study to produce the results they wish to obtain, or they may only publicize information that supports their viewpoint.

Researcher bias often takes the form of a self-fulfilling prophecy. A researcher who is strongly inclined toward one point of view may communicate that attitude through questions and reactions in such a way that the subject fulfills the researcher's expectations. Most often this phenomenon is seen in the classroom where a teacher, treating a child as an intellectual inferior, elicits from that child behavior that conforms to the teacher's view (Rosenthal and Jacobson, 1966). Researchers in sociology can also fall into this trap and pull the subjects in with them. For example, a researcher who is trying to prove an association between poverty and antisocial behavior might question low-income subjects in a way that would indicate a low regard for their social attitudes. The subjects, perceiving the researcher's bias, might react with hostility and thus fulfill the researcher's expectations.

Sociologist Lenore Weitzman may have displayed researcher bias in her book *The Divorce Revolution* (1985). Weitzman theorized that changes in divorce laws resulting in an increase of no-fault divorces had resulted in the systematic impoverishment of divorced women and children. Weitzman argued that men usually make more money than women and that in divorce women usually get the children; therefore, treating men and women equally in divorce cheats the wife and children. This argument seems reasonable, and Weitzman presented statistics to prove it. She noted that on the average divorced women experience a 73 percent decline in their standard of living in the first year of divorce while divorced men experience a 42 percent rise in their standard of living.

Greg Duncan and Saul Hoffman (1988), two researchers who had been tracking the effect of divorce on income for two decades, found the changes following divorce nowhere near as dramatic as Weitzman described. They found only a 30 percent decline in women's living standards and a ten–fifteen percent improvement in men's living standards. In addition, five years after divorce, the average woman's living standard was actually higher, mainly because many of them had remarried.

What baffled Duncan and Hoffman most was that Weitzman had used their methods to arrive at her numbers. They were not able to duplicate her findings and noted as much. A Census Bureau study eventually confirmed Duncan and Hoffman's study (Bianchi, 1991).

The problem with Weitzman's data may have been that her sample was small—228 divorced men and women all taken from the Los Angeles County divorce court. In this way it was not representative of the whole country. In addition a good deal of the subjects' financial information came from their personal recollections, a notoriously unreliable source of research data (Falaudi, 1991).

One of the standard means for dealing with research bias is to use **blind investigators,** *or investigators who do not know whether a specific subject belongs to the group of actual cases being investigated or to a comparison group.* For example, in a study on the causes of child abuse, the investigator looking at the children's family background would not be told which children had been abused and which were in the non-abused comparison group. Sometimes double–blind investigators are used. **Double–blind investigators** *are kept uninformed not only of the kinds of subjects (case subjects or comparison group subjects) they are studying but also of the hypotheses being tested.* This eliminates any tendency on their part to find cases that support—or disprove—the research hypothesis.

Analyze the Data and Draw Conclusions

In its most basic sense, **analysis** *is the process through which large and complicated collections of scientific data are organized so that comparisons can be made and conclusions drawn.* It is not unusual for a sociological research project to result in hundreds of thousands of individual pieces of information. By itself this vast array of data has no particular meaning. The analyst must find ways to organize such data into useful categories so that the relationships that exist can be determined. In this way the hypotheses forming the core of the research can be tested, and new hypotheses can be formulated for further investigation. (One important device to aid in the analysis of data is the table, which is explained in the box "How to Read a Table.")

Sociologists often summarize their data by calculating central tendencies or averages. Actually, there are three different types of averages used by sociologists: the mean, the median, and the mode. Each type is calculated differently, and each can result in a different figure. Suppose you are studying a group of ten college students whose verbal SAT scores are as follows:

| 450 | 690 | 280 | 450 | 760 |
| 540 | 520 | 450 | 430 | 530 |

Although you can report the information in this form, a more meaningful presentation would give some indication of the *central tendency* of the 10 SAT scores. There are three measures of central tendency: the mean, median, and mode.

The *mean* is what is commonly called the *average*. To calculate the mean, you add up all the figures and divide by the number of items. In our example the SAT scores add up to 5,100. Dividing by 10 gives a mean of 510.

The *median* is the figure that falls midway in a series of numbers—there are as many numbers above it as below it. Because we have 10 scores—an even number—in our example, the median is the mean (the average) of the fifth and sixth figures, the two numbers in the middle. To calculate the median, rearrange the data in order from the lowest to highest (or vice versa). In our example you would list the scores as follows: 280, 430, 450, 450, 450, 520, 530, 540, 690, 760. The median is 485—midway between the fifth score (450) and the sixth score (520).

The *mode* is the number that occurs most often in the data. In our example the mode is 450.

The three different measures are used for different reasons, and each has its advantages and disadvantages. The mean is most useful when a narrow range of figures exists, as it has the advantage of including all the data. It can be misleading, however, when one or two scores are much higher or lower than the rest. The median deals with this problem by not allowing extreme figures to distort the central tendency. The mode enables researchers to show which number occurs most often. Its disadvantage is that it does not give any idea of the entire range of data. Realizing the problems inherent in each average, sociologists often state the central tendency in more than one form.

Scientists usually are careful in drawing conclusions from their research. One of the purposes of drawing conclusions from data compiled in the course of research is the ability to apply the information gathered to other, similar situations. Problems thus may develop if there are faults in the research

design. For example, the study must show **validity**—that is, *the study must actually test what it was intended to test.* If you want to say one event is the cause of another, you must be able to rule out other explanations to show that your research is valid. Suppose you conclude that marijuana use leads to heroin use. You must show that it is marijuana use and not some other factor, such as peer pressure or emotional problems, that leads to heroin use.

The study must also demonstrate **reliability**—that is, *the findings of the study must be repeatable.* To demonstrate reliability we must show that research can be replicated—repeated for the purpose of determining whether initial results can be duplicated. Suppose you conclude from a study that whites living in racially integrated housing projects, who have contact with blacks in the same projects, have more favorable attitudes toward blacks than do whites living in racially segregated housing projects. If you or other researchers carry out the same study in housing projects in various cities throughout the country and get the same results, the study is reliable.

It is highly unlikely that any single piece of research will provide all the answers to a given question. In fact, good research frequently leads to the discovery of unanticipated information requiring further research. One of the pleasures of research is that ongoing studies keep opening up new perspectives and posing further questions.

Prepare the Research Report

Research that goes unreported is wasted. Scientific progress is made through the accumulation of research that tests hypotheses and contributes to the ongoing process of bettering our understanding of the world. Therefore, it is usual for agencies that fund research to insist that scientists agree to share their findings.

Scientists generally publish their findings in technical journals. If the information is relevant to the public, many popular and semiscientific publications will report these findings as well. It is especially important that research in sociology and other social sciences be made available to the public, because much of this research has a bearing on social issues and public policies.

Unfortunately, the general public is not always cautious in interpreting research findings. Special interest groups, politicians, and others who have a cause to plead are often too quick to generalize from specific research results, frequently distorting them beyond recognition. This happens most often when the research focuses on something of national

TAKING THE SOCIOLOGICAL PERSPECTIVE

How to Read a Table

Statistical tables are used frequently by sociologists both to present the findings of their own research and to study the data of others. We will use the accompanying table to outline the steps to follow in reading and interpreting a table.

1. *Read the title.* The title tells you the subject of the table. This table presents data on life expectancy at birth in various countries.

2. *Check the source.* At the bottom of a table you will find its source. In this case the source is the *Statistical Abstract of the United States: 1991.* Knowing the source of a table can help you decide whether the information it contains is reliable. It also tells you where to look to find the original data and how recent the information is. In our example the source is both reliable and recent. If the source were the 1958 *Abstract,* it would be of limited value in telling you about life expec-

TABLE 2.2

Life Expectancy at Birth for Selected Countries

Country	Expectation of Life at Birth, 1990
Angola	43.8
Burma	54.5
Canada	77.3
Ghana	54.2
India	57.7
Japan	79.3
Kenya	64.5
Poland	72.5
*Soviet Union	69.5
Syria	68.9
United States	75.6

*Data collected prior to the break up of the Soviet Union. Present-day nations represented by this data include the Commonwealth of Independent States, the Baltic States (Estonia, Latvia, and Lithuania), and Georgia.

Source: Statistical Abstract of the United States: 1991. 111th ed. Washington, DC, 1991, pp. 834–35.

tancy in those countries today. Improvements in health care, control of epidemic diseases, or national birth-control programs all are factors that may have altered life expectancy drastically in several countries since 1958. Likewise, consider a table of data about the standard of living of black people in South Africa. If its source were an agency of the South African government (which might be trying to "prove" how well-off blacks are in that country), you might well be

or emotional concern. It is therefore important to double check reports of sociological research appearing in popular magazines with the original research.

OBJECTIVITY IN SOCIOLOGICAL RESEARCH

Max Weber believed that the social scientist should describe and explain what *is,* rather than prescribe what should be. His goal was a value-free approach to sociology. More and more sociologists today, however, are admitting that completely value-free

research may not be possible. In fact, one of the trends in sociology today that could ultimately harm the discipline is that some sociologists who are more interested in social reform than social research have abandoned all claims to objectivity.

Sociology, like any other science, is molded by factors that impose values on research. Gunnar Myrdal (1969) lists three such influential factors: (1) the scientific tradition within which the scientist is educated, (2) the cultural, social, economic, and political environment within which the scientist is trained and engages in research, and (3) the scientist's own temperament, inclinations, interests, concerns, and experiences. These factors are especially skeptical about the reliability of the information in the table.

3. *Look for headnotes.* Many tables contain headnotes directly below the title. These may explain how the data were collected, why certain variables (and not others) were studied, why the data are presented in a particular way, whether some data were collected at different times, and so on. In our table on life expectancy the headnote explains that the numbers in the table refer to the average number of additional years a person can expect to live at birth.

4. *Look for footnotes.* Many tables contain footnotes that explain limitations or unusual circumstances surrounding certain data. For example, in this table, the footnote explains that the data for life expectancies in the Soviet Union was collected *before* the 1991 break-up of that republic into several independent nations.

5. *Read the labels or headings for each row and column.* The labels will tell you exactly what information is contained in the table. It is essential that you understand the labels—both the row headings on the left and the column heading at the top. Here the row headings tell you the names of the countries being compared for life expectancy. For each group, life expectancy is given. Note the units being used in the table. In this case the units are years. Often the figures represent percentages or rates. Many population and crime statistics are given in rates per 100,000 people.

6. *Examine the data.* Suppose you want to find the life expectancy of a newborn baby in the United States. First look down the row at the left until you come to "United States." Then look across the columns until you come to a number. Reading across you discover that on average, a newborn baby in the United States can expect to live another 75.6 years.

7. *Compare the data.* Compare the data in the table both horizontally and vertically. Suppose you want to find in which country people can expect to live longest from birth. Looking down the life expectancy column we find that people born in Japan can expect to live longest—79.3 years. Among these eleven nations life expectancies of people born in the United States ranks third behind Japan and Canada. A person born in Angola has the shortest life expectancy—only 43.8 years.

8. *Draw conclusions.* Draw conclusions about the information in the table. After examining the data in the table, you might conclude that a person born in a relatively developed country (Canada, Japan, Poland, United States) is likely to live much longer than someone born in a poorer nation (Angola, Burma, Ghana, India, Kenya).

9. *Pose new questions.* The conclusions you reach might lead to new questions that could prompt further research. Why, you might want to know, do people in Angola have shorter life expectancies than people in the U.S.? What causes the gap in life expectancy between the rich and poor nations?

strong in sociological research because the researcher usually is part of the society being studied.

Does this mean that all science—sociology in particular—is hopelessly subjective? Is objectivity in sociological research an impossible goal? There are no simple answers to these questions. The best sociologists can do is strive to become aware of the ways in which these factors influence them and to make such biases explicit when sharing the results of their research. We may think of this as disciplined, or "objective," subjectivity, and it is a reasonable goal for sociological research.

Another problem of bias in sociological research relates to the people being studied rather than to the researchers themselves. The mere presence of investigators or researchers may distort the situation and produce unusual reactions from subjects who now feel special because of their selection for study.

ETHICAL ISSUES IN SOCIOLOGICAL RESEARCH

All research projects raise fundamental questions. Whose interests are served by the research? Who will benefit from it? How might people be hurt? To what degree do subjects have the right to be told

Do Early Calls of Election Results Influence Voter Behavior

It is 6 P.M. in California and 9 P.M. in New York on the first Tuesday in November in 1996—election day with the office of the president of the United States up for grabs. As the polls close in each state, the three major networks and the Cable News Network project the winner of the presidential race. Within a short time—minutes at most—it becomes clear to voters on the West Coast that the race has been decided—that one candidate has enough electoral votes to be the next president. Trouble is, millions of West Coast voters have not yet gone to the polls. Although polls have closed in New York, Boston, Miami, and Hartford, closing time in Los Angeles, Portland, Tacoma, and San Diego is three hours away. On the basis of network news projections, millions of people who might have voted for the president do not bother because they already know who won.

Are these early calls of election results fair in a society that gives nearly every adult an equal voice at the polls? As you will see, opinions are divided, although the law is clear: Networks have the right to make projections as polls close in each state—even in national races where projections are made before polls close in the West. "That's how we elect a president—by going across the electoral college," said Mary Klette, Director of Election Unit Operations at NBC. "There are no restrictions in place on the federal or state level to prevent networks from making these projections on a state-by-state basis. If there were, these laws would violate the constitutional right to freedom of the press" (Interview with Klette, June 23, 1988).

When the state of Washington passed a law preventing the press from conducting exit polls, which ask people for whom they voted as they leave the voting place, the law was overturned as a violation of this basic freedom. In 1985, the networks signed a pledge to avoid "projections, characterizations, or any other uses of exit polling data that would indicate the winner of the election before polls in a given state were closed." Although this agreement went a long way toward minimizing the influence network projections have on voter behavior, it still did not solve

about the research design, its purposes, and possible applications? Who should have access to and control over research data after a study is completed—the agency that funded the study, the scientists, the subjects? Should research subjects have the right to participate in the planning of projects? Is it ethical to manipulate people without their knowledge in order to control research variables? To what degree do researchers owe it to their subjects not to invade their privacy and to keep secret (and, therefore, not report anywhere) things that were told in strict confidence? What obligations do researchers have to the society in which they are working? What commitments do researchers have in supporting or subverting a political order? Should researchers report to legal authorities any illegal behavior discovered in the course of their investigations? Is it ethical to expose subjects to such risk by asking them to participate in a study?

In the 1960s the federal government began to prescribe regulations for "the protection of human subjects." These regulations are designed to force scientists to consider one central issue: how to judge and balance the intellectual and societal benefits of scientific research against the actual or possible physical and emotional costs of the people being studied. This issue creates three potential dilemmas for the researcher.

The first situation concerns the degree of permissible risk, pain, or harm. Suppose a study that temporarily induces severe emotional distress promises significant benefits. The researcher may justify the study. However, we may wonder whether the benefits will be realized or whether they justify the potential dangers to the subjects, even if the volunteers know what to expect and all possible protective measures have been taken.

A second dilemma is the extent to which subjects should be deceived in a study. It is now necessary for researchers to obtain, in writing, the "informed consent" of the people they study. Questions still arise, however, about whether subjects are informed about the true nature of the study and whether, once informed, they can freely decline to participate.

the problem faced by West Coast voters in a presidential election year.

The main argument against early calls of election based on polling data is that the calls will discourage voters from showing up at the polls; it is human nature not to bother to vote if you already know who won. But the effect may be limited. According to Seymour Sudman, professor of marketing at the University of Illinois, studies have shown that "the only time the exit polls can have an effect is when they change voters' perceptions about the closeness of the race."

Exit polls, in particular, are subject to error and manipulation. Many voters lie to the pollsters or refuse to answer pollsters' questions, thus limiting the size of the sample. Or political hacks may try to stack the deck by finding out where the poll is being conducted, hiring people to go in and out of voting places without actually voting, and then telling the pollster that they voted for a particular candidate. Realizing the possibility of this type of manipulation, many polling organizations do not base their calls on exit polls, but rely instead on projections, which are based on votes actually cast as the count is tabulated in different precincts throughout a state. Unlike exit polls, projections have nothing to do with what voters tell the pollsters.

Freedom of the press aside, the arguments against the restraint of early election calls are substantial. Burns W. Roper, chairman of The Roper Organization, makes these points:

"I have never seen any convincing evidence that demonstrates that an early call here affects the outcome of an election there. Moreover, logic . . . argues against the thesis that an early call will change the outcome. If in 1980 you were for Ronald Reagan and I was for Jimmy Carter and we both heard early calls before we went to the polls, it seems to me the effect on us would be equal. You might be tempted not to vote because it is now clear that Ronald Reagan no longer needs your vote. I might be tempted not to vote because it is now clear my vote for Carter can't help him."

To deal with the public perception that West Coast voters are being cheated of their right to participate fully in the election of the president, legislation has been proposed for a uniform poll closing time throughout the country. That is, if the polls close at 9 P.M. in California, they would close at 6 P.M. in New York. Meanwhile, voters can take some comfort in knowing that there is little solid research on exactly what the effect of early calls is.

Sources: Seymour Sudman, "Do Exit Polls Influence Voting Behavior?" *Public Opinion Quarterly*, Spring 1985, pp. 332–33; Burns W. Roper, "Early Election Calls: The Larger Dangers." *Public Opinion Quarterly*, Spring 1985, pp. 5–6.

A third problem in research studies concerns the disclosure of confidential or personally harmful information. Is the researcher entitled to delve into personal lives? What if the researcher uncovers some information that should be brought to the attention of the authorities? Should confidential information be included in a published study (Gans, 1979)?

Every sociologist must grapple with these questions and find answers that apply to particular situations. However, two general points are worth noting. The first is that social research rarely benefits the research subject directly. Benefits to subjects tend to be indirect and delayed by many years—as when new government policies are developed to correct problems discovered by researchers. Second, most subjects of sociological research belong to groups with little or no power. It is hardly an accident that poor people are the most studied, rich people the least. Therefore, research subjects typically have little control over how research findings are used, even though such applications may affect them greatly. This means that sociologists must accept responsibility for the fact that they have recruited research subjects who may be made vulnerable as a result of their cooperation. It is important that researchers establish safeguards limiting the use of their findings, protecting the anonymity of their data, and honoring all commitments to confidentiality made in the course of their research.

The ideal relationship between scientist and research participant is characterized by openness and honesty. Deliberately lying in order to manipulate the participant's perceptions and actions goes directly against this ideal. Yet often researchers must choose between deception and abandoning the research. With few, if any, exceptions, social scientists regard deception of research participants as a questionable practice to be avoided if at all possible. It diminishes the respect due to others and violates the expectations of mutual trust upon which organized society is based. When the deceiver is a respected scientist, it may have the undesirable effect of modeling deceit as an acceptable practice. Conceivably, it may contribute to the growing climate of cynicism and mistrust bred by widespread use of deception by important public figures.

Research Fraud

The history of science is replete with examples of frauds. Some of these were quickly discovered and forgotten, but others have damaged the reputations of individuals or even entire fields of study. Perhaps the hoax that has had the most devastating consequences for the social sciences was the IQ fraud perpetrated by the British psychologist Sir Cyril Burt.

Over a period of 60 years, beginning in 1912, Burt published a great many books and articles "proving" that intelligence is largely inherited. The basis of this so-called proof was his analysis and comparison of some 53 pairs of identical twins who had been orphaned and raised apart.

Though Burt's work was attacked by sociologists, anthropologists, and geneticists, he was defended by his fellow psychologists, and in 1946 was knighted for his service to British education. When he died in 1971, at the age of 88, colleagues called him "a born nobleman" and "a man of Renaissance proportions." The *London Times* eulogized him, stating: "For over forty years he had been the leading figure in . . . the application of psychology to education and the development of children, and to the assessment of mental qualities."

In 1969, when Arthur Jensen published an article in the *Harvard Educational Review* in which he implied that blacks are innately less intelligent than whites, he acknowledged his great debt to Burt by citing 10 of Burt's studies. It now is known that all 10 studies were fraudulent. Apparently Burt was so convinced that intelligence was determined by a person's genetic endowment and that upper-class Britons were the most generously endowed of all that he simply invented the existence of pairs of twins raised in different environments to prove his point.

Burt's prestige was so great that it was not until five years after his death that accusations of fraud were raised publicly. It was then discovered that no one except Burt's colleague, a Ms. Conway, had ever seen any of the twins who figured in Burt's studies. After an investigation it turned out that Ms. Conway, in fact, never existed.

Why Burt—a man of undoubted intelligence and ability—spent a lifetime deliberately publishing fraudulent studies is a question to which no one really knows the answer. Whatever the reason, the fraud Burt perpetrated has had an incalculably negative impact on thousands, perhaps even millions, of young children. In Britain, Burt's research was used to develop a national education policy that "tracked" youngsters from a very early age and systematically excluded many of them from obtaining the necessary skills that would lead them up the social and economic ladder. In the United States, Burt's studies were cited over and over again as a justification for shifting federal funds away from day care and Head Start programs. Many programs were closed down, and thousands of children were deprived of what might have been enriching educational experiences.

It is useful for human beings to seek to understand themselves and the social world in which they

The research fraud that Sir Cyril Burt perpetrated had an incalculably negative impact on thousands of children by influencing the shifting away of federal funds from Head Start programs.

live. Sociology has a great contribution to make to this endeavor, both in promoting understanding for its own sake and in providing social planners with scientific information with which well-founded decisions can be made and sound plans for future development adopted. However, sociologists must also shoulder the burden of self-reflection—of seeking to understand the role they play in contemporary social processes while at the same time assessing how these social processes affect their findings (Gouldner, 1970).

PART

II

THE INDIVIDUAL IN SOCIETY

CHAPTER 3   *Culture*

CHAPTER 4   *Socialization and Development*

CHAPTER 5   *Social Interaction and Social Groups*

CHAPTER 6   *Deviant Behavior and Social Control*

Now that you've seen how sociologists study society, it's time to develop your sociological imagination by applying the sociological perspective to the analysis of human behavior in groups. It seems appropriate to begin by asking "What makes us human?" That is, what makes us different from other animal species, and what makes human society unique? Chapter 3 provides the answer: culture. Culture, you will see, is a system of meaning that humans impose on the world because we generally lack instinctual programming of our social behavior. Thus humans are compelled to create themselves and their societies in a symbolic, interpreted fashion. You will discover that it is this very symbolic nature of humans that permits societies to vary so dramatically from one another in their basic beliefs and social practices. Moreover, even within a single society a variety of different ideas, outlooks, and practices may be found. Yet, despite the enormous variation among human cultures, you will find that they all seem to have certain forms and categories in common.

But how do individuals develop and learn to use their symbolic capacities? The answer is through the process of socialization, which you will explore in Chapter 4. Here you will discover that each human being is a complex mixture of nature, or biological heritage, and nurture, or the entire social-ization experience. You will explore the common mechanisms by which each human develops a unique personality and social identity. In Chapter 4 you will encounter some of the major theories about how and why children develop as they do. You will also find out how socialization continues to play a role throughout our lives.

Assuming that individuals have developed the skills through the socialization process, how do humans interact with one another? Are there rules that guide our behavior? How do these rules differ in different situations? How does the context of the interaction (for example, size, setting, level of intimacy) affect the nature, quality, and dynamics of interaction? These issues are explored in Chapter 5 where you will investigate the various types of elements of human interaction. You will also examine the dynamics of human behavior in groups—groups that range from two people, to large formal associations, to impersonal bureaucracies, to social institutions like the family, the economy, or the political system.

Social interaction is not random; it is clearly organized. But how is that organization achieved? How are the rules for social interaction enforced? And what happens when individuals violate social expectations? This is the topic of deviant behavior and social control, which you will explore in Chapter 6. Here you will discover that what is appropriate and inappropriate behavior is socially defined in each society and subculture and, perhaps somewhat surprisingly, that deviant behavior, or a violation of social expectations, is not only inevitable, but also useful and even necessary in society. You will examine the leading sociological theories for deviant behavior and critically scrutinize the formal system for dealing with deviance in the United States: our system of law and criminal justice.

When you have completed this section of the book, you should have a solid understanding of what it means to be human in society, how humans construct and alter each other's behavior in various contexts, and how deviant behavior is defined and dealt with. You will then be ready to move on to an investigation of the structural factors—which are often beyond individual control—that shape the context of human life and social interaction.

CHAPTER
▪ 3 ▪
Culture

The Concept of Culture
Culture and Biology
Culture Shock
Ethnocentrism and Cultural Relativism

Components of Culture
Material Culture
Normative Culture
Cognitive Culture
Language and Culture

The Symbolic Nature of Culture
Signs, Symbols, and Culture

Culture and Adaptation
Human Evolution: Biological and
    Cultural
Culture as an Adaptive Mechanism
Mechanisms of Cultural Change
Cultural Lag

Animals and Culture

Subcultures
Types of Subcultures

Universals of Culture
The Division of Labor
The Incest Taboo, Marriage, and the
    Family
Rites of Passage
Ideology

Culture and Individual Choice

Shokore ole Meyoki, a member of the Maasai tribe in Kenya, is a short strange-looking man in his sixties. He has forbidding features, a rough complexion and heavy eyelids that give his face an unexpected Oriental appearance. He usually wears the same outfit, a buttoned wool overcoat with the collar turned up, and his bare legs sticking out below. His expression suggests shrewdness and the feeling that he is keeping some dark secrets. This expression, however, is a cover for a deeper sense of life's disappointments.

He is having trouble with his two wives, particularly Njisha, whose pregnancy seems suspicious to him. His other wife, Nterue, drinks too much. His two wives have been quarreling among themselves. Shokore blames the situation on development. "Before, there were no roads in Maasailand, and a man could keep an eye on his wives. Now the women go everywhere!"

He believes that men today have to beat their wives more than their fathers ever had to, and they have to use a bigger stick. "Women have their own affairs—nobody respects father anymore," he notes wistfully. Earlier in the day Shokore had beaten Njisha for napping instead of washing clothes. He also is angry that Njisha has several boyfriends, one of whom is probably responsible for her pregnancy.

How are we to respond to a society in which men have several wives whom they beat regularly? As we study other cultures we will encounter value systems that conflict with ours. To deal with this problem we must first recognize that all human societies, whether technologically primitive or sophisticated, have complex ways of life that differ greatly from one to the other. These ways have come to be known as *culture*. In 1871 Edward Tylor gave us the first definition of this concept. "Culture," he noted, "is that complex whole which includes knowledge, belief, art, law, morals, custom, and other capabilities and habits acquired by man as a member of society" (Tylor, 1958). Robert Bierstadt simplified Tylor's definition by stating, "Culture is the complex whole that consists of all the ways we think and do and everything we have as members of society" (Bierstadt, 1974).

Most definitions of culture emphasize certain features. Namely, culture is shared; it is acquired, not inborn; the elements make up a complex whole; and it is transmitted from one generation to the next (Sagarin, 1978).

THE CONCEPT OF CULTURE

We will define **culture** *as all that human beings learn to do, to use, to produce, to know, and to believe as they grow to maturity and live out their lives in the social groups to which they belong.* Culture is basically a blueprint for living in a particular society. In common speech, people often refer to a "cultured person" as someone with an interest in the arts,

Native Americans often wish to follow the traditional practices and customs of their culture. At the same time the culture of the larger society urges them to adopt the conventions of mainstream American society.

literature, or music, suggesting that the individual has a highly developed sense of style or aesthetic appreciation of the "finer things." To sociologists, however, every human being is "cultured." All human beings participate in a culture, whether they are Harvard educated and upper class, or illiterate and living in a primitive society. Culture is crucial to human existence.

When sociologists speak of culture, they are referring to the general phenomenon that is a characteristic of all human groups. However, when they refer to *a* culture, they are pointing to the specific culture of a particular group. In other words, all human groups have a culture, but it often varies considerably from one group to the next. Take the concept of time, which we accept as entirely natural. To Westerners, "time marches on" steadily and predictably, with past, present, and future divided into units of precise duration (minutes, hours, days, months, years, and so on). In the culture of the Sioux Indians, however, the concept of time simply does not exist apart from ongoing events: Nothing can be early or late—things just happen when they happen. For the Navajo Indians, the future is a meaningless concept—immediate obligations are what count. For natives of the Pacific island of Truk, however, the past has no independent meaning—it is a living part of the present. These examples of cultural differences in the perception of time point to a basic sociological fact—each culture must be investigated and understood on its own terms before it is possible to make valid cross-cultural comparisons (Hall, 1981).

In every social group, culture is transmitted from one generation to the next. Unlike other creatures, human beings do not pass on many behavioral patterns through their genes. Rather, culture is taught and learned through social interaction.

Culture and Biology

Human beings, like all other creatures, have basic biological needs. We must eat, sleep, protect ourselves from the environment, reproduce, and nurture our young—or else we could not survive as a species. In most other animals, such basic biological needs are met in more or less identical ways by all the members of a species through inherited behavior patterns or instincts. These instincts are specific for a given species as well as universal for all members of that species. Thus, instinctual behaviors, such as the web spinning of specific species of spiders, are constant and do not vary significantly from one individual member of a species to another. This is not true of humans, whose behaviors are highly variable and changeable, both individually and culturally. It is through culture that human beings acquire the means to meet their needs.

For example, the young, or larvae, of hornets or yellow jackets are housed in paper-walled, hexagonal chambers that the young scrape against with their heads when hungry. This is a signal to workers to immediately feed the young tiny bits of undigested insect parts (Wilson, 1975). Neither the larvae nor the worker learns these patterns of behavior: They are instinctual. In contrast, although human infants cry when hungry or uncomfortable, the responses to those cries vary from group to group and even from person to person. In some groups, infants are breast-fed; in others, they are fed prepared milk formulas from bottles; and in others they are fed according to the mother's preference. Some groups breast-feed children for as long as five or six years; others for no more than 10 to 12 months. Some mothers feed their infants on demand—whenever they seem hungry; other mothers hold their infants to a rigid feeding schedule. In some groups, infants are picked up and soothed when they seem unhappy or uncomfortable. Other groups believe that infants should be left "to cry it out." In the United States, mothers differ in their approaches to feeding and handling their infants, but most are influenced by the practices they have observed among members of their families and their social groups. Such habits, shared by the members of each group, express the group's culture. They are learned by group members and are kept more or less uniform by social expectations and pressures.

Culture Shock

Every social group has its own specific culture, its own way of seeing, doing, and making things, its own traditions. Some cultures are quite similar to one another; others are very different. When individuals travel abroad to countries with cultures different from their own, the experience can be quite upsetting. Meals are scheduled at different times of day, "strange" or even "repulsive" foods are eaten, and the traveler never quite knows what to expect from others or what others in turn may expect. Local customs may seem "charming" or "brutal." Sometimes travelers are unable to adjust easily to a foreign culture; they may become anxious, lose their appetites, or even feel sick. Sociologists use the term **culture shock** to describe *the difficulty people have adjusting to a new culture that differs markedly from the one they are used to.*

Anthropologist Napoleon A. Chagnon (1977)

experienced culture shock when he went to live with a group of people known as the Yanomamo (the entire word is nasalized and pronounced "Yah-no-mama"). The Yanomamo are approximately 10,000 South American Indians who live in 125 villages in southern Venezuela and northern Brazil.

My first day in the field illustrated to me what my teachers meant when they spoke of "culture shock." I had traveled in a small, aluminum rowboat propelled by a large outboard motor for two and a half days . . . We arrived at the village, Bissaai-teri, about 2:00 p.m. . . . I looked up and gasped when I saw a dozen burly, naked, filthy, hideous men staring at us down the shafts of their drawn arrows! Immense wads of green tobacco were stuck between their lower teeth and lips making them look even more hideous, and strands of dark green slime dripped or hung from their noses. We arrived at the village while the men were blowing a hallucinogenic drug up their nose. The mucus is always saturated with the green powder and the Indians usually let it run freely from their nostrils. My next discovery was that there were a dozen or so vicious, underfed dogs snapping at my legs, circling me as if I were going to be their next meal. I just stood there holding my notebook, helpless and pathetic. Then the stench of the decaying vegetation and filth struck me and I almost got sick. I was horrified.

Culture shock can also be experienced within a person's own society. Picture the army recruit having to adapt to a whole new set of behaviors, rules, and expectations in basic training—a new cultural setting.

Ethnocentrism and Cultural Relativism

People often make judgments about other cultures according to the customs and values of their own, a practice sociologists call **ethnocentrism.** Thus, an American might call a Guatemalan peasant's home filthy because the floor is made of packed dirt or believe that the family organization of the Watusi (of East Africa) is immoral because a husband may have several wives. Ethnocentrism can lead to prejudice and discrimination and often results in the repression or domination of one group by another.

Immigrants, for instance, often encounter hostility when their manners, dress, eating habits, or religious beliefs differ markedly from those of their new neighbors. Because of this hostility and because of their own ethnocentrism, immigrants often establish their own communities in their adopted country. Many Cuban Americans, for example, have settled in Miami where they have built a power base through strength in numbers. In Dade County alone,

Marriage to a Yanomamo Woman— Kenneth Good

In the 1960s Napoleon Chagnon went to live with the Yanomamo. The Yanomamo are approximately 10,000 South American Indians who live in 125 villages in southern Venezuela and northern Brazil. When Chagnon first visited them, they had had almost no contact with the outside world. Chagnon named them the "fierce people" because of the importance aggression and fighting played in their culture. He claimed that each village was in a constant state of war with the others.

In terms of their material and technological culture, the Yanomamo stand out for their primitiveness. They have no system of numbers; they manage with "one," "two," and "many." Their only calendar is the waxing and waning of the moon. On treks they carry everything they own on their backs; they have not yet invented the wheel. Until recently

Kenneth Good and his Yanomamo wife, Yarima. Photo copyright © by Kenneth Good.

they made fire with fire drills, the rubbing together of two sticks.

Traditionally the Yanomamo wear no clothes; they paint their bodies in serpentine and circular designs using red onoto seed paste. Girls and women adorn their faces by inserting slender sticks through holes in the lower lip at either side of the mouth and

which includes Miami, there are about 700,000 Cuban Americans.

To avoid ethnocentrism in their own research, sociologists are guided by the concept of **cultural relativism**, *the recognition that social groups and cultures must be studied and understood on their own terms before valid comparisons can be made.* Cultural relativism frequently is taken to mean that social scientists never should judge the relative merits of any group or culture. This is not the case. Cultural relativism is an approach to doing objective cross-cultural research. It does not require researchers to abdicate their personal standards. In fact, good social scientists will take the trouble to spell out exactly what their standards are so that both researchers and readers will be alert to possible bias in their studies.

American Moshe Rubinstein encountered the contrasting values between American and Arab culture after a traditional Arabic dinner. Rubinstein was presented with a parable by his host Ahmed. "Moshe," he said, putting his fable in the form of a question, "imagine that you, your mother, your wife, and your child are in a boat, and it capsizes. You can save yourself and only one of the remaining three. Whom will you save?" For a moment Moshe froze, while thoughts raced through his mind. No matter what he might say, it would not be right from someone's point of view, and if he refused to answer he might be even worse off. Moshe was stuck. So he tried to answer by thinking aloud as he progressed to a conclusion, hoping for salvation before he said what came to his mind as soon as the question was posed, namely, save the child.

in the middle, and through the pierced nasal septum. Yanomamo life is characterized by persistent aggression among village mates and perpetual warfare between antagonistic groups. They are supposedly given to club fighting, gang rape, and murder.

This was Kenneth Good's understanding of these people when he first read about them in an anthropology course as an undergraduate at Pennsylvania State University in 1969, and it was still his understanding six years later when, as a graduate student, he went off to do a 15-month stint of field work among them to confirm and elaborate on Chagnon's findings. Here is Good's description of his experience:

Contrary to all my initial intentions, I did not leave the Yanomamo when the 15 months were up. To my great surprise I had found among them a way of life that, while dangerous and harsh, was also filled with camaraderie, compassion, and a thousand daily lessons in communal harmony. In time I learned to speak their language. I learned to walk in their forest and to hunt, fish, and gather. I discovered

what it meant to be a nomad. As more time passed I was adopted into the lineage of my village and given a wife, Yarima, according to Yanomamo custom and in keeping with the wishes of the great shamen-headman.

As I began to understand the Yanomamo better I became increasingly upset with Chagnon's "fierce people" portrayal. The man had clearly taken one aspect of Yanomamo behavior out of context and in so doing had sensationalized it. In the process he had stigmatized these remarkable people as brutish and hateful.

By 1982 Kenneth Good found that the young girl Yarima who had been given to him as a wife was having a profound effect on him.

I'm in love. Unbelievable, intense emotion, almost all the time. In the morning when she gets up to start the day, when I see her come in from the gardens with a basket of plaintains, especially when we make love. Sure it's universal, except that being in love in Yanomamo culture with a Yanomamo girl is different, a different game, different rules. But the feelings, they're universal.

In my wildest dreams it had never occurred to me to marry an Indian woman in the Amazon jungle. I was from suburban Philadelphia. I had no intention of going native. But, down deep, all I really did want was to find some way to make a living and to get back into the jungle. Not only to study the Indians—I already had enough data for three books—but to live with them. More especially to live with Yarima. That was what I had come to, after all these years of struggling to fit into the Yanomamo world, to speak their language fluently, to grasp their way of life from the inside. My original purpose—to observe and analyze this people as an anthropological researcher—had slowly merged with something far more personal.

Eventually Kenneth Good brought his wife, Yarima, out of the Amazon jungle. Today they have two children and live in Rutherford, New Jersey. Good teaches anthropology at Jersey City State college.

Source: Kenneth Good, with David Chanoff, *Into the Heart.* New York: Simon & Schuster, 1991.

Ahmed was very surprised. Moshe had flunked the test. As Ahmed saw it, there was only one correct answer. "You see," he said, "you can have more than one wife in a lifetime, you can have more than one child, but you have only one mother. You must save your mother!" (Rubinstein, 1975).

This example shows us how the value of individuals such as children, spouses, and mothers can vary greatly from one culture to the next. We can see how what we might consider to be a natural way of thinking is not the case at all in another culture.

Cultural relativism requires that behaviors and customs be viewed and analyzed within the context in which they occur. The packed-dirt floor of the Guatemalan house should be noted in terms of the culture of the Guatemalan peasant, not in terms of suburban America. Researchers, however, may find

that dirt floors contribute to the incidence of parasites in young children and may, therefore, judge such construction to be less desirable than wood or tile floors.

COMPONENTS OF CULTURE

The concept of culture is not easy to understand, perhaps because every aspect of our social lives is an expression of it, and also because familiarity produces a kind of nearsightedness toward our own culture, making it difficult for us to take an analytical perspective toward our everyday social lives. Sociologists find it helpful to break down culture into separate components: material culture (objects), normative culture (rules), cognitive culture (shared beliefs), and language (Hall, 1990).

The King of Akure in Nigeria appears in the palace court with some of his 156 wives during the festival of Ifa. The mores of our society do not allow this type of behavior. Cultural relativism would require that we not judge this practice from the standpoint of our culture alone.

Material Culture

Material culture *consists of human technology—all the things human beings make and use from small hand-held tools to skyscrapers.* Without material culture our species could not long survive, for material culture provides a buffer between humans and their environment. Using it, humans can protect themselves from environmental stresses, as when they build shelters and wear clothing to protect themselves from the cold or from strong sunlight. Even more important, humans use material culture

Housing is an aspect of material culture that can vary widely, as can be seen by comparing this elaborate home in Saudi Arabia, and these thatched huts in Nigeria.

to modify and exploit the environment. They build dams and irrigation canals, plant fields and forests, convert coal and oil into energy, and transform ores into versatile metals. Using material culture, our species has learned to cope with the most extreme environments and to survive and even thrive on all continents and in all climates. Humans have walked on the floor of the ocean and on the surface of the moon. No other creature can do this: none has our flexibility. Material culture has made human beings the dominant life-form on earth.

Normative Culture

Every society also has a **nonmaterial culture** *which represents the totality of knowledge, beliefs, values, and rules for appropriate behavior.* **Normative culture** *consists of the rules people follow for doing things.* Normative culture is structured by such institutions as the family, religion, education, economy, and government.

While material culture is made up of things that have a physical existence (they can be seen, touched, and so on), the elements of nonmaterial culture are the ideas associated with their use. Although engagement rings and birthday flowers have a material existence, they also reflect attitudes, beliefs, and values that are part of our culture. There are rules for their appropriate use in specified situations.

Norms are central elements of normative culture. **Norms** *are the rules of behavior that are agreed upon and shared within a culture which prescribe limits of acceptable behavior.* They define "normal" expected behavior and help people achieve predictability in their lives. For example, Edward T. Hall (1966) found that Americans follow many unwritten rules concerning public behavior. As soon as an individual stops or is seated in a public place, a small, invisible sphere of privacy that should not be violated develops around the person. The size will vary with the degree of crowding, the age, sex, and importance of the person, and the general surroundings. Anyone who enters this zone and stays there is intruding. In order to overcome this personal-space barrier, a person who intrudes for a specific purpose will usually acknowledge the intrusion by beginning with a phrase like, "Pardon me, but can you tell me. . . ?"

On the other hand, pushing and shoving in public places is a characteristic of Middle Eastern culture, a characteristic that, unlike the attitude in Western cultures, is not considered rude behavior. For the Arab, there is no such thing as an intrusion of space in public. Occupying a given spot does not give you any special rights to that area at all. If, for example, person A is standing on a street corner and person B wants that spot, it is perfectly all right for person B to try to make person A uncomfortable enough to move.

Arabs also have a completely different set of assumptions regarding the body and the rights associated with it than do Westerners. Arabs do not have any concept of a private zone outside the body. In the Western world, the person is synonymous with the individual inside the skin, and you usually need permission to touch the body and even the clothes if you are a stranger. For the Arab, however, the location of the person in relation to the body is quite different. The person exists somewhere down inside the body, protected from touch. Touching

According to the norms of American culture, a common way for people to greet each other is to shake hands. In Japan, people greet each other by bowing.

the outside of the body—skin and clothes—is not really touching the person.

Arabs also believe that sharing smells is an act of friendship and to deny the smell of your breath to your friends is interpreted as an act of shame. So it is that Americans, trained as they are not to breathe in people's faces, automatically communicate shame to the Arabs (Hall, 1966).

Mores (*pronounced more-ays*) *are strongly held norms that usually have a moral connotation and are based on the central values of the culture.* Violations of mores produce strong negative reactions, which are often supported by the law. Desecration of a church or temple, sexual molestation of a child, rape, murder, incest, and child beating all are violations of American mores.

Not all norms command such absolute conformity. Much of day-to-day life is governed by traditions, or **folkways**, *which are norms that permit a wide degree of individual interpretation as long as certain limits are not overstepped.* People who violate folkways are seen as peculiar or possibly eccentric, but rarely do they elicit strong public response. For example, a wide range of dress is now acceptable in most theaters and restaurants. A man may wear clothes ranging from a business suit, shirt, and tie to jeans, an open-necked shirt, or sweater. A woman may choose a cocktail dress and high-heeled shoes or, like the man, a more casual look. However, extremes in either direction will cause a reaction. Many establishments limit the extent of informal dress: Signs may specify that no one with bare feet or without a shirt may enter. On the other hand, a person in extremely formal attire might well attract attention and elicit amused comments in a fast-food restaurant.

Good manners in our culture also show a range of acceptable behavior. A man may or may not open a door or hold a coat for a woman, who may also choose to open a door or hold a coat for a man—all four options are acceptable behavior and cause neither comment nor negative reactions from people.

These two examples illustrate another aspect of folkways: They change with time. Not too long ago a man was *always* expected to hold a door open for a woman, and a woman was *never* expected to hold a coat for a man.

Folkways also vary from one culture to another. In the United States, for example, it is customary to thank someone for a gift. To fail to do so is to be ungrateful and ill-mannered. Subtle cultural differences can make international gift giving, however, a source of anxiety or embarrassment to well-meaning business travelers. For example, if you give

a gift on first meeting an Arab businessman, it may be interpreted as a bribe. If you give a clock in China, it is considered bad luck.

In Latin America you will have a problem if you give knives or handkerchiefs. The former connotes the end of a friendship; the latter is associated with sadness.

The Japanese are maniacal gift givers. Gift giving is so prevalent in the Japanese culture that they often practice something called *taraimawashi*. This ritual involves giving a gift so utterly useless that the recipient can then give it to someone else, who in turn passes it on (New York Times, December 6, 1981).

Norms are specific expectations about social behavior, but it is important to add that they are not absolute. Even though we learn what is expected in our culture, there is room for what might be called "slippage" in individual interpretations of these norms that deviate from the ideal norm.

Ideal norms *are expectations of what people should do under perfect conditions.* These are the norms we first teach our children. They tend to be simple, making few distinctions and allowing for no exceptions. That drivers should "stop at red lights" is an ideal norm in American society. So is the norm that a marriage will last "until death do us part."

In reality, however, nothing about human beings is ever that dependable. For example, if you interviewed Americans about how drivers respond to red lights, you would get answers like: Ideally, drivers should stop at red lights. But in actual fact, drivers sometimes run red lights. So even though you can pretty much count on a driver stopping for a red light, it pays to be careful. And if it looks like a driver is not going to stop for a light, you had better play it safe and slow down. In other words, people recognize that drivers usually do feel they should stop when a traffic light is red, but they also acknowledge that there are times when a driver will not stop for a red light. The driver may be in a hurry, drunk, upset, or simply not paying attention. **Real norms** *are norms that are expressed with qualifications and allowances for differences in individual behavior.* They specify how people actually behave. They reflect the fact that a person's behavior is a function not only of norm guidance but also of situational elements, as exemplified by the driver who does not always stop at a red light if no car appears to be coming from the other direction.

The concepts of ideal and real norms are useful for distinguishing between mores and folkways. For mores, the ideal and the real norms tend to be very close, whereas folkways can be much more loosely connected: Our mores say *thou shalt not kill* and really mean it, but thou might violate a folkway by neglecting to say thank you without provoking general outrage. More important, the very fact that a culture legitimizes the difference between ideal and real expectations allows the individual room to interpret norms to a greater or lesser degree according to his or her own personal disposition.

Cognitive Culture

Cognitive culture *is the thinking component of culture, which consists of shared beliefs and knowledge of what the world is like—what is real and what is not, what is important and what is trivial.* The beliefs need not even be true or testable as long as they are shared by a majority of people. Cognitive culture is like a map that guides us through society. Think of a scout troop on a hike in the wilderness. The troop finds its way by studying a map showing many of the important features of the terrain. The scouts who use the map share a mental image of the area represented by the map. Yet just as maps differ, each perhaps emphasizing different details of the terrain or using different symbols to represent them, so do cultures differ in the ways in which they represent the world. It is important not to confuse any culture's representation of reality with what ultimately is real—just as a map is not the actual terrain it charts.

Values *are a culture's general orientations toward life—its notions of what is good and bad, what is desirable and undesirable.* Values themselves are abstractions. They can best be found by looking

Certain aspects of the material culture, such as the invention of the telephone, produce profound and lasting changes.

for the recurring patterns of behavior that express them.

Language and Culture

Language enables humans to organize the world around them into labeled cognitive categories and use these labels to communicate with one another. Language, therefore, makes possible the teaching and sharing of the cognitive and normative cultures we just discussed. It provides the principal means through which culture is transmitted and the foundation on which the complexity of human thought and experience rests.

Language allows humans to transcend the limitations imposed by their environment and biological evolution. It has taken tens of millions of years of biological evolution to produce the human species. On the other hand, in a matter of decades, cultural evolution has made it possible for us to travel to the moon. Biological evolution had to work slowly through genetic changes, but cultural evolution works quickly through the transmission of information from one generation to the next. In terms of knowledge and information, each human generation, because of language, is able to begin where the previous one left off. Each generation does not have to begin anew, as is the case in the animal world.

Every person is shaped by the **selectivity** *of their culture, a process by which some aspects of the world are viewed as important while others are virtually neglected.* The language of a culture reflects this selectivity in its vocabulary and even its grammar. Therefore, as children learn a language, they are being molded to think and even to experience the world in terms of one particular cultural perspective.

This view of language and culture, known as the **Sapir-Whorf hypothesis,** *argues that the language a person uses determines his or her perception of reality* (Whorf, 1956; Sapir, 1961). This idea caused some alarm among social scientists at first, for it implied that people from different cultures never quite experience the same reality. Although more recent research has modified this extreme view, it remains true that different languages classify experiences differently—that language is the lens through which we experience the world. The prominent anthropologist Ruth Benedict (1961) pointed out, "We do not see the lens through which we look."

The category corresponding to one word and one thought in language A may be regarded by language B as two or more categories corresponding to two or more words or thoughts. For example,

The Inuit Eskimos would have a much easier time describing the subtleties of this snow scene than would the average American. With nearly forty words for snow, it is clear that snow is much more important to them than it is to us.

we have only one word for water, but the Hopi Indians have two words—*pahe* (water in a natural state) and *keyi* (water in a container). On the other hand, the Hopi have only one word to cover everything that flies, except birds. Strange as it may seem to us, they call a flying insect, an airplane, and a pilot by the same word. The Inuit (Eskimos) must find it very odd indeed to learn that we have only one word for snow. For them falling snow, slushy snow, loose snow, hard-packed snow, wind-driven snow, and so on, clearly are different, and the Inuit language uses different words for each. In contrast, the ancient Aztecs of Mexico used only one word for cold, ice, and snow. Verbs also are treated differently in different cultures. In English we have one verb *to go*. In New Guinea, however, the Manus language has three verbs that distinguish between direction, distance, and whether the going is up or down.

A bit closer to home, consider today's urban American youngsters, who casually use many words and expressions pertaining to technology. Technological terms even are used to describe states of mind—*tuned in, tuned out, turned on,* or *turned off,* for instance. This use of language reflects the preoccupation of American culture with technology. In contrast, many Americans are at a loss for words when asked to describe nature: varieties of snow, wind, or rain; kinds of forests; rock formations; earth colors and textures; or vegetation zones. Why? Because these things are not of great importance in urban American culture.

The translation of one language into another often presents problems. Direct translations are often impossible because (1) words may have a variety of meanings and (2) many words and ideas are culture-bound.

An extreme example of the first type of these translation problems occurred near the end of World War II. After Germany surrendered, the Allies sent Japan an ultimatum to surrender. Japan's premier responded that his government would *mokusatsu* the surrender ultimatum. *Mokusatsu* has two possible meanings in English: "to consider" or "to take notice of." The premier meant that the government would consider the surrender ultimatum. The English translators, however, used the second interpretation "to take notice of" and assumed that Japan had rejected the ultimatum. This belief that Japan was unwilling to surrender led to the atomic bombing of Hiroshima and Nagasaki. Most likely the bombing would still have taken place even with the other interpretation, but this example does demonstrate the problems in translating words and ideas from one language into another (Samovar, Porter, and Jain, 1981).

These examples demonstrate the uniqueness of language. No two cultures represent the world in exactly the same manner, and this cultural selectivity, or bias, is expressed in the form and content of a culture's language.

THE SYMBOLIC NATURE OF CULTURE

All human beings respond to the world around them. They may decorate their bodies, make drawings on cave walls or canvases, or mold likenesses in clay. These all act as symbolic representations of their society. All complex behavior is derived from the ability to use symbols for people, events, or places. Without the ability to use symbols to create language, culture could not exist.

Signs, Symbols, and Culture

What does it mean to say that culture is symbolic? In order to answer this question we first must distinguish between signs and symbols. **Signs** *are objects or things that can represent other things because they share some important quality with them.* A clenched fist can be a sign of anger, because when people are angry they may use their fists to beat one another. Wrinkling one's nose can be a sign that something is undesirable because that is what people do when something smells bad.

Few travelers would think of going abroad without taking along a dictionary or phrase book to help them communicate with the people in the countries they visit. Although most people are aware that gestures are the most common form of cross-cultural communication, they do not realize that the language of gestures can be just as different, just as regional, and just as likely to cause misunderstanding as the spoken word.

After a good meal in Naples, a well-meaning American tourist expressed his appreciation to the waiter by making the "A-okay" gesture with his thumb and forefinger. The waiter was shocked. He headed for the manager. The two men seriously discussed calling the police and having the hapless tourist arrested for obscene behavior in a public place.

What had happened? How could such a seemingly innocent and flattering gesture have been so misunderstood? In American culture the "A-okay" sign is used confidently in public by everyone from astronauts to politicians to signify that everything is fine. In France and Belgium, however, it means "You're worth zero," while in Greece and Turkey it is an insulting or vulgar sexual invitation. In parts of southern Italy, it is an offensive and graphic reference to a part of the anatomy. It is no small wonder that the waiter was shocked.

There are, in fact, dozens of gestures that take on totally different meanings as you move from one country to another. Is "thumbs up" always a positive gesture? It is in the United States and most of western Europe. When it was displayed by the Emperor of Rome, the upright thumb gesture spared the lives of gladiators in the Coliseum. However, don't try it in Sardinia and Northern Greece, for there the gesture means, "Up yours."

The same naivete that can lead Americans into trouble in foreign countries also may work in reverse. After paying a call on Richard Nixon, Soviet leader Leonid Brezhnev stood on a balcony at the White House and saluted the American public with his hands clasped together in a gesture many people

The communication system of many animals involves a series of signs, as does this courtship dance of the male seagull. The little boy's shrug is a symbol because it conveys an agreed-upon meaning.

interpreted as meaning "I am the champ," or "I won." What many Americans perceived as a belligerent gesture was really just the Russian gesture for friendship (Ekman, Friesen, and Bear, 1984).

The communication systems of many animal species consist of more or less complicated systems of signs. For example, a worker bee returning to its hive can communicate accurately to other bees the location of pollen-rich plants by performing a complicated dance. Careful research by the German biologist Karl von Frisch (1967) showed that this is accomplished when the bee, in effect, acts out a miniature version of its flight. The direction of the dance is the direction of the flight, and the duration of the dance is proportional to the distance of the pollen-rich flowers from the hive. Most important, a bee can dance only to communicate where pollen is to be found, not about anything else, such as imminent danger from an approaching bear.

Symbols *are objects that, like signs, represent other things; however, unlike signs, symbols need not share any quality at all with whatever they represent.* Symbols stand for things simply because people agree they do. Hence, when two or more individuals agree about the things a particular object represents, that object becomes a symbol by virtue of its shared meaning for those individuals. When Betsy Ross sewed the first American flag, she was creating a symbol.

The important point about the meanings of symbols is that they are entirely arbitrary, a matter of cultural convention. Each culture attaches its own meanings to things. Thus, in the United States mourners wear black to symbolize their sadness at a funeral. In the Far East people wear white. In this case the symbol is different but the meaning is the same. On the other hand, the same object can have different meanings in different cultures. Among the Sioux Indians the swastika (a cross made with ends bent at right angles to its arms) was a religious symbol; in Nazi Germany its meaning was political.

Looking at culture from this point of view, we would have to say that all aspects of culture—nonmaterial and material—are symbolic. Thus, culture may be said to consist of shared patterns of meanings expressed in symbols (Geertz, 1973). This means that virtually everything we say and do and use as group members has some shared meaning beyond itself. For example, wearing lipstick is more than just coloring one's lips; smoking a cigarette is more than just filling one's lungs with smoke, and wearing high-heeled shoes is more than just trying to be taller. All these actions and artifacts are part of American culture and are symbolic of sexuality and adulthood, among other things. Even a person's clothes and home—material possessions—are not only means of protection from the environment, they are symbolic of that person's status in the social class structure. An automobile for many people is more than just a means of transportation—it is symbolic of their socioeconomic status.

CULTURE AND ADAPTATION

Over time, cultures adjust to the demands of the environment. Although **environmental determinism**—*the belief that the environment dictates cul-*

tural patterns—is no longer accepted, there must be some degree of "fit" between environment and culture. Whereas other species adapt to their environment through the long, slow process of evolution and natural selection, culture has allowed humans to adapt relatively quickly to many different habitats and become the most flexible species on earth.

Human Evolution: Biological and Cultural

Because most of human behavior is not instinctive but is learned (see Chapter 4) and depends on culture, much can be learned about human development by tracing the evolution of culture.

The earliest evidence of culture found thus far is in Africa. In Tanzania, Kenya, and Ethiopia, fist-sized stone tools have been found dating from 1.5 to 2.9 million years ago. These very simple tools were made by knocking several flakes off pieces of flint to produce an implement with which animals could be killed and butchered. The creatures that produced these tools stood upright and walked on their hind legs as we do, were between four and five feet tall, and weighed between 80 and 150 pounds. However, their heads were still very apelike.

These ancestors of ours subsisted on a varied diet of plants and small game, and evidence suggests they were able to hunt larger animals. In order to protect themselves against dangerous meat-eating predators and to successfully hunt big game they probably developed some form of communication and social organization (This is a reasonable assumption, as modern apes and monkeys, our closest primate relatives, also live in organized social groups).

Sometime between 1 and 1.5 million years ago our immediate ancestors—*Homo erectus*—evolved. *Homo erectus* resembled the modern human in all respects except for its head, which still was quite primitive. The jaws were large, the eyes protected by heavy ridges, the forehead still slanted sharply back. However, the brain had grown significantly, averaging 1,000 cubic centimeters—a little over two-thirds that of modern humans.

Homo erecti were very versatile. Their bands moved out of the tropics and subtropics, venturing forth across the vast expanses of Africa, Europe, and Asia as far north as Germany and Beijing. They lived in caves and skin huts on windswept plains, braving cold winters in their pursuit of big game—mammoth, horse, rhinoceros, deer, and oxen. *Homo erecti* lived in nomadic, well-organized bands, and their tools and weapons were well adapted to the different environments they inhabited.

We have learned a great deal about primitive cultures from cave paintings such as this one found in Niaux, France.

Human culture and subsistence activities changed significantly around 70,000 years ago. By this time the Neanderthal, an early form of our own species, had already been in existence for several hundred thousand years. The cultural changes that came about at this time seem to have been in response to human populations moving ever farther north, right up to the ice-age glaciers. Here humans became even more skillful hunters than their ancestors. Stone tools were made in a new process that involved shaping a piece of flint carefully before the final tool was split off. The process resulted in the production of a great variety of specialized tools including spear points. But the most dramatic cultural developments were in other areas. There is evidence that Neanderthals practiced crude surgery, cared for the aged and crippled, and buried their dead according to rituals that included tying corpses into a fetal position, sprinkling them with red powder, placing offerings of food beside them, and sometimes even covering them with flower petals (Solecki, 1971). This evidence suggests that Neanderthal people were intelligent, developed strong feelings for each other, and had ideas about death and possibly even about an afterlife.

By 35,000 to 40,000 years ago, stone-tool technology had reached its highest stage of development. Tool kits featured many forms of choppers, scrapers, chisels, points, and blades. In southern Europe, beginning around 25,000 B.C., we find the emergence of sophisticated art forms: engravings, wall paintings, abstract designs, and even three-dimensional sculptures of animals and humans. Hunter-gatherers—nomadic people who moved around in small groups living off whatever game or plants they happened to come upon—were responsible for these advances. It was bands of these versatile

and creative hunter-gatherers that crossed the last frontiers into Australia and the Americas (where they arrived probably around 40,000 years ago).

By 10,000 B.C. the agricultural revolution was beginning, and on this base civilizations were built— societies that were to push forward the evolution of culture at an ever-accelerating pace.

Culture As an Adaptive Mechanism

Culture probably has been part of human evolution since the time, some 15 million years ago, when our ancestors first began to live on the ground. As we have stressed throughout this chapter, humans are extraordinarily flexible and adaptable. This adaptability, however, is not the result of being biologically fitted to the environment; in fact, human beings are remarkably unspecialized. We do not run very fast, jump very high, climb very well, or swim very far. But we are specialized in one area: We are culture producing, culture transmitting, and culture dependent. This unique specialization is rooted in the size and structure of the human brain and in our physical ability both to speak and to use tools.

Culture, then, is the primary means by which human beings adapt to the challenges of their environment. Thus, using enormous machines we strip away layers of the earth to extract minerals, and using other machines we transport these minerals to yet more machines, where they are converted to a staggering number of different products. Take away all our machines and American society would cease to exist. Take away all culture and the human species would perish. Culture is as much a part of us as our skin, muscles, bones, and brains.

Adaptation *is the process by which human beings adjust to changes in their environment.* Adap-

The extraordinary conditions of the Andes produced a specialized type of cultural adaptation as seen in these ancient ruins known as Machu Picchu. The terraces were built into the nearly vertical mountainside so that they could collect soil and moisture for gardening. The beveled building stones were so well fitted that they survived many earthquakes.

tation can take two different forms: specialization and generalized adaptability. Most cultures make use of both these means. **Specialization** *involves developing ways of doing things that work extremely well in a particular environment or set of circumstances.* For example, the Inuit (Eskimo) igloo is a specialized way of building a shelter. It works in the Arctic but would fail miserably in the Sahara desert or in a Florida swamp. An American brick apartment building is also specialized. It is fine where the ground is solid and bricks can be delivered by truck or train, but in swamps, deserts, or where people must move around a great deal in order to subsist, the brick apartment building is of no use whatsoever.

Generalized adaptability *involves developing more complicated yet more flexible ways of doing things.* For example, industrial society has very elaborate means of transportation, including trucks, trains, planes, and ships. Industrialized transportation is complex, much more so than, say, the use of camels by desert nomads. At the same time, industrial transportation is a much more flexible transportation system, adaptable to every climate on earth. As such, it displays the quality of generalized adaptability as long as our environment continues to provide enough resources to meet its needs. Should we ever run out of rubber, metals, oil, and the other resources necessary for the operation of this technology, it will have lost its adaptive value. Then the camel might look like a very tempting means of transportation, and our "adaptable" technology would be as overspecialized as the dinosaur, with about the same probability of survival.

Mechanisms of Cultural Change

Cultural change takes place at many different levels within a society. Some of the radical changes that have taken place often become obvious only in hindsight. When the airplane was invented, few people could visualize the changes it would produce. Not only did it markedly decrease the impact of distance on cultural contact, but it had enormous impact on such areas as economics and warfare.

It is generally assumed that the number of cultural items in a society (including everything from toothpicks to structures as complex as government agencies) has a direct relation to the rate of social change. A society that has few such items will tend to have few **innovations,** *any new practice or tool that becomes widely accepted in a society.* As the number of cultural items increases, so do the innovations, as well as the rate of social change. For example, an inventory of the cultural items—from tools to religious practices—among the hunting and gathering Shoshone Indians totals a mere three thousand. Modern Americans who also inhabit the same territory in Nevada and Utah are part of a culture with items numbering well into the millions. Social change in American society is proceeding rapidly, while Shoshone culture, as revealed by archeological excavations, appears to have changed scarcely at all for thousands of years.

Two simple mechanisms are responsible for cultural evolution: innovation and diffusion. Innovation is the source of all **cultural traits**—that is, *items of a culture such as tools, materials used, beliefs, values, and typical ways of doing things.*

When people of one society come in contact with people of another society, cultural diffusion takes place, as evidenced by this display of Valentine's Day candy representing a holiday indigenous to the United States.

Innovation takes place in several different ways, including recombining in a new way elements already available to a society (invention), discovering new concepts, finding new solutions to old problems, and devising and making new material objects.

Diffusion *is the movement of culture traits from one culture to another.* It almost inevitably results when people from one group or society come into contact with another, as when immigrant groups take on the dress or manners of already established groups and in turn contribute new foods or art forms to the dominant culture. Rarely does a trait diffuse directly from one culture into another. Rather, diffusion is marked by reformulation, *in which a trait is modified in some way so that it fits better in its new context.* This process of reformulation can be seen in the transformation of black folk-blues into commercial music such as rhythm and blues and rock 'n' roll. Or, consider moccasins—the machine-made, chemically waterproofed, soft-soled cowhide shoes—which today differ from the Native American originals and usually are worn for recreation rather than as part of basic dress, as they originally were. Sociologists would say, therefore, that moccasins are an example of a cultural trait that was reformulated when it diffused from Native American culture to industrial America.

Cultural Lag

Although the diverse elements of a culture are interrelated, some may change rapidly while others lag behind. William F. Ogburn (1964) coined the term **cultural lag** to describe *the phenomenon where new patterns of behavior may emerge, even though they conflict with traditional values.* Ogburn observed that technological change (material culture) is typically faster than change in nonmaterial culture—a culture's norms and values—and technological change often results in cultural lag. Consequently, stresses and strains among elements of a culture are more or less inevitable. For example, although it is now possible to determine if a baby is genetically normal before birth, the Catholic Church, as well as other religious groups, are opposed to using this technology. Similarly, although thousands of babies have been born through in-vitro fertilization, a process in which the egg and sperm are joined outside the mother's body, the Church opposes this type of human reproduction.

Or, consider the warning recently issued to commuters between Kuala Lumpur, the capital of Malaysia, and the town of Port Kelang. Workers building a modern bridge apparently consulted local religious leaders who declared that human heads were needed to appease dangerous spirits during the construction. Commuters were alerted that headhunters had been busy trying to supply them.

Other instances of cultural lag have considerably greater and more widespread negative effects. Advances in medicine have led to lowered infant mortality and greater life expectancy, but there has been no corresponding rapid worldwide acceptance of methods of birth control. The result is a potentially disastrous population explosion—our planet may not be able to support all the people being born and living longer.

ANIMALS AND CULTURE

Do animals have culture? Not long ago most scholars would have said "no." Language and the production and use of tools are central elements of nonmaterial and material culture. Thus, species that lack language and tools would also lack culture. For years scientists reported that animals used their calls simply to announce identity, gender, species, location, and readiness to fight or mate. Some scientists claimed that this is all animals need to express, as life in the wild is simple. Or is it? Could it be that animals use symbols in other ways that we have overlooked? Is it possible to find the roots of human language in animal language?

A number of experiments—the earliest dating back to the mid-1960s—have shown that apes are able to master some of the most fundamental aspects of language. Apes, of course, cannot talk. Their mouths and throats simply are not built to produce speech, and no ape has been able to approximate more than four human words. However, efforts to teach apes to communicate by other means have met with a fair amount of success.

The first and most widely known experiment in ape language research began in 1966 under the direction of Alan and Beatrix Gardner of the University of Nevada, with a chimpanzee named Washoe. This experiment consisted of teaching Washoe the American Sign Language (ASL), a hand gesture language used by deaf people. Washoe learned more than 130 distinct signs and was able to ask for food, name objects, and make reference to her environment. The Gardners replicated their results with four other chimpanzees.

Today Washoe lives with four other signing chimpanzees at Central Washington University under the direction of Roger and Debbie Fouts. She now has an adopted son named Loolis. Loolis is not being taught any signs by humans, and the Fouts are observing him to see whether he will acquire signs from the other chimps. To date he has learned 41 signs.

Another female chimp, Lana, has been taught to communicate by pressing different-shaped buttons in a particular series to obtain a desired goal. These buttons represent individual words, and Lana has mastered quite a few of them. She can even distinguish among nouns, verbs, adjectives, and adverbs.

One of the most successful experiments involves a female gorilla named Koko. Francine Patterson has been working with Koko for the last 13 years. Koko uses approximately 400 signs regularly and another 300 occasionally. She understands several hundred spoken words (so much so that Patterson has to spell such words as "candy" in her presence). In addition Koko invents signs or creates sign combinations to describe new things. She tells Patterson when she is happy or sad, refers to past and future events, defines objects, and insults her human companions by calling them such things as "dirty toilet," "nut," and "rotten stink."

Koko has taken several I.Q. tests, including the Stanford-Binet, and scores just below average for a human child—between 85 and 95 points. However, as Patterson points out, the IQ tests have a cultural bias toward humans, and the gorilla may be more intelligent than the test indicates. For example, one item instructs the subject to "point to two things that are good to eat." The choices are a block, an apple, a shoe, a flower, and an ice cream sundae. Reflecting her tastes, Koko pointed to the apple and the flower. She likes to eat flowers and has never seen an ice cream sundae. Although these answers are correct for Koko, they are wrong for humans and were scored incorrect.

Patterson claims that Koko uses signs to swear, gossip, rhyme, and lie. If she is right, these findings represent the most sophisticated results anyone has ever achieved with an ape.

Recently, however, some social scientists have raised serious questions as to whether apes truly are using language (Terrace et al., 1979; Greenberg, 1980). They argue that although apes can acquire large vocabularies, they cannot produce a sentence and are not using the equivalent of human language. For now the implications of language use by apes remains unclear, and the evidence continues to mount on both sides.

In the last two decades a variety of research has also challenged the idea that animals lack toolmaking capabilities. For example, Jane van Lawick-Goodall (1971) discovered that chimpanzees living in the wild not only use tools but produce them first and then carry them to where they will use them. These chimps break twigs off trees, strip them of leaves and bark, then carry them to termite mounds where, after wetting them with spit, they poke them into tunnels and pull them out again all covered with delicious termites ready to be licked off. Sea otters search out flat pieces of rock and, while floating on their backs, place the rocks on their stomachs and crack shellfish open against them.

In view of this research, does it make sense to say that culture is limited to human beings? Although scientists disagree in their answers to this question, they do agree that humans have refined culture to a far greater degree than any other animals and that humans depend on culture for their survival much more than any other creatures.

SUBCULTURES

In order to function, every social group must have a culture of its own—its own goals, norms, values, and ways of doing things. As Thomas Lasswell (1965) pointed out, such group culture is not just a "partial or miniature" culture. It is a full-blown, complete culture in its own right. Every family, clique, shop, community, ethnic group, and society has its own culture. Hence, every individual participates in a number of different cultures in the course of a day. Meeting social expectations of various cultures is often a source of considerable stress for individuals in complex, heterogeneous societies like ours. Many college students, for example, find that the culture of the campus varies significantly from the culture of their family or neighborhood. At home they may be criticized for their musical taste, their clothing, their anti-establishment ideas, and for spending too little time with the family. On campus they may be pressured to open up their minds and experiment a little, or to reject old-fashioned values.

Sociologists use the term *subculture* to refer to *the distinctive lifestyles, values, norms, and beliefs of certain segments of the population within a society.* The concept of *subculture* originated in studies of juvenile delinquency and criminality (Sutherland, 1924), and in some contexts the *sub* in subculture still has the meaning of inferior. However, sociologists increasingly use *subculture* to refer to the cultures of discrete population segments within a society (Gordon, 1947). The term is primarily applied to the culture of ethnic groups (Italian-Americans, Jews, Native Americans, and so on) as well as to social classes (lower or working, middle, upper, and so on). Certain sociologists reserve the term *subculture* for marginal groups—that is, for groups that differ significantly from the so-called dominant culture.

Some theorists, stressing the adaptive function of culture, view subcultures as specialized approaches to solving the particular problems faced by specific groups (Cohen, 1955). For example, they note that chronic unemployment or underemployment among inner-city residents evokes criminal behavior that is reinforced by social interactions and eventually becomes normal for certain inner-city groups. Once this happens, a deviant subculture begins to flourish.

Types of Subcultures

Several groups have been studied at one time or another by sociologists as examples of subcultures. These can be classified roughly as follows.

ETHNIC SUBCULTURES Many immigrant groups have maintained their group identities and sustained their traditions while at the same time adjusting to the demands of the wider society. Though originally distinct and separate cultures, they have become American subcultures. America's newest immigrants, Asians from Vietnam, Japan, the Philippines, Taiwan, India, and Cambodia, have maintained their values by living together in tight-knit communities in New York, Los Angeles and other large cities while, at the same time, encouraging their children to achieve success by American terms.

OCCUPATIONAL SUBCULTURES Certain occupations seem to involve people in a distinctive lifestyle even beyond their work. For example, New York's Wall Street is not only the financial capital of the world, it is identified with certain values such as materialism, greed, or power. Construction workers, police, entertainers, and many other occupational groups involve people in distinctive subcultures.

RELIGIOUS SUBCULTURES Certain religious groups, though continuing to participate in the wider society, nevertheless practice lifestyles that set them apart. These include Christian evangelical groups, Mormons, Muslims, Jews, and many religious splinter groups.

Sometimes the lifestyle may separate the group from the culture as a whole as well as the subculture of their immediate community. In a drug-ridden area of Brooklyn, New York, for example, a group of Muslims follows an anti-drug creed in a community filled with addicts, drug dealers and crack houses. Their religious beliefs set them apart from the general society while their attitude toward drugs separates them from many other community members.

POLITICAL SUBCULTURES Small, marginal political groups may so involve their members that their entire way of life is an expression of their political convictions. Often these are so-called left-wing and right-wing groups that reject much of what they see in American society, but remain engaged in society through their constant efforts to change it to their liking.

GEOGRAPHICAL SUBCULTURES   Large societies often show regional variations in culture. America has several geographical areas known for their distinctive subcultures. For instance, the South is known for its leisurely approach to life, its broad dialect, and its hospitality. The North is noted for "Yankee ingenuity," commercial cunning, and a crusty standoffishness. California, or "the Coast," is known for its trendiness and ultrarelaxed or "laid-back" lifestyle. And New York stands as much for an anxious, elitist, arts-and-literature-oriented subculture as for a city.

SOCIAL CLASS SUBCULTURES   Although social classes cut horizontally across geographical, ethnic, and other subdivisions of society, to some degree it is possible to discern cultural differences among the classes. Sociologists have documented that linguistic styles, family and household forms, and values and norms applied to child rearing are patterned in terms of social class subcultures. (See Chapter 8 for a discussion of social class in the United States.).

DEVIANT SUBCULTURES   As we mentioned above, sociologists first began to study subcultures as a way of explaining juvenile delinquency and criminality. This interest expanded to include the study of a wide variety of groups that are marginal to society in one way or another and whose lifestyles clash with that of the wider society in important ways. Some of the deviant subcultural groups studied by sociologists include prostitutes, strippers, swingers, pool hustlers, pickpockets, drug users, and a variety of other criminals.

UNIVERSALS OF CULTURE

In spite of their individual and cultural diversity, their many subcultures and countercultures, human beings are members of one species with a common evolutionary heritage. Therefore, people everywhere must confront and resolve certain common, basic problems such as maintaining group organization and overcoming difficulties originating in their social and natural environments. **Cultural universals** *are certain models or patterns that have developed in all cultures to resolve these problems.*

Among those universals that fulfill basic human needs are the division of labor, the incest taboo, marriage, family organization, rites of passage, and ideology. It is important to keep in mind that although these *forms* are universal, their specific *contents* are particular to each culture.

The Division of Labor

Many primates live in social groups in which it is typical for each adult group member to meet most of his or her own needs. The adults find their own food, prepare their own sleeping places, and, with the exception of infant care, mutual grooming, and some defense-related activities, generally fend for themselves (DeVore, 1965; Kummer, 1971).

This is not true of human groups. In all societies—from the simplest bands to the most complex industrial nations—groups divide the responsibility for completing necessary tasks among their members. This means that humans constantly must rely on one another; hence they are the most cooperative of all primates (Lancaster and Whitten, 1980).

The variety of ways in which human groups divide their tasks and choose the kinds of tasks they undertake reflects differences in environment, history, and level of technological development. Yet there are certain commonalities in the division of labor. All cultures distinguish between females and males and between adults and children, and these distinctions are used to organize the division of labor. Thus, in every society there are adult-female tasks, adult-male tasks, and children's tasks. In the last two decades in America, these role distinctions have been changing quite rapidly, a topic we shall explore in Chapter 10.

The Incest Taboo, Marriage, and the Family

All human societies regulate sexual behavior. Sexual mores vary enormously from one culture to another, but all cultures apparently share one basic value: sexual relations between parents and their children are to be avoided. (There is evidence that some primates also avoid sexual relations between males and their mothers.) In most societies it is also wrong for brothers and sisters to have sexual contact (notable exceptions being the brother-sister marriages among royal families in ancient Egypt and Hawaii, and among the Incas of Peru). *Sexual relations between family members is called* **incest,** and because in most cultures very strong feelings of horror and revulsion are attached to incest, it is said to be forbidden by taboo. *A* **taboo** *is the prohibition of a specific action.*

The presence of the incest taboo means that individuals must seek socially acceptable sexual relationships outside their families. All cultures provide definitions of who is or is not an acceptable candidate for sexual contact. They also provide for institutionalized marriages—ritualized means of

Certain patterns of behavior, such as marriage, are found in every culture but take various forms. The marriage ceremony, for example, varies greatly among different cultures.

publicly legitimizing sexual partnerships and the resulting children. Thus, the presence of the incest taboo and the institution of marriage results in the creation of families. Depending on who is allowed to marry—and how many spouses each person is allowed to have—the family will differ from one culture to another. However, the basic family unit consisting of husband, wife, and children (called the nuclear family) seems to be a recognized unit in almost every culture, and sexual relations among its members (other than between husband and wife) are almost universally taboo. For one thing, this helps keep sexual jealousy under control. For another, it prevents the confusion of authority relation-

ships within the family. Perhaps most important, the incest taboo ensures that family offspring will marry into other families, thus recreating in every generation a network of social bonds among families that knits them together into larger, more stable social groupings.

Rites of Passage

All cultures recognize stages through which individuals pass in the course of their lifetimes. Some of these stages are marked by biological events, such as the start of menstruation in girls. However, most of these stages are quite arbitrary and culturally

Japanese Culture: To Be Emulated or Rejected?

It should not surprise anyone if we claim that Japanese culture is unique. We are willing to admit that the past 250 years of American history, which include revolution, settling the frontier, subjugating Indians, slavery, and absorbing vast numbers of immigrants, have given the United States a distinctive set of values. Therefore, it is certainly conceivable that 2,500 years of isolation on a few small islands might have given the Japanese a peculiar culture.

In recent years we have come to admire aspects of Japanese society and to contrast them with facets of American society. Beyond the much discussed successes of the Japanese economy, Japan seems different and better in those details of daily life that reflect consideration and duty. A thousand times a day in modern society your life is made easier or harder, depending on the care

with which someone else has done his or her job. In general, can you count on others to do their best? In Japan you can.

From bureaucrats at the Ministry of Foreign Affairs to department-store package-wrappers, the Japanese seem invulnerable to the idea that discharging one's duty to others might be considered "just a job." Tipping is virtually unknown in Japan; from the Japanese perspective it seems vulgar, because it implies that the recipient will not do his best unless he is bribed.

Most of Japan is extremely crowded. It is common for 100,000 people to live within a half-mile radius. Yet, in the evening one can walk through the alleyways and notice that the neighborhoods are totally quiet. The restraint and reserve of Japanese life can seem suffocating if you are used to something different, but they are also admirable

and necessary, if so many people are to coexist so harmoniously in such close quarters.

With a very low crime rate and its economic miracle, is this not truly Japan's golden age? Everything is working, Japan is taking a proud place in the world, there are no serious domestic divisions, and the drugs, corruption, and similar disorders that blight the rest of the world barely exist there. It appears that Japan has figured out what is still puzzling everybody else.

The same culture that produces so many of the above-mentioned admirable traits also has some very deeply ingrained dilemmas. The most serious of these is an attitude of racial exclusion. Rather than talking about race—as white Americans did when enslaving blacks and excluding "inferior" immigrants—the Japanese talk about "purity." Their society is different from others in being

defined. All such stages—whether or not corresponding to biological events—are meaningful only in terms of each group's culture.

Rarely do individuals drift from one such stage to another; every culture has established **rites of passage,** *or standardized rituals marking major life transitions.* The most widespread—if not universal—rites of passage are those marking the arrival of puberty (often resulting in the individual's taking on adult status), marriage, and death. Typical rites of passage celebrated in American society include baptisms, bar and bas mitzvahs, confirmations, major birthdays, graduation, showers (for brides-to-be), stag parties (for grooms-to-be), wedding ceremonies, major anniversaries, retirement parties, and funerals and wakes. Such rituals accomplish several important functions, including helping the individual achieve a sense of social identity, mapping out the individual's life course, and aiding the

individual in making appropriate life plans. Finally, rites of passage provide people with a context in which to share common emotions, particularly with regard to events that are sources of stress and intense feelings such as marriage and death.

Ideology

A central challenge that every group faces is how to maintain its identity as a social unit. One of the most important ways that groups accomplish this is by promoting beliefs and values to which group members are firmly committed. Such **ideologies,** *or strongly held beliefs and values* are the cement of social structure.

Ideologies are found in every culture. Some are religious, referring to things and events beyond the perception of the human senses. Others are more secular—that is, nonreligious and concerned with purer; it consists of practically none but Japanese. What makes the subject so complicated is the overlap between two different kinds of purity, that of culture and that of blood.

The significant point is that as far as the Japanese are concerned, they are inherently different from other people, and are all bound together by birth and blood. The United States is built on the principle of a voluntary fraternity; in theory, anyone can become an American. A place in Japanese society is open only to those who are born Japanese. Being born Japanese means being born with the right racial background, not merely on rocky Japanese soil. One of Japan's touchiest problems is the second- and third-generation Koreans, descended from the people who were brought to Japan for forced labor in the fascist days. They are still known as Koreans even though they were born in Japan, speak the language like natives, and in many cases are physically indistinguishable from everyone else. They have long-term "alien resi-

dence" permits but are not citizens—and in principle they and their descendants never will be (obtaining naturalized Japanese citizenship is nearly impossible). They must register as aliens and be fingerprinted by the police.

The Japanese public has a voracious appetite for *Nihonjinron*—the study of traits that distinguish them from everyone else. Hundreds of works of self-examination are published each year. This discipline involves perfectly reasonable questions about what makes Japan unique as a social system, but it easily slips into inquiries about what makes the Japanese people special as a race. One popular book was *The Japanese Brain*. This book contends that the Japanese have brains that are organized differently from those of the rest of humanity. Many Japanese believe that their thoughts and emotions are different from those of anyone else in the world.

The United States has tried, albeit inconsistently and with limited success, to assimilate people from different backgrounds and

parts of the world. It could be argued that this ethnic mixture has helped us in our dealings with other countries. The Japanese, in contrast, have suffered grievously from their lack of any built-in understanding of foreign cultures. Sitting off on their own, it is easy for them to view the rest of the world as merely a market. A homogeneous population with no emotional ties to the rest of the world acts even more narcissistically than others.

Professor Edward Seidensticker, after living in Japan many years, noted that the Japanese "are not like other people. They are infinitely more clannish, insular, parochial, and one owes it to one's self-respect to preserve a feeling of outrage at the insularity." Even as Japan steadily rises in influence, the idea that it should be the new world model is difficult to accept.

Source: Excerpted and adapted from James Fallows, "The Japanese Are Different from You and Me." *Atlantic Monthly,* September 1986, pp. 35–41.

the everyday world. In the end all ideologies rest on untestable ideas rooted in the basic values and assumptions of each culture. There is a story (Geertz, 1973) about a researcher who challenged the assertion of a native of India that the world is supported on the back of an elephant. "Well," he snorted, "what's the elephant standing on?"

"He's standing on the back of a turtle," came the native's confident reply.

"And what's the turtle standing on?"

"From there"—the Indian smiled—"it's turtles . . . turtles all the way down."

Even though ideologies rest on untestable assumptions, their consequences are very real. They give direction and thrust to our social existence and meaning to our lives. The power of ideologies to mold passion and behavior is well known. History is filled with both horrors and noble deeds people have performed in the name of some ideology:

thirteenth-century Crusaders, fifteenth-century Inquisitors, pro-states rights and pro-union forces in nineteenth-century America, abolitionists, prohibitionists, trade unionists, Nazis and fascists, communists, segregationists, civil rights activists, feminists, consumer activists, environmentalists. These and countless other groups have marched behind their ideological banners, and in the name of their ideologies they have changed the world, often in major ways.

CULTURE AND INDIVIDUAL CHOICE

Very little human behavior is instinctual or biologically programmed. In the course of human evolution, genetic programming gradually was substituted by culture as the source of instructions about what to do, how to do it, and when it should be done. This means that humans have a great deal of individual freedom of action—probably more than any other creature.

However, as we have seen, individual choices are not entirely free. Simply by being born into a particular society with a particular culture, every human being is presented with a limited number of recognized or socially valued choices. Every society has means of training and of social control that are brought to bear on each person, making it difficult for individuals to act or even think in ways that deviate too far from their culture's norms. In order to get along in society, people must keep their impulses under some control and express feelings and gratify needs in a socially approved manner at a socially approved time. This means that humans inevitably feel somewhat dissatisfied, no matter to which group they belong (Freud, 1930). Coming to terms with this central truth about human existence is one of the great tasks of living. Perhaps it is especially important to consider at the present time, for a society that sets out to meet all personal needs is doomed to failure. Sociology, therefore, has an opportunity to make a contribution to setting goals for the future, for only if these goals are grounded solidly on the nature of society and culture will it be possible to make realistic plans that have a chance of succeeding in the long run.

CHAPTER

·4·

Socialization and Development

Becoming a Person: Biology and Culture
Nature versus Nurture: A False Debate
Deprivation and Development

The Concept of Self
Dimensions of Human Development

Theories of Development
Charles Horton Cooley (1864–1929)
George Herbert Mead (1863–1931)
Sigmund Freud (1856–1939)
Erik H. Erikson (1902–   )
Daniel Levinson (1920–   )

Early Socialization in American Society
The Family
The School
Peer Groups
The Mass Media

Adult Socialization
Marriage and Responsibility
Parenthood
Career Development: Vocation and
Identity
Aging and Society

A dramatic moment was about to take place. Tony Milasi of Binghamton, New York, and Roger Brooks of Miami, Florida were about to meet for the first time. They were 24-year-old identical twins who had been separated at birth and reared apart.

Born to a destitute and unmarried woman who could not support them, Tony and Roger were offered to an immigrant couple named Milasi. Unfortunately the couple could only give Tony a secure home.

Roger was not so lucky. He spent his early years in a foster home, a hospital, and an orphanage. Roger did not learn to walk until he was 18 months old, whereas Tony was walking at 12 months. At the age of two Roger was judged to be five months retarded. His youth was marked by disruption and instability. Before dropping out of high school to join the air force, he attended eight schools.

By an amazing coincidence, a man who had worked with Tony in New York happened to spot Roger in a restaurant in Florida. This chance meeting eventually led to the twins being reunited.

Once they were brought together the comparisons began. They certainly appeared to be alike physically, but there were other unexpected similarities. They used the same after-shave lotion, smoked the same brand of cigarettes, used the same obscure brand of toothpaste, and held a pen in the same awkward fashion. They had each joined the military within eight days of each other, liked the same sports, and liked to perform before an audience.

There were, however, substantial differences in personality and emotional development. Tony, who had benefited from a secure family life, was the more venturesome and extroverted of the two twins with an optimistic, happy-go-lucky approach to life. He was a natural salesman with great confidence in his ability.

Roger, on the other hand, possibly as an outgrowth of his difficult childhood, readily empathized with the problems of others. He was very security-

69

Hinaus mit allen Störenfrieden!

Einheit der Jugend in der Hitlerjugend!

Just as the young are socialized to accept the values of American society, they were also socialized into accepting those that were part of the Nazi society. This poster proclaims the glory of the Nazi youth movement as it seeks to rid Germany of those people who are seen as disruptive. Notice how the people representing the threatening groups are made to seem like fleeing rodents or insects.

conscious and willing to endure long hours and boring work in a factory in order to save for the future.

The twins saw each other every day, but their personalities remained quite different. Tony continued to be outgoing and quickly became the dominant "big brother." The quieter Roger worked with the mentally handicapped.

Alike in many ways, but so different in others, the twins reveal some of the complex influences our social environment has in shaping us (Lindeman, 1969).

A macaque monkey reaches maturity in 4 to 6 years, a chimpanzee in 6 to 10, but a human being takes 10 to 15 years to reach sexual maturity and usually even longer to come of age socially. This long period of dependency allows enough time for parents and society to mold and indoctrinate children, creating the differences seen between Tony

and Roger. *This process of social interaction which teaches the child the intellectual, physical, and social skills needed to function as a member of society is called* **socialization.** It is through socialization that children learn the culture of the society into which they have been born. In the course of this process each child slowly acquires a **personality**—that is, *the patterns of behavior and ways of thinking and feeling that are distinctive for each individual.* Contrary to popular wisdom, nobody is a born salesman, a criminal, or a military officer. These things are learned as part of the socialization process.

BECOMING A PERSON: BIOLOGY AND CULTURE

Every human being is born with a set of **genes**, *inherited units of biological material.* Half the genes are inherited from the mother, half from the father. No two people have exactly the same genes, except for identical twins. Genes are made up of complicated chemical substances, and a full set of genes is found in every body cell. Scientists still do not know how many different genes a human body contains, but certainly they number in the tens of thousands.

What makes genes so special is that they influence the chemical processes in our bodies and completely control some of them. For example, such things as blood type, the ability to taste the presence of certain chemicals, and some people's inability to distinguish certain shades of green and red are completely under the control of genes. Most of our body processes, however, are the result of the interaction of genes and the environment (physical, social, and cultural). Thus, how tall you are depends on the genes that control the growth of your legs, trunk, neck, and head, and also on the amount of protein, vitamins, and minerals in your diet. Genes help determine your blood pressure, but so does the amount of salt in your diet, the frequency with which you exercise, and the amount of stress under which you live.

Nature versus Nurture: A False Debate

For over a century, sociologists, educators, and psychologists have argued about which is more important in determining a person's qualities: inherited characteristics (nature) or socialization experiences (nurture). After Charles Darwin (1809–1882) published *On the Origin of Species* in 1859, human beings were seen as a species similar to all others in the animal kingdom. Because most animal behavior seemed to the scholars of that time to be governed by inherited factors, they reasoned that human behavior similarly must be determined by **instincts**—*biologically inherited patterns of complex behavior.* Eventually over 10,000 human instincts were catalogued by researchers (Bernard, 1924).

Then, at the turn of the century, a Russian scientist named Ivan Pavlov (1834–1936) made a startling discovery. He found that if a bell rang just before dogs were fed, that eventually the dogs began to salivate at the ringing of the bell itself, even when no food was served. The experiment led Pavlov to an inescapable conclusion. *So-called instinctual behavior could be molded or* **conditioned** *through a series of repeated experiences linking a desired reaction with a particular object or event.* Dogs could be taught to salivate. Pavlov's work quickly became the foundation on which a new view of human beings was built—one that stressed their infinite capacity to learn and be molded. The American psychologist John B. Watson (1878–1958) conditioned a little boy to be afraid of a rabbit by startling him with a loud noise every time the boy saw the animal. Watson had linked a certain reaction (fear) with an object (the rabbit) through the repetition of the experience. Watson claimed that if he were given complete control over the environment of a dozen healthy infants, he could train each one to be whatever he wished—a doctor, lawyer, artist, merchant, even beggar or thief (Watson, 1925). Among certain psychologists, conditioning became the means by which human behavior could be explained.

Tony Milasi and Roger Brooks reveal some of the issues generated by the tug-of-war between genes and environment in shaping us. By studying identical twins separated at birth we may be able to find out which behaviors are controlled by genes we inherit and which are controlled by external factors such as our family. A study of identical twins separated at birth at the University of Minnesota suggests that traits such as vulnerability to stress may be inherited, while a desire for achievement and aggressiveness are the result of environmental factors. A tendency to develop certain phobias seems to be inherited. Of 15 pairs of twins in the study, three shared one or more phobias.

SOCIOBIOLOGY The debate over nature versus nurture took a new turn with the emergence of sociobiology. The discipline of **sociobiology** *uses biological principles to explain the behavior of all social beings, both animal and human.* For example, when an especially harsh and prolonged winter leaves an Eskimo family without food supplies, they must break camp and quickly find a new site in order to survive. Occasionally an elderly member of the family, often a grandmother, who may slow down the others and require some of the scarce food, will stay behind and face certain death. From the viewpoint of a sociobiologist such as Edward O. Wilson (1975, 1979), this would be an example of altruism, which might ultimately have a biological component.

Wilson believes that behavior can be explained in terms of the ways in which individuals act to increase the probability that their genes and the genes of their close relatives will be passed on to the next generation. Proponents of this view, known as sociobiologists, believe that social science will one day be a mere subdivision of biology. Sociobiologists would claim that the grandmother, in sacrificing her own life, is improving her kin's chances of survival. She has already made her productive contribution to the family. Now the younger members of the family must survive to ensure the continuation of the family and its genes into future generations.

Many researchers disagree with the sociobiological viewpoint. Biologist-geologist Stephen Jay Gould (1976) proposed another, equally plausible scenario, one that discounts the existence of a particular gene programmed for altruism. He perceives the grandmother's sacrifice as an adaptive cultural trait. (As discussed in Chapter 3, culture is a major adaptive mechanism for humans.) Gould posits that the elders remain behind because they have been socially conditioned from earliest childhood to the possibility and appropriateness of this choice. They grew up hearing the songs and stories that praised the elders who stayed behind. Such self-sacrificers were the greatest heroes of the clan. Families whose elders rose to such an occasion survived to celebrate the self-sacrifice, but those families without self-sacrificing elders died out.

Wilson nonetheless makes several major concessions to Gould's viewpoint, acknowledging that among human beings, "the intensity and form of altruistic acts are to a large extent culturally determined" and that "human social evolution is obviously more cultural than genetic." He also leaves the door open to free will admitting that even though our genetic coding may have a major influence, we still have the ability to choose an appropriate course of action (Wilson, 1978). However, Wilson insists the underlying motivation remains genetic, no matter how it is altered or reinforced by cultural influences.

Gould agrees that human behavior has a biological, or genetic, base. He does, however, distinguish between genetic determinism (the sociobiological viewpoint) and genetic potential. What the genes prescribe is not necessarily a particular behavior but the capacity to develop certain behaviors. Although the total array of human possibilities is inherited, which of these numerous possibilities a particular person displays depends on his or her experience in the culture.

Although both nature and nurture are important, the debate over the relative contribution of each continues. However, just as a winter snowfall is the result of both the temperature and the moisture in the air, so must the human organism and human behavior be understood in terms of both genetic inheritance and the effects of environment. **Nurture**—that is, *the entire socialization experience*—is as essential a part of "human nature" as are our genes. It is from the interplay between genes and environment that each human being emerges.

Deprivation and Development

Some unusual events and interesting research indicate that human infants need more than just food and shelter if they are to function effectively as social creatures.

EXTREME CHILDHOOD DEPRIVATION
There are only a few recorded cases of human beings who have grown up without any real contact with other humans. One such case took place in January of 1800, when hunters in Aveyron, France, captured a boy who was running naked through the forest. He seemed to be about 11 years old and apparently had been living alone in the forest for at least five or six years. He appeared thoroughly wild and was subsequently exhibited in a cage from which he escaped several times. Finally, he was examined by "experts" who found him an incurable "idiot" and placed him in an institute for deaf-mutes. But a young doctor, Jean-Marc Itard, thought differently. After close observation he discovered the boy was neither deaf, mute, nor an idiot. Itard believed the boy's wild behavior, lack of speech, highly developed sense of smell, and poor visual attention span were all the result of having been deprived of human contact. The crucial socialization provided by a family had been denied him. Though human, the boy had learned little about how to live with other people. Itard took the boy into his house, named him Victor, and tried to socialize him. He had little success. Although Victor slowly learned to wear clothes, to speak and write a few simple words, and to eat with a knife and fork, he ignored human voices unless they were associated with food, developed no relationships with people other than Dr. Itard and

Children need to understand that other people care about them. This, in turn, teaches them to have feelings for others.

the housekeeper who cared for him, and died at the age of 40 (Itard, 1932; Shattuck, 1980).

Psychologist Bruno Bettleheim (1967) believes that children such as Victor are really autistic—that is, they never develop the capacity to relate to others in a human way because of a prolonged early period of deprivation. The case of Anna sheds more light on this subject.

Anna grew up in the 1930s and had the misfortune of being born illegitimately to the daughter of an extremely disapproving family. Her mother tried to place Anna with foster parents, but was unable to do so and brought her back home. In order to quiet the family's harsh criticism, the young mother hid Anna away in the attic, where she was kept out of sight and even forgotten by the family. Anna remained in the attic for almost six years, ignored by the entire family, including her mother, who did the very minimum to keep her alive. Finally, social workers discovered Anna. The six-year-old girl was unable to sit up, to walk, or to talk. In fact, she was so withdrawn from human beings that at first she appeared to be deaf, mute, and brain damaged. However, after being placed in a special school, Anna learned to communicate a little, to walk awkwardly, to care for herself, and even play with other children. Unfortunately, she died at the age of 10 (Davis, 1940).

A more recent example is Genie, who came to the attention of authorities in California in 1970. From the age of 20 months until 13 and a half years old, genie lived in nearly total isolation. Genie's 70-year-old father kept her restrained day and night in a harness he fashioned for her. She had nothing to do and could only move her hands and feet. Her brother fed her milk and baby food and followed his father's instruction not to talk to her.

When Genie was hospitalized she was malformed, unsocialized and severely malnourished. She was unable to speak or even stand upright. After four years of care, Genie learned some social skills, took a bus to school, began to express some feelings toward others, and achieved the intellectual development of a nine-year-old. There were still, however, serious problems with her language development that could not be corrected no matter how involved the instruction (Curtiss et al., 1977).

These three examples of extreme childhood isolation point to the fact that none of the behavior we think of as typically human arises spontaneously. Humans must be taught to stand, walk, talk, even to think. Human infants must develop **social attachments**—*they must learn to have feelings for others and must see evidence that other people care for them.* This seems a basic need of all primates, as the research by Harry F. Harlow shows.

In a series of experiments with rhesus monkeys, Harlow and his coworkers demonstrated the importance of body contact in social development (Harlow, 1959; Harlow and Harlow, 1962). In one experiment, infant monkeys were taken from their mothers and placed in cages where they were raised in isolation from other monkeys. Each cage contained two substitute mothers: One was made of hard wire and contained a feeding bottle; the other was covered with soft terry cloth but did not have a bottle. Surprisingly, the baby monkeys spent much more time clinging to the cloth mothers than to the wire mothers, even though they received no food at all from the cloth mothers. Apparently the need to cling to and to cuddle against even this miserable substitute for a real mother was more important to them than being fed.

Other experiments with monkeys have con-

firmed the importance of social contact in behavior. Monkeys raised in isolation *never* learn how to interact with other monkeys or even how to mate. If placed in a cage with other monkeys, they either withdraw or become violent and aggressive—threatening, biting, and scratching the others.

Monkeys who are raised without affection make wretched mothers. After being artificially impregnated and giving birth, such monkeys either ignored their infants or displayed a pattern of behavior described by Harlow as "ghastly."

> When an infant attempted to make contact with its mother, she would literally scrape it from her body and abuse it by various sadistic devices. The mother would push the baby's face against the floor and rub it back and forth. Not infrequently, the mother would encircle the infant's head with her jaws, and in one case an infant's skull was crushed in this manner (*Science News*, 1972).

Most times the researchers were able to stop the battering and abuse, but in a few instances the mothers were so violent that the infants were killed before the researchers could intervene. For obvious ethical reasons, similar experiments have never been carried out with human babies.

As with all animal studies, we must be very cautious in drawing inferences for human behavior. After all, we are not monkeys. Yet Harlow's experiments show that without socialization, monkeys do not develop normal social, emotional, sexual, or maternal behavior. Because human beings rely on learning even more than monkeys do, it is likely that the same is true of us.

It is obvious that the human organism needs to acquire culture to be complete; it is very difficult, if not impossible, for children who have been isolated from other people during the crucial years of development to catch up. They apparently suffer permanent damage, although human beings do seem more adaptable than the monkeys studied by Harlow.

INFANTS IN INSTITUTIONS Studies of infants and young children in institutions confirm the view that human developmental needs include more than the mere provision of food and shelter. Psychologist Rene Spitz (1945) visited orphanages in Europe and found that in those dormitories where children were given routine care but were otherwise ignored, they were slow to develop and were withdrawn and sickly. In sociological language these children's needs for **affiliation** (*meaningful interaction with others*) were not met.

In another example, 75 children in an American institution were studied (Provence and Lipton,

1962). The infants, who received minimal physical care but were otherwise neglected in their first year of life, became severely retarded, socially and emotionally. Although they improved when given more attention or when they were brought back into their families, they continued to show long-lasting emotional problems. Like Harlow's monkeys, they found it difficult to form relationships with others, and were unable to control their aggressive impulses.

As the studies we have cited show, human infants need more than just food and shelter if they are to grow and develop normally. Every human infant needs frequent contact with others who demonstrate affection, who respond to attempts to interact, and who themselves initiate interactions with the child. Infants also need contact with people who find ways to interest the child in his or her surroundings and who teach the child the physical and social skills and knowledge needed to function. In addition, in order to develop normally, children need to be taught the culture of their society—to be socialized into the world of social relations and symbols that are the foundation of the human experience.

THE CONCEPT OF SELF

Every individual comes to possess a social identity by occupying **statuses**—*culturally and socially defined positions*—in the course of his or her socialization. This social identity changes as the person moves through the various stages of childhood and adulthood recognized by his or her society. New statuses are occupied; old ones are abandoned. Picture a teenage girl who volunteers as a "candystriper" in a community hospital. She leaves that position to attend college, joins a sorority, becomes a premedical major, and graduates. She goes to medical school, completes an internship, becomes engaged, then enters a program for specialized training in surgery. Perhaps she marries; possibly she has a child. All along the way she moves through different social identities, often assuming several at once. When, many years later, she returns to the hospital where she was a teenage volunteer, she will have an entirely new social identity: adult woman, surgeon, wife (perhaps), mother (possibly).

The above description of the developing girl was from the outside, the way that other members of the society experience her social transitions, or what sociologists would call changes in her social identity. *A* **social identity** *is the total of all the statuses that define an individual.* But what of the person herself? How does this human being who is growing and developing physically, emotionally, intellectually, and socially experience these changes? Is there something constant about a person's experience that allows one to say, "I am that changing person—changing, but yet somehow the same individual?" In other words, do all human beings have personal identities separate from their social identities? Most social scientists believe the answer is yes. *This changing yet enduring personal identity is called the* **self.**

The self develops when the individual becomes aware of his or her feelings, thoughts, and behaviors as separate and distinct from those of other people. This usually happens at a young age when children begin to realize that they have their own history, habits, and needs, and begin to imagine how these

The process of socialization involves trying on a variety of roles that will eventually make up the self.

might appear to others. By adulthood the concept of self is fully developed. Most researchers would agree that the concept of self includes (1) an awareness of the existence, appearance, and boundaries of one's own body (you are walking among the other members of the crowd, dressed appropriately for the occasion, and trying to avoid bumping into people as you chat), (2) the ability to refer to one's own being by using language and other symbols ("Hi, as you can see from my name tag, I'm Harry Hernandez from Gonzales, Texas"), (3) knowledge of one's personal history ("Yup, I grew up in Gonzales. My folks own a farm there, and since I was a small boy I've wanted to study farm management"), (4) knowledge of one's needs and skills ("I'm good with my hands all right, but I need the intellectual stimulation of doing large-scale planning"), (5) the ability to organize one's knowledge and beliefs ("Let me tell you about planning crop rotation. . ."), (6) the ability to organize one's experiences ("I know what I like and what I don't like"), and (7) the ability to take a step back and look at one's being as others do, to evaluate the impressions one creates, and to understand the feelings and attitudes one stimulates in others ("It might seem a little funny to you that a farmer like me would want to come to a party for the opening of a new art gallery. Well, as far back as I can remember, I always kinda enjoyed art, and now that I can afford to indulge myself, I thought maybe I'd buy some paintings") (see Cooley, 1909; Erikson, 1964; Gardner, 1978; Mead, 1934).

Dimensions of Human Development

The development of the self is a complicated process. It involves many interacting factors, including the acquisition of language and the ability to use symbols. There are three dimensions of human development tied to the emergence of the self: cognitive development, moral development, and gender identity.

COGNITIVE DEVELOPMENT For centuries most people assumed that a child's mind worked exactly the same way as an adult's. The child was thought of as a miniature adult who simply lacked information about the world. Swiss philosopher and psychologist Jean Piaget (1896–1980) was instrumental in changing that view through his studies of the development of intelligence in children. His work has been significant to sociologists because the processes of thought are central to the development of identity and, consequently, to the ability to function in society.

Piaget found that children move through a series of predictable stages on their way to logical thought, and some never attain the most advanced stages. From birth to age two, during the *sensorimotor stage,* the infant relies on touch and the manipulation of objects for information about the world, slowly learning about cause and effect. At about the age of two, the child begins to learn that words can be symbols for objects. In this, the *preoperational stage* of development, the child cannot yet see the world from another person's point of view.

The *operational* stage is next and lasts from the age of seven to about the age of 12. During this period the child begins to think with some logic and can understand and work with numbers, volume, shapes, and spatial relationships. With the onset of adolescence, the child progresses to the most advanced stage of thinking—*formal logical thought.* People at this stage are capable of abstract, logical thought and can develop ideas about things that have no concrete reference, such as infinity, death, freedom, and justice. In addition, they are able to anticipate possible consequences of their acts and decisions. Achieving this stage is crucial to developing an identity and an ability to enter into mature interpersonal relationships (Piaget and Inhelder, 1969).

MORAL DEVELOPMENT Every society has a **moral order**—that is, a *shared view of right and wrong.* Without moral order a society would soon fall apart. People would not know what to expect from themselves and one another, and social relationships would be impossible to maintain. Therefore, the process of socialization must include instruction about the moral order of an individual's society.

The research of Lawrence Kohlberg (1969) suggests that not every person is capable of thinking about morality in the same way. Just as our sense of self and our ability to think logically develop in stages, our moral thinking develops in a progression of steps as well. To illustrate this, Kohlberg asked children from a number of different societies (including Turkey, Mexico, China, and the United States) to resolve moral dilemmas such as the following: A man's wife is dying of cancer. A rare drug might save her, but it costs $2,000. The man tries to raise the money but can come up with only $1,000. He asks the druggist to sell him the drug for $1,000. The druggist refuses. The desperate husband then breaks into the druggist's store and steals the drug. Should he have done so? Why or why not?

Kohlberg was more interested in the *reasoning*

behind the child's judgment than in the answer itself. Based on his analysis of this reasoning, he believed that changes in moral thinking progress step by step through six qualitatively distinct stages (although most people never go beyond stages 3 or 4):

Stage 1: *Orientation toward punishment.* Those who thought the man should steal, (pros), said he could get into trouble if he just let his wife die. Those who said he should not steal (cons) stressed that he might be arrested for the crime.

Stage 2: *Orientation toward reward.* The pros said that if the woman lived, the man would have what he wanted. If he got caught in the act of stealing the drug, he could return the drug and would probably be given only a light sentence. The cons said that the man should not blame himself if his wife died, and if he got caught, she might die before he got out of jail so he would have lost her anyway. Stealing would not pay.

Stage 3: *Orientation toward possible disapproval by others.* The pros observed that nobody would think the man was bad if he stole the drug but that his family would never forgive him if his wife died and he had done nothing to help her. The cons pointed out that not only would the druggist think of the man as a criminal, but the rest of society would, too.

Stage 4: *Orientation toward formal laws and fear of personal dishonor.* The pros said that the man would always feel dishonored if he did nothing and his wife died. The cons said that even if he saved his wife by stealing, he would feel guilty and dishonored for having broken the law.

Stage 5: *Orientation toward peer values and democracy.* The pros said that failure to steal the drug would cost the man his peers' respect because he would have acted out of fear rather than out of consideration of what was the logical thing to do. The cons countered that the man would lose the respect of the community if he were caught because he would show himself as a person who acted out of emotion rather than according to the laws that govern everybody's behavior.

Stage 6: *Orientation toward one's own set of values.* The pros focused on the man's conscience, saying he would never be able to live with himself if his wife died and he had done nothing. The cons argued that although others might not blame the man for stealing the drug, in doing so he would have failed to live up to his own standards of honesty.

Kohlberg found that although these stages of moral development correspond roughly to other aspects of the developing self, most people never progress to stages 5 and 6. In fact, Kohlberg subsequently dropped stage 6 from his scheme as a result of widespread criticism that it was elitist and culturally biased. Kohlberg himself could find no evidence that any of his long-term subjects ever reached this stage (Muson, 1979). At times people regress from a higher stage to a lower one. For example, when Kohlberg analyzed the explanations that Nazi war criminals of World War II gave for their participation in the systematic murder of millions of people who happened to possess certain religious (Jewish), ethnic (gypsies), or psychological (mentally retarded) traits, he found that none of the reasons were above stage 3 and more were at stage 1—"I did what I was told to do, otherwise I'd have been punished" (Kohlberg, 1967). However, many of these war criminals had been very responsible and successful people in their pre–war lives and presumably in those times had reached higher stages of moral development.

GENDER IDENTITY   One of the most important elements of the sense of self is our **identity,** *the view of ourselves resulting from our gender.* Certain aspects of gender identity are rooted in biology. Males tend to be larger and stronger than females, but females tend to have better endurance than males do. Females also become pregnant and give birth to infants and usually can nurse infants with their own milk. However, gender identity is mostly a matter of cultural definition. There is nothing inherently male or female about a teacher, a pilot, a carpenter, or a typist other than what our culture tells us. As we shall see in Chapter 10, "gender identity and sex roles" are far more a matter of nurture than of nature.

THEORIES OF DEVELOPMENT

Among scholars who have devised theories of development, Charles Horton Cooley, George Herbert Mead, Sigmund Freud, and Erik Erikson stand out because of the contributions they have made to the way sociologists today think about socialization. Cooley and Mead saw the individual and society as partners. They were symbolic interactionists (see Chapter 1) and as such believed that the individual develops a self solely through social relationships— that is, through interaction with others. Cooley and Mead believed that all our behaviors, our attitudes, even our ideas of self, arise from our interactions with other people. Hence they were pure environmentalists in that they believed that social forces rather than genetic factors shape the individual.

If a child's need for meaningful interaction with others is not met, the development of a social identity will be delayed.

Freud, on the other hand, tended to picture the individual and society as enemies. He saw the individual as constantly having to yield reluctantly to the greater power of society, to keep internal urges (especially sexual and aggressive ones) under strict control.

Erikson presented something of a compromise. He thought of the individual as progressing through a series of stages of development that express internal urges, yet are greatly influenced by societal and cultural factors.

Charles Horton Cooley (1864–1929)

Cooley believed that the self develops through the process of social interaction with others. This process begins early in life and is influenced by such primary groups as the family. Later on, peer groups become very important. Cooley used the phrase **looking-glass self** to describe *the three-stage process through which each of us develops a sense of self.* First, we imagine how our actions appear to others.

Second, we imagine how other people judge these actions. Finally, we make some sort of self-judgment based on the presumed judgments of others. In effect, other people become a mirror or looking glass for us (1909).

In Cooley's view, therefore, the self is entirely a social product—that is, a product of social interaction. Each individual acquires a sense of self in the course of being socialized and continues to modify it in each new situation throughout life. Cooley believed that the looking-glass self constructed early in life remains fairly stable and that childhood experiences are very important in determining our sense of self throughout our lives.

One of Cooley's principal contributions to sociology was his observation that although our perceptions are not always correct, what we believe is more important in determining our behavior than what is real. This same idea was expressed by sociologist W. I. Thomas (1928) when he noted, "If men define situations as real, they are real in their consequences." If we can understand the ways in which people perceive reality, we can begin to understand their behavior.

George Herbert Mead (1863–1931)

Mead was a philosopher and a well-known social psychologist at the University of Chicago. His work led to the development of the school of thought called symbolic interactionism (described in Chapter 1). Mead was a student of Cooley. He built on Cooley's ideas, tracing the beginning of a person's awareness of self to the relationships between the care giver (usually the mother) and the child (1934).

The self becomes the sum total of a person's beliefs and feelings about themselves. The self is composed of two parts, the "I" and the "me." *The "I" portion of the self wishes to have free expression, to be active and spontaneous.* The "I" wishes to be free of the control of others and to take the initiative in situations. It is the part of the individual that is unique and distinctive. *The "me" portion of the self is made up of those things learned through the socialization process from the family, peers, school, and so on.* The "me" makes normal social interaction possible, while the "I" prevents it from being mechanical and totally predictable.

Mead used the term "significant others" to refer to those individuals who are most important in our development, such as parents, friends, and teachers. As we continue to be socialized we learn awareness of the views of the generalized others. *These **generalized others** are the viewpoints, attitudes, and expectations of society as a whole or of a general* community of people that we are aware of and who are important to us. We may believe it is important to go to college for example, because significant others have instilled this viewpoint in us. While at college we may be influenced by the views of selected generalized others who represent the community of lawyers we hope to join one day as we progress with our education.

Mead believed the self develops in three stages (1934). The first, or *preparatory stage,* is characterized by the child's imitating the behavior of others, which prepares the child for learning social role expectations. In the second or *play stage* the child has acquired language and begins not only to imitate behavior but also to formulate role expectations: playing house, cops and robbers, and so on. In this stage the play will feature many discussions among playmates about the way things "ought" to be. "I'm the boss," a little boy may announce. "The daddy is the boss of the house." "Oh no," his friend might counter, "Mommies are the real bosses. . ." In the third, or *game stage,* the child learns that there are rules that specify the proper and correct relationship among the players. For example, in a baseball game rules apply to the game in general as well as to a series of expectations about how each position should be played. During the game stage, according to Mead, we learn the expectations, positions, and rules of society at large. Throughout life, in whatever position we occupy, we must learn the expectations of the various positions with which we interact as well as the expectations of the general audience, if our performance is to go smoothly.

Thus, for Mead the self is rooted in, and begins to take shape through, the social play of children, and is well on its way to being formed by the time the child is eight or nine years old. Therefore, like Cooley, Mead regarded childhood experience as very important to charting the course of development.

Sigmund Freud (1856–1939)

Freud was a pioneer in the study of human behavior and the human mind. He was a doctor in Vienna, Austria, who gradually became interested in the problem of understanding mental illness. Once he turned his attention to this area, he charted new pathways of scholarship and thought, and today is regarded as one of the most creative and original thinkers of the nineteenth and twentieth centuries.

Over his lifetime, Freud developed a body of thought about the mind that is called psychoanalytic theory. **Psychoanalytic theory** *holds that the human mind and human behavior is shaped by two main*

forces: *unconscious impulses and the resistance or repression of those unconscious impulses.* (**Psychoanalysis** *is a method developed by Freud for treating mental illness in which a patient's unconscious wishes and fears are brought into the conscious mind.*) Psychoanalytic theory rests on two basic hypotheses: (1) **Psychic determinism,** *or the view that every human act has a psychological cause or basis.* Because no human behavior comes about as the result of chance, "slips" of the tongue, moments of clumsiness, and unexpected moods all are explainable as events in the person's mind. (2) The existence of the **unconscious,** *or the view that people are aware of only a small part of the thoughts and feelings that exist in their minds.*

In Freud's view, the self has three separately functioning parts: the id, the superego, and the ego. *The* **id** *consists of the drives or instincts that Freud believed every human being inherits but for the most part remain unconscious.* Of these instincts two are most important: the aggressive drive and the **libido,** *or sexual drive.* Every feeling derives from these two drives. The superego is the internal censor. It is not inherited biologically, like the id, but is learned in the course of a person's socialization. The superego keeps trying to put the brakes on the so-called **pleasure principle,** *or the id's impulsive attempts to satisfy its drives.* Another way to describe this is to

Sigmund Freud believed that even though the individual needs society, society's restrictive norms are a constant source of discontent.

say that the **superego** in each of us *represents society's norms and moral values as learned primarily from our parents.* So, for instance, the superego must hold back the id's unending drive for sexual expression (Freud, 1920, 1923). The id and superego, then, are eternally at war with each other. Fortunately, there is a third functional part of the self called the **ego** *that tries not only to mediate in the eternal conflict between id and superego, but also to find socially acceptable ways for the id's drives to be expressed.* Unlike the id, the ego is guided by the **reality principle,** *a process by which the ego constantly evaluates social realities and looks for ways to adjust to them.* For example, the ego finds socially appropriate sexual partners with whom the individual can satisfy sexual drives. Thus, just as the id works on the pleasure principle, the ego works on the reality principle (Freud, 1920, 1923).

Freud pictured the individual as constantly in conflict: The instinctual drives of the id (essentially sex and aggression) push for expression, while at the same time the demands of society set certain limits on the behavior patterns that will be tolerated. Even though the individual needs society, society's restrictive norms and values are a source of ongoing discontent (Freud, 1930). Freud's theories suggest that society and the individual are enemies, with the latter yielding to the former reluctantly and only out of compulsion.

Erik H. Erikson (1902–   )

In 1950 Erikson, an artist-turned-psychologist who studied with Freud in Vienna, published an influential book called *Childhood and Society* (1963). In it he built on Freud's theory of development but added two important elements. First, he stressed that development is a lifelong process and that a person continues to pass through new stages even during adulthood. Second, he paid greater attention to the social and cultural forces operating at each step along the way.

In Erikson's view, human development is accomplished in eight separate stages (see Table 4.1). Each stage amounts to a crisis of sorts brought on by two factors: biological changes in the developing individual and social expectations and stresses. At each stage the individual is pulled in two opposite directions to resolve the crisis. In normal development the individual resolves the conflict experienced at each stage somewhere toward the middle of the opposing options. For example, very few people are entirely trusting, and very few trust nobody at all. Most of us are able to trust at least some people

and thereby form enduring relationships while at the same time staying alert to the possibility of being misled.

Erikson's view of development has proved useful to sociologists because it seems to apply to many societies. In a later work (1968) he focused on the social and psychological causes of the "identity crisis" so prevalent among American and European youths. Erikson's most valuable contribution to the study of human development has been to show that socialization continues throughout a person's life and does not stop with childhood. There is indeed development after 30—and after 60 and 70 as well. The task of building the self is lifelong; it can be considered our central task from cradle to grave. We construct the self—our identity—using the materials made available to us by our culture and our society.

Daniel Levinson (1920–   )

A fascinating blend of sociology and psychology has taken place in the area of adult development. Through research in this field we have come to

According to Erik Erikson, adolescence is a time when the teenager must develop an identity, as well as the ability to establish close personal relationships with others.

TABLE 4.1

Erikson's Eight Stages of Human Development

Stage	Age Period	Characteristic to Be Achieved	Major Hazards to Achievement
Trust versus mistrust	Birth to 1 year	Sense of trust or security—achieved through parental gratification of needs and affection.	Neglect, abuse, or deprivation; inconsistent or inappropriate love in infancy; early or harsh weaning.
Autonomy versus shame and doubt	1 to 4 years	Sense of autonomy—achieved as child begins to see self as individual apart from his/her parents.	Conditions that make the child feel inadequate, evil, or dirty.
Initiative versus guilt	4 to 5 years	Sense of initiative—achieved as child begins to imitate adult behavior and extends control of the world around him/her.	Guilt produced by overly strict discipline and the internalization of rigid ethical standards that interfere with the child's spontaneity.
Industry versus inferiority	6 to 12 years	Sense of duty and accomplishment—achieved as the child lays aside fantasy and play and begins to undertake tasks and school work.	Feelings of inadequacy produced by excessive competition, personal limitations, or other events leading to feelings of inferiority.
Identity versus role confusion	Adolescence	Sense of identity—achieved as one clarifies sense of self and what he/she believes in.	Sense of role confusion resulting from the failure of the family or society to provide clear role models.
Intimacy versus isolation	Young adulthood	Sense of intimacy—the ability to establish close personal relationships with others.	Problems with earlier stages that make it difficult to get close to others.
Generativity versus stagnation	30s to 50s	Sense of productivity and creativity—resulting from work and parenting activities.	Sense of stagnation produced by feeling inadequate as a parent and stifled at work.
Integrity versus despair	Old age	Sense of ego integrity—achieved by acceptance of the life one has lived.	Feelings of despair and dissatisfaction with one's role as a senior member of society.

Source: Adapted from Erik H. Erikson, *Childhood and Society*. 2nd ed. New York: W.W. Norton, copyright renewed by author, 1978.

recognize that there are predictable age-related developmental periods in the adult life cycle, just as there are in the developmental cycles for children and adolescents. These periods are marked by a concerted effort to resolve particular life issues and goals.

Daniel Levinson and his colleagues have contributed important research in this area (1978). Levinson recruited 40 men, age 35 to 45, from four occupational groups: factory workers, novelists, business executives, and academic biologists. Each subject was interviewed several times during a two- to three-month period and again, if possible, in a follow-up session two years later.

From this study Levinson developed the founda-tion of his theory. He proposed that adults are periodically faced with new but predictable developmental tasks throughout their life and that working through these challenges is the essence of adulthood. Levinson believes the adult life course is marked by a continual series of building periods, followed by stable periods, then followed again by periods in which attempts are made to change some of the perceived flaws in the pervious design.

Levinson's model describes the periods in the adult life cycle:

I. *Early Adult Period (age 18 to 22)*
   Leaving the family of origin is the major task of this period. A great deal of energy is expended

in trying to reduce dependence on the family for support or authority. Peer support often becomes critical to this task.

II. *Getting Into the Adult World (age 22 to 28)*
This period is marked by the exploration and beginning commitment to adult roles, responsibilities, and relationships. Career advancement may become a major focal point. This period produces an initial life structure including marriage and occupation. The individual may also form a *dream* that serves as a guiding force and provides images of future life structures.

III. *Transitional Period (age 28 to 32)*
At this point the individual begins to perceive some of the "flaws" in his or her initial life structure and sets out to correct them. Divorce and job changes are common during this period. This is a time of internal instability, in which many aspects of the individual's life are questioned and examined.

IV. *Settling Down (age 33 to 40)*
Having reworked some of the aspects of one's life during the previous period, the individual is now ready to seek order and stability. There is a strong desire for achievement and an earnest attempt to make the dream a reality. The individual wants to "sink roots."

V. *Transitional Period (age 38 to 42)*
This is a major transitional period representing the turning point between young and middle adulthood. The individual starts to see a difference between the dream and the reality of his or her life, leading to a great deal of soul searching. Divorce and career changes once again become real possibilities. The individual may start to give up certain aspects of the dream and become less achievement and advancement oriented.

VI. *Beginning of Middle Adulthood (age mid-40s)*
The previous period of turmoil has produced a greater acceptance of oneself. The individual is less dominated by the need to win or to achieve external rewards and more concerned with enjoying his or her life and work. The individual also has a greater concern for other people than before.

Levinson did not study people beyond age 45, though he does believe that the developmental process continues throughout the entire life course. The model is particularly interesting to sociologists because it appears to show a close relationship between individual development and one's position in society at a particular time.

There are however, problems with being too quick to embrace this type of theory. Levinson's theory of adult development is what is commonly referred to as a "stage theory." Stage theories describe a series of changes that follow an orderly sequential pattern. These theories have been criticized for being too rigid, for assuming that the changes are always in one direction, and for assuming that the stages are universal. Critics note that we can apply stages of development to children, but when we do so with adults, we leave little room for individual differences, social change, and specific cohort experiences (Neugarten, 1979). Levinson's theory has also been criticized as not being relevant to women. Since the model is based on a study only including men, it is not clear whether all the stages also apply to women. Barnett and Baruch (1979) argue that women's roles involve varying life structures that are not so centrally tied to chronological age as men's are. Women may experience various combinations of career, marriage, and children throughout their lives. Some women may not enter the world of work until their children have started school. Their ability to reassess their career commitments at age 40 may involve different issues than those important to men.

Rossi (1985) notes that the stage theorists may have merely described the life pattern of a particular cohort. Most of the subjects in these studies were born before and during the Depression, were predominantly white and upper-middle class. What was true for this group may not hold for today's 30 and 40 year olds, born after World War II. She points out that the men in the studies may have burned out at a premature age, rather than reflecting a normal developmental process all men go through."

EARLY SOCIALIZATION IN AMERICAN SOCIETY

Children are brought up very differently from one society to another. Each culture has its own child-rearing values, attitudes, and practices. No matter how children are raised, however, each society must provide certain minimal necessities to ensure normal development. The infant's body must, of course, be cared for. But more than care is required. Children need speaking social partners (some evidence suggests that a child who has received no language stimulation at all in the first five to six years of life will be unable ever to acquire speech [Chomsky, 1975]). They also need physical stimulation, objects they can manipulate, space and time to explore, activity to initiate, time to be alone, and finally,

TAKING THE SOCIOLOGICAL PERSPECTIVE

Are Geniuses Born or Created?

On approximately six Sundays a year, a new group of 80 people arrives on the campus of The Institute for the Advancement of Human Potential in Philadelphia to take a week-long course on how to turn their children into geniuses.

Marjorie Bennett has been using the regime taught in this course with her son Jeremy, age six. While many of Jeremy's peers are struggling through their first primer, Jeremy is breezing through the *Wall Street Journal, Newsweek,* and selected works by Longfellow. He likes knock-knock jokes in addition to history, paleontology, geography, and astronomy.

Jeremy's interests are not confined to books. He just signed up for an advanced gymnastics class, and he plays the piano and sings.

Since Jeremy was barely out of the womb, his mother has been teaching him reading, math, science, and music. Marjorie Bennett recently quit her job so she can spend even more time leading Jeremy to what she hopes will be the fast track to success.

Not so long ago, most parents wanted their children to be like everybody else. They were often as upset if their children were advanced as they were if the children were slow. Now all that appears to have changed. For many parents today there is no such thing as going too fast, and their major concern is that their children stay ahead of the pack.

Perhaps the most controversial and evangelical proponent of the "start-them-young-and-push-them-hard" philosophy is Glenn Doman, founder of the Philadel-

phia institute mentioned above. He has written such books as *Teach Your Baby Math, How To Teach Your Baby to Read,* and *How to Multiply Your Baby's Intelligence.*

At Doman's institute, children as young as seven months are "reading" in three languages, one-year-olds study musical notation, and 18-month-olds begin violin lessons. Doman, who has been teaching parents how to teach their babies for the past 40 years, believes that early education can lead to a "golden age" for society and an end to war, poverty, and hunger.

Psychologist David Elkind believes the major consequence of this new parenting is that many contemporary parents are putting tremendous pressure on children to perform at ever-earlier ages.

---

limits and prohibitions that organize their options and channel development in certain culturally specified directions (Provence, 1972).

Every society provides this basic minimum care in its own culturally prescribed ways. A variety of agents are used to mold the child to fit into the society. Once again, these agents vary from culture to culture. Here we consider some of the most important agents of socialization in American society.

The Family

For young children in most societies—and certainly in American society—the family is the primary world for the first few years of life. The values, norms, ideals, and standards presented are accepted by the child uncritically as correct—indeed, as the only way things could possibly be. Even though later experiences lead children to modify much of what they have learned within the family, it is not unusual for individuals to carry into the social relationships of adult life the role expectations that

characterized the family of their childhood. It is hardly insignificant that we joke about such things as a newlywed wife not being able to cook her husband's favorite meal as well as his mother did, or that a daughter may take on many of the characteristics of her mother.

Every family, therefore, socializes its children to its own particular version of the society's culture. In addition, however, each family exists within certain subcultures of the larger society: It belongs to a geographical region, a social class, one (or two) ethnic groups, and possibly a religious group or other subculture. Families differ with regard to how important these factors are in determining their lifestyle and their child-rearing practices. For example, some families are deeply committed to an ethnic identification such as African-American, Hispanic, Asian-American, Native American, Italian American, Polish American, or Jewish. Much of the family life may revolve around participation in social and religious events of the community and may include speaking a language other than standard English.

Clearly, there is nothing wrong with wanting children to do their best. It is not the normal healthy desire of parents to have successful children that is the problem, but the excessive pressure some parents are putting on children.

What is behind this push for excellence? Elkind believes it is related to the fact that parents today are having fewer children. The pressure to have "a child to be proud of" is therefore greater. Parents who have been successful in their own careers see no reason why they should not ensure the same success for their children. The gifted children become proof of their own success.

Elkind believes many parents become far too intrusive and deprive children of the opportunity to take responsibility for their mistakes and credit for their achievements. These parents run the risk of producing children who are dependent and lack self-esteem. Instead of superkids,

Elkind notes, the parents may end up with super problems.

Glenn Doman disagrees. He believes that every human infant has within him or her the seeds of genius. He notes, "Genius is available to each human infant both genetically . . . and environmentally (because intelligence can be either created or throttled, increased or decreased, in each individual human infant)."

Doman believes that what we call genius, a uniquely human capacity, is no gift at all but is instead a human birthright common to us all, out of which we have been cheated by our lack of knowledge—a superb opportunity which has been stolen from us. Every human mother has the capacity to nurture the seeds of genius within her infant.

Studies of gifted and successful adults give no support to the idea that early formal instruction creates intellectual giftedness or creative talent. Autobiographical

statements from such adults note that their parents were careful not to impose their own priorities on them. Instead, these parents allowed their children to lead and then provided the necessary support and encouragement.

We must also ask "What is gained by ballet lessons?" The child is forced to adjust to another adult, another set of standards, another group of people, another set of rules. Is this activity being done for the convenience of the parents or out of interest for the child? We should remember that childhood is the springtime of life, not spring training.

Sources: Glenn Doman, *How to Multiply Your Baby's Intelligence* (Garden City, New York: Doubleday, 1984); David Elkind, "Superkids and Super Problems," *Psychology Today,* May 1987, pp. 60–61; David Elkind, *Miseducation: Preschoolers at Risk* (New York: Alfred A. Knopf, 1987).

There is also evidence that social class and parents' occupations influence the ways in which children are raised in America. Parents who have white-collar occupations are used to dealing with people and solving problems. As a consequence, white-collar parents value intellectual curiosity and flexibility. Blue-collar parents have jobs which involve machines, require obeying orders and being on time. They are likely to reward obedience to authority, punctuality, and mechanical ability in their children (Kohn and Schooler, 1983).

The last two decades have seen major changes

Every family socializes its children to its own particular version of the society's culture. The values and world view of a boy raised on a dairy farm in Wisconsin are likely to be different from those of a child born and raised in an urban center such as Los Angeles or New York City.

in the structure of the American family. High divorce rates, the dramatic increase in the number of single-parent families, and the common phenomenon of two-worker families, has meant that the family as the major source of socialization of children is being challenged. Child-care providers have also become a major influence in the lives of many young children. (For a discussion of the effects on day-care of the socialization of children see the box on Page 88, "Is Day Care Harmful to Children?")

The School

The school is an institution intended to socialize children in selected skills and knowledge. In recent decades, however, the school has been assigned additional tasks. For instance, in poor communities and neighborhoods, school lunch (and breakfast) programs are an important source of balanced nutrition for children. There is also a more basic problem the school must confront. As an institution the school must resolve the conflict in values between the local community and state and regional officials whose job it is to determine what should be taught. For example, in many schools of the rural American South, the theory of evolution is not taught, even though it represents a body of knowledge that most American scholars accept as valuable and important. In other instances, education officials are able to ramrod curriculum changes into the classroom despite the complaints of parents, whose objections are dismissed as ignorant or tradition-bound.

An example of such a conflict involves the addition of AIDS education to the curriculum in many schools. Some parents have objected to teaching young children about condoms and sexual activity despite the health risk that ignorance could pose. Many school boards have taken the position that the schools have a responsibility to provide this information even when large numbers of parents object.

In coming to grips with their multiple responsibilities, many schools have established a philosophy of education that encompasses socialization as well as academic instruction. According to the philosophy adopted by one school, for instance, its aim is to help students develop to their fullest capacity, not only intellectually, but also emotionally, culturally, morally, socially, and physically. By exposing the student to a variety of ideas, teachers attempt to guide the development of the whole student in interests and abilities unique to each. Students are expected to learn how to analyze these ideas critically and reach their own conclusions. The ultimate goal of the school is to produce a "well-integrated" person who will become socially responsible and a good neighbor and citizen. Two questions arise: Is such an ambitious, all-embracing educational philosophy working? And is it an appropriate goal for our schools?

In a way the school is a model of much of the adult social world. Interpersonal relationships are not based on individual love and affection for one another. Rather, they are impersonal and predefined by the society with little regard for each particular individual who enters into them. Children's adjustment to the school's social order is a preview of what will be expected as they mature and attempt to negotiate their way into the institutions of adult society (job, political work, organized recreation, and so on). Of all the functions of the school, this may be the most important. (The role of the school in socialization will be discussed more extensively in Chapter 13.)

Peer Groups

Peers *are individuals who are social equals.* From early childhood until late adulthood we encounter a wide variety of peer groups. No one will deny that they play a powerful role in our socialization. Often their influence is greater than any other socialization source.

Within the family and the school, children are in socially inferior positions relative to figures of authority (parents, teachers, principals). As long as the child is small and weak, this social inferiority seems natural, but by adolescence a person is almost fully grown, and arbitrary submission to authority is not so easy to accept. Hence, many adolescents withdraw into the comfort of social groups com-

Peer groups provide valuable social support for adolescents.

posed of peers. In the United States, school-age children spend twice as much time with their peers, on the average, than they do with their parents (Bronfenbrenner, 1970).

It appears that parents play a major role in the teaching of basic values and the desire to achieve long-term goals. Peers have the greatest influence in life-style issues, such as appearance, social activities, and dating (Sebald, 1986).

Peer groups provide valuable social support for adolescents who are moving toward independence from their parents. As a consequence peer-group values often run counter to those of the older generation. New group members are quickly socialized to adopt symbols of group membership such as styles of dress, use and consumption of certain material goods, and stylized patterns of behavior. It is ironic that although adolescents often proclaim their freedom from the conformity of their parents, within their peer groups they are themselves slaves to group fashion.

A number of studies have documented the increasing importance of peer-group socialization in America. One reason for this is that parents' life experiences and accumulated wisdom may not be very helpful in preparing young people to meet the requirements of life in a society that is changing constantly. Not infrequently adolescents are better informed than their parents about such things as sex, drugs, and technology. In her study of the generation gap, Margaret Mead (1970) likened youth to pioneers exploring not a new land but rather a new time.

Peer group influence for many inner-city youths can lead to wasted lives and violence. For many, gangs—kids banding together for identity, status, criminal activity, and mutual protection—often involves drug abuse. In Dallas, for example, cocaine is traded in many high schools, and attempts to emphasize the dangers of drugs fall on deaf ears.

The negative effects of peer pressure are felt on college campuses as well as in the ghetto. Peer pressure has led to deaths from hazing activities in college fraternities. An 18-year-old freshman at Rutgers University in New Jersey died when he consumed more than 20 ounces of liquor in 30 to 45 minutes as part of a hazing ritual to initiate new members into the fraternity. The student's need for being accepted by his peers overcame his sense of reason, even when he realized that the alcohol was making him sick (Rangel, *New York Times*, May 4, 1988).

As the authority of the family diminishes under the pressures of social change, peer groups move into the vacuum and substitute their own morality for that of the older generation. Peer groups are most effective in molding the behavior of those adolescents whose parents do not provide consistent standards, a principled moral code, guidance, and emotional support (Baumrind, 1975; Elder, 1975). Elkins (1981) has expressed the view that the power of the peer group is in direct proportion to the extent that the adolescent feels ignored by the parents. In fact, four decades ago sociologist David Riesman, in his classic work *The Lonely Crowd* (1950), already thought that the peer group had become the single most powerful molder of many adolescents' behavior, and that striving for peer approval had become the dominant concern of an entire American generation—adults as well as adolescents. He coined the term *other directed* to describe those who are overly concerned with finding social approval.

The Mass Media

It is possible that today Riesman would review his thinking somewhat. Over the past 25 to 30 years, the mass media—television, radio, magazines, films, newspapers—have become important agents of socialization in America. It is almost impossible in our society to escape from the images and sounds of television or radio; even in most private homes, especially those with children, the media are constantly visible and/or audible.

The **mass media** *are an impersonal means of transmitting information to great numbers of people in a very short period of time.* For the most part, the communication is one way, creating an audience conditioned to receive passively what is sometimes called *mass culture* (Rosenberg and White, 1971), consisting of whatever news, messages, programs, or events are brought to them.

Because young children are so impressionable and because in so many American households the television is used as an unpaid mechanical babysitter, social scientists have become increasingly concerned about the socializing role played by the mass media in our society.

Today 98.2 percent of all households in the United States have television sets, with an average of two sets per home. Most children become regular watchers of television between the ages of three and six. School children watch an average of two-and-one-half hours of television a day on school days and an average of four hours and twenty minutes during the weekend. Their favorite programs in order of most frequently watched are evening situation comedies, cartoons, music videos, sports, game shows, talk shows, and soap operas. One study

People have become increasingly concerned about the socializing role played by the mass media.

concluded that by the time most people reach the age of 18, they will have spent more waking time watching television than doing anything else—talking with parents, spending time with friends, or even going to school (*Statistical Abstract of the United States: 1991*). What effect does this have on children?

For one thing, today's children receive an enormous amount of information. They are instantly informed of new fads and styles, new activities, and new products. Many people consider this blatant exploitation, because young children have no way of evaluating the merits of advertising programs.

This is not to say that all children's television programming is exploitive. Programs such as "Sesame Street," a production of the Children's Television Workshop, are designed to help preschoolers develop the intellectual, social, and emotional skills needed to succeed in school. Although "Sesame Street" teaches children their letters and numbers, an equally important aim is to help young children understand and adjust to the relationships around them.

Some researchers (Mayrowitz, 1984) believe the impact of the media has been enhanced because the United States has shifted from a book culture to a television culture. The television set opens up a whole new world that is largely beyond the control of parents. Children get to see adults acting in ways that their parents may disapprove of, such as committing violence, stealing, engaging in adultery, or taking drugs. The children are also forced to confront issues (AIDS, abortion, racial violence, or

suicide) that they may have been sheltered from during previous eras. As the role of the media in the socialization process increases, the role of the parents decreases.

The influence of television on behavior is of special concern to those who believe that the prevalence of violence depicted on TV and in films produces violent crime and aggression in children. A study by the National Institute of Mental Health (1982) came to the conclusion that there was "overwhelming" evidence of a clear relationship between televised violence and antisocial behavior. The study concluded that television is not innocuous entertainment and that we must be aware of its negative impact.

Other research places in doubt some of the views about this relationship. Cullingford (1984) believes that children are not really paying that much attention to what they watch and that they are better at separating fact from fiction than we may think. We now believe that the relationship between violent acts and antisocial behavior is much more complicated than originally thought. For both adults and children, the social context, peer influence, and values and attitudes all play at least as important a role in determining their behavior as television.

Children are also exposed to attitudes toward authority figures and criminal behavior on television. Two researchers (Lichter and Lichter, 1984) analyzed three decades of television programming and found that contemporary TV is laced with antiestablishment and antiauthority themes. The public is being socialized to a particular view of society through entertainment programming.

The Lichters found that criminals on prime time TV are usually middle- or upper-class white males over 30. In fact, wealthy individuals are portrayed as criminals twice as often as the middle-class or poor. The criminals we are less likely to see on television are the juvenile delinquents or the youth gangs. We are infrequently exposed to the culture of poverty that is directly or indirectly responsible for a great deal of crime.

There is also a possible link between homicides and suicides and television presentations of these acts. It has been shown (Bollen and Phillips, 1982) that homicides tend to increase immediately after a widely publicized heavyweight boxing match, and that suicides increase during the 10 days after the reported suicide of a well-known person.

Recent waves of adolescent suicides have focused attention on the effects of fictional accounts of suicide and television news coverage of subsequent "imitation suicides." At the moment it is not clear that there is a proven statistical link between these suicides and the television programs. According to Harvard medical School psychiatrist Leon Eisenberg, however, it is time "to ask whether there are measures that should be undertaken to limit media coverage of suicide" (*Science News,* October 3, 1987).

ADULT SOCIALIZATION

A person's primary socialization is completed when he or she reaches adulthood. **Primary socialization** *means that individuals have mastered the basic information and skills required of members of a society.* They have (1) learned a language and can think logically to some degree, (2) accepted the basic norms and values of the culture, (3) developed the ability to pattern their behavior in terms of these norms and values, and (4) assumed a culturally appropriate social identity.

There is still much to learn, however, and there are many new social identities to explore. **Adult socialization** *is the process by which adults learn new statuses and roles.* Adult socialization differs from primary socialization in two ways.

First, adults are much more aware of the processes through which they are being socialized. In fact, they deliberately engage in programs such as advanced education or on-the-job training in which socialization is an explicit goal. Second, adults often have more control over how they wish to be socialized and therefore can mobilize more enthusiasm for the process. Whether going to business school, taking up a new hobby, or signing up for the Peace Corps, adults can decide to channel their energy into making the most effective use of an opportunity to learn new skills or knowledge.

An important aspect of adult socialization is **resocialization,** which involves *exposure to ideas or values that in one way or another conflict with what was learned in childhood.* This is a common experience for college students who leave their homes for the first time and encounter a new environment in which many of their family's cherished beliefs and values are held up to critical examination. Changes in religious and political orientation are not uncommon during the college years, and often lead to a time of stress for students and their parents.

Erving Goffman (1961a) discussed the major resocialization that takes place in **total institutions**—*environments such as prisons or mental hospitals in which the participants are physically and socially isolated from the outside world.* Goffman noted several factors that make for effective resocialization. These include (1) isolation from the outside

world, (2) spending all of one's time in the same place with the same people, (3) shedding individual identity by giving up old clothes and possessions for standard uniforms, (4) a clean break with the past, and (5) loss of freedom of action. Under these circumstances there is usually a major change in the individual along the lines prescribed by those controlling the resocialization.

The methods used by various religious cults to indoctrinate their members can be seen as a conscious attempt at resocialization. The Unification Church, headed by the Reverend Sun Myung Moon, is one example of such resocialization that has received widespread criticism. Many potential members of Reverend Moon's church are first approached on the street. Once the new recruits have been convinced to attend the training sessions, the "Moonies" begin applying selected resocialization techniques. Upon arriving at the retreat, the potential members are met with balloons and a banner reading, "Welcome Home Brothers and Sisters." Complete strangers start hugging and welcoming the recruits, and without thinking, the newcomers hug back. Even the most reluctant recruit feels pressure to join in. This friendliness is actually a subtle form of intimidation, which makes any nonparticipation conspicuous.

Every minute of the 16- to 18-hour days are filled with tightly controlled activities. The "Moonies" stress the church's importance over all else, especially relationships outside the group, whether they be with parents, friends, or lovers. This theme is repeated in tightly controlled discussion groups in which the "Moonies" maintain the image of a warm communal family with no harsh words or rejection. For many recruits, the "Moonie" way eventually is accepted under the stress of mental and physical exhaustion.

Resocialization is complete when the new recruit is swept up in the communal spirit. Group pressures start to become so strong that major personality changes take place, and new value systems replace the ones learned previously. Consequently, friends and family members may feel that they no longer recognize a person who as been resocialized.

The Moonies defend their program as simply a means through which they try to get people to rid themselves of old ideas and replace them with new ones (MacRobert, 1977). It is not unusual for those undergoing resocialization experiences to become confused and depressed and to question whether they have chosen the right course. Some drop out; others eventually stop resisting and accept the values of their instructors.

Most agents of adult socialization are not as obvious as the above example, however. In the

CONTROVERSIES IN SOCIOLOGY

Is Day Care Harmful to Children?

Our culture sends conflicting messages to mothers about child-rearing. On the one hand, mothers are still viewed as the principal caretakers of children. Yet on the other hand, they are now also expected to expand fully as individuals and develop their own potentials and needs (Rubinstein, 1988).

A variety of demographic and social changes have produced serious conflicts for parents with respect to child-care arrangements. The mothers who were born after World War II are far more likely to be working when their children are preschoolers than were women in the past. The National Research Council (Hayes, Palmer, and Zaslow, 1990) projects that 80 percent of school-age children and 70 percent of preschool-age children will have mothers in the labor force by the year 2000.

There are 8.2 million children under five whose mothers work. These children are usually in one of three types of child-care. About 31 percent of the children are cared for in their own homes (principally by their fathers). In the second type of arrangement, usually referred to as "family day care," a woman takes four to six

unrelated young children into her home on a regular basis. Thirty-seven percent of child-care is of this type. The remaining 23 percent of the children are enrolled in day-care centers. Another eight percent are cared for by their mother while she is working (See Figure 4.1). (Bureau of the Census, Statistical Brief, May 1987).

Recognizing the growing need for child-care, Congress passed legislation known as Child-Care and Development Block Grants which authorizes expenditures of $750 million in 1991, $825 million in 1992, and $925 million in 1993 for child-care services (Gill, 1991).

With one in four parents putting their preschoolers in organized child-care, we must ask whether this arrangement is serving the children as well as traditional child-rearing does.

Sociologists and psychologists begin to answer this question by noting that just as all parenting is not uniformly good, neither is all day care mediocre. High-quality day care does exist and can be a suitable substitute for home parenting. Unfortunately, poor quality care which threatens the child with serious physical and

psychological harm is also readily available.

According to Edward Zigler, one of the architects of Project Head Start, "We have all the knowledge necessary to provide absolutely first-rate child-care in the United States. What's missing is the commitment and the will." (Trotter, 1987). Zigler believes we must convince people that when a family uses a day-care center, they are not just dropping the child off so they can work. These families are selecting an environment that will have an enormous impact on the development of their child.

Many experts agree that one way to improve child-care standards is to ensure that no adult be allowed to care for more than three infants at a time. Currently only three states—Kansas, Massachusetts, and Maryland—adhere to this standard. KinderCare, a national chain of day-care centers, staffs its centers according to state-mandated ratios which for infants in Connecticut, for example, is one to four; in Alabama this ratio is one to six, and in Ohio, it is one to eight. For three-year-olds, some states allow a ratio of one worker to 15 children (Magnet, 1983).

following section we will discuss four common events in adult socialization: marriage, parenthood, work, and aging.

Marriage and Responsibility

As Ruth Benedict (1938) noted in a now-classic article on socialization in America, ". . . our culture goes to great extremes in emphasizing contrasts between the child and the adult." We think of childhood as a time without cares, a time for play.

Adulthood, on the other hand, is marked by work and responsibility. One of the great adult responsibilities in our society is marriage.

Ours is a time of uncertainty and experimentation. Indeed, many of the traditional role expectations of marriage are no longer accepted uncritically by today's young adults. Even so, marriage still retains its primacy as a life choice for adults. Although divorce has become acceptable in most circles, marriage is still treated seriously as a public statement that both partners are committed to each

Problems also arise in centers where the staff is underpaid and where there is a high staff turnover, a situation all too common. Many children going to day-care centers do not encounter enduring stable relationships with child-care workers (Gill, 1991). For example, a 1988 National Center for Health Statistics Study found that ¼ of children in day care switched centers within the previous 12 months. This was apart from changes in child-care workers within a specific center.

In addition to the impact that two-worker families have on children and child-care arrangements, there is also a substantial effect on the parents themselves. Women are likely to experience considerable role conflict and role strain as they try to meet the obligations of the job and the family. In the traditional role of mother, women are considered responsible for the well-being of the children. If the children have problems, it is assumed to be her fault. Mothers are vulnerable to self-blame when their children show signs of distress (Barnett and Baruch, 1987). One way to alleviate this guilt is to have the father take a more active role in the child-care.

When the fathers take an active role in child-care, however, new problems may arise. In one study of 160 fathers, their wives, and their children, it was found that although fathers who participated in child-care and home chores extensively felt more competent as parents, they also were likely to report having too little time for their careers and complained that their family responsibilities were interfering with their work (Baruch and Barnett, 1986). These fathers were also more critical of their wife's performance as a mother.

At least in the short run then, one of the costs of changing family care arrangements is increased marital strain.

Because day care is now becoming a reality for a large segment of the nation's preschoolers, the issue that needs to be addressed is how to make it a positive socialization experience. Clearly this requires well-trained staff and a properly supervised environment. If we can create that type of environment, then the fear of damaging experiences will be minimized.

FIGURE 4.1

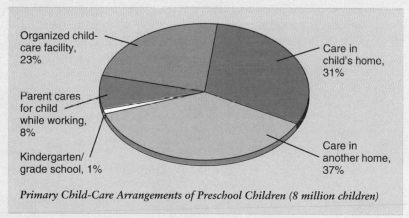

Organized child-care facility, 23%

Care in child's home, 31%

Parent cares for child while working, 8%

Kindergarten/grade school, 1%

Care in another home, 37%

Primary Child-Care Arrangements of Preschool Children (8 million children)

Source: Bureau of the Census, *Statistical Brief,* May 1987.

other and to stability and responsibility. (We will discuss marriage and alternative lifestyles in greater detail in Chapter 11.)

Once married, the new partners must define their relationships to each other and to the demands of society. This is not as easy today as it used to be when tradition largely determined these choices. Although friends, parents, and relatives usually are only too ready to instruct the young couple in the "shoulds" and "should nots" of married life, increasingly such attempts are resented by young people who wish to chart their own courses. One choice they must make is whether or not to become parents.

Parenthood

Once a couple has a child, their responsibilities increase enormously. They must find ways to provide the care and nurturing necessary to the healthy development of their baby, and at the same time they must work hard to keep their own relationship intact, because the arrival of an infant inevitably is accompanied by stress. This requires a reexamination of the role expectations each partner has of the other, both as a parent and as a spouse.

Of course, most parents anticipate some stresses and try to resolve them before the baby is born. Financial plans are made, living space is created, baby care is studied. Friends and relatives are asked for advice, and their future baby-sitting services are secured. However, not all the stresses of parenthood are so obvious. One that is frequently overlooked is the fact that parenthood is itself a new developmental phase.

The psychology of being and becoming a parent is extremely complicated. The birth of the child brings forth new feelings in the parents, many of which can be traced to the parents' own experiences as infants. As their child grows and passes through all the stages of development we have described, parents relive their own development. In psychological terms parenthood can be viewed as "a second chance": Adults can bring to bear all they have learned in order to resolve the conflicts not resolved when they were children. For example, it might be possible for some parents to develop a more trusting approach to life while observing their infants as they grapple with the conflict of basic trust and mistrust (Erikson's first stage).

Career Development: Vocation and Identity

Taking a job is more than finding a place to work. It means stepping into a new social context with its own statuses and roles, and it requires that a person be socialized to meet the needs of the situation. This may even include such basics as learning how to dress appropriately. For example, a young management trainee in a major corporation was criticized for wearing his keys on a ring snapped to his belt. "Janitors wear their keys," his supervisor told him. "Executives keep them in their pockets." The keys disappeared from his belt.

Aspiring climbers of the occupational ladder may even have to adjust their personalities to fit the job. In the 1950s and 1960s, corporations looked for quiet, loyal, tradition-oriented men to fill their management positions—men who wouldn't "upset the applecart" (Whyte, 1956)—and most certainly not women. Since the late 1960s, however, the trend has been toward recruiting men and women who show drive and initiative and a capacity for creative thinking and problem solving.

Some occupations require extensive resocialization. Individuals wishing to become doctors or nurses, for example, must overcome their squeamishness about blood, body wastes, genitals, and the inside of the body. They must also learn to accept the undemocratic fact that they will receive much of their training while caring for poor patients (usually ethnic minorities). Well-to-do patients receive care mostly from fully trained personnel.

The armed forces use basic training to socialized recruits to obey orders without hesitating, and to accept killing as a necessary part of their work. For many people such resocialization can be quite painful.

For some, career and identity are so intertwined that job loss can lead to personal crisis. Many people who lost their jobs during the recession of 1991 and 1992 experienced such a predicament. For many, unemployment meant reevaluation and a new direction. For others it meant spending months looking for a new job and realizing that it would be difficult to earn as much as they did before.

Aging and Society

In many societies age itself brings respect and honor. Older people are turned to for advice, and their opinions are valued because they reflect a full measure of experience. Often older people are not required to stop their productive work simply because they have reached a certain age. Rather, they work as long as they are able, and their tasks may be modified to allow them to continue to work virtually until they die. In this way people maintain their social identities as they grow old—and their feelings of self-esteem as well.

This is not the case in the United States. Most employers retire their employees automatically once they reach age 70, and social security regulations restrict the amount of nontaxable income retired persons may earn.

Perhaps the biggest concern of the elderly is where they will live and who will take care of them when they get sick. The American family is not ordinarily prepared to accommodate an aging parent who is sick or whose spouse has recently died. Apartment rents are high, and the cost of an extra room may be more than the family can afford. Most suburban houses are not designed to meet the needs of the elderly. In the typical house, for example, none of the bedrooms are at the same level as the kitchen or living room, and the family room frequently is down a flight of stairs. As a result, those older people who have trouble moving around or caring for themselves often find themselves with no choice but to live in homes for the aged or nursing homes. They have little access to their

In many societies, older people are turned to for advice, and their opinions are valued because they are based on life experiences.

families and are deprived of the pleasure of seeing their grandchildren grow up. (The grandchildren also are deprived of the pleasure of getting to know their grandparents.)

This means that late in life, many people are forced to acquire another social identity. Sadly, it is not a valued one, but rather one of social insignificance (de Beauvoir, 1972). This can be very damaging to older people's self-esteem, and it may even hasten them to their graves. The last few years have seen some attempts at reform to address these issues. Age discrimination in hiring is illegal, and some companies have extended or eliminated specified retirement ages. However, the problem will not be resolved until the elderly once again achieve a position of respect and value in American culture.

Even though aging is itself a biological process, becoming old is a social and cultural one. Only society can create a "senior citizen." From infancy to old age, both biology and society play important parts in determining how people develop over the course of their lives.

Social Interaction and Social Groups

Understanding Social Interaction
   Contexts
   Norms

Types of Social Interaction
   Nonverbal Behavior
   Exchange
   Cooperation
   Conflict
   Competition

Elements of Social Interaction
   Statuses
   Roles
   Role Sets
   Role Strain
   Role Conflict
   Role Playing

The Nature of Groups
   Primary and Secondary Groups
   Characteristics of Groups
   Reference Groups

Small Groups

Large Groups: Associations
   The Formal Structure
   The Informal Structure

Bureaucracy
   Weber's Model of Bureaucracy
   Bureaucracy Today: The Reality
   The Iron Law of Oligarchy

Institutions and Social Organization
   Social Institutions
   Social Organization

Have you ever wondered why people kiss? There are parent-child kisses, friendly greeting kisses, and passionate kisses. Yet it seems a strange way of sending a message to another person. Some social scientists believe that kissing is an outgrowth of the practice of a mother passing pre-chewed food to her infant during the weaning process. This practice, which still exists in many cultures, was associated with the feeling of comfort, security and a loving relationship that existed between the mother and child.

From this beginning people in societies throughout the world have broadened the meaning and practice of kissing. Today we find people kissing others' hands, feet, shoulders, cheeks, brows, eyes, and the hems of their clothings. In France the president kisses a man on both cheeks in formal ceremonies. There is no kissing between males in the United States except between fathers and young sons or in a homosexual relationship. *How* you kiss someone also conveys information. Kissing an adult on the head or forehead may be condescending, as that is how we kiss babies or children. Some societies, such as certain African cultures, do not engage in kissing at all and find the act revolting.

There is no doubt that kissing is a social interaction, but so are the countless other behaviors we engage in each day. If we accept the fact that all social interaction has a message of value, then it follows that no matter how one may try, one cannot *not* send a message. There is no way *not* to interact with others. Activity or inactivity, words or silence, all contain a message. They influence others and others respond to these messages. The mere absence of talking or taking notice of each other is no exception, because there is a message in that behavior also. Social interaction has no opposite.

When sociologists study human behavior, they are primarily interested in how people affect each other through their actions. They look at the overt behaviors that produce responses from others as well the subtle cues that may result in unintended consequences. Human social interaction is flexible and unlike that of the social animals, such as monkeys or geese.

UNDERSTANDING SOCIAL INTERACTION

Max Weber (1922) was one of the first sociologists to stress the importance of social interaction in the study of sociology. He argued that the main goal of sociology was to explain what he called **social action,** *a term he used to refer to anything people are conscious of doing because of other people.* Weber claimed that in order to interpret social actions, we have to put ourselves in the position of the people we are studying and try to understand their thoughts and motives. The German word Weber used for this is *Verstehen,* which can be translated as "sympathetic understanding."

Weber's use of the term social action identifies only half the puzzle because it simply deals with one individual taking others into account before acting. *A* **social interaction** *involves two or more people taking each other into account.* It is the interplay between the actions of individuals. In this respect, social interaction is a central concept to understanding the nature of social life.

In this chapter we shall explain how sociologists investigate social interaction. We shall start with the basic types of social interaction, verbal and nonverbal. Next we shall examine how social interaction affects those involved in it. Then we will broaden our focus and move to groups and social interactions within them. Finally, we will examine large groupings of people that make social life possible and ultimately comprise the social structure. In other words, we shall start with social behavior at the most basic level and move outward to evermore complicated levels of social interaction.

Contexts

Where a social interaction takes place makes a difference in what it means. Edward T. Hall (1974) identified *three elements* that, *taken together, define* the **context** *of a social interaction: (1) the physical setting or place, (2) the social environment, and (3) the activities surrounding the interaction*—preceding it, happening simultaneously with it, and coming after it. Without knowledge of these elements it is impossible to know the meaning of even the simplest interaction. For example, Germans and Americans treat space very differently. Hall (1969) noted that in many ways the difference between German and American doors gives us a clue about the space perceptions of these two cultures. In Germany, public and private buildings usually have double doors that create a soundproof environment. Germans feel that American doors, in contrast, are flimsy and light, inadequate for providing the privacy that Germans require. In American offices, doors are usually kept open; in German offices they are kept closed. In Germany the closed door does not mean the individual wants to be left alone or that something is being planned that should not be seen by others. Germans simply think that open doors are sloppy and disorderly. As Hall explained:

Social interaction is a central concept to understanding the nature of social life.

Where a social interaction takes place makes a difference in what it means.

I was once called in to advise a firm that has operations all over the world. One of the first questions asked was, "How do you get the Germans to keep their doors open?" In this company the open doors were making the Germans feel exposed and gave the whole operation an unusually relaxed and unbusinesslike air. Closed doors, on the other hand, gave the Americans the feeling that there was a conspiratorial air about the place and that they were being left out. The point is that whether the door is open or shut, it is not going to mean the same thing in the two countries (Hall, 1969).

The English, particularly those of the middle and upper classes, are at the opposite extreme from the Germans in their requirements for privacy. They are usually brought up in a nursery shared with brothers and sisters. The oldest has a room to himself or herself that is vacated when he or she leaves for boarding school. However, many children in England may never have a room of their own and seldom expect one or feel entitled to one. Even members of Parliament have no offices and often conduct their business in the open. The English are

consequently puzzled by the American need for a secure place—an office—in which to work. Americans working in England often are annoyed that they are not given an appropriately enclosed workplace (Hall, 1969). These markedly different views of the use of space are culturally determined, and it is important to be aware of these differences in order to interpret correctly the context of an interaction.

Norms

Human behavior is not random. It is patterned and, for the most part, quite predictable. What makes human beings act predictably in certain situations? For one thing, there is the presence of **norms**—*specific rules of behavior that are agreed upon and shared which prescribe limits of acceptable behavior.* Norms tell us the things we should do and not do. In fact, our society's norms are so much a part of us that we often are not aware of them. In the United States our norms tell us that it is proper to drive on the right, to look at someone when speaking to him or her, and to stand for the national anthem. Likewise, they tell us that when two people meet, one of the ways of greeting is shaking hands. Yet in most Asian countries, people have learned to bow to express this same idea.

We also have norms that guide us in how we present ourselves to others. We realize that how we dress, how we speak, and the objects we possess relay information about us. In this respect Americans are a rather outgoing group of people. The Japanese have learned that it is a sign of weakness to disclose too much of oneself by overt actions. They are taught very early in life that touching, laughing, crying, or speaking loudly in public are not acceptable ways of interacting.

Not only can the norms for behavior differ considerably from one culture to another, but they also can differ within our own society. Conflicting interpretations of action have been shown to exist among men and women in our society when a stranger joins them at a public table, such as in a library. It has been found that men prefer to position themselves across from others they like, whereas women prefer to position themselves next to someone they like (Byrne, 1971). On the basis of this information, Fisher and Byrne (1975) reasoned that females thus would respond more negatively than males would to a side-by-side invasion of their personal space, and males would respond more negatively to face-to-face invasions.

An experiment was conducted using males and females sitting alone in a library. An "invader" was sent to sit either across or next to the subjects. After five minutes, the invader left and an experimenter arrived to ask the subjects some questions. Regardless of the invader's gender, the males felt negatively about the invader when he or she sat across from them but did not seem to have those feelings about a side-by-side invader. The females responded negatively when the invader sat next to them but not when he or she sat across from them.

It was hypothesized this difference results from gender-role socialization in which males are taught to be relatively competitive and hence more sensitive to competitive cues. Sitting across from a male may tend to signal a competitive situation, and males tend to prefer a trusted or nonthreatening person in that location. Females are thought to be more sensitive to affiliative or friendship cues. Sitting adjacent to a female tends to be interpreted as an affiliative demand, and so females tend to respond negatively to this cue when the person occupying the seat is a stranger or someone with whom they do not wish to be intimate.

Sociologists thus need to understand the norms that guide people's behavior, as without this knowledge it is impossible to understand social interaction.

TYPES OF SOCIAL INTERACTION

When two individuals are in each other's presence, they inevitably affect each other. They may do so intentionally, as when one person asks the other for change of a dollar, or they may do so unintentionally, as when two people drift toward opposite sides of the elevator. Whether intentional or unintenional, both represent types of social interaction.

Nonverbal Behavior

In recent years many researchers have focused our attention on how we communicate with one another by using body movements. This study of body movements, known as *kinesics*, attempts to examine how such things as slight head nods, yawns, postural shifts, and other nonverbal cues, whether spontaneous or deliberate, affect communication.

Many of our movements relate to an attitude that our culture has, consciously or unconsciously, taught us to express in a specific manner. In the United States, for example, we show a status relationship in a variety of ways. The ritualistic nonverbal movements and gestures in which we engage to see who goes through a door first or who sits or stands first are but a few ways our culture uses movement to communicate status. In the Middle East, status is underscored nonverbally by which

The use of hand and arm movements, eye contact, and norms of nonverbal behavior are markedly different for these Arab Bedouins than they are for Americans.

individual you turn your back to. In Asian cultures, bowing and backing out of a room are signs of status relationships. Humility might be shown in the United States by a slight downward bending of the head, but in many European countries this same attitude is manifested by dropping one's arms and sighing. In Samoa, humility is communicated by bending the body forward.

The use of hand and arm movements as a means of communicating also varies among cultures. We all are aware of the different gestures for mockery. For some European cultures it is a closed fist with the thumb protruding between the index and middle fingers. The Russian expresses this same attitude by moving one index finger horizontally across the other.

In the United States, we can indicate that things are OK by making a circle with one's thumb and index finger while extending the others. In Japan this gesture signifies "money." Among Arabs if you accompany this gesture with a baring of the teeth, it displays extreme hostility.

In the United States you say good-bye or farewell by waving the hand and arm up and down. If you wave in this manner in South America, you may discover that the other person is not leaving, but moving toward you because in many countries this gesture means "come."

Eye contact is another area in which some interesting findings have appeared. In the United

Language and Social Interaction in the Courtroom

People tend to think of our court system as a forum in which unbiased men and women come together to discover truth. Far from being an unbiased fact-finding mission though, a trial is more likely to be a maze of language in which the words of the lawyers and witnesses are designed to create obstacles for juries seeking to reach an accurate understanding of conflicting information.

Each of us has a style of speaking which has an effect on others. Some effects of our language are intentional, others are inadvertent. In the courtroom people who speak rapidly or have a standard accent are seen as more competent than people who speak slowly or with an unusual accent. Those whose native language is not English leave jurors with a bad impression.

One anthropologist, William O'Barr, studied language in the courtroom and concluded that minor differences in phraseology, tempo, and length of answers can have a major effect on jurors. Some witnesses use a powerless style of speech which is marked by such examples as (1) tentative phrases ("I think ...," "It ap-

pears to have been ...," "Maybe ...," (2) a rising intonation at the end of declarative statements, as for example when trying to recall the time of an incident: "Eight, eight-thirty?" and (3) intensifiers, saying, "I saw him very often," instead of "I saw him often."

O'Barr took the same testimony and recorded it once in a powerless style, then again in a powerful style with tentative phrases, rising intonations, and intensifiers removed. Jurors tended to rate the powerful speakers, whether male or female, more convincing, competent, intelligent and trustworthy than the powerless speakers.

Speech provides clues about the status, trustworthiness and believability of the speaker. Listeners may see the powerful style as high status and tend to think more favorably of such individuals.

A witness is often seen as more credible if he or she testifies in a narrative style, rather than with fragmented statements interrupted by numerous questions from the lawyer. When the witness was allowed to testify narratively, listeners believed the lawyer thought the witness was more

intelligent, more competent and assertive, and they tended to judge the witness the same way.

A lawyer's style of speaking can also mean the difference between winning and losing a case. One study found that winning prosecutors asked more questions of witnesses, spoke longer and made more assertive statements than losing ones.

Speaking lucidly and understandably was not a plus, which may explain why attorneys often sound pompous and jargon-laden when they get going. Successful defense attorneys use more abstract language, more legal jargon, and more ambiguous words than losers. The more they confused the jury the better the attornies did.

In the past, people settled disputes through means which favored the physically strong or powerful. Today we settle disputes through means that favor those who are best able to manipulate words and other social interactive cues.

Source Adapted from Lori B. Andrews, "Exhibit A: Language." *Psychology Today*, February 1984, 18(2) pp. 28–33.

States the following has been noted: (1) We tend to look at the person we are speaking to more when we are listening than when we are talking. If we are at a loss for a word we frequently look into space, as if to find the words imprinted somewhere out there. (2) The more rewarding we find the speaker's message to be, the more intensely we will look at that person. (3) How much eye contact we maintain with other people is determined in part by how high

we perceive their status. When we address someone we regard as having high status, we maintain a modest-to-high degree of eye contact. On the other hand, when we address a person of low status, we make very little effort to maintain eye contact. (4) Eye contact must be regularly broken, because we feel uncomfortable if someone gazes at us for longer than ten seconds at a time.

These notions of eye contact found in the United

States differ from those of other societies. In Japan and China, for example, it is considered rude to look into another person's eyes during conversation. Arabs, on the other hand stand very close to the person they are talking to and stare directly into their eyes. Arabs believe the eyes are a key to a person's being, and looking deeply into another's eyes allows one to see that person's soul.

The proscribed relationships between males and females in a culture also influence eye behavior. Asian cultures, for example, consider it a taboo for women to look straight into the eyes of men. Therefore, most Asian men, out of respect for this cultural characteristic, do not stare directly at women. French men accept staring as a cultural norm and often stare at women in public (Samovar, Porter, and Jain, 1981).

Spontaneous cooperation, which arises from the needs of a particular situation, is the oldest and most natural form of cooperation.

Exchange

When people do something for each other with the express purpose of receiving a reward or return, they are involved in an **exchange interaction.** Most employer—employee relationships are exchange relationships. The employee does the job and is rewarded with a salary. The reward in an exchange interaction, however, need not always be material; it can also be based on emotions such as gratitude. For example, if you visit a sick friend, help someone with a heavy package at the market, or help someone solve a problem, you probably will expect these people to feel grateful to you.

Sociologist Peter Blau pointed out that exchange is the most basic form of social interaction:

> Social exchange can be observed everywhere once we are sensitized . . . to it, not only in market relations but also in friendship and even in love. . . Neighbors exchange favors; children, toys; colleagues, assistance; acquaintances, courtesies; politicians, concessions; discussants, ideas; housewives, recipes (Blau, 1964).

Cooperation

A **cooperative interaction** *occurs when people act together to promote common interests or achieve shared goals.* The members of a basketball team pass to one another, block opponents, rebound, and assist one another to achieve a common goal—winning the game. Likewise, family members cooperate to promote their interests as a family—husband and wife both may hold jobs as well as share in household duties, and children may help out by mowing the lawn and washing the dishes. College students often cooperate by studying together for tests.

Sociologists Robert A. Nisbet and Robert Perrin (1977) describe four types of cooperation: spontaneous, traditional, directed, and contractual. The oldest, most natrual, and most common form of cooperaton is **spontaneous cooperation,** which *arises from the needs of a particular situation.* For example, when the calm of a rainy May evening in Chepachet, Rhode Island was broken by the sound and sight of a girl being dragged into the woods by a masked abductor, five of the girl's neighbors pursued and cornered the kidnapper until the police arrived. Said one of the rescuers, who may have saved the young girl's life, "It all went click, click, with everybody doing their part. Around here, people notice if somethings's not right" (*Newsweek*, July 4, 1988.)

Traditional cooperation which held together earlier preindustrial societies, *is tied to custom and is passed on from one generation to the next.* Examples of this form of cooperation are the barn raisings and quilting bees of American farming communities.

Modern societies rely less on traditional cooperation than on directed and contractual cooperation. **Directed cooperation** *is a joint activity under the control of people in authority.* It is planned in advance and requires leadership. When President John F. Kennedy announced the United States would put a person on the moon before 1970, he initiated large-scale directed cooperation that achieved its goal. After the *Challenger* space shuttle disaster killed seven astronauts in January 1986, more than $2 billion was spent over a two year period to rebuild the system and make it safer. There were approximately 600 system improvements involving

An Amish barn raising is an example of traditional cooperation that carries the weight of custom and is passed on from one generation to the next.

workers in dozens of private aerospace corporations, as well as government agencies.

Contractual cooperation is also planned, but in **contractual cooperation** *people agree to cooperate in certain specified ways, with each person's obligations clearly spelled out.* The author of this text and the publisher signed a formal contract and met their specific obligations to produce the book you are now reading.

Conflict

In a cooperative interaction, people join forces to achieve a common goal. By contrast, *people in* **conflict** *struggle against one another for some commonly prized object or value* (Nisbet and Perrin, 1977). In most conflict relationships, a person gains at someone else's expense. Conflicts arise when people or groups have incompatible values or when the rewards or resources available to a society or its members are limited. Thus, conflict always involves an attempt to gain or use power.

The fact that conflict often leads to unhappiness and violence causes many people to view it negatively. However, conflict appears inevitable in human society. A stable society is not a society without conflicts but one that has developed methods for resolving its conflicts by justly or brutally suppressing them temporarily. For example, Lewis Coser (1956, 1967) pointed out that conflict can be a positive force in society. The American civil rights movement in the 1950s and 1960s may have seemed threatening and disruptive to many people at the time, but it helped bring about important social changes that may have led to a greater social stability.

Coercion *is a special kind of conflict that occurs when one of the parties in a conflict is much stronger than the other and imposes its will on the weaker,* as in the case of a parent using the threat of punishment to impose a curfew on an adolescent child. Coercion can rest on force or the threat of force, but usually operates more subtly.

Competition

The fourth type of social interaction, **competition,** *is a form of conflict in which individuals or groups confine their conflict within agreed-upon rules.* Competition is a common form of interaction in the modern world—not only on the sports field but in the marketplace, the education system, and the political system. Our presidential elections, for example, are based on competition. Candidates for each party compete through the primaries, and eventually one candidate is selected to represent each of the major parties. The competition grows even more intense as the remaining candidates battle directly against each other to persuade a nation of voters they are the best person for the presidency.

One type of relationship may span an entire range of interactions: An excellent example is marriage. Husbands and wives cooperate in household chores and responsibilities (an interaction discussed earlier). They also engage in exchange interactions. Married people often discuss their problems with each other—the partner whose role is listener at one time will expect the other spouse to provide a sympathetic ear at another time. Married people also experience conflicts in their relationship. A couple may have a limited amount of money set aside, and each may want to use it for a different purpose. Unless they can agree on a third, mutually desirable use for the money, one spouse will gain at the other's expense, and the marriage may suffer. The husband and wife whose marriage is irreversibly damaged may find themselves in direct competition. If they wish to separate or divorce, their conflict will be regulated according to legal and judicial rules.

Through the course of a lifetime people constantly are involved in many types of social interaction because most of their time is spent in some kind of group situation. How we behave in these situations is generally determined by two factors—the statuses we occupy and the role we play—which together constitute the main components of what sociologists call social organization.

ELEMENTS OF SOCIAL INTERACTION

People do not interact with each other as anonymous beings. They come together in the context of specific environments, with specific purposes. Their interactions involve behavior associated with defined statuses and particular roles. These statuses and roles help to define our social interactions and provide predictability.

Statuses

Statuses *are socially defined positions that people occupy in a group or society and in terms of which they interact with one another.* Common statuses may pertain to religion, education, ethnicity, and occupation—for example, Protestant, college graduate, African American, and teacher. Statuses exist independent of the specific people who occupy them (Linton, 1936). For example, our society recognizes the status of rock musician. Many people occupy that status, including Madonna, Hammer, Sting, Rod Stewart, Tracy Chapman, and Michael Jackson. New musicians appear; others retire or lose popularity. But the status, as the culture defines it, remains essentially unchanged. The same is true for all other statuses: occupational statuses such as doctor, computer analyst, bank teller, police officer, butcher, insurance adjuster, thief, and prostitute; as well as nonoccupational statuses such as son and daughter, jogger, friend, Little League coach, neighbor, gang leader, and mental patient.

It is important to keep in mind that from a sociological point of view, status does not refer—as it does in common usage—to the idea of prestige, even though different statuses often do contain differing degrees of prestige. In America, for example, research has shown that the status of Supreme Court Justice has more prestige than that of lawyer, which in turn has more prestige than does the status of sociologist (Hodge et al., 1964).

People generally occupy more than one status at a time. Consider yourself, for example: You are someone's daughter or son, a full-time or part-time college student, perhaps also a worker, a licensed car driver, a member of a church or synagogue, and so forth. Often, one of a person's statuses may become a master status. **A master status** *is one of the multiple statuses a person occupies that seems to dominate the others in patterning that person's life.* For example, George Bush has occupied a number of diverse statuses: husband, father, vice-president, and presidential candidate. After January 20, 1989, however, his master status was that of president of the United States, as it governed his actions more than did any other status he occupied at the time.

A person's master status will change many times in the course of his or her life. Right now your master status probably is that of college student. Five years from now it may be graduate student, artist, lawyer, spouse, or parent. Figure 5.1 illustrates the different statuses occupied by a 35-year-old woman who is an executive at a major television network. Although she occupies many statuses at once, her master status is that of vice-president for programming.

In some situations, a person's master status may have a negative influence on that person's life. For example, people who have followed what their culture considers a deviant lifestyle may find that their master status is labeled according to their deviant behavior. Those who have been identified as ex-convicts are likely to be so classified no matter what other statuses they occupy: they will be thought of as ex-convict painters, ex-convict machinists, ex-convict writers, and so on. Their master status has a negative effect on their ability to fulfill the roles of the statuses they would like to occupy. Ex-convicts who are good machinists or house painters may find employers unwilling to hire them because of their police records. Because the label "criminal" can stay with individuals throughout their lives, the criminal justice system is reluctant to label juvenile offenders or to open their records to the courts. Juvenile court files are usually kept secret and often permanently sealed when the person reaches age 18.

Some statuses, called **ascribed statuses** *are conferred upon us by virtue of birth or other socially significant factors not controlled by our own actions or decisions.* Certain family positions—daughter, son—are typical ascribed statuses, as are one's gender and ethnic or racial identity. Other statuses, called **achieved statuses** *are occupied as a result of the individual's actions.* A student, professor, garage mechanic, race driver, hobo, artist, prisoner, bus driver, husband, wife, mother, or father are all achieved statuses.

Roles

Statuses alone are static—nothing more than social categories into which people are placed. Roles bring statuses to life, making them dynamic. As Linton (1936) observed, you occupy a status but you play a role. **Roles** *are the culturally defined rules for proper behavior that are associated with every status.* Roles may be thought of as collections of

FIGURE 5.1

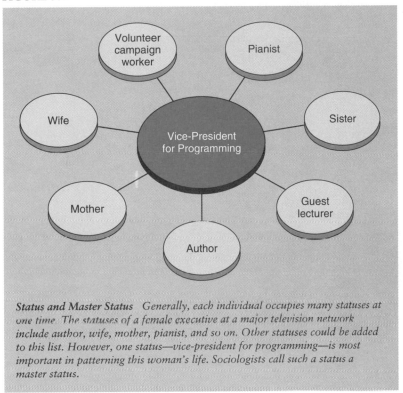

Status and Master Status   Generally, each individual occupies many statuses at one time. The statuses of a female executive at a major television network include author, wife, mother, pianist, and so on. Other statuses could be added to this list. However, one status—vice-president for programming—is most important in patterning this woman's life. Sociologists call such a status a master status.

rights and obligations. For example, to be a race car driver you must become well versed in these rights and obligations, as your life might depend on them. Every driver has the *right* to expect other drivers not to try to pass when the race has been

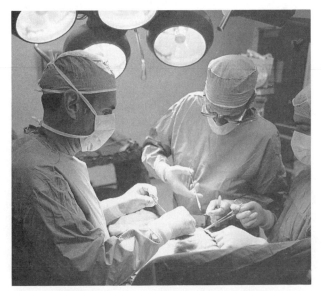

These surgeons have the ascribed status of "male." Their achieved status is "doctor."

interrupted by a yellow flag because of danger. Turned around, each driver has the *obligation* not to pass other drivers under yellow-flag conditions. A driver also has a *right* to expect race committee members to enforce the rules and ensure spectators stay off the raceway. On the other hand, a driver has an *obligation* to the owner of the car to try hard to win.

In the case of our television executive, she has the *right* to expect to be paid on time, to be provided with good-quality scripts and staff support, and to make decisions about the use of her budget. On the other hand, she has the *obligation* to act in the best interests of the network, to meet schedules, to stay within her budget, and to treat her employees fairly. What is important is that all these rights and obligations are part of the roles associated with the status of vice-president for programming. They exist without regard to the particular individuals whose behavior they guide (see Figure 5.2).

A status may include a number of roles, and each role will be appropriate to a specific social context. For example, the president of the United States must be a host at diplomatic dinners, a leader at cabinet sessions, and a policy setter for his staff. Sociologists use the concept of role sets to explain this phenomenon.

FIGURE 5.2

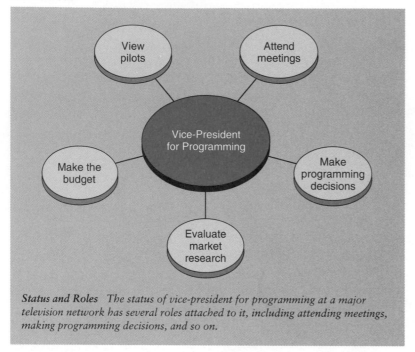

Status and Roles *The status of vice-president for programming at a major television network has several roles attached to it, including attending meetings, making programming decisions, and so on.*

Role Sets

All roles attached to a single status are known collectively as a **role set**. However, not every role in a particular role set is enacted all the time. An individual's role behaviors depend on the statuses of the other people with whom he or she is interacting. For example, as a college student you behave one way toward other students and another way toward professors. Similarly, professors behave one way toward other professors, another way toward students, and yet a third way toward deans. So the role behavior we expect in any given situation depends on the pairs of statuses occupied by the interacting individuals. This means that role behavior really is defined by the rights and obligations assigned to statuses when they are paired with one another (see Figure 5.3). It would be difficult to describe the wide-ranging, unorganized assortment of role behaviors associated with the status of television vice-president for programming. Sociologists find it more useful to describe the specific behavior expected of a network television vice-president for programming interacting with different people. Such a role set would include:

vice-president for programming/network president;
vice-president for programming/other vice-presidents;
vice-president for programming/script writer;
vice-president for programming/secretary;

vice-president for programming/television star;
vice-president for programming/journalist;
vice-president for programming/producer;
vice-president for programming/sponsor.

The vice-president's role behavior in each case would be different, meshing with the role behavior of the individual(s) occupying the other status in each pairing (Merton, 1968).

Role Strain

Even though most people try to enact their roles as expected, they sometimes find it difficult. *When a single role has conflicting demands attached to it, individuals who play that role experience* **role strain** (Goode, 1960). For example, the captain of a freighter is expected to be sure the ship sails only when it is in safe condition, but the captain is also expected to meet the company's delivery schedule, because a day's delay could cost the company thousands of dollars. These two expectations may exert competing pulls on the captain. The stress of these competing pulls is not due to the captain's personality but rather is built into the nature of the role expectations attached to the captain's status. Therefore, sociologists describe the captain's experience of stress as role strain.

Role Conflict

An individual occupying more than one status at a time who is unable to enact the roles of one

FIGURE 5.3

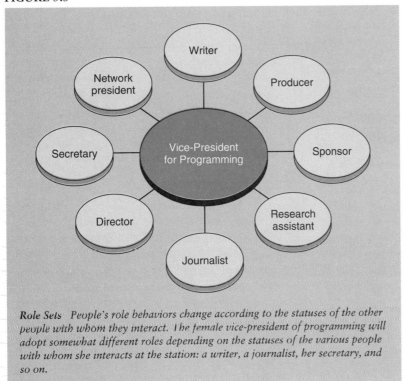

Role Sets   People's role behaviors change according to the statuses of the other people with whom they interact. The female vice-president of programming will adopt somewhat different roles depending on the statuses of the various people with whom she interacts at the station: a writer, a journalist, her secretary, and so on.

status without violating those of another status is encountering **role conflict.**

Military wives who want to pursue their own careers are often in a role conflict situation. Traditionally, military wives volunteer for a variety of activities on the base and take part in an endless number of social events to help further their husband's careers. When a wife has a career of her own, she no longer has the time for volunteer work—the makings of role conflict. "The message to the wives all along has been, 'Play the game or your husband will suffer,' " said Carolyn Becraft, an Army colonel's wife. The message to the husbands is, "Control your wife—or your career is over." The role conflict was so great for the wife of Colonel Michael Langston that the colonel resigned from the Air force and left 20 years of service and a promising career behind. The colonel felt he had no choice but to resign when his wife, a top media consultant, refused to relocate overseas along with him (*U.S. News and World Report*, August 18, 1988).

Not too long ago pregnancy was considered "women's work." An expectant father was expected to get his wife to the hospital on time and pace the waiting room anxiously awaiting the nurse's report on the sex of the baby and its health. Today men are encouraged and sometimes even expected to participate as fully as possible in the pregnancy period and the birth of the child. A role conflict, however, arises in that while the new father is expected to be involved, his involvement is defined along male gender role lines. He is expected to be helpful, supportive, and essentially a stabilizing force. He is not really allowed to indicate that he is frightened, nervous or possible angry about the baby. His role as a male, even in 1990s American society, conflicts with his feelings as a new expectant father (Shapiro, 1987).

As society becomes more complex, individuals occupy increasingly larger numbers of statuses. This increases the chances for role conflict, which is one of the major sources of stress in modern society.

Role Playing

The roles we play can have a profound influence on both our attitudes and our behavior. Playing a new social role often feels awkward at first, and we may feel we are just acting—pretending to be something we are not. However, many sociologists feel that the roles a person plays are the person's only true self. Peter Berger's (1963) explanation of role playing goes further: The roles we play can transform not only our actions but ourselves as well.

One feels more ardent by kissing, more humble by kneeling and more angry by shaking one's fist. That is, the kiss not only expresses ardor but manufactures it. Roles carry with them certain actions and emotions and attitudes that belong to these actions. The professor putting on an act that pretends to be wisdom comes to feel wise.

THE NATURE OF GROUPS

A good deal of social interaction takes place in the context of a group. In common speech the word *group* is often used for almost any occasion when two or more people come together. In sociology, however, there are several terms used for various collections of people, not all of which are considered groups. A **social group** *consists of a number of people who have a common identity, some feeling of unity, and certain common goals and shared norms*. In any social group, individuals interact with one another according to established statuses and roles. The members develop expectations of proper behavior for people occupying different positions in the social group. The people have a sense of identity and realize they are different from others who are not members. Social groups have a set of values and norms that may or may not be similar to those of the larger society.

Our description of a social group contrasts with our definition of a **social aggregate**, which *is made up of people temporarily in physical proximity to each other, but who share little else*. Consider passengers riding together in one car of a train. They may share a purpose (traveling to Des Moines) but do not interact or even consider their temporary association to have any meaning. It hardly makes sense to call them a group—unless something more happens. If it is a long ride, for instance, and several passengers start a card game, the cardplayers will have formed a social group: They have a purpose, share certain role expectations and attach importance to what they are doing together. Moreover, if the cardplayers continue to meet one another every day (say on a commuter train), they may begin to feel special in contrast with the rest of the passengers, who are just "riders."

A social group, unlike an aggregate, does not cease to exist when its members are away from one another. Members of social groups carry the fact of their membership with them and see the group as a distinct entity with specific requirements for membership. A social group has a purpose and is therefore important to its members, who know how to tell an "insider" from an "outsider." It is a social entity that exists for its members apart from any other social relationships that some of them might share. Members of a group interact according to established norms and traditional statuses and roles. As new members are recruited to the group, they move into these traditional statuses and adopt the expected role behavior—if not gladly, then as a result of group pressure.

Consider, for example, a tenants' group that consists of the people who rent apartments in a building. Most such groups are founded because tenants feel a need for a strong, unified voice in dealing with the landlord on problems with repairs, heat, hot water, and rent increases. Many members of a tenants' group may have never met one another before; others may be related to one another; and some may belong to other groups such as a neighborhood church, the PTA, a bowling league, or political associations. The group's existence does

Even if people are aware of one another, it is still not enough to make them a social group. In a social group, people are involved with each other in some patterned way.

not depend on these other relationships, nor does it cease when members leave the building to go to work or away on vacation. The group remains even when some tenants move out of the building and others move in. Newcomers are recruited, told of the group's purpose, and informed of its meetings; they are encouraged to join committees, take leadership responsibilities, and participate in the actions the group has planned. Members who fail to support the group action (such as withholding rent) will be pressured and criticized and may even receive threats of violence or expulsion from the group.

People are sometimes defined as being part of a specific group because they share certain characterisitics. If these characteristics are unknown or unimportant to those in the category, it is not a social group. People with similar characteristics do not become a social group unless concrete, dynamic interrelations develop among them (Lewin, 1948). For example, although all left-handed people fit into a group, they are not a social group just because they share this common characteristic. A further interrelationship must also exist. They may, for instance, belong to Left-Handers International, an organization that champions the rights of left-handers by addressing issues of discrimination and analyzing new products designed for use by left-handers. About 23,000 left-handers belong to this group.

Even if people are aware of one another, it is still not enough to make them a social group. We may be classified as Democrats, college students, upper class, or suburbanites. Yet for many of us who fall into these categories, there is no group. We may not be involved with the others in any patterned way that is an outgrowth of that classification. In fact, we personally may not even define ourselves as members of the particular category, even if someone else does.

Social groups can be large or small, temporary or long lasting: Your family is a group, as is your bowling club, any association to which you belong, or the clique with which you hang around. In fact, it is difficult for you to participate in society without belonging to a number of different groups.

In general, social groups, regardless of their nature, have the following characteristics: (1) permanence beyond the meetings of members—that is, even when members are dispersed, (2) means for identifying members, (3) mechanisms for recruiting new members, (4) goals or purposes, (5) social statuses and roles (that is, norms for behavior), and (6) means for controlling members' behavior.

The traits we described are features of many groups. A baseball team, a couple about to be married, a work unit, a weekly poker game, members of a family, or a town planning board may all be described as groups. Yet being a member of a family is significantly different from being a member of a work unit. The family is a primary group, whereas most work units are secondary groups.

Primary and Secondary Groups

The difference between primary and secondary groups lies in the kinds of relationships their members have with one another. Charles Horton Cooley (1909) defined primary groups as groups that are characterized by:

> intimate face-to-face association and cooperation. They are primary in several senses, but chiefly in that they are fundamental in forming the social nature and ideas of the individual. The result of intimate association, psychologically, is a certain fusion of individualities in a common whole, so that one's very self, for many purposes at least, is the common life and purpose of the group. Perhaps the simplest way of describing this wholeness is by saying that it is a "we"; it involves the sort of sympathy and mutual identification for which "we" is the natural expression (p. 23).

Cooley called primary groups the nursery of human nature because they have the earliest and most fundamental impact upon the individual's socialization and development. He identified three basic primary groups: the family, children's play groups, and neighborhood or community groups.

Primary groups *involve interaction among members who have an emotional investment in one another and in a situation, who know one another intimately and interact as total individuals rather than through socialized roles.* For example, members of a family are emotionally involved with one another and know one another well. In addition, they interact with one another in terms of their total personalities, not just in terms of their social identities or statuses as breadwinner, student, athlete, or community leader.

A secondary group, in contrast, is characterized by much less intimacy among its members. It usually has specific goals, is formally organized, and is impersonal. Secondary groups tend to be larger than primary groups, and their members do not necessarily interact with all other members. In fact, many members often do not know one another at all—to the extent that they do, rarely do they know more about one another than about their respective social identities. Members feelings about, and behavior toward, one another are patterned mostly by their statuses and roles rather than by personality characteristics. The chairman of the board of General Motors, for example, is treated respectfully by all General Motors employees—regardless of the chariman's sex, age, intelligence, habits of dress, physical fitness, temperament, or qualities as a parent or spouse. In secondary groups, such as political parties, labor unions, and large corporations, people *are* very much what they *do*. Table 5.1 outlines the major differences between primary and secondary groups.

Characteristics of Groups

In order to function properly, all groups—both primary and secondary—must (1) define their boundaries, (2) choose leaders, (3) make decisions, (4) set goals, (5) assign tasks, and (6) control members' behavior.

DEFINING BOUNDARIES Group members must have ways of knowing who belongs to their group and who does not. Sometimes devices for marking boundaries are obvious symbols such as the uniforms worn by athletic teams, lapel pins worn by Rotary Club members, rings worn by Masons, and styles of dress. Other ways in which group boundaries are marked include the use of gestures (think of the special handshakes often used by many African Americans) and language (dialect differences

often mark people's regional origin and social class). In some societies (including our own), skin color sometimes mark's boundaries between groups. The idea of the British school tie that, by its pattern and colors, signals exclusive group membership, has been adopted by businesses ranging from banking to brewing.

CHOOSING LEADERS All groups must grapple with the issue of leadership. A **leader** *is someone who occupies a central role or position of dominance and influence in a group.* In some groups, such as large corporations, leadership is assigned to individuals by those in positions of authority. In other groups, such as adolescent peer groups, individuals move into positions of leadership through the force of personality or through particular skills such as athletic ability, fighting, or debating. In still other groups, including political organizations, leadership is awarded through the democratic process of nominations and voting. Think of the long primary process that presidential candidates must endure in order to amass enough votes to carry their party's nomination for the November election.

Leadership need not always be held by the same person within a group. It can shift from one individual to another in response to problems or situations that the group encounters. In a group of factory workers, for instance, leadership may fall on different members depending on what the group

TABLE 5.1

Relationships in Primary and Secondary Groups

	Primary	Secondary
Physical Conditions	Small number	Large number
	Long duration	Shorter duration
Social Characteristics	Identification of ends	Disparity of ends
	Intrinsic valuation of the relation	Extrinsic valuation of the relation
	Intrinsic valuation of other person	Extrinsic valuation of other person
	Inclusive knowledge of other person	Specialized and limited knowledge of other person
	Feeling of freedom and spontaneity	Feeling of external constraint
	Operation of informal controls	Operation of formal controls
Sample Relationships	Friend–friend	Clerk–customer
	Husband–wife	Announcer–listener
	Parent–child	Performer–spectator
	Teacher–pupil	Officer–subordinate
Sample Groups	Play group	Nation
	Family	Clerical hierarchy
	Village or neighborhood	Professional association
	Work–team	Corporation

Source: Kingsley Davis, *Human Society.* New York: Macmillan, 1949.

plans to do—complain to the supervisor, head to a tavern after work, or organize a picnic for all members and their families.

Politicians and athletic coaches often like to talk about individuals who are "natural leaders." Although attempts to account for leadership solely in terms of personality traits have failed again and again, personality factors may determine what kinds of leadership functions a person assumes. Researchers (Bales, 1958; Slater, 1966) have identified two types of leadership roles: (1) **instrumental leadership** *in which a leader actively proposes tasks and plans to guide the group toward achieving its goals*, and (2) **expressive leadership**, *in which a leader works to keep relations among group members harmonious and morale high*. Both kinds of leadership are crucial to group success.

Sometimes both functions are fulfilled by one person as they were in the case of Bear Bryant, former football coach at the University of Alabama. Ken Stabler, who went on to become quarterback of the Oakland Raiders and New Orleans Saints, described Bryant's leadership style in this way:

Coach Bryant had a way of being very, very tough, while still making you love him. He was doing it to make you a better player and ultimately a better man. . . . He was the sort of man who had his own way of doing things, and that was the only way things got done. . . . I think Coach Bryant's strong suit was motivation. He knew how to make an overachiever out of everybody. . . . There was a certain amount of intimidation in his style, but the main thing always was respect. He kept his distance, yet somehow you felt close to him. I still don't know how he managed to do that (Stabler, *Esquire*, June 1986).

When one person cannot be found to take both leadership functions, these functions are often distributed among several group members. The individual with knowledge of the terrain who leads a group of airplane crash survivors to safety is providing instrumental leadership. The group members who think of ways to keep the group from giving in to despair are providing expressive leadership. The group needs both to survive.

There are three types of instrumental leaders: *An* **authoritarian leader** *makes decisions and gives orders; a* **democratic leader** *attempts to encourage group members to reach a consensus; and a* **laissez-faire leader** *is a leader in name or title only and does little actively to influence group affairs*.

When Pakistani President General Mohammed Zia ul-Haq decided unilaterally in 1988 to dismiss civilian government and dissolve the national assembly, he demonstrated the power of an authoritarian

leader. In the corporate arena, Lee Iacocca, Chairman of Chrysler Corporation, tends also to exercise an authoritarian form of leadership. Says Iacocca: "You have to be a decision maker. After all the information has been gathered, somebody has to decide. That's what being in charge is all about." (*U.S. News and World Report*, May 20, 1985) On the whole, Americans are biased toward democratic leaders. Much of this is due to an ideological opposition to authoritarian political systems.

In most situations a democratic style of leadership promotes greater satisfaction among group members and more effective group functioning than either the authoritarian or laissez-faire style. The authoritarian type of leader may be generally disliked in times of normal operations. However, there are certain group situations in which the authoritarian form of leadership is more effective than the democratic form. For example, when speed and efficiency are important, an authoritarian leader can be quite useful. An authoritarian leader may take charge very effectively during emergencies, whereas the democratic leader might be highly valued during routine operations but find it more difficult to assume a strong leadership role when the situation demands it.

MAKING DECISIONS Closely related to the problem of leadership is the way in which groups make decisions. In many early hunting and food-gathering societies, important group decisions were reached by consensus—talking about an issue until everybody agreed on what to do (Fried, 1967). Today, occasionally, town councils and other small governing bodies operate in this way. Because this takes a great deal of time and energy, many groups opt for efficiency by taking votes or simply letting one person's decision stand for the group as a whole. Bales and Strodtbeck (1951) identified four stages in group decision making: (1) *orientation*—in which a situation that has disrupted the group's equilibrium is identified and information is gathered, (2) *evaluation*—in which the information is assessed and possible courses of action are proposed, (3) *decision*—in which the group chooses a course of action, and (4) *restoration of equilibrium*—in which the group once more takes up its normal activities.

SETTING GOALS As we pointed out before, all groups must have a purpose, a goal, or a set of goals. The goal may be very general, such as spreading peace throughout the world, or it may be very specific, such as playing cards on a railroad train. Group goals may change. For example, the cardplayers might discover they all share a concern about the use of nuclear energy and decide to organize a political-action group.

ASSIGNING TASKS   Establishing boundaries, defining leadership, making decisions, and setting goals are not enough to keep a group going. In order to endure, a group must do something, if nothing more than ensure that its members continue to make contact with one another. Therefore, it is important that group members know what needs to be done and who is going to do it. This assigning of tasks in itself can be an important group activity—think of your family discussions about sharing household chores. By taking on group tasks, members not only help the group reach its goals but also show their commitment to one another and to the group as a whole. This leads members to appreciate one another's importance as individuals and the importance of the group in all their lives—a process that injects life and energy into a group.

CONTROLLING MEMBERS' BEHAVIOR   If a group cannot control its members' behavior, it will cease to exist. For this reason, failure to conform to group norms is seen as dangerous or threatening, whereas conforming to group norms is rewarded—if only by others' friendly attitudes. Groups not only encourage but often depend for survival on conformity of behavior. A member's failure to conform is met with responses ranging from coolness to criticism, or even ejection from the group. Anyone who has ever tried to introduce changes into the constitution of a club or to ignore long-standing conventions, such as ways of dressing, rituals of greeting, or the assumption of designated responsibilities, probably has experienced group hostility.

Primary groups tend to be more tolerant of members' deviant behavior than secondary groups (Lee, 1966). For example, families often will conceal the problems of a member who suffers from chronic alcoholism or drug abuse. Even primary groups, however, must draw the line somewhere, and they will invoke negative sanctions (see Chapter 6) if all else fails to get the deviant member to show at least a willingness to *try* to conform. When primary groups finally act, their punishments can be far more severe or harsh than those of secondary groups. Thus, an intergenerational conflict in a family can result in the commitment of a teenager to an institution or treatment center.

Secondary groups tend to use formal, as opposed to informal, sanctions and are much more likely than primary groups simply to expel, or push out, a member who persists in violating strongly held norms: corporations fire unsatisfactory employ-

ees, the army discharges soldiers who violate regulations, and so on. Even though primary groups are more tolerant of a member's behavior, people tend to conform more closely to their norms than to those of secondary groups. This is because people value their membership in a primary group, with its strong interpersonal bonds, for its own sake. Secondary group membership is valued mostly for what it will do for the people in the group, not because of any deep emotional ties. Because primary group membership is so desirable, its members are more reluctant to risk expulsion by indulging in behavior that might violate the group's standards, or norms, than are secondary group members.

Usually group members will want to conform as long as the group is perceived as important. Solomon Asch (1955) showed just how far group members will go to promote group solidarity and conformity. In a series of experiments, he formed groups of eight people and asked each member to match one line against three other lines of varying lengths (see Figure 5.4). Each judgment was announced in the presence of the other group members. The groups were composed of one real subject and seven of Asch's confederates, whose identities were kept secret from the real subject. The confederates had previously met with Asch and had been instructed to give a unanimous but incorrect answer at certain points throughout the experiment. Asch was interested in finding out how the individual who had been made a minority of one in the presence of a unanimous majority would respond. The subject

FIGURE 5.4

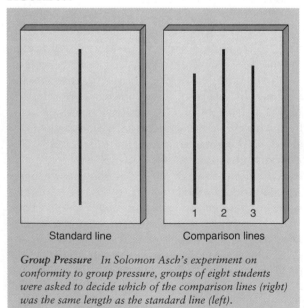

| Standard line | Comparison lines |

Group Pressure   In Solomon Asch's experiment on conformity to group pressure, groups of eight students were asked to decide which of the comparison lines (right) was the same length as the standard line (left).

was placed in a situation in which a group unanimously contradicted the information of his or her senses. Asch repeated the experiment many times. He found that 32 percent of the answers by the real subjects were identical with, or in the direction of, the inaccurate estimates of the majority. This was quite remarkable, because there were virtualy no incorrect answers in the control groups that lacked Asch's accomplices, ruling out the possibility of optical illusion. What we have here is an instance in which individuals are willing to give incorrect answers in order not to appear out of step with the judgments of other group members.

Reference Groups

Groups are more than just bridges between the individual and society as a whole. We spend much of our time in one group or another, and the impact these groups have on us continues even when we are not actually in contact with its members. The norms and values of groups to which we belong or with which we identify serve as the basis for evaluating our own and others' behavior.

A **reference group** *is a group or social category that an individual uses to help define beliefs, attitudes, and values to guide behavior.* They provide a comparison point against which persons measure themselves and others. A reference group is often a category with which we identify, rather than a specific group to which we belong. For example, a communications major may identify with individuals in the media without having any direct contact with them. In this respect, anticipatory socialization is taking place, in that the individual may alter his or her behavior and attitudes toward those they perceive as part of the group they plan to join. For example, people who become bankers soon feel themselves part of a group and assume ideas and lifestyles that help them identify with that group. They tend to dress in a conservative, "bankerish" fashion, even buying their clothes in shops that other bankers patronize to make sure they have the "right" clothes from the "right" stores. They join certain organizations such as country clubs and alumni associations so that they can mingle with other bankers and clients. Eventually the norms and values they adopted when they joined the bankers group become internalized and they see and judge the world around them as bankers.

We can also distinguish between positive and negative reference groups. Positive reference groups are made up of people we want to emulate. Negative reference groups provide a model we do not wish to follow. Therefore, a writer may identify positively

with those writers who produce serious fiction while thinking of journalists who write for gossip publications as a negative reference group.

Even though groups are in fact composed of individuals, individuals are created to a large degree by groups to which they belong through the process of socialization (see Chapter 4). Of these groups, the small group usually has the strongest impact on an individual.

SMALL GROUPS

The term **small group** *refers to many kinds of social groups, such as families, peer goups, and work groups, that actually meet together and contain few enough members so that all members know one another.* The smallest group possible is a **dyad**, *which contains only two members.* an engaged couple is a dyad, as are the pilot and copilot of an aircraft.

Georg Simmel (1950) was the first sociologist to emphasize the importance of the size of a group on the interaction process. He suggested that small groups have distinctive qualities and patterns of interaction that disappear when the group grows larger. For example, dyads resist change in their group size: on the one hand, the loss of one member destroys the group leaving the other member alone; but on the other hand a **triad**, *or the addition of a third member,* creates uncertainty because it introduces the possibility of two-against-one alliances.

Triads are more stable in those situations when one member can help resolve quarrels between the other two. When three diplomats are negotiating offshore fishing rights, for example, one member of the triad may offer a concession that will break the deadlock between the other two. If that does not work, the third person may try to analyze the arguments of the other two in an effort to bring about a compromise. The formation of shifting pair-offs within triads can help stabilize the group. When it appears that one group member is weakening, one of the two paired members will often break the alliance and form a new one with the individual who had been isolated (Hare, 1976). This is often seen among groups of children engaged in games. In triads in which there is no shifting of alliances and the configuration constantly breaks down into two against one, the group will become unstable and may eventually break up. In Aldous Huxley's novel *Brave New World*, the political organization of the earth was organized into three eternally warring political powers. As one power seemed to be losing, one of the others would come to its aid

Triads are usually unstable groups because there is always the possibility of two-against-one alliances.

in a temporary alliance, thereby ensuring worldwide political stability while also making possible endless warfare. No power could risk the total defeat of another because the other surviving power might then become the stronger of the surviving dyad.

As a group grows larger, the number of relationships within it increases, which often leads to the formation of **subgroups**—*splinter groups within the larger group.* Once a group has more than five to seven members, spontaneous conversation becomes difficult for the group as a whole. Then there are two solutions available: The group can split into subgroups (as happens informally at parties), or it can adopt a formal means of controlling communication (use of *Robert's Rules of Order,* for instance). For these reasons, small groups tend to resist the addition of new members because increasing size threatens the nature of the group. In addition, there may be a fear that new members will resist socialization to group norms and thereby undermine group traditions and values. On the whole, small groups are much more vulnerable than large groups to disruption by new members, and the introduction of new members often leads to shifts in patterns of interaction and group norms.

LARGE GROUPS: ASSOCIATIONS

Although all of us could probably identify and describe the various small groups to which we

belong, we might find it difficult to follow the same process with the large groups that affect us. As patrons or employees of large organizations and governments, we function as part of large groups all the time. Thus, sociologists must study large groups as well as small groups in order to understand the workings of society.

Much of the activity of a modern society is carried out through large and formally organized groups. Sociologists refer to these groups as associations. **Associations** *are purposefully created special-interest groups that have clearly defined goals and official ways of doing things.* Associations include such organizations as government departments and agencies, businesses and factories, labor unions, schools and colleges, fraternal and service groups, hospitals and clinics, and clubs for various hobbies from gardening to antique collecting. Their goals may be very broad and general, such as helping the poor, healing the sick, or making a profit, or quite specific and limited, such as manufacturing automobile tires, or teaching people to speak Chinese. Although an enormous variety of associations exists, they all are characterized by some degree of formal structure with an underlying informal structure.

The Formal Structure

In order for associations to function, the work that must be accomplished is assessed and broken down into manageable tasks that are assigned to specific individuals. In other words, associations are run according to some type of formal organizational structure that consists of planned, highly institutionalized, and clearly defined statuses and role relationships. The formal organizational structure of large associations in contemporary society is best exemplified by the organizational structure called bureaucracy.

A college or university must have a highly developed organizational structure. Fulfilling its main purpose of educating students requires far more than simply bringing together students and teachers. Funds must be raised, buildings constructed, qualified students and instructors recruited, programs and classes organized, materials ordered and distributed, grounds kept up, and buildings maintained. Messages need to be typed, copied, and filed; lectures must be given; and seminars must be led. To accomplish all these tasks, the school must create many different positions: president, deans, department heads, registrars, public relations staff, grounds keepers, maintenance personnel, purchasing agents, secretaries, faculty, and students. Every member of the school has clearly spelled out tasks that are organized in relation to one another: Students are taught and evaluated by faculty, faculty must answer to department heads or deans, deans to the president, and so on. Yet, underlying these clearly defined assignments are procedures that are never written down but are worked out and understood by those who must get the job done.

The Informal Structure

Sociologists recognize that formal associations never operate entirely according to their stated rules and procedures. Every association has an informal structure consisting of networks of people who help out one another by "bending" rules and taking procedural shortcuts. No matter how carefully plans are made, no matter how clearly and rationally roles are defined and tasks assigned, every situation and its variants cannot be anticipated. Sooner or later, then, individuals in associations are confronted with situations in which they must improvise and even persuade others to help them do so.

As every student knows, no school ever runs as smoothly as planned. For instance, "going by the book"—that is, following all the formal rules—often gets students tied up in long lines and red tape. Enterprising students and instructors find shortcuts. For example, a student who wants to change from Section A of Sociology 100 to Section E might find it very difficult or time-consuming to change sections

(add-and-drop) officially. However, it may be possible to work out an informal deal—the student stays registered in Section A but attends and is evaluated in Section E. The instructor of Section E then turns the grade over to the instructor of Section A who hands in that grade with all the other Section A grades—as if the student had attended Section A all along. The formal rules have been "bent," but the major purposes of the school (educating and evaluating students) have been served.

In addition, human beings have their own individual needs even when they are on "company time," and these needs are not always met by attending single-mindedly to assigned tasks. To accommodate these needs, people often try to find extra break time for personal business by getting jobs done faster than would be possible if all the formal rules and procedures were followed. To accomplish these ends, individuals in associations find it useful to help one another by "covering" for one another, "looking the other way" at strategic moments, and offering one another useful information about office politics, people, and procedures. Gradually the reciprocal relationships among members of these informal networks become institutionalized: "Unwritten laws" are established, and a fully functioning informal structure evolves (Selznick, 1948).

At the same time as the goals of associations have given rise to an informal structure for job performance, they have also spawned an organizational structure that often increases the formality of procedures. This formal organizational structure, called bureaucracy has an impact on the informal structure.

BUREAUCRACY

Associations evolved along with literacy and the rise of cities some 5,500 years ago, but bureaucracy emerged as the organizational counterpart of the Industrial Revolution only two centuries ago. Although in ordinary usage the term suggests a certain rigidity and red tape, it has a somewhat different meaning to sociologists. Robert K. Merton (1968) defined **bureaucracy** as *"a formal, rationally organized social structure [with] clearly defined patterns of activity in which, ideally, every series of actions is functionally related to the purposes of the organization."*

Max Weber, the German sociologist introduced in Chapter 1, provided the first detailed study of the nature and origins of bureaucracy. Although much has changed since he first developed his theories,

Weber's basic description of bureaucracy remains essentially accurate to this day.

Weber's Model of Bureaucracy

Weber viewed bureaucracy as the most efficient— although not necessarily the most desirable—form of social organization for the administration of work. He studied examples of bureaucracy in history and in contemporary times and noted the elements they had in common. From this work he developed a model of bureaucracy, or an ideal type. *An **ideal type** is a simplified, exaggerated model of reality used to illustrate a concept.* When Weber presented his ideal type of bureaucracy, he combined into one those characteristics found in one form or another in a variety of organizations. It is unlikely that we ever would find a bureaucracy with all the traits in Weber's ideal type. However, his presentation can help us understand what is involved in bureaucratic systems. It is also important to recognize that Weber's ideal type is in no way meant to be "ideal" in the sense that it presents a desired state of affairs. In short, an ideal type is an exaggeration of a situation that is used in order to convey a set of ideas. Weber outlined six characteristics of bureaucracies:

1. *A clear-cut division of labor.* The activities of a bureaucracy are broken down into clearly defined, limited tasks, which are attached to formally defined positions (statuses) in the organization. This structure permits a great deal of specialization and a high degree of expertise. For example, a small-town police department might consist of a chief, a lieutenant, a detective, several sergeants and a dozen officers. The chief issues orders and assigns tasks; the lieutenant is in charge when the chief is not around; the detective does investigative work; the sergeants handle calls at the desk and do the paperwork required for formal booking procedures; and the officers walk or drive through the community, making arrests and responding to emergencies. Each member of the department has a defined status and duty as well as specialized skills appropriate to his or her position.

2. *Hierarchical delegaton of power and responsibility.* Each position in the bureaucracy is given sufficient power so that the individual who occupies it can do assigned work adequately and compel subordinates to follow instructions. Such power must be limited to what is necessary to meet the requirements of the position. For example, a police chief can order an officer to walk a specific beat but cannot insist that the officer join the Lions Club.

3. *Rules and regulations.* The rights and duties attached to various positions are clearly stated in writing and govern the behavior of all individuals who occupy them. In this way all members of the organizational structure know what is expected of them, and each person is held accountable for his or her behavior. For example, the regulations of a police department might state, "No member of the department shall drink intoxicating liquors while on duty." Such rules make the activities of bureaucracies predictable and stable.

4. *Impartiality.* The organization's written rules and regulations apply equally to all members.

Modern bureaucracies have an organizational structure that makes it clear to all members what rights and duties are attached to the various positions and what behavior is expected.

Can A Case Be Made for Bureaucracy?

Mass media depictions of bureaucracy display a surprisingly uniform picture. Writers, cartoonist, and commentators of every shade of opinion seem to share a common consensus on this "evil" worldwide phenomenon.

The bureaucrat is inevitably depicted as lazy or snarling, or both. The office occupied by this sow feeding at the public trough is bungling or inhumane, or both. The overall department is portrayed as overstaffed, inflexible, unresponsive, and power-hungry, all at once.

Here are a few examples of the excesses of bureaucracies taken from recent news reports:

- Several years ago, federal government officials put together a 700-page document outlining standards for a "rodent elimination device"—usually referred to as a mousetrap.
- A Chicago woman undergoing medical treatment applied for Medicare. She received a computer-printed letter informing her that she was ineligible because she had died the previous April.
- The Department of Energy set out to declassify millions of documents inherited from the Atomic Energy Commission. Eight of the released documents contained the basic design principles for the hydrogen bomb.
- A unit of what is now the Department of Health and Human Services sent 15 chimpanzees to a Texas laboratory to start a chimp-breeding program. All were males.

- In New York City, fire department scuba divers were prevented from searching for survivors of a helicopter crash in the East River by police commanders in charge of the rescue mission. The reason: a bitter bureaucratic rivalry between the two uniformed forces that had little to do with public safety. One man died who might have been saved had divers found him sooner.

In each of these examples, it appears that the ultimate goal of serving the community is lost in a tangle of rules, regulations, and incompetence.

Is it possible to make any sort of case in defense of bureaucracy? Yes, says Charles T. Goodsell, an expert on bureaucracy, who has written an entire book doing just that.

First, he points out, we should notice that most bureaucratic horror stories are usually short (we presented five here). They stress the citizen's anguish and the incident's adverse effects. Little information is given about the bureaucracy's side of the story.

Second, he says, the cases described are usually bizarre, reinforce stereotypes, and strike a responsive chord. Anyone old enought to read this has experienced incidents in which officials have acted in a baffling and frustrating way. So it is little wonder we can personally relate to bureaucratic horror stories.

But be honest. How can *all* bureaucracies be inefficient, secretive, rigid, oppressive, undemo-

cratic, alienating, and discriminatory *all* the time?

Goodsell notes that, contrary to popular images, the majority of ordinary citizens, when asked to rate their experiences with specific bureaucracies, find them to be "satisfactory" or "acceptable."

The "bureaucrat mentality" also seems to disappear when researchers look for it. Bureaucrats tend to be just like the general population in all respects. Small wonder. Some probably live next door to you.

The low-prestige image of the bureaucrat is most common among upper-middle-class Americans. Could it be that the antibureaucracy sentiment is an elitist bias?

Critics of bureaucracies too often assume that the dissatisfaction voiced by some indicates widespread disapproval. But this is not necessarily true. Goodsell argues that most people are quite satisfied with present bureaucracies and are reluctant to press for change that may, at best, benefit a relative few.

Bureaucracy is often presented as an alien force—"us" against "them." Actually, bureaucracy is very much a part of us. It is every public institution operating in our community: the staff at our children's schools, the officials who run our towns. It is collective action on our behalf. In a very real sense, *we* are bureaucracy.

Source: Charles T. Goodsell, *The Case for Bureaucracy*, 2nd ed., Chatham, NJ: Chatham House, 1985.

No exceptions are made because of social or psychological differences among individuals. Also, people occupy positions in the bureaucracy only because they are assigned according to formal procedures. These positions "belong to" the organization itself; they cannot become the personal property of those who occupy them. For example, a vice-president of United States Steel Corporation is usually not permitted to pass on that position to his or her children through inheritance.

5. *Employment based on technical qualifications.* People are hired because they have the ability and skills to do the job, not because they have personal contacts within the company. Advancement is based on how well a person does the job. Promotions and job security go to those who are most competent.

6. *Distinction between public and private spheres.* A clear distinction is made between the employees' personal lives and their working lives. It is unusual for employees to be expected to take business calls at home. At the same time their family life has no place in the work setting.

Although many bureaucracies strive at the organizational level to attain the goals that Weber proposed, most do not achieve them on the practical level.

Bureaucracy Today: The Reality

Just as no building is ever identical with its blueprint, no bureaucratic organization fully embodies all the features of Weber's model. Studies of organizations around the world reveal that such elements as degree of hierarchical organization, adherence to rules and regulations, and job specialization vary widely—both between and within organizations (Udy, 1959; Hall, 1963–1964). One thing that most bureaucracies have in common is a structure that separates those whose responsibilities include keeping in mind the overall needs of the entire organization from those whose responsibilities are much more narrow and task oriented. Visualize a modern industrial organization as a pyramid. Management (at the top of the pyramid) plans, organizes, hires, and fires. Workers (in the bottom section) make much smaller decisions limited to carrying out the work assigned. A similar division cuts through the hierarchy of the Roman Catholic church. The bishops are at the top, along with archbishops, cardinals, and the pope; the clergy are below. Only bishops can ordain new priests, and they plan the church's worldwide activities. The priests administer parishes, schools, and missions; their tasks are quite narrow and

confined. Figure 5.5 illustrates the organizational structure of a university.

Although employees of bureaucracies may enjoy the privileges of their position and guard them jealously, they may be adversely affected by the system in ways they do not recognize. Alienation, adherence to unproductive ritual, and acceptance of incompetence are some of the results of a less-than-ideal bureaucracy.

Robert Michels, a friend of Weber's, also was concerned about the depersonalizing effect of bureaucracy. His views, formulated at the beginning of this century, are still pertinent today.

The Iron Law of Oligarchy

Michels (1911) came to the conclusion that the formal organization of bureaucracies inevitably leads to **oligarchy**, *under which organizations originally idealistic and democratic eventually come to be dominated by a small, self-serving group of people who achieved positions of power and responsibility.* This can occur in large organizations because it becomes physically impossible for everyone to get together every time a decision has to be made. Consequently, a small group is given the responsibility of making decisions. Michels believed that the people in this group would become enthralled with their elite positions and more and more inclined to make decisions that protect their power rather than represent the will of the group they are supposed to serve. In effect Michels was saying that bureaucracy and democracy do not mix. Despite any protestations and promises that they would not become like all the rest, those placed in positions of responsibility and power often come to believe that they too are indispensable, and more knowledgeable than those they serve. As time goes on, they become further removed from the rank and file.

This may have occurred during the Iran-Contra scandal of 1987–1988 when Oliver North, John Poindexter and other members of the National Security Council were accused of illegally selling arms to Iran and diverting the profits to the Nicaraguan Contras. They were accused of doing this despite laws prohibiting such actions and without the consent of the President or Congress.

The Iron Law of Oligarchy suggests that organizations wishing to avoid oligarchy should take a number of precautionary steps. They should make sure that the rank and file remain active in the organization and that the leaders not be granted absolute control of a centralized administration. As long as there are open lines of communication and

FIGURE 5.5

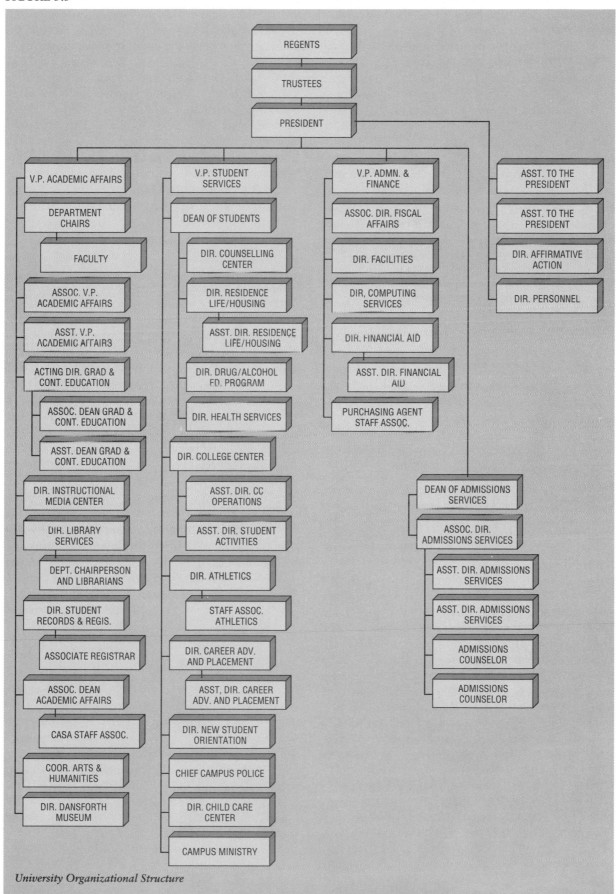

University Organizational Structure

shared decision making between the leaders and the rank and file, an oligarchy cannot easily develop.

Clearly, the problems of oligarchy, of the bureaucratic depersonalization described by Weber, and of personal alienation all are interrelated. If individuals are deprived of the power to make decisions that affect their lives in many or even most of the areas that are important to them, withdrawal into narrow **ritualism** (*overconformity to rules*) and apathy are likely responses. Such withdrawals seemed to constitute a chronic condition in some of the highly centralized socialist countries. However, there are many signs of public apathy in the United States, too. For example, in 1964 about 70 percent of those eligible to vote for president did so. In each of the succeeding national elections this figure has dropped, and in 1988 it was only 50 percent.

INSTITUTIONS AND SOCIAL ORGANIZATION

Anyone who has traveled to foreign countries knows that different societies have different ways of doing things. The basic things that get done actually are quite similar—food is produced and distributed; people get married and have children; and children are raised to take on the responsibilities of adulthood. The vehicle for accomplishing the basic needs of any society is the social institution.

Social Institutions

Sociologists usually speak of five areas of society in which basic needs have to be fulfilled: the family sector, the education sector, the economic sector, the religious sector, and the political sector. For each of these areas social groups and associations carry out the goals and meet the needs of society. The behavior of people in these groups and associations is organized or patterned by the relevant **social institutions**—that is, *the ordered social relationships that grow out of the values, norms, statuses, and roles that organize those activities that fulfill society's fundamental needs*. Thus, economic institutions organize the ways in which society produces and distributes the goods and services it needs; educational institutions determine what should be learned and how it should be taught; and so forth.

Of all social institutions, the family is the most basic. A stable family unit is the main ingredient necessary for the smooth functioning of society. For instance, sexual behavior must be regulated and children must be cared for and raised to fit into society. Hence, the institution of the family provides a system of continuity from one generation to the next. Although nothing in society is completely static, social institutions normally are among the most slowly changing aspects of any society. Thus, particular businesses may come and go, but basic economic institutions persist. Political power may change hands, but usually according to the rules and within the context of a society's political institution. It is important, therefore, to keep clear the distinction between the concept of group and the concept of institution. A group is a collection of specific, indentifiable people. *An* **institution** *is a system for organizing standardized patterns of social behavior*. In other words, a group consists of people, and an institution is the standardized ways in which people do certain things. For example, when sociologists discuss *a* family (say the Smith family), they are referring to a particular group of people. When they discuss *the* family, they are referring to the family as an instituion—a cluster of statuses, roles, values, and norms that organize the standardized patterns of behavior we expect to find within family groups. Thus, the family as an American institution typically embodies several master statuses: those of husband, wife, and, possibly, father, mother, and child. It also includes the statuses of son, daughter, brother, and sister. These statuses are organized into well-defined, patterned relationships: Parents have authority over their children; spouses have a sexual relationship with each other (but not with the children); and so on. However, specific family groups may not conform entirely to the ideals of the institution. There are single-parent families, families in which the children appear to be running things, and families in which there is an incestuous parent-child relationship. Although a society's institutions provide what can be thought of a a "master plan" for human interaction in groups, *actual* behavior and *actual* group organization often deviate in varying degrees from this plan.

Social Organization

If we step back from a mosaic, the many multicolored stones are seen to compose a single, coordinated pattern or picture. Similarly, if we step back and look at society, the many actions of its members fall into a pattern or series of interrelated patterns. These consist of social interactions and relationships expressing individual decisions and choices. These choices, however, are not random; rather, they are an outgrowth of a society's social organization. **Social organization** *consists of the relatively stable pattern of social relationships among individuals and groups in society*. These relationships are based

Relatively rapid social change is making less predictable the types of behavior that should go along with gender roles.

upon systems of social roles, norms, and shared meanings that provide regularity and predictability in social interaction. Social organization differs from one society to the next. Thus, Islam allows a man to marry up to four wives at any given time, whereas in our society, with its Judeo-Christian religious tradition, such plural marriage is not acceptable. Just as statuses and roles exist within ordered relationships to one another, social institutions also exist in patterned relationships with one another in the context of society. All societies have their own patterning for these relationships. For example, a society's economic and political institutions often are closely interrelated. So, too, are the family and religious institutions. Thus, a description of American social organization would indicate the presence of monogamy along with Judeo-Christian values and norms and the institutionalization of economic competition and of democratic political organizations.

A society's social organization tends to be the most stable aspect of society. The American social organization, however, may not be as static as that of many other societies. Our society is experiencing relatively rapid social change because of its complexity and because of the great variety of people that are part of it. This complexity makes life less predictable because new values and norms being introduced from numerous quarters result in changes in our social organization. For example, ideas about the behavior that should go along with female gender roles have changed considerably over the last two decades. Not long ago it was assumed that most married women would not work but would stay home and attend to the rearing of children. Today the majority of American women are working outside the home, and views on what roles mothers should play in the lives of their children are in flux.

CHAPTER

▪ 6 ▪

Deviant Behavior and Social Control

Defining Normal and Deviant Behavior
   Making Moral Judgments
   The Functions of Deviance
   The Dysfunctions of Deviance

Mechanisms of Social Control
   Internal Means of Control
   External Means of Control: Sanctions

Theories of Crime and Deviance
   Biological Theories of Deviance
   Psychological Theories of Deviance
   Sociological Theories of Deviance

The Importance of Law
   The Emergence of Laws

Crime in the United States
   Crime Statistics

Kinds of Crime in the United States
   Juvenile Crime
   Violent Crime
   Property Crime
   White-Collar Crime
   Organized Crime
   Victimless Crime

Criminal Justice in the United States
   The Police
   The Courts
   Prisons

What would you think of a man who graduated from Harvard College but repudiated his degree? A man who never married, but loved children and was forever taking them out on forays in the woods and fields? A man who lived all his life at home with his parents and sisters and who subsisted by taking odd jobs? What would you think of a man who for two years lived alone in a one-room cabin by a pond in the woods in a section of town where drunks and lowlifes of one sort or another often took refuge? A man who waded chest deep into the swamps and waited there all morning observing frogs and fish? Sometimes this man felt that he actually ceased to be and that he was suspended above the earth. He described his profession as that of a mystic and natural philosopher. This man often boasted that he was happy living in this manner, that he was right and the world was wrong and that "The mass of men live lives of quiet desperation."

Was he a deviant? Ralph Waldo Emerson described this man as "the bachelor of thought and nature." Some described him in political terms, as the founder of the passive-resistance movement, some in philosophical terms, as the only real transcendentalist. Some think of him as an essayist, some as a naturalist (Mitchell, 1990).

The man was Henry David Thoreau. Thoreau was responsible for an important essay on civil disobedience that influenced the likes of Leo Tolstoy of Russia, Mahatma Ghandi of India, and the leaders of the American civil rights movement. Thoreau's Walden Pond in Concord, Massachusetts, stands as a tribute to his life and ideas. His belief that people should refuse to obey any law they believe is unjust became the center of a major controversy when developers attempted to erect an office building on the site. Instead of being seen as someone engaged in deviant behavior, Thoreau has been marked by history as a great thinker and idealist.

119

DEFINING NORMAL AND DEVIANT BEHAVIOR

What determines whether a person's actions end up being seen as deviance or creativity? Why will two men walking hand-in-hand in downtown Minneapolis cause raised eyebrows but pass unnoticed in San Francisco or in Provincetown, Massachusetts? Why do Britons waiting to enter a theater stand patiently in line, whereas people from the Middle East jam together at the turnstile? In other words, what makes a given action—supporting segregation, men holding hands, cutting into a line—"normal" in one case but "deviant" in another?

The answer is culture—more specifically, the norms and values of each culture (see Chapter 3). Together, norms and values make up the **moral code** of a culture—*the symbolic system in terms of which behavior takes on the quality of being "good" or "bad," "right" or "wrong."* Therefore, in order to

Sociologists believe that deviant behavior fails to conform to the norms of the group. This man has no shirt on and is lying on the sidewalk in the middle of the winter. Would this behavior conform to the standards of any group?

decide whether any specific act is "normal" or "deviant," it is necessary to know more than only *what* a person did. One also must know who the person is (that is, the person's social identity) and the social and cultural context of the act. For example, if Thoreau had practiced his doctrine of *civil disobedience* and refusal to pay poll taxes not as a protest against slavery but as a protest against democracy, would we still find his ideas so enlightening? Of course not.

For sociologists, then, **normal behavior** *is behavior that conforms to the rules or norms of the group in which it occurs.* **Deviant behavior** *is behavior that fails to conform to the rules or norms of the group in question* (Durkheim, 1960a). Therefore, when we try to assess an act as being normal or deviant, we must identify the group by whose terms the behavior is judged. Moral codes differ widely from one society to another. For that matter, even within a society there exist groups and subcultures whose moral codes differ considerably. Watching television is normal behavior for most Americans, but it would be seen as deviant behavor among the Amish of Pennsylvania.

Making Moral Judgments

As we stated sociologists take a culturally relative view of normalcy and deviance and evaluate behavior according to the values of the culture in which it takes place. Ideally, they do not use their own values to judge the behavior of people from other cultures. Even though social scientists recognize that there is great variation in normal and deviant behavior and that no science can determine what acts are inherently deviant, there are certain acts that are almost universally accepted as being deviant. For example, parent-child incest is severely disapproved of in nearly every society. Genocide, the willful killing of specific groups of people—as occurred in the Nazi extermination camps during World War II—also is considered to be wrong even if it is sanctioned by the government or an entire society. The Nuremberg trials that were conducted after World War II supported this point. Even though most of the accused individuals claimed they were merely following orders when they murdered or arranged for the murder of large numbers of Jews and other groups, many were found guilty. The reasoning was that there is a higher moral order under which certain human actions are wrong, regardless of who endorses them. Thus, despite their desire to view events from a culturally relative standpoint, most sociologists find certain actions wrong, no matter what the context.

What forms of dress and what types of behavior are considered deviant depends on who is doing the judging and what the context might be.

The Functions of Deviance

Emile Durkheim observed that deviant behavior is "an integral part of all healthy societies" (1895, 1958). Why is this the case? The answer, Durkheim suggested, is that in the presence of deviant behavior, a social group becomes united in its response. In other words, opposition to deviant behavior creates

opportunities for cooperation essential to the survival of any group. For example, let us look at the response to a scandal in a small town as Durkheim described it:

> [People] stop each other on the street, they visit each other, they seek to come together to talk of the event and to wax indignant in common. From all the similar

In this photo from France at the end of World War II, the woman whose head has been shaven is jeered by the crowd as she is escorted out of town. She had been a Nazi collaborator during the war. Durkheim believed that deviant behavior performs an important function by focusing people's attention on the values of the group. The deviance represents a threat to the group and forces it to protect itself and preserve its existence.

impressions which are exchanged, from all the temper that gets itself expressed, there emerges a unique temper . . . which is everybody's without being anybody's in particular. That is the public temper (1895).

When social life moves along normally, people begin to take for granted one another and the meaning of their social interdependency. A deviant act, however, reawakens their group attachments and loyalties, because it represents a threat to the moral order of the group. The deviant act focuses people's attention on the value of the group. Perceiving itself under pressure, the group marshals its forces to protect itself and preserve its existence.

It appears, as Kai T. Erikson (1966) found, that unless the rhythm of group life is "punctuated by occasional moments of deviant behavior . . . social organization . . . [is] impossible."

Deviance also offers society's members an opportunity to rededicate themselves to their social controls. In some cases, deviant behavior actually helps teach society's rules by providing illustrations of violation. Knowing what is wrong is a step toward understanding what is right.

Deviance, then, may be functional to a group in that it (1) causes the group's members to close ranks, (2) prompts the group to organize in order to limit future deviant acts, (3) helps clarify for the group what it really does believe in, and (4) teaches normal behavior by providing examples of rule violation. Finally, (5) in some situations, tolerance of deviant behavior acts as a safety valve and actually prevents more serious instances of nonconformity. For example, the Amish, a religious group that does not believe in using such "modern" examples of contemporary society as cars, radios, televisions, and fashion oriented clothing, allows its teenagers a great deal of latitude in their behaviors before they are fully required to follow the dictates of the community. This prevents a confrontation that could result in a major battle of wills.

The Dysfunctions of Deviance

Deviance, of course has a number of dysfunctions as well, which is why every society attempts to restrain deviant behavior as much as possible. Included among the dysfunctions of deviant behavior are the following. (1) It is a threat to the social order because it makes social life difficult and unpredictable. (2) It causes confusion about the norms and values of that society. People become confused about what is expected, what is right and wrong. The variety of social standards compete with each other causing tension among the different segments of society. (3) Deviance also undermines trust. Social relationships are based on the premise that people will behave according to certain rules of conduct. When people's actions become unpredictable, the social order is thrown into disarray. (4) Deviance also diverts valuable resources. In order to control widespread deviance vast resources must be called upon and shifted from other social needs.

MECHANISMS OF SOCIAL CONTROL

In any society or social group it is necessary to have **mechanisms of social control**, *or a way of directing or influencing members' behavior to conform to the group's values and norms.* Sociologists distinguish between internal and external means of control.

Internal Means of Control

As we already observed in Chapters 3 and 5, people are socialized to accept the norms and values of their culture, especially in the smaller and more personally important social groups to which they belong, such as the family. The word *accept* is important here. Individuals conform to moral standards not just because they *know* what they are, but also because they have *internalized* these standards. They experience discomfort, often in the form of guilt, when they violate these norms. In other words, in order for a group's moral code to work properly it must be internalized and become part of each individual's emotional life as well as his or her thought processes. As this occurs, individuals begin to pass judgment on their own actions. In this way the moral code of a culture becomes an **internal means of control**—*that is, it operates on the individual even in the absence of reactions by others.*

External Means of Control: Sanctions

External means of social control *consist of other people's responses to a person's behavior*, that is, rewards and punishments. They include social forces external to the individual that channel behavior toward the culture's norms and values.

Sanctions *are rewards and penalties by a group's members used to regulate an individual's behavior.* Thus all external means of control use sanctions of one kind or another. *Actions that encourage the individual to continue acting in a certain way are called* **positive sanctions.** *Actions that discourage the repetition or continuation of the behavior are* **negative sanctions.**

POSITIVE AND NEGATIVE SANCTIONS   Sanctions take many forms, varying widely from group to group and from society to society. For example, an American audience might clap and whistle enthusiastically to show its appreciation for an excellent artistic or athletic performance, but the same whistling in Europe would be a display of strong disapproval. Or consider the *absence* of a response. In America a professor would not infer public disapproval because of the absence of applause at the end of a lecture—such applause by students is the rarest of compliments. In many universities in Europe, however, students are expected to applaud after every lecture (if only in a rhythmic, stylized manner). The absence of such applause would be a horrible blow to the professor, a public criticism of the presentation.

Most social sanctions have a symbolic side to them. Such symbolism has a powerful impact on people's self-esteem and sense of identity. Consider the positive feelings experienced by Olympic gold medalists or those elected to Phi Beta Kappa, the national society honoring excellence in undergraduate study. Or imagine the negative experience of being given the "silent treatment" such as that imposed on cadets who violate the honor code at the military academy at West Point (to some this is so painful that they drop out).

Sanctions often have important material qualities as well as symbolic meanings. Nobel Prize winners receive not only public acclaim but also a hefty check. The threat of loss of employment may accompany public disgrace when an individual's deviant behavior becomes known. In isolated, preliterate societies, social ostracism can be the equivalent of a death sentence.

Both positive and negative sanctions work only to the degree that people can be reasonably sure that they will actually take place as a consequence of a given act. In other words, they work on people's expectations. Whenever such expectations are not met, sanctions lose their ability to mold social conformity.

On the other hand, it is important to recognize a crucial difference between positive and negative sanctions. When society applies a positive sanction, it is a sign that social controls are successful: The desired behavior has occurred and is being rewarded. When a negative sanction is applied, it is due to the failure of social controls: The undesired behavior has not been prevented. Therefore, a society that frequently must punish people is failing in its attempts to promote conformity. A school that must expel large groups of students or a government that must frequently call out troops to quell protest and riots should begin to look for the weaknesses in its own system of internal means of social control to promote conformity.

FORMAL AND INFORMAL SANCTIONS   **Formal sanctions** *are applied in a public ritual—as in the awarding of a prize or an announcement of expulsion—and are usually under the direct or indirect control of authorities.* For example, in order to enforce certain standards of behavior and protect members of society, our society creates laws. Behavior that violates these laws may be punished through formal negative sanctions. Not all sanctions are formal, however. Many social responses to a person's behavior involve **informal sanctions**, *or actions by group members that arise spontaneously with little or no formal direction.* Gossip is an informal sanction that is used universally. Congratulations are offered to people whose behavior has approval. In teenage peer groups, ridicule is a powerful, informal, negative sanction. The anonymity and impersonality of urban living, however, decreases the influence of these controls except when we are with members of our friendship and kinship groups.

A TYPOLOGY OF SANCTIONS   Figure 6.1 shows the four main types of social sanctions, produced by combining the two sets of sanctions we have just discussed: informal and formal, positive and negative. Although formal sanctions might appear to be strong influences on behavior, informal sanctions actually have a greater impact on people's self-images and behavior. This is so because informal sanctions usually occur more frequently and come from close, respected associates.

1. **Informal positive sanctions** *are displays people use to spontaneously express their approval of*

FIGURE 6.1

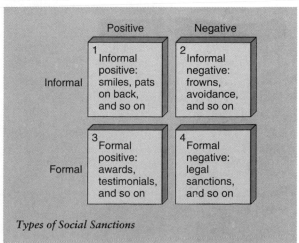

	Positive	Negative
Informal	1 Informal positive: smiles, pats on back, and so on	2 Informal negative: frowns, avoidance, and so on
Formal	3 Formal positive: awards, testimonials, and so on	4 Formal negative: legal sanctions, and so on

Types of Social Sanctions

another's behavior. Smiles, pats on the back, handshakes, congratulations, and hugs are informal positive sanctions.

2. **Informal negative sanctions** *are spontaneous displays of disapproval or displeasure,* such as frowns, damaging gossip, or impolite treatment directed toward the violator of a group norm.

3. **Formal positive sanctions** *are public affairs, rituals, or ceremonies that express social approval of a person's behavior.* These occasions are planned and organized. In our society they include such events as tickertape parades like the one that took place after the Persian Gulf War, the presentation of awards or degrees, and public declarations of respect or appreciation (sports banquets, for example). Awards of money are a form of formal positive sanctions.

4. **Formal negative sanctions** *are actions that express institutionalized disapproval of a person's behavior.* They usually are applied within the context of a society's formal organizations—schools, corporations, the legal system, for example—and include expulsion, dismissal, fines, and imprisonment. They flow directly from decisions made by a person or agency of authority, and frequently there are specialized agencies or personnel (such as a board of directors, a government agency, or a police force) to enforce them.

THEORIES OF CRIME AND DEVIANCE

Criminal and deviant behavior has been found throughout history. It has been so troublesome and so persistent that much effort has been devoted to understanding its roots. Many dubious ideas and theories have been developed over the ages. For example, a medieval law specified that "if two persons fell under suspicion of crime, the uglier or more deformed was to be regarded as more probably guilty" (Wilson and Herrnstein, 1985). Modern day approaches to deviant and criminal behavior can be divided into the general categories of biological, psychological, and sociological explanations.

Biological Theories of Deviance

The first attempts to provide "scientific" explanations for deviant and criminal behavior centered around the importance of inherited factors and downplayed the importance of environmental influences. From this point of view, deviant individuals are born, not made.

Cesare Lombroso (1835–1901) was an Italian doctor who believed that too much emphasis was being put on "free will" as an explanation for

Normally it would be considered deviant to paint your body and appear in public. During certain festivals, however, it is quite acceptable.

deviant behavior. While trying to discover the anatomical differences between deviant and insane men, he came upon what he believed was an important insight. As he was examining the skull of a criminal he noticed a series of features, recalling an apeish past rather than a human present:

> . . . At the sight of that skull, I seemed to see all of a sudden, lighted up as a vast plain under a flaming sky, the problem of the nature of the criminal—an atavistic being who reproduces in his person the ferocious instincts of primitive humanity and the inferior animals (Taylor et al., 1973, p. 4).

According to Lombroso, criminals were evolutionary throwbacks whose behavior is more apelike than human. They are driven by their instincts to engage in deviant behavior. These people can be identified by certain physical signs that betray their savage nature. Lombroso spent much of his life studying and dissecting dead prisoners in Italy's jails and concluded that their criminality was associated with an animal-like body type that revealed an inherited primitiveness (Lombroso-Ferrero, 1972). He also believed that certain criminal types could be identified by their head size, facial characteristics (size and shape of the nose, for instance), and even hair color. His writings were met with heated criticism from scholars who pointed out that perfectly normal-looking people have committed violent acts. (Modern social scientists would add that by confining his research to the study of prison inmates, Lombroso used a biased sample, thereby limiting the validity of his investigations.)

In this century William H. Sheldon and his coworkers carried out body measurements of thousands of subjects to determine whether personality traits are associated with particular body types. They found that human shapes could be classified as three particular types (see Figure 6.2): *endomorphic* (round and soft), *ectomorphic* (thin and linear), and *mesomorphic* (ruggedly muscular) (Sheldon and Tucker, 1940). They also claimed that certain psychological orientations are associated with body type. They saw endomorphs as being relaxed creatures of comfort; ectomorphs as being inhibited, secretive, and restrained; and mesomorphs as being assertive, action oriented, and uncaring of others feelings (Sheldon and Stevens, 1942).

Sheldon did not take a firm position on whether temperamental dispositions are inherited or are the outcome of society's responses to individuals based on their body types. For example, Americans expect heavy people to be good-natured and cheerful,

FIGURE 6.2

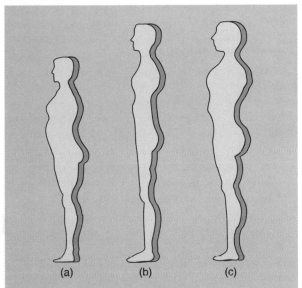

(a)   (b)   (c)

Sheldon's Body Types William Sheldon identified three basic body types (a) Endomorph: soft, round, and fat. (b) Ectomorph: skinny, fragile, and with a sensitive nervous system. (c) Mesomorph: muscular, agile, and physically strong. Sheldon believed mesomorphs were more inclined toward criminal behavior than the other two types, but subsequent research has cast considerable doubt on this conclusion.

skinny people to be timid, and strongly muscled people to be physically active and inclined toward aggressiveness. Anticipating such behaviors, people often encourage them. In a study of delinquent boys, Sheldon and his colleagues (1949) found that mesomorphs were more likely to become delinquents than were boys with other body types. Their explanation of this finding emphasized inherited factors, although they acknowledged social variables. The mesomorph is quick to anger and lacks the ectomorph's restraint, they claimed. Therefore, in situations of stress, the mesomorph is more likely to get into trouble, especially if the individual is both poor and not very smart. Sheldon's bias toward a mainly biological explanation of delinquency was strong enough for him to have proposed a eugenic program of selective breeding to weed out those types predisposed toward criminal behavior.

In the mid 1960s, further biological explanations of deviance appeared linking a chromosomal anomaly in males, know as XYY, with violent and criminal behavior. Typically males receive a single X chromosome from their mothers and a Y chromosome from their fathers. Occasionally, a child will receive two Y chromosomes from his father. These individuals will look like normal males; however, based on limited observations, a theory developed that these individuals were prone to commit violent crimes. The simplistic logic behind this theory is that since males are more aggressive than females and possess a Y chromosome that females lack, this Y chromosome must be the cause of aggression: A double dose means double trouble. One group of researchers (Jarvik, 1972) noted: "It should come as no surprise that an extra Y chromosome can produce an individual with heightened masculinity, evinced by characteristics such as unusual tallness . . . and powerful aggressive tendencies."

Today the XYY chromosome theory has been discounted. It has been estimated (Chorover, 1979) that 96 percent of XYY males lead ordinary lives with no criminal involvement. A maximum of 1 percent of all XYY males in the United States may spend any time in a prison (Pyeritz et. al., 1977). No valid theory of deviant and criminal behavior can be devised around such unconvincing data.

The biological basis for deviant behavior is still being investigated today. These investigations have yielded conflicting data and conclusions so that the existence of biologically, or at least genetically, determined deviant behavior is still far from proven.

Psychological Theories of Deviance

Psychological explanations of deviance downplay biological factors and emphasize instead the role of parents and early childhood experiences, or behavioral conditioning, in producing deviant behavior. Although such explanations stress environmental influences, there is a significant distinction between psychological and sociological explanations of deviance. Psychological orientations assume that the seeds of deviance are planted in childhood and that adult behavior is a manifestation of early experiences rather than an expression of ongoing social or cultural factors. The deviant individual therefore is viewed as a "psychologically sick" person who has experienced emotional deprivation or damage during childhood.

PSYCHOANALYTIC THEORY Psychoanalytic explanations of deviance are based on the work of Sigmund Freud and his followers. Psychoanalytic theorists believe that the *unconscious,* the part of us consisting of irrational thoughts and feelings of which we are not aware, causes us to commit deviant acts.

As we saw in Chapter 4, according to Freud, our personality has three parts: the id, our irrational drives and instincts; the superego, our conscience and guide as internalized from our parents and other

authority figures; and the ego, the balance among the impulsiveness of the id, the restrictions and demands of the superego, and the requirements of society. Because of the id, all of us have deviant tendencies, but through the socialization process we learn to control our behavior, driving many of these tendencies into the unconscious. In this way most of us are able to function effectively according to our society's norms and values. For some, however, the socialization process is not what it should be. As a result, the individual's behavior is not adequately controlled by either the ego or superego, and the wishes of the id take over. Consider, for example, a situation in which a man has been driving around congested city streets looking for a parking space. Finally he spots a car that is leaving and pulls up to wait for the space. Just as he is ready to park his car, another car whips in and takes the space. Most of us would react to the situation with anger. We might even roll down the car window and direct some angry gestures and strong language at the offending driver. There have been cases, however, in which the angry driver has pulled out a gun and shot the offender. Instead of simply saying, "I'm so mad I could kill that guy," the offended party acted out the threat. Psychoanalytic theorists might hypothesize that in this case, the id's aggressive drive took over, because of an inadequately developed conscience.

Psychoanalytic approaches to deviance have been strongly criticized because the concepts are very abstract and cannot easily be tested. For one thing, the unconscious can be neither seen directly nor measured. Also there is an overemphasis on innate drives at the same time that there is an underemphasis on social and cultural factors that bring about deviant behavior.

BEHAVIORAL THEORIES According to the behavioral view, people adjust and modify their behavior in response to the rewards and punishments their actions elicit. If we do something that leads to a favorable outcome, we are likely to repeat that action. If our behavior leads to unfavorable consequences, we are not eager to do the same thing again (Bandura, 1969). Those of us who live in a fairly traditional environment are likely to be rewarded for engaging in conformist behavior, such as working hard, dressing in a certain manner, or treating our friends in a certain way. We would receive negative sanctions if our friends found out that we had robbed a liquor store. For some people, however, the situation is reversed. That is, deviant behavior may elicit positive rewards. A 13-year-old who associates with a delinquent gang and is rewarded with praise for shoplifting, stealing, or vandalizing a school is being indoctrinated into a deviant lifestyle. The group may look with contempt at the "straight" kids who study hard, make career plans, and do not go out during the week. According to this approach, deviant behavior is learned by a series of trials and errors. One learns to be a thief in the same way that one learns to be a sociologist.

CRIME AS INDIVIDUAL CHOICE James Q. Wilson and Richard Herrnstein (1985) have devised a theory of criminal behavior that is based on an analysis of individual behavior. Sociologists, almost by definition, are suspicious of explanations that emphasize individual behavior, because they believe such theories neglect the setting in which crime occurs and the broad social forces that determine levels of crime. However, Wilson and Herrnstein argue that whatever factors contribute to crime— the state of the economy, the competence of the police, the nurturance of the family, the availability of drugs, the quality of the schools—they must affect the behavior of *individuals* before they affect crime. They believe that if crime rates rise or fall, it must be due to changes that have occurred in areas that affect individual behavior.

Wilson and Herrnstein believe that individual behavior is the result of rational choice. A person will choose to do one thing as opposed to another because it appears that the consequences of doing it are more desirable than the consequences of doing something else. At any given moment, a person can choose between committing a crime and not committing it. The consequences of committing the crime consist of rewards and punishments. The consequences of not committing the crime also entail gains and losses. Crime becomes likely if the rewards for committing the crime are significantly greater than those for not committing the crime. The net rewards of crime include not only the likely material gain from the crime but also intangible benefits such as obtaining emotional gratification, receiving the approval of peers, or settling an old score against an enemy. Some of the disadvantages of crime include the pangs of conscience, the disapproval of onlookers, and the retaliation of the victim.

The benefits of not committing a crime include avoiding the risk of being caught and punished, and not suffering a loss of reputation or the sense of shame afflicting a person later discovered to have broken the law. All of the benefits of not committing a crime lie in the future, whereas many of the benefits of committing a crime are immediate. The consequences of committing a crime gradually lose their ability to control behavior in proportion to

how delayed or improbable they are. For example, millions of cigarette smokers ignore the possibility of fatal consequences of smoking because they are distant and uncertain. If smoking one cigarette caused certain death tomorrow, we would expect cigarette smoking to drop dramatically.

Sociological Theories of Deviance

Sociologists have been interested in the issue of deviant behavior since the pioneering efforts of Emile Durkheim in the late nineteenth century. Indeed, one of the major sociological approaches to understanding this problem derives directly from his work. It is called anomie theory.

ANOMIE THEORY Durkheim published *The Division of Labor in Society* in 1893. In it he argues that deviant behavior can be understood only in relation to the specific moral code it violates: "We must not say that an action shocks the common conscience because it is criminal, but rather that it is criminal because it shocks the common conscience" (1960a).

Durkheim recognized that the common conscience, or moral code, has an extremely strong hold on the individual in small, isolated societies where there are few social distinctions among people and everybody more or less performs the same tasks. Such *mechanically integrated* societies, he believed, are organized in terms of shared norms and values: All members are equally committed to the moral code. Therefore, deviant behavior that violates the code is felt by all members of the society to be a personal threat. As society becomes more complex— that is, as work is divided into more numerous and increasingly specialized tasks—social organization is maintained by the interdependence of individuals. In other words, as the division of labor becomes more specialized and differentiated, society becomes more *organically integrated*. It is held together less by moral consensus than by economic interdependence. A shared moral code continues to exist, of course, but it tends to be broader and less powerful in determining individual behavior. For example, political leaders among the Cheyenne Indians led their people by persuasion and by setting a moral example (Hoebel, 1960). In contrast with the Cheyenne, few modern Americans actually expect exemplary moral behavior from their leaders, despite the public rhetoric calling for it. We express surprise, but not outrage when less than honorable behavior is revealed about our political leaders. We recognize that political leadership is exercised through formal institutionalized channels, and not through model behavior.

In highly complex, rapidly changing societies such as our own, some individuals come to feel that the moral consensus has weakened. Some persons lose their sense of belongingness, the feeling of participating in a meaningful social whole. Such individuals feel disoriented, frightened, and alone. Durkheim used the term **anomie** to refer to *the condition of normlessness, where values and norms have little impact and the culture no longer provides adequate guidelines for behavior.* Durkheim found that anomie was a major cause of suicide, as we discussed in Chapter 1. Robert Merton built on this concept and developed a general theory of deviance in American society.

STRAIN THEORY   Robert Merton (1938, 1968) believes that American society pushes individuals toward deviance by overemphasizing the importance of monetary success while failing to emphasize the importance of using legitimate means to achieve that success. Those individuals who occupy favorable positions in the social-class structure have many legitimate means at their disposal to achieve success. However, those who occupy unfavorable positions lack such means. Thus the goal of financial success combined with the unequal access to important environmental resources creates deviance.

As you can see in Figure 6.3, Merton identified four types of deviance that emerge from this strain. Each type represents a mode of adaptation on the part of the deviant individual. That is, the form of deviance a person engages in depends greatly on the position he or she occupies in the social structure. Specifically, it depends on the availability to the individual of legitimate, institutionalized means for achieving success. Thus some individuals called **innovators** *accept the culturally validated goal of success but find deviant ways of going about reaching it.* Con artists, embezzlers, bank robbers, fraudulent advertisers, drug dealers, corporate criminals, crooked politicians, cops on the take—each is trying to "get ahead" using whatever means are available.

Ritualists *are individuals who reject or deemphasize the importance of success once they realize they will never achieve it and instead concentrate on following and enforcing rules more precisely than was ever intended.* Because they have a stable job with a predictable income, they remain within the labor force but refuse to take risks that might jeopardize their occupational security. Many ritualists are often tucked away in large institutions such as governmental bureaucracies. Here they cross each *t* and dot each *i*, following and enforcing rules more precisely (and mindlessly) than ever was intended. Their deviance is in giving up the belief in being able to move beyond their present level of attainment.

Another group of people also lacks the means to attain success but does not have the institutional security of the ritualists. **Retreatists** *are people who pull back from society altogether and cease to pursue culturally legitimate goals.* They are the drug and alcohol addicts who can no longer function—the hobos, panhandlers, and so-called street people who live on the fringes of society.

FIGURE 6.3

Mode of adaption		Culture's goals	Institutionalized means
Conformists		Accept	Accept
Deviants	Innovators	Accept	Reject
	Ritualists	Reject	Accept
	Retreatists	Reject	Reject
	Rebels	Reject/Accept	Reject/Accept

Merton's Typology of Individual Modes of Adaptation: Conforming and Deviant   Conformists accept both (a) the goals of the culture and (b) the institutionalized means of achieving them. Deviants reject either or both. Rebels are deviants who may reject the goals or the institutions of the current social order and seek to replace them with new ones that they would then embrace.

Finally, there are the rebels. **Rebels** *reject both the goals of what to them is an unfair social order and the institutionalized means of achieving them.* Rebels seek to tear down the old social order and build a new one with goals and institutions they can support and accept.

Merton's theory has become quite influential among sociologists. It is useful because it emphasizes external causes of deviant behavior that are within the power of society to correct. The theory's weakness is its inability to account for the presence of certain kinds of deviance that occur among all social strata and within almost all social groups in American society: for example, juvenile alcoholism, drug dependence, and family violence (spouse beating and child abuse).

CONTROL THEORY In control theory social ties among people are important in determining their behavior. Instead of asking what causes deviance, control theorists ask: What causes conformity? They believe that what causes deviance is the absence of what causes conformity. In their view conformity is a direct result of control over the individual. Therefore, the absence of social control causes deviance. According to this theory, people are free to violate norms if they lack intimate attachments with parents, teachers, and peers. These attachments help them establish values linked to a conventional lifestyle. Without these attachments and acceptance of conventional norms, the opinions of other people do not matter and the individual is free to violate norms without fear of social disapproval This theory assumes that the disapproval of others plays a major role in preventing deviant acts and crimes.

According to Travis Hirschi (1969), one of the main proponents of control theory, we all have the potential to commit deviant acts. Most of us never commit these acts because of our strong bond to society. Hirschi believes there are four ways in which individuals become bonded to society and conventional behavior:

1. *Attachment to Others.* People form intimate attachments to parents, teachers, and peers who display conventional attitudes and behavior.
2. *A Commitment to Conformity.* Individuals invest their time and energies in conventional types of activities, such as getting an education, holding a job, or developing occupational skills. At the same time, people show a commitment to achievement through these activities.
3. *Involvement in Conventional Activities.* People spend so much time engaged in conventional activities that they have no time to commit or even think about deviant activities.

4. *A Belief in the Moral Validity of Social Rules.* Individuals have a strong moral belief that they should obey the rules of conventional society.

If these four elements are strongly developed, the individual is likely to display conventional behavior. If these elements are weak, deviant behavior is likely.

TECHNIQUES OF NEUTRALIZATION Most of us think we act logically and rationally most of the time. In order to violate the norms and moral values of society, we must have **techniques of neutralization,** *a process that makes it possible for us to justify illegal or deviant behavior* (Sykes and Matza, 1957). In the language of control theory, these techniques provide a mechanism by which people can break the ties to the conventional society that would inhibit them from violating the rules. Techniques of neutralization are learned through the socialization process. They can take several forms:

1. *Denial of Responsibility.* The person argues that he or she is not responsible for their actions; forces beyond their control drove them to commit the act, such as a troubled family life, poverty, poor schools, or being drunk at the time of the incident. In any event, the responsibility for what they did lies elsewhere. For example, criminologist Kathleen Heide notes that 40 percent of the delinquents she studied did not see themselves as responsible for their crime. Many even blamed the victim (*U.S. News and World Report,* August 24, 1987).
2. *Denying the Injury.* The individual argues that the action did not really cause any harm. Who really got hurt when they illegally copied some computer software and sold it to their friends? Who is really hurt in illegal betting on a football game?
3. *Denial of the Victim.* The victim is seen as someone who "deserves what he or she got." The man who made an obscene gesture to us on the highway deserved to be assaulted when we caught up with him at the next traffic light. It is all right to cheat the large utility company, since it tries to cheat the public. The angry white mob that chased Michael Griffith, a black man, to his death in Howard Beach, New York, claimed he should not have been in the neighborhood in the first place.
4. *Condemnation of the Authorities.* Deviant or criminal behavior is justified since those who are in positions of power or are responsible for enforcing the rules are dishonest and corrupt

themselves. Political corruption and police dishonesty leave us with little respect for these authority figures, since they are more dishonest than we are.

5. *Appealing to Higher Principles or Authorities.* We claim our behavior is justified since we are adhering to standards that are more important than abstract laws. Acts of civil disobedience against the government are justified because of the government's misguided policy of supporting nuclear power plants. Our behavior may be technically illegal, but the way everyone does things in this business requires that we do it also.

Using these techniques of neutralization people are able to break the rules without feeling morally unworthy. They may even be able to put themselves on a higher plain specifically because of their willingness to rebel against rules. They are basically redefining the situation in favor of their actions.

CULTURAL TRANSMISSION THEORY This theory relies strongly on the concept of learning, growing out of the work of Clifford Shaw and Henry McKay, who received their training at the University of Chicago. They became interested in the patterning of delinquent behavior in that city when they observed that Chicago's high-crime areas remained the same over the decades—even though the ethnic groups living in those areas changed. Further, they found that as members of an ethnic group moved out of the high-crime areas, the rate of juvenile delinquency in that group fell; at the same time the delinquency rate for the newly-arriving ethnic group rose. Shaw and McKay (1931, 1942) discovered that delinquent behavior was taught to newcomers in the context of junvenile peer groups. And because such behavior occurred, on the whole, only in the context of peer-group activities, youngsters gave up their deviant ways when their families left the high-crime areas.

Edwin H. Sutherland and his student Donald R. Cressey (1978) built a more general theory of juvenile delinquency on the foundation laid by Shaw and McKay. This **theory of differential association** *is based on the central notion that criminal behavior is learned in the context of intimate groups* (see Table 6.1). When criminal behavior is learned, it includes two components: (1) criminal techniques (such as how to break into houses) and (2) criminal attitudes (rationalizations that justify criminal behavior). In this context, people who become criminals are thought to do so when they associate with the rationalizations for breaking the law more than with the arguments for obeying the law. They

TABLE 6.1

Sutherland's Principles of Differential Association

1. Deviant behavior is learned.
2. Deviant behavior is learned in interaction with other persons in a process of communication.
3. The principal part of the learning of criminal behavior occurs within intimate personal groups.
4. When deviant behavior is learned, the learning includes (a) techniques of committing the act, which are sometimes very complicated or sometimes very simple, and (b) the specific direction of motives, drives, rationalizations, and attitudes.
5. The specific direction of motives and drives is learned from definitions of the legal codes as favorable or unfavorable. That is, a person learns reasons for both obeying and violating rules.
6. A person becomes deviant because of an excess of definitions favorable to violating the law over definitions unfavorable to violating the law.
7. Differential associations may vary in frequency, duration, priority, and intensity.
8. The process of learning criminal behavior by association with criminal and anticriminal patterns involves all the mechanisms used in any other learning.
9. Although criminal behavior is an expression of general needs and values, it is not explained by those general needs and values, because noncriminal behavior is an expression of the same needs and values.

Source: Adapted from Edwin H. Sutherland and Donald R. Cressey, *Criminology.* 10th ed. Philadelphia: Lippincott, 1978, pp. 80–82.

acquire these attitudes through long-standing interactions with others who hold these views. Thus, among the estimated 70,000 gang members in Los Angeles County, status is often based on criminal activity and drug use. Even arrests and imprisonment are events worthy of respect. A youngster exposed to and immersed in such a value system will associate with it, if only in order to survive. In many respects, differential association theory is quite similar to the behavioral theory we discussed earlier. Both emphasize the learning or socialization aspect of deviance. Both also point out that deviant behavior emerges in the same way that conformist behavior emerges; it is merely the result of different experiences and different associations.

LABELING THEORY Under the **labeling theory** *there is a shift of focus from the deviant individual to the social process by which a person comes to be labeled as deviant and the consequences of such labeling for the individual.* This view emerged in the 1950s from the writings of Edwin Lemert (1972). Since then many other sociologists have elaborated on the labeling approach.

Labeling theorists note that although we all break rules from time to time, we do not necessarily think of ourselves as deviant—nor are we so labeled by others. However, some individuals, through a series of circumstances, do come to be defined as deviant by others in society. Paradoxically, this labeling process actually helps bring about more deviant behavior.

Being caught and branded as deviant has important consequences for one's further social participation and self-image. The most important consequence is a drastic change in the individual's public identity. Committing an improper act and being publicly caught at it places the individual in a new status, and he or she may be revealed as a different kind of person than formerly thought to be. Such people may be labeled as thieves, drug addicts, lunatics, or embezzlers, and treated accordingly.

To be labeled as a criminal, one need commit only a single criminal offense. Yet the word carries a number of connotations of other traits characteristic of anyone bearing the label. A man convicted of breaking into a house and thereby labeled criminal is presumed to be a person likely to break into other houses. Police operate on this premise and round up known offenders for investigation after a crime has been committed. In addition, it is assumed that such an individual is likely to commit other kinds of crimes as well, because he or she has been shown to be a person without "respect for the law." Therefore, apprehension for one deviant act increases the likelihood that this person will be regarded as deviant or undesirable in other respects.

Even if no one else discovers the deviance or enforces the rules against it, the individual who has committed it acts as an enforcer. Such individuals may brand themselves as deviant because of what they did and punish themselves in one way or another for the behavior (Becker, 1963).

There appear to be at least three factors that determine whether a person's behavior will set in motion the process by which he or she will be labeled as deviant: (1) the importance of the norms that are violated, (2) the social identity of the individual who violates them, and (3) the social context of the behavior in question. Let us examine these factors more closely.

1. *The importance of the violated norms.* As we noted in Chapter 3, not all norms are equally important to the people who hold them. The most strongly held norms are mores, and their violation is likely to cause, in short order, the culprit to be labeled deviant. The physical assault of elderly persons is an example. For less strongly held norms, however, much more nonconformity is tolerated, even if the behavior is illegal. For example, running red lights is both illegal and potentially very dangerous, but in some American cities it has become so commonplace that even the police are likely to "look the other way" rather than pursue violators.

2. *The social identity of the individual.* In all societies there are those whose wealth or power (or even force of personality) enable them to ward off being labeled deviant despite behavior that violates local values and norms. Such individuals are buffered against public judgment and even legal sanction. A rich or famous person caught shoplifting or even using narcotics has a fair chance of being treated indulgently as an "eccentric" and let off with a lecture by the local chief of police. Conversely, there are those marginal or powerless individuals and groups, such as welfare recipients or the chronically unemployed, toward whom society has a "hair-trigger" response, with little tolerance for nonconformity. Such people quickly are labeled deviant when an opportunity presents itself and are much more likely to face criminal charges.

3. *The social context.* The social context within which an action takes place is important. In a certain situation an action might be considered deviant, whereas in another context it will not. Notice that we say social context, not physical location. The nature of the social context can change even when the physical location remains the same. For example, for most of the year the New Orleans police manage to control open displays of sexual behavior, even in the famous French Quarter. However, during the week of Mardi Gras, throngs of people freely engage in what at other times of the year would be called lewd and indecent behavior. During Mardi Gras the social context invokes norms for evaluating behavior that do not so quickly lead to the assignment of a deviant label.

Labeling theory has led sociologists to distinguish between primary and secondary deviance. **Primary deviance** *is the original behavior that leads to the application of the label to an individual.* **Secondary deviance** *is the behavior that people develop as a result of having been labeled as deviant* (Lemert, 1972). For example, a teenager who has experimented with illegal drugs for the first time and is arrested for it may be labeled as a drug addict and face ostracism by peers, family, and school authorities. Such negative treatment may cause this person to turn more frequently to using illegal drugs and to associating with other drug users and pushers, resorting to robberies and muggings to get enough money to buy the drugs. Thus the primary deviant behavior and the labeling resulting from it lead the teenager to slip into an even more deviant lifestyle. This new lifestyle would be an example of secondary deviance.

Labeling theory has proved quite useful. It explains why society will label certain individuals deviant but not others, even when their behavior is similar. There are, however, several drawbacks to labeling theory. For one thing, it does not explain primary deviance. That is, even though we may understand how labeling may produce future, or secondary, acts of deviance, we do not know why the original, or primary, act of deviance took place. In this respect, labeling theory explains only part of the deviance process. Another problem is that labeling theory ignores the instances when the labeling process may deter a person from engaging in future acts of deviance. It looks at the deviant as a misunderstood individual who really would like to be an accepted, law-abiding citizen. Clearly, this is an overly optimistic view.

It would be unrealistic to expect any single approach to explain deviant behavior fully. In all likelihood some combination of the various theories discussed is necessary to gain a fuller understanding of the emergence and continuation of deviant behavior.

THE IMPORTANCE OF LAW

As discussed earlier in this chapter some interests are so important to a society that folkways and mores are not adequate enough to ensure orderly social interaction. Therefore laws are passed to give the state the power of enforcement. These laws become a formal system of social control which is exercised when other informal forms of control are not effective.

It is important not to confuse a society's moral code with its legal code, nor to confuse deviance with crime. Some legal theorists have argued that the legal code is an expression of the moral code, but this is not necessarily the case. For example, although 41 states and at least 300 municipalities have enacted some sort of antismoking law, smoking is not an offense against morals. Conversely, it is possible to violate American "moral" sensibilities without breaking the law.

What, then, is the legal code? *The **legal code** consists of the formal rules, called **laws**, adopted by a society's political authority.* The code is enforced through the use of formal negative sanctions when rules are broken. Ideally, laws are passed to promote conformity to those rules of conduct that the authorities believe are necessary for the society to function and that will not be followed if left solely to people's internal controls or the use of informal sanctions. Others argue that laws are passed to benefit or protect specific interest groups with political power, rather than society at large (Quinney, 1974).

One of the questions sociologists ask is "When do we reach the point where norms are no longer voluntary and need to be codified and given the power of authority for enforcement?"

The Emergence of Laws

How is it that laws come into society? How do we reach the point where norms are no longer voluntary and need to be codified and given the power of authority for enforcement? Two major explanatory approaches have been proposed, the consensus approach and the conflict approach.

The **consensus approach** *assumes that laws are merely a formal version of the norms and values of the people.* There is a general consensus among the people on these norms and values and the laws reflect this consensus. For example, people will generally agree that it is wrong to steal from another person. Therefore, laws emerge formally stating this fact and provide penalties for those caught violating the law.

The consensus approach is basically a functionalist model for explaining a society's legal system. It assumes that social cohesion will produce an orderly adjustment in the laws. As the norms and values in society change, so will the laws. Therefore "blue laws," which were enacted in many states 100 to 200 years ago, and which prohibited people from working or opening shops on Sunday, have been changed, and now vast shopping malls do an enormous amount of business on Sunday.

The conflict approach to explaining the emergence of laws sees dissension and conflict between various groups as a basic aspect of society. The conflict is resolved when the groups in power achieve control. *The* **conflict approach** *to law assumes that the elite use their power to enact and enforce laws that support their own economic interests and go against the interests of the lower classes.* As Chambliss (1973) notes:

> Conventional myths notwithstanding, the history of criminal law is *not* a history of public opinion or public interest. . . . On the contrary, the history of the criminal law is everywhere the history of legislation and appellate-court decisions which in effect (if not in intent) reflect the interests of the economic elites who control the production and distribution of the major resources of the society.

The conflict approach to law is supported by Richard Quinney (1974) when he notes "Law serves the powerful over the weak . . . moreover, law is used by the state . . . to promote and protect itself."

Chambliss used the development of vagrancy laws as an example of how the conflict approach to law works. He believes the emergence of such laws parallel the need of landowners for cheap labor in England during a time when the system of serfdom was breaking down. Later, when cheap labor was no longer needed, vagrancy laws were not enforced. Then, in the sixteenth century, the laws were modified to focus on those who were suspected of being involved in criminal activities and interfering with those engaged in the transportation of goods. Chambliss (1973) notes, "Shifts and changes in the law of vagrancy show a clear pattern of reflecting the interests and needs of the groups who control the economic institutions of the society. The laws change as these institutions change."

There are two types of law, criminal law and civil law. Criminal law deals with violations against the interests of society, while civil law deals with violations against the individual. The distinction is not as clear as it sounds. Many actions which are punishable under criminal law because they are a threat to society are also directed against individuals. For example, rape is an action against a specific individual, but is also a threat to general safety. In the next section we will examine crimes, those actions which are punishable under criminal law.

CRIME IN THE UNITED STATES

Crime *is behavior that violates a society's criminal laws.* In the United States what is criminal is specified in written law, primarily state statutes. Federal, state, and local jurisdictions often vary in their definitions of crimes, though they seldom disagree in their definitions of serious crimes.

A distinction is often made between violent crimes and property crimes. *A* **violent crime** *is an unlawful event such as homicide, rape, and assault that may result in injury to a person.* Robbery is also a violent crime because it involves the use or threat of force against the person.

A **property crime** *is an unlawful act that is committed with the intent of gaining property but that does not involve the use or threat of force against an individual.* Larceny, burglary, and motor vehicle theft are examples of property crimes.

Criminal offenses are also classified according to how they are handled by the criminal justice system. In this respect most jurisdictions recognize two classes of offenses: felonies and misdemeanors. Felonies are not distinguished from misdemeanors in the same way in all areas, but *most states define* **felonies** *as offenses punishable by a year or more in state prison.* Although the same act may be classified as a felony in one jurisdiction and as a misdemeanor in another, the most serious crimes are never misdemeanors, and the most minor offenses are never felonies.

Crime Statistics

It is very difficult to know with any certainty how many crimes are committed in America each year. There are two major approaches taken in determining the extent of crime. One measure of crime is provided by the FBI through its *Uniform Crime Reporting* program (UCR). Since 1930 the FBI has been receiving monthly and annual reports from law enforcement agencies throughout the country, currently representing 98 percent of the national population. There are eight crimes that make up the *Uniform Crime Reports.* They are *murder and nonnegligent manslaughter, forcible rape, robbery, aggravated assault, burglary, larceny-theft, motor vehicle theft,* and *arson.* Not included are federal offenses—political corruption, tax evasion, bribery, or violation of environmental-protection laws, among others.

Sociologists and critics in other fields note that for a variety of reasons, these statistics are not always reliable. For example, each police department compiles its own figures, and so definitions of the same crime vary from place to place. Other factors affect the accuracy of the crime figures and rates published in the *Reports*—for example, a law-enforcement agency or a local government may change its method of reporting crimes, so that the new statistics reflect a false increase or decrease in the occurrence of certain crimes. These changes may even be deliberate: The government or agency may want to stress its achievements or gain some other benefit (Reid, 1979).

A second measure of crime is provided through the *National Crime Victimization Survey,* which began in 1973 to collect victimization data from households across the country. Unlike the *UCR, NCVS* measures both reported and unreported crimes.

Six crimes are measured in the *National Crime Victimization Survey*: *rape, robbery, assault, household burglary, personal larceny,* and *motor vehicle theft.* The similarity between these crimes and the *Uniform Crime Reports* is obvious and intentional. Two crimes are missing from the *National Crime Victimization Survey* that appear in the *Uniform Crime Reports. Murder* cannot be measured through victim surveys because obviously the victim is dead. *Arson* cannot be measured well through such surveys because the victim may in fact have been the criminal. A professional is often needed to determine whether a fire was actually arson.

Whereas the *Uniform Crime Reports* depends on police departments' records of reported crimes, the *National Crime Victimization Survey* attempts to assess the total number of crimes committed. The *NCVS* obtains its information by asking a national sample of 47,000 households, representing 95,000 people over the age of twelve, about their experiences as victims of crime during the previous six months.

Of the 34,404,000 crimes that took place in 1990, the *National Crime Victimization Survey* estimated that only 38 percent were reported to the police. The specific crimes most likely to be reported were motor vehicle theft (75 percent) and aggravated assault (59 percent). The crime least likely reported was household larceny (27 percent).

The particular reason most frequently mentioned for *not* reporting a crime was that it was not important enough. For violent crimes the reason most often given for not reporting was that it was

It is difficult to know with certainty how many crimes are committed each year.

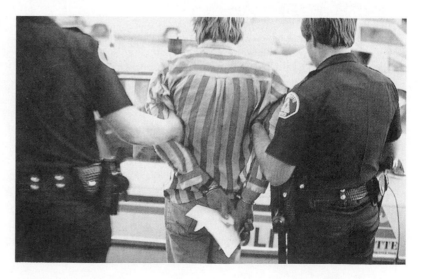

a private or personal matter. For an example of the reporting rates for a variety of crimes, see Figure 6.4.

Each survey is subject to the kinds of errors and problems typical to its method of data collection. Despite their respective drawbacks, they are both valuable sources of data on nationwide crime.

KINDS OF CRIME IN THE UNITED STATES

It should be obvious that the crime committed can vary considerably in terms of the impact it has on the victim and on the self-definition of the perpetrator of the crime. White-collar crime is as different from street crime as organized crime is from juvenile crime. In the next section we shall examine these differences.

Juvenile Crime

Juvenile crime *refers to the breaking of criminal laws by individuals under the age of eighteen.* Regardless of the specific statistics reliability, one thing is clear: Serious crime among our nation's youth is a matter of great concern. Hardcore youthful offenders—perhaps 10 percent of all juvenile criminals—are responsible, by some estimates, for two-thirds of all serious crimes. Although the vast majority of juvenile delinquents commit only minor violations, the juvenile justice system is overwhelmed by these hard-core criminals.

Serious juvenile offenders are predominantly male, are disproportionately minority group members—compared with their proportion in the population—and are typically disadvantaged economically. They are likely to exhibit interpersonal difficulties and behavioral problems both in school and on the job. They are also likely to come from one-parent families or families with a high degree of conflict, instability, and inadequate supervision.

Arrest records for 1989 show that youths under age 18 accounted for 15.5 percent of all arrests (*Statistical Abstract of the United States: 1991*). Arrests, however, are only a general indicator of criminal activity. The greater number of arrests among young people may be due partly to their lack of experience in committing crimes and partly to their involvement in the types of crimes for which apprehension is more likely; for example, theft versus fraud. In addition, because youths often commit crimes in groups, the resolution of a single crime may lead to several arrests (see Table 6.2 for arrest rates by age).

Indeed, one of the major differences between juvenile and adult offenders is the importance of gang membership and the tendency of youths to engage in group criminal activities. Gang members are more likely than are other young criminals to engage in violent crimes, particularly robbery, rape, assault, and weapons violations. Gangs that deal in the sale of crack cocaine have become especially violent in the last few years.

There is conflicting evidence on whether juve-

FIGURE 6.4

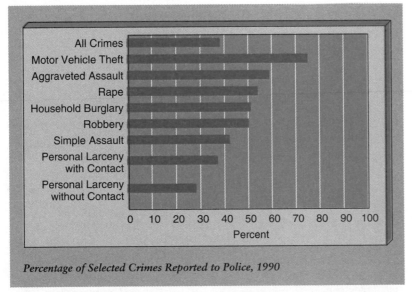

Percentage of Selected Crimes Reported to Police, 1990

Source: United States Department of Justice, Bureau of Justice Statistics Bulletin, "Criminal Victimization, 1990," Washington, DC: United States Government Printing Office, 1991, p. 5.

Arrest records show that youths under age 18 account for 15.5 percent of all arrests. Juvenile crime has turned some schools into fortresses patrolled by the police.

niles tend to progress from less to more serious crimes. The evidence suggests that violent adult offenders began their careers with violent juvenile crimes; thus they began as and remained serious offenders. However, minor offenses of youths are often dealt with informally and may not be recorded in crime statistics (U.S. Dept. of Justice, 1983).

The juvenile courts—traditionally meant to treat, not punish—have had limited success in coping with such juvenile offenders (Reid, 1979). Strict rules of confidentiality, aimed at protecting juvenile offenders from being labeled as criminals,

make it difficult for the police and judges to know the full extent of a youth's criminal record. The result is that violent youthful offenders who have committed numerous crimes often receive little or no punishment.

Defenders of the juvenile courts contend, nonetheless, that there would be even more juvenile crime without them. Others, arguing from learning and labeling perspectives, charge that the system has such a negative impact on children that it actually encourages **recidivism,** that is, *repeated criminal behavior after punishment* (Paulsen, 1967). All who are concerned with this issue agree that the juvenile courts are less than efficient, especially in the treatment of repeat offenders. One reason for this is that perhaps two-thirds of juvenile court time is devoted to processing children guilty of what are called **status offenses,** *behavior that is criminal only because the person involved is a minor* (examples are truancy and running away from home). Recognizing that status offenders clog the courts and add greatly to the terrible overcrowding of juvenile detention homes, states have sought ways to deinstitutionalize status offenders. One approach, known as **diversion**—*steering youthful offenders away from the juvenile justice system to nonofficial social agencies*—has been suggested by Edwin M. Lemert (1981).

Violent Crime

In 1989 there were 3,951 violent crimes per 100,000 population reported in Atlanta, 2,401 in Detroit, 2,246 in Los Angeles, and 2,300 in New York City. If we keep in mind that only about 48 percent of all violent crimes are reported to the police we can

TABLE 6.2

Age Distribution of Arrests, 1989

Age Group	Percentage of U.S. Population	Percentage of Persons Arrested
Age 12 and younger	19.1%	1.7%
13–15	4.0	6.3
16–18	4.3	12.4
19–21	4.5	13.6
22–24	4.6	11.9
25–29	8.7	18.4
30–34	8.9	14.1
35–39	7.9	9.0
40–44	6.8	5.3
45–49	5.4	3.0
50–54	4.6	1.7
55–59	4.3	1.1
60–64	4.4	0.7
Age 65 and older	12.5	0.7

Source: Kathleen Maguire and Timothy J. Flanagan, eds., *Sourcebook of Criminal Justice Statistics—1990.* United States Department of Justice, Bureau of Justice Statistics, Washington, DC: United States Government Printing Office, 1991, p. 414.

SOCIOLOGY AT WORK

Interview with Jack Levin: Serial Murderers and Mass Murderers

What used to be a rare occurrence in the United States is now becoming increasingly commonplace. There are now two or three mass murders every month in the United States. In fact, seven of the ten largest mass killings in American history have taken place in the last decade. Many people want to know what makes these individuals kill. Sociologist Jack Levin is one of the nation's best known authorities on this problem.

Levin points out that contrary to popular assumptions, mass murderers do not just "snap" or "go crazy." Their killing spree is methodical and extremely well planned, and the motive usually is to get even. Mass murderers seek revenge against those individuals they feel are responsible for their problems. Levin notes, "The mass killer may be depressed, disillusioned, despondent, or desperate, but not deranged."

There are two types of multiple homicides. First are the mass killings often in the news. Here the individual kills a number of people within a short period of time. It could take place at the killer's last place of employment, in a restaurant, or at home. Serial killings differ in that instead of a violent outburst, the murderer kills one victim at a time over a period of days, weeks, years, and even decades.

Mass killers tend to be white, middle-class, middle-aged males. Levin believes it takes a prolonged period of frustration to produce the kind of rage necessary for this type of brutal eruption. Mass killers have seen their lives go down hill for decades. Their relationships with others have fallen apart. Many cannot hold a job. They are trying to survive with their many problems but then a catastrophic event puts them over the edge.

On the surface serial murderers seem the same in that they are also likely to be white, middle-aged males. The difference is that serial murderers love to kill. Killing becomes a pleasurable end in itself. Most importantly, killing gives the serial killer a feeling of power. Levin notes that serial murderers have a great need for dominance and control which they satisfy by taking the last breath from their victims. Very few will use a gun because they want physical contact with the victim. They are sadistic.

Levin believes it is incorrect to characterize serial killers as insane. These people know what they are doing is wrong; they simply do not care. Levin notes, "They do not have a defect of the mind, they have a defect of character. They are not mad, they are bad. They are not crazy, they are very crafty. They are not sick, they are sickening." They do not feel guilty about their actions. "The secret to serial murderers' success lies in the fact that they do not look like the monsters they are. They are thoroughly familiar with the rules of society, but they do not feel the rules apply to them."

When it comes to the issue of whether there should be a death penalty for these killers, Levin points out that in many ways mass murderers are dead already. They want to die and often kill themselves right after their violent binge. For the serial killers, Levin believes we should "lock them up and throw away the key. These people cannot be rehabilitated."

Mass murders and serial murders are a growing, but still rare phenomenon. Levin points out that all told about 500 people die a year at the hand of a mass killer or serial killer. This is quite small compared to the 23,000 single victim homicides a year. Levin reminds us that, "You are still more likely to contract leprosy or malaria than you are to be murdered by a serial killer or mass killer." We cannot suspect everyone around us of being a killer. Our goal should be to understand the basis for mass killings and serial killings so we may one day be able to prevent them.

see how high the incidence of violent crime really is (*Statistical Abstract of the United States: 1991*).

Whereas the majority of violent crimes used to occur among people who knew one another—in families, among relatives and social acquaintances—violence committed against strangers has risen in the last few years. This has added greatly to a growing "terror of the night," because people feel that violence may strike them anonymously and unpredictably.

The United States violent crime rate also includes the highest homicide rate in the industrialized world. There are more murders in any one of the cities of New York, Detroit, Los Angeles, or Chicago each year than in all of England and Wales combined.

The U.S. homicide rate averages 10.8 per 100,000 people in the population. In some cities this rate is significantly higher. For example, Detroit has a homicide rate of 60.0 per 100,000 population; for Dallas it is 35.2, for Baltimore it is 34.3, and for Atlanta it is 57.7 (*Statistical Abstract of the United States, 1991*).

In contrast the average homicide rate in Australia is 1.9 homicides per 100,000 people, Israel 1.8, Japan 1.0, and England and Wales, 0.4 (Barlow, 1987).

In addition to homicide, rape, aggravated assault, and robbery are other violent crimes that have an impact on American households. In 1990, 130,000 households reported a rape, 1,601,000 reported an aggravated assault, and 1,150,000 reported a robbery (Bureau of Justice Statistics Bulletin, "Criminal Victimization 1990," October 1991). (See Figure 6.5 for the percentage of households experiencing a rape, aggravated assault, or robbery on a yearly basis.)

Property Crime

Of all crime in the United States, 90 percent is what is referred to as crime against property, as opposed to crime against a person. In all instances of crime against property the victim is not present and is not confronted by the criminal.

The most significant nonviolent crimes are burglary, auto theft, and larceny-theft. In 1990, 4,557,000 households reported a burglary, 1,825,000 reported an auto theft, and 7,199,000 reported a household theft (BJS Bulletin, 1991). Keep in mind that only about 27 percent of all household thefts are reported (*Statistical Abstract of the United States: 1991*).

White-Collar Crime

The term **white-collar crime** *was coined by Edwin H. Sutherland (1940) to refer to individuals who, while occupying positions of social responsibility or high prestige, break the law in the course of their work, for the purpose of illegal personal or organizational gain.* Another term often used to refer to what typically are nonviolent crimes by "respectable"

FIGURE 6.5

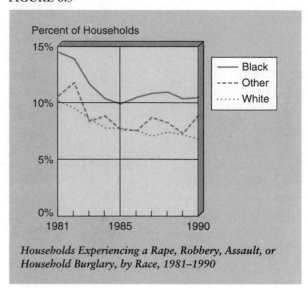

Households Experiencing a Rape, Robbery, Assault, or Household Burglary, by Race, 1981–1990

Source: United States Department of Justice, Bureau of Justice Statistics Bulletin, "Crime and the Nation's Households, 1990," August 1991.

individuals is *upper-world crime.* White-collar crimes include such illegalities as embezzlement, bribery, fraud, theft of services, kickback schemes, and others in which the violator's position of trust, power, or influence has provided the opportunity to use lawful institutions for unlawful purposes. White-collar offenses frequently involve deception.

Although white-collar offenses are often less visible than crimes such as burglary and robbery, the overall economic impact of crimes committed by such individuals as Charles Keating (convicted of banking crimes), or Michael Milken (convicted of investment fraud), are considerably greater. Among the white-collar cases filed by U.S. Attorneys in 1985, more than 140 persons were charged with offenses estimated to involve over $1 million each, and 64 were charged with offenses valued at over $10 million each. In comparison, losses from all bank robberies reported to the police in that year were under $19 million, and losses from all robberies reported to the police totaled $313 million (Bureau of Justice Statistics, Special Report, "White Collar Crime," September 1987).

Not only is white-collar crime very expensive, it is a threat to the fabric of society. Sutherland (1961) has argued that because white-collar crimes involve a violation of public trust, it contributes to a disintegration of social morale and threatens the social structure. This problem is compounded by the fact that in the few cases in which white-collar criminals actually are prosecuted and convicted,

A white-collar computer criminal can transfer vast sums of money into unauthorized accounts, stealing far more money than a daring bank robber ever could.

punishment usually is relatively light. For example, only about 40 percent of convicted white-collar criminals are given prison terms compared to 54 percent of nonwhite-collar offenders. In addition, those who do receive prison terms receive shorter average sentences (29 months) than other Federal offenders (50 months). (BJS, 1987)

New forms of white-collar crime involving political and corporate institutions have emerged in the past decade. For example, the dramatic growth in high technology has brought with it sensational accounts of computerized "heists" by sophisticated criminals seated safely behind computer terminals. The possibility of electronic crime has spurred widespread interest in computer security, by business and government alike.

Organized Crime

Organized crime *refers to structured associations of individuals or groups who come together for the purpose of obtaining gain mostly from illegal activities.* Organized crime groups possess some of the following characteristics:

They conduct their activities in a methodical, systematic, or highly disciplined and secret fashion.

In at least some of their activities they commit or threaten to commit acts of violence or other acts that are likely to intimidate.

They insulate their leadership from direct involvement in illegal activities by their intricate organizational structure.

The distribution and sale of drugs used to be a major organized crime activity. In the last decade, other groups have taken over this lucrative criminal activity.

They attempt to gain influence in government, politics, and commerce through corruption, graft, and legitimate means (United States Department of Justice, 1983).

Organized crime makes most of its money through providing illegal goods and services. Prohibition gave it the ability to organize nationwide, because for the first time there was a uniform national demand for illegal goods: alcoholic beverages. Today organized crime profits from illegal activities that include gambling, the smuggling and sale of illicit drugs, the production and distribution of pornography, prostitution, and loan sharking. In order to be able to account for and spend their wealth, the families of organized crime have bought controlling interests in innumerable "legitimate" businesses in which their funds can be "laundered" and additional, legitimate profits can be made. For example, profits from an illegal gambling operation can show up on the books of a legitimate, cash-oriented business such as a restaurant or vending-machine enterprise.

Organized crime was dominated by Irish Americans in the early part of the twentieth century, and by Jewish Americans in the 1920s. Beginning in the 1930s organized crime has been dominated by those of Italian ancestry. This has changed within the last decade and other ethnic groups are gaining a significant foothold. The power of these groups varies from city to city. In Miami, Cubans control illegal gambling and Canadians dominate loan-sharking and money laundering. In Detroit, organized crime members are Lebanese or black. In New York, Koreans run illegal massage parlors and Russian immigrants are involved in extortion and contract murder. Police call this trend the "internationalization of crime" in the United States (*U.S. News and World Report*, January 18, 1988).

Victimless Crime

Usually we think of crimes as involving culprits and victims—that is, individuals who suffer some loss or injury as a result of a criminal act. But there are a number of crimes that do not produce victims in any obvious way, and so some scholars have coined the term *victimless crime* to refer to them.

Basically, **victimless crimes** *are acts that violate those laws meant to enforce the moral code.* Usually they involve the use of narcotics, illegal gambling, public drunkenness, the sale of sexual services, or status offenses by minors. If heroin and crack addicts can support their illegal addiction legitimately, then who is the victim? If prostitutes provide sexual gratification for a fee, who is the victim? If a person bets $10 or $20 per week with the local bookmaker, who is the victim? If someone staggers drunk through the streets, who is the victim? If a teenager runs away from home because conditions there are intolerable, who is the victim?

Some legal scholars argue that the perpetrators themselves are victims: Their behavior damages their own lives. This is, of course, a value judgment, but the concept of deviance depends on the existence of values and norms (Schur and Bedau, 1974). Others note that such offenses against the public order do in fact contribute to the creation of victims, if only indirectly: Heroin addicts rarely can hold jobs and eventually are forced to steal to support themselves; prostitutes are used to blackmail people and to rob them; chronic gamblers impoverish themselves and bring ruin on their families; drunks drive and get into accidents and may be violent at home, and so on.

Clearly the problems raised by the existence of victimless crimes are complex. In recent years, American society has begun to recognize that at least some crimes truly are victimless and should therefore be decriminalized. Two major activities that have been decriminalized in many states and municipalities are the smoking of marijuana (though not its sale) and sex between unmarried, consenting adults of the same gender.

CRIMINAL JUSTICE IN THE UNITED STATES

Every society that has established a legal code has also set up a **criminal justice system**—*personnel and procedures for arrest, trial, and punishment to deal with violations of the law.* The three main categories of our criminal justice system are the police, the courts, and the prisons.

The Police

The police system developed in the United States is a highly decentralized one. It exists on three levels: federal, state, and local. On the federal level, the United States does not have a national police system. There are, however, federal laws enacted by Congress. These laws govern the District of Columbia and all states when a "federal" offense has been committed, such as kidnapping, assassination of a president, mail fraud, bank robbery, and so on. The Federal Bureau of Investigation (FBI) enforces these laws and also assists local and state law enforcement authorities in solving local crimes. If a nonfederal

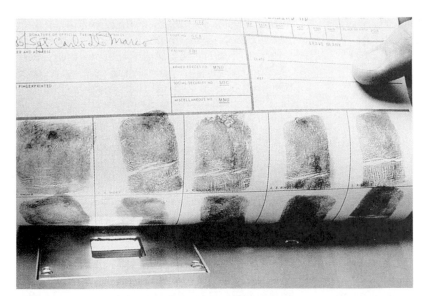

Today's police use sophisticated devices to track criminals, such as this finger matrix machine, which speeds up the process of analyzing fingerprints.

crime has been committed, the FBI must be asked by local or state authorities to aid in the investigation. If a particular crime is a violation of both state and federal law, state and local police often cooperate with the FBI to avoid unnecessary duplication of effort.

The state police patrol the highways, regulate traffic, and have primary responsibility for the enforcement of some state laws. They provide a variety of other services, such as a system of criminal identification, police training programs, and computer-based records systems to assist local police departments.

The jurisdiction of police officers at the local level is limited to the state, town, or municipality in which the person is a sworn officer of the law. Some problems inevitably result from such a highly decentralized system. Jurisdictional boundaries sometimes result in overlapping, communication problems, and difficulty in obtaining assistance from another law enforcement agency.

August Vollmer, a recognized authority on police administration, dramatized the high expectations society has of the police by noting that we expect the police officer

> ... to have the wisdom of Solomon, the courage of David, the patience of Job and the leadership of Moses, the kindness of the Good Samaritan, the strategy of Alexander, the faith of Daniel, the diplomacy of Lincoln, the tolerance of the Carpenter of Nazareth, and, finally, an intimate knowledge of every branch of the natural, biological and social sciences (Quoted in Pray, 1987).

Such expectations are, of course, unrealistic. Historically police in the United States have been young white males with a high school education (or less). Most still come from working-class backgrounds. In recent years attempts have been made to raise the educational levels of the police, as well as produce a more heterogeneous distribution including women and minorities.

The Courts

The United States has a dual court system consisting of state and federal courts, with state and federal crimes being prosecuted in the respective courts. Some crimes may violate both state and federal statutes. About 85 percent of all criminal cases are tried in the state courts.

The state court system varies from one state to the other. Lower trial courts exist for the most part to try misdemeanors and petty offenses. Higher trial courts can try felonies and serious misdemeanors. All states have appeal courts. Many have only one court of appeal, which is often known as the state supreme court. Some states have intermediate appeal courts.

The federal court system consists of three basic levels, excluding such special courts as the United States Court of Military Appeals. The United States *district courts* are the trial courts. Appeals may be brought from these courts to the *appellate courts*. There are eleven courts at this level, referred to as *circuit courts*. Finally, the highest court is the *Supreme Court*, which is basically an appeal court, although it has original jurisdiction in some cases.

The lower federal courts and the state courts are separate systems. Cases are not appealed from a state court to a lower federal court. A state court is not bound by the decisions of the lower federal court in its district, but it is bound by decisions of the United States Supreme Court (Reid, 1979).

Prisons

Prisons are a fact of life in the United States. As much as we may wish to conceal them, and no matter how unsatisfactory we think they are, we cannot imagine doing without them. They represent such a fundamental defense against crime and criminals that we now keep a larger portion of our population in prisons than any other nation with the exception of South Africa, and for terms that are longer than in many countries. Small wonder that we Americans invented the prison.

Before prisons serious crimes were redressed by corporal or capital punishment. Jails existed, but mainly for pretrial detention. The closest thing to the modern prison was the workhouse. This was a place of hard labor designed almost exclusively for minor offenders, derelicts, and vagrants. The typical convicted felon was either physically punished or fined, but not incarcerated. Today's system of imprisonment for a felony is an historical newcomer.

GOALS OF IMPRISONMENT Prisons exist in order to accomplish at least four goals: (1) separation of criminals from society, (2) punishment of criminal behavior, (3) deterrence of criminal behavior, and (4) rehabilitation of criminals.

1. *Separation of criminal from society.* Prisons accomplish this purpose once convicted felons reach the prison gates. Inasmuch as it is important to protect society from individuals who seem bent on repeating destructive behavior, prisons are one logical choice among several others, such as exile and capital punishment (execution). The American criminal justice system relies principally on prisons to segregate convicts from society, and in this regard they are quite efficient.

2. *Punishment of criminal behavior.* There can be no doubt that prisons are extremely unpleasant places in which to spend time. They are crowded, degrading, boring, and dangerous. Not infrequently prisoners are victims of one another's violence. Inmates are constantly supervised, sometimes harassed by guards, and deprived of normal means of social, emotional, intellectual, and sexual expression. Prison undoubtedly is a severe form of punishment.

3. *Deterrence of criminal behavior.* The rising crime figures cited earlier suggest that prisons have failed to achieve the goal of deterring criminal behavior. There are good reasons for this. First, by their very nature, prisons are closed to the public. Few people know much about prison life, nor do they often think about it. Inmates who return to society frequently brag to their peers about their prison experiences in order to recover their self-esteem. To use the prison experience as a deterrent, the very unpleasant aspects of prison life would have to be constantly brought to the attention of the population at large. To promote this approach, some prisons have allowed inmates to develop programs introducing high school students to the horrors of prison life. From the scanty evidence available to date, it is unclear whether such programs deter people from committing crimes. Another reason that prisons fail to deter crime is the funnel effect, discussed later. No punishment can deter undesired behavior if the likelihood of being punished is minimal. Thus the argument regarding the relative merit of different types of punishment is pointless until there is a high probability that whatever forms are used will be applied to all (or most) offenders.

4. *Rehabilitation of criminals.* Many Americans believe that rehabilitation—the resocialization of criminals to conform to society's values and norms and the teaching of usable work habits and skills—should be the most important goal of imprisonment. It is also the stated goal of almost all corrections officials. Yet there can be no doubt that prisons do not come close to achieving this aim. According to the FBI, about 70 percent of all inmates released from prison are arrested again for criminal behavior (Bureau of Justice, 1988).

Sociological theory provides ample explanations for this fact. For example, Sutherland's ideas on cultural transmission and differential association point to the fact that inside prisons, the society of inmates has a culture of its own, in which obeying the law is not highly valued. New inmates are quickly socialized to this peer culture and adopt its negative attitudes toward the law. Further, labeling theory tells us that once somebody has been designated as deviant, his or her subsequent behavior often conforms to that label. Prison inmates who are released find it difficult to be accepted in the society at large and to find legitimate work. Hence former inmates quickly take up with their old acquaintances, many of whom are active criminals. It thus becomes only a matter of time before they are once more engaged in criminal activities.

This does not mean that prisons should be torn down and all prisoners set free. As we have indicated, prisons do accomplish important goals, though certain changes are needed. Certainly it is clear that the entire criminal justice system needs to be made more efficient and that prison terms as well as other forms of punishment must follow predictably the commission of a crime. Another idea, which gained some approval in the late 1960s but seems of late to have declined in popularity, is to create "halfway" houses and other institutions in which the inmate population is not so completely locked away from society. This way, they are less likely to be socialized to the prison's criminal subculture. Labeling theory suggests that if the process of delabeling former prisoners were made open, formal, and explicit, released inmates might find it easier to win reentry into society. Finally, just as new prisoners are quickly socialized into a prison's inmate culture, released prisoners must be resocialized into society's culture. This can be accomplished only if means are found to bring ex-inmates into frequent, supportive, and structured contact with stable members of the wider society (again, perhaps, through halfway houses). The simple separation of prisoners from society undermines this goal.

To date, no society has been able to come up with an ideal way of confronting, accommodating, or preventing deviant behavior. Although much attention has been focused on the causes of and remedies for deviant behavior, no theory, law, or social-control mechanism has yet provided a fully-satisfying solution to the problem.

A SHORTAGE OF PRISONS Today's criminal justice system is in a state of crisis over prison crowding. Even though our national prison capacity has expanded, it has not kept up with demands. The National Institute of Justice estimates we must add 1000 prison spaces a week just to keep up with the growth in the criminal population.

Compounding the problem is the fact that many states have mandated prison terms for drunk drivers and for those who commit gun crimes. Yet nearly every community will have an angry uprising if the legislature suggests building a new prison in their town.

Given state financial pressures, community resistance, and soaring construction costs, people face a difficult choice. They must either build more prisons, or let most convicted offenders go back into the community. Letting them go back to the community has been a common choice lately.

A key consideration in sending a person to prison is money. The custodial cost of incarceration in a medium-security prison is $15,000 a year. The cost is closer to $25,000 once you add the cost of actually building the prison, and additional payments to dependent families. You can see why judges are quick to use probation as an alternative to imprisonment, particularly when the prisons are already overcrowded.

The other side of the question, however, is how much does it cost us not to send this person to prison? While it is easy to calculate the cost of an offender's year in prison, it is considerably more difficult to figure the cost to society of letting that individual roam the streets.

One study suggests that it is more expensive to release an offender, than to incarcerate him when you weigh the value of crime prevented through imprisonment.

Hardened, habitual criminals can be one-person crime waves. When inmates were studied in California, Michigan, and Texas, it was found that each inmate averaged between 187 and 287 crimes per year, exclusive of drug deals. Ten percent of the inmates *each* committed more than 600 crimes per year. That is almost two crimes per day. Can there be doubt in anybody's mind that it is cheaper to incarcerate these individuals than to let them pursue their trade on society (Bureau of Justice Statistics, 1988)?

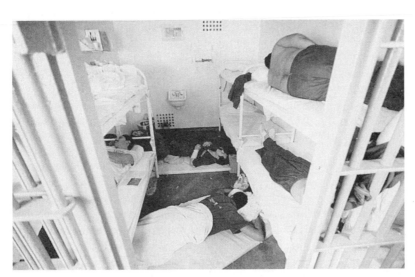

The National Institute of Justice estimates we must add 1,000 prison spaces a week just to keep up with the growth in the criminal population.

The Continuing Debate Over Capital Punishment: Does It Deter Murderers?

Of the 36 States and the Federal Government with capital punishment laws, 11 states executed 23 prisoners during 1990, bringing the total number of executions to 143 since 1976, the year the U.S. Supreme Court reinstated the death penalty. Although 23 prisoners were executed in 1990, another 244 were given the death sentence that year bringing the total to 2,356 prisoners on death row, a 5 percent increase over those awaiting the penalty at the end of 1989. It seems obvious that the vast majority of inmates with a death sentence will not be executed.

Capital punishment has been opposed for many years and for many reasons. Amnesty International, U.S.A., calls capital punishment a "horrifying lottery" where the penalty is death and the odds of escaping it are determined more by politics, money, race, and geography than by the crime committed. They base their impression on the fact that black men are more likely to be executed than white men; southern states including Texas, Florida, Louisiana, Georgia, and Virginia account for the vast majority of executions that have taken place since the Supreme Court reinstituted the death penalty in 1976.

Yet the arguments for capital punishment continue to mount centering mainly around the issue of deterrence. As professor Ernest Van Den Haag notes: "If by executing convicted murderers there is any chance, even a mere possibility, of deterring future murderers, I think we should execute them. The life of even a few victims who may be spared seems infinitely precious to me. The life of the convicted murderer has negative value. His crime has forfeited it (Van Den Haag, 1986).

This brings us back to the age-old question: Does the death penalty deter homicide? Until the 1970s, social scientists continued to argue that they could find no evidence that it did. In 1975, however, Isaac Erlich presented information based on sophisticated statistical techniques showing that the death penalty was an enormous deterrent on murder. In fact, he concluded that eight additional homicides were prevented by every execution. That

FIGURE 6.6

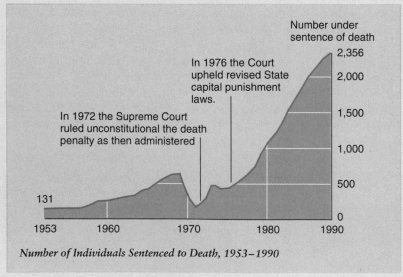

Number of Individuals Sentenced to Death, 1953–1990

Source: United States Department of Justice, Bureau of Justice Statistics Bulletin, "Capital Punishment 1990," September 1991, p. 2.

Just in case anyone still needs to be convinced, let us see how much each crime costs the public. The National Institute of Justice has come up with a figure of $2,300 per crime. This number undoubtedly overestimates the value of petty larce-

nies, and underestimates the value of rapes, murders, and serious assaults. It is an average however, and it does give us some way of comparing the costs of incarceration with the costs of freedom.

Using this number we find that a typical inmate

FIGURE 6.7

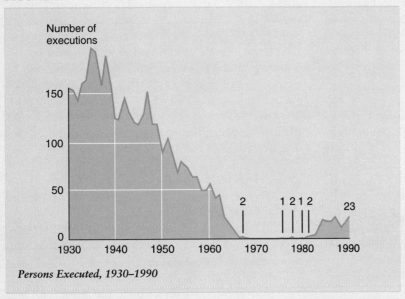

Persons Executed, 1930–1990

Source: United States Department of Justice, Bureau of Justice Statistics Bulletin, "Capital Punishment, 1990," September 1991, p. 12.

is, eight people escape being the homicide victims of future murderers every time an execution takes place. A more recent study by economists Stephen K. Layson concludes that every execution of a convicted murderer prevents 18 future murders. Therefore putting a murderer to death saves many additional lives (Layson, 1985).

There may be more involved in deterrence than we think. Plato believed we were deterred from committing crimes by seeing others punished. He was referring to punishments administered in public where everyone could see the gory details of torture and execution. Fortunately, today executions are not held in public and only a small number of people witness them. In place of actually seeing the execution we now have mass media reports that become our "eyes." Therefore deterrence should be related to how much an execution is publicized (Stark, 1987).

Using this approach, one researcher (Phillips, 1980) argued that deterrence does not depend on how many executions actually occur, but rather on how much publicity they generate. One well-publicized execution has a far greater deterrent effect than several little-known executions. Indeed it was shown that the greater the number of inches a newspaper devoted to an execution the greater the drop in the homicide rate during that week.

Even so, the deterrent effect of an execution is short-lived. The drop in the homicide rate only lasts for about two weeks. At that point homicides climb back to the pre-execution level (Phillips, 1980).

If by some chance we could arrange to hold and publicize an execution every two weeks, the deterrent effect would probably still wear off. We would then become so used to hearing about executions that they would have little impact on potential murderers.

With public support for the death penalty increasing, and with no broad legal challenges to capital punishment being waged, we can expect executions to continue to take place.

Source: United States Department of Justice, Bureau of Justice Statistics Bulletin, "Capital Punishment 1990." September 1991. David P. Phillips, "The Deterrent Effect of Capital Punishment: New Evidence on an Old Controversy." *American Journal of Sociology*, Vol. 86, pp. 139–48. Isaac Ehrlich, "The Deterrent Effect of Capital Punishment: A Question of Life and Death." *American Economic Review*, 1975, pp. 397–417.

committing 187 crimes (the low estimate) is responsible for $430,000 in crime costs per year. Sending 1,000 additional offenders to prison, instead of putting them on probation, would cost an additional $25 million per year. The crimes averted however, by taking these individuals out of the community, would save society $430 million. (Bureau of Justice Statistics, 1988)

This approach merely gives us a dollars and cents way of making a comparison. It does not in any way account for the personal anguish and trauma to the victim of crime that would be averted.

Looking at the issue from this perspective overwhelmingly supports the case for more prison space. It costs communities more in real losses, social damages, and security measures than it does to incarcerate offenders who are crowded out by today's space limitations.

WOMEN IN PRISON As prison reform began in this country, the practice was to segregate women into sections of the existing institutions. There were few women inmates, a fact that was used to "justify" not providing them with a matron. Vocational training and educational programs were not even considered. In 1873, the first separate prison for women, the Indiana Women's Prison, was opened, with its emphasis on rehabilitation, obedience, and religious education.

In contrast with institutions for adult males, institutions for adult women are generally more aesthetic and less secure. Women inmates are usually not considered high security risks, nor have they proved as violent as male inmates. Women are more likely to commit property crimes—such as larceny, forgery, fraud, and embezzlement—or drug offenses (Bureau of Justice Statistics, *Special Report*, 1991). There are some exceptions, but on the whole women's institutions are built and maintained with the view that their occupants are not great risks to themselves or to others. Women inmates also usually have more privacy than men do while incarcerated, and they usually have individual rooms. With the relatively smaller number of women in prison, there is a greater opportunity for the inmates to have contact with the staff, and a greater chance for innovation in programming (Reid, 1981).

The number of women in Federal or State prisons in 1989 reached a record of 40,556. Although the female inmate population has grown by more than 27,000 since 1980, an increase of over 200 percent, females still comprise a relatively small segment of the prison population—5.7 percent at the end of 1989.

Female, as compared with male, inmates appear to have greater difficulty adjusting to the absence of their families, especially to the absence of their children. More than three-fourths of women in prison are mothers, and the vast majority (88 percent) of their children are under 18. It was estimated that in 1989 there were 37,600 children in this country who had mothers in prison. Only 22 percent of these children were cared for by their father while their mother was in prison. Most of the children lived with a grandparent.

THE "FUNNEL" EFFECT One complaint voiced by many concerned with our criminal justice system is the existence of the **funnel effect**, *in which many crimes are committed, but few ever seem to be punished.* The funnel effect begins with the fact that of all the crimes committed, the *National Crime Victimization Survey* reports that in 1990 only 38 percent were reported to the police (Bureau of Justice Bulletin, 1991). Only about 26 percent lead to an arrest. Next, false arrests, lack of evidence, and plea bargaining (negotiations in which individuals arrested for a crime are allowed to plead guilty to a lesser charge of the crime, thereby saving the criminal justice system the time and money spent in a trial) considerably reduce the number of complaints that actually are brought to trial.

In one Bureau of Justice study of 532,000 felony arrests in 11 States, 84 percent of those adults arrested were prosecuted; 62 percent were convicted; 36 percent were sentenced to incarceration, and 13 percent were imprisoned for more than one year (Bureau of Justice Statistics Bulletin, January, 1988). (See Figure 6.8 for the typical outcome of 100 felony arrests.)

Ernest van den Haag and others contend from such figures that crime goes unchecked because street-wise criminals know that their chance of being caught and punished is very small, indeed; therefore punishment has lost its force as a negative sanction.

[In New York City] police and city officials have tacitly agreed to allow certain kinds of criminal behavior to go on without harassment or punishment. The authorities have enlarged the scope of unchallenged criminal behavior to include not only quality-of-life offenses such as aggressive panhandling, smoking in the subway, drunkenness, brawling, urinating on sidewalks and in the subways, but also certain muggings, burglaries, narcotics transactions, purse snatchings, car thefts, and larcenies.

There is neither the manpower nor the courtroom space available for police to make the kinds of disorderly-conduct arrests they routinely made in the past. If outraged citizens complain strenuously enough, a patrolman will try to move the violators along or issue a summons. These summonses are not really supposed to be a deterrent to the offender so much as a pacifier for the angry citizen (Pileggi, 1981).

To be fair, the situation is not quite as bad as it appears. In regard to serious crimes, the number of arrests is considerably more than it is for crimes in general.

What about punishment? Those who criticize the system in terms of its "funnel" effect seem to regard only a term in prison as an effective

FIGURE 6.8

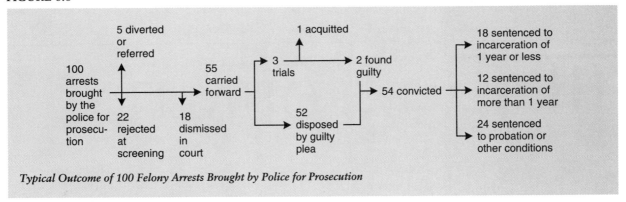

Typical Outcome of 100 Felony Arrests Brought by Police for Prosecution

Source: United States Department of Justice, Bureau of Justice Statistics, *BJS Data Report, 1988,* April 1989, p. 53.

punishment. Yet the usual practice is to send to prison only those criminals whose terms of confinement are set at over one year. After declining through the 1960s, the number of American prisoners rose sharply through the 1970s, 1980s and 1990s (see Figure 6.9). Many thousands of other criminals receive shorter sentences and serve them in municipal and county jails. Thus, if the number of people sent to local jails as well as to prison are counted, the funnel effect is less severe than often is portrayed. The question then becomes one of philosophy: Is a jail term of less than one year an adequate measure for the deterrence of crime? Or should all convicted criminals have to serve longer sentences in federal or state prisons, with jails used primarily for pretrial detention?

FIGURE 6.9

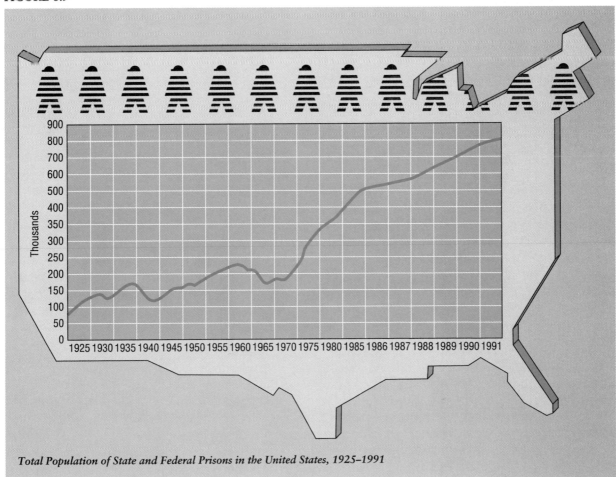

Total Population of State and Federal Prisons in the United States, 1925–1991

Source: United States Department of Justice, Bureau of Justice Statistics.

PART

III

SOCIAL INEQUALITY

CHAPTER 7   *Social Stratification*

CHAPTER 8   *Social Class in the United States*

CHAPTER 9   *Racial and Ethnic Minorities*

CHAPTER 10   *Gender and Age Stratification*

As humans interact in groups and organizations, they do not always do so as equals. In many cases, some actors possess more resources than others. Why is this so? On what basis are valued assets distributed unequally? And, for that matter, who decides what assets or personal characteristics will be valued in a particular society and who gets to establish the basis for distributing these precious goods?

This topic of social inequality is dealt with in Part III of this book. In Chapter 7 you will learn that all societies make distinctions among people, but only under certain conditions are these distinctions differentially evaluated, resulting in systems of unequal privilege, rewards, opportunities, power, prestige, and influence. When these inequalities are solidified into ranks or levels that are perpetuated by major institutions in society, we speak of a system of social stratification. In Chapter 7 you will examine the social bases for stratification, different historical stratification systems, and the possibilities people have for changing their location within the social hierarchy. You also will explore the major theories sociologists have developed to explain social stratification.

But how do these somewhat abstract concepts of stratification apply to our society? How can we go about getting an accurate picture of the extent of inequality in the United States? This is the subject of Chapter 8. Here you will examine various approaches to the study of stratification and look at one of the most commonly accepted models of social class in the U.S. Next you will investigate the extent of economic inequality in this country. How are income and wealth distributed? How is poverty determined? Who are the poor? And how does the amount of economic inequality in the U.S. compare to that in other countries? Finally, how does inequality affect the life chances of individuals? All of these issues will be explored in Chapter 8.

Social class, though, is not the only form of social inequality. Race or ethnic background, gender, and age also have been used historically as a basis for unequally distributing rewards and privileges. Chapter 9 examines the dynamics of racial and ethnic inequality and the position of major ethnic groups and racial minorities in the contemporary U.S. stratification system. Chapter 10 looks at inequality on the basis of gender and age. How are definitions of gender related to biological differences between the sexes? Why are gender distinctions made at all, and how are they perpetuated? What are the implications of these distinctions, both for individuals and society? How do we socially define and interpret the aging process? Given that our population is, on the average, getting older, how is our society likely to be different in the future? These issues will all be addressed in Chapter 10.

This section of the book will provide you with an understanding of the basic dimensions of inequality in the United States. When you have completed it, you will be prepared to explore the salient organizational features of American society.

Social Stratification

The Nature of Social Stratification
  Social Mobility

Stratification Systems
  The Caste System
  The Estate System
  The Class System

The Dimensions of Social Stratification
  Economics
  Power
  Prestige

Theories of Stratification
  The Functionalist Theory
  Conflict Theory
  Modern Conflict Theory
  The Need for Synthesis

Let us go back to early periods in the history of civilization when hunting and gathering societies were widespread. By and large, families in hunting and gathering societies were nearly equal—equally poor, equally rich, equal in number of possessions. Both men and women performed important economic duties. Everyone worked hard and there was little in the way of economic surplus. To be sure, some people stood out because they possessed outstanding abilities that were directly beneficial to the tribe. An outstanding male hunter may have been rewarded with a larger share of the food for his family. A female who was good at hunting small game would also gain extra benefits. They may also have commanded greater respect when it came to making important tribal decisions. In essence this was the beginning of stratification. Once abilities and rewards were distributed unequally within a society, economic, political, and social stratification began. Compared to what we are used to however, the stratification in a hunting and gathering society was quite limited. After all, those with special abilities have no way of guaranteeing this superiority to future generations. It is difficult to pass on hunting abilities, and hunters and gatherers have little in the way of tangible possessions to leave future generations (Rossides, 1990). So we can begin to see that stratification depends on the unequal distribution of valued attributes or assets. What is valued changes over time and from one society to another.

THE NATURE OF SOCIAL STRATIFICATION

Every society makes distinctions among its people. These differences are not always accompanied by qualitative judgments, however. For example, a five-year-old child is very different from an infant, but is not necessarily viewed as being superior because of the age difference. Although a society may not value a five-year-old more highly than an infant, it might place a value on old people. Compare, for example, the attitude of respect for the elderly in Japan with the attitude toward senior citizens in the United States.

Values placed on physical characteristics and personality habits also vary from one society to another. For example, among Europeans and Americans, body hair on adult males is considered to be "manly" and acceptable, but it is seen by the Japanese as "ugly." Americans promote competitiveness and individualism; the !Kung San of the Kalahari Desert in southern Africa value cooperativeness and modesty (Lee, 1980). Individuals who have characteristics favored by their culture have an advantage over those who do not. It is easier for them to win respect and prestige, to make friends, to find a mate, and to achieve positions of leadership. In all societies there are some people who are favored, who have more prestige, and who are admired; there are others who are avoided and looked down on. In addition all groups—even hunters and food gatherers, the most equal-minded of societies—make distinctions on the basis of age and gender. **Social evaluation,** *the process of making qualitative judgments on the basis of individual characteristics or behaviors,* leads to social inequality. **Social inequality** *is the uneven distribution of privileges, material rewards, opportunities, power, prestige, and influence among individuals or groups.* When social inequality becomes part of the social structure and is transmitted from one generation to the next, social stratification exists.

Social stratification, *the division of society into levels, steps, or positions,* is perpetuated by the major institutions of society such as the economy, the family, religion, and education. Even though no formal social stratification policy exists in the United States, there is stratification based on wealth, gender, race, and age. Certain groups have greater access than others to better education, medical care, and jobs, and these advantages perpetuate their privileged position in our society.

Social Mobility

Social mobility *is the movement of an individual or a group from one social status to another.* The extent of social mobility varies from one society to another. An **open society** *attempts to provide equal opportunity to everyone to compete for desired roles and statuses, regardless of race, religion, gender, or family history. In a* **closed society** *the various aspects of people's lives are determined at birth and remain fixed.*

There are no purely open or completely closed societies. Even the most democratic societies make a practice of assigning some roles and statuses, and even the most closed societies have a certain amount of mobility. For example, in the United States, an open society, minorities and women continue to struggle against job discrimination. On the other hand, even in a closed society, such as the estate system of medieval Europe, a wealthy merchant whose social position was low could buy his way into the nobility and consolidate his family's new social status by marrying his children off to landed aristocracy.

Social inequality involves the uneven distribution of privileges, material rewards, and power.

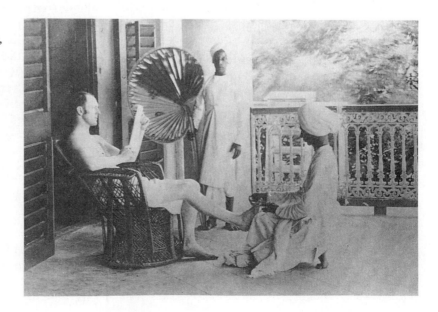

In some Middle Eastern societies, women are expected to cover themselves in public. Such a situation can help to perpetuate inequality between men and women.

Mobility may come about as a result of changing one's occupation, marrying into a certain family, and so on. *Movement that involves a change in status with no corresponding change in social class is known as* **horizontal mobility.** For example, Adriane G. Berg started her career as an attorney. Within 15 years, she made a number of horizontal career moves, none of which appreciably changed her position in the social hierarchy. She became a financial planner, a stock broker, an author of a number of successful books on financial planning, a college instructor, and finally, a radio talk-show host. Although each of these career moves was extremely important to Berg, from a sociological point of view, they are perceived as involving little or no change in prestige, power, or wealth and hence, little mobility.

Movement up or down in the social hierarchy that results in a change in social class is known as **vertical mobility.** The United States is filled with success stories of vertical mobility. Often it involves **intergenerational mobility,** that is, *a change in social status that takes place over two or more generations.* The Kennedy family offers a prime example of this type of vertical mobility. Patrick Joseph Kennedy, the grandfather of John F. Kennedy, started life in relative poverty. He had to borrow money from family members to buy a Boston saloon. His son, Joseph P. Kennedy, became an enormously wealthy—and often unscrupulous—business ty-

coon. John F. Kennedy achieved the pinnacle of success and respectability in this culture be becoming president of the United States.

Another type of vertical mobility is **intragenerational mobility,** *or a change in social status that occurs during the lifetime of one individual.* There are many examples of men and women who have experienced upward intragenerational mobility. Steven P. Jobs and Stephen G. Wozniak started Apple Computer on approximately $1,200 in Jobs's garage. William Gates made hundreds of millions while still in his twenties as head of the Microsoft Corporation. George E. Johnson, founder and president of Johnson Products Company, started his empire with $500, half of which was borrowed. Today, he is the head of a multimillion dollar company that manufactures hair-care products and cosmetics for African Americans.

Unfortunately downward intragenerational mobility is common also. Ivan Boesky and Dennis Levine were self-made millionaires convicted of insider trading on Wall Street. They lost prestige, power, and wealth, as well as their freedom when they were sent to prison for their wrongdoings.

Usually a person's social rank in the stratification hierarchy is consistent and comparatively easy to identify. However, many people do not fit neatly into one social category—their situations are examples of status inconsistency. **Status inconsistency** *refers to situations in which people rank differently (higher or lower) on certain stratification characteristics than on others.* A person whose great wealth is known or suspected to have been acquired illegally will probably not become part of the accepted social establishment. An African American physician, despite the high prestige of the profession, may in certain circles be denied a higher social position because of racial prejudice.

FACTORS AFFECTING SOCIAL MOBILITY   In the United States people believe that if individuals work hard enough they can become upwardly mobile—that is, they will become part of the next higher social class. In fact there are several other factors that affect social mobility. For example, there may be social structural factors, such as the state of the economy, that may either help or hinder social mobility.

During periods of economic expansion the number of professional and technical jobs increases. These white-collar jobs can often be filled by upwardly mobile members of other classes. When the supply of jobs increases, one group can no longer determine who will get all the jobs. Consequently people from lower social classes who have the necessary education, talent, and skills are able to fill some of the positions without having any inside connections. During periods of economic contraction, however, the opposite is true. Getting a job depends on factors that go beyond talent or experience, such as family ties or personal friendships.

Demographic factors also affect upward mobility. With the number of people entering the workforce declining during the 1990s, it will be easier for people with the right education, skills, and experience to get a job and advance than during the 1970s when the opposite was the case.

Societies also differ in terms of how much they encourage social mobility. The values and norms of American society encourage upward mobility. In fact, Americans are expected to try to succeed and better their status in life. We often look with contempt at those who have no desire to move up the social-class ladder or, worse yet, are downwardly mobile.

What is it that produces mobility? Level of education appears to be an extremely important factor. As would be expected, the greater the level of education attained by the children, the stronger the probability of their upward movement. It can even be claimed that the impact of education on occupational status is greater than that of parent's occupational status. It is difficult to separate these two factors, however, because the parent's occupation often has an impact on the amount of education received by the children.

The degree of social mobility in a society thus depends in great measure on the type of stratification system that exists.

STRATIFICATION SYSTEMS

There are two major ways in which stratification can come about: (1) People can be assigned to societal roles according to an ascribed status—some easily identifiable characteristic, such as sex, age, family name, or skin color, over which they have no control. This will produce the caste and estate systems of stratification. Or (2) People's positions in the social hierarchy can be based to some degree on their achieved statuses (see Chapter 5), gained through their individual, direct efforts. This is known as the class system.

The Caste System

*The **caste system** is a rigid form of stratification based on ascribed characteristics, such as skin color*

or family identity, that determine a person's prestige, occupation, residence, and social relationships. People are born into, and spend their entire lives within, a caste, with little chance of leaving it.

Contact between castes is minimal and governed by a set of rules or laws. If interaction must take place, it is impersonal, and examples of the participants' superior or inferior status are abundant. Access to valued resources is extremely unequal. A set of religious beliefs often justifies a caste system. The caste system as it existed for centuries in India before the 1950s is a prime example of how this kind of inflexible stratification works.

The Hindu caste system, in its traditional form in India, consisted of four *varnas* ("grades of being"), each of which corresponded to a body part of the mythical Purusa, whose dismemberment gave rise to the human species. Purusa's mouth issued forth priests (Brahmans), and his arms gave rise to warriors (Kshatriyas). His thighs produced artisans and merchants (Vaisyas), and his feet brought forth menial laborers (Sudras). Hindu scripture holds that each person's *varni* is inherited directly from his or her parents and cannot change during the person's life (Gould, 1971).

In a caste system, people are born into, and spend their entire lives within, a caste, with little chance of leaving.

Each *varna* had clearly defined rights and duties attached to it. Hindus believed in reincarnation of the soul *(karma)* and that to the extent that an individual followed the norms of behavior of his or her *varna,* the state of the soul increased in purity, and the individual could expect to be born to a higher *varna* in a subsequent life. (The opposite was also true, in that failure to act appropriately according to the *varna* resulted in a person's being born to a lower *varna* in the next life.)

This picture of India's caste system is complicated by the presence of thousands of subcastes, or *jatis.* Each of these *jatis* corresponds in name to a particular occupation (leather worker, shoemaker, cattle herder, barber, potter, and so on). Only a minority within each *jati* actually perform the work of that subcaste; the rest find employment when and where they can.

It is important to note that the Hindus have never placidly accepted the caste system. Scholars have frequently noted continuous changes during the centuries of the caste system's development. Even today, changes in the caste system are taking place. *Varnas* are all but nonexistent, and officially the Indian caste system is outlawed, although it still exists informally.

The Estate System

The **estate system** *is a closed system of stratification in which a person's social position is defined by law and membership is determined primarily by inheritance.* Because the estate system is a closed system involving ascribed statuses, it is similar to a caste system, although not as extreme. Some mobility is present, but by no means as much as exists in a class system.

The estate system of medieval Europe is a good example of how this type of stratification system works. *An* **estate** *is a segment of a society that has legally established rights and duties.* The three major estates in Europe during the Middle Ages were the nobility, the clergy, and, at the bottom of the hierarchy, the peasants. A royal landholding family at the top had authority over a group of priests and the secular nobility, who were quite powerful in their own right. The nobility were the warriors; they were expected to be brave and give military protection to the other two estates. The clergy not only ministered to the spiritual needs of all the people but were often powerful landowners as well. The peasants were legally tied to the land, which they worked in order to provide the nobles with

food and a source of wealth. In return, the nobles were supposed to provide social order, not only with their military strength, but also as the legal authorities who held court and acted as judges in disputes concerning the peasants who belonged to their land. The peasants had little freedom or economic standing, low social status, and almost no power. Just above the peasants was a small but growing group, the merchants and craftsmen. They operated somewhat outside the estate system in that although they might achieve great wealth and political influence, they had little chance of moving into the estate of the nobility of warriors. It is worth noting that it was this marginal group, which was less constricted by norms governing the behavior of the estates, that had the flexibility to gain power when the Industrial Revolution undermined the estate system, starting in the eighteenth century. Individuals were born into one of the estates and remained there throughout their lives. Under unusual circumstances people could change their estate, as for example when peasants—using produce or livestock saved from their own meager supply or a promise to turn over a bit of land that by some rare fortune belonged to them outright—could buy a position in the church for a son or daughter. For most, however, social mobility was difficult and extremely limited because wealth was permanently concentrated among the landowners. The only solace for the poor was the promise of a better life in the hereafter (Vanfossen, 1979).

The Class System

A **social class** *consists of a category of people who share similar opportunities, similar economic and vocational positions, similar lifestyles, and similar attitudes and behaviors. A society that contains several different social classes and permits greater social mobility than a caste or estate system is said to be based on a* **class system** *of stratification.* Class boundaries are maintained by limitation of social interaction, intermarriage, and mobility into that class. Some form of class system is usually present in all industrial societies, whether they be capitalist or communist. Mobility in a class system is greater than that in either a caste or an estate system. This mobility is often the result of an occupational structure that supposedly opens up higher-level jobs to anyone with the education and experience required. A class society encourages striving and achievement. Here in the United States we should find this concept familiar, for ours is basically a class society.

THE DIMENSIONS OF SOCIAL STRATIFICATION

There are many things that can produce authority, status or position in a society. If we look closely we will see that most of the valued attributes that produce stratification fall into three categories: economics, power, and prestige.

Economics

The total economic assets of an individual or a family are known as wealth. For people in the United States, wealth includes income, monetary assets, and various holdings that can be converted into money. These holdings include stocks, bonds, real estate, automobiles, precious metals and jewelry, and trusts (Jeffries and Ransford, 1980).

Information on income and wealth in the United States shows that there continues to be a high concentration of wealth in the hands of a relatively small number of people. This point is highlighted by the fact that the richest one percent of the American population owns about 20 percent of the

nation's wealth. This figure was as high as 36 percent in 1929 and illustrates dramatically the extent to which the nation's wealth is controlled by a very few (United States Department of Commerce, 1987).

There are also differences between whites, blacks, and Hispanics with respect to the amount of wealth each possesses (see Figure 7.1).

Power

One of the most widely used definitions of power in sociology is a variation of one suggested by Max Weber. **Power** *is the ability of an individual or group to attain goals, control events, and maintain influence over others—even in the face of opposition.*

In the United States, ideas about power often have their origins in the struggle for independence. It is a cliche of every Fourth of July speech that the colonists fought the Revolutionary War because of a desire to have a voice in how they were governed and how they were taxed. The colonists were also making revolutionary political demands on their own political leaders as well, by insisting that special conventions be elected to frame constitutions and

FIGURE 7.1

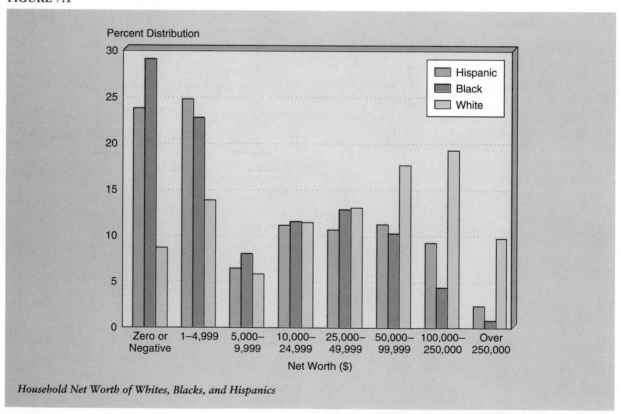

Household Net Worth of Whites, Blacks, and Hispanics

Source: United States Bureau of the Census, *Statistical Abstract of the United States: 1991.* 111th ed. Washington, DC, 1991, p. 469.

that the constitutions be ratified by a vote of all free white males without regard to property ownership. In the past, governments had been founded on the power of religious leaders, kings, self-appointed conventions, or parliaments. It was the middle classes' resolve for a voice in the decision-making process during the revolutionary period that succeeded in changing our thinking about political representation. The revolutionary period helped develop the doctrine that "power" in the United States should belong to "the people."

Every society has highly valued experiences and material objects. It can be assumed that most people in society would like to have as great a share as possible of these experiences and objects. Those who end up having the most of what people want are then, by inference, the powerful (Domhoff, 1983).

In almost all societies the distribution of power is institutionalized so that some groups consistently have more power than others. In 1956, C. Wright Mills, in his book *The Power Elite*, attacked the view that American democracy meant that simply by voting all citizens could exercise power over the major decisions that affected their lives. Mills claimed that most Americans in fact are quite powerless and that power in America is held by a relatively small segment of society from whose ranks the leaders of government, industry, and the military usually come. He further argued that it is the leaders of these three interrelated hierarchies who shape the course of events in America.

Mills took great pains to explain that America does not have a single ruling class, an aristocracy of noble families who inherit great power. But that does not mean that membership in the class called the **power elite**—*the group of people who control policymaking and the setting of priorities* in America—is open to all:

> The bulk of the very rich, the corporate executives, the political outsiders [those high-ranking planners and bureaucrats who survive in power even as different administrators come and go], the high military, derive from, at least, the upper third of the income and occupational pyramids. Their fathers were at least of the professional and business strata, and very frequently higher than that. They are native-born Americans of native parents, primarily from urban areas, and, with the exceptions of the politicians among them, overwhelmingly from the East. They are mainly Protestants, especially Episcopalian or Presbyterian. In general, the higher the position, the greater the proportion of men within it who have derived from and who maintain connections with the upper classes (Mills, 1956).

Mills showed that members of the power elite typically are graduates from a small number of prestigious colleges, belong to certain exclusive social and country clubs, and frequently marry within elite circles.

In addition, G. William Domhoff found what he called a "governing class" in America, defined in terms of economic (wealth and income) and social (education, club membership) variables. This governing class numbers about 0.5 percent of the total U.S. population. Although it is less tightly organized than the power elite suggested by Mills, its members are, nevertheless, very rich, do intermarry, spend their time in the same clubs, attend the same schools, and are extremely powerful. Despite their political party registration, the members of this governing class agree on the value of free enterprise, the profit motive, and the private ownership of property.

Domhoff suggests that even with recent changes in society,

> there continues to be a small upper class that owns 20 to 25 percent of all privately held wealth and 45 to 50 percent of all privately held corporate stock, sits in seats of formal power from the corporate community to the federal government, and wins much more often than it loses on issues ranging from the nature of the tax structure to the stifling of reform in such vital areas as consumer protection, environmental protection, and labor law (Domhoff, 1983).

Some sociologists disagree with Mills's and Domhoff's views of power in America, observing that a large number of groups compete for power. Each group is out for itself, and cooperation between them is minimal. Hence there can be no "power elite." A major proponent of this position, Arnold Rose, presented his ideas in *The Power Structure* (1967). He believes that there are power structures within every organized area of society. Within each of these power structures there is a small elite that has unusual influence. However, there are so many power structures and so many elites that it is wrong to assume that they ordinarily have any power beyond their specific spheres. Their power, moreover, is institutionally limited. At times, however, the power of one elite segment may expand (for instance, as a result of changing political regimes, the military may gain or lose influence over government spending for defense and policy decisions).

Most likely, however, the truth is somewhere in the middle. For example, in both the military and the arts there is a small elite that exerts great influence in its particular group. However, whereas the military elite's decisions and its ability to control events virtually affect the lives and futures of all Americans, the same cannot be said of the arts. The influence of the art elite is felt primarily in its own sphere and in fact can be overridden by other power elites—the government, for instance, which can withhold financial support for different areas of the arts, thus affecting the kinds, number, and quality of artistic presentations. Rose seems to have ignored the fact that often there is cooperation between different power structures—the political elite and large corporations, for example.

Prestige

Prestige *consists of the approval and respect an individual or group receives from other members of society.* There are two types of prestige. To avoid confusion we can call the first type *esteem,* which is

potentially open to all. It consists of the appreciation and respect a person wins in his or her daily interpersonal relationships. Thus, for example, among your friends there are some who are looked up to for their outgoing personalities, athletic abilities, reliability, and so on.

The second form of prestige is much more difficult for many people to achieve. This is the honor that is associated with specific statuses (social positions) in a society. Regardless of personality, athletic ability, or willingness to help others, individuals such as Supreme Court justices, state governors, physicians, physicists, and foreign service diplomats acquire prestige simply because they occupy these statuses. Access to prestigious statuses usually is difficult: Generally speaking, the greater the prestige a status has, the more difficult it is to gain it. For example, few positions carry as much prestige as

TABLE 7.1

Prestige Ratings of Various Occupations

Occupation	Prestige	Occupation	Prestige
Physician	95.8	Private secretary	60.9
Mayor	92.2	Floor supervisor in a hospital	60.3
Lawyer	90.1	Supervisor of telephone operators	60.3
College professor	90.1	Plumber	58.7
Architect	88.8	Police officer	58.3
City superintendent of schools	87.8	Manager of a supermarket	57.1
Owner of a factory employing 2000 people	81.7	Car dealer	57.1
Stockbroker	81.7	Practical nurse	56.4
Advertising executive	80.8	Dental assistant	54.8
Electrical engineer	79.5	Warehouse supervisor	54.2
Building construction contractor	78.9	Assembly-line supervisor in a manufacturing plant	53.8
Chiropractor	75.3	Carpenter	53.5
Registered nurse	75.0	Locomotive engineer	52.9
Sociologist	74.7	Stenographer	52.6
Accountant	71.2	Office secretary	51.3
High school teacher	70.2	Inspector in a manufacturing plant	51.3
Manager of a factory employing 2000 people	69.2	Housewife	51.0
Office manager	68.3	Bookkeeper	50.0
Administrative assistant	67.8	Florist	49.7
Grade school teacher	65.4	Tool machinist	48.4
Powerhouse engineer	64.5	Welder	46.8
Hotel manager	64.1	Wholesale salesperson	46.2
Circulation director of a newspaper	63.5	Telephone operator	46.2
Social worker	63.2	Auto mechanic	44.9
Hospital lab technician	63.1	Typist	44.9
Artist	62.8	Keypunch operator	44.6
Electrician	62.5	Typesetter	42.6
Insurance agent	62.5		

This chart shows how Americans have ranked the prestige of various occupations. Generally, the more prestigious jobs are those that require the greatest number of years of formal education and those that pay the highest income.

that of president of the United States—and few positions are as hard to attain.

OCCUPATIONAL STRATIFICATION Occupations are perhaps the most visible statuses to which prestige is attached in industrial society. Table 7.1 shows the prestige rankings of selected occupations in the United States. These rankings, first undertaken in the 1940s by the National Opinion Research Center, have remained quite stable since then.

During the last 30 years, women have had a dramatic impact on the American labor force. As of 1989, about 56 million women were working outside the home. This is more than a 200 percent increase over the number of working women at the end of World War II. During that same period, the number of men in the labor force has increased by

only 51 percent (*Statistical Abstract of the United States: 1991*).

The types of jobs held by working women has been changing, although there is still a great deal of occupational segregation. There are certain occupations that are heavily dominated by women. These include schoolteachers (73.3 percent female in 1989), cashiers (81.1 percent), librarians (83.3 percent), registered nurses (94.2 percent), and secretaries (99.1 percent). In contrast very few women are firefighters (3.9 percent), construction workers (2.1 percent), mechanics (3.1 percent), police officers (12.6 percent), and engineers (7.6 percent).

Even with the persistence of occupational segregation, the representation of women in a number of occupations is growing rapidly. These occupations include lawyers (22.2 percent in 1989, compared to 5 percent in 1970), doctors (17.9 percent versus 10

TABLE 7.1 CONTINUED

Prestige Ratings of Various Occupations

Occupation	Prestige	Occupation	Prestige
Post office clerk	42.3	Person who repairs shoes	26.0
Beautician	42.4	Fruit harvester, working for own family	26.0
Piano tuner	41.0	Blacksmith	26.0
Landscape gardener	40.5	Housekeeper	25.3
Truck driver	40.4	Flour miller	25.0
House painter	39.7	Stock clerk	24.4
Hairdresser	39.4	Coal miner	24.0
Pastry chef in a restaurant	39.4	Boardinghouse keeper	23.7
Butcher in a shop	38.8	Warehouse clerk	22.4
Washing-machine repairman	38.8	Waitress/waiter	22.1
Automobile refinisher	36.9	Short-order cook	21.5
Someone who sells shoes in a store	35.9	Baby-sitter	18.3
Cashier	35.6	Rubber mixer	18.1
File clerk	34.0	Feed grinder	17.8
Dress cutter	33.6	Garbage collector	16.3
Cattledriver working for own family	33.0	Box packer	15.1
Cotton farmer	32.4	Laundry worker	14.7
Metal-container maker	31.4	Househusband	14.5
Hospital aide	29.5	Salad maker in a hotel	13.8
Fireman in a boiler room	29.2	Janitor	12.5
Floor finisher	28.8	Yarn washer	11.8
Assembly-line worker	28.3	Maid (F)/household day worker (M)	11.5
Book binder	28.2	Bellhop	10.6
Textile-machine operator	27.9	Hotel chambermaid (F)/hotel bedmaker (M)	10.3
Electric-wire winder	27.6	Carhop	8.3
Vegetable grader	27.4	Person living on welfare	8.2
Delivery truck driver	26.9	Parking lot attendant	8.0
Shirtmaker in a manufacturing plant	26.6	Rag picker	4.6

Source: Christine E. Bose and Peter H. Rossi, *American Sociological Review.* June, 1983, pp. 327–28.

During World War II many job opportunities were created for women. After the war it became difficult for women to hold on to these jobs, but the long-term effect on the female work force was undeniable.

percent), college and university professors (38.7 percent versus 29 percent), mathematical and computer scientists (35.7 percent versus 14 percent), and architects (20.6 percent versus 4 percent). As of 1989, women made up the majority of professional employees in the United States (*Statistical Abstract of the United States: 1991*).

One of the key issues determining labor force participation of women is the ability to combine work and family commitments. The United States has been slow in alleviating problems in this area. Sweden, on the other hand, has been quite innovative encouraging the entry of women into the labor force.

Sweden has instituted a network of government-supported day-care centers designed to ease child-care responsibilities. The government has also produced legislation that makes it easier for women to work and have children. The Swedish parent can receive up to nine months maternity or paternity leave at 90 percent of full pay, with a guaranteed job on returning to work. The government also mandates that a worker will receive full-time pay for a shortened workday (six hours) until a child's eighth birthday. Under these measures, 66 percent of all women work. This is the highest female labor force participation rate among the industrialized

Sweden has instituted a network of government-supported day-care centers that has eased child-care responsibilities considerably.

nations. In the United States, 57.4 percent of all women work (*Statistical Abstract of the United States: 1991*).

THEORIES OF STRATIFICATION

Social philosophers have long tried to explain the presence of social inequality—that situation in which the very wealthy and powerful coexist with the poverty-stricken and socially ineffectual. In this section we shall discuss the theories that try to explain this phenomenon.

The Functionalist Theory

Functionalism is based on the assumption that the major social structures contribute to the maintenance of the social system (see Chapter 1). The existence of a specific pattern in society is explained in terms of the benefits that society receives because of that situation. In this sense the function of the family is the socialization of the young, and the function of marriage is to provide a stable family structure.

The functionalist theory of stratification as presented by Kingsley Davis and Wilbert Moore (1945) holds that social stratification is a social necessity. Every society must select individual members to fill a wide variety of social positions (or statuses) and then motivate those people to do what is expected of them in these positions, that is, fulfill their role expectations. For example, our society needs teachers, engineers, janitors, police officers,

managers, farmers, crop dusters, assembly-line workers, firefighters, textbook writers, construction workers, sanitation workers, chemists, inventors, artists, bank tellers, athletes, pilots, secretaries, and so on. In order to attract the most talented individuals to each occupation, society must set up a system of differential rewards based on the skills needed for each position.

> If the duties associated with the various positions were all equally pleasant . . . all equally important to social survival, and all equally in need of the same ability or talent, it would make no difference who got into which positions. . . . But actually it does make a great deal of difference who gets into which positions, not only because some positions are inherently more agreeable than others, but also because some require special talents or training and some are functionally more important than others. Also, it is essential that the duties of the positions be performed with the diligence that their importance requires. Inevitably, then, a society must have, first, some kind of rewards that it can use as inducements, and, second, some way of distributing these rewards differentially according to positions. The rewards and their distribution become part of the social order, and thus give rise to stratification (Davis and Moore, 1945).

According to Davis and Moore, (1) different positions in society make different levels of contributions to the well-being and preservation of society; (2) filling the more complex and important positions in society often requires talent that is scarce and has a long period of training; and (3) providing unequal rewards ensures that the most talented and best-

According to functionalist explanations of stratification, providing unequal rewards for jobs ensures that the most talented and best-trained individuals will fill the roles of greatest importance to society. Conflict theorists would disagree.

trained individuals will fill the roles of greatest importance. In effect, Davis and Moore mean that those people who are rich and powerful are at the top because they are the best qualified and are making the most significant contributions to the preservation of society (Zeitlin, 1981).

Many scholars, however, disagree with Davis and Moore (Tumin, 1953), and their arguments generally take two forms. The first argument questions the morality of stratification. The second questions the functional usefulness of stratification. Both criticisms share the belief that social stratification does more harm than good—that is, stratification is dysfunctional, rather than functional.

THE IMMORALITY OF SOCIAL STRATIFICATION On what grounds, one might ask, is it morally justifiable to give widely different rewards to different occupations, when all occupations contribute to society's ongoing functioning? How can we decide which occupations contribute more? After all, without assembly-line workers, mail carriers, janitors, seamstresses, auto mechanics, nurses aides, construction laborers, truck drivers, secretaries, shelf stockers, sanitation workers, and so on, our society would grind to a halt. How can the $1,000,000-a-year incomes of a select few be justified when the earnings of nearly 12 percent of the American population fall below the poverty level determined by the federal government, and many others have trouble making ends meet? Why are the enormous resources of our society not more evenly distributed?

Many people find the moral arguments against social stratification convincing enough. But there are other grounds on which stratification has been attacked, namely, that it is destructive for individuals and the society as a whole.

THE NEGLECT OF TALENT AND MERIT Regardless of whether social stratification is morally "right" or "wrong," many critics contend that it undermines the very functions that its defenders claim it promotes. A society divided into social classes (with limited mobility between them) is deprived of the potential contributions of many talented individuals born into the lower classes. From this point of view it is not necessary to do away with differences in rewards for different occupations. Rather, it is crucial to put aside all the obstacles to achievement that currently handicap the children of the poor.

BARRIERS TO FREE COMPETITION It can also be claimed that access to important positions in society is not really open. That is, those members of society who occupy privileged positions allow only a small number of people to enter their circle. Thereby, shortages are created artifically. This, in turn, increases the perceived worth of those who are in the important positions. For example, the American Medical Association (AMA) is a wealthy and powerful group that exercises great control over the quality and quantity of physicians available to the American public. Historically, the AMA has had a direct influence on the number of medical schools in the United States and thereby the number of doctors that are produced each year, effectively creating a scarcity of physicians. A direct result of this influence is that medical care costs and physicians' salaries have increased more rapidly than has the pace of inflation.

This situation is beginning to change, however. The allure of high earnings along with changing demographic characteristics will mean that in the future there will be a surplus of physicians. In addition, as more and more doctors fight for the same patient dollars, earnings have begun to suffer. Although physicians earn considerably more than most other professionals, the rise in their median income has started to fall short of the rate of inflation in recent years (Statistical Abstract of the United States: 1991). Thus, while barriers to free competition exist in our society, often the marketplace overrules them in the end.

Of course, the same market forces will probably create a shortage of doctors by the year 2010. With today's talented young people realizing that there are better (and certainly easier) ways of earning a living than medicine, medical school enrollments may drop, once again creating a shortage just when the baby boom generation needs a doctor most (Schloss, 1988).

FUNCTIONALLY IMPORTANT JOBS When we examine the functional importance of various jobs, we become aware that the rewards attached to jobs do not necessarily reflect the essential nature of the functions. Why should a Hollywood actor receive an enormous salary for starring in a film and a child-protection worker receive barely a living wage? It is difficult to prove empirically which positions are most important to society or what rewards are necessary to persuade people to want to fill certain positions.

Conflict Theory

As we saw, the functionalist theory of stratification assumes society is a relatively stable system of

Critics of functionalist theory would ask on what grounds is it morally justifiable to give widely different rewards to different occupations when they are all important to making society work?

interdependent parts in which conflict and change are abnormal. Functionalists maintain that stratification is necessary for the smooth functioning of society. Conflict theorists, on the other hand, see stratification as the outcome of a struggle for dominance. Current views of the conflict theory of stratification are based on the writings of Karl Marx. Max Weber developed many of his ideas in response to Marx's writings.

KARL MARX In order to understand human societies, Karl Marx believed, one must look at the economic conditions surrounding production of the necessities of life. Stratification emerges from the power struggles for scarce resources.

> The history of all hitherto existing society is the history of class struggles. [There always has been conflict between] freeman and slave, patrician and plebeian, lord and serf, guild-master and journeyman, in a word, oppressor and oppressed . . . (Marx and Engels, 1961).

Those groups who own and/or control the means of production within a society also have the power to shape or maintain aspects of society to best favor their interests. They are determined to maintain their advantage. They do this by setting up political structures and value systems that support their position. In this way the legal system, the schools, and the churches are shaped in ways that benefit the ruling class. As Marx and Engels put it, "The ruling ideas of each age have always been the ideas of its ruling class" (1961). Thus the pharaohs of ancient Egypt ruled because they claimed to be gods. And in the first third of this century, America's capitalist class justified its position by misusing Darwin's theory of evolution: They adhered to the

idea of Social Darwinism (see Chapter 1), which states that those who rule do so because they are the most "fit" to rule, having won the evolutionary struggles that promote the "survival of the fittest."

Marx was most interested in the social impact of the capitalist society which was based on industrial production. In a capitalist society there are two great classes, the **bourgeoisie,** *the owners of the means of production or capital,* and the **proletariat,** *or working class.* The working class has no resources other than their labor, which they sell to the capitalists. In all class societies there is exploitation of one class by another.

Marx believed the moving force of history was class struggle, or class conflict. This conflict grows out of differing class interests. As capitalism develops, two conflicting trends emerge. On the one hand, the capitalists try to maintain and strengthen their position. The exploitative nature of capitalism is found in the fact that the capitalists pay the workers only a bare minimum wage, below the value of what the workers actually produce. The remainder is taken by the capitalists as profit and adds to their capital. This capital, which rightfully belongs to the workers, is then used to build more factories, machines, or anything else to produce more goods. As Marx saw it, "Capital is dead labor, that vampire-like, only lives by sucking living labor, and lives the more, the more labor it sucks" (Marx, 1906).

Eventually, in the face of continuing exploitation, the working classes find it in their interest to overthrow the dominant class and establish a social order more favorable to their interests. Marx believed that with the proletariat in power, class conflict would finally end. The proletariat would have no class below it to exploit. The final stage of advanced communism would include an industrial society of plenty where all could live in comfort.

Marx was basically a materialist. He believed that people's lives are centered on how they deal with the material world. The key issue is how wealth is distributed among the people. There are at least four ways by which wealth can be distributed:

1. *To each according to need.* In this system, the basic economic needs of all the people are satisfied. These needs include food, housing, medical care, and education. Extravagant material possessions are not basic needs and have no place in this system.
2. *To each according to want.* Here wealth will be distributed according to what people desire and request. Material possessions beyond the basic needs are now included.
3. *To each according to what is earned.* People who live according to this system become themselves the source of their own wealth. If they earn a great deal of money, they can lavish extravagant possessions upon themselves. If they earn little, they must do without.
4. *To each according to what can be obtained—by whatever means.* Under this system everyone ruthlessly attempts to acquire as much wealth as possible without regard for the hardships that might be brought on others because of these actions. Those who are best at exploiting others become wealthy and powerful, and the others become the exploited and poor (Cuzzort and King, 1980).

In Marxist terms, the first of these four possibilities is what would happen in a socialist society. Although many readers will believe that the third possibility describes our society (according to what is earned), Marxists would say that a capitalist society is characterized by the last choice—the capitalists obtain whatever they can get in any possible way.

MAX WEBER Marx's ideas about class were expanded by Max Weber into a multidimensional view of stratification. Weber agreed with Marx on many issues related to stratification including the following:

1. Group conflict is a basic ingredient of society.
2. People are motivated by self-interest.
3. Those who do not have property can defend their interests less well than can those who have property.
4. Economic institutions are of fundamental importance in shaping the rest of society.

5. Those in power promote ideas and values that help them maintain their dominance.
6. Only when exploitation becomes extremely obvious will the powerless object.

From those areas of agreement Weber went on to add to and modify many of Marx's basic premises. Weber's view of stratification went beyond the material or economic perspective of Marx. Weber included status and power as important aspects of stratification as well.

Weber was not interested in society as a whole but in the groups formed by self-interested individuals who compete with one another for power and privilege. Weber rejected the notion that conflict between the bourgeoisie and proletariat was the only, or even the most important, conflict relationship in society.

Weber believed there were three sources of stratification: economic class, social status, and political power. Economic classes arise out of the unequal distribution of economic power, a point on which both Marx and Weber agreed. Weber went further, however, maintaining that social status is based on prestige or esteem—that is, status groups are shaped by lifestyle, which is in turn affected by income, value system, and education. People recognize others who share a similar lifestyle and develop social bonds with those who are most like themselves. From this inclination comes an attitude of exclusivity: Others are defined as being not as good as those who are a part of the status group. Weber did recognize that there is a relationship between economic stratification and social-status stratification. Typically, those who have a high social status also have great economic power.

Inequality in political power exists when groups are able to influence events in their favor. For example, representatives from large industries lobby at the state and federal levels of government for legislation favorable to their interests and against laws that are unfavorable. Thus the petroleum industry has pushed for lifting restrictions on gasoline prices; the auto industry lobbied for quotas on imported cars. In exchange for "correct" votes, a politician is often promised substantial campaign contributions from wealthy corporate leaders or endorsement and funding by a large labor union whose members' jobs will be affected by the government's decisions. The individual consumer who will pay the price for such political arrangements is powerless to exert any influence over these decisions.

Class, status, and power, though related, are not the same. One can exist without the others. To Weber they are not always connected in some

CONTROVERSIES IN SOCIOLOGY

Why is the Black Underclass Growing?

Information about black America is often depressing. The proportion of blacks living in poverty in 1990 was 31.9 percent, higher than in 1969 and nearly three times the white rate. Forty-five percent of black children live in poverty, compared to 15 percent of white children. Even though blacks constitute 12 percent of the population, they made up 47 percent of the prison inmates in 1990, and African Americans are about six times more likely to be the victims of murder than are whites (*Violent Crime in the United States*, March 1991). As bad as these figures may seem, within the black community a relatively small but growing underclass has problems beyond these just cited. They can be termed "the poorest of the poor."

The source of the growth in the black underclass is not exactly clear. Is it that blacks are being absorbed into the underclass as they become poorer and are caught up in a culture of illegitimacy, drugs, and joblessness? Or are children simply being born into the underclass and failing to escape? Most likely the two possibilities are related.

How the underclass developed and what should be done about it are issues that are fiercely debated within the social sciences. There are basically three major approaches to the issue: the "welfare school" theory, the "structural unemployment/social isolation" theory, and the "culture of poverty" theory.

Charles Murray's "welfare school" approach was presented in his 1984 book *Losing Ground*, in which he argued that the liberal policies of the 1960s, such as increases in social spending, the loosening of welfare regulations, and the lowering of academic and discipline standards in public schools, are the cause of current problems. These policies made it possible for black girls to have illegitimate babies while unemployed and to see no disadvantage to this practice. Murray claims that these policies destroyed the work ethic and made it harder for blacks to learn how to get out of poverty.

William Julius Wilson proposed the "structural unemployment/social isolation" thesis in his 1987 book *The Truly Disadvantaged*. He argued that, with the deindustrialization of the American economy and the movement of jobs to the suburbs beginning in the early 1970s, unskilled young ghetto males became increasingly unemployable and undesirable as prospects for marriage. As middle-class and working-class blacks left for work elsewhere, the ghettos became "communities of the underclass . . . plagued by massive joblessness, flagrant and open lawlessness, and low achieving schools. . . ." Wilson further noted that residents of these areas ". . . have become increasingly socially isolated from mainstream patterns of behavior."

In his "culture of poverty" thesis, Glenn Loury notes that Murray and Wilson put too much emphasis on economic conditions, and not enough on the breakdown of values in the ghetto and the failure of prominent blacks to help restore them. Status in the ghetto is gained from becoming a drug dealer or a mother. Loury believes black leaders need to get the message across that this is not what it means to be "cool."

Which of the three proposals are correct? Probably all of them, to some extent. Social policies have contributed to a breakdown in the black family, industry has left the inner city, and more affluent blacks have left the ghetto.

While researchers argue over the growth of the underclass, little is being done to address the problem. At the moment there is no concerted policy to stop this growth. The more this problem is ignored the worse it will get.

Source: Morton M. Kondracke, "The Two Black Americas." *The New Republic*, February 6, 1989, pp. 17–20.

predictable fashion, nor are they always tied into the economic mode of production. A southern "aristocratic" family may be in a state that is often labeled "genteel poverty," but the family name still elicits respect in the community. This kind of status is sometimes denied to the rich, powerful labor leader whose family connections and school ties are not acceptable to the social elite. In addition, status and power are often accorded to those who have no relationship to the mode of production. Henry

Kissinger, for example, controlled no industry, nor did he have any great personal wealth; yet his influence was felt by the heads of state the world over.

Whereas Marx was somewhat of an optimist in that he believed that conflict, inequality, and exploitation could eventually be eliminated in future societies, Weber was much more pessimistic about the potential for a more just and humane society.

Modern Conflict Theory

Conflict theorists assume that people act in their own self-interest in a material world in which exploitation and power struggles are prevalent. There are five aspects of modern conflict theory:

1. Social inequality emerges through the domination of one or more groups by other groups. Stratification is the outgrowth of a struggle for dominance in which people compete for scarce goods and services. Those who control these items gain power and prestige. Dominance can also result from the control of property, as others become dependent on the landowners.
2. Those who are dominated have the potential to express resistance and hostility toward those in power. While the potential for resistance is there, it sometimes lies dormant. Opposition may not be organized because the subordinated groups may not be aware of their mutual interests. They

may also be divided because of racial, religious, or ethnic differences.
3. Conflict will most often center on the distribution of property and political power. The ruling classes will be extremely resistant to any attempts to share their advantage in these areas. Economic and political power are the most important advantages in maintaining a position of dominance.
4. What are thought to be the common values of society are really the values of the dominant groups. The dominant groups establish a value system that justifies their position. They control systems of socialization, such as education, and impose their values on the general population. In this way the subordinate groups come to accept a negative evaluation of themselves and believe those in power have a right to that position.
5. Because those in power are engaged in exploitative relationships, they must find mechanisms of social control to keep the masses in line. The most common mechanism of social control is the threat or the actual use of force, which can include physical punishment or the deprivation of certain rights. However, more subtle approaches are preferred. By holding out the possibility of a small amount of social mobility for those who are deprived, the power elite will try to induce them to accept the system's basic assumptions. Thus the subordinate masses will come to believe

TABLE 7.2

Functionalist and Conflict Views of Social Stratification: A Comparison

The Functionalist View	The Conflict View
1. Stratification is universal, necessary, and inevitable.	1. Stratification may be universal without being necessary or inevitable.
2. Social organization (the social system) shapes the stratification system.	2. The stratification system shapes social organizations (the social system).
3. Stratification arises from the societal need for integration, coordination, and cohesion.	3. Stratification arises from group conquest, competition, and conflict.
4. Stratification facilitates the optimal functioning of society and the individual.	4. Stratification impedes the optimal functioning of society and the individual.
5. Stratification is an expression of commonly shared social values.	5. Stratification is an expression of the values of powerful groups.
6. Power is usually legitimately distributed in society.	6. Power is usually illegitimately distributed in society.
7. Tasks and rewards are equitably allocated.	7. Tasks and rewards are inequitably allocated.
8. The economic dimension is subordinate to other dimensions of society.	8. The economic dimension is paramount in society.
9. Stratification systems generally change through evolutionary processes.	9. Stratification systems often change through revolutionary processes.

Source: Arthur L. Stinchcombe, "Some Empirical Consequences of the Davis-Moore Theory of Stratification," in Jack L. Roach, Llewellyn Gross, and Orville R. Gursslin, eds., *Social Stratification in the United States*, Englewood Cliffs, NJ: Prentice-Hall, 1969, p. 55.

that by behaving according to the rules, they will gain a better life (Vanfossen, 1979).

The Need for Synthesis

Any empirical investigation will show that neither the functionalist nor the conflict theory of stratification is entirely accurate. This does not mean that both are useless in understanding how stratification operates in society. Ralf Dahrendorf (1959) suggests that the two theories are really complementary rather than opposed to each other. (Table 7.2 compares the two.) We do not need to choose between the two but instead should see how each is qualified to explain specific situations. For example, functionalism may help explain why differential rewards are needed to serve as an incentive for a person to spend many years training to become a lawyer. Conflict theory would help explain why the offspring of members of the upper classes study at elite institutions and end up as members of prestigious law firms, while the sons and daughters of the middle and lower classes study at public institutions and become overworked district attorneys in a minority district court.

In the next chapter we will look at the issue of social stratification further by focusing specifically on social class in the United States.

Social Class in the United States

Studying Social Stratification
  Objective Approach
  Reputational Approach
  Subjective Approach

Social Class in the United States
  The Upper Class
  The Upper-Middle Class
  The Lower-Middle Class
  The Working Class
  The Lower Class

Income Distribution

Poverty
  The Feminization of Poverty
  How Do We Count the Poor?
  Myths About the Poor

Government Assistance Programs

Worldwide Comparisons

Consequences of Social Stratification

Tabitha Morrison is a petite, African American, fifteen-year-old high school student who lives in a poor section of Dallas. Her mother works as a waitress and her father left when she was three. She plans to go to medical school and become a surgeon. Her grades are fair and she is taking a remedial science course. She has a boyfriend but says she does not want to marry until she has a secure job. Last month she had a pregnancy scare. She states emphatically "I want to be successful, to make money, to have cars." In fact, her main reason for wanting to be a doctor is "primarily for the money."

Beth Percy is a white sixteen-year-old high-school junior who lives with her parents in an affluent New England college town. She has three brothers, two older and one younger. Her mother is a librarian, her father a stockbroker. She attends a top-notch public high school and hopes to study drama in college, possibly at Yale, "like Meryl Streep." She would like to live and act in England for a time, possibly doing Shakespeare. By the age of 25 she plans to live in New York City and develop her acting career. She wants to have "a great life," be "really independent," and have "everything that's mine—crazy furniture, everything my own style" (Sidel 1990).

Jose Gaitan, 39, grew up in one of Seattle's worst neighborhoods. He is the son of an illegal Salvadoran immigrant father who was deported when Jose was five and an American-born heroin-addicted mother. Growing up on welfare, Gaitan remembers that food was scarce and that one Thanksgiving he shared two turkey TV dinners with his mother and younger brother. At the Baptist church Jose attended, the minister took an interest in him and encouraged him to work hard in school. The minister's concern had an impact and Jose's grades won him a scholarship to Linfield College in Oregon. After graduating in 1973, he returned to Seattle and worked his way through the University of Washington's School of Law. In 1982 he opened a private law practice. Today his firm grosses more than $2 million a year and he employs 13 other lawyers (Money Magazine, October 1991).

These three stories have a good deal of information in them about the social class of the main characters. The subject of social class in the United States is a touchy one, indeed. As Americans, we like to think that class is a minor issue. After all, we do not have inherited ranks, titles, or honors. We do not have coats of arms or rigid caste rankings. Besides, equality among men—and women—is an ideal guaranteed by our Constitution and summoned forth regularly in speeches from podiums and lecterns across the land.

Yet, who do you think has a greater chance of reaching her dream, Tabitha or Beth? If you say Beth, what does Jose tell us about movement between the social classes? What we will begin to see in this chapter is that social stratification is quite complex and open to many subtle variations. It does not always fit neatly into our stereotypes.

STUDYING SOCIAL STRATIFICATION

It would come as no surprise to anyone if we noted that we live in a country characterized by extreme wealth and equally extreme poverty. Although many people are reluctant to talk about it, there are class distinctions in America based on race, education, family name, occupation, and income. These remain despite legislation, free public education, and political idealism. In his book *Inequality in an Age of Decline* (1980), Paul Blumberg went so far as to call the idea of class America's "forbidden thought." Although the thought may at times be forbidden, the reality of a class structure is a hallmark of our society that will be explored in this chapter.

A common way of measuring social stratification in a society is to divide people into a specified number of social classes. How do we decide what social class somebody belongs to? Social classes vary in many distinctive ways, and there is considerable disagreement among sociologists as to what is most important in determining social class. For example, if we were to define social class solely in terms of income, a number of problems would immediately become obvious. In many large cities a sanitation worker may receive a higher starting pay than a public school teacher. Thus, if income were our sole criterion for determining social class, we would have to admit that the trash collector belongs to a higher social class than the public school teacher. By the same token we would have to assign upper-class

status to organized-crime figures who "earn" hundreds of thousands of dollars a year. Obviously, we must find a system of measurement that will avoid some of these problems. Sociologists have devised three approaches to measuring social class: the objective approach, the reputational approach, and the subjective approach.

Objective Approach

*When using the **objective approach** to measure social class researchers determine a set number of classes in advance and then assign people to each one based on given criteria.* This method was first instituted by August Hollingshead (1949) in his study of the residents of New Haven, Connecticut. Using criteria that included occupation, level of education, and residence, Hollingshead grouped people into one of five categories which are similar to the social classes we will discuss.

Proponents of this method see it as an objective, relatively precise assessment tool which does not rely on subjective feelings and attitudes, and thus can be used to assign social class levels to large populations. Critics disagree. They point to the fact that researchers arbitrarily determine the number of social classes and the characteristics that put a person into each. Clearly, there may be—and often are—differences of opinion among sociologists concerning these characteristics, making this method less objective than its label implies.

Reputational Approach

*The **reputational approach** of determining social class relies on the opinions the community members have of one another.* This approach was first used by W. Lloyd Warner and Paul Lunt (1941) in their study of a town in Massachusetts. Through personal contact with many community residents, researchers analyze the social categories into which community members place one another. For example, while some people are perceived as "high society," others are viewed as "trash," and still others are looked upon as "good old boys." From these judgments researchers are able to categorize community members into specific social classes. This method suffers from the need for subjective judgments from both researchers and local residents. In addition, it can be used only in a small community where most people either know or know of one another.

Subjective Approach

*With the **subjective approach** of measuring social class, individuals are asked to place themselves into* *one of several categories.* There may be as few as three—upper, middle, and lower class—or as many as ten. No matter how many categories are used, the middle category is the one most often selected—a tendency that reduces the method's accuracy and usefulness. In addition, judgments are influenced greatly by the wording of the questions and by researcher attitudes. People also tend to play down the presence and importance of social classes in their lives, and as a result, often do not treat the issue very seriously.

SOCIAL CLASS IN THE UNITED STATES

There is little agreement among sociologists as to how many social classes exist in the United States and what their characteristics may be. However, for our purposes, we will follow the relatively common approach of assuming that there are five social classes in the United States: upper class, upper middle class, lower-middle class, working class, and lower class (Rossides, 1990; Kahl, 1960). Table 8.1 presents stratification data for each of these classes.

The Upper Class

Members of the upper class have great wealth, often going back for many generations. They recognize one another and are recognized by others by reputation and lifestyle. They usually have high prestige and a lifestyle that excludes those from other classes. Members of this class often influence our society's basic economic and political structure. The upper class usually isolates itself from the rest of society by residential segregation, private clubs, and private schools. They are most likely to be Protestant, especially Episcopalian or Presbyterian. It is estimated that in the United States, the upper class consists of from one to three percent of the population.

During the last decade, the upper class has also come to include society's new entrepreneurs—people who have often made many millions—and sometimes billions—in business. In many respects these people do not resemble the upper class of the past. Included are people like David Packard, a pioneer in computers and electronics who founded Hewlett-Packard Company and is now worth some $2.56 billion; William Gates, the 34-year-old chief executive officer of the Microsoft Corporation, who has a $1.2 billion net worth, and Ted Turner, the founder of the 24-hour cable news network, whose net worth exceeds $1 billion (*Newsweek*, May 30, 1988).

Not all billionaires lead such an opulent lifestyle, and many in the upper class would not approve of this display of wealth. More fitting of upper class

TABLE 8.1

Social Stratification in the United States by Occupation

Class	Occupation	Education	Children's Education
Upper class	Corporate ownership; upper-echelon politics; honorific positions in government and the arts	Liberal arts education at elite schools	College and postcollege
Upper-middle class	Professional and technical fields; managers; officials; proprietors	College and graduate school training	College and graduate school training
Lower-middle class	Clerical and sales positions; small-business owners; semiprofessionals; farmers	High school; some college	Option of college
Working class	Skilled and semiskilled manual labor; craftspeople; foremen; nonfarm workers	Grade school; some or all of high school	High school; vocational school
Lower class	Unskilled labor and service work; private household work and farm labor	Grade school; semi-illiterate	Little interest in education; high school dropouts

Source: Adapted from United States Department of Commerce, Bureau of the Census, *Statistical Abstract of the United States: 1981.* Washington, DC: United States Government Printing Office, 1981.

Members of the upper class recognize one another and are recognized by others by reputation and life-style.

acceptance are the Main Street billionaires like Sam Walton, who made their money in the heartland and continued to live there. Walton, the founder of Wal-Mart Stores, made his fortune through retailing geared to middle America. Another example is Leslie Wexner, founder of The Limited, a women's retailing chain, who lives and works in Columbus, Ohio. His $2.1 billion fortune has enabled him to contribute nearly $50 million to local charities, making him the city's largest benefactor (Conant, 1988).

One of the upper class's quaintest institutions is a little-known address and telephone book called the *Social Register*. It lists the names and various addresses of about 65,000 families and single adults, as well as information concerning each person's membership in clubs and ancestral societies, colleges and universities attended, and year of graduation. Social scientists can obtain a great deal of information about the upper class from this source.

The *Social Register* association does not really decide who is and who is not a member of the upper class, they merely decide who should be listed. The *Social Register* is essentially a telephone book. It should be remembered, though, that the venture has persisted since 1887. Tens of thousands of families send their forms in each year. This at least gives some small measure of proof to the fact that a self-conscious group of members of the upper class does exist in America.

The Upper-Middle Class

The upper-middle class is made up of successful business and professional people and their families.

They are usually just below the top in an organizational hierarchy but still command a reasonably high income. Many aspects of their lives are dominated by their careers, and continued success in this area is a long-term consideration. These people often have a college education, own property, and have a savings reserve. They live in comfortable homes in the more exclusive areas of a community, are active in civic groups, and carefully plan for the future. They are very likely to belong to a church. The most common denominations represented are Presbyterian, Episcopalian, Congregationalist, Jewish, and Unitarian. Of the United States population 10 to 15 percent fall into this category.

A large percentage of the new upper-middle class are two-income couples, both of whom are college educated and employed as corporate executives, high government officials, business owners, or professionals. These relatively affluent individuals are changing the face of many communities. They are gentrifying run-down city neighborhoods with their presence and their money

The Lower-Middle Class

The lower-middle class shares many characteristics with the upper-middle class, but they have not been able to achieve the same kind of lifestyle because of economic or educational shortcomings. Usually high school graduates with modest incomes, they are the lesser professionals, clerical and sales workers, and upper-level manual laborers. They emphasize respectability and security, have some savings, and are politically and economically conservative. They are often dissatisfied with their standard of living,

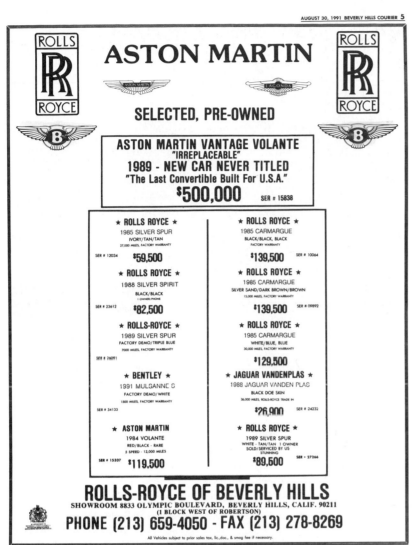

Certain members of the upper class wish to display their wealth through material possessions. Others consider such displays crass and typical of the newly rich.

jobs, and family incomes. Religiously they are likely to be represented among the Protestant denominations such as Baptist, Methodist, Lutheran, or Greek Orthodox or Catholic. They make up 25 to 30 percent of the United States population.

The Working Class

The working class is made up of skilled and semi-skilled laborers, factory employees and other blue-collar workers. These are the people who keep the country's machinery going. They are assembly-line workers, auto mechanics, and repair personnel. They are the most likely to be buffeted by economic downturns. More than half belong to unions.

Working class people live adequately but with little left over for luxuries. They are less likely to vote than higher classes and feel politically powerless. Although they have little time to be involved in civic organizations, they are very much involved with

their extended families. The families are likely to be patriarchal with sharply segregated gender roles. They stress obedience and respect for elders. Many of them have not finished high school. More than 50 percent of this group is likely to be Catholic. They represent 25 to 35 percent of the United States population.

The Lower Class

These are the people at the bottom of the economic ladder. They have little in the way of education or occupational skills and are consequently either unemployed or underemployed. Lower-class families often have many problems, including broken homes, illegitimacy, criminal involvement, and alcoholism. Members of the lower class have little knowledge of world events, are not involved with their communities, and do not usually identify with other poor people. They have low voting rates.

We tend to think of the lower class as an urban population. Yet a substantial portion of this population is rural.

Because of a variety of personal and economic problems, they often have no way of improving their lot in life. For them, life is a matter of surviving from one day to the next. Their drop out rate from school is high, and they have the highest rates of illiteracy of any of the groups. The lower class is disproportionately African American and Hispanic, but it is not defined by race or even poverty. Rather, it is a set of characteristics and conditions that are part of a broader lifestyle. Lower class people often belong to fundamentalist or revivalist sects. Fifteen to twenty percent of the population falls into this class.

Money, power, and prestige are unequally distributed among these classes. However, a desire to advance and achieve success is shared by members of all five, which makes them believe that the system is just and that upward mobility is open to all. Therefore the lower classes tend to blame themselves for lack of success and for material need (Vanfossen, 1979).

INCOME DISTRIBUTION

The United States Census Bureau has published annual estimates of the distribution of family income since 1947. These figures show a highly unequal distribution of wealth. In 1989, for example, the richest one-fifth of families received $9.70 of income for every $1.00 received by the poorest one-fifth.

Without further elaboration this information allows us to imagine that the richest one-fifth of families consists of millionaire real estate moguls, wall street professionals, and CEOs of major companies. The image is somewhat misleading. In 1990 the richest one-fifth included all families with incomes of $61,490 or more (see Table 8.2). Keep in mind that this is family income derived from jobs held by husbands, wives, and all other family members. Family incomes for the richest five percent of the population begin at $102,358 (Levy, 1987; *Statistical Abstract of the United States: 1991*).

This is not to imply, though, that there is not a significant difference in the distribution of wealth in the United States. Table 8.2 also shows that the richest 20 percent of the population receives 44.6 percent of the total income, and the poorest 20 percent receives only 4.6 percent of the total income. Income is only part of the picture. Total wealth—in the form of stocks, bonds, real estate, and other holdings are even more unequally distributed. The richest 20 percent of American families own more than three-fourths of all the country's wealth. In fact, the richest five percent of all families own more than half of America's wealth.

There is also evidence to support the old adage that "the rich get richer, and the poor get poorer." The number of people in poverty grew from 24.5 million in 1978 to 33.6 million in 1990 (United States Department of Commerce *News*, 1991).

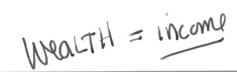 Wealth = income

TABLE 8.2

Family Income Distribution, 1990

	Income Amount	Percent of Total Income Received By All Families
Richest 5 percent	$102,358 and above*	17.9
Fifth quintile	61,490 and above	44.6
Fourth quintile	42,040–61,489	23.7
Third quintile	29,044–42,039	16.5
Second quintile	16,846–29,043	10.6
First quintile	16,845 or below	4.6

*Richest five percent is contained in fifth quintile.

Source: United States Census Bureau, Congressional Budget Office, House Ways and Means Committee, *World Almanac.*

POVERTY

On a very basic level, poverty refers to a condition in which people do not have enough money to maintain a standard of living that includes the basic necessities of life. Depending on which official or quasi-official approach one uses, it is possible to document that anywhere from 14 million to 45 million Americans are living in poverty. The actual fact is we do not really have an unequivocal way of determining how many poor people there are in the United States.

Poverty seems to be present among certain groups much more than among others. In 1990, 13.5 percent of all Americans lived below the poverty level. While 10.7 percent of all whites were living in poverty, 31.9 percent of all blacks and 28.1 percent of all those of Spanish origin fell into this group (see Figure 8.1). People living in certain regions of the United States are much more likely to live in poverty than those living elsewhere. In the South, for example, the percentage of people living below the poverty level is 12.5 percent, while in the Northeast, it is 8.1 percent (*Statistical Abstract of the United States: 1991*).

These figures reflect the fact that the level of poverty in rural areas is actually higher than it is in our cities. Thirty percent of the nation's poor live in rural America—a fact often overlooked by those who focus only on the problems of the urban poor. Even worse, the economic conditions of the rural poor are expected to deteriorate along with the decline of unskilled manufacturing jobs and changes in the mining, agriculture, and oil industries.

The problem is especially acute for those with little education or marketable job skills. For example, more than 11,000 sugar workers in southern Louisiana, almost all of whom are black and many of whom are illiterate, have lost their jobs over the past ten years due to mechanization. With nowhere to turn and with no other jobs available, many lead desperate lives in poverty (*New York Times*, June 3, 1988.

The Feminization of Poverty

Different types of families also have different earning potentials. In 1989, a family with both a husband and wife present had a median income of $34,700.

FIGURE 8.1

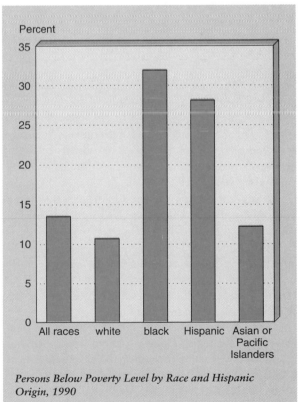

Persons Below Poverty Level by Race and Hispanic Origin, 1990

Source: United States Department of Commerce News, "1990 Median Household Income Dips, Census Bureau Reports in Annual Survey," September 26, 1991.

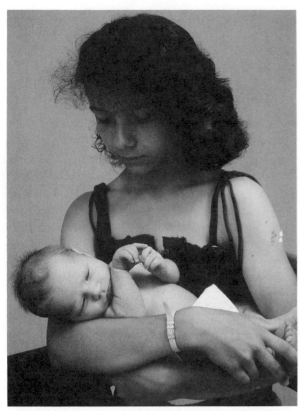

Seventy percent of all out-of-wedlock births occur to young women between the ages of 15 and 24. Only 53 percent of them have a high school diploma. This situation has contributed to the feminization of poverty.

counterparts? Of all out-of-wedlock births, 70 percent occur to young women between the ages of 15 and 24. They are on average ten years younger than divorced mothers. Never-married mothers are also, on average, much less educated. Only 53 percent have a high school diploma. Thus, inexperience and lack of education combine to give these women much poorer job prospects (Besharov and Quin, 1987).

How Do We Count the Poor?

In order to put a dollar amount on what constitutes poverty, the federal government has devised a poverty index of specific income levels, below which, people are considered to be living in poverty. Many people use this index to determine how many poor people there are in the United States. According to the poverty index, the minimum income level for a family of four in 1990 was $13,359 (see Table 8.3). The poverty-level income figures do not include income received in the form of noncash benefits, such as food stamps, medical care, and subsidized housing.

The official definition of poverty that we use for the poverty index was developed by the Social Security Administration in 1964. It was calculated in the following way. First, it estimated the national average dollar-cost of a frugal, but adequate diet. Then, because a 1955 study found that families of

For male-headed families, the figure was $24,804, though for female-headed families, the figure was $14,620 (*Statistical Abstract of the United States: 1991*). This has caused some sociologists to refer to the "feminization of poverty," a phrase referring to the disproportionate concentration of poverty among women.

If present trends continue, 60 percent of all children born today will spend part of their childhood in a family headed by a mother who is divorced, separated, unwed, or widowed. There is substantial evidence that women in such families are often the victims of poverty. Almost half of all female-headed families with children under the age of 18 are below the poverty line.

Not all female-headed families are the same, however. The feminization of poverty is both not as bad as, and much worse than, the above statement suggests. Families headed by divorced mothers are doing better than the 50 percent figure, while families headed by never-married mothers are doing much worse.

What accounts for the fact that never-married mothers are so much poorer than their divorced

TABLE 8.3

Poverty Levels Based on Income for Families and Unrelated Individuals: 1989

Size of Unit	Income
1 person	$6,652 (1990)
Under 65	6,451
Over 65	5,947
2 persons	8,076
Under 65	8,343
Over 65	7,501
3 persons	9,885
4 persons	13,359 (1990)
5 persons	14,990
6 persons	16,921
7 persons	19,162
8 persons	21,328
9 persons	26,848 (1990)

Source: United States Department of Commerce, Bureau of the Census, *Statistical Abstract of the United States: 1991.* Washington, DC: United States Government Printing Office, 1991, p. 430; United States Department of Commerce News, "1990 Median Household Income Dips, Census Bureau Reports in Annual Survey," September 26, 1991.

three or more people spent about one-third of their income on food, food costs were multiplied by three to estimate how much total cash income was needed to cover food and other necessities. The "poverty index" was not originally intended to certify that any individual or family was in "need." In fact, the government has specifically warned against using the index for administrative use in any specific program. Despite this warning people continue to use, or misuse, the poverty index and variations of it for a variety of purposes for which it was not intended. For example, those wanting to show that current government programs are inadequate for the poor will try to inflate the numbers of those living in poverty. Those trying to show that government policies are adequate for meeting the needs of the poor will try to show that the number of poor people is decreasing.

The poverty index has become less and less meaningful over time. However, its continued existence over the years has given it somewhat of a sacred character. Few people who cite it know how it is calculated and choose to assume it is a fair measure for determining the number of poor in the country.

The poverty index has never been a sufficiently precise indicator of need to make it an indisputable test of which individuals and families were poor and which were not. Regional differences in cost of living by themselves were enough to throw off the index's accuracy substantially. The federal government uses the same poverty level figures for every part of the country. That means the poverty threshold is the same in rural Mississippi as it is in Manhattan (O'Hare, 1988).

TABLE 8.4

Number of Poor and Poverty Rate

Year	Number of people in Poverty	Percent Below Poverty Level
1960	39,851,000	22.2
1965	33,185,000	17.3
1970	25,559,000	12.6
1975	25,877,000	12.3
1980	29,272,000	13.0
1985	33,272,000	14.0
1987	32,500,000	13.5
1989	31,500,000	12.8
1990	33,600,000	13.5

Source: United States Department of Commerce, Bureau of the Census, *Statistical Abstract of the United States: 1991.* Washington, DC: United States Government Printing Office, 1991, p. 462. United States Department of Commerce News, "1990 Median Household Income Dips, Census Bureau Reports in Annual Survey," September 26, 1991.

Adding to the problem of the poverty index is the fact that food typically accounts for a considerably smaller proportion of family expenses today than it did previously. If we were to try to develop a poverty index today we would probably have to multiply minimal food costs by a factor of five instead of three (Dukert, 1983).

When the federal government developed the poverty index in 1964, about one-quarter of federal welfare benefits were in the form of goods and services. Today noncash benefits account for about two-thirds of welfare assistance (O'Hare, 1988). For example, there are now about eight million

Poverty statistics may not adequately count homeless families who have no permanent address.

households who receive food stamps, valued at ten billion dollars, which is not considered "income" under existing poverty-index rules. Complicating the issue further, the market value of in-kind benefits, such as housing subsidies, school lunch programs, and health care services, among others, has been multiplied by a factor of forty. Including noncash benefits in any measure of poverty would require that we convert these benefits into income, an extremely difficult task.

The number of people living in poverty is also distorted by the fact that the Census Bureau's Current Population Survey is derived from households. It excludes all those people who do not live in traditional housing, specifically the growing numbers of the homeless which is estimated at anywhere from 350,000 to 2.5 million. People in nursing homes and other types of institutions are also not included in the poverty figures because of surveying techniques (O'Hare, 1988).

This is not to downplay the number of poor people in the United States. The basic fact is that trying to determine how many poor people there are depends on who you ask and what type of statistical maneuvering is involved.

Myths About the Poor

We are presented with a variety of views on poverty and what should be done about it. One side argues that more government aid and the creation of jobs is needed to combat what has been produced by structural changes in the national economy (Harrington, 1984). The other side contends that government assistance programs launched with the war on poverty in the mid-1960s have encouraged many of the poor to remain poor and should be eliminated for the able-bodied poor of working age (Murray, 1984).

Our perceptions of the poor shape our views of the various government programs available to help them. It is important that we have a clear understanding of who the poor are in order to direct public policy intelligently. There are a number of common myths about the poor that many Americans believe. Let us try to clear some of them up.

Myth 1: People Are Poor Because They Are Too Lazy to Work. Most of the able-bodied poor of working age are working or looking for work. Many of the poor adults who do not work have good reasons for not working. Many of them are ill or disabled, while many others are going to school (mostly teenagers in high school from poor families). There are also over two million poor who are retired.

In 1990, 40.3 percent of poor persons 15 years and over worked and 9.4 percent worked year round (United States Department of Commerce *News*, 1991). However, a person working forty hours a week, every week of the year at minimum wage, will not earn enough to lift a family of three out of poverty. The numbers of the working poor are increasing at an alarming rate. There are several reasons for this growth. First, although there are more jobs in the economy than ever before, many of these jobs are in low-paying service industries. A janitor or a cook at a fast food restaurant earns no more than minimum wage.

Secondly, the better jobs the poor formerly held are no longer part of the U.S. economy. Many companies, seeking sources of cheap labor, have set up manufacturing operations overseas, in order to increase their ability to compete in the world market. Finally, many of the working poor are women or young people with few marketable skills. Often, they are forced to settle for poorly paid, part-time work.

In many ways, the working poor are worse off than those on welfare. For example, a mother on welfare may be eligible for public housing and a variety of services that a working poor two-parent family may not be able to receive.

It is easy for the government to ignore the plight of the working poor. Scattered throughout the country and with no single voice to protest, they are relatively invisible and, therefore, easily forgotten.

Myth 2: Most Poor People Are Black and Most Black People Are Poor. Neither of these statements is true. Most poor people are white, not black. There are more than two times as many white poor people as black poor people. The poverty rate however, remains nearly three times higher for blacks than whites (31.9 versus 10.7 percent in 1990). (*Statistical Abstract of the United States: 1991.*)

One of the reasons that blacks are associated with the image of poverty is that they make up over half of the long-term poor. Another reason is that the war on poverty was motivated in part and occurred simultaneously with the civil rights movement of the 1960s (O Hare, 1987).

Myth 3: Most Poor People Live in Female-Headed Households. While it is true that a disproportionate share of poor households are headed by women, and that the poverty rate for female-headed families is extremely high, the majority of people in poverty do not live in female-headed families. In 1988, 16.2 million poor people lived in female-headed families, but 12.1 million lived in married-couple or male-headed families. The remainder of the poor, 14.9 million, live by themselves or with people not related to them (*Statistical Abstract of the United States: 1991*).

Myth 4: Most People in Poverty Live in Inner-City Ghettos. Nearly 36 percent of the poor live in central cities. About 26 percent of all poor families live in the suburbs, while 39 percent live in nonmetropolitan or rural areas.

Poverty is growing rapidly in areas not typically identified as poor. Many white suburbanites have been added to the poor, accounting for one-fourth of the growth in poverty in recent years (O'Hare, 1986).

GOVERNMENT ASSISTANCE PROGRAMS

The public appears to be quite frustrated and upset about perceived soaring welfare costs and growing poverty. Much of this frustration, however, stems from a misconception of what programs are behind the escalating government expenditures, a misunderstanding about who is receiving government assistance, and an exaggerated notion of the amount of assistance going to the typical person in poverty. Most government benefits go to the middle class. Many of the people reading this book would be surprised to know that they or their families may actually receive more benefits than those people typically defined as poor. The value of benefits going to the poor has actually fallen in recent years, while those going to the middle class have actually risen.

Government programs which provide benefits to families or individuals can be divided into three categories: (1) social insurance, (2) means-tested cash assistance, and (3) noncash benefits (see Table 8.5).

Social insurance benefits are not means-tested, meaning that you do not have to be poor to receive them. They go primarily to the middle class. Many people receiving payments from social insurance programs, such as Social Security retirement and unemployment insurance, feel they are simply get-

TABLE 8.5

Expenditures for Major Federal Government Assistance Programs, 1989

Social Insurance (Non-means Tested)	Billions	Means-Tested Cash Assistance	Billions
Social Security Retirement (Established in 1935 to provide cash payments to retired workers and their dependents)	230.8*	Education Aid (Student loans, college work-study programs, Head Start, and Pell grants)	10.0* (1988)
Social Security Disability Insurance (Cash payments to disabled workers over 50 and their dependents)	24.1*	**Means-Tested Noncash Benefits**	
Unemployment Insurance (Provides partial wage-replacement payments to workers who lose their jobs involuntarily)	13.2*	Medicaid (Covers most medical costs for individuals in AFDC families or eligible for Supplemental Security Income)	30.6 (1988)
		Housings Benefits (Provides public housing or subsidizes rent in non-public housings)	14.7 (1988)
Non-means Tested Cash Benefits		Food Stamps (Distributes coupons redeemable for food to individuals and families with incomes 130 percent of the poverty line)	13.3 (1988)
Medicare (Covers most medical costs for individuals eligible for Social Security retirement and disability payments)	98.3*	Subsidized School Lunches (Provides free and reduced lunches to students from low income families)	3.1 (1988)
Means-Tested Cash Assistance		* Indicates recipients of benefits are predominantly middle class	
Aid to Families with Dependent Children (Provides cash payments to needy families where one parent is absent or incapacitated)	10.3 (1988)	Amount Going to Predominantly Middle-Income Recipients ———376.4 billion Amount Going to Low-Income Recipients———82.3 billion	
Supplemental Security Income (Provides cash payments to needy, aged, blind, and disabled persons)	10.3 (1988)	*Source:* United States Bureau of the Census, *Statistical Abstract of the United States: 1991.* Washington, DC, 1991, pp. 359–63.	

About one-quarter of all children are dependent on welfare payments.

ting back the money they put into these programs. They accuse those of receiving benefits from means-tested programs of "getting something for nothing." This is not exactly true when we recognize that many social insurance recipients receive back far more than they put in, and the poor, the majority of whom work, pay taxes which contribute to their own mean-tested benefits.

Social insurance programs account for the overwhelming majority of federal cash assistance expenditures, and their share has been rising rapidly. Female-headed families in poverty, often portrayed as a heavy drain on the government treasury, accounted for only two percent of the federal outlays for human resources. In contrast, Social Security for the retired elderly, the vast majority of whom are middle class, accounted for 38 percent.

Means-tested cash assistance programs go mainly to the poor and include such items as Aid to Families with Dependent Children (AFDC), and Supplemental Security Income (SSI). As social insurance cash assistance has been rising, means-tested cash assistance to the poor has been falling. Between 1975 and 1985, the average annual payment per recipient in Social Security retirement benefits which are indexed to rise with inflation increased by 20 percent in constant dollars. Meanwhile, the average annual federal expenditure per family in the AFDC program, which is not indexed, fell by 20 percent in constant dollars.

Noncash assistance programs include items which are both means-tested such as Medicaid, food stamps, subsidized housing, free or reduced-price school lunch programs, and non-means-tested, such Medicare and subsidized lunches for all students in participating schools. The middle class again wins out in federal noncash assistance. Medicare outlays

are at least 50 percent more than the combined expenditures for the four above mentioned major noncash benefit programs for the poor.

WORLDWIDE COMPARISONS

It appears that economic rewards are more unequally distributed in the United States than elsewhere in the Western industrialized world. In addition, the United States experiences more poverty than other capitalist countries with similar standards of living. In one international study the poverty rates for children, working-age adults, and the elderly were tabulated for a variety of countries.

The results show (see Table 8.6) that the United States has been moderately successful in holding down poverty among the elderly. The American elderly experience far less poverty than the elderly in Great Britain, approximately the same as the old in Norway and West Germany, and much higher poverty than the elderly in Canada and Sweden.

The United States has been much less successful in keeping children and working-age adults out of poverty. The U.S. child poverty rate is 60 percent higher than the rate in Great Britain, nearly 80 percent higher than the rate in Canada, and more than double the rate in the other three countries.

How has it happened that the United States has made progress in combating poverty among the elderly, but not among other groups? Since 1960 a variety of social policies have been enacted that have improved the standard of living of the elderly relative to that of the younger population. Social Security benefits were significantly increased and protected against the threat of future inflation, medicare provided the elderly with national health insurance,

TABLE 8.6

Poverty Rates Among Children, Working-Age Adults, and the Elderly in Six Nations

Country	Children	Working-Age Adults	The Elderly
United States	19.0% (1989)	12.8% (1989)	11.4% (1989)
United Kingdom	10.7	6.9	37.0
Canada	9.6	7.5	4.8
West Germany	8.2	6.5	15.4
Norway	7.6	7.1	18.7
Sweden	5.1	6.7	2.1

Source: Timothy Smeeding, Barbara Doyle Torrey, and Martin Rein, "Patterns of Income and Poverty: The Economic Status of the Young and the Old in Six Countries," Paper presented at the Conference on the Well-Being of Children and the Aged, the Urban Institute, February 1987 *(Statistical Abstract of the United States: 1991).*

while Supplemental Security Income provided a guaranteed minimum income, special tax benefits for the elderly protected their assets during the later years, and the Older American's Act supported an array of services specifically for this age group. As a consequence of these measures, poverty among the elderly has declined substantially. While 24.6 percent of those families 65 and over lived below the poverty level in 1970, only 6.6 percent did so in 1989. By contrast 14.9 percent of families age 25–34 lived below the poverty level in 1989 *(Statistical Abstract of the United States: 1991).*

To achieve this dramatic improvement in the condition of the elderly it has been necessary to increase greatly the federal money spent on this age group. Currently, expenditures on the population over age 65 capture 30 percent of the annual federal budget. This is for a population that currently represents 13 percent of the country. If these arrangements are maintained, projections show about 60 percent of the federal budget going to the elderly by the year 2030. A group that has suffered particularly under this shift in expenditures to the elderly is the young. While 14 percent of children lived in poverty in 1970, 19 percent do so today (Uhlenberg, 1987; *Statistical Abstract of the United States: 1991).*

It would also surprise many people if we noted that not only are the elderly as a group not poor, but that they are actually better off than most Americans. They are more likely than any age group to possess money market accounts, CDs, U.S.

The elderly in the United States tend to be better off than their counterparts in the United Kingdom, but worse off than the elderly in Canada and Sweden.

The Elderly—Rich or Poor

Special-interest groups in Washington claim that millions of older adults could be thrown into poverty if there are cuts in Social Security. Meanwhile, cruise-ship companies, automobile manufacturers, and land developers present images of energetic, attractive, silver-haired couples with substantial amounts of money.

Which of these two images is correct? Both of these presentations are accurate depictions of some older Americans. The special interest groups are talking about the poorest 20 percent of households containing the elderly. These households have an average net worth of about $3,400. Luxury cruise lines are interested in the richest 20 percent, who are worth almost 90 times as much.

Some of the confusion over the economic condition of older Americans stems from the unique ways in which they use and store money. The median income of the average American household peaks between the ages of 45 and 54. The incomes of households age 65 and older are two-fifths as high, on average. This would seem to indicate that older Americans are significantly less well off than younger Americans.

Yet lower incomes do not necessarily mean less spending power. Although the median income of households headed by people aged 65 and older is only about 40 percent that of households headed by 45-to-54 year-olds, the older group has a much smaller average household size, so their per capita discretionary income is actually higher than it is among the younger group.

To get a more accurate picture we should not focus on income, but instead on the financial condition of older Americans (for example, net worth, or the market value of all assets minus all debts). Older adults can finance major purchases by cashing in on stocks, real estate or other assets. This gives a more realistic picture of wealth than just income alone.

A Census Bureau survey found that median net worth rises from about $6,000 for a householder younger than 35 to $32,200 for those 35 to 44, to $57,500 for those aged 45 to 54, and just over $80,000 for those aged 55 to 64. The highest net worth is among those aged 65 to 69 ($83,500). From this point on it starts to drop.

Looking at net worth shows us that the oldest households con-

trol more wealth than do households in the highest-income age group. Moreover, the share of wealth controlled by working-age Americans is eroding, while the share controlled by the elderly is increasing.

Three factors have caused the elderly to control a substantial and increasing portion of the nation's wealth. First, the share of households headed by the elderly has been increasing, thereby increasing the aggregate wealth of older Americans. Second, the stock market growth has benefitted the affluent elderly who control a large portion of individual stock holdings. Finally, the escalation in home values in many states has boosted the net worth of the elderly because most older Americans own their homes.

These facts paint a picture different than normally thought to be the case. It all appears to depend on which factors one considers most important in understanding the issue.

Source: Excerpted and adapted from Charles F. Longino Jr., and William H. Crown, "Older Americans: Rich or Poor?" *American Demographics,* August 1991, pp. 48–53.

government securities, and municipal and corporate bonds. Their median household net worth is the second highest of any age group, surpassed only by the 55 to 64 year olds. They have the highest rate of homeownership of any age group. Seventy-seven percent of those 65 to 74 own homes, and most of these homes are fully paid for.

CONSEQUENCES OF SOCIAL STRATIFICATION

Studies of stratification in the United States have shown that social class affects many factors in a person's life. Striking differences in health and life expectancy are apparent among the social classes, especially between the lower-class poor and the other social groups. As might be expected, lower class people are sick more frequently than are others. For example, in Harlem, a predominantly African American ghetto of New York City, the rate of infection with tuberculosis is more than thirteen times the national average. The only other area in the Western hemisphere to exceed this rate is Haiti (*Newsweek*, February 22, 1988).

Tuberculosis is especially common among the homeless who are forced to live in city shelters. Even if treated properly and promptly, the treatment method makes the problem unlikely to go away. Sufferers are required to take several antibiotics daily over a period of a year—a regimen that is difficult for many of the poor and uneducated to follow. As a result, only about four in ten TB patients in New York City public hospitals get all the medication they need for a complete recovery (*Newsweek*, February 22, 1988).

Social class differences also affect the infant mortality rate. According to the Public Voice for Food and Health Policy, the 320 poorest rural counties in the country have an infant mortality rate that is 45 percent higher than the national average. African American teenagers between fifteen and nineteen who become pregnant are more than twice as likely as white teenagers to have the baby die. In addition, a black mother is more than three times as likely to die giving birth than a white mother (Statistical Abstract of the United States: 1991).

Diet and living conditions also give a distinct advantage to the upper classes because they have access to better and more sanitary housing and can afford more balanced and nutritious food. A direct consequence of this situation is seen in each social class's life-expectancy pattern. Not surprisingly, lower class people do not live as long as do those in the upper classes. White males born in 1989 have a life expectancy over five years longer than that for black males, many of whom are concentrated in the lower-income brackets (*Statistical Abstract of the United States: 1991*).

Family, childbearing, and child-rearing patterns also vary according to social class. Women in the higher-income groups who have more education tend to have fewer children than do lower-class women with less schooling. Women more often head the family in the lower class, compared with women in the other groups. Middle-class women discipline their children differently than do working-class mothers. The former will punish boys and girls alike for the same infraction, whereas the latter

There is a direct relationship between a person's social class and the possibility of his or her arrest, conviction, and sentencing if accused of a crime.

often have different standards for sons and daughters. Also, middle-class mothers will judge the misbehaving child's intention, whereas working-class women are more concerned with the effects of the child's action.

There is a direct relationship between a person's social class and the possibility of his or her arrest, conviction, and sentencing if accused of a crime. For the same criminal behavior the poor are more likely to be arrested; if arrested, they are more likely to be charged; if charged, more likely to be convicted; if convicted, more likely to be sentenced to prison; and if sentenced, more likely to be given longer prison terms than members of the middle and upper classes.

The poor are singled out for harsher treatment at the very beginning of the criminal justice system. Although many surveys show that almost all people admit to having committed a crime for which they could be imprisoned, the police are prone to arrest a poor person and release, with no formal charges, a higher-class person for the same offense. A well-to-do teenager who has been accused of a criminal offense is frequently just held by the police at the station house until the youngster can be released to the custody of the parents; poorer teenagers who have committed the same kind of crime more often are automatically charged and referred to juvenile court.

The poor tend to commit violent crimes and crimes against property—they have little opportunity to commit such white-collar crimes as embezzlement, fraud, or large-scale tax evasion—and they are much more severely punished for their crimes than upper-class criminals are for theirs. Yet white-

SOCIOLOGICAL CONTROVERSY

What Produces the Gap Between the Rich and the Poor?

There are approximately 663,000 families that fall into that lofty category of being in the top one percent of income earners in the United States. Even though it takes a family income of $232,320 to be part of the top one percent, the average for this group is considerably higher and stood at $515,600 in 1990. The average family incomes for these people nearly doubled between 1980 and 1990.

Before 1973, incomes rose equally for poor, middle class and wealthy families. Since that time the economy of the 1980s helped lift the incomes of the rich, but not the poor. As the wealth of the rich doubled during the 1980s, the poor watched their already low incomes slide five percent to a 1990 average of $9,800. This helped make the gap between the rich and the poor its widest in decades.

How did this happen? As with so many social issues the answers are not all that easy and include a number of possible explanations.

Many people are inclined to say that the rich grew richer at the expense of the poor. This view is difficult to support. The poor had so little to begin with that it is impossible for them to account for the dollar gains of the rich. There are three trends we can point to that converged to widen income inequality.

1. *Growth of Underclass.* The 1980s saw a substantial growth in the underclass, much of it minority and young. For example, the number of unwed mothers who make up the poorest families of all increased tenfold from 1970 to 1990 to 2.8 million. Politicians may argue over why the underclass is growing, but it appears that these people have fallen so far behind that an upward turn in our economy cannot help them.

2. *Investment Earnings.* Investment opportunities and financial speculation fueled during the 1980s helped increase the wealth of the rich. Census Bureau figures show that 99 percent of all families—even the well-off upper-middle class—depend on work salaries for most of their income. Not so for the top one percent of families who make the majority of their income from interest, dividends, and other investment income.

3. *Need for Educated Workers.* Our society has become very dependent on an educated workforce, and in the middle class there has been a noticeable split between the earnings of the highly skilled and unskilled. This is due to the decline in American manufacturing and blue-collar jobs. The median weekly wage of blue-collar workers has dropped almost 10 percent in the last decade. At the same time the earnings of college graduates have risen sharply in comparison with high-school graduates. Incomes of college educated families have increased nearly as much as those of the top one percent group. Families with only high-school degrees have watched theirs fall (U.S. Bureau of Census).

Unless there are dramatic changes, the trend points in the direction of a nation with drastically greater inequities between the well-to-do and those who are unable to obtain the staples of the American Dream.

collar crimes are far more damaging and costly to the public than poor-people crimes. It has been estimated by the government that white-collar crimes cost over $40 billion a year—more than ten times the total amount of all reported thefts and over 250 times the amount taken in all bank robberies!

Even the language used to describe the same crime committed by an upper-class criminal and a poor one reflects the disparity in the treatment they receive. The poor thief who takes $2,000 is accused of stealing and usually receives a stiff prison sentence. The corporate executive who embezzles $200,000 merely has "misappropriated" the funds and is given a token punishment, such as a suspended sentence or even no arrest at all on the promise to make restitution. A corporation often can avoid criminal prosecution by signing a "consent decree," which is in essence a statement that it has done nothing wrong and promises never to do it again. Were this ploy available to ordinary burglars, the police would have no need to arrest them; a burglar

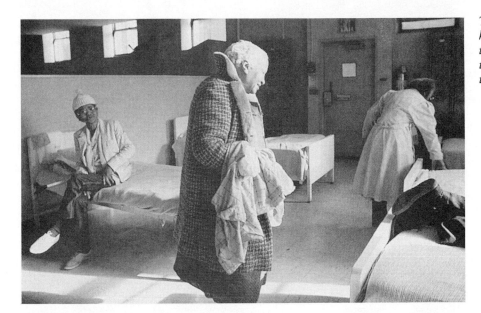

The mentally ill among the homeless are the least likely to reach out for help and the most likely to remain on the streets.

would merely need to sign a statement promising never to burgle again and file it with the court.

Once charged, the poor are usually dependent on court-appointed lawyers or public defenders to handle their cases. The better off rely on private lawyers who have more time, resources, and personal interests for defending their cases.

If convicted of the same kind of crime as a well-to-do offender, the poor criminal is more likely to be sentenced and will generally receive a longer prison term. A study of individuals with no prior records convicted in federal courts showed that 84 percent of the nonpoor were recommended for probation, whereas only 73 percent of the poor were so treated. As for prison terms, the sentence for burglary, a crime of the poor, is generally over twice as long as that for fraud, while a robber will draw an average sentence more than six times longer than an embezzler. The end result is a prison system heavily populated by the poor (Reimann, 1979).

Another serious consequence of social stratification is mental illness. The types of mental illness suffered seem to be correlated with social class, as is the likelihood of spending time in a mental hospital (Hollingshead and Redlich, 1958; Bottomore, 1966; Jencks et al., 1972). Studies have also shown that at least one-third of all homeless people suffer from schizophrenia, manic-depressive psychosis, or other mental disorders. These people are the least likely to reach out for help and the most likely to remain on the streets in utter poverty and despair year after year (Torrey, 1988).

Thus, social class has very real and immediate consequences for individuals. In fact, class membership affects the quality of people's lives more than any other single variable.

CHAPTER

▪ 9 ▪

Racial and Ethnic Minorities

The Concept of Race
  Genetic Definitions
  Legal Definitions
  Social Definitions

The Concept of Ethnic Group

The Concept of Minorities

Problems in Race and Ethnic Relations
  Prejudice
  Discrimination
  Institutionalized Prejudice and
    Discrimination

Patterns in Racial and Ethnic Relations
  Assimilation
  Pluralism
  Subjugation
  Segregation
  Expulsion
  Annihilation

**Racial and Ethnic Immigration to the
  United States**
  Illegal Immigration

**Racial and Ethnic Groups in the United
  States**
  White Anglo-Saxon Protestants
  African Americans
  Hispanics
  Jews
  Asian Americans
  Native Americans (Indians)

Prospects for the Future

Paul and Philip Malone, twin brothers, wanted to join the Boston Fire Department back in 1977. The only problem was that the brothers received scores of 69 and 57 respectively on the written portion of the test, when the passing grade was 82.

During this same period, Boston was under pressure to increase its minority population within the Fire Department, and had separate, and lower, passing grades for non-whites.

Although Paul and Philip were aware of the fact that they had a great-grandmother who was African American, they had not given the issue of race much thought. They decided to apply again, only this time they described themselves as African American on the application. Their new scores were considered passing because the city had imposed lower passing grades for minorities. The Malones were hired and listed in the records as black.

The Malones did their job well for ten and a half years, and then, in 1988 decided to apply for promotion. As their applications were reviewed, questions arose about their race. They continued to insist that their claim to being black was legitimate and produced photos of their great-grandmother. Their protests were to no avail, however, and they were fired for misrepresenting their race on the original application (*The Boston Herald*, September 26, 1988).

A similar case took place in Stockton, California. In a close election Ralph Lee White, a black man, lost his seat on the City Council to Mark Linton Stebbins, a pale-skinned, blue-eyed man with kinky reddish-brown hair. White claimed Stebbins would not represent the minority district because he was white. Stebbins claimed he was black.

Birth records indicated that Stebbins' parents and grandparents were white. He has five sisters and one brother, all of whom are white. Yet, when asked to declare his race he noted: "First, I'm a human being, but I'm black."

Stebbins did not deny that he was raised as a white person. He said he only began to consider himself black after he moved to Stockton. "As far as a birth certificate goes, then I'm white, but I am black. There is no question about that."

Stebbins now belongs to a black Baptist church and to the NAACP. Most of his friends are black. He has been married three times, first to a white woman, and then to two black women. He has three children from the first two marriages; two are being raised as whites, the third as black. He considers himself black—"culturally, socially, genetically."

Ralph Lee White remained unconvinced, especially with his council seat lost to Stebbins. Stebbins, however, believes the issue of race is tied to identifying with a community in terms of beliefs, aspirations, and concerns. He notes that a person's racial identity depends on much more than birth records.

These two examples, which on the one hand may seem slightly humorous, are at the same time related to some very serious issues. Throughout history, people have gone to great lengths to determine what race a person belonged to. In many states laws were devised to determine race, particularly in the case of mixed ancestry, such as the Malones. Usually these laws existed for the purpose of discriminating against certain minority groups. In this chapter we will explore these and other issues related to race and ethnicity as we try to understand how people come to be identified with certain groups and what that membership means.

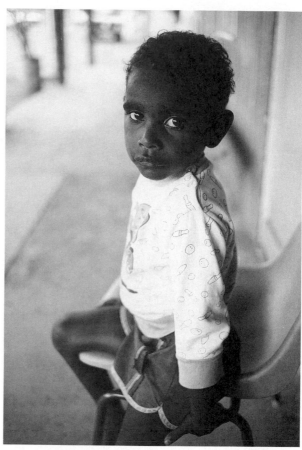

Throughout history, races have been defined along genetic, legal, and social lines, each presenting its own set of problems.

THE CONCEPT OF RACE

While the origin of the word is not known, the term *race* has been a highly controversial concept for a long time. Many authorities suspect that it is of Semitic origin, coming from a word that some translations of the Bible render as "race," as in the "race of Abraham" but that is otherwise translated as "seed" or "generation." Other scholars trace the origin to the Czech word *raz*, meaning "artery" or "blood;" others to the Latin *generatio* or the Basque *arraca* or *arraze*, referring to a male stud animal. Some trace it to the Spanish *ras*, itself of Arabic derivation, meaning "head" or "origin." In all these possible sources, the word has a biological significance that implies descent, blood, or relationship.

We shall use the term **race** to refer to *a category of people who are defined as similar because of a number of physical characteristics.* Often it is based on an arbitrary set of features chosen to suit the labeler's purposes and convenience. As long ago as

1781, German physiologist Johann Blumenbach realized that racial categories did not reflect the actual divisions among human groups. As he put it, "When the matter is thoroughly considered, you see that all [human groups] do so run into one another, and that one variety of mankind does so sensibly pass into the other, that you cannot mark out the limits between them" (Montagu, 1964). Blumenbach believed racial differences were superficial and changeable, and modern scientific evidence seems to support this view.

Throughout history, races have been defined along genetic, legal and social lines, each presenting its own set of problems.

Genetic Definitions

Geneticists define race by noting differences in gene frequencies among selected groups. The number of distinct races that can be defined by this method depends on the particular genetic trait under investigation. Differences in traits, such as hair and nose type, have proved of no value in making biological classifications of human beings. In fact, the physiological and mental similarities among groups of people appear to be far greater than any superficial differences in skin color and physical characteristics. Also, the various so-called racial criteria appear to be independent of one another. For example, any form of hair may occur with any skin color—a narrow nose gives no clue to an individual's skin pigmentation or hair texture. Thus, Australian aborigines have dark skin, broad noses, and an abundance of curly-to-wavy hair; Asiatic Indians have dark skin, narrow noses, and straight hair. Likewise, if head form is selected as the major criterion for sorting, an equally diverse collection of physical types will appear in each category thus defined. If people are sorted on the basis of skin color, therefore, all kinds of noses, hair, and head shapes will appear in each category.

Legal Definitions

By and large, legal definitions of race have not been devised to determine who was black or of another race, but who was *not white*. The laws were used in instances in which separation and different treatments were applied to members of certain groups. Segregation laws are an excellent example. If railroad conductors had to assign someone to either the black or white cars, they needed fairly precise guidelines for knowing whom to seat where. Most legal definitions of race in the United States were devices to prevent blacks from attending white schools, serving on juries, holding certain jobs, or patronizing certain public places. The official guidelines could then be applied to individual cases. The common assumption that "anyone not white was colored," although imperfect, did minimize ambiguity.

There has been, however, very little consistency among the various legal definitions of race that have been devised. The state of Missouri, for example, made "one-eighth or more Negro blood" the criterion for nonwhite status. Georgia was even more rigid in its definition and noted:

> The term "white person" shall include only persons of the white or Caucasian race, who have no ascertainable trace of either Negro, African, West Indian, Asiatic Indian, Mongolian, Japanese, or Chinese blood in their veins. No person, any of whose ancestors [was] . . . a colored person or person of color, shall be deemed to be a white person.

Virginia had a similar law but made exceptions for individuals with one-fourth or more Indian "blood" and less than one-sixteenth Negro "blood." These Virginians were regarded as Indians as long as they remained on an Indian reservation, but if they moved, they were regarded as blacks (Novit-Evans and Welch, 1983; Berry and Tischler, 1978).

Most of these laws are artifacts of the segregation era. However, if people think that all vestiges have disappeared, they are wrong. As recently as 1982 a dispute arose over a Louisiana law requiring anyone of more than one-thirty-second African descent to be classified as black. Louisiana's one-thirty-second law is actually of recent vintage, having been passed in 1971. Before this, racial classification depended on what was referred to as "common repute." The 1971 law was intended to eliminate racial classifications by gossip and inference. In September, 1982, Susie Guillory Phipps, having noticed that her birth certificate classified her as "colored," filed to have her classification changed to white. The state objected and produced an eleven-generation family tree tracing Phipps's ancestry back to an early eighteenth-century black slave and a white plantation owner (Novit-Evans and Welch, 1983).

Social Definitions

The social definition of race, which is the decisive one in most interactions, pays little attention to an individual's physical features or to blood lines. According to social definitions of race, if a person presents himself or herself as a member of a certain race and others respond to that person as a member of that race, then it makes little sense to say that he or she is not a member of that race.

In Latin American countries, having black ancestry or black features does not automatically define an individual as black. For example, in Brazil many individuals are listed in the census as, and are considered to be, white by their friends and associates even if they had a grandmother who was of pure African descent. It is much the same in Puerto Rico, where anyone who is not obviously black is classified as either mulatto or white. The Republic of South Africa has historically used sharp distinctions between the races to control access to economic and political power. The white Afrikaners and descendants of English settlers were at the top of the ladder, and blacks at the very bottom. South Africa's two other legally recognized races, Asians and coloreds (people of mixed racial heritage) held social positions intermediate to the dominant whites and subordinant blacks. Although the dismantlement of apartheid began in 1992, the vestiges of such long-term institutionalized prejudice and discrimination are likely to remain for decades to come.

The U.S. Census relies on self-definition for racial classification and does not apply any legal or genetic rules. In the 1990 census the term *race* did not appear, though respondents were asked an open-ended question about their ancestry, with 15 possible groups listed. If a person of mixed racial parentage could not provide a single response to the question, the race of the person's mother was used. If a single response could not be provided for the mother, then the first race listed was used.

THE CONCEPT OF ETHNIC GROUP

An **ethnic group** *is a group with a distinct cultural tradition with which its own members identify and which may or may not be recognized by others* (Glazer and Moynihan, 1975). An ethnic group need not necessarily be a numerical minority within a nation (although the term sometimes is used that way).

Many ethnic groups form subcultures (see Chapter 3). They usually possess a high degree of internal loyalty and adherence to basic customs, making for similarity in family patterns, religion, and cultural values. They often possess distinctive folkways and mores; customs of dress, art, and ornamentation; moral codes and value systems; and patterns of recreation. There is usually something to which the whole group is devoted, such as a monarch, a religion, a language, or a territory. Above all there is a feeling of association. The group's members are aware of a relationship because of a shared loyalty to a cultural tradition. The folkways may change, the institutions may become radically altered, and the object of allegiance may shift from one trait to another, but loyalty to the group and the consciousness of belonging remain as long as the group exists.

Political unification is not an essential feature of ethnic groups. An ethnic group may or may not have its own separate political unit; it may have had one in the past; it may aspire to have one in the future; or its members may be scattered through existing countries. Accordingly, despite their unique cultural features, many ethnic groups—Arabs, French Canadians, Flemish, Scots, Jews, and Pennsylvania Dutch, for example—are part of larger political and cultural units.

THE CONCEPT OF MINORITIES

Whenever race and ethnicity are discussed, it is usually assumed that the object of the discussion is a minority group. Technically this is not always

Many ethnic groups form subcultures with a high degree of internal loyalty and adherence to basic customs.

true, as we shall see shortly. A minority is often thought of as being small in number. The concept of minority, rather than implying a small number, should be thought of as implying differential treatment and exclusion from full social participation by the dominant group in a society. In this sense we shall use Louis Wirth's definition of a **minority** as *a group of people who, because of physical or cultural characteristics, are singled out from others in the society in which they live for differential and unequal treatment, and who therefore regard themselves as objects of collective discrimination* (Linton, 1945).

In his definition, Wirth speaks of "physical and cultural characteristics" and not of gender, age, disability, or undesirable behavioral patterns. It is obvious he is referring to racial and ethnic groups in his definition of minorities. Some writers have suggested, however, that many other groups are in the same position as those more commonly thought of as minorities and endure the same sociological and psychological problems. In this light, women, homosexuals, adolescents, the aged, the handicapped, the radical right or left, and intellectuals can be thought of as minority groups.

PROBLEMS IN RACE AND ETHNIC RELATIONS

All too often when people with different racial and ethnic identities come together, frictions develop. People's suspicions and fears are often aroused by those whom they feel to be "different."

Prejudice

There are many definitions of prejudice. Prejudice, one popular way of putting it states, is being down on something you are not up on, the implication being that prejudice results from a lack of knowledge of or familiarity with the subject. People, particularly those with a strong sense of identity, often have feelings of prejudice toward others who are not like themselves. Literally, *prejudice* means a "prejudgment." According to Louis Wirth (1944), prejudice is "an attitude with an emotional bias." But there is a problem with this definition. All of us, through the process of socialization, acquire attitudes, which may not be in response only to racial and ethnic groups but also to many things in our environment. We come to have attitudes toward cats, roses, blue eyes, chocolate cheesecake, television programs, and even ourselves. These attitudes run the gamut from love to hate, from esteem to contempt, from loyalty

to indifference. How have we developed these attitudes? Has it been through the scientific evaluation of information, or by other, less logical means?

For our purposes we shall define **prejudice** as *an irrationally based negative, or occasionally positive, attitude toward certain groups and their members.*

Although exploring the cause of prejudice is beyond the scope of this book, we can list some of the uses to which prejudice is put and the social functions it serves. First, a prejudice, simply because it is shared, helps draw together those who hold it. It promotes a feeling of "we-ness," of being part of an in-group—and it helps define group boundaries. Especially in a complex world, belonging to an in-group and consequently feeling "special" or "superior" can be an important social identity for many people.

Mexicans who live in the provinces have a we/them attitude with respect to those who live in Mexico City, the country's capital. They complain that "guachos," as Mexico City natives are called, are a "plundering species" which, according to author Jose Teheran, is "contemptuous of the habits and customs of others; indifferent, impudent, infallible, and excessively cunning of tongue; underhanded, greedy and capable of anything." In truth, residents of Mexico City have a more aggressive, competitive lifestyle than other Mexicans—a lifestyle that makes them objects of prejudice, disdain, and sometimes violence. A nine-year-old boy, who moved from the capital to a small provincial city, died after he was beaten by his classmates (Rohter, 1988).

Second, when two or more groups are competing against one another for access to scarce resources (jobs, for example), it makes it easier if one can write off his or her competitors as somehow less than human or inherently unworthy. Nations at war consistently characterize each other negatively, using terms that seem to deprive the enemy of any humanity whatsoever.

Third, psychologists suggest that prejudice allows us to project onto others those parts of ourselves that we do not like and therefore try to avoid facing. For example, most of us feel stupid at one time or another. How comforting it is to know that we belong to a group that is inherently more intelligent than another group! Who does not feel lazy sometimes? But how good it is that we do not belong to that group—the one everybody knows is lazy!

Of course, prejudice also has many negative consequences, or *dysfunctions*. For one thing, it limits our vision of the world around us, reducing social complexities and richness to a sterile and empty caricature. Aside from this individual effect, prejudice also has negative consequences for the whole of society. Most notably, prejudice is the necessary ingredient of discrimination, a problem found in many societies—including our own.

Discrimination

Prejudice is a subjective feeling, whereas discrimination is an overt action. **Discrimination** *refers to the differential treatment, usually unequal and injurious, accorded to individuals who are assumed to belong to a particular category or group.* At one time or another, most minorities in this country have been subjected to differential treatment limiting opportunity (McBride, 1988).

Prejudice does not always result in discrimination. Although our attitudes and our overt behavior are closely related, they are neither identical nor dependent on each other. We may have feelings of antipathy without expressing them overtly or even giving the slightest indication of their presence. This simple fact—namely, that attitudes and overt behavior vary independently—has been applied by Robert Merton to the classification of racial prejudice and discrimination. There are, he believes, the following four types of people.

UNPREJUDICED NONDISCRIMINATORS

These people are neither prejudiced against the members of other racial and ethnic groups nor do they practice discrimination. They believe implicitly in the American ideals of justice, freedom, equality of opportunity, and dignity of the individual. Merton recognizes that these people are properly motivated to spread the ideals and values of this creed and to fight against those forms of discrimination that make a mockery of it. At the same time, unprejudiced nondiscriminators have their shortcomings. They enjoy talking to one another, engaging in mutual exhortation and thereby giving psychological support to one another. They believe their own spiritual house is in order, thus they do not feel pangs of guilt and accordingly shrink from any collective effort to set things right.

UNPREJUDICED DISCRIMINATORS

This type includes those who constantly think of expediency. Though they themselves are free from racial prejudice, they will keep silent when bigots speak out. They will not condemn acts of discrimination but will make concessions to the intolerant and will accept discriminatory practices for fear that to do otherwise would hurt their own position.

PREJUDICED NONDISCRIMINATORS

This category is for the timid bigots who do not accept the tenets of equality for all but conform to it and give it lip service when the slightest pressure is applied. Here belong those who hesitate to express their prejudice when in the presence of those who

Ku Klux Klan members are an example of what Robert Merton refers to as prejudiced discriminators.

are more tolerant. Among them are employers who hate certain minorities but hire them rather than run afoul of affirmative-action laws and labor leaders who suppress their personal racial bias when the majority of their followers demand an end to discrimination.

PREJUDICED DISCRIMINATORS   These are the bigots, pure and unashamed. They do not believe in equality, nor do they hesitate to give free expression to their intolerance both in speech and action. For them there is no conflict between attitude and behavior. They discriminate, believing that it is not only proper but in fact their duty to do so (Berry and Tischler, 1978).

Knowing a person's attitudes does not mean that that person's behavior always can be predicted. Attitudes and behavior are frequently inconsistent because of the nature and magnitude of the social pressures in a particular situation. The influence of situational factors on behavior can be traced in Figure 9.1.

Institutionalized Prejudice and Discrimination

Sociologists also tend to distinguish between individual and institutionalized prejudice and discrimination. When individuals display prejudicial attitudes and discriminatory behavior, it is often based on the assumption of the out-group's inferiority. By contrast, when there is **institutionalized prejudice and discrimination,** this *refers to complex societal arrangements that restrict the life chances and choices of a specifically defined group, in comparison with those of the dominant group.* In this way, benefits are given to one group and withheld from another. Society is structured in such a way that people's values and experiences are shaped by a prejudiced social order. Discrimination is seen as a by-product of a purposive attempt to maintain social, political, and economic advantage (Davis, 1979).

Some people argue that institutionalized prejudice and discrimination are responsible for the substandard education that many blacks receive in

FIGURE 9.1

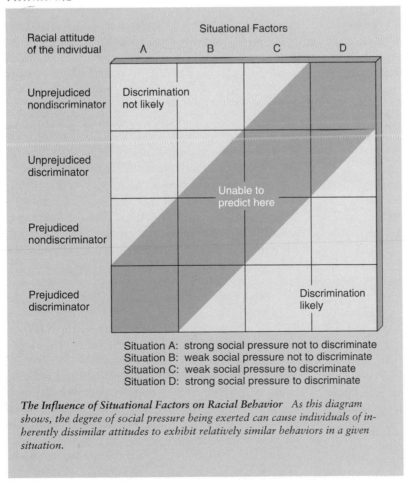

Situation A: strong social pressure not to discriminate
Situation B: weak social pressure not to discriminate
Situation C: weak social pressure to discriminate
Situation D: strong social pressure to discriminate

The Influence of Situational Factors on Racial Behavior   As this diagram shows, the degree of social pressure being exerted can cause individuals of inherently dissimilar attitudes to exhibit relatively similar behaviors in a given situation.

the United States. Schools that are predominantly black tend to be inferior to schools that are predominantly white. The facilities for blacks are usually of poorer quality than are those for whites. Many blacks also attend unaccredited black colleges where the teachers are less likely to hold advanced degrees and are poorly paid. The poorer education that blacks receive is one of the reasons they generally are in lower occupational categories than whites are. In this way, institutionalized prejudice and discrimination combine to keep blacks in a disadvantaged social and economic position (Duberman, 1976).

PATTERNS IN RACIAL AND ETHNIC RELATIONS

Relations among racial and ethnic groups seem to include an infinite variety of human experiences. They range from curiosity and hospitality, at one extreme, to bitter hostility at the other. Although relations between different ethnic and racial groups appear to be utterly unpredictable and capricious, there is actually a limited number of outcomes when such groups come into contact. These include assimilation, pluralism, subjugation, segregation, expulsion, and annihilation. In some cases, these categories overlap—for instance, segregation can be considered a form of subjugation—but each has distinct traits that make it worth examining separately.

Assimilation

Assimilation *is the process whereby groups with different cultures come to share a common culture.* It refers to more than just dress or language and includes less tangible items such as values, sentiments, and attitudes. We are really referring to the fusion of cultural heritages.

The transfer of culture from one group to another is a highly complex process, often involving the rejection of ancient ideologies, habits, customs, language, and attitudes. It also includes the elusive problem of selection. Of the many possibilities presented by the other culture, which ones will be adopted? Why did the American Indians, for example, when confronted with white civilization, take avidly to guns, horses, rum, knives, and glass beads, while showing no interest in certain other features to which whites themselves attached the highest value?

In the process of assimilation, one society sets the pattern, for the give and take of culture seems never to operate on a fifty-fifty basis. Invariably one group has a much larger role in the process than the other does. Usually one society enjoys greater prestige than the other, giving it an advantage in the assimilation process, or one is better suited for the environment than the other, or one has greater numerical strength than the other. Thus the pattern for assimilation in the United States was set by the British colonists, and other groups were asked to adapt to their standards. This process has often been referred to as **Anglo conformity**—*the renunciation of the ancestral culture in favor of Anglo-American behavior and values* (Gordon, 1964; Berry and Tischler, 1978).

Although assimilation frequently has been a professed political goal in the United States, it has seldom been fully achieved. For example, consider the case of Native Americans (Indians). In 1924 they were granted full United States citizenship. Nevertheless, the federal government's policies regarding the integration of Native Americans into American society wavered back and forth until the Hoover Commission Report of 1946 became the guideline for all subsequent administrations. The report stated that:

> A program for the Indian peoples must include progressive measures for their complete integration into the mass of the population as full, tax-paying [members of the larger society].... Young employable Indians and the better cultured families should be encouraged and assisted to leave the reservations and set themselves up on the land or in business (Shepardson, 1963).

However, to this day, Native American groups remain largely unassimilated into mainstream American life. About 55 percent live on or near reservations, and most of the rest live in impoverished urban ghettos. In addition, many Native Americans who left the reservation for greater opportunity in America's cities are returning again. Despite the economic and lifestyle hardships they face on the reservation, their ethnic pride overrides any desire to assimilate (*Newsweek*, May 2, 1988).

Other groups, whether or not by choice, have also resisted assimilation. The Amish, for instance, have steadfastly maintained their subculture in the face of constant pressure to conform.

China provides an interesting example of what might be called reverse assimilation. Usually it is the defeated minority groups who are assimilated into the culture of the politically dominant group. In the seventeenth century, however, Mongol invaders conquered China and installed themselves as rulers. The Mongols were originally nomadic pastoralists;

however, they were so impressed with the advanced achievements of Chinese civilization that they gave up their own ways and took on the trappings of Chinese culture: language, manners, dress, and philosophy. During their rule, the Mongols were fully assimilated into Chinese culture.

Pluralism

Pluralism *or the development and coexistence of separate racial and ethnic group identities within a society,* is a philosophical viewpoint that attempts to produce what is considered to be a desirable social situation. When people use the term *pluralism* today, they believe they are describing a condition that seems to be developing in contemporary American society. They often ignore the ideological foundation of pluralism.

The person principally responsible for the development of the theory of cultural pluralism was Horace Kallen, born in the area of Germany known as Silesia. He came to Boston at the age of five and was raised in an orthodox Jewish home. As he progressed through the Boston public schools, he underwent a common second-generation phenomenon. He started to reject his home environment and religion and developed an uncritical enthusiasm for the United States. As he put it, "It seemed to me

Pluralism is a reaction against assimilationism and encourages minorities to celebrate their differences.

that the identity of every human being with every other was the important thing, and that the term American should nullify the meaning of every other term in one's personal makeup . . ."

While Kallen was a student at Harvard, he experienced a number of shocks. Working in a nearby social settlement, he came in contact with liberal and socialist ideas and observed people expressing numerous ethnic goals and aspirations. This exposure caused him to question his definition of what it meant to be an American.

This quandary was compounded by his experiences in the American literature class of Professor Barrett Wendell, who believed that Puritan traits and ideals were at the core of the American value structure. The Puritans, in turn, had modeled themselves after the Old Testament prophets. Wendell even suggested that the early Puritans were largely of Jewish descent. These ideas led Kallen to believe that he could be an unassimilated Jew and still belong to the core of the American value system.

After discovering that he could be totally Jewish and still be American, Kallen came to realize that the application could be made to other ethnic groups as well. All ethnic groups, he felt, should preserve their own separate culture without shame or guilt. As he put it, "Democracy involves not the elimination of differences, but the perfection and conservation of differences."

Pluralism is a reaction against assimilationism and the "melting-pot" idea. It is a philosophy that not only assumes that minorities have rights but also considers the lifestyle of the minority group to be a legitimate, and even desirable, way of participating in society. The theory of pluralism celebrates the differences among groups of people. The theory also implies a hostility to existing inequalities in the status and treatment of minority groups. Pluralism has provided a means for minorities to resist the pull of assimilation, by allowing them to claim that they constitute the very structure of the social order. From the assimilationist's point of view, the minority is seen as a subordinate group that should give up its identity as quickly as possible. Pluralism, on the other hand, assumes that the minority is a primary unit of society, and that the unity of the whole depends on the harmony of the various parts.

Switzerland provides an example of balanced pluralism that so far has worked exceptionally well (Kohn, 1956). After a short civil war between the Catholics and the Protestants in 1847, a new constitution—drafted in 1848—established a confederation of cantons (states), and church-state relations were left up to the individual cantons. The three major languages—German, French, and Italian—were declared official languages for the whole nation, and their respective speakers were acknowledged as political equals (Petersen, 1975).

Switzerland's linguistic regions are culturally distinctive. Italian-speaking Switzerland has a Mediterranean flavor; French-speaking Switzerland has obvious vestiges of the culture of France, and German-speaking Switzerland is distinctly Germanic. However, all three linguistic groups are fiercely pro-Swiss, and the German-speaking Swiss especially have strong anti-German sentiments.

Subjugation

In theory we could assume that two groups may come together and develop an egalitarian relationship. However, there are few cases in which racial and ethnic groups have established such a relationship. One of the more common consequences of the interaction between such groups has been subjugation—*the subordination of one group and the assumption of a position of authority, power, and domination by the other.* The members of the subordinate group may for a time accept their lower status and even devise ingenious rationalizations for it.

For the most part subjugation occurs because there are few instances in which group contact has been based on the complete equality of power. Differences in power will invariably lead to a situation of superior and inferior position. The greater the discrepancy in the power of the groups involved, the greater the extent and scope of the subjugation will be.

Why should different levels of power between two groups lead to the domination of one by the other? Gerhard Lenski (1966) proposed that it is because people have a desire to control goods and services. No matter how much they have, they are never satisfied. In addition, high status is often associated with the consumption of goods and services. Therefore, demand will exceed supply, and as Lenski claims, a struggle for rewards will be present in every human society. The outcome of this struggle thus will lead to the subjugation of one group by the other.

According to Lenski's argument, in many cases the efforts of one group to dominate another group are motivated by a desire to control goods and services. When a racial or ethnic group is placed in an inferior position, its people are often eliminated as competitors. In addition, their subordinate position may increase the supply of goods and services available to the dominant group.

Segregation

Segregation *is actually a form of subjugation, which refers to the act, process, or state of being set apart.* Segregation places limits and restrictions on the contact, communication, and social relations among groups. Many people think of segregation as a negative phenomenon—a form of ostracism imposed on a minority by a dominant group—and this is most often the case. However, for some groups, such as the Amish or Chinese, who wish to retain their ethnicity, segregation is voluntary.

The practice of segregating people is as old as the human race itself. There are examples of it in the Bible and in preliterate cultures. American blacks were originally segregated by the institution of slavery and later by both formal sanction and informal discrimination. Although some blacks formed groups that preached total segregation from whites as an aid to black cultural development, for most it is an involuntary and degrading experience. The word ghetto is derived from the segregated quarter of a city where the Jews in Europe were often forced to live. Today, **ghetto** is used to describe *any kind of segregated living environment.* Native-American tribes were often forced to choose segregation on a reservation in preference to annihilation or assimilation.

Expulsion

Expulsion *is the process of either indirectly or directly forcing a group to leave the territory in which it resides.* Indirect expulsion is usually accomplished by making life increasingly unpleasant for a group, as the Germans did for Jews after Adolf Hitler was appointed chancellor in 1933. Over the following six years, Jews were stripped of their citizenship, made ineligible to hold public office, removed from the professions, and forced out of the artistic and intellectual circles to which they had belonged. In 1938 Jewish children were barred from the public schools. At the same time the government encouraged acts of violence and vandalism against Jewish communities. These actions culminated in *Kristallnacht,* November 9, 1938, when the windows in Jewish homes, businesses and synagogues across Germany were shattered and Jewish individuals were beaten. Under these conditions, Jews left Germany by the thousands. In 1933 there were some 500,000 Jews in Germany; by 1940, before Hitler began his "final solution" (the murder of all remaining Jews) only 220,000 remained (Robinson, 1976).

Expulsion can also be accomplished through **forced migration,** *the relocation of a group through*

Orlando Patterson on Slavery and Freedom

When Harvard sociologist Orlando Patterson was in grade school in the West Indies, much was made of the May 24 observance of Empire Day. At the end of the day's festivities there was patriotic singing. Patterson was always struck by the last lines of 'Rule Britannia,' ("For Britons never, never, never shall be slaves").

It was back then, as a child in Jamaica, that Patterson's interest in the relationship between slavery and freedom was sparked. This interest eventually led him to write a doctoral dissertation at the London School of Economics on slavery in 18th-century Jamaica.

Patterson continued to be intrigued with the subject of slavery and what he believed was a "strange and troubling relationship between slavery and freedom." Patterson's fascination with the topic culminated in the book Freedom: Freedom in the Making of Western Culture (1991), which won the 1991 National Book Award for nonfiction. His book follows the relationship between slavery and freedom from the era of the Greeks and Romans through the rise of Christianity until the Middle Ages. Patterson argues that freedom became a quintessential value in Western culture because of the centrality of slavery in Western society. Patterson postulates that the concept of human freedom is distinctive to the West and evolved from slavery. In the following interview, Orlando Patterson discusses his views on slavery and freedom.

Most people in the West think that all humans desire freedom. That's also the way we think about all the things we value greatly. We make the assumption that they are natural, innate desires. If you test the assumption that everybody around the world naturally desires freedom, you are generally surprised to find that it's not the case. That's the basis of my book: It's an examination of our deep belief that it's natural to want freedom. That's not borne out if you study societies around the world, which has serious implications for how we deal with other countries—for example, China and some Southeast Asian societies.

If we believe that something like freedom is really good, what do we do when we discover that there are parts of the world where freedom is not even in their world view, parts of the world where freedom is not within the cultural or idealistic framework? In societies like those we have a problem. We can say to another country, "Freedom is good. You may not know it's good, but we do, and we're going to try to persuade you that it's good and maybe even pressure you to accept it." In effect, that's what we're doing when we say to the Chinese or the Islamic fundamentalists in Algeria, "You need freedom whether you think you do or not." The Chinese leaders may reply, "We have thousands of years of history, longer than yours, and we don't think that this thing freedom is an important part of our history and culture." At that point we can say, "Too bad, we

think freedom is better, and we're going to try to pressure you to become free."

Some societies hold certain values above freedom. Look at what's happening in Algeria, with the fundamentalist Islamic society. We know what their values are: the worship of Allah, obedience to the laws of the Koran, having a theocracy, a society that is not secularized. They want a collectivist ethos rather than a highly individualized one. Those are ideals, and who's to say that they are any worse or better than ours. We may find some of their laws abhorrent—cutting off hands to punish thieves, for example. We may deplore their laws concerning women. But if we look deeper than that, you see that their ideals are in fundamental conflict with the libertarian ideals of the West.

This is true for the Chinese also. The Chinese leadership has said that their society is superior to the ideals of a society that celebrates personal freedom. Especially personal freedom in its worst aspects such as greed, selfishness, alienation, poverty in the midst of affluence—those are all closely related to the value of personal freedom. So those are all valid criticisms. The Chinese are very articulate about them. And we can't be smug about those criticisms.

Sources: Charles E. Claffey, "Rewriting the Book on Slavery and Freedom," The Boston Globe, December 3, 1991, p. 61; D.C. Denison, "Orlando Patterson," The Boston Globe Magazine, February 23, 1992, pp. 8–9.

direct action. For example, forced migration was a major aspect of the United States government's policies toward Native-American groups in the nineteenth century. For example, when the army needed to protect its lines of communication to the West Coast, Colonel "Kit" Carson was ordered to move the Navajos of Arizona and New Mexico out of the way. He was instructed to kill all the men who resisted and to take everybody else captive. He accomplished this in 1864 by destroying their cornfields and slaughtering their herds of sheep, thereby confronting the Navajos with starvation. After a last showdown in Canyon de Chelly, some 8,000 Navajos were rounded up in Fort Defiance. They were marched on foot 300 miles to Fort Sumner, where they were taught the ways of "civilization" (Spicer, 1962).

Although expulsion is an extreme attempt to eliminate a certain minority from an area, annihilation is the most extreme action one group can take against another.

Annihilation

Annihilation *refers to the extermination of a racial or ethnic group,* most often through purposeful and deliberate action. In recent years it has also been referred to as *genocide,* a word coined to describe the crimes committed by the Nazis during World War II—crimes that induced the United Nations to draw up a convention on genocide.

Sometimes annihilation occurs as an unintended result of new contact between two groups. For example, when the Europeans arrived in the Ameri-

cas, they brought smallpox with them. Native American groups, the Blackfeet, the Aztecs, and the Incas, among many others, who had no immunity against this disease, were nearly wiped out (McNeill, 1976). In most cases, however, the extermination of one group by another has been the result of deliberate action. The native population of Tasmania, a large island off the coast of Australia, was exterminated by Europeans in the 250 years after the country was discovered in 1642.

The largest, most systematic program of ethnic extermination was the murder of 11 million people—close to six million of whom were Jews—by the Nazis before and during World War II. In each country occupied by the Germans, the majority of the Jewish population was killed. Thus, in the mid-1930s, before the war, there were about 3.3 million Jews in Poland, but at the end of the war in 1945 there were only 73,955 Polish Jews left (Baron, 1976). Among them, not a single known family remained intact.

Although there have been recent attempts to portray the holocaust as a secret undertaking of the Nazi elite that was not widely supported by the German people, historical evidence suggests otherwise. For example, during a wave of anti-Semitism (anti-Jewish prejudice, accompanied by violence and repression) in Germany in the 1880s—long before the Nazi regime—only 75 German scholars and other distinguished citizens protested publicly. During the 1930s the majority of German Protestant churches endorsed the so-called "racial" principles that were used by the Nazis to justify first the disenfranchisement of Jews, then their forced depor-

The Jews in this photo are arriving at the Nazi concentration camp known as Auschwitz. Most of these people were murdered and cremated within a few weeks as part of the German policy of genocide against the Jews.

tation, and finally their extermination (Jews were blamed for a bewildering combination of "crimes," including "polluting the purity of the Aryan race," and causing the rise of communism while at the same time manipulating capitalist economies through their "secret control" of banks).

It would seem, then, that the majority of Germans supported the Nazi racial policies, or at best were apathetic (Robinson, 1976). Although in 1943 both the Catholic church and the anti-Nazi Confessing church finally condemned the murder of innocent people and pointedly stated that race was no justification for murder, it is fair to say that even this opposition was "mild, vague, and belated" (Robinson, 1976). The very fact that such objections were raised points out that the Nazis' plan was not a well-kept military secret. The measure of its success is that some 60 percent of all Jews in Europe—36 percent of all Jews in the world—were slaughtered (computed from figures in Baron, 1976).

Another "race" also slated for extermination by the Nazis were the Gypsies, a people made up of small wandering groups who appear to be the descendants of the Aryan invaders of India and Central Eurasian nomads. For the last thousand years or so, Gypsy bands had spread throughout the continents, largely unassimilated (Ulc, 1975). In Europe they were widely disliked and constantly accused of small thefts and other criminal behavior.

The sheer magnitude and horror of the Nazi attempt at genocide provoked outrage and attempts by the nations of the world to prevent such circumstances from arising again. On December 11, 1946, the General Assembly of the United Nations passed by unanimous vote a resolution affirming that genocide was a crime under international law and for the commission of which both principals and accomplices alike would be held accountable and would be punished. The assembly called for the preparation of a convention on genocide that would define the offense more precisely and provide enforcement procedures for its repression and punishment. After two years of study and debate, the draft of the convention on genocide was presented to the General Assembly, and it was adopted. Article II of the convention defines genocide as:

> . . . any of the following acts committed with intent to destroy, in whole or in part, a national, ethnical, racial or religious group as such:
> 1. Killing members of the group;
> 2. Causing serious bodily or mental harm to members of the group;
> 3. Deliberately inflicting on the group conditions of life calculated to bring about its physical destruction in whole or part;
> 4. Imposing measures intended to prevent births within the group;
> 5. Forcibly transferring children of the group to another group.

The convention furthermore provided that any of the contracting parties could call on the United Nations to take action under its charter for the "prevention and suppression" of acts of genocide. In addition, any of the contracting parties could bring charges before the International Court of Justice.

Here in the United States, President Harry Truman submitted the resolution to the Senate on June 16, 1949, for ratification. However, the Senate did not act on the measure, and the United States did not sign the document. In 1984 President Ronald Reagan again requested the Senate to hold hearings on the convention so that it could be signed. The United States finally signed the document in 1988.

In the more than 40 years of its existence, the Genocide Convention has never been used to bring charges of genocide against a country, although numerous examples of genocide have occurred during that period. It appears to serve more of a symbolic purpose (asking nations to go on record that they are opposed to genocide), than it does as an effective means of actually dealing with actual instances (Berry and Tischler, 1978).

RACIAL AND ETHNIC IMMIGRATION TO THE UNITED STATES

Since the settlement of Jamestown in 1607, well over 45 million people have immigrated to the United States. Up until 1882, the policy of the United States was almost one of free and unrestricted admittance. The country was regarded as the land of the free, a haven for those oppressed by tyrants, and a place of opportunity. The words of Emma Lazarus, inscribed on the Statue of Liberty, were indeed appropriate:

> Give me your tired, your poor,
> Your huddled masses yearning to breathe free;
> The wretched refuse of your teeming shore.
> Send these, the homeless, tempest-tost to me,
> I lift my lamp beside the golden door!

To be sure, there were those who had misgivings about the immigrants. George Washington wrote to John Adams in 1794: "My opinion with respect to immigration is that except for useful mechanics and some particular descriptions of men or professions,

Between 1892 and 1924 some 16 million immigrants came through Ellis Island outside of New York City on the way to their new life in the United States.

there is no need for encouragement." Thomas Jefferson was even more emphatic in expressing the wish that there might be "an ocean of fire between this country and Europe, so that it would be impossible for any more immigrants to come hither." Such fears, however, were not widely felt. There was the West to be opened, railroads to be built and canals dug; there was land for the asking. People poured across the mountains, and the young nation was eager for population.

Immigration of white ethnics to the United States can be viewed from the perspective of *old migration* and *new migration*. The *old migration* consisted of people from northern Europe who came before the 1880s. The *new migration* was much larger in numbers and consisted of people from southern and eastern Europe who came between 1880 and 1920. The ethnic groups that made up the *old migration* included the English, Dutch, French, Germans, Irish, Scandinavians, Scots, and Welsh. The *new migration* included Poles, Hungarians, Ukrainians, Russians, Italians, Greeks, Portuguese, and Armenians.

Figure 9.2 shows the number of immigrants that came to the United States in each year from 1820 to 1990. The *new migration* sent far more immigrants to the United States than the *old migration*. The earlier immigrants felt threatened by the waves of unskilled and uneducated newcomers whose appearance and culture were so different from their own. Public pressure for immigration restriction increased. After 1921 quotas were established limiting the number of people that could arrive from any particular country. The quotas

were specifically designed to discriminate against potential immigrants from the southern and eastern European countries. The discriminatory immigration policy remained in effect until 1965 when a new policy was established.

In Table 9.1 you will see a listing of the people that have been excluded from immigrating to the United States during various periods. As you can see, we were much more lenient during the early days of our history. However, even with our periods of restrictive immigration, the United States has had one of the most open immigration policies in the world, and we continue to take in more legal immigrants than the rest of the world combined (Kotkin and Kishimoto, 1988).

In contrast to the stereotype of the European immigrant arriving at Ellis Island as in previous eras, today's immigrant is likely to be from the Orient and arrive by plane. Since 1970, Asian immigrants have been rising rapidly both in number and as a percentage of all immigrants to the United States. In fact, the United States's Asian immigrant population is increasing faster than the foreign-born population from Mexico, Central America, the Caribbean, and Canada combined. Europe, on the other hand, no longer sends many of its natives to our shores. Even with the massive immigration from Europe during our early history, only 26 percent of today's foreign born population came from Europe, and only 13 percent of them have arrived since 1980 (Woodrow, Passel, and Warren, 1987).

During the 1980s, six million legal immigrants entered the United States, up from 4.2 during the 1970s and 3.2 million during the 1960s. Immigra-

FIGURE 9.2

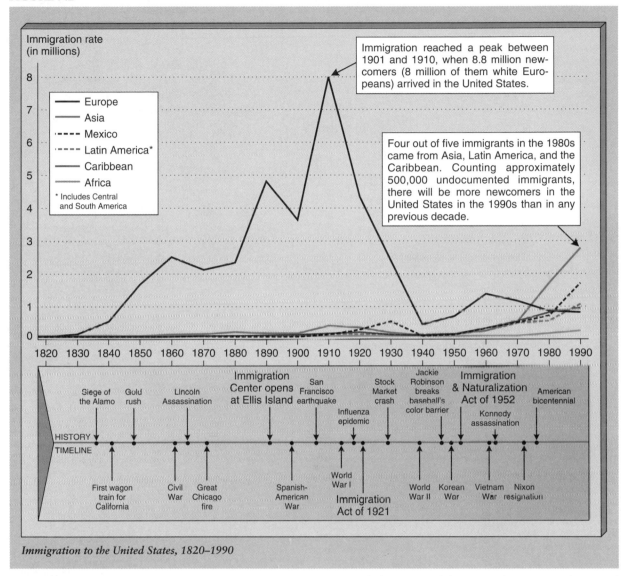

Immigration reached a peak between 1901 and 1910, when 8.8 million newcomers (8 million of them white Europeans) arrived in the United States.

Four out of five immigrants in the 1980s came from Asia, Latin America, and the Caribbean. Counting approximately 500,000 undocumented immigrants, there will be more newcomers in the United States in the 1990s than in any previous decade.

Immigration to the United States, 1820–1990

Source: Chart by Neil Pinchin, published in the October 13, 1991, issue of *The Boston Globe*. Copyright © 1991 and reprinted courtesy of *The Boston Globe*.

tion during the 1990s will be even greater. The Immigration and Naturalization Service estimates more than 700,000 immigrants per year starting in 1992. A contributing factor will be the 1990 law that allows people who have no family in the United States to immigrate if they have highly prized work skills, or if they are willing to make a significant business investment (Riche, 1991).

Illegal Immigration

Since 1970 illegal immigrants have figured prominently in the ethnic makeup of certain regions of the United States. It is estimated that there are anywhere between 2.5 and 4.7 million illegal immi-

grants in the United States, and the number is growing by 200,000 a year. It is estimated that 55 percent of the illegal immigrants are from Mexico. Latin America as a whole accounts for 77 percent. Of the remainder about 10 percent come from Asia, 8.5 percent from Europe and Canada, and slightly over four percent from the rest of the world.

The vast majority (71 percent) of illegal immigrants are between ages 15 and 39. Very few are over 65. About half of all illegal immigrants live in California. Other states likely to attract illegal immigrants are New York, Texas, Illinois, and Florida.

In 1986 Congress passed the Immigration Reform and Control Act, a law designed to control

TABLE 9.1

United States Immigration Restrictions

1769–1875	No restrictions Open-door policy
1875	No convicts No prostitutes
1882	No idiots No lunatics No persons likely to need public care Start of head tax
1882–1943	No Chinese
1885	No gangs of cheap contract laborers
1891	No immigrants with dangerous contagious diseases No paupers No polygamists Start of medical inspections
1903	No epileptics No insane persons No beggars No anarchists
1907	No feeble-minded No children under 16 unaccompanied by parents No immigrants unable to support themselves because of physical of mental defects
1917	No immigrants from most of Asia or the Pacific Islands No adults unable to read and write Start of literacy tests
1921	No more than 3 percent of foreign-born of each nationality in U.S. in 1910; total about 350,000 annually
1924–1927	National Origins Quota Law; no more than 2 percent of foreign-born of each nationality already in U.S. in 1890: total about 150,000 annually
1940	Alien Registration Act; all aliens must register and be fingerprinted
1950	Exclusion and deportation of aliens dangerous to national security
1952	Codification, nationalization, and minor alterations of previous immigration laws
1965	National Origins Quota system abolished. No more than 20,000 from any one country outside Western Hemisphere: total about 170,000 annually. Start of restrictions on immigrants from other Western Hemisphere countries; no more than 120,000 annually. Preference to refugees, aliens with relatives here, and workers with skills needed in U.S.

Source: Smithsonian Institution.

the flow of illegal immigrants into the United States. The new law makes it a crime for employers, even individuals hiring household help, to knowingly employ an illegal immigrant.

The same law also provides legal status to illegal immigrants who entered the United States before 1982 and who have lived here continuously since then. This part of the law changed the status of more than two million formerly illegal immigrants.

RACIAL AND ETHNIC GROUPS IN THE UNITED STATES

What is America's racial and ethnic composition today? The United States is perhaps the most racially and ethnically diverse country in the world. Unlike many other countries, it has no ethnic group that makes up a numerical majority of the population. In the following discussion, we shall examine the major groups in American society.

White Anglo-Saxon Protestants

About 63,000,000 people claim some English, Scottish, or Welsh origin. These Americans of British origin are often grouped together as white Anglo-Saxon Protestants (WASPs). Although in numbers they are a minority within the total American population, they have been in America the longest (with the exception of Native Americans) and, as a group, have always had the greatest economic and political power in the country (Mills, 1963). As a result, white Anglo-Saxon Protestants often have acted as the ethnic majority in America, influencing other ethnic groups to assimilate or acculturate to their way of life, the ideal of Anglo conformity (Cole and Cole, 1954).

The Americanization of immigrant groups has been the desired goal of the dominant white Anglo-Saxon Protestants during many periods in American history. Contrary to the romantic sentiments expressed on the base of the Statue of Liberty, immigrant groups who came to America after the

Many illegal immigrants to the United States travel across the Rio Grande River into Texas.

British Protestants met with considerable hostility and suspicion.

The 1830s and 1840s saw the rise of the "native" American movement, directed against recent immigrant groups (and especially Catholics). In 1841 the American Protestant Union was founded in New York City to oppose the "subjugation of our country to control of the Pope of Rome, and his adherents" (Leonard and Parmet, 1971). Protestant religious organizations across America joined forces and urged "native" Americans to organize in order to offset "foreign" voting blocs. They also conducted intimidation campaigns against "foreigners" and attempted to persuade Catholics to renounce their religion for Protestantism (Leonard and Parmet, 1971).

As the twentieth century dawned, American sentiments against immigrants from Southern and Eastern Europe ran high. In Boston, the Immigration Restriction League was formed, which directed its efforts toward keeping out racially "inferior" groups—who were depicted as inherently criminal, mentally defective, and marginally educable. The league achieved its goals in 1924 when the government adopted a new immigration policy that set quotas on the numbers of immigrants to be admitted from various nations. Because the quotas were designed to reflect (and reestablish) the ethnic composition of America in the 1890s, they heavily favored the admission of immigrants from Britain, Ireland, Germany, Holland, and Scandinavia. This new policy was celebrated as a victory for the "Nordic" race (Krause, 1966).

Another expression of Anglo conformity was the Americanization Movement, which gained strength from the nationalistic passions brought on by World War I. Its stated purpose was to promote the very rapid acculturation of new immigrants. Thus federal agencies, state government, municipali-

About 63 million Americans proclaim some English, Scottish, or Welsh ancestry.

ties, and a host of private organizations joined in the effort to persuade the immigrant to learn English, take out naturalization papers, buy war bonds, forget his former origins and culture, and give himself over to "patriotic hysteria" (Gordon, 1975).

From World War II until the early 1960s, Anglo conformity was mostly an established ideal of the American way of life. In the last decades, there has been a strong organized reaction among other ethnic groups against Anglo conformity. Blacks led the way in the later 1960s with the Black Power Movement, and they were joined by Italian Americans, Mexican Americans (Chicanos), Puerto Ricans, Native Americans, and others. America once again is focusing on its ethnic diversity, and the assumptions of Anglo conformity are being questioned.

African Americans

African Americans represent the second largest racial group in the United States. According to the 1990 Census, there were approximately 29,986,060 blacks living in the country, accounting for 12.1 percent of the total population of 253,600,000 (U.S. Department of Commerce News, March 12, 1991 and January 1, 1992). In reality, the African-American population may be closer to 32 million because the Census Bureau estimates that nearly two million were missed in the 1990 count. The current percent of African Americans in the U.S. population is the largest since 1880. During the 1980s, the African-American population grew by more than 13 percent—double the growth of the white population (six percent) (O'Hare, Pollard, Mann, and Kent, 1991).

Roughly 84 percent of all African Americans live in urban areas, and about 53 percent live in the southern states (Bureau of the Census, 1990 Census data). This is a significant shift from the 1940s, when roughly 80 percent of American blacks lived in the South and worked in agriculture.

Black immigrants have been accounting for a greater share of all blacks in the United States in recent years. The majority of these black immigrants have come to the United States from the West Indian countries of Jamaica, Haiti, the Dominican Republic, Barbados, and Trinidad. In addition, a significant number of African blacks are also entering the United States each year. As a result of this trend, the percentage of black immigrants in the total black population is now greater than the percentage of nonblack immigrants in the total nonblack population. In some cities such as Miami,

Black immigrants have been accounting for an increasingly greater share of all blacks in the United States in recent years.

black immigrants have become a clearly distinguishable segment of the black population.

Still, there are only about 825,000 blacks born abroad, plus their descendants living in the United States, compared to the native-born black population of 30 million. Assuming an annual immigration of about 72,000 per year, projections would place the number of black immigrants and their descendants in the United States by the year 2000 at 2.5 million in a total black population of 33 million. By 2030, their numbers should nearly double to 4.8 million, whereas native-born blacks and their descendants would account for 37 million (American Demographics, 1984).

In 1989, the median annual income for African-American families was $20,200, a six percent rise over the 1980 figure after adjusting for inflation. The white family income has been increasing more rapidly however, and the ratio of African-American to white earnings has actually fallen from 61 percent in 1969 to 56 percent in 1989.

Why have African-American families lost ground over the last two decades? A major reason is the growth in female-headed families who earn only one-third the annual income of African-American married-couple families. Another factor is that the average African-American family has fewer members in the labor force than white families. Even if African Americans and whites held comparable jobs and earned equal pay, the higher number of wage earners per family for whites would still keep the average African-American family income below that of whites (O'Hare, Pollard, Mann and Kent, 1991).

Hispanics

The number of Hispanics in the United States grew 53 percent between 1980 and 1990, more than five times faster than the U.S. population as a whole. The 22,354,059 Hispanics in the United States in 1990 form the nation's second-largest minority. They are not a very well understood segment of the population. First, no one knows exactly how many Hispanics have crossed the border from Mexico as illegal immigrants. Second, many Americans of Hispanic descent do not identify themselves as "Hispanic" on census forms and are not counted as such.

The Hispanic population in the United States is made up of 13.5 million people of Mexican origin (60 percent of all Hispanics); 2.7 million of Puerto Rican origin (12 percent); 5.1 million of Other Hispanic origin (22.8 percent) and one million of Cuban origin (4.5 percent). (United States Department of Commerce *News*, June 12, 1991.)

According to one set of Census Bureau projections, there should be twice as many Hispanics in the United States as there are now shortly after the year 2000. At that point, the Spanish-origin population would be growing by one million people per year. Continuing at this pace, the Hispanic population would be four times its present size in the year 2030 and larger than the black population (See Figure 9.3). (Exter, 1987.)

The greatest concentrations of Hispanics live in Texas and California, but they are also found in large numbers in Arizona, New Mexico, Florida and in such northern cities as Denver; Hartford, Connecticut; Union City, New Jersey; and New York City. Interestingly, although the vast majority of Hispanics come from rural areas, 90 percent settle in America's industrial cities and surrounding

FIGURE 9.3

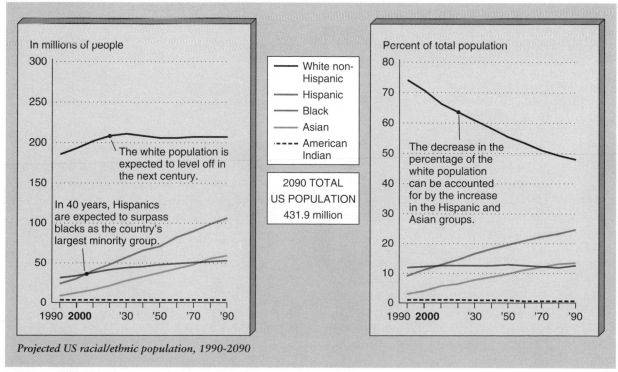

Projected US racial/ethnic population, 1990-2090

Source: Population Studies Center at The Urban Institute.

suburbs. Living together in tightly knit communities, they share their common language and customs. There are problems associated with this isolation, though (*U.S. News and World Report,* August 10, 1987). Seven out of ten Hispanic students attended segregated schools, up dramatically 55 percent from twenty years ago. This increase occurred at the same time as the percentage of blacks attending predominantly minority schools dropped from 76 percent to 63 percent. In addition, the need to master English is lessened by the fact that nearly everyone in the community speaks Spanish. As a result, more than half of all Hispanic adults are illiterate in English. Without needed language skills and with high school drop-out rates two to three times the rate of other students, nearly 25 percent of all Hispanic families have incomes below the poverty level. (Carmody, 1988).

MEXICAN AMERICANS   Hispanics of Mexican descent, also known as *Chicanos,* make up the majority of the Spanish speaking population in the United States. The main reason is proximity. The 1,936 mile border we share with Mexico is the site of millions of legal and illegal crossings each year.

The term *Chicano* is somewhat controversial. It has long been used as a slang word in Mexico to refer to people of low social class. In the United States the word came to be used to describe Mexicans who illegally crossed the border in search of work. Recently, however, many Mexican Americans have taken to using the term themselves to suggest a tough breed of individuals of Mexican ancestry who are committed to achieving success in this country and are willing to fight for it (Madsen, 1973).

In his study of Mexican Americans in Texas, William Madsen (1973) notes that among them, three levels of "acculturation" may be distinguished. Although American technology is appreciated by most Mexican Americans, one group has retained its Mexican peasant culture, at least in regard to values. Another group consists of persons torn between the traditional culture of their parents and grandparents on the one hand, and Anglo-American culture (learned in American schools) on the other. Many individuals in this group suffer crises of personal and ethnic identity. Finally there are those Mexican Americans who have acculturated fully and achieved success in Anglo-American society. Some remain proud of and committed to their ethnic origins, but others would just as soon forget them and assimilate fully into the Anglo-American world.

Mexican Americans have been exploited for many years as a source of cheap agricultural labor. Their median family income is $21,025, two-thirds of the income for whites (*Statistical Abstract of the United States: 1991*). In addition, 19 percent of all Mexican-American families are headed by women, compared to nine percent of all white families, and nearly a quarter of all births are out of wedlock (Chavez, 1988). Like blacks, Mexican Americans have yet to achieve true equality in the United States.

PUERTO RICANS   Another group included under the category of Hispanics are Puerto Ricans. In 1898

Mexican Americans have been exploited for many years as a source of cheap agricultural labor. Others have achieved various levels of success in Anglo-American society.

the United States fought a brief war with Spain and, as a result, took over the former Spanish colonies in the Pacific (the Philippines and Guam) and the Caribbean (Cuba and Puerto Rico). Puerto Ricans were made full citizens of the United States in 1917. Although government programs improved their education and dramatically lowered the death rate, rapid population growth helped keep the Puerto Rican people poor. American business took advantage of the large supply of cheap, nonunion Puerto Rican labor and built plants there under very favorable tax laws.

There are 2,728,000 Puerto Ricans in the United States. Many have migrated to the American mainland seeking better economic opportunities. Most make their homes in the New York City area but return frequently to the island to visit family and friends.

Puerto Ricans living in the United States have the lowest median family income of any Hispanic group. The median income of Puerto Rican families is $18,932 (Statistical Abstract of the United States: 1991). Ironically, the poverty of Puerto Rican families is due in part to the ease with which they can travel back and forth between their homeland and the United States. The desire to one day return permanently to Puerto Rico interferes with a total commitment to assimilate into American culture (*Time*, July 8, 1985).

CUBAN AMERICANS   Cuban Americans, for the most part, have come to the United States relatively recently. Only in the 1970s did they begin to have a visible cultural and economic impact on the cities where they have settled in sizable numbers.

Many Cubans came to the United States as a result of the 1959 revolution that catapulted Fidel Castro into power. At that time the rebel forces of Castro overthrew the Fulgencio Batista government. Castro, a Marxist, soon began a process of restructuring the social order, including the appropriation by the state of privately owned land and property. Professionals and business people who were part of the established Cuban society, felt threatened by these changes and fled to the United States. More than 155,000 Cubans immigrated to the United States between 1959 and 1962. As a whole, these immigrants have done extremely well in American society, having the distinct advantage of coming to the United States with marketable skills and money.

The second wave of Cuban immigration occurred in 1980 when Castro allowed people to leave Cuba by way of Mariel Harbor. The result was a flotilla of boats bringing 125,000 refugees to the United States. This second wave of immigration was poorer and less-well educated than the first. It also included several thousand prisoners and mental patients, many of whom were imprisoned in the United States as soon as they got off the boat. Others fled into Miami and other cities. Serious friction exists between these two waves of immigrants because of differences in background and social class.

Cubans are relatively recent immigrants, and

Miami, with 652,000 Cubans, has become known as "little Havana." Many shops and businesses cater to this Cuban population.

the first-generation foreign-born predominate. They are exiles who came to the United States not so much because they preferred the U.S. way of life, but because they felt compelled to leave their country. For these reasons most Cuban immigrants fiercely attempt to retain the culture and way of life they knew in Cuba. Of all the Hispanic groups, they are the most likely to speak Spanish in the home: Eight out of ten families do so.

Cubans are found largely in a few major cities. Nearly 65 percent live in Miami, which, with its 652,000 Cubans, and with Latins making up a larger percentage of the population than whites, has become a distinctively Cuban city. Most other Cubans live in New York City, Jersey City and Newark, Los Angeles, and Chicago, all of which are large centers for Hispanics in general.

Acculturation and assimilation has been slow in Miami in light of the fact that the Cuban community is so self-sufficient and has such a large base. There also appears to be a lack of social and cultural integration between Cubans and other Hispanic groups in U.S. cities with sizable and differentiated Spanish-speaking populations. Of the major Hispanic groups, only the Cubans have come as political exiles, and this has resulted in social, economic, and class differences. In the New York City area, Cubans and Puerto Ricans maintain a distinct social distance. Many Cubans feel or perceive that they have little in common with Puerto Ricans, Mexican Americans, or Dominicans.

The more than one million Cubans who live in the United States have fared better than any other Hispanic immigrant group. The median family income of Cubans is $26,858, a third higher than the earnings of the average Hispanic family. At the current rate of growth, the Cuban income could surpass the national median income within a few years.

Why have Cubans done so well? Some point to the fact that many Cubans who immigrated to the U.S. were middle-class educated people. They brought money and skills with them, as well as a determination to build a good life in the United States (Schwartz, 1988).

Jews

There is no satisfactory answer to the question "What makes the Jews a people?" other than the fact that they see themselves—and are seen by others—as one. Judaism is a religion, of course, but many Jews are nonreligious. Some think of Jews as a race, but their physical diversity makes this notion absurd. For more than two thousand years, Jews have been dispersed around the world. Reflecting this geographic separation, three major Jewish groups have evolved, each with its own distinctive culture: the *Ashkenazim*—the Jews of Eastern and Western Europe (excluding Spain); the *Sephardim*— the Jews of Turkey, Spain, and western North Africa; and the "Oriental" Jews of Egypt, Ethiopia, the Middle East, and Central Asia. Jews are not united linguistically. In addition to speaking the language of whatever nation they are living in, many Jews speak one or more of three Jewish languages: Hebrew, the language of ancient and modern Israel; Yiddish, a Germanic language spoken by Ashkenazi Jews; and Ladino, an ancient Romance language spoken by the Sephardim.

The first Jews came to America from Brazil in 1654, but it was not until the mid-1800s that large numbers of Jews began to arrive. These were mostly German Jews, refugees from European anti-Semitism. Then, with especially violent anti-Semitism erupting in Eastern Europe in the 1880s, there was a massive increase in Jewish immigration to America. It came in two waves: in the last two decades of the nineteenth century and in the first two decades of the twentieth.

Jewish immigration was similar to that of other groups, in that it consisted overwhelmingly of young people, though Jewish immigration also had some unique features. First, it was much more a migration of families than was that of other European immigrants, who were mostly single males. Second, Jewish immigrants were much more committed to staying here: Two-thirds of all immigrants to the United States between 1908 and 1924 remained, but 94.8 percent of the Jewish immigrants settled here permanently. Third, the Jewish immigrant groups contained a higher percentage of skilled and urban workers than did other groups. And fourth, especially after the turn of the century, there were many scholars and intellectuals among Jewish immigrants, which was not true of other immigrant groups (Howe, 1976).

These differences account for the fact that even though Jews encountered at least as much hostility from white Anglo-Saxon Protestants as did other immigrant groups (and also were subject to intense prejudice from Catholics), they have been relatively successful in pulling themselves up the socioeconomic ladder. Of the approximately six million Jews in America today, 53 percent of those working are in the professions and business (versus 25 percent for the nation as an average).

Asian Americans

Most Asian Americans are concentrated in the major metropolitan areas. Their percentage of the total

These Japanese Americans are about to be taken to Seattle by a special ferry, which will connect with a train to California, as part of their evacuation and internment during World War II.

population in these cities varies from 29.1 in San Francisco to 0.8 percent in Detroit. In Honolulu, 70.5 percent of the population is Asian or Pacific Islander (Statistical Abstract of the United States: 1991).

The first Asians to settle in America in significant numbers were the Chinese. Some 300,000 Chinese migrated here between 1850 and 1880 in order to escape the famine and war that plagued their homeland. Initially they settled on the West Coast, where they took back-breaking jobs mining and building railroads. However, they were far from welcome and were subjected to a great amount of harassment. In 1882 the government limited further Chinese immigration for 10 years. This limitation was extended in 1892 and again in 1904, before it was finally repealed in 1943. The state of California set special taxes on Chinese miners, and most labor unions fought to keep them out of the mines because they took jobs from white workers. In the late 1800s and early 1900s, numerous riots and strikes were directed against the Chinese, who withdrew into their "Chinatowns" for protection. The harassment proved successful. In 1880 there were 105,465 Chinese in the United States. By 1900 the figure had dropped to 89,863 and by 1920, to 61,729. The Chinese population in the United States began to rise again only after the 1950s (U.S. Bureau of the Census, 1976). The 1990 Census showed there were 1,645,472 ethnic Chinese in the United States

(United States Department of Commerce *News*, June 12, 1991), making them the largest group of Asian origin.

Japanese immigrants began arriving in the United States shortly after the Chinese—and quickly joined them as victims of prejudice and discrimination. Feelings against the Japanese ran especially high in California, where one political movement attempted to have them expelled from the United States. In 1906 the San Francisco Board of Education decreed that all Asian children in that city had to attend a single, segregated school. The Japanese government protested, and after negotiations, the United States and Japan reached what became known as a "gentlemen's agreement." The Japanese agreed to discourage emigration, and President Theodore Roosevelt agreed to prevent the passage of laws discriminating against Japanese in the United States.

Initially, Japanese immigrants were minuscule in number: In 1870 there were only 55 Japanese in America and in 1880 a mere 148. By 1900, however, there were 24,326, and their numbers have grown steadily. By 1970 they surpassed the Chinese (U.S. Bureau of the Census, 1976), but later figures showed that despite a sharp increase since 1970, the number of ethnic Japanese was far fewer than the number of Chinese (United States Department of Commerce *News*, June 12, 1991).

Japanese Americans were subjected to especially

vicious mistreatment during World War II. Fearing espionage and sabotage from among the ethnic minorities with whose home countries the United States was at war, President Franklin D. Roosevelt signed Executive Order 9066 empowering the military to "remove any and all persons" from certain regions of the country. Although before the United States entered World War II, many German Americans actively demonstrated on behalf of Germany, no general action was taken against them as a group. Nor was any general action taken against Italian Americans. Nonetheless, General John L. DeWitt ordered that *all* individuals of Japanese descent be evacuated from three West Coast states and moved inland to "relocation" camps for the duration of the war. In 1942, 120,000 Japanese, including some 77,000 who were American citizens, were moved and imprisoned solely because of their national origin—even though not a single act of espionage or sabotage against the United States ever was attributed to one of their number (Simpson and Yinger, 1972). Many lost their homes and possessions in the process. Included in those who were relocated were members of the 442nd Regimental Combat Team, a fighting group comprised solely of Japanese-Americans, who fought valiantly in Europe until they were interned.

In 1988, President Ronald Reagan signed legislation apologizing for this wartime action. The legislation moved to "right a great wrong" by establishing a $1.25 billion trust fund as reparation for the imprisonment. Each eligible person was to receive a $20,000 tax-free award from the government. The president noted as he signed the legislation: "Yes, the nation was then at war, struggling for its survival. And it's not for us today to pass judgment upon those who may have made mistakes while engaging in the great struggle. Yet we must recognize that the internment of Japanese-Americans was just that, a mistake" (*New York Times,* August 11, 1988).

Compared to the earlier group of Asian immigrants who came primarily from China and Japan, the current wave includes many Asians from Vietnam, the Philippines, Korea, India, Laos, Cambodia, and Singapore. Approximately 250,000 new Asian immigrants are added each year to the five million who already call the United States their home. Within twenty years there will probably be twice as many Asians in the United States as there are today.

The vast majority of Asian immigrants are middle-class and highly educated. More than a third have a college degree, twice the rate of Americans born here (immigrants from Vietnam, Cambodia and other Indochinese countries are the exception).

The education, occupations, and income attainments of Asian Americans have been far above the national average. Although Asian Americans make up only two percent of the total U.S. population, they comprise nearly 12 percent of the freshman class at Harvard and 20 percent at the University of California at Berkeley. They have achieved stunning success in science and business. As a group they have the highest rate of business ownership of any minority group in the United States. For every one thousand Asians in the population, nearly fifty-five own a business. For Hispanics the rate is 17 per 1,000, while for blacks it is 12.5 per 1,000 (Manning and O'Hare, 1988).

Native Americans (Indians)

Early European colonists encountered Native-American societies that in many ways were as advanced as their own. Especially impressive were their political institutions. For example, the League of the Iroquois, a confederacy that ensured peace among its five member nations and was remarkably successful in warfare against hostile neighbors, was the model on which Benjamin Franklin drew when he was planning the Federation of States (Kennedy, 1961).

The colonists and their descendants never really questioned the view that the land of the New World was theirs. They took land as they needed it—for

More than half of all Native Americans live on or near reservations administered by the government's Bureau of Indian Affairs.

The Battle Over English

Which of the following statements is true?

1. English is the official language of the United States.

2. English is the official language of California, South Carolina, Georgia, and Illinois.

The first statement is false. In a recent survey, 64 percent of the population thought English was made our national language 200 years ago by the Constitution. They are wrong. The United States has no official language.

The second statement, however, is true. More than a dozen states have made English their official language, and another nineteen have legislation pending to do likewise.

Why is there such a strong movement to make English our official language today, when our founding fathers did not think it necessary to do so 200 years ago? One reason is that by 1990, Hispanic-Americans whose native language was not English, had become the second largest minority group in the United States.

On one side we have U.S. English, a national public interest group that campaigns actively in support of English as our official language and has the blessing of all those who fear that the United States will become a modern-day Tower of Babel.

They point to the fact that in less than one generation, no single ethnic group will be a majority in California—the nation's most populous state. In less than four generations, about one-third of

all Americans will be post-1980 immigrants and their descendants. English as a common language, they maintain, will be the only glue that can hold this diversity together.

On the other side we have opponents who argue that whenever a majority insists on a rigid monolingualism, it means that language is being used as a strategy for keeping the minority in its place.

The debate is an outgrowth of the fact that over the past two decades, the federal government has promoted bilingual education, at the same time it has downplayed the importance of learning English for full participation in the political, economic, or social life of the country.

This approach came at a time when immigration was at an historic high and when, for the first time in American history, a majority of immigrants spoke one particular language other than English—namely Spanish.

In response to this perceived bilingual bias, people started to point out that just as it is not the government's role to promote or preserve any religion, it is also not the government's role to promote and preserve ethnic or racial traditions. The government has no more business helping Mexican-American children learn Spanish or appreciate mariachi music, they say, than it does telling the children of Italians they must speak Italian and play bocce.

Bilingual education has also

been promoted as a tool for producing better learning among immigrant children. Proponents claim that the goal is a speedier integration of the students into American society, not the maintenance of native cultures.

It is thought that children who speak English as a second language learn more easily if they are taught in their native tongue.

Yet there is little proof of the effectiveness of bilingual education. Most programs seem perpetuated for political, not educational, reasons. They give jobs and legitimacy to political opportunists in non-English-speaking communities. More often than not, these individuals wish to build a power base for reasons that have nothing to do with education.

The real political forces behind bilingual education tend to promote cultural separatism; the bilingual programs they espouse rarely are transitional and even more rarely make facility in English their primary goal. Bilingual programs hold students prisoners in their native languages and ensure students a prolonged "second-class" status.

So, who are the real racists? Those who use glib rhetoric to promote a linguistic ghetto, or those who want non-English speakers to be part of the American dream as soon as possible?

Sources: American Demographics, February 1987, p. 7. *American Demographics,* April 1987, pp. 52, 54.

agriculture, for mining, and later for industry—and drove off the native groups. Some land was purchased, some acquired through political agreements, some through trickery and deceit, and some through violence. In the end, hundreds of thousands of Native Americans were exterminated by disease, starvation, and deliberate massacre. By 1900 only some 250,000 Indians remained (perhaps one-eighth of their number in pre-Colonial times). (McNeill, 1976.) In recent years, however, their numbers have grown dramatically.

According to the 1990 United States Census figures there were 1,878,000 Native Americans (up from 1,479,000 in 1980, representing a 38 percent increase) (Fost, 1991). About 55 percent of all American Indians live on or near reservations administered fully or partly by the federal government's Bureau of Indian Affairs (BIA). Many of the others are living in Indian enclaves in urban areas. Oklahoma, California, Arizona, and New Mexico, in that order, are the states with the largest American Indian populations.

Interestingly, more than seven million Americans claim American Indian ancestry. That is about one in 35 United States residents. Yet under two million identified themselves as American Indians in the 1990 census. Most people who claimed American Indian ancestry did so in combination with another ancestry group such as the English or Irish. The 38 percent increase in the American Indian population is not due to a baby boom, but rather the increasing likelihood of people to identify with their American Indian heritage.

On the whole, Native Americans are at the bottom of the American socioeconomic ladder. Their family income is only 60 percent that of whites, and their life expectancy two-thirds of the national average. One-third of all adults are illiterate; 74 percent use contaminated water; and most live in overcrowded conditions (averaging 5.4 occupants in two rooms, against the national average of 2.4 people in four rooms). (*Statistical Abstract of the United States: 1991.*)

Conditions on the reservation leave most Native Americans in despair. For example, at Pine Ridge, a 5000 square mile reservation in South Dakota on which 18,000 Indians live, more than eight out of ten adults are unemployed and many are chronic alcoholics. As a result of these conditions, the suicide rate on the reservation is up to four times the national average (*Newsweek*, May 2, 1988). Other reservations are similarly blighted. Seven out of ten Puyallup Indians of Washington State are unemployed (*The New York Times*, August 29, 1988).

PROSPECTS FOR THE FUTURE

As should be evident by now, the many racial and ethnic groups in the United States present a complex and constantly changing picture. Some trends in intergroup relations can be discerned and are likely to continue—new ones may emerge as new groups gain prominence. The resurgence of ethnic-identity movements will probably spread and may be coupled with more collective protest movements among disaffected ethnic and racial minorities, who are demanding they be given equal access to the opportunities and benefits of American society.

It is important to realize that the old concept of the United States as a "melting pot" is both simplistic and idealistic. Many groups have entered the United States. Most encountered prejudice, some severe discrimination, and others the pressures of Anglo conformity. Contemporary American society is the outcome of all these diverse groups coming together and trying to adjust. Indeed, if these groups are able to interact on the basis of mutual respect, this diversity may offer America strengths and flexibility not available in a homogeneous society.

Gender and Age Stratification

Are the Sexes Separate and Unequal?
  Historical Views
  Religious Views
  Biological Views
  Sociological Views: Cross-Cultural
    Evidence

What Produces Gender Inequality?
  The Functionalist Viewpoint
  The Conflict Theory Viewpoint

Gender-Role Socialization
  Childhood Socialization
  Adolescent Socialization
  Adult Socialization
  Gender Differences in Social Interaction

Gender Inequality and Work
  Job Discrimination

Gender Roles and the Future
  Changes in Attitudes

Age Stratification
  Composition of the Older Population
  Aging by Sex Ratio
  Aging by Race
  Aging by Marital Status

Theories of Aging
  Disengagement Theory
  Activity Theory
  Modernization Theory

Future Trends in Age Stratification

John Wilson has some very distinct memories of he and his brother being indoctrinated with proper gender-role behaviors. After all, they were sons of an Air Force general and spent their youth on a variety of military bases. When John's younger brother Charlie was about three years old, he had a favorite toy, a rag doll. Charlie loved this doll and carried it everywhere. His father, appalled and embarrassed by the sight of his little son with a doll, went to great lengths to wean Charlie from the toy but had no success. The father had a little uniform especially made for Charlie so that he could look just like Dad, hoping that it would take his mind off the doll. Charlie took to the uniform immediately and spent a good portion of day marching around the house, but always clutching the doll under his left arm. John recently found a packet of photos of his dad and Charlie in their uniforms, and each one shows Charlie grasping the doll and Dad standing next to him with a pained expression on his face. It took another year of coaxing, threatening and cajoling before Dad was able to get Charlie to reluctantly and tearfully part with the doll.

In such innocuous and ordinary ways gender-role socialization takes place. Three-year-old Charlie was not acting as the boy his father wanted him to be. The father responded by dressing Charlie just like Dad, creating a message that even a three-year-old could not miss. But the carefully orchestrated attempt at gender-role socialization was not successful, at least not at first. Eventually Charlie learned that being a boy in his father's eyes meant he had to surrender an important part of himself. In this way he learned there were appropriate behaviors not just for males, but also for military officer's sons (Wertsch, 1991).

In this chapter we will look at some of the differences between the sexes, examine cross-cultural variations in gender roles, and try to understand how a gender identity is acquired. In the process we will begin to understand the changes taking place in gender roles in American society.

ARE THE SEXES SEPARATE AND UNEQUAL?

Sociology makes an important distinction between sex and gender. **Sex** *refers to the physical and biological differences between men and women.* In general, sex differences are made evident by distinctions in anatomical, chromosomal, hormonal, and physiological characteristics. At birth the differences are most evident in the male and female genitalia.

Gender *refers to the social, psychological, and cultural attributes of masculinity and femininity that are based on the above biological distinctions.* Gender pertains to the socially learned patterns of behavior and the psychological or emotional expressions of attitudes that distinguish males from females. Ideas about masculinity and femininity are culturally derived and pattern the ways in which males and females are treated from birth onward. Gender is an important factor in shaping people's self-images and social identities. Whereas sex refers to an ascribed status, in that a person is born either a male or female, gender is learned through the socialization process and thus is an achieved status.

Are gender-role differences innate? The dominant view in many societies is that gender identities are expressions of what is "natural." People tend to assume that acting masculine or feminine is the result of an innate, biologically determined process rather than the result of socialization and social-learning experiences. In order to support the view that gender-role differences are innate, people have sought evidence from religion and the biological and social sciences. Whereas most religions tend to support the biological view, both biology and the social sciences provide evidence which suggests that what is "natural" about sex roles expresses both innate and learned characteristics.

Historical Views

The third-century Chinese scholar Fu Hsuan penned these lines about the status of women in his era:

> Bitter indeed it is to be born a woman,
> It is difficult to imagine anything so low!
> Boys can stand openly at the front gate,
> They are treated like gods as soon as they are born . . .
> But a girl is reared without joy or love,
> And no one in her family really cares for her,
> Grown up, she has to hide in the inner rooms,
> Cover her head, be afraid to look others in the face,
> And no one sheds a tear when she is married off . . .
> (Quoted in Bullough, 1973).

 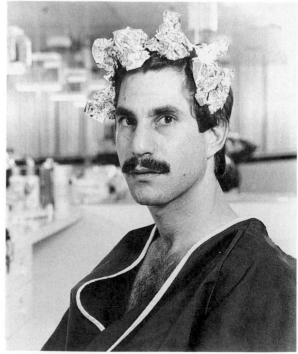

Society causes us to expect certain gender role behaviors from males and females. A changing society, however, produces changes in how these roles are carried out.

In traditional Chinese society, women were subordinate to men. Chinese women were often called "Nei Ren," or "inside person." To keep women in shackles, Confucian doctrine created what was known as the three obediences and the four virtues. The three obediences were "obedience to the father when yet unmarried, obedience to the husband when married, and obedience to the sons when widowed." Thus, traditionally, Chinese women were placed under the control of males from the cradle to the grave.

The four virtues were: (1) "women's ethics," meaning a woman must know her place and act in every way in compliance with the old ethical code; (2) "women's speech," meaning a woman must not talk too much, taking care not to bore people; (3) "woman's appearance," meaning a woman must pay attention to adorning herself with a view to pleasing men; and (4) "woman's chores," meaning a woman must willingly do all the chores in the home.

In nineteenth-century Europe, attitudes toward women had not improved appreciably. The father of modern sociology, Auguste Comte (1851), in constructing his views of the perfect society also dealt with questions about women's proper role. Comte saw women as the "mental and physical inferiors of men." In all kinds of force, whether physical, intellectual, or practical, it is certain that man surpasses women in accordance with the general law prevailing throughout the animal kingdom." Comte did grant women a slight superiority in the realms of emotion, love, and morality.

Comte believed women should not be allowed to work outside the home, to own property, or to exercise political power. Their gentle nature required that they remain in the home as mothers tending to their children and as wives tending to their husbands' emotional, domestic, and sexual needs.

Comte viewed equality as a social and moral danger to women. He felt progress would result only from making the female's life "more and more domestic; to diminish as far as possible the burden of out-door labour." Women in short, were to be the pampered slaves of men.

Religious Views

Many religions have overtly acknowledged that men are superior to women. For example, the Judeo-Christian story of creation presents a God-ordained sex-role hierarchy, with man created in the image of God and woman a subsequent and secondary act of creation. Thus, the man is superior to the woman, who was created to assist man and bear his children. This account has been used as the theological justification for a **patriarchal ideology**, *or the belief that men are superior to women and should control all important aspects of society.* This kind of legitimation of male superiority is displayed in the following passage.

For a man indeed ought not to have his head veiled, forasmuch as he is the image and glory of God: but the woman is the glory of the man: for neither was the man created for the woman but the woman for the man: for this cause ought the woman to have a sign of authority on her head (I Cor. 11:3–10).

Models for proper gender role behavior are widespread within society. In addition to our experiences with others, art, literature, and music play important roles in transmitting appropriate behavior to us.

In traditional India, the Hindu religion conceived of women as strongly erotic and thus a threat to male asceticism and spirituality. Women were cut off physically from the outside world. They wore veils and voluminous garments and were never seen by men who were not members of the family. Only men were allowed access to and involvement with the outside world.

Womens' precarious and inferior position in traditional India is illustrated further by the ancient Manu code, drawn up between 200 B.C. and A.D. 200. The code states that if a wife had no children after eight years of marriage, she would be banished; if all her children were dead after 10 years, she could be dismissed, and if she had produced only girls after 11 years, she could be repudiated.

Stemming from the Hindu patriarchal ideology was the practice of prohibiting women from owning and disposing of property. The prevalent practice in traditional Hindu India was that property acquired by the wife belonged to the husband. Similar restrictions on the ownership of property by women also prevailed in ancient Greece, Rome, Israel, China, and Japan. Such restrictions are still followed by fundamentalist Muslim states like Saudi Arabia and Iran.

Even in Pakistan, a relatively modern Moslem country, women have far less value than men. In a court of law, for example, the testimony of women is given half the weight of the testimony of men. According to a Moslem clergyman, this rule is necessary because of the emotional and irrational nature of women—a nature that makes women intellectually inferior. From the court's point of view, women have the same value as "the blind, handicapped, lunatics, and children" (*New York Times,* June 17, 1988).

Biological Views

Supporters of the belief that the basic differences between males and females are biologically determined have sought evidence from two sources: studies of other animal species, including nonhuman primates—monkeys and apes—and studies of the physiological differences between men and women. We shall examine each in turn.

ANIMAL STUDIES AND SOCIOBIOLOGY
Ethology *is the scientific study of animal behavior.* Ethologists have observed sexual differences in behavior throughout much of the nonhuman animal world. Evidence indicates these differences are biologically determined—that in a given species, members of the same sex behave in much the same way and perform the same tasks and activities. Popularized versions of these ideas, such as those of Desmond Morris in *The Human Zoo* (1970) or Lionel Tiger and Robin Fox in *The Imperial Animal* (1971), generalize from the behavior of nonhuman primates to that of humans. They maintain that in all primate species, including *Homo sapiens,* there are fundamental differences between males and females. They try to explain human male dominance and the traditional sexual division of labor in all human societies on the basis of inherent male or female capacities. They even have extended their analysis to explain other human phenomena such as war and territoriality through evolutionary comparisons with other species. A more sophisticated treatment of this same theme is found in the field of sociobiology (see Chapter 1), the study of the genetic basis for social behavior (Wilson, 1975, 1978).

Sociobiologists believe that much of human social behavior has a genetic basis. Patterns of social organization such as family systems, organized aggression, male dominance, defense of territory, fear of strangers, the incest taboo, and even religion are seen to be rooted in the genetic structure of our species. The emphasis in sociobiology is on the inborn structure of social traits.

Critics note that sociobiologists overlook the important role learning plays among nonhuman primates in their acquisition of social and sexual behavior patterns (Montagu, 1973). They also observe that by generalizing from animal to human behavior, fundamental differences between human and nonhuman primates, such as the human use of a complex language system, are not taken into account. While freely acknowledging the biological basis for sex differences, these critics claim that among humans, social and cultural factors overwhelmingly account for the variety in the roles and attitudes of the two sexes. Human expressions of maleness and femaleness, they argue, although influenced by biology, are not determined by it; rather, gender identities acquired through social learning provide the guidelines for appropriate gender-role behavior and expression.

GENETIC AND PHYSIOLOGICAL DIFFERENCES
Even ardent critics cannot deny that certain genetic and physiological differences exist between the sexes—differences that influence health and physical capacity. Accordingly, the study of gender roles must take into account differences such as size and muscle development (both usually greater in males), longevity (females, with few exceptions, live longer in nearly every part of the world, some-

times as much as nine years longer on average), and susceptibility to disease and physical disorders (generally greater in males). As you can see from the following tables, men and women are afflicted by extremely different chronic conditions. Even though women are sick more often than men and suffer from a greater variety of problems, men are more likely to die or suffer serious disability from their illnesses than women (see Table 10.1).

The genetic and physiological differences between the sexes influence but do not determine, the ease with which members of each sex can learn to perform certain tasks. Some researchers believe, for example, that gender differences account for the edge males appear to have in math. One study of Scholastic Aptitude Test Scores of more than 10,000 gifted junior high school students (Benbow and Stanley, 1980) found that the vast majority of the those particularly gifted in math were boys. Benbow and Stanley speculated that this talent might be linked to the male sex hormone, testosterone. Other studies have shown that males hold a clear advantage in determining visual-spatial relationships—an ability that emerges at around age eight and persists throughout life.

Not everyone believes the causes of these differences are genetic. Some sociologists suggest there is a self-fulfilling prophecy at work. Boys do better in math than girls because that is what is expected of them. Girls, at the same time are doing what is expected of them when they do not do well in math.

RESPONSES TO STRESS   Gender differences also influence the way men and women react to stress, the "fight or flight" reaction that is thought to play a part in heart disease, stroke, coronary-artery disease, among other ailments. In earlier days, when primitive man was threatened by wild animals while hunting, testosterone enabled him to react quickly to danger. This intense type of reaction is no longer

TABLE 10.1

Prevalence of Fatal and Nonfatal Illness among Men and Women

Women	Percent Greater*	Men	Percent Greater*
Nonfatal		*Nonfatal*	
Thyroid diseases	551	Visual impairments	49
Bladder infection disorders	382	Hearing impairments	46
Anemias	378	Paralysis, complete or partial	25
Bunions	335	Tinnitus	21
Spastic colon	305	Hernia of abdominal cavity	18
Frequent constipation	253	Intervertebral disk disorders	14
Varicose veins	233	Hemorrhoids	5
Migraine headaches	175		
Diverticulitis of intestines	152	*Fatal*	
Chronic enteritis and colitis	111	Emphysema	59
Sciatica	85	Atherosclerosis	54
Trouble with corns, calluses	82	Ischemic heart disease	51
Neuralgia and neuritis	79	Cerebrovascular disease	32
Gallstones	64	Liver disease, including cirrhosis	23
Arthritis	59	Other selected heart diseases	3
Dermatitis	59	Ulcer of stomach, duodenum	3
Gastritis and duodenitis	54		
Heart rhythm disorders	43		
Diseases of retina	32		
Fatal			
Asthma	41		
High blood pressure**	8		

 * Percentages indicate the higher prevalence of each disorder among that sex compared to the other.

 ** A risk factor for fatal circulatory diseases. Women's higher prevalence rates are thought to reflect earlier diagnosis and control, compared with men. For younger, premenopausal women, high blood pressure is less common than among men, and more men die from the disease because of damage done to their blood vessels at the younger age, when they do contract it in higher proportions.

 Source: U.S. News & World Report, August 8, 1988, p. 53. Basic data from Lois Verbrugge of University of Michigan and unpublished data from the National Health Interview Surveys, 1983–1985.

important today and may be part of the reason men suffer more heart attacks than women. Women, it appears, react more slowly to stress, putting less pressure on the blood vessels and the heart. While learned behavior may play a role in women's response to stress, biology is no less important (*U.S. News and World Report,* August 8, 1988).

Although many differences between males and females have a biological basis, other physical conditions may be tied to cultural influences and variations in environment and activity. Men react differently to psychological stress than women do: Each sex develops severe but dissimilar symptoms. Changing cultural standards and patterns of social behavior have had a pronounced effect on other traits formerly thought to be sex linked. For example, the rising incidence of lung cancer among women—a disease historically associated primarily with men—can be traced directly to changes in social behavior and custom, not biology: Women now smoke as freely as men.

In summary, differing learned behaviors do contribute to the relative prevalence of certain diseases and disorders in each sex. But as has been pointed out, not all male-female differences in disease and susceptibility can be attributed to these factors. In addition to genetically linked defects, differences in some basic physiological processes such as metabolic rates and adult secretion of gonadal hormones may make males more vulnerable than females to certain physical problems.

Sociological Views: Cross-Cultural Evidence

Most sociologists believe the way people are socialized has a greater effect on their gender identities than do biological factors. Cross-cultural and historical research offers support for this view, revealing that different societies allocate different tasks and duties to men and women, and that males and females have culturally patterned conceptions of themselves and of one another.

Until the pioneering work of anthropologist Margaret Mead (1901–1978) was published in the 1930s, it was widely believed that gender identity (what then was called sex temperament) was a matter of biology alone. It never occurred to Westerners to question their culture's definitions of "male" and "female" temperament and behavior, nor did most people doubt these were innate properties. In 1935 Mead published a refutation of this assumption in *Sex and Temperament,* which became a classic. While doing research among isolated tribal groups on the island of New Guinea, she found three societies with widely differing expectations of male and female behavior. The Arapesh were characterized as gentle and home loving, with a belief that men and women were of equivalent temperament. Both adult men and women subordinated their needs to those of the younger or weaker members of the society. The Mundugamor, by contrast, assumed a natural hostility between members of the same sex and only slightly less hostility between the sexes. Both sexes were expected to be tough, aggressive, and competitive. The third society, the Tchambuli, believed that the sexes were temperamentally different, but the gender roles were reversed relative to the Western pattern.

> I found . . . in one, both men and women act as we expect women to act—in a mild parental responsive way; in the second, both act as we expect men to act—in a fierce initiative fashion, and in the third, the men act according to our stereotype for women—are catty, wear curls and go shopping, while the women are energetic, managerial, unadorned partners (Mead, 1935).

Although Mead's findings are interesting and suggestive, anthropologists have cautioned against overinterpreting them. They point out Mead's research was limited to a matter of months and that her then husband and collaborator Reo Fortune rejected her view that the Arapesh did not distinguish between male and female temperaments. Furthermore, research (Maccoby and Jacklin, 1975) points out four areas of difference between the sexes—in girls and boys, at least:

1. Girls have greater verbal ability than boys.
2. Boys excel in visual-spatial ability.
3. Boys excel in mathematical ability.
4. Boys are more aggressive than girls.

Most sociologists tend to agree that even in preliterate societies, culture is central to the patterning of gender roles. Nevertheless, biological factors may play a more prominent part in structuring gender roles in societies less technologically developed than our own. Anthropologist Clellan S. Ford (1970) believes that for preindustrial peoples, "the single most important biological fact in determining how men and women live is the differential part they play in reproduction." The woman's life is characterized by a continuing cycle of pregnancy, childbearing, and nursing for periods of up to three years. By the time the child is weaned, the mother is likely to be pregnant again. Not until menopause, which frequently coincides with the end of the woman's life itself, is her reproductive role over. In these circumstances it is not surprising that such activities as hunting, fighting, and forest clearing usually are defined as male tasks, gathering and preparing small game, grains, and vegetables; tending gardens and building shelters are typically female activities, as is caring for the young.

In an early study George Murdock (1937) provided data on the division of labor by sex in 224 preliterate societies. Such activities as metalworking, making weapons, woodworking and stoneworking, hunting and trapping, building houses and boats, and clearing the land for agriculture were tasks performed by men. Women's activities included grinding grain, gathering and cooking herbs, roots, seeds, fruits, and nuts, weaving baskets, making pottery, and making and repairing clothing. In a review of the cross-cultural literature (D'Andrade, 1966), it was concluded that the division of labor by sex occurs in all societies. Generally, male tasks require vigorous physical activity or travel, whereas female tasks are less physically strenuous and more sedentary.

The almost universal classification of women to secondary status has had a profound effect on their work and family roles. Anthropologist Sherry Ortner (1974) observed that "everywhere, in every known culture, women are considered in some degree inferior to men." One important result of this attitude is the exclusion of women from participation in, or contact with, those areas of the particular society believed to be most powerful, whether they be religious or secular. We see these exclusionary patterns in our own society. There are no female priests in the Catholic Church nor women rabbis in orthodox Judaism. No woman has ever run for President, and there are very few women chief executive officers of major U.S. corporations.

Another anthropologist, Michelle Rosaldo (1974), believes "women's status will be lowest in those societies where there is a firm differentiation between domestic and public spheres of activity and where women are isolated from one another and placed under a single man's authority in the home." She believes that the time-consuming and emotionally compelling involvement of a mother with her child is unmatched by any single involvement and commitment by a man. The result is that men are free to form broader associations in the outside world through their involvement in work, politics, and religion. The relative absence of women from these public spheres results in their lack of authority and power. Men's involvements and activities are viewed as important, and the cultural systems accord authority and value to men's activities and roles. In turn, women's work, especially when it is confined to domestic roles and activities, tends to be oppres-

sive and lacking in value and status. Women are seen to gain power and a sense of value only when they are able to transcend the domestic sphere of activities. This differentiation is most acute in those societies that practice sexual discrimination. Societies in which men value and participate in domestic activities tend to be more egalitarian.

Nevertheless, even though physiological factors tend to play an influential part in gender-role differences, biology does not determine these differences. Rather, people acquire much of their ability to fulfill their gender roles through socialization.

WHAT PRODUCES GENDER INEQUALITY?

Sociologists have devoted much thought and research to answering this question. Two major theoretical approaches have been used to explain male dominance and gender inequality: functionalism and conflict theory.

The Functionalist Viewpoint

From Chapter 1 you may recall that functionalists (or structural functionalists, to be more precise) believe that society consists of a system of interrelated parts that all work together to maintain the smooth operation of society. Functionalists argue that it was quite useful to have men and women fulfill different roles in preindustrial societies. The society was more efficient when tasks and responsibilities were allocated to particular individuals who were socialized to fulfill specific roles.

The fact that the human infant is helpless for such a long time makes it necessary that someone look after the child. It is logical that the mother who gives birth to the child and nurses it is also the one to take care of it. Because, in preindustrial societies, women spent their time near the home, they took on the duties of preparing the food, cleaning clothes, and attending to the other necessities of daily living. To the male fell the duties of hunting, defending the family, and herding. He also became the one to make economic and other decisions important to the family's survival.

This division of labor created a situation in which the female was largely dependent on the male for protection and food, and so he became the dominant partner in the relationship. This dominance, in turn, caused his activities to be more highly regarded and rewarded. Over time, this pattern came to be seen as natural and was thought to be tied to biological sex differences.

Men increasingly are playing expressive roles as well as instrumental roles within the family.

Talcott Parsons and Robert Bales (1955) are known for applying functionalist theory to the modern family. They argue that the division of labor and role differentiation by sex are universal principles of family organization and are also functional to the modern family. They believe the family functions best when the father assumes the *instrumental role,* which focuses on relationships between the family and the outside world. The instrumental role mainly involves supporting and protecting the family. The mother concentrates her energies on the *expressive role,* which focuses on relationships within the family and requires the mother to provide the love and support needed to sustain the family. The male is required to be dominant and competent, and the female should be passive and nurturant.

As can be imagined, there has been much criticism of the functionalist position. The view that gender roles and gender stratification are inevitable does not fit with cross-cultural evidence and the changing situation in American society (Crano and Aronoff, 1978). Critics contend that industrial society can be quite flexible in assigning tasks to males and females. Furthermore, the functionalist model was developed during the 1950s, an era of very traditional family patterns, and rather than being predictive of family arrangements, it is merely representative of the era during which it became popular.

The Conflict Theory Viewpoint

While functionalist theory may explain why gender-role differences emerged, it does not explain why they persisted. According to the conflict theory, males dominate females because of their superior power and control over key resources. A major consequence of this domination is the exploitation of women by men. By subordinating women, men gain greater economic, political, and social power. According to conflict theory, as long as the dominant group benefits from the existing relationship, it has little incentive to change it. The resulting inequalities are therefore perpetuated long after they may have served any functional purpose. In this way, gender inequalities resemble race and class inequalities.

Conflict theorists believe the main source of gender inequality is the economic inequality between men and women. Economic advantage leads to power and prestige. If men have an economic advantage in society, it will produce a superior social position in both the society and the family.

Friedrich Engels (1884) linked gender inequalities to capitalism, contending that primitive, noncapitalistic hunting and gathering societies without private property were egalitarian. As these societies developed capitalistic institutions of private property, power came to be concentrated in the hands of a minority of men who used it to subordinate women and to create political institutions designed to maintain that power. Engels also believed that to free women from subordination and exploitation, society must abolish private property and other capitalistic institutions. Engels believed that socialism was the only solution to gender inequality.

Today many conflict theorists accept the view that gender inequalities may have evolved because they were initially functional. Many functionalists also agree that gender inequalities are becoming more and more dysfunctional. They agree that the origins for gender inequalities are more social than biological.

GENDER-ROLE SOCIALIZATION

Gender-role *socialization is a lifelong process whereby people learn the values, attitudes, motivations, and behavior considered appropriate to each sex by their culture.* In our society, as in all others, males and females are socialized differently. In addition, each culture defines gender roles differently. This process is not limited to childhood but continues through adolescence, adulthood, and into old age.

Childhood Socialization

Even before a baby is born, its sex is a subject of speculation, and the different gender-role relationships it will form from birth on already are being decided.

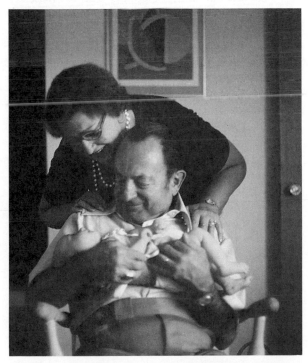

Parents and grandparents respond differently to boys and girls right from the beginning, and they carry in their minds images of what the child should be like, how it should behave, and what it should be in later life.

A scene from the early musical "Carousel" epitomizes (in somewhat caricatured form) some of the feelings that parents have about bringing up sons as opposed to daughters. A young man discovers he is to be a father. He rhapsodizes about what kind of son he expects to have. The boy will be tall and tough as a tree, and no one will dare to boss him around; it will be all right for his mother to teach him manners but she mustn't make a sissy out of him. He'll be good at wrestling and will be able to herd cattle, run a riverboat, drive spikes, etc. Then the prospective father realizes, with a start, that the child may be a girl. The music changes to a gentle theme. She will have ribbons in her hair; she will be sweet and petite (just like her mother) and suitors will flock around her. There's a slightly discordant note, introduced for comic relief from sentimentality, when the expectant father brags that she'll be half again as bright as girls are meant to be; but then he returns to the main theme: She must be protected, and he must find enough money to raise her in a setting where she will meet the right kind of man to marry (Maccoby and Jacklin, 1975).

Parents carry in their minds images of what girls and boys are like, how they should behave, and what they should be in later life. Parents respond differently to girls and boys right from the beginning. After studying the behavior of parents and their infants, Michael Lewis (1972) reported that there are significant differences in the very early socialization of males and females. Thus, girls are caressed more than boys, but boys are jostled and roughhoused more. Mothers talk more to their daughters, and fathers interact more with their sons.

A variety of research studies (Lynn, 1969; Maccoby and Jacklin, 1975) reveal that there are persistent differences in the parental gender-role socialization of children. These differences are reinforced by other socializing agents—siblings, peers, educational systems, and the mass media. Indeed, R. J. Stoller (1967), director of the UCLA Gender Research Clinic, states that "by the first two or three years of life, core gender identity—the sense of maleness or femaleness—is established as a result of the parents' conviction that their infant's assignment at birth to either the male or female sex is correct."

The pervasive manner in which the individual is socialized into the appropriate gender role can be best illustrated by cases in which an erroneous gender assignment was made at birth. For example, consider the case of Frankie, who, mistakenly classified as a male at birth, was socialized as a male. At the age of five, "he" was brought to the hospital for examination and was diagnosed then as a female whose clitoris had been mistaken for a small penis. Lindesmith and Strauss (1956), in a report based on an unpublished document made available to them by one of the nurses assigned to the case, state that Frankie showed a decided preference for the company of little boys in the children's ward and a disdain for little girls and their "sissy" activities. After the child's real sex had been determined, the nurses were required to treat Frankie as a little girl. One of the nurses observed that this was not easy:

> This didn't sound too difficult—until we tried it. Frankie simply didn't give the right cues. It is amazing how much your response to a child depends on that child's behavior toward you. It was extremely difficult to keep from responding to Frankie's typically little boy behavior in the same way that I responded to other boys in the ward. And to treat Frankie as a girl was jarringly out of key. It was something we all had to continually remind ourselves to do. Yet the doing of it left all of us feeling vaguely uneasy as if we had committed an error. . . . About the same time Frankie became increasingly aware of the change in our attitude toward her. She seemed to realize that behavior which had always before brought forth approval was no longer approved. It must have been far more confusing to her than it was to us, and certainly it was bad enough for us. Her reaction was strong and violent. She became extremely belligerent and even less willing to accept crayons, color books and games which she simply called "sissy" and threw on the floor (Lindesmith and Strauss, 1956).

Adolescent Socialization

Most societies have different expectations for adolescent girls and boys. Erik Erikson (1968) believes the most important task in adolescence is the establishment of a sense of identity. He believes that during the adolescent stage, both boys and girls undergo severe emotional crises centered on questions of who they are and who they will be. If the adolescent crisis is satisfactorily resolved, a sense of identity will be developed, if not, role confusion will persist. According to Erikson, adolescent boys in our society generally are encouraged to pursue role paths that will prepare them for some occupational commitment, whereas girls generally are encouraged to develop behavior patterns designed to attract a suitable mate. Erikson observes that it is more difficult for girls than for boys to achieve a positive identity in Western society. This is because women are encouraged to be more passive and less achievement oriented than men and to stress the development of interpersonal skills—traits not highly valued in our society. Males, on the other hand, are encouraged to be competitive, to strive for achievement, to assert autonomy and independence—char-

acteristics held in high esteem in our competitive society.

The result of the adolescent gender-role socialization process becomes evident during young adulthood (ages 18 to 21). This is a period of transition from the earlier economic and psychological dependence on one's parents to the beginning of independent living. Research shows that during this period, young men experience more stress and less satisfaction with their lives than do young women (Frieze et al., 1978). Men at this age seem more burdened and concerned by the expectations and demands of their socialization process. Much of this anxiety arises from the pressure that young men face in choosing an occupation, a decision they feel will be the prime determinant of their adult lives—affecting their future economic resources, social expectations, and friendship networks as well as defining their future work activities.

Traditionally, the pressure to choose a lifelong occupation has not been as severe for women at this age because their socialization emphasized marriage as their central adult role. Outside employment was seen as a temporary occupation subordinate to, and contingent on, marriage and future familial roles. The choice of a husband, not a job, was women's primary concern.

The predominant personality characteristics of young women during this period included a strong dependency on others for support, approval, and direction. Their sense of self is less clearly defined than that of men, and there is a tentativeness in their quest for personal identity. Many of these personality characteristics are associated with their marriage goals.

Nonetheless, female gender roles are changing rapidly, although traditional attitudes toward careers and marriage undoubtedly still remain part of the thinking of many people in our society. Girls are being encouraged not to limit themselves to these stereotyped roles and attitudes. More and more young women expect to pursue careers before and during marriage and child rearing. Marriage is no longer considered the only desirable goal for a woman, nor is it any longer even considered necessary to a woman's success and happiness.

Adult Socialization

Gender-role socialization continues into adulthood. Three personality characteristics associated with adult sex differences are gender identity, self-esteem, and achievement motivation (Mandle, 1979). Because of cultural socialization, women are less likely to have an independent gender identity than men. That is, they tend to see their female identity as largely defined by, and dependent on, the characteristics of their husbands and children.

According to Mandle, low self-esteem, the second personality trait characteristic of adult women, is associated with psychological feelings of inadequacy and even self-hatred. One manifestation of this is that both men and women consistently devalue the attributes of women. In one study (Goldberg, 1968), a psychologist asked female college students to read a number of professional articles from each of six fields and to rate them for persuasive impact, profundity, writing style, professional competency, and overall value. Half the women received articles purportedly written by a male author (for example, John T. McKay), and half got the identical articles supposedly written by a woman (for example, Joan T. McKay). The women gave consistently lower ratings to the identical articles when they were attributed to a female author than when they were attributed to a male author.

The third personality characteristic believed to be typical of women is low achievement motivation. Women are socialized to deemphasize qualities that are highly regarded in our society—competition, independence, intellectual achievement, and leadership (of course, these personality traits, like most others, are not intrinsically "good" or "bad"—the value placed on each is culturally determined. Judith Bardwick and Elizabeth Douvan (1971) point out that the result of these factors is that very few women have succeeded in traditionally masculine roles, not only because of disparagement and prejudice, but largely because women have not been fundamentally equipped and determined to succeed.

The job fields that women dominate are those that utilize skills of nurturance and empathy and that deemphasize such traits as aggressiveness and competitiveness or treat them as largely dysfunctional. These jobs include teaching, nursing, and secretarial work. It should be noted that all these occupations pay poorly compared with many male-dominated positions.

Gender-role socialization also is fostered by a society's concepts of proper public behavior—its rules of etiquette, or good manners. In traditional social behavior between the sexes in public places and in everyday life—the rules by which men are expected to open doors for women, walk on the outside of pavements (possibly to protect women from being splashed or pelted by garbage), and ask women for permission to smoke in their presence—the recurrent pattern is for men to defer to women. Underlying these deferential patterns is an imputa-

Gender role stereotyping takes place in the media in many subtle and not so subtle ways.

tion of women's helplessness, weakness, and frailty. Supporters of traditional rules of etiquette fail to see that these deferential patterns are in reality forms of social control that perpetuate and reinforce the power of men.

Daryl and Sandra Bem, a husband-and-wife team of psychologists, have devised two passages that expose the accepted ideological rationalization that women and men have complementary but equal positions in our society.

Both my wife and I earned Ph.D. degrees in our respective disciplines. I turned down a superior academic post in Oregon and accepted a slightly less desirable position in New York where my wife could obtain a part-time teaching job and do research at one of the several other colleges in the area. Although I would have preferred to live in a suburb, we purchased a home near my wife's college so that she could have an office at home where she would be when the children returned from school. Because my wife earns a good salary, she can easily afford to pay a maid to do her major household chores. My wife and I share all other tasks around the house equally. For example, she cooks the meals, but I do the laundry for her and help her with many of her other household tasks (Bem and Bem, 1976).

At first glance, the man speaking in this passage seems to express an egalitarian gender-role relationship that rejects traditional sexist ideology. But Bem and Bem point out that such a marriage may not be an instance of interpersonal equality at all. There may be hidden assumptions about the "natural" role of women that are based on traditional ideology. These unconscious assumptions become clear in the comparison passage in which the roles of the husband and wife are reversed:

> Both my husband and I earned Ph.D. degrees in our respective disciplines. I turned down a superior academic post in Oregon and accepted a slightly less desirable position in New York where my husband could obtain a part-time teaching job and do research at one of the several other colleges in the area. Although I would have preferred to live in a suburb, we purchased a home near my husband's college so that he could have an office at home where he would be when the children returned from school. Because my husband earns a good salary, he can easily afford to pay a maid to do his major household chores. My husband and I share all other tasks around the house equally. For example, he cooks the meals, but I do the laundry for him and help him with many of his other household tasks (Bem and Bem, 1976).

This reversal of characters vividly illustrates that the first passage, rather than representing an egalitarian ideology, in fact perpetuates a sexist one. Why is it "her" maid, "her" laundry, "her" household tasks, and so forth? The first passage is an example of the subtlety of a nonconscious ideology. On the other hand, the second passage sounds absurd because it goes counter to the same nonconscious sexist ideology. As Sandra and Daryl Bem (1976) put it, "A truly equalitarian marriage would permit both partners to pursue careers or outside commitments which carry equal weight when all important decisions are to be made."

Gender Differences in Social Interaction

There are some interesting differences in how men and women think about the future and solve problems. In one study researchers (Maines and Hardesty, 1987) asked undergraduates to describe what they expected would happen to them over the next ten years. For both male and female undergraduates today, work appears to be a universal expectation. Likewise, the kinds of jobs wanted are nearly identical. Both groups mention jobs in business, law, hospital administration, and the computer industry. Further education was anticipated by more than half of the men and women. The vast majority

(94 percent) also see themselves as eventually married with a family.

Thus, at first glance a striking similarity appears in men and women's future plans. They express the desire for marriage, children, and work, and the desire for higher education is equally present. However, there are significant gender differences in expectations of *how* family, work, and education will be integrated. Men and women have different assumptions and tactics for achieving the similarly desired events in their lives.

Men operate in what Maines and Hardesty call a *linear temporal world*. When they try to project what the future might hold for them they almost always define it in terms of career accomplishments—lawyer, doctor, college professor, business executive, and so on. Education is seen as something which is pursued in order to attain the desired career.

Men see a family as desirable and not much of an issue in terms of pursuing career goals. They see little problem in coordinating career and family demands. Many expect to have a traditional division of labor in their families which will provide a support system for their career pursuit. Mostly, the problems of family living are viewed as being resolved rather easily, and typically there is no mention of career adjustments to the wife's and children's needs.

Young women, on the other hand, operate in *contingent temporal worlds*. Work, education, and family are all seen as having to be balanced against each other. Careers are seen as pursuits that may have to be suspended or halted at certain points. The vast majority of women envision problems in their career pursuits, and they see family responsibilities as a major issue. Nearly half say they will quit work for a few years as a solution to family/work demands. Instead of a clear vision of steps needed to accomplish their career goals, women become much more tentative about their future, since they expect it to entail adjustments and compromises.

Young men seem to take their autonomy for granted. They assume they will be able to accomplish what they set out to do if they have the necessary education, skill, and good fortune. Women, on the other hand, feel much more limited in the control of their future, even with the necessary education and skill. The problems surrounding the integration of family and career lend an element of uncertainty to their ability to accomplish their future goals. Women plan to be flexible in order to adjust to career and family needs. This flexibility gives them only partial autonomy in controlling their lives.

This element of tentativeness about the future, the willingness to be flexible and adjust to the needs of others, and the realization that goals cannot easily be achieved without compromise, evidently produces a difference in how men and women approach issues. This has led Carol Gilligan (1982) to believe that men and women think differently when it comes to problem solving.

Men often think that the highest praise they can bestow on a woman is to compliment her for "thinking like a man." That usually means that the woman has been decisive, rational, firm, and clear. To think like a "woman" in our society has always had negative overtones, being characterized as fuzzy, indecisive, unpredictable, tentative, and softheaded.

Carol Gilligan challenged the value judgments made about male, versus female, styles of reasoning, especially in the area of moral decision making. She argues that a woman's perspective on things is not inferior to a man's; it is simply different.

To illustrate her point, Gilligan describes the different responses that 11-year-old boys and girls made to an example used by Lawrence Kohlberg (discussed more fully in Chapter 4). In the example, Heinz, a fictional character, is caught up in a complex moral question. Heinz's wife is dying of cancer. The local pharmacist has discovered a drug that might cure her, but it is very expensive. Heinz has done all he can to raise the money necessary to buy the drug but can come up with only half the amount, and the druggist demands the full price. The question is: Should Heinz steal the drug?

Boys and girls differ significantly on how they answer this question. Boys often see the problem as the man's individual moral choice, stating that Heinz should steal the drug, as the right to life supersedes the right to property. Case closed.

The girls Gilligan questioned always seemed to get bogged down in peripheral issues. No, they maintained, Heinz should not steal the drug, because stealing is wrong. Heinz should have a long talk with the pharmacist and try to persuade him to do what is right. Besides, they point out, if Heinz steals the drug, he might be caught and go to jail. Then what would happen to his wife? What if there were children?

Instead of labeling this tentativeness as a typical example of women's inability to make firm decisions, Gilligan sees it as an attempt to deal with the consequences of actions rather than simply with "what is right." For women, moral dilemmas involving people have a greater complexity and therefore a greater ambiguity.

If your morality stresses the importance of not hurting others, as seems to be the case with most women, you will often face failure. As one of the men Gilligan interviewed said, making a moral decision is often a matter of "choosing the victim." There is "violence inherent in choice," Gilligan writes, and "the injunction not to hurt can paralyze women."

If you base your decision on an absolute principle (for example, abortion is murder; therefore it is wrong), you may then act with the decisiveness so admired by both men and women. If you base your decision on what you imagine is likely to happen (for example, if this child would be born with no father; if the fetus is likely to be seriously defective; if the mother's life would be endangered by the birth, and so on), you will often face uncertainty. Women, whose value systems are more focused on people than on principles, consequently find themselves wrestling with the problems that might result from their decisions.

Gilligan hopes that by ceasing to label a man's perspective as right and a woman's wrong, we can begin to understand that each may be valuable, though different. For this to happen, according to Gilligan, girls and women must gain confidence in their own ethical perspectives. Indeed, Gilligan feels, if society finally accepted a women's moral view of the interconnectedness of actions and relationships, it could have enormous consequences for everything from scholarship to politics to international relations.

GENDER INEQUALITY AND WORK

Women's numerical superiority over men has not enabled them as yet to avoid discrimination in many spheres of American society. In this discussion we shall focus on economic and job-related discrimination, because these data are easily quantified and serve well to highlight the problem. It should be remembered, though, that discrimination against women in America actually is expressed in a far wider range of social contexts and institutions.

Job Discrimination

As of 1990, 57.5 percent of all American women were part of the paid labor force. It is projected that this percentage will reach 61.5 percent in the year 2000. Figure 10.1 shows the steady rise in women's labor force participation rates over the last century (Spain, 1988).

SOCIOLOGY AT WORK

Deborah Tannen—Communication Between Men and Women

Deborah Tannen, a sociolinguist, is the author of the best-seller *You Just Don't Understand: Women and Men in Conversation* (1990). Tannen believes gender differences are widespread in everyday speech, and in many ways men and women are living in different worlds when they try to communicate with each other. Men and women use language for different purposes and differ in what they are willing to talk about. Tannen believes women use language primarily to create connections with others. They use it to create intimacy. For women language is the glue that holds relationships together.

Men, on the other hand, use language mainly to convey information. For men activities are the

Deborah Tannen.

things that hold people together, and in the absence of doing something with others, talking about an activity is the next best thing. This involves talking about concrete events or facts. This explains the tendency among men to engage in endless discussions about sporting events, batting averages and so on. Men are acutely aware of the status differences implied by knowledge or in one way of speaking or another. For men language and information are used to attain status, not intimacy.

Tannen also notes that women engage in "troubles talk," or talking about the day's problems. Confronted with this type of talk, a man is likely to offer advice or solutions and get on with it. Women are not looking for this response. More typically when one woman mentions a problem, someone else will give an example of a similar problem. Women are looking for agreement and mutual understanding. When someone offers advice or a solution, it creates "oneupsmanship". It is no longer a situation where two people are in similar circumstances but become two people jockeying for status.

Tannen tells a joke about a man whose wife wants to divorce him for not talking to her for two years. At the divorce hearing the judge asks the man why he has

not talked to her for this time. He answers that he did not want to interrupt her. This joke implies that women talk more than men. Upon closer observation, though, we must distinguish between speaking in public situations and speaking at home. Men seem more comfortable with the language used in a public setting while women find the language used in private settings more natural. Essentially the public language is about information and one person attempting to attain status with knowledge, whereas private language is about personal feelings and sharing those with others. It therefore seems understandable that men talk more in public settings while women talk more in the home. Men feel they do not need to talk much at home as their status is established. They use language when they are struggling for status. The home is not such a place.

Can people change their conversational styles? Tannen believes they can, if they want to. But even if no one changes, understanding these gender differences improves relationships. Once people realize that their partners have different conversational styles, they are inclined to accept differences without blaming themselves, their partners, or their relationships.

Presence in the labor force, however, does not mean full-time work. In 1989, 74.5 percent of all women were working full-time compared to 90 percent of all men (*Statistical Abstract of the United States: 1991*).

Working women as a group consistently earn less than working men. In 1989 the median weekly income for working men was $468, and for working women it was $328 (*Statistical Abstract of the United States: 1991*).

FIGURE 10.1

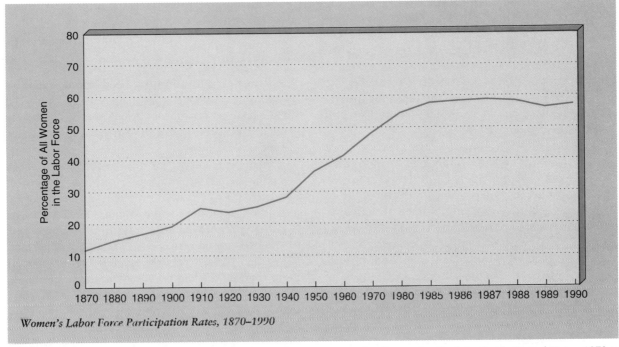

Women's Labor Force Participation Rates, 1870–1990

Sources: United States Bureau of the Census, 1943, "Population: Comparative Occupation Statistics for the United States, 1870 to 1940," Table XIV, *Sixteenth Census of the United States: 1940*; Suzanne M. Bianchi and Daphne Spain, 1986, *American Women in Transition*, Table 5.2, New York: Russell Sage Foundation; United States Bureau of the Census, 1986c, *Statistical Abstract of the United States: 1987*, 107th ed., Table 639; United States Bureau of the Census 1987b, *Statistical Abstract of the United States: 1991*, Table 608; *Monthly Labor Review III*, June 1988, p. 77; cited in Spain, Radcliffe Conferences, December 1988.

Women and men are concentrated in different occupational groups. Some would argue that the income and earnings differences between them result from pay differences across occupations rather than sex. However an analysis of 503 occupations showed that controlling for occupations makes little difference in the wage gap. Women working in the same occupations as men earn approximately 70 percent of what men earn (Bianchi and Spain, 1986). For example, male machine operators earned $19,200 in 1989, compared to $10,845 for female operators. Male executives, administrators, and managers earned $36,696 while women in the same professions earned $21,551 (*Statistical Abstract of the United States: 1991*).

Could it be these salary differences result from educational disparities between men and women? It does not seem like that is the answer, either. In 1988, male high-school graduates who worked full-time year-round had an average salary of $27,139, while women had an average salary of $17,336. For college graduates the average salaries were $40,415 for men and $25,674 for women (*Statistical Abstract of the United States: 1991*).

A striking fact in the above information is that not only are the average earnings for women lower than for men, but male high-school graduates average more than female college graduates. One possible explanation for this disparity is that the less skilled jobs men hold are typically unionized, such as construction, for example, and therefore pay better. Women who hold less skilled jobs, on the other hand, such as waitressing, are not unionized (Bianchi and Spain, 1986).

Job discrimination against women is a pervasive and complicated phenomenon. One study of business firms identified three ways in which women experience discrimination in the business world: (1) during the hiring process, when women are given jobs with lower occupational prestige than are men with equivalent qualifications; (2) through unequal wage policies, by which women receive less pay than men do for equivalent work; and (3) in awarding promotions—women find it more difficult than men to advance up the career ladder (Staires, Quin, and Shepard, 1976).

Discrimination against women in the economic sector is often quite subtle. Women are more or less channeled away from participation in occupations that are socially defined as appropriate to men. For example, it cannot really be argued that women bank presidents are paid less than men; instead, there are almost no women bank presidents. Women and men often do not perform equal work; therefore the phrase "equal pay for equal work" has little relevance. In some instances, similar work is performed by men and women, but there may be two job titles and two pay scales—for example, administrative assistant and executive secretary. The first may be a male or female; the second is usually a female and is likely to be paid less (Davidson and Gordon, 1979).

Having painted a somewhat pessimistic picture here we should note that there has been some improvement in recent years. During the 1970s, the share of women managers and administrators grew from 16 percent to 27 percent; women accountants and auditors were up from 25 percent to 38 percent.

In 1980, men outnumbered women by 3.8 million in higher-paying managerial and professional occupations. Women outnumbered men by 9.8 million in technical, sales, and administrative support jobs. But between 1975 and 1985, the number of women managers and professionals increased 77 percent while the number of men in these positions increased by only 26 percent (Taeuber and Valdisera, 1987).

Despite this progress women still dominate low-paying fields. Five of the top ten occupations employing women are secretaries, bookkeepers, cashiers, salesworkers, and typists. The two professional positions they dominate are relatively low-paying, namely nursing and elementary school teaching (Taeuber and Valdisera, 1987).

GENDER ROLES AND THE FUTURE

Earlier in this chapter we alluded to certain conditions in contemporary society that have had great significance and impact on gender roles and family relations. Demographic changes, lengthened life spans, the decline in infant and child mortality and in maternal deaths during childbirth, lower birthrates, the dissociation of reproduction from sexual activities, and the shorter period of time devoted to maternity in relation to women's total life expectancy—all have contributed to changes in attitudes and behavior in the family.

Throughout the twentieth century, women have been gaining legal equality. Changes in women's legal status include the right of suffrage, rights of separation and divorce, and rights of equal employment and opportunity. Although equality has not been fully realized, there has been marked improvement in the power and status of women

compared with their position during the nineteenth century. The result has been the growth of female independence.

Changes in Attitudes

The Roper Organization has been asking a nationally representative sample of men and women the same questions for the last fifteen years. The results show a significant shift in the attitudes and lifestyles of men and women.

When the impact of the feminist movement began to be felt around 1970, only 38 percent of women and 40 percent of men believed women were looked on with more respect than a decade earlier. By 1985, after the feminist movement became a part of mainstream society, 60 percent of women and 61 percent of men believed women were respected more than during the previous decade.

With these changes has come the realization that gender equality benefits not only women, but men and children as well. As corporations face a shrinking work force in the 1990s, they will be forced to respond to the needs of workers for a variety of benefits including child care, unpaid maternity leaves, flexible working hours, job sharing and part-time work.

For the first time, the concerns of women for adequate child-care and maternity leave are being shared by men. As a result, both men and women are pressing corporations and government to respond to the needs of the family. When the Du Pont Corporation surveyed 3,300 male employees in 1985, they found that only 18 percent were interested in part-time work to give them more time with their children. By 1988, the percentage had jumped to 33 percent. Similarly, in 1985, only 11 percent expressed interest in a period after the birth of a child in which they could work fewer hours. Three years later the percentage climbed to 28 percent. Clearly, in those three years, the issue of child-care evolved from a female issue into a concern of both men and women (*U.S. News and World Report*, June 20, 1988).

We should not assume that economic conditions are forcing women to go to work. When women are asked if they would continue working if they were financially secure, 70 percent of women in all age groups claim they would. The same percentage of men responded similarly to the same question. Education appears to be a deciding factor in continuing to work. Women who have dropped out of high school are most likely to not work if they do not have to, while those with some college education are the least likely to leave the work force if they are financially secure. The least likely of all to leave the work force are women in households with the highest incomes.

The vast majority of both men and women think that marriage is the best way to live. But the type of marriage that people want is different than the marriage of the past. In 1974, about half of all men and women thought a traditional marriage where the husband worked and the wife stayed home and took care of the house and children was ideal. By 1985, only 37 percent of women and 43 percent of men wanted this type of arrangement. The majority of men and women thought the most satisfying marriage was one where husband and wife share work, housekeeping, and child-care. It should also come as no surprise that younger women are the most likely to want an egalitarian lifestyle (Walsh, 1986).

Women's employment changed the ways in which women and men define marital and parental roles. As women become less dependent and are able to buy services, marital and parental roles may become less stressful. However, some new stresses may emerge. Employed women are likely to redefine involvement in child rearing and expect more equal participation from their husbands. This situation may produce heightened marital tensions.

It appears that nontraditional gender roles produce a gain in power and control for women. Some believe this accounts for the lower levels of depression among working women in nontraditional marriages compared to women in traditional home-maker roles. At the same time this change may produce less control for men in such marriages and the potential for higher levels of depression. At least in the short term, marital strain may be one of the costs for the current redefinitions of family roles (Barnett, and Baruch, 1987).

Like so many other areas of American life, gender roles are undergoing rapid change. Traditional distinctions are becoming blurred and obsolete in response to new social and economic demands, but experts on the whole expect strong family bonds to survive.

AGE STRATIFICATION

For the first time in our history, there are more people aged 65 and over in the population than there are teenagers. By 1990 the number of older citizens surpassed 31 million, whereas the teenaged population dropped to 23 million.

When the first United States Census was taken in 1790, there were about 50,000 Americans over the age of 65, representing two percent of the population of 2.5 million. One hundred years later, the over-65 population had grown to 2.4 million or just under four percent of the population. The rate of increase in the older population really started to rise after 1920, and by 1989 there were 30.1 million older Americans making up 12.4 percent of the population (*Statistical Abstract of the United States, 1991*). (See Figure 10.2.)

According to projections, the number of persons 65 and over will increase sharply beginning in 2010, and by the year 2030 there will be 64.6 million older people representing 21.1 percent of the total population. Projections for the future are usually conservative and do not take into account declines in mortality that produce longer life spans.

There are several basic reasons for the growth in the older population. First, a large number of people who were born when the birthrate was high are now reaching age 65. Secondly, many people who immigrated to the United States before World War II are also reaching age 65. Thirdly, improvements in medical technology have created a dramatic increase in life expectancy.

Composition of the Older Population

People tend to think of the older population as a homogeneous group with common concerns and problems. This is not the case. We can divide the older population into three groups: the *young-old*

For the first time in our history, there are more people aged 65 and over in the population than there are teenagers.

FIGURE 10.2

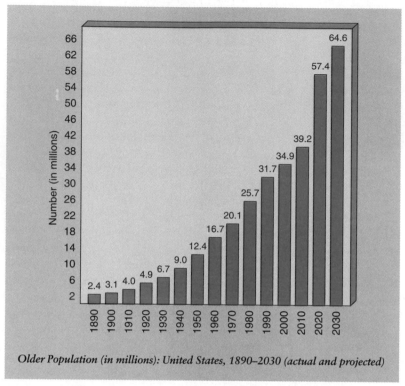

Older Population (in millions): United States, 1890–2030 (actual and projected)

Source: United States Bureau of the Census, 1984b.

(age 65–74), the *middle-old* (age 75–84), and the *old-old* (age 85 and over). The older population as a whole is itself getter older. Whereas in 1960 about one-third of the older population was over 75, by the year 2000, fifty percent of the older people will be over 75. In that same period of time the *old-old* (those over 85) will have nearly tripled in numbers.

Aging by Sex Ratio

The mortality rate for both men and women has been declining, but it has been declining much more rapidly for women. Women at any age of life are less likely to die than men. This decline has helped produce a substantial sex ratio imbalance in the over 65 group that continues to become more apparent as we move further up the age scale. By the year 2000 there will be 65 men per 100 women over age 65. Among those over age 85, however, there will be only 38 men per 100 women (National Center for Health Statistics, 1986).

Aging by Race

About 90 percent of the older population of the United States is white, 8.2 percent is African Ameri-

can, and the remaining 1.8 percent is made up of Asian American, American Indian, and a smattering of other groups. The African-American percentage of the over 65 group is lower than might be expected. That is, if African Americans make up 12 percent of the total population, then we would expect them to also make up 12 percent of the older population. This is caused by the higher birthrate among African Americans, as well as the fact that life expectancy is lower for that group than it is for whites.

Aging by Marital Status

Women in the United States outlive men by about 7.3 years. The older a woman becomes, the more likely she is to be a widow. Seventy percent of women over the age of 75 are widows, while less than 20 percent of men that age are widowers. In addition to the longer life expectancy of women, men tend to marry women younger than themselves. Because of the discrepancy in life expectancy, a widow will find few older men available to marry, whereas a widower has many older women available to remarry, making it more likely that those older people living alone or in institutions are women.

THEORIES OF AGING

The study of the social aspects of aging is almost exclusively a twentieth century United States phenomenon. Most theories about aging have been put forth since 1950 and little effort has been made to apply them cross-culturally. Generating theories of aging has been a process very much related to the changing perceptions of aging and emerging social policies.

Disengagement Theory

Disengagement theory *states that aging involves an inevitable withdrawal, or disengagement from positions of social responsibility as part of the orderly operation of society* (Cumming and Henry, 1961). The process may be initiated by the individual or other people or groups. Disengagement theory implies that this process is the way in which society and the individual gradually prepare for the ultimate withdrawal of the person through death. Disengagement involves giving up the major roles in life. These include the role of parent, as well as occupational positions.

An underlying assumption of disengagement theory is that both the individual and society are happy about this process. The individual is pleased to be relieved of societal pressures for continued productivity. Society is pleased because the withdrawal of older members allows younger, more energetic and competent members to fill the vacated roles. There would be a considerable amount of social disruption if roles were only vacated through death or incompetence. Disengagement allows an orderly transition to take place.

Disengagement theory has a strong functionalist theory bias because it assumes that everyone benefits from a smooth transfer of power from the old to the young. Older people are granted greater freedom of behavior with little expected in return, while society experiences an orderly changing of the guards.

Activity Theory

Activity theory *assumes that satisfaction in later life is related to the level of activity the person engages in* (Burgess, 1953–1954). Activity theory assumes inactivity is closely related to low levels of happiness, little sense of purpose, and a generally inadequate

One of the values present in middle-class American society is that being active and productive is desirable for a successful life.

adjustment to the senior years. The theory assumes that successful aging is dependent on maintaining an optimal level of activity. An individual's identity throughout life is built on a variety of statuses and roles, and satisfaction in later life depends on maintaining this social identity.

One of the values present in middle-class American society is that being active and productive is desirable for a successful life. Middle-class children are encouraged to get involved in as many activities as possible from music lessons to little league, scouts, and religious schools. Adult life is a continuation of this pattern with work and a whole host of activities consuming most of the hours in a day. By the time these people reach retirement, there is likely to be a good deal of ambivalence about disengaging from work and social responsibilities.

One problem with activity theory is that if we accept the belief that everyone should remain active in later life, then those people, who cannot maintain an active lifestyle because of physiological limitations that are part of the aging process, are likely to experience considerable frustration and guilt at not meeting up to the standards. The theory imposes a certain value system on the lifestyle needs of a diverse population.

Modernization Theory

Modernization theory *assumes there is a direct relationship between the extent of modernization in a society and the status and condition of the elderly.* According to this theory, loss of status is a universal experience in all cultures in which modernization processes occur. Cowgill and Holmes (1972) studied fifteen societies and offered the following correlations:

1. The concept of old age is relative to the degree of modernization. A person is classified as old at an earlier chronological age in primitive society than in a modern society.
2. Longevity is directly related to degree of modernization.
3. Modernized societies have higher proportions of old people.
4. The status of the aged is high in primitive societies and lower and more ambiguous in modern societies.
5. The status of the aged is high when there are few of them and declines as their numbers and proportions increase.
6. Retirement is a modern invention and is found chiefly in modern high-productivity societies.
7. Disengagement is not characteristic of the aged in primitive or agrarian societies, but appears to accompany modernization.

One study done in the 1970s (Palmore and Whittington, 1971) found that not only did the elderly have a lower status than the young, but also that there had been a significant decline in the status of the aged relative to the rest of the population between 1940 and 1969. The decline in status was continuing and would get worse in the future.

Critics of modernization theory charge that the correlation between the status of the elderly and modernization is not real, and that modernization theorists have romanticized a "golden age" in the past. They charge that most people in that past never reached old age by today's standards and that it is therefore incorrect to assume their status was higher then.

FUTURE TRENDS IN AGE STRATIFICATION

Relatively stagnant birthrates and big jumps in life expectancy have contributed to the growth in the older population. In addition, the enormous baby-boom generation, born between 1946 and 1964, which now represents about one third of the population, is moving into middle age. The number of people between the ages of 30 and 44 has surged to 20 percent and totals 60 million (U.S. Bureau of Census).

As the baby boom population ages, its large numbers will cause cycles of relative growth and decline at each stage of life. The aging of the baby-boom generation will push the median age, now at 31 years, to over 38 years by 2010, and almost to 42 years by 2050.

The years from 1985 through 2020 cover the most economically productive years for the baby-boom generation. In 2010 the oldest members of the baby boom will be nearing 65, while the youngest will have just passed 45.

As the baby-boom cohorts begin to reach age 65 starting in 2011, the number of elderly persons will rise dramatically.

In about 2030, the final phase of the elderly explosion caused by the baby boom will begin. At that point the population aged 85 and over will be the only older age group still growing and will have increased from 2.7 million now to 8.6 million in 2030, to over 16 million by 2050 (U.S. Bureau of Census). (See Table 10.2)

To put it another way, today one in 100 people is 85 years or older; in 2050, one in twenty persons could be so old. Persons 85 and older could constitute close to one-quarter of the older population by then.

Concerns associated with problems of the older population are exacerbated by the large excess of women over men in the older ages. Among the

Increased longevity and the aging of the baby-boom generation will mean that many people will find themselves caring for very old persons after they themselves have reached retirement age.

CONTROVERSIES IN SOCIOLOGY

Euthanasia—What is the "Good Death?"

It is the scene modern men and women dread. They are in a hospital, desperately ill and alone. By their side is a respirator, supplementing breathing with a regular sigh of its own. Tubes run into their nose and stomach, carrying vital fluids needed for life. As death approaches, control of one's life has been lost.

Modern medicine affords marvelous cures; it keeps men and women alive longer than they could have hoped for even half a century ago. Yet when life is prolonged, there is all the more chance that it will end in debilitation, dementia and dependence. The old who used to be snatched away by pneumonia, or by a heart attack, now can be cured with antibiotics, and stopped hearts can be pounded back to life with cardio-pulmonary resuscitation. Death can be cheated.

But the cheating brings with it a crowd of questions. Should people be kept alive who, without intervention, would surely die? Should patients be allowed to choose for themselves whether or not to go on living? Should doctors become ministers, not of cures, but of easeful death? How are life and death to be valued?

All religions and legal codes have long upheld the principle that life is sacred and ought to be preserved. To that, hospitals and institutions of medicine add their conviction that death is a failure. These presumptions still carry enormous weight, both in courts and on the wards. To put it in bluntly secular form, the state

has an interest in preserving its subjects. . . .

Yet what are a patient's best interests, and how are they to be discovered? Against the principle of state interest looms the equally weighty principle of autonomy: a person's right to privacy and the direction of his own life. In the end, autonomy decides most cases of "right-to-die," but it is a principle that may sometimes lean towards life, not death. Can anyone say, on behalf of a patient unable to speak for themselves, that their life is not worth living?

Euthanasia, in Greek, means "the good death"—the active intervention of a doctor, usually at the patient's request, to bring that patient's life to an end. Even when asked for, euthanasia is illegal everywhere. In the United States it counts as assistance in a suicide; in Britain it is classed as attempted murder. In Holland, where since 1973 the practice has been winked at, the statutory penalty is up to twelve years in prison.

Yet a majority of people in all these countries (70 percent in America, 75 percent in Britain) approves of being "helped to die" in *extremis*, and judgements in the courts are coming to reflect that softer attitude.

Society has a legitimate interest in death. Not many years ago a whole village, not just the dying person's family, gathered round to give strength. If societies can no longer agree on the meaning or purpose of death (or whether it has any meaning at all), they can still construct sensible and

comforting legislation to allay the fears of the dying.

First, they could recognize the right of the terminally ill to decide their own treatment. This would be done by a standardized document, filled in on admission to hospital if not before, by the routine appointment of a proxy with durable power of attorney, and by continuing consultation with a doctor, so that the dying could always change their minds. When there can be no statement of intention (as with infants), the basis of decision would be the balance of burdens and benefits to the patient of a certain course of treatment.

The patient's right to decide treatment would stop short of the right to request death. If no extraordinary means were used to prolong life, death would not be unnecessarily delayed. The patient's life would be made as comfortable as possible.

To civilize death, to bring it home and to make it no longer a source of dread, is one of the great challenges of the age. These changes would be a first step on that road. The road leads not to total control of dying (as it should not), but to acceptance and understanding. Gradually, dying may come to hold again the place it used to occupy in the midst of life: not a terror, but a mystery so deep that people would no more wish to cheat themselves of it than to cheat themselves of life.

Source: Adapted and excerpted from "Euthanasia, What is the 'Good Death'?" *The Economist*, July 20, 1991, pp. 21–22, 24.

TABLE 10.2

Average Annual Rate of Growth of the U.S. Population, 1980–2010 and 2010–2030

	1980–2010	2010–2030
Preschool (Under 5)	+0.3	*
School Age (5–17)	*	+0.1
Young Adult (18–34)	−0.2	−0.1
Adult (35–44)	+1.4	+0.5
Middle Aged (45–64)	+2.5	−0.4
Young Old (65–74)	+1.0	+3.5
Old Old (75+)	+2.9	+3.0

Source: U.S. Bureau of Census, *Statistical Brief*, December 1986.

aged, women outnumber men three to two. That imbalance increases to more than two to one for persons 85 and over.

Increased longevity and the aging of the baby-boom generation will mean that many people will find themselves caring for very old persons after they themselves have reached retirement age. Assuming that generations are separated by about 25 years, persons 85, 90, or 95 would have children who are anywhere between 60 and 70 years old. It is estimated that every third person 60 to 74 years old will have a living elderly parent by 2010.

Now there are more than twice as many children as there are elderly persons. By 2030, the proportion of children will have shrunk and the proportion of elderly will have grown until these two groups are approximately equal at just over one-fifth of the population each (U.S. Bureau of Census).

There are few certainties about the future, but the demographic outlook seems relatively clear, at least for persons already born. Careful consideration of the impact of our aging population can be an important tool in planning for the future.

PART IV

INSTITUTIONS

CHAPTER 11 *Marriage and Alternative Family Lifestyles*

CHAPTER 12 *Religion*

CHAPTER 13 *Education*

CHAPTER 14 *Political and Economic Systems*

Every society has standardized ways of dealing with basic social needs. Sociologists call these patterned activities that fulfill society's fundamental needs social institutions. Humans fashion their social institutions in accordance with their society's dominant norms and values. At the same time, well-defined institutional patterns mold and channel individual behavior and awareness. Social institutions, however, are not monolithic; tensions, defects, and countervailing pressures within them mirror conflicts and controversies in society at large.

In this section of the book you will explore four major institutions in American society. The first of these is the family. Why do humans live in families? What functions does the family fulfill? What different forms does the family take? How are families formed—that is, what are the rules and practices surrounding marriage? How is the family changing in today's society? All of these questions will be dealt with in Chapter 11.

We also will examine the religious institution. Chapter 12 explores the elements and major types of religious belief. Here you will be introduced to a sociological analysis of religion: competing perspectives on the functions of religious belief for individuals and groups, description and analysis of the social organization of religious life, and examination of religious trends in contemporary American society.

Education is about the acquisition of skills and knowledge. But what else is it? What else goes on in our classrooms and our schools? Indeed, what should be going on there? As you have already seen in examining other issues, functionalists and conflict theorists have different views of why certain features of our society exist and whose interests those features serve. This is also true with regard to education, and in Chapter 13 you will examine these contrasting perspectives on the organization and operation of our educational system. You will also investigate some of the most important social issues facing American education today.

Every society must have mechanisms for making decisions about important issues. These mechanisms are organized into the political institution, which is the subject of Chapter 14. Some of the questions you will explore in this chapter include: What is power? How is it exercised legitimately? How and why is government organized the way it is? How does the economic system influence politics and the government, and vice versa? How does political change occur?

When you have completed Part IV of this book, you should have a comprehensive picture of how American society is organized. You will then be ready to explore some important social issues facing our society and our world as we move into the next century.

Marriage and Alternative Family Lifestyles

The Nature of Family Life
  Functions of the Family
  Family Structures

Defining Marriage
  Romantic Love
  Marriage Rules
  Marital Residence
  Mate Selection

The Transformation of the Family
  Changes in the Marriage Rate
  Childless Couples
  Changes in Household Size
  Premarital Sex
  Working Women
  Family Violence
  Divorce

Alternative Lifestyles
  The Growing Single Population
  Single-Parent Families
  Stepfamilies
  Cohabitation
  Homosexual and Lesbian Couples

The Future: Bright or Dismal?

There is no single description of the American family. The family of the 1950s with a husband who worked outside the home and wife who cared for two or more well-scrubbed children is gone for most Americans. In its place is a montage of family types—a diversity that adds strength to the American social landscape.

John Edwards, 29, and his wife Elaine have decided to remain childless. John notes: "This world is a crazy place to raise children. Some day we may all blow ourselves up." Elaine adds: "If we wanted to help the poor in the ghetto, how could we with a child? Now nothing holds us back."

Seventeen-year-old Vincent Sowell has not yet had a full shave. Yet he is already the father of a 3-month-old baby daughter and another child is on the way. Vincent's children have two different mothers, both teenagers. "I know I've got responsibilities," says Vincent, who earns $5.50 an hour working for a landscaping firm.

Elizabeth Perkins did everything right. At 38, she is a well-established lawyer who spent her 20s in college and law school. Although she acquired impressive credentials, she had no time to date and never married. She now feels she may have waited too long.

These vignettes give us an idea of the diversity in family life in the United States and the many forms the family can take. The American family will continue to evolve and change even more during the next decade. By the year 2000, the U.S. will have 19 million more households than it does today, but the households of the turn of the century will be even less traditional than the households of today. Families will comprise only two out of three households and married couples will live in just over half of all households (U.S. Bureau of Census, 1986).

Has the American family always been in such flux? Although information about family life during the earliest days of our country is not very precise, it does appear clear, beginning with the 1790 census, that the American family was quite stable. Divorce and family breakup were not common. If a marriage ended because of desertion, death, or divorce, it was seen as a personal and community tragedy.

The American family has always been small. There has never been a strong tradition here of the extended family, where relatives and several generations lived within the same dwelling. Even in the 1700s, the American family consisted of a husband, wife, and approximately three children. This private, inviolate enclave made it possible for the family to endure severe circumstances and to help build the American frontier.

By the 1960s, radical changes were becoming evident. The marriage and birth rate began to fall, and the divorce rate, which had been fairly level, began accelerating upward.

This trend is continuing. In 1989 there were 2.4 million marriages, though there were also 1.16 million divorces. This information is even more striking when we realize that divorce statistics do not include desertion or other forms of marital breakup, such as annulment or legal separation.

There also are other signs of change and family instability. Of all children born in 1988, 25.7 percent were born to single women. Among African-Americans, the percentage of children born out of wedlock was 63.5 percent (*Statistical Abstract of the United States: 1991*).

The inescapable conclusion is that the American family is in a state of transition. But transition to what? In this chapter we shall study the institution of the family and look more closely at current trends and what they forecast for the future.

THE NATURE OF FAMILY LIFE

For a long time, social scientists defined the family in a way that reflected "common knowledge." For example, in his classic study of social organization and the family, anthropologist George P. Murdock (1949) defined the family as:

> a social group characterized by common residence, economic cooperation, and reproduction. It includes adults of both sexes, at least two of whom maintain a socially approved sexual relationship, and one or more children, own or adopted, of the sexually cohabiting adults.

This definition has proved too limited. For one thing, it excludes many kinds of social groups that seem, on the basis of the functions they serve, to deserve the label of family. For example, in America, single-parent families are widely recognized. If we expand our perspective to include other societies, we find that quite a few seem to lack the kind of group described by Murdock. For example, in 1954, Melford Spiro, an anthropologist, studied Israeli *kibbutzim* (pronounced kee-boots-eem)—agricultural communities with communal living, collective

Anthropologist George P. Murdock defined the family as a social group characterized by common residence, economic cooperation, and reproduction.

ownership of all property, and the communal rearing of children. In some *kibbutzim,* the children sleep apart from their parents in "children's houses" and are cared for in peer groups by child care workers assigned by the *kibbutz.* Spiro's studies at first seemed to indicate that the institution of the family did not exist within the *kibbutz,* that the psychological and social functions of the family were provided by the *kibbutz* as a whole. However, as Spiro himself later pointed out (1960), many features typical of the family do exist in the *kibbutz:* Couples marry and plan for children; parents call only their own children "son" and "daughter," and parents and children together form identifiable subgroups within the *kibbutz,* even though the children live in the children's houses. Furthermore, one of the most valued times of day is the late afternoon when children of all ages return to their parents' rooms for several hours of uninterrupted socializing. So even in the *kibbutz,* the family exists as a significant social group.

Despite Murdock's restricted definition of the family, it was his 1949 study of kinship and family in 250 societies that led social scientists to believe that some form of the family is found in every known human society.

Perhaps a better understanding of the concept of the family may be gained by examining the various functions it performs in society.

Functions of the Family

Social scientists often assign to the fundamental family unit—married parents and their offspring— a number of the basic functions that it serves in most, if not all, societies. Although in many societies the basic family unit serves some of these functions, in no society does it serve all of them completely or exclusively. For example, among the Nayar of India, a child's biological father is socially irrelevant. Generally another man takes on the social responsibility of parenthood (Gough, 1952). Or consider the Trobrianders, a people living on a small string of islands north of New Guinea. There, as reported by anthropologist Bronislaw Malinowski (1922), the father's role in parenthood is not recognized, and the responsibility for raising children falls to the family of their mother's brother.

Nor is the basic family always the fundamental unit of economic cooperation. Among artisans in preindustrial Europe, the essential economic unit was not the family but rather the household, typically consisting of the artisan's family plus assorted apprentices and even servants (Laslett, 1965). In some societies, members of the basic family group need not necessarily even live in the same household. Among the Ashanti of western Africa, for example, husbands and wives each live with their own mother's relatives (Fortes et al., 1947). In the United States a small but growing number of two-career families is finding it necessary to set up separate households in different communities—sometimes hundreds of miles apart. Husband and wife travel back and forth between these households to be with each other and the children on weekends and during vacations.

In all societies, however, the family does serve the basic social functions discussed below.

REGULATING SEXUAL BEHAVIOR No society permits random sexual behavior. All societies have an **incest taboo,** *which forbids sexual intercourse among closely related individuals*—although *who* is considered closely related varies widely. Almost universally, incest rules prohibit sex between parents and their children and between brothers and sisters. But there are exceptions: The royal families of ancient Egypt, the Inca nation, and Hawaii did allow sex and marriage between brothers and sisters. In the United States, marriage between parents and children, brothers and sisters, grandparents and grandchildren, aunts and nephews, and uncles and nieces is defined as incest and is forbidden. In addition, approximately 30 states prohibit marriage between first cousins. The incest taboo usually applies to members of one's family (however the family is defined culturally) and thus it promotes marriage and consequently social ties among members of different families.

PATTERNING REPRODUCTION Every society must replace its members. By regulating where and with whom individuals may enter into sexual relationships, society also patterns sexual reproduction. By permitting or forbidding certain forms of marriage (multiple wives or multiple husbands, for example) a society can encourage or discourage reproduction.

ORGANIZING PRODUCTION AND CONSUMPTION In preindustrial societies, the economic system often depended on each family producing much of what it consumed. In almost all societies, the family consumes food and other necessities as a social unit. Therefore, a society's economic system and family structures often are closely correlated.

SOCIALIZING CHILDREN Not only must a society reproduce itself biologically, it must also ensure that its children are encouraged to accept the lifestyle it favors, to master the skills it values, and to perform the work it requires. In other words, a society must provide predictable social contexts within which its children are to be socialized (see Chapter 4). The family provides such a context, at least during the period when the child is dependent on the constant attention of others. The family is ideally suited to this task because its members know the child from birth and are aware of its special abilities and needs.

PROVIDING CARE AND PROTECTION Every human needs food and shelter. In addition, we all need to be among people who care for us, who help us with the problems that arise in daily life, and who back us up when we come into conflict with others. Although many kinds of social groups are capable of meeting one or more of these needs, the family often is the one group in a society that meets them all.

PROVIDING SOCIAL STATUS Simply by being born into a family, each individual inherits both material goods and a socially recognized position defined by ascribed statuses (see Chapter 5). These statuses include social class or caste membership and ethnic identity. Our inherited social position, or family background, probably is the single most important social factor affecting the predictable course in our lives.

Thus, we see that Murdock's definition of the family, based primarily on structure, is indeed too restrictive. A much more productive way of defining the family would be to view it as a universal institution that generally serves the functions discussed above, although the way it does so may vary greatly from one society to another. The different ways in which various social functions are fulfilled by the institution of the family depend, in some instances, on the form the family takes.

Family Structures

The **nuclear family** *is made up of a married couple and their biological or adopted children.* The nuclear family is found in all societies, and it is from this form that all other (composite) family forms derive.

There are two major composite family forms: polygamous and extended families (see Figure 11.1). **Polygamous families** *are nuclear families linked together by multiple marriage bonds, with one central individual married to several spouses. The family is* **polygynous** *when the central person is male and the multiple spouses are female. The family is* **polyandrous** *when the central person is female and*

the multiple spouses are male. Polyandry is known to exist only in a very few societies.

Extended families *include other relations and generations in addition to the nuclear family, so that along with married parents and their offspring there may be the parents' parents, siblings of the parents, the siblings' spouses and in-laws.* All the members of the extended family live in one house or in homes close to one another, forming one cooperative unit.

Families, whether nuclear or extended, trace their relationships through generations in several different ways. Under the **patrilineal system,** *the generations are tied together through the males of a family;* all members trace their kinship through the father's line. Under the **matrilineal system,** *the generations are tied together through the females of a family.* Under the **bilateral system,** *descent passes through both females and males of a family.* Although in American society, descent is bilateral, the majority of the world's societies are either patrilineal or matrilineal (Murdock, 1949).

In patrilineal societies, social, economic, and political affairs are usually organized around the kinship relationships among men, and men tend to dominate public affairs. Polygyny often is permitted, and men also tend to dominate family affairs. Sociologists use the term **patriarchal family** *to describe situations in which most family affairs are dominated by men. The* **matriarchal family,** *in which most family affairs are dominated by women, is relatively uncommon.* Typically matriarchal families emerge in matrilineal societies. The matriarchal family is becoming increasingly more common in American society, however, with the rise of single-parent families (most often headed by mothers).

Whatever form the family takes and whatever functions it serves, it generally requires a marriage in order to exist. Like the family, marriage varies from society to society in its forms.

DEFINING MARRIAGE

Marriage *is the socially recognized, legitimized, and supported union of individuals of opposite sexes.* It is an institution found in all societies. It differs from other unions (such as friendships) in that (1) it takes place in a public (and usually formal) manner; (2) it includes sexual intercourse as an explicit element of the relationship; (3) it provides the essential condition for legitimizing offspring (that is, it provides newborns with socially accepted statuses); and (4) it is intended to be a stable and enduring relationship. Thus, although almost all societies

FIGURE 11.1

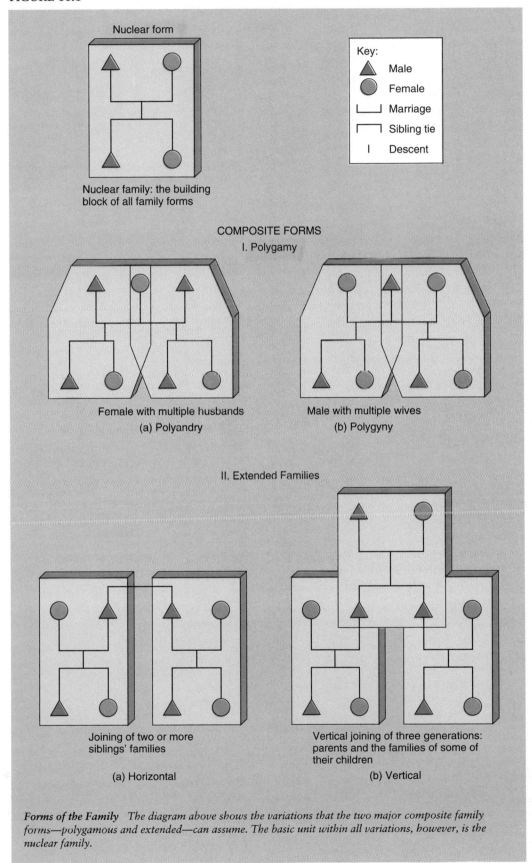

Forms of the Family *The diagram above shows the variations that the two major composite family forms—polygamous and extended—can assume. The basic unit within all variations, however, is the nuclear family.*

Under the patrilineal system, the generations are tied together through the males of the family.

allow for divorce—that is, the breakup of marriage—no society endorses it as an ideal norm.

Romantic Love

Our culture is relatively unique in regarding romantic love and the institution of marriage as compatible. Not only do we believe they are compatible, we also generally expect that they coexist. Our culture implies that without the prospect of marriage, romance is immoral and that without romance, marriage is empty. This view underlies most romantic fiction and media presentations.

Romantic love can be defined in terms of five dimensions: (1) idealization of the loved one, (2) the notion of a one and only, (3) love at first sight, (4) love winning out over all, and (5) an indulgence of personal emotions (Lantz, 1982).

Throughout most of the world, romantic love is unknown or is seen as a strange maladjustment. It may exist, but it has nothing to do with marriage. Marriage in these societies is an institution that organizes or patterns the establishment of economic, social, and even political relationships among families. Three families are ultimately involved in a marriage. The two spouses' **families of orientation,** that is, *the family in which one was born and raised,* and the **family of procreation**—*the family created by the union of the spouses.* Differing rules for marriage and for residence after marriage result in the creation of very different household and family forms.

Throughout most of history and in most of the world's societies, romantic love is unknown or is seen as a strange maladjustment.

Marriage Rules

In every society, marriage is the binding link that makes possible the existence of the family. All societies have norms or rules governing who may marry whom and where the newlywed couples should live. These rules vary, but there are certain typical arrangements that occur in many societies around the world.

Almost all societies have two kinds of marriage norms or rules: **rules of endogamy** *limit the social categories from within which one can choose a marriage partner.* For example, many Americans still attempt to instill in their children the idea that one should marry one's "own kind," that is, someone within the ethnic, religious, or economic group of one's family of origin.

Rules of exogamy, *on the other hand, require an individual to marry someone outside his or her culturally defined group.* For example, in many tribal groups, members must marry outside their lineage. In the United States there are laws forbidding the marriage of close relatives, although the rules are variable.

Although these norms vary widely across cultures, they serve the same basic social functions. Rules of exogamy determine the ties and boundaries between social groups, linking them through the institution of marriage and whatever social, economic, and political obligations go along with it. Rules of endogamy, by requiring people to marry within specific groups, reinforce group boundaries and perpetuate them from one generation to the next.

Marriage rules also determine how many spouses a person may have at one time. Among many groups—Europeans and Americans, for example—marriage is **monogamous**—*that is, each person is allowed only one spouse at a time.* However, many societies allow **multiple marriages,** *in which an individual may have more than one spouse* (polygamy). Polygyny, the most common form of polygamy, is found among such diverse peoples as the Swazi of Africa, the Tiwi of Australia, and, formerly, the Blackfeet Indians of the United States. Polyandry is extremely rare. Murdock (1949) lists only three societies that practice polyandry, from among his sample of 250: the Toda of India, the Sherpa of Nepal, and the Marquesan Islanders of the South Pacific.

As Marvin Harris (1975) notes, "Some form of polygamy occurs in 90 percent of the world's cultures." But within each such society only a minority of people actually can afford it. In addition, the Industrial Revolution favored monogamy for reasons we shall discuss shortly. Therefore, monogamy is the most common and widespread form of marriage in the world today.

Marital Residence

Once two people are married, they must set up housekeeping. In most societies strongly held norms influence where a couple lives. **Marital residence rules** *are rules that govern where a newly married couple settles down and lives.* **Patrilocal residence** *requires the new couple to settle down near or within the husband's father's household*—as among Greek villagers and the Swazi of Africa. **Matrilocal residence** *requires the new couple to settle down near or within the wife's mother's household*—as among the Hopi Indians of the American Southwest.

Some societies allow for **bilocal residence** *where the new couple may choose whether to live with the husband's or wife's family of origin.* In modern industrial society, newlyweds typically have even more freedom, and neolocal residence is common. *With* **neolocal residence,** *the couple may choose to live virtually anywhere, even thousands of miles from their families of origin.* In practice, however, it is not unusual for American newlyweds to set up housekeeping near one of their respective families.

Marital residence rules play a major role in determining the compositions of households. With patrilocal residence, groups of men remain in the familiar context of their father's home, and their sisters leave to join their husbands. In other words, after marriage the women leave home to live as "strangers" among their husband's kinfolk. With matrilocal residence just the opposite is true: Women and their children remain at home, and husbands are the "outsiders." In many matrilocal societies, this situation often leads to considerable marital stress, with husbands going home to their own mothers' families when domestic conflict becomes intolerable.

Bilocal residence and neolocal residence allow greater flexibility and a wider range of household forms because young couples may move to places in which the social, economic, and political advantages may be greatest. One disadvantage of neolocal residence is that a young couple cannot count on the immediate presence of kinfolk to help out in times of need or with demanding household chores (including the raising of children). In the United States today, a new phenomenon, the surrogate, nonkin "family," made up of neighbors, friends, and colleagues at work, may help fill this void (Wolfe, 1981). In other societies, polygynous neolocal families help overcome such difficulties, with a number of wives cooperating in the division of household work.

Mate Selection

Like our patterns of family life, America's rules for marriage, which are expressed through mate selection, spring from those of our society's European forebears. Because we have been nourished, through songs and cinema, by the notions of "love at first sight," "love is blind," and "love conquers all," most of us probably are under the impression that in the United States there are no rules for mate selection. Research shows, however, that this is not necessarily true.

If we think statistically about mate selection, we must admit that in no way is it random. Consider for a moment what would happen if it were: Given the population distribution of the United States, blacks would be more likely to marry whites than members of their race; upper-class individuals would have a greater chance of marrying a lower-class person; and various culturally unlikely but statistically probable combinations of age, education, and religion would take place. In actual fact, **homogamy**—*the tendency to choose a spouse with a similar racial, religious, ethnic, educational, age, and socioeconomic background*—is much more the rule.

There are numerous ways in which homogamy can be achieved. One way is to let someone older and wiser, such as a parent or matchmaker, pair up appropriately suited individuals. Throughout history, this has been one of the most common ways by which marriages have taken place. The role of the couple in question can range from having no choice at all to having some sort of veto power. This tradition is quite strong in Islamic countries such as Pakistan. Benazir Bhutto, an outspoken political leader and daughter of a former Pakistani prime minister, agreed to an arranged marriage despite her Western education and feminist leanings. She submitted to Islamic cultural traditions where dating is not considered acceptable behavior for a woman (*New York Times*, June 17, 1988).

In the United States, most people who get married do not use the services of a matchmaker, though the end result in terms of similarity of background is so highly patterned that it could seem as if a very conscious homogamous matchmaking effort were involved.

AGE In American society, people generally marry within their own age range. There are comparatively few marriages in which there is a wide gap between the ages of the two partners. In addition, only 23.2 percent of American women marry men who are younger than themselves. On the average, in a first marriage for both the man and the woman, the man tends to be 2.6 years older than the woman. This is, however, related to age at the time of marriage. For example, 20-year-old men marry women with a median age only one month younger. Twenty-five-year-old men marry women with a median age 11 months younger. For 30–34 year-old men, the median age for wives is 2.8 years younger, while for men over 65, the median age for wives is nearly 10 years younger (Statistical Abstract of the United States: 1991).

In 1890, the estimated median age at first marriage was 26.1 years for men and 22.0 years for women. At that time, a decline in the median age at first marriage began that did not end until 1956 when the median age reached a low of 20.1 years for women and 22.5 years for men. This 66-year decline was reversed between 1956 and 1990, as the median returned to the 1890 level of 26.1 years for men and an even higher 23.6 median for women (Marital Status and Living Arrangements: March 1990, 1991).

There are also regional differences in the average age of marriage. Southern women marrying for the first time are the youngest, while eastern brides are the oldest (Wilson and London, 1987).

Age homogamy appears to hold for all groups within the population. Studies show that it is true for blacks as well as whites and for professionals as well as laborers. (Leslie, 1979; Hollingshead, 1951; Glick and Landau, 1950).

RACE Homogamy is most obvious in the area of race. As late as 1966, 19 states sought to ban interracial marriage through legislation. The laws varied widely. In Arizona before 1967, it was illegal for a white person to marry a black, Hindu, Malay, or Asian. The same thing was true in Wyoming, and residents of that state were also prohibited from marrying mulattos.

In 1966 the state of Virginia's Supreme Court of Appeals had to decide on the legality of a marriage between Richard P. Loving, a white man, and his part-Indian and part-black wife, Mildred Loving. The court unanimously upheld the state's ban on interracial marriages. The couple appealed the case to the United States Supreme Court, which agreed to decide whether state laws prohibiting racial intermarriage were constitutional. Previously, all courts had ruled that the laws were not discriminatory because they applied to both whites and non-

As late as 1966, nineteen states sought to stop interracial marriage through legislation.

whites. However, on June 12, 1967, the Supreme Court ruled that states could not outlaw racial intermarriage.

Since that time, the number of couples in interracial marriages has risen from 0.7 percent of all married couples in 1970 to 1.6 percent in 1986. Yet, interracial unions represent less than two of every 100 married couples (*Statistical Abstract of the United States, 1991*).

The most common type of interracial marriage is one between a white husband and a wife of a race other than African American. The next most common is between a white woman and a man of a race other than African American. These types of interracial marriages have been increasing substantially, while black/white interracial marriages appear to be leveling off.

Interracial marriages are more likely to involve at least one previously married partner than are marriages between spouses of the same race. In addition, brides and grooms who married interracially tend to be older than the national average.

The degree of education of the participants also differs in interracial marriages. White grooms in interracial marriages are more likely to have completed college than white grooms who marry within their race. In all-white couples, 18 percent of the grooms hold college degrees. In a marriage involving a white groom and a black bride, 24 percent of the men finished college. Among black men married to

women of other races only five percent had completed college, whereas 13 percent of black men married to white brides had done so. Nine percent of black men whose spouses were also black held college degrees.

Although the rate of interracial marriage is growing, the proportions vary widely by state. Hawaii has the distinction of having both the highest number and the greatest proportion of interracial marriage. Almost one-fourth of all marriages there are interracial, the majority of which are Asian-Caucasian unions. Florida runs a distant second in the number of interracial marriages. Illinois is unusual in that the 1,173 interracial marriages include 665 white brides marrying black grooms—the highest number of marriages of that combination in any state. The record for the reverse combination—black brides marrying white grooms—is held by New Jersey. Alaska comes second to Hawaii in the proportion of interracial marriages. Thirteen percent of the state's marriages are interracial. None of the other states come close to these percentages.

Even though their total numbers are still small, racially mixed marriages have become increasingly common in America's melting pot.

RELIGION Religious homogamy is not nearly as widespread as racial homogamy, though most marriages still do involve people of the same religion. Unlike many European nations, none of the American states has ever had legislation restricting interreligious marriage.

Attitudes toward religious intermarriage vary somewhat from one religious group to another. Almost all religious bodies try to discourage or control marriage outside the religion, but vary in the extent of their opposition. Prior to 1970 the Roman Catholic Church would not allow a priest to perform an interreligious marriage ceremony unless the non-Catholic partner promised to raise the children of the union as Catholics, and the Catholic partner promised to encourage the non-Catholic to convert. However, in the late 1960s the Catholic church softened its policy, and since 1970 the Pope has allowed local bishops to permit mixed marriages to be performed without a priest and has also eliminated the requirement that the non-Catholic partner promise to rear the children as Catholics. Nevertheless, the Catholic partner must still promise to *try* to have the children raised as Catholic.

Protestant denominations and sects also differ with regard to the barriers they place on the intermarriage of their members. At one extreme are the

Rules of endogamy encourage a person to choose a marriage partner from a certain ethnic or religious group.

Mennonites, who excommunicate any member who marries outside the faith. At the other are numerous bodies that may encourage their members to marry within the faith, but provide no formal penalties for those who do not (Heer, 1980).

Jewish religious bodies also differ in their degree of opposition to religious intermarriage. Orthodox Jews are the most adamantly opposed to intermarriage, while Conservative and Reform Jews, while by no means endorsing it, are more tolerant. Jewish intermarriage rates have been increasing dramatically in recent years, with nearly 40 percent of all Jews marrying someone of another religion.

Religious leaders are often concerned about religious intermarriage for a variety of reasons. Some claim that one or both intermarrying parties are lost to the religion; others believe the potential for marital success is decreased greatly. Studies have shown there are several complex factors in intermarriage and that simplistic and unequivocal predictions are not warranted. For example, a study in Iowa of Catholic-Protestant marriages concluded that though there was a slightly higher divorce rate among intermarried couples, the results did not justify predictions of marital problems. Moreover, the study also showed that Presbyterians, Methodists, and Baptists who married persons of other Protestant denominations had higher marital survival rates than did those who married within their denomination (Burchinal and Chancellor, 1963).

Although most marriages still involve religious homogamy, there is a clear trend of more religious intermarriages in the United States today.

SOCIAL STATUS Level of education and type of occupation are two measures of social status. In these areas there is usually a great deal of similarity between people who marry each other. Men tend to marry women who are slightly below them in education and social status, though these differences are within a narrow range. Wide-ranging differences in social status often contain an element of exploitation. One partner may either be trying to make a major leap on the social class ladder or be looking for an easy way of taking advantage of the other partner because of unequal power.

The typical high school environment often plays a major role in maintaining social status homogamy. In high school, students start making plans about their future careers. Some may go to college, others may plan on working immediately after graduation. This process divides students into two groups: the college-bound and the work force-bound. Although the lines separating the two are by no means impenetrable, in many high schools these two groups maintain separate social activities. In this way barriers against dating and future marriage between those of unlike social status are set up. After graduation, those who attend a college are more likely to associate with other college students and choose their mates from that pool. Those who have joined the work force are more likely to choose their mates from that environment.

As with several items we have discussed already, education, social class, and occupation produce a similarity of experience and values among people. Just as growing up in an Italian family may make one feel comfortable with Italian customs and traits, going to college may make one feel comfortable with those who have experienced that environment. Similarities in social status, then, are as much a result of socialization and culture as conscious choice. We most likely will marry a person we feel comfortable with—a person who has had experiences similar to our own.

Coming to terms with limitations on mate selection can be a sobering experience: What we thought to be freedom of choice is revealed instead to be governed by rules and patterns.

THE TRANSFORMATION OF THE FAMILY

Most scholars agree that the Industrial Revolution had a strong impact on the family. In his influential study of family patterns around the world, William J. Goode (1963) showed that the modern, relatively isolated nuclear family with weak ties to an extensive kinship network is well adapted to the pressures of industrialism.

First, industrialism demands that workers be geographically mobile so that a work force is available wherever new industries are built. The modern nuclear family, by having cut many of its ties to extended family networks, is freer to move. Extended kinship ties first weakened among families of laborers. Only in the last few decades have middle- and upper-class families become similarly isolated.

Second, industrialism requires a certain degree of social mobility (see Chapter 8) so that talented workers may be recruited to positions of greater responsibility (with greater material rewards and increased prestige). A family that is too closely tied to other families in its kinship network will find it difficult to "break free" and climb into a higher social class. On the other hand, if families in the higher social classes are too tightly linked by kinship ties, newly arriving families will find it very difficult to fit into their new social environment. Hence the isolated nuclear family is well suited to the needed social mobility in an industrial society.

A third point is that the modern nuclear family allows for inheritance and descent through both sides of the family. Further, material resources and social opportunities are not inherited mainly by the oldest males (or females), as in some societies. This means that all children in a family will have a chance to develop their skills, which in turn means that industry will have a larger, more talented, and flexible labor force from which to hire workers.

By the early twentieth century, then, the nuclear family had evolved fully among the working classes of industrial society. It rested on (1) the child-centered family; (2) **companionate marriage** *(that is, marriage based on romantic love)*; (3) increased equality for women; (4) decreased links with extended families or kinship networks; (5) neolocal residence and increased geographical mobility; (6) increased social mobility; and (7) the clear separation between work and leisure. In addition, most work during the period was boring and alienating, and the nuclear family was expected to fulfill the function of providing emotional support for its members.

The World War II years also had a profound effect on the American family, by accelerating a process that began in the Depression. The war made it necessary for hundreds of thousands of women to work outside the home in order to support their families. They often had to take jobs vital to the American economy that had been vacated when their husbands went to fight overseas. After the war, an effort was made to "defeminize" the work force. Nevertheless, many women remained on the job, and those who left now knew what it was like to work for compensation outside the home. Things were never the same again for the American family.

The initial changes were not all that apparent.

In 1946 (the year this photo was taken), the median family income was $2,800, television was in its infancy, and only 12.5 percent of people ages 18 to 22 went to college. In the years following World War II, a radical transformation took place in our society and in the family.

On the contrary, by the 1950s the United States had entered the most family-oriented period in its history. This was the beginning of the baby boom, and couples were marrying at the youngest ages in recorded American history. During the 1950s, 96 percent of those people in the child-bearing years married (Blumstein and Schwartz, 1983). The war years experiences also paved the way for secondary groups and formal organization (see Chapter 5) gradually to take over many of the family's traditional activities and functions. As social historian Christopher Lasch (1977) points out, this trend was supported by public policymakers who came to see the family as an obstacle to social progress. Because the family preserved separatist cultural and religious traditions and other "old-fashioned" ideas that stood in the way of "progress," social reformers sought to diminish the family's hold over its children. Thus the prime task of socializing the young was shifted from the family to centrally administered schools. Social workers entered the home, offering constantly expanding welfare services to families by outside agencies. The juvenile court system expanded in the belief that deficiencies in families of youthful offenders caused crime among children.

Thus, the modern period has seen what sociologists refer to as the *transfer of functions* from the family to other, outside institutions. This transfer has had a great effect on the family and underlies the trends currently troubling many people.

There are several problems in trying to assess the prevailing state of the family. Some feel the family is deteriorating, citing examples of divorce rates and single-parent families. Others think of the family as an institution in transition but just as stable as ever. Was the family of the past a stable extended family unit with everyone working for the betterment of the whole? Or has the family structure changed throughout history in response to the economic and political changes within society. In this section we shall explore these views and attempt to clarify the current direction of family life.

Changes in the Marriage Rate

Are fewer people marrying now than in the past? The answer depends on how you evaluate the data. One way to look at it is to ask how many actual marriages there are. In 1989 there were 2.4 million marriages (see Figure 11.2).

Another way to look at it is to calculate the marriage rate, the proportion of the total population marrying. The 2.4 million marriages in 1989, divided by total population of 247.3 million Americans, yields a marriage rate of 9.7 per 1,000 people in the population. According to the marriage rate, the institution is holding its own with a rate close to the mid-1970s level (see Figure 11.3).

The third way to get a true picture of marriage in the United States is to examine the marriage rate of eligible women (women age 15 and older) marrying for the first time. As of 1989 this rate was 58.9 per 1,000 (see Figure 11.4). The rate for never married men is 48.8. With these rates, about six percent of all eligible women and men marry each year.

Since 1960, the number of marriages and the marriage rate has been high because the pool of eligible adults kept expanding. Hidden in these numbers, though, is the fact that a rising share of eligible people are choosing not to marry. Even though the number of marriages increased from 1.5 million in 1960 to 2.4 million in 1989, the marriage

FIGURE 11.2

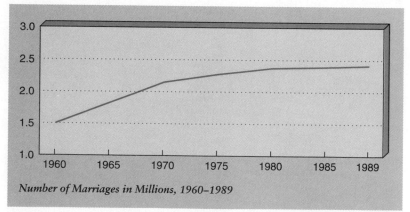

Number of Marriages in Millions, 1960–1989

Source: National Center for Health Statistics; *Statistical Abstract of the United States: 1991.*

FIGURE 11.3

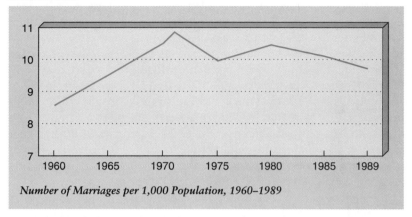

Number of Marriages per 1,000 Population, 1960–1989

Source: National Center for Health Statistics; *Statistical Abstract of the United States: 1991.*

rate for never married women fell from 93.4 per 1,000 in 1970 to 58.9 in 1987.

The proportion of eligible women who marry has shown a steady decline since 1970. It appears that people are less inclined to marry than they once were (Wilson and London, 1987).

Childless Couples

A significant trend in the last fifteen years has been the growth in the number of childless couples. There are currently six million married women aged 18 to 44 who have no children. While the number of couples with children increased by only eight percent between 1968 and 1985, the number of childless couples increased by 75 percent during that period (Bloom, 1986).

This trend appears to be an outgrowth of an increase in the number of women who are delaying marriage, which produces a substantial number of women who are well educated and have progressed in a career at the time of marriage. Many of these women decide to forego childbearing. Statistics show that the more educated the woman, the less likely she is to want children. Only seven percent of women aged 30 to 34 with less than twelve years of schooling expect to be childless; 11 percent of high school graduates expect no children, and fully 19 percent of college graduates expect to be childless (U.S. Bureau of Census, 1985). In addition, since fertility decreases with age, many of these women who marry later become childless involuntarily.

Religion also relates to whether women have children. Among married women aged 35 to 44, 21 percent of those who do not practice a religion are childless, compared to 11 percent of Protestants, and just six percent of Catholics (Bloom and Bennett, 1986).

FIGURE 11.4

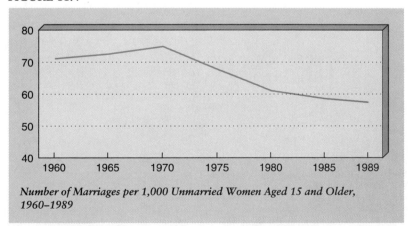

Number of Marriages per 1,000 Unmarried Women Aged 15 and Older, 1960–1989

Source: National Center for Health Statistics; *Statistical Abstract of the United States: 1991.*

Changes in Household Size

Although changes in household size may be neither a positive nor a negative change, some social scientists use this point to support a negative view of the future of the family. The American household of 1790 had an average of 5.8 members. By 1989 the average number had dropped to 2.63 (Statistical Abstract of the United States, 1991). The same trend also has been evident in other parts of the world. The average rural household in Japan in 1660 often had 20 or more members, but by the 1960s the rural Japanese household averaged only 4.5 members. It has been suggested that one reason for the reduction in size of the American household is that today it is very unlikely for us to house unrelated people (Cohen, 1981). Until the 1940s, for a variety of reasons, it was common for people to have nonkin living with them, either as laborers in the fields or as boarders who helped with the rent payment.

The reduction in the number of nonrelatives living with the family explains only part of the continuing reduction in the average household size. Another reason that has often been cited is a rapid decrease in the number of aging parents living with grown children and their families. Some point to this as evidence of the fragmentation and loss of intimacy present in the contemporary family. At the turn of the century over 60 percent of those 65 or older lived with one or more of their children; today this figure is below 10 percent.

How can we account for so many more old people living apart from their families? Although we might be tempted to say that the family has become so self-centered and so unable to fulfill the needs of its members that the elderly have become the first and most obvious castoffs, this trend can also be seen as a result of the increasing wealth of the population, including the elderly. The percentage of the total population living in poverty rose from 12.6 percent in 1970 to 12.9 percent in 1989. In contrast there was a substantial drop for the number of elderly living in poverty during that same period, from 24.5 percent to 11.4 percent, indicating that their position relative to that of the general population has improved greatly (Statistical Abstract of the United States, 1991).

This change in the elderly's economic position is more likely to be responsible for their living apart from their children than is any supposed deterioration in family life—older people themselves are choosing to live independently.

Another reason for the change in the size of the households is the increasing divorce rate. As more families separate legally and move apart physically, the numbers of people living under one roof have fallen.

A further explanation for the smaller families of today is the tendency of young people to postpone marriage and the increase in the number of working women. As people marry later, they have fewer children. Many couples are also deciding to have no children; as more and more women become involved in work and careers, they tend to defer marriage and limit the number of children they bear.

All these factors point to what, according to 1990 census data, are the most significant causes of the sharp decline in the average size of the American

Older people prefer to remain independent and live apart from their adult children.

household: The decrease in the number of children per family and the increase in the number of people living alone (Herbers, 1981). These facts will ultimately have important consequences for the entire structure of society.

Premarital Sex

The revolution in attitudes toward premarital sex was triggered by the social upheavals of the 1960s and 1970s, the accompanying changes in the gender roles, and, of course, the development and accessibility of effective contraceptives. Studies (NORC, 1977) reflect this radical change in attitudes. In 1963, 80 percent of the people surveyed felt that premarital sex was wrong. Twenty-one years later, in a study of 5,237 students from universities in Arkansas, Louisiana, Oklahoma, and Texas, nearly 55 percent said they have or would engage in sexual intercourse before marriage, while 31.8 percent said they hadn't or wouldn't. Seventy-two percent indicated that it is not acceptable to experience sexual intercourse without the love of one's partner (Martin and Martin, 1984).

Other research indicates the enormous change in the female sexual experience in that period—there was a far greater increase in premarital sex among teenage girls and women than among men (Zelnik and Kantner, 1972, 1979). Part of the reason for this increase was the widespread use of the birth control pill as well as the legalization of abortion. Women became less fearful of becoming pregnant and of being forced into marriage because of pregnancy.

Recent widespread concern about sexually transmitted diseases such as AIDS (Acquired Immune Deficiency Syndrome) and genital herpes may have a profound effect on reversing these trends. However, it is still too early for research to substantiate this trend.

Working Women

The period since World War II has seen a dramatic change in the labor force participation rates of American women. Fifty-six million women were working in 1989, representing more than a 200 percent increase in 45 years. The number of men in the labor force during this same period increased by only 50 percent. The change in the labor force is probably the single most important recent change that has taken place in American society.

This change is a result of a number of factors. After World War II, many women who took jobs in record numbers to ease labor shortages during the war remained on the job. Their numbers increased the social acceptability of the working woman. Widespread use of contraceptives was a second important factor. Effective contraception gave women the freedom of deciding whether and when to have children. As a result many women postponed childbearing and continued their educations. Baby boomers also had different economic expectations when they entered the workforce. Having two incomes became important to ensure the lifestyle and standard of living they had come to expect.

Occupational segregation is still present even through the types of jobs women are holding has been changing. Women still dominate such jobs as schoolteaching (73.3 percent women in 1989), retail saleswork (81.8 pecent), librarians (83.3 percent), nursing (96.1 percent), and secretaries (98.3 percent).

Women, however, have been making progress in entering traditionally male occupations. Progress is evident among lawyers (22.3 percent women, up from five percent in 1970), doctors (17.9 percent, up from 10 percent), architects (20.6 percent, up from four percent), computer scientists (32.4 percent, up from 14 percent), and college and university professors (38.7 percent, up from 29 percent). (See Figure 11.5.)

Women have also been successful in entering the ranks of business managers and executives. Thirty-six percent of executives, administrators, and managers are women, even though 45 percent of American workers are women. The vast majority of the top executive positions are held by men. The proportion of women who are managers is rising though, and now stands at 36 percent, up from 27 percent in 1972.

It has been noted that women who reach the executive ranks have different managerial styles. They tend to be more participatory and nurturant. The upper echelons of American companies are dominated by men, possibly making it difficult for women to initiate the management styles they find desirable. But as women continue to enter these ranks they will add diversity to American management (Bloom, 1986).

Family Violence

According to a recent nationwide survey (Straus, Gelles, and Steinmetz, 1980), every year some 8 million Americans are assaulted by members of their own families. Spouses attack each other, parents attack children, even children attack and hurt both their parents and one another. Every year, 16 percent

SOCIOLOGY AT WORK

Arlie Hochschild on Working Parents

The last twenty-five years have seen a revolution in the job market and at home as the majority of women have entered the workplace. For working parents today, there is a second shift, which involves the job they do before they get to the office and after they return home. In many marriages, it is this job that tears the family apart. Sociologist Arlie Hochschild studied these families over an eight year period.

My research associates and I started our research on working families by sending a questionnaire on work and family life to every thirteenth name of a personnel roster of a large manufacturing company. At the end of the questionnaire, we asked members of working couples raising children under six and working full-time jobs if they would be willing to talk to us in greater depth. For the next eight years we interviewed these couples, their neighbors and friends, their children's teachers, daycare workers, and baby-sitters.

The women I interviewed seemed far more deeply torn between the demands of work and family than were their husbands. It was a woman who first proposed to me the metaphor, borrowed from industrial life, of the "second shift." She strongly resisted the *idea* that homemaking was a "shift." Her family was her life and she did not want it reduced to a job. But as she put it, "You're on duty at work. You come home, and you're on duty. Then you go back to work and you're on duty." That was the real story and that was the real problem.

One reason women take a deeper interest than men in the problems of juggling work with family life is that even when husbands happily shared the hours of work, their wives felt more *responsible* for home and children. They were more likely to think about their children while at work and to check in by phone with the baby-sitter.

Partly because of this, more women felt torn between one sense of urgency and another, between the need to soothe a child's fear of being left at daycare, and the need to show the boss she's "serious" at work. More women than men questioned how good they were as parents, or if they did not, they questioned why they weren't questioning it. More often than men, women alternated between living in their ambition and standing apart from it.

All in all, if in this period of American history, the two-job family is suffering from a speed up of work and family life, working mothers are its primary victims. It is ironic, then, that often it falls to women to be the "time and motion expert" of family life. Watching inside homes, I noticed it was often the mother who rushed children saying, "Hurry up! It's time to go," "Finish your cereal now," "You can do it later," "Let's go!" Sadly enough, women are more often the lightening rods for family aggressions aroused by the speed-up of work and family life. They are the "villains" in a process of which they are also the primary victims. More than the longer hours, the sleeplessness, and feeling torn, this is the saddest cost to women.

The happiest two-job marriages I saw were between men and women who did not load the former role of the housewife-mother onto the woman, and did not devalue it as one would a bygone "peasant" way of life. They shared the role between them. What couples called "good communication" often meant that they were good at saying thanks for one tiny form or another of taking responsibility for the "upstairs." These were the silver and gold of marital exchange. Up until now, the woman married to the "new man" has been one of the lucky few. But as the government and society shape a new gender strategy, as the young learn from example, many more women and men will be able to enjoy the leisurely bodily rhythms and freer laughter that arise when family life is family life and not a second shift.

Source: Arlie Hochschild, with Anne Machung, *The Second Shift: Working Parents and the Revolution at Home*, New York: Viking Penguin, 1989.

FIGURE 11.5

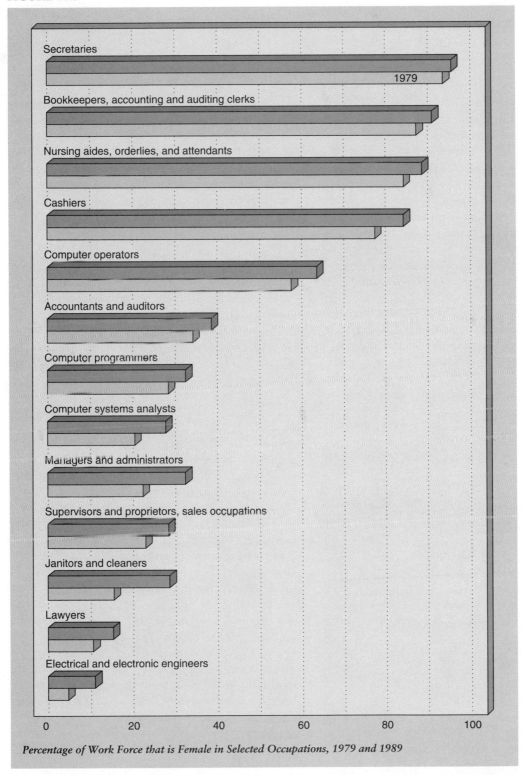

Percentage of Work Force that is Female in Selected Occupations, 1979 and 1989

Source: *Statistical Abstract of the United States: 1991*, pp. 395–97.

of all couples come to blows with each other, and more than a third of the time these violent confrontations include severe punching, kicking, and even biting. Three percent of all children are punched, kicked, or bitten by parents; over a third of all siblings assault one another severely.

In general, research has shown the incidence of family violence to be highest among urban lower-class families. It is high among families with more than four children and in those in which the husband is unemployed. Families in which child abuse occurs tend to be socially isolated, living in crowded and otherwise inadequate housing. Research on family violence has tended to focus on lower socioeconomic groups, but scattered data from school counselors and mental health agencies suggest that family violence is also a serious problem among America's more affluent households. In fact, two sociologists found that the highest incidence of violence was in families in which both husband and wife were high school graduates. A related finding was that the children most likely to act violently toward their siblings were those whose parents had had some college education (Kenney, 1980). Other research indicates that violence often begins when couples are dating (Parke and Collmer, 1975). Some believe that the more money a woman has, the less likely she is to report abuse (*Christian Science monitor,* July 14, 1988). In addition, in homes where the wife is battered, the children are more likely to be

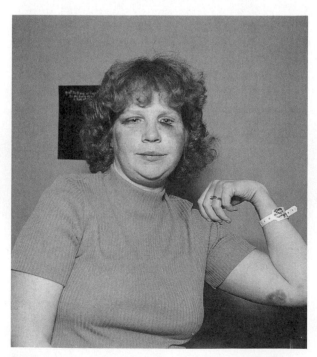

Every year some 8 million Americans are assaulted by members of their own families.

battered, too. It is apparent from these observations that more research focused on family violence in the middle and upper classes is needed.

Sociologists have not yet been able to answer the following questions: Is family violence on the rise in American society? Or is it simply being reported and recorded more accurately than it used to be? Certainly some researchers feel that family violence is an accepted, pervasive attribute of American life (Kenney, 1980). Is family violence more prevalent in the United States than in other industrial societies or in nonindustrial societies? What are the causes of family violence? These questions must be studied before it is possible to assess what can be done to help prevent the occurrence of this disturbing aspect of family life in America.

Divorce

Of all the changes apparent in modern American family life, the increasing incidence of divorce is one of the most prominent. The rate of divorce in America has risen fivefold since 1910. In 1970, of all American males, 2.5 percent were divorced. These figures more than doubled, to 7.2 percent, in 1990. The figures for women are higher, though roughly proprotional, at 2.9 percent and 9.3 percent for 1970 and 1990, respectively. For certain age groups, the figures are considerably higher. For example, among 40 to 44-year-old males and females, the percentage divorced is 11.3 and 15.8, respectively (U.S. Bureau of the Census, *Current Population Reports,* 1991).

The likelihood of divorce varies considerably with several factors. For example, education levels seem to have a strong effect on divorce rates (see Figure 11.6). The likelihood of a first marriage ending in divorce is nearly 60 percent for those people with some college education but no bachelor's degree. Those people who have a college degree but no graduate school training have nearly a 40 percent chance of divorce and are the least divorce-prone. We could argue that those people, with the personality traits and family background that lead them to achieve a college degree, are also those most likely to achieve marital stability.

Women who have gone on to graduate school have a greater likelihood of divorce than some less-educated women: Approximately 53 percent of them will divorce. The problem for these women is the difficulty of combining career, marriage, and child rearing with the necessary societal supports for these often competing roles. As more and more women earn graduate degrees and as some of the barriers impeding women in combining professional

FIGURE 11.6

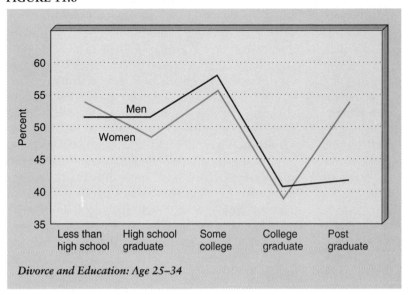

Divorce and Education: Age 25–34

Source: Paul C. Glick, "How American Families Are Changing," *American Demographics,* 6(1), January 1984, p. 24.

and personal lives are removed, the higher rate of divorce for these women may also decline.

Divorced men are more likely to remarry than divorced women. Divorced men usually marry women who are at least five years younger than they are. In this way divorced men end up having a larger pool of potential partners than do divorced women, for whom the pool of potential partners decreases as they age.

For divorced women in their thirties, the likelihood of remarriage declines with increasing levels of education. Those women with no college education remarry rather quickly, whereas those with more

education wait longer or remain unmarried (Norton and Moorman, 1987).

Although the divorce rate has been rising fairly steadily since 1970, it has shown signs of leveling off in recent years. In 1989 the divorce rate per 1,000 people was 4.7, the lowest it has been since 1975 (see Figure 11.7).

Even though the divorce rate may be leveling off, there is little evidence to suggest that it will decline. The United States still has the highest divorce rate in the world. Current divorce rates imply that half of all marriages will end in divorce. Many argue that society cannot tolerate such a high

FIGURE 11.7

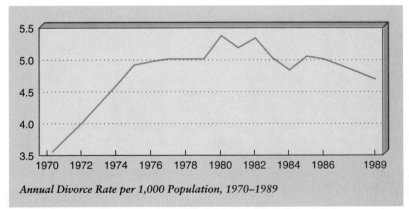

Annual Divorce Rate per 1,000 Population, 1970–1989

Source: National Center for Health Statistics; *Statistical Abstract of the United States: 1991.*

rate of marital disruptions, although 30 years ago, few would have believed society could tolerate even one-third of all married couples divorcing, but that level already has been reached by some marriage cohorts.

Even though divorce rates were lower in 1910, 1930, and 1950 than they are today, can we assume that family life then was happier or more stable? Divorce during those periods was expensive, legally difficult, and socially stigmatized. Many who would have otherwise considered divorce remained married because of these factors. Is it thus accurate to say that it was better for the children and society for the partners to maintain these marriages?

It should be pointed out that the higher incidence of divorce in no way implies a general disillusionment with the institution of marriage. About 75 percent of divorced women and 85 percent of divorced men remarry (Reiss, 1980). Nor are children an impediment to remarriage since 71 percent of the divorces involve children (Norton and Moorman, 1987).

The large number of divorces is itself a force that keeps the divorce rate high. A large majority of divorced people remarry. These remarriages then have a higher overall risk of divorce and thus an impact on the overall divorce rate.

As divorce becomes more common, it also becomes more visible, and such visibility can actually produce more divorces. The model of people suffering in an unhappy marriage is being replaced by one in which people start new lives after dissolving a marriage. Divorce also may be encouraged by the increasing tendency, mentioned earlier, for outside social institutions to assume traditional family functions that once helped hold the family together. Then again, divorce has become a viable option because people can look forward to living longer today, and they may be less willing to endure a bad marriage if they feel there is time to look for a better way of life.

Another reason for today's high divorce rate is that we have come to expect a great deal from marriage. It is no longer enough, as it might have been at the turn of the century, for the husband to be a good provider and the wife to be a good mother and family caretaker. We now look to marriage as a source of emotional support in which each spouse complements the other in a variety of social, occupational, and psychological endeavors.

Divorce rates have also increased because the possibilities for women in the work force have improved. During earlier eras, divorced women had great problems contending with the financial realities of survival, and many were discouraged from seeking a divorce because they could not envision a realistic way of supporting themselves. With their greater economic independence, many women can now consider divorce as an option.

Today's high divorce rates can also be traced to a number of legal changes that have taken place to make divorce a more realistic possibility for those couples who are experiencing difficulties. Many states have instituted "no-fault" divorce laws, and many others have liberalized the grounds for divorce to include mental cruelty and incompatibility, rather vague terms that can be applied to many problem marriages. Even changes by the American Bar Association, which now allow lawyers to advertise, contribute to the increased divorce rate. Advertisements that state an uncomplicated divorce will cost only $150 put this option within the reach of many couples.

These legal changes are but a reflection of society's changing attitudes toward divorce. We are a far cry from a generation ago when divorce was to be avoided at all costs, and when it did occur, it became a major source of embarrassment for the entire extended family. The fact that Ronald Reagan was divorced and remarried had little impact on his election to the presidency in 1980 and 1984. With so little public concern being shown we can be sure that the role of peer group and public opinion in preventing divorce has been greatly diminished.

DIVORCE LAWS In an analysis of the implications of recent changes in divorce laws, Lenore Weitzman and Ruth Dixon (1980) emphasize that the laws governing divorce reflect society's definition of marriage, provide guidelines for appropriate marriage behavior, and spell out the reciprocal rights and obligations of marriage partners. Divorce laws also define the continued obligations that the formerly married couple have to each other after they divorce. As Weitzman and Dixon explain:

One can generally examine the way a society defines marriage by examining its provisions for divorce, for it is at the point of divorce that a society has the opportunity to reward the marital behavior it approves of, and to punish spouses who have violated its norms.

Given this viewpoint, the authors assert that a study of changing divorce laws will reveal changes in family and gender-role patterns. For this reason they chose to examine no-fault divorce laws to demonstrate how "this new legislation seeks to alter the definition of marriage, the relationship between husbands and wives, and the economic and social obligations of former spouses to each other and to their children after divorce."

No-fault divorce laws were first introduced in California in 1970, and now are in effect in every state but South Dakota. **No-fault divorce** *laws allow couples to dissolve their marriage without either partner having to assume blame for the failure of the marriage.*

Weitzman and Dixon argue that no-fault divorce reflects changes in the traditional view of legal marriage. By eliminating the fault-based grounds for divorce and the adversary process, no-fault divorce laws recognize that frequently both parties are responsible for the breakdown of the marriage.

No-fault divorce laws advocate that the financial aspects of marital dissolution are to be based on equity, equality, and economic need rather than on fault- or gender-based role assignments. The new laws seek to reflect the changing circumstances of women and their increased participation in the labor force. By so doing, they encourage women in their efforts to become self-supporting. Under no-fault divorce law, husbands are not automatically expected to continue to support their ex-wives throughout their lives.

Some see no-fault divorce legislation as a redefinition of the traditional marital responsibilities of men and women by the institution of a new norm of equality between the sexes. Husbands are no longer automatically designated as the head of the household solely responsible for support, nor are wives alone expected to assume the responsibility of domestic household activities and child rearing. These changes are reflected most clearly in new considerations for alimony allocation. In addition, property is divided on an equal basis. Finally, child-support expectations and the standards for child custody also reflect the new egalitarian criteria for no-fault divorce legislation. Under new laws, both father and mother are expected to be equally responsible for the financial support of their children after divorce. Mothers are no longer to receive custody of the child automatically; rather, a sex-neutral standard instructs judges to award custody in the best interests of the child.

Weitzman (1985) began her 10-year study of no-fault divorce assuming that the new law was an improvement for women and families. A decade later she ended her study, disillusioned. She felt that while no-fault has worked well for some couples, it has had devastating consequences for many others. Among the problems she found were older homemakers married 35 years or more, lacking any labor-force experience or skills whatever, awarded short-term settlements, ordered to sell the family home, and instructed by the court to pursue job training. Similarly mothers with toddlers were routinely left with virtually full responsibility for their support. Weizman concluded that "divorce is a financial catastrophe for most women." She points to evidence from her study showing that while men's standard of living rose 42 percent in the year following divorce, women's standard of living dropped 73 percent—even counting child-support and alimony payments.

No-fault divorce laws are based on an idealized picture of women's social, occupational, and economic gains in achieving an equality that in fact may not reflect their actual conditions and circumstances. This discrepancy between reality and the ideal can have extremely detrimental effects on women's ability to become self-sufficient after divorce.

CHILD-CUSTODY LAWS   Child custody is one of the areas of divorce law in which the gap between the ideal and the reality still is apparent. Until recently, divorce laws generally discriminated against fathers in custody cases. Although no-fault legislation approaches the question of child custody in a gender-neutral way, mothers still are awarded legal custody of children in about 90 percent of American divorce cases (Weiss, 1979b).

However, there has been an increased recognition of fathers' rights regarding custody, reflecting the changing role of American fathers. In addition to giving more fathers custody of their children, the courts are now beginning to view joint custody as another legal option.

In 1979 only six states had statutes with express joint-custody provisions. Today more than thirty states have replaced traditional sole-custody laws with joint-custody statutes, and legislation is pending in many other jurisdictions. In a legal sense, joint custody means that parental decision-making authority is given equally to both parents after a divorce. It implies that neither parent's rights will be considered paramount. Both parents will have an equal voice in the children's education, upbringing, and general welfare.

Joint legal custody is not a determinant of physical custody or postdivorce living arrangements. It is, however, often confused with complicated situations in which parents share responsibility for the physical day-to-day care of the children. Such arrangements usually require children to alternate between the respective parent's residences every few days, weeks, or months.

While alternating living environments may accompany joint-custody decisions, in most instances they do not. In 90 to 95 percent of joint-custody awards, the living arrangements are exactly the same as those under sole-custody orders, namely, the child physically resides with only one parent. However, both parents make decisions regarding the welfare of the child.

Advocates of joint custody note that sole-custody arrangements, which almost always involve the child living with the mother, weaken father-child relationships. They create enormous burdens for the mothers and tend to exacerbate hostilities between the custodial parent and the "visiting" parent. They continue to perpetuate outmoded sex-role stereotyping. Studies also show that sole-custody arrangements are associated with poverty, antisocial behavior in boys, depression in children, lower academic performance, and juvenile delinquency.

Such arguments assume that by giving fathers the opportunity to be available as nurturers, to be accessible, they will begin to participate more in the lives of their children—furthermore, that such participation will have beneficial effects on children.

Before we too quickly assume that joint custody alleviates problems and produces benefits, we should note that it is far from being a panacea. If couples have trouble communicating and agreeing on things before the divorce, there is no reason to assume they will have an easier time afterwards. Most joint-custody orders are vague and do not decide at what point the joint custodial parent's rights end and those of the parent with the day-to-day care of the child begin. What sorts of responsibilities can one parent require of the other parent? Issues such as these can easily erupt into disputes, particularly when a history of disagreement and distrust has preceded the joint-custody arrangement. In order to solve serious disputes, the parents must return to court where they engage in litigation to prove that one or the other is "unfit"—the very process that awarding joint custody was to have avoided.

As the divorce rate continues to remain at a high level, and laws change in favor of joint custody, this arrangement will become more prevalent. Joint custody appears to work best with those parents who have the capacity, desire, and energy to make it work—and for the children whose characteristics and desires allow them to expend the effort necessary to make it work and to thrive under it.

ALTERNATIVE LIFESTYLES

A number of options are increasingly available to people who, for various reasons, find the traditional form of marriage impractical or incompatible with their lifestyles. More young people are selecting cohabitation as a permanent alternative to marriage (although many consider it more as a prelude to marriage). In addition, some older men and women are opting to live together in a permanent relationship without getting married. These people choose cohabitation primarily for economic reasons—many would lose sources of income or control of their assets if they entered into a legal marriage. Several other options are discussed below.

The Growing Single Population

Americans have traditionally been the marrying kind. In 1990, nearly 70 percent of American men and nearly 78 percent of American women over the age of 15 were married. Younger people, however, may be rejecting this tradition. In 1970, only 11 percent of the women and 19 percent of the men between the ages of 25 and 29 had never been married. In 1990, 31.1 percent of the women and 45.2 percent of men that age had never been married (U.S. Bureau of the Census, Current Population reports, 1991).

Even though the number of people living alone doubled between 1970 and 1990, this trend may mean only that more young people are postponing marriage. On the other hand, it could mean that a growing proportion of adults are staying single permanently. In fact, as we mentioned earlier in this chapter, there are studies that show the marriage rate declining.

There are a number of reasons why people are choosing not to marry. Working women do not need the financial security that a traditional marriage brings, and sex outside of marriage has become much more widespread. Moreover, many singles view marriage as merely a prelude to divorce and are unwilling to invest in a relationship that is likely to fail. As sociologist Frank Furstenburg notes: "Men who weren't married by their late 20's in the 60s were oddballs. Now they're just successful 29-year olds."

Clearly, many singles would gladly change their marital status if the right person came along. But a large group of female baby boomers may never marry. The reality is that there are far more of them than there are available men. For the post baby-boom group, the reverse is true and this trend may just be concentrated among a certain segment of the population.

The elderly comprise a significant proportion of the single-person households. Currently 39 percent of one-person households are maintained by persons aged 65 and older, and fully 80 percent of them are elderly women. About 6.5 million women aged 65 or older live alone, but fewer than 1.6 million men of that age do so (see Table 11.1 for the percentage of single people in various age categories).

Single-Parent Families

There has been a significant increase in the number of single-parent families in the United States. Today, only 72.5 percent of children live with both biological parents compared with 85 percent in 1970. Even more dramatic is the proportion of children who will live in a single-parent household sometime during their youth: 42 percent of white children and 86 percent of black children.

The increase in the divorce rate is the major cause of the increase in single-parent families. Most divorced parents now set up new households, whereas in earlier times many of them would have returned to their own parents' household.

Some single-parent families arise from illegitimate births, when the mother decides against putting her child up for adoption. More than 23 percent of all births between July 1989 and June 1990 involved an unmarried woman. For black women the figure was 56.7 percent (U.S. Bureau of the Census, 1991).

Single parents initially do not intend to change the remaining family relationship radically, though they soon discover that things cannot be done as before. Single parents do not have the same resources, time, or money available to two-parent families. The children eventually become junior partners in the family and end up having to be much more responsible and independent than before.

Outsiders looking at a single-parent family often interpret this independence as the result of excessive permissiveness by the single parent.

The parent-child relationship in a single-parent family is often closer than in the traditional nuclear family. A second parent is not available to establish a close relationship with the children. To the single parent, the children are what is left of the previous family. The children become extremely important emotionally to the single parent. Taking care of and raising the children properly often become the most important aim. In single-parent families consisting of a mother and daughter, it is common to hear their relationship described as similar to that existing between two sisters.

This close parent-child relationship can have some negative effects as well. For example, a single parent may become extremely dependent on the relationship. As the child matures, it may be difficult to continue the relationship at its previous level of intensity. Often the parent begins to feel isolated, while the grown child ends up feeling guilty. However, children usually adjust reasonably well to single-parent situations, and it would be wrong to assume that they are at a marked disadvantage compared with children in two-parent families (Weiss, 1979a).

Stepfamilies

It should come as little surprise that with divorce and remarriage rates so high, stepfamilies are becoming a

TABLE 11.1

Marital Status of Population by Sex and Age, 1990

Age	Percent Distribution							
	Single		Married		Divorced		Widowed	
	M	F	M	F	M	F	M	F
15–17	99.8	98.5	.1	1.5	—	—	—	—
18–19	96.8	90.3	3.4	10.4	—	.4	—	—
20–24	79.3	62.8	21.0	37.5	1.1	2.8	—	.1
25–29	45.2	31.1	52.8	66.3	4.7	7.1	.1	.4
30–34	27.0	16.4	68.8	77.6	7.9	10.5	.2	.8
35–39	14.7	10.4	78.0	78.9	10.9	13.8	.4	1.4
40–44	10.5	8.0	81.2	78.7	11.3	15.8	.5	2.3
45–54	6.3	5.0	85.0	79.9	11.1	14.4	1.2	5.3
55–64	5.8	3.9	86.1	71.9	8.1	9.9	3.3	17.2
65–74	4.7	4.6	82.2	55.3	6.0	6.2	9.2	36.1
75–84	3.3	5.2	76.4	30.6	3.3	3.6	19.5	62.0
85 years and over	3.5	6.2	55.2	11.1	2.0	3.4	43.4	79.8

Source: U.S. Bureau of the Census, "Marital Status and Living Arrangements: March 1990," *Current Population Reports*, series P-20, No. 450, Washington, DC: U.S. Government Printing Office, 1991, p. 17.

permanent part of the social landscape. Currently, one out of every six children under the age of 18 has a stepparent. By the year 2000, this figure will jump to about one in four. Stepfamilies are changing such businesses as the greeting card industry (we now have birthday wishes to stepmothers and thank you cards to stepfathers). Schools must now ask for information on stepparents as well as biological parents.

Stepfamilies, also known as blended families, are transforming basic family relationships. Where there were once two sets of grandparents, there now may be four; an only child may obtain siblings when his mother remarries a man with children.

Stepparents take on roles formerly held by biological parents. They stay up nights with sick children, attend class recitals, and engage in heated battles over such essential issues of child rearing as curfews, TV, homework, and rights to the family car. But in the minds of most children, stepparents can never take the place of their real father or mother—a fact that often leads to intrafamily problems. Studies have shown that it takes at least four years for children to accept a stepparent in the same way they do their biological parents. Researcher James H. Bray has noted this acceptance is harder for girls than boys. "Although divorce appears harder on elementary school-age boys, remarriage appears harder on girls" (Kutner, 1988).

At the heart of most stepfamily relationships are children who, like their parents, are casualties of divorce. In the best stepfamily relationship, all adults work together to meet the needs of the children, realizing that, all too often, no matter what they do, there will still be problems. In reality, stepfamilies are torn apart by many of the same pressures that divide intact families. Financial problems can be especially acute when parents must support children from different marriages. Resentment builds quickly when stepparents feel they have little power or authority in their own houses. The most difficult stage in forming a blended family is the early years. Once stepparents realize that relationships with stepchildren build over time and that their potential network of allies includes all other adults in the stepfamily relationship, the adjustment for all will be faster and healthier.

Cohabitation

Cohabitation *refers to unmarried couples living together out of wedlock*. It is a phenomenon that may well have an impact on the American family. Although we have a great deal of information on marriages, we have very little on cohabitation in the

The increasing incidence of cohabitation is a phenomenon that may well have an impact on the American family.

United States within the last fifteen years, and almost no information about it before that time.

The number of unmarried-couple households has grown 80 percent during the 1980s, from 1.6 million in 1980 to 2.9 million in 1990. An unmarried-couple household, as defined by the Census Bureau, contains only two adults with or without children under 15 years of age present. To fit the Census' definition, the adults must be of the opposite sex and not related to one another.

Even though the percentage of cohabiting couples in the total population is relatively small, the proportion of such couples in certain age groups is quite striking. If we look at couples in which the man is under 25, the percentage of cohabitors is 7.4. Although this figure is still considerably lower than in some countries (such as Sweden where the cohabitation rate is about 12 percent), it may be indicative of a trend (Cherlin, 1981).

Clayton and Voss (1977) found that 18 percent of American men had at one time lived with a woman for six months or more without being married, though only five percent of those men were living with a woman when they were interviewed. Cohabitation was more common among black men than among white and more prevalent among urban residents than among rural. The majority of cohabiting men had been married.

It is unlikely that the increase in cohabitation will continue indefinitely. If it did, cohabitation would start to become more common than marriage.

However, now that cohabitation does not produce as much disapproval as it once did, it is likely it will become more common and visible.

Cohabitation should not be seen as a rejection of traditional marriage. There are a number of characteristics regarding cohabiting couples that are quite different from those of traditionally married couples. First of all, cohabitation is primarily a *childless* lifestyle. Nearly 70 percent of cohabiting couples in 1985 did not have any children living with them. When cohabitors consider adding children to their unit, they are very reluctant to do so without marriage.

It is not clear whether cohabitation leads to a lifetime commitment. Most of the men in the Clayton and Voss study did *not* plan to marry their present partners and in fact did not do so (Blumstein and Schwartz, 1983). Other research during the 1980s showed that 44 percent of all couples who ultimately married had lived together (Bumpass and Sweet, 1988).

Homosexual and Lesbian Couples

A phenomenon that is not new but has become more and more visible is the household consisting of a homosexual or lesbian couple. Before 1970 almost all gay people wished to avoid the risks that would come with a disclosure of their sexual preference.

Traditionally, researchers and the media have concentrated on ways in which gays and lesbians are different from heterosexuals. Little attention has been paid to the fact that gay men and lesbian women form long-term relationships and have problems similar to those of heterosexual couples.

Blumstein and Schwartz (1983) believe that homosexual couples follow family patterns typical of each era. During the 1950s when the traditional gender roles in marriage went unchallenged (husband as provider, wife as homemaker and nurturer), same-sex couples fell into a similar pattern of role playing. The terms butch and femme, which were part of lesbian terminology, reflected a stringent division between masculine and feminine roles. A *butch* woman was expected to perform male tasks and be more involved in the couple's financial support, and the *femme* was expected to act along more traditionally feminine lines. Although gay men did not use the same terms, there was also an expectation that one partner would be more masculine and the other more feminine.

Traditional role playing is no longer common in same-sex couples. The women's movement and the reevaluation of gender roles in our society have affected lesbian women and gay men just as much as they have affected heterosexuals.

The desire to form a relationship with another person appears to be quite strong among gays and lesbians. A Kinsey study in the late 1960s found that 71 percent of their sample of gay men between the ages of 36 and 45 were living with a partner. In the 1970s, Bell and Weinberg found that one-fourth of the lesbians in their study stated that being in a permanent relationship was the "most important thing in life," and another 35 percent believed that it was very important. Eighty-two percent of the women they interviewed were living with someone. By and large, gay men and lesbian women who were not in a relationship reported that they had been in one previously and believed that they would be in one again in the future. There is no doubt that "couplehood," as either a reality or an aspiration, is as strong among gay men and lesbian women as it is among heterosexuals (Blumstein and Schwartz, 1983).

Gay men and lesbian women form long-term relationships and have problems similar to those of heterosexual couples.

THE FUTURE: BRIGHT OR DISMAL?

Given all these changes in the American family, should we be concerned that marriage and family life as we know it will one day disappear? Probably not.

Despite claims to contrary, there is little evidence that the family as an institution is in decline,

CONTROVERSIES IN SOCIOLOGY

Should Unmarried Partners Get Married Benefits?

Some people who consider themselves family members do not fall within the legal definition of the term. That is why a small but growing number of U.S. cities are recognizing the familial bonds that exist between unrelated people.

In 1990, Seattle's city council granted sick and bereavement leave to city employees who have domestic partners. The ordinance also gives unmarried partners access to the city's health insurance plan. Similar laws are on the books in Toronto, Ontario, and Takoma Park, Maryland. But the leaders are in California, where four cities (Berkeley, Santa Cruz, West Hollywood, and Laguna Beach) and one county (San Mateo) extend family leaves to unmarried employees and health insurance to their partners.

Much of the lobbying for domestic partnership ordinances has come from gay and lesbian groups. The number of insured domestic partners is still insignificant. But these local governments may be on the cutting edge of a trend that could greatly expand employee benefits. Some 4.6 percent of U.S. households contain unrelated people who live together, up from 3.6 percent in 1980, according to the Current Population Survey. Another 15 percent of households are headed by single parents, many of whom have unmarried partners. If enough laws change, employers could find themselves supporting a new kind of beneficiary.

Minneapolis's city council has been debating a domestic partnership ordinance for over a year. The main issue is cost. It is estimated that extending health benefits to domestic partners would cost the city an extra $300,000 a year. Some people would rather use that money for other city services.

Seattle's decision to grant sick and bereavement leave came with a price. Several of the city's insurance carriers refused to extend coverage to unmarried partners. As a result the city is partially self-insured.

San Francisco voters defeated a ballot proposition that would have granted health insurance to partners of city employees, but did approve a law that allows citizens to register domestic partnerships. A similar law exists in Madison, Wisconsin. For a $25 fee, any couple in Madison can receive a certificate of domestic partnership. So far, thirty-six nontraditional families have registered. Most are gay and lesbian couples, although heterosexual couples are also eligible. The ordinance guarantees family rates at the city's YMCA. That is about the extent of the benefits.

Although we are still a long way from fully recognizing all the types of nontraditional families that exist, a growing number of cities are taking the first steps.

Source: Excerpted and adapted from Jan Larson and Brad Edmondson, "Should Unmarried Partners Get Married Benefits?" *American Demographics*, March 1991, p. 47.

---

or any weaker today than a generation ago. Nor is there any indication that people place less value on their own family relationships, or on the role of the family within society at large, than they once did.

The "traditional" family is being replaced by family arrangements that better suit today's lifestyles: There are fewer full-time housewives because more women are in the work force. Nonfamily households have increased from 5 million in 1950 to more than 22 million today. The "typical family" with a working dad, housewife mom, and two or more kids accounts for only six percent of all households today (Schwartz, 1987).

The institutions of marriage and the family have proved both extremely flexible and durable and have flourished in all human societies under almost every imaginable condition. As we have seen, these institutions take on different forms in differing social and economic contexts, and there is no reason to suspect that they will not continue to do so. Therefore, to make predictions about the future of the American family is equivalent to making predictions about the future of American society in particular and industrial society in general. This is extremely difficult to do, given the social, economic, political, and ecological problems facing us. However, for the foreseeable future, it seems reasonable to assume that the forces of industrialism and public policy that helped the current nuclear family in its one-parent and two-parent forms will persist. And there- fore the contemporary nuclear family will continue to provide the basic context within which American society will reproduce itself for several generations to come.

CHAPTER

·12·

Religion

The Nature of Religion
   The Elements of Religion

Magic

Major Types of Religion
   Supernaturalism
   Animism
   Theism
   Monotheism
   Abstract Ideals

A Sociological Approach to Religion
   The Functionalist Perspective
   The Conflict Theory Perspective

Organization of Religious Life
   The Universal Church
   The Ecclesia
   The Denomination
   The Sect
   Millenarian Movements

Aspects of American Religion
   Widespread Belief
   Secularism
   Ecumenism
   Television Evangelism

Major Religions in the United States
   Protestantism
   Catholicism
   Judaism
   Islam

Social Correlates of Religious Affiliation

The belief in one God is a basic tenet of Christianity and the cornerstone of Judaism. Islam also proclaims, "There is no God but Allah and Muhammad is His Prophet."

Hinduism, on the other hand, does not have one creed, one founder, one prophet or one central moment of revelation. Its theology rests on a very different concept—the "manyness" of God. Hinduism is an expression of five thousand years of religious and cultural development in Asia and the assimilation of many ideas and ideologies. In Hinduism, whether there is one God or many gods is unimportant. Rather than worshiping a single God, Hinduism involves the worshiping of one God at a time. Each Hindu is free to choose his or her own god or goddess.

The idea of the "manyness" of God is an idea alien not only to Western religion, but also to Western culture. At the same time that monotheism teaches us to believe in One Truth, it conditions us to believe that there is a "best" or "ultimate" in many areas, whether it be the best car, the best university, or the ultimate religion (Goldman, 1991).

In his book, *All Religions Are True,* Mohandas Karamchand Gandhi wrote:

> . . . it has been a humble but persistent effort on my part to understand the truth of all the religions of the world, and adopt and assimilate in my own thought, word, and deed all that I have found to be best in those religions.

Gandhi's acceptance of diversity, however, has a down side. If all religions are true, then they are all imperfect. After all, if any one religion were perfect, it would be better than all others.

The important thing to realize is that although religion assumes many different forms, it is a universal human institution. To appreciate the many possible kinds of religious experiences, from the belief in one God to the belief in many Gods, requires an understanding of the nature and functions of religion in human life and society.

THE NATURE OF RELIGION

Religion *is a system of beliefs, practices and philosophical values shared by a group of people that defines the sacred, helps explain life, and provides salvation from the problems of human existence.* It is recognized as one of society's important institutions.

In his classic study *The Elementary Form of Religious Life,* first published in 1915, Emile Durkheim observed that all religions divide the universe into two mutually exclusive categories: the profane and the sacred. The **profane** *consists of all empirically observable things, that is, things that are knowable through common, everyday experiences.* In contrast, the **sacred** *consists of things that are awe inspiring and knowable only through extraordinary experience.*

Sacred traits or objects symbolize important values. They may consist of almost anything: objects fashioned just for that purpose (like a cross), a geographical location (Mount Sinai), a place constructed for religious observance (a temple), a word or phrase ("Our Father, who art in heaven . . ."), or even an animal (the cow to Hindus, for example). To devout Muslims the sabbath, which falls on Friday, is a sacred day of the week. To Hindus the cow is holy, not to be killed or eaten. These are not ideas open for debate—they simply exist as unchallengeable truths. Similarly, to Christians, Jesus of Nazareth was the Messiah; to Muslims, Jesus was a prophet; to sociologists, Jesus is a religious symbol. Religious symbols acquire their particular sacred meanings through the religious belief system of which they are a part.

Durkheim believed every society must distinguish between the sacred and the profane. This distinction is essentially between the social and nonsocial. What is considered sacred has the capacity to represent shared values, sentiments, power, or beliefs. The profane is not supported in this manner; it may have utility to one or more individuals, but it has little public relevance.

We may look at Babe Ruth's bat as an example of the transformation of the profane to the sacred. At first it was merely a profane object that had little social value in itself. Today, however, one of Babe Ruth's bats is enshrined in baseball's Hall of Fame. It is no longer used in a profane way but instead is seen as an object that represents the values, sentiments, power, and beliefs of the baseball community. The bat has gained some of the qualities of a sacred object, thus changing from a private object to a public object.

In addition to sacred symbols and a system of belief, religion also includes specific rituals. **Rituals** *are patterns of behavior or practices that are related to the sacred.* For example, the Christian ritual of Holy Communion is much more than eating wafers and drinking wine. To many participants these objects *are* the body and blood of Jesus Christ. Similarly, the Sun Dance of the Plains Indians was more than merely a group of braves dancing around a pole to which they were attached by leather thongs that pierced their skin and chest muscles. It was a religious ritual in which the participants were seeking a personal communion.

The Elements of Religion

All of the world's religions contain certain shared elements, including ritual and prayer, emotion, belief, and organization.

RITUAL AND PRAYER All religions have formalized social rituals, but many also feature private rituals such as prayer. Of course, the particular events that make up rituals vary widely from culture to culture and from religion to religion.

All religions include a belief in the existence of

All religions provide a means for communicating with supernatural beings or forces.

beings or forces that are beyond the ability of human beings to experience. Hence, they also include **prayer,** *or a means for individuals to address or communicate with supernatural beings or forces,* typically by speaking aloud while holding the body in a conventionalized posture or making stylized movements or gestures.

EMOTION   One of the functions of ritual and prayer is to produce an appropriate emotional state. This may be done in many ways. In some religions, participants in rituals deliberately attempt to alter their state of consciousness through the use of drugs, fasting, sleep deprivation, and induction of physical pain. Thus Scandinavian groups ate mushrooms that caused euphoria, as did many native Siberian tribes. Various American Indian religions feature the use of peyote, a buttonlike mushroom that contains a hallucinogenic drug. And for a while in the late 1960s, a number of countercultural groups in America relied on LSD and other drugs to induce religious experiences.

Although not every religion attempts to induce altered states of consciousness in believers, all reli-

One of the functions of ritual and prayer is to produce an appropriate emotional state.

gions do recognize that such states may happen and believe that they may be the result of divine or sacred intervention in human affairs. Religions differ in the degree of importance they attach to such happenings. Prophets, for example, are thought by many religions to be the result of such divine intervention.

BELIEF   All religions endorse a belief system that usually includes a supernatural order and a set of values to be applied to daily life.

Belief systems can vary widely. Some religions believe that a valuable quality can flow from a sacred object—animate or inanimate, part or whole—to a lesser object. Numerous Christian sects, for instance, practice the "laying on of hands," whereby a healer channels divine energy into afflicted people and thus heals them. Some Christians also believe in the power of relics to work miracles simply because these objects once were associated physically with Jesus or one of the saints. Such beliefs are quite common among the world's religions: Native Australians have their sacred stones, and shamans from among African, Asian, and North American societies heal through sympathetic touching. In some religions the source of the valued quality is a personalized deity. In others it is a reservoir of supernatural force that is tapped.

Members of the St. John Neumann Roman Catholic Church in Lubbock, Texas, are drawn together by the belief that God's spirit is actually present in their worship. In 1988, this belief brought some 12,000 worshipers to the small church after several parishioners claimed to have received messages from the Virgin Mary. Many of those who came hoped for a miracle that would cure their ills. Others wanted to receive their own messages from Mary, to see visions of Jesus, or to strengthen their faith (Belkin, 1988).

ORGANIZATION   Many religions have an organizational structure through which specialists can be recruited and trained, religious meetings conducted, and interaction facilitated between society and the members of the religion.

The organization also will promote interaction among the members of the religion in order to foster a sense of unity and group solidarity. Rituals may be performed in the presence of other members. They may be limited to certain locations such as temples, or they may be processions from one place to another. Although some religious behavior may be carried out by individuals in private, all religions demand some public, shared participation.

MAGIC

In some societies, magic serves some of the functions of religion, though there are essential differences between the two. **Magic** *is an active attempt to coerce spirits or to control supernatural forces. It differs from other types of religious beliefs in that there is no worship of a god or gods.* Magic is used to manipulate and control matters that seem to be beyond human control and that may involve danger and uncertainty. It is usually a means to an end, whereas religion is usually an end in itself, although prayer may be seen as utilitarian when a believer asks for some personal benefit. In most instances, religion serves to unify a group of believers, whereas magic is designed to help the individual who uses it. Bronislaw Malinowski (1954) notes:

> We find magic wherever the elements of chance and accident, and the emotional play between hope and fear have a wide and extensive range. We do not find magic wherever the pursuit is certain, reliable, and well under the control of rational methods.

Stark and Bainbridge (1985) note that a belief in magic has always been a major part of Christian faith. A common theme throughout the centuries has been the effort of organized religion to prohibit unorthodox practices and practitioners and to monopolize magic. Nonchurch magic was identified as "superstition." Serious efforts to root out magic once and for all emerged in the fifteenth century. Eventually, as many as 500,000 people may have been executed for witchcraft. Stark and Bainbridge write:

> In order to monopolize religion, a church must monopolize all access to the supernatural . . . But if the church is to deny others access to the supernatural, it must remain in the magic business. The demand for magic is too great to be ignored . . . Thus the Catholic Church remained deeply involved in dispensing magic. Immense numbers of magical rites and procedures were developed . . . Saints and shrines that performed specialized miracles proliferated, and new procedures for seeking saintly intercession abounded. Many forms of illness, especially mental illness, were defined as cases of possession, and legions of official exorcists appeared to treat them.

Stark and Bainbridge note that magic's respectability has decreased as more scientific attitudes have proliferated. Magic, and especially magical healing, is now found mostly among sectarians and cultists. This fact makes the religious beliefs of sects and cults particularly vulnerable to criticism and refutation (Beckwith, 1986).

MAJOR TYPES OF RELIGION

The earliest available evidence for religious practice comes from the Middle East. In Shanidar Cave in Iraq, archaeologist Ralph Solecki (1971) found remains of burials of Neanderthals—early members of our own species, *Homo sapiens,* once believed to be brutish but now recognized as fully human—dating between 60,000 and 45,000 years ago (see Chapter 3). Bodies were tied in a fetal position, buried on their sides, provided with morsels of food placed at their heads, and covered with red powder and sometimes with flower petals. These practices—the food and the ritual care with which the dead were buried—point to a belief in some kind of existence after death.

Using studies of present-day cultures as well as historical records, sociologists have devised a number of ways of classifying religions. One of the simplest and most broadly inclusive schemes recognizes four types of religion: supernaturalism, animism, theism, and abstract ideals. Despite the profound differences in their basic assumptions, each of these belief systems is recognized as a religion because of certain shared basic attributes.

Supernaturalism

Supernaturalism *postulates the existence of nonpersonalized supernatural forces that can and often do influence human events.* These forces are thought to inhabit animate and inanimate objects alike—people, trees, rocks, places, even spirits or ghosts—and can come and go at will. The Melanesian/Polynesian concept of *mana* is a good example of the belief of an impersonal supernatural power.

Mana *is a diffuse, nonpersonalized force that acts through anything that lives or moves,* although inanimate objects such as an unusually shaped rock also may possess mana. The proof that a person or thing possesses mana lies in its observable effects. A great chief, merely by virtue of his position of power, must possess mana, as does the oddly shaped stone placed in a garden plot that then unexpectedly yields huge crops. Although it is considered dangerous because of its power, mana is neither harmful nor beneficial in itself, but sometimes may be used by its possessors for either good or evil purposes. An analogy in our culture might be the scientific phenomenon of nuclear power, which is a natural force that intrinsically is neither good nor evil but can be turned to either end by its possessors. We must not carry the analogy too far, however, because we are able to account for nuclear power according to natural, scientific principles and can predict its effects reliably without resorting to supernatural explanations. A narrower, less comprehensive, but more appropriate analogy in Western society is our idea of "luck," which can be good or bad, and over which we feel we have very little control.

Although on the one hand certain objects possess mana, taboos may exist in relation to other situations. *A religious taboo is a sacred prohibition against touching, mentioning, or looking at certain objects, acts, or people.* Violating a taboo results in some form of pollution. A person who becomes a victim of some misfortune may be accused of having violated a taboo and may also become stigmatized.

Taboos exist in a wide variety of religions. Polynesians believed that their chiefs and noble families were imbued with powerful mana that could be deadly to commoners. Hence, elaborate precautions were taken to prevent physical contact between commoners and nobles. The families of the nobility intermarried (a chief often would marry his own sister), and chiefs actually were carried everywhere to prevent them from touching the ground (thereby killing the crops). Many religions forbid the eating of selected foods. Jews and Muslims have taboos against eating pork at any time, and until fairly recently, Catholics were forbidden to eat meat on Fridays. Most cultures forbid sexual relations between parents and children and between siblings (the incest taboo).

Supernatural beings fall into two broad categories: those of nonhuman origin, such as gods and spirits, and those of human origin, such as ghosts and ancestral spirits. Chief among those of nonhuman origin are the gods who are believed to have created themselves and may have created or given birth to other gods. Although gods may create, not all peoples attribute the creation of the world to them.

Many of those gods thought to have participated in creation have retired, so to speak. Having set the world in motion, they no longer take part in day-to-day activities. Other creator gods remain involved in ordinary human activities. Whether or not a society has creator gods, many other affairs are left to lesser gods. For example, the Maori of New Zealand have three important gods: a god of the sea, a god of the forest, and a god of agriculture. They call upon each god for help in the appropriate area.

The unnamed spirits are below the gods in prestige but often closer to the people. Some of these gods offer constructive assistance, others take pleasure in deliberately working evil for people.

Ghosts and ancestral spirits represent the supernatural beings of human origin. Many cultures believe that everyone has a soul, or several souls, which survive after death. Some of these souls remain near the living and continue to be interested in the welfare of their kin (Ember and Ember, 1981).

Animism

Animism *is the belief in animate, personalized spirits or ghosts of ancestors that take an interest in and actively work to influence human affairs.* Such spirits may inhabit the bodies of people and animals as well as inanimate phenomena such as winds, rivers, or mountains. They are discrete beings with feelings, motives, and a will of their own. Unlike mana, these spirits may be intrinsically good or evil. Although they are powerful, they are not worshiped as gods, and because of their humanlike qualities, they can be manipulated—wheedled, frightened away, or appeased—by using the proper magic rituals. For example, among many Native American and South American Indian societies (as well as many other cultures in the world), sickness is thought to be caused by evil spirits. Shamans, or medicine men or women, are able to effect cures because of their special relationships with these spirits and their knowledge of magic rituals. If the shamans are good at their jobs, they are able to persuade or force the evil spirit to leave the sick person or to discontinue exerting its harmful influence. In our own culture, there are people who consult mediums, spiritualists, and Ouija boards in an effort to contact the spirits and ghosts of departed loved ones.

Theism

Theism *is the belief in divine beings—gods and goddesses—who shape human affairs.* Gods are powerful beings worthy of being worshiped. Most theistic societies practice polytheism, the belief in a number of gods. Each god or goddess usually has particular spheres of influence such as childbirth, rain, or war, and there is generally one who is more powerful than the rest and oversees the others' activities. In the ancient religions of Mexico, Egypt, and Greece, for instance, we find a **pantheon**, *or a host of gods and goddesses.*

Monotheism

Monotheism *is the belief in the existence of a single one god.* Only three religions are known to be monotheistic: Judaism and its two offshoots, Christianity and Islam. Yet these three religions have the greatest number of believers worldwide (see Figure 12.1). Even these faiths are not purely monotheistic, however, for they include in their tenets a belief in such divine or semidivine beings as angels, a devil, saints, and the Virgin Mary. Nevertheless, because all three religions promote such a strong belief in the supremacy of one all-powerful being, they are considered monotheistic.

Abstract Ideals

Some religions are based on abstract ideals rather than a belief in supernatural forces, spirits, or divine beings. **Abstract ideals** *focus on the achievement of personal awareness and a higher state of consciousness through correct ways of thinking and behaving, rather than by manipulating spirits or worshiping gods.* Such religions promote devotion to religious rituals and practices and adherence to moral codes of behavior. Buddhism is an example of a religion based on abstract ideals. The Buddhist's ideal is to become "one with the universe," not through worship or magic, but by meditation and correct behavior.

Only three religions are known to be monotheistic: Judaism, Christianity, and Islam.

FIGURE 12.1

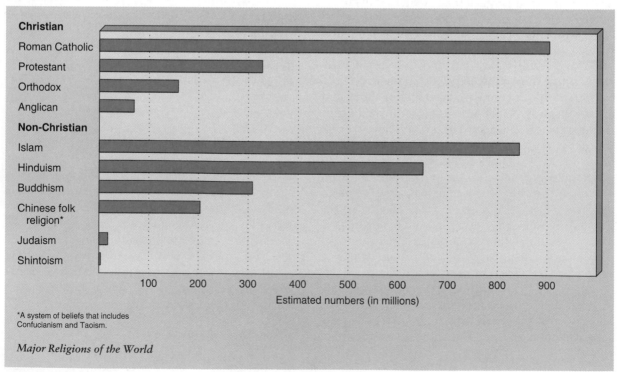

*A system of beliefs that includes Confucianism and Taoism.

Major Religions of the World

Source: David B. Barrett, editor, *World Christian Encyclopedia.*

A SOCIOLOGICAL APPROACH TO RELIGION

When sociologists approach the study of religion, they focus on the relationship between religion and society. Functionalist sociologists examine the utility of religion in social life. Conflict theorists, on the other hand, view religion as a means for justifying the political status quo. In the following section we will examine each of these approaches in detail.

The Functionalist Perspective

Since at least 60,000 years ago, as indicated by the Neanderthal burials at Shanidar Cave, religion has played a role in all known human societies. The question that interests us here is, what universal functions does religion have? Sociologists have identified four categories of religious function: satisfying individual needs, promoting social cohesion, providing a world view, and acting as a form of social control.

SATISFYING INDIVIDUAL NEEDS Religion offers individuals ways to reduce anxiety and promote emotional integration.

Although Sigmund Freud (1918, 1928) thought religion to be irrational, he saw it as helpful to the individual in restraining impulses that induce guilt and anxiety. Freud argued that a belief in lawgiving, powerful deities can help people reduce their anxieties by providing strong, socially reinforced inducements for controlling dangerous or "immoral" impulses.

Further, in times of stress, individuals can calm themselves by appealing to deities for guidance and even outright help, or they can calm their fears by "trusting in God." In the face of so many things that are beyond human control and yet may drastically affect human fortunes (such as droughts, floods, or other natural disasters), life can be terrifying. It is comforting to "know" the supernatural causes of both good fortune and bad. Perhaps this is why former first lady Nancy Reagan appealed to astrology—the belief that the position of the planets determines human fate—to plan her husband's schedule when he was president. Mrs. Reagan's belief in astrology became particularly intense following the attempted assassination of her husband in March 1981. By following the astrological charts, Mrs. Reagan expressed concern for her husband's welfare and attempted to control the outcome of his activities (Sperling, 1988).

Another very different example occurs each year in the state of Orissa in India, as people walk barefoot through a trench filled with glowing coals to test their faith in the power of Kali (the mother goddess) to protect them. Their success in accomplishing this feat unharmed proves the active and protective role played by Kali in the villagers' daily lives (Freeman, 1974).

SOCIAL COHESION Emile Durkheim, one of the earliest functional theorists, noted the ability of religion to bring about group unity and cohesion. According to Durkheim, all societies have a continuing need to reaffirm and uphold their basic sentiments and values. This is accomplished when people come together and communally proclaim their acceptance of the dominant belief system. In this way people are bound to one another, and as a result the stability of the society is strengthened.

Not only does religion in itself bring about social cohesion, but often the hostility and prejudice directed at its members by outsiders helps strengthen their bonds. For example, during the 1820s, Joseph Smith, a young farmer from Vermont, claimed that he had received visits from heavenly beings that enabled him to produce a six-hundred-page history of the ancient inhabitants of the Americas, known as the Book of Mormon. Shortly after the establishment of the Mormon church, Smith had a revelation that "Zion," the place where the Mormons would prepare for the millennium, was to be established in Jackson County, Missouri. Within two years, 1,200 Mormons had bought land and settled in Jackson County. Other residents in this area became concerned about the influx and in 1833 published their grievances in a document that became known as the "manifesto," or secret constitution. They charged the Mormons with a variety of transgressions and pledged to remove them from Jackson County. Several episodes of conflict followed that eventually forced the Mormons to move into an adjoining county. These encounters with a hostile environment produced a sense of collective identity at a time when it was desperately needed. Their church was less than two years old and included individuals from diverse religious backgrounds. There was a great deal of internal discord, and if it had not been for the unity that resulted from the conflict with the townspeople, the group might have disappeared altogether (MacMurray and Cunningham, 1973).

Durkheim's interest in the role of religion in society was aroused by his observation that religion, like the family, seemed to be a universal human institution. This universality meant that religion must serve a vital function in maintaining the social order. Durkheim felt he could best understand the social role of religion by studying what he considered one of the simplest religions—the totemism of the aboriginal Australian. *A* **totem** *is an ordinary object such as a plant or animal that has become a sacred symbol to and of a particular group or clan, who not only revere the totem but also identify with it.* Thus, reasoned Durkheim, religious symbols such as totems, as well as religion itself, arose from society itself, not outside it. When people recognize or worship supernatural entities, they are really worshiping their own society. They do not realize their religious feelings are actually the result (a crowd reaction) of the intense emotions aroused when people gather together at a clan meeting, for example. They look for an outside source of this emotional excitement and may settle on a nearby, familiar object as the symbol of both their religion and their society. Thus society—the clan—is the origin of the clan members shared religious beliefs, which in turn help cement their society together.

Durkheim sees religious ritual as an important part of this "social cement." Religion, through its rituals, fulfills a number of social functions: it brings people together physically, promoting social cohesion; it reaffirms the group's beliefs and values;

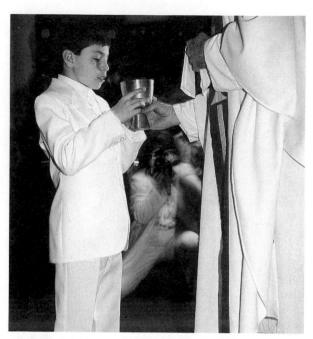

Religious rituals fulfill a number of social functions. They bring people together physically, promote social cohesion, and reaffirm a group's beliefs and values.

Émile Durkheim believed that when people recognize or worship supernatural entities, they are really worshipping their own society.

it helps maintain norms, mores, and prohibitions so that violation of a secular law—murder or incest, for instance—is also a violation of the religious code and may warrant ritual punishment or purification; it translates a group's cultural heritage from one generation to the next, and it offers emotional support to individuals during times of stress and important stages in their life cycle, such as puberty, marriage, and death (see Figure 12.2).

Although many sociologists today take issue with Durkheim's explanation of the origins of religion based on totemism, they nevertheless recognize the value of his functional approach in understanding the vital role of religion in society.

Secular society depends on external rewards and pressures for results, whereas religion depends on the internal acceptance of a moral value structure. Durkheim believed that because religion is effective in bringing about adherence to social norms, society usually presents these as an expression of a divine order. For example, in ancient China, as in France until the late eighteenth century, political authority—the right to rule absolutely—rested securely on the notion that emperors and kings ruled because it was divine will that they do so—"the divine right of kings." In Egypt, the political authority of pharaohs, was unquestioned because they were more than just kings; they were believed to be gods in human form.

But religion serves to legitimize more than just political authority. Although many forms of

FIGURE 12.2

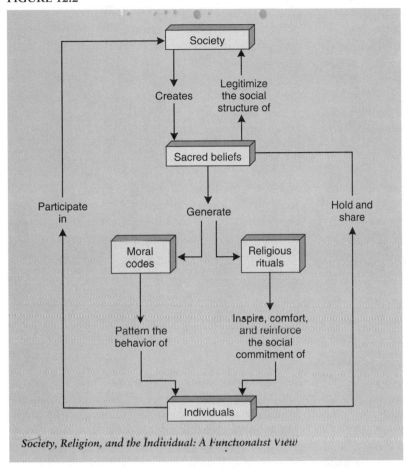

Society, Religion, and the Individual: A Functionalist View

institutionalized inequality do not operate to the advantage of the subgroups or individuals affected by them, they help perpetuate the larger social order and often are justified by an appeal to sacred authority. In such situations, although religion serves as a legitimator of social inequality, it does function to sustain societal stability. Thus the Jews in Europe were kept from owning land and were otherwise persecuted because "they had killed Christ" (Trachtenberg, 1961), and even slavery has been defended on religious grounds. In 1700 Judge John Saffin of Boston wrote of

> the Order that God hath set in the world, who hath Ordained different degrees and orders of men, some to the High and Honorable, some to be Low and Despicable . . . yea, some to be born slaves, and so to remain during their lives, as hath been proved (Montagu, 1964a).

Religions do not *always* legitimize secular authority. In feudal Europe the church had its own political structure, and often tension existed between church and state. Indeed, just as the church often

legitimized monarchs, it also excommunicated those who failed to take its wishes into account. However, the fact remains that religious institutions usually do dovetail quite neatly with other social institutions, legitimizing and helping sustain them. For example, though church and state in medieval Europe were separate structures and often conflicted, the church nonetheless played an important role in supporting the entire feudal system.

ESTABLISHING WORLD VIEWS   According to Max Weber in his classic book *The Protestant Ethic and the Spirit of Capitalism*, religion responds to the basic human need to understand the purpose of life. In doing so, religion must give meaning to the social world within which life takes place. This means creating a world view that can have social, political, and economic consequences. Take, for example, the issue of whether salvation is achieved through active mastery (hard work, for example) or through passive contemplation (meditation). The first philosophy is at the heart of Calvinism, and the second approach is evident in several of the Eastern religions.

Weber theorized that Calvinism fostered the Protestant ethic of hard work and asceticism and that Protestantism in turn was an important influence on the development of capitalism. Calvinism is rooted in the concept of predestination, which holds that before they are born, certain people are selected for heaven and others for hell. The Calvinists consequently were anxious to find out whether they were among those chosen for salvation. Worldly success, especially the financial success that grew out of strict discipline, hard work, and self-control, was seen as proof that a person was among the select few. Money was accumulated not to be spent but to be displayed as proof of one's chosenness. Capitalist virtues became Calvinist virtues. It was Weber's view that even though capitalism existed before Calvinist influence, it blossomed only with the advent of Calvinism.

Weber's analysis has been criticized from many standpoints. Calvinist doctrines were not so uniform as Weber pictured them, nor was the work ethic confined to the Protestant value system. Rather, it seems to have been characteristic of the times, promoted by Catholics as well as Protestants. Finally, one could just as well argue the reverse: that the social and economic changes leading to the rise of industrialism and capitalism stimulated the emergence of the new Protestantism—a position that Marxist analysts have taken. Today it is generally agreed that although religious beliefs did indeed affect economic behavior, the tenets of Protestantism and capitalism tended to support each other. However, the lasting value of Weber's work is his demonstration of how religion creates and legitimizes world views and how important these views are to human social and political life.

ADAPTATIONS TO SOCIETY Religion can also be seen as having adaptive consequences for the society in which it exists. For example, many would view the Hindu belief in the sacred cow, which may not be slaughtered, as a strange and not particularly adaptive belief. The cows are permitted to wander around freely and defecate along public paths.

Marvin Harris (1966) has suggested there may be some beneficial economic consequences in India from not slaughtering cattle. The cows and their offspring provide a number of resources that could not easily be provided in other ways. For example, a team of oxen is essential to India's many small farms. Oxen could be produced with fewer cows, but in order to do so, food production would have to be devoted to feeding those cows. With the huge supply of sacred cows, although they are not well

fed, the oxen are produced at no cost to the economy.

Cow dung is also necessary in India for cooking and as a fertilizer. It is estimated that dung equivalent to 45 million tons of coal is burned annually. Alternative sources of fuel, such as wood or oil, are scarce and/or costly.

Although the Hindus do not eat beef, those cattle that die naturally or are slaughtered by non-Hindus are eaten by the lower castes. Without the Hindu taboo against eating beef, these other members of the Indian hierarchy would not have access to this food supply. Therefore, because the sacred cows do not compete with people for limited resources and because they provide a cheap source of labor, fuel, and fertilizer, the taboo against slaughtering cattle may be quite adaptive.

When societies are under great stress or attack, their members sometimes fall into a state of despair analogous, perhaps, to a person who becomes depressed. Institutions lose their meaning for people, and the society is threatened with what Durkheim called *anomie*, or "normlessness." If this continues, the social structure may break down, and the society may be absorbed by another society, unless the culture can regenerate itself. Under these conditions revitalization movements sometimes emerge. **Revitalization movements** *are powerful religious movements that stress a return to the traditional religious values of the past, and many of them can be found in the pages of history and are even in existence today.*

In the 1880s, the once free and proud Plains Indians lived in misery, crowded onto barren reservations by soldiers of the United States government. Cheated out of the pitiful rations promised them, they lived in hunger—and with memories of the past. Then a Paiute by the name of Wovoka had a vision, and he traveled from tribe to tribe to spread the word and demonstrate his Ghost Dance. "Give up fighting," he told the people. "Give up all things of the white man. Give up guns, give up European clothing, give up alcohol, give up all trade goods. Return to the simple life of the ancestors. Live simply—and dance! Once the Indian people are pure again, the Great Spirit will come, all Indian ancestors will return, and all the game will return. A big flood will come, and after it is gone, only Indians will be left in this good time."

Wovoka's Ghost Dance spread among the defeated tribes. From the Great Plains to California, Indian communities took up the slow, trancelike dance. Some believed that the return of the ancestors would lead to the slaughter of all whites. For others, the dance rekindled pride in their heritage. But for whatever reasons, the Ghost Dance could not be contained, despite the government soldiers' attempts to ban it.

On December 28, 1890, the people of a Sioux village camped under federal guard at Wounded Knee, South Dakota, and began to dance. They ignored orders to stop and continued to dance until suddenly someone fired a shot. The soldiers opened fire, and soon more than 200 of the original 350 Sioux men, women, and children were killed. Twenty-nine soldiers were killed, mostly from the bullets and shrapnel of their own comrades. This slaughter was the last battle between the Indians of the Plains and soldiers of the dominant Anglo society (Brown, 1971).

The Conflict Theory Perspective

Karl Marx argued that "the ruling ideas of each age have always been the ideas of the ruling class" (Marx and Engles, 1961). From this belief it was a small step to his claim that the dominant religion of a society is that of the dominant class, an observation that has been borne out by historical evidence. Marxist scholars emphasize religion's role in justifying the political status quo, by cloaking political authority with sacred legitimacy and thereby making opposition to it seem immoral.

The concept of alienation is an important part of Marx's thinking, especially in his ideas of the origin and functions of religion. **Alienation** *is the process by which people lose control over the social institutions they themselves invented.* People begin to feel like strangers—aliens—in their own world. Marx further believed that religion is one of the most alienating influences in human society, affecting all other social institutions and contributing to a totally alienated world.

According to Marx, "Man makes religion, religion does not make man" (Marx, 1967). The function of God thus was invented to serve as the model of an ideal human being. People soon lost sight of this fact, however, and began to worship and fear the ideal they had created as if it were a separate, powerful supernatural entity. Thus religion, because of the fear people feel for the nonexistent god they themselves have created, serves to alienate people from the real world.

Marx saw religion as the tool that the upper classes used to maintain control of society and to dominate the lower classes. In fact, he referred to it as the "opiate of the masses," believing that through religion, the masses were kept from actions that might change their relationship with those in power. The lower classes were distracted from taking steps for social change by the promise of happiness through religion—if they followed the rules established by religion, they would receive their reward in heaven, and so they had no reason to try to change or improve their condition in this world. These religious beliefs made it easy for the ruling classes to continue to exploit the lower classes: Religion served to legitimize upper-class power and authority. Although modern political and social thinkers do not accept all of Marx's ideas, they recognize his contribution to the understanding of the social functions of religion.

While religion performs a number of vital functions in society—helping maintain social cohesion and control while satisfying the individual's need for emotional comfort, reassurance, and a world view—it also has negative, or dysfunctional, aspects.

Karl Marx would be quick to point out a major dysfunction of religion: Through its ability to make it seem that the existing social order is the only conceivable and acceptable way of life, it obscures the fact that people construct society and therefore can change society. Religion, by imposing the acceptance of supernatural causes of conditions and events, tends to conceal the natural and human causes of social problems in the world. In fact, in its role of justifying, or legitimating the status quo, religion may very well hinder much-needed changes in the social structure. By diverting attention from injustices in the existing social order, religion discourages the individual from taking steps to correct these conditions.

An even more basic and subtle dysfunction of religion is its insistence that only one body of knowledge and only one way of thinking are sacred and correct, thereby limiting independent thinking and the search for further knowledge.

ORGANIZATION OF RELIGIOUS LIFE

Several forms or types of organization of religious groups are found in society.

The Universal Church

A **universal church** *includes all the members of a society within one united moral community* (Yinger, 1970). It is fully a part of the social, political, and economic status quo and therefore accepts and supports (more or less) the secular culture. In preliterate societies, in which religion is not a differentiated institution but rather permeates the entire fabric of social life, a person belongs to the church simply by being a member of the society. In more complex societies, this religious form cuts across divisions of the social structure, such as social classes and ethnic groups, binding all believers into one moral community. A universal church, however, does not seek to change any conditions of social inequality created by the secular society and culture, and indeed, may even legitimize them. (An example is the Hindu religion of India, which perpetuates a rigid caste system.)

The Ecclesia

An **ecclesia** *is a church that shares the same ethical system as the secular society and has come to represent and promote the interest of the society at large.* Like the universal church, an ecclesia extends itself to all members of a society, but because it has so completely adjusted its ethical system to the political structure of the secular society, it comes to represent and promote the interests of the ruling classes. In this process the ecclesia loses adherents among the lower social classes, who increasingly reject it for membership in sects, be these sacred or "civil" (Yinger, 1970). The Russian Orthodox Church, for example, must be seen as an ecclesia. With the rise of political and religious turmoil in Russia early in this century, the church tied itself firmly to the interests of the czar and the aristocracy. After the 1917 Bolshevik revolution, the church was subdued and dispersed.

The Denomination

A **denomination** *tends to limit its membership to a particular class, ethnic group, or regional group, or at least to have its leadership positions dominated by members of such a group.* It has no official or unofficial connection with the state, and any political involvement is purely a matter of choice by the denomination's leaders, who may either support or oppose any or all of the state's actions and political positions. Denominations do not withdraw themselves from the secular society. Rather, they participate actively in secular affairs and tend to cooperate with other religious groups. These two characteristics distinguish them from sects, which are separatist and unlikely to tolerate other religious persuasions (Yinger, 1970). (For that matter, universal churches, by their very nature, also typically dismiss other religions.) In America, Lutheranism, Methodism,

In the U.S., Lutheranism, Methodism, Catholicism, and Judaism each embodies the characteristics of a denomination.

other Protestant groups, Catholicism, and Judaism embody the characteristics of a denomination.

The Sect

A **sect** *is a small group that adheres strictly to religious doctrine that often includes unconventional beliefs or forms of worship.* Sects generally represent a withdrawal from secular society and an active *rejection* of secular culture (Yinger, 1970). For example, the Dead Sea Scrolls show clearly that the beliefs of both early Christian and Jewish sects such as the Essenes were rooted in a disgust with society's self-indulgent pursuit of worldly pleasures and in a rejection of the corruption perceived in the prevailing religious hierarchy (Wilson, 1969).

Early in their development, sects often are so harsh in their rejection of society that they invite persecution. Some actually thrive on martyrdom, which causes members to intensify their fervent commitment to the faith. (Consider, for example, the Christian martyrs in Rome before the conversion to Christianity of the Emperor Constantine in 313.)

Millenarian Movements

Millenarian *movements typically prophesize the end of the world, the destruction of all evil people and their works, and the saving of the just.* Millenarian (from the Latin word for "thousand") prophesies are often linked with the symbolic number of 1000—from which the name originated.

Throughout human history in times of stress, religious leaders have emerged, foretelling the end of the world, and asking everyone to stop whatever they are doing to follow the bearers of the message. In the early 1950s, in the midwestern town of Lake City (a fictitious name), several people formed a group around a middle-aged woman named Mrs. Keech. This woman, who had the remarkable ability to "tune in" to communication from extraterrestrial beings, had recently received an urgent message: On December 21, 1955, the earth would be destroyed, and only the "elect" would be taken aboard a spacecraft and saved.

On the night of December 21, the faithful gathered around Mrs. Keech, took off all their jewelry, ripped zippers from pants and hooks from bras (metal could not be worn on space journeys), and waited for their saviors. When the ships failed to come, Mrs. Keech received a message setting a new date for the Reckoning. But most of the followers became disheartened, and the group slowly drifted apart (Festinger, Rieken, and Schachter, 1956).

How can we understand Mrs. Keech's group? Although on television, it is much in style to portray the 1950s as "happy days," this was hardly the case. Less than a decade earlier, America had dropped two atomic bombs on cities in Japan—and from then on, the world lived with the real possibility of the extermination of all human life through nuclear warfare. The 1950s brought their own age of anxiety: the Berlin blockade, the Soviet development of their own atomic bomb, and the Korean War.

ASPECTS OF AMERICAN RELIGION

The Pilgrims of 1620 sought to build a sanctuary where they would be free from religious persecution, and the Puritans who followed 10 years later intended to build a community embodying all the virtues of "pure" Protestantism, a community that would serve as a moral guide to others. Thus religion pervaded the social and political goals of the early English-speaking settlers and played a major role in shaping the nature of colonial society. Today the three main themes that characterize religion in America are widespread belief, secularism, and ecumenism.

Widespread Belief

Americans generally take religion for granted. Although they differ widely in religious affiliation and degree of church attendance, almost all Americans claim to believe in God. Nine out of every ten Americans have a religious preference, even if they maintain no formal church affiliation, and four out of every ten American adults attend either church or synagogue each week.

Evidence as to whether America is experiencing a "religious revival," as some have claimed, is contradictory. When asked if they feel they have a personal relationship with God, 82 percent of Catholics, 86 percent of Protestants, and 97 percent of Evangelicals responded yes (Gallup and Castelli, 1987). Church attendance, however, has declined. In 1960, 47 percent of the people questioned said they had attended a church or synagogue during the

When asked if they felt they have a personal relationship with God, 82 percent of American Catholics responded yes.

week before they were polled. This figure dropped to 42 percent in 1985.

More than half of all religiously affiliated individuals in the United States belong to a Protestant denomination, clearly reflecting America's colonial history. But other denominations are also well represented, especially Catholicism and Judaism. There are well over 200 formally chartered religious organizations in America today. Such pluralism is not typical of other societies and has resulted primarily from the waves of European immigrants who arrived in the postcolonial era. Traditional tolerance of religious diversity in the United States can also be seen as a reflection of the constitutional separation of church and state, so that no one religion is recognized officially as better or more acceptable than any other.

Secularism

Many scholars have noted that modern society is becoming increasingly **secularized,** that is *less influenced by religion.* Religious institutions are being confined to ever-narrowing spheres of social influence, while people turn to nonreligious sources for moral guidance (Berger, 1967). This shift is reflected in the reactions of Americans who, for the most part, are notoriously indifferent to, and ignorant of, the basic doctrines of their faiths. Stark and Glock (1968) report that a poll of Americans found that 67 percent of Protestants and 40 percent of Catholics could not correctly identify Father, Son, and Holy Spirit as constituting the Holy Trinity; 79 percent of Protestants and 86 percent of Catholics could not correctly identify a single prophet from the Old Testament, and finally, 41 percent of Protestants and 81 percent of Catholics could not identify the first book of the Bible.

Of course, social and political leaders still rely on religious symbolism to influence secular behavior. The American Pledge of Allegiance tells us that we are "one nation, under God, indivisible . . ." and our currency tells us that "In God We Trust." Since the turn of the century, however, modern society has turned increasingly to science, rather than religion, to point the way. Secular political movements have emerged that attempt to provide most, if not all, of the functions for their followers that traditionally have been fulfilled by religion. For example, communism prescribes a belief system and an organization that rival those of any religion. Like religions, communism offers a general conception of the nature of all things and provides symbols that, for its adherents, establish powerful feelings and attitudes and supply motivation toward action.

Thus, some political movements lack only a sacred or supernatural component to qualify as religions. But in this increasingly secular, modern world, sacred legitimacy appears unnecessary for establishing meaning and value in life.

Ecumenism

Ecumenism *refers to the trend among many religious communities to draw together and project a sense of unity and common direction.* Ecumenism is partially a response to secularism and is a tendency especially evident among many of the religions in the United States.

Unlike religious groups in Europe, where issues of doctrine have fostered sect-like hard-line separatism among denominations, in America most religious groups have focused on ethics, that is, how to live the good and right life. There is less likelihood of disagreement over ethics than over doctrine. Hence, American Protestant denominations typically have had rather loose boundaries, with members of congregations switching denominations rather easily and churches featuring guest appearances from ministers of other denominations. In this context, ecumenism has flourished in the United States far more than in Europe.

Television Evangelism

The share of Americans who attend religious services from their living rooms now rivals the share who go to church. A recent survey showed that 45 percent of Americans watch religious programs on television or listen to them on the radio at least monthly. Nine percent watch or listen daily. Listenership is higher among Protestants than Catholics, and black Protestants are more likely to tune in than white Protestants. In fact, black Protestants are more likely to watch or listen to a religious program than attend church (American Demographics, 1986).

The growth of the electronic church in America is truly remarkable, with four religious TV networks, 35 religious TV stations, and an estimated 1,400 religious radio stations currently in operation.

Prior to a number of scandals that rocked the electronic church, televangelists like Jerry Falwell, Jimmy Swaggart, Jim Bakker, Oral Roberts, Pat Robertson, and Robert Schuller broadcast prayers and sermons to their flock as they built empires with viewer donation. At the height of his popularity, Jimmy Swaggart drew an audience of more than two million households. Pat Robertson's "700 Club" program drew more than 4.4 million viewers a day. The twelve most popular ministries together collected annual sums totaling $1 billion (*Newsweek,* July 17, 1988).

Even with a number of well publicized scandals, more people than ever are tuning in to TV ministers. In 1988, 25 percent of American adults watched religious programs, up from 18 percent in 1983 (The Gallup Report, 1988).

The typical weekly viewer of religious television programs is over 50 years of age, female, Baptist, not a high school graduate, lives in the South, and has a household income below $15,000. Despite their low income, they are likely to donate more than $300 a year to the television ministry (*Statistical Abstract of the United States: 1987, 1986*).

Some pastors have expressed concern that the electronic church will decrease involvement in local churches, or worse yet, keep prospective members from joining a church. Others are concerned that the electronic media may make religion too easy and comfortable and encourage individualized religion. The notion of turning religion into "show business" has also drawn criticism.

In their defense, we must note that religious programs reach a vast number of people who might not be reached otherwise, especially the elderly, the infirm, and the handicapped. It is also possible that these programs raise the level of awareness of the unchurched and make them more likely to become involved in their religious communities (Gallup Organization, 1981).

MAJOR RELIGIONS IN THE UNITED STATES

Nowhere is the diversity of the American people more evident than in their religious denominations. There are more than one thousand different religious groups in the United States, which vary widely in religious practices, moral views, class structure, family values, and attitudes. A recent survey found surprisingly large and persistent differences among even the major religious groups.

The national census is prohibited from asking about religion. However, the National Opinion Research Center has been conducting the General Social Survey since 1972 which gives us a basis for examining American religious attitudes and practices. This group has correlated information on a variety of issues with religious affiliation. Some of its findings are summarized below.

It is useful to think of American Protestant religious denominations as ranked on a scale as to their degree of traditionalism. Conservative Protes-

tant denominations include fundamentalists (Pentecostals, Jehovah's Witnesses, etc.), Southern Baptists, and other Baptists. Moderates include Lutherans, Methodists, and inter- or non-denominationalists. Liberal Protestants are represented by Unitarians, Congregationalists, Presbyterians, and Episcopalians. The various branches of Protestantism often differ so markedly in their attitudes, especially toward social issues, that they resemble other religions more than the various denominations of one religion.

For example, with respect to the hereafter, nearly 90 percent of the fundamentalists and Baptists believe in an afterlife. This falls to 80 percent among the moderate and liberal denominations. Catholics are similar to liberal Protestants in that 75 percent believe in an afterlife. Among people with no religious affiliation 46 percent believe in an afterlife.

A strong belief in sin and a more literal interpretation of the Bible is typical of Fundamentalists and Baptists. As a result, they strongly condemn extramarital and premarital sex, homosexuality, and favor laws against pornography and abortion. There is greater sexual permissiveness among the moderate denominations and considerably more so among the liberal elite. Catholics tend to resemble Protestant moderates, regarding sexual permissiveness, and Jews tend to be more liberal than the liberal Protestant denominations. Attitudes toward drugs and alcohol follow the same pattern. Smoking, drinking, or the frequenting of bars is least common among Fundamentalists and Baptists.

There are substantial social class differences among the major Protestant denominations. The average annual household income for non-black Fundamentalists and Southern Baptists is less than $15,000. For Lutherans it is $16,300, for Methodists $17,000, Catholics $17,400, Presbyterians $20,500, Episcopalians $21,700, and Jews $23,300. The average annual household income for people with no religious affiliation is $17,600. The pattern is the same for occupational prestige and education, with Jews and Episcopalians averaging three more years of education than Fundamentalists and Baptists.

Given the wide differences in values and attitudes among religious groups, the relative proportion of the population that belongs to each group helps determine the shape of society. Protestants make up about 64 percent of the adult population, according to data from the General Social Survey. Among the five major Protestant families, Baptists account for 21 percent of the adult population, Methodists 12 percent, and Lutherans eight percent. Roman Catholics, representing about one-quarter of the adult population, are the largest single religious denomination. Jews make up 2 to 3 percent of the population followed by a host of religions such as Eastern Orthodox, Muslim, Hindu, Sufi, and Baha'i, which add up to a little over one percent.

These percentages are in a constant state of flux, however, since demographic factors such as birthrates and migration patterns may influence the number of people of any given religion. Religious conversion can also affect percentages. Fundamentalism, for example, is becoming increasingly popular among the young.

Despite trends toward ecumenicalism, it seems the magnitude of religious differences, the persistence of established faiths, and the continual development of new faiths will ensure continued religious diversity (Smith, 1984).

Protestantism

Because American Protestantism is so fragmented, many sociologists simply classify all non-Catholic Christian denominations in the general category of "Protestant." It should be kept in mind, however, that there are differences—of greater or lesser significance—among the various denominations.

Since the 1960s there has been a 10 percent drop in the membership of the United Methodists and United Presbyterians, and the Episcopalians have seen a 15 percent decline. At the same time, the more conservative denominations have increased dramatically. In the same period of time there has been an 18 percent increase in the number of Baptists, a 37 percent increase among the Assemblies of God, and a 34 percent increase among Seventh-Day Adventists.

At the present time fundamentalists and evangelical Christians have become an extremely visible and vocal segment of the Protestant population, with a strong presence in the media and the political arena. Why are the fundamentalist and evangelical churches gaining such popularity? Some of their appeal may lie in the sense of belonging and the comfort in a well-defined and self-assured religious doctrine—no ambiguities and hence few moral choices to be made.

The growth of these churches reflects religion's role as a social institution, changing over time and from place to place, partly in response to concurrent social and cultural changes and partly acting alone as an agent of social change.

Catholicism

One of the most striking things about Catholics in the United States is their youth: Twenty-nine percent

are under 30, 36 percent are between 30 and 49, and 35 percent are over 50. In contrast, 24 percent of Protestants are under 30 and 41 percent are over 50. The higher birth rate among Catholics in the "baby boom" generation, especially among Hispanic Catholics, accounts for a large part of this difference. Another part of the explanation is the difficulty mainline Protestant denominations have had in retaining young people.

American Catholics have long been an immigrant people, a tradition continuing today. One in five Catholics is a member of a minority group. Hispanics now make up 16 percent of American Catholics. Another three percent are black. Another three percent describe themselves as "nonwhite." Since very few Hispanics identify themselves as "nonwhite," this suggests the influx of Catholic immigrants from Southeast Asia is starting to show in national surveys. While the percentage of blacks among Protestants is five times that among Catholics, a higher percentage of Catholics overall come from minority groups.

Since the mid-1960s, Catholics have equaled Protestants in education and income levels. However, the overall figures for Protestants mask significant differences between denominations. When we compare Catholics with individual denominations, we find them still ranking behind Presbyterians and Episcopalians on education and income, about on par with Lutherans and Methodists, and well ahead of Baptists. This comparison is striking in light of the fact that large numbers of lower-income minorities are included in the overall Catholic figures.

Catholics remain an urban people, with only one in four living in rural areas. A higher percentage of Catholics (39 percent) than of any major denomination live in central cities, and 35 percent live in suburbs. The vast majority of Catholics are concentrated in the Northeast and Midwest.

Catholics have historically favored larger families than other Americans, but by 1985 the difference in ideal family size between Catholics and Protestants had disappeared, with both groups considering two children the ideal family size. Despite the Catholic Church's condemnation of artificial means of birth control, American Catholics have favored access to contraceptives and information about them in the same proportion as the rest of the population since the 1950s (Gallup and Castelli, 1987).

One of the most important developments in the recent history of Catholicism was the ecumenical council (Vatican II) called by Pope John XXIII, which met from 1962 to 1965. This council thoroughly reexamined existing Catholic doctrine, which in turn led to many changes, often referred to as "liberalization," including the substitution of common language for Latin in the Mass. One unintended consequence of Vatican II was that the centralized authority structure of the Catholic Church was called into question. Laypersons and priests felt free to dispute the doctrinal pronouncements of bishops and even of the pope himself. During the same period, the percentage of Catholics using some form of birth control rose from under 60 percent to 75 percent, despite the church's prohibition (Westoff and Jones, 1977).

Under the leadership of Pope John Paul II, the Catholic Church has experienced a more conservative turn. It continues to condemn all forms of birth control except the rhythm method and rejects technological aids to conception, such as artificial insemination, in vitro fertilization, or surrogate motherhood. The call for a greater role for women in the church or possible ordination to priesthood has been rejected. Women have been told to seek meaning in their lives through motherhood and giving love to others (Suro, 1988).

Judaism

There is a strong identification among Jews on both a cultural and a religious level. This sense of connectedness is an important aspect in understanding current trends within the religion.

The state of Israel has played a major role in shaping current Jewish thinking. For many Jews, identification with, and support for, the state of Israel is important to the development of their cultural and/or religious ties. For some, identification with Israel has come to be a secular replacement of religiosity. To many Jews, the continued existence of Israel guarantees a homeland that can help defend world Jewry from the unwarranted attacks (such as the Holocaust) that have occurred throughout history.

Jews can be divided into three groups, based on the manner in which they approach traditional religious precepts. Orthodox Jews observe traditional religious laws very closely. They maintain strict dietary laws and do not work, drive, or engage in other everyday practices on the Sabbath. Women are not permitted to be ordained as rabbis. Reform Jews, on the other hand, allow for major reinterpretations of religious practices and customs, often in response to changes in society. Conservative Jews represent a compromise between the two extremes. They are less traditional than the Orthodox Jews, but not as willing to make major modifications in religious observance as the Reform Jews. Both Reform and Conservative Jews have permitted women to become rabbis. In addition, a large secularized segment of the Jewish population still identifies itself as Jewish but refrains from formal synagogue affiliation.

As among Protestants, there are social-class differences among the various Jewish groups. Reform Jews are the best educated and have the highest incomes. Orthodox Jews emphasize religious over secular education. They have the lowest incomes and the least amount of secular education. As might be expected, Conservative Jews fall between the two extremes.

Recent surveys (1992) estimate there are 5.98 million Jews in the United States, about the same as in 1977. Demographers predict the population will decline by five to 17 percent by the end of the century. The American Jewish community is thus facing a crisis.

A common fear is that a further decline in the number of American Jews would lessen their ability to defend their political interests. Others suggest

At the Wailing Wall in Jerusalem, thousands of Jews gather each day to pray and mourn the destruction of the second temple by the Romans in 70 A.D.

that we would lose the contributions of Jewish scientists, artists and performers. Even though Jews account for roughly between 2.0 and 2.5 percent of the U.S. population, they represent 20 percent of U.S. Nobel laureates.

Reasons for the lack of growth in the Jewish community are varied. First, Jews in the U.S. aren't bearing enough children to replace themselves: The Jewish fertility rate is estimated at between 1.3 to 1.7 per lifetime—well below the replacement rate of 2.1. Also, the Jewish population is quite old. About 40 percent of the American Jewish population has a remaining life expectancy of 20 years or less. Finally, substantial numbers of young Jews (about 40 percent) are choosing to marry outside the faith, although this does not always lead to a loss of Jewish identity. Jewish immigration from Russia and Israel has helped somewhat, but is unpredictable.

Whether or not there is a population erosion, and what should be done about it, is an ongoing debate in the American Jewish community. Jewish religious groups have attempted to liberalize the definition of who is a Jew, and—in a radical break with tradition—change their attitude toward and seek converts to Judaism. For example, the Reform movement's outreach (comparative religion discussion groups in which introductory classes in Judaism are available to interfaith couples, as well as converts) goes against centuries of Jewish tradition in which proselytizing has been disdained (Putka, 1984).

While many of the reasons for the shrinking of the population are demographic in nature, the issue of how to stem the tide has been the cause of some major rifts between the various branches of the religion. Recent statistics, for example, put the rate of Jewish intermarriage at 40 percent. Strictly observant Jews blame their more liberal co-religionists for this high percentage. No doubt, the liberal Reform movement is quite tolerant of intermarriages. Interfaith couples today have little difficulty finding rabbis willing to officiate at the marriage ceremony.

A subject that has provoked even more controversy is the Reform movement's break with the tradition of matrilineal, or motherly descent. In 1983, the Reform movement declared that a person could be considered Jewish if either the father or mother was Jewish. Prior to that time, Judaism could only be passed on to the child from the mother.

Islam

A Moslem is someone who has accepted the Islamic creed that "there is no god but Allah, and Mohammed is his prophet." Like Jews and Christians, Moslems are monotheists, and all three share in common the prophets of the Old Testament.

From its roots in the Arab world, Islam has spread in virtually every direction, as far west as the Atlantic Coast of Africa and as far east as Indonesia. There are an estimated 984 million Moslems in the world, and almost one-fourth of the world population may be Moslem after the turn of the century if current high levels of fertility exist. Among the five most populous nations in the world, the United States has by far the fewest Moslems. It

Islamic pilgrims to Mecca must circle the flat-roofed kaaba seven times and, at its east corner, kiss the Black Stone. The Black Stone is said to have been received by Adam when he fell from paradise.

is, however, very difficult to ascertain exactly how many Moslems there are in the United States. Islam does not require attendance for formal membership in the way that many Christian groups do, and there is no major minority group that can be identified as being predominantly Moslem.

One way to estimate the Moslem population in the United States is to consider that there are 600 mosques or Islamic centers in the United States, and that informal counts of the number of people coming to pray and to break the fast during Ramadan exceed two million. In the absence of more certain information, it is probably reasonable to assume that the Moslem population of the United States is between three to four million (Weeks, 1988).

All religions and denominations are affected by the current mood of the country. A heightened social consciousness results in demands for reform, whereas stressful times often produce a movement toward the personalization of religion. In any event, while traditional forms and practices of religion may be changing in the United States, religion itself is likely to continue to function as a basic social institution.

SOCIAL CORRELATES OF RELIGIOUS AFFILIATION

Religious affiliation seems to correlate strongly with many other important aspects of people's lives: Direct relationships can be traced between membership in a particular religious group and a person's politics, professional and economic standing, educational level, family life, social mobility, and attitudes toward social issues. For example, Jews, who in the 1990 census represented only 2.5 percent of the total population, are proportionally the best-educated group; they also have higher incomes in general than Christians, and a greater proportion are represented in business and the professions. Despite their high socioeconomic and educational levels, however, Jews, like Catholics, occupy relatively few of the highest positions of power in the corporate world and politics: These fields generally are dominated by white Anglo-Saxon Protestants. Among Christian groups, the same correlation appears among denomination, social and professional prestige, and income level. For example, Episcopalians, the smallest Protestant denomination, consistently rank highest in social prestige and income.

Other studies show equally interesting relationships between politics and religious affiliation. Studies of the major religious faiths in the United States show that about 58 percent of Jews are Democrats and only nine percent are Republicans (1982). A lower proportion of Catholics, but still almost 44 percent, are Democrats, and 29 percent are Republicans. Protestants have the lowest proportion of Democrats (40 percent) and the highest proportion (38 percent) of Republicans (1985).

Attitudes toward social policy also seem to correlate, to some extent, with religious affiliation. Fundamentalist and evangelical Protestant sects generally are more conservative on key issues than are major Protestant sects. According to a Gallup

There has been a steady increase in interfaith marriages as religious prejudices have declined.

Are Religious Cults Dangerous?

Although a sect often develops in response to a rejection of certain religious doctrine or ritual within the larger religious organization, a cult usually introduces totally new religious ideas and principles. Cults generally have charismatic leaders who expect total commitment. Members of cults, who are usually motivated by an intense sense of mission, often must give up individual autonomy and decision making. Many cults require resocialization practices so strong as to make the member seem unrecognizable in personality and behavior to former friends and relatives. Included among the best known contemporary religious cults are the Unification Church, the Church of Scientology, Church Universal and Triumphant, and The Way International.

Because the activities and excesses of some cults have taken over the headlines in recent years, we may tend to forget or even dismiss the fact that many major religions began as cults and sects.

Some contemporary religious cults have been referred to as destructive cults because of the effects they have on their members. According to Steve Hassan, an ex-cult member who helps people leave such cults, destructive religious cults have the following characteristics:

1. *The Doctrine is reality* The doctrine is the TRUTH, it is perfect and absolute. Any flaw in it is viewed as a reflection of the believer's own imperfection. The doctrine becomes a master program for all thoughts, feelings, and actions.
2. *Reality is presented in simple polar terms* Cult doctrines reduce reality into two basic poles: black verses white, good verses evil, spiritual world verses physical world, us verses them. The cult recognizes no outside group as having any validity because such recognition would threaten the cult's monopoly on the truth.
3. *Elitist mentality* Members are made to feel part of an elite group. They consider themselves better, more knowledgeable, and more powerful than anyone else. This carries a heavy burden of responsibility, however, because if members are told they are not fully performing their duty, they are thus made to feel they are a failure.
4. *Group goals over individual goals* The self must be subordinated to the will of the group. Absolute obedience to superiors is a common theme in many cults. Conformity to the group is good.
5. *Continued acceptance depends on good performance* One of the most attractive qualities of a cult is its sense of community. But to remain part of this community the cult member learns that he or she must meet group goals, whether they be in the area of recruitment, collecting money, allegiance to the leader, or proper behavior.
6. *Manipulation through fear and guilt* The cult member lives within a narrow corridor of fear, guilt, and shame. Problems are due to the member's weakness, lack of understanding, evil spirits, and so forth. The cult member constantly feels guilty for not being "good" enough. The devil is always lurking just around the corner, waiting to tempt or seduce the cult member.
7. *Changes in time orientation* The past, present, and future are seen in a different light. The cult member looks back on his past life in a distorted way and sees it as totally negative. The present is marked by a sense of urgency in terms of the work that needs to be done. The future is a time when you will be either rewarded or punished for what you have done to help the cause.
8. *No legitimate reason for leaving* The cult does not recognize a person's right to choose to move on. Members are made to believe that the only reason people leave is because of weakness, insanity, brainwashing (deprogramming), pride, or sin. The cult stresses that if they ever leave, terrible things will happen to them, their families, or the world.

Source: Steven Hassan, *Combatting Cult Mind Control*, Rochester, VT: Park Street Press, 1988.

Opinion poll (1985), 66 percent of the Evangelicals said they would favor a constitutional amendment to ban abortion except for rape, incest, and threat to the mother's life; 59 percent of the Catholics agreed, along with 51 percent of the Protestants (Gallup and Castelli, 1987).

Interestingly, Fundamentalists, despite their conservative views on marriage and family issues, are more likely to have unstable marriages than nonfundamentalists (Chi and Houseknecht, 1985). It appears that Fundamentalists are more likely than Protestants or Catholics in general to be unhappy with their marriage if their spouses have different religious beliefs.

Dissatisfaction arises from discrepancies between "real" and "ideal" family life as perceived through interpretations of the scriptures. "Among Fundamentalists, the wife is expected to submit to her husband as her head, even if her husband is not a good Christian or is an "unbeliever," note Chi and Houseknecht. This often creates marital problems. Problems also arise when the wife must work outside the home. Labor force participation is considered "a distortion of God's plan." Nevertheless, Fundamentalist women are as likely to work as other Protestant or Catholic women.

Although it is clear that religious associations show definite correlations with political, social, and economic demographics, we must be careful not to ascribe a cause-and-effect relationship to such data, which at most can be considered an indicator of an individual's attitudes and social standing.

CHAPTER

▪ 13 ▪

Education

Education: A Functionalist View
  Socialization
  Cultural Transmission
  Academic Skills
  Innovation
  Child Care
  Postponing Job Hunting

The Conflict Theory View
  Social Control
  Screening and Allocation: Tracking
  The Credentialized Society

Issues in American Education
  Unequal Access to Education
  High School Dropouts
  Violence in the Schools
  Standardized Testing
  The Gifted

It is June 24, graduation day for Seward Park High School in New York City, and teacher Jessica Siegel has a pocketbook full of bobby pins and tissues. The bobby pins are for her students. The tissues are for herself.

The high school sits empty and silent in the late afternoon, a breeze nudging litter down the street outside, for the commencement is being held eighty blocks farther north in Manhattan, at Hunter College. Here the streets unfold with boutiques and diplomatic mansions and elegant apartment buildings, with awnings and doormen and gilt doors that glint in the summer sun.

With footsteps both urgent and tentative, the students and their families arrive. Six rise from the Lexington Avenue subway, palms shading their eyes. Five pile out of a Dodge Dart piloted by an uncle. Four emerge from the gypsy cab on which they have splurged, with its smoked windows and air freshener. All of them pause to gape, and the cabbie, too, waits an extra moment before driving on, leaning out the window to admire the promised land. Their world is the Lower East Side, its streets crammed with tenements and bodegas and second-story sweatshops, its belly bursting with immigrants, its class and tongues and customs so foreign here at Hunter, only twenty minutes from home.

The seniors have traveled to a border, to a frontier. Some will never cross it. They will have their diplomas and shrink back southward, back to the comforting, familiar things, back to the many menaces. But others will wield their diplomas as passports and will step into the new, the strange, the almost inconceivable. A few will even attend college (Freedman, 1990).

Jessica Siegel was thrilled to see so many of her students graduate from high school, a major accomplishment that took place largely because of her dedication and effort. By helping these students get an education, she had accomplished her goals. But what are those goals specifically? It may sound like a simple question, but if you were asked why people should get an education, what would you say? The most common answer people across the country give is to get a "better job," or "a better paying job" (42 percent). Very few people mention things like "acquire knowledge" (10 percent), "to learn basic skills" (3 percent), "to develop an understanding and appreciation for culture" (1 percent), or "to develop critical thinking skills" (1 percent) (The Gallup Report, 1986).

Clearly, our education system is geared to more than job training. After all it does not really take 12 years of schooling to prepare for many jobs. You can take short courses that prepare you to be a bartender, tractor trailer driver, or hairdresser. Something else is taking place during those years as the school prepares children to become members of society. In this chapter we will examine the complex social institution of education by contrasting the functionalist and conflict perspectives. Functionalists stress the importance of education in socializing the young, transmitting culture, and developing skills. Conflict theorists, on the other hand, note that education preserves social class distinctions, maintains social control, and promotes inequality. We will also examine the impact of some of the contemporary issues facing education.

Our educational system is geared to more than job training; it does not take 12 years of schooling to prepare for most jobs. Socialization is also an important aspect of education.

EDUCATION: A FUNCTIONALIST VIEW

What social needs does our educational system meet? What are its tasks and goals? Education has several manifest functions (Chapter 1), that is, intended and predetermined goals such as the socialization of the young or the teaching of academic skills. Education also has latent functions, or unintended consequences. These may include child care, the transmission of ethnocentric values, and respect for the American class structure.

Socialization

In the broadest sense, all societies must have an educational system. That is, they must have a way of teaching the young the tasks likely expected of them as they develop and mature into adulthood. If we accept this definition of an educational system, then we must believe there really is no difference between education and socialization. And as Margaret Mead (1943) observed, in many preliterate societies, no such distinction is made. Children learn most things informally, almost incidentally, simply by being included in adult activities.

Traditionally the family has been the main agent of socialization. As societies have become more complex, the family has been unable to fulfill all aspects of socialization. Thus, there is a need for a formal educational system that extends the socialization process started in the family.

In modern industrialized societies, a distinction is made between education and socialization. In ordinary speech, we differentiate between socialization and education by talking about "bringing up" and "educating" children as two separate tasks. Whereas rearing children is an informal activity, education or schooling is formal. The role prescriptions that determine interactions between students and teachers are clearly defined, and the curriculum taught is explicit. Obviously, the educational process goes far beyond just formalized instruction. In addition, children also learn things in their families and among their peers. In school, children's master status (see Chapter 5) is that of student, and their primary task is to learn what is taught.

Schools, as differentiated, formal institutions of education, emerged as part of the evolution of civilization. However, until about two hundred years ago, education did not help people become more productive in practical ways, and thus was a luxury that very few could afford. This changed dramatically with the industrialization of Western culture. Workers with specialized skills were re-

Handwritten margin notes (top): I ndustrialized society → Formal education / Institution / separated from family / Guidelines standards

Until about 200 years ago, education was a luxury that few could afford. Schools, as we known them today, arose out of a need to create a skilled work force.

Handwritten margin notes (left): Industrialization: Functions on skills + : Level of democracy Reflects level of education

quircd for production jobs, as were professional, well-trained managers. When the Industrial Revolution moved workers out of their homes and into factories, the labor force consisted not only of adults but also of children. Subsequently, child labor laws were passed to prohibit children from working in factories. These laws created a need for places outside the home to care for children. Schools, as we know them today, arose out of this need and the need to create a skilled work force.

Cultural Transmission

The most obvious goal of education is **cultural transmission,** *in which major portions of a society's knowledge are passed from one generation to the next.* In relatively small, homogeneous societies, in which almost all members share the same norms,

values, and perspectives, cultural transmission is a matter of consensus and needs few specialized institutions. But in a complex, pluralistic society like ours, with competition among ethnic and other minority groups for economic and political power, the decision as to what aspects of culture will be transmitted is the outgrowth of a complicated process.

For a society to hold together, there must be certain "core" values and goals—some common traits of culture—that its constituent social elements share to a greater or lesser degree (see Chapter 4). In America, it seems this "core culture" itself is in a period of rapid change.

A school's curriculum often reflects the ability of organized groups of concerned citizens to impose their views on an educational system, whether local, statewide, or nationwide. Thus it was a political

A school's curriculum often reflects the ability of organized groups of concerned citizens to impose their views on an educational system.

Handwritten: Politics sets standard

process that caused black history to be introduced into elementary, high school, and college curricula during the 1960s. Similarly, political activism caused the creation of women's studies in many colleges. And even though the concept of evolution is a cornerstone of modern scientific knowledge, political pressure (from Christian fundamentalists) causes textbooks to refer to the "theory" of evolution, and prevents the theory from being taught outright in certain states. Also, in some states the pressure has led to government insistence that teachers give equal time to other creation theories.

In recent years, bilingual education is one of the most dominant educational and political issues. Proponents believe that it is critical for children to receive instruction in their primary language. They believe that by acknowledging students' native languages, the school system is helping them make the transition into the all-English mainstream—and is also helping to preserve the diversity of American culture. Others see a danger in these programs. They believe many bilingual education programs never provide for the transition into English—a fact that leaves many youngsters without the basic skills needed to earn a living and participate in our society.

In the end, the debate centers on how closely our sense of who we are as a nation hinges on the language our children speak in school. For the time being, the only agreement between the two sides is that language is the cornerstone for cultural transmission (Molotsky, 1988).

Many people would agree that citizen input into school curricula is important because it ensures what is taught reflects cultural values. In keeping with this viewpoint, during the 1960s under President Lyndon B. Johnson, the federal government financed the creation of community boards to give poor people some control over local school curricula and the hiring and firing of teachers. State and local courts and legislatures followed this lead, and in many cities mandated community-based school boards and advisory groups with significant political power. But a 1979 study commissioned by the National Institute of Education (NIE) cast doubt on the usefulness of this approach. Investigating the impact of community boards on schools in Boston, Atlanta, and Los Angeles, the institute found that their actual impact had been minor. The research found these groups typically recruited from among the poor, who themselves were inadequately educated and hence lacked many of the skills necessary to effect substantial changes. Also, community groups typically are controlled by city governments, and educational bureaucracies have found ways to limit their influence. Perhaps for these reasons, such

community groups have tended to focus on narrow and minor issues rather than on major school policies. Nor have they produced any major educational leaders who could introduce wide-ranging reforms. In fact, given the overall lack of effectiveness of community boards, the (NIE) study recommended eliminating federal and state program policies requiring them.

Academic Skills

Another critical function of schools is to equip children with the academic skills needed to function as adults—to hold down a job, to balance a checkbook, to evaluate political candidates, to read a newspaper, to analyze the importance of a scientific study, and so on. Have the schools been successful in this area? Most experts believe they have not.

In 1983, the National Commission on Excellence on Education issued a report entitled "A Nation at Risk," which bitterly attacked the effectiveness of American education. The message of the report was clear and sobering: "The educational foundations of our society are presently being eroded by a rising tide of mediocrity that threatens our very future."

As a result of this report, reforms were instituted in all fifty states which stressed the teaching of the "three Rs" and the elimination of frivolous electives that waste valuable student and teacher time. In addition, high school graduation requirements were raised in forty states. In nineteen states, students must pass minimum competency tests, demonstrating the mastery of basic skills, in order to receive their high school diplomas. Forty-eight states also

A particularly troubling aspect of American education is that student performance in math and science does not match that of students in other countries.

require new teachers to prove their competence by passing a standardized test.

Although the back-to-basics movement has worked, its success has been limited. Five years after "A Nation at Risk" appeared, a follow-up report was issued entitled "American Education: Making It Work" (1988). According to the report, "the precipitous downward slide of previous decades has been arrested and we have begun the long climb back to reasonable standards." However, despite this progress, especially among minority groups, the report condemned the performance of American schools as unacceptably low. "Too many students do not graduate from our high schools, and too many of those who do graduate have been poorly educated. . . . Our students know little, and their command of essential skills is too slight."

Particularly troublesome is student performance in math and science. According to a study done by the Nation's Report Card (1988), an assessment group that is part of the Educational Testing Service, the math performance of 17-year-olds is "dismal." The study found that although half the nation's 17-year-olds have no trouble with junior high-school math, fewer than one in fifteen students was able to solve multistep high-school level problems or those involving algebra or geometry. At fault might be the very back-to-basics movement supposed to rescue our educational system from failure in the early 1980s. While rote learning has helped improve the scores of the lowest level students, it leaves others totally unprepared to analyze complex problems.

The Nation's Report Card also found American students' understanding of science "distressingly low." The report found that most 17-year-olds did not have the skills to handle today's technologically based jobs and that only seven percent could cope with college-level science courses.

Perhaps the most disheartening evidence of the failure of our schools to prepare Americans with essential academic skills is the astonishingly high number of functionally illiterate adults found throughout America. Some 23 to 27 million adults, roughly 10 percent of the nation's population, cannot read and write well enough to hold down a job or otherwise function properly in society (*U.S. News and World Report*, June 20, 1988).

This failure will become even more critical as businesses place greater demands on workers. Studies predict that by the year 2000, almost all new jobs will require more than a high school education and literacy skills to match. Right now millions of workers are unable to meet these basic literacy standards. Some 14 million workers read at a fourth-grade level and an additional 23 million at an eighth-grade level, despite the fact that 70 percent of all work-related documents are written at the ninth-grade level or above. This type of functional illiteracy costs businesses millions of dollars each year in poor productivity, low product quality, on-the-job accidents, and absenteeism (Daniels, 1988).

In the early 1990s, great momentum was building for the establishment of national performance standards for students, a notion which was previously unacceptable. As a result of a meeting between President Bush and various state governors, national goals for students were developed. These goals were not federal standards for which the states would be held accountable, but rather goals that would be implemented and monitored by the individual states. The next few years will determine whether these standards will be adopted.

Innovation

A primary task of educational institutions is to transmit society's knowledge, and part of that knowledge consists of the means by which new knowledge is to be sought. Learning how to think independently and creatively is probably one of the most valuable tools the educational institution can transmit. This is especially true in the scientific fields in institutions of higher education. Until well into this century, scientific research was undertaken more as a hobby than a vocation. Gregor Mendel (1822–1884), who discovered, by breeding peas, the principles of genetic inheritance, worked alone in the gardens of the monastery where he lived. And Albert Einstein supported himself between 1905 and 1907 as a patent office employee while making several trail-blazing discoveries in physics, the most widely known of which is the "special theory of relativity."

Today, science is regarded as a socially useful pursuit and is no longer the province of part timers. Modern scientific research typically is undertaken by highly trained professionals, many of whom frequently work as teams. The technology needed has become so expensive that most research is possible only under the aegis of extensive government or corporate funding. In 1989 the federal government spent 142 billion dollars on research and development funding (*Statistical Abstract of the United States: 1991*). In research and development, the areas of national defense, space exploration, and health research receive by far the greatest amount of support. In research alone, the leading three areas are life sciences (biological sciences and agriculture), engineering, and the physical sciences.

The importance of the contributions to science

Learning how to think independently and creatively is probably one of the most valuable tools our educational systems can transmit.

by higher academic institutions cannot be overestimated. First, there could be no scientific innovations—no breakthroughs—without the training provided by these schools. In the United States alone, 13,184 doctorates were awarded in 1988 in the biological and physical sciences, mathematics, computer science, and engineering. During 1988, the combined fields of science and engineering employed 101,800 scientists in institutions of higher education (*Statistical Abstract of the United States: 1991*). Second, universities of the highest caliber continue to serve as the point of origin for some of the most significant research currently undertaken in both the biological and the physical sciences.

Child Care

In addition to their manifest or intended functions, the schools in America have come to fulfill a number of functions they were not originally designed to serve.

One latent function of many public schools is to provide child care outside the nuclear family. This has become increasingly important since World War II, when women began to enter the labor force in large numbers. As of 1989, 73.2 percent of married females with school-age children (ages 6 to 17) were in the labor force, as well as 85.0 percent of divorced women with children that age (*Statistical Abstract of the United States: 1991*).

A related service of schools is to provide children with at least one nutritious meal a day. In 1975 25,289,000 public school pupils in the United States participated in federally funded school lunch programs at a cost of $1.28 billion. By 1988 the number of pupils in the school lunch program had dropped

to 11,700,000, at a cost of $3.06 billion (*Statistical Abstract of the United States: 1991*). Recent federal reductions have established new and stringent criteria limiting eligibility for such programs. In addition, government subsidization has been appreciably reduced.

Despite federal cutbacks, a move is on to make free or reduced cost breakfasts available to a larger number of students. Proponents of this program claim a positive relationship between early morning nutrition and improved learning and performance. Many children are forced to fend for themselves early in the morning and, all too often, leave home without breakfast.

Postponing Job Hunting

More and more young American adults are choosing to continue their education after graduating from high school. In 1989, 37.9 percent of male and 41.5 percent of female high school graduates were enrolled in college (*Statistical Abstract of the United States: 1991*). Even though some of these individuals also work at part-time and even full-time jobs, an important latent function of the American educational system is to slow down the entry of young adults into the labor market. This helps keep down unemployment, as well as competition for low-paying unskilled jobs.

Originally two factors seemed to indicate that college enrollments would not continue to increase. Because of low birth rates, the number of high school graduates peaked at 3.2 million in 1977 and began a 15-year decline. There were 16 percent fewer high school graduates in 1987 than 1977, and the number dropped another 11 percent by 1992.

CONFLICT
1. CURRICULUM
2. Segragation/Integration/Boundries/District
3. Tracking

Another concern and possible cause of decreased enrollments is the rigor now applied to government subsidization of student loans. Strict new criteria for loan eligibility are being enforced, and in addition, higher interest rates and shorter repayment periods may mean that thousands of students from all socioeconomic levels will be unable to afford a college education or graduate studies.

Colleges and universities, in anticipation of potential enrollment problems, have embarked on concerted efforts to ward off disaster. Through hard work and luck they have succeeded. Despite the loss of half a million high school graduates in the last decade, total enrollment in two- and four-year colleges rose from 11.5 million in 1977 to 13.04 million in 1988.

Colleges have also benefitted from the fact that the U.S. economic base has shifted from manufacturing jobs to service jobs, causing the demand for professionals and technicians to grow. The salaries for service positions are considerably higher than manufacturing jobs. In one study of the average annual incomes of 25- to 34-year-old men, those with college degrees earned 40 percent more than high school graduates and 93 percent more than high school dropouts. Small wonder that the most common reason given today for going to college is "to get a better job" (Edmondson, 1987).

Colleges have also benefitted from two other trends: the increase in the number of women going to college and in the number of older students. Since 1980 women have represented the majority of college students. In 1988, 54.6 percent of college students were female, compared to 45.4 percent male. This trend is an outgrowth of changing attitudes about the status of women in our society and the breakdown in gender role stereotypes (see Chapter 10).

Older students (25 and over) represent the most rapidly growing group of college students, accounting for 45 percent of all undergraduate and graduate students. Women are again overrepresented in this group, as are part-time students.

THE CONFLICT THEORY VIEW

To the conflict theorist, society is an arena for conflict, not cooperation. In any society, certain groups come to dominate others, and social institutions become the instruments by which those in power are able to control the less powerful. The conflict theorist thus sees the educational system as a means for maintaining the status quo, and it is able to carry out this task in a variety of ways. The educational system socializes students into values dictated by the powerful majority. Schools are seen as systems which stifle individualism and creativity in the name of maintaining order. To the conflict theorist the function of school "is to produce the kind of people the system needs, to train people for the jobs the corporations require and to instill in them the proper attitudes and values necessary for the proper fulfillment of one's social role" (Szymanski and Goertzel, 1979).

Social Control

In the United States, schools have been assigned the function of developing personal control and social skills in children. Although the explicit, formally defined school curriculum emphasizes basic skills such as reading and writing, much of what is taught is in fact oriented away from practical concerns. Many critics point out that much of the curriculum (other than in special professional training programs) has little direct, practical application to everyday life. This has led conflict theorists and others to conclude that the most important lessons learned in school are not those listed in the formal curriculum but, rather, involve a hidden curriculum. *The* **hidden curriculum** *refers to the social attitudes and values taught in school that prepare children to accept the requirements of adult life and to "fit into" the social, political, and economic statuses the society provides.*

In order to succeed in school, a student must learn both the official (academic) curriculum and the hidden (social) curriculum. The hidden curriculum is often an outgrowth of the structure within which the student is asked to learn. Within the framework of mass education, it would be impossible to provide instruction on a one-to-one basis or even in very small groups. Consequently, students are usually grouped into relatively larger classes. Because this system obviously demands a great deal of social conformity by the children, those who divert attention and make it difficult for the teacher to proceed are punished. In many respects the hidden curriculum is a lesson in being docile. For example, an article in *Today's Education,* the journal of the National Education Association, gives an experienced teacher's advice to new teachers: "During the first week or two of teaching in an inner-city school, I concentrate on establishing simple routines, such as the procedure for walking downstairs. I line up the children, and . . . have them practice walking up and down the stairs. Each time the group is allowed to move only when quiet and orderly."

Social skills are highly valued in American

society, and a mastery of them is widely accepted as an indication of a child's maturity. The school is a "miniature society," and many individuals fail in school because they are either unable or unwilling to learn or use the values, attitudes, and skills contained in the hidden curriculum. We do a great disservice to these students when we make them feel that they have failed in education, when they have in fact only failed to conform to the school's socialization standards.

Some authors (Bowles and Gintis, 1976) go so far as to assert that the idea of educational success being determined by merit or intelligence is an illusion fostered in the schools. Educational success, they claim, is much more likely to be determined by the possession of appropriate personality traits, and by conformity to school norms. These traits are acquired in the family and home environments. The educational system, while claiming to reward those who demonstrate objective displays of merit, in fact is rewarding behavioral characteristics already possessed by individuals from specific social class backgrounds, for example, the middle class.

Screening and Allocation: Tracking

From its beginning, the American school system *in principle* has been opposed to **tracking**, *or the stratification of students by ability, social class, and various other categories.* Legislators saw in compulsory public education a way to diminish the grip of inherited social stratification by providing the means for individuals to rise as high as their achieved skills would allow. In the words of Horace Mann, an influential American educator of the late nineteenth century, public education was to be "the great equalizer of the conditions of men." The second goal of mass education, closely related to the first, was the desired "Anglo-conformity" of the crowds of immigrants whose ethnic and cultural diversity was seen by many as a dangerous source of potential social chaos (see Chapter 9). The third aim of universal public education was to give workers a wide range of skills to match the requirements of an increasingly complex industrial economy.

Despite the principles on which it is based, the American educational system depends on tracking in ways less formal but no less real than the Swiss system. Although tracking in American education is not as formally structured or as irreversible as in most other industrial societies, it is influenced by many factors, including socioeconomic status, ethnicity, and residence. It is also consistently expressed in the differences between public and private schools as well as in the difference among public schools (in New York City, for example, there are highly competitive math, science-oriented, and arts-oriented high schools, neighborhood high schools, and vocational high schools). And of course, tracking occurs in higher education in the selection of students by private as well as state colleges and universities.

Tracking begins in first grade when students are assigned to "fast," "average," and "slow" groups. It can be difficult for a student to break out of an assigned category because teachers come to expect a certain level of performance from that individual.

As societies have become more complex, a greater need has developed for the formal educational system to extend the socialization process that starts in the family.

In turn, the student, sensing this expectation, will often give the level of performance expected. In this way, tracking becomes a self-fulfilling prophecy.

In one study of this phenomenon, Rosenthal and Jacobson (1966) gave IQ tests to 650 lower-class elementary school pupils. Their teachers were told that the test would predict which of the students were expected to "bloom" intellectually during the next year. In other words, the tests would identify the superior students in the class. This approach was in fact not the one employed. Twenty percent of the students were randomly selected to be designated as "superior," even though there was no measured difference between them and the other 80 percent of the school population. The point of the study was to determine whether the teacher's expectations would have any effect on the "superior" students. At the end of the first year, all the students were tested again. There was a significant difference in the gain in IQ scores between the "superior" group and the control group. This gain was most pronounced among those students in the first and second grades. Yet the following year, when these students were promoted to another class and assigned to teachers who had not been told that they were "superior," they no longer made the sorts of gains evidenced during the previous year. Nonetheless, the "superior" students in the upper grades did continue to gain during their second year, showing long-term advantages from positive teacher expectations. Apparently the younger students needed continuous input to benefit from teacher expectations, whereas older students needed less.

The Credentialized Society

Conflict theorists would also argue that we have become a "credentialized society" (Collins, 1979) in the last thirty years. A degree or certificate has become necessary to perform a vast variety of jobs. This credential may not necessarily cause the recipient to perform the job better. Even in professions such as medicine, engineering, or law, most knowledge is acquired by performing tasks on the job. However, credentials have become a rite of passage and a sign that a certain process of indoctrination and socialization has taken place. Therefore colleges and universities act as gatekeepers, allowing those who are willing to play by the rules to succeed, while barring those who may disrupt the existing social order.

At the same time advanced degrees are undergoing constant change and becoming less specialized. Obtaining a law degree from Harvard, Yale, or Columbia is less an indication of the quality of the training of a particular candidate, but rather provides a basis upon which leading corporations, major public agencies, and important law firms can recruit those who will maintain the status quo. The degree signifies the candidate has forged links with the established networks and achieved a grade necessary to obtain a degree.

Colleges and universities are miniature societies more than centers of technical and scientific education. In these environments students learn how to operate within the established order and to accept traditional social hierarchies. In this sense they provide the power structure with a constantly replenishing army of defenders of the established order. At the same time those who could disrupt the status quo are not permitted to enter positions of power and responsibility.

ISSUES IN AMERICAN EDUCATION

How well have American schools done in educating the population? The answer to this question depends on the standards one applies. Americans take for granted that everyone has a basic right to an education and that the state should provide free elementary and high school classes. The United States pioneered this concept long before similar systems were introduced in Europe.

As we have attempted to provide formal education to everyone, we have also had to contend with a wide variety of problems stemming from the diverse population. In this section we will examine some of the concerns in contemporary American education.

Unequal Access to Education

American minorities have sought equal access to public schools for two centuries. Tracing these efforts over the generations reveals a pattern of dissatisfaction with integrated, as well as with segregated schools.

Black parents attributed the ineffective instruction at the schools attended by their children to one of two causes. If the schools were all-black, failure was attributed to the racially segregated character of those schools. If whites were attending these schools, black parents concluded, conditions would be better. This has been the predominant theme both in the nineteenth and twentieth centuries.

Discontent has also occurred when black children have attended predominantly white schools. In those instances the racially integrated character of

SOCIOLOGY AT WORK

Jonathan Kozol on Unequal Schooling

Jonathan Kozol, author of *Savage Inequalities* and *Death at an Early Age,* notes that four decades after the Supreme Court ordered America to integrate its schools, the country has established two separate and unequal school systems, divided by class and race, with the gap between them growing larger each year.

Kozol studied 30 schools and found children going to schools in Third World conditions a short bus ride away from beautiful, well-equipped school campuses.

"These children have done nothing wrong. They have committed no crime. They are too young to have offended us in any way. One searches for some way

Jonathan Kozol

to understand why a society so rich would leave them in squalor for so long, and with so little public indignation."

Kozol notes that the gaps in school funding are so consistent from one metropolitan area to another—with rich schools in many areas spending more than twice per pupil as poor schools—that it suggests a deliberate pattern. He points out that students in suburban New Trier High School, outside Chicago, "will compete against each other and against graduates of other schools attended by rich children. They will not compete against the poor, few of whom will graduate from high school; fewer still will go to college; scarcely any will attend good colleges. There will be more spaces for children of New Trier as a consequence."

While their children enjoy richer schools, bolstered by higher property tax bases and federal deductions for property taxes and mortgage payments, suburban parents are lulled by politicians who claim spending more money on inner-city schools will not make any difference.

Kozol traces the country's retreat from equal public education to two crucial Supreme Court decisions—the *Rodriquez* decision in 1974, a Texas case in which

the Court declared that disparities in public education were not a Constitutional issue, and the *Milliken* decision a year later, a Michigan case in which the Court exempted white suburban schools from urban school desegregation programs.

Kozol points out that "there is a deep-seated reverence for fair play in the United States, but this is not the case in education, health care, or inheritance of wealth. In these elemental areas we want the game to be unfair and we have made it so."

For many poor students, dropping out of school appears a rational strategy, given how little they are getting and how depressing their schools are. If large numbers of dropouts ever did return to school, most urban school systems, already stretched to the breaking point, would have no room for them.

Kozol notes that "conservatives are often the first to rise to protest an insult to the flag. But they soil the flag in telling us to fly it over ruined children's heads in ugly segregated schools. Flags in these schools hang motionless and gather dust, and are frequently no cleaner than the schools themselves. Children in a dirty school are asked to pledge a dirtied flag."

the school was seen as a problem because white students were favored by the teachers.

In the 1954 case *Brown v. Board of Education,* of Topeka, Kansas, the Supreme Court ruled that school segregation was illegal. The Court held that "In the field of public education, the doctrine of

separate but equal has no place. Separate educational facilities are inherently unequal." Segregating black school children from white school children was a violation of the equal protection clause of the Constitution. However, while the Court's verdict banned **de jure segregation,** *or laws prohibiting one*

The facilities and education available at some elite, private high schools are better than those found at many colleges.

racial group from attending school with another, it had little effect on **de facto segregation,** *or segregation resulting from residential patterns.* For example, many minorities often live in areas of a city where there are few, if any, whites. Consequently, when children attend neighborhood schools, they are usually taught in a racially segregated environment.

Ten years after the 1954 ruling, the federal government attempted to document the degree to which equality of education among all groups had been achieved. It financed a cross-sectional study of 645,000 children in grades 1, 3, 6, 9, and 12 attending some four thousand different schools across the country. The results, appearing in James S. Coleman's now-famous report *Equality of Educational Opportunity* (1966), supported unequivocally the conclusion that American education remains largely unequal in most parts of the country, including those where "Negroes form any significant proportion of the population." Coleman noted further that on all tests measuring pupil skills in areas critical to job performance and career advancement, not only did Native Americans, Mexican Americans, Puerto Ricans, and blacks score significantly below whites but also that the gaps widened in the higher grades. Although there are acknowledged wide inequalities of educational opportunity throughout the United States, the discrepancies between the skills of minorities and those of their white counterparts could not be accounted for in terms of how much money was spent on education per pupil, quality of school buildings, number of labs or libraries, or even class sizes. In spite of good intentions, a school presumably cannot usually outweigh the influence of the family backgrounds of its individual students and of the family background

of its student population as a whole. The Coleman study thus provided evidence that schools per se do not play as important a role in student achievement as was once thought. It appears that the home environment, the quality of the neighborhood, and the types of friends and associates one has are much more influential in school *achievement* than is the quality of the school facilities or the skills of teachers. In effect, then, the areas that schools have least control over—the areas of social influence and development—are the most important in determining how well an individual will do in school.

The Coleman report did, however, point out that lower-class nonwhite students showed better school achievement when they went to school with middle-class whites. Racial segregation, therefore, hindered the educational attainments of nonwhites.

A direct outgrowth of the Coleman report pointing to the harm of de facto segregation was the busing of children from one neighborhood to another in order to achieve racial integration in the schools. The fundamental assumption underlying school busing was that it would bring about improved academic achievement among minority groups. Nationwide, many parents, both black and white, responded negatively to the idea that their school-age children must leave their home neighborhoods. For all practical purposes, busing is no longer a major issue today. Those schools that needed to desegregate have done so, and other less disruptive approaches to desegregation are attempted.

One factor that has increased the difficulty of integrating public schools is so-called *white flight,* the continuing exodus of white Americans by the hundreds of thousands from the cities to the suburbs. White flight has been prompted partly by the migration of blacks from the South to the inner cities of the North and Midwest during the past two decades, but some authorities strongly maintain that it is also closely related to school-desegregation efforts in the large cities.

For example, in a later view of desegregation attempts (1977), James Coleman vastly revised his position in his 1966 report, stating that urban desegregation has in some instances had the self-defeating effect of emptying the cities of white pupils. Some authorities (Pettigrew and Green, 1975), however, took exception to the Coleman thesis, and others believe that what may appear to be flight is more directly related to the characteristic tendency of the American middle class to be "upwardly mobile" and to constantly seek a better lifestyle. Even though some evidence exists of a countertrend in which middle-class whites are beginning to "regentrify" inner cities, there seems to be no abating of this migration. Nor have most established communities relinquished the ideal of self-determination as embodied in the right to maintain "neighborhood" schools.

Since the Coleman report was issued, the integration of our schools has continued to be a critical problem, especially in urban areas where the vast majority of minority group members live. According to a study by the National School Boards Association, there has been "no significant progress on the desegregation of black students in urban districts since the mid-1970s," and some areas have shown "severe increases in racial isolation" (Fiske, 1988). Schools in Atlanta and Detroit, for example are more segregated now than a decade ago.

Only about three percent of the nation's white students attend one of the central city schools. As a result, these schools "have become almost irrelevant to the nation's white population." There are currently many more minority and far fewer white students in our public schools than in the past (Fiske, 1988).

As whites are leaving the inner city schools, they are being replaced by blacks, Hispanics, Asian-Americans and other immigrants. A large share of Hispanic, Asian, and immigrant students usually means a large share of non-English-speaking students. A recent count showed ninety-three different languages were spoken by the students in the Los Angeles schools. In 1989, 38 percent of the elementary students in Los Angeles County public schools were enrolled in English as a Second Language (ESL) classes. Not only are special language programs costly, but ESL students miss out on regular classroom instruction while they are in language class (Griffith, Frase, and Ralph, 1989).

Colleges and universities have had mixed results in increasing minority enrollment. Between 1980 and 1985, the number of blacks enrolled as undergraduates was on a steady decline before rising again slightly in 1986. Many qualified students do not apply because their families cannot afford tuition, despite the fact that complete aid packages are available. To overcome this problem, many schools have taken an aggressive recruitment stance, believing that once they find qualified candidates, they can convince them to attend. For example, at Guilford College in Greensboro, North Carolina, the tuition and living expenses of needy minority students are covered in full. At Harvard University, where 214 blacks were accepted to the freshman class in 1988—the largest number in the school's history—no student is turned away because of financial need.

Still, thousands of qualified minority students never attend college and many who do attend fail to graduate. The reasons for low graduation rates include financial problems, poor preparation, and the feeling that they are not really welcome. Many cannot afford the loss of income that comes with being a full-time student. For many, family survival depends on the money they contribute. Others are victims of inadequate schools. They simply do not have the skills needed to complete college. Still others drop out because they feel out of place in the predominantly white world of higher education.

High School Dropouts

Dropping out of high school has long been viewed as a serious educational and social problem. By leaving high school before graduation, dropouts risk serious educational deficiencies that severely limit their economic and social well-being.

Over the last seventy-five years, the proportion of people in the adult population who have failed to finish high school has decreased substantially (see Figure 13.1). In 1910 the proportion of the adult population (age 25 and over) that had completed at least four years of high school was 13.5 percent. It stood at 24.5 percent in 1940, at 55.2 percent in 1970, and at 76.9 percent in 1989. Among young people (age 25 to 29) the drop is even more striking with 86.6 percent having completed high school in 1989 (*Statistical Abstract of the United States: 1991*).

Despite these long-term declines in dropout rates, interest in the problem has increased substantially among educators and policymakers in recent years. For example, the "Dropout Prevention and Re-entry Act" passed in 1986 authorizes fifty million

FIGURE 13.1

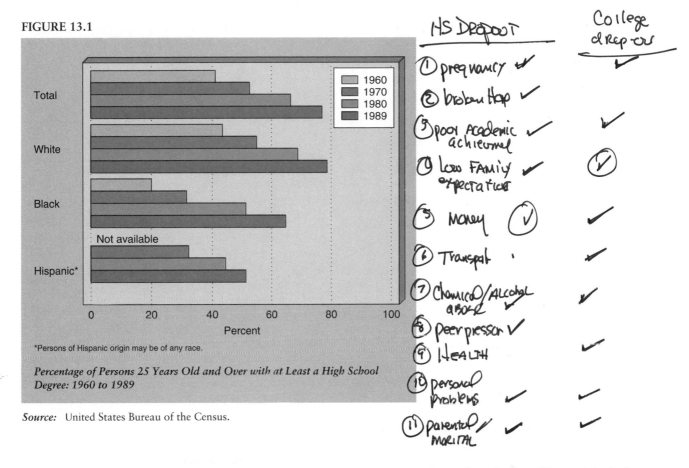

Percentage of Persons 25 Years Old and Over with at Least a High School Degree: 1960 to 1989

Source: United States Bureau of the Census.

[Handwritten annotations:

HS Dropout   College dropout

① pregnancy ✓
② broken home ✓
③ poor academic achievemt ✓   ✓
④ low family expectation ✓   ⨀
⑤ money ⨀   ✓
⑥ transport   ✓
⑦ chemical/alcohol abuse   ✓
⑧ peer pressure ✓
⑨ health   ✓
⑩ personal problems ✓   ✓
⑪ parental marital ✓   ✓]

dollars a year in federal funds for dropout-plagued school systems. In New York City, thirty-eight million dollars a year goes into dropout prevention programs (Finn, 1987).

If dropout rates are declining, why has the concern for this problem increased? First, although the long-term trend of dropping out has declined, the short-term trend has remained steady and even increased for some groups. A second reason is that minority populations, who have always had higher dropout rates than whites, are increasing as a proportion of the public high school population. Racial and ethnic minorities now represent the majority of students enrolled in most large U.S. cities and more than 90 percent of all students in such cities as Newark, Atlanta, and San Antonio (Plisko and Stern, 1985).

Dropout rates are higher for members of racial, ethnic, and language minorities, higher for males than females, and higher for persons from the lower socioeconomic classes. Hispanics have the highest dropout rates—19.1 percent, compared to 17.2 percent for blacks, and 13.0 percent for whites. Among Hispanics, Puerto Ricans have the highest dropout rates, followed by Mexican Americans and Cubans. Dropout rates are also particularly high among American Indians.

Factors associated with dropping out include low educational and occupational attainment levels of parents, low family income, speaking a language other than English in the home, single-parent families, and poor academic achievement. The influence of peers is also important, but has not received much attention in previous research. Many dropouts have friends who are also dropouts, but it is not clear to what extent and in what ways a student's friends and peers influence the decision to leave school (Rumberger, 1987).

Dropping out of high school affects not only those who leave school, but also society at large. In addition, the social consequences go beyond the economic and psychological impact on the dropout. In a comprehensive study of the dropout problem, Levin (1972) identified seven social consequences of dropping out of high school:

1. A loss of national income because dropouts earn less than graduates;
2. A loss of tax revenues because of the lower earnings of dropouts;
3. Increased demand for social services including welfare, medical assistance, and unemployment compensation;
4. Increased crime;

Schools act as gatekeepers, allowing those who are willing to play by the rules to succeed and barring those who may disrupt the existing social order.

5. Reduced political participation;
6. Reduced intergenerational mobility;
7. Poorer levels of health.

Levin estimates that every dollar invested in dropout programs would produce six dollars in national income and almost two dollars in tax revenues. A more recent study estimated the costs of dropout prevention programs in Chicago are only one percent of the benefits derived from increased tax revenues, reduced welfare payments, and reduced crime (Hess and Lauber, 1985).

Given these facts it is small wonder that the U.S. Department of Education has focused an increasing amount of attention on how to improve high school completion rates.

Violence in the Schools

Nothing undermines the effectiveness of our educational system more than unsafe schools. Books, pencils, and papers have been replaced by drugs, guns, knives, and other paraphernalia of destruction. In New York City, there were about 1,400 incidents involving weapons in the schools in 1987. In some high schools, metal detectors are used to reduce the number of weapons brought into the schools. In some Chicago schools, where gangs freely sell drugs to students within school buildings, principals chain doors to keep dealers out and students in. Philadelphia has schools where students are afraid to use filthy school bathrooms because of the gang members who hang out there.

The violence that fills America's inner-city schools came to the public's attention when Joe Clark, principal of Eastside High in Paterson, New Jersey, graced the cover of *Time* magazine. When Clark took over Eastside in 1982, he found deplorable conditions that he was determined to change. In response:

> "Clark chained doors against pushers and threatened any strays that might leak through with a baseball bat ... Bellowing through the bullhorn and the school's P.A. system, he banned loitering, mandated keep-to-the-right and keep-moving rules for the corridors, and set up a dress code forbidding hats and any gangish ... clothing. Students who got to school late or cut class could expect latrine or graffiti-scrubbing duty" (*Time*, February 8, 1988, p. 52).

Although Clark's methods have been severely criticized by many educators and government officials throughout the country, and praised by others including former President Reagan, his actions showed the desperate conditions of inner-city schools and the measures some are willing to take to improve them. Inner-city schools are made up primarily of minority students, have high dropout rates, high assault rates, and a staff that expects failure and violence.

Standardized Testing

In American schools, the standardized test is the most frequently used means of evaluating student aptitude and ability. Every year more than 100 million standardized tests are administered to individuals from nursery school to graduate school.

Children encounter standardized tests almost from the first day they come to school. Usually their first experience with testing takes the form of an intelligence test given to more than two million youngsters each year. Students are also required to take a number of achievement tests, beginning in elementary school. High school and college seniors take college admissions tests that decide whether they will be accepted at universities and graduate schools.

The Educational Testing Service's (ETS) Scholastic Aptitude Test (SAT) which is required by about 1,200 colleges and universities is the best-known college admissions test. Another 2,800 American colleges require or recommend the American College Test (ACT). Students wishing to go to graduate school are required to take other exams which are tailored to measure the ability and skills used in the field they wish to enter.

The ETS claims to be meticulous in its test construction. It hires college students, teachers, and professors to assist its staff in writing questions. Each of the approximately three thousand questions that are created each year are reviewed by about fifteen people for style, content, or racial bias.

Much criticism, however, has been leveled against standardized tests. Many claim that all standardized tests are academically invalid and biased against minorities. The average black or Hispanic youngster encounters references and vocabulary on a test that is likely to be more familiar to white middle-class students. Many others oppose the secrecy surrounding the test companies. Groups have pushed for "truth in testing," meaning that the test makers must divulge all exam questions and answers shortly after the tests are given. This would enable people to evaluate the tests more closely for cultural bias and possible scoring errors. The testing industry is opposed to such measures, as it would force the creation of totally new tests for each administration, without the possibility of reusing valid and reliable questions.

No one would claim that standardized tests are perfect measuring instruments. At best they can provide an objective measure to be used in conjunction with grades and teacher comments. At worst, they may discriminate against minorities or not validly measure potential ability. Yet college admissions officers insist that results from standardized college admissions tests give them a significant tool to use in evaluating students from a variety of backgrounds and many different parts of the country.

As you can see from Figure 13.2, more students are taking the SAT than ever before, a fact that might be expected to result in lowered scores. Instead, average combined SAT scores have risen sixteen points since 1980, reversing a trend that saw scores drop ninety points since 1963. In part, higher scores can be attributed to the more rigorous standards of the back-to-basics movement—a movement bringing about modest gains among poor performers.

The Gifted

The term *gifted* is emotionally loaded. The word may evoke feelings that range from admiration to resentment and hostility. Throughout history, people have displayed a marked ambivalence toward the gifted. It was not unusual to view giftedness as either divinely or diabolically inspired. Genius was

FIGURE 13.2

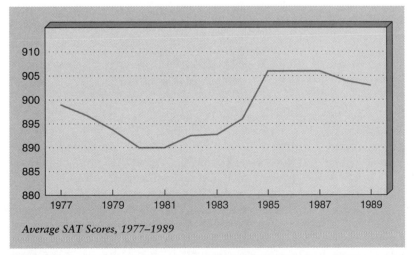

Average SAT Scores, 1977–1989

Source: College Entrance Examination Board, *National College-Bound Senior,* annual, New York.

CONTROVERSIES IN SOCIOLOGY

Does TV Make Kids Stupid?

Critics of television claim that instead of reading and doing homework, today's kids settle in front of the tube with vacant minds, mesmerized and numbed by constant movement and visual change. The evils of television are said to be reduced attention span, hyperactivity, loss of creativity and imagination, poor reading ability and even deterioration of the left half of the brain. Can it really be that bad?

After examining more than 165 studies on the topic from the time of television's inception to the present, researchers Daniel R. Anderson and Patricia A. Collins found almost no scientific evidence that television has a negative effect on the intellectual ability of children.

Some of the questions they asked were:

1. *Are children mesmerized by TV?* Not really. Children between five and 11 years old actually only look at the TV about two-thirds of the time. They are usually doing something else while they are watching and look away from the set over 100 times an hour.
2. *Do children have blank minds when they watch TV?* Not likely. Studies show that children actively try to comprehend what they are watching, make judgements about it, and try to anticipate the outcome. This is very similar to what a child does when reading or listening to the radio.
3. *Does TV replace other valuable intellectual activities?* Not really. The studies note that television replaces other entertainment media, such as movies, radio and comic books. There is virtually no reduction in the reading of books or magazines due to television. This should not be surprising. The typical American child did very little reading outside of school before television arrived, and the situation is no different today.
4. *Does TV reduce attention span?* Educational programs such as "Sesame Street" and "Mister Rogers" appear to have positive effects, while violent action programs, music videos, and programs with rapidly changing scenes have a negative effect.
5. *Does TV impair reading ability?* Poor readers spend more time watching TV than reading, but that does not mean TV produces poor readers. Most studies have shown there is no effect.
6. *Does television have any positive effects on intellectual development?* Preschool children learn some vocabulary from television and educational programs can educate. On the whole, however, there is little evidence that television either enhances or detracts from development of the intellect.

Anderson and Collins go on to point out that this does not mean that television is good for children. It does shape their thinking about the world. If society is depicted as violent and people are depicted as motivated by greed, children will learn these messages. Thus, while the medium may be neither good nor bad, the messages may have an undesirable effect.

Source: Daniel R. Anderson and Patricia A. Collins, "Does TV Make Kids Stupid?," *The Boston Globe,* January 15, 1989, pp. A21, A23.

often seen as one aspect of insanity. Aristotle's observation that "There was never a great genius without a tincture of madness" continues to be believed as common folklore.

People also tend to believe that intellectualism and practicality are incompatible, as expressed in sayings such as "too smart for his (or her) own good" or "It's not smart to be too smart." High intelligence is often also assumed to be incompatible with happiness.

There is little agreement on what constitutes giftedness. The most common measure is performance on a standardized test. All who score above a certain level are defined as gifted, though serious problems occur when this criterion alone is used. Arbitrary approaches to measuring giftedness tend to ignore the likelihood that active intervention could increase the number of candidates among females, the disabled, and selected minorities, groups that are often underrepresented among the gifted.

Women tend to be underrepresented among the gifted because popular culture deems that high intelligence is incompatible with femininity; thus some girls quickly learn to deny, disguise, or repress their abilities. Minorities are hindered by the fact that commonly used assessment tools discriminate against ethnic groups whose members have had different cultural experiences or use English as a second language. The intellectual ability of disabled youngsters is often overlooked. Their physical handicaps may mask or divert attention away from their mental potential, particularly when communication is impaired, as this is a key factor in assessment procedures.

Teachers often confuse intelligence with unrelated school behaviors. Children who are neat, clean, and well mannered, have good handwriting, or manifest other desirable but irrelevant classroom traits may often be thought to be very bright. Teachers often associate giftedness with children who come from prominent families, have traveled widely, and have had extensive cultural advantages. Teachers are likely to discount high intelligence when it might be present in combination with poor grammar, truancy, aggressiveness, or learning disabilities.

Public education's first attempt to deal with the gifted took place in St. Louis schools in 1868. The program involved a system of flexible promotions enabling high-achieving students not to have to remain in any grade for a fixed amount of time. By the early 1900s, special schools for the gifted appeared.

There has never been a consistent, cohesive national policy or consensus on how to educate the gifted. Those special programs instituted have reached only a small fraction of those who conceivably could benefit from them. A serious problem with the education of the gifted arises from philosophical considerations. Many teachers are reluctant to single out the gifted for special treatment, as they feel the children are already naturally privileged. Sometimes, attention given to gifted children is seen as antidemocratic.

No matter now inadequate it may seem, the effort to provide for the educational needs of learning-disabled children has far exceeded that expended for the gifted. Similarly, the time and money spent on research for educating the slower children far outstrip that set aside for research on materials, methodology for teaching, and so on, for the gifted.

When schools do have enrichment programs, their effectiveness is rarely monitored. Enrichment programs are often provided by teachers untrained in dealing with the gifted, for it is assumed that anyone qualified to teach is presumably capable of teaching the gifted. Yet most basic teacher certification programs do not require even one hour's exposure to information on the theory, identification, or methodology of teaching such children. Most administrators do not have the theoretical background or practical experience necessary to establish and promote successful programs for the gifted.

There is some evidence that the nation's population of gifted children—and possibly, prodigies—is growing. Researchers who test large numbers of children have detected a startling proportion in the 170 to 180-IQ range.

But while psychologists would agree that early exceptional ability should be nurtured in order to thrive, they do not necessarily think the current movement to produce "superbabies" by force-feeding a diet of mathematics and vocabulary to infants is a good idea. Pediatricians have begun seeing children with backlash symptoms—headaches, tummy-aches, hair-tearing, anxiety, depression—as a result of this pressure to perform.

History has shown that being an authentic child prodigy creates enough problems of its own. The fine line between nurturing genius and trying to force a bright, but not brilliant child to be something he is not, is clearly one that must be walked with care.

It appears that there are more than 2.5 million schoolchildren in the United States that can be described as gifted, or about three percent of the school population. Giftedness is essentially *potential*. Whether these children will achieve their potential intellectual growth will depend on many factors, not the least of which is the level of educational instruction they receive. We must question why we continue to show such ambivalence toward the gifted and why we are willing to tolerate incompetence and waste in regard to such a valuable resource (Baskin and Harris, 1980).

CHAPTER

▪ 14 ▪

Political and Economic Systems

Politics, Power, and Authority
Power
Political Authority

Government and the State
Functions of the State

The Economy and the State
Capitalism
The Marxist Response to Capitalism
Command Economies
Socialism
The Capitalist View of Socialism

Types of States
Autocracy
Totalitarianism
Democracy
Democracy and Socialism
Democratic Socialism

Functionalist and Conflict Theory Views
of the State

Political Change
Institutionalized Political Change
Rebellions
Revolutions

The American Political System
The Two-Party System
Voting Behavior
Special-Interest Groups

Larry Hawkins has no objection to being considered an avatar of social reform. For more than a decade, as a Dade County, Florida commissioner and before that as a state legislator, he has championed child-care issues. In 1992, a Hawkins-sponsored measure requiring Dade County businesses to establish family leave policies went into effect.

Mr. Hawkins's measure requires companies with fifty or more employees and companies of any size that do business with the county to allow unpaid leaves of up to ninety days every two years for such things as child birth, adoption or caring for a sick relative. Miami is home to several large employers, including the Ryder Corporation and Burger King. Opposition to the measure from the business community was deep because they were worried that once unpaid leave was established, paid leave would be next. Critics charged that most large employers already have leave policies, many more generous than the minimum standard set by Dade County. President George Bush, too, voiced his view that mandating policies like family leave was too costly and intrusive on business. (Noble, 1992)

In most societies what laws get passed, or not passed, depend to a large extent on which categories of people have power. The powerful in a society work hard to pass laws to their liking. In this chapter we will look at the social institution known as the political system. **Politics** *is the process by which power is distributed and decisions are made.* This chapter will help clarify what is unique about our two-party system and where the American political system fits into the whole spectrum of political institutions.

POLITICS, POWER, AND AUTHORITY

There are more than 800 candidates for the House of Representatives every other year. Americans also vote for senators, governors, and a host of other offices on a regular basis. Candidates ring our doorbells, shake our hands, stuff our mailboxes, and exhort us through our television sets. They make promises they often cannot keep. This is politics, American style. Small wonder it has been said that politics, like baseball, is the great American pastime. Hence, running for president of the United States is a political activity. So is enacting legislation. So is taxing town property owners to subsidize the digging of sewers. So is going to war. The study of the political process, then, is the study of power.

Power

Max Weber (1958a) referred to **power** *as the ability to carry out one person's or group's will, even in the presence of resistance or opposition from others.* In this sense, power is the capability of making others comply with one's decisions, often exacting compliance through the threat or actual use of sanctions, penalties, or force.

In some relationships the division of power is spelled out clearly and defined formally. Employers have specific powers over employees, army officers over enlisted personnel, ship captains over their crews, professors over their students. In other relationships, the question of power is less clearly defined and may even shift back and forth, depending on individual personalities and the particular situation: between wife and husband, among sisters and brothers, or among friends in a social clique.

Power is an element of many types of relationships and covers a broad spectrum of interactions. At one pole is **authority**—*power that is regarded as legitimate by those over whom it is exercised, who also accept the authority's legitimacy in imposing sanctions or even in using force if necessary.* For example, here in the United States few people are eager to pay income taxes; yet most do so regularly. Most taxpayers accept the authority of the government not only to demand payment but also to impose penalties for nonpayment.

At the other extreme is **coercion**—*power that is regarded as illegitimate by those over whom it is exerted.* In coercion, compliance is based on fear of reprisals that are not recognized as falling within the range of accepted norms.

Power based on authority is quite stable, and obedience to it is accepted as a social norm. Power based on coercion, on the other hand, is unstable. People will obey only out of fear, and any opportunity to test this power will be taken. Power based on coercion will fail in the long run.

The American Revolution, for example, was preceded by the erosion of the legitimacy of the existing system. The authority of the King of England was questioned and his power, based increasingly on coercion rather than on acceptance as a social norm, inevitably crumbled.

Political Authority

An individual's authority often will apply only to certain people in certain situations. For example, a professor has the authority to require students to write term papers, but no authority to demand the students' votes should he or she run for public office.

In the same sense Max Weber pointed out that the most powerful states do not impose their will by the use of physical force alone, but by ensuring that their authority is seen as *legitimate.* In such a state people accept the idea that the allocation of power is as it should be and that those who hold power do so legitimately.

Max Weber (1957) identified three kinds of authority: legal-rational authority, traditional authority, and charismatic authority.

[*LEGAL-RATIONAL AUTHORITY*] **Legal-rational authority** *is authority derived from the understanding that specific individuals have clearly defined rights and duties to uphold and implement rules and procedures impersonally.* Indeed, this is the key: Power is vested not in individuals but in particular positions or offices. There usually are rules and procedures designed to achieve a broad purpose. Rulers acquire political power by meeting requirements for office, and they hold power only as long as they themselves obey the laws that legitimize their rule. Found in most modern corporations and organizations, legal-rational authority emphasizes *rationally purposeful action.*

[*TRADITIONAL AUTHORITY*] **Traditional authority** *is rooted in the assumption that the customs of the past legitimate the present*—that things are as they always have been and basically should remain that way. Usually both the rulers and the ruled recognize and support the tradition that legitimizes such political authority. Typically traditional authority is hereditary, although this is not always the case. For example, throughout most of English history the English crown was the property of various families. As long as tradition was followed, the authority was accepted.

[*CHARISMATIC AUTHORITY*] **Charismatic authority** *derives from a ruler's ability to inspire*

Power based on authority is quite stable, and obedience to it is accepted as a social norm.

passion and devotion among followers. Weber noted that a charismatic leader—who is most likely to emerge during a period of crisis—will emerge when followers (1) perceive a leader as somehow supernatural; (2) blindly believe the leader's statements; (3) unconditionally comply with the leader's directives; and (4) give the leader unqualified emotional commitment. Others have added (Willner, 1984) that charismatic leaders must also perform seemingly extraordinarily feats and possess outstanding speaking ability.

Sitting Bull and Red Cloud, for example, were charismatic leaders of the Sioux Indians. Their people followed them because they led by example and inspired personal loyalty. However, individuals were free to disagree, to refuse to participate in planned undertakings, even to leave and look for a group led by people with whom they were more likely to agree (Brown, 1974). This was not true in Rome under Augustus, in Russia under Lenin, in Germany under Hitler, or in Iran under the Ayatollah Khomeini. These men all were charismatic rulers but also had the political authority necessary to enforce obedience or conformity to their demands.

Charismatic authorities and rulers emerge when people lose faith in their social institutions. Lenin led the Russian Revolution in the chaos left in the wake of World War I. Hitler rose to power in a

Germany that had been defeated, humiliated in World War I, and whose economy was shattered. Khomeini rose to power in a country in which rapid modernization had undercut traditional Islamic norms and values, in which great poverty and great wealth existed side by side, and in which fear of the Shah's secret police left the populace constantly anxious for its personal safety.

The great challenge facing all charismatic rulers is to sustain their leadership after the crisis subsides and to create political institutions that will survive their death or retirement. Weber pointed out that if the program the leader has implemented is to be sustained, the leader's charisma will have to be "routinized" in some form. For example, after Christ's death—and after it became apparent that his return to earth was not imminent—the apostles began to set up the rudiments of a religious organization with priestly offices.

GOVERNMENT AND THE STATE

Governments vary according to the relationship that exists between the rulers and the ruled. In some societies, political power is shared among most or all adults. This is true of the Mbuti pygmies and the !Kung San of Africa, for instance. The group is its

The power of a charismatic leader derives from the ruler's force of personality and his ability to inspire passion and devotion among his followers. President John F. Kennedy was the closest the United States has come to having a charismatic leader.

own authority and decisions are made by a consensus among adults. Among such societies the concept of government is meaningless. But in modern societies, government is necessary.

In complex societies the **state** *is the institutionalized way of organizing power within territorial limits.* Just as a true government is nonexistent in some societies, so too is the state limited to certain societies. Its presence indicates a high level of social and political development.

Modern thought regarding the nature of government and its forms is derived directly from the ideas of three Greek philosophers: Socrates, his student Plato, and Plato's student Aristotle. In the *Republic,* written around 365 B.C., Plato was concerned with the form of government that would be most just. Athens had been through a period of political upheaval and Plato was concerned with the problem of maintaining social order. He rejected democracy, or rule by the majority, because he believed that this form of government would lead to chaos. He also rejected **autocracy,** *or rule by one person,* because he thought that no single person could be wise or competent enough to make decisions for a whole society. Rather, he favored what he called **aristocracy** *(a form of oligarchy) or rule by a select few.*

Plato called his proposed ruling class the guardians of society. The guardians, he argued, should be bred from the most exemplary parents but separated from them at birth. They should live in poverty for 30 years while being trained in mind and body, and then they should fill positions of government in which they would execute their responsibilities wisely and without favoritism. (It is important not to confound Plato's use of the term aristocracy with the modern usage. Plato explicitly rejected the ideal of inherited political power, which he believed inevitably results in power falling to unqualified individuals—leading to an unjust society.)

Aristotle (384–322 B.C.) was the tutor of Alexander the Great and a political scholar. Unlike Plato, he recognized that even in just societies, social-class interests produce class conflicts, which are the business of the state to control. Aristotle favored centering political power in the middle class (consisting of merchants, artisans, and farmers), but he insisted on defining the rights and duties of the state in a legal constitution (Laslett and Cummings, 1967).

Functions of the State

Although a preindustrial society can exist without an organized government, no modern industrial society can thrive without those functions that the state performs: establishing laws and norms, providing social control, ensuring economic stability, setting goals, and protecting against outside threats.

ESTABLISHING LAWS AND NORMS The state has the power to establish laws that formally specify what is expected and what is prohibited in the society. Such laws often represent a codification of specific norms; for example, one should not steal or commit violent crimes against others. The establishment of laws also brings about the enactment of penalties for violating the laws.

PROVIDING SOCIAL CONTROL In addition to establishing laws, the state also has the power to enforce them. The police, courts, and various government agencies make sure that the violations of laws are punished. In the United States, the Internal Revenue Service seeks out tax evaders, the courts sentence criminals to prison, and the police attempt to maintain order.

ENSURING ECONOMIC STABILITY In the modern world, no individual can provide entirely for his or her own needs. Large work forces must be mobilized to build roads, dig canals, and erect dams. Money must be minted, and standards of weights and measures must be set and checked; merchants must be protected from thieves and consumers from fraud. The state tries to ensure that a stable system of distribution and allocation of resources exists within the society.

SETTING GOALS The state sets goals and provides a direction for society. If a society is to curtail its use of oil, for instance, the government must promote this as a goal. It must encourage conservation and the search for alternative energy sources and must discourage (perhaps through taxation or rationing) the use of oil. But how is the government able to accomplish these tasks? How can it bring about individual and organizational compliance? Obviously, it would be best if the government could rely on persuasion alone, but this course seldom is enough. In the end the government usually needs the power to compel compliance.

PROTECTING AGAINST OUTSIDE THREATS Historic data leave little doubt that the rise of the state was accompanied almost everywhere by the intensification of warfare (Otterbein, 1970, 1973). As early as the fourteenth century, Ibn Khaldun (1958), a brilliant Islamic scholar of the time, noted

One of the tasks a state must perform is to protect itself from outside threats, especially those of a military nature.

CAPITALISM
1. PRIVATE PROPERTY
2. Freedom of CHOICE
3. Freedom of Competition
4. Little / NO gov't interference

this connection and even attributed the rise of the state to the needs of sedentary farmers to protect themselves from raids by fierce nomads. His views were echoed by Ludwig Gumplowicz (1899): "States have never arisen except through the subjugation of one stock by another, or by several in alliance." In any event, it is clear that one of the tasks of maintaining a society is to protect it from outside threats, especially those of a military nature. Hence governments build and maintain armies. Although the lack of military preparedness may invite an expansionist attack from a neighboring society, it does not follow that such preparedness necessarily will prevent attack.

Although there is widespread agreement that the functions just described are tasks that the state should and usually does perform, not all social scientists agree that the state emerged because of the need for these functions.

THE ECONOMY AND THE STATE

Politics and economics are intricately linked, and the political form a state takes is tied to the economy. In its simplest terms, *the* **economy** *is the social institution that determines how a society produces, distributes, and consumes goods and services.* Money, goods and services do not flow of their own accord. People work at particular jobs, manufacture particular products, distribute the fruits of their labor, purchase basic necessities and luxury items, and decide to save or spend their money.

A very simple society may only produce and distribute food, water, and shelter. As a society becomes more complex and productive, the products produced and distributed become increasingly more elaborate. To be useful, all these goods and services must be distributed throughout the society. We depend on impersonal distribution systems to bring us such essential items as food, water, housing, clothing, health care, transportation, and communication, all of which we consume according to our ability to pay for them.

The political problem for any society is to decide how much to be involved in the production and distribution of goods and services. In most economies, *markets* play the major role in determining what gets produced, how, and for whom. The market determines whether there is a demand for something, who is willing to produce it and how much people are willing to pay for it. Economies that do not allow markets to function are known as command economies.

Capitalism

In its classic form, **capitalism** *is an economic system based on private ownership of the means of production, and in which resource allocation depends largely on market forces.* The government plays only a minor role in the marketplace, which works out its own problems through the forces of supply and demand.

There are two basic premises behind capitalism. The first, as Max Weber noted, is production "for the pursuit of profit and ever renewed profit." Capitalism notes that people are entitled to pursue their own self-interest, and this activity is desirable and eventually benefits society through what is known as the "invisible hand" of capitalism. For example, pharmaceutical companies may have no other goal in mind than profit when they develop new drugs. The fact that their products eventually benefit society is an indirect benefit brought about by this invisible hand.

The second basic premise behind capitalism is that the free market will determine what is produced and at what price.

Adam Smith, regarded as the father of modern capitalism, set forth his ideas in his book *The Wealth of Nations* (1776), which is still used today as a yardstick for analyzing economic systems in the Western world. According to Smith, capitalism has four features: private property, freedom of choice, freedom of competition, and freedom from government interference.

PRIVATE PROPERTY Smith believed the ability to own private property acts as an incentive for people to be thrifty and industrious. These motivations, although selfish, will benefit society, because those who own property will respect the property rights of others.

FREEDOM OF CHOICE Along with the right to own property is the right to do with it what one pleases as long as it does not harm society. Consequently, people are free to sell, rent, trade, give away, or retain whatever they possess.

FREEDOM OF COMPETITION Smith believed society would benefit most from a free market in which there is unregulated competition for profits. Supply and demand would be the main factors determining the course of the economy.

FREEDOM FROM GOVERNMENT INTERFERENCE Smith believed government should promote competition and free trade and keep order in society.

It should not regulate business or commerce. The best thing the government can do for business is leave it alone. *This view that government should stay out of business is often referred to as* **laissez-faire capitalism** (the French words *laissez-faire* are translated as "allow to act").

Laissez-faire capitalism and command economies are completely opposite ways for societies to deal with the distribution of goods and services. In the United States the government does play a vital role in the economy. Therefore, the U.S. system cannot be seen as an example of pure capitalism. Rather, many have referred to our system as modified capitalism, also known as a mixed economy (Rachman, 1985).

A **mixed economy** *combines free-enterprise capitalism with governmental regulation of business, industry, and social-welfare programs.* Although private property rights are protected, the forces of supply and demand are not allowed to operate with total freedom. The distribution of resources takes place through a combination of market and governmental forces. Because there are few nationalized industries in this country (the Tennessee Valley Authority and Amtrak are two exceptions), the government uses its regulatory power to guard against private-industry abuse. Our government is also involved in such areas as antitrust violations, the environment, and minority employment. Ironically, this involvement may be even greater than it is in some of the more socialistic European countries.

Most countries have a mixed economy. Some countries such as the United States and Hong Kong are closer to the free market end of the continuum, while China and Cuba are closer to the command economy end. The absolute extremes of a pure command economy or a pure capitalistic economy do not exist, whether it be in Cuba or the United

Adam Smith believed that government should promote competition and free trade and keep order in society; it should not regulate business or commerce.

States. Command economy countries let consumers choose some of the goods they buy, and allow private agricultural markets to some extent. In the United States, in addition to government regulation of economic activity through minimum wage levels, safety standards for the workplace, antitrust laws, and farm price supports, the federal government has also assumed partial or total control of privately owned businesses when their potential collapse would have had a significant impact on the people. Two examples include the government involvement in Amtrak and the savings and loan industry.

ROBRIGUEZ

The Marxist Response to Capitalism

Adam Smith believed that ordinary people would thrive under capitalism. Not only would their needs for goods and services be met, but they would also benefit by being part of the marketplace. In contrast, Karl Marx was convinced that capitalism produces a small group of well-to-do individuals, while the masses suffer under the tyranny of those who exploit them for their own profit.

RICHARD

Karl Marx argued that capitalism causes people to be alienated from their labor and from themselves. Under capitalism, the worker is not paid for part of the value of the goods produced. Instead this "surplus value" is taken by the capitalist as profit at the expense of the worker.

Workers are also alienated by doing very small specific jobs, as on an assembly line, and not feeling connected to the final product produced. The worker feels no relationship or pride in the product and merely works to obtain a pay check and survive—a far cry from work being the joyous fulfillment of self that Marx believed it should be.

Karl Marx believed nineteenth-century capitalism contained several contradictions that were the seeds of its own destruction. The main problem with capitalism, he contended, is that profits will decline as production expands. This in turn will force the industrialist to exploit the laborers even further, paying them less in order to continue to make a profit. As workers are paid less or are fired, they are less able to buy the goods being produced. This, then, causes profits to fall even further, leading to bankruptcies, greater unemployment, and even full-scale economic depression. After an increasingly severe series of depressions, Marx predicted that workers would rise up and take control of the state. Workers would then create a socialist form of government in which private property is abolished and turned over to the state. In the end, workers would control the means of production and thus end the exploitation of labor.

The reality of capitalism has not matched Marxist expectations. As we mentioned earlier, capitalist economies have really become mixed economies. The progressive impoverishment of the worker that Marx predicted has been avoided, and labor unions have been able to obtain higher wages and better working conditions for the labor force—something Marx thought could only come about through revolution. Labor-saving machinery has also led to higher profits without the predicted unemployment, and the production of goods to meet consumer demands has increased accordingly.

Marxists have offered a number of explanations for capitalism's continued success. Some have suggested that capitalism has survived because Western societies are able to sell their excess goods to developing countries and these sales enable capitalists to maintain high prices and profits. However, Marxists see this as only a temporary solution to the inevitable decline of capitalism. Eventually the whole world will be industrialized, and the contradictions in capitalism will be revealed. Marxists believe the movement toward socialism has not been avoided, only postponed.

Command Economies
SOCIALISM
→ GOVT DICTATES

In a **command economy** *the government makes all the decisions about production and consumption. A government planning office decides what will be produced, as well as how and for whom it will be produced.*

Just as there are no pure capitalist economies, there are no pure command economies where all allocation is done by others. There is, however, a large dose of central direction and planning in communist countries, where the state owns factories and land and makes many of the decisions about what people should consume and how much they should work.

To appreciate the immensity of the task of central planning, try to imagine what it would be like if the city in which you live were run by command. Think of the food, clothing, and housing allocations you would have to make for everyone. Then consider how you would know who should get what and how it should be produced. These decisions are currently being made by the market.

Often, this planning fails to deliver the goods and services needed by the population. Although, for example, the former Soviet Union had more farmers than all Western nations and Japan combined, its farm output was dismal; Soviet farmers produced only one quarter as much food and fiber as their Western counterparts. As a result, grocery store shelves were poorly stocked and, to control demand, consumers were issued rationing coupons. Even these were ineffective in controlling food shortages, though, and milk, sour cream, sugar, sausage, and other staples of the diet were often absent from store shelves (Keller, 1988). In addition, rigidity often blocks efficiency. Afraid to try new technologies, command economy bureaucrats stick with the old tried-and-true methods for much too long.

Socialism

Socialism is one type of command economy that is an alternative to, and a reaction against, capitalism. Whereas capitalism views profit as the ultimate goal of economic activity, socialism is based on the belief that economic activity should be guided by public needs rather than private profit. **Socialism** *is an economic system in which the government owns the sources of production—including factories, raw materials, and transportation and communication systems—and sets production and distribution goals.* Production and distribution are oriented toward output rather than profit. This ensures that key industries run smoothly and that the public "good" is met. Individuals are heavily taxed in order to support a range of social-welfare programs that benefit every member of the society. Many socialist countries are described as having a "cradle-to-grave" welfare system.

Socialists believe that major economic, social, and political decisions should be made by elected representatives of the people in conjunction with the broader plans of the state. Instead of relying on the marketplace to determine prices, prices for major goods and services are set by government agencies. The aim is to influence the economic system so that wealth and income are distributed as equally as possible. The belief is that everyone should have such essentials as food, housing, medical care, and education before some people can have luxury items, such as cars and jewelry. Accordingly, in socialist societies, nonessential consumer items are very expensive, whereas basic commodities are inexpensive by Western standards.

The Capitalist View of Socialism

Capitalists view the centrally planned economies of the socialist societies as inefficient and concentrating power in the hands of one group whose authority is based on party position. Workers are controlled both economically and politically and have very little opportunity to improve their lifestyles or partic-

ipate in political decisions. Any worker disagreement or organized effort to change policies is interpreted as disloyalty to the state.

Capitalists also question socialist approaches to production and distribution. For example, if essential goods and services are subsidized by the state and the consumers do not pay their full cost, what will prevent them from using more than they are entitled to and taking advantage of the system? If the producers of goods and services are immune from competition and have few incentives, what will encourage them to produce high-quality products?

TYPES OF STATES

In today's shrinking world different types of states exist side by side and must deal with one another constantly. To comprehend their relationships, it is helpful to understand the structure of each main form of government—autocracy, totalitarianism, democracy, and socialism.

Autocracy

In an **autocracy** *the ultimate authority and rule of the government rest with one person, who is the chief source of laws and the major agent of social control.* For example, the pharaohs of ancient Egypt were autocrats. More recently the reigns of Ferdinand Marcos of the Philippines, and the Perons of Argentina have been autocratic.

In an autocracy the loyalty and devotion of the people are required. To ensure this requirement is met, dissent and criticism of the government and the person in power are prohibited. The media are often controlled by the government, and terror may be used to prevent or suppress rebellion. For the most part, however, no great attempt is made to control the personal lives of the people. A strict boundary is set up between private and public behavior. Individuals have a wide range of freedom in pursuing such private aspects of their lives as religion, the family, and many other traditional elements of life. At the same time, it should be pointed out that virtually all present-day autocracies have witnessed exploitation of the poor by the rich and powerful—a situation supported by the respective governments.

Totalitarianism

In a **totalitarian** **government,** *one group has virtually total control of the nation's social institutions.* Any other group is prevented from attaining power.

[handwritten annotation at top:] U.S. / mixed economy / SOCIALIST COMMAND ECONOMY / Capitalist/MARKet Driven

Religious, educational, political, and economic institutions all are managed directly or indirectly by the state. Typically, under totalitarian rule, several elements interact to concentrate political power.

1. *A single political party* controls the state apparatus. It is the only legal political party in the state. The party organization is itself controlled by one person or by a ruling clique.
2. *The use of terror* is implemented by an elaborate internal security system that intimidates the populace into conformity. It defines dissenters as enemies of the state and often chooses, arbitrarily, whole groups of people against whom it directs especially harsh oppression (for instance, the Jews in Nazi Germany or minority tribal groups in several of the recently created African states).
3. *The control of the media* (television, radio, newspapers, and journals) is in the hands of the state. Differing opinions are denied a forum. The media communicate only the official line of thinking to the people.

4. *Control over the military apparatus* ensures the use of weapons are monopolized by those in power.
5. *Control of the economy* is wielded by the government, which sets goals for the various industrial and economic sectors and determines both the prices and the supplies of goods.

6. *An elaborate ideology,* in which previous sociopolitical conditions are rejected, legitimizes the current state and provides more or less explicit instructions to citizens on how to conduct their daily lives. This ideology offers explanations for nearly every aspect of life, often in a simplistic and distorted way (Friedrich and Brzezinski, 1965).

Two distinct types of totalitarianism are found in the modern world. Though they share the same basic political features described above, they differ widely in their economic systems. *Under* **totalitarian socialism,** *in addition to almost total regulation of all social institutions, the government controls and owns all major means of production and distribution: There is little private ownership or free enterprise. Totalitarian socialist forms of government are more commonly known as* **communism.**

Totalitarian capitalism, *on the other hand, denotes a system under which the government, while retaining control of social institutions, allows the means of production and distribution to be owned and managed by private groups and individuals. However, production goals usually are dictated by the government, especially in heavy industry.*

Hitler's Germany is a good example of totalitarian capitalism. The mammoth Krupp industrial complex was owned and managed by the family of that name, but the government had the company gear its efforts toward producing munitions and heavy equipment to further the nation's political and militaristic aims. *Totalitarian capitalism is often referred to as* **fascism.**

One of the problems faced by totalitarian governments is that because their total control over their citizenry allows no organized independent opposition, they are never sure whether the populace's conformity to the laws is based on its acceptance of the government's legitimate authority or is motivated primarily by fear or coercion by a ruling power it considers illegitimate. This inability to judge accurately its citizens' perceptions of its legitimacy is considered by many observers a source of great anxiety and explains some of the oppressive actions of totalitarian governments, such as imprisoning artists and intellectuals.

Democracy

As a form of government, democracy has not always been regarded as the best. People often approved of the aims of democracy, yet argued that democracy was impossible to attain. Others argued that it was logically unsound. Today, however, there is hardly a government anywhere in the world which does not claim to have some sort of democratic authority. In the United States we regard our political system as democratic, and the same claim is made by leaders in communist countries. The word *democracy* seems to have so many different meanings today that we face the problem of distinguishing democracy from other political systems.

Democracy comes from two Greek words— *demos,* meaning people, and *kratia,* meaning authority. By *democracy,* then, the Greeks were referring to a system in which the rule was by the people rather than a few selected individuals. Because of the growth in population, industrialization, and specialization, it has become impossible for citizens to participate in politics today as they did in ancient Athens. Today **democracy** *refers to a political system operating under the principles of constitutionalism, representative government, majority rule, civilian rule, and minority rights.* **Constitutionalism** *means that government power is limited by law.* Various agencies of the government can act only in specified legal ways. Individuals possess rights—such as freedom of speech, press, assembly, and religion—that the government cannot take away.

[handwritten annotation:] Follow The Constitution

One of the most important ways for people to participate in the political life of the country is to vote.

A basic feature of democracy is that it is rooted in **representative government,** *which means that the authority to govern is achieved through, and legitimized by, popular elections.* Every government officeholder has sought, in one way or another, the support of the **electorate** *(those citizens eligible to vote)* and has persuaded a large enough portion of that group to grant its support (through voting). The elected official is entitled to hold office for a specified term and generally will be reelected as long as that body of voters is satisfied that the officeholder is adequately representing their interests.

Representative institutions can operate freely only if certain other conditions prevail. First, there must be what sociologist Edward Shils (1968) calls *civilian rule.* That is, every qualified citizen has the legal right to run for and hold an office of government. Such rights do not belong to any one class (say, of highly trained scholars, as in ancient China), caste, sect, religious group, ethnic group, or race. Further, there must be public confidence in the fact that such organized agencies as the police and the military will not intervene in, or change the outcome of, elections (as happened in Greece during the "rule of the colonels" in the 1960s, in Chile with the overthrow of President Salvadore Allende in 1973, and in Pakistan with the overthrow and eventual execution of President Ali Bhutto in 1979).

In addition, *majority rule* must be maintained. Because of the complexity of a modern democracy it is not possible for "the people" to rule. One of the most important ways for people to participate in the political life of the country is to vote. In order for this to happen people must be free to assemble, to express their views and seek to persuade others, to engage in political organizing, and to vote for whomever they wish.

Democracy also assumes that *minority rights* must be protected. The majority may not always act wisely and may be unjust. The minority abides by the laws as determined by the majority, but the minority must be free to try to change these laws.

Democratic societies contrast markedly with totalitarian societies. Ideally, they are open and culturally diverse; dissent is not viewed as disloyalty; there are two or more political parties; and terror and intimidation are not an overt part of the political scene.

The economic base of democratic societies can vary considerably. Democracy can be found in a capitalistic country like the United States and in a more socialistic one like Sweden. However, it appears necessary for the country to have reached an advanced level of economic development before democracy can evolve. Such societies are most likely to have the sophisticated population and stability necessary for democracy (Lipset, 1960).

Democracy and Socialism

Critics of capitalism argue that "true" democracy is an impossible dream in capitalistic society. They claim that although in theory all members of a capitalist society have the same political rights, in fact capitalist societies are inherently stratified, and therefore wealth, social esteem, and even political power of necessity are unequally distributed (see Chapter 7). Because of this, some critics contend, "true" democracy can be achieved only under socialism—when the government owns and controls the

*Legal-Rational: The status that has authority
Regardless of the individual occupying it.*

major means of production and distribution (Schumpeter, 1950).

As we have noted, there is no obvious reason that socialist societies cannot be democratic. In fact, though, many societies whose economies are socialist tend to be communist states. One reason is that historically, socialist societies often have been born in revolution. Political revolutions by definition mean a redistribution of power (see the discussion of political change later in this chapter). One group seizes power from another and then tries to prevent the old group from retaking it. Lenin argued that in order to consolidate power, it is necessary for the new group to use strong repressive measures against the old—in fact, to build a dictatorship. *A **dictatorship** is a totalitarian government in which all power rests ultimately in one person. This person, or dictator, generally heads the only recognized political party, at least until all the economic resources of the old group are seized, its links to all political agencies are broken, and its claims to political legitimacy are wiped out.* Lenin (1949) quoted Marx to support this point:

> Between capitalist and communist society lies the period of the revolutionary transformation of the one into the other. Corresponding to this is also a political transition period in which the state can be nothing but *the revolutionary dictatorship of the proletariat* [the working class].

Lenin (1949) put it more graphically himself:

> The proletariat needs state power, a centralized organization of force, and organization of violence, both to crush the resistance of the exploiters and to *lead* the enormous mass of the population . . . in the work of organizing a socialist economy.

In China, Cuba, and more recently in African and Southeast Asian countries, socialist revolutions all have resulted in dictatorships. Families of the previous ruling classes have been executed, jailed, "reeducated," or exiled, and their properties have been seized and redistributed. The dictatorships have not proved to be temporary, nor has the state gradually "withered away," as Marx and Engels predicted it would after socialism was firmly established. Many Marxists claim that this will happen in the future, especially once capitalism has been defeated all around the globe and socialist states no longer need to protect themselves against "counterrevolutionary" subversion and military threats by capitalist nations. However, it is fair to observe that even the ancient Greeks knew that power corrupts and that those groups who have power are unlikely

ever to give it up voluntarily. So we may expect that at least in the foreseeable future, socialist states that have emerged through revolution will—despite their disclaimers—remain totalitarian communist dictatorships.

Democratic Socialism

Democratic socialism *is a convergence of capitalist and socialist economic theory in which the state assumes ownership of strategic industries and services, but allows other enterprises to remain in private hands.* In Western Europe, democratic socialism has evolved as a political and economic system that attempts to preserve individual freedom in the context of social equality and a centrally planned economy.

Social democrats have been able to win representation in the government through election rather than revolution by attempting to appeal to middle-class workers and highly trained technicians as well as to industrial workers.

This type of government flourishes to varying degrees in the Scandinavian countries, in Great

Under democracy people possess rights—such as freedom of speech, press, assembly, and religion—which the government cannot take away.

Britain, and in Israel. These countries all have a strong private (that is, capitalist) sector in their economies, but they also have extensive government programs to ensure the people's well-being.

Under democratic socialism the state assumes ownership of only strategic industries and services, such as airlines, railways, banks, TV and radio stations, medical services, colleges, and important manufacturing enterprises. Other enterprises remain in private hands as long as government policies can ensure they are responsive to the nation's common welfare. High tax rates prevent excessive profits and the concentration of wealth. In return the population receives extensive welfare benefits, such as free medical care, free college education, or subsidized housing.

The convergence of capitalist and socialist economic theories is a trend that has been evident for some time now. Capitalist systems such as the United States have seen an ever-greater introduction of state planning and government programs, and socialist systems have seen the introduction of market forces and the profit motive. The growing economic interdependence of the world's nations will help continue this trend.

FUNCTIONALIST AND CONFLICT THEORY VIEWS OF THE STATE

Functionalists and conflict theorists hold very different ideas about the function of the state. As our discussion of social stratification in Chapter 7 revealed, functionalist theorists view social stratification—and the state that maintains it—as necessary devices that provide for the recruitment of workers to perform the tasks necessary to sustain society. Individual talents must be matched to jobs that need doing, and those with specialized talents must be given sufficiently satisfying rewards. Functionalists therefore maintain that the state emerged because society began to get so large and complex that only a specialized, central institution (that is, the state) could manage society's increasingly complicated and intertwined institutions (Davis, 1949; Service, 1975).

Marxists and other conflict theorists take a different view. They argue that technological changes resulting in surplus production brought about the production of commodities for trade (as opposed to products for immediate use). Meanwhile, certain groups were able to seize control of the means of production and distribution of commodities, thereby succeeding in establishing themselves as powerful ruling classes that dominated and exploited workers and serfs. Finally, the state emerged as a means of coordinating the use of force, by means of which the ruling classes could protect their institutionalized supremacy from the resentful and potentially rebellious lower classes. As Lenin (1949) explained, "The state is a special organization of force: It is an organization of violence for the suppression of some class."

There is evidence to support this view of the state's origins. The earliest legal codes of ancient states featured laws protecting the persons and properties of rulers, nobles, landholders, and wealthy merchants. The Code of Hammurabi of Babylon, dating back to about 1750 B.C., prescribed the death penalty for burglars and for anybody who harbored a fugitive slave. The code regulated wages, prices, and fees to be charged for services. It provided that a commoner be fined six times as much for striking a noble or a landholder as for striking another commoner. And it condemned to death housewives who were proved by their husbands to be uneconomical in managing household resources (Durant, 1954).

Nevertheless, the functionalist view also has value. The state provides crucial organizational functions such as carrying out large-scale projects and undertaking long-range planning, without which complex society probably could not exist. Because it provides a sophisticated organizational structure, the state can—and does—fulfill many other important functions. In most modern societies, the state supports a public school system to provide a basic, uniform education for its members. The health and well-being of its citizens also have become the concern of the state. In our own country, as in many others, the government provides some level of medical and financial support for its young, old, and disabled at the same time that it sponsors scientific and medical research for the ongoing welfare of its people. Regulating industry and trade to some degree also has become a function of the modern state, and it has devised ways (different for each kind of state) of establishing, controlling, and even safeguarding the civil rights and liberties of its citizens. And certainly one of the most important functions of any state is the protection of its people. Long gone are the days when cavedwellers, lords of the manor, or frontiersmen themselves defended their territories and other members of their groups from attack or encroachment; the state now provides such protection through specialized agencies: armies, militias, and police forces.

When groups in a society develop sufficient dissatisfaction with their present system of government and achieve the strength to influence the direction of that system, changes in government can take place. After such changes the state may perform the same functions, but it may do so in a different way and under different leadership.

POLITICAL CHANGE

Political change can occur when there is a shift in the distribution of power among groups in a society. It is one facet of the wider process of social change, the topic of the last part of this book. Political change can take place in a variety of different ways depending on the type of political structure the state has and the desire for change present among the people. People may attempt to produce change through established channels within the government, or they may rise up against the political power structure with rebellion and revolution. Here we shall consider briefly three forms of political change: institutionalized change, rebellion, and revolution.

Institutionalized Political Change

In democracies, the institutional provision for the changing of leaders is implemented through elections. Usually, candidates representing different parties and interest groups must compete for a particular office at formally designated periods of time. There may also be laws that prevent a person from holding the same office for more than a given number of terms. If a plurality or a majority of the electorate is dissatisfied with a given officeholder, they are given the opportunity to vote the incumbent

out of office. Thus the laws and traditions of a democracy ensure the orderly changeover of politicians and, usually, of parties in office.

In dictatorships and totalitarian societies, if a leader unexpectedly dies, is debilitated, or is deposed, a crisis of authority may occur. In dictatorships, illegal, violent means must often be used by an opposition to overthrow a leader or the government, as there is no democratic means by which legally to vote a person or group out of power. Thus, we should not be surprised that revolutions and assassinations are most likely to occur in developing nations that have dictatorships. Established totalitarian societies, such as China, are more likely than dictatorships to offer normatively prescribed means by which a ruling committee decides who should fill a vacated position of leadership.

Rebellions

Rebellions *are attempts—typically through armed force—to achieve rapid political change not possible within existing institutions.* Rebellions typically do not call into question the legitimacy of power but, rather, its uses. Thus, rebellions do not change the society's political and class structure. For example, consider Shays's Rebellion. Shortly after the American colonies won their independence from Britain, the colonies were hit by an economic depression followed by raging inflation. Soon, in several states, paper money lost almost all its value. As the states began to pay off their war debts (which had been bought by speculators), they were forced to increase

People may attempt to produce change through established channels within the government, or they may rise up against the political power structure.

the taxation of farmers, many of whom could not afford to pay these new taxes and consequently lost their land. Farmers began to band together to prevent courts from hearing debt cases, and state militias were called out to protect court hearings. Desperate farmers in the Connecticut Valley region armed themselves under Daniel Shays, an ex-officer of the Continental Army (Blum et al., 1981). This armed band was defeated by the Massachusetts militia, but its members eventually were pardoned and the debt laws were loosened somewhat (Parkes, 1968). Shays's Rebellion did not intend to overthrow the courts or the legislature; it was aimed at effecting changes in their operation.

▶ Revolutions

In contrast to rebellions, **revolutions** *are attempts to rapidly and dramatically change a society's previously existing structure.* Sociologists further distinguish between political and social revolutions.

▶ POLITICAL REVOLUTIONS *Relatively rapid transformations of state or government structures that are not accompanied by changes in social structure or stratification are known as* **political revolutions** (Skocpol, 1979). The American War of Independence is a good example of a political revolution. The colonists were not seeking to change the structure of society nor even necessarily to overthrow the ruling order. Their goal was to put a stop to the abuse of power by the British. After the war the colonists created a new form of government, but they did not attempt to change the fact that landowners and wealthy merchants held the reins of political power—just as they had before the shooting started. In the American Revolution, then, a lower class did not rise up against a ruling class. Rather, it was the American ruling class going to war in order to shake loose from inconvenient interference by the British ruling class. The initial result, therefore, was political, but not social, change.

▶ SOCIAL REVOLUTIONS *In contrast,* **social revolutions,** *are rapid and basic transformations of a society's state and class structures.* They are accompanied and in part carried through by class-based revolts (Skocpol, 1979). Hence they involve two simultaneous and interrelated processes: (1) the transformation of a society's system of social stratification brought about by upheaval in the lower class(es); and (2) changes in the form of the state. Both processes must reinforce each other for

a revolution to succeed. The French Revolution of the 1790s was a true social revolution. So were the Mexican Revolution of 1910, the Russian Revolution of 1917, the Chinese Revolution of 1949, and the Cuban Revolution of 1959. In all these revolutions, class struggle provided both the context and the driving force. The old ruling classes were stripped of political power and economic resources, wealth and property were redistributed, and state institutions were thoroughly reconstructed (Wolf, 1969).

Although the American Revolution did not arise from class struggle and did not result immediately in changes in the social structure, it did mark the beginning of a form of government that eventually modified the social stratification of eighteenth-century America.

THE AMERICAN POLITICAL SYSTEM

Growing out of a strong commitment to a democratic political process and the influence of a capitalist economy, the United States political system is unique in a number of ways. It has many distinctive features of particular interest to sociologists. In this section we will examine the role of the electorate and how influence is exerted on the political process.

The Two-Party System

Few democracies have only two main political parties. Besides the United States, only Canada, Australia, New Zealand, and Austria operate on a two-party system. Other democracies all have more than two major parties, thus providing proportional representation for a wide spectrum of divergent political views and interests. For example, in most European democracies, if a political party receives 12 percent of the vote in an election, they are allocated 12 percent of the seats in the national legislature. Such a system ensures that minority parties are represented.

The American two-party political system, however, operates on a "winner-take-all" basis. Therefore, groups with differing political interests must face not being represented if their candidates lose. Conversely, candidates must attempt to gain the support of a broad spectrum of political interest groups, because a candidate representing a narrow range of voters cannot win. This system forces accommodations between interest groups on the one hand and candidates and parties on the other.

Few, if any, individual interest groups (like the

National Organization for Women, the National Rifle Association, or the Moral Majority), represent the views of a majority of an electorate, be it local, state, or national. Hence, it is necessary for interest groups to ally with political parties in which other interest groups are involved as well, hoping thereby to become part of a majority that can succeed in electing one or more candidates. Each interest group then hopes that the candidate(s) it has helped elect will represent its point of view. But for most interest groups to achieve their ends more effectively, they must find a common ground with their allies in the party they have chosen to support. And in doing so they often have to compromise some strongly held principles. Hence party platforms often tend to be composed of mild and noncontroversial issues, and party principles tend to adhere as closely as possible to the center of the American political spectrum.

When either party attempts to move away from the center to accommodate a very strong interest group with left- or right-wing views, the result generally is disaster at the polls. This happened to the Republican party in 1964, when the politically conservative (or right-wing) Barry Goldwater forces gained control of its organizational structure and led it to a landslide defeat: In that year's presidential election the Democrats captured 61.1 percent of the national vote. Eight years later the Democratic party made the same mistake. It nominated George McGovern, a distinctly liberal (or left-wing) candidate who, among other things, advocated a federally subsidized minimum income. The predictable landslide brought the Republicans and Richard Nixon 60.7 percent of the vote. In 1984 when the Democrats put a woman, Geraldine Ferraro, on the ticket as the vice-presidential nominee, the Republicans won 58.8 percent of the vote and swept every state except Minnesota, the home of the presidential nominee, Walter Mondale (*Statistical Abstract of the United States: 1991*).

The candidates themselves have other problems. In order to gain support within their parties, they must somehow distinguish themselves from other candidates. In other words, they must stake out identifiable positions. Yet in order to win state and national elections, they must appeal to a broad political spectrum. To do this, they must soften the positions that first won them party support. Candidates thus often find themselves justly accused of "double-talk" and vagueness as they try to finesse their way through this built-in dilemma. It is no accident that once they have their party's nomination, some presidential candidates may express themselves differently and far more cautiously than before.

Voting Behavior

In totalitarian societies, strong pressure is put on people to vote. Usually there is no contest between the candidates, as there is no alternative to voting for the party slate. Dissent is not tolerated, and nearly everyone votes.

In the United States there is a constant progression of contests for political office, and in comparison with many other countries, voter turnout is quite low. Since the 1920s, only about 50 to 70 percent of all eligible voters turn out for presidential elections. Considering the emphasis Americans place on living in a democratic society, it is interesting that participation in national elections is declining steadily, a cause of grave concern to social scientists and political observers alike.

Voting rates vary with the characteristics of the people. For example, those over 45 years old and with a college education and a white-collar job have high rates of voter participation. Hispanics, the young, and the unemployed have some of the lowest voter participation rates (see Table 14.1 for voter participation by selected characteristics).

The Democratic party has tended to be the means through which the less privileged and the unprivileged have voted for politicians whom they hoped would advance their interests. Since 1932 the Democratic party has tended to receive most of its votes from the lower class, the working class,

TABLE 14.1

Voter Participation by Selected Characteristics, 1988

Characteristic	Percentage Voting
Male	56.4
Female	58.3
White	59.1
Black	51.5
Hispanic	28.8
18–20 years old	33.2
21–24 years old	38.3
25–34 years old	48.0
35–44 years old	61.3
45–64 years old	67.9
65 and over	68.8
Less than eight years of education	36.7
High school graduate	54.7
College graduate	77.6
Unemployed	38.6
Employed	58.4

Source: U.S. Bureau of the Census, *Statistical Abstract of the United States: 1991*, Washington, DC, 1991, p. 268.

blacks, Southern and Eastern Europeans, Hispanics, Catholics, and Jews (Cummings and Wise, 1981). Thus, almost all the legislation passed to aid these groups has been promoted by the Democrats and opposed by the Republicans. Democrats have sponsored legislation supporting unions, social security, unemployment compensation, disability insurance, antipoverty legislation, medicare and medicaid, civil rights, and consumer protection.

The Republican party has tended to receive most of its votes from the upper-middle and lower-middle classes, Protestants, and farmers. Americans under 30 tend to vote the Democratic ticket, and those over 49 tend to vote for the Republican party, even though the Democratic party has been responsible for almost all the legislation to benefit older citizens. These voting patterns are, of course, generalizations and may change during any specific election.

The politicians of both parties tend to be most responsive to the needs of the best-organized groups with the largest sources of funds or blocks of votes. Thus, we would expect the Republicans to represent best the interests of large corporations and well-funded professional groups (such as the American Medical Association). The Democrats, on the other hand, would be more closely aligned with the demands of unions.

There has been a steady increase in the number of black elected officials over the last two decades.

Factors other than the social characteristics of voters and the traditional platforms of parties may also affect the way people vote (Cummings and Wise, 1981). Indeed, the physical attributes, social characteristics, and personality of a candidate may prompt some to vote against the party they usually support. More importantly, current events may cause voters to vote against the party with which they usually identify. When people are frustrated by factors such as war, recession, inflation, and other international or national events, they often blame the incumbent president and the party he or she represents.

Recently there have been efforts to increase the number of minority members who register to vote and to improve their voting rate. The greater prominence of minority candidates, such as Jesse Jackson in 1988, has helped some, as minority groups are more likely to vote if they feel the elections are relevant to their lives. As minority voting rates increase, minorities also become more successful in electing members of their groups. Figure 14.1 shows the consistent rise, from 1970 to 1990, in the number of black elected officials. There were nearly five times as many African Americans in office in 1990 than in 1970.

In the political arena blacks are not just another interest group. Blacks experience deep-seated economic differences that make them skeptical of political promises. These differences have made blacks leery of white Democrats, no matter how liberal their voting records (Robey, 1984).

Hispanics make up less than four percent of all registered voters in the population, yet their votes are critical in many presidential elections. The main reason is the geographical distribution of the voters. Approximately eight million Hispanic voters are registered in six major states—New York, New Jersey, Florida, Illinois, Texas, and California—which together can give a presidential candidate most of the electoral votes he needs to win the election.

Hispanic voters are overwhelmingly Democratic. Hispanics tend to support Democratic candidates because of the support these candidates give to social programs that help the poor. The fact that Hispanics, like blacks, have a harder time climbing the socio-economic ladder keeps them in the Democratic camp.

With the Hispanic population expected to grow rapidly over the next few decades, both Democrats and Republicans will be paying more attention to the needs of this group. It is also likely that Hispanics will elect greater numbers of Hispanic candidates to political office (Franchi, 1988).

FIGURE 14.1

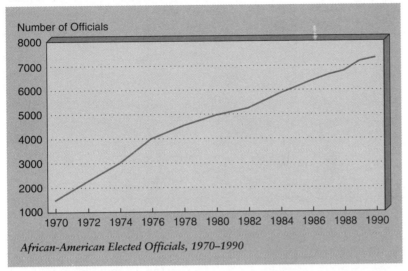

African-American Elected Officials, 1970–1990

Source: United States Bureau of the Census, *Statistical Abstract of the United States: 1991*, Washington, DC, 1991, p. 266.

Women have also been successful in increasing their representation in state legislatures. Figure 14.2 shows that the number of women holding such offices doubled between 1975 and 1990.

Despite these advances, Congress is still overwhelmingly represented by white males over 40 years of age. In 1990 the Senate had only two women and no blacks; the other 98 percent were white males. The lack of women and blacks in the House of Representatives was also striking (see Table 14.2 for a description of selected characteristics of members of Congress).

It would be wrong to conclude from the figures cited that Americans are politically inactive. There is more to political activity than voting. A study of American political behavior identified four different modes of participation (Verba, 1972): (1) Some 21 percent of Americans eligible to vote do so more or less regularly in municipal, state, and national elections but do not engage in other forms of political behavior. (2) Roughly four percent of the American electorate not only vote but also make the effort to communicate their concerns directly to government officials in an attempt to influence the officials' actions. (3) Some 15 percent of the electorate vote and also periodically take part in

FIGURE 14.2

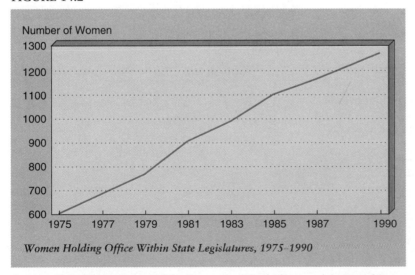

Women Holding Office Within State Legislatures, 1975–1990

Source: United States Bureau of the Census, *Statistical Abstract of the United States: 1991*, Washington, DC, 1991, p. 267.

Do the Media Have Too Powerful a Role in Elections?

No sooner had Governor Clinton achieved national recognition in his bid for the presidency than the mass media focused on facts that diverted all attention from the issues Clinton wanted to address in his campaign.

Instead of having to do battle with other Democrats, Clinton had to fend off the media, which had launched an intensive investigation of his affair with a woman, and his avoidance of the draft during the Viet Nam War.

This situation is an example of how the mass media have contributed to a radical transformation of election campaigns in the United States. This transformation involves changes in how po-

litical candidates communicate with the voters, and in the information journalists provide about election campaigns.

On one side we have candidates who are trying to present self-serving and strategically designed images of themselves and their campaigns. On the other side are television and print journalists who believe they should be detached, objective observers, motivated primarily by a desire to inform the U.S. public accurately.

Although this norm is often violated, there is no doubt that the journalistic perspective is markedly different from that of the candidate. Campaign coverage is far more apt to be critical and unfavorable toward a candi-

date than favorable. Journalists strive to reveal a candidate's flaws and weaknesses and to uncover tasty tidbits of hushed-up information.

Journalists exercise considerable political power in four important ways. The first and most obvious way they exert power involves deciding how much coverage to give a campaign and the candidate involved.

A candidate who is ignored by the media has a difficult time becoming known to the public and acquiring important political resources such as money and volunteers. Such candidates have little chance of winning.

In the beginning stages of presidential nomination cam-

political campaigns. However, they do not involve themselves in ongoing local political affairs. (4) Finally, about 20 percent of eligible voters are relatively active in ongoing community politics. They vote but do not get involved in political campaigns.

Special-Interest Groups

Because the government spends so much money and engages in so much regulating, special-interest groups constantly attempt to persuade the government to support them financially or through favorable regulatory practices. **Lobbying** *refers to attempts by special-interest groups to influence government policy.* Farmers lobby for agricultural subsidies, labor unions for higher minimum wages and laws favorable to union organizing and strike actions, corporate and big business interests lobby for favorable legislation and less government control of their practices and power, the National Rifle Association lobbies to prevent the passage of legislation requiring the registration or licensing of firearms, consumer-

protection groups lobby for increased monitoring of corporate practices and product quality, the steel industry lobbies for legislation taxing or limiting imported steel, and so on.

TABLE 14.2
Selected Characteristics of Members of Congress, 1990

	Senators	Representatives
Male	98	405
Female	2	27
White	100	381
African-American	0	24
Married	90	371
Under 40	–	34
40–49 years old	25	159
50–59 years old	45	132
60–69 years old	22	84
70–79 years old	6	19
Over 80 years old	2	4

Source: U.S. Bureau of the Census, *Statistical Abstract of the United States: 1991,* Washington, DC, 1991, p. 263.

paigns, for example, a candidate's goal is typically to do something that will result in news coverage and stimulate campaign contributions. These contributions can then be used for further campaigning, helping to convince the press and the public that the candidate is both credible and newsworthy.

Secondly the media decide which of many possible interpretations to give to campaign events. Since an election is a complex and ambiguous phenomenon, there are different conclusions drawn about its meaning. Here the journalists help us to form specific impressions of the candidates.

For example, presidential candidates are always concerned with how the results of presidential primaries are interpreted. Candidates want to be seen as winners who are gaining momentum—but at the same time, to be seen as the frontrunner too early leaves you open for being shot down later.

The media also exercise discretion in how favorably candidates are presented in the news. Although norms of objectivity and balance prevent most campaign coverage from including biased assertions, a more subtle and pervasive "slant" or "theme" to campaign coverage is possible and can be significant.

Finally, journalists also may officially endorse a candidate. This can be particularly important to the candidate, if the newspaper is one of the major national publications.

Politicians need the mass media to get the coverage they need to win. At the same time they can very easily fall victim to the intense scrutiny that is likely to result.

Although a great deal has been written about the "power of the press," little is known about the upper echelons of the newspaper hierarchy—the top decision makers or the boards of directors of newspaper-owning corporations. Much of what is known about these individuals comes from official and unofficial biographies of publishers, histories of particular newspapers, and journalistic accounts. Though these studies suggest that publishers and board members can have an influence on the general tone of a paper as well as on specific stories, there has been little systematic research on the characteristics of these people and how (or if) they are connected to other sectors of the U.S. power structure.

LOBBYISTS Of all the pressures on Congress, none has received more publicity than the role of the Washington-based lobbyists and the groups they represent. The popular image of a lobbyist is an individual with unlimited funds trying to use devious methods to obtain favorable legislation. The role of today's lobbyist is far more complicated.

The federal government now has tremendous power in many fields, and changes in federal policy can spell success or failure for special-interest groups. With the expansion of federal authority into new areas and the huge increase in federal spending, the corps of Washington lobbyists has grown markedly. As of 1986 there were 8,200 registered lobbyists, more than twice as many as in 1976. There also may be as many as 20,000 unregistered lobbyists (Thomas, 1986).

Lobbyists usually are personable and extremely knowledgeable about every aspect of their interest group's concerns. They cultivate personal friendships with officials and representatives in all branches of the government, and they frequently have conversations with these government people, often in a semisocial atmosphere, such as over drinks or dinner.

The pressure brought by lobbyists usually has self-interest aims, that is, to win special privileges or financial benefits for the groups they represent. On some occasions the purpose may be more objective, as when the lobbyist tries to further an ideological goal or to put forth a group's particular interpretation of what is in the national interest.

Certain liabilities are associated with lobbyists. The key problem is that they may lead Congress to make decisions that benefit the pressure group but may not serve the interests of the public at large. A group's influence may be based less on the arguments for their position than on the size of their membership, the amount of their financial resources, or the number of lobbyists and their astuteness.

Lobbyists might focus their attention not only on key members of a committee but also on the committee's professional staff. Such staffs can be extremely influential, particularly when the legislation involves highly technical matters about which the member of Congress may not be entirely knowl-

The media have contributed to a radical transformation in politics in the United States.

edgeable. Lobbyists also exert their influence through testimony at congressional hearings. These hearings may give the lobbyist access to key Congress members who could not have been contacted in any other way. The lobbyists may rehearse their statements before the hearing, ensure a large turnout from their constituency for the hearing, and may even give leading questions to friendly committee members so that certain points can be made at the hearing.

Lobbyists do perform some important and indispensable functions, including helping inform both Congress and the public about specific problems and issues that normally may not get much attention, stimulating public debate, and making known to

Congress who would benefit and who would be hurt by specific pieces of legislation (*Congressional Quarterly*, 1980). Many lobbyists believe their most important and useful role, both to the groups they represent and to the government itself, is the research and detailed information they supply. And in fact, many members of the government find the data and suggestions they receive from lobbyists valuable in studying issues, making decisions, and even in voting on legislation.

POLITICAL ACTION COMMITTEES *Special-interest groups, called* **political action committees (PACs),** *often are concerned with a single issue and usually represent corporate, trade, or labor interests.*

Lobbyists usually attempt to win special privileges or financial benefits for the groups they represent.

There are thousands of PACs in operation, and they are an extremely influential special-interest group. Between 1987 and 1988, PACs contributed $364.2 million to politicians and political campaigns.

Several criticisms have been leveled at PACs. Among the most prominent is that they represent neither the majority of the American people nor all social classes. Most PACs represent groups of affluent and well-educated individuals or big organizations. Only about 10 percent of the population is in a position to exert this kind of pressure on the government. Disadvantaged groups—those who most need the ear of the government—have no access to this type of political action (Cummings and Wise, 1981).

PACs also tend to favor incumbents. Two-thirds of all PAC committee contributions in recent elections have gone to incumbents. Challengers therefore end up being much more dependent on the small donations from individuals or from the Democratic and Republican National Committees. PACs may ultimately diminish the role of the individual voter with their increasing control over political contributions.

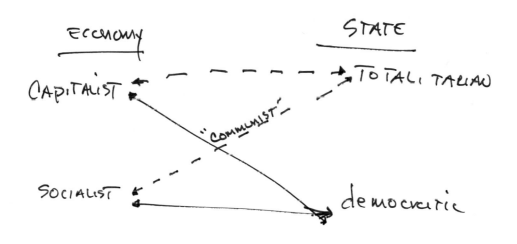

• STATE CAN HAVE EITHER TYPE OF ECONOMY.

• SOCIALIST TOTALITARIAN GOV'T IS LEAST LIKED BY U.S /WORLD. Free

PART

V

SOCIAL CHANGE AND SOCIAL ISSUES

CHAPTER 15 *Population and Demography*

CHAPTER 16 *Urban Society*

CHAPTER 17 *Health and Health Care*

CHAPTER 18 *Collective Behavior and Social Movements*

CHAPTER 19 *Social Change*

At this point in your voyage of sociological discovery you have mapped out much of the structure of society, and you have discovered many important characteristics of the natives who inhabit it: human beings. What remains is to explore some of the most compelling social issues within contemporary society—problems and situations that demand attention and represent driving forces of social change. How we address these issues will undoubtedly affect the quality of life in our future societies. But in order to successfully inhibit damaging trends and enhance productive ones, we must not only understand the problems themselves, but the process of social change as well. Only then can we hope to reshape society in ways that effectively promote human growth and development.

Chapter 15 deals with the dynamics of human populations. How do we measure such things as population growth, stability, and decline? What social factors influence each trend? Do we face a problem of overpopulation on this planet? In this chapter you will see, once again, that there are competing definitions and explanations for a given social problem. The perspective we adopt, obviously, affects the solutions we generate.

One important trend in population dynamics is urbanization: the increasing tendency of humans to live in cities and for urban culture and urban concerns to dominate national agendas, particularly in industrialized societies. In Chapter 16 you will examine this phenomenon, as well as some of the most significant urban problems in the United States today: central-city decay, suburban sprawl, and homelessness.

Staying healthy is an important human issue. Who gets sick, however, is powerfully influenced by social factors such as gender, race, social class, and age. In addition, access to health care is affected by the same factors. These are some of the issues you will investigate in Chapter 17. Additionally, you will explore two of the most compelling health issues in the world today: the spread of AIDS, and the tenuous health of mothers and children in developing countries.

You have seen throughout this book that humans are social animals. How do humans behave in large groups? How and why does group size make a difference? In Chapter 18 you will explore several sociological theories of collective behavior, and you will examine a variety of collective behaviors: crowds, fads, rumors, public opinion, mass hysteria, and social movements. In the latter case you will be looking at how people consciously and collectively organize themselves to make change. The final chapter of this book will introduce you to major theories and significant sources of social change in contemporary society.

When you have finished Part V of this book, you will have completed your maiden voyage of sociological exploration. The knowledge and insight that you have gained to this point should be immensely useful in navigating through your society and daily social interactions. As an educated citizen of your society and the world, however, the challenge that now lies ahead is to continue to expand your knowledge and insight in order to act more intelligently and effectively within those contexts, both as an individual and in concert with your fellow citizens. Bon voyage!

·15·

Population and Demography

Population Dynamics
   Fertility
   Mortality
   Migration

Theories of Population
   Malthus's Theory of Population
      Growth
   Marx's Theory of Population Growth
   Demographic Transition Theory
   A Second Demographic Transition

Current Population Trends: A Ticking
   Bomb?
   Determinants of Fertility
   Problems of Overpopulation
   Predictions of Ecological Disaster
   Sources of Optimism

The Chinese words *wan, xi, shao* mean later, longer, fewer. Later marriage, longer periods of time between pregnancies, and fewer children.

Just a few years ago that slogan launched a birth control campaign—unprecedented in scale in all of history—in the People's Republic of China. Posters proclaiming the message appeared virtually everywhere, even in the smallest village outposts.

At first the goal was not specified, but a three-child family was considered an acceptable limit. Then the government encouraged a two-child family. Now the emphasis is on the last word: shao, *fewer:* as few as possible, as fast as possible.

Shao has been reinterpreted three times from the original "fewer" to "one is best" and finally to "one is enough."

In the 1970s, the average Chinese woman of childbearing age was giving birth to six children. The Chinese government decided to take drastic action to ensure future survival by setting a goal for a population of no more than 1.2 billion people by the year 2000. To accomplish this goal, China instituted a nationwide campaign to convince couples to follow the government's guidelines.

To promote acceptance of the one-child limit, the government devised a reward-punishment system that makes daily life easier and richer for those who comply and burdensome for those who do not. A nationwide campaign to promote the one-child family features the Glorious One Child Certificate, under which couples sign an agreement to limit their family to a single child in exchange for extensive benefits.

As long as they only have one child, an urban couple receives a monthly bonus of $5 (Chinese dollars, equal to $3.50 American). As the average working family income is only $30 to $35 (Chinese dollars) a month, the bonus amounts to an extra 15 percent in income.

A one-child couple may also choose between two other types of preferential treatment. They can opt for free child care until the child is 7 years old or for free medical care for the child until age 14. They also receive preferential treatment in living accommodations, food allowances, and work assignments.

Couples who have two children—spaced over a long period of time—are neither punished nor rewarded. They receive no extra money, no extra work points, and no free education or medical benefits for the second child. They must assume the extra cost of raising the second child themselves.

Penalties are harsh for those who have a third child. Ten percent of their pay or work points will be deducted from the time of the fourth month of pregnancy until the third child is 14 years old. The same penalties are imposed on couples who have their second child in fewer than four years and on women who have a child out of wedlock (McLaughlin, 1980).

An additional punishment for the three-or-more-child couple is denial of any job promotion and loss of all work bonuses for at least three years. This is to make sure that couples who exceed the state limit for children do so at the price of personal sacrifice. They cannot prosper from extra work.

Are these policies working? By 1984, the fertility rate for women of childbearing age had dropped to 1.94. This is just below the number required for the population to remain stable. By 1986, the fertility rate had started to move up again, due to a less stringent interpretation of the one-couple, one-child rule.

POPULATION DYNAMICS

Chinese leaders have given the one-child policy top priority, ahead of competing social goals because population growth overshadows all other issues in that country. As of 1991 approximately 1.2 billion people lived in China, 21.2 percent of the world's habitants. The dramatic impact the one-child policy can have on population growth can be seen if we compare population projections based on a three-child family and a one-child family. If for the next 100 years, couples were to have an average of only three children, China's population would reach 4.2 billion by the year 2080. If, on the other hand, the planned one-child family were to prevail over that period of time, China could bring its population way down to a socially and economically manageable 370 million by 2080—a number still 130 million greater than the United States today in a land area virtually the same size.

China is responding to a basic demographic fact. Population problems become progressively more pressing because of what is referred to as *exponential growth*. The yearly increase in population is determined by a continuously expanding base. Each successive addition of one million people to a

Most of the world's population growth in the next few decades will occur in the developing countries.

population requires less time than the previous addition even if the birth rate does not increase. The best way to demonstrate the effects of exponential growth is to use a simple example. Let us assume that you have a job that requires you to work eight hours a day, every day, for thirty days. At the end of that time, your job is over. Your boss offers you a choice of two different methods of payment. The first choice is to be paid $100 a day for a total of $3,000 dollars. The second choice is somewhat different. The employer will pay you 1 cent for the first day, 2 cents for the second day, 4 cents for the third, 8 cents on the fourth, and so on. Each day you will receive double what you received the day before. Which form of payment will you choose? The second form of payment will yield a significantly higher total payment, in fact so high that no employer could realistically pay the amount. Through this process of successive doubling, you would be paid $5.12 for your labor on the tenth day. Only on the fifteenth day would you receive more than the flat $100 a day you could have received from the first day under the alternative payment plan: The amount that day would be $163.84. However, from that day on, the daily pay increase is quite dramatic. On the twentieth day you would receive $5,242.88, and on the twenty-fifth day your daily pay would be $167,772.16. Finally, on the thirtieth day, you would be paid $5,368,708.80, bringing your total pay for the month to more than $10 million.

This example demonstrates how the continual doubling in the world's population produces enormous problems. The annual growth rate in the world's population has declined from a peak of 2.04 percent in the late 1960s to 1.7 percent today. This difference between global birth and death rates means that the world's population now doubles every 42 years instead of every 35 years. Although this is an improvement for the world as a whole, many regions are still experiencing an increase rather than decrease in growth rates. In some countries in Africa, national fertility rates have actually increased in the past decade. In Kenya, for example, the average woman now has eight children. This fact combined with the declining infant mortality rate could push the country's population from its present 22 million to 160 million in the year 2050. Rwanda, Zambia, and Tanzania are three other African countries for which enormous growth has been projected. Africa has the most rapid population growth of anywhere in the world. For the continent as a whole, the yearly percentage increase in population is three percent, which means the population

of the entire continent will double in 23 years and will be ten times larger than it is today within 77 years (see Table 15.1 for projected yearly population growth percentages for selected countries).

Most of the world's growth in population in the next few decades will take place in the developing countries. The population of the richer countries will increase by 200 million by the year 2050, while the developing areas will increase by about six billion (see Figure 15.1).

Symbolizing the shift in population from the developed to the less-developed world is Sao Paulo, Brazil. In 1950, this city was smaller than Manchester, England, but by the year 2000, Sao Paulo could have a population of 25.8 million, which would make it one of the largest cities in the world. By contrast, London, which was the second largest city

TABLE 15.1

Population Projections for Selected Countries

Country	Estimated Annual Percentage Increase, 1990–2000
Afghanistan	4.7
Brunei	4.1
Iraq	3.7
Kenya	3.6
Zambia	3.6
Saudi Arabia	3.8
Tanzania	3.4
Ethiopia	3.2
Malawi	2.5
Guatemala	2.3
Philippines	2.2
Mozambique	2.1
El Salvador	2.0
Brazil	1.7
Israel	1.5
Argentina	1.1
United States	0.7
Poland	0.3
Japan	0.3
Italy	0.2
United Kingdom	0.2
Germany	0.2
Greece	0.1
Grenada	−0.1

Note: A four percent yearly increase means population doubles every 18 years. A three percent yearly increase means population doubles every 23 years. A two percent yearly increase means population doubles every 35 years.

Source: Statistical Abstract of the United States: 1991, Washington, DC, 1991, pp. 830–32.

FIGURE 15.1

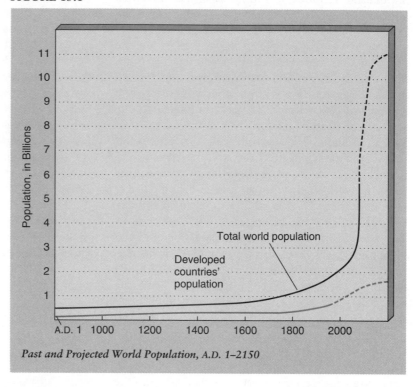

Past and Projected World Population, A.D. 1–2150

in the world in 1950, will not be in the top 25 largest cities in 2000 if current growth trends continue.

Demography *is the study of the size and composition of human populations, as well as the causes and consequences of changes in these factors.* Demography is influenced by three major factors: *fertility, mortality, and migration.*

The fertility rate is linked to industrialization and tends to decline with modernization.

Fertility

Fecundity *is the physiological ability to have children.* Most women between the ages of 15 and 45 are capable of bearing children. During this time, a woman could potentially have up to 30 children; however, the realistic maximum number of children a woman can have is about 15. This is a far cry

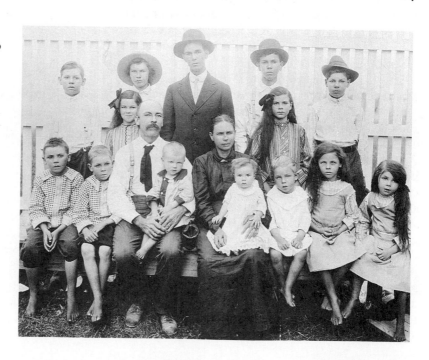

from real life, though, where health, culture, and other factors act as a limit on childbearing. Even in countries with high birth rates, the average woman rarely has more than eight children (McFalls, 1991).

Where fecundity refers to the biological potential to bear children, **fertility** *refers to the actual number of births in a given population.* One common way of measuring fertility is by using the **crude birthrate,** *the number of annual live births per 1000 people in a given population.* The crude birthrate for the United States fell from 24.1 in 1950 to 17 in 1990. Births since 1985 have been at their highest level since the mid-1960s, causing the population to increase by 1.0 percent in 1991 (U.S. Department of Commerce *News,* January 1, 1992).

Another indicator of reproductive behavior is the **fertility rate,** *the number of annual births per 1000 women of childbearing age, usually defined as ages 15 to 44.* In 1990, fertility rates ranged from an average of 1.3 children per woman in Italy, to 8.1 children per woman in Rwanda. In the United States, the average is 2.1 children per woman.

As we will see later in this chapter, the fertility rate is linked to industrialization. Fertility declines with modernization, but not immediately. This lag is a source of tremendous population pressure in developing nations that have benefitted from the introduction of modern medical technology, which immediately lowers mortality rates.

Mortality

Mortality *is the frequency of actual deaths in a population.* The most commonly used measure of mortality is the **crude death rate,** *that is, the annual number of deaths per 1,000 people in a given population.* In 1990, 2.2 million Americans died, producing a crude death rate of nine per 1000. Demographers also look at **age-specific death rates,** *which measure the annual number of deaths per 1,000 people in a population at specific ages.* For example, one measure used is the **infant mortality rate,** *which measures the number of children who die within the first year of life per 1000 live births.* Some countries have extremely high infant mortality rates. In Mali, for example, 174 out of every 1,000 infants die before age one. In Ethiopia the figure is 168 (World Bank, 1987).

In the United States the infant mortality rate dropped from 47.0 in 1940 to 10.0 in 1988. This rate does not apply to all infants, however. In 1940 the infant mortality rate among whites was 43.2 (below the national average), while among African Americans it was 73.8. In 1988 the rates were 8.5 for whites and 17.6 for blacks (*Statistical Abstract*

of the United States: 1991). These figures suggest that good infant medical care is not equally available to all Americans. Cultural differences in childrearing may also affect infant mortality.

Although the infant mortality rate in the United States is considerably lower than the rates of developing countries, it is higher than that of twenty-three nations including Japan and Hong Kong, as well as most countries in Northern Europe. The lowest infant mortality rates in the world are found in Japan and Switzerland, where only six infants out of every 1000 die before their first birthday (*U.S. News and World Report,* August 8, 1988).

Mortality is reflected in **life expectancy,** *the average number of years a person born in a particular year can expect to live* (see Table 15.2 for life expectancies in selected countries). In 1990, the average life expectancy at birth in the United States was 75 years. The Japanese have the world's longest life expectancy at 79 years. The shortest life expectancies are for the West African countries of Sierra Leone, Guinea, and Guinea-Bissau at 42 years (McFalls, 1991).

Life expectancy is usually determined more by infant than adult mortality. Once an individual survives infancy, his or her life expectancy improves

TABLE 15.2	
Life Expectancy for Children Born in 1990	
Country	Years
Japan	79.3
Spain	78.2
Italy	78.0
Canada	77.3
Australia	76.6
Denmark	75.7
United States	75.6
Chile	73.2
Mexico	71.8
China—Mainland	68.4
Saudi Arabia	65.4
Morocco	64.0
Peru	63.9
India	57.7
Zambia	56.2
Bolivia	53.9
Nepal	50.1
Nigeria	48.5
Afghanistan	46.6
Angola	43.8
Guinea	42.4

Source: Statistical Abstract of the United States: 1991, Washington, DC, 1991, pp. 834–35.

dramatically. In the United States, for example, only when individuals reach their sixties do their chances of dying approximate those of their infancy (Bureau of the Census, 1987).

Though often overlooked, the rapid increase in population growth in the Third World countries is caused by sharp improvements in life expectancy, *not* by a rise in the birth rate. Disease also took a dramatic toll on life expectancy in the United States in the not too distant past. For example, Abraham Lincoln's mother died when she was thirty-five (he was nine). Prior to her death she had three children: Lincoln's brother died in infancy and his sister died in her early twenties. Of the four sons born to Abraham and Mary Todd Lincoln, only one survived to maturity.

In developing countries, the proportion of infant and child deaths is quite high, resulting in a significantly lower life expectancy than that in developed countries. In Bangladesh, infant deaths account for over one-third of all deaths. In the United States that figure is about one percent. The high proportion of infant deaths in developing countries can be attributed to impure drinking water and unsanitary conditions. In addition, the diet of pregnant women and nursing mothers often lacks proper nutrients, and babies and children are not fed a healthy diet. Flu, diarrhea, and pneumonia are common, as are typhoid, cholera, malaria, and tuberculosis. Many children are not immunized against common childhood diseases, such as polio, measles, diphtheria, and whooping cough, and the parents' income is often so low that when the children do fall ill, they cannot provide medical care (World Bank, 1984).

A good example of a country which has experienced a decline in mortality, but no decrease in fertility, is Kenya. Kenya has experienced an incredible population growth rate of four percent a year. If this rate of increase continues, Kenya's population of 22 million people will double in eighteen years (Haub, 1987).

Migration

Migration *is the movement of populations from one geographical area to another.* We call it **emigration** *when a population leaves an area* and **immigration** *when a population enters an area.* All migrations, therefore, are both emigrations and immigrations.

Of the three components of population change—fertility, mortality, and migration—migration historically exerts the least impact on population growth or decline.

Most countries of the world do not encourage immigration. When it is permitted it is often viewed as a way to provide needed skilled labor, or to provide unskilled labor for jobs the resident population no longer wishes to do. Exceptions to this trend are the traditional receiver countries, such as the United States, Australia, and Canada. These countries owe much of their growth to immigrant populations. In recent years, the United States has experienced an influx of illegal immigrants from Mexico.

Where migration is a significant factor, it is necessary to take the age and sex of the immigrants and emigrants into account, as well as the number of migrants. These characteristics tell us the number of potential workers among the migrants, the number of women of childbearing age, the number of school-age children, the number of elderly, and other factors affecting society.

Sometimes it is important to distinguish between those movements of populations that cross national boundary lines from those that are entirely within a country. In order to make this distinction, sociologists use the term **internal migration** *for movement within a nation's boundary lines*—in contrast with immigration, in which boundary lines are crossed.

Since 1970, population growth in the United States has been greatest in the sunbelt states, reflecting continued migration patterns toward the

Life expectancy in many Scandinavian countries is longer than it is in the United States.

South and West. California, Texas, and Florida are growing significantly faster than the United States as a whole because they attract many northeastern and midwestern residents. There is some indication, however, that internal migration patterns may be starting to change. Typically northern and midwestern migrants moved to the three major sunbelt states and then distributed themselves to the surrounding states. It now appears that future migration patterns in the U.S. could resemble an enormous cyclone, with a long westward flow to California from the Northeast and Midwest, and a series of shorter eastward flows through the South beginning in California and continuing to Florida and back up the Atlantic coast (Sanders and Long, 1987).

THEORIES OF POPULATION

The study of population is a relatively new scholarly undertaking, as it was not until the eighteenth century that populations as such were carefully examined. The first person to do so, and perhaps the most influential, was Thomas Malthus.

Malthus's Theory of Population Growth

Thomas Robert Malthus (1776–1834) was a British clergyman, philosopher, and economist who believed that population growth is linked to certain natural laws. The core of the population problem, according to Malthus, is that populations will always grow faster than the available food supply. With a fixed amount of land, farm animals, fish, and other food resources, agricultural production can be increased only by cultivating new acres, catching more fish, and so on—an additive process that Malthus believed would increase the food supply in an arithmetic progression (1, 2, 3, 4, 5, and so on). Population growth, on the other hand, increases at a geometric rate (1, 2, 4, 8, 16, and so on) as couples have 3, 4, 5, and more children. (A stable population requires that two individuals produce no more than 2.1 children: two to replace themselves and 0.1 to make up for those people who remain childless.) Thus, if left unchecked, human populations are destined to outgrow their food supplies and suffer poverty and a never-ending "struggle for existence" (a term coined by Malthus that later became a cornerstone of Darwinian and evolutionary thought).

Malthus recognized the presence of certain forces limiting population growth and grouped these into one of two categories: preventive checks and positive checks. **Preventive checks** *are practices that would limit reproduction.* Preventative checks include celibacy, the delay of marriage, and such practices as contraception within marriage, extramarital sexual relations, and prostitution (if the latter two are linked with abortion and contraception). **Positive checks** *are events that limit reproduction either by causing the deaths of individuals before they reach reproductive age or by causing the deaths of large numbers of people, thereby lowering the overall population.* Positive checks include famines, wars, and epidemics. Malthus's thinking was assuredly influenced by the plague that wiped out so much of Europe's population during the fourteenth and fifteenth centuries.

Malthus refuted the theories of the *utopian socialists,* who advocated a reorganization of society in order to eliminate poverty and other social evils. Regardless of any planning, Malthus argued, misery and suffering are inevitable for most people. On the one hand, there is the constant threat that population will outstrip the available food supplies; on the other, there are the unpleasant and often devastating checks on this growth, which result in death, destruction, and suffering.

History proved Malthus wrong, at least for the developed countries. Technological breakthroughs

According to Thomas Robert Malthus, populations will always grow faster than the available food supply.

in the 19th century enabled Europe to avoid many of his predictions. The newly invented steam engine used energy more efficiently; labor production was increased through the factory system. An expanded trade system provided raw materials for growing industries and food for workers. Fertility declined and emigration eased Europe's population pressures. By the end of the nineteenth century, Malthus and his concerns had been all but forgotten.

Marx's Theory of Population Growth

Karl Marx and other socialists rejected Malthus's view that population pressures and their attendant miseries are inevitable. Marxists argue that the sheer number of people in a population is not the problem. Rather, industrialism (and in particular, capitalism) creates the social and economic problems associated with population growth. Industrialists need large populations to keep the labor force adequate, available, flexible, and inexpensive. In addition, the capitalistic system requires constantly expanding markets, which can be assured only by an ever-increasing population. As the population grows, large numbers of unemployed and underemployed people compete for the few available jobs, which they are willing to take at lower and lower wages. Therefore, according to Marxists, the norms and values of a society that encourage population growth are rooted in its economic and political systems. Only by reorganizing the political economy of industrial society in the direction of socialism, they contended, is there any hope of eliminating poverty and the miseries of overcrowding and scarce resources for the masses.

Demographic Transition Theory

Sweden has been keeping records of birth and deaths longer than any other country. Throughout the centuries Sweden's birth and death rates fluctuated widely. Periods of rapid population growth were followed by periods of slow growth, and even population declines during famines. In the late 1800s, Sweden's death rate began a sustained decline while the birth rate remained high. Eventually Sweden's birth rate also declined, so that today its births and deaths are virtually in balance.

The shift in Sweden's population can be explained by a theory of population dynamics developed by Warren Thompson. According to the **demographic transition theory,** *societies pass through four stages of population change from high fertility and high mortality to relatively low fertility and low mortality.* During stage 1, high fertility rates are counterbalanced by a high death rate due to disease, starvation, and natural disaster. The population tends to be very young, and there is little or no population growth. During stage 2, populations rapidly increase as a result of continued high fertility linked to the increased food supply, development of modern medicine, and public health care. Slowly, however, during stage 3 the traditional institutions and religious beliefs that support a high birthrate are undermined and replaced by values stressing individualism and upward mobility. Family planning is introduced, and the birthrate begins to fall. Eventually population growth begins to decline. Finally, in stage 4, both fertility and mortality are relatively low, and population growth once again is stabilized (see Figure 15.2).

APPLICATIONS TO INDUSTRIAL SOCIETY

The first wave of declines in the world's death rate came in countries experiencing real economic progress. These declines gradually gained momentum as the Industrial Revolution proceeded. Advances in agriculture, transportation, and commerce made it possible for people to have a better diet, and advances in manufacturing made adequate clothing and housing more widely available. A rise in people's real income facilitated improved public sanitation, medical science, and public education.

Although the preceding explanation applies well to Western society, it does not explain the population trends in the underdeveloped areas of today's world. Since 1920 these areas have experienced a much faster drop in death rates than Western societies without a comparable rate of increase in economic development due primarily to the application of medical discoveries made and financed in the industrial nations. For example, the most important source of death being eliminated is infectious disease. These diseases have been controlled through the introduction of vaccines, antibiotics and other medical advances developed in the industrial nations. Those of us who are used to paying high costs for private medical care will find it hard to believe that preventive public health measures in underdeveloped countries can save millions of lives at costs ranging from a few cents to a few dollars per person.

Because the mortality rates in underdeveloped countries have been significantly reduced, the birthrate, which has not fallen as fast or as consistently, has become an increasingly serious problem. Often this problem persists and worsens despite monumental government efforts at disseminating birth control information and contraceptive devices. In India, for example, despite the government's commitment to

FIGURE 15.2

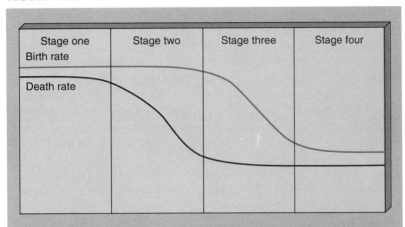

Stage one	Stage two	Stage three	Stage four

Birth rate

Death rate

The Demographic Transition The demographic transition theory states that societies pass through four stages of population change. Stage 1 is marked by high birth rates and high death rates. In stage 2, populations rapidly increase as death rates fall, but birth rates stay high. In stage 3, birth rates begin to fall. Finally, in stage 4, both fertility and mortality rates are relatively low.

controlling population size through birth control and sterilization, the population is expected to increase from 717 million in 1982 to 994 million in the year 2000 (World Bank, 1984).

These failures have shown the birthrate can be brought down only when attention is paid to the complex interrelationships of biological, social, economic, political, and cultural factors. For example, a mother in India may reject sterilization because four of her five children may be girls. With no social security, private pension plans or other forms of social insurance for the elderly, parents know they will need at least one son to take care of them in old age. India's high infant mortality rate creates the belief that parents should have two or three sons to ensure that at least one will survive (Freed and Freed, 1985).

A Second Demographic Transition

The original demographic transition theory ends with the final stage involving an equal distribution of births and deaths and a stable population. Some people (Van de Kaa, 1987) have suggested that Europe has gone beyond the original theory and entered a second demographic transition, which started at the arbitrarily set date of 1965. The principle feature of this transition is the decline in fertility to a level well below replacement.

If fertility stabilizes below replacement, as seems likely in most of Europe (barring major changes in immigration), the population of these countries will decline. As of 1985 this second demographic

transition was already taking place in four countries: Austria, Denmark, Germany, and Hungary.

The United States is not expected to experience a population decline in the near future. United Nations population projections to the year 2025 indicate that the United States will continue to grow modestly, even with continued low fertility and reduced immigration levels (Teitelbaum and Winter, 1985).

The principal feature of the second demographic transition is a decline in fertility to a level well below replacement.

The causes of the second demographic transition center around a strong desire for individual advancement and improvement. In European societies, as in American society, this advancement is dependent on education, and a commitment to develop and use one's talents. This holds for both men and women. Getting married and having children presents a number of tradeoffs, especially for women. A child may interrupt career plans, as well as add to the financial costs of the family. In European societies children are no longer either expected or required to support the parents in old age or help with the family finances. Therefore, the emotional satisfaction of parenthood can usually be satisfied by having either one or perhaps two children. Multiplied on a large scale, this trend produces births per woman that are below replacement level.

PRONATALIST POLICIES In most of this chapter, we presented information about population growth rates that appear to be out of control. Yet the second demographic transition in Europe is producing government policies in some countries that are designed to encourage people to have children.

Fewer births than deaths is already a reality in Germany and other European countries. Some have projected that there will be only half as many Europeans in 100 years as there are today. Declining populations will threaten European economies, defense systems, and even national identities.

Some countries have adopted measures that make it difficult to obtain contraceptives or to resort to abortion. Others have tried to provide incentives for having children. Since 1964 in Czechoslovakia, women with five or more children are entitled to their old-age pension at 53, those with three or four children at 54, those with two at 55, those with one at 56, and the childless at 57. Also in Czechoslovakia, newlywed couples receive low-interest loans which do not have to be paid back if they have enough children (Pavlik, 1986).

Other pronatalist incentives include full-paid maternity leave of up to twenty-six weeks and subsidized leave thereafter (up to the child's third birthday in Hungary), subsidized nurseries and kindergartens, educational and transportation grants, tax rebates, free medical care during pregnancy and delivery, and so on.

Studies of pronatalist policies have shown that they hardly ever lead to spectacular long-term effects on the birth rate. They may, however, contribute toward slowing down the fertility decline and improving the living conditions of the parents and their children.

CURRENT POPULATION TRENDS: A TICKING BOMB?

Every minute, 150 babies are born in the world. That means about 220,000 new human beings a day—80 million a year who need to be fed, clothed, sheltered, educated, and employed. At this rate the six billionth person will arrive before the year 2000. Another billion people will be added every 11 to 13 years until the middle of the 21st century. It took all of human history for the world's population to reach the first billion. Now a new billion people are added in just over a decade.

Along with the prediction of the six billionth person are some of the following troublesome predictions:

• In the year 2000, at least nineteen of the poorest nations will be unable to grow enough food to feed their people even if they use new technology.

• By the year 2000, poor countries will have half the water per person that they had in 1975, and the availability of water will be halved again by 2035.

• Six hundred million new jobs will be needed in developing countries by the year 2000 just to employ persons already born and soon to enter the work force.

• Many cities in poor countries face a doubling in population by the year 2000 (Population Reference Bureau, 1986).

Robert S. McNamara, former secretary of defense and president of the World Bank, noted that "Short of nuclear war itself, population growth is the gravest issue that the world faces over the decade ahead. . . Both can and will have catastrophic consequences. If we do not act, the problem will be solved by famine, riot, insurrection, war."

Like many other specialists in this field, he believes that overpopulation is now threatening the basic fabric of world order.

The problem is underscored by the increasing speed with which the world's population is multiplying. During the first two to five million years of human existence, the world population never exceeded ten million people. The death rate was about as high as the birth rate, so there was no population growth. Population growth began around 8000 B.C. when humans began to farm and raise animals. In 1650 there were an estimated 510 million people in the entire world. One hundred years later there were 710 million, an increase of some 39 percent. By 1900 there were 1.6 billion. Only 92 years later the world population had spiraled to 5.5 billion. The World Bank estimates that in the year 2025, the global population will be

a pattern of many children born close together, weakening both the mother and babies and producing more infant mortality.

In the short term, the prevention of ten infant deaths may produce only one to five fewer births. Initially, lower infant and child mortality will lead to somewhat larger families and faster rates of population growth than before. However, the long-term effects are most important. With improved chances of survival, parents give greater attention to their children and are willing to spend more on their children's health and education. Eventually the lower mortality rates help parents achieve and desire a smaller family with fewer births.

GENDER PREFERENCES

The effect of gender preference on fertility is actually more complicated than it might appear at first glance. In most countries throughout the world there is a strong preference for male children, although logic would predict otherwise. In most of the underdeveloped countries daughters typically help their mothers with household chores. One would think this would increase their worth to the family. Clearly, there must be countervailing factors to reduce the desire for daughters. It has been suggested that it may be tied in with the expense of a dowry or the early loss of the daughter's help through marriage (Mason, 1987). The Philippines is actually one of the few countries in the world where daughters are preferred over sons (Williamson, 1983).

The preference for sons, however, may not be that important in countries with high fertility rates. In Bangladesh, for example, the preference for sons is extremely strong, but the fact that couples desire large families, combined with little practice of contraception, has more of an impact on fertility than gender preference (Ahmed, 1981).

In countries with declining fertility rates the preference for sons may cause the fertility rate to level off above replacement level. Couples may continue to have children until they have the desired son.

BENEFITS AND COSTS OF CHILDREN

In underdeveloped countries the benefits of having children have generally been greater for an individual family than the costs. The costs and benefits change with each successive child a couple has.

For a rural sample in the Philippines three-quarters of the costs involved in rearing a third child come from buying goods and services; the other quarter comes from costs in time (or lost wages). But receipts from child earnings, work at home, and old age support offset 46 percent of the total. The remaining 54 percent, the net cost of a child, is equivalent to about six percent of a husband's annual earnings.

By contrast, a study of urban areas of the United States showed that almost half the costs of a third child are time costs. Receipts from the child offset only four percent of all costs.

Only economic costs and benefits are taken into account in these calculations. To investigate social and psychological costs, other researchers have examined how individuals perceive children. Economic contributions from children are clearly more important in the Philippines, where fertility is higher

In underdeveloped countries, the benefits of having children have generally been greater than the costs for the individual family.

than in Korea or the United States; concern with the restrictions children impose on parents, on the other hand, is clearly greatest in the United States.

In all three countries, however, couples demonstrate a progression in the values they emphasize as their families grow. The first child is important to cement the marriage and bring the spouses closer together, as well as to have someone to carry on the family name. In describing the first child, couples also stress the desire to have someone to love and care for, as well as the child's bringing play and fun into their lives.

In considering a second child, parents emphasize more the desire for a companion for the first child. They also place more weight on the desire to have a child of the opposite sex from the first. Similar values are prominent in relation to third, fourth, and fifth children; emphasis is also given to the pleasure derived from watching children grow.

Beyond the fifth child economic considerations predominate. Parents speak of the sixth or later children in terms of their helping around the house, contributing to the support of the household, and providing security in old age. For first to third children, the time taken away from work or other pursuits is the main drawback; for fourth and later children, the direct financial burden is more prominent than the time costs (The World Bank, 1984).

CONTRACEPTION Apart from the factors already mentioned, fertility rates are tied to the increasing use of contraception. Use of contraception is partly a function of a couple's wish to avoid or delay having children and partly related to its costs. People have regulated family size for centuries, through abortion, abstinence, even infanticide. However, the costs, whether economic, social, or psychological, in preventing a birth may be greater than the risk of having another child.

Use of contraception varies widely with rates of 10 percent or fewer for married women in almost all of sub-Saharan Africa to usage rates between 70 and 80 percent for women in Europe and the United States (Population Reports, 1985).

Contraception is most likely to be effective when such programs are publicly subsidized. Not only do such programs address the economic costs in providing contraception, they also help promote the idea that birth control is possible. These programs offer information about the private and social benefits of smaller families, which helps reduce the desired family size.

The support given to family planning programs differs dramatically from country to country. At one end of the family planning spectrum are the governments of India and China, which provide birth control information and devices and actively support the termination of pregnancy through abortion. At the other end are countries such as Bolivia and the Philippines whose large Roman Catholic populations follow the anti-birth control and anti-abortion teachings of the church (Helmore, 1988). (See Table 15.4 for the impact of government support for family planning to slow population growth.)

INCOME LEVEL It is a well-established fact that people with higher incomes want fewer children. However, it is not the higher income itself but rather

The support given to family planning programs differs dramatically from country to country. The government of India is active in providing birth-control information and devices, while Roman Catholic countries follow anti-birth-control policies.

TABLE 15.4

Government Supported Family Planning Programs and Population Growth

Country	Year Policy Adopted	Annual Percentage Growth Rate	
		1960–1965	1985–1990
India	1951	2.26	2.07
Pakistan	1960	2.69	3.44
Republic of Korea	1961	2.64	0.95
China	1962	2.07	1.45
Fiji	1962	3.27	1.78
Egypt	1965	2.51	2.39
Mauritius	1965	2.64	1.17
Singapore	1965	2.81	1.25
Sri Lanka	1965	2.43	1.33
Turkey	1965	2.49	2.08

Source: Dorothy Nortman, *Population and Family Planning Programs: A Compendium through 1981,* 11th ed., New York: The Population Council, 1982, table 6; United Nations, "1990 Revision of World Population Prospects: Computerized Data Base and Summary Tables," New York: United Nations, May 1990.

the life changes it brings about that lowers fertility. Alternative uses of time, such as earning money, developing or using skills, and pursuing leisure activities, become more attractive, particularly to women. The children's economic contributions become less important to the family welfare, as the family no longer needs to think of children as a form of social security in old age.

The relationship between income and fertility holds true only for those with an income above a certain minimum level. If people are extremely poor, increases in income will actually increase fertility. In the poorest countries in Africa and Asia, families are often below this threshold. Above the threshold, though, the greatest fertility reduction with rising income will take place among low-income groups.

EDUCATION OF WOMEN One of the strongest factors in reducing fertility is the education of women. The number of children that women have declines substantially as their level of education increases. The differences can sometimes be quite large; for example, in Colombia, women in the lowest educational group have, on the average, four more children than do women in the highest educational group.

Studies also show that women's level of education has a greater impact on fertility than does that of men. There are a number of reasons for this fact. In most instances, children have a greater impact on women, in terms of time and energy, than they do on men. The more educated a woman is, the more opportunities she may encounter that conflict with having children. Education also appears to

delay marriage, which in itself lowers fertility. In ten out of fourteen developing countries, women with seven or more years of education marry at least 3.5 years later than do women with no education. Educated women are also more likely to know about and adopt birth control methods. In Mexico, 72 percent of those women with nine or more years of education are likely to use contraception, whereas only 31 percent of those with five or fewer years of education are likely to do so.

URBAN OR RURAL RESIDENCE Urban fertility in developing countries tends to be lower than rural fertility, although it still is at least twice as high as fertility in developed countries (Salas, 1987). Urban dwellers usually have access to better education and health services, a wider range of jobs, and more avenues for self-improvement and social mobility than do their rural counterparts. They are exposed to new consumer goods and are encouraged to delay or limit their childbearing in order to increase their incomes. They also face higher costs in raising children. As a result, urban fertility rates are usually one to two children lower than are rural fertility rates.

The urban woman marries on the average at least one and one-half years later than the rural woman. She is more likely to accept the view that fertility should be controlled, and the means for doing so are more likely to be at her disposal.

Population officials in China are hoping the dramatic increase in the number of people moving into cities will help slow the country's growth. Between 1983 and 1988, the Chinese population changed from a predominantly rural population to one that is evenly split between urban and rural areas (Gargan, 1988).

Problems of Overpopulation

As long as many of the developing nations remain in stage 2 of demographic transition (high fertility but falling mortality), they will continue to be burdened by overpopulation, which slows economic development and creates widespread hunger.

Overpopulation undermines economic growth by disproportionately raising the **dependency ratio**, *the number of people of nonworking age in a society for every 100 people of working age.* Because populations at stage 2 have a high proportion of children, as compared with adults, they have fewer able-bodied workers than they need. For example, 49.5 percent of Kenya's population is below the age of 15, compared with 21.6 percent in the United States (*Statistical Abstract of the United States: 1991*). The economic development of countries with high dependency ratios is slowed further by the channeling of capital away from industrialization and technological growth toward mechanisms for feeding their expanding populations.

How will these problems be resolved in the future? Neo-Malthusians paint a gloomy picture of what lies ahead, contending that as we head toward the end of this century the population inevitably will outpace the available supply of food. Others believe we have the technological means to provide all the world's people with food. They speak of a "Green Revolution" in which new breeds of grain and improved fertilizers will raise harvest yields and eliminate the threat of a food shortage. The only thing holding back the revolution is international cooperation in planning the production and distribution of food.

However, the Green Revolution, widely proclaimed in the 1970s, has failed to materialize, owing to a number of serious limitations (Brown, 1974; Brown and Eckholm, 1974; Crossen, 1975). For one thing, there are inherent limits to the land, water, fertilizer, and energy available for food production. The total availability of land, for example, is declining as the climatic drying trend we have seen in recent decades reduces millions of acres of previously arable land to desert (hundreds of thousands of people in northern Africa face starvation because of this problem). In addition, an unhappy paradox links today's increased agricultural production to the possibility of a smaller food production capacity tomorrow. Overfarming and the indiscriminate destruction of forests have increased erosion, and excess fertilization has polluted rivers and lakes, killing fish and threatening the entire food chain. These factors indicate that the problem of widespread hunger is more complicated than the sole fact of a rising world population.

Predictions of Ecological Disaster

A group of some one hundred scientists, businesspeople, and academics known as the Club of Rome created great controversy with their predictions of

There are inherent limits to the land, water, fertilizer, and energy available for food production. Overfarming and the indiscriminate destruction of forests have produced deserts. Proper use of the land, as seen in this example of terrace farming, can save many people from starvation.

Paul Ehrlich on the Population Explosion

Paul R. Ehrlich is the Bing Professor of Population Studies at Stanford University. An expert on population, he has published several hundred scientific papers and a series of textbooks in the field. In 1968, his bestseller, The Population Bomb, *warned against the catastrophic consequences of unchecked population growth and helped to launch the environmental movement.*

Slightly over one billion people, less than a quarter of the world's population, live in nations whose standard of living—health, education, diet, housing, and quantity of material possessions—has improved dramatically over what the vast majority of the world's population enjoyed a century ago. But the standards for some four billion people haven't. They live in nations where average per-capita wealth is only about a fifteenth of that of the rich nations and where their babies are some five to twenty times as likely to die by the age of one. Of those, nearly a billion live in "absolute poverty"—defined as being too poor to buy enough food to maintain health or perform a job.

Rich and poor nations also differ drastically in their rates of population increase. The poor nations, except China, are growing at an average rate of 2.4 percent a year, which, if continued, would double their populations in about 29 years. The poorest populations are among the fastest growing ones. In contrast, the populations of rich nations are growing at only approximately 0.6 percent annually, which gives a doubling time of some 120 years. These numbers are, remember, averages—they conceal considerable differences among nations within these groups, just as national statistics do not show the very different states of individuals within countries.

We must always also keep in mind that buried in dry statistics about differences between rich and poor is an enormous amount of human misery, an endless series of almost incomprehensible tragedies. But, even if you don't care about starving children and overburdened parents who live without hope for a future, selfishness alone demands attention to the problems of the poverty-stricken. That is because the plight of the underprivileged of Earth is probably the single most important barrier to keeping our planet habitable.

Without the cooperation of the poor, the most important global environmental problems cannot be solved; at the moment the poor have precious little reason to listen to appeals for cooperation. Many of them are well aware that the affluent are mindlessly using up humanity's common inheritance—even as they yearn to help us do it. And all poor people are aware that the rich have the ability to bear the suffering of the poverty-stricken with a stiff upper lip. To remove such attitudes and start helping the less fortunate (and themselves), the rich must understand the plight of the poor not just intellectually but also emotionally.

The United States and India, the rich and the poor, face the same basic choice: either to shift in an orderly, planned way to a sustainable human life-support system or to be brutally forced into that shift by nature—through the untimely deaths of large numbers of human beings. Population control in both rich and poor nations is absolutely essential. If that were achieved, and the rich chose to restrain themselves and to help the poor, the remaining nonrenewable resources could be used to build a bridge to reach that sustainable future. At the same time, the damage currently being done to nominally replenishable resources would have to be curbed and their replenishment encouraged. Otherwise, those resources will be capable of supporting even fewer people in the future.

In short, human beings and human behavior must be brought into line with the constraints placed upon *Homo sapiens* by the limits of the Earth and the laws of nature. People who think those can be ignored or evaded are living in a dream world. They haven't reflected on the four *million* years it took for humanity to build a population of two billion people, in contrast to the 46 years in which the second two billion appeared and the 22 years it will take for the arrival of the third two billion. They have overlooked the most important trend of their time.

Source: Paul R. Ehrlich and Anne H. Ehrlich, *The Population Explosion,* New York: Simon and Schuster, 1990.

CONTROVERSIES IN SOCIOLOGY

What Causes the High U.S. Infant Mortality Rate?

We like to think of ourselves as the most medically advanced country in the world. Yet our infant mortality rate is embarrassingly high. Nicholas Eberhardt is a researcher at Harvard University's Center for Population and Development Studies. He disagrees with those people who claim our high infant mortality rate is due to poverty or lack of adequate health care.

Over the past 20 years, a succession of presidents and Congresses have voiced alarm over America's level of infant mortality and have authorized programs and policies to bring it down. But the American infant mortality problem endures—and by some measures, seems to be worsening.

To be sure, the proportion of babies dying before their first birthday has been declining in the U.S. Yet in relative terms, America's pace of progress has been so slow that many countries have surpassed us. According to the Department of Health and Human Services, the U.S. infant mortality rate is higher than that of twenty-three other industrialized countries, and is twice as high as that of Japan.

Washington's infant mortality "strategy" has been a plan for battle in a bygone world. By and large, our public health policies presume that high infant mortality levels are due to poverty or lack of medical services—qualities a government can supply. These are hardly the only threats to infant survival—and may not be the major ones.

The economic data cannot explain why some poorer groups of Americans have lower infant mortality rates than some richer groups. By the Census Bureau's most recent estimates, for example, Asians and Pacific Islanders have a higher poverty rate than U.S. whites, yet their infant mortality rate is substantially lower. By the same token, infant mortality rates for Hispanic Americans and non-Hispanic whites are just about the same, even though the poverty rate for Hispanic children is more than twice as high.

Inadequate medical care is another less than fully satisfactory explanation for the problem. In Western societies, the great majority of infant deaths occur within days of birth; the lower the baby's birthweight, the greater the risk. America's infant mortality problem has less to do with the survival chances of any low-birthweight baby than with the unusually large numbers of infants born into high-risk categories. Among blacks, the incidence of low birthweight (defined as 5.5 pounds or less at delivery) is not only higher than that of virtually any other Western population, but also twice as high as that of U.S. whites. Yet the incidence among U.S. whites is high as well—nearly twice that of Norway, for example. When one considers that infant mortality rates are roughly 20 times higher for low-birthweight babies than for those above 5.5 pounds, the significance of America's disposition toward low birthweight becomes deadly clear.

Why does America produce so many low-birthweight babies? The answer may have much to do with the behavior of parents-to-be. Evidence suggests that the attitudes, practices, and lifestyles of many American parents—including many who are neither poor nor poorly educated—are exposing U.S. babies to unfamiliar and unnecessary hazards.

Data shows that one of the maternal characteristics most strongly associated with low birthweight is out-of-wedlock childbearing. Regardless of a mother's race or age, her child is more likely to be of low birthweight if illegitimate. And regardless of a mother's race or age, infant mortality is higher for out-of-wedlock births.

Drug use and smoking are also much higher among mothers of out-of-wedlock children. Unfortunately, traditional social policy tools are not easily applied against dangerous parental behavior. Education can be highly effective when lack of knowledge is a constraint; it fares less well when the problem is lack of motivation.

Medical advances and increased health expenditures promise the continuation of progress against U.S. infant mortality. Unless the problem of hazardous parental behavior is controlled, however, the infant mortality rate is likely to remain needlessly high. It may well be that our government and legal system, which prize liberty, are not particularly suited to enforce model behavior upon negligent parents-to-be.

Source: Excerpted from Nicholas Eberstadt, "America's Infant Mortality Problem: Parents," *The Wall Street Journal,* January 20, 1992, p. A14.

worldwide economic and ecological collapse due to continuing population growth (Meadows et al., 1972). Using elaborate computer models developed at the Massachusetts Institute of Technology, they concluded that current worldwide trends in population, production, and pollution were on a direct collision course with the production limits imposed by natural resources and the pollution-absorbing capacity of the environment.

This "doomsday model" of the future asserts that modern technology is inevitably headed toward the exhaustion of the earth's natural resources. It assumes that we will eventually run out of oil, coal, copper, silver, arable land, and other items vital to production. Further, this model argues that modern technology also is heavily dependent on the environment for waste disposal. Eventually the increased waste from the increased production will go beyond the environment's absorptive capacity. At this point we will not be able to live with our own pollution. The Club of Rome concluded that if current trends continue, the limits of growth on this planet will be reached within the next one hundred years. The result will be a sudden and uncontrollable decline in population and production capacity:

> . . . We have tried in every doubtful case to make the most optimistic estimate of unknown qualities, and we have also ignored discontinuous events such as wars or epidemics, which might act to bring an end to growth even sooner than our model would indicate. In other words, the model is biased to allow growth to continue longer than it probably can continue in the real world. We can thus say with some confidence that under the assumption of no major change in the present system, population and industrial growth will certainly stop within the next century, at the latest (Meadows et al., 1972).

Sources of Optimism

The gloomy predictions presented by the Club of Rome have sparked a great deal of controversy and criticism. Critics point to a number of logical fallacies in its reasoning. Julian Simon and Herman Kahn (1984) argue that these dire predictions ignore the role of the marketplace in helping to produce adjustments that bring population, resources, and the environment back in balance. They cited evidence that the prices of goods have fallen rather than risen over the long run, and listed the inventions

that human ingenuity has produced in response to population growth.

In their optimistic view, population growth is a stimulus, not a deterrent, to economic advance. If imbalances exist it is because markets are not allowed to operate freely to permit innovators, investors, and entrepreneurs to provide solutions.

Others have questioned the basic assumptions of the "doomsday model," namely, exponential growth in population and production and absolute limits on natural resources and technological capabilities. The following (McConnell, 1977) are some of these counterarguments.

1. *Wider application of existing technology.* Greater efficiency and wider application of technology on a worldwide basis could continue to supply the world's needs far into the future. For example, it is estimated that greater efficiency in land cultivation would result in increased capacity to feed the world's population for many years. Many poorer countries that now find their agricultural output limited by pest infestation would see rapid improvement if modern technology were applied.
2. *Discovery of new resources.* Some critics also argue that the supply of natural resources is not really as fixed as the doomsday predictors claim. These critics maintain that technological advances can create new uses for formerly worthless substances. In this way new resources come into play that were not previously anticipated. Therefore technology will stay ahead of resource use.
3. *Exponential increase in knowledge.* It is further argued that just as doomsday predictors claim there will be an exponential growth in population and production, there will also be an exponential growth in knowledge that will enable societies to solve the problems associated with growth. New technological information and discoveries will alleviate new problems as they arise.

Population issues will continue to have an impact on the developed and developing areas of the world. There is a strong trend toward an improving situation. In the next decade we will see whether this trend is developing fast enough to prevent further outbreaks of famine and misery for millions of people.

Urban Society

The Development of Cities
  The Earliest Cities
  Preindustrial Cities
  Industrial Cities

Urbanization
  Classification of Urban Environments
  The Structure of Cities

The Nature of Urban Life
  Gemeinschaft to *Gesellschaft*
  Mechanical and Organic Solidarity
  Social Interaction in Urban Areas
  Urban Neighborhoods
  Urban Decline
  Homelessness

**Future Urban Growth in the
    United States**
  Surburban Living
  The Exurbs

. . . They tell me you are wicked and I believe
    them, for I have seen your painted women
    under the gas lamps luring farm boys.
And they tell me you are crooked and I
    answer: Yes, it is true I have seen the
    gunman kill and go free to kill again.
And they tell me you are brutal and my reply
    is: On the faces of women and children I
    have seen the marks of wanton hunger.
And having answered so I turn once more to
    those who sneer at this my city, and I give
    them back the sneer and say to them:
Come and show me another city with lifted
    head singing so proud to be alive and
    coarse and strong and cunning . . .
  Carl Sandburg, *Chicago Poems*, 1916.

Stand in your window and scan the sights,
On Broadway with its bright white lights.
Its dashing cabs and cabarets,
Its painted women and fast cafes.
That's when you really see New York.
Vulgar of manner, overfed,
Overdressed and underbred.
Heartless and Godless, Hell's delight,
Rude by day and lewd by night.

The two poems you have just read display the range of responses to the city. We are fascinated by them as well as terrified and revolted by them at the same time. Most of us now live in urban environments and we have found ways of adjusting to city life. In this chapter we will attempt to gain a better understanding of our urban society and the impact it has on people.

THE DEVELOPMENT OF CITIES

According to archaeologists, people have been on the earth for a couple of million years. During the vast majority of these years, human beings lived without cities. In spite of the fact that today we accept cities as a basic part of human life, cities are a relatively recent addition to the story of human evolution, appearing only within the last 7,000 to 9,000 years.

The city's dominance in social, economic, and cultural affairs is even more recent. Nonetheless, what we label as the period "civilization" only emerged during the time span that coincides with the city. The whole history of human triumphs and tragedies is encompassed within this period. The very terms "civilization" and "civilized" come from the Latin *civis,* which means a "person living in a city."

The cities of the past were still very unusual in an overwhelmingly rural world of small villages. In the year 1800, 97 percent of the world lived in rural areas of fewer than 5000 people. By the year 1900, 86 percent of the world still lived in rural areas (Palen, 1987). England was the first country to undergo an urban transformation. One hundred years ago it was the only predominantly urban country. It was not until 1920 that the United States held the same distinction.

Today we are on the threshold of living in a world that will for the first time be more urban than rural. Currently, some 45 percent of the world's population is urban. By the year 2000 it will increase to over half (Hauser and Gardner, 1982). Not all of the world is urbanizing at the same pace, though. In the more industrialized areas of the world—North America, Europe, and the former Soviet Union—urban growth has either stopped or slowed considerably (Spates and Macionis, 1987). For example, in 1970, 73.5 percent of the United States population lived in urban areas, while in 1990 it had increased to 75.2 percent (United States Department of Commerce News, December 18, 1991).

The area of greatest urban growth is now in the non-industrial world, such as Latin America, Africa, the Middle East, and Asia. In fact, the ten countries with the highest urban growth rates are all in these four areas, while the ten with the *lowest* are all, with one exception (Uruguay in South America), in Western Europe (Kurian, 1984). Already there are 118 cities of over one million people in the less developed countries. Most of us have never heard the names of more than a few of these cities. The United Nations projects that by the year 2000 there will be 284 such cities. By that year the population projections for Mexico City are 26.3 million, for Sao Paulo, Brazil, 24 million, and for Calcutta, India, 16.6 million (Palen, 1987).

The rapid transformation from a basically rural to a heavily urbanized world, along with the urban life styles that accompany this shift, are having a dramatic impact on the world's peoples. In this chapter we will examine the historical development of cities and urbanization trends.

The Earliest Cities

Two requirements had to be met in order for cities to emerge. The first was that there had to be a surplus of food and other necessities. Farmers had to be able to produce more food than their immediate families needed to survive. This surplus made it possible for some people to live in places where they could not produce their own food and had to depend on others to supply their needs. These settlements could become relatively large, densely populated, and permanent. The second requirement was some form of social organization beyond the family. Even though there might be a surplus of food, there was no guarantee it would be distributed to those in need of it. Consequently, a form of social organization adapted to these kinds of living environments had to emerge.

The world's first fully-developed cities arose in the Middle East, mostly in what is now Iraq, which was the site of the Sumerian civilization. The land is watered by the giant Tigris and Euphrates rivers, and it yielded an abundant food surplus for the people who farmed there. In addition, this area (called Mesopotamia) lay at the crossroads of the trade networks that already, 6,000 years ago, tied together East and West. Not only material goods but also the knowledge of technological and social innovations traveled along these routes.

Sumerian cities were clustered around temple compounds raised high up on brick-sheathed mounds called *ziggurats.* The cities and their sur-

Artists' conceptions of the early cities were often not very flattering. Pieter Bruegel painted this "Tower of Babel" scene to depict the fifth-century B.C. ziggurat of Babylon.

rounding farmlands were believed to belong to the city god, who lived inside the temple and ruled through a class of priests who organized trade caravans and controlled all aspects of the economy. In fact, these priests invented the world's first system of writing, as well as numerical notation late in the fourth millennium B.C. in order to keep track of their commercial transactions. Because warfare both among cities and against marauders from the deserts was chronic, many of these early cities were walled and fortified, and they maintained standing armies. In time the generals who were elected to lead these armies were kept permanently in place, and their positions evolved into that of hereditary kingship (Frankfort, 1956).

These early Sumerian cities had populations ranging between 7,000 and 20,000. However, one Sumerian city, Uruk, extended over 1,100 acres and contained as many as 50,000 people (Gist and Fava, 1974). By today's standards, the populations of these early cities seem rather small. They do, however, present a marked contrast with the small nomadic and seminomadic bands of individuals that existed prior to the emergence of these cities. Within the next 1,500 years, cities arose across all of the ancient world. Memphis was built around 3200 B.C. as the capital of Egypt, and between 2500 and 2000 B.C. major cities were built in what is now Pakistan. The two largest, Harappa and Mohenjo-Daro, were the most advanced cities of their day. They were carefully planned in a modern grid pattern with central grain warehouses and elaborate water systems, including wells and underground drainage.

The houses of the wealthy were large and multistoried, built of fired brick in neighborhoods separated from the humble dried-mud dwellings of the common laborers. Like the Sumerian cities, they were supported by a surplus-producing agricultural peasantry organized around central temple complexes.

By 2400 B.C. cities were established in Europe, and by 1850 B.C., in China. No fully developed cities were erected in the Americas until some 1,500 years later during the so-called Late Preclassic times (300 B.C. to A.D. 300). In Africa, cities of prosperous traders appeared around A.D. 1000 in Ghana and Zimbabwe (formerly Rhodesia).

Preindustrial Cities

Preindustrial cities—*cities established prior to the Industrial Revolution*—often were walled for protection and densely packed with residents whose occupations, religion, and social class were clearly evident from symbols of dress, heraldic imagery, and manners. Power typically was shared between the feudal lords and religious leaders. Preindustrial cities housed only five to 10 percent of a country's population. In fact, most had populations under 10,000.

These cities often served as the seats of political power and as commercial, religious, and educational centers. Their populations were usually stratified into a broad-based pyramid of social classes: A small ruling elite sat at the top; a small middle class of entrepreneurs rested just beneath, and a very large, impoverished class of manual laborers (artisans and peasants) slaved at the bottom. Religious institutions were strong, well established, and usually tightly interconnected with political institutions, the rule of which they supported and justified in theological terms. Art and education flowered (at least among the upper classes), but these activities were strongly oriented toward expressing or exploring religious ideologies.

Gideon Sjoberg (1965) has noted that three things were necessary for the rise of preindustrial cities. First, it was necessary that there be a favorable physical environment. Second, some advanced technology in either agricultural or nonagricultural areas had to have developed in order to provide a means of shaping the physical environment—if only to produce the enormous food surplus necessary to feed city dwellers. Finally, a well-developed system of social structures had to emerge so that the more complex needs of society could be met: An economic system, a system of social control, and a political system were needed.

Industrial Cities

Industrial cities *are cities established during or after the Industrial Revolution and are characterized by large populations that work primarily in industrial and service-related jobs.*

We use the term *Industrial Revolution* to refer to the application of scientific methods to production and distribution, wherein machines were used to perform work formerly done by humans or farm animals. Food, clothing, and other necessities could be produced and distributed quickly and efficiently, freeing some people—the social elites—to engage in other activities.

The Industrial Revolution of the nineteenth century forever changed the face of the world. It created new forms of work, new institutions and social classes, and multiplied many times over the speed with which humans could exploit the resources of their environment. In England, where the Industrial Revolution began in about 1750, the introduction of the steam engine was a major stimulus for such changes. This engine required large amounts of coal, which England had, and made it possible for cities to be established in areas other than ports and trade centers. Work could take place wherever there were coal deposits; industries grew and workers streamed to fill the resulting jobs. Thus, industrial cities arose, cities with populations that were much larger than those of preindustrial times.

Nineteenth-century urban industrialization produced industrial slums which were seen as some of the worst results of capitalism. Fredrich Engels, a close associate of Karl Marx, described the horrors of one of these areas.

The view from this bridge—mercifully concealed from smaller mortals by a parapet as high as a man—is quite characteristic of the entire district. At the bottom the irk flows, or rather stagnates. It is a narrow, coal-black stinking river full of filth and garbage which it deposits on the lower-lying bank. In dry weather, an extended series of the most revolting blackish green pools of slime remain standing on this bank, out of whose depths bubbles of miasmatic gases constantly

The Industrial Revolution created new forms of work. In this photo, taken in 1911, a young woman is seen taking home piecework.

rise and give forth a stench that is unbearable even on the bridge forty or fifty feet above the level of the water.

Modern-day industrial cities are large and expansive, often with no clear physical boundary that separates them from surrounding towns and suburbs. Like the preindustrial cities before them, industrial cities are divided into neighborhoods that reflect differences in social class and ethnicity (see Table 16.1 for a comparison of the preindustrial and industrial city).

The industrial cities of today have become centers for banking and manufacturing. Their streets are designed for autos and trucks as well as for pedestrians, and they feature mass transportation systems. They are stratified, but class lines often become blurred. The elite is large and consists of business and financial leaders as well as some professionals and scientists. There is a large middle class consisting of white-collar salaried workers and professionals such as sales personnel, technicians, teachers, and social workers.

Formal political bureaucracies with elected political officeholders at the top govern the industrial city. Religious institutions no longer are tightly intertwined with the political system, and the arts and education are secular with a strong technological orientation. Mass media disseminate news and pattern the consumption of material goods as well as most aesthetic experiences. Subcultures proliferate, and ethnic diversity often is great. As the industrial city grows, it spreads out, creating a phenomenon known as *urbanization*.

URBANIZATION

The vast majority of the people in the United States live in urban areas. We should not confuse urban areas with cities. In fact, there are several terms that often are used inappropriately when cities or urban areas are discussed that should be clarified. Thus, when we discuss cities, we are referring to something that has a legal definition. *A city is a unit that typically has been incorporated according to the laws of the state within which it is located.* Legal and political boundaries may be quite arbitrary, however, and a "city-type," or urban, environment

TABLE 16.1

Comparison of the Preindustrial City and the Industrial City

	Preindustrial City	Industrial City
Physical characteristics	A small, walled, fortified, densely populated settlement, containing only a small part of the population in the society	A large, expansive settlement with no clear physical boundaries, containing a large proportion of the population in the society
Transportation	Narrow streets, made for travel by foot or horseback	Wide streets, designed for motorized vehicles
Functions	Seat of political power; commercial, religious, and educational center	Manufacturing and business center of an industrial society
Political structure	Governed by a small, ruling elite, determined by heredity	Governed by a larger elite made up of business and financial leaders and some professionals
Social structure	A rigid class structure	Less rigidly stratified but still containing clear class distinctions
Religious institutions	Strong, well established, tightly connected with political and economic institutions	Weaker, with fewer formal ties to other social institutions
Communication	Primarily oral, with little emphasis on record keeping beyond mercantile data; all records handwritten	Primarily written, with extensive record keeping; use of mechanized print media
Education	Religious and secular education for upper-class males	Secular education for all classes but with differences related to social class

may exist in an area that is not officially known as a city. For example, in New England there are places known as towns—such as Framingham, Massachusetts, with a population of nearly 70,000—that for all practical purposes should be known as cities. Yet they do not adopt the city form of government with a mayor, a city council, and so on because of an attachment to the town council form of government.

Classification of Urban Environments

The legal boundaries of a city seldom encompass all the people and businesses that have an impact on that city. The U.S. Bureau of the Census has realized that for many purposes it is necessary to consider the entire population in and around the city that may be affected by the social and economic aspects of an urban environment. As a result, the bureau recognized the need for a complex set of terms to describe and classify urban environments. As of 1982, the terms the Bureau of Census applies to urban data include urbanized area, urban population, metropolitan statistical area, primary metropolitan statistical area, and consolidated metropolitan statistical area (Federal Committee on Standard Metropolitan Statistical Areas, 1979).

An **urbanized area** *contains a central city and the continuously built-up, closely settled surrounding territory that together have a population of 50,000 or more.* The term thus refers to the actual urban population of an area regardless of the political boundaries such as county or state lines. This term is often confused with **urbanization,** *which refers to the process whereby a population becomes concentrated in a specific area because of migration patterns.* More simply, *urbanized area* refers to a certain

place, and *urbanization* refers to a set of events that are taking place. **Urban population** *refers to the inhabitants of an urbanized area and the inhabitants of incorporated or unincorporated areas with a population of 2,500 or more.*

As a result of the 1990 census, 33 new urbanized areas were recognized, bringing the total number of urbanized areas in the United States to 396. When an area receives the urbanized area designation, it generally becomes recognized as having a large enough urban population concentration to warrant extra attention by government planners and business marketers (United States Department of Commerce News, August 16, 1991).

A **metropolitan area** *is an area that has a large population nucleus, and adjacent communities that are economically and socially integrated into that nucleus* (U.S. Department of Commerce, 1983). A metropolitan area emerges as an industrial city expands ever outward, incorporating towns and villages into its systems of highways, mass transportation, industry, and government.

A **metropolitan statistical area** **(MSA)** *has either one or more central cities, each with a population of at least 50,000, or a single urbanized area that has at least 50,000 people and that is part of an MSA with a total population of 100,000.* Each MSA also contains at least one central county; more than half the population of an MSA resides in these central counties. There also may be outlying counties that are more rural but have close economic and social ties to the central counties, cities, and urbanized areas in the MSA (see Table 16.2). *A* **primary metropolitan statistical area** **(PMSA)**, *is a large, urbanized county or cluster of counties that is part of an MSA with one million people or more.*

Expanding metropolitan areas draw on sur-

The legal boundaries of a city seldom encompass all the people and businesses that depend on the city or have an impact on it. The U.S. Bureau of the Census has realized that it is necessary to consider the entire population in and around the city.

TABLE 16.2

The 20 Largest U.S. Metropolitan Areas, 1990

Metropolitan Area	Size (Millions)	Rank 1970	Rank 1990
New York	18.1	1	1
Los Angeles	14.5	2	2
Chicago	8.1	3	3
San Francisco	6.3	6	4
Philadelphia	5.9	4	5
Detroit	4.7	5	6
Boston	4.2	7	7
Washington, D.C.	3.9	8	8
Dallas	3.9	12	9
Houston	3.7	13	10
Miami	3.2	16	11
Atlanta	2.8	18	12
Cleveland	2.8	9	13
Seattle	2.6	17	14
San Diego	2.5	22	15
Minneapolis-St. Paul	2.5	15	16
St. Louis	2.4	11	17
Baltimore	2.4	14	18
Pittsburgh	2.2	10	19
Phoenix	2.1	34	20

Source: U.S. Bureau of the Census, 1970, and United States Department of Commerce News, "Half of the Nation's Population Lives in Large Metropolitan Areas," February 21, 1991.

rounding areas for their labor pool and other resources to such an extent that all levels of planning—from the building of airports, sports complexes, and highway and railroad systems to the production of electric power and the zoning of land for industrial use—must increasingly be undertaken with their possible effects on entire regions kept in mind. In America, the most dramatic examples of this trend are the Los Angeles metropolitan area, the Dallas–Fort Worth area, and the so-called 500 mile northeast corridor from Washington, D.C., to Boston, Massachusetts ("Boswash"), which is forming one enormous metropolis including 60 million people—sometimes called a megalopolis—with New York City as its hub. A **megalopolis** *is a metropolitan area with a population of one million or more that consists of two or more smaller metropolitan areas.* The federal government *uses the phrase* **Consolidated Metropolitan Statistical Area (CMSA)** *to refer to a megalopolis.*

Despite the much-heralded flow of population to nonmetropolitan areas, more than one-third of all Americans live in the country's 23 megalopolises or CMSAs. New York–Northern New Jersey–Long Island ranks first among the CMSAs in population size, and it will continue to be number one well into the future. However, the Houston–Galveston–Brazoria, Texas area should experience the most rapid rate of population growth of any CMSA.

Basically, then, the United States can be seen as a three-tiered system of metropolitan areas: 257 freestanding MSAs; 78 larger PMSAs; and 23 very large CMSAs.

The Structure of Cities

Before a city grows outward to form a metropolitan area or become part of a megalopolis, it has gone through certain internal developments that establish the placement of various types of industrial, commercial, and residential areas.

The community and the city have been two of the primary areas of study ever since the beginning of American sociology. In the 1920s, classical *human ecology* blossomed under the leadership of Robert Park and Ernest Burgess at the University of Chicago.

The early human ecologists attempted to systematically apply the basic theoretical scheme of plant and animal ecology to human communities. Theories of human communities were developed that were analogous to theories explaining plant and animal development. For example, if you were to drive from the mountains to the desert, you would find that different soil, water, and climate conditions produce entirely different types of vegetation. By analogy, driving from a city's business district to its suburbs, you will also notice different types of communities based on a competition for specific types of land uses.

In fact, the human ecologists told us, human communities can be understood from a Darwinian perspective. Communities and cities have evolved and changed as a consequence of competition for prime space, invasion, succession, and segregation of new groups.

Park and Burgess and other members of the Chicago school of sociologists studied the internal structure of cities as revealed by what they called the ecological patterning (or spatial distribution) of urban groups. In investigating the ways in which cities are patterned by their social and economic systems and by the availability of land, these sociologists proposed a theory based on concentric circles of development.

CONCENTRIC ZONE MODEL The concentric zone model, sometimes irreverently called the bull's-eye model, is illustrated in Figure 16.1 (Park, Bur-

FIGURE 16.1

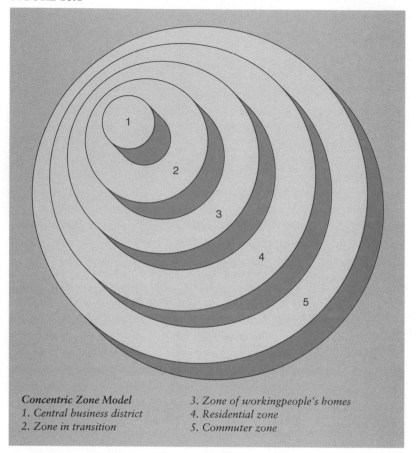

Concentric Zone Model
1. *Central business district*
2. *Zone in transition*
3. *Zone of workingpeople's homes*
4. *Residential zone*
5. *Commuter zone*

gess, and McKenzie, 1925). *The* **concentric zone model** *is a theory of city development in which the central city is made up of a business district, and radiating from this district are zones of (1) low-income, crowded but unstable, residential housing with high crime rates, prostitution, gambling, and other vices; (2) a working-class residential zone; (3) a middle-class residential zone; and (4) an upper-class residential zone in what we would now think of as the suburbs.* These zones reflect the fact that urban groups are in competition for limited space and that not all space is equally desirable in terms of its location and resources.

The concentric zone model initially was quite influential in that it did reflect the structure of certain cities, especially those like Chicago that developed quickly early in the Industrial Revolution, before the development of mass transportation and the automobile introduced the complicating factor of increased mobility. It did not, however, describe many other cities satisfactorily, and other models were needed.

SECTOR MODEL In the 1930s Homer Hoyt (1943) developed a modified version of the concen-

tric zone model that attempted to take into account the influence of urban transportation systems. He agreed with the notion that a business center lies at the heart of a city but abandoned the tight geometrical symmetry of the concentric zones. Hoyt suggested that the structure of the city could be better represented by a **sector model**, *in which urban groups establish themselves along major transportation arteries (railroad lines, waterways, and highways).* Then, as the city becomes more crowded and desirable land is even farther from its heart, each sector remains associated with an identifiable group but extends its boundaries toward the city's edge (see Figure 16.2).

MULTIPLE-NUCLEI MODEL A third ecological model, developed at roughly the same time as the sector model, stresses the impact of land costs, interest-rate schedules, and land-use patterns in determining the structure of cities. This multi-nuclei model (Harris and Ullman, 1945) emphasizes the fact that different industries have different land-use and financial requirements, which determine where they establish themselves (see Figure 16.3). Thus, *the* **multi-nuclei model** *holds that as similar indus-*

FIGURE 16.2

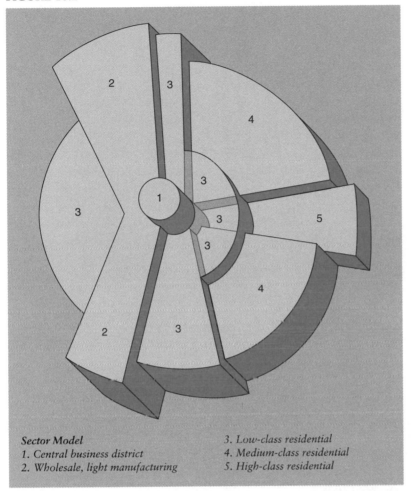

Sector Model
1. *Central business district*
2. *Wholesale, light manufacturing*
3. *Low-class residential*
4. *Medium-class residential*
5. *High-class residential*

tries are established near one another, the immediate neighborhood is shaped by the nature of its typical industry, becoming one of a number of separate nuclei that together constitute the city. For example, some industries, such as scrap metal yards, need to be near railroad lines. Others, such as plants manufacturing airplanes or automobiles, need a great deal of space. Still others, such as dressmaking factories, can be squeezed into several floors of central business district buildings. In this model, a city's growth is marked by an increase in the number and kinds of nuclei that compose it.

The limitations of the ecological approach to studying urban structure is that it downplays variables that often strongly influence urban residential and land-use patterns. For instance, the ethnic composition of a city may be a powerful influence on its structure: a city with but one or two resident ethnic groups will look very different from a city with many. Another important variable is the local culture—the history and traditions that attach certain meanings to specific parts of the city. For

example, the North End of Boston has become the Italian section of the city. People who normally might leave the city and move to the suburbs have remained in this city neighborhood because of strong ties to the traditions associated with that area. Indeed, cultural factors are important contributors to the continuing trend of urbanization.

The early ecologists could not predict some of the trends that have taken place since World War II. Since that time our Eastern and Midwestern cities have declined in population while the sprawling Sun Belt cities of the South and West have gained population and business. In addition, cities everywhere are more decentralized because of the automobile. The central business districts of cities have become less important over time. As the cities spread out, urban areas become linked to one another in a more complex manner than the early ecologists could have imagined.

Contemporary urban ecologists (Exline, Peters and Larkin, 1982; Hawley, 1981; Berry and Kasarda, 1977) have developed more advanced theories

FIGURE 16.3

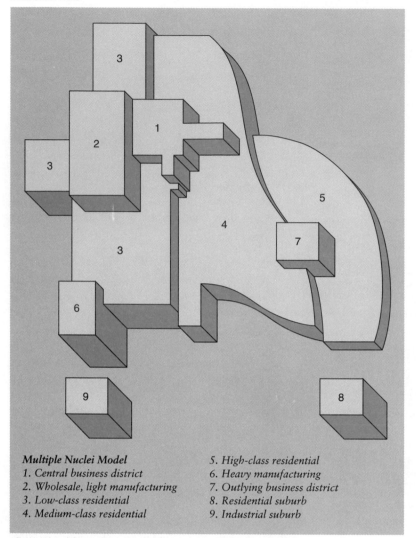

Multiple Nuclei Model
1. *Central business district*
2. *Wholesale, light manufacturing*
3. *Low-class residential*
4. *Medium-class residential*
5. *High-class residential*
6. *Heavy manufacturing*
7. *Outlying business district*
8. *Residential suburb*
9. *Industrial suburb*

that take into account some of the contemporary developments. Computers and modern statistical techniques are now used to analyze the variables that influence the growth and development of a city.

THE NATURE OF URBAN LIFE

Ever since sociologists began writing about communities, they have been concerned with differences between rural and urban societies and with changes that take place as society moves away from small homogeneous settlements to modern-day urban centers. These changes have been accompanied by a shift in the way people interact and cooperate with one another.

The "Chicago school" of sociology, as it was called, produced a large number of studies dealing with human interaction in city communities. The researchers were interested in discovering how the sociological, psychological, and moral experiences of city life were a reflection of the physical environment.

Gemeinschaft to *Gesellschaft*

The Chicago sociologists in their studies of the city were using some of the concepts developed by Ferdinand Tonnies (1865–1936), a German sociologist. In his book *Gemeinschaft und Gesellschaft*, Tonnies examined the changes in social relations attributable to the transition from rural society (organized around small communities) to urban society (organized around large impersonal structures).

Tonnies noted that in a **Gemeinschaft** *(community), relationships are intimate, cooperative, and personal. The exchange of goods is based on reci-*

procity and barter, and people look out for the well-being of the group as a whole. *In a* **Gesellschaft** *(society), relationships are impersonal and independent.* People look out for their own interests, goods are bought and sold, and formal contracts govern economic exchanges. Modern urban society is, in Tonnies's terms, typically a *Gesellschaft,* whereas rural areas retain the more intimate qualities of *Gemeinschaft.*

For example, among the Amish there is such a strong community spirit that should a barn burn down, members of the community will quickly come together to rebuild it. In just a matter of days a new barn will be standing—the work of community members who feel a strong tie and responsibility to another community member who has encountered some misfortune.

In a *Gesellschaft,* everyone is seen as an individual who may be in competition with others who happen to share a living space. Tonnies saw *Gesellschaft* as the end product of mid-nineteenth-century social changes that grew out of industrialization in which people no longer automatically want to help one another or to share freely what they have. There is little sense of identification with others in a *Gesellschaft,* in which each individual strives for advantages and regards the accumulation of goods and possessions as more important than the qualities of personal ties.

In small, rural communities and preliterate societies, the family provided the context in which people lived, worked, were socialized, were cared for when ill or infirm, and practiced their religion. In contrast, modern urban society has produced many secondary groups in which these needs are met. It also offers far more options and choices than did the society of Tonnies's *Gemeinschaft:* educational options, career options, lifestyle options, choice of marriage partner, choice of whether to have children, and choice of where to live. In this sense, the person living in today's urban *Gesellschaft* is freer.

Mechanical and Organic Solidarity

Tonnies wrote about communities and cities from the standpoint of what we described in Chapter 5 as an "ideal type," in that no community or city could completely conform to the definitions Tonnies presented. Rather the concepts are used to help us understand the differences between the two. In the same sense, Emile Durkheim devised ideas about mechanical and organic solidarity.

According to Durkheim, every society has a **collective conscience**—*a system of fundamental beliefs and values.* These beliefs and values define for its members the characteristics of the "good society," which is one that meets needs for individuality, security, superiority over others, and for any of a host of other values that could become important to the people in that society. **Social solidarity** *emerges from the people's commitment and conformity to the society's collective conscience.*

A **mechanically integrated society** *is one in which a society's collective conscience is strong and there is a great commitment to that collective conscience.* In this type of society, members have common goals and values and a deep and personal involvement with the community. A modern-day example of such a society is that of the Tasaday, a food-gathering community in the Philippines. Theirs is a relatively small, simple society, with little division of labor, no separate social classes, and no permanent leadership or power structure.

In contrast, *in an* **organically integrated society,** *social solidarity depends on the cooperation of individuals in many different positions who perform specialized tasks.* The society can survive only if all the tasks are performed. With organic integration such as is found in the United States, social relation-

A small town is likely to produce a Gemeinschaft, *in which relationships are intimate, cooperative, and personal; a city is likely to produce a* Gesellschaft, *in which relationships are impersonal and people look out for their own interests.*

William H. Whyte on the Role of the City Center

William H. Whyte is best known for his classic book The Organization Man. *Since that time his interests have moved into the area of urban environments and the impact changes in that environment have on people and cities themselves. In this section William H. Whyte discusses the blurring of lines between suburban office centers and city centers.*

Suburban office centers are imitating the center city. The center city is imitating suburban office parks. Where will the center go? There are two contrary trends. On the one hand there are cities that are tightening up their downtown, reinforcing the role of the street, and in general reasserting the dominance of the center. But a growing number are growing in the opposite direction. They are loosening up the structure, gearing it more to the car, taking the pedestrian off the street, and retailing, too. They are doing almost everything, indeed, to eliminate the structured advantages of the center they inherited.

As a way of distinguishing which camp a city is in, I have prepared a checklist of eight questions. No one city scores yes on all eight, but quite a number score high. Conversely, some cities score very low. There seems to be a strong tendency to move decisively in one direction or in the other.

1. Was much of downtown successfully razed under urban renewal?
2. Is at least half of downtown devoted to parking?
3. Have municipal and county offices been relocated to a campus?
4. Have streets been de-mapped for superblock developments?
5. Have the developments included an enclosed shopping mall?
6. Have they been linked together with skyways?
7. Have they been linked together with underground concourses?
8. Is an automated people-mover system being planned?

The higher the score, the more likely the city is to be one that has lost its ego, its sense and pride of place, its awareness of where it has come from and where it is going. It is a city with so little assurance that it is prey to what could be billed as bold new approaches, and to architectural acrobatics of all kinds.

Small and medium-sized cities seem particularly vulnerable. Their downtowns, for one thing, are more subject to the dominance of the freeways than are very large cities.

The worst discontinuity is parking. It is usually ugly, though it need not be. The blight of parking lies in what is not there—people, activity, function. The daytime storage of vehicles is not a highest and best use but is treated as if it were.

In some American cities, so much of the center has been cleared to make way for parking that there is more parking than there is city. If they clear away any more of what is left, there would not be much reason to go there and park.

In their zeal to woo the car, developers and municipalities grabbed off some of the best-located parcels of downtown. But so much of the surrounding area of downtown is given over to parking that it is hard to envision further progress without some garage clearance.

Supply has so conditioned demand that parking has become an end in itself, with people's bondage to it more psychological than physical. But suppose, just suppose, that Americans were to extend their walking radius by only a few hundred feet. The result could be the emancipation of downtown. Instead of being sequestered for the storage of vehicles, prime space would be released for positive activities.

In our wastefulness, in sum, lies opportunity. There is really a great deal of space in the city if we have the wit to see it.

Source: William H. Whyte, *City: Rediscovering the Center,* New York: Doubleday, 1988, pp. 310–16.

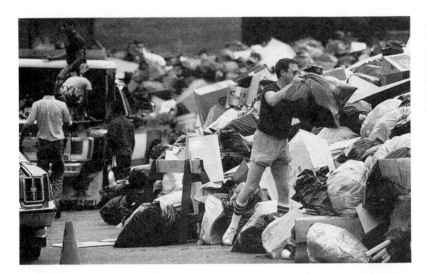

A organically integrated society depends on the cooperation of individuals in many different positions who perform specialized tasks. When one group does not do its job, as in a garbage strike, many others suffer.

ships are more formal and functionally determined than are the close, personal relationships of mechanically integrated societies.

Although we may take the movement from Gemeinschafts to Gesellschafts, or mechanically integrated to organically integrated societies for granted, it is only relatively recently in the course of human history that cities have become the dominant type of living arrangement.

Social Interaction in Urban Areas

The anonymity of social relations and the cultural heterogeneity of urban areas give the individual a far greater range of personal choices and opportunities than typically are found in rural communities. People are less likely to inherit their occupations and social positions. Rather, they can pick and choose and even improve their social position through education, career choice, or marriage. Urbanism makes for a complicated multidimensional society with people involved in many different types of jobs and roles.

Louis Wirth proposed what is now a widely accepted definition of *city* in his classic essay "Urbanism as a Way of Life" (1938). Wirth defined the city as a "relatively large, dense, and permanent settlement of socially heterogeneous individuals." For years urban studies tended to accept Wirth's view of the city as an alienating place where, because of population density, people hurry by one another without personal contact. However, in *The Urban Villagers* (1962), Herbert Gans helped refocus the way sociologists see urban life. Gans showed that urbanites can and do participate in strong and vital community cultures, and a number of subsequent studies have supported this view. For

example, researchers in Britain found that people who live in cities actually have a greater number of social relationships than do rural folk (Kasarda and Janowitz, 1974). Other investigators have discovered that the high population density typical of city neighborhoods need not be a deterrent to the formation of friendships; under certain circumstances, city crowding may even enhance the likelihood that such relationships will occur. Gerald Suttles (1968) showed that in one of the oldest slum areas of Chicago, ethnic communities flourish with their own cultures—with norms and values that are well adapted to the poverty in which these people live.

Of course, increased population size can lead to increased superficiality and impersonality in social relations. People interact with one another because they have practical rather than social goals in mind. For example, adults will patronize neighborhood shops primarily to purchase specific items rather than to chat and share information. As a result, urbanites rarely know a significant number of their neighbors. As Georg Simmel (1955) noted, in rural society, people's social relationships are rich because they interact with one another in terms of several role relationships at once (a neighbor may be a fellow farmer, the local banker, and a member of the town council, and so on). In urban areas, by contrast, people's relationships tend to be confined to one role set at a time (see Chapter 5).

With increasing numbers of people it also becomes possible for segments or subgroups of the population to establish themselves—each with their own norms, values, and lifestyles—as separate from the rest of the community. Consequently, the city becomes culturally heterogeneous and increasingly complex. As people in an urban environment come into contact with so many different types of people, typically they also become more tolerant of diversity than do rural people.

Although urban areas may be described as alienating places in which lonely people live in crowded, interdependent, social isolation, there is another side to the coin, one that points to the existence of vital community life in the harshest urban landscapes. Further, urban areas still provide the most fertile soil for the arts in modern society. The close association of large numbers of people, wealth, communications media, and cultural heterogeneity are an ideal context for aesthetic exploration, production, and consumption.

Urban Neighborhoods

People sometimes talk of city neighborhoods as if they were all single, united communities, such as Spanish Harlem or Little Italy in New York City, or Chinatown in San Francisco. These communities do display a strong sense of identity, but to some extent this notion is rooted in a romantic wish for the "good old days" when most people still lived in small towns and villages that were in fact communities that gave their residents a sense of belonging. Yet, although the sense of community that does develop in urban neighborhoods is not exactly like that in small, closely knit rural communities, it is very much present in many sections throughout a city. Urban dwellers have a mental map of what different parts of their city are like and who lives in them.

Gerald Suttles (1972) found that people living in the city draw arbitrary (in terms of physical location) but socially meaningful boundary lines between local neighborhoods, even though these lines do not always reflect ethnic group composition, socioeconomic status, or other demographic variables (see Chapter 19). In Suttle's view, urban neighborhoods attain such symbolic importance in the local culture because they provide a structure according to which city residents organize their expectations and their behavior. For example, in New York City, the neighborhood of Harlem (once among the most fashionable places to live) "begins" east of Central Park on the north side of Ninety-sixth Street and is a place that has symbolic significance for all New Yorkers. Whites tend to think of it as a place where they are not welcome and which is inhabited by black and Spanish-speaking people. For many blacks and Hispanics, on the other hand, Harlem represents the "real" New York City and is the place where most of their daily encounters take place.

Even those urban neighborhoods that are well known, that have boundaries clearly drawn by very distinctive landmarks, and that have local and even national meaning are not necessarily homogeneous communities. For example, Boston's Beacon Hill neighborhood is divided into four (or possibly five) subdistricts (Lynch, 1960), and New York's Greenwich Village consists of several communities defined in terms of ethnicity, lifestyle (artists), and subculture (especially homosexual).

On the whole, Jane Jacobs observations in *The Death and Life of American Cities* (1961) generally seem to hold true. She argues that the social control of public behavior and the patterning of social interactions in terms of what might be called community life are to be found on the level of blocks rather than entire neighborhoods. Once city dwellers venture beyond their own block, they tend to lose their feelings of identification. In fact, one of the typical features of urban life is the degree to which people move through many neighborhoods in their daily comings and goings—rushing here and there without much attention or attachment to their surroundings. Occasionally a city as a whole may have meaning to all or most of its residents and may, for this reason, assume some communitylike qualities. Consider, for example, the community spirit expressed in spontaneous celebrations for homecoming World Series or Super Bowl winners.

The vast majority of the people in the United States live in urban areas.

Although urban blocks and neighborhoods may offer a rich context for community living, there are some inescapably unpleasant facts about urban America that make many people decide to live elsewhere. Cities and urban areas in general can be crowded, noisy, and polluted; they can be dangerous, and they may have poorer schools than those in the suburbs. Consequently, many families, especially those with children, choose the suburbs as an alternative to urban life. Other city dwellers, such as the elderly living on fixed incomes, may be forced to remain despite their wish to move.

Urban Decline

A grim circle of problems threatens to strangle urban areas. Since World War II there has been a migration of both white and black middle-class families out of the cities and into the suburbs. The number of black middle-class families moving to the suburbs increased sharply in the aftermath of the civil rights movement of the 1960s. This migration has led to a greater concentration of poor people in the central cities, which is reflected in the loss of revenues that many large cities have experienced. As the more affluent families leave urban areas, so do their tax dollars and the money they spend in local businesses. In fact, many businesses have followed the middle class to the suburbs, taking with them both their tax revenues and the jobs crucial to the survival of urban neighborhoods. This has resulted in a shrinking tax base for central cities at the same time that conditions are growing (such as unemployment) that force people to rely on government assistance. It is not easy to entice suburbanites to move back into cities, even though the U.S. Department of Housing and Urban Development has created several financial incentive programs designed to do so. Because most United States suburbs were created in the last forty years, their facilities and physical plants (schools and hospitals) are still relatively new, clean, and attractive. So are the shopping centers that continue to mushroom across the country offering their suburban patrons local outlets of prestigious "downtown" stores as well as supermarkets, discount warehouses, specialty shops, and even entertainment centers. In the central cities many buildings are old, and apartment dwellers must pay higher rents for accommodations that are inferior to those of their suburban counterparts.

Gans (1977) suggests that if we are to save the central cities, we can do so only by mobilizing resources at the national level and raising central-city residents themselves to middle-class economic status. He believes this is more likely to succeed than trying to convince suburbanites to move back into urban areas. Many people believe, however, that the vicious circle outlined is a sinking spiral and that some of our cities have already spun downward and out of control. They see no way of resurrecting them and forecast their gradual demise as the population spreads itself out across the country, particularly into the sunbelt of the South and Southwest.

A small countertrend has been noticed. Many middle-class young adults have begun to find urban life attractive again. Most of these people are single or married with no children. This trend has produced an upgrading of previously marginal urban areas and the replacement of some poor residents with middle-class ones, a process known as gentrification. Critics contend that gentrification depletes the housing supply for the poor. Others counter that it improves neighborhoods and increases a city's tax base. So far, however, this trend has been limited to a handful of cities. The trend may be short lived, because these young adults may once again abandon the city once they start having children if they find city life unsuitable for child rearing. If it continues and grows, however, it clearly will have a major impact on the future of urban life and could serve as a convincing argument against doomsday predictions about the city.

Homelessness

A decade ago every city had its "skid row" with "bums," "derelicts," and "vagrants." Aside from the occasional story about the executive who became an alcoholic and ended up sleeping in "flop houses," little interest or sympathy was expressed for the denizens of these marginal areas of the city. Today, not only have the words we use to describe these people changed, so has our thinking and attitudes about them. The "bum" or "hobo" of the past has become today's "homeless person." The sense of personal responsibility for their fate attributed to them before, has now been replaced with a view that the homeless are the victims of a selfish, even ruthless society.

What has really changed? Has society become more heartless and created more victims, or have we become more compassionate and aware of the problem? Have the numbers of homeless gone up so much that we are forced to recognize the issue?

The movement to the suburbs of post-World War II America emphasized the suburban ideal of a single-family home. The city was where one worked during the day and once nightfall came one left for the safety of the suburban community.

If the movement to the suburbs required abandoning the downtown streets at nightfall, there were many people who did not leave the central city. There are, of course, the working-class neighborhoods of the older cities where family life goes on in close proximity to the central business district, under somewhat less private and more crowded conditions than in the suburbs. There are also the marginal people for whom downtown provided alternatives not available elsewhere. Commercial and industrial areas, as well as fringe areas in decaying working-class districts, have tended to provide the housing stock vital to poor persons not living in conventional families. Single-room occupancy hotels, rooming houses, and even skid row flophouses all have provided low-cost single accommodations for those who might not be able to come by them elsewhere.

Downtowns in many older cities have also traditionally contained the cities' skid rows and red-light districts, which provided shelter and a degree of tolerance for deviant individuals and activities. Being close to transportation and requiring little initial outlay (often renting by the week), single-room housing has traditionally been utilized by the elderly poor, the seasonally employed, the addicted, and the mentally handicapped.

In the United States there are more than 150 skid rows, but the number and size of such areas has been decreasing. There are two principal reasons for the decrease. First, the economy no longer requires large numbers of unskilled migratory workers; second, the land occupied by skid rows is being converted by real estate developers to other uses (Palen, 1987). As old skid rows decrease in size or disappear, the traditional skid row inhabitants of single older men are being supplemented with large numbers of people of both sexes, many of whom were released from mental hospitals during the 1970s. The process of deinstitutionalization caused many of those who previously would have been committed to institutions to become homeless street people. Others who have reached adulthood since then have never been institutionalized, but would have been during previous decades. Estimates from neutral sources claim that the mentally ill account for anywhere from 30-40 percent or more of the homeless, making them the largest single category. They are not necessarily physically dangerous, but rather are disturbed or marginally competent individuals without supportive families.

Homelessness was not the intended result of this process. The original idea was to free the patients from the wretched and abusive conditions in mental hospitals and allow them instead to be treated in the community. However, community treatment never materialized and many ended up on the streets, uncared for and unable to care for themselves.

Advocates for the homeless often claim that these people are out on the streets because of a lost job, a low minimum wage, or a lack of affordable housing—all things outside the control of the homeless. Certainly there are many situations where that is the case, particularly among those homeless for a short spell. However, for the broader category of the homeless, we will find very few auto-workers laid off from well-paying jobs. Most homeless individuals will have histories of chronic unemployment, poverty, family disorganization, illiteracy, crime, mental illness, and welfare dependency—problems that cannot be corrected by quick or simple economic measures. According to one study (Sosin, 1986) three factors differentiate the homeless from the poor in general: extreme poverty, fewer years of schooling, and less family support.

It is also unclear how many homeless people there are. Because the homeless are so difficult to find and to count, estimates range widely. Advocates claim the population ranges from two to three million and will rise to 18 million by the end of the century. The media often use the two to three million figure, which represents about one percent of the population even though no study has ever supported this contention. A little thought would show that it is ridiculous to claim that one percent of the U.S. population is homeless. At the other end, the Department of Housing and Urban Development did a study which estimated the homeless population at a drastically lower 250,000 to 350,000.

Both estimates are probably wrong: The HUD figure because it was a poorly executed study, and the advocates figure because of the lack of any study.

Advocates for the homeless justify their inflated numbers by referring to the "hidden homeless" who cannot be located, and the "borderline homeless" who are living with relatives because they cannot afford suitable housing. However, sociologist Peter Rossi of the University of Massachusetts, himself an advocate for more public spending on the homeless, notes "we have never been able to locate any data from which these numbers were derived. There is no evidence that they are anything but guesses" (*Insight*, May 18, 1988).

In recent years, the downtown sections of many American cities have undergone extensive renovation and revitalization. This "back to the city" or "gentrification" movement has been both hailed as an urban renaissance and condemned for disrupting urban neighborhoods and displacing inner-city residents. As city land becomes more desirable, it has an effect on what is usually considered to be the nation's least desirable housing stock, namely single-room occupancy hotels, rooming houses, and shelters. Although these places have long been seen as the very symbols of urban decay, they serve the vital needs of people with few resources or alternatives. Gentrification has placed these powerless people in direct competition for inner-city space. The results may be at least a partial explanation for the growing ranks of the homeless on the streets of many cities.

The deinstitutionalized, the ex-offender, the addicted, the poor, the sick, and the elderly all bring to the central city a lifestyle incompatible with that of the new urban middle class. Yet these people will not go away simply because their housing is eliminated. They remain on our streets and tax the strained resources of the remaining shelters. Unlike the suburb, the newly gentrified inner city cannot close its gates to marginal members of society. It therefore becomes imperative that new alternatives be provided.

FUTURE URBAN GROWTH IN THE UNITED STATES

What will metropolitan areas look like in the year 2000? Which cities will grow the most? Which cities will lose the most population?

One way to answer such questions would be simply to extend into the future the trends of the 1970s, 1980s, and early 1990s. A forecast of this sort would show only modest growth for the economy, with decreased reliance on manufacturing and increased service and energy-producing activities.

Regionally, such a forecast would indicate that metropolitan areas in the industrial Northeast and Midwest would stagnate. The economic vitality those cities once had would continue to be drained as population and jobs were lost. The migration of American families in the previous two decades to rapidly growing cities in the West and South would suggest that the manufacturing centers of the country would no longer lead economic recoveries as they had in the not so distant past.

Historically, the United States population has become increasingly more urban as people moved from rural areas to find employment in industrial centers. The growth in the population of urban areas at the expense of population in the surrounding rural areas has long been considered a trademark of advancing societies. However, during the 1970s and 1980s, the percentage of Americans living in metropolitan areas did not grow significantly, moving from 76.0 percent in 1970 to 77.5 percent in 1990 (United States Department of Commerce *News*, February 21, 1991). Hidden in these figures is the fact that rural areas not classified as metropolitan in 1970 were included, because of revised definitions, in the figures in 1990. Therefore we could argue that there has actually been a decline in the population of metropolitan areas.

The percentage of people living in metropolitan areas is also expected to decline in the future. By the year 2000 it is expected to be 74.8 percent. This slowdown in the growth of metropolitan areas relative to the surrounding countryside is new to the United States. The last time such a slowdown in urban growth occurred was early in the nineteenth century when the country's land area expanded rapidly (Holdrich, 1984).

The decline in the urban population is due to the fact that employment opportunities in all metropolitan areas together are expected to remain stable throughout the end of the century. Approximately 78 percent of all United States jobs will be located in urban areas, though the types of jobs available in the metropolitan areas are changing. By the year 2000, metropolitan areas are expected to support only 77 percent of all manufacturing jobs (Holdrich, 1984).

Manufacturing jobs for the nation as a whole have been growing less rapidly in recent years because of international competition and increased productivity, which reduce the amount of labor required to produce goods. In fact, manufacturing has been supplanted by the service sector as the largest employer of American workers, indicating a major shift in the economy.

Metropolitan trends vary widely according to region. Some metropolitan areas are expected to maintain high growth rates over the next two decades. These are primarily in the South and West. Ninety percent of the nation's population growth since 1980 can be accounted for by the rapid growth rate in these regions. Between 1980 and 1985, the population of the South grew by 6.7 million, while that of the West grew by 4.7 million. The Northeast increased by 724,000, the Midwest by only 331,000. The South in particular has experienced substantial growth. "Between 1970 and 1980, overall net migration to the South was twice that to the West. Spurred by a substantial increase in migration from the Midwest, net migration to the South between 1980 and 1985 increased to nearly three times that to the West" (Kasarda, Irwin, and Hughes, 1986). (See

Figure 16.4 for a comparison of growth rates for the various regions of the United States.)

Although many of the cities in the South and West have grown rapidly, constraints to this expansion are appearing. The rate of growth for Houston and other southern and western metropolitan areas should slow somewhat, and the same pattern will be seen in most other sunbelt areas.

Suburban Living

Suburbs *consist of those territories that are part of an MSA but outside the central city.* According to this definition, 60 million people lived in the suburbs in 1960, 74 million in 1970, and over 100 million in 1990. In fact, most people now living in metropolitan areas live in suburbs rather than in the central cities.

Suburbanites inhabited a territory which did not fit any traditional definition of city or country. Originally, the small-scale agriculture of suburban gardeners was mocked by farmers, and city newspa-

per editors derided the lack of cultural facilities in the suburbs.

We accept the sprawling landscape of single-family houses on small lots without question today and assume that suburbs have always been with us. We give little thought to their origin.

Suburbs, as we know them, developed relatively recently and largely without planning. They were a direct response to changes that made commuting easier. Well-surfaced roads and hundreds of new bridges began to appear in the early nineteenth century. The steamship also changed matters dramatically in the New York City region. Individuals discovered a new lifestyle that included steaming down the Hudson in the early morning and cruising slowly upstream in early evening. Railroads were also instrumental in the development of the suburbs. Trains made it possible to travel in all kinds of weather prompting thousands of upper-class Americans to use them. Originally, the railroad companies discouraged short-haul commuting, but eventually demand created the commuter train. Suburbs began

FIGURE 16.4

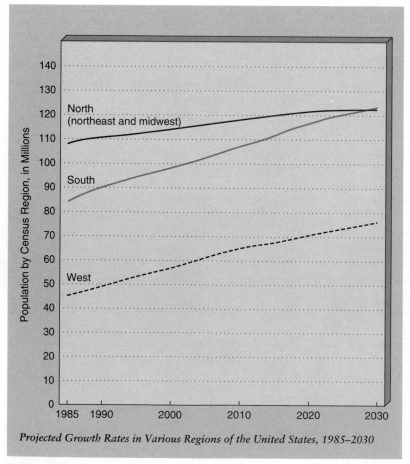

Projected Growth Rates in Various Regions of the United States, 1985–2030

Source: *American Demographics*, June 1986, p. 39.

One characteristic of suburbs is that they tend to be homogeneous with respect to the stage of development of families in their natural life cycle. While children will be represented, there will be few older families.

to blossom all along the railroad routes that lead to the city. Thousands of middle-income families settled in these suburbs which offered the advantages of both rural and urban living.

The typical suburban house, part farmhouse and part urban residence, reflected a desire for open space, sanitation and security. It usually had many large closets, a large cellar, an attic, a pantry, a back hall—even guest rooms. Suburbanites also started to copy the front lawn which was typical of estates, and English country homes. The lawn mower appeared in the 1880s, and magazines explained the use of the new machines. By the 1920s the idea of a smooth, green lawn became widely accepted. Lawn-mower manufacturers determined that grass height should be about one and one-half inches, and suburbanites were quick to follow the recommendation.

Suburban growth slowed during the Depression and the subsequent war years when gasoline rationing took place. Once the war ended, however, suburban growth resumed. By the mid-1950s, the automobile made it possible for suburbs to exist far beyond the range of railroads and trolleys. Popular television shows such as "I Love Lucy" and "Leave it to Beaver" responded to the public sentiment which was turning against the city and shifted their locales to the suburbs.

The way in which homes were purchased also influenced the growth of the suburbs. Before the 1920s, a home-buyer borrowed 30 to 40 percent of the cost of the property. Mortgage interest payments of 5 or 6 percent were made semiannually. At the end of anywhere from three to eight years the principal was repaid in one lump sum or the mortgage was renegotiated. After the 1920s, savings

and loan associations replaced the informal, individual-lender.

After World War II, the government guaranteed mortgages to veterans. Ex-GIs needed only the smallest of down payments to purchase a home, and a building boom emerged. For the children of these families, the suburbs represented the world—a world ruled by women, more than men. Men went to work in the city and returned every evening to the suburban landscape. As commuting time increased, the fathers looked for jobs in the suburbs and began deserting the city altogether. When white-collar workers started to appear in the suburbs in large numbers, suburbs entered their present stage.

The suburbs of today are markedly different from those that existed three decades ago. A declining birthrate changed the nature of many residential neighborhoods and forced the closing of many schools. The vast increase in the number of women working outside the home caused many suburban areas to appear uninhabited during the week day. Today, many suburban areas really are urban areas that have grown horizontally rather than vertically and these areas experience many of the same concerns and problems as large cities do (Stulgoe, 1984).

In many respects, at least until recently, suburbs have served as a dramatic contrast to city life. Suburbs generally are cleaner than cities, less crowded, less noisy, and less crime ridden. Often their school systems are newer and better. Many characteristics of urban life, however, have followed people to the suburbs.

Suburbs increasingly are suffering from some of the serious problems that used to be thought of as exclusively urban in nature. Perhaps the most dramatic of these is the sharp rise in juvenile

Levittown, Pennsylvania, became the symbol of the post-World War II suburban building boom. With little to no money down and low monthly payments attracting former GIs and their families, the U.S. urban landscape and society were changed.

alcoholism, drug addition, and delinquency. At least one reason for this seems to be that suburban areas typically have few resources that address the needs of youth. There is little for teenagers to do, few places for them to go. Consequently they often are bored. Furthermore, as the middle class finds itself suffering more and more from economic strain, suburban populations are less willing to spend tax money on social services to address these problems, and even the public buildings and areas of many suburbs are beginning to show signs of "urban" decay.

In the last 20 years the fastest-growing areas have been the exurbs, an area where development is much less dense, located in a newer, second ring beyond the old suburbs.

One characteristic that still separates suburban from city neighborhoods is that suburbs tend to be homogeneous with regard to the stage of development of families in their natural life cycle. For example, in the suburbs, retired couples rarely live among young couples who are just starting to have children. Aside from the rather dulling "sameness" of many suburban tracts that results from this, it also creates problems in the planning of public works. For example, a young suburb might well invest money in school buildings, which, some twenty years later, are likely to stand empty when the children leave home.

Gradually the suburban "dream life" is showing signs of strain. Although many wealthy suburbs are still not experiencing these problems, less affluent suburbs—with diminishing resources, obsolete structures resulting from poor planning, and a seeming inability to solve such problems as adolescent boredom and the provision of services for the elderly—appear to be heading for a period of reassessment by those seeking a better life.

The Exurbs

For the last twenty years the fastest growing areas appear to be located in the **exurbs,** *a newer, second ring beyond the old suburbs.* Exurbs have been designated by some as the "new heartland," a mixture of urban, rural, and suburban living (Herbers, 1986).

The exurb is taking shape largely within metropolitan boundaries, but it differs sharply from the traditional suburb. Development in the exurbs is much less dense, emerging near farms and rural land in the remotest fringes of metropolitan areas (see Table 16.3 for a comparison of growth rates in cities of various sizes). While suburbs traditionally depend on the city for jobs and services, the exurb

TABLE 16.3				

Number of U.S. Cities by Population Size, 1960–1988

	Number of Cities			
Population Size	1960	1970	1980	1988
1,000,000 or more	5	6	6	7
500,000–1,000,000	16	20	16	17
250,000–500,000	30	30	34	37
100,000–250,000	79	97	116	125
50,000–100,000	180	232	254	300
25,000–50,000	366	455	529	575
10,000–25,000	978	1,127	1,278	1,323
Under 10,000	16,434	16,699	16,892	16,868

Source: U.S. Bureau of the Census, *Statistical Abstract of the United States; 1991,* Washington, DC, 1991, p. 34.

CONTROVERSIES IN SOCIOLOGY

Are Cities Inherently Unhealthy?

A favorite Spanish toast is *salud, amor y pesetas:* "Health, love and money." Many add: "and the time to enjoy them all."

Increasingly, people recognize that their health is largely a matter of their own choosing. One choice we make is where to live and work, and most of us choose metropolitan areas. Computers and communications have in theory reduced our need for cities, yet we still cluster together to do business and socialize. Where we choose to be does seem to affect our health.

Over the years people have migrated to the big cities even though polls show people would rather live in small country towns. The post-World War II compromise was to live in suburbia and work in the city, but with commuting times up to three hours a day, the widespread separation of homes from workplace has become a serious problem that has increased stress—a negative for health.

In some ways cities are healthier than rural areas. For example, the quality of drinking water is high in most cities, while a significant fraction of rural dwellers drink from polluted wells. City dwellers have prompt access to nearby emergency health services; rural dwellers must resort to distant emergency rooms. While the air is polluted in many cities—ozone particularly continues to be a disturbing problem—country dwellers are more threatened by insecticides and ticks. Congestion is much higher in the cities—an annoyance, but one that contributes to a lower rate of traffic fatalities than in the faster-moving vehicles on country roads and highways.

Above all, country dwellers lack the range and challenge offered by the city's best jobs, as well as the companionship and constant stimulation of urban social and cultural life. From the perspective of mental health, cities offer diversion that potentially makes it easier to break dependence on cigarettes or alcohol. (Alcohol overindulgence is a common hazard in rural areas, especially during the inactive winters.)

John Tepper Marlin tried to determine which U.S. cities are the healthiest. A quick way to do this is to ask: "In which cities do people live the longest?" Marlin looked at cities in terms of how many people die in each metropolitan area in relation to the area's average age. Why is the average age important? Because when we identify the cities where people die at a higher rate, we come upon the unenlightening fact that many, like Fort Lauderdale or Tampa-

creates its own economic base in its shopping malls, office complexes, and decentralized manufacturing plants. Although the earlier wave of fringe development may have been an expansion of the city, the new areas may be anticity (Townsend, 1987). By and large, the people moving there are white, relatively wealthy, highly educated, and professional.

Why are so many people moving still further out from the central city? Recent research suggests a variety of reasons, but, on the whole, reasons that are not very surprising when we consider the suburban exodus of the early postwar era. When people are asked why they moved to the exurbs, typical responses are "retirement," "because my job is there or nearby," "because I have friends or family in the area," and "because I want to get out of the city" (Fuguitt, 1984).

Herbers suggests that the state of North Carolina could be the prototype for America's future.

St. Petersburg, seem simply to be the ones with more older inhabitants. For each year added to the median age of a city, the number of deaths increases by about 0.2 per 1000 residents.

To allow for the fact that some cities have a younger population, we have factored out the influence of age on mortality rates by calculating what is left over, the "residual death rate," when the age factor is removed. The interesting cities are the ones with high residuals in either direction. Miami, Bridgeport, Denver, Honolulu, Salt Lake City, Charlotte, and Anchorage have *lower* death rates than one would predict from their median ages. They are the healthiest cities. But Buffalo, Worcester, Toledo, Newark and Flint have *higher* death rates than one would expect. They are the least healthy cities.

Source: John Tepper Marlin, *The Livable Cities Almanac,* New York: HarperCollins Publishers, 1992.

TABLE 16.4

Health Rankings of U.S. Cities

Most Healthy		Least Healthy	
Metro Area	Residual Death Rate	Metro Area	Residual Death Rate
1. Honolulu	−3.42	1. Buffalo	4.23
2. Anchorage	−3.24	2. Toledo	3.70
3. Denver-Aurora-Boulder	−3.00	3. Worcester-Fitchburg	3.43
4. Charlotte	−2.84	4. Newark, N.J.	2.77
5. Bridgeport-Stamford	−2.63	5. Flint	2.72
6. Washington, D.C.	−2.48	6. Jersey City	2.53
7. Salt Lake City	−2.46	7. Springfield, Ma.	2.50
8. Seattle	−2.22	8. Portland, Me.	2.48
9. Miami-Hialeah	−2.04	9. Shreveport	2.14
10. Sacramento	−1.95	10. Pittsburgh	1.75

Source: John Tepper Marlin, *The Livable Cities Almanac,* New York: HarperCollins Publishers, 1991, pp. 2–3.

North Carolina offers scenic beauty alongside economic vitality, thanks in part to a conscious policy of dispersed development. To avoid the problems of large urban areas, the state decentralized the university system over sixteen campuses, improved roads even in the remotest areas, and encouraged scattered industrial development. As a result, North Carolina is a leading manufacturing state, but has no city larger than Charlotte, with 350,000 people (Herbers, 1986).

In short, the exurb, like the suburb before it, is seemingly another step in the quest for the American dream.

Urbanism has become an American way of life. Although the shape and form of metropolitan areas continue to change, their influence continues to dominate the manner in which we interact with our environment.

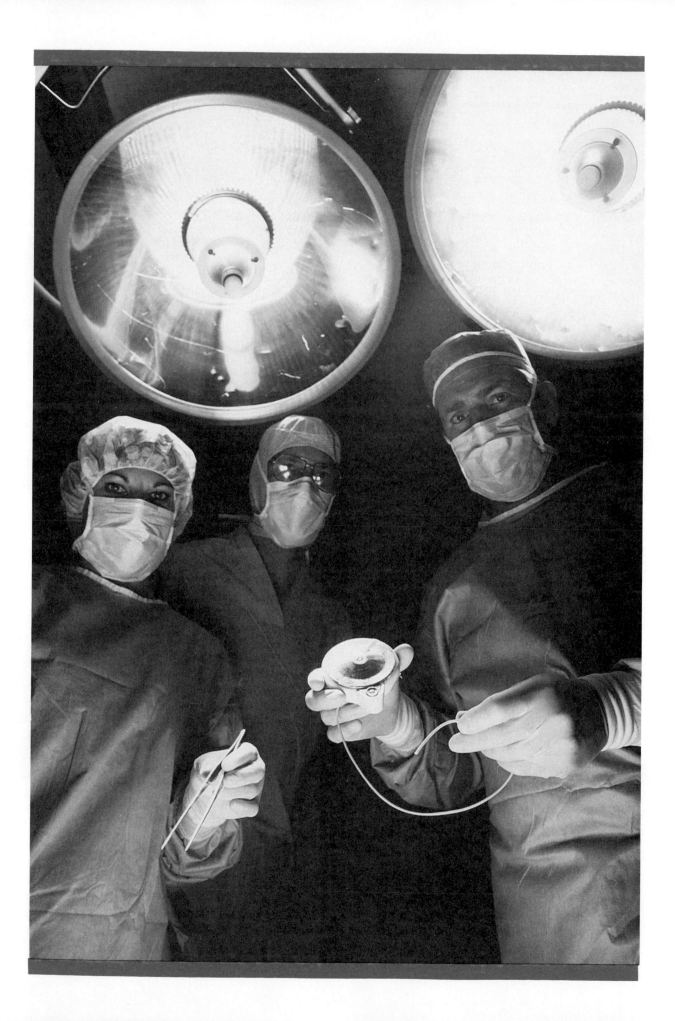

· 17 ·

Health and Health Care

The Experience of Illness

Health Care in the United States
   Gender and Health
   Race and Health
   Social Class and Health
   Age and Health

*Contemporary Health Care Issues
in the United States*
   Acquired Immunodeficiency Syndrome
   (AIDS)
   Health Insurance
   Preventing Illness

World Health Trends
   The Health of Infants and Children in
   Developing Countries

In the book, *Mother India*, anthropologist Katherine Mayo describes a woman being assisted in childbirth. The scene is a dark, unventilated room with a dirt floor in which a smoky fire burns to ward off evil spirits. The midwives, or *dhai*, come from the lowest class of "untouchables." As Mayo notes:

> If the delivery is at all delayed, the dhai is expected to explore the reason for the delay. She thrusts her long, unwashed hand, loaded with dirty rings and bracelets and encrusted with untold living contaminations, into the patient's body, pulling and twisting at what she finds there. If the delivery is long delayed and difficult . . . the dhai resorts to all her traditions. She kneads the patient with her fists, stands her against the wall and butts her with her head, props her upright on the bare ground, seizes her hands and shoves against her thighs with gruesome bare feet . . . Also, she makes balls of strange substances, such as hollyhock roots, or dirty string, or rags full of quince-seeds, or earth or earth mixed with cloves, butter and marigold flowers, or nuts, or spices—any irritant—and thrusts them into the uterus, to hasten the event. In some parts of the country goats' hair, scorpions' stings, monkey-skulls, and snakeskins are considered valuable applications (Cited in Goldman, 1991).

By this time many of you may be grimacing at the thought of such unsanitary and medically questionable procedures being applied to the birth of a child. Even though it may seem disgusting to Western eyes, it has validity for Hindus, and even makes the experience holy for them. Most likely, our antiseptic, high-tech delivery rooms seem terribly impersonal and intrusive to Indian peasants.

Medicine and health-care issues are intertwined with social and cultural customs and reflect the society they are a part of. In this chapter we will examine society's influence on health and illness, and the influence of health and illness on society. We will also examine health-care delivery systems.

THE EXPERIENCE OF ILLNESS

Illness not only involves the body, but it also affects the individual's social relationships, self-image, and behavior. Being defined as "sick" has consequences independent of any physiological effects. Talcott Parsons (1951) suggests that in order to prevent the potentially disruptive consequences of illness on a group or society, there exists a sick role. The **sick role** *is a shared set of cultural norms that legitimates deviant behavior caused by illness and channels the individual into the health care system.* According to Parsons, the sick role has four components. First, the sick person is excused from normal social responsibilities, except to the extent that they are supposed to do whatever is necessary to get well. Secondly, the sick person is not held responsible for his or her condition and is not expected to recover by an act of will. Third, the sick person must recognize that being ill is undesirable and must want to recover. Finally, the sick person is obligated to seek medical care and cooperate with the advice of the designated experts, notably the physicians. In this sense, sick people are not blamed for their illness, but they must work toward regaining their health.

The sick-role concept is based on the perspective that all roads lead to medical care. It tends to create a "doctor-centered" picture where the illness is viewed from outside the individual. Some (Strauss and Glaser, 1975; Schneider and Conrad, 1983) have suggested that the actual subjective experience of being sick should be examined more closely. These researchers suggest that we should focus more on individual perceptions of illness, one's interactions with others, and the effects of the illness on the person's identity.

HEALTH CARE IN THE UNITED STATES

The United States has the most advanced health care resources in the world. Health expenditures per person per year came to $2,354 in 1989, up from $205 per person in 1965. In 1988 we had 6,927 hospitals, 612,500 highly-trained physicians, and 1,648,000 nurses *(Statistical Abstract of the United States: 1991).* We are prepared to treat illlness and injury with the most modern techniques available. We can scan a brain for tumors, reconnect nerve tissues, reattach severed limbs through microsurgery, and eliminate diseases like poliomyelitis that crippled a president. (Table 17.1 reflects how the major medical advances have increased life expectancy and reduced infant and maternal deaths). We can do all this and much more; yet many would consider our health care system wholly inadequate to meet the needs of *all* Americans. These critics maintain that the current U.S. health care system is one that pays off only when the patient can pay.

The American health care system has been described as "... acute, curative, [and] hospital based ..." (Knowles, 1977). This statement implies that our approach to medicine is organized around

The United States has the most advanced health-care resources in the world, yet Americans are not the healthiest people.

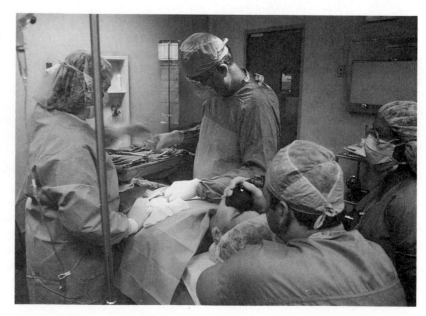

TABLE 17.1

Changes in U.S. Mortality Rates, 1920–1988

Mortality Data	1920	1950	1980	1985	1988
Death rates (per 1,000 population)	13.0	9.6	8.8	8.5	8.8
Life expectancy	54.1	68.2	73.7	74.9	74.9
Infant mortality (per 1,000 live births)	*	29.2	12.6	10.6	10.1
Maternal mortality (per 1,000 live births)	*	83.3	9.2	7.8	8.4

*Data not available
Source: *Mortality Statistics 1950,* Department of HEW, National Center for Health Statistics; *Monthly Vital Statistics Report,* 22(13), June 27, 1974; *U.S. National Health Survey,* Series B-10 and Series 10, No. 95., U.S. Department of Commerce, Census Bureau, *Current Population Reports,* and *Statistical Abstract of the United States: 1991,* Washington, D.C.: Government Printing Office, 1991.

the cure and/or control of serious diseases and repairing physical injuries, rather than "caring" for the sick or "preventing" disease. The American medical care system is highly technological, specialized, and increasingly centralized.

Medical care workers include some of the highest paid employees in our nation (physicians), and some of the lowest paid. About three-quarters of all medical workers are women, although the majority of doctors are men. Many of the workers are members of minority groups, and most come from lower-middle class backgrounds. The majority of the physicians are white and from the upper-middle class.

The medical care workforce can be pictured as a broad-based triangle, with a small number of highly-paid physicians and administrators at the very top. These people control the medical care services. As one moves toward the bottom of the triangle, there are increasing numbers of significantly lower-paid workers with little or no authority in the health care organization. This triangle is further layered with more than 300 licensed occupational categories of medical workers. There is practically no movement of workers from one category to another, because each requires its own specialized training and qualifications (Conrad and Kern, 1986).

Even with our large investment in health care, Americans are not the healthiest people in the world. The high death rate among African Americans causes the United States to rank 20th in infant mortality out of 22 members of the Organization for Economic Cooperation and Development. United States life expectancy ranks in the lower half of the scale. In addition, the health of U.S. citizens is heavily influenced by such factors as gender, race, social class, and age.

Gender and Health

You are probably aware of the striking differences in life expectancy among men and women. Male death rates exceed female death rates at all ages and for the leading causes of death such as heart disease, cancer, cerebrovascular diseases, accidents, and pneumonia. Women suffer from illness and disability more frequently than men, but their health problems are usually not as life threatening as those encountered by men. Women, of course, do suffer from most of the same diseases as men. The difference is at what point in their life they encounter them. For example, coronary heart disease is the leading cause of death for women after age 66, but for men it is the number one killer after age 39.

It appears that both biological and sociological factors contribute to the lower life expectancies of men. Men are born at a biological disadvantage to women, as seen by the higher mortality rates from the prenatal and neonatal (newborn) stages onward. Although the percentages may vary from year to year, the chances of dying during the prenatal stage are approximately 12 percent greater among males than females, and 130 percent greater during the newborn stage. Neonatal disorders common in males but not female babies include respiratory diseeases, digestive diseases, certain circulatory disorders of the aorta and pulmonary artery, and bacterial infections. Thus the male seems more vulnerable than the female, even before being exposed to the different social roles and stress situations of later life.

There are a number of sociological factors that also play an important role in different life expectancies for men and women. Men are more likely to place themselves in dangerous situations during both work and leisure. Men are concentrated in some of the most dangerous jobs, such as structural steel workers, lumberjacks, bank guards, coal miners, and state police. Alcohol use, high-speed driving, and participation in violent sports are also much higher among men than women (Cockerham, 1989). Therefore it should be no surprise that accidents cause more deaths among men than women.

While men have shorter life expectancies, women appear to be sick more often. Women have high rates of acute illnesses, such as infectious and parasitic diseases, digestive problems, and respiratory conditions, as well as chronic illnesses, such as hypertension, arthritis, diabetes, and colitis. Some have suggested that women may not be sick more often, but may in fact be more sensitive to bodily discomforts and more willing to report them to a doctor.

According to the National Institute of Mental Health, men are just as vulnerable to psychiatric problems as women. Earlier studies found higher rates among women, partly because alcoholism, drug dependence and antisocial personality disorders were not included. Still, there are some gender differences in mental disorders. Men, when emotionally disturbed, are likely to act out through drugs, liquor, and antisocial acts, while women display behaviors that show an internalization of their problems such as depression or phobias (Riche, 1987).

One concern for women is breast cancer. In January 1991, The American Cancer Society announced that a woman's odds of getting breast cancer had risen to 1 in 9. In the flood of news stories about the disease, women heard that breast cancer was inexplicably on the rise, and that the risk to young women was going up. Many women panicked after hearing this information, and talked about "time bombs" in their bodies.

Much of the fear was unwarranted, however. The 1-in-9 figure is the cumulative probability that any woman will develop breast cancer sometime between birth and age 110. A woman's risk during most of her life is much lower. Because breast cancer is most common in older women, it is incorrect to calculate risk without talking about age. Even women in their 80s do not face a 1-in-9 risk of getting breast cancer the next year. For women under age 50, the risk is closer to 1 in 1,000. In fact, even under the highest possible risk conditions, the probability of getting breast cancer in any given year is rarely greater than one percent (Blakeslee, 1992). This is just one example of the myths that appear surrounding health care issues.

Race and Health

There are significant differences in the health of the various racial groups in the United States. Asian Americans have had the best health profile, followed by whites. Blacks and Native Americans have the worst health profile.

There are glaring disparities in childhood mortality of the white and black populations. The infant mortality rate for blacks stood at 17.6 per 1,000 births in 1988. This was more than twice as high as the white infant mortality rate, which was 8.5 per 1,000. In some cities, such as Washington, D.C., the infant mortality rate is higher than in less developed countries such as Cuba, Costa Rica, and Chile (*Statistical Abstract of the United States: 1991*).

Many of the same problems that face mothers in less developed countries are factors in the high infant mortality rate among United States blacks. For example, black women giving birth are two and one-half times as likely as white mothers to be under age 18; nearly one third have less than twelve years of education, and 40 percent have not received prenatal care during the crucial first trimester of pregnancy. Consequently, low-birth-weight babies are more than twice as common among blacks than whites.

Life expectancies for whites and blacks also differ markedly. The black male has the lowest life expectancy of any racial category. In 1989, a black male baby had a life expectancy of 65.2 years. For the white male baby it was 72.6 years. The data for white and black females are 79.1 and 74.0 respectively (*Statistical Abstract of the United States: 1991*). (See Table 17.2.)

The health situation for black men is particularly bad. Black men age 15 to 29 die at a higher rate than any other group except those 85 and older.

TABLE 17.2

Expectation of Life at Birth, 1900 to 1989

Year	White Male	White Female	Black Male	Black Female
1900	46.6	48.7	32.5	33.5
1960	67.4	74.1	61.1	66.3
1970	68.0	75.6	60.0	68.3
1980	70.7	78.1	63.8	72.5
1989	72.6	79.1	65.2	74.0

Source: U.S. Bureau of the Census, *Current Population Reports*, Series P-25, No. 1018; U.S. Center for Health Statistics, *Vital Statistics of the United States*, annual; *Statistical Abstract of the United States: 1991*.

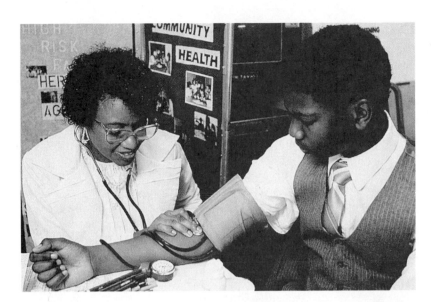

The black male has the lowest life expectancy of any racial group.

Over the last decade black men are the only group of Americans to actually have an average decrease of two months in life expectancy. Every other group, including black women, gained from three to six years (Coleman, 1992).

A major health problem among black Americans is hypertension or high blood pressure. Even though blacks constitute about 12 percent of the United States population, they account for 21 percent of the diagnosed cases. Between the ages of 25 and 44, hypertension kills black males 15.5 times more frequently than it does white males. Black women in that age category are seventeen times as likely to die of the disease (Cockerham, 1989).

Health statistics for blacks and whites also show higher ratios of deaths among blacks as a result of heart disease, cancer, diabetes, accidents, and homicide. AIDS is another disease that is killing African Americans at a disproportional rate. In 1990, 31.7 percent of all AIDS victims were black (*Statistical Abstract of the United States: 1991*).

The health situation for Hispanic Americans is also worse than that for Anglo Americans. Studies show that Hispanic Americans have a higher infant mortality rate, a shorter life expectancy, and higher rates of death from influenza, pneumonia, diabetes, and tuberculosis than whites. However, Hispanic death rates for heart disease and cancer are lower than those for whites.

Native Americans have shown an improvement in their overall health in the last forty years. Native Americans have the lowest cancer rates in the United States, and their mortality rates from heart disease are lower than the general population as well. There are other areas where Native Americans fare much worse than other groups. Their mortality rates from

diabetes are 2.3 times that of the general population. The complications from diabetes take a further toll by increasing the probability of kidney disease and blindness. Native Americans also suffer from high rates of venereal disease, hepatitis, tuberculosis, alcoholism and alcohol-related diseases such as cirrhosis of the liver, gastrointestinal bleeding, and dietary deficiency.

Native Americans have suicide rates 20 percent higher than the general population. Native American suicide victims are generally younger than those of other groups—their suicide rate peaks between ages 15 and 39. For the general population suicide peaks after age 40 (Cockerham).

Social Class and Health

Some of the health problems afflicting minority groups have a genetic basis—hypertension, diabetes and sickle cell anemia being prime examples. Many others, however, are the result of environmental factors related to poverty. Poverty contributes to disease and a shortened life span both directly and indirectly. It is estimated that some 25 million Americans do not have enough money to feed themselves adequately, and as a result suffer from serious nutritional deficiencies that lead to illness and death.

Poverty also produces living conditions that encourage illness. Pneumonia, influenza, alcoholism, drug addiction, tuberculosis, whooping cough, and even rat bites are much more common in poor minority populations than among middle-class ones. Inadequate housing, heating, and sanitation all contribute to these acute medical problems, as does the

Many health problems are the result of environmental factors related to poverty.

U.S. fee-for-service system that links medical care to the ability to pay.

An example of how social class can account for race differences with respect to health issues can be seen by examining the health data of Asian Americans. Asian Americans have the highest levels of income, education, and employment of any racial or ethnic minority in the United States, often exceeding the general white population. At the same time, the lowest age-adjusted mortality rates in the United States are among Asian Americans. Even though heart disease is the leading cause of death for Asians, mortality from this disease is less than that for whites and other minorities. Deaths from homicide and suicide are particularly low for Asian Americans. Infant mortality rates for Asian Americans ranging between five and six per 1,000 (depending on the group) are also lower than those for whites. Although infant mortality rates are only one indicator of health within a group, they are nevertheless an important measure of the quality of life experienced by that population.

Studies of life expectancy show that on every measure, social class influences longevity. A statisti-cal investigation (Antonovsky, 1972) of approximately thirty studies of mortality rates in the United States and Europe found that with the exception of heart disease, the upper socioeconomic classes had longer life expectancies. Since the time of this study, rates of coronary heart disease have declined dramatically. The decline has been the greatest among the upper middle classes. The result is that coronary heart disease is now also more concentrated among the poor. The lower classes have higher rates of obesity, smoking, stress, hypertension, engage in less exercise and have poorer diets (Susser et al., 1983). The inescapable conclusion appears to be that social class and life expectancy are correlated.

Age and Health

As advances in medical science prolong the life span of most Americans, the problem of medical care for the aged is becoming more acute. Since the turn of the century, the median age of Americans has risen from 22.9 to 32.6 in 1989. In 1900 there were only 3.1 million Americans aged 65 or older, a group that constituted a mere four percent of the total population. But by 1989 there were 31 million Americans aged 65 or older—a full 12.5 percent of the total population. This change in the age structure of the American population has had important consequences for health and health care in the United States.

At the turn of the twentieth century, more Americans were killed by pneumonia, influenza, tuberculosis, infections of the digestive tract, and other microorganism diseases than by any other cause. By comparison, only eight percent of the population died of heart disease and four percent of cancer. Today, this situation is completely reversed. Heart diseases, cancer, stroke and related disorders are now the three most common causes of death. These diseases are tied to the bodily deterioration that is a natural part of the aging process.

The result of these changes in health patterns is increased hospitalization for those over 65. Only one percent of all Americans are institutionalized in medical facilities. But of those 65 and older, five percent are institutionalized in convalescent homes, homes for the aged, hospitals, and mental hospitals. The elderly are 30 times as likely to be in nursing homes than are people under 65 and unfortunately their care is often wholly inadequate.

Little therapy is provided for nursing home residents: Only 15 percent are offered recreational therapy, 10 percent physical therapy, and six percent occupational therapy. For those who have been residents for over a year. 13 percent had not seen a physician for at least six months, and almost nine percent had not seen a physician for at least a year (Enos and Sultan, 1977).

CONTEMPORARY HEALTH CARE ISSUES IN THE UNITED STATES

The American health care system is among the best in the world. The United States invests a large amount of social and economic resources in medical care. It has some of the world's finest physicians, hospitals, and medical schools. It is no longer plagued by infectious dieseases, and is in the forefront in developing medical and technological advances for the treatment of disease and illness.

At the same time, there are a large number of issues that the American health care system must deal with. In this section we will discuss a few of them.

Acquired Immunodeficiency Syndrome (AIDS)

The Centers for Disease Control (CDC) defines AIDS as a specific group of diseases or conditions which are indicative of severe immunosuppression related to infection with the human immunodeficiency virus (HIV). As of May 31, 1991, the CDC reported a cumulative 179,136 AIDS cases in the United States. AIDS, a disease now known virtually everywhere, was only identified in 1981, and the retrovirus that causes it was only discovered in 1983. Yet this disease could transform the global future in ways no one imagined even a few years ago. It appears that the impact of this disease in the 1990s could be as great as a major war unless a vaccine or cure can be developed soon (see Figure 17.1 for U.S. AIDS deaths).

AIDS is caused by the human immunodeficiency virus (HIV). HIV is a member of the retrovirus family. HIV gradually incapacitates the immune system by infecting at least two types of white blood cells. The depletion of white blood cells leaves the infected person vulnerable to a multitude of infections and certain types of cancer. These infections and cancers rarely occur, or produce only mild illness, in individuals with normally functioning immune systems. The virus also causes disease directly by doing damage to the central nervous system.

HIV is transmitted through sexual contact, piercing the skin by HIV-contaminated instruments, transfusion of contamined blood products, and the transplantation of contaminated tissue. An infected

FIGURE 17.1

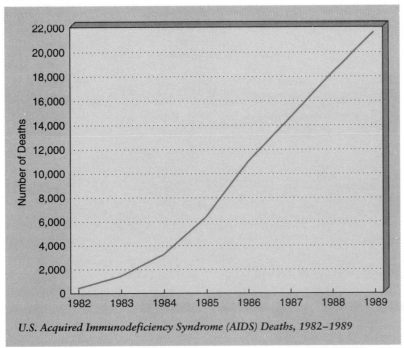

U.S. Acquired Immunodeficiency Syndrome (AIDS) Deaths, 1982–1989

Source: *Statistical Abstract of the United States: 1991*, Washington DC: United States Government Printing Office, 1991, p. 83.

mother can transmit the virus to her child before, during, or shortly after giving birth. There is no evidence that HIV is transmitted by casual contact.

According to the CDC, a part of the U.S. Public Health Service, the majority of AIDS cases have occurred among homosexual or bisexual males (58.9%) or heterosexual intravenous drug users (22.2%) (Centers for Disease Control, 1991). (See Figure 17.2.) The vast majority of those infected are young adults who do not realize they are infected, and the numbers are increasing dramatically. In six to ten years, half of those infected will have developed AIDS. Death follows within a few years after the disease emerges. Almost all of those infected will be contagious to others for the rest of their lives and will eventually die of AIDS-related diseases.

Initially, the majority of U.S. victims of AIDS were male homosexuals. AIDS, however, is not a gay disease; the virus that causes AIDS can be transmitted between any two people of any sex by the exchange of infected blood, semen, or vaginal secretions. Heterosexual transmission of the HIV virus is becoming another significant form of transmission. It was the fastest growing exposure category during 1989, with those types of cases increasing 36 percent over 1988.

The AIDS virus can also be transmitted nonsexually, as through the sharing of infected needles among drug users and accidental contact with infected blood. The spread of HIV among intravenous-drug users is now becoming a major cause of concern in many communities. The mayors of several cities have made attempts to institute a needle exchange program to stop the sharing of needles among drug users as a way of stopping the spread of HIV.

The Centers for Disease Control estimates that there are about one million people infected with the HIV virus in the United States, and they are expected to eventually develop AIDS within 10 to 15 years. Although AIDS is found throughout the United States, a number of cities have been particularly hard hit. In New York City, for example, which has 30 percent of all cases and deaths from the disease, the rates are ten times higher than nationally. In that city it is assumed that about one in three men under 50 may be infected. AIDS has become the leading cause of death in New York City for both men and women in their thirties (Centers for Disease Control, Quarterly Data Report, 1992).

Infection through drug abuse has made the disease a severe problem in prison. Estimates are that AIDS is fourteen times higher in state and federal prisons than on the outside. There are 202 AIDS cases per 100,000 inmates compared to 14.65 cases per 100,000 people in the general population (Weiner and Anno, 1992).

As the death rate from AIDS increases it could have an impact on life expectancy figures. The total deaths of young men already infected could reach one million within the next decade, which would be greater than the deaths from all our wars.

AIDS is not just a U.S. problem though. The World Health Organization (WHO) has reports on AIDS from 113 countries. Africa appears to be particularly hard hit with over six million cases. That is 60 percent of the world's cases in a continent with 12 to 13 percent of the population. Central African countries, such as Zaire and Uganda, have

FIGURE 17.2

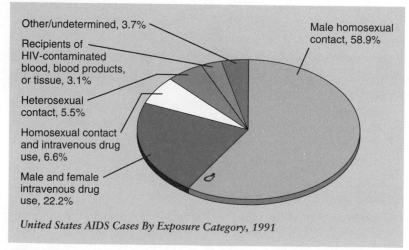

Other/undetermined, 3.7%

Recipients of HIV-contaminated blood, blood products, or tissue, 3.1%

Heterosexual contact, 5.5%

Homosexual contact and intravenous drug use, 6.6%

Male and female intravenous drug use, 22.2%

Male homosexual contact, 58.9%

United States AIDS Cases By Exposure Category, 1991

Source: Centers for Disease Control, *HIV/AIDS Surveillance Report,* June 1991.

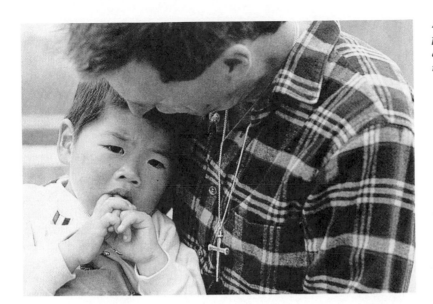

AIDS can be transmitted from parents to children. This child acquired the disease from his mother.

the highest incidence rates with the Eastern African countries of Kenya and Tanzania following. As many as one million children have been infected by the disease and two million have been orphaned because of it.

Unlike the United States, the predominant means of HIV infection in Africa has been through heterosexual contact. The male-to-female AIDS case ratio in Africa is virtually one to one. In the United States nine men get it for every one woman. Nearly 90 percent of AIDS cases in the United States thus far have occurred among homosexual/bisexual males or intravenous drug users. In Africa, AIDS patients rarely report intravenous drug use or homosexuality.

Asia is the next area of the world that is likely to feel the AIDS crisis. By some estimates, by the mid-1990s there will be more HIV-infected Asians than HIV-infected people in all of the industrialized world, including the United States, Canada, Western Europe, Australia, and New Zealand.

Asian countries have approached the disease in ways ranging from draconian measures to denial. Malaysia, with about 1,400 known HIV carriers in a population of 18 million, has resorted to rounding up the HIV-infected and putting them into isolation camps, similar to leper colonies. Other Malaysian plans include issuing special identification cards to HIV carriers, and beatings and lengthy prison sentences to those caught bringing AIDS-infected prostitutes into the country.

The Japanese tend to think of AIDS as an affliction of foreigners and refer to it as *taigan no kaji*—"the fire across the river." Public awareness and government concern about AIDS is still very low. The country is starting to put money into AIDS research and screening for HIV carriers, but there is no massive public education campaign to explain how the disease is transmitted and how it can be avoided. In Japan, there is a great stigma attached to the disease, victims are treated as pariahs and shunned by family and friends.

Other Asian countries where the AIDS virus is spreading quickly—notably India, the Philippines, Sri Lanka, and Indonesia—are simply too poor, or have too many other pressing social ills, to cope with the disease. With 55 percent of the world's population, Asia is likely to have the greatest number of AIDS victims by the next century (Nickerson, 1991).

The World Health Organization estimates that the total worldwide deaths from AIDS in the 1990s could be 50 million. The number infected could double several more times after that, particularly in the poorer countries, before vaccines or drugs are developed.

The Black Death swept through Europe along the trade routes from Italy to Sweden between 1347 and 1350, killing some 30 million people out of a population of 75 million in four years. Some believe AIDS has the potential to do the same. The main difference with AIDS is that its long period of incubation could cause it to be the Black Death in slow motion (Platt, 1987).

The question of when the AIDS epidemic will level off is the crucial issue in the total impact of AIDS. If AIDS continues its present course, most of humanity will still survive, but by then we will see the development of new social structures and new behaviors.

TAKING THE SOCIOLOGICAL PERSPECTIVE

How Did the AIDS Epidemic Begin?

Some gay-bashers believe it is God's way of punishing homosexuals. Some Africans suspect it is just another of the white man's weapons of genocide. Others have suggested that it was hatched in a biological-weapons laboratory. There has been no shortage of theories about the origins of the virus that caused the current worldwide AIDS epidemic, but most have ranged from truly bizarre to scientifically implausible at best.

African monkeys are almost certainly the source of the deadly virus. Just how the virus made the leap from its simian host to people is still hotly debated, however, and the most likely explanations are far more complex, involving shifts in African society that turned an isolated disease into a plague.

Researchers got their first hint that monkeys were the source of the AIDS virus in the mid-1980s, when it was discovered that a group of Asian monkeys used for biomedical research had fallen ill with a virus picked up from other captive monkeys from Africa. The germ turned out to be simian AIDS virus, and subsequent research showed that in the wild at least six species of African monkeys carry their own strain of the virus. It does not make the African monkeys sick, but it proved deadly to the Asian monkeys.

Though researchers initially resisted the idea that human AIDS also came from African monkeys, that fact now seems well established. In 1991, convincing evidence was presented that the simian virus that infects sooty mangabeys, a type of monkey found in West Africa, carries virtually the same genetic material as HIV-2, one of the two strains of human AIDS virus.

One theory of how the virus traveled from monkeys to humans is based on reports that certain West African tribes injected monkey blood into their backs and thighs to heighten sexual arousal. Other researchers have referred to bizarre (not to mention unsuccessful) attempts by European doctors in the 1920s to boost the flagging sexual powers of aging men with injections of monkey testicles.

The most compelling explanation for the spread of the AIDS virus is cultural as well as biological. The actual transfer of the virus from monkeys to humans may have involved something as prosaic as a monkey bite or a monkey hunter's nick on the hand while butchering his quarry. Some experts believe that AIDS might have died out with that hunter, or perhaps with his isolated village, had profound cultural changes not come to Africa. Over the last 30 years, the population of sub-Saharan Africa, the region hardest hit by AIDS, became increasingly urban. As in the United States, infection rates appear far higher in African cities than in rural areas. Urbanization brings many diverse people together. It appears that the AIDS virus is approximately 40 years old. That places its origin right at the beginning of the period of rapid African urban development.

As with the history of plagues, tracing the precise movements of the AIDS virus through various populations is exceedingly difficult. In the end, the origin of AIDS is not the real problem; the real problem is where the disease is going.

Source: Shannon Brownlee, Karen Schmidt, and Eric Ransdell, "Origin of a Plague," U.S. News and World Report, March 30, 1992, p. 50.

Health Insurance

Most people pay for their health services through some form of health insurance. In 1989 Americans paid almost $200 billion in insurance premiums (Statistical Abstract of the United States: 1991). Poor people, however, cannot afford these premiums or the out-of-pocket expenses required before insurance coverage begins. They receive coverage through government-sponsored Medicare and Medicaid programs.

Most of the money spent on medical care in the United States comes by way of third-party payments as differentiated from direct or out-of-pocket payments. Third-party payments are those made through some form of public or private insurance or charitable organization. Essentially, insurance is a form of "mass financing" that ensures that medical care providers will be paid and people will be able to obtain the medical care they need. Insurance involves collecting small amounts of money from a large number of people. That money is put into a pool, and when any of the insured people get sick, that pool pays for the medical services.

The United States has two types of private insurance organizations: nonprofit tax-exempt Blue Cross and Blue Shield plans and for-profit commercial insurance companies. Blue Cross and Blue Shield emerged out of the Depression of the 1930s as a mechanism to provide for the payment of medical bills to hospitals and physicians. People made regular monthly payments, and if they became sick, their hospital bills were paid directly by the insurance plan. Blue Cross and Blue Shield originally set the cost of insurance premiums by what was called "community rating," giving everybody within a community the chance to purchase insurance at the same price. Commercial insurance companies appeared after World War II and based their prices on "experience rating." Experience rating bases the price of insurance premiums on the statistical likelihood of the individual needing medical care. People more likely to need medical care are charged more than those less likely to need it. Eventually Blue Cross and Blue Shield had to follow the path of the commercial insurers in order to compete.

One unfortunate result of the use of experience ratings was that those who most needed insurance coverage—the old and the sick—were least able to afford or obtain it. Medicare and Medicaid were created by Congress in 1965 to help with this problem. Medicare pays for medical care for people over sixty-five years of age, while Medicaid pays for the care of those who qualify as too poor to pay their own medical costs.

Even with these forms of government insurance, many people believe the way health care is delivered in the United States produces problems. Critics point to the fact that the United States is the only leading industrial nation that does not have an organized, centrally planned health care delivery system.

In addition, despite attempts to form comprehensive national health insurance that would guarantee all Americans access to medical care, no plan as yet exists. The care that the poor receive is inferior to that received by the more affluent. Many doctors will not accept Medicare or Medicaid assignments, requiring patients to reimburse them for the difference between the insurance coverage and their bill. Moreover, most doctors will not practice in poor neighborhoods, so the poor are relegated to overcrowded, demeaning clinics staffed by young, inexperienced doctors and residents. Under conditions like these it is no surprise that the poor generally wait longer before seeking medical care than do more affluent patients, and many seek medical advice only when they are seriously ill and intervention is already too late.

The American Medical Association has been a leading opponent of national health insurance. In essence, because of pressures from the American Medical Association and other sectors of the medical establishment, the United States health care system focuses primarily on benefits received by doctors. The fee-for-service system of remuneration gives doctors a vested interest in pathology rather than

Critics of the U.S. health care system claim it only pays off when the patient can pay.

in good health. Instead of emphasizing preventive medical care, the American health care system emphasizes cure (Friedman and Friedman, 1980).

▶ One problematic result of this orientation is the very uneven geographic distribution of doctors and the overabundance of specialists. In 1988, for example, only 11.8 percent of the nation's physicians were in general practice, even though many more general practictioners are needed to treat the total population, especially the poor and elderly. This is partially due to the fact that general practitioners earn less than specialists. In 1988 the average gross earning for a general practitioner was $143,900. For an obstetrician, it was $317,700, and for a plastic surgeon, it was $398,800 (*Statistical Abstract of the United States, 1991*).

Preventing Illness

Our cultural values cause us to approach health and medicine from a particular vantage point. In the United States we are conditioned to distrust nature and assume that aggressive medical procedures work better than other approaches. This situation has caused about one quarter of all births in the United States to be by Caesarean section. The rate of hysterectomy in the United States is twice that in England and three times that in France. Sixty percent of these hysterectomies are performed on women under 44. Our rate of coronary bypass operations is five times that of England. We tend to be a can-do society in which doctors emphasize the risk of doing nothing, and minimize the risk of doing something. This approach is then coupled with the fact that Americans want to be in perfect health. The result is far more surgery being performed than in any other country. We tend to think that if something is removed, then our health will return (Payer, 1988).

Yet, our experience with heart disease has shown that significant benefits can be obtained from such things as changing diets and engaging in healthier practices. At the moment, the best way to deal with the AIDS crisis is through prevention techniques that limit the spread of the illness.

If the health care system is to reorient itself from an approach of "cure" to "prevention," it must place greater emphasis on sociological issues. Illness and disease are socially as well as biophysiologically produced. During the last century, the medical system has devoted a great deal of effort to combating germs and viruses that cause specific illnesses. We are starting to see limitations to this viewpoint. We must now investigate environments, lifestyles, and social structures for the causes of disease with the same commitment we have shown to investigating germ theory. This is not to say we should ignore established biomedical knowledge, but rather we should focus greater attention on the interaction of social environments and human physiology.

At first glance most of the factors that come forth when thinking about preventing disease are little more than healthy habits. For example, if people adopt better diets, with more whole grains and less red meat, sugar, and salt, and stop smoking, exercise regularly and keep their weight down, they will surely prevent much illness. While these things are important in preventing illness, we must also think of prevention of illness as involving at least three levels: medical, behavioral, and structural (see Table 17.3). Medical prevention is directed at the individual's body; behavioral prevention is directed at changing people's behavior; and structural prevention is directed at changing the society or environments within which people work and live.

We hear a great deal about trying to prevent disease on a behavioral level. While this is an important level of prevention, we have little knowledge about *how* to change people's unhealthy habits. Education is not sufficient. Most people are aware of the health risks of smoking or not wearing seat belts, yet roughly 30 percent of Americans smoke and 80 percent do not use seat belts regularly.

TABLE 17.3

Types of Illness Prevention

Level of Prevention	Type of Intervention	Site of Intervention	Examples of Intervention
Medical	Biophysiological	Individual's body	Vaccinations; Medical procedures
Behavioral	Social psychological	Individual's behavior or lifestyle	Change of habits or behaviors
Structural	Sociological	Social structure and social systems	Legislative conrols; Environmental changes

Source: Peter Conrad and Rochelle Kern, eds., *The Sociology of Health and Illness*, 2d ed., New York: St. Martins Press, 1986.

Sometimes individual habits are responses to complex social situations, such as coping mechanisms to stressful and alienating work environments. Behavioral approaches to prevention focus on the individual and place the burden of change on the individual.

The structural factors related to health care in the United States do not get as much attention as the medical and behavioral factors. We have discussed the issues of gender, race, and class earlier in this chapter. Increasingly, people are realizing that health care and the prevention of illness take place on a number of different levels.

WORLD HEALTH TRENDS

The World Health Organization defines **health** as *"a state of complete mental, physical, and social well-being."* This concept may appear straightforward, but it does not easily lend itself to measurement. Consequently, to describe the state of health in the world, we must look at trends. When we look at human health from this perspective we find that the twentieth century has seen unprecedented gains in health and survival. On a worldwide basis, the average life expectancy for a newborn baby more than doubled from 30 years in 1900 to 64 years in 1989. For a country like China this has meant moving from conditions at the turn of the century, when scarcely 60 percent of newborns reached their fifth birthday, to the present, when more than 60 percent can expect to reach their 70th birthday.

Health advances in some countries have reached the point where it appears that the population is approaching the upper limit of average life expectancy. In Japan, where life expectancy is 79 years, a newborn has only a four in 1,000 chance of dying before its first birthday, and a less than a one in 1,000 risk of dying by age 40.

Unfortunately, the same cannot be said for less developed countries. More than 300 million people live in twenty-four countries where life expectancy is less than 50 years. In these countries one out of ten newborns die by age one. In some African villages, deaths among infants and young children occur ten times more frequently than among the aged.

Currently 80 percent of the world's population does not have access to any health care. Malnutrition, parasitic, and infectious diseases are the principal causes of death and disability in the poorer nations. The problems these diseases cause are largely preventable and most of these conditions could be dramatically reduced at a relatively modest cost.

The Health of Infants and Children in Developing Countries

When we look at infant and child health from a global perspective, we find that deaths among children is overwhelmingly a problem of the developing countries in Africa, Asia, and Latin America. These countries account for 98 percent of the world's deaths among children under five. To make matters

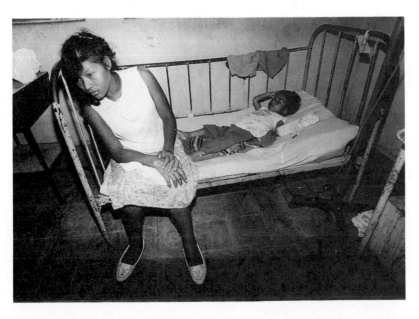

More than 300 million people live in 24 countries where life expectancy is less than 50 years.

CONTROVERSIES IN SOCIOLOGY

Is Disease Caused by Our State of Mind?

Sociologists and psychologists often differ in terms of their views on the causes of disease. In this section psychologist Blair Justice suggests that disease is the result of our state of mind. Sociologist Arthur Frank, on the other hand, believes that these disease theories merely provide comfort to those who are not sick and help them to deal with the unpredictable nature of health.

Psychologist Blair Justice believes "an expanded explanation of disease is emerging that is 'bio-psycho-social,' meaning that a person's mind, body, and environment together determine whether he or she gets sick. Disease, he notes, is not so much the effect of noxious, external forces—the 'bugs,' both literal and figurative, in our lives—as it is the faulty efforts of our minds and bodies to deal with them. Most of the 'bugs,' the literal kind, already reside in our bodies. When our responses to problems in life are excessive or deficient, the central nervous system and hormones act on our immune defenses in such a way that the microbes aid and abet disease. The balance is upset between us and the resident pathogens."

Justice notes that "if we have poor coping skills, deficient social support and high stress, then the internal balance of our bodies may be easily upset and our resistance lowered. Illness or disease occurs more from our vulnerability than from external agents that are 'the cause' of our health problems. The more vulnerable we are, the more risk we run of getting sick. The factors that place us at risk range from our attitudes and appraisals in coping with stress to the kind of food we eat and the genes we inherit."

Sociologist Arthur Frank believes that those who tell people who are sick that their disease is caused by their personalities present themselves as comforters, but are really accusers. Society has aways had personality theories to explain the diseases it feared and did not understand. The healthy want to believe that disease does not "just happen." They want to believe that they control their health and that they earned it. Those who are sick must have done something wrong, which the healthy can then avoid. The sick person must have participated in illness by choosing to have a disease-prone personality. Otherwise illness is an intolerable reminder of how risky life is.

Frank notes that if we believe that the ill person has a disease-prone personality, then the world is less fragile, less risky, for everyone else. Even many ill people would rather believe they have done something wrong than believe disease just happened to them; guilt may be preferable to uncertainty.

Personality theories will persist, because they have a payoff for everyone. On the one hand the ill person is accused, but on the other she is comforted. Perhaps by changing her personality she can recover; it is never too late. Those around the ill person can rest assured that she got sick because she was that sort of person, different from themselves. The genius of the disease-prone personality argument Frank notes is that it means nothing has to change. The fault and the fear are safely contained, locked up inside the patient. Cigarette companies stay in business, polluters can pollute and those who enjoy good health can believe they have earned it. Only the ill are left to feel guilty.

Source: Blair Justice, *Who Gets Sick*, Los Angeles: Jeremy P. Tarcher, 1988. Arthur Frank, *At the Will of the Body: Reflections on Illness*, Boston: Houghton Mifflin, 1991.

---

worse, UNICEF estimates that of the 14.5 million infant and child deaths in 1990, 95 percent were preventable. Let us examine the causes for these deaths.

MATERNAL HEALTH   Infant and child survival is critically dependent upon the nurturing provided by the mother during pregnancy and childhood. When an expectant mother suffers from illness or malnutrition during pregnancy, it is more likely that she will have a low birth-weight baby. In developing countries, about 17 percent of the births involve low birth-weight. In addition to maternal malnutrition, other causes of low birth-weight babies are exces-

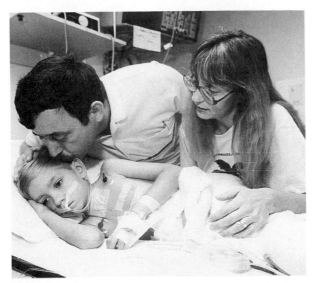

Unlike developing countries where 95 percent of infant and child deaths are preventable, a sick child in the United States will usually receive proper medical care.

sively heavy work, malaria infection, severe anemia related to an iron deficient diet, and hookworm infestation.

MATERNAL AGE   Infants are at high health risk if their mothers are in their teens or over age 40, if they have had more than seven births, or when the interval between births is less than two years. The interval between births is the most important factor in infant and child mortality. Infants born to mothers at less than two-year intervals between births were 80 percent more likely to die than children born at birth intervals of two to three years.

This information suggests that family planning programs that also discourage early childbearing can substantially reduce infant and child mortality by preventing births to high-risk mothers. When childbearing is spread out, the woman has more time and energy to devote to her own health and the care of her other children.

MATERNAL EDUCATION   Children's chances of surviving improve as their mother's education increases. An increase of three years of education produces 20 to 30 percent declines in the mortality of children under age five. A mother's education affects her child's health in a number of ways. Better educated mothers know more about good diets and hygiene. These mothers are also more likely to use maternal and child health services—specifically prenatal care, delivery care, childhood immunization, and other therapies (Cleland and Ginneken, 1988).

BREAST-FEEDING   In developing countries it is much safer for infants to be breastfed during the first six months of life than to be bottlefed. Bottlefed babies are three to six time more likely to experience respiratory infections or diarrhea than breastfed babies. Bottlefeeding has been introduced into developing countries by hospitals that are trying to follow Western practices, as well as commercial concerns that aggressively promote breastmilk substitutes. The World Health Organization and UNICEF have tried to combat this trend with limited success.

In this chapter we have seen that just as disease influences society, so do social factors affect the manifestation of disease. There are patterns in the incidence and rate of disease, and there are always reasons why one group (rather than another) falls victim to an illness, even if those reasons are not immediately apparent. Genetic and constitutional factors play an important role in the incidence of disease, but so does the interaction of social and cultural factors.

CHAPTER

• 18 •

Collective Behavior and Social Movements

Theories of Collective Behavior
  Contagion (Mentalist) Theory
  Emergent Norm Theory
  Convergence Theory
  Value-Added Theory

Crowds: Concentrated Collectivities
  Attributes of Crowds
  Types of Crowds
  The Changeable Nature of Crowds

Dispersed Collective Behavior
  Fads and Fashions
  Rumors
  Public Opinion
  Mass Hysterias and Panics

Social Movements
  Relative Deprivation Theory
  Resource-Mobilization Theory
  Types of Social Movements
  The Life Cycle of Social Movements

Under an eerie sky choked with smoke, Los Angeles officials fought to regain control of their city after three days of widespread violence that left 53 dead and more than 2,200 injured.

Ignited by the acquittal of four white Los Angeles police officers in the beating of black motorist Rodney King, mobs looted and burned parts of their own poor urban neighborhoods despite repeated official appeals for order. The beating of King had been videotaped by a bystander and the 81 seconds were broadcast repeatedly nationwide.

The rioting began two hours after a mostly white suburban jury acquitted the officers of assault charges in the March 1991 beating, and the violence spread through the night. It was the worst outbreak of violence in the city since Watts went up in flames in 1965.

State officials called in 4,000 National Guard troops and dispatched many into South Central Los Angeles, where hundreds of fires gutted houses, stores, and cars. Looters, undeterred by daylight or television cameras, stole food, videos, car tires, and anything else they could carry.

Mayor Tom Bradley declared a dusk-to-dawn curfew for the entire city, which was under a state of emergency. "We cannot and will not tolerate any violence," Bradley said at a news conference. "We are going to enforce the law."

However, large numbers of people wandered the streets after the curfew began. Wide-scale looting continued, and the violence showed little sign of abating.

Parts of the city all but shut down. Officials canceled bus service, rerouted some flights and closed portions of freeways. Thousands of schools and businesses closed, and professional sports events were postponed.

A crowd becomes a social entity greater than the sum of its parts.

How can we begin to explain the violence, looting and hysteria of the Los Angeles riots? These actions fall under the general category of collective behavior.

By this time you have probably noticed that sociology makes us aware of the fact that most social behavior is patterned and follows agreed upon rules. We may interact with each other based on specific social statuses and roles, or participate in rituals of social solidarity. At other times, however, it appears that people act in ways that seem to escape the control of common expectations, and their behavior strikes us as bizarre and unpredictable. How can we begin to explain the violence and hysteria of the Salem witch trials? Or the willingness of people to participate in a mass wedding ceremony to spouses they hardly know? These actions fall under the general category of collective behavior.

Collective behavior refers to relatively spontaneous social actions that occur when people respond to unstructured and ambiguous situations. Collective behavior has the potential for causing the unpredictable, and even the improbable, to happen. Collective actions are capable of unleashing surprisingly powerful social forces that catch us by surprise and change our lives, at times temporarily, but at other times even permanently. We tend to remember the more dramatic forms of collective behavior: riots, mass hysterias, lynchings, or panics. Fads, fashion, and rumor, however, are also forms of collective behavior.

THEORIES OF COLLECTIVE BEHAVIOR

There are two ways of approaching the topic of collective behavior. We could think of such collective behavior as riots, demonstrations, and religious revivals as a means for improving society. These actions provide the needed push to overcome the inertia of established institutions in dealing with human problems. Social reform comes about when the system is pushed by the pressure of large groups of people. Thus it can be argued that the civil rights legislation of the 1960s occurred only because legislators were pushed by the protest demonstrations of that period.

On the other hand, we can argue that collective behavior is pathological and destructive to the fabric of society. Gustav LeBon espoused this view when he viewed "the crowd" as something of a reversion to the bestial tendency in human nature. People are swept away in the contagious excitement of the crowd. Civilized members of society who would never engage in antisocial acts as individuals, engage in just such acts under the cloak of anonymity provided by the crowd.

In the next section we will examine several theories devised to account for crowd behavior. These include the contagion (or "mentalist") theory, the emergent norm theory, the convergence theory, and the value-added theory.

Contagion (Mentalist) Theory

Gustave Le Bon (1841–1931) was a French sociologist whose major interest was the role played by collective behavior in shaping historical events such as the storming of the Bastille in 1789, a turning point in the launching of the French Revolution. In 1895 Le Bon published his classic work *The Psychology of Crowds* (1960), in which he argued that once individuals experience the sense of anonymity in a crowd, they are transformed. Hence, they think, feel, and act quite differently than they would alone. They acquire a crowd mentality, lose their characteristic inhibitions, and become highly receptive to group sentiments. Concerns for proper behavior or norms disappear, and individuals give up their personal moral responsibilities to the will of the crowd. When this happens, the crowd becomes a social entity greater than the sum of its individual parts.

Herbert Blumer (1946) explains the contagion that sweeps through a crowd as what he calls the "circular reaction" that typifies crowd behavior. In his view, a crowd begins as a collectivity of people more or less waiting for something to happen. Sooner or later an "exciting event" stirs them, and people react to it without the kind of caution and critical judgment they would ordinarily use if they were experiencing the event alone. Individuals become excited, the excitement spreads, the original event is invested with even greater emotional significance, and people give in to the "engulfing mood, impulse, or form of conduct." In this manner, a crowd can spiral out of control, as when casual onlookers observing the arrest of a drunken driver are transformed into a crowd of rioters.

There are a number of problems with the contagion theory. Le Bon did not specify under what conditions contagion would sweep through a crowd. In addition, the theory does not account for events that could limit the spread of contagion or for the fact that contagion may affect only one portion of a crowd. Finally, research has not borne out Le Bon's basic premise that the average person can be transformed through crowd dynamics from a civilized being into an irrational and violent person.

Emergent Norm Theory

Rather than viewing the formation of crowd sentiments and behavior as inherently irrational, as Le Bon and Blumer did, Ralph H. Turner (1964), as well as other sociologists, espouse the emergent norm theory of collective behavior. This theory implies that crowd members have different motives for participating in collective behavior. They acquire common standards by observing and listening to one another. In this respect, contagion does play a role in establishing the crowd's norms. A few leaders may help in the emergence of these norms by presenting the crowd with a particular interpretation of events. However, even without leaders, the crowd still can develop shared expectations about what behavior is appropriate.

The emergent norm theory provides the basis for analyzing the factors that push a crowd in one direction or another. If people bring with them into a crowd situation a set of expectations about the norms that are likely to be established, then the emergence of such norms will not be just a matter of the collective processes of the moment (Lang and

According to Herbert Blumer, a crowd is a collectivity of people more or less waiting for something to happen. Eventually something stirs them, and they react without the kind of caution and critical judgment they would normally use.

Lang, 1961). Thus, many hockey fans attending Bruins games in Boston Garden expect to vent hostile feelings against opposing players, expect that members of the crowd will throw beer cans and other debris, and expect that management will encourage this fanaticism by playing "Charge!" music on the public address system, by flashing violence-oriented slogans on the scoreboard, and by selling alcoholic beverages. In other words, the fans expect to become frenzied. Predictably, fights often occur in the stands; sportswriters from out of town are subjected to abuse, and players from opposing teams are harassed. As one journalist put it, "A sense of hostility ... pervades the arena ..." (Fischler, 1980).

Convergence Theory

Whereas contagion theory assumes that a crowd mentality arises when people are gathered in a specific area and interact in ways that produce common perceptions and common behavior, **convergence theory** *views collective behavior as the outcome of situations in which people with similar characteristics, attitudes, and needs are drawn together*. In contrast with contagion theory, it is not the crowd situation that produces unusual behavior but, rather, that certain kinds of people who are predisposed to certain kinds of actions have been brought together. Consequently, if violent or unusual collective behavior takes place during and after a rap or heavy metal concert, it is because people who are predisposed to this type of behavior have been drawn to the event.

Convergence theory is helpful because it stresses the role of the individual and points out that no matter how powerful a group's influence may be, not everyone will respond to it. Therefore, it is unlikely that a group of conservative bankers attending the above concert would be part of any unusual collective action.

The problem with convergence theory is that it cannot explain why crowds often pass through a number of stages, from disorganized milling to organized action against specific targets. If the participants' characteristics do not change, what produces the changes in crowd behavior? Convergence theory also does not tell us which events will ignite a crowd with common characteristics into action and which events will thwart collective behavior.

Value-Added Theory

Of all the attempts to understand collective behavior, the value-added theory of sociologist Neil Smelser (1962) is in many ways the most comprehensive. It attempts to explain whether collective behavior will occur and what direction it will take. Smelser suggests that when combined, the following six conditions shape the outcome of collective behavior:

1. *Structural conduciveness.* This refers to the conditions that may promote or encourage collective behavior. Structural conduciveness is tied to the arrangement of the existing social order. For example, in the chapter opening example of the Los Angeles riots, the fact that the news media were quick to report on the progress of the trial and its outcome was important. The people in the South Central Los Angeles black neighborhoods were also able to gauge each other's reactions to the verdict. All of this provided a fertile ground for collective action.

2. *Structural strain.* When a group's ideals conflict with its everyday realities, structural strain occurs. For the black community in Los Angeles the disparity between their hopes and dreams and the reality of their lives produced structural strain.

3. *Growth and spread of a generalized belief.* People develop explanations for the structural strains under which they must struggle to exist. When these explanations are clearly expressed and widely shared, collective behavior may take the shape of well-organized social movements, such as the civil rights and labor movements. The less clearly these explanations are expressed or the more competing explanations that exist, the more likely it is that collective behavior will emerge in an unstructured form, a riot, for example. In the Los Angeles black community the widely shared beliefs included a strong resentment of the police and the hope that a guilty verdict for the four policemen accused of beating Rodney King would be forthcoming. At the same time many people suspected that an all-white jury would not produce a fair verdict for a black man. Once the outcome of the trial was known and the fact that any other types of structured collective behavior were not likely to change the verdict, conditions leading to the riot began to appear.

4. *Precipitating factors.* In all cases of collective behavior there is an event, or a related set of events, that triggers a collective response. In the Los Angeles riots, it was the news of the not-guilty verdict that caused people to unite and take action.

5. *Mobilization for action.* A group of people must be mobilized or organized into taking action.

When there are no previously recognized leaders to take charge, a group is easily swayed by its more boisterous members. In Los Angeles, the not-guilty verdict mobilized people into unplanned, expressive acts that included scattered fires, looting, and random destruction. By the time community leaders attempted to intervene, the riot had escalated out of control.

6. *Mechanism of social control.* At this point the course that collective behavior follows depends on the various ways those in power respond to the action in order to reestablish order. In the Los Angeles riot, Mayor Bradley imposed a curfew and had the National Guard brought in, while President George Bush sent in federal troops. This show of force was eventually enough to quell the riot.

According to Smelser, the final outcome of collective behavior depends on how each of the six determinants has built on the previous one. Each becomes a necessary condition and an important part of the next determinant.

CROWDS: CONCENTRATED COLLECTIVITIES

A crowd is a temporary concentration of people who focus on some thing or event but who also are attuned to one another's behavior. There is a magnetic quality to a crowd: It attracts passersby who often will interrupt whatever they are doing to join. Think, for example, of the crowds that gather "out of nowhere" at fires or accidents. Crowds fascinate social scientists because crowds always have within them the potential for unpredictable behavior and group action that erupts quickly and often seems to lack structure or direction—either from leaders or from institutionalized norms of behavior.

Attributes of Crowds

In his study *Crowds and Power* (1978), social psychologist Elias Canetti attributed to crowds the following traits:

1. *Crowds are self-generating.* Crowds have no natural boundaries. When boundaries are imposed—for example, by police barricades intended to isolate a street demonstration—there is an ever-present danger that the crowd will erupt and spill over the boundaries, thereby creating chaos. So, in effect, crowds always contain threats of chaos, serious disorder, and uncontrollable force.

2. *Crowds are characterized by equality.* Social distinctions lose their importance within crowds. Indeed, Canetti believes that people join crowds specifically to achieve the condition of equality with one another, a condition that carries with it a charged and exciting atmosphere.

3. *Crowds love density.* The circles of private space that usually surround each person in the normal course of events shrink to nothing in crowds. People pack together shoulder to shoulder, front to back, touching each other in ways normally reserved for intimates. Everyone included within the body of the crowd must relinquish a bit of his or her personal identity in order to experience the crowd's fervor. With a "we're all in this together" attitude, the crowd discourages isolated factions and detached onlookers.

4. *Crowds need direction.* Many crowds are in motion. They may physically move from place to place as they do in a marching demonstration or psychologically as at a rock concert. The direction of movement is set by the crowd's goals, which become so important to crowd members that individual and social differences lessen or disappear. This constant need for direction contains the seeds of danger: Having achieved or abandoned one goal the crowd may easily seize on another, perhaps destructive one. The direction that a crowd will take depends on the type of crowd involved.

Types of Crowds

In his essay on collective behavior, Herbert Blumer (1946) classified crowds into four types: acting, expressive, conventional, and casual.

ACTING CROWDS An acting crowd is a crowd in its most frightening form. *An **acting crowd** is a group of people whose passions and tempers have been aroused by some focal event. who come to share a purpose, and who feed off one another's arousal often erupting into spontaneous acts of violence.* When members of the studio audience of the *Geraldo Show* saw black activist Roy Innis get so angry at a neo-Nazi for calling him an Uncle Tom that he began choking the neo-Nazi on camera, the audience stormed the set and joined in the violence by hurling punches and epithets and throwing chairs (*Newsweek*, November 14, 1988).

Acting crowds can become violent and destructive as 400 million worldwide television viewers discovered in the summer of 1985. Sixty thousand soccer fans had assembled in Brussels to watch the European Cup Finals between Italy and Great

Britain. Verbal taunts quickly turned into rocks and bottles being thrown. Suddenly British fans stormed the fence and surged toward the Italian fans, trampling hundreds of helpless spectators. Before the horror could be stopped thirty-eight people were dead and another four hundred injured (*Time*, 1985).

THREATENED CROWDS *A **threatened crowd** is an acting crowd that is in a state of alarm, believing some kind of danger is present.* A threatened crowd created havoc when a busboy accidentally ignited an artificial palm at the Coconut Grove Night Club in Boston on November 28, 1942, spreading fire instantaneously through the rooms of the club. The fire lasted only 20 minutes, but 488 people died. Most died needlessly when panic gripped the crowd. Fire investigators found that the club's main entrance—a revolving door—was jammed by hundreds of terrified patrons. With their escape route blocked, these people died of burns and smoke inhalation only feet away from possible safety (Veltfort and Lee, 1943). In this as well as other threatened crowds, there is a lack of communication regarding escape routes.

California officials must attempt to minimize the widespread panic that could erupt during a major earthquake.

EXPRESSIVE CROWDS *An **expressive crowd** is drawn together by the promise of personal gratification through active participation in activities and events.* For example, many rock concert audiences are not content simply to listen to the music and watch the show. In a very real sense they want to be part of the show. Many dress in clothing calculated to draw attention to themselves, take drugs during the performance, dance in the aisles and in packed masses up against the stage, scream and chant, sometimes in unison, and delight in giving problems to security personnel.

CONVENTIONAL CROWDS *A **conventional crowd** is a gathering in which people's behavior conforms to some well-established set of cultural norms and gratification results from a passive appreciation of an event.* Such crowds include the audiences attending lectures, plays, and classical music concerts, where it is expected that everybody will follow traditional norms of etiquette.

CASUAL CROWDS A casual crowd is the inevitable outgrowth of modern society in which large numbers of people live, work, and travel closely together. *A **casual crowd** is any collection of people who just happen, in the course of their private activities, to be in one place at the same time and focus their attention on a common object or event.* On Fifth Avenue in New York City at noon, many casual crowds gather to watch the construction of a new building, an accident, a purse snatcher, or a theatrical performer. A casual crowd has the potential of becoming an acting crowd or an expressive crowd; the nature of a crowd can change if events change.

The Changeable Nature Of Crowds

Although the typology presented is useful for distinguishing among kinds of crowds, it is important to recognize that any particular crowd can shift from one type to another. For example, if a sidewalk musician starts playing a violin on Fifth Avenue, part of the aggregate walking by will quickly consolidate into a casual crowd of onlookers. Or, an expressive crowd at a rock concert will become a threatened crowd if a fire breaks out.

Changing times may also affect the nature of crowds. For example, until the 1970s, British soccer matches generally attracted conventional crowds who occasionally would turn into expressive crowds chanting team songs. In the last decade or so, however, British soccer fans have become active crowds: fighting in the stands is epidemic, charging onto the field to assault players and officials has become common, and near rioting has taken place. In 1988, when British fans traveled to west Germany to watch their national team take part in the European championships, four nights of street fighting followed between the English and West German fans that resulted in 500 arrests (Raines, 1988).

Because they are relatively concentrated in place and time, crowds present rich materials for sociological study (even if much of the data must be tracked down after the dust has settled). However, when collective behavior is widely dispersed among large numbers of people whose connection with one another is minimal or even elusive, the sociologist must then deal with phenomena that are extremely difficult to study, including fads and fashions, rumors, public opinion, panics, and mass hysteria.

DISPERSED COLLECTIVE BEHAVIOR

In this age of mass media, with television and other systems of communication spreading information instantaneously throughout the entire population, collective behavior shared by large numbers of people who have no direct knowledge of one another has become commonplace. Sociologists use the term **mass** to describe *a collection of people who, although physically dispersed, participate in some event either physically or with a common concern or interest.*

A nationwide television audience watching a presidential address or a Superbowl game is a mass. So are those individuals who rush out to buy the latest best-selling record and the fashion-conscious whose hemlines, lapel widths, and designer jeans always reflect the "in" look. In other words, dispersed forms of collective behavior seem to be universal.

Fads and Fashions

Fads and fashion are transitory social changes (Vago, 1980), patterns of behavior that are widely dispersed among a mass but that do not last long enough to become fixed or institutionalized. Yet it would be foolish to dismiss fads and fashions as unimportant just because they fade relatively quickly. In modern society, fortunes are won and lost trying to predict fashions and fads—in clothing, in entertainment preferences, in eating habits, in choices of investments, and so on.

Probably the easiest way to distinguish between a fad and a fashion is to look at their typical patterns of diffusion through society. *Fads are social changes with a very short life span marked by a rapid spread and an abrupt drop from popularity.* This was the fate of the Hula Hoop in the 1950s and the dance known as the "twist" in the 1960s. The roller-skating fad that emerged in 1979 rolled off into the pages of history sometime in the 1980s, as did the Rubik's cube, and Coleco, the company that made cabbage-patch dolls, went bankrupt in 1988. *A fad*

Fashions relate to standards of dress and manners during a particular time. They spread more slowly and last longer than fads.

that is especially short-lived may be called a craze. The mohawk hairstyle, among both young males and females was a relatively short-lived craze, as was streaking, or running naked down a street or through a public gathering, in 1974.

At the peak of their popularity, fads and crazes may become competitive activities. For example, when streaking was a craze, individual streaking was followed by group streaking, streaking on horseback, and parachuting naked from a plane.

Fashions relate to the standard of dress or manners in a given society at a certain time. They spread more slowly and last longer than fads. In his study of fashions in European clothing from the eighteenth to the present century, Alfred A. Kroeber (1963) shows that though minor decorative features come and go rapidly (that is, are faddish), basic silhouettes move through surprisingly predictable cycles that can be correlated with degrees of social and political stability. In times of great stress, fashions change erratically, but in peaceful times they seem to oscillate slowly in cycles lasting about 100 years.

Georg Simmel (1957) believed that changes in fashion (such as dress or manners) are introduced or adopted by the upper classes who seek in this way to keep themselves visibly distinct from the lower classes. Of course, those immediately below them observe these fashions and also adopt them in an attempt to identify themselves as "'upper crust." This process repeats itself again and again, with the fashion slowly moving down the class ladder, rung by rung. When the upper classes see that their fashions have become commonplace, they take up new ones, and the process starts all over again.

Blue jeans have shown that this pattern may no longer be true today. Jeans started out as sturdy work pants worn by those engaged in physical labor. Young people then started to wear them for play and everyday activities. College students wore them to class. Eventually fashion designers started to make fancier, higher-priced versions worn by the middle and upper classes. In this way the introduction of blue jeans into the fashion scene represents movement in the opposite direction from what Simmel noted.

Of course, the power of the fashion business to shape consumer taste cannot be ignored. Fashion designers, manufacturers, wholesalers, and retailers earn money only when people tire of their old clothes and purchase new ones. Thus, they shift hemlines up and down and widen and narrow lapels to create new looks, which consumers purchase.

Indeed, the study of fads and fashions provides sociologists with recurrent social events through which to study the processes of change. Because they so often use concrete and quantifiable objects, such as consumer goods, fads and fashions are much easier to study and count than are rumors, another common form of dispersed collective behavior.

Rumors

*A **rumor** is information that is shared informally and spreads quickly through a mass or a crowd.* It arises in situations that, for whatever reasons, create ambiguity with regard to their truth or their meaning. Rumors may be true, false, or partially true, but characteristically they are difficult or impossible to verify.

Rumors are generally passed from one person to another through face-to-face contact, but they can be started through television, radio, and newspaper reports as well. However, when the rumor source is the mass media, the rumor still needs people-to-people contact to enable it to escalate to the point of causing widespread concern (or even panic).

Sociologists see rumors as one means through which collectivities try to bring definition and order to situations of uncertainty and confusion. In other words, rumors are "improvised news" (Shibutani, 1966). Recognizing this, sociologists have been able to help prevent riots in a number of potentially inflammable situations. For example, a national motorcycle race was planned for the Labor Day weekend at Upper Marlboro, Maryland, in the summer of 1965. But earlier that summer, after the national championship motorcycle races in Laconia, New Hampshire, on July 4, the nearby resort town of Weir Beach had erupted into riot. Planners for the Labor Day races were worried that it might happen again—a fear strengthened when three Hells Angels motorcyclists (who had been arrested and jailed for disorderly conduct) threatened to "tear up the county." Two sociologists offered their services to law-enforcement officials planning crowd control. Among other things they set up a system for investigating all rumors and quickly disseminating correct information. In their analysis of "the riot that didn't happen" the sociologists credited the continuous flow of accurate information as being one of the major factors in keeping the crowds—which at times were quite unstable—from erupting into serious violence (Shellow and Roemer, 1965).

Some rumors die more easily than others. Hard-to-believe rumors usually disappear first, but this is not always the case. For 103 years, Proctor and Gamble used the symbol of the moon and thirteen stars as a company logo on its products. Around 1979 a rumor started to circulate that this symbol indicated a connection between the giant corporation and satanic religion. There was no evidence to substantiate this rumor, yet, unable to dispel the rumor, the company finally removed the logo from its products in 1985 (Koenig, 1985).

Public Opinion

The term *public* refers to a dispersed collectivity of individuals concerned with or engaged in a common problem, interest, focus, or activity. An *opinion* is a strongly held belief. Thus, **public opinion** *refers to the beliefs held by a dispersed collectivity of individuals about a common problem, interest, focus, or activity.* It is important to recognize that a public that forms around a common concern is not necessarily united in its opinions regarding this concern. For example, Americans concerned with the issue of abortion are sharply divided into pro and con camps.

Whenever a public forms, it is a potential source of support for, or opposition to, whatever its focus is. Hence, it is extremely important for politicians, market analysts, public relations experts, and others who depend on public support to know the range of public opinion on many different topics. These individuals often are not willing to leave opinions to chance, however. They seek to mold or influence public opinion, primarily in the area of consumption. They may create a "need" where there was none, as they did with fabric softeners, or they may try to convince consumers that one product is better than another when there is actually no difference at all. *Advertisements of a political nature, seeking to mobilize public support behind one specific party, candidate, or point of view technically are called* **propaganda** (but usually by only those in disagreement). For example, radio broadcasts from the former Soviet Union were habitually called "propaganda blasts" in the American press, but similar "Voice of America" programs were called "news" or "informational broadcasts."

Opinion leaders *are socially acknowledged experts to whom the public turns for advice.* The more conflicting sources of information there are on an issue of public concern, the more powerful the position of opinion leaders becomes. They weigh various news sources and then provide an interpretation in what has been called the two-step flow of communication. These opinion leaders can have a great influence on collective behavior, including voting (Lazarsfeld et al., 1968), patterns of consumption, and the acceptance of new ideas and inventions. Typically, each social stratum has its own opinion leaders (Katz, 1957). Jesse Jackson, for example, is an opinion leader in the black community. The mass media have made news anchors like Dan Rather, Tom Brokaw, and Peter Jennings accepted opinion leaders for a broad portion of the American public.

When rumor and public opinion grip the public imagination so strongly that "facts" no longer seem to matter, terrifying forces may be unleashed. Mass hysteria may reign, and panic may set in.

Mass Hysterias and Panics

On a Wednesday in June, 1962, reports began emerging from a small Southern town of a mysterious illness that had stricken workers in a local clothing plant. According to the 6 p.m. news, at least 10 female employees were hospitalized after complaining of feeling nauseated. While no hard evidence was available, the broadcast blamed the outbreak on some kind of "bug" that may have found its way into the country on a shipment of cloth from England. By the time the 11 p.m. news aired, the stricken workers had narrowed the cause of their illness to the bite of a small insect. They quickly labeled this insect the "June Bug."

Two days later, experts from the U.S. Public Health Service Communicable Disease Center in Atlanta, Georgia, arrived at the plant to investigate the cause of the mysterious outbreak. They set up a task force of community and health service officials to search the plant for the small black bug most employees believed was responsible for the outbreak. Their efforts were fruitless. The only bugs they found in the entire plant were a housefly, a black ant, a mite, and several entirely innocent gnats and beetles. Even though the investigators reported that they could not find the cause of the illness (indeed, no cause was ever found), the outbreak continued. By the time it ended, 62 people were stricken in what sociologists believe was a case of mass hysteria (Kerckhoff and Back, 1968).

Mass hysteria *occurs when large numbers of people are overwhelmed with emotion and frenzied activity or become convinced that they have experienced something for which investigators can find no discernible evidence. A* **panic** *is an uncoordinated group flight from a perceived danger,* as in the public reaction to Orson Welles's 1938 radio broadcast of H. G. Wells's "War of the Worlds," and to the 508-point drop in stock prices that occurred in October 1987.

According to Irving Janis and his colleagues (1964), people generally do not panic unless four conditions are met. First, they must feel that they are trapped in a life-threatening situation. Second, they must perceive a threat to their safety that is so large they can do little else but try to escape. Third, they must realize their escape routes are limited or inaccessible. Fourth, there must be a breakdown in communication between the front and rear of the crowd. Driven into a frenzy by fear, people at the rear of the crowd make desperate attempts to reach the exit doors, their actions often completely closing off the possibility of escape.

The perception of danger that causes a panic may come from rational as well as irrational sources. A fire in a crowded theater, for example, can cause people to lose control and trample one another in their attempt to escape. This happened when fire broke out in the Beverly Hills Supper Club on May 28, 1977. In their attempt to escape the overcrowded, smoke-filled room, people blocked the exit doors and 164 people died.

Such bizarre events are not very common but do occur often enough to present a challenge to social scientists, some of whom believe there is a rational core behind what at first glance appears to be wholly irrational behavior (Rosen, 1968). For example, sociologist Kai Erickson (1966) looked for the rational core behind the wave of previously discussed witchcraft trials and hangings that raged through the Massachusetts Bay Colony beginning in 1692. Erickson joins most other scholars in viewing this troublesome episode in American history as an instance of mass hysteria (Brown, 1954). He accounts for it as one of a series of symptoms, suggesting that the colony was in the grip of a serious identity crisis and needed to create real and present evil figures who stood for what the colony was not—thus enabling the colony to define its identity in contrast and build a viable self-image.

Mass hysterias account for some of the more unpleasant episodes in history. Of all social phenomena they are among the least understood creating a serious gap in our knowledge of human behavior.

SOCIAL MOVEMENTS

A **social movement** *is an important form of collective behavior in which large numbers of people are organized or alerted to support and bring about, or to resist, social change.* By their very nature, social movements are an expression of dissatisfaction with the way things are, or with changes that are about to take place.

Participation in a social movement is for most people only informal and indirect. Usually large numbers of sympathizers identify with and support

For people to join a social movement, they must think that their own values, needs, goals, or beliefs are being stifled or challenged by the social structure or by specific individuals.

the movement and its program without joining any formal organizations associated with the movement. For people to join a social movement they must think that their own values, needs, goals, or beliefs are being stifled or challenged by the social structure or specific individuals. The people feel the situation is undesirable and that something must be done to "set things right." Some catalyst, however, is needed to actually mobilize the discontent people feel. Relative deprivation theory and resource-mobilization theory are two major theories that attempt to explain how social movements emerge.

Relative Deprivation Theory

First used by Samuel A. Stouffer (1950), relative deprivation refers to a situation where deprivation or disadvantage is measured not by objective standards, but by comparison with the condition of others with whom one identifies or thinks of as a reference group.

Thus, **relative deprivation theory** *assumes social movements are the outgrowth of the feeling of* *relative deprivation among large numbers of people who believe they lack certain things they are entitled to*—such as better living conditions, working conditions, political rights, or social dignity.

From the standpoint of relative deprivation theory, the actual degree of deprivation people suffer is not automatically related to whether people will feel deprived and therefore join a social movement to correct the situation. Rather deprivation is considered unjust when others with whom the people identify do not suffer the deprivation (Gurr, 1970).

Karl Marx expressed this view when he noted:

> A house may be large or small; as long as the surrounding houses are equally small it satisfies all social demands for a dwelling. But let a palace arise beside the little house, and it shrinks from a little house to a hut ... Our desires and pleasures spring from society; we measure them therefore, by society and not by the objects which serve for their satisfaction. Because they are of a social nature, they are of a relative nature (Marx, 1968).

There is a flaw in the theory of relative deprivation in that often the people who protest a situation or condition may not be deprived themselves. Sometimes people protest because a situation violates their learned standards of justice. The white civil rights marchers in the 1960s were not personally the victims of anti-black discrimination. We could however, argue that they were experiencing deprivation in the sense that reality was not judged to be what it ought to be. They were experiencing a moral, as opposed to a material or personal, social deprivation (Rose, 1982).

Resource-Mobilization Theory

The **resource-mobilization theory** *assumes that social movements arise at certain times and not at others because some people know how to mobilize and channel the popular discontent.* Although discontent exists virtually everywhere, a social movement will not emerge until specific individuals actually mobilize resources available to a group. They do this by persuading people to contribute time, money, information, or anything else that might be valuable to the movement. An organizational format must also be developed for allocating these resources.

Leadership, therefore, becomes a crucial ingredient for the emergence of a social movement. Ideally, such leadership formulates the resources and ideology in such an attractive fashion that many others join the movement. It is not enough to make speeches and distribute flyers; the messages have to strike a responsive chord in others (Ferree and Hess, 1985).

Leadership is an important ingredient in the emergence of a social movement.

One of the most successful people in terms of resource mobilization was Saul Alinsky, an activist who devoted his life to developing "people's organizations" at the neighborhood level to combat exploitation and poor living conditions. Alinsky was not the sort of man people were impartial about. He was abrasive, forceful, witty, antagonistic, irreverent, and not above shocking or lying to people. Some saw him as a menace. Corporations hired detectives to follow him. What people were really responding to was not Alinsky the person but the method of community organizing that came to be associated with him.

In order to accomplish his goals, Alinsky followed a number of guidelines. First, he believed the professional organizer was the key catalyst for social change. Community organizing is difficult and requires crucial and correct decisions. He believed democracy was important, but the organizer was even more so. Secondly, the goal was to win using any tactics necessary. The end justified the means, Alinsky counseled. For example, Alinsky described the tactics used by one of his organizations in the following way:

> When [they have] a bunch of housing complaints they don't forward them to the building inspector. They drive forty or fifty members—the blackest ones they can find—to the nice suburb where the slumlord lives and they picket his home. Now we know the picket line isn't going to convert the slumlord. But we also know what happens when his white neighbors get after him and say, "We don't care what you do for a living— all we're telling you is to get those niggers out of here or you get out." That's the kind of jujitsu operation that forces the slumlord to surrender and gets repairs made in the slum (Quoted in Fisher, 1984).

Throughout his life Alinsky was involved in countless organizing efforts, and his methods were adopted by a vast array of groups. He was a clear example of a leader who knew how to mobilize and channel the deprivation and dissatisfaction existing among the poor.

Types of Social Movements

In the politics chapter we discussed rebellions and revolutions, which certainly qualify as social movements, but there are other kinds of social movements as well. Scholars differ as to how they classify social movements, but some general characteristics are well recognized. We shall discuss these characteristics according to William Bruce Cameron's (1966) four social-movement classifications: reactionary, conservative, revisionary, and revolutionary. In addi-

tion, we shall examine the concept of expressive social movements first developed by Herbert Blumer (1946).

Although this classification is useful to sociologists in their studies of social movements, in practice it is sometimes difficult to place a social movement in only one category. In reality any social movement may possess a complex set of ideological positions in regard to the many different features of the society, its institutions, the class structure, and the different categories of people within that society.

REACTIONARY SOCIAL MOVEMENTS Reactionary social movements *embrace the aims of the past and seek to return the general society to yesterday's values.* Using slogans like the "good old days" and our "grand and glorious heritage," reactionaries abhor the changes that have transformed society and are committed to recreating a set of valued social conditions they believe existed at an earlier point in time. Reactionary groups, such as the neo-Nazis and the Ku Klux Klan, hold a set of racial, ethnic, and religious values that are more characteristic of a previous historic period. The Klan has sought to uphold white dominance and traditional morality. To accomplish this, it has threatened, flogged, mutilated, and, on occasion, murdered. The main purpose of the Klan has been to defend and restore what they conceive as traditional cultural values. Their values legitimize prejudice and discrimination based on race, ethnicity, and religion—patterns that are now neither culturally legitimate nor legal (Chalmers, 1980).

Recently, this kind of reactionary fanaticism has been displayed by organized groups of teenagers who are part of a neo-Nazi political movement. The teens, known as skinheads, are white supremacists who are committing a variety of hate crimes against blacks, immigrants, and Jews across the country.

CONSERVATIVE SOCIAL MOVEMENTS Conservative social movements *seek to maintain society's current values by reacting to change or threats of change they believe will undermine the status quo.* Many of the Evangelical religious groups are associated with conservative social movements. For example, they often are opposed to the forces that promulgate equal rights for women. In order to preserve what they consider traditional values of the family and religion, these groups have threatened to boycott advertisers that sponsor television programs containing sex and violence and have mounted successful campaigns to defeat political candidates who oppose their views.

Although both revolutionary and revisionary social movements seek change in society, they differ in the degree of change they seek.

Conservative movements are most likely to arise when traditional-minded people perceive a threat of change that might alter the status quo. Reacting to what might happen if another movement achieves its goals, members of conservative movements mobilize an "anti" movement crusade. Thus, antigun control groups have waged political war against any group seeking to restrict the public's access to handguns. Although reactive in nature, conservative movements are far different from true reactionary movements, which attempt to restore values that have already changed.

REVISIONARY SOCIAL MOVEMENTS Revisionary social movements *seek partial or slight changes within the existing order but do not threaten the order itself.* The women's movement, for example, seeks to change the institutions and practices that have imposed prejudice and discrimination on women. The civil rights movement, the antinuclear movement, and the ecology movement are all examples of revisionary social movements.

REVOLUTIONARY SOCIAL MOVEMENTS Revolutionary social movements *seek to overthrow all or nearly all of the existing social order and replace it with an order they consider more suitable.* For example, the black guerrilla movement in Zimbabwe (formerly Rhodesia) was a revolutionary movement. Through the use of arms and political agitation, the guerrillas were successful in forcing the white minority to turn over political power to the black majority, and also in creating a new form of government that guaranteed 80 of the 100 seats in the country's legislative body would be held by blacks.

Although both revolutionary and revisionary social movements seek change in society, they differ in the degree of change they seek. The American Revolution, for example, which sought to overthrow

Expressive social movements typically arise to fill some void or to distract people from some dissatisfaction with their lives.

CONTROVERSIES IN SOCIOLOGY

Why Do People Join Cults?

Every year thousands of people abruptly turn their backs on family, friends, and future to join one or another of an estimated 2,500 communal groups in North America whose values, dress, and behavior seem totally alien to everything the joiner has previously stood for. Such radical departures are a cultural phenomenon that has inspired more fear, agony, anger, disgust—and misinterpretation—than almost any other movement. Parents and friends of young people who join such cults as the Moonies, or Hare Krishnas, are often hurt, angry, or baffled by the joiner's decision.

In seeking to account for such behavior, people have resorted to a variety of explanations: The joiners were troubled, academic failures, loners from embattled homes, drug addicts, or simply gullible innocents who have been brainwashed. One researcher, who studied members of such groups, found a much more benign explanation for what seems to be a radical move.

Researcher Saul V. Levine found that, by and large, people who joined such ideological groups came right out of solid middle-class backgrounds. After intensively studying more than 400 subjects, he concluded there were no more signs of pathology among joiners than among any other group of young people. These people came from warm, concerned families that had given them every material, social, and intellectual benefit.

Why, then, were they prompted to make such a drastic decision? To understand what makes them different, one must examine what normally happens to teenagers in our society.

In our middle-class culture, we strongly believe that during the adolescent years, teenagers must separate from their families and establish their individuality. As children become teenagers, parents begin to diminish control. At the same time, parents also make it clear to high school students that adult responsibilities loom ahead. They are asked to think about college and to make tentative career choices; most are expected to leave home. As parents withdraw control, their children also withdraw the uncondi-

tional love and faith that typify childhood. But because they cannot proceed into adulthood without love and faith, they seek intimacy with friends and lovers. That is the normal course of events.

Among radical departers, however, the process is especially difficult. Few of these young people are able to separate gradually to everyone's satisfaction. All of them are still so closely tied to their parents that they resemble children, despite their true age. Few have been involved in relationships that were more than exploitive or tentative. None felt committed to a value system at the time they joined an ideological group. Joiners look to belief as a way to avoid their personal dilemma. Feeling little self-esteem, they can't shoulder the responsibility of perhaps making the wrong moral choice and thereby feeling even more worthless. They are looking for ideology that will bolster whatever is admirable in them, and purge whatever is bad.

Just at this critical period in their lives, they are offered what

---

British colonial rule and led to the formation of our own government, differed significantly from the women's movement, which seeks change within existing judicial and legislative structures.

EXPRESSIVE SOCIAL MOVEMENTS Though other types of movements tend to focus on changing the social structure in some way, **expressive social movements** *stress personal feelings of satisfaction or well-being and typically arise to fill some void or to distract people from some great dissatisfaction in*

their lives. Movements—such as the "Hare Krishnas" and the "Moonies" of the Unification church—are religious examples of expressive social movements.

The Life Cycle of Social Movements

Social movements, by their nature, do not last forever. They rise, consolidate, and eventually succeed, fail, or change. Armand L. Mauss (1975) suggested that social movements typically pass seems a magical situation: separation without the pain, loneliness, self-doubt, and disillusion that usually accompanies the passage to adulthood. It is very common for such a young person to join an ideological group while away from home, sometimes for the first time. These people wish to be back at home, safe from the frightening freedom of travel, but then how can they be separate? The departure is a compromise solution to this conflict.

Despite the public perception that people are somehow tricked into joining radical groups, the initial encounter is actually only the beginning of a screening process that will sort out those who do belong from those who might be alien to the group. In fact, only about five out of every 100 people approached will agree to a first visit with the group; fewer than 10 percent who are then invited to a two- or three-day retreat will ultimately decide to join. But this screening process is so accurate that, while only one in 500 of those originally approached choose to join, those who do join usually stay at least six months.

A sense of belonging is the key to understanding cults. The group is made up of people all doing the same things, believing the same beliefs, speaking the same stock phrases, eating the same food, wearing the same clothes, and working for the same cause. For the period of their commitment, joiners give up the usual adolescent struggle to form an independent self and instead participate with relief in a flawless group self.

But one of Levine's most fascinating findings about radical departure is that despite this intense commitment to the group, nine out of ten members leave their group within two years. After a period of some months, subtle but unmistakable changes begin. Dogmatic attitudes relax; there are fewer unequivocal opinions and less inflexible faith. This is quickly followed by a siege of doubt about the perfection of the group and its leader, an upwelling of longing for the family, and, finally, a return to the world.

Radical departures, then, may be seen as a rehearsal for separation, practice for the real task of growning up. While the group members appear to be passively frozen into their narrow mold of commitment, they are, in fact, actively rehearsing for their coming out. The group has served its purpose, and the joiner is now psychologically fortified to deal with the conflicts posed by the passage to adulthood.

But some parents, reluctant to wait for this process to naturally run its course, resort to extreme measures to get their children back. In Levine's estimation, this is a serious mistake. Deprogramming, he says, works against the possibility that the joiner will resolve their conflicts, and interferes with the natual rhythm of a radical departure. It can, in fact, drive the person back into the group, or into a pattern of cult-hopping, for years.

While no one claims that having a child or friend join a cult is a painless experience, Levine suggests that the best approach may be to wait it out. By understanding what it is that joiners seek, why they find commitment gratifying, and—most important—how the experience is of genuine use to them, we are in a better position to judge what we as a society should do to enable people to emancipate themselves and find meaning in their lives.

Saul V. Levine, "Radical Departures," *Psychology Today*, August 1984, pp. 21–27.

---

through a series of five stages: (1) incipiency, (2) coalescence, (3) institutionalization, (4) fragmentation, and (5) demise. However, these stages are by no means common to all social movements.

INCIPIENCY   The first stage of a social movement, termed **incipiency**, *begins when large numbers of people become frustrated about a problem and do not perceive any solution to it through existing institutions.* This occurred in the nineteenth century when American workers, desperate over worsening working conditions, formed the U.S. labor movement.

Disruption and violence may mark a social movement's incipiency. In 1886 and 1887, for example, as the labor movement grew, workers battled private Pinkerton agents and state militiamen, and called nationwide strikes. Although physically beaten, the workers continued to organize.

Incipiency is also the time when leaders emerge. Various individuals offer competing solutions to the perceived problem, and some are more persuasive than others. According to Max Weber (see Chapter 14), many of the more successful leaders have charismatic qualities derived from exceptional personal characteristics. Samuel Gompers, who launched the American Federation of Labor (AFL) in 1881, was such a leader, as was Martin Luther King.

COALESCENCE   During the second stage, known as **coalescence,** *groups form around leaders, to promote policies, and to promulgate programs.* Some groups join forces, others are defeated in the competition for new members. Gradually a dominant group or coalition of groups emerges that is able to establish itself in a position of leadership. Its goals become the goals of many; its actions command wide participation, and its policies gain influence. This occurred in the labor movement when, in 1905, William D. Haywood organized the Industrial Workers of the World (IWW), which led its increasingly dissatisfied members in a number of violent strikes. Labor coalescence continued in 1935 when such militant industrial union leaders as John L. Lewis of the United Mine Workers and David Dubinsky of the International Ladies' Garment Workers founded the Committee for Industrial Organization (CIO), which rapidly organized the steel, automobile, and other basic industries. Thus, through coalescence, the labor movement gradually created several large, increasingly powerful organizations.

INSTITUTIONALIZATION   During the third stage, known as **institutionalization,** *social movements reach the peak of their strength and influence and became firmly established.* Their leadership no longer depends on the elusive quality of charisma to motivate followers. Rather, it has established formal, rational organizations (see Chapter 5) that have the power to effect lasting changes in the social order. At this point, the organizations themselves become part of the normal pattern of everyday life.

When the institutionalization of the U.S. labor movement became formalized with the legalization of unions in the 1930s, union leaders no longer used the revolutionary rhetoric that was necessary when unions were neither legitimate nor legal. Instead, they talked in pragmatic terms, worked within the political power structure, and sought reforms within the structure of the existing democratic, capitalistic system.

Not all social movements become institutionalized. In fact, social movements fail and disappear more often than they reach this stage. Institutionalization depends, to a great degree, on how the members feel about the movement—whether it reflects their goals and has been successful in achieving them—and on the extent to which the movement is accepted or rejected by the larger society.

Ironically, the acceptance of a social movement may also mark its end. Many members drop out or lose interest once a movement's goals have been reached. It can be argued that a certain amount of opposition from those in power reminds the members that they still must work to accomplish their goals. Movement leaders often hope for a conformation that will clarify the identity of the opposition and show the members against what and whom they must fight. Movements that evoke an apathetic or disinterested response from the institutions controlling the power structure have few resources with which to unite their membership.

*FRAGMENTATION   **Fragmentation** refers to the fourth stage of a social movement, when the movement gradually begins to fall apart.* Organizational structures no longer seem necessary because the changes they sought to bring about have been institutionalized or the changes they sought to block have been prevented. Disputes over doctrine may drive dissident members out, as when the United Auto Workers (UAW) and the Teamsters left the AFL-CIO. Also, demographic changes may transform a once strong social movement into a far less powerful force. Economic changes have been largely responsible for the fragmentation of the American labor movement. As was pointed out earlier, unions now represent the smallest share of the labor force since World War II, even though the work force continues to expand. Their lost power is due, in part, to a sharp decrease in the percentage of more easily unionized blue-collar workers in the labor force and a dramatic increase in the percentage of white-collar employees who are largely resistant to unionization.

*DEMISE   **Demise,** the last stage, refers to the end of a social movement.* The organizations they created and the institutions they introduced may well survive—indeed, their goals may become official state policy—however, they are no longer set apart from mainstream society. Transformed from social movements into institutions, they leave behind well-entrenched organizations that guarantee members the goals they sought. This pattern of social-movement demise has occurred in parts of the American labor movement. The United Auto Workers, for example, is no longer a social movement fighting for the rights of its members from the outskirts of the power structure. Rather, it is now an institutionalized part of society. But all unions have not followed this course. Labor is still very much a social movement, for it is trying to organize such previously unorganized groups as farm workers, nonunionized clerical and professional workers, and all workers in the traditionally nonunion South. The American Federation of State, County, and Municipal Employees is a recent example of the labor movement's continued organizational efforts.

CHAPTER

·19·

Social Change

Society and Social Change

Sources of Social Change
   Internal Sources of Social Change
   External Sources of Social Change

Theories of Social Change
   Evolutionary Theory
   Conflict Theory
   Functionalist Theory
   Cyclical (Rise and Fall) Theory

Modernization: Global Social Change
   Modernization: An Overview
   Modernization in the Third World
   Modernization and the Individual

Social Change in the United States
   Technological Change
   The Workforce of the Future

On May 3, 1990, in an investigation using the most accessible information system available, Bill McKibben had friends record the entire 24-hour broadcasting output of ninety-three stations on the mammoth Media General Cable television system of Fairfax, Virginia. McKibben spent almost an entire year viewing and analyzing the over 1,700 hours of shows from that one day of broadcasting. He then withdrew to a mountain retreat and subjected himself to another day's worth of programming. McKibben's goal was to find out exactly what could be learned if these programs were the *only* source of information people had.

While watching the seemingly endless hours of video, McKibben endured a steady stream of "The Brady Bunch," fishing shows, situation comedies, hyperactive game shows, infomercials for devices with unknown uses, evangelists begging for money, shopping programs, and sporting events. He noted that we believe we live in an "age of information." We speak of the information explosion and even an information "revolution." McKibben, however, raised a basic question: Does having access to more information than ever mean that we *know* more than ever? How has the world and our lives changed as a result of the vast amount of information that we have access to now (McKibben, 1992)?

Twenty-five centuries ago the Greek philosopher Heraclitus lectured on the inevitability of change. "You cannot step into the same river twice," he said, "for . . . waters are continually flowing on." Indeed, he observed, ". . . everything gives way and nothing stays fixed" (Wheelright, 1959).

The same is true for society. As you will see in this chapter, technology is one of the primary sources of social change—and it is also one of the primary sources of social stress. The beliefs, norms, and values that regulate our lives are all being tested by the pace of change. In the last two decades, we have seen an impressive number of technological innovations, and the social changes growing out of them are still evolving. In this chapter we will examine how, why, and in what specific directions societies are likely to change.

SOCIETY AND SOCIAL CHANGE

What, exactly, is social change? The best way to analyze how sociologists define social change is through example. The invention of the steam locomotive was not in itself a social change, but the acceptance of the invention and the spread of railroad transportation were. Martin Luther's indictments of the Catholic church nailed to the door of Wittenberg Cathedral in 1517 were not in themselves social change, but they helped give rise to one of the major social changes of all time, the Protestant Reformation. Adam Smith's great work, *An Inquiry Into the Nature and Causes of the Wealth of Nations* (first published in 1776), was not in itself social change, but it helped initiate a social change that altered the world—the Industrial Revolution. Thus, individual discoveries, actions, or works do not themselves constitute social change, but they may lead to alterations in shared values or patterns of social behavior or even to the reorganization of social relationships and institutions. When this happens, sociologists speak of social change. Hans Gerth and C. Wright Mills (1953) define social change as "whatever happens in the course of time to the roles, the institutions, or the orders comprising a social structure, their emergence, growth and decline." To put it simply, using terms we defined in Chapter 5, **social change** *consists of any modification in the social organization of a society in any of its social institutions or social roles.*

Some social changes may be violent and dramatic, like the French Revolution of 1789 or the 1917 Russian Revolution. However, not all cases of violent social or collective behavior are instances of social change. Thus, the United States' race riots of the late 1960s and early 1970s were not in themselves examples of social change. For that matter, not all social change need be violent. For example, the transformation of the family into its modern forms over the last 200 years represents an enormous social change that has profoundly affected both the general nature of society and each person's childhood and adult experiences. Similarly, the rise of computer technology and developments in telecommunications over the last few decades has resulted in the emergence of what sociologist Edward Shils (1971) describes as "mass society," in which vast numbers of individuals share collectively in the community and in a common language.

It would be a mistake to think of social change only in terms of the social structure. Morris Ginsberg (1958) observed that "the term social change must also include changes in attitudes and beliefs, insofar as they sustain institutions and change with them." In addition, individual motivation always plays a vital but immeasurable role in social change.

SOURCES OF SOCIAL CHANGE

What causes social change? Sociologists have linked several factors to social change. These factors, which we shall consider here, are categorized as internal and external sources of change.

Internal Sources of Social Change

Internal sources of social change *include those factors that originate within a specific society and that singly or in combination produce significant alterations in its social organization and structure.* The most important internal sources of social change are technological innovation, ideology, cultural conflicts, and institutionalized structural inequality.

TECHNOLOGICAL INNOVATION Technological change in industrial society is advancing at a dizzying pace, carrying social organizations and institutions along with it. Computer and communications-based electronic information technology has

The invention of the airplane was not in itself social change, but the acceptance of the invention and the spread of air travel were.

already transformed American life as we know it in the home, family, workplace, and school.

Homes have been turned into technological workstations in which people both work and live. By receiving and sending information through computer terminals and fax machines, workers have less need to establish a base of work operations in a separate office.

Already, signs of these trends are plentiful. We can deposit funds and pay bills through electronic banking centers without ever handling money. Home computers are already in millions of American homes. Even crime patterns have been changed by the computer. Clever thieves have diverted funds using computer codes in banks. In fact, so much about society is changing so quickly as a result of advanced computer technology that scholars are beginning to worry whether humans have the psychological resilience to adapt to the social changes that must follow.

IDEOLOGY The term **ideology** *is most often used to refer to a set of interrelated religious or secular beliefs, values, and norms that justify the pursuit of a given set of goals through a given set of means.* Throughout history, ideologies have played a major role in shaping the direction of social change.

Conservative *(or* **traditional***) ideologies are ideologies that try to preserve things as they are.* Indeed, conservative ideologies may slow down social changes that technological advances are promoting.

Liberal ideologies *seek limited reforms that do not involve fundamental changes in the social structure of society.* Affirmative-action programs, for example, are intended to redress historical patterns of discrimination that have kept women and minority groups from competing for jobs on an equal footing with white males. Although far-reaching, such programs do not attempt to change the economic system that more radical critics believe is at the heart of job discrimination.

Radical (or revolutionary) ideologies reject liberal reforms as mere tinkerings that simply make the structural inequities of the system more bearable and therefore more likely to be maintained. Like the socialist political movement described in Chapter 14, **radical ideologists** *seek major structural changes in society.* Interestingly, radicals sometimes share the objectives of conservatives in their opposition to liberal reforms that would lessen the severity of a problem, thereby making major structural changes less likely to occur. For example, conservative as well as many radical groups bitterly attacked President Franklin D. Roosevelt's New Deal policies in which federal funds were used to create jobs and bring the country out of the Depression. Conservatives attacked the New Deal as "creeping socialism," and radicals saw it as a desperate (and successful) attempt to save the faltering capitalist system and stave off a socialist revolution.

CULTURAL CONFLICTS AND INSTITUTIONAL STRUCTURAL INEQUALITY Structural conflict promotes social change as society attempts to accommodate itself to a wide variety of demands for social, economic, political, and cultural reforms. These demands stem from cultural conflict and institutionalized structural inequality.

Cultural conflict exists in America in a variety of forms. African Americans, Hispanics, and other minorities, for example, are often the victims of institutionalized inequality. As these groups have asserted their rights to equality, institutions have been forced to change. For example, federal, state, and local laws have been passed making it illegal to discriminate against minorities in voting, education, employment, housing, and other sectors of American life. Cultural conflicts institutionalized in the form of structural inequality have caused a strong movement toward change. The labor and civil rights movement, for example, arose because of structural inequalities in American society.

External Sources of Social Change

As noted in Chapter 3, diffusion, the process of transmitting traits from one culture to another, occurs when groups with different cultures come

Technology is one of the primary sources of social change. The personal computer has had a dramatic impact on society.

Cultural diffusion inevitably results when people from one group or society come into contact with another.

into contact and exchange items and ideas with one another. Diffusion is thus an example of an **external source of social change**, *changes within a society produced by events external to that society.* It does not take the diffusion of many culture traits to result in profound social changes, as anthropologist Lauriston Sharp (1952) demonstrated with regard to the introduction of steel axes to the Yir Yoront, a Stone Age tribe inhabiting southeastern Australia. Before European missionaries brought steel axes to the Yir Yoront, these tools were made by chipping and grinding stone, a long, laborious process. Axes were very valuable, had religious importance, and also were the status symbol of tribal leaders. Women and young men had to ask permission from a leader to use an ax, which reinforced the patriarchal authority structure. However, anybody could earn a steel ax from the missionaries simply by impressing them as being "deserving." With women and young men thus having direct access to superior tools, the symbols representing status relations between male and female as well as young and old were devalued, and the norms governing these traditional relationships were upset. In addition, introducing into the tribe valuable tools that did not have religious sanctions governing their use led to a drastic rise in the incidence of theft. In fact, the entire moral order of the Yir Yoront was undermined because their myths explained the origins of all important things in the world—but did not account for the arrival of steel axes. This, as Sharp observed, caused conditions fertile for the introduction of a new religion, a happy circumstance for the missionaries.

Diffusion occurs wherever and whenever different cultures come into contact, though direct contact is not essential for diffusion to take place. For example, Native American groups below the Arctic smoked tobacco long before the arrival of the Europeans. But in Alaska, the Inuit (Eskimos) knew nothing of tobacco's pleasures. European settlers brought tobacco back to Europe, where it immediately became popular and diffused eastward across Central Europe and Eurasia, up into Siberia, and eventually across the Bering Strait to the Inuit.

Today, of course, when so many of the world's peoples increasingly are in contact with one another through all forms of mass communication, cultural traits spread easily from one society to another. But the *direction* of diffusion rarely is random or balanced among societies. In general, traits diffuse from more powerful to weaker peoples, from the more technologically advanced to the less so. *A social change that is imposed by might or conquest on weaker people is called* **forced acculturation.**

Why does social change occur? Different theories offer some important insights into the process of social change.

THEORIES OF SOCIAL CHANGE

The complexity of social change makes it impossible for a single theory to explain all its ramifications. Because each theory views social change from an entirely different perspective, contradictions are common. For example, functionalist and conflict theories are diametrically opposed, but this does not make one theory "right" and the other "wrong."

Modernization produces a complex set of social changes.

Rather, they are complementary views that must be analyzed together in order to understand the total theoretical framework of social change.

Evolutionary Theory

By the middle of the nineteenth century, the concept of **evolution**—*the continuous change from a simpler condition to a more complex state*—was the dominant concern of European scholars in a variety of disciplines. The most influential evolutionary theorist was Charles Darwin, who, in his 1859 volume, *On the Origin of Species*, described what he believed to be the biological evolutionary process that moved populations of organisms toward increasing levels of biological complexity.

Darwin's evolutionary theory influenced the work of sociologist Herbert Spencer, who used terms like "survival of the fittest" and "struggle for existence" to explain the superiority of Western cultures over non-Western ones. In Spencer's view, Western cultures had reached higher levels of cultural achievement because they were better adapted to compete for scarce resources and to meet other difficult challenges of life.

Late nineteenth-century and early twentieth-century philosophers continued to be influenced by what has come to be known as social-evolutionary thought. Although using different names, the theories they developed proposed similar stages through which societies progress. Two of the more influential social-evolutionary theorists, Emile Durkheim and Ferdinand Tonnies, were discussed in Chapter 16.

Durkheim argued that evolutionary changes affect the way society is organized, particularly with regard to work. Small, primitive societies whose members share a set of common social characteristics, norms, and values come together in a bond of solidarity Durkheim called *mechanical solidarity*. These people tend to be of the same ethnicity and religion and share similar economic roles. As society grows larger, it develops a more complex division of labor. People play different economic roles; a more complex class structure develops, and members of the society increasingly do not share the same beliefs, values, and norms. However, they must still depend on one another's efforts in order that all may survive. Durkheim called the new advanced form of cohesion *organic solidarity*.

Ferdinand Tonnies's views of social evolution parallel those of Durkheim. In his view societies shift from the intimate, cooperative relationships of small societies, characterized by *Gemeinschaft* to *Gesellschaft*—the specialized impersonal relationships typical of large societies. Tonnies did not believe that these changes always brought progress (a feeling shared by Durkheim). Rather, he saw social fragmentation, individual isolation, and a general weakening of societal bonds as the direct results of the movement toward individualization and the struggle for power that characterize urban society.

Much of early evolutionary theory has been harshly criticized by contemporary sociologists who charge that it uses the norms and values of one culture as absolute standards for all cultures. In response to these problems, modern evolutionists propose sequences of evolutionary stages that are much more flexible in allowing for actual historical variation among societies. Anthropologist Julian H. Steward (1955) proposes that social evolution is "multilineal," by which he means that the evolution of each society or cultural tradition must be studied independently and must not be forced into broad, arbitrary, "universal" stages. Marshall D. Sahlins and Elman R. Service (1960) distinguish between "general" evolution (the trend toward increasing differentiation) and "specific" evolution (social changes in each specific society that may move either in the direction of greater simplicity or greater complexity).

Sociologists today realize that change occurs in many different ways and does not necessarily follow a specific course. Nor does change necessarily mean progress (Lenski and Lenski, 1982). All evolutionary theories suffer to a greater or lesser degree from an inability to give a convincing answer to the question, "Why do societies change?" One approach that attempts to deal with this question is conflict theory (Gerhard Lenski and Jean Lenski, 1982).

Conflict Theory

According to conflict theory, conflicts rooted in the class struggle between unequal groups lead to social change. This, in turn, creates conditions that lead to new conflicts.

Modern conflict theory is rooted in the writings of Karl Marx, whose theory of society and social conflict we introduced in Chapter 1. In *Das Kapital*, first published in 1867, Marx argued that social-class conflict is the most basic and influential source of all social change. Classes are in conflict because of the unequal allocation of goods and services. Those with money may purchase these products, those without cannot. To Marx, it is a division between the exploiting and exploited classes.

Europe's transition from a feudal to a capitalistic society gave Marx the source of his model for social change. "Without conflict no progress: this is the law which civilization has followed to the present day" (Marx, 1959).

Several modern conflict theorists have modified Marx's theories of class conflict in light of recent historical events. Ralf Dahrendorf (1959), one of the foremost contemporary conflict theorists, sees the view that all social change is the outgrowth of class conflict as too simplistic. He believes that conflict and dissension are present in nearly every part of society. For example, nonsocial-class conflict may involve religious groups, political groups, or even nations. Dahrendorf does accept, however, that social conflict and social change are built-in structural features of society—a basic principle of conflict theory.

Conflict theory accounts for some of the major sources of social change within a society: the changing means of production and class conflict. Marx believed that social change within a capitalist society would occur through a violent revolution of the workers against the capitalists. However, Marx did not foresee that those who controlled the means of production would tolerate the legalization of unions, collective bargaining, strikes, and integration of the less privileged into legal, reform-oriented parties of the Left. Marx also did not foresee that those who controlled the means of production would accept government regulation of corporations, welfare legislation, civil rights legislation, and other laws aimed at protecting employees and consumers.

Functionalist Theory

Functionalists view society as a **homeostatic system,** *that is, an assemblage of interrelated parts that seeks to achieve and maintain a settled or stable state* (Davis, 1949). A system that maintains a stable state is said to be in equilibrium. Because society is inherently an open system subject to influence from its natural and social environments, complete equilibrium never can be achieved. Rather, functionalists describe society as normally being in a condition of *dynamic* or *near equilibrium*, constantly making small adjustments in response to shifts or changes in its internal elements or parts (Homans, 1950).

Probably the best-known spokesman for functionalist theory in America was Talcott Parsons (1951, 1954, 1966), who saw society as a "homeostatic action system" that seeks to integrate its elements and whose patterns of actions are maintained by its culture. According to Parsons, it is the role of society to fulfill six basic needs: (1) member replacement, (2) member socialization, (3) production of goods and services, (4) preservation of internal order, (5) provision and maintenance of a sense of purpose, and (6) protection from external attack. These needs are in a constant state of equilibrium with one another, and when one changes, the others must accommodate. For example, when industrialization shifted the burden of socializing young people from the family to the school, schools enlarged their educational function to include the education of the whole child. Parent–teacher associations were established, and guidance counselors were hired to coordinate the function of the school with those of the family and other institutions. Thus, when the family became more specialized, the schools stepped in to fill the vacuum. In this case, as in all others, argued Parsons (1951, 1971), change promotes adaptation, equilibrium, and eventual social stability.

As functionalist theory developed, it began to trace the cause of social change to people's dissatisfactions with social conditions that personally affect them. Consider the area of medicine. Technological advances in medical science have made the practice of general medicine all but impossible and encouraged the development of medical subspecialites. Patients, who were forced to see a different specialist for almost every one of their health care needs, quickly became dissatisfied, even though the technical ability of each subspecialist was greater than that of the general practitioner. Responding to this dissatisfaction and to patients' conviction that their all-around health care was suffering as a result of the system of medical subspecializations, the medical profession created the "new" specialty of family medicine. Thus, the needs met by the old "family doctor" are once again being addressed by the new "family medicine specialist."

Another example of the functionalist view of social change is the American civil rights movement of the 1960s, which gained strength outside the normal channels of political action. Hundreds of thousands of individuals joined in street protests, and many thousands were arrested. Occurring against the backdrop of race riots in Watts and other inner-city neighborhoods (see Chapter 18), the civil rights movement threatened society with widespread rebellion and chaos. In response, political and social leaders launched a series of important adjustments that functioned to reform the society's institutional structure. These structural changes included the passage of the Civil Rights Act of 1964, which was intended to eliminate discrimination in public accommodations and in the labor force. Affirmative-action programs were established to integrate blacks into the labor force and provide equal access to higher education. The Voting Rights Act of 1965 was passed to attack discrimination in voting, in particular in voter registration procedures in the South. In 1968, Congress passed the first laws to attack discrimination in housing. Institutions that did not comply with these new federal rulings faced the possible withdrawal of all federal funds. Hence, though American society was pushed toward disequilibrium in the 1960s and early 1970s, greater equilibrium was reestablished through selected institutional adjustments that diminished organized expressions of discontent.

Functionalist theory successfully explains moderate degrees of social change, such as the adjustments that diffused the civil rights movement in America. The concepts of equilibrium and homeostatics are not very helpful, however, in explaining major structural changes (Bertalanffy, 1968). This criticism was summed up by Gnessous (1967) when he said that "an equilibrium theory like that of Parsons can neither explain the occurrence of radical changes in society nor account for the phenomena that accompany them; it says nothing about what happens when a social system is in disequilibrium . . . it is tied to the image of a society whose historical development holds no surprises."

William F. Ogburn's (1964) concept of *cultural lag* attempts to deal with these criticisms and explain social change in functionalist terms (see Chapter 3). Although all elements of a society are interrelated, Ogburn asserted, some elements may change rapidly and others lag behind. According to Ogburn, technological change typically is faster than change in the nonmaterial culture, that is, the beliefs, norms, and values that regulate people's day-to-day lives in friendship and kinship groups and in religion. Therefore, he argued, technological change often results in culture lag. New patterns of behavior may emerge, even though they conflict with traditional values. When the birth control pill was developed, for example (a product of our material culture), orthodox religious norms forbade its use. Catholic women who wanted to limit their family size thus were on the horns of a dilemma. If they took the pill, they would violate the dictum of the church. If they did not, they would face additional pregnancies and the concomitant economic and family stress. Thus, even though Ogburn adopts a functionalist approach to social change, his theories incorporate the idea that stresses and strains, or "lack of fit" among the parts of the social order, are inevitable.

Popular during the 1940s and 1950s, the functionalists theory of social change has been criticized widely in recent times. Aside from those points we have mentioned, critics argue further that functionalism is a conservative theory that overestimates the amount of consensus in society and underestimates the effects of social conflict.

Cyclical (Rise and Fall) Theory

Inherent in cyclical theories of social change is the assumption that the rise and fall of civilizations is inevitable and the notion that social change may not be for the good. Shocked by the devastation of World War I, people began to see social progress as the decline of society rather than as its enhancement. These feelings were crystallized in the works of Oswald Spengler, Arnold Toynbee, and Pitirim Sorokin.

In his controversial work *The Decline of the West* (1932), German historian Oswald Spengler theorized that every society moves through four stages of development: childhood, youth, mature adulthood, and old age. Spengler felt that Western society had reached the "golden age" of maturity during the Enlightenment of the eighteenth century, and since then had begun the inevitable crumbling and decline that go along with old age. Nothing, he believed, could stop this process. Just as the great civilizations of Babylon, Egypt, Greece, and Rome had declined and died, so too would the West.

British historian Arnold Toynbee (1946) theorized that the rise and fall of civilizations were explicable through the interrelated concepts of societal *challenge* and *response*. Every society, he observed, faces both natural and social challenges from its environments. Are its natural resources plentiful or limited? Are its boundaries easy or difficult to defend? Are important trade routes readily accessible or difficult to reach? Are its neighbors warlike or peaceful? When a society is able to fashion adequate responses to these challenges, it survives and grows. When it cannot, it falls into a spiral of decline. According to Toynbee, as each challenge is met, new challenges arise, placing the society in a constant give-and-take interaction with its environments.

Pitirim A. Sorokin (1889–1968) theorized that cultures are divided into two groups: **ideational cultures**, *which emphasize spiritual values*, and **sensate cultures**, *which are based on what is immediately apparent through the senses*. In an ideational culture, progress is achieved through self-control and adherence to a strong moral code. In a sensate culture, people are dedicated to self-expression and the gratification of their immediate physical needs.

Sorokin believed societies are constantly moving between the two extremes. The main reason for this back and forth movement is that neither sensate nor ideational culture provides the basis for a perfect society. As one culture begins to deteriorate, its weaknesses and excesses become apparent, and there is a movement in the opposite direction. Occasionally, however, a culture may reach an intermediate place between these extremes. Sorokin called this *the* **idealistic point**, *at which sensate and ideational values coexist in a harmonious mix.*

Although cyclical, or "rise and fall," theories offer an interesting perspective on social change, they assume social change cannot be truly controlled by those who experience it. There is a supposedly inevitable cycle that all societies follow. The actions of people all are part of an elaborate, predetermined cyclical progression of events that has a life of its own. This may well be true of the ways in which many individuals experience social changes. However, such changes are clearly rooted in concrete decisions made by many individuals. The study of modernization allows us to examine the dominant form of social change in the world today and reveals both social and intrapersonal dynamics at work.

Oswald Spengler believed that the disappearance of the Egyptian civilization was part of the inevitable crumbling and decline that is part of the life cycle of any society.

SOCIOLOGY AT WORK

George Ritzer on the McDonaldization of Society

*S*ociologist George Ritzer believes the fast-food restaurant chain McDonald's is undoubtedly one of the most influential creations of twentieth-century America. This is true not just as a fast-food restaurant, but also as a model for many other institutions, and for its principles that have been widely adopted throughout American society and much of the rest of the world.

George Ritzer uses the term *McDonaldization* to describe the process by which the principles of the fast-food restaurant are coming to dominate more and more sectors of American society, as well as the rest of the world. McDonaldization is not only affecting the restaurant business, but also education, work, travel, leisure-time activities, dieting, politics, religion, the family, and virtually every other sector of society. Ritzer believes McDonaldization has shown every sign of being an irresistible process as it sweeps through institutions and parts of the world that one would have thought impervious to it.

McDonald's has achieved its exalted position in the world as a result of the fact that virtually all Americans, and many people from other countries, have passed through its "golden arches." Furthermore, Ritzer notes, we have been bombarded by commercials extolling McDonald's virtues. Thus, in a survey of school children, 96 percent were able to identify Ronald McDonald, making him second only to Santa Claus in name recognition.

Ritzer notes that McDonald's model has succeeded because it offers the consumer efficiency and predictability, and because it seems to offer the diner a good value. It has also flourished because it has been able to exert control through non-human technologies over both employees and customers, getting them to behave the way the organization wishes them to. The substitution of non-human for human technologies has also allowed the fast-food restaurant to deliver its fare increasingly more efficiently and predictably. Thus, there are good, solid reasons why the process of McDonaldization continues unabated.

Ritzer notes that the McDonaldization process as it permeates many areas of modern society also has a downside to it. We can think of efficiency, predictability, quantification, and control through non-human technology as the basic components of a *rational* system. However, rational systems often spawn irrationalities. Another way of saying this is that rational systems may serve to deny human reason.

Ritzer points out that the fast-food restaurant is often a dehumanizing setting in which to eat and work. People lining up for a burger, or waiting in the drive-through line, often feel like they are dining on an assembly-line. Assembly-lines are hardly human settings in which to eat, and they have been shown to be inhuman settings in which to work.

Ritzer believes we should question the headlong rush toward McDonaldization in our society and throughout the world. True, there are great gains to be made from McDonaldization. But there are great costs and enormous risks, Ritzer points out. Ultimately, we must ask whether in creating rationalized systems, we are not also creating an even greater number of irrationalities. At the minimum, Ritzer would like us to be aware of the costs associated with McDonaldization.

Source: George Ritzer, *The McDonaldization of Society*, Newbury Park, CA: Pine Forge Press, 1993.

MODERNIZATION: GLOBAL SOCIAL CHANGE

Modernization *refers to a complex set of changes that take place as a traditional society becomes an industrial one.* Modernization as we know it today is a phenomenon that first began with the Industrial Revolution some two centuries ago. Whereas the modernization of Western society evolved steadily over that time, the modernization of Third World nations is proceeding at a much more rapid pace.

Modernization: An Overview

As modernization progresses, many different changes occur. In the first stages of modernization, farmers move beyond subsistence farming to produce surplus food, which they sell in the market for money instead of bartering for goods and services. In addition, a few limited cash crops and natural resources are exploited, bringing a steady flow of money into the economy. Simple tools and traditional crafts are replaced by industrialized technology and applied scientific knowledge. And whenever possible, human physical power is replaced by machines.

As modernization continues, work becomes increasingly specialized. New jobs—often requiring special training—are created, and people work for wages rather than living from the products of their labor. The economic system is freed from the traditional restraints and obligations rooted in kinship relations, and money becomes the medium of exchange. Educational institutions become differentiated from family life, and the population becomes increasingly literate. Cities rise as industrial and commercial centers attract migrants from rural areas. Thanks to modern medicine, the death rate of the population falls, but the birthrate stays the same (at least in the early stages of modernization), creating overcrowding.

Modernization reduces the role of the family in the socialization of young children. Nuclear families are cut off from extended kinship networks, and many traditional constraints on behavior, such as notions of family pride and religious beliefs, lose their potency. Frequently, social equality between men and women increases as new social statuses and roles allow for changes in institutionalized behavior. Wealth is unequally distributed between the upper and lower classes (Dalton, 1971; Moore, 1965; Smelser, 1971). As you may have noted, many of these developments are separate facets of the overall pattern of increasing differentiation, which is a key trait of modernizing societies.

Modernization in the Third World

Whereas modernization was indigenous to most of Europe, it was forced on Third World nations by conquering armies, missionaries, plantation managers, colonial administrators, colonist groups, and industrial enterprises. Colonial administrators did not hesitate to destroy existing political structures whenever they seemed to endanger their rule. Missionaries used the threat of military force, bribery, and even good deeds (such as the construction of hospitals and schools) to draw people away from their traditions. The stamped out practices of which they did not approve (such as polygamy) and arbitrarily imposed European customs. Occasionally these missionary activities had comic consequences,

as when women, unaccustomed to covering their breasts, simply cut holes in the fronts of their missionary-issued T-shirts. Other results were less humorous: People in tropical climates suffered skin infections after missionaries convinced them to dress in Western clothes but neglected to introduce soap.

Until recently, modernization and "Westernization" were thought of as more or less the same thing. A developing country that wanted to adopt Western technology had to accept its cultural elements at the same time. However, as Third World nations have gained some measure of economic control over their resources, many have asserted political independence and insisted that modernization be guided by their own traditional values. One need only think of oil-rich Islamic countries to realize the different directions that the modernization of developing countries is now taking.

The goals and methods of modernization in the Third World vary widely from region to region and even from one nation to another. Nevertheless, because of the extreme abruptness and pervasiveness of the social changes created by modernization, certain common problems confront many of the developing nations.

Modernization and the Individual

Modernization has given people in developed countries improved health, increased longevity, more

There is virtually no area of life in the United States that has not changed since the relatively simple days of the 1950s.

leisure time and affluence. Poverty, malnutrition, and disease, which were problems of Western nations as recently as 1890, have been eliminated or reduced dramatically for the bulk of the population. Life expectancy at birth increased from 47.6 years in 1900 to 75.6 years, and the workweek has been reduced from about 62 hours in 1890 to about 37 hours today. Indeed, modernization has given many in Western society the "luxury" of turning their attention to the problems of affluence, including anxiety, obesity, degenerative diseases, divorce, high taxes, inflation, and pollution.

The positive psychological effects of modernization were demonstrated by sociologists Alex Inkeles and David H. Smith (1974), who interviewed factory workers in Argentina, Bangladesh, Chile, India, Israel, and Nigeria. These researchers found that attending school and going to work in a factory had been a valued, liberating experience for many of these workers. They had improved their standards of living, overcome their fears of new things and foreign people, become more flexible about trying new ways of doing things, and adopted a more positive and action-oriented attitude toward their own lives.

Despite these benefits, modernization is not without costs. Max Weber, who valued modernization as a means for making society more rational and efficient, nevertheless was painfully aware of its emotional costs, of its damaging impact on the spirit of the individual:

> Already now, throughout private enterprise in wholesale manufacture, as well as in all other economic enterprises run on modern lines . . . rational calculation . . . is manifest at every stage. By it, the performance of each individual worker is mathematically measured, each man becomes a little cog in the machine and, aware of this, his one preoccupation is whether he can become a bigger cog (Weber, 1956).

Anthropologists and others have documented the severe psychological dislocation suffered by many peoples around the world as a result of modernization. The collapse of traditional cultures under the pressures of modernization has left individuals emotionally adrift in a world they do not understand and cannot control. Probably the most horrifying account is Colin Turnbull's (1972) of the Ik, a hunting and food-gathering people of Uganda who were relocated and forced to become farmers. Within five years their society, including its basic family unit, had disintegrated. Unable to feed themselves or their families in their traditional way, individuals starved, became demoralized, and lost their ability to empathize with one another.

Thus, it is clear that modernization has a profound psychological effect on people's lives. The *degree* of personal stress and dislocation that individuals experience as their society modernizes depends on many things, including the historical traditions of the culture, the conditions under which modernization is introduced, and the degree to which the masses are allowed to share in the material benefits of the change.

SOCIAL CHANGE IN THE UNITED STATES

There is virtually no area in the United States that has not changed in some respect since the relatively simple days of the 1950s. In addition, the pace of change will quicken even more as the turn of the century approaches. The following are a few of the major forces that are shaping future life in the United States.

Technological Change

In the past dozen years the personal computer has transformed the workplace and our lives; videocassette recorders are now present in 66 percent of all households (American Demographics, 1988); compact discs have added dramatically to home entertainment activities, and biotechnology has helped us discover genetically engineered vaccines and a host of other benefits. What could possibly top what has already happened and the changes that have been produced?

The answer is that the technological innovations about to take place will be part of a new era which one author (Bylinsky, 1988) has called *The Age of Insight*, in which advances will help us understand how things work and how to make them work better. The immediate future will produce not just more and more data but also some startling new discoveries. The computer is being transformed from a number cruncher into a machine for insight and discovery.

The Age of Insight will help us understand the workings of the human body in a way never before possible. Deciphering the body's own healing mechanisms and the underlying causes of disease will allow us to develop new drugs and novel methods of treatment. Researchers will increasingly tap the body itself as a new source of medications that genetic engineers can copy and improve on. New insights into human diseases should essentially make it possible to prevent such autoimmune diseases as rheumatoid arthritis, multiple sclerosis, and insulin-dependent diabetes, in which the body mistakenly attacks its own tissue (Bylinsky, 1988).

Many changes have already taken place in the area of telecommunications. Telecommunications experts see a world linked by vast computerized networks that process voice, data, and video with equal ease. Desktop workstations will have the power of what we now know as supercomputers.

Even the individual scientist can now conduct research impossible just a short time ago. With a personal computer and newly developed compact computer disks that hold enormous amounts of information, huge databases can be tapped (Crispell, 1987). Additional databases can be accessed via the telephone lines, making hard-to-find information available in minutes.

Supercomputers themselves are expected to advance to the point where they will enable scientists to "see" objects on a smaller scale than microscopes can. This should make a vital contribution to chemistry, chemical engineering, molecular biology, and other fields. Supercomputers will also be able to describe complex events, such as the chemistry involved in photosynthesis, in greater detail than is possible with today's instruments.

"Visual computing" in effect mathematically reproduces the world around us within a computer, allowing objects to be both seen and manipulated in all sorts of ways. A researcher can then describe the nature and behavior of an object or phenomenon with equations and present it visually. The objects simulated can include anything from the wing of an airplane to the interior of the sun. This kind of computing will create new areas of scientific inquiry as well as the development of new consumer products (Bylinsky, 1988).

When sociologists examine technological change, they often refer to **technological determinism**, *the view that technological change has an important effect on society and impacts its culture, social structure, and even its history.* For example, the printing press, the automobile, the jet engine, and nuclear weapons have all had a phenomenal social impact on us.

We must be careful to realize that technology *influences* rather than determines social change. Technological innovation always occurs in the context of other forces—political, economic, or historical—which themselves help shape technology and its uses. Technological innovation only takes hold when there is a need and a social acceptance for it. Technology itself is neutral; people decide whether and how to use it (Rybczynski, 1983).

The Workforce of the Future

Technological change will produce changes in the workforce. According to projections from the Bureau of Labor Statistics, the United States will have 21 million more workers in the year 2000 than it did in 1986. This represents an 18 percent increase but points to a slowing down in the rate of growth achieved in the 1972–1986 period when the labor force increased by almost 31 million (or 35 percent).

The rapid growth during the past fifteen years was the result of the coming of age of the baby-

Technological innovation takes hold only when there is some need and social acceptance for it.

Many believe we are on the brink of "The Age of Insight," a period in which advances will help us understand how things work and how to make them work better. This is a computer image of the air flow below a vertical-takeoff-and-landing jet aircraft. This sophisticated technology makes it possible to design high-speed aircraft.

boom generation and the rapid increase in the number of women entering the labor force. The effects of these two trends will be less in the future as the number of young people ready to enter the labor force declines, and the entry of women into the labor force slows.

The labor force in the year 2000 will have more minority and female workers and fewer young workers than it does today. Although the number of white men in the labor force will grow by five million, this is an increase of only 8.8 percent. Other groups will grow at much faster rates. African-American labor force participation, for example, is expected to increase 23 percent, adding 3.6 million members to the labor force. The number of women in the labor force is projected to rise 25 percent, up more than 13 million. Asians, American Indians, and members of other racial groups will add 2.4 million workers (Kutscher, 1988).

Hispanics represent one of fastest growing segments of the labor force today. They are expected to increase by 74 percent or six million by the year 2000. In fact, African Americans, Asians and other races, women, and Hispanics will account for more than 90 percent of all labor force growth. In addition, as many as 23 percent of the new workers will be immigrants (U.S. Bureau of Labor Statistics, 1987).

Service-producing industries will account for nearly all projected growth. The finance, insurance, and real estate industry is projected to add more than 1.6 million jobs. This number, however, represents a considerable slowing in this sector when compared with the nearly 2.4 million jobs added over the previous fourteen years. The service industries themselves will expand by more than 10 million jobs. Health care services and business services will be important contributors as they continue to produce new services that greatly add to their overall demand and employment growth (U.S. Bureau of Labor Statistics, 1987).

There will be a number of effects from the expected changes in the growth and composition of the labor force. For example, as the number of jobseekers aged 16 to 19 declines, the unemployment rate for this group, which has been historically high, should also decline. There will also be a much smaller market for goods and services primarily targeted at 16 to 24 year olds (Kutscher, 1988).

Five occupational groups are projected to grow faster than average between now and the year 2000. These include technicians, service workers, professional workers, sales workers, and executive and managerial employees. Some groups—agriculture, forestry, fishing workers, and private household workers—are expected to decline (see Figures 19.1 and 19.2 for the fastest growing and fastest declining occupations).

In certain parts of the country the shape of future employment is already quite clear. On the West Coast and in New England a great concentration of high-tech industries has produced a demand for a large workforce in science, engineering, and technical occupations. In fact, in California, Massachusetts, Washington, Connecticut, New Hampshire, and New Jersey at least 13.5 percent of the workforce now operates in those areas (Giese and Testa, 1988).

FIGURE 19.1

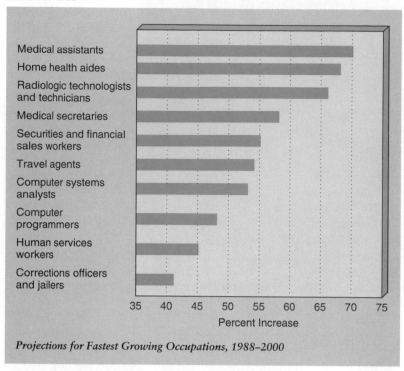

Projections for Fastest Growing Occupations, 1988–2000

Source: United States Bureau of the Census, *Statistical Abstract of the United States: 1991,* Washington, DC, 1991, p. 398.

The occupational projections are related to education. For the most part, occupations which require the most education will grow the most rapidly. There will still be plenty of jobs available for those with only a high school degree. However, the prospects for someone with less than a high school education will be dim (Kutscher, 1988).

FIGURE 19.2

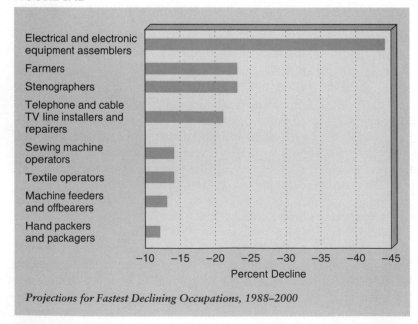

Projections for Fastest Declining Occupations, 1988–2000

Source: United States Bureau of the Census, *Statistical Abstract of the United States: 1991,* Washington, DC, 1991, p. 398.

CONTROVERSIES IN SOCIOLOGY

Are We Experiencing Information Anxiety?

For hundreds of years, the production of information increased in sedate increments. Then, in the late 1950s, the advent of new technology made possible the almost instantaneous pooling of information. This, along with the increase in the number of people involved in data production and processing, and the low cost of collecting it, caused the rate at which information was produced to soar. The amount of available information now doubles every five years; soon it will double every four.

With new information comes new demands on our faculties. We must learn new concepts and new vocabularies. Today, the English language contains roughly 500,000 useable words, five times more than during the time of Shakespeare. The number of books in top libraries doubles every fourteen years, giving new meaning to the words "keep up with your reading."

To survive in the workplace and even to function in society in general, we are forced to assimilate a body of knowledge that is expanding by the minute. For evidence, think of the ever-higher pile of periodicals, books, brochures, office memos, and annual reports that accumulate on people's desks.

Information has become the driving force of our lives, and the ominous threat of this ever-increasing pile demanding to be understood has made most of us anxious. Information anxiety is produced by the ever-widening gap between what we understand and what we think we should understand. Information anxiety is the black hole between data and knowledge.

Our relationship to information is not the only source of information anxiety. We are also made anxious by the fact that our access to information is often controlled by other people. We are dependent on those who design information, on the news editors and producers who decide what news we will receive, and by decision makers in the public and private sectors who can restrict the flow of information. We are also made anxious by other people's expectations of what we should know, be they company presidents, peers, or even parents.

Almost everyone suffers from information anxiety to some degree. We read without comprehending, see without perceiving, hear without listening. It can also be manifested as a chronic malaise, a pervasive fear that we are about to be overwhelmed by the very material we need to master in order to function in this world.

Source: Richard Saul Wurman, *Information Anxiety*, New York: Doubleday, 1989.

▪ GLOSSARY ▪

Abstract ideals Aspects of a religion that focus on correct ways of thinking and behaving rather than on a belief in supernatural forces, spirits, or beings.

Achieved statuses Statuses obtained as a result of individual efforts.

Acting crowd A group of people whose passions and tempers have been aroused by some focal event, who come to share a purpose, who feed off one another's arousal, and who often erupt into spontaneous acts of violence.

Activity theory The view that satisfaction in later life is related to the level of activity the person engages in.

Adaptation The process by which human beings adjust to the changes in their environment.

Adult socialization The process by which adults learn new statuses and roles. Adult socialization continues throughout the adult years.

Affiliation Meaningful interaction with others

Age-Specific death rates The annual number of deaths per 1,000 population at specific ages.

Alienation The sense of loss and disconnectedness that is claimed to be present among workers in capitalistic societies.

Analysis The process through which scientific data are organized so comparisons can be made and conclusions drawn.

Anglo conformity A form of assimilation that involves the renuciation of the ancestral culture in favor of Anglo-American behavior and values.

Animism The belief in animate, personalized spirits or ghosts of ancestors that take an interest in, and actively work to influence, human affairs.

Annihilation The deliberate practice of trying to exterminate a racial or ethnic group. Also known as genocide.

Anomie The feeling of some individuals that their culture no longer provides adequate guidelines for behavior; a condition of "normlessness" in which values and norms have little impact.

Aristocracy Rule by a select few; a form of oligarchy.

Ascribed statuses Statuses conferred on an individual at birth or on other occasions by circumstances beyond the individual's control.

Assimilation The process whereby groups with different cultures come to have a common culture.

Associations Purposefully created special interest groups that have clearly defined goals and official ways of doing things.

Authoritarian leader A type of instrumental leader who makes decisions and gives orders.

Authority Power regarded as legitimate by those over whom it is exercised, who also accept the authority's legitimacy in imposing sanctions or even in using force, if necessary.

Autocracy A political system in which the ultimate authority rests with a single person.

Bilateral descent system A descent system that traces kinship through both female and male family members.

Bilocal residence Marital residence rules allowing a newly married couple to live with either the husband's or wife's family of origin.

Blind investigator A researcher who does not know whether a specific subject belongs to the group of actual cases being investigated or to a comparison group. This is done to eliminate researcher bias.

Bourgeoisie The term used by Karl Marx to describe the owners of the means of production and distribution in capitalist societies.

Bureaucracy A formal, rationally organized social structure with clearly defined patterns of activity in which, ideally, every series of actions is fundamentally related to the organization's purpose.

Capitalism An economic system based on private ownership of the means of production in which resource allocation depends largely on market forces.

Caste system A rigid form of social stratification based on ascribed characteristics that determines its members' prestige, occupation, residence, and social relationships.

Casual crowd A crowd made up of a collection of people who, in the course of their private activities, happen to be in the same place at the same time.

Charismatic authority The power deriving from a ruler's force of personality. It is the ability to inspire passion and devotion among followers.

City A unit typically incorporated according to the laws of the state within whch it is located.

Class system A system of social stratification containing several social classes in which greater social mobility is permitted than in a caste or estate system.

Closed society A society in which the various aspects of people's lives are determined at birth and remain fixed.

Coalescence The second stage in the life cycle of a social movement when groups begin to form around leaders, promote policies, and promulgate programs.

Coercion A form of conflict in which one of the parties is much stronger than the others and imposes its will because of that strength.

Cognitive culture The thinking component of culture consisting of shared beliefs and knowledge of what the world is like—what is real and what is not, what is important and what is trivial. One of the two categories of nonmaterial culture.

Collective behavior Relatively spontaneous social actions that occur when people respond to unstructured and ambiguous situations.

Collective conscience A system of fundamental beliefs and values.

Command economy An economy in which the government makes all the decisions about production and consumption.

Communism The name commonly given to totalitarian socialist forms of government.

Companionate marriage Marriage based on romantic love.

Competition A form of conflict in which individuals or groups confine their conflict within agreed-upon rules.

Concentric zone model A theory of city development in which the central city is made up of a business district and, radiating from this district, zones of low-income, working-class, middle-class, and upper-class residential units.

Conditioning the molding of behavior through a series of repeated experiences that link a desired reaction with a particular object or event.

Conflict The opposite of cooperation. People in conflict struggle against one another for some commonly prized object or value.

Conflict approach An approach to law which assumes that the elite use their power to enact and enforce laws that support their own economic interests and go against the interests of the lower classes.

Conflict theory This label applies to any of a number of theories which assume that society is in a constant state of social conflict, with only temporarily stable periods, and that social phenomena are the result of this conflict.

Consensus approach An approach to law which assumes that laws are merely a formal version of the norms and values of the people.

Conservative ideologies Ideologies that try to preserve things as they are.

Conservative social movement A social movement that seeks to maintain society's current values.

Consolidated metropolitan statistical area (CMSA) A metropolitan area with a population of one million or more that consists of two or more smaller metropolitan areas.

Constitutionalism The rule of the government is limited. The various agencies of government can act only in specific legal ways.

Context The conditions under which an action takes place, including the physical setting or place, the social environment, and the other activities surrounding the action.

Contractual cooperation Cooperation in which each person's specific obligations are clearly spelled out.

Conventional crowd A crowd in which people's behavior conforms to some well-established set of cultural norms and in which people's gratification results from a passive appreciation of an event.

Convergence theory Collective behavior is the outcome of situations in which people with similar characteristics, attitudes, and needs are drawn together.

Cooperation A form of social interaction in which people act together to promote common interests or achieve shared goals.

Craze A fad that is especially short-lived.

Crime Behavior that violates a society's legal code.

Cross-sectional study An examination of a population at a given point in time.

Crowd A temporary concentration of people who focus on some thing or event but who also are attuned to one another's behavior.

Crude birthrate The number of annual births per 1,000 population.

Crude death rate The annual number of deaths per 1,000 population.

Cult A religious movement that often introduces totally new religious ideas and principles, and involves an intense sense of mission. Cults usually have charismatic leaders who expect a total commitment from the cult members.

Cultural lag A situation that develops when new patterns of behavior conflict with traditional values. Cultural lag may occur when technological change (material culture) is more rapid than are changes in norms and values (nonmaterial culture).

Cultural relativism The position that social scientists doing cross cultural research should view and analyze behaviors and customs within the cultural context in which they occur.

Cultural traits Items of a culture such as tools, materials used, beliefs, values, and typical ways of doing things.

Cultural transmission The transmission of major portions of a society's knowledge, norms, values, and perspectives from one generation to the next. Cultural transmission is an intended function of education.

Cultural universals Forms or patterns for resolving common, basic human problems that are found in all cultures. Cultural universals include the division of labor, the incest taboo, marriage, the family, rites of passage, and ideology.

Culture All that human beings learn to do, to use, to produce, to know, and to believe as they grow to maturity and live out their lives in the social groups to which they belong.

Culture shock The reaction people may have when encountering cultural traditions different from their own.

De facto segregation Segregation of community or neighborhood schools that results from residential patterns in which minority groups often live in areas of a city where there are few whites or none at all.

De jure segregation Segregation that is an outgrowth of local laws that prohibit one racial group from attending school with another.

Demise The last stage in the life cycle of a social movement when the movement comes to an end.

Democracy A political system operating under the principles of constitutionalism, representatve government, majority rule, civilian rule, and minority rights.

Democratic leader A type of instrumental leader who attempts to encourage group members to reach a consensus.

Democratic socialism A political system that exhibits the dominant features of a democracy, but the control of the economy is vested in the government to a greater extent than under capitalism.

Demographic transition theory A theory that explains population dynamics in terms of four distinct stages from high fertility and high mortality to relatively low fertility and mortality.

Demography The study of the dynamics of human populations.

Denomination A religious group that tends to draw its membership from a particular "socially acceptable" class, or ethnic group, or at least to have its leadership positions dominated by members of such a group.

Dependency ratio The number of people of nonworking age in a society, for every 100 people of working age.

Dependent variable A variable that changes in response to changes in the independent variable.

Deviant behavior Behavior that fails to conform to the rules or norms of the group in which it occurs.

Dictatorship A totalitarian government in which all power rests ultimately in one person, who generally heads the only recognized political party.

Diffusion One of the two mechanisms responsible for cultural evolution. Diffusion is the movement of cultural traits from one culture to another.

Directed cooperation Cooperation characterized by a joint effort under the control of people in authority.

Discrimination Differential treatment, usually unequal and injurious, accorded to individuals who are assumed to belong to a particular category or group.

Disengagement theory Aging involves an inevitable withdrawal, or disengagement from positions of social responsibility as part of the orderly operation of society.

Diversion Steering youthful offenders away from the juvenile justice system to nonofficial social agencies.

Double-blind investigator A researcher who does not know either the kind of subject being investigated or the hypothesis being tested.

Dramaturgy The study of the roles people play in order to create a particular impression in others.

Ecclesia A church that shares the same ethical system as the secular society and that has come to represent and promote the interests of the society at large.

Economy An institution whose primary function is to determine the manner in which a society produces, distributes, and consumes goods and services.

Ecumenism The trend among many religions to draw together and project a sense of unity and common direction.

Ego In Freudian theory, one of the three separate functioning parts of the self. The ego tries to mediate in the conflict between the id and the superego and find socially acceptable ways for the id's drives to be expressed. This part of the self constantly evaluates social realities and looks for ways to adjust to them.

Electorate Those citizens eligible to vote.

Empirical question A question that can be answered by observation and analysis of the world as it is known.

Empiricism The view that generalizations are valid only if they rely on evidence observed directly or verified through our senses.

Endogamy Societal norms that limit the social categories from within which one can choose a marriage partner.

Environmental determinism The belief that the environment dictates cultural patterns.

Estate A segment of a society that has legally established rights and duties.

Estate system A closed system of stratification in which social position is defined by law, and membership is based primarily on inheritance. A very limited possibility of upward mobility exists.

Ethnic group A group that has a distinct cultural tradition with which its own members identify and which may or may not be recognized by others.

Ethnocentrism The tendency to judge other cultures in terms of one's own customs and values.

Ethology The scientific study of animal behavior.

Ethomethodology A study of the sets of rules or guidelines people use in their everyday living practices. This approach provides information about a society's unwritten rules for social behavior.

Evolution The continuous change from a simpler condition to a more complex state.

Exchange interaction An interaction involving one person doing something for another with the express purpose of receiving a reward or return.

Exogamy Societal norms that require an individual to marry someone outside his or her culturally defined group.

Experiment An investigation in which the variables being studied are controlled and the researcher obtains the results through precise observation and measurement.

Expressive crowd A crowd that is drawn together by the promise of personal gratification for its members through active participation in activities and events.

Expressive leadership A form of leadership in which a leader works to keep relations among group members harmonious and morale high.

Expressive social movement A social movement that stresses personal feelings of satisfaction or well-being and that typically arises to fill some void or to distract people from some great dissatisfaction in their lives.

Expulsion The process of forcing a group to leave the territory in which it resides.

Extended families Families that include, in addition to nuclear family members, other relatives such as the parents' parents, the parents' siblings, and in-laws.

External means of social control The ways in which others respond to a person's behavior that channel his or her behavior along culturally approved lines.

External sources of social change Changes within a society produced by events external to that society.

Exurbs The fast growing area located in a newer, second ring beyond the old suburbs.

Fad A transitory social change that has a very short life span marked by a rapid spread, and an abrupt drop from popularity.

Family of orientation The nuclear family in which one is born and raised. Also known as family of origin.

Family of procreation The family created by marriage.

Fascism A political-economic system characterized by totalitarian capitalism.

Fashion A transitory change in the standards of dress or manners in a given society.

Felonies Offenses punishable by a year or more in a state prison.

Fertility The actual number of births in the population.

Fertility rate The number of annual births per 1,000 women of childbearing age in a population.

Folkways Norms that permit a rather wide degree of individual interpretation as long as certain limits are not overstepped. Folkways change with time and vary from culture to culture.

Forced acculturation The situation that occurs when social change is imposed by might or conquest on weaker peoples.

Forced migration The relocation of a group of people through direct action.

Formal negative sanctions Actions that express institutionalized disapproval of a person's behavior, such as expulsion, dismissal, or imprisonment. They are usually applied within the context of a society's formal organizations, including schools, corporations, and the legal system.

Formal positive sanctions Actions that express social approval of a person's behavior, such as public gatherings, rituals, or ceremonies.

Formal sanctions Sanctions that are applied in a public ritual, usually under the direct or indirect leadership of social authorities. Examples: the award of a prize or the announcement of an expulsion.

Fragmentation The fourth stage in the life cycle of a social movement when the movement gradually begins to fall apart.

Functionalism (Structural Functionalism) One of the major sociological perspectives which assumes that society is a system of highly interrelated parts that operate (function) together harmoniously.

Funnel effect The situation in our criminal justice system where many crimes are committed, but few criminals seem to be punished.

Gemeinschaft A community in which relationships are intimate, cooperative, and personal.

Gender The social, psychological, and cultural attributes of masculinity and femininity that are based on biological distinctions.

Gender identity The view of ourselves resulting from our sex.

Gender-role socialization The lifelong process whereby people learn the values, attitudes, and behavior considered appropriate to each sex by their culture.

Generalized adaptation One of the two forms of adaptation. Generalized adaptation involves developing more complicated yet more flexible ways of doing things.

Generalized others The viewpoints, attitudes, and expectations of society as a whole or of a general community of people that we are aware of and who are important to us.

Genes The set of inherited units of biological material with which each individual is born.

Gentrification A trend that involves young, middle-class people, moving to marginal urban areas, upgrading the neighborhood and displacing some of the poor residents who become priced out of the available housing.

Gesellschaft A society in which relationships are impersonal and independent.

Ghetto A term originally used to refer to the segregated quarter of a city where the Jews in Europe were often forced to live. Today it is used to refer to any kind of segregated living environment.

Group A collection of specific, identifiable people.

Hidden curriculum The social attitudes and values learned in school that prepare children to accept the requirements of adult life and to "fit into" the social, political, and economic statuses of adult life.

Homeostatic system An assemblage of interrelated parts that seeks to achieve and maintain a settled or stable state.

Homogamy The tendency to choose a spouse with a similar racial, religious, ethnic, educational, age, and socioeconomic background.

Horizontal mobility Movement that involves a change in status with no corresponding change in social class.

Hypothesis A testable statement about the relationship between two or more empirical variables.

I The portion of the self that wishes to have free expression, to be active, and to be spontaneous.

Id In Freudian theory, one of the three separately functioning parts of the self. The id consists of the unconscious drives or instincts that Freud believed every human being inherits.

Ideal norms Expectations of what people should do under perfect conditions. The norm that marriage will last "until death do us part" is an ideal norm in American society.

Ideal type A simplified, exaggerated model of reality used to illustrate a concept.

Idealistic point A term developed by Pitirim A. Sorokin to refer to the situation where sensate and ideational values coexist in a harmonious mix.

Ideational culture A term developed by Pitirim A. Sorokin to describe a culture in which spiritual concerns have the greatest value.

Ideologies Strongly held beliefs and values to which group members are firmly committed and which cement the social structure.

Ideology A set of interrelated religious or secular beliefs, values, and norms justifying the pursuit of a given set of goals through a given set of means.

Immigration The movement of a population into an area.

Incest The term used to describe sexual relations within families. Most cultures have strict taboos against incest, which is often associated with strong feelings of horror and revulsion.

Incest taboo A societal prohibition that forbids sexual intercourse among closely related individuals.

Incipiency The first stage in the life cycle of a social movement when large numbers of people perceive a problem without an existing solution.

Independent variable A variable that changes for reasons that have nothing to do with the dependent variable.

Industrial cities Cities established during or after the Industrial Revolution, characterized by large populations that work primarily in industrial or service-related jobs.

Infant mortality rate The number of children who die within the first year of life per 1,000 live births.

Informal negative sanctions Spontaneous displays of disapproval of a person's behavior. Impolite treatment is directed toward the violator of a group norm.

Informal positive sanctions Spontaneous actions such as smiles, pats on the back, handshakes, congratulations, and hugs, through which individuals express their approval of another's behavior.

Informal sanctions Responses by others to an individual's behavior that arise spontaneously with little or no formal leadership.

Innovation Any new practice or tool that becomes widely accepted in a society.

Innovators Individuals who accept the culturally validated goal of success but find deviant ways of reaching it.

Instincts Biologically inherited patterns of complex behavior.

Institutionalization The third stage in the life cycle of a social movement when the movement reaches its peak of strength and influence and becomes firmly established.

Institutionalized prejudice and discrimination Complex societal arrangements that restrict the life chances and choices of a specifically defined group.

Instrumental leadership A form of leadership in which a leader actively proposes tasks and plans to guide the group toward achieving its goals.

Intergenerational mobility Changes in the social level of a family through two or more generations.

Internal means of social control A group's moral code becomes internalized and becomes part of each individual's personal code of conduct that operates even in the absence of reactions by others.

Internal migration The movement of a population within a nation's boundary lines.

Internal sources of social change Those factors that originate within a specific society and that singly or in combination produce significant alterations in its social organization and structure.

Interview A conversation between an investigator and a subject for the purpose of gathering information.

Intragenerational mobility Changes in the social level of a family through two or more generations.

Labeling theory A theory of deviance that assumes the social process by which an individual comes to be labeled a deviant contributes to causing more of the deviant behavior.

Laissez-faire capitalism The view of capitalism which espouses that government should stay out of business.

Laissez-faire leader A type of instrumental leader who is a leader in name or title only and does little actively to influence group affairs.

Latent function One of two types of social functions identified by Robert Merton referring to the *unintended* or not readily recognized consequences of a social process.

Leader Someone who occupies a central role or position of dominance and influence in a group.

Legal code The formal body of rules adopted by a society's political authority.

Legal-rational authority Authority that derives from the fact that specific individuals have clearly defined rights and duties to uphold and implement rules and procedures.

Liberal ideologies Ideologies that seek limited reforms that do not involve fundamental changes in the structure of society.

Libido One of the two basic instincts of the id. According to Freud, the libido controls the erotic or sexual drive.

Life expectancy The average number of years that a person born in a particular year can expect to live.

Lobbying Attempts by special-interest groups to influence government policy.

Longitudinal research A research approach in which a population is studied at several intervals over a relatively long period of time.

Looking-glass self A theory developed by Charles Horton Cooley to explain how individuals develop a sense of self through interaction with others. The theory has three stages: (1) we imagine how our actions appear to others, (2) we imagine how other people judge these actions, and (3) we make some sort of self-judgment based on the presumed judgments of others.

Magic Interaction with the supernatural. Magic does not involve the worship of a god or gods, but is rather an attempt to coerce spirits or control supernatural forces.

Majority rule The right of people to assemble to express their views and seek to persuade others, to engage in political organizing, and to vote for whomever they wish.

Mana A Melanesian/Polynesian concept of the supernatural that refers to a diffuse, nonpersonalized force that acts through anything that lives or moves.

Manifest function One of two types of social functions identified by Robert Merton referring to an *intended* and recognized consequence of a social process.

Marital residence rules Rules that govern where a newly married couple settles down and lives.

Marriage The socially recognized, legitimized, and supported union of individuals of opposite sexes.

Mass A collection of people who, although physically dispersed, participate in some event either physically or with a common concern or interest.

Mass hysteria A condition in which large numbers of people are overwhelmed with emotion and frenzied activity or become convinced that they have experienced something for which investigators can find no discernible evidence.

Mass media Methods of communication, including television, radio, magazines, films, and newspapers, that have become some of society's most important agents of socialization.

Master status One of the multiple statuses a person occupies that dominates the others in patterning that person's life.

Material culture All the things human beings make and use, from small hand-held tools to skyscrapers.

Matriarchal family A family in which most family affairs are dominated by women.

Matrilineal system A descent system that traces kinship through the females of the family.

Matrilocal residence Marital residence rules that require a newly-married couple to settle down near or within the wife's mother's household.

Me The portion of the self that is made up of those things learned through the socialization process from the family, peers, school, and so on.

Mechanically integrated society A type of society in which members have common goals and values and a deep and personal involvement with the community.

Mechanisms of social control Processes used by all societies and social groups to influence or mold members' behavior to conform to group values and norms.

Megalopolis Another term for Consolidated Metropolitan Statistical Area. See CMSA for definition.

Metropolitan area An area that has a large population nucleus, together with the adjacent communities that are economically and socially integrated into that nucleus.

Metropolitan statistical area (MSA) An area that has either one or more central cities, each with a population of at least 50,000, or a single urbanized area that has at least 50,000 people and that is part of an MSA with a total population of 100,000.

Middle-range theories Theories concerned with explaining specific issues or aspects of society instead of trying to explain how all of society operates.

Migration The movement of populations from one geographical area to another.

Millenarian movements Religious movements that prophesy the end of the world, the destruction of all evil people and their works, and the saving of the just.

Minority A group of people who, because of physical or cultural characteristics, are singled out from others in the society in which they live for different and unequal treatment and who therefore regard themselves as objects of collective discrimination.

Minority rights The minority has the right to try to change the laws of the majority.

Mixed economy An economy that combines free-enterprise capitalism with government regulation of business, industry, and social-welfare programs.

Modernization The complex set of changes that take place as a traditional society becomes an industrial society.

Modernization theory There is a direct relationship between the extent of modernization in a society and the status and condition of the elderly.

Monogamous marriage The form of marriage in which each person is allowed only one spouse at a time.

Monotheism The belief in the existence of only one god.

Moral code The symbolic system, made up of a culture's norms and values, in terms of which behavior takes on the quality of being "good" or "bad," "right" or "wrong."

Moral order A society's shared view of right and wrong.

Mores Strongly held norms that usually have a moral connotation and are based on the central values of the culture.

Multiple marriage A form of marriage in which an individual may have more than one spouse (polygamy).

Multiple nuclei model An theory of city development that emphasizes the fact that different industries have different land-use and financial requirements, which determine where they establish themselves. As similar industries are established close to one another, the immediate neighborhood is strongly shaped by the nature of its typical industry, becoming one of a number of separate nuclei that together constitute the city.

Negative sanctions Responses by others that discourage the individual from continuing or repeating the behavior.

Neolocal residence Marital residence standards which allow a newly married couple to live virtually anywhere, even thousands of miles from their families or origin.

Nonmaterial culture The totality of knowledge, beliefs, values, and rules for appropriate behavior that specifies how a people should interact and how they may solve their problems.

Normal behavior Behavior that conforms to the rules or norms of the group in which it occurs.

Normative culture One of the two categories of nonmaterial culture. Normative culture consists of the rules people follow for doing things. Norms, mores, and folkways are the central elements of normative culture.

Norms Specific rules of behavior that are agreed upon and shared within a culture to prescribe limits of acceptable behavior.

Nuclear family The most basic family form, made up of parents and their children, biological or adopted.

Nurture The entire socialization experience.

Objective approach The approach to measuring social stratification in which researchers decide in advance that a certain number of social classes will be used and then determine what criteria will be used for assigning people to each class.

Oligarchy Rule by a few individuals who occupy the highest positions in an organization.

Open society A society that provides equal opportunity to everyone to compete for the role and status desired, regardless of race, religion, gender, or family history.

Operational definition A definition of an abstract concept in terms of the observable features that describe the things being investigated.

Opinion leaders Socially acknowledged experts to whom the public turns for advice.

Organically integrated society A type of society in which solidarity depends on the cooperation of individuals in many different positions who perform specialized tasks.

Organized crime Structured associations of individuals or groups who come together for the purpose of obtaining gain mostly from illegal activities.

Panic An uncoordinated group flight from a perceived danger.

Pantheon The hierarchy of deities in a religious belief system.

Paradigm A basic model for explaining events that provides a framework for the questions that generate and guide research.

Participant observation A research technique in which the investigator enters into a group's activities while, at the same time, studying the group's behavior.

Patriarchal family A family in which most family affairs are dominated by men.

Patriarchal ideology The belief that men are superior to women and should control all important aspects of society.

Patrilineal system A descent system that traces kinship through the males of the family.

Patrilocal residence Marital residence rules that require a newly-married couple to settle down near or within the husband's father's household.

Peers Individuals who are social equals.

Personality The patterns of behavior and ways of thinking and feeling that are distinctive for each individual.

Pleasure principle A Freudian principle that explains the id's impulsive attempts to satisfy its drive for sexual expression.

Pluralism The development and coexistence of separate racial and ethnic group identities in a society in which no single subgroup dominates.

Political action committee (PAC) A fundraising and lobbying committee that has been set up to represent a single-issue group.

Political revolutions Relatively rapid transformations of state or government structures that are not accompanied by changes in social structure or stratification.

Politics The process by which power is distributed and decisions are made.

Polyandrous family A polygamous family unit in which the central figure is female and the multiple spouses are male.

Polygamous families Nuclear families linked together by multiple marriage bonds, with one central individual married to several spouses.

Polygynous family A polygamous family unit in which the central person is male and the multiple spouses are female.

Polytheism The belief in a number of gods.

Positive checks Events, described by Thomas Robert Malthus, that limit reproduction either by causing the deaths of individuals before they reach reproductive age or by causing the deaths of large numbers of people, thereby lowering the overall population. Examples: famines, wars, and epidemics.

Positive sanctions Responses by others that encourage the individual to continue acting in a certain way.

Power The ability of an individual or group to attain goals, control events, and maintain influence over others—even in the face of opposition.

Power elite The group of people who control policy making and the setting of priorities.

Prayer A religious ritual that enables individuals to communicate with supernatural beings or forces.

Preindustrial cities Cities established prior to the Industrial Revolution. These cities were usually walled for protection and power was typically shared between feudal lords and religious leaders.

Prejudice An irrationally based negative, or occasionally positive, attitude toward certain groups and their members.

Prestige The approval and respect an individual or group receives from other members of society.

Preventive checks Practices, described by Thomas Robert Malthus, that limit reproduction. Examples: contraception, prostitution, and other vices.

Primary deviance A term used in labeling theory to refer to the original behavior that leads to the individual being labeled as deviant.

Primary group A group that is characterized by intimate face-to-face association and cooperation. Primary groups involve interaction among members who have an emotional investment in one another and who interact as total individuals rather than through specialized roles.

Primary metropolitan statistical area (PMSA) A large urbanized county or cluster of counties that is part of a metropolitan statistical area with one million people or more.

Primary socialization The process by which children master the basic information and skills required of members of society.

Profane All empirically observable things that are knowable through ordinary everyday experiences.

Proletariat The label used by Karl Marx to describe the mass of people in society who have no other resources to sell than their labor.

Propaganda Advertisements of a political nature seeking to mobilize public support behind one specific party, candidate, or point of view.

Property crime An unlawful act that is committed with the intent of gaining property but does not involve the use or threat of force against an individual.

Psychoanalysis The form of therapy developed by Sigmund Freud for treating mental illness.

Psychoanalytic theory A body of thought developed by Sigmund Freud that rests on two basic hypotheses: (1) every human act has a psychological cause or basis, and (2) every person has an unconscious mind.

Public opinion The beliefs held by a dispersed collectivity of individuals about a common concern, interest, focus, or activity.

Race A category of people who are defined as similar because of a number of physical characteristics.

Radical ideologies Ideologies that seek major structural changes in society.

Random sample A sample selected purely on the basis of chance.

Reactionary social movement A social movement that embraces the aims of the past and seeks to return the general society to yesterday's values.

Real norms Norms that allow for differences in individual behavior. Real norms specify how people actually behave, not how they should behave under ideal circumstances.

Reality principle A Freudian principle that explains the ego's attempts to adjust to the socially appropriate demands of the real world.

Rebellions Attempts to achieve rapid political change that is not possible within existing institutions.

Rebels Individuals who reject both the goals of what to them is an unfair social order and the institutionalized means of achieving them. They propose alternative societal goals and institutions.

Recidivism Repeated criminal behavior after punishment.

Reference group A group or social category that an individual uses to help define beliefs, attitudes, and values, and to guide behavior.

Reformulation The process in which traits passed from one culture to another are modified to fit better in their new context.

Relative deprivation theory A theory that assumes social movements are the outgrowth of the feeling of relative deprivation among large numbers of people who believe they lack certain things to which they believe they are entitled.

Reliability The ability to repeat the findings of a research study.

Religion A system of beliefs, practices, and philosophical values shared by a group of people that defines the sacred, helps explain life and provides salvation from the problems of human existence.

Replication Repetition of the same research procedure or experiment for the purpose of determining whether earlier results can be duplicated.

Representative government The authority to govern is achieved through, and legitimized by, popular elections.

Representative sample A sample that has the same distribution of characteristics as the larger population from which it is drawn.

Reputational approach The approach to measuring social stratification in which social class is determined by the opinions of other community members about an individual.

Research process A sequence of steps in the design and implementation of a research study, including defining the problem, reviewing previous research, determining the research design, defining the sample and collecting data, analyzing and interpreting the data, and preparing the final research report.

Researcher bias The tendency for researchers to select data that support their hypothesis and to ignore data that appear to contradict it.

Resocialization An important aspect of adult socialization that involves being exposed to ideas or values that in one way or another conflict with what was learned in childhood.

Resource-mobilization theory A theory that assumes that social movements arise at certain times and not at others because some people know how to mobilize and channel popular discontent.

Retreatists Individuals who have pulled back from society altogether and who do not pursue culturally legitimate goals, such as drug addicts, alcoholics, hobos, and panhandlers.

Revisionary social movement A social movement that seeks partial or slight changes within the existing order but does not threaten the order itself.

Revitalization movement Powerful religious movements that stress a return to the religious values of the past. These movements spring up when a society is under great stress or attack.

Revolutionary social movement A social movement that seeks to overthrow all or nearly all of the existing social order and replace it with an order it considers to be more suitable.

Revolutions Relatively rapid transformations that produce change in a society's existing power structure.

Rites of passage Standardized rituals that mark the transition from one stage of life to another.

Ritualism Overconformity to rules.

Ritualists Individuals who deemphasize or reject the importance of success once they realize they will never achieve it and instead concentrate on following and enforcing rules more precisely than was ever intended.

Rituals Patterns of behavior or practices related to the sacred.

Role conflict The situation in which an individual who is occupying more than one status at the same time is unable to enact the roles of one status without violating those of another.

Role sets The roles attached to a single status.

Role strain The stress that results from conflicting demands within a single role.

Roles Culturally defined rules for proper behavior associated with every status.

Rumor Information that is shared informally and spreads quickly through a mass or a crowd.

Sacred Things that are awe inspiring and knowable only through extraordinary experience. Sacred traits or objects symbolize important values.

Sample The particular subset of a larger population that has been selected for study.

Sampling A research technique in which a manageable number of subjects (a sample) is selected for study from a larger population.

Sampling error The failure to select a representative sample.

Sanctions Rewards and penalties used to regulate an individual's behavior. All external means of control use sanctions.

Sapir-Whorf hypothesis A hypothesis that argues that the language a person uses determines his or her perception of reality.

Science A body of systematically arranged knowledge that shows the operation of general laws. The term also refers to the logical, systematic methods by which that knowledge is obtained.

Scientific method The approach to research which involves observation, experimentation, generalization, and verification.

Secondary deviance A term used in labeling theory to refer to the deviant behavior that emerges as a result of having been labeled as deviant.

Secondary group A group that is characterized by an impersonal, formal organization with specific goals. Secondary groups are larger and much less intimate than are primary groups, and the relationships among members are patterned mostly by statuses and roles rather than by personality characteristics.

Sect A small religious group that adheres strictly to religious doctrine involving unconventional beliefs or forms of worship.

Sector model A modified version of the concentric zone model in which urban groups establish themselves along major transportation arteries around the central business district.

Secularization The process by which religious institutions are confined to ever-narrowing spheres of social influence, while people turn to secular sources for moral guidance in their everyday lives.

Segregation A form of subjugation that refers to the act, process, or state of being set apart.

Selectivity A process that defines some aspects of the world as important and others as unimportant. Selectivity is reflected in the vocabulary and grammar of language.

Self The personal identity of each individual that is separate from his or her social identity.

Semistructured (open-ended) interview An interview in which the investigator asks a list of questions but is free to vary them or make up new ones that become important during the course of the interview.

Sensate culture A term developed by Pitirim A. Sorokin to describe a culture in which people are dedicated to self-expression and the gratification of their immediate physical needs.

Sex The physical and biological differences between men and women.

Sick role The sick role legitimates the deviant behavior caused by the illness and channels the individual into the health care system.

Significant others Those people who are most important in our development, such as parents, friends, and teachers.

Signs Objects or things that can represent other things because they share some important quality with them. A clenched fist, for example, can be a sign of anger because fists are used in physical arguments.

Small group A relative term that refers to the many kinds of social groups that actually meet together and contain few enough members so that all members know one another.

Spontaneous cooperation Cooperation that arises from the needs of a particular situation.

Social action Anything people are conscious of doing because of other people.

Social aggregate People who happen to be in the same place but share little else.

Social attachments The emotional bonds that infants form with others that are necessary for normal development. Social attachments are a basic need of human beings and all primates.

Social change Any modification in the social organization of a society in any of its social institutions or social roles.

Social class A category of people within a stratification system who share similar economic positions, similar lifestyles, and similar attitudes and behavior.

Social Darwinism The attempt to apply the evolutionary theories of animal and plant development proposed by Charles Darwin to social phenomena.

Social evaluation The process of making qualitative judgments on the basis of individual characteristics or behaviors.

Social function A social process that contributes to the ongoing operation or maintenance of society.

Social group A number of people who have a common identity, some feeling of unity, and certain common goals and shared norms.

Social identity The statuses that define an individual. Social identity is determined by how others see us.

Social inequality The uneven distribution of privileges, material rewards, opportunities, power, prestige, and influence among individuals or groups.

Social institutions The ordered social relationships that grow out of the values, norms, statuses, and roles that organize those activities that fulfill society's fundamental needs.

Social interaction The interplay between the actions of one individual and those of one or more other people.

Social mobility The movement of an individual or a group from one social status to another.

Social movement A form of collective behavior in which large numbers of people are organized or alerted to support and bring about, or to resist social change.

Social organization The web of actual interactions among individuals and groups in society that defines their mutual rights and responsibilities and differs from society to society.

Social revolutions Rapid and basic transformations of a society's state and class structures that are accompanied, and in part carried through, by class-based revolts.

Social sciences All those disciplines that apply scientific methods to the study of human behavior. The social sciences include sociology, cultural anthropology, psychology, economics, history, and political science.

Social solidarity People's commitment to a society's collective conscience.

Social stratification The division of society into levels, steps, or positions that is perpetuated by the major institutions of society such as the economy, the family, religion, and education.

Social structure The stable, patterned relationships that exist among social institutions within a society.

Socialism An economic system under which the government owns and controls the major means of production and distribution. Centralized planning is used to set production and distribution goals.

Socialization The long and complicated processes of social interaction through which a child learns the intellectual, physical, and social skills needed to function as a member of society.

Sociobiology An approach that tries to use biological principles to explain the behavior of social beings.

Sociology The scientific study of human society and social interactions.

Specialization One of the two forms of adaptation. Specialization is developing ways of doing things that work extremely well in a particular environment or set of circumstances.

State The institutionalized way of organizing power within territorial limits.

Statement of association A proposition that changes in one thing are related to changes in another, but that one does not necessarily cause the other.

Statement of causality A proposition that one thing brings about, influences, or changes something else.

Statistical significance A mathematical statement about the probability that some event or relationship is not due to change alone.

Status inconsistency Situations in which people rank differently (higher or lower) on certain stratification characteristics than on others.

Status offenses Behavior that is criminal only because the person involved is a minor.

Statuses The culturally and socially defined positions occupied by individuals throughout their lifetime.

Stratified random sample A technique to make sure that all significant variables are represented in a sample in proportion to their numbers in the larger population.

Structural conduciveness One of sociologist Neil Smelser's six conditions that shape the outcome of collective behavior, structural conduciveness refers to the conditions within society that may promote or encourage collective behavior.

Structural strain One of sociologist Neil Smelser's six conditions that shape the outcome of collective behavior, structural strain refers to the tension that develops when a group's ideals conflict with its everyday realities.

Structured interview An interview with a predetermined set of questions that are followed precisely with each subject.

Subculture The distinctive lifestyles, values, norms, and beliefs of certain segments of the population within a society.

Subjective approach The approach to measuring social stratification in which the people being studied are asked to put themselves into one of several categories.

Subjugation The subordination of one group and the assumption of a position of authority, power, and domination by the other.

Suburbs Those territories that are part of a metropolitan statistical area but outside the central city.

Superego In Freudian theory, one of the three separately functioning parts of the self. The superego consists of society's norms and values, learned in the course of a person's socialization, that often conflict with the impulses of the id. The superego is the internal censor.

Supernaturalism A belief system that postulates the existence of impersonal forces that can influence human events.

Survey A research method in which a population or a sample is studied in order to reveal specific facts about it.

Symbolic interactionism A theoretical approach that stresses the meaning people place on their own and one another's behavior.

Symbols Objects that represent other things. Unlike signs, symbols need not share any of the qualities of whatever they represent and stand for.

Taboo A sacred prohibition against touching, mentioning, or looking at certain objects, acts, or people.

Techniques of neutralization A process that makes it possible to justify illegal or deviant behavior.

Technological determinism The view that technological change has an important effect on a society and has an impact on its culture, social structure, and even its history.

Theism A belief in divine beings—gods and goddesses—who shape human affairs.

Theory of differential association A theory of juvenile delinquency based on the position that criminal behavior is learned in the context of intimate groups. People become criminals as a result of associating with others who engage in criminal activities.

Threatened crowd A crowd that is in a state of alarm, believing itself to be in some kind of danger.

Total institutions Environments, such as prisons or mental hospitals, in which the participants are physically and socially isolated from the outside world.

Totalitarian capitalism A political-economic system under which the government retains control of the social institutions, but allows the means of production and distribution to be owned and managed by private groups and individuals.

Totalitarian government A government in which one group has virtually total control of the nation's social institutions.

Totalitarian socialism In addition to almost total regulation of all social institutions, the government controls and owns all major means of production and distribution.

Totem An ordinary object, such as a plant or animal, that has become a sacred symbol to a particular group which not only reveres the totem but identifies with it.

Tracking The stratification of students by ability, social class, and various other categories.

Tracks The academic and social levels typically assigned to and followed by the children of different social classes.

Traditional authority Power rooted in the assumption that the customs of the past legitimize the present.

Traditional cooperation Cooperation that is tied to custom and is passed on from one generation to the next.

Traditional ideology An ideology that tries to preserve things as they are.

Unconscious The view that people are aware of only a small part of the thoughts and feelings that exist in their minds.

Universal church A church that includes all the members of a society within one united moral community.

Urban population The inhabitants of an urbanized area and the inhabitants of incorporated or unincorporated areas with a population of 2,500 or more.

Urbanization A process whereby a population becomes concentrated in a specific area because of migration patterns.

Urbanized area An area that contains a central city and the continuously built-up and closely settled surrounding territory that together have a population of 50,000 or more.

Validity The ability of a research study to test what it was designed to test.

Values A culture's general orientations toward life—its notion of what is good and bad, what is desirable and undesirable.

Variable Anything that can change (vary).

Vertical mobility Movement up or down in the social hierarchy that results in a change in social class.

Victimless crime Acts that violate those laws meant to enforce the moral code.

Violent crime Crimes that involve the use of force or the threat of force against an individual.

White collar crime Crime committed by individuals who, while occupying positions of social responsibility or high prestige, break the law in the course of their work for illegal, personal, or organizational gain.

▪ REFERENCES ▪

Andrews, Lori B. 1984 "Exhibit A: Language." *Psychology Today*, Vol. 18, No. 2, Feb., pp. 28–33.

Antonovsky, Aaron. 1972. "Social Class, Life Expectancy and Overall Mortality." In E. Gatly Jaco, ed., *Patients, Physicians and Illness*, 2nd. ed. New York: Free Press, pp. 5–30.

Arenson, Karen W. 1982. "Services: Bucking the Slump." *The New York Times*, May 18, p. D1.

Asch, Solomon. 1955. "Opinions and Social Press." *Scientific American*, 193, pp. 31–35.

———. 1951. "Effects of Group Pressure Upon the Modification and Distortion of Judgements." In H. Guptzkow, ed., *Groups, Leadership and Men*. Pittsburgh: Carnegie Press.

Bales, R. F. 1958. "Task Roles and Social Roles in Problem-Solving Groups." In E. E. Maccoby, T. M. Newcomb, and E. L. Hartley, eds., *Readings in Social Psychology*. 3rd ed. New York: Holt, Rinehart and Winston.

Bales, R. F. and F. L. Strodbeck. 1951. "Phases in Group Problem Solving." *Journal of Abnormal and Social Psychology*, 46, pp. 485–95.

Bandura, A. 1969. *Principles of Behavior Modification*. New York: Holt, Rinehart and Winston.

Bardwick, Judith W. and Elizabeth Douvan. 1971. "Ambivalence: The Socialization of Women." In Vivian Gornick and Barbara K. Moran, eds., *Women in Sexist Society: Studies in Power and Powerlessness*. New York: Basic Books.

Barlow, Hugh D. 1987. *Introduction to Criminology*. 4th ed. Boston: Little, Brown.

Barnett, Rosalind C. and Grace K. Baruch. 1987. "Social Roles, Gender, and Psychological Distress." In Rosalind C. Barnett, Lois Biener, and Grace K. Baruch, eds., *Gender and Stress*. New York: Free Press.

Baron, Salo W. 1976. "European Jewry Before and After Hitler." In Yisrael Gutman and Livia Rothkirchen, eds., *The Catastrophe of European Jewry*. Jerusalem: Yad Veshem.

Baskin, Barbara H. and Karen Harris. 1980. *Books for the Gifted Child*. New York: R. R. Bowker.

Baumrind, Diane. 1975. "Early Socialization and Adolescent Competence." In Sigmund E. Dragastin and Glen H. Elder, Jr., eds., *Adolescence in the Life Cycle*. New York: Halsted Press.

Becker, Howard. 1963. *Outsiders: Studies in the Sociology of Deviance*. New York: Free Press.

Beckwith, Burnham P. 1986. "Religion: A Growing or Dying Institution?" *The Futurist*, Vol. 20, No. 4, July/Aug., pp. 24–25.

Bell, Alan P., Martin S. Weinberg, and Sue Kiefer Hammersmith. 1981. *Sexual Preference: Its Development in Men and Women*. Bloomington, IN: Indiana University Press.

Bell, D. 1973. *The Coming of the Post-Industrial Society: A Venture in Social Forecasting*. New York: Basic Books.

Bem, Sandra L. and Daryl J. Bem. 1976. "Case Study of a Nonconscious Ideology: Training the Woman to Know Her Place." In Sue Cox, ed., *Female Psychology: The Emerging Self*. Chicago: Science Research Associates.

Bendix, R. 1962. *Max Weber: An Intellectual Portrait*. Garden City, NY: Doubleday/Anchor.

Benedict, Ruth. 1961 (1934). *Patterns of Culture*. Boston: Houghton Mifflin.

———. 1938. "Continuities and Discontinuities in Cultural Conditioning." *Psychiatry*, 1, pp. 161–67.

Bennis, W. 1971. "Beyond Bureaucracy." In S. G. McNall, ed., *The Sociological Perspective*. 2nd ed. Boston: Little, Brown, pp. 225–33.

Bentsen, Cheryl. 1989. *Maasai Days*. New York: Summit Books.

Berger, Peter. 1967. *The Sacred Canopy*. New York: Doubleday.

———. 1963. *Invitation to Sociology: A Humanistic Perspective*. New York: Doubleday.

Bernard, L. L. 1924. *Instinct*. New York: Holt, Rinehart and Winston.

Berry, Brewton and Henry L. Tischler. 1978. *Race and Ethnic Relations*. 4th ed. Boston: Houghton Mifflin.

Berry, Brian J. and John D. Kasarda. 1977. *Contemporary Urban Ecology*. New York: Macmillan.

Bertalanffy, Ludwig Von. 1968. *General System Theory*. New York: George Braziller.

Besharov, Douglas J. and Alison J. Quin. 1987. "Not all Female-Headed Families are Created Equal." *The Public Interest*, Fall, No. 89, pp. 48–56.

Bettleheim, B. 1967. *The Empty Fortress*. New York: Free Press.

Bianchi, Suzanne M. 1991. "Family Disruption and Economic Hardship." U.S. Bureau of the Census, March, Series P–70 No. 23.

Bianchi, Suzanne M. 1991. "Family Disruption and Economic Hardship." U.S. Bureau of the Census, March, Series P–70, No. 23.

Bierstadt, Robert. 1974. *The Social Order*. 4th ed. New York: McGraw-Hill.

Bishop, Katherine. 1988. "Neo-Nazi Activity is Arising Among U.S. Youth." *The New York Times*, June 13, p. A12.

Blakslee, Sandra. 1992. "Faulty Math Heightens Fears of Breast Cancer." *The New York Times*, March 15, Sec. 4, pp. 1,6.

Blau, Peter M. 1964. *Exchange and Power in Social Life*. New York: John Wiley.

Blau, Peter M. and M. W. Meyer. 1971. *Bureaucracy in Modern Society*. 2nd ed. New York: Random House.

Blau, Peter M. and O. D. Duncan. 1967. *The American Occupational Structure*. New York: John Wiley.

Bloom, David E. 1986. "Women and Work." *American Demographics*, Sept., pp. 24–30.

Bloom, David and Neil G. Bennett. 1986. "Childless Couples." *American Demographics*, Aug., pp. 22–25, 54.

Blum, John M., Edmund S. Morgan, Willie Lee Rose, Arthur M. Schlesinger, Jr., Kenneth M. Stamp, and C. Van Woodard. 1981. *The National Experience: A History of the United States.* 5th ed. New York: Harcourt Brace Jovanovich.

Blumberg, Paul. 1980. *Inequality in an Age of Decline.* New York: Oxford University Press.

Blumer, Herbert. 1946. "Collective Behavior." In Alfred McClung Lee, ed., *Principles of Sociology.* New York: Barnes & Noble.

Blumstein, Phillip and Pepper Schwartz. 1983. *American Couples.* New York: Morrow.

Bollen, Kenneth and David P. Phillips. 1982. "Imitative Suicides: A National Study of the Effects of Television News Stories." *American Sociological Review*, 47(6), pp. 802–09.

Bose, Christine E. and Peter H. Rossi. 1983. "Gender and Jobs: Prestige Standings of Occupations as Affected by Gender." *American Sociological Review*, June, pp. 316–30.

Bottomore, T. B. 1966. *Classes in Modern Society.* New York: Pantheon.

Bowles, Samuel and Herbert Gintis. 1976. *Schooling in Capitalist America: Educational Reform and the Contradictions of Economic Life.* New York: Basic Books.

Bronfenbrenner, U. 1970. *Worlds of Childhood.* New York: Russell Sage Foundation.

Brown, Dee. 1978. *Bury My Heart at Wounded Knee.* New York: Holt, Rinehart and Winston.

Brown, Lester R. 1974. *In the Human Interest.* New York: Norton.

Brown, Lester R. and Erik P. Eckholm. 1974. *By Bread Alone.* New York: Praeger.

Brown, Roger W. 1954. "Mass Phenomena." In Gardner Lindzey, ed., *Handbook of Social Psychology.* Cambridge, MA: Addison-Wesley.

Brown, Susan. 1984. "Changes in Laws Governing Divorce: An Evaluation of Joint Custody Presumptions." In *Journal of Family Issues*, 5(2) June, pp. 200–23.

Brownlee, Shannon, Karen Schmidt, and Eric Ransdell. 1992. "Origin of a Plague." *U.S. News and World Report*, March 30, p. 50.

Bullough, Vern L. 1973. *The Subordinate Sex.* Chicago: University of Chicago Press.

Bumpass, Larry and James Sweet. 1988. "Preliminary Evidence on Cohabitation." University of Wisconsin, Center for Demographic Ecology, Working Paper #2.

Burchinal, Lee G. and Loren E. Chancellor. 1963. "Survival Rates Among Religiously Homogamous and Interreligious Marriages." *Social Factors*, 41, pp. 353–62.

Burgess, Ernest W. 1953–1954. "Social Relations, Activities, and Personal Adjustment." *American Journal of Sociology*, 59, pp. 352–60.

Bylinski, Gene. 1988. "Technology in the Year 2000." *Fortune*, July 18, pp. 92–98.

Byrne, D. 1971. *The Attraction Paradigm.* New York: Academic Press.

Caldwell, John C. 1976. "Toward a Restatement of Demographic Transition Theory. *Population and Development Review*, 2.

Cameron, William Bruce. 1966. *Modern Social Movements: A Sociological Outline.* New York: Random House.

Canetti, Elias. 1978. (1960). *Crowds and Power.* New York: Seabury Press.

Cantril, Hadley. 1940. *The Invasion from Mars: A Study in the Psychology of Panic.* Princeton, NJ: Princeton University Press.

Capdevielle, P. and D. Alvarez. 1981. "International Comparisons of Trends in Productivity and Labor Costs." *Monthly Labor Review*, Dec., p. 15.

Centers for Disease Control. 1991. *HIV/AIDS Surveillance Report.* June.

Chalmers, David. 1980. "The Rise and Fall of the Invisible Empire of the Ku Klux Klan." *Contemporary Review*, 237, Aug., pp. 57–64.

Chambliss, William J. 1973. "Elites and the Creation of Criminal Law." In William J. Chambliss, ed., *Sociological Readings in the Conflict Perspective.* Reading, MA: Addison-Wesley.

Cherlin, Andrew. 1981. *Marriage, Divorce and Remarriage.* Cambridge, MA: Harvard University Press.

Chi, Kenneth S. and Sharon K. Houseknecht. 1985. "Protestant Fundamentalism and Marital Success: A Comparative Approach." *Sociology and Social Research*, Vol. 69, No. 3, pp. 351–75.

Chomsky, N. 1975. *Language and Mind.* New York: Harcourt Brace Jovanovich.

Claffey, Charles E. 1991. "Rewriting the Book on Slavery and Freedom." *The Boston Globe*, Dec. 3, p. 61.

Clayton, Richard B. and Harwin L. Voss. 1977. "Shacking Up: Cohabitation in the 1970s." *Journal of Marriage and the Family*, 39(2), May, pp. 273–83.

Cleland, John G. and Jerome K. van Ginneken. 1988. "Maternal Education and Child Survival in Developing Countries: The Search for Pathways of Influence." *Social Science and Medicine*, Vol. 27, No. 12, pp. 1357–68.

Cohen, Albert K. 1955. *Delinquent Boys: The Culture of the Gang.* Glencoe, IL: Free Press.

Cohen, Majorie A. and Diane E. Vigars. 1991. *Reported Missing Children in New York State, 1990.* New York: New York State Division of Criminal Justice Services.

Cohen, Yehudi A. 1981. "Shrinking Households." *Society*, 18(2), Jan.–Feb., p. 51.

———. 1974. "Pastoralism." In Y. A. Cohen, ed., *Man in*

Adaptation: The Cultural Present. 2nd ed. Chicago: Aldine.

Cole, Steward G. and Mildred Wiese Cole. 1954. *Minorities and the American Promise.* New York: Harper & Row.

Coleman, Daniel. 1992. "Black Scientists Study the 'Pose' of the Inner City." *The New York Times,* April 21, p. C1, C7.

Coleman, James S. 1977. *Parents, Teachers, and Children.* San Francisco: San Francisco Institute for Contemporary Studies.

———. 1966. *Equality of Educational Opportunity.* Washington, DC: U.S. Government Printing Office.

Collins, Randall. 1979. *The Credential Society: An Historical Sociology of Education and Stratification.* New York: Academic Press.

———. 1975. *Conflict Sociology: Toward an Explanatory Science.* New York: Academic Press.

Comte, Auguste. 1968 (1851). *System of Positive Policy.* Vol. 1, Trans. John Henry Bridges. New York: Burt Franklin.

Conrad, Peter and Rochelle Kern, eds. 1986. *The Sociology of Health and Illness.* 2nd ed. New York: St. Martin's Press.

Cooley, C. H. 1909. *Social Organization.* New York: Scribner.

Coser, L. A. 1977. *Masters of Sociological Thought.* 2nd ed. New York: Harcourt Brace Jovanovich.

———. 1967. *Continuities in the Study of Social Conflict.* New York: Free Press.

———. 1956. *The Functions of Social Conflict.* Glencoe, IL: Free Press.

Cowgill, Donald O. 1986. *Aging Around the World.* Belmont, CA: Wadsworth.

Cowgill, Donald O. and Lowell Holmes. 1972. *Aging and Modernization.* New York: Appleton-Century-Crofts.

Crano, William D. and Joel Aronoff. 1978. "A Cross-Cultural Study of Expressive and Instrumental Role Complementarity in the Family." *American Sociological Review,* 43, Aug., pp. 463–71.

Cressey, D. R. 1969. *Theft of the Nation: The Structure and Operations of Organized Crime in America.* New York: Harper Torchbooks.

Crispell, Diane. 1987. "Navigating With Ship." *American Demographics,* Sept., p. 56.

Crossen, Pierre R. 1975. "Institutional Obstacles to Expansion of World Food Production." *Science,* 188, pp. 519–24.

Cullingford, Cedric. 1984. *Children and Television.* New York: St. Martin's Press.

Cumming, Elaine and William H. Henry. 1961. *Growing Old.* New York: Basic Books.

Cummings, Milton C. and David Wise. 1981. *Democracy Under Pressure: An Introduction to the American Political System.* 4th ed. New York: Harcourt Brace Jovanovich.

Curtiss, S. 1977. *Genie: A Psycholinguistic Study of a Modern-Day Wild Child.* New York: Academic Press.

Cuzzort, R. P. and E. W. King. 1980. *Twentieth Century Social Thought.* 3rd ed. New York: Holt, Rinehart and Winston.

Dahrendorf, R. 1959. *Class and Conflict in Industrial Society.* Stanford, CA: Stanford University Press.

———. 1958. "Out of Utopia: Toward a Reorientation of Sociological Analysis." *American Journal of Sociology,* 64, Sept., pp. 158–64.

Dalton, George. 1971. *Modernizing Village Economics.* Toronto: Addison-Wesley Module.

D'Andrade, Roy G. 1966. "Sex Differences and Cultural Institutions." In Eleanor Emmons Maccoby, ed., *The Development of Sex Differences.* Stanford, CA: Stanford University Press.

Darwin, Charles. 1964 (1859). *On the Origin of Species.* Cambridge, MA: Harvard University Press.

Davidson, Laurie and Laura Kramer Gordon. 1979. *The Sociology of Gender.* Chicago: Rand McNally.

Davis, F. James. 1979. *Understanding Minority-Dominant Relations.* Arlington Heights, IL: AHM Publishing.

Davis, Kingsley. 1976. *America's Children.* Washington, DC: National Council of Organizations for Children and Youth.

———, ed. 1973. *Cities: Their Origin, Growth and Human Impact.* San Francisco: W. H. Freeman.

———. 1966. "The World's Population Crisis." In Robert K. Merton and Robert Nisbet, eds., *Contemporary Social Problems.* 2nd ed. New York: Harcourt Brace Jovanovich.

———. 1949. *Human Society.* New York: Macmillan.

———. 1940. "Extreme Social Isolation of a Child." *American Journal of Sociology,* 45, pp. 554–65.

Davis, Kingsley and W. W. Moore. 1945. "Some Principles of Stratification." *American Sociological Review,* 10, pp. 242–49.

Denison, D. C. 1992. "Orlando Patterson." *The Boston Globe Magazine,* Feb. 23, pp. 8–9.

DeVore, I., ed. 1965. *Primate Behavior: Field Studies of Monkeys and Apes.* New York: Holt, Rinehart and Winston.

Domhoff, G. William. 1983. *Who Rules America Now?* Englewood Cliffs, NJ: Prentice-Hall.

———. 1967. *Who Rules America?* Englewood Cliffs, NJ: Prentice-Hall.

Duberman, Lucile. 1976. *Social Inequality.* New York: Harper & Row.

Dukert, Joseph M. 1983. "Who Is Poor? Who is Truly Needy?" *Public Welfare* 41(1) Winter, pp. 17–22.

Duncan, Greg J. and Saul D. Hoffman. 1988. "What are the Economic Consequences of Divorce?" *Demography,* 25(4) Nov., p. 641.

Durant, Will. 1954. "Our Oriental Heritage." *The Story of Civilization.* Vol. I. New York: Simon & Schuster.

———. 1944. *Caesar and Christ.* New York: Simon & Schuster.

Durkheim, Émile. 1961 (1915). *The Elementary Forms of Religious Life.* New York: Collier Books.

———. 1960a (1893). *The Division of Labor in Society.* Trans. G. Simpson. New York: Free Press.

———. 1960b. (1893). *Montesquieu and Rousseau.* Ann Arbor, MI: University of Michigan Press.

———. 1958 (1895). *The Rules of Sociological Method.* Glencoe, IL: Free Press.

———. 1954 (1917). *The Elementary Forms of Religious Life.* Trans. J. W. Swain. New York: Free Press.

———. 1951 (1897). *Suicide: A Study in Sociology.* Trans. J. A. Spaulding and G. Simpson. New York: Free Press.

———. 1950 (1894). *Rules of Sociological Method.* New York: Free Press.

Eberstadt, Nicholas. 1992. "America's Infant Mortality Problem: Parents." *The Wall Street Journal*, Jan. 20, p. A14.

The Economist. 1991. "Euthanasia, What is the 'Good Death?'" July 20, pp. 21–22, 24.

Edmundson, Brad. 1986. "The Political Sell." *American Demographics*, Nov., pp. 26–29, 63–69.

Ehrlich, Isaac. 1975. "The Deterrent Effect of Capital Punishment: A Question of Life and Death." *American Economic Review*, pp. 397–417.

Ehrlich, Paul R. and Anne H. Ehrlich. 1990. *The Population Explosion.* New York: Simon and Schuster.

Ehrlich, Paul and Anne H. Ehrlich. 1972. *Population, Resources, Environment.* San Francisco: W. H. Freeman.

Ehrlich, Paul and S. Shirley Feldman. 1978. *The Race Bomb: Skin Color, Prejudice, and Intelligence.* New York: Quadrangle.

Elder, Glen H. 1975. "Adolescence in the Life Cycle: An Introduction." In Sigmund E. Dragastin and Glen H. Elder, Jr., eds., *Adolescence in the Life Cycle.* New York: Halsted Press.

Elkind, David. 1981. *The Hurried Child.* Reading, MA: Addison Wesley.

Ember, Carol R. and Melvin Ember. 1981. *Anthropology.* 3rd ed. Englewood Cliffs, NJ: Prentice-Hall.

Engels, Friedrich. 1973. *The Condition of the Working Class in England in 1844.* Moscow: Progress Publishers.

———. 1942 (1884). *The Origin of the Family, Private Property and the State.* New York: International Publishing.

Erikson, Erik H. 1968. *Identity, Youth and Crisis.* New York: Norton.

———. 1964. *Childhood and Society.* New York: Norton.

Erikson, Kai T. 1966. *Wayward Puritans: A Study in the Sociology of Deviance.* New York: John Wiley.

Exter, Thomas. 1987. "How Many Hispanics?" *American Demographics*, May, pp. 36–39, 67.

Exter, Thomas and Frederick Barber. 1986. "The Age of Conservatism." *American Demographics*, Nov., pp. 30–37.

Ferree, Myra Marx and Beth B. Hess. 1985. *Controversy and Coalition: The New Feminist Movement.* Boston: G. K. Hall.

Festinger, Leon, Henry W. Rieken, and Stanley Schacter.

1956. *When Prophesy Fails.* New York: Harper Torchbooks.

Finn, Chester E., Jr. 1987. "The High School Dropout Puzzle." *The Public Interest*, Spring, No. 87, pp. 3–22.

Firth, Raymond. 1963. *Elements of Social Organization.* Boston: Beacon Press.

Fisher, Jeffrey D. and D. Byrne. 1975. "Too Close for Comfort: Sex Differences in Response to Invasions of Personal Space." *Journal of Personality and Social Psychology*, 32, pp. 15–21.

Fisher, Robert. 1984. *Let the People Decide: Neighborhood Organizing in America.* Boston: G. K. Hall.

Flannery, Kent V. 1968. "Archaeological Systems Theory and Early Mesopotamia." In Betty J. Meggars, ed., *Anthropological Archaeology in the Americas.* Washington, DC: Anthropological Society of Washington.

———. 1965. "The Ecology of Early Food Production in Mesopotamia." *Science*, 147, pp. 1247–56.

Ford, Clellan S. 1970. "Some Primitive Societies." In Georgene H. Seward and Robert C. Williamson, eds., *Sex Roles in Changing Society.* New York: Random House.

Fortes, M., R. W. Steel, and P. Ady. 1947. "Ashanti Survey, 1945–46: An Experiment in Social Research." *Geographical Journal*, 110, pp. 149–79.

Frank, Arthur. 1991. *At the Will of the Body: Reflections on Illness.* Boston: Houghton Mifflin.

Frankfort, H. 1956 (1951). *The Birth of Civilization in the Near East.* Garden City, NY: Doubleday/Anchor.

Frederickson, George M. 1971. *The Black Image in the White Mind.* New York: Harper & Row.

Freed, Stanley A. and Ruth S. Freed. 1985. "One Son is No Sons." *Natural History*, Jan., p. 10.

Freedman, James M. 1974. "Trial by Fire." *Natural History*, Jan., pp. 54–63.

Freedman, Samuel G. 1990. *Small Victories.* New York: Harper & Row.

Freitag, Peter. 1975. "The Cabinet and Big Business: A Study of Interlocks." *Social Problems*, 2, Dec. 23, pp. 137–52.

Freud, Sigmund. 1930. "Civilization and its Discontents." In *Standard Edition of the Complete Psychological Works of Sigmund Freud.* Vol. 29. London: Hogarth Press.

———. 1928. *The Future of an Illusion.* New York: Horace Liveright and the Institute of Psycho-Analysis.

———. 1923. "The Ego and the Id." In *Standard Edition of the Complete Psychological Works of Sigmund Freud.* Vol. 19. London: Hogarth Press.

———. 1920. "Beyond the Pleasure Principle." In *Standard Edition of the Complete Psychological Works of Sigmund Freud.* Vol. 14. London: Hogarth Press.

———. 1918. *Totem and Taboo.* New York: Moffat, Yard.

Fried, Morton. 1967. *The Evolution of Political Society.* New York: Random House.

Friedman, Milton and Rose Friedman. 1980. *Free to Choose: A Personal Statement.* New York: Harcourt Brace Jovanovich.

Friedrich, Carl J. and Zbigniew Brzezinski. 1965. *Totalitarian Dictatorship and Autocracy*. Vol. 2. Cambridge, MA: Harvard University Press.

Frieze, Irene H., J. E. Parsons, P. B. Johnson, Diana N. Ruble, and Gail L. Zellman. 1975. *Women in Sex Roles: A Social Psychological Perspective*. New York: Norton.

Fuguitt, Glenn V. 1984. "The Nonmetropolitan Population Turnaround." *Annual Review of Sociology*, Vol. 21, pp. 259–80.

Gallup, George, Jr. and Jim Castelli. 1987. *The American Catholic People: Their Beliefs, Practices, and Values*. Garden City, NY: Doubleday.

The Gallup Report. 1988. "Religion in America." No. 259. Gallup Opinion Index. Princeton, NJ: Gallup Organization and Princeton Research Center.

Gans, Herbert J. 1979. "Deception and Disclosure in the Field." *The Nation*, 17, May, pp. 507–12.

———. 1977. "Why Exurbanites Won't Reurbanize Themselves." *The New York Times*, Feb. 12, p. 21.

———. 1968. *People and Plans*. New York: Basic Books.

———. 1962. *The Urban Villagers*. New York: Free Press.

Gardner, Howard. 1978. *Developmental Psychology*. Boston: Little, Brown.

Garfinkel, Harold. 1972. "Studies of the Routine Grounds of Everyday Activities." In David Snow, ed., *Studies in Social Interaction*. New York: Free Press.

———. 1967. *Studies in Ethnomethodology*. Englewood Cliffs, NJ: Prentice-Hall.

Gargan, Edward A. 1988. "Beijing Admits Easing of Birth Limits." *The New York Times*, Nov. 2, p. A3.

Geertz, C. 1973. *The Interpretation of Cultures*. New York: Basic Books.

Gerth, Hans and C. Wright Mills. 1953. *Character and Social Structure*. New York: Harcourt Brace Jovanovich.

Giese, Alenka S. and William A. Testa. 1988. "Targeting High Tech." *American Demographics*, May, pp. 38–41, 59.

Gill, Richard T. 1991 "Day Care or Parental Care?" *The Public Interest*, Fall.

Gilligan, Carol. 1982. *In a Different Voice*. Cambridge: Harvard University Press.

Ginsberg, Morris. 1958. "Social Change." *British Journal of Sociology*, 9(3), pp. 205–29.

Gist, Noel P. and Sylvia Fleis Fava. 1974. *Urban Society*. 6th ed. New York: Crowell.

Glazer, Nathan and Daniel P. Moynihan, eds. 1975. *Ethnicity: Theory and Experience*. Cambridge, MA: Harvard University Press.

Glick, Paul C. 1984. "How American Families are Changing." *American Demographics*, 6(1), Jan., p. 24.

———. 1979. "The Future of the American Family." *Current Population Reports Series P-23*, no. 78. Bureau of the Census, Special Studies. Washington, DC: U.S. Government Printing Office.

Glick, Paul C. and Emmanuel Landau. 1950. "Age as a Factor in Marriage." *American Sociological Review*, 15, Aug., pp. 517–29.

Glick, Paul C. and Arthur J. Norton. 1977. "Marrying, Divorcing, and Living Together in the United States Today." *Popular Bulletin*, 32, Oct., pp. 1–39.

Gnessous, Mohammed. 1967. "A General Critique of Equilibrium Theory." In Wilburt E. Moore and Robert M. Cooke, eds., *Readings on Social Change*. Englewood Cliffs, NJ: Prentice-Hall.

Goffman, E. 1971. *Relations in Public*. New York: Basic Books.

———. 1963. *Behavior in Public Places*. New York: Free Press.

———. 1961a. *Asylums: Essays on the Social Situation of Mental Patients and Other Inmates*. Chicago: Aldine.

———. 1961b. *Encounters: Two Studies in the Sociology of Interaction*. Indianapolis: Bobbs-Merrill.

———. 1959. *The Presentation of Self in Everyday Life*. Garden City, NY: Doubleday.

Goldberg, Phillip. 1968. "Are Women Prejudiced Against Women?" *Transaction*, 5, pp. 28–30.

Goldman, Ari L. 1991. *The Search for God at Harvard*. New York: Times Books.

Good, Kenneth. 1991. *Into the Heart*. New York: Simon and Schuster.

Goode, W. J. 1963. *World Revolution and Family Patterns*. New York: Free Press.

———. 1960. "A Theory of Role Strain." *American Sociological Review*, Aug. 25, pp. 902–14.

Gordon, Milton M. 1975 (1961). "Assimilation in America: Theory and Reality." In Norman R. Yetman and C. Hoy Steele, eds., *Majority and Minority: The Dynamics of Racial and Ethnic Relations*. Boston: Allyn & Bacon.

———. 1964. *Assimilation in American Life*. New York: Oxford University Press.

———. 1947. "The Concept of Subculture and Its Application." *Social Forces*, 26, pp. 40–42.

Gough, Kathleen. 1961. "Nayar: Central Kerela." In David M. Schneider and Kathleen Gough, eds., *Matrilineal Kinship*. Berkeley and Los Angeles: University of Claifornia Press.

———. 1952. "Changing Kinship Usages in the Setting of Political and Economic Change Among the Nayars of Malabor." *Journal of Royal Anthropological Institute of Great Britain and Ireland*, 82, pp. 71–87.

Gould, H. 1971. "Caste and Class: A Comparative View." *Module*, 11, pp. 1–24.

Gould, Stephen Jay. 1976. "The View of Life: Biological Potential versus Biological Determinism." *Natural History Magazine*, 85, May, pp. 34–41.

Gouldner, Alvin W. 1970. *The Coming Crisis of Western Sociology*. New York: Avon.

Granfield, Mary. 1991. "Five All-American Ways to Make it Big." *Money Magazine*, Oct., pp. 148–57.

Greeley, Andrew M., William McCready, and Kathleen McCourt. 1975. *Catholic Schools in a Declining Church*. New ed. Mission, KS: Sheed, Andrews & McMeel.

Greenberg, J. 1980. "Ape Talk: More Than Pigeon English?" *Science News*, 117(19), pp. 298–300.

Griffith, Jeanne E., Mary J. Frase, and John H. Ralph. 1989. "American Education: The Challenge of Change." *Population Bulletin*, Vol. 44, No. 4, Dec.

Gumplowicz, Ludwig. 1899. *The Outlines of Sociology*. Philadelphia: American Academy of Political and Social Sciences.

Gurr, Ted Robert. 1970. *Why Men Rebel*. Princeton, NJ: Princeton University Press.

Hall, Edward T. 1974. *Handbook for Proxemic Analysis*. Washington, DC: Society for the Anthropology of Visual Communication.

———. 1969. *The Hidden Dimension*. New York: Doubleday.

Hall, Edward T. and Mildred Reed Hall. 1990. *Hidden Differences*. New York: Anchor Books.

Hall, R. H. 1963–1964. "The Concept of Bureaucracy: An Empirical Assessment." *American Journal of Sociology*, 69, pp. 32–40.

Hare, Paul A. 1976. *Handbook of Small Group Research*. 2nd ed. New York: Free Press.

Harlow, Harry F. 1975. "Review." *Science News*, 108, Dec. 20, pp. 389–90.

———. 1959. "Love in Infant Monkeys." *Scientific American*, June, pp. 68–74.

Harlow, Harry F. and M. Harlow. 1962. "The Heterosexual Affectional System in Monkeys." *American Psychologist*, 17, 1–9.

Harris, C. D. and E. L. Ullman. 1945. "The Nature of Cities." *Annals of the American Academy of Political and Social Science*, 242, p. 12.

Harris, Marvin. 1980. *Cultural Materialism: The Struggle for a Science of Culture*. New York: Random House.

———. 1975. *Culture, People, and Nature: An Introduction to General Anthropology*. 2nd ed. New York: Crowell.

———. 1966. "The Cultural Ecology of India's Sacred Cattle." *Current Anthropology*, 7, pp. 51–63.

Harris, Sarah. 1971. *Father Divine*. New York: Macmillan.

Hart, C. W. M. and Arnold R. Pilling. 1960. *The Tiwi of North Australia*. New York: Holt, Rinehart and Winston.

Haub, Carl. 1987. "Understanding Population Projections." *Population Bulletin*, Dec.

Hauser, Phillip and Robert Gardner. 1982. "Urban Future: Trends and Prospects." In Philip Hauser, et al. *Population and the Urban Future*. U.N. Fund for Population Activities. Albany, NY: SUNY Press.

Hawley, Amos. 1981. *Urban Society*. 2nd. ed. New York: John Wiley.

Hayes, Cheryl D., John L. Palmer, and Martha J. Zaslow, eds., 1990. "Who Cares for America's Children?" *Child-Care Policies for the 1990s*. Washington, DC: National Academy Press.

Heer, David M. 1980. "Intermarriage." *Harvard Encyclopedia of American Ethnic Groups*. Cambridge, MA: Harvard University Press, pp. 513–21.

Helmore, Kristin. 1988. "In Third World, Desire to Limit Family Size Far Exceeds Available Help." *The Christian Science Monitor*, July 21, p. 10.

Herbers, John. 1986. *The New Heartland*. New York: Times Books.

———. 1981a. "1980 Census Finds Sharp Decline in Size of American Households." *The New York Times*, May 5, pp. A1, A18.

———. 1981b. "Census Finds More Blacks Living in Suburbs of Nation's Large Cities." *The New York Times*, May 31, pp. 1, 48.

Hochschild, Arlie, with Anne Machung. 1989. *The Second Shift: Working Parents and the Revolution at Home*. New York: Viking Penguin.

Hodge, R. W., P. M. Siegel, and P. H. Rossi. 1964. "Occupational Prestige in the United States." *American Journal of Sociology*, 70, pp. 286–302.

Hodge, R. W., D. J. Treiman, and P. H. Rossi. 1966. "A Comparative Study of Occupational Prestige." In R. Bendix and S. M. Lipset, eds., *Class, Status and Power*. 2nd ed. New York: Free Press.

Hoebel, E. Andamson. 1960. *The Cheyennes: Indians of the Great Plains*. New York: Holt, Rinehart and Winston.

Hoffman, Abbie. 1968. *Revolution for the Hell of It*. New York: Dial Press.

Hollingshead, August B. 1951. "Age Relationships and Marriage." *American Sociological Review*, 16, Aug., pp. 492–99.

———. 1949. *Elmtown's Youth*. New York: John Wiley.

Hollingshead, A. B. and F. C. Redlich. 1958. *Social Class and Mental Illness*. New York: John Wiley.

Homans, G. C. 1950. *The Human Group*. New York: Harcourt.

Howe, Irving. 1976. *World of Our Fathers*. New York: Simon & Schuster.

Hoyt, H. 1943. "The Structure of American Cities in the Post-war Era." *American Journal of Sociology*, 48, pp. 475–92.

Inkeles, Alex and David H. Smith. 1974. *Becoming Modern: Individual Changes in Six Developing Countries*. Cambridge, MA: Harvard University Press.

Itard, J. 1932. *The Wild Boy of Aveyron*. Trans. G. Humphrey and M. Humphrey. New York: Appleton-Century-Crofts.

Jacobs, J. 1961. *The Death and Life of Great American Cities*. New York: Vintage.

Jacobson, Paul. 1959. *American Marriage and Divorce*. New York: Holt, Rinehart and Winston.

Janis, I. and L. Mann. 1976. *Decision Making*. New York: Free Press.

Janis, I., Dwight W. Chapman, John P. Gillin, and John P. Spiegel. 1964. "The Problem of Panic." In Duane P. Schultz, ed., *Panic Behavior*. New York: Random House.

Jeffries, V. and H. E. Ransford. 1980. *Social Stratification:*

A Multiple Hierarchy Approach. Boston: Allyn & Bacon.

Jencks, C., M. Smith, H. Acland, J. J. Bane, D. Cohen, H. Gintis, B. Heyns, and S. Michelson. 1972. *Inequality: A Reassessment of the Effect of Family and Schooling in America*. New York: Holt, Rinehart and Winston.

Jensen, A. R. 1969. "How Much Can We Boost I.Q. and Scholastic Achievement?" *Harvard Educational Review*, 39(1), Winter, pp. 1–123.

Johnson, Nicholas. 1971. "Television and Violence: Perspectives and Proposals." In Bernard Rosenberg and David Manning White, eds., *Mass Culture Revisited*. New York: Van Nostrand.

Joslyn, Richard. 1984. *Mass Media and Elections*. Reading, MA: Addison-Wesley.

Judson, David and David Olson. 1984. "Birth Records Say Stebbins Kin Whites." *Stockton Record*, Jan. 17, pp. 1, 4.

———. 1984a. "Uproar Over Stebbins Roots Echoes Far from District 9." *Stockton Record*, Apr. 1, pp. 1, 4.

Justice, Blair. 1988. *Who Gets Sick*. Los Angeles: Jeremy P. Tarcher.

Kahl, J. A. 1960. *The American Class Structure*. New York: Holt, Rinehart and Winston.

Kasarda, John D., Michael D. Irwin, and Holly L. Hughes. 1986. "The South is Still Rising." *American Demographics*, June, pp. 32–35, 38–39, 70.

Kasarda, J. D. and M. Janowitz. 1974. "Community Attachment in Mass Society." *American Journal of Sociology*, 48, pp. 328–39.

Katz, Elihu. 1957. "The Two-Step Flow of Communication: An Up-To-Date Report on an Hypothesis." *Public Opinon Quarterly*, 21, pp. 61–78.

Kennedy, John F. 1961. "Introduction." In William Brandon, ed., *The American Heritage Book of Indians*. New York: Dell.

Kerlinger, F. N. 1973. *Foundation of Behavioral Research*. 2nd ed. New York: Holt, Rinehart and Winston.

Khaldun, Ibn. 1958. *The Mugaddimah*. Bollingen Series XLIII. Princeton, NJ: Princeton University Press.

Koenig, Frederick. 1985. *Rumor in the Marketplace: The Social Psychology of Commercial Heresy*. Dover, MA: Auburn House.

Kohlberg, Lawrence. 1969. "Stage and Sequence: The Cognitive-Developmental Approach to Socialization." In David A. Goslin, ed., *Handbook of Socialization Theory and Research*. Chicago: Rand McNally.

———. 1967. "Moral and Religious Education in the Public Schools: A Developmental View." In T. Sizer, ed., *Religion and Public Education*. Boston: Houghton Mifflin.

Kohn, Hans. 1956. *Nationalism and Liberty: The Swiss Example*. London: Allen and Unwin.

Kohn, Melvin L. 1969. *Class and Conformity*. Homewood, IL: Dorsey Press.

Kohn, Melvin L. and Carmi Schooler. 1983. *Work and Personality: An Inquiry Into the Impact of Social Stratification*. New York: Ablex Press.

Kotkin, Joel and Yoriko Kishimoto. 1988. *The Third Century: America's Resurgence in the Asian Era*. New York: Crown.

Krause, Aurel. 1956. *The Tlingit Indians*. Seattle: University of Washington Press.

Krause, Michael. 1966. *Immigration: The American Mosaic*. New York: Van Nostrand Reinhold.

Kroeber, Alfred A. 1963 (1923). *Anthropology: Culture Patterns and Processes*. New York: Harcourt Brace Jovanovich.

Kroeber, T. 1961. *Ishi in Two Worlds*. Berkeley and Los Angeles: University of California Press.

Kummer, H. 1971. *Primate Societies: Group Technologies of Ecological Adaptation*. Chicago: Aldine.

Kurian, George T. 1984. *The New Book of World Rankings*. New York: Facts on File Publications.

Kuter, Lawrence. 1988. "For Children and Step-parents War Isn't Inevitable." *The New York Times*, June 30, p. C8.

Kutscher, Ronald E. 1988. "An Overview of the Year 2000," *Occupational Outlook Quarterly*, Vol. 32, No. 1, Spring, pp. 3–9.

Lang, Kurt and Gladys Lang. 1961. *Collective Dynamics*. New York: Crowell.

Lantz, Herman R. 1982. "Romantic Love in the Pre-Modern Period: A Sociological Commentary." *Journal of Social History*, Spring, pp. 349–70.

Larson, Jan and Brad Edmondson. 1991. "Should Unmarried Partners Get Married Benefits?" *American Demographics*, March, p. 47.

Lasch, Christopher. 1979. *The Culture of Narcissism*. New York: Warner Books.

———. 1977. *Haven in a Heartless World: The Family Besieged*. New York: Basic Books.

Laslett, P. 1965. *The World We Have Lost: England Before the Industrial Age*. New York: Scribner's.

Laslett, P. and Phillip W. Cummings. 1967. "History of Political Philosophy." In Paul Edwards, ed., *The Encyclopedia of Philosophy*. Vols. 5, 6. New York: Macmillan.

Lasswell, Thomas. 1965. *Class and Stratum*. Boston: Houghton Mifflin.

Latane, K. Williams and S. Harkins. 1979. "Many Hands Make Light the Work: The Causes and Consequences of Social Loafing." *Journal of Personality and Social Psychology*, 37, pp. 822–32.

Lazarsfeld, Paul F. 1971. "Introduction." In Bernard Rosenberg and David Manning White, eds., *Mass Culture Revisited*. New York: Van Nostrand.

Lazarsfeld, Paul F., Bernard Berelson, and Hazel Gaudet. 1968. *The People's Choice*. 3rd ed. New York: Columbia University Press.

Leakey, Richard E. 1981. *The Making of Mankind*. New York: Dutton.

Leakey, Richard E. and Roger Lewin. 1977. *Origins*. New York: Dutton.

Le Bon, Gustave. 1960 (1895). *The Crowd: A Study of the Popular Mind*. New York: Viking.

Lee, Alfred McClung. 1978. *Sociology for Whom?* New York: Oxford University Press.

Lee, Gary, R. 1981. "Marriage and Aging." *Society*, 18(2), Jan.–Feb., pp. 70–71.

Lee, M. 1966. *Multivalent Man*. New York: George Braziller.

Lee, Richard Borshay. 1980. *The !KungSan*. Berkeley and Los Angeles: University of California Press.

———. 1969a. "!Kung Bushmen Subsistence: An Input-Output Analysis." In A. P. Vayda, ed., *Environment and Cultural Behavior*. Garden City, NY: Natural History Press.

———. 1969b. "A Naturalist at Large: Eating Christmas in the Kalahari." *Natural History*, Dec., p. 5.

Lemert, Edwin. 1972. *Human Deviance, Social Problems and Social Control*. 2nd ed. Englewood Cliffs, NJ: Prentice-Hall.

Lenin, Vladimir I. 1949 (1917). *The State and Revolution*. Moscow: Progress Publishers.

Lenski, Gerhard. 1966. *Power and Privilege: A Theory of Social Stratification*. New York: McGraw-Hill.

Lenski, Gerhard and Jean Lenski. 1982. *Human Societies*. 4th ed. New York: McGraw-Hill.

Leonard, Ira M. and R. D. Parmet. 1972. *American Nativism: 1830–1860*. New York: Van Nostrand-Reinhold.

Leslie, Gerald R. 1979. *The Family in Social Context*. 4th ed. New York: Oxford University Press.

Levine, Adeline and Janice Crumrine. 1975. "Women and the Fear of Success: A Problem in Replication." *American Journal of Sociology*, 80, pp. 964–74.

Levine, Irving M. and Judith Herman. 1974. "The Life of White Ethnics." In Charles H. Anderson, ed., *Sociological Essays and Research*. Homewood, IL: Dorsey Press.

Levinson, Daniel J., with Charlotte N. Darrow, Edward B. Klein, Maria H. Levinson, and Braxton Mckee. 1978. *The Seasons of a Man's Life*. New York: Ballantine.

Levy, Frank. 1987. "The Middle Class: Is It Really Vanishing?" *The Brookings Review*, Summer, pp. 17–21.

Lewin, Kurt. 1948. *Resolving Social Conflicts*. New York: Harper.

Lewis, Michael. 1972. "Culture and Gender Roles: There's No Unisex in the Nursery." *Psychology Today*, 5, pp. 54–57.

Lewis, O. 1960. *Tepoztlan: Village in Mexico*. New York: Holt, Rinehart and Winston.

———. 1951. *Life in a Mexican Village: Tepoztlan Revisited*. Urbana, IL: University of Illinois Press.

Lindesmith, Alfred R. and Anselm L. Strauss. 1956. *Social Psychology*. New York: Holt, Rinehart and Winston.

Linton, R. 1936. *The Study of Man*. New York: Appleton-Century-Crofts.

———. 1915. *The Cultural Background of Personality*. Westport, CN: Greenwood Press.

Lipset, Seymour M. 1960. *Political Man*. Garden City, NY: Doubleday.

Lipsey, R. G. and P. D. Steiner. 1975. *Economics*. New York: Harper & Row.

Lombroso-Ferrero, Gina. 1972. *Criminal Man*. Reprint ed. Montclair, NJ: Patterson Smith.

Longino, Charles F., Jr. and William H. Crown. 1991. "Older Americans: Rich or Poor?" *American Demographics*, Aug., pp. 48–53.

Lynch, K. 1960. *The Image of the City*. Cambridge, MA: MIT Press.

Lynn, David B. 1969. *Parental and Sex Role Identification: A Theoretical Formulation*. Berkeley, CA: McCutchan.

Maccoby, Eleanor Emmons and Carol Nagy Jacklin. 1975. *The Psychology of Sex Differences*. Stanford, CA: Stanford University Press.

Macmurry, V. D. and P. H. Cunningham. 1973. "Mormons and Gentiles." In Donald E. Gelfand and Russell D. Lee, eds., *Ethnic Conflicts and Power: A Cross National Perspective*. New York: John Wiley.

Madsen, William. 1973. *The Mexican-Americans of South Texas*. 2nd ed. New York: Holt, Rinehart and Winston.

Maguire, Kathleen and Timothy J. Flanagan, eds. 1991. *Sourcebook of Criminal Justice Statistics—1990*. U.S. Department of Justice, Bureau of Justice Statistics. Washington, DC: U.S. Government Printing Office.

Malinowski, Bronislaw. 1954. *Magic, Science and Religion*. New York: Free Press.

———. 1922. *Argonauts of the Western Pacific*. New York: Dutton.

Mandle, Joan D. 1979. *Women and Social Change in America*. Princeton, NJ: Princeton Books.

Manning, Wendy and William O'Hare. 1988. "The Best Metros for Asian-American Businesses." *American Demographics*, Aug., pp. 34–37, 59.

Marlin, John Tepper. 1992. *The Livable Cities Almanac*. New York: HarperCollins.

Martin, K. M. 1976. "The Evolution of Social Forms." In D. E. Hunter and P. Whitten, eds., *The Study of Anthropology*. New York: Harper and Row.

———. 1974. "The Foraging Adaptation: Uniformity or Diversity?" Addison-Wesley Modular Publication No. 56. Reading, MA: Addison-Wesley.

Martin, K. M. and B. Voorhies. 1975. *The Female of the Species*. New York: Columbia University Press.

Marx, Karl. 1968. "Wage, Labour and Capital." In Karl Marx and Friedrich Engels, *Selected Works in One Volume*. New York: International Publishers.

———. 1967 (1867). *Capital: A Critique of Political Economy*. Ed. by Friedrich Engels. New York: New World.

———. 1967 (1867). *Das Kapital*. 3 vols. Ed. by Friedrich Engels. New York: International Publishing.

———. 1964 (1844). *The Economic and Philosophical Manuscripts of 1844*. New York: International Publishers.

———. 1959. (1847). *Class and Class Conflict in Industrial Society*. Stanford, CA: Stanford University Press.

Marx, Karl and Friedrich Engels. 1961 (1848). "The Communist Manifesto." In Arthur P. Mendel, ed., *Essential Works of Marxism*. New York: Bantam Books.

Mason, Karen Oppenheim. 1987. "The Impact of Women's Social Position on Fertility in Developing Countries." *Sociological Forum*, Vol. 2, No. 4, Fall, pp. 363–72.

Mauss, Armand I. 1975. *Social Problems of Social Movements*. Philadelphia: Lippincott.

McKibben, Bill. 1992. *The Age of Missing Information*. New York: Random House.

McLaughlin, Loretta. 1980. "China's Last Word on Children: One." *Boston Globe*, Sept. 6, pp. 1, 2.

McNeill, William H. 1976. *Plagues and People*. New York: Anchor/Doubleday.

Mead, G. H. 1934. *Mind, Self, and Society*. Ed. by C. W. Morris. Chicago: University of Chicago Press.

Mead, Margaret. 1970. *Culture and Commitment*. New York: Doubleday.

———. 1943. "Our Educational Emphases in Primitive Perspectives." *American Journal of Sociology*, 48, pp. 633–39.

———. 1935. *Sex and Temperament in Three Primitive Societies*. New York: Morrow.

Meadows, Donelle H., Dennis L. Meadows, Jorgan Randers, and William W. Behrens, III. 1972. *The Limits of Growth: A Report of the Club of Rome's Project on the Predicament of Mankind*. New York: Universe Books.

Merton, R. K. 1968 (1949). *Social Theory and Social Structure*. 2nd ed. New York: Free Press.

———. 1938. "Social Structure and Social Action." *American Sociological Review*, 3, pp. 672–82.

Merton, R. K., Leonard Broom, and Leonard S. Cottrell, Jr. 1959. *Sociology Today: Problems and Prospects*. New York: Basic Books.

Michels, R. 1966 (1911). *Political Parties*. Trans. Eden Paul and Adar Paul. New York: Free Press.

Mills, C. Wright. 1963. *Power, Politics and People*. New York: Ballantine.

———. 1959. *The Sociological Imagination*. New York: Oxford University Press.

———. 1956. *The Power Elite*. New York: Oxford University Press.

Mills, T. M. 1967. *The Sociology of Small Groups*. Englewood Cliffs, NJ: Prentice-Hall.

Mitchell, John Hanson. 1990. *Living at the End of Time*. Boston: Houghton Mifflin.

Molotsky, Irvin. 1988. "New and Old School Chiefs Differ on Issues and Styles." *The New York Times*. Sept. 22, p. A22.

Montagu, Ashley, ed. 1973. *Man and Aggression*. 2nd ed. London: Oxford University Press.

———, ed. 1964a. *The Concept of Race*. New York: Collier Books.

———, 1964b. *Man's Most Dangerous Myth: The Fallacy of Race*. New York: Meridian.

Moore, Wilbert E. 1965. *The Impact of Industry*. Englewood Cliffs, NJ: Prentice-Hall.

Morris, Desmond. 1970. *The Human Zoo*. New York: McGraw-Hill.

Mosca, Gaetano. 1939. *The Ruling Class*. New York: McGraw-Hill.

Moskos, C. C., Jr. 1975. "The American Combat Soldier in Vietnam." *Journal of Social Issues*, 31, pp. 25–37.

Murdock, George P. 1949. *Social Structure*. New York: Macmillan.

———. 1937. "Comparative Data on the Division of Labor by Sex." *Social Forces*, 15, pp. 551–53.

Muson, H. 1979. "Moral Thinking—Can it be Taught?" *Psychology Today*, Feb., pp. 26–29.

Myrdal, Gunnar. 1969. *Objectivity in Social Research*. New York: Pantheon.

———. 1944. *An American Dilemma*. New York: Harper.

National Institute of Mental Health. 1982. *Television and Behavior: Ten Years of Scientific Progress and Implications for the Eighties*. Vols. I and II, Washington, DC: U.S. Government Printing Office.

Neugarten, Bernice L. 1979. "Timing, Age, and The Life Cycle." *American Journal of Psychiatry*, 136, pp. 887–94.

Nickerson, Colin. 1991. "Thailand, India Hardest Hit." and "AIDS is Shrugged Off as 'Foreigners' Disease.'" *The Boston Globe*, Nov. 25, pp. 33, 34, 36.

Nisbet, R. A. and R. G. Perrin. 1977. *The Social Bond: An Introduction to the Study of Sociology*. 2nd ed. New York: Knopf.

Novak, Michael. 1972. *The Rise of the Unmeltable Ethnics*. New York: Macmillan.

Novit-Evans, Bette and Ashton Wesley Welch. 1983. "Racial and Ethnic Definition as Reflections of Public Policy." *Journal of American Studies*, 17(3), pp. 417–35.

Ogburn, William, F. 1964. *On Culture and Social Change*. Chicago: University of Chicago Press.

———. 1964 (1950). *Social Change: With Respect to Culture and Original Nature*. Magnolia, MA: Peter Smith.

O'Hare, William. 1988. "How to Read Poverty Statistics." *American Demographics*, May, pp. 42–43.

———. 1987. "Separating Welfare Fact From Fiction." *The Wall Street Journal*, Dec. 14, p. 24.

———. 1986. "The Eight Myths of Poverty." *American Demographics*, May, pp. 22–25.

Ortner, Sherry. 1974. "Is Female to Male as Nature is to Culture?" In Michelle Zimbalist Rosaldo and Louise Lampheres, eds., *Woman, Culture and Society*. Stanford, CA: Stanford University Press.

Otterbein, Keith, 1973. "The Anthropology of War." In John J. Honigmann, ed., *Handbook of Social and Cultural Anthropology*. Chicago: Rand McNally.

———. 1970. *The Evolution of War*. New Haven, CN: Human Relations Area Files.

Ouchi, William G. 1981. *Theory Z: How American Business Can Meet the Japanese Challenge.* Reading, MA: Addison-Wesley.

Palen, John J. 1987. *The Urban World.* New York: McGraw-Hill.

Palmore, Erdman B. and Frank Whittington. 1971. "Trends in the Relative Status of the Aged." *Social Forces,* 50, Sept., pp. 84–91.

Park, R., E. Burgess, and R. McKenzie, eds. 1925. *The City.* Chicago: University of Chicago Press.

Parke, R. D. and C. W. Collmer. 1975. "Child Abuse: An Interdisciplinary Analysis." In E. M. Hetherington, ed., *Review of Child Development Research.* Vol. 5. Chicago: University of Chicago Press.

Parkes, Henry Bamford. 1968. *The United States of America: A History.* 3rd ed. New York: Knopf.

Parmet, Ira M. and Robert D. Parmet. 1971. *American Nativism, 1830–1860.* New York: Van Nostrand.

Parsons, Talcott. 1971. *The System of Modern Societies.* Englewood Cliffs, NJ: Prentice-Hall.

———. 1966. *Societies: Evolutionary and Comparative Perspectives.* Englewood Cliffs, NJ: Prentice-Hall.

———. 1954. *Essays in Sociological Theory.* Rev. ed. New York: Free Press.

———. 1951. *The Social System.* New York: Free Press.

———. 1937. *The Structure of Social Action.* New York: McGraw-Hill.

Parsons, Talcott and Robert F. Bales. 1955. *Family Socialization and Interaction Process.* New York: Free Press.

Parsons, Talcott and E. A. Shils. 1951. *Toward a General Theory of Action.* Cambridge, MA: Harvard University Press.

Paulsen, Monrad. 1967. "Role of Juvenile Courts." *Current History,* 53, Aug., p. 72.

Pavlik, Z. 1986. *Family Policy and Population Climate in the CSSR.* Conference on the Demographic Impact of Political Action, March.

Pavlov, I. P. 1927. *Conditional Reflexes.* Trans. G. V. Anrep. New York: Oxford University Press.

Payer, Lynn. 1988. *Medicine and Culture.* New York: Henry Holt.

Peter, L. F. and R. Hull. 1969. *The Peter Principle.* New York: Morrow.

Petersen, William. 1975. "On the Subnations of Western Europe." In Nathan Glazer and Daniel P. Moynihan, eds., *Ethnicity: Theory and Experience.* Cambridge, MA: Harvard University Press.

Pettigrew, Thomas F. and Robert C. Green. 1975. "School Desegregation in Large Cities: A Critique of the Coleman White Flight Thesis." *Harvard Educational Review,* 46(1), pp. 1–53.

Phillips, David P. 1980. "The Deterrent Effect of Capital Punishment: New Evidence on an Old Controversy." *American Journal of Sociology,* Vol. 86, pp. 139–48.

Piaget, J. and B. Inhelder. 1969. *The Psychology of the Child.* New York: Basic Books.

Pileggi, N. 1981. "Open City." *New York Magazine,* Jan. 19, pp. 20–26.

Platt, John. 1987. "The Future of AIDS." *The Futurist,* Nov.–Dec., pp. 10–17.

Postman, Neil. 1985. *Amusing Ourselves to Death.* New York: Viking.

Provence, Sally. 1972. "Psychoanalysis and the Treatment of Psychological Disorders of Infancy." In S. Wolman, ed., *A Handbook of Child Psychoanalysis: Research, Theory, and Practice.* New York: Van Nostrand.

Provence, Sally and R. Lipton. 1963. *Infants in Institutions.* New York: International University Press.

Public Opinion. 1980. Dec.–Jan., p. 35.

———. 1978. Nov.–Dec., p. 33.

Putka, Gary. 1984. "As Jewish Population Falls in U.S., Leaders Seek to Reverse Trend." *The Wall Street Journal,* Apr. 13, pp. 1, 10.

Quinney, Richard. 1974. *Critique of Legal Order.* Boston: Little Brown.

Raines, Howell. 1988. "British Government Devising Plan to Curb Violence by Soccer Fans." *The New York Times,* June 17, p. A1.

Reid, Sue Titus. 1981. *The Correctional System.* New York: Holt, Rinehart and Winston.

———. 1979. *Crime and Criminology.* 2nd ed. New York: Holt, Rinehart and Winston.

Reinisch, June M. 1990. *The Kinsey Institute New Report on Sex.* New York: St. Martin's Press.

Reinmann, Jeffrey H. 1979. "The Rich Get Richer and the Poor Get Prison." In *Ideology, Class, and Criminal Justice.* New York: John Wiley, pp. 95–128.

Reiss, Ira L. 1980. *Family Systems in America.* 3rd ed. New York: Holt, Rinehart and Winston.

Riche, Martha Farnsworth. 1991. "We're All Minorities Now." *American Demographics,* Oct., pp. 26–34.

———. 1987. "Behind the Boom in Mental Health Care." *American Demographics,* Nov., pp. 34–37, 60–61.

Riesman, D. 1950. *The Lonely Crowd.* New Haven, CN: Yale University Press.

Ritzer, George. 1993. *The McDonaldization of Society.* Newbury Park, CA: Pine Forge Press.

Robey, Bryant. 1984. "Black Votes, Black Money." *American Demographics,* May, pp. 4–5.

Robinson, Jacob. 1976. "The Holocaust." In Yisrael Gutman and Livia Rothkirchen, eds., *The Catastrophe of European Jewry.* Jerusalem: Yad Veshem.

Robinson, John P. 1979. "Toward a Postindustrious Society." *Public Opinion,* Aug.–Sept., pp. 41–46.

Rogers, Willard L. and Arland Thornton. 1985. "Changing Patterns of First Marriage in the United States." *Demography,* 22, pp. 265–79.

Roper, Burns W. 1985. "Early Election Calls: The Larger Dangers." *Public Opinion Quarterly,* Spring, pp. 5–6.

Rosaldo, Michelle Zimbalist. 1974. "Woman, Culture and Society: A Theoretical Overview." In Michelle Zimbalist Rosaldo and Louise Lamphere, eds.,

Woman, Culture and Society. Stanford, CA: Stanford University Press.

Rose, A. 1967. *Power Structure: Political Process in American Society*. New York: Oxford University Press.

Rose, Jerry D. 1982. *Outbreaks: The Sociology of Collective Behavior*. New York: Free Press.

Rosen, George. 1968. *Madness in Society*. New York: Harper Torchbooks.

Rosenberg, Bernard and David Manning White, eds. 1971. *Mass Culture Revisited*. New York: Van Nostrand.

Rosenthal, R. and L. Jacobson. 1966. "Teachers Expectancies: Determinants of Pupils I.Q. Gain." *Psychological Reports*, 18, pp. 115–18.

Ross, Catherine. 1972. "Sex-Role Socialization in Picture Books for Pre-School Children." *American Journal of Sociology*, 77, May, pp. 1125–50.

Rossi, Alice. 1977. "A Biosocial Perspective on Parenting." *Daedalus*, 106, pp. 1–31.

———. 1985. *Gender and the Life Course*. New York: Aldine.

Rossides, Daniel W. 1990. *Social Stratification*. Englewood Cliffs, NJ: Prentice-Hall.

———. 1976. *The American Class System*. Boston: Houghton Mifflin.

Rumberger, Russell W. 1987. "High School Dropouts: A Review of Issues and Evidence." *Review of Educational Research*, Summer, Vol. 57, No. 2, pp. 101–21.

Sagarin, Edward. 1978. *Sociology: The Basic Concepts*. New York: Holt, Rinehart and Winston.

Sahlins, Marshall D. 1972. *Stone Age Economics*. Chicago: Aldine.

Sahlins, Marshall D. and Elman R. Service, eds. 1960. *Evolution and Culture*. Ann Arbor, MI: University of Michigan Press.

Salas, Rafael M. 1987. "Urban Population Growth: Blessing or Burden?" *USA Today*, Vol. 116, No. 2506, July, pp. 74–77.

Samovar, Larry A., Richard Porter, and Nemi C. Jain. 1981. *Understanding Intercultural Communication*. Belmont, CA: Wadsworth.

Samuelson, Paul A. 1976. *Economics*. 10th ed. New York: McGraw-Hill.

Sandburg, Carl. 1916. *Chicago Poems*. New York: Henry Holt.

Sanders, Alvin J. and Larry Long. 1987. "New Sunbelt Migration Patterns." *American Demographics*, Jan., pp. 38–41.

Sapir, Edward. 1961. *Culture, Language and Personality*. Berkeley and Los Angeles: University of California Press.

Schneider, Joseph W. and Peter Conrad. 1983. *Having Epilepsy: The Experience and Control of Illness*. Philadelphia: Temple University Press.

Schumpeter, Joseph A. 1950. *Capitalism, Socialism and Democracy*. 3rd ed. New York: Harper Torchbooks.

Schur, Edwin M. and Hugo A. Bedau. 1974. *Victimless Crimes: Two Sides of a Controversy*. Englewood Cliffs, NJ: Prentice-Hall.

Schwartz, Allan J. 1990. "The Epidemiology of Suicide Among Students at Colleges and Universities in the United States." In Leighton C. Whitaker and Richard E. Slimak, eds., *College Student Suicide*. New York: The Haworth Press.

Schwartz, Joe. 1988. "Hispanics in the Eighties." *American Demographics*, Jan., pp. 42–45.

Sebold, Hans. 1986. "Adolescents Shifting Orientation Toward Parents and Peers: A Curvilinear Trend Over Recent Decades." *Journal of Marriage and the Family*, Feb., pp. 5–13.

Seligman, Daniel. 1984. "Pay Equity is a Bad Idea." *Fortune*, 109(10), May 14, pp. 133–40.

Selznick, P. 1948. "Foundations of the Theory of Organization." *American Sociological Review*, 13, pp. 25–35.

Service, Elman R. 1975. *Origins of the State and Civilization*. New York: Norton.

Shapiro, Jerrold Lee. 1987. "The Expectant Father." *Psychology Today*, Jan., pp. 32–34.

Sharp, Lauriston. 1952. "Steel Axes for Stone-Age Australians." *Human Organization*, 11, pp. 17–22.

Shattuck, R. 1980. *The Forbidden Experiment*. New York: Farrar, Straus & Giroux.

Shaw, Clifford R. and Henry D. Mckay. 1942. *Juvenile Delinquency and Urban Areas*. Chicago: University of Chicago Press.

———. 1931. "Social Factors in Juvenile Delinquency." Vol. 2. In *National Committee on Law Observance and Law Enforcement, Report on the Causes of Crime*. Washington, DC: U.S. Government Printing Office.

Sheldon, W. H., E. M. Hartl, and E. Mcdermott. 1949. *The Varieties of Delinquent Youth*. New York: Harper.

Sheldon, W. H. and S. S. Stevens. 1942. *The Variety of Temperament*. New York: Harper.

Sheldon, W. H. and W. B. Tucker. 1940. *The Varieties of Human Physique*. New York: Harper.

Shellow, Robert and Derek V. Roemer. 1965. "The Riot That Didn't Happen." *Social Problems*, 14, pp. 221–33.

Shepardson, Mary. 1963. *Navajo Ways in Government*. Manasha, WI: American Anthropological Association.

Shibutani, Tamotsu. 1966. *Improvised News: A Sociological Study of Rumor*. Indianapolis: Bobbs-Merrill.

Shils, Edward. 1971 (1960). "Mass Society and Its Culture." In Bernard Rosenberg and David Manning, eds., *Mass Culture Revisited*. New York: Van Nostrand.

———. 1968. *Political Development in the New States*. The Hague: Mouton.

———. 1950. "Primary Groups in the American Army." In R. K. Merton and P. F. Lazarsfeld, eds., *Continuities in Social Research*. New York: Free Press.

Shin-Shan, Henry Tsai. 1986. *The Chinese Experience in America*. Bloomington, IN: Indiana University Press, pp. 157–58.

Sidel, Ruth. 1990. *On Her Own: Growing Up in the Shadow of the American Dream*. New York: Viking Penguin.

Silberman, C. E. 1978. *Criminal Violence—Criminal Justice: Criminals, Police, Courts and Prisons in America*. New York: Random House.

———. 1971. *Crisis in the Classroom: The Remaking of American Education*. New York: Random House.

Simmel, Georg. 1957. "Fashion." *American Journal of Sociology*, 62, pp. 541–88.

Simon, Julian L. and Herman Kahn, eds. 1984. *The Resourceful Earth: A Response to Global 2000*. New York: Basil Blackwell.

Simpson, George E. and Milton Yinger. 1972. *Racial and Cultural Minorities: An Analysis of Prejudice and Discrimination*. 4th ed. New York: Harper & Row.

Sjoberg, Gideon. 1965. *Preindustrial City: Past and Present*. New York: Free Press.

Skocpol, Theda. 1979. *States and Social Revolutions*. New York: Cambridge University Press.

Slater, P. 1970. *The Pursuit of Loneliness: American Culture at the Breaking Point*. Boston: Beacon Press.

———. 1966. *Microcosm: Structural, Psychological, and Religious Evolution in Groups*. New York: John Wiley.

Smelser, Neil J. 1971. "Mechanisms of Change and Adjustment to Change." In George Dalton, ed., *Economic Development and Social Change*. Garden City, NY: Natural History Press.

———. 1962. *Theory of Collective Behavior*. New York: Free Press.

Smith, Adam. 1969 (1776). *An Inquiry into the Nature and Causes of the Wealth of Nations*. 2 vols. Chicago: University of Chicago Press.

Smith, Tom. 1984. "America's Religious Mosaic." *American Demographics*, June, pp. 19–23.

Snyder, Z. 1971. "The Social Environment of the Urban Indian." In Jack O. Waddell and Michael Watson, eds., *The American Indian in Urban Society*. Boston: Little, Brown.

Solecki, Ralph. 1971. *Shanidar: The First Flower People*. New York: Knopf.

Sorokin, Pitirim A. 1937. *Social and Cultural Dynamics*. New York: American Books.

Sosin, Michael. 1986. *Homelessness in Chicago*. Chicago: School of Social Service Administration, University of Chicago.

Spain, Daphne. 1988. "Women's Demographic Past, Present and Future." Radcliffe Conferences on Women in the 21st Century, Cambridge, MA, Dec.

Spates, James L. and John J. Macionis. 1987. *The Sociology of Cities*. Belmont, CA: Wadsworth.

Spengler, Oswald. 1932. *The Decline of the West*. New York: Knopf.

Spicer, Edward H. 1962. *Cycles of Conquest*. Tucson, AZ: University of Arizona Press.

Spiro, Melford E. 1960. "Addendum, 1958." In Norman W. Bell and Ezra F. Vogel, eds., *A Modern Introduction to the Family*. Glencoe, IL: Free Press.

Spitz, Rene A. 1945. "Hospitalism: An Inquiry Into the Genesis of Psychiatric Conditions in Early Childhood." In Anna Freud, et al., eds., *The Psychoanalytic Study of the Child*. New York: International Universities Press.

Squire, Peverill. 1988. "Why the 1936 Literary Digest Poll Failed." *Public Opinion Quarterly*, Vol 52. Spring, pp. 125–33.

Stabler, Ken. 1986. "Bear Bryant." *Esquire*, June, p. 67.

Staires, Graham L., Robert P. Quinn, and Linda J. Shepard. 1976. "Occupational Sex Discrimination." *Industrial Relations*, 15, pp. 88–98.

Stark, Rodney and William Sims Bainbridge. 1985. *The Future of Religion: Secularization, Revival, and Cult Formation*. Berkeley, CA: University of California Press.

Stark, Rodney and Charles Y. Glock. 1968. *American Piety: The Nature of Religious Commitments*. Berkeley and Los Angeles: University of California Press.

Steward, Julian H. 1955. *The Theory of Culture Change: The Methodology of Multilineal Evolution*. Urbana, IL: University of Illinois Press.

Stoller, R. J. 1967. "Effects of Parents' Attitudes on Core Gender Identity." *International Journal of Psychiatry*, March, p. 57.

Stoner, James A. F. 1982. *Management*. 2nd ed. Englewood Cliffs, NJ: Prentice-Hall.

Stouffer, Samuel A., ed. 1950. *The American Solider*. Princeton, NJ: Princeton University Press.

Straus, Murray A., Richard J. Gelles, and Suzanne K. Steinmetz. 1980. *Behind Closed Doors*. New York: Anchor/Doubleday.

Strauss, Anselm and Barney Glaser. 1975. *Chronic Illness and the Quality of Life*. St. Louis: C.V. Mosby.

Stulgoe, John R. 1984. "The Suburbs." *American Heritage*, 35(2), Feb.–March, pp. 21–36.

Sudman, Seymour. 1985. "Do Exit Polls Influence Voting Behavior?" *Public Opinion Quarterly*, Spring, pp. 332–33.

Sullivan, Joseph F. 1979. "New Jersey: Assaults are a Daily Occurrence." *The New York Times*, Oct. 23, p. 6E.

Sumner, W. G. 1906. *Folkways: A Study of the Sociological Importance of Usages, Manners, Customs, Mores, and Morals*. Boston: Ginn.

Susser, Mervyn W., Kim Hopper, and Judith Richman. 1983. "Society, Culture and Health." In D. Mechanic, ed., *Handbook of Health, Health Care, and the Health Professions*. New York: The Free Press, pp. 23–49.

Sutherland, Edwin H. 1961. *White Collar Crime*. New York: Holt, Rinehart and Winston.

———. 1940. "White Collar Criminality." *American Sociological Review*, 40, pp. 1–12.

———. 1924. *Criminology*. New York: Lippincott.

Sutherland, Edwin H. and D. R. Cressey. 1978. *Principles of Criminology*. 10th ed. Chicago: Lippincott.

Suttles, G. 1972. *The Social Construction of Communities*. Chicago: University of Chicago Press.

———. 1968. *The Social Order of the Slum*. Chicago: University of Chicago Press.

Szymanski, Albert T. and Ted George Goertzel. 1979. *Sociology: Class, Consciousness, and Contradictions*. New York: Van Nostrand.

Taeuber, Cynthia M. and Victor Valdisera. 1987. "Women in the American Economy." *Current Population Reports*, Special Studies, Series P-23, No. 146. Washington, DC: U.S. Government Printing Office.

Tannen, Deborah. 1990. *You Just Don't Understand: Women and Men in Conversation*. New York: William Morrow.

Teitelbaum, Michael S. and Jay M. Winter. 1985. *The Fear of Population Decline*. Orlando, FL: Academic Press.

Terrace, H. S., L. A. Petitto, R. J. Sanders, and T. G. Bever. 1979. "Can an Ape Create a Sentence?" *Science*, 206, pp. 891–902.

Thomas, W. I. 1928. *The Child in America*. New York: Knopf.

Thompson, Laura. 1950. *Culture in Crisis*. New York: Harper.

Thompson, Warren S. 1929. "Population." *American Journal of Sociology*, 34, pp. 959–75.

Tiger, Lionel and Robin Fox. 1971. *The Imperial Animal*. New York: Holt, Rinehart and Winston.

Töennies, Ferdinand. 1963. *Community and Society*. New York: Harper and Row. (Originally published in German as *Gemeinschaft und Gesellschaft* in 1887.)

Toffler, Alvin. 1970. *Future Shock*. New York: Random House.

Torrey, E. Fuller. 1988. "Homelessness and Mental Illness." *USA Today Magazine*, March, pp. 26–30.

Townsend, Bickley. 1987. "Back to the Future." *American Demographics*, March, p. 10.

Toynbee, Arnold. 1946. *A Study of History*. New York and London: Oxford University Press.

Trachtenberg, Joshua. 1961. *The Devil and the Jews*. New York: Meridian Books.

Treiman, Donald J. 1977. *Occupational Prestige in Comparative Perspective*. New York: Academic Press.

Turnbull, Colin. 1972. *The Mountain People*. New York: Simon & Schuster.

Turner, Ralph H. 1964. "Collective Behavior." In R. E. L. Faris, ed., *Handbook of Modern Sociology*. Chicago: Rand McNally.

Turner, Ralph H. and Lewis M. Killian. 1972. *Collective Behavior*. 2nd ed. Englewood Cliffs, NJ: Prentice-Hall.

Tylor, E. 1958 (1871). *Primitive Culture: Researches into the Development of Mythology, Philosophy, Religion, Art and Custom*. Vol. 1. London: John Murray.

———. 1889. "On a Method of Investigating the Development of Institutions Applied to Laws of Marriage and Descent." *Journal of the Royal Anthropological Institute*, 18, pp. 245–69.

Udy, S. H., Jr. 1959. "Bureaucracy and Rationality in Weber's Organizational Theory: An Empirical Study." *American Sociological Review*, 24, pp. 791–95.

Uhlenberg, Peter. 1987. "How Old is Old Age?" *The Public Interest*, Summer, No. 88, pp. 67–79.

Ulc, Otto. 1975 (1969). "Communist National Minority Policy: The Case of the Gypsies in Czechoslovakia." In Norman R. Yetman and C. Hoy Steele, eds., *Majority and Minority: The Dynamics of Racial and Ethnic Relations*. Boston: Allyn & Bacon.

U.S. Bureau of the Census. 1991. "Marital Status and Living Arrangements: March 1990." Current Population Reports, Series P-20, No. 450, p. 17.

U.S. Bureau of the Census. 1991. Current Population Reports, Series P-25, No. 1018.

U.S. Bureau of the Census. 1991. *Statistical Abstract of the United States: 1991*. Washington, DC: U.S. Government Printing Office.

———. 1988. "Statistical Brief, December 1986." *Occupational Outlook Quarterly*, Spring.

U.S. Bureau of Census. 1986. "Age Structure of the U.S. Population in the 21st Century." Statistical Brief, Dec.

U.S. Bureau of Labor Statistics. 1985. *Monthly Labor Review*. Nov.

U.S. Center for Health Statistics. *Vital Statistics of the United States*. Annual.

U.S. Department of Commerce News. 1991. "1990 Median Household Income Dips, Census Bureau Reports in Annual Survey," Sept. 26.

U.S. Department of Commerce, Bureau of the Census. 1989. *Statistical Abstract of the United States, 1989*. Washington, DC: U.S. Government Printing Office.

U.S. Department of Commerce, Bureau of the Census. 1988. *Statistical Abstract of the United States, 1987*. Washington, DC: U.S. Government Printing Office.

———. 1988. *Uniform Crime Report*. Preliminary Annual Release. Washington, DC: U.S. Government Printing Office.

———. 1989. *Uniform Crime Report, 1988*. Washington, DC: U.S. Government Printing Office.

U.S. Department of Justice. 1991. "Capital Punishment 1990." *Bureau of Justice Statistics Bulletin*, Sept.

U.S. Department of Justice. 1990. "Black Victims." *Bureau of Justice Statistics Special Report*, April.

U.S. Department of Justice. 1991. *Bureau of Justice Statistics*. Washington, DC: U.S. Government Printing Office.

U.S. Department of Justice. 1991. "Criminal Victimization 1990." *Bureau of Justice Statistics Bulletin*. Washington, DC: U.S. Government Printing Office.

U.S. Department of Justice. 1988. "Households Touched by Crime, 1987." *Bureau of Justice Statistics Bulletin*, May.

U.S. Department of Justice. 1988. *BJS Data Report*. Bureau of Justice Statistics, Jan.

U.S. Department of Justice. 1987. "Lifetime Likelihood of Victimization." *Bureau of Justice Statistics, Technical Report*, March.

U.S. News & World Report. 1988. "Internationalization of Crime in the United States." Jan. 18.

———. 1988. "The Rochester Experiment: School Reform, School Reality." June 20, pp. 58–63.

Useem, Michael. 1984. *The Inner Circle: Large Corporations and the Rise of Business Political Activity in the U.S. and U.K.* New York: Oxford University Press.

Vago, Steven. 1980. *Social Change.* New York: Holt, Rinehart and Winston.

Van de Kaa, Dirk J. 1987. "Europe's Second Demographic Transition." *Population Bulletin,* March.

Vanfossen, Beth E. 1979. *The Structure of Social Inequality.* Boston: Little, Brown.

Van Lawick-Goodall, J. 1971. *In the Shadow of Man.* Boston: Houghton Mifflin.

Veltford, Helen and George E. Lee. 1943. "The Coconut Grove Fire: A Study in Scapegoating." *Journal of Abnormal and Social Psychology,* Clinical Supplement, 38, April, pp. 138–54.

Verba, Sidney. 1972. *Small Groups and Political Behavior: A Study of Leadership.* Princeton, NJ: Princeton University Press.

———. 1975. *Sociobiology: The New Synthesis.* Cambridge, MA: Harvard University Press.

Walsh, Doris L. 1986. "What Women Want." *American Demographics,* p. 60.

Warner, W. L. P. Lunt. 1941. *The Social Life of a Modern Community.* New Haven, CT: Yale University Press.

Warren, R. L. 1972. *The Community in America.* 2nd ed. New York: Rand McNally.

Watson, J. B. 1925. *Behavior.* New York: Norton.

Weber, Max. 1968 (1922). *Economy and Society.* Trans. Ephraim Fischoff. New York: Bedminster Press.

———. 1962. *Basic Sociology.* Secaucus, NJ: Citadel Press.

———. 1958a (1921). *The City.* New York: Collier.

———. 1958b. "Class, Status, and Party." In Hans H. Gerth and C. Wright Mills, eds., *Max Weber: Essays in Sociology,* New York: Oxford University Press.

———. 1957. *The Theory of Social and Economic Organization.* New York: Free Press.

———. 1956. "Some Consequences of Bureaucratization." In J. P. Mayer, Trans., *Max Weber and German Politics,* 2nd ed. New York: Free Press.

———. 1949. *Max Weber on the Methodology of the Social Sciences.* Trans. and ed. Edward A. Shils and Henry A. Finch. New York: Free Press.

———. 1947. *Max Weber: Essays in Sociology.* New York: Oxford University Press.

———. 1930 (1920). *Protestant Ethic and the Spirit of Capitalism.* Trans. Talcott Parsons. New York: Scribner.

Weeks, John R., 1988. "The Demography of Islamic Nations." *The Population Bulletin,* Vol. 43. No. 4, Dec. Washington, DC: Population Reference Bureau.

Weiner, Janet and B. Jaye Anno. 1992. "The Crisis in Correctional Health Care: The Impact of the National Drug Control Strategy on Correctional Health Services." *Annals of Internal Medicine,* Vol. 117, No. 1, July 1, pp. 71–77.

Weisman, Steven R. 1988. "Pakistani Women Take Lead in Drive Against Islamization." *The New York Times,* June 17, pp. A1, A10.

Weiss, Robert S. 1979a. *Going It Alone: The Family Life and Social Situation of the Single Parent.* New York: Basic Books.

———. 1979b. "Issues in the Adjudication of Custody When Parents Separate." In George Levinger and Oliver C. Moles, eds., *Divorce and Separation: Context, Causes, and Consequences.* New York: Basic Books.

Weissberg, Robert. 1981. *Understanding American Government.* Alternate ed. New York: Holt, Rinehart and Winston.

Weitzman, Lenore J. 1985. *The Divorce Revolution: The Unexpected Social and Economic Consequences for Women and Children in America.* New York: Free Press.

Weitzman, Lenore J., Deborah Eitler, Elizabeth Hokada, and Catherine Ross. 1972. "Sex-Role Socialization in Picture Books for Preschool Children." *American Journal of Sociology,* May, pp. 1125–50.

Weitzman, Lenore J. and Ruth B. Dixon. 1980. "The Transformation of Legal Marriage Through No-Fault Divorce." In Arlene S. Skolnick and Jerome H. Skolnick, eds., *Family in Transition: Rethinking Marriage, Sexuality, Child Rearing and Family Organization.* 3rd ed. Boston: Little, Brown.

Wertsch, Mary Edwards. 1991. *Military Brats.* New York: Harmony Books, p. 145.

Westoff, Charles F. and Elise F. Jones. 1977. "The Secularization of Catholic Birth Control Practice." *Family Planning Perspectives,* 9, Sept.–Oct., pp. 96–101.

Wheelwright, Philip. 1959. *Heraclitus.* Princeton, NJ: Princeton University Press.

White, Theodore H. 1982. *America in Search of Itself: The Making of the President, 1956–80.* New York: Harper & Row.

White, W. F. 1943. *Street Corner Society.* Chicago: University of Illinois Press.

Whorf, B. 1956. *Language, Thought, and Reality.* Cambridge, MA: MIT Press.

Whyte, W. H. 1956. *The Organization Man.* New York: Simon & Schuster.

Williamson, Nancy E. 1983. "Parental Sex Preferences and Sex Selection." In N.G. Bennett, ed., *Sex Selection of Children.* New York: Academic Press.

Willner, Ann Ruth. 1984. *The Spellbinders: Charismatic Political Leadership.* New Haven, CT: Yale University Press.

Wilson, Barbara Foley. 1984. "Marriage's Melting Pot." *American Demographics,* 6(7), July, pp. 34–37, 45.

Wilson, Barbara Foley and Kathryn A. London. 1987. "Going to the Chapel." *American Demographics,* Dec., pp. 26–31.

Wilson, Edmund. 1969. *The Dead Sea Scrolls 1947–1969.* Rev. ed. London: W. H. Allen.

Wilson, Edward O. 1979. *Sociobiology.* 2nd ed. Cambridge, MA: Belknap.

——. 1978. *On Human Nature.* Cambridge, MA: Harvard University Press.

Wilson, James Q. 1980. *American Government.* Lexington, MA: Health.

Wilson, John. 1973. *Introduction to Social Movements.* New York: Basic Books.

Wirth, Louis. 1944. "Race and Public Policy." *Scientific Monthly,* 58(4), March, p. 303.

——. 1938. "Urbanism as a Way of Life." *American Journal of Sociology,* 64, pp. 1–24.

Wolf, Eric. 1969. *Peasant Wars of the Twentieth Century.* New York: Harper & Row.

Wolfe, Linda. 1981. "The Good News." *New York Magazine,* Dec. 28, pp. 33–35.

Wolfgang, Marvin, Robert M. Figlio, and Thorsten Sellin. 1972. *Delinquency in a Birth Cohort.* Chicago: University of Chicago Press.

Woodrow, Karen A., Jeffrey S. Passel, and Robert Warren. 1987. "Recent Immigration to the United States—Legal and Undocumented: An Analysis of Data From the June 1986 Current Population Survey." Paper presented at the meetings of the Population Association of America, Chicago.

World Bank. 1987. *World Development Report 1987.* Washington, DC: World Bank.

——. 1984. *World Development Report, 1984.* New York: Oxford University Press.

——. 1984. *The Development Data Book.* Washington, DC: World Bank.

—— 1984. "Measuring the Value of Children." *World Development Report 1984.* New York: Oxford University Press, pp. 122–23.

Wurman, Richard Saul. 1989. *Information Anxiety.* New York: Doubleday.

Yinger, J. Milton. 1970. *The Scientific Study of Religion.* New York: Macmillan.

——. 1960. "Contraculture and Subculture." *American Sociological Review,* 25, pp. 625–35.

Zeitlin, I. M. 1981. *Social Condition of Humanity.* New York: Oxford University Press.

Zelnik, Melvin and Robert Kantner. 1979. "Probabilities of Intercourse and Conception Among U.S. Teenage Women 1971 and 1976." *Family Planning Perspectives,* 2, May–June, pp. 177–83.

——. 1972. "Sexuality, Contraception and Pregnancy Among Young Unwed Females in the United States." In *U.S. Commission on Population Growth and the American Future, Demographic and Social Aspects of Population Growth.* Washington, DC: U.S. Government Printing Office.

Zimbardo, P. G. 1972. "Pathology of Imprisonment." *Society,* April 9, p. 4.

■ CREDITS ■

Advertisement reprinted courtesy of Rolls-Royce of Beverly Hills.

"The Battle Over English." Sourced and reprinted with permission © *American Demographics*, February 1987, p. 7; and April 1987, pp. 52 and 54.

"Euthanasia: What is a Good Death?" From *The Economist*, July 21, 1991, issue, pp. 21, 22, 24. Copyright © 1991, *The Economist, Ltd.* Distributed by the New York Times Special Features. Reprinted by permission.

Daniel Anderson and Patricia A. Collins. "Does TV Make Kids Stupid?" Appeared in *The Boston Globe*, January 15, 1989. Copyright © 1989 and reprinted by permission of the authors.

Lori B. Andrews. "Exhibit A: Language." Reprinted with permission from PSYCHOLOGY TODAY Magazine. Copyright © 1984 (Sussex Publishers, Inc.). Issue date February 1984.

Christine E. Bose and Peter H. Rossi. "Prestige Ratings of Various Occupations." From "Gender and Jobs: Prestige Standings of Occupations as Affected by Gender," *American Sociological Review* 48:316–330 (1983), Table 4. Reprinted by permission of the American Sociological Association and the authors.

Shannon Brownlee, Karen Schmidt, and Eric Ransdell. "Origin of a Plague," *U.S. News and World Report*, issue date March 30, 1992, p. 50. Reprinted courtesy of *U.S. News and World Report.*

Donald R. Cressey and Edwin H. Sutherland. A table from CRIMINOLOGY, 10e. Copyright © 1978. Reprinted courtesy of Elaine S. Cressey.

Kingsley Davis. A table from "Relationships in Primary and Secondary Groups." Copyright © 1949. Reprinted by permission of Kingsley Davis, Senior Research Fellow, Hoover Institution.

Nicholas Eberstadt. "America's Infant Mortality Problem: Parents." January 20, 1992, issue date, p. A-14. Copyright © 1992. Reprinted by permission of *The Wall Street Journal.*

Paul R. Ehrlich and Anne H. Ehrlich. THE POPULATION EXPLOSION. Copyright © 1990 by Paul R. Ehrlich and Anne H. Ehrlich. Reprinted by permission of SIMON & SCHUSTER.

Erik H. Erikson. Adapted from CHILDHOOD AND SOCIETY, Second Edition, by Erik H. Erikson, by permission of W. W. Norton & Company, Inc. Copyright 1950, © 1963 by W. W. Norton & Company, Inc. Copyright renewed 1978, 1991 by Erik H. Erikson.

James Fallows. Adapted from "The Japanese Are Different from You and Me," by James Fallows. Originally appeared in *Atlantic Monthly*, September 1986, pp. 35–41. Reprinted by permission of the author and publisher.

Paul C. Glick. Table from "How American Families Are Changing," January 1984 issue, p. 24. Reprinted with permission © *American Demographics*.

Ken Good and David Chanoff. From INTO THE HEART. Copyright © 1991 by Ken Good and David Chanoff. Reprinted by permission of SIMON & SCHUSTER.

Charles T. Goodsell. From THE CASE FOR BUREAUCRACY, 2e, by Charles T. Goodsell. Copyright © 1985. Reprinted by permission of Chatham House Publishers, Inc.

Steve Hassan. COMBATTING CULT MIND CONTROL. Published 1988 by Park Street Press, a division of Inner Traditions International, Rochester, VT.

Arlie Hochschild and Ann Machung. Adapted from THE SECOND SHIFT, by Arlie Hochschild and Ann Machung. Copyright © 1989 by Arlie Hochschild. Used by permission of Viking Press, a division of Penguin Books, USA, Inc.

Jan Larson and Brad Edmondson. Adaptation of "Should Unmarried Partners Get Married Benefits?" March 1991, p. 47. Reprinted with permission © *American Demographics*.

Charles Longino, Jr., and William Crown. "Older Americans: Rich or Poor?" August 1991, pp. 48–53. Reprinted by permission © *American Demographics*.

John Marlin. Table from THE LIVABLE CITIES ALMANAC by John Marlin. Copyright © 1992 by John Marlin. Reprinted by permission of HarperCollins Publishers.

Neil Pinchin. Graphic on U.S. Immigration by racial/ethnic group by Neil Pinchin, *The Boston Globe Magazine*, October 13, 1991. Reprinted courtesy of the Boston Globe.

Allan J. Schwartz. "The Epidemiology of Suicide Among Students at Colleges and Universities." From COLLEGE STUDENT SUICIDE, copyright © 1990. Reprinted by permission of Haworth Press.

William Whyte. From CITY. Copyright © 1989 by William Whyte. Used by permission of Doubleday, a division of Bantam Doubleday Dell Publishing Group, Inc.

Richard Saul Wurman. From INFORMATION ANXIETY by Richard Saul Wurman. Copyright © 1989 by Richard Saul Wurman. Used by permission of Doubleday, a division of Bantam Doubleday Dell Publishing Group, Inc.

PHOTO CREDITS

p. 2   © 91 Andrew Holbrooke/Black Star
p. 5   J. Brown/Offshoot Stock
p. 8   T. Howarth/Woodfin Camp & Associates
p. 10   Giraudon/Art Resource
p. 11   The Bettmann Archive
p. 12   The Bettmann Archive
p. 13   The Bettmann Archive
p. 14   The Bettmann Archive
p. 15   Brown Brothers
p. 16   NASA
p. 17   Harvard University News Office
p. 19   Andrew Holbrooke/Black Star
p. 21   M. Gibson/The Stock Market
p. 24   Garry Gay/The Image Bank
p. 27   Jan Doyle
p. 28   Stacy Pick/Stock, Boston
p. 29   © Candace Barbot/The Miami Herald
p. 31   Konner/Anthro-Photo
p. 32   P. Fusco/Magnum Photos
p. 33   UPI/Bettmann
p. 40   Laura Dwight/Peter Arnold, Inc.
p. 44   Guido A. Rossi/The Image Bank
p. 46   © 1977 John Running/Black Star
p. 48   Copyright © Kenneth Good
p. 50   (top) M & E Bernheim/Woodfin Camp
       & Associates
p. 50   (bottom left) Minosa-Scorpio/Sygma
p. 50   (bottom right) G. Holton/Photo Researchers,
       Inc.
p. 51   Charles Gupton/Stock, Boston
p. 53   The Bettmann Archive
p. 54   K. Galvin/Bruce Coleman
p. 55   (top) Frans Lanting/Photo Researchers, Inc.
p. 55   (bottom) © David Burnett/Contact Press Images
p. 57   T. McHugh/Photo Researchers, Inc.
p. 58   D. Mason/The Stock Market
p. 59   J. Brown/Offshoot Stock
p. 63   (top) T. Braise/The Stock Market
p. 63   (bottom) B. Bear/Woodfin Camp & Associates
p. 68   Wayne Floyd/Unicorn Stock Photos
p. 70   Bundesarchiv
p. 72   Joseph A. Dichello, Jr.
p. 74   J.W. Myers/The Stock Market
p. 77   Boston Filmworks
p. 78   The Bettmann Archive
p. 79   Boston Filmworks
p. 83   Robert Frerck/TSW-Click/Chicago
p. 84   Bob Daemmrich/Stock, Boston
p. 86   © Joel Gordon 1979
p. 91   B. Daemmrich/The Image Works
p. 92   Dennis Barnes
p. 94   P. Damien/TSW-Click/Chicago
p. 95   Joan Liftin/Actuality Inc.
p. 96   © Frank Siteman/Stock, Boston
p. 98   Ben Bernhart/Offshoot Stock
p. 99   Dennis Barnes
p. 101   © 1987 Anthony Suau/Black Star

p. 104   G. Hiller/Black Star
p. 110   C. Harbutt/Actuality Inc.
p. 112   T. Thai/Sygma
p. 117   (left) Laura Dwight/Peter Arnold, Inc.
p. 117   (right) Steven McCurry/Magnum
p. 118   © 1991 Matt Herron
p. 120   © Carey/The Image Works
p. 121   (top left) Henry K. Kaiser/Leo de Wys, Inc.
p. 121   (top right) Boston Filmworks
p. 121   (bottom) Robert Cappa/Magnum
p. 124   J. Curtis/Offshoot Stock
p. 132   B. Stanton/Magnum
p. 134   H. Halberstadt/Photo Researchers, Inc.
p. 136   Sudhir/The Picture Group
p. 139   (top) R. Scheipman/Offshoot Stock
p. 139   (bottom) Tannenbaum/Sygma
p. 141   Courtesy of Finger Matrix
p. 143   M. Richards/The Picture Group
p. 150   © 1991 Viviane Moos/Photoreporters, Inc.
p. 152   The Bettmann Archive
p. 153   Andrew Holbrooke/Black Star
p. 154   John Bryson/The Image Bank
p. 160   (top) Bettmann Newsphotos
p. 160   (bottom) J. Rodriguez/Black Star
p. 161   (left) © H. Mark Weidman
p. 161   (right) Ted Horowitz/The Stock Market
p. 163   J.T. Miller/The Stock Market
p. 168   © 1991 Arni Katz/Unicorn Stock Photos
p. 172   Bob Krist
p. 173   Ad. courtesy of ROLLS-ROYCE of Beverly
       Hills. © ROLLS-ROYCE of Beverly Hills.
p. 174   B. Gallery/Stock, Boston
p. 176   © Jeff Albertson/Stock, Boston
p. 177   C. Gupton/TSW-Click/Chicago
p. 180   G. Peress/Magnum
p. 181   G. Palmer/The Stock Market
p. 183   Frances M. Roberts
p. 185   O. Franken/Stock, Boston
p. 186   © Richard B. Levine
p. 188   Russell Schleipman 1987/Offshoot Stock
p. 190   B. Kliewe/The Picture Group
p. 192   M. Greenlar/The Picture Group
p. 195   Alex Webb/Magnum
p. 198   Brown Brothers
p. 200   AP/Wide World Photos
p. 203   (top) © 1984 Phil Huber/Black Star
p. 203   (bottom) Peter Arnold, Inc.
p. 204   Paula M. Lerner/The Picture Cube
p. 206   M. Winter/The Picture Group
p. 207   J.P. Laffont/Sygma
p. 209   Brown Brothers
p. 210   Russell Schleipman 1987/Offshoot Stock
p. 214   Mike Kirkpatrick/ProFiles West
p. 216   (left) Eve Arnold/Magnum
p. 216   (right) Owen Franken/Sygma
p. 217   T. Eakin/SuperStock/Three Lions
p. 222   Boston Filmworks

■ AUTHOR INDEX ■

Adams, J., 199
Ahmed, N., 345
Alexander, 312
Alinsky, S., 404
Allende, S., 318
Anderson, D.R., 306
Andrews, L.B., 97
Anno, B.J., 384
Antonovsky, A., 382
Appelbaum, R.P., 22
Aristotle, 306, 312
Aronoff, J., 222
Asch, S., 108-109
Augustus, 311

Bainbridge, W.S., 272
Bales, R.F., 107, 222
Bandura, A., 126
Bardwick, J., 225
Barlow, H.D., 138
Barnett, R.C., 81, 89, 231
Baron, S.W., 198, 199
Baruch, G.K., 81, 89, 231
Baskin, B.H., 307
Batista, F., 207
Baumrind, S., 85
Bear, J., 55
Becker, H., 131
Beckwith, B.P., 272
Becraft, C., 103
Bedau, H.A., 140
Belkin, 271
Bell, A.P., 265
Bem, D., 225, 226
Bem, S., 225, 226
Benbow, 219
Benedict, R., 53, 88
Bennett, N.G., 253
Berg, A.G., 153
Berger, P., 103, 282
Bernard, L.L., 71
Berry, B., 13, 189, 193, 194, 199
Berry, B.J., 361
Bertalanffy, L.V., 417
Besharov, D.J., 176
Best, F., 3
Bettleheim, B., 72
Bhutto, A., 318
Bhutto, B., 248
Bianchi, S.M., 34, 229
Bierstadt, R., 45-46
Black, K.W., 401
Blakeslee, S., 380
Blau, P., 98

Bloom, D.E., 253, 255
Blum, J.M., 322
Blumberg, P., 170
Blumenbach, J., 188
Blumer, H., 395, 397, 404
Blumstein, P., 252, 265
Boesky, I., 153
Bollen, K., 86
Bose, C.E., 159
Bottomore, T.B., 185
Bowles, S., 298
Bradley, T., 393, 397
Bray, J.H., 264
Brezhnev, L., 55
Brokaw, T., 401
Bronfenbrenner, U., 85
Brown, D., 279
Brown, L.R., 311, 348
Brown, R.W., 402
Brownlee, S., 386
Bruegel, P., 355
Brzezinski, Z., 317
Bullough, V.L., 216
Bumpass, L., 265
Burchinal, L.G., 250
Burgess, E.W., 17, 233, 359-360
Burt, C., 40
Bush, G., 100, 295, 309, 397
Bylinsky, G., 421, 422
Byrne, D., 95

Cameron, W.B., 404
Canetti, E., 397
Carmody, D., 206
Carson, C. "Kit," 198
Castelli, J., 281, 284, 289
Castro, F., 207
Chagnon, N.A., 47, 48
Chalmers, D., 404
Chambliss, W.J., 133
Chancellor, L.E., 250
Chanoff, D., 49
Chavez, C., 206
Cherlin, A., 264
Chi, K.S., 289
Chomsky, N., 81
Chorover, 126
Claffey, C.E., 197
Clark, J., 304
Clayton, R.B., 264, 265
Cleland, J.G., 391
Clinton, B., 327
Cockerham, W.C., 380, 381
Cohen, A.K., 61

Cohen, M.A., 3
Cohen, Y.A., 254
Cole, M.W., 202
Cole, S.G., 202
Coleman, D., 381
Coleman, J.S., 301-302
Collins, P.A., 306
Collins, R., 18, 23, 299
Collmer, C.W., 258
Comte, A., 11, 13, 15, 22, 217
Conant, 172
Conrad, P., 378, 379, 388
Cooley, C.H., 75, 76, 77, 78, 105
Coser, L.A., 16, 23, 99
Cowgill, D.O., 234
Crano, W.D., 222
Cressey, D.R., 130
Crispell, D., 422
Crossen, P.R., 348
Crown, W.H., 182
Cullingford, C., 86
Cumming, E., 233
Cummings, M.C., 324, 328
Cummings, P.W., 312
Cunningham, P.H., 275
Curtiss, S., 73
Cuzzort, R.P., 164

Dahrendorf, R., 23, 167, 416
Dalton, G., 420
D'Andrade, R.G., 221
Daniels, N., 295
Darwin, C., 71, 163, 415
Davidson, L., 230
Davis, F.J., 193
Davis, K., 73, 106, 161-162, 320, 416
De Beauvoir, S., 91
Denison, D.C., 197
DeVore, I., 62
DeWitt, J.L., 210
Dixon, R., 260, 261
Doman, G., 82, 83
Domhoff, G.W., 157
Douglas, J.D., 22
Douvan, E., 225
Duberman, L., 194
Dubinsky, D., 408
Dukert, J.M., 177
Duncan, G., 34
Durant, W., 320
Durkheim, E., 12, 13-15, 17, 18, 120, 121-122, 127, 128, 270, 275-276, 278, 363, 415

Eberstadt, N., 350
Eckholm, E.P., 348
Edmondson, B., 266, 297
Ehrlich, A.H., 349
Ehrlich, P.R., 349
Einstein, A., 295
Eisenberg, L., 87
Ekman, P., 55
Elder, G.H., 85
Elkind, D., 82-83
Elkins, S.M., 85
Ember, C.R., 273
Ember, M., 273
Emerson, R.W., 119
Engels, F., 163, 222, 279, 319, 356
Enos, D.D., 383
Erikson, E.H., 75, 76-77, 79, 80, 90
Erikson, K.T., 122, 402
Erlich, I., 144
Exline, 361
Exter, T., 205

Falaudi, S., 34
Fallows, J., 65
Fava, S.F., 355
Ferraro, G., 323
Ferree, M.M., 403
Festinger, L., 31, 281
Finn, C.E., Jr., 303
Fischler, S., 396
Fisher, J.D., 95
Fisher, R., 404
Fiske, E.B., 302
Flanagan, T.J., 136
Ford, C.S., 220
Fortes, M., 243
Fortune, R., 220
Fost, 212
Fouts, D., 60
Fouts, R., 60
Fox, R., 218
Franchi, S., 324
Frank, A., 390
Frankfort, H., 355
Franklin, B., 210
Frase, M.J., 302
Fredrickson, G.M., 13
Freed, R.S., 341
Freed, S.A., 341
Freedman, S.G., 291
Freeman, J.M., 275
Freud, S., 66, 76, 77, 78-79, 126, 275
Fried, M., 107
Friedman, M., 388
Friedman, R., 388
Friedrich, C.J., 317
Friesen, W.V., 55
Frieze, I.H., 224

Fuguitt, G.V., 374
Fu Hsuan, 216
Furstenburg, F., 262

Gallup, G., 33
Gallup, G., Jr., 281, 284, 289
Gandhi, M.K., 119, 269
Gans, H.J., 31, 39, 365, 367
Gardner, A., 60
Gardner, B., 60
Gardner, H., 75
Gardner, R., 354
Garfinkel, H., 19, 20-21
Gargan, E.A., 348
Gates, W., 153, 171
Geertz, C., 56, 65
Gelles, R.J., 255
Gerth, H., 412
Giese, A.S., 423
Gill, R.T., 88, 89
Gilligan, C., 227
Ginsberg, M., 412
Gintis, H., 298
Gist, N.P., 355
Glaser, B., 378
Glazer, N., 190
Glick, P.C., 248, 259
Glock, C.Y., 282
Gnessous, M., 417
Goertzel, T.G., 297
Goffman, E., 19, 21, 87
Goldberg, P., 225
Goldman, A.L., 269, 377
Goldwater, B., 323
Gompers, S., 408
Good, K., 48-49
Goodall, J. See Van Lawick-Goodall
Goode, W.J., 102, 251
Goodsell, C.T., 113
Gordon, L., 230
Gordon, M.M., 61, 194, 204
Gough, K., 243
Gould, H., 154
Gould, S.J., 71
Gouldner, A.W., 17, 23, 41
Green, R.C., 302
Greenberg, J., 60
Griffith, J.E., 302
Griffith, M., 129
Gross, L., 166
Gumplowicz, L., 313
Gurr, T.R., 403
Gursslin, O.R., 166

Hall, E.T., 46, 49, 51, 52, 94-95
Hall, R.H., 114
Hammurabi, 320
Hardesty, D., 226

Hare, P.A., 109
Harlow, H.F., 73, 74
Harlow, M., 73
Harrington, M., 178
Harris, C.D., 360
Harris, K., 307
Harris, M., 247, 278
Hassan, S., 288
Haub, C., 338
Hauser, P., 354
Hawkins, L., 309
Hawley, A., 361
Hayes, C.D., 88
Haywood, W.D., 408
Heer, D.M., 250
Heide, K., 129
Helmore, K., 346
Henry, W.H., 233
Heraclitus, 411
Herbers, J., 255, 373, 375
Herrnstein, R., 124, 127
Hess, B.B., 304, 403
Hirschi, T., 129
Hitler, A., 196, 311
Hochschild, A., 256
Hodge, R.W., 100
Hoebel, E.A., 127
Hoffman, S., 34
Holdrich, M., 369
Hollingshead, A.B., 170, 185, 248
Holmes, L., 234
Homans, G.C., 416
Houseknecht, S.K., 289
Howe, I., 208
Hoyt, H., 360
Hughes, H.L., 369
Huxley, A., 109

Iacocca, L., 107
Inherder, B., 75
Inkeles, A., 421
Innis, R., 397
Irwin, M.D., 369
Itard, J., 72

Jacklin, C.N., 220, 223
Jackson, J., 324, 401
Jacobs, J., 366
Jacobson, L., 34, 299
Jain, N.C., 54, 98
Janis, I., 401
Janowitz, M., 365
Jefferson, T., 200
Jeffries, V., 156
Jencks, C., 185
Jennings, P., 401
Jensen, A., 40
Jobs, S.P., 153

John XXIII, Pope, 284
John Paul II, Pope, 285
Johnson, G.E., 153
Johnson, L.B., 294
Jones, E.F., 285
Justice, B., 390

Kahl, J.A., 171
Kahn, H., 351
Kallen, H., 195
Kantner, R., 255
Kasarda, J.D., 361, 365, 369
Katz, E., 401
Keating, C., 138
Keller, S., 316
Kennedy, J.F., 98, 153, 210, 311
Kennedy, J.P., 153
Kennedy, P.J., 153
Kenney, M., 258
Kent, 204, 205
Kerckhoff, A.C., 401
Kern, R., 379, 388
Khaldun, I., 312
Khomeini, A., 311
King, E.W., 164
King, M.L., Jr., 408
King, R., 393, 396
Kinsey, A.C., 25
Kishimoto, Y., 200
Kissinger, H., 165-166
Klette, M., 38
Knowles, A., 378
Koenig, F., 401
Kohlberg, L., 75-76, 227
Kohn, H., 195
Kohn, M.L., 83
Kondracke, M.M., 165
Kotkin, J., 200
Kozol, J., 300
Krause, M., 203
Kroeber, A.A., 400
Kummer, H., 62
Kurian, G.T., 354
Kutner, L., 264
Kutscher, R.E., 423, 424

Lancaster, J.B., 62
Landau, E., 248
Landers, A., 33-34
Landon, A.E., 32, 33
Lang, G., 396
Lang, K., 395
Langston, M., 102
Lantz, H.R., 246
Larkin, 361
Larson, J., 266
Lasch, C., 252
Laslett, P., 243, 312

Lasswell, T., 61
Lauber, J., 304
Layson, S.K., 145
Lazarsfeld, P.F., 401
Lazarus, E., 199
LeBon, G., 394, 395
Lee, A.M., 17
Lee, G.E., 398
Lee, M., 108
Lee, R.B., 152
Lemert, E.M., 131, 136
Lenin, V.I., 311, 319, 320
Lenski, G., 196, 416
Lenski, J., 416
Leonard, I.M., 203
Leslie, G.R., 248
Levin, 303
Levin, J., 137
Levine, D., 153
Levine, S.V., 406-407
Levinson, D., 79-81
Levy, F., 174
Lewin, K., 105
Lewis, J.L., 408
Lewis, M., 223
Lichter, D.R., 86
Lincoln, A., 338
Lincoln, M.T., 338
Lindeman, 70
Lindesmith, A.R., 223, 224
Linton, R., 100, 191
Lipset, S.M., 318
Lipsey, R.G., 12
Lipton, R., 73
Logino, C.F., Jr., 182
Lombroso, C., 124-125
Lombroso-Ferrero, G., 125
London, K.A., 248, 253
Long, L., 339
Longfellow, W.W., 82
Loury, G., 165
Loving, M., 248
Loving, R.P., 248
Lunt, P., 170
Luther, M., 412
Lynch, K., 366
Lynn, D.B., 223

Maccoby, E.E., 220, 223
Machung, A., 256
Macionis, J.J., 354
MacMurray, V.D., 275
MacRobert, A., 87
Madsen, W., 206
Magnet, M., 88
Maguire, K., 136
Maines, 226
Malinowski, B., 243, 272
Malthus, T.R., 339-340

Mandle, J.D., 224-225
Mann, 204, 205
Mann, H., 298
Manning, W., 210
Marcos, F., 316
Marlin, J.T., 374-375
Martin, 255
Marx, K., 12-13, 15, 16, 18, 163-
    164, 166, 279, 315, 319, 340,
    356, 403, 416
Mason, K.O., 345
Matza, D., 129
Mauss, A.L., 406
Mayo, K., 377
Mayrowitz, 86
McBride, 192
McConnell, J.V., 351
McFalls, 337
McGovern, G., 323
McKay, H., 130
McKenzie, R., 360
McKibben, B., 411
McLaughlin, L., 334
McNamara, R., 342
McNeill, W.H., 198, 212
Mead, G.H., 19-20, 75, 76, 77-78
Mead, M., 85, 220, 292
Meadows, D.H., 351
Mendel, G., 295
Merrick, T.W., 344
Merton, R.K., 17, 18, 23, 102, 111,
    128-129, 192
Michels, R., 114
Milken, M., 138
Mills, C.W., 5, 17, 23, 157, 202,
    412
Mitchell, J.H., 119
Molotsky, I., 294
Mondale, W., 323
Montagu, A., 188, 218, 277
Moon, S.M., 87
Moore, W.E., 161-162, 420
Moorman, 259, 260
Morris, D., 218
Moynihan, D.P., 190
Murdock, G.P., 221, 242, 243, 244,
    247
Murray, C., 165, 178
Muson, H., 76
Myrdal, G., 36

Neugarten, B.L., 81
Nickerson, C., 385
Nisbet, R.A., 98, 99
Nixon, R., 55, 323
Noble, 309
North, O., 114
Nortman, D., 347

Norton, 259, 260
Novit-Evans, B., 189

O'Barr, W., 97
Ogburn, W.F., 59, 417
O'Hare, W., 177, 178, 179, 204, 205, 210
Ortner, S., 221
Otterbein, K., 312

Packard, D., 171
Palen, J.J., 354, 368
Palmer, J.L., 88
Palmore, E.B., 234
Park, R.E., 17, 359-360
Parke, R.D., 258
Parkes, H.B., 322
Parmet, R.D., 203
Parsons, T., 17, 18, 222, 378, 416-417
Passel, J.S., 200
Patterson, F., 60
Patterson, O., 197
Paulsen, M., 136
Pavlik, Z., 342
Pavlov, I., 71
Payer, L., 388
Perrin, R., 98, 99
Peters, T.J., 361
Petersen, W., 196
Pettigrew, T.F., 302
Phillips, D.P., 86, 145
Phipps, S.G., 189
Piaget, J., 75
Pileggi, N., 146
Pinchin, N., 201
Plato, 145, 312
Platt, J., 385
Plisko, 303
Poindexter, J., 114
Pollard, 204, 205
Porter, R., 54, 98
Pray, 141
Provence, S., 73, 82
Putka, G., 286
Pyeritz, 126

Quin, A.J., 176
Quin, R.P., 229
Quinney, R., 132, 133

Rachman, D., 314
Raines, H., 399
Ralph, J.H., 302
Ransdell, E., 386
Ransford, H.E., 156

Rather, D., 401
Reagan, N., 275
Reagan, R., 199, 210, 260, 304
Red Cloud, 311
Redlich, F.C., 185
Reid, S.T., 134, 136, 142, 146
Rein, M., 181
Reinisch, J., 25-26
Reiss, I.L., 260
Riche, M.F., 201, 380
Rieken, H.W., 31, 281
Riesman, D., 85
Ritzer, G., 419
Roach, J.L., 166
Robey, B., 324
Robinson, J., 196, 199
Roemer, D.V., 400
Rohter, 191
Roosevelt, F.D., 33, 210, 413
Roosevelt, T., 209
Roper, B.W., 39
Rosaldo, M., 221
Rose, A., 157, 158
Rose, J.D., 403
Rosen, G., 402
Rosenberg, B., 85
Rosenblatt, 28
Rosenthal, R., 34, 299
Ross, B., 56
Rossi, A., 81
Rossi, P., 368
Rossi, P.H., 159
Rossides, D.W., 151, 171
Rubin, 27, 28
Rubinstein, 88
Rubinstein, M., 48-49
Rumberger, R.W., 303
Rybczynski, W., 422

Saffin, J., 277
Sagarin, E., 46
Sahlins, M.D., 416
Saint-Simon, H., 11
Salas, R.M., 347
Samovar, L.A., 54, 98
Sandburg, C., 353
Sanders, A.J., 339
Sapir, E., 53
Schacter, S., 31, 281
Schloss, 162
Schmidt, K., 386
Schneider, J.W., 378
Schooler, C., 83
Schumpeter, J.A., 319
Schur, E.M., 140
Schwartz, A.J., 15
Schwartz, J., 208
Schwartz, P., 252, 265, 266

Sebald, H., 85
Seidensticker, E., 65
Selznick, P., 111
Service, E.R., 320, 416
Shapiro, J.L., 103
Sharp, L., 413
Shattuck, R., 72
Shaw, C., 130
Shays, D., 322
Sheldon, W.H., 125
Shellow, R., 400
Shepard, L.J., 229
Shepardson, M., 194
Shibutani, T., 400
Shils, E., 318, 412
Sidel, R., 169
Simmel, G., 109, 365, 400
Simon, J., 351
Simpson, G.E., 210
Sitting Bull, 311
Sjoberg, G., 356
Skocpol, T., 23, 322
Slater, P., 107
Slimak, R.E., 15
Smeeding, T., 181
Smelser, N.J., 396, 397, 420
Smith, A., 314, 315, 412
Smith, D.H., 421
Smith, J., 275
Smith, T., 284
Socrates, 312
Solecki, R., 56, 272
Sorokin, P., 418
Sosin, M., 368
Spain, D., 227, 229
Spates, J.L., 354
Spencer, H., 13, 15, 18, 415
Spengler, O., 418
Spicer, E.H., 198
Spiro, M., 242, 243
Spitz, R., 73
Squire, P., 33
Stabler, K., 107
Staires, G.L., 229
Stanley, J., 219
Stark, R., 145, 272, 282
Starr, P., 23
Stebbins, M.L., 187, 188
Steiner, P.D., 12
Steinmetz, S.K., 255
Stern, 303
Stevens, S.S., 125
Steward, J.H., 416
Stinchcombe, A.L., 166
Stoller, R.J., 223
Stouffer, S.A., 402
Straus, M.A., 255
Strauss, A.L., 223, 224, 378
Strodtbeck, F.L., 107
Stulgoe, J.R., 371

Sudman, S., 39
Sultan, P., 383
Suro, 285
Susser, M.W., 382
Sutherland, E.H., 61, 130, 138, 142
Suttles, G., 365, 366
Sweet, J., 265
Sykes, G., 129
Szymanski, A.T., 297

Taeuber, C.M., 230
Tannen, D., 228
Taylor, G., 125
Teheran, J., 191
Teitelbaum, M.S., 341
Terrace, H.S., 60
Testa, W.A., 423
Thomas, E., 326
Thomas, W.I., 17, 77
Thompson, W., 340
Thoreau, H.D., 119
Tiger, L., 218
Tilly, C., 23
Tischler, H.L., 13, 189, 193, 194, 199
Tolstoy, L., 119
Tonnies, F., 362-363, 415
Torrey, B.D., 181
Torrey, E.F., 185
Townsend, B., 374
Toynbee, A., 418
Trachtenberg, J., 277
Trotter, R.J., 88
Truman, H., 33, 199
Tucker, W.B., 125
Tumin, M., 162
Turnbull, C., 421
Turner, R.H., 395
Turner, T., 171
Tylor, E., 45

Udy, S.H., Jr., 114
Uhlenberg, P., 181
Ulc, O., 199
Ullman, E.L., 360

Vago, S., 399
Valdisera, V., 230
Van De Kaa, D.J., 341
Van Den Haag, E., 144, 146
Vanfossen, B.E., 155, 167, 174
Van Ginneken, J.K., 391
Van Lawick-Goodall, J., 60
Veltford, H., 398
Verba, S., 325
Vernon, G., 8
Vigars, D.E., 3
Vollmer, A., 141
Von Frisch, K., 55
Voss, H.L., 264, 265

Wallerstein, J.S., 23
Walsh, D.L., 231
Walton, S., 172
Warner, W.L., 170
Warren, R., 200
Washington, G., 199
Watson, J.B., 71
Weber, M., 12, 15 16, 17, 36, 94, 111-112, 114, 156, 163, 164-166, 277-278, 310, 311, 313, 408, 421
Weeks, J.R., 287
Weinberg, M., 265
Weiner, J., 384
Weiss, R.S., 261, 263
Weitzman, L., 34, 260, 261
Welch, A.W., 189
Welles, O., 401

Wells, H.G., 401
Wendell, B., 195
Wertsch, M.E., 215
Westoff, C.F., 285
Wexner, L., 172
Wheelright, P., 411
Whitaker, L.C., 15
White, D.M., 85
White, R.L., 187, 188
Whitten, P., 62
Whittington, F., 234
Whorf, B., 53
Whyte, W.F., 31
Whyte, W.H., 90, 364
Williamson, N.E., 345
Willner, A.R., 311
Wilson, B.F., 248, 253
Wilson, E., 280
Wilson, E.O., 47, 71, 218
Wilson, J.Q., 124, 127
Wilson, W.J., 165
Winter, J.M., 341
Wirth, L., 191, 365
Wise, D., 324, 328
Wolf, E., 322
Wolfe, L., 247
Woodrow, K.A., 200
Wovoka, 278
Wozniak, S.G., 153
Wurman, R.S., 425

Yinger, J.M., 210, 279, 280

Zaslow, M.J., 88
Zelnik, M., 255
Zia ul-Haq, M., 107
Zigler, E., 88

■ SUBJECT INDEX ■

Abortion, 255
Abstract ideals, 274
Academic skills, schools and, 294-295
Acculturation, forced, 414
Achieved statuses, 100
Achievement, educational, 301
Achievement motivation, 225
Acquired Immunodeficiency Syndrome. *See* AIDS
ACT. *See* American College Test
Acting crowd, 397-398
Activity theory, 233
Adaptation, 56-60, 57
   and cultural traits, 71
   religion and social, 278-279
   strain theory and, 128
Adolescence, 79
Adolescents
   peer groups and, 84-85
   socialization of, 224
Adult(s). *See also* Aging; Older adults; Older Americans
   illiteracy of, 295
   socialization of, 224-226
Adult development, 79-80
Adult life cycle model, 80-82
Adult socialization, 87-91
Affiliation, 73
Africa. *See also* Developing countries
   AIDS in, 385
   immigration from, 201
African Americans, 187-188, 204-205. *See also* Race
   death rate among, 379
   educational equality and, 299-302
   health and, 380-381
   immigration to U.S. of, 204-205
   intelligence and, 40
   Social Darwinism and, 13
   as underclass, 165
   voting and, 324, 325
   wealth of, 156
Afrikaners, 189
Age
   and health, 382-383
   and marriage, 248
   maternal, 391
Age-specific death rates, 337
Age stratification, 231-236
   trends in, 234, 236
Aggregate, social, 104

Aging, 232
   by marital status, 232
   by race, 232
   by sex ratio, 232
   and society, 90-91
   theories of, 233-234
Agricultural revolution, 57
AIDS (Acquired Immunodeficiency Syndrome), 255, 383-386
   and African Americans, 381
   origins of epidemic, 386
Aid to Families with Dependent Children, 179
Alcoholism, perspectives on, 9
Alienation, 279
   in urban areas, 366
Alternative lifestyles, 262-265
Altruistic suicide, 14-15
America. *See* United States
American College Test (ACT), 305
American culture, and Arab culture, 48-49
"American Education: Making It Work," 295
American Federation of Labor (AFL), 408
American Federation of State, County, and Municipal Employees, 409
Americanization Movement, 203-204
American Medical Association (AMA), 162
   national health insurance and, 387-388
American Sign Language (ASL), animal research with, 60
American society, early socialization in, 81-87
American Sociological Association, and sociology as career, 7
Amnesty International, U.S.A., 144
Analysis, 26, 34-35
Ancestral spirits, 273
Anglo conformity, 194, 204
   education and, 298
Anglo-Saxon Protestants, immigration to U.S. of, 202-204
Animals
   communication systems of, 55-56
   and culture, 60-61
   gender roles and, 218
   language research with, 60-61
Animism, 273

Annihilation, 198-199
Anomic suicide, 15
Anomie, 128, 278
   theory of, 127-128
Anthropology
   cultural, 8
   gender role views of, 221
Antinuclear movement, 405
Anti-Semitism, 198, 208
Apartheid, 189-190
Apes, language work with, 60
Appellate courts, 141
Applied sociology, 6-7
Arab Bedouins, 96
Arab culture, 51-52
   and American culture, 48-49
Arapesh, 220
Aristocracy, 312
Arrests, 136. *See also* Crime
Ascribed statuses, 100
Ashanti people, 243
Ashkenazim, 208
Asia. *See also* Developing countries
   AIDS in, 385
   immigration from, 200, 201
Asian Americans, 208-210
   social class, health, and, 382
Asians, race and, 189
Assault, 138
Assimilation, 194-195
Assistance programs
   in United States, 179-180
   worldwide, 181-182
Association, statement of, 29
Associations, 110-111
   formal structure of, 110
   informal structure of, 111
Auschwitz, 198
Authoritarian leader, 107
Authority, 310
   charismatic, 310-311
   legal-rational, 310
   traditional, 310
Autism, 72
Autocracy, 312, 316
Averages, 35
Aztecs, 198

Baby-boom generation, and future workforce, 422-423
Behavior. *See also* Deviant behavior; Norms
   conditioned, 71

Behavior (*Cont.*)
  criminal. *See* Criminal justice system
  of group members, 108-109
  instincts and, 71
  nature vs. nurture and, 70-72
  normal vs. deviant, 120-122
  norms and, 51
Behavioral theory, and deviance, 126-127
Behavior patterns, 46-47
Belief, religion and, 271
Beliefs, spread of, and collective behavior, 396
Benefits, to unmarried couples, 266
Beverly Hills Supper Club, panic in, 402
Bias
  objectivity and, 36-37
  researcher, 34
Bilateral system, 244
Bilingual education, 211, 294. *See also* English as a Second Language
Bilocal residence, 247
Biological theories, of deviance, 124-126
Biology
  culture and, 46-47
  sociobiology and, 71-72
Bio-psycho-social health, 390
Birth, health and, 377
Birth control, 255, 341
Birth control policies, 346
Birthrate, 334-336, 340-341
  crude, 337
  population trends and, 342-344
Blackfeet, 198
Blacks. *See* African Americans; Race
Blended families, 264
Blind investigators, 34
Blue Cross and Blue Shield, 387
Body contact, 73
Body types, 125
Bonding, deviant behavior and, 129
Boundaries, groups and, 105-106
Bourgeoisie, 163
Brave New World, 109
Breast cancer, 380
Breast-feeding
  as fertility determinant, 344
  and infant health, 391
Brown v. *Board of Education*, 300
Buddhism, 274
Bureaucracy, 111-116
Bureau of Indian Affairs (BIA), 212
Business services, 423

Cambodia, immigrants from, 210

Cancer, breast, 380
Capitalism, 313-315
  democratic socialism and, 320
  laissez-faire, 314
  Marxist response to, 315
  and socialism, 316
  sociology and, 12
  totalitarian, 317
Capital punishment, 144-145
Career development, 90
Careers
  gender differences and, 226-227
  as sociologist, 6-7
Caribbean, immigration from, 200, 201
Caste system, 154-155
Casual crowd, 398
Catholics. *See also* St. John Neumann Roman Catholic Church
  contraception and, 346
  taboos of, 273
  in U.S., 284-285
Causality, statement of, 29
Centers for Disease Control, AIDS and, 384
Change
  cultural, 58-59
  political, 321-322
Charismatic authority, 310-311
Cheyenne Indians, 127
Chicago, University of, 17, 77
  delinquent behavior and, 130
Chicago school, 17, 77
  cities and, 359
Childbearing, in China, 333-334
Child care, schools and, 296
Child-Care and Development Block Grants, 88
Child-custody laws, 261-262
Childhood and Society, 79
Childless couples, 253
Child mortality, as fertility determinant, 344-345
Child prodigy, 307
Children. *See also* Population growth
  benefits and costs of, 345-346
  day care and, 88-89
  deprivation, development, and, 72-73
  family, socialization, and, 243-244
  socialization of, in U.S., 81-87
  world health trends and, 389-391
Children's Television Workshop, 86
China
  assimilation in, 194-195
  immigrants from, 209
  population growth in, 333-334

Choice
  crime and individual, 127
  freedom of, 314
  individual, 65-66
Christianity: *See also* Religion
  magic and, 272
  monotheism of, 274
Chromosomes, and crime, 125-156
Church, universal, 279-280. *See also* Religion; religious groups by name
Church attendance, and social class, 172, 173
Church of Scientology, 288
Church Universal and Triumphant, 288
CIO. *See* Committee for Industrial Organization
Circuit courts, 141
City, 354-358, 357
City. *See also* Urbanized area
  concentric zone model of, 359-360
  definition of, 365
  earliest, 354-355
  industrial, 356-357
  modernization and, 420
  multi-nuclei model of, 360-361
  preindustrial, 355-356
  sector model of, 360
  structure of, 359-362
Civil disobedience, 119, 120
Civilian rule, 318
Civilization
  meaning of term, 354
  rise and fall of, 418
Civil Rights Act (1964), 417
Civil rights movement, 405
  and functionalist theory of social change, 417
  Thoreau and, 119
Civil War, 13
Class, educational separation and, 300. *See also* Social stratification
Classical theorists, 11-16
Class system, 155
Closed society, 152
Club of Rome, 351
CMSA. *See* Consolidated Metropolitan Statistical Area
Coalescence, and social movements, 408
Code of Hammurabi, 320
Coercion, 98, 310
Cognitive culture, 53
Cognitive development, 75
Cohabitation, 264-265
  insurance benefits and, 266
Coleman report, 301-302

Collective behavior, 394
    contagion (mentalist) theory of, 395
    convergence theory and, 396
    dispersed, 399-402
    emergent norm theory and, 395-396
    fads and fashions and, 399-400
    mass hysteria, panics, and, 401-402
    public opinion and, 401
    rumors and, 400-401
    and social movements, 393-409
    value-added theory and, 396-397
Collective conscience, 363
College entrance examinations, 305
Colleges and universities
    and credentialized society, 299
    enrollment in, 297
College students, sampling of, 32
Colored people. *See* African Americans
Command economy, 314-316, **315**
Committee for Industrial Organization (CIO), 408
Common sense, sociology and, 7-8
Communication
    language and, 53-54
    nonverbal behavior and, 96-98
    symbolism and, 55-56
Communism, 317. *See also* Command economy; Marxist economic philosophy
Community organizing, 404
Companionate marriage, 251
Competition, 99
    freedom of, 314
    social stratification as barrier to, 162
Computer, 421-422
Concentric zone model, of cities, 359-360
Conditioned behavior, 71
Conflict, 99
    cultural, 413
Conflict theory, 13, **18**, 21-23
    education and, 297-299
    and functionalism, 19
    and gender inequality, 222-223
    Neo-Marxists and, 23
    religion and, 279
    and social change, 416
    social stratification and, 161, 162-167
    and state, 320-321
Conformity, 108, 129
    and assimilation, 194
Congress, members of, 325
Consensus approach, to laws, 133

Conservative (traditional) ideologies, **413**
Conservative Jews, 285
Consolidated Metropolitan Statistical Area (CMSA), **359**
Constitutionalism, 317-318
Consumption (economic), 313
Contagion (mentalist) theory, of collective behavior, 395
Context, 94-95
    social, 131
Contingent temporal world, 226
Contraception, as fertility determinant, 346
Contractual cooperation, 99
Control theory, 129
Conventional crowd, 398
Convergence theory, of collective behavior, 396
Conversation, men's and women's styles of, 228
Cooperation, 98-99
Cooperative interaction, 98-99
Cornerville, 31
Corporations, sociology careers in, 7
Courts, 141-142
    juvenile, 136
Craze, **400**
Credentialized society, 99
Crime, 133-141. *See also* Criminal justice system
    and deviance 124-133
    felonies, 133
    of hate, 404
    juvenile, **135-136**
    kinds of, in U.S., 135-140
    law and, 132-133
    organized, 139-140
    poverty and, 183-184
    property, 133, 138
    reporting of, 134-135
    statistics, 134-135
    victimless, 140
    violent, 133, 136-138
    white-collar, 138-139
Criminal behavior. *See* Crime
Criminal justice system, **140**-147
Criminals, treatment of, 142-146
"Criminal Victimization," 138
Cross-cultural comparisons, 46
Cross-cultural gender differencs, 220-221
Cross-sectional study, **30**
Crowds, **394**. *See also* Collective behavior
    acting, 397-398
    attributes of, 397
    casual, 398
    changeable nature of, 398-399

    as concentrated collectivities, 397-399
    conventional, 398
    expressive, 398
    at sporting events, 396, 397-398
    threatened, 398
    types of, 397-398
Crowds and Power, 397
Crude birthrate, **337**
Crude death rate, **337**
Cuban Americans, 47-48, 207-208
Cults, 288
    reasons for joining, 406-407
Cultural anthropology, 8
Cultural change, 58-59
Cultural conflicts, and institutional structural inequality, 413
Cultural diffusion, 414
Cultural lag, **69**, 417
Cultural relativism, 47-49, **48**
Cultural traits, 58
Cultural transmission, 293-294
    theory of, 130
Cultural universals, **62**-65
Culture, 43, 45-66, **46**. *See also* Communication
    and adaptation, 56-60
    animals and, 60-61
    and biology, 46-47
    cognitive, 53
    components of, 49-54
    definition of, 45-46
    early signs of, 56
    gender roles and, 215-236
    and individual choice, 65-66
    language and, 53-54
    material, 53
    norms and values of, 120
    selectivity of, 53
    symbolic nature of, 54-56
Culture of poverty theory, 165
Culture shock, **47**
Curriculum, 293-294. *See also* Education; School
    hidden, 297
Cyclical (rise and fall) theory, of social change, 417-418
Czechoslovakia, pronatalist policies in, 32

Data
    analysis of, 34-35
    collection of, 32-34
Day care, 88-89, 160
Dead Sea Scrolls, 280
Death and Life of American Cities, The, 366
Death at an Early Age, 300
Death rate, 335, 337-338

Decision making, in groups, 107
Decline of the West, 418
Decriminalization, 140
De facto segregation, 301
Degrees (college), 299
De jure segregation, 300-301
Delinquents, 129. *See also* Deviant
behavior
Demise, and social movements,
408-409
Democracy, 317-320
and socialism, 318-319
Democratic leader, 107
Democratic party, 323-324
Democratic socialism, 319-320
Demographic factors, and social mo-
bility, 154
Demographic transition theory,
340-342
Demography, 336. *See also* Popula-
tion; Population growth; Pop-
ulation trends
population and, 333-351
Demonstrations, 394
Denomination, 280
Dependency ratio, 348
Dependent variable, 29
Deprivation
childhood, 72-73
and development, 72-74
Determinism, environmental, 56
Deterrence
capital punishment and, 144-145
of criminal behavior, 142
Developing countries
health of infants and children in,
389-391
mortality in, 338
population growth in, 335-336
Development
deprivation and, 72-74
dimensions of human, 75-76
Erikson's stages of, 79, 80
socialization and, 69-91
stages of, 77
theories of, 76-81
Deviant behavior, 43, 108. *See also*
Crime
biological theories of, 124-126
crime and, 124-133
defining, **120-122**
dysfunctions of, 122
functions of, 121-122
law and, 132-133
primary and secondary, 131-132
psychological theories of, 126-
127
and social control, 119-147
sociological theories of, 127-132
Deviant subcultures, 61, 62

Dictatorships, 321
Differential association theory, 130
Diffusion, 59, 414
Directed cooperation, 98-99
Disadvantaged, blacks as, 165
Disapproval, and moral develop-
ment, 76
Disclosure, and confidentiality, 39
Discrimination, 192-193
economic, 229-230
institutionalized, 193-194
job, 227-230
Disease. *See also* Health
mental health and, 390
prevention of, 388-389
and world health trends, 389
Disengagement theory, 233
**Dispersed collective behavior, 399-
402**
Distribution (economic), 313
District courts, 141
Diversion, 136
Division of labor, 62, 221
in bureaucracy, 112
Division of Labor in Society, The,
15, 127
Divorce, 258-262
and child-custody laws, 261-262
laws about, 260-261
Doctors, earnings of, 388
"Doomsday model," of ecological
disaster, 351
Double-blind investigators, 34
Downtown sections, homelessness
and, 368
Dramaturgy, 19, 21
Dress, 399-400
behavior and, 121
Drives, instinctual, 79
"Dropout Prevention and Re-entry
Act," 302
Dropouts, high school, 302-304
Drug abuse, AIDS and, 384
Dyad, 109
Dysfunctional behavior, deviance
as, 122
Dysfunctions, of prejudice, 191-192

Earnings, of men and women, 227-
230
Ecclesia, 280
Ecological disaster, and population
growth, 348-351
Ecological patterning, and cities,
359
Ecology
human, 359
movement, 405

Economic conditions, social mobility and, 153-154
Economic discrimination, gender
and, 229-230
Economics, 9
social stratification, 156
Economic stability, government establishment of, 312
Economic systems
capitalism, 313-315
family and, 243
modernization and, 420
political systems and, 309-328
Economy
command, 314-316
mixed, 314
and politics, 313-316
socialism and, 316
Ectomorphic types, 125
Ecumenism, 282
Education, 291-307, 423. *See also*
Occupation; Social class
academic skills and, 294-295
bilingual, 211, 294
for career in sociology, 6-7
child care and, 296
conflict theory view of, 297-299
credentials and, 299
cultural transmission and, 293-
294
functionalist view of, 292-297
gifted, 305-307
high school dropouts and, 302-
304
and innovation, 295-296
intelligence studies and, 40-41
issues in, 299-307
and jobs, 296-297
level of, 302, 303
and marriage, 250
maternal, 391
purposes of, 292
standardized testing and, 304-
305
tracking in, 298-299
unequal access to, 299-302
of workforce, 184
Education aid program, 179
Educational Testing Service (ETS),
305
Egoistic suicide, 14
Egyptian civilization, disappearance
of, 418
Elderly, 181, 182
health of, 382-383
Elections. *See also* Presidential elections
media role in, 326-327
two-party system and, 322-323
voting and, 323-326

Electorate, 318
Electronic crime, 139
Elementary Forms of Religious Life, The, 15, 270
Ellis Island, 200
Emergent norm theory, 395-396
Emigration, 338
Emotion, and religion, 271
Empirical question, 26-27
Empiricism, 8
Employment. *See* Labor force
Endogamy, 247, 250
Endomorphic types, 125
English as a Second Language (ESL) classes, 302
English language, and bilingual education, 211
English people, 95
Enrichment programs, 307
Environment, social. *See* Socialization
Environmental determinism, 56
Environmental factors, and health, 382
Equality of Educational Opportunity, 301
Equilibrium theory, 416, 417
Eskimos. *See* Inuit (Eskimos)
ESL. *See* English as a Second Language
Estate, 155
Estate system, 155
Esteem, 158
Ethical issues, 37-41
Ethnic group, concept of, 190. *See also* Social class
Ethnic minorities
    bilingualism and, 211
    patterns in relations of, 194-199
    racial minorities and, 187-212
Ethnic subcultures, 61
Ethnocentrism, 47-49
Ethnomethodology, 19, 20-21
Ethology, 218
Etiquette, gender inequality and, 225
ETS. *See* Educational Testing Service
Europe
    and demographic transition, 340-342
    immigration from, 200, 201, 203
Euthanasia, 235
Evaluation, in decision making, 107
Evangelism, television, 282-283
Evolution, 415
    human, 56-57
Evolutionary theory, and social change, 415-416
Exchange interaction, 98

Exit polls, 39
Exogamy, 247
Experiment, 31-32
Exponential growth, of population, 334
Expressive crowd, 398
Expressive leadership, 107
Expressive role, in family, 222
Expressive social movements, 405, 406
Extended families, 244, 245
External means of social control, 122-124
External source of social change, 413-414
Eye contact, 97-98

Fads, 399-400
Families of orientation, 246
Family
    alternative lifestyles and, 262-265
    blended, 264
    Catholics and, 284
    child care and, 88-89
    and divorce, 258-262
    forms of, 245
    functions of, 243-244
    future of, 265-267
    household size and, 254-255
    income distribution and, 175
    marriage and, 244-262
    modernization and, 420
    religious affiliation and, 289
    single-parent, 263
    socialization and, 292
    structures of, 244
    transformation of, 250-262
    in United States, 82-84
    violence, 255-258
    and working parents, 256
Family life
    nature of, 242-244
    U.S., 241-242
Family of procreation, 246
Family planning, and population growth, 347
Family unit, 63
Farming, modernization and, 419-420
Fascism, 317
Fashions, 399-400
Fast-food business, social impact of, 419
Fathers, child care and, 89
FBI (Federal Bureau of Investigation), 134
Fecundity, 336

Fecundity rate, 337
Federal courts, 141-142
Federal government assistance programs, 179
Felonies, 133
Feminization of poverty, 175-176
Fertility, 337
    determinants of, 344-348
    and second demographic transition, 341-342
Fertility rate, and industrialization, 336, 337, 340-341
Folkways, 51
Food stamps program, 179
Food surpluses, modernization and, 420
Forced acculturation, 414
Forced migration, 196-198
Formal logical thought stage, of cognitive development, 75
Formal negative sanctions, 124
Formal positive sanctions, 124
Formal sanctions, 123
Fragmentation, and social movements, 408
Fraud, research, 40-41
Freedom, 197
    of action, 66
    of choice, 314
    of competition, 314
    from government interference, 314-315
Freedom: Freedom in the Making of Western Culture, 197
Free market, 314
French Revolution, 412
    social changes and, 10
Functionalism, 15, 18, 21-23
    and conflict theory, 19
    education and, 292-297
    and gender inequality, 221-222
    and religon, 275-279
    and social change, 416-417
    social stratification and, 161-162, 166
    and state, 320-321
Fundamentalists, 283
Funnel effect, 146
Future, concept of, 46

Game stage, of development, 78
Gangs, 135
Gatekeepers, schools as, 304
Gemeinschaft, 362-363, 365, 415
Gender, 216
    and health, 379-380
    and social interaction, 226-227
    stratification by, 215-231

Gender identity, 76, 224-225
Gender inequality
    causes of, 221-223
    in family, 222
    and work, 227-230
Gender preference, as fertility determinant, 345
Gender roles
    biological views of, 218-219
    and future, 230-231
    genetic differences and, 218-220
    physiological differences and, 218-219
    religious views of, 217-218
    sociological views of, 220-221
Gender-role socialization, **223-227**
Generalizations, 8
Generalized adaptability, 58
Generalized others, 77-78
General Social Survey, 283
Generational mobility, 153
Genes, 70. *See also* Behavior
Genetic definitions, of race, 188-189
Genetics, gender roles and, 218-219
Genius, 82-83
    and gifted education, 307
Genocide, 120, 198
Genocide Convention, 199
Gentrification, 367. *See also* Regentrification
Geographical subcultures, 62
German people, 94-95
Germany, Jews in, 196, 198-199
Gesellschaft, 363, 365, 415
Gestures, 96-98
Ghetto, 196
Ghost Dance, 278-279
Ghosts, 273
Gifted children, 82-83
    education for, 305-307
Gift giving, 52
Goals
    government establishment of, 312
    of groups, 107-108
Goods and services, 313
Gorillas, language work with, 60
Governing class, 157
Government
    economic regulation by, 314-315
    forms of, 317-320
    freedom from interference by, 314-315
    functions of, 312-313
    Greek derivation of, 312
    representative, 318
    sociology careers in, 6-7
    and state, 311-313
Government assistance programs, in United States, 179-180

"Green Revolution," 348
Groups, 4
    associations, 110-111
    characteristics of, 106-109
    culture and, 46
    division of labor in, 62
    large, 110-111
    leadership of, 106-107
    primary and secondary, 105-106
    small, 109-110
    social, 104-111
    social interaction and, 93-117
Gypsies, annihilation and, 199

Hare Krishnas, 406
Harlem, 366
Hate crimes, 404
Health, 182-183, **389.** *See also*
    AIDS; Social stratification
    age and, 382-383
    and city life, 374-375
    gender and, 379-380
    and health care, 377-391
    and illness, 378
    maternal, 390-391
    and mortality rates, 337-338
    preventive medicine and, 388-389
    race and, 380-381
    social class and, 381-382
    U.S. cities ranked by, 375
Health care
    insurance and, 386-388
    issues in U.S., 383-389
    in U.S., 378-389
    world trends, 389-391
Health care services, 423
Health insurance, 386-388
Hidden curriculum, 297
Hierarchy. *See* Bureaucracy
High school, dropouts from, 302-304
High-tech industries, 423-424
Hindu religion, 269. *See also* Religion
    caste system and, 154-155, 280
    cows and, 278
    and women, 218
Hispanic Americans, health of, 381
Hispanics
    immigration to U.S. of, 205-208
    in labor force, 423
    voting and, 324
    wealth of, 156
History, 9
HIV (human immunodeficiency virus), 383-384
Hobos, 367
Homelessness, 367-369

Homeostatic system, 416
Homicide, 138. *See also* Crime
Homo erectus, 56
Homogamy, 248
Homosexuals, 386. *See also* AIDS
    couples, 265
Honor and dishonor, and moral development, 76
Horizontal mobility, 153
Household, size changes in, 254-255
Housing, 50
Housing benefits program, 179
Human development, dimensions of, 74-76
Human ecology, 359
Human evolution, 56-57
Human immunodeficiency virus. *See* HIV
Human Zoo, The, 218
Hunger, and population growth, 348
Hunter-gatherers, 57
Husbands. *See* Men
Hypothesis, 28-29
Hysteria. *See* Mass hysteria

"I", 77
Id, 78, 79
Idealistic point, 418
Ideal norms, 52
Ideal type, 112, 114
Ideational cultures, 418
Identity
    gender, **76**
    social, 131
    in urban neighborhoods, 366
    vocation and, 90
Ideology, 64-65
    and social change, **413**
Illegal immigrants, 201-202
Illegal immigration, 338
Illegitimate child-bearing, and infant mortality, 350
Illiteracy, 295
Illness, 378. *See also* Disease; Mental health
    of men and women, 379-380
    prevention of, 388-389
Immigrants, ethnocentrism of, 47
Immigration, 338
    of African Americans to U.S., 204-205
    illegal, 338
    racial and ethnic to U.S., 199-202
    restrictions on, 202
    sources of, 200-202

Immigration and Naturalization Service, 201
Immigration Restriction League, 203
Immunization, and mortality, 338
Impartiality, in bureaucracy, 112, 114
Imperial Animal, The, 218
Imprisonment, goals of, 142-143
Incas, 198
Incest taboo, 62-63, **243**
Incipiency, and social movements, 407-408
Income. *See also* Social class
distribution of (United States), 174, 175
poverty levels and, 176-178
social stratification and, 156
Income gap, 184
Income level, as fertility determinant, 346-347
Independent variable, 29
India
caste system in, 154-155
cows in, 278
immigrants from, 210
Nayar of, 243
women in, 218
Indiana Women's Prison, 146
Indians, American. *See* Native Americans
Individual. *See also* Culture
modernization and, 420-421
in society, 42
Individual actions, and social forces, 5-6
Individual choice, 65-66
crime and, 127
Individual needs, religion and, 275
Indochina, immigrants from, 210
Industrial cities, 356-357
modern, 357
and preindustrial cities, 357
Industrialization, population growth and, 340
social impact of, 14-15
Industrial organization, 114
Industrial Revolution
and growth of cities, 356-357
and marriage, 250-251
Industrial society, demographic transition theory and, 340-341
Industrial Workers of the World (IWW), 408
Industries, growth of, 423-424
Inequality
institutional structural, 413
social, 149, 152
Inequality in an Age of Decline, 170

Infant mortality, 337-338
as fertility determinant, 344-345
in U.S., 350, 379
Infants
in institutions, 73-74
world health trends and, 389-390
Informal negative sanctions, 124
Informal positive sanctions, 123-124
Informal sanctions, 123
Information anxiety, 425
Inner-city schools, violence in, 304
Innovations, 58-59
education and, 295-296
Innovators, 128
Inquiry Into the Nature and Causes of the Wealth of Nations, An, 412
Insiders, 104
Instincts, 47, 71
Institute for the Advancement of Human Potential (Philadelphia), 82
Institution, 116
Institutionalization, and social movements, **408**
Institutionalized prejudice and discrimination, 193-194
Institutional structural inequality, cultural conflicts and, 413
Institutions
marriage as, 241-262
resocialization in, 87
and social organization, 116-117
Instrumental leadership, 107
Instrumental role, in family, 222
Insurance, health, 386-388
Insurance benefits, to unmarried couples, 267
Integration, racial, 299-302
Intelligence, fraud in study of, 40
Interaction, social groups and, 93-117. *See also* Affiliation
Interactionist perspective, 18-21, 19, 21-23
Interest groups, 323
Interfaith marriages, 286, 287
Intergenerational mobility, 153
Internal means of control, 122
Internal migration, 338-339, 369-370
Internal sources of social change, 412
International Ladies Garment Workers, 408
Interracial marriage, 248-249
Interreligious marriage. *See* Jews and Judaism; Protestantism
Interview, 30
structured, 30

Intimacy, conversation and, 228
Intragenerational mobility, 153
Inuit (Eskimos), 414
language of, 54
shelter of, 58
Investment earnings, 184
Invisible hand, 313-314
IQ, and gifted education, 307
IQ fraud, 40
IQ tests, and educational tracking, 299
Iron Law of Oligarchy, 114, 116
Islam. *See also* Religion
monotheism of, 274
in United States, 286-287
Israel, 285
kibbutz family life in, 242-243
IWW. *See* Industrial Workers of the World

Jamestown, 199
Japan
AIDS in, 385
culture of, 64-65
gift giving in, 52
household size in, 254
language during World War II and, 54
Japanese Brain, The, 65
Japanese immigrants, 209-210
Jews and Judaism, 208. *See also* Religion
annihilation of, 198-199
and interreligious marriage, 250
monotheism and, 274
and Nazi Germany, 196
pluralism and, 195-196
taboos of, 273
in U.S., 285-286
Job discrimination, 227-230
in future, 230
Job hunting, education and postponement of, 296-297
Jobs, in future, 422-424. *See also* Occupations
Job training, education for, 292
Journalists, 326-327
Juvenile courts, 136
Juvenile crime, 135-136

Kamikaze, 15
Kenya, mortality in, 338
Kibbutz, family life in, 242-243
Kinesics, 96
Kinsey Institute for Sex Research, 25
Kinsey Institute New Report on Sex, The, 25
Kinship, and marriage, 251

Knowledge, increase in, and future, 351
Korean immigrants, 210
Koreans, Japanese and, 65
Kristallnacht, 196
Kuala Lumpur, cultural lag and, 59
Ku Klux Klan, 192, 404

Labeling theory, 130-132
Labor, division of, 62
Labor force
  growth of, 423-424
  women in, 227-230
Labor movement, 407-409
Laissez-faire capitalism, 314
Laissez-faire leader, 107
Language
  bilingualism and, 211
  in courtroom, 97
  and culture, 53-54
  social class subcultures and, 62
  translation of, 54
Laos, immigrants from, 210
Large groups, associations, 110-111
Latent functions, 17
Latin America. *See also* Developing
    countries
  immigration from, 200, 201
  racial classifications in, 189
Laws, 132-133. *See also* Crime; De-
    viant behavior
  divorce, 260-261
  emergence of, 133
  establishment of, 312
Leader, 106-107
  crowd behavior and, 395-396
Leadership, in social movements,
    403-404
Learned behavior, 219-220
Learning theory, cultural transmis-
    sion theory and, 130
Legal code, 132
Legal-rational authority, 310
Legitimate authority, 310
Lesbian couples, 265
Less developed countries. *See* Third
    World
Liberal ideologies, 413
Liberal Protestants, 283
Libido, 78
Life cycle, of social movements,
    407-409
Life cycle model, adult, 80-82
Life expectancy, 337-338
  of men and women, 379-380
  and social class, 381-382
Lifestyles, alternative, 262-265
Linear temporal world, 226
Literary Digest, 32-33

Living standards. *See* Standards of
    living
Lobbying, 326
Lobbyists, 326-328
Lonely Crowd, The, 85
Longitudinal research, 30
Looking-glass self, 77
Los Angeles, rioting in, 393-394,
    417
Los Angeles County public schools,
    ESL classes in, 302
Losing Ground, 165
Love
  defining and measuring, 27-28
  romantic, 245
Lower class, 171, 173-174
Lower-middle class, 171, 172-173

Maasai tribe, 45
Machu Picchu, 58
Magic, 271
Majority rule, 318
Malaysia
  AIDS in, 385
  cultural lag and, 59
Malnutrition, 389
Malthus's theory of population
    growth, 339-340
Mana, 272
Manifest functions, 17
Manners, 52, 399-400
Maori, 273
Marginal groups, 61
Marital residence, 247-248
Marital status
  aging by, 232
  of U.S. population, 263
Markets (economic), 313
  free, 314
Marriage, 99, 241-262, **244**
  age of, 344
  alternatives to, 262-265
  gender equality in, 231
  institutionalized, 63
  interfaith, 286, 287
  interracial, 248-249
  interreligious, 286
  love and, 27
  and mate selection, 248-249
  monogamous, 247
  multiple, 247
  patterns of, 5
  postponement of, 254
  responsibility and, 88-89
  rules of, 247
  survey of sex and, 33-34
Marriage rate, 252-253
Marxist theory, 163-166
  economic philosophy, 315

of population growth, 340
and social change, 416
state and, 320
Mass, 399
Mass hysteria, 401-402
Mass media, socialization and, 85-
    87
Mass murderers, 137
Master status, 100
Matchmaker, and marriage, 247
Mate, selection of, 248-249
Material culture, 50-51, 52
Maternal health, 390-391
Matriarchal family, 244
Matrilineal system, 244
Matrilocal residence, 247
McDonaldization of society, 419
"Me", 77
Mean (statistical), 35
Means of production, ownership of,
    15-16
Measures of central tendencies, 34
Mecca, 286
Mechanically integrated society,
  127, **363**
Mechanical solidarity, 415
Mechanisms of social control, 122-
  124
Media, election role of, 326-327.
    See also Presidential elections
Median, 35
Medicaid, 179, 387
Medicare, 179, 387
Medicine
  doctors and, 388
  and euthanasia, 235
  health and, 377
  health insurance and, 386-387
  and infant mortality rate, 350
  and life expectancy, 337-338
  medical care workers, 379-389
Megalopolis, 359
Melanesian/Polynesian religion,
    272-273
Melting-pot idea, 195
Men. *See also* Gender; Gender in-
    equality; Gender roles
  conversation styles of, 228
  divorce and, 258-262
  health of, 379-380
  and linear temporal world, 236
  reasoning styles of, 227
Mental health, and disease, 390
Mental illness, poverty and, 185
Mentalist theory, of collective behav-
    ior, 395
Mercy killing. *See* Euthanasia
Merton's typology, 128-129
Mesomorphic types, 125
Mesopotamia, 354

Metropolitan area, **358**
future growth of, 369
list of largest U.S., 359
Metropolitan statistical area (MSA), **358**
suburbs and, 370
Mexican Americans, 206
Mexicans, prejudice and, 191
Mexico, immigration from, 200, 201
Middle East, city development in, 354-355
Middle Eastern culture, 51
Middle-old population, 232
Middle-range theories, **23**
Migration, **338-339**
internal, 338-339, 369-370
old and new, 200
Millenarian movements, **280-281**
Minorities
concept of, 190-191
democracy and rights of, 318
educational equality and, 299-302
and giftedness, 307
in labor force, 423
racial and ethnic, 187-212
voting and, 324
Minority workers, 423
Mixed economy, **314**
Mobility
social, 152-154, 153
Mode, 35
Moderate Protestants, 283
Modernization, **419-421**
individual and, 420-421
Modernization theory, **234**
Monogamous marriage, **247**
Mongols, assimilation of, 194-195
Monkeys, social contact and, 73
Monotheism, **273-274**
Moonies, 87, 406
Moral code, **120**
Moral decisions, gender approaches to making, 227
Moral development, 75-76
Moral judgments, 120
Moral order, **75**
Mores, **52**
Mormon church, 275
Mortality, **337-338**
Mortality rates, 340
changes in U.S., 379
Moslems. See also Islam; Religion
taboos of, 273
in United States, 266-287
women and, 218
Mother India, 377
Mothers. See also Women
child care and, 89
health of, 390-391

Movement, social, 153
Movements and gestures, 96-98
MSA. See Metropolitan statistical area
Multi-nuclei model, of cities, **360-362**
Multiple marriages, **247**
Mundugamor, 220
Murder, 144-145
Murderers. See Crime; Violent crime

National Commission on Excellence on Education, 294
National Crime Victimization Survey, 134, 146
National Education Association, 297
National health insurance, 387-388
National Institute of Education (NIE), 294
National Institute of Justice, 144, 145
Nationalism, 203-204
National Rifle Association, 326
"Nation at Risk, A," 294-295
Nation's Report Card, 295
Native American movement, 203
Native Americans, 210-212
animism and, 273
annihilation of, 198
assimilation of, 194
Cheyenne, 127
college students, 32
culture of, 46
expulsion of, 198
peyote and, 271
Plains Indians, 278-279
segregation of, 196
Shoshone, 58
Sioux, 56, 311
Social Darwinism and, 13
in South America, 47
Nature vs. nurture, 70-72
Navajo Indians, 46
Nayar, of India, 243
Nazis, 70, 121, 196, 198-199
genocide and, 120
neo-Nazis, 404
swastika and, 56
Neanderthal people, 57
burials of, 275
Negative sanctions, **122-123**
formal, 124
informal, 124
Negroes. See African Americans
Neighborhoods, urban, 366-367. See also City
Neo-Malthusians, 348

Neo-Marxists, 23
Neo-Nazis, 404
Neutralization techniques, and deviant behavior, 129-130
New migration, 200
New York City, Harlem and, 366
New Zealand, Maori in, 273
NIE. See National Institute of Education
Nigeria
cultural relativism and, 50
housing in, 50
Nobles, 155
No-fault divorce, 261
Nomadic peoples, 57
Non-industrial world, urban growth in, 354
Nonmaterial culture, **51**
Nonverbal behavior, 96-98
Normal behavior, **120-122**
Normative culture, **51**
Norms, **51**, 79, 95-96
government establishment of, 312
ideal, 52
real, 52-53
violated, 131
Nuclear family, **244**, 245, 251
Nursing homes, 382
Nurture, nature vs. **70-72**
Nutrition, 381-382

Objective approach, to measuring social class, **170**
Objectivity, in sociological research, 36-37
Obligations, 101
Observation, 26
participant, 30-31
Occupational groups, growth of, 423-424
Occupational segregation, 255
Occupational subcultures, 61
Occupations
and marriage, 250
prestige ratings of, 158-159
social stratification by (United States), 171
stratification by, 159-161
Older adult, in college, 297. See also Aging; Older Americans
Older Americans, 231-236
health and, 382-383
population composition of, 231-232
Older American's Act, 181
Old-old population, 232
Oligarchy, **114**, 312
law of, 114, 116
On the Origin of Species, 71

Open-ended interview, 30
Open society, 152
Operational definition, 28
Operational stage, of cognitive development, 75
Opinion leaders, 401
Organically integrated society, 127, 363-365
Organization
    of religion, 271
    university structure and, 115
Organization Man, The, 364
Organized crime, 139-140
Orientation
    in decision making, 107
    families of, 246
Orthodox Jews, 285
Other directed, 85
Outsiders, 104
Overpopulation, 348

PACs. *See* Political action committees
Paiute, 278
Pakistan, women in, 218
Panic, 401-402
Pantheon, 273
Paradigms, 17
Parenthood, 89-90
Parents, working, 256. *See also* Family
Participant observation, 30-31
Passage, rites of, 63-64
Patriarchal family, 244
Patriarchal ideology, 217
Patrilineal family, 246
Patrilineal system, 244
Peasants, 155
Peers, 84-85
Peer values, and moral development, 76
Personal computer, 421
Personality, 70
    and disease, 390
Peyote, 271
Physicians, earnings of, 388
Physiology, gender roles and, 218-219
Plains Indians, 278-279
Pleasure principle, 78
Pluralism, 195-196
PMSA. *See* Primary metropolitan statistical area
Police system, 140-141
Policymaking, as sociology career, 6-7
Political action committees (PACs), 328-329

Political authority, 310
    religion and, 276-277
Political change, 321-322
    institutionalized, 321
Political revolutions, 322
Political science, 9-10
Political subcultures, 61
Political systems
    American, 322-328
    and economic systems, 309-328
    government, state, and, 311-313
Politics, 309
    media and, 326-327
    power, authority, and, 309-311
    and religious affiliation, 287-289
Polls, and presidential elections, 38-39. *See also* Research; Surveys
Polyandrous families, 244
Polyandry, 245
Polygamous families, 244
Polygamy, 245
Polygynous families, 244
Polygyny, 245
Polynesian religion, 272-273
Poor. *See also* Poverty
    myths about, 178-179
    number of, 176-178
Population
    and age stratification, 231-236
    and demography, 333-351
    dynamics of, 334-339
    fertility and, 336-337
    growth of U.S., 236
    marital status of, 263
    migration and, 338-339
    mortality and, 337-338
    number of U.S. cities by, 373
    projected, for selected countries, 335
    single, 262-263
    theories of, 339-342
    urban, 358
    urban decline and, 369
Population explosion, 343, 349. *See also* Population growth
Population growth, 334-335
    in China, 333-334
    cultural lag and, 59
    demographic transition theory and, 341-342
    family planning and, 347
    Malthus's theory of, 339-340
    Marxist theory of, 340
    pronatalist policies and, 342
    urban areas, social interaction, and, 365-366
Population trends, 342-351
    ecological disaster and, 348-351
    ecological disaster predictions and, 348-351

fertility determinants and, 344 - 348
    optimism and, 351
    overpopulation, 348
Positive checks, 339
Positive sanctions, 122-123
    formal, 124
Poverty, 170
    and crime, 183-184
    elderly and, 181, 182
    feminization of, 175-176
    government assistance programs and, 179-180
    and health, 381-382
    and population explosion, 349
    in United States, 175-179
    worldwide comparisons of, 180-182
Poverty index, 176-178
Power, 156, 310. *See also* Social class
    delegation of, in bureaucracy, 112
    and social stratification, 156-158
Power elite, 157
Power Elite, The, 157
Power Structure, The, 157
Prayer, 270-271
Pregnancy, poverty and, 176, 183
Preindustrial cities, 355-356
    and industrial cities, 357
Prejudice, 191-192
    institutionalized, 193-194
Prejudiced discriminators, 193
Prejudiced nondiscriminators, 192-193
Premarital sex, 255
Preparatory stage, of development, 78
Presidential elections
    media and, 326-327
    projections and, 38-39
    sampling error and (1936, 1948), 33
Prestige, 158-161
    occupational ratings by, 158-159. *See also* Social class
Preventive checks, 339
Primary deviance, 131-132
Primary groups, 105-106
    deviant behavior in, 108
Primary metropolitan statistical area (PMSA), 358
Primary socialization, 87
Principles of Sociology, 13
Prisons, 142-147
    populations of, 147
    shortage of, 143-146
    women in, 146-147
Private property, 314

Problem, definition of, 26-28
Procreation, families of, 246
Production (economic), 313
   and consumption, family and, 243
   ownership of, 15-16
Profane, 270
Proletariat, 163
Pronatalist policies, 342
Propaganda, 401
Property, private, 314
Property crime, 133, 138
Protection
   family and, 244
   government establishment of, 312-313
Protestant Ethic and the Spirit of Capitalism, The, 16, 277
Protestantism, in United States, 281, 283-284. *See also* Religion
   and interreligious marriage, 249-250
Psychiatric illnesses, 380
Psychic determinism, 78
Psychoanalysis, 78
Psychoanalytic theory, 77-78
   and deviance, 126
Psychological dislocation, and modernization, 421
Psychological theories, of deviance, 126-127
Psychology, 8-9
Psychology of Crowds, The, 395
Psycho-social health, 390
Public opinion, 401
Public schools. *See* Education; Schools
Puerto Ricans, 206-207
Puerto Rico, race in, 189
Punishment
   of criminal behavior, 142, 146-147
   and moral development, 76
Puritan values, 195

Quality of life, in cities, 374-375
Questions
   empirical, 26-27
   and previous research, 28

Race. *See also* African Americans
   aging by, 232
   of Catholics in U.S., 284
   concept of, 187, 188-190
   educational separation and, 300
   genetic definitions of, 188-189
   and health, 380-381
   legal definitions of, 189

   and marriage, 248
   social definitions of, 189-190
Racial and ethnic minorities, immigration to United States of, 199-202
Racial exclusion, in Japan, 64-65
Racial integration, in schools, 299-302
Racial minorities
   bilingualism and, 211
   and ethnic minorities, 187-212
   patterns in relations of, 194-199
Radical ideologists, 413
Rape, 138
Ratings, and health insurance, 387
Reactionary social movements, 404
Reality, culture and, 53-54
Reality principle, 79
Real norms, 52-53
Reasoning, male vs. female styles of, 227
Rebellions, 321-322
Rebels, 129
Recidivism, 136
Reference group, 109
Reform Jews, 285
Reformulation, 59
Regulations, in bureaucracy, 112
Rehabilitation, of criminals, 142-143
Relative deprivation theory, 402-403
Reliability, 35
Religion, 269-289, 270. *See also* Specific religion
   abstract ideals and, 274
   affiliation with, 281-282
   animism and, 273
   conflict theory view of, 279
   cults and, 288, 406-407
   drugs and, 271
   functionalist view of, 275-279
   Hindu, 269
   Judaism as, 208
   list of major, 274
   magic and, 272
   and marriage, 249-250
   monotheism and, 273-274
   nature of, 270-272
   as "opiate to the people," 16
   organization of, 271
   organization of religious life, 279-281
   social correlates of, 287-289
   sociological approach to, 275-279
   supernaturalism and, 272-273
   theism and, 273
   types of, 272-274
   in United States, 281-283

   women's roles and, 217-218
Religious groups, in U.S., 282-287
Religious subcultures, 61
Religious taboo, 273
Relocation, 196-198
Relocation camps, 210
Reports, research, 35-36
Representative government, 318
Representative sample, 32
Reproduction, family and, 243
Republic, 312
Republican party, 323-324
Reputational approach, to measuring social class, **170**
Research
   dilemmas in, 38-39
   ethical issues in, 37-41
   experiments and, 31-32
   fraud in, 40-41
   longitudinal, 30
   objectivity in, 36-37
   participant observation and, 30-31
   subjects of, 38-39
Research design, 29
Researcher bias, 34
Research jobs, as sociology career, 6
Research methods, 25-41
   surveys, 29-30
Research process, 26-36
   hypotheses in, 28-29
   research design and, 29
   steps in, 27
Research report, preparing, 35-36
Residence, fertility and, 347-348
   and marriage, 247-248
Residential patterns, segregation and, 300-301
Resocialization, 87
Resource allocation, 313
Resource-mobilization theory, 403-404
Resources, new, 351
Responsibility, marriage and, 88-89
Retreatists, 128
Revisionary social movements, 405
Revitalization movements, 278
Revivals, and collective behavior, 394
Revolutionary social movements, 405-406
Revolutions, 322, 412
   political, 322
   social, 322
Reward, and moral development, 76
Right and wrong, 75-76
Right-to-die, 235
Riots, 394
   in Los Angeles, 393-394

Rise and fall theory, of social change, 417-418
Rites of passage, 63-64
Ritual
    formal sanctions and, 123
    religious, 276
Ritualism, 116
Ritualists, 128
Rituals, 270-271
Robbery, 138
Robert's Rules of Order, 110
Role conflict, 102-103
Role playing, 103
Roles, 100-104
    gender, 216
Role set, 102, 103
Role strain, 102
Roman Catholic Church
    hierarchy in, 114
    interreligious marriage and, 249
Roman Catholics. *See* Catholics
Romantic love, 245
Rulers and ruled, 311-312. *See also* Government
Rules. *See also* Roles
    in bureaucracy, 112
    ritualism and, 114.
Rules of endogamy, 247
Rules of exogamy, 247
Rumor, 400-401
Rural residence, fertility and, 347-348
Russian Orthodox Church, 280
Russian Revolution, 412

St. John Neumann Roman Catholic Church, 271
St. Louis schools, gifted education in, 307
Salary, gender differences in, 228-230
Sampling, 32-34
Sampling error, 32
Sanctions, 122-124
    typology of, 123-124
Sapir-Whorf hypothesis, 53
SAT. *See* Scholastic Aptitude Test
Saudi Arabia, housing in, 50
Savage Inequalities, 300
Scholastic Aptitude Test (SAT), 305
School boards, 294
Schools. *See also* Education
    evolution of, 292-293
    socialization and, 84
    violence in, 304
Science, education and, 295-296
    sociology and, **8**

Scientific method, 8
Scientology, 288
Screening, education and, 298-299
Secondary deviance, 131-132
Secondary groups, 105, 106
    deviant behavior in, 108
Sect, 280
Sector model, of cities, 360
Secularized society, 282. *See also* Religion
Segguku, 15
Segregation, 196-198
Selectivity, 53
Self, 74
    concept of, 74-76
Self-esteem, gender inequality and, 225
Semistructured (open-ended) interview, 30
Senior citizens, 91
Sensate cultures, 418
Sensorimotor stage, of cognitive development, 75
Sephardim, 208
Serial murderers, 137
Service industries, 423
"Sesame Street," 86
Sex, 216. *See also* Gender
Sex, premarital, 255.
Sex and Temperament, 220
Sex ratio, aging by, 232
Sex roles, 216
Sexual behavior, family regulation of, 243
Sexual Behavior in the Human Female, 25
Sexual Behavior in the Human Male, 25
Sexual relations, incest and, 62-63
Shamans, 273
Shanidar Cave, burials at, 275
Shays's Rebellion, 321-322
Sheldon's body types, 125
Shelter, 58
Shoshone Indians, 58
Signs, 55
Singapore, immigrants from, 210
Single (unmarried) Americans, 262-263
Single-parent families, 263
Sioux Indians, 279, 311
    swastika and, 56
Skid row, 367, 368
Skills, academic, 294-295
Slavery, 197
Small group, 109-110
Social aggregate, 104
Social attachments, 73
Social change, 411-425
    conflict theory and, 416

cyclical (rise and fall) theory of, 417-418
    evolutionary theory and, 415-416
    external sources of, 413-414
    functionalist theory and, 416-417
    global modernization and, 419-421
    internal sources of, 412-413
    society and, **412**
    sources of, 412-414
    theories of, 414-418
    in United States, 421-423
Social characteristics, of voters, 323-326
Social class, 155
    child-raising and, 83
    and health, 381-382
    among Jews, 285
    lower-middle class, 172-173
    among Protestant denominations, 283
    subcultures, 62
    in United States, 169-185
    upper class, 171-172
    upper-middle class, 171, 172
    working class, 173-174
Social class subcultures, 62
Social cohesion, religion and, 275-277
Social contact, 72-74
Social context, deviant behavior and, 131
Social control
    and collective behavior, 397
    deviant behavior and, 119-147
    education and, 297-298
    government establishment of, 312
    mechanisms of, 122-124
Social Darwinism, 13, 163
Social evaluation, 152
Social-evolutionary thought, 415
Social expectations, 47
Social functions, 17
Social group, 104-111
    characteristics of, 105
    social interaction and, 93-117
Social identity, 74, 131
Social inequality, 149, 152
Social institutions, 116-117
Social interaction, 43, 46
    competition and, 99
    conflict and, 99
    contexts of, 94-95
    cooperation and, 98-99
    in courtroom, 97
    elements of, 100-103
    gender differences in, 226-227

nonverbal behavior as, 96-98
and social groups, 93-117
in urban areas, 365-366
Socialism, 315, **316**
democracy and, 318-319
democratic, 319-320
totalitarian, 317
Social issues, sociological perspective on, 9
Socialists, utopian, 339
Socialization, 43, **70**
adolescent, 224
adult, 87-91, 224-226
and development, 69-91
early, in American society, 81-87
education and, 292-293
family and, 82-84, 243-244
and gender roles, 220-221, 223-227
mass media and, 85-87
peer groups and, 84-85
school and, 84
self and, 74
Social mobility, 152-154
Social movements, **402-409**
collective behavior and, 393-409
expressive, 405, 406
labor movement as, 407-409
life cycle of, 407-409
reactionary, 404
relative deprivation theory of, 402-403
resource-mobilization theory of, 403-404
revisionary, 405
revolutionary, 405-406
types of, 404-406
Social organization, **116**-117
institutions and, 116-117
Social policy, 3
and religious affiliation, 287-289
Social psychology, 9
Social Register, 172
Social revolutions, **322**
Social sciences, **8-10**
sociology as, 1
Social Security Disability Insurance program, 179
Social Security Retirement program, 179
Social solidarity, **363**
Social status
family and, 244
and marriage, 250
Social stratification, 151-167, **152**
consequences of, 182-185
dimensions of, 156-161
educational tracking and, 298-299

immorality of, 162
by occupation (United States), 171
by occupational prestige, 159-161
social class and, 169-185
systems of, 154-155
theories of, 161-167
Social System, The, 17
Social Theory and Social Structure, 17
Social work, 10
Society. See also Culture; City
aging and , 90-91
improvement of, by sociology, 22
individual in, 42
needs met by, 416
religion and adaptation to, 278-279
and social change, 412
study of, 4-5
urban, 353-375
Sociobiology, **71-72**, 218
Sociological imagination, 5-7
Sociological research. See Research
Sociological theory, of deviance, 127-132
Sociologist, 5
career as, 6-7
classical theorists as, 11-16
Sociology, **4**
applied, 6-7
as common sense, 7-8
contemporary theory and, 21-23
development of, 10-17
ethical issues in, 37-41
gender role views of, 220-221
objectivity in, 36-37
perspective of, 3-23
as point of view, 1, 4-8
research methods in, 25-41
and science, 8
as social science, 8-10
societal improvement and, 22
theoretical perspectives on, 17-23
South Africa, race in, 189-190
South America. See Developing countries
South American Indians, 47
Soviet Union, command economy in, 315-316
Space, as cultural context, 94-95
Special-interest groups, 326-329
Specialization, **58**
Specialization of labor, 420
Spirits (religious), 273
Spontaneous cooperation, **98**
Sporting events, crowd behavior at, 396, 397-398, 399

Stage theory, 81
Standardized testing, educational, 304-305
Standards of living, and population explosion, 349
State (governmental body), 311-313, **312**
autocracy as, 316
conflict theory view of, 320
democracy and, 317-320
economy and, 313-316
forms of, 317-320
functionalist view of, 320
functions of, 312-313
totalitarianism and, 316-317
State courts, 141-142
Statement of association, **29**
Statement of causality, **29**
Statistics
analyzing, 34-37
crime, 134-135
reading tables, 36-37
Statuses, **74**, 100-102, 158-159
eye contact and, 97
Status inconsistency, **153**
Status offenses, **136**
Stepfamilies, 263-264
Sterilization, 341
Stone age, 57
Strain theory, 128-129
Stratification
by age, 231-236
gender, 215-231
social, 151-167
systems of, 154-155
Stratified random sample, **32**
Street Corner Society, 31
Stress, gender and, 219-220
Structural changes, functionalist view and, 417
Structural conduciveness, and collective behavior, 396
Structural inequality, institutional, 413
Structural strain, and collective behavior, 396
Structural unemployment/social isolation theory, 165
Structured interview, **30**
Structure of Social Action, The, 17
Students, minority, 299-302. See also; Education; Schools
Subculture, **61-62**
ethnic group as, 190
Subgroups, **110**
Subjective approach, to measuring social class, **170**-171
Subjugation, **196**
Subsidized school lunch program, 179

Suburbs, 364, **370-373**
  homelessness and, 367-368
Suicide, 14-15
  among college students, 15
  mass media and, 86-87
Sumer, 354-355
Sunbelt states, 338-339
Supercomputers, 422
Superego, 79
Supernatural, 271
Supernaturalism, 272-273
Supplemental Security Income, 179, 181
Supreme Court, 141
  Brown v. *Board of Education* and, 300
  Milliken decision and, 300
  Rodriquez decision and, 300
Survey, 29-30
  of sex after marriage, 33-34
  of working women, 33
Swastika, as symbol, 56
Switzerland, pluralism in, 195-196
Symbolic interactionism, 21-23, 19-20, 76-77
Symbolism, culture and, 54-56
Symbols, 43, 56
  religious, 276

Tables, reading, 36-37
Taboo, 62-63
  incest, 62-63, 243
  religious, 273
Talent, and social stratification, 162
Taraimawashi, 52
Task assignment, in groups, 108
Tasmania, annihilation of population in, 198
Tchambuli, 220
Teachers. *See* Education
Teaching, as sociology career, 6
Teach Your Baby Math, 82
Techniques of neutralization, 129- 130
Technological innovation, 421-422
  and social change, 411-412, 412-413
Technology, 421-422
  future application of, 351
  and language, 54
Teenagers
  and age stratification, 231
  premarital sex among, 255
Telecommunications, 422
Television, 85-87
  evangelism and, 282-283
  impact on children, 306
Television networks. *See* Presidential elections

Testing, educational, 304-305
Theism, 273
Theories. *See* theories by name
Theory of differential association, 130
Thinking skills, 295-296
Third World, modernization and, 420
Threatened crowds, 398
Time, perception of, 46
Total institutions, 87
Totalitarian capitalism, 317
Totalitarian government, 316-317
Totalitarian socialism, 317
Totalitarian societies, 321
Totem, 276
Tracking, educational, 298-299
Traditional authority, 310
Traditional cooperation, 98
Traditions, 47
Traits
  cultural, 58
  of social groups, 105
Translation, language, 54
Triad, 109-110
Trobrianders, 243
Truk island, 46
Truly Disadvantaged, The, 165
Twins, socialization, development, and, 69-70, 71
Two-party system, 322-323

Unconscious, 78
  deviant behavior and, 126
Underclass, 184
  blacks as, 165
Underdeveloped countries. *See* Developing countries; Fertility; Third World
Unemployment Insurance program, 179
Unification Church, 288
Uniform Crime Reports (UCR), 134
United Auto Workers (UAW), 408-409
United Mine Workers, 408
United States. *See also* Education; Family
  bilingual education in, 211
  changes in mortality rates in, 379
  demographic transition and, 341
  family in, 251-262
  government assistance programs in, 179-180
  health care in, 378-389
  health ranking of cities in, 375
  immigration to, 199-202
  infant mortality in, 337, 350

  number of cities in, by population, 373
  political system in, 322-328
  racial and ethnic groups in, 202-212
  religion in, 280-283
  social change in, 421-423
  social class in, 169-185
  socialization of children in, 81-87
  social stratification consequences in, 181-185
  sociological development in, 16-17
  University of Chicago and sociology in, 17
  urban growth in future, 369-375
Universal church, 279-280
Universality, of religion, 275-276
University, organizational structure of, 115. *See also* Colleges and universities
University of Chicago, 77
  development of sociology at, 17
Unprejudiced discriminators, 192
Unprejudiced nondiscriminators, 192
Upper class (United States), 171-172
Upper-middle class, 171, 172
Upper-world crime, 138
Urban ecology, 361-362
Urban environments, suburbs and, 364
Urban growth, 369-375
"Urbanism as a Way of Life," 365
Urbanization, 357-362, 358
Urbanized area, 358
  classification of, 358-359
Urban life
  decline of, 367
  exurbs and, 373-375
  Gemeinschaft to Gesellschaft, 362-363
  health and, 374
  homelessness and, 367-369
  mechanical and organic solidarity in, 363-365
  nature of, 362-369
  neighborhoods and, 366-367
  social interaction and, 365-366
  in U.S. cities, 374
Urban neighborhoods, 366-367
Urban population, 358
  decline in, 369
Urban residence, fertility and, 347-348
Urban society, 353-375
Urban Villagers, The, 31, 365
Utopian socialists, 339
Utopian vision, of society, 22

Validity, 35
Value-added theory, of collective behavior, 396-397
Values, 53, 79
  and assimilation, 194
  cultural lag and, 59
  education and, 293-294
  and moral development, 76
  religion and, 276
  and social stratification, 151-152
Value systems, 45
Variable, 28, 29
Varnas, 154-155
Venereal disease, 255
Vertical mobility, 153
Victimization. See Crime
Victimless crimes, 140
Vietnamese immigrants, 210
Violence
  family, 255-258
  mass media and, 86
  in schools, 304
Violent crime, 133, 136-138
  poverty and, 183-184
Violent Crime in the United States, 165
Vocation, and identity, 90
Voting, 323-326
  participation in, 323

Walden Pond, 119
Warfare, government and, 312-313
Watts riots, 417
Way International, The, 288
Wealth, 174, 175
  social impact of, 15-16
  social stratification and, 156
Wealth of Nations, The, 314
Weber's model of bureaucracy, 112-114

Welfare, 179-180
Welfare school theory, 165
West (U.S.), migration to, 338-339
West End, 31
White-collar crime, 138-139
White flight, 201
Whites. See also Race
  immigration to U.S. of, 202-204
  wealth of, 156
WHO. See World Health Organization
Wives. See Women
Women. See also Gender; Gender inequality; Gender roles; Sex roles
  child care and, 89
  and childlessness, 253
  in college, 297
  and contingent temporal worlds, 226
  conversation styles of, 228
  divorce and, 258-262
  education and fertility of, 347
  flexibility of, 226-227
  gender inequality and, 221-223
  gender-role socialization and, 223-227
  among gifted, 307
  health of, 379-380
  job discrimination and, 227-230
  in labor force, 423
  occupational status of, 160
  poverty and, 175-176
  premarital sex and, 255
  in prison, 146-147
  reasoning styles of, 227
  religion and, 217-218
  survey of, 33
  voting and, 325
  working, and family, 255

Women's movement, 405
Work
  gender inequality and, 227-230
  specialization and, 420
Work force, education and, 292-293
  technology and, 422-424
Working class, 171, 173
  nuclear family and, 251
Working parents, 256
Working Woman, subscriber survey of, 33
World Health Organization (WHO), 384, 385
  world health trends and, 389-391
World hunger, 348
World views, religion and, 277-278
World War II, and family (U.S.), 251-252
Wounded Knee, South Dakota, 279

XYY chromosomal anomaly, 125-126

Yanomamo people, 47, 48-49
Yir Yoront, 414
You Just Don't Understand: Women and Men in Conversation, 228
Young-old population, 231-232

Ziggurats, 355
Zimbabwe black guerilla movement, 405

STUDY
GUIDE

CHAPTER SUMMARY

Sociology as a Point of View

We are constantly bombarded today with information about social issues. Much of it, however, comes from sources that have an interest in getting people to support a particular point of view (like special interest groups) or that wish to attract attention and maintain high ratings (like journalists and talk show hosts). Sociology, on the other hand, seeks an accurate and scientific understanding of society and social life.

Sociology also asks us to broaden our perspective and to see the world through the eyes of others. Thus sociology's scientific understanding goes beyond the knowledge gained by each individual from their own everyday experience. Though this personal experiential knowledge may serve us quite well on a day-to-day basis, it does not provide us with enough accurate information to develop an understanding of the broader social picture. Moreover, "common sense" experiential knowledge can be either misleading or can fail to help us understand the conditions under which human interaction takes place.

The focus of sociology is the group and not the individual. A sociologist tries to understand the forces that operate throughout the society—forces that mold individuals, shape their behavior, and thus determine social events. Social theorist C. Wright Mills referred to this perspective as the sociological imagination. Many possibilities exist for applying sociological understanding and insight to the solution of social problems, and the demand for applied sociology is growing.

Sociology is one of the social sciences, which means it relies upon empirical evidence, or evidence directly observed by the senses, organized and interpreted by theories. Though there is some overlap in goals and procedures, each of the social sciences has its own areas of concern. Cultural anthropology, psychology, economics, history, political science, and social work all have things in common with sociology, but each has its own distinct focus, objectives, theories, and methods.

The Development of Sociology

The science of sociology emerged in Europe during the nineteenth century—a time of rapid and dramatic social change. In an effort to understand the effects of the Industrial Revolution on the fabric of society and the life style of individuals, scholars such as Auguste Comte turned to methods of the natural sciences to discover the underlying principles of society. It was Comte who coined the term *sociology.*

Karl Marx, Herbert Spencer, Émile Durkheim, and Max Weber, known as the classical theorists, were all instrumental in shaping the development of sociology.

Marx believed the history of human societies could be viewed as a history of class struggles, or conflicts between those who own and control the means of production and those who work for them. Marx was committed not only to investigating social problems but also to working to change the social system.

Spencer was the first to define the subject matter of sociology, and he developed many of the standard concepts and terms of the field. Spencer was also a proponent of the doctrine of Social Darwinism, which argued that people who could not successfully compete in modern society were poorly adapted to their environment and therefore inferior. For this he has been justly criticized.

Durkheim was the first professor of sociology. He held that individuals are exclusively the product of their social environment. Durkheim set out to prove this theory through the study of suicide, an individual act. He identified three major types of suicide: egoistic, altruistic, and anomic. All of them, he argued, were in some way the result of social influence.

Weber was interested in understanding—rather than changing—human behavior. Much of his work was an attempt to clarify, criticize, or modify the ideas of Marx. Weber proposed that ideologies could influence the economic system, and was a pioneer in the study of bureaucracy.

In the United States, sociology developed in the early twentieth century. Initially it was largely concerned with social reform. Under the leadership of the Chicago School, the goals and methods of sociology were refined. Other sociologists, such as Talcott Parsons and Robert Merton, developed the theoretical perspective of functionalism. Merton is best known for his distinction between manifest functions, or the intended consequences of social processes, and latent functions, or their unintended consequences.

Theoretical Perspectives

Scientists need a set of working assumptions to guide them in their professional activities. These models, or frameworks, are known as paradigms. Sociologists have developed several paradigms to help them investigate social processes. Functionalism sees society as a system of interrelated structures that work together harmoniously. Conflict theory regards society as continuously changing in response to conflict over persistent social inequality. Social order, in this view, is maintained by coercion.

The interactionist perspective focuses on how, in the process of social interaction, individuals makes sense of, or interpret, the social world. This perspective consists of a number of loosely linked approaches. Symbolic interactionism is concerned with the meanings people place on their own and one another's behavior. Ethnomethodology attempts to discover and describe the unwritten rules that guide the behavior of individuals and groups in society. Dramaturgy looks at how people play roles in order to create and manage a desired impression among others.

Contemporary sociology has both built on and modified the insights of these three theoretical perspectives. Many sociologists today focus on developing middle-range theories, which try to explain specific issues or aspects of society rather than how the whole society operates.

Sociological theory gives meaning to sociological practice. Theory must inform data collection, and data must be collected in order to test the adequacy of theories.

CHAPTER OUTLINE

Sociology as a Point of View
What is unique about the sociological point of view?

THE SOCIOLOGICAL IMAGINATION
What is the sociological imagination? Why might it be useful?

IS SOCIOLOGY COMMON SENSE?
In what way is sociology different from common sense?

SOCIOLOGY AND SCIENCE
Why can sociology be called a science?

SOCIOLOGY AS A SOCIAL SCIENCE
Why is sociology a social science?

Cultural Anthropology
What is the most significant difference between sociology and cultural anthropology?

Psychology
What is the most significant difference between sociology and psychology?

Economics
What is the most significant difference between sociology and economics?

History
What is the most significant difference between sociology and history?

Political Science
What is the most significant difference between sociology and political science?

Social Work
What is the most significant difference between sociology and social work?

The Development of Sociology
When did sociology emerge as a field of study? Why did it emerge at that time?

AUGUSTE COMTE (1798–1857) (oh GYOOST KOHMT)
What role did Comte play in the development of sociology?

CLASSICAL THEORISTS
What is the importance of the Classical Theorists?

Karl Marx (1818–1883)
What is the most important contribution of Karl Marx to the field of sociology?

Herbert Spencer (1820–1903)
Why is Herbert Spencer important in the development of the discipline of sociology?

Émile Durkheim (1858–1917) (aay MEEL Derk HIGHM)
What did Émile Durkheim contribute to the development of sociology?

Max Weber (1864–1920) (Mahks VAY ber)
What are Max Weber's most important contributions to the field of sociology?

THE DEVELOPMENT OF SOCIOLOGY IN THE UNITED STATES
How and when did sociology develop in the United States?

Theoretical Perspectives
What are theoretical perspectives and why are they important?

FUNCTIONALISM
What are the basic assumptions of functionalism?

CONFLICT THEORY
What are the basic assumptions of conflict theory?

THE INTERACTIONIST PERSPECTIVE
What are the basic assumptions of the interactionist perspective?

Symbolic Interactionism
What is the focus of symbolic interactionism?

Ethnomethodology
What is ethnomethodology?

Dramaturgy
How does dramaturgy look at social behavior?

CONTEMPORARY SOCIOLOGY
What is significant about contemporary sociology?

THEORY AND PRACTICE
What is the relationship between theory and practice?

LEARNING OBJECTIVES

After studying this chapter you should be able to:

■ *Understand and explain the sociological point of view.*

Sociology is _____.

The main goal of sociology is to _____.

The sociological imagination is the process of _____.

While an understanding of society and social interaction based on common sense is useful, its main weakness is that it _____.

◼ *Explain how the sociological point of view differs from that of journalists and talk show hosts.*

Choose a contemporary social issue (for example, teenage pregnancy, the AIDS epidemic, child abuse, the crisis in education, capital punishment, and so on). _____.

What questions would a talk show host ask about this problem?

What questions would a sociologist ask about the same problem?

◼ *Explain why sociology is a social science.*

What does it mean to say that science is empirical?

Define social sciences:

How does sociology fit this definition?

◼ *Compare and contrast sociology with the other major social sciences.*

Cultural Anthropology

   Similarities:

   Differences:

Psychology

   Similarities:

   Differences:

Economics

Similarities:

Differences:

History

Similarities:

Differences:

Political Science

Similarities:

Differences:

Social Work

Similarities:

Differences:

■ *Trace the early development of sociology from its origins in nineteenth-century Europe.*

List five historical changes in nineteenth-century Europe that led to the development of sociology.

1.

2.

3.

4.

5.

Describe two contributions of Auguste Comte to the development of sociology.

1.

2.

■ *Summarize the major contributions of sociology's classical theorists: Marx, Spencer, Durkheim, and Weber.*

	Major Focus of Theorist	Major Contribution
Marx		
Spencer		
Durkheim		
Weber		

■ *Describe the early development of sociology in the United States.*

For what is the Chicago School best known?

	Major Focus of Theorist	Major Contribution
Parsons		
Merton		

■ *Contrast functionalism and conflict theory, explaining the distinctive way in which each theory would understand the same phenomenon.*

Why are public schools organized the way that they are? Compare and contrast functionalist and conflict theory views.

The functionalist perspective of schooling:

The conflict theory perspective of schooling:

Crucial differences:

■ *Discuss the major contemporary interactionist perspectives: symbolic interactionism, ethnomethodology, and dramaturgy.*

How would a sociologist from each of the interactionist perspectives go about studying behavior in a singles bar? What questions would each ask; what approach would each take?

Symbolic interactionist approach to behavior in a singles bar:

Ethnomethodological approach to behavior in a singles bar:

Dramaturgical approach to behavior in a singles bar:

■ *Explain the connection between theory and practice.*

Practice (sociological research) without theory would be _____.

_____.

Theory without practice (research to test it) is _____.

_____.

KEY CONCEPTS

■ *Match each concept with its definition, illustration, or explication below.*

a. empiricism	j. egoistic suicide	s. class conflict
b. paradigm	k. altruistic suicide	t. symbolic interactionism
c. applied sociology	l. interactionist perspective	u. science
d. the Protestant Ethic	m. functionalism	v. latent function
e. middle-range theories	n. the social sciences	w. manifest function
f. the scientific method	o. sociology	x. conflict theory
g. the Chicago School	p. ethnomethodology	y. the sociological imagination
h. Social Darwinism	q. social function	z. dramaturgy
i. anomic suicide	r. value-free perspective	

_____ **1.** the scientific study of human society and social interactions.

_____ **2.** the process of looking at all types of human behavior patterns and discerning unseen connections among them.

_____ **3.** applying sociology to the solution of "real world" problems.

_____ **4.** a body of systematically arranged knowledge that shows the operation of general laws.

_____ **5.** the building of knowledge through systematic observation, experimentation, generalization, and verification.

_____ **6.** the view that generalizations are valid only if they rely on evidence observed directly through our senses.

_____ **7.** those disciplines that apply scientific methods to the study of human behavior.

_____ **8.** conflict between those who own and control the means of production and the workers.

_____ **9.** the notion that people who cannot successfully compete in modern society are poorly adapted to their environment and therefore inferior.

_____ **10.** a type of suicide caused by low group solidarity.

_____ **11.** a type of suicide caused by a very high level of group solidarity.

_____ **12.** a type of suicide caused by a disconnectedness from society's values.

_____ **13.** a religious value system that encourages rational, disciplined, hard work.

_____ **14.** group of early U.S. sociologists who developed empirical methods for studying urban neighborhoods and ethnic areas.

_____ **15.** processes that contribute to the ongoing operation or maintenance of society.

_____ **16.** intended and recognized consequences of social processes.

_____ **17.** unintended or not readily recognized consequences of social processes.

_____ **18.** a perspective that restricts itself to describing and explaining rather than attempting to suggest what should be.

_____ **19.** a model or framework for organizing the questions that generate and guide research.

_____ **20.** a view of society as a system of highly interrelated parts that operate together rather harmoniously.

_____ **21.** a view of society that sees it constantly changing in response to social inequality and the resulting conflict.

_____ **22.** a view that focuses on how individuals make sense of the social world.

_____ **23.** a view that is concerned with the meanings that people place on their own and one another's behavior.

_____ **24.** the study of the rules that individuals use to initiate, respond to, and modify behavior in social things.

_____ **25.** the study of the way that individuals use roles to create impressions in social settings.

_____ **26.** theories that are concerned with explaining specific issues or aspects of society rather than how the whole society operates.

KEY THINKERS

■ *Match each thinker with their main idea or contribution.*

a. Harold Garfinkel
b. Talcott Parsons
c. Karl Marx
d. Erving Goffman
e. C. Wright Mills
f. George Herbert Mead

g. Max Weber
h. Auguste Comte
i. Robert K. Merton
j. Herbert Spencer
k. Émile Durkheim

_____ 1. developed the concept of the sociological imagination.

_____ 2. coined the term sociology.

_____ 3. pioneered the conflict theory approach to sociology.

_____ 4. developed many of the standard terms and concepts of sociology and wrote them down in the first sociology textbook.

_____ 5. the first professor of sociology, he produced the first true sociological study, in which he explained the individual act of suicide as a result of social forces.

_____ 6. pioneered the study of bureaucracy.

_____ 7. an early U.S. sociologist, he elaborated the functionalist perspective.

_____ 8. developed the distinction between manifest and latent functions.

_____ 9. first developed the symbolic interactionist perspective.

_____10. invented the ethnomethodological approach to studying social behavior.

_____11. developed dramaturgy as a way of studying social interaction.

CRITICAL THINKING/APPLICATION QUESTIONS

1. Your college or university is thinking about eliminating departments due to a severe budget crunch. Sociology is one of the departments slated to be disbanded. You disagree. Explain to the administration why a sociological perspective is valuable and necessary in the college or university's educational program and in society.
2. Imagine a panel consisting of Marx, Spencer, Durkheim, and Weber convened to discuss the problem of missing children. How would each theorist approach this issue? What criticisms might they offer of the others' viewpoints?
3. In 1992, a major civil disorder occurred in south central Los Angeles after a group of white police officers were found not guilty of assaulting Rodney King, an African American, whose beating by the police had been captured on videotape and broadcast nationwide. How would sociologists using each major theoretical perspective (functionalist, conflict, and the three interactionist perspectives) look at and interpret this civil disorder?
4. Review the data on suicide among college students presented in Table 1.1. As an exercise in applied sociology, what specific policies would you propose to your college or university administration as a way of dealing with this social phenomenon?

SUGGESTED READINGS
DISCOVERING SOCIOLOGY

C. Wright Mills, *The Sociological Imagination* (New York: Oxford University Press, 1959). Most of this book is a critique of sociological theory, some of it is a bit dated. Nonetheless, much of it remains a lively critique of the field, and the first chapter, entitled "The Promise," is still by far the best description of the sociological imagination.

Peter L. Berger, *Invitation to Sociology: A Humanistic Perspective* (Garden City, NY: Doubleday Anchor Books, 1963). A timeless classic, in which readers are invited in a friendly way to go along on the sociological voyage of discovery.

Zygmunt Bauman, *Thinking Sociologically* (Cambridge, MA: Basil Blackwell, 1990). A very personal introduction to the value of understanding sociology. The author's contention is that, at its best, sociology is exciting and subversive, and should serve the "cause of freedom." Bauman demonstrates just how sociology could do so by examining many of the pressing issues of contemporary life.

Anthony Giddens, *Sociology: A Brief But Critical Introduction,* 2nd ed. (San Diego, CA: Harcourt Brace Jovanovich, 1987). A brief introduction to the field by one of the most important contemporary sociological theorists. This book is unique in that its approach is theoretical, historical, and comparative.

Lewis A. Coser, ed., *The Pleasures of Sociology* (New York: New American Library, 1980). A collection of thirty-six highly readable essays by outstanding sociologists that show the field at its most insightful and intriguing best.

THE CLASSICAL THEORISTS

Randall Collins and Michael Makowsky, *The Discovery of Society,* 2nd ed. (New York: Random House, 1978). Profiles over a dozen classical theorists in an approach that provides excellent social and historical context as well as comparison and contrast among the thinkers. It is brief and well-written.

Lewis A. Coser, *Masters of Sociological Thought: Ideas in Historical and Social Context,* 2nd ed. (New York: Harcourt Brace Jovanovich, 1977). Provides a fairly comprehensive social, intellectual, and personal biographical context for about fifteen major sociological theorists.

Peter Worsley, *Marx and Marxism* (London: Tavistock, 1982). Part of the *Key Sociologists* series, this is a brief but sophisticated introduction to the historical and intellectual context and the main ideas of Marx.

Jonathan H. Turner, *Herbert Spencer: A Renewed Appreciation* (Beverly Hills, CA: Sage, 1985). An attempt to recognize Spencer's pioneering contributions as well as show their relevance to today's world.

Kenneth Thompson, *Émile Durkheim* (London: Tavistock, 1982). Part of the *Key Sociologists* series, this is a brief but sophisticated introduction to the historical and intellectual context and the main ideas of Weber.

Frank Parkin, *Max Weber* (London: Tavistock, 1982). Part of the *Key Sociologists* series, this is a brief but sophisticated introduction to the historical and intellectual context and the main ideas of Weber.

CONTEMPORARY SOCIOLOGY

R.P. Cuzzort and E.P. King, *Twentieth-Century Social Thought,* 4th ed. (Fort Worth, TX: Holt, Rinehart and Winston, 1989). A highly-readable survey of 13 major contemporary theorists, including G.H. Mead, Merton, Mills, Goffman, and Garfinkel.

ANSWER KEY

KEY CONCEPTS

1. o	14. g
2. y	15. q
3. c	16. w
4. u	17. v
5. f	18. r
6. a	19. b
7. n	20. m
8. s	21. x
9. h	22. l
10. j	23. t
11. k	24. p
12. i	25. z
13. d	26. e

KEY THINKERS

1. e	7. b
2. h	8. i
3. c	9. f
4. j	10. a
5. k	11. d
6. g	

CHAPTER SUMMARY

The Research Process

To produce a valid study of the social world, we cannot approach it solely on the basis of personal experience and perceptions, rather we must do so scientifically. Science has two main goals: (1) to describe in detail particular things or events, and (2) to propose and test theories that help us understand these things or events. The scientific research process involves a number of specific steps that must be followed to produce a valid study. Only when this is done faithfully can we have any confidence in the results of the study.

The research process begins by defining a problem in such a way that it can be observed and objectively measured. This is called an operational definition. Then the researcher attempts to find out as much as possible about previous studies on the same topic. The next step is to develop one or more hypotheses, or testable statements about the relationship between two or more empirical (that is, measurable) variables. Here the researcher must distinguish between statements of causality and statements of association. The first refers to a declaration that something causes, influences, or determines something else. The second says only that changes in one thing are related to changes in another thing without any causal connection.

Hypotheses often propose relationships between a dependent variable and an independent variable. A dependent variable changes in response to changes in the independent variable, but an independent variable changes for reasons that have nothing to do with the dependent variable. Hypotheses are tested by constructing a research design, or a strategy for collecting appropriate data. Sociologists use three main research designs: surveys, participant observation, and experiments.

A survey is a research method in which a population, or a portion thereof, is questioned in order to reveal specific facts about itself. The questions asked can be structured (predetermined and rigid) or unstructured (open-ended and flexible). Data is gathered either by a conversation with each research subject, called an interview, or by distributing the questions to subjects and asking these people to answer and return them.

In participant observation, researchers enter into a group's activities and observe the group members in order to obtain a detailed portrait of a selected group of people. The success of this method is highly dependent upon the relationship that develops between the researcher and the research subjects.

An experiment is an investigation in which the variables studied are controlled and the researcher obtains the results through precise observation and measurement. Although some aspects of small-group interaction have been studied experimentally, this method remains the least-used research design in sociology because most social events cannot be studied in controlled circumstances.

When collecting data, sociologists often choose to examine a manageable subset, or sample, of the larger population. In order to be fully representative of that larger population, however, the sample must be selected randomly—that is, each member of the population must have an equal chance of being chosen. Failure to obtain a representative sample is known as sampling error. To prevent certain groups from being under- or over-represented in a sample, researchers divide the population into relevant categories like age, sex, or ethnicity, draw random samples from each group, then combine these subsamples in the appropriate proportions to obtain the final sample.

One of the most serious problems in data collection is researcher bias—the tendency for researchers to select data that support, and ignore data that seem to go against, their hypothesis. A researcher who is strongly inclined toward one point of view may communicate that attitude through questions and reactions in such a way that the subjects fulfill the researcher's expectations. This is known as a self-fulfilling prophecy. A way of avoiding this problem is through the technique of blind or double-blind investigations, in which data collectors are kept unaware of information that could bias their perceptions.

After the data have been collected, the researcher analyzes the many pieces of information and then determines what conclusions can be drawn. In developing conclusions the researcher will want to demonstrate that the study has validity and reliability—that it tested what it was intended to test and that its method is repeatable. Finally, the scientist prepares a research report for the relevant audiences.

Objectivity in Sociological Research

Sociology, like any other science, is molded by factors that impose values on research. Thus, completely value-free research may not be possible. Nevertheless, objectivity, or a kind of disciplined subjectivity, is a reasonable goal for sociological research. This means that researchers strive to become aware of the ways in which values influence them, and to make such biases explicit when sharing the results of their research.

Ethical Issues in Sociological Research

The central ethical concern in research on human subjects is how to judge and balance the intellectual and societal benefits of scientific research against the actual or possible physical and emotional costs paid by the research subjects. One dilemma concerns the degree of permissible risk, pain, or harm to the subjects. Another dilemma is the extent to which the subjects should be deceived during the study. A third problem has to do with the disclosure of confidential or personally harmful information. In grappling with these questions, sociologists must keep in mind that social research rarely benefits the subjects directly and that most subjects of social research belong to groups with little or no power. These conditions place an added responsibility on sociologists to protect their subjects.

Research fraud, or conscious deceit in the collection or reporting of data, creates a climate of mistrust and cynicism and can damage individuals far beyond those in the immediate study.

CHAPTER OUTLINE

The Research Process

What are the aims of the research process in sociology? Why are they important?

DEFINE THE PROBLEM

What is involved in defining the problem?

REVIEW PREVIOUS RESEARCH

What is to be gained by reviewing previous research?

DEVELOP ONE OR MORE HYPOTHESES

How does a researcher develop a hypothesis?

DETERMINE THE RESEARCH DESIGN

What is the role of the research design?

Surveys

What are the important features of the survey method?

Participant Observation

How do sociologists do participant observation?

Experiments

What is the basic feature of experiments in sociology?

DEFINE THE SAMPLE AND COLLECT DATA

How are samples defined?

Researcher Bias

How does researcher bias occur?

ANALYZE THE DATA AND DRAW CONCLUSIONS

How do sociologists analyze data? What criteria guide the type of conclusions drawn?

PREPARE THE RESEARCH REPORT
For whom is the research report prepared?

Objectivity in Sociological Research
Is objectivity in social research possible?

Ethical Issues in Sociological Research
What is the most important ethical issue in sociological research?

RESEARCH FRAUD
What are the implications of research fraud?

LEARNING OBJECTIVES

After studying this chapter you should be able to:

■ *Explain the steps in the sociological research process.*

Step in the Process	Two Typical Questions Asked
1.	a.
	b.
2.	a.
	b.
3.	a.
	b.
4.	a.
	b.
5.	a.
	b.
6.	a.
	b.
7.	a.
	b.

■ *Translate questions into testable hypotheses.*

Suppose you wanted to study the problem of crime in contemporary society.

Develop an empirical question about crime:

In what ways can this question be answered with observable data?

Identify two factors that you hypothesize (that is, have an educated guess about) are associated with or influence the occurrence of crime.

Factor 1 _____

Factor 2 _____

State your hypothesis about the relationship between these two factors and crime:

Is this a statement of causality? _____   or   a statement of association? _____

State the reason for your choice:

Develop an operational definition for each of the variables in your hypothesis.

Operational definition of crime:

Operational definition of your first variable (Factor 1):

Operational definition of your second variable (Factor 2):

■ *Identify independent and dependent variables in statements of causation.*

Identify the independent and dependent variables in the following hypotheses:
Poverty produces low self-esteem.

independent variable: _____

dependent variable: _____

Higher unemployment causes an increase in the rate of divorce.

independent variable: _____

dependent variable: _____

Inflexible, uncreative children are the products of authoritarian socialization.

independent variable: _____

dependent variable: _____

■ *Identify the strengths and weaknesses of competing research designs.*
Survey

Major Strength:

Major Weakness:

Participant Observation

Major Strength:

Major Weakness:

Experiment

Major Strength:

Major Weakness:

■ *Understand the process of sampling and the importance of obtaining a representative sample.*

Suppose you wanted to survey the attitudes of your classmates in this introductory sociology course. To save time and effort, you decide to study a sample of the larger population. Explain why each of the following samples is, or is not, a representative sample of everyone enrolled in the course.

• Students occupying the first ten desks in your classroom:

• Every tenth name on an alphabetically-arranged course roster:

• Every student whose last name happens to begin with the most-frequently occurring letter:

• Ten names drawn out of a hat containing the shuffled names of everyone enrolled in the course:

■ *Recognize researcher bias and understand how it can affect the outcome of research studies.*

Suppose a sociologist is convinced that genuine sexual harassment does not occur very frequently, and that many reported cases are a product of media hype and/or active, feminist-inspired imaginations of women. List and explain three ways this particular opinion may potentially bias this researcher's investigation of sexual harassment in the workplace.

1.

2.

3.

■ *Understand the strengths and weaknesses of the various measures of central tendency.*

Here are the annual incomes of seven hypothetical families:

| $1,000,000 | $50,000 | $20,000 | $10,000 |
| $70,000 | $40,000 | $20,000 | |

What is the mean income of these families? $ _____.

What is the median income of these families? $ _____.

What income represents the mode of this group? $ _____.

Which measure provides the most accurate description of this group of families? Why?

■ *Read a table and appropriately interpret its contents.*

Turn to Table 8.6, "Poverty Rates Among Children, Working-Age Adults, and the Elderly in Six Nations," in Chapter 8 and answer the following questions about it.

Summarize what this table is about:

How important is it that the data in this table be current? Are the data, in fact, current?

Do you consider the source of the data to be reliable? Why or why not?

In what units are the data in the table reported? (that is, what do the numbers mean?)

Which country has the highest poverty rate among children? _____

Which country has the lowest poverty rate among working-age adults? _____

Which country has the highest poverty rate among the elderly? _____

Which country seems to have the greatest variation in poverty rates among the three groups? _____

Summarize what you think is the most significant conclusion you can draw from the data in this table:

List two questions for further research that are prompted by the data in this table.

1.

2.

■ *Explain the concepts of reliability and validity in sociological research.*

A sociologist concludes that left-handed people are more likely to be criminals, based upon a single study of a dozen people cited for littering in a public park.

What can you say about the reliability of this study?

What can you say about the validity of this study?

■ *Understand the ethical problems that arise in sociological research.*

In a famous sociological study, Laud Humphries investigated the characteristics of homosexual men who had sexual encounters in public restrooms. He discovered the identities of these men by posing as a willing "lookout" in the restrooms, then following the men back to their cars and surreptitiously writing down their license numbers. Through the state Bureau of Motor Vehicles, Humphries obtained the names and addresses of the men he had observed and eventually went to their homes to interview them. The police were very interested in Humphries' research notes, of course, because they recorded the identities of persons participating in illegal activities. Humphries successfully resisted turning any information over to the authorities.

Consider the merits of this research in light of the need to balance the protection of human subjects against the desirability of obtaining data on every kind of human interaction. More specifically, evaluate the study in terms of the following three ethical dilemmas:

1. Degree of permissible risk, pain, or harm to the subjects

2. Extent to which the subjects are deceived by the researcher

3. Potential for the disclosure of confidential or personally harmful information

Conclusion: Was it ethical for Humphries to conduct this research?

KEY CONCEPTS

■ *Match each concept with its definition, illustration, or explication below.*

a. longitudinal study
b. stratified random sample
c. dependent variable
d. structured interview
e. median
f. validity
g. survey
h. operational definition
i. semistructured interview
j. self-fulfilling prophecy
k. statement of causality
l. blind and double-blind investigators
m. representative sample
n. participant observation
o. reliability
p. variable

q. statement of association
r. cross-sectional study
s. research process
t. mean
u. mode
v. ethical issues
w. randomness
x. experiment
y. analysis
z. sampling error
aa. hypothesis
bb. researcher bias
cc. empirical question
dd. independent variable
ee. objectivity
ff. sampling

_____ 1. a sequence of steps followed when designing a research project.

_____ 2. an issue posed in such a way that it can be studied by observation.

_____ 3. a specific statement about an abstract concept in terms of the observable features of the phenomenon being investigated.

_____ 4. a testable statement about the relationships between two or more empirical variables.

_____ 5. any factor that can change or take on different values.

_____ 6. a declaration that changes in one variable are related to changes in another, but that one does not necessarily bring about or induce changes in the other.

_____ 7. a declaration that some factor brings about, influences, or changes something else.

_____ 8. the phenomenon studied by the researcher—that is, the variable for which an explanation is sought.

_____ 9. a factor that changes for reasons having nothing to do with the dependent variable.

_____10. a research method in which a population, or a portion thereof, is questioned in order to reveal specific facts about itself.

_____11. an examination of a population at a given point in time.

_____12. research that investigates a population over a period of time.

_____13. a form of research conversation in which a questionnaire is followed rigidly.

_____14. a form of research conversation in which the investigator is free to vary the questions or even to make up new ones if the situation warrants.

_____15. research based upon precise observation and measurement and extensive control of the variables being studied.

_____16. researchers enter into a groups' activities as a method for investigating the group.

_____17. a technique in which researchers study a manageable subset of people selected from the population under study.

_____18. a subset of the population that exhibits, in correct proportion, the significant characteristics of the population as a whole.

_____19. method for choosing a representative sample by ensuring that each individual in the population has an equal chance of being selected.

_____20. the result of failing to achieve a representative sample.

_____21. a method used to prevent certain groups from being under- or over-represented in a sample.

_____22. the tendency for researchers to select data that support, and to ignore data that seem to go against, their hypotheses.

_____23. a phenomenon produced when a researcher who is strongly inclined toward a particular point of view communicates that attitude through questions and reactions such that the subject winds up fulfilling the researcher's expectations.

_____24. a method of avoiding bias in which potentially prejudicial information about the subjects and/or the study is withheld from the investigators during data collection.

_____25. the process through which scientific data are organized so that comparisons can be made and conclusions drawn.

_____26. the number that occurs most often in a data set.

_____27. the figure that falls in the exact middle of a ranked series of scores.

_____28. the average of a set of numbers.

_____29. the characteristic of a study which indicates that it is repeatable.

_____30. the extent to which a study tests what it was intended to test.

_____31. a kind of disciplined subjectivity in which researchers strive to make their biases explicit and to become aware of how these biases influence their research.

_____32. questions about how to balance the intellectual and societal benefits of research against the actual or possible harm to the people being studied.

CRITICAL THINKING/APPLICATION QUESTIONS

1. Suppose you wanted to evaluate the teaching effectiveness of your instructor. How would you do so using each of the research methods discussed in this chapter?
2. Many popular magazines include tear-out surveys, which readers are asked to fill out and return. Often many thousands of readers do so. From the point of view of representative sampling, what is wrong with these surveys?
3. Locate a report of some sociological research in a popular magazine or newspaper. Based on the information provided, what can you say about the reliability, validity, and sampling procedures of the study? Do you have enough information to make this determination? If not, what else do you need to know?
4. Micro-miniature electronics and sophisticated computers made it possible for some people to gather and store extensive information on the private lives of fellow citizens. There is great potential here for productive social research, as well as abuse. Where do we draw the line? By what values shall we decide? Who should get to decide?

SUGGESTED READINGS

THE RESEARCH PROCESS

Earl R. Babbie, *Social Research for Consumers* (Belmont, CA: Wadsworth, 1982). One of the few research methods books available that specifically addresses itself to students as *consumers* of scientific research and data. Written in a very conversational style.

Paul D. Leedy, *How To Read Research and Understand It* (New York: Macmillan, 1981). A relatively brief paperback that systematically demystifies all aspects of the presentation of research findings.

Lucy Horwitz and Lou Ferleger, *Statistics for Social Change* (Boston: South End Press, 1980). One of the best introductions to statistics, designed to be used for self-study, and written in a conversational style.

Herman W. Smith, *Strategies of Social Research, 3rd ed.* (Fort Worth, TX: Holt, Rinehart and Winston, 1991). An up-to-date survey of research strategies that is very comprehensive in its coverage of different methods.

OBJECTIVITY IN SOCIOLOGICAL RESEARCH

William Foote Whyte, in collaboration with Kathleen King Whyte, *Learning From the Field: A Guide From Experience* (Beverly Hills, CA: Sage, 1984). A passionate argument for the overriding importance of an applied, reflexive social research approach. Written by a justly famous sociologist, based upon his experience as a pioneer in a number of fields of sociological research.

ETHICAL ISSUES IN SOCIOLOGICAL RESEARCH

Paul D. Reynolds, *Ethics and Social Science Research* (Englewood Cliffs, NJ: Prentice Hall, 1982). An introduction to the ethical dilemmas faced by social scientists when they do research. Includes possible solutions.

ANSWER KEY

KEY CONCEPTS

1.	s	18.	m
2.	cc	19.	w
3.	h	20.	z
4.	aa	21.	b
5.	p	22.	bb
6.	q	23.	j
7.	k	24.	l
8.	c	25.	y
9.	dd	26.	u
10.	g	27.	e
11.	r	28.	t
12.	a	29.	o
13.	d	30.	f
14.	i	31.	ee
15.	x	32.	v
16.	n		
17.	ff		

CHAPTER SUMMARY

The Concept of Culture

Human societies differ—often greatly—in their ways of life and in their understandings of themselves and others. Each society has its own unique blueprint for living. Sociologists call this blueprint *culture*, which they define as all that human beings learn to do, to use, to produce, to know, and to believe as they grow to maturity and live out their lives in the social groups to which they belong. Unlike other creatures, humans do not pass on many behavioral patterns through their genes; rather, culture is taught and learned through social interaction. The result is a much wider variation of behavior among humans than other animal species.

Because human cultures vary so widely, people often have difficulty adjusting to a culture that differs markedly from their own. Sociologists call this culture shock. In addition, people often make judgments about other cultures according to the customs and values of their own. This practice, called ethnocentrism, can lead to prejudice and discrimination and, often, the repression or domination of one group by another. To avoid ethnocentrism in their research, sociologists are guided by the concept of cultural relativism, or the recognition that social groups and cultures must be understood on their own terms before valid comparisons can be made.

Components of Culture

Sociologists view culture as having four major components: material culture, normative culture, cognitive culture, and language. Material culture consists of all the things that humans learn to make and use in order to modify and exploit their environment. Due to its great flexibility, material culture has made humans the dominant life-form on earth.

Normative culture consists of society's norms, or the rules of behavior that are agreed upon and shared and which prescribe limits of acceptable behavior. Strongly held norms that have a moral connotation and are based on the central values of the culture are known as mores. Violation of mores produce strong negative reactions, which are frequently codified in laws. Folkways are conventions of everyday life which permit a rather wide degree of individual interpretation, as long as certain limits are not overstepped. Ideal norms are expectations of what people should do under perfect conditions; real norms are expressed with qualifications and allowances for differences in individual behavior.

Cognitive culture consists of shared beliefs and knowledge of what the world is like—what is real and what is not, what is important and what is trivial. Notions of what a culture considers good and bad, desirable and undesirable, are known as values. These general orientations toward life are usually expressed in recurring patterns of behavior.

Language enables humans to organize the world around them into labeled cognitive categories and to use these labels to communicate with one another. Language makes possible the teaching and sharing of cognitive and normative culture; it is also the vehicle that allows humans to transcend the limitations imposed by their environment and biological evolution. Each culture selects, and identifies as important, only certain aspects of the world. The language of each culture, then, becomes the lens through which its members view and experience the world.

The Symbolic Nature of Culture

Language, and indeed all of culture, is based upon the use of symbols, which are arbitrary representations. Unlike signs—objects that represent other things because they share some important quality with them—symbols need not share any quality at all with whatever they represent. Their meaning is simply a matter of cultural convention.

Culture and Adaptation

Without instincts to guide them, humans must use culture to adapt to the challenges of their environment. Adaptation can take the form of specialization, which involves developing ways of doing things that work extremely well in a particular environment, or generalized adaptability, more complicated yet flexible ways of doing things. The evolution of human culture is driven by innovation and diffusion. Innovation, comprising invention and discovery, creates new cultural traits. Diffusion is the movement of cultural traits from one culture to another. In this process the original cultural trait is often reformulated to better fit into its new context. When some parts of the culture change more rapidly than other parts, it creates a situation known as cultural lag.

Animals and Culture

Language and the production of tools are central elements of culture. Evidence exists that nonhuman animals engage, or can be taught to engage, in both of these activities. Does this mean that they have culture? Scientists disagree about how to interpret the evidence. Without question, however, it can be said that humans have refined culture to a far greater degree than other animals and are far more dependent upon it for survival.

Subcultures

Within the broad culture of a society may be found a number of subcultures, or distinctive lifestyles, values, norms, and beliefs associated with certain segments of the population. Sociologists speak of ethnic, occupational, religious, political, geographical, social class, and deviant subcultures, among others.

Universals of Culture

Certain models or patterns that have developed in all cultures are known as cultural universals. Among them are the division of labor, the incest taboo, marriage, family organization, rites of passage, and ideology. Though the forms are universal, the content is unique to each culture.

Culture and Individual Choice

Due to a lack of instinctual or biolgical programming, humans have a great deal of flexibility and choice in their activities. Individual freedom of action is limited, however, by the existing culture. Moreover, social pressure to act, think, and feel in socially-approved ways inevitably generates some individual dissatisfaction. There is thus a tension between the individual and society. Sociology can enlighten us about this tension and assist in constructing realistic goals and plans.

CHAPTER OUTLINE

The Concept of Culture
To what does the concept of culture refer?

CULTURE AND BIOLOGY
What is the relationship between culture and biology?

CULTURE SHOCK
What does it mean to experience culture shock?

ETHNOCENTRISM AND CULTURAL RELATIVISM
What is the relationship between ethnocentrism and cultural relativism?

Components of Culture
What are the major components of culture?

MATERIAL CULTURE
Of what does material culture consist?

NORMATIVE CULTURE
What is the role of normative culture?

COGNITIVE CULTURE
What is the basic feature of cognitive culture?

LANGUAGE AND CULTURE
How is language related to culture?

The Symbolic Nature of Culture
What does it mean to say that culture is symbolic?

SIGNS, SYMBOLS, AND CULTURE
What are signs and symbols? What is their role in a society's culture?

Culture and Adaptation
What is the role of culture in adaptation?

HUMAN EVOLUTION: BIOLOGICAL AND CULTURAL
What is the relationship between human biological and cultural evolution?

CULTURE AS AN ADAPTIVE MECHANISM
How does culture function as an adaptive mechanism?

MECHANISMS OF CULTURAL CHANGE
What are the major mechanisms of cultural change?

CULTURAL LAG
What does it mean to experience cultural lag?

Animals and Culture
Do animals have culture?

Subcultures
How do subcultures arise?

TYPES OF SUBCULTURES
What are the major types of subcultures?

Ethnic Subcultures
Where have ethnic subcultures come from?

Occupational Subcultures
Why do occupational subcultures arise?

Religious Subcultures
What is the basis for religious subcultures?

Political Subcultures
What groups are likely to be political subcultures?

Geographical Subcultures
Why do geographical subcultures arise?

Social Class Subcultures
What is the basis for social class subcultures?

Deviant Subcultures
How are deviant subcultures defined?

Universals of Culture
What determines the universals of culture?

THE DIVISION OF LABOR
What does it mean to have a division of labor?

THE INCEST TABOO, MARRIAGE, AND THE FAMILY
Why do the incest taboo, marriage, and the family exist?

RITES OF PASSAGE
What is the role of rites of passage?

IDEOLOGY
What is the primary purpose of an ideology?

Culture and Individual Choice
How does culture affect individual choice?

LEARNING OBJECTIVES

After studying this chapter you should be able to:

■ *Understand how culture makes possible the variation in human societies.*

Why don't all human societies have the exact same culture?
Compose an answer to this question by addressing each of the following features of culture:

Culture is symbolic (that is, it is composed of symbols).

Culture is acquired, not inborn.

\

Culture is adaptive (that is, it is a product of adaptation).

Culture is shared.

■ *Distinguish between ethnocentrism and cultural relativism, and understand why social science must be based upon the latter.*

Your text recounts Napoleon Chagnon's and Kenneth Good's experiences with the Yanomamö. Reflect upon your own encounters with other cultures or subcultures, whether through actual experience or through your reading (including works of fiction). Chose one of those cultural encounters and do the following exercise.

Describe this culture in ethnocentric terms:

Describe this culture from the point of view of cultural relativism:

Which description is more likely to lead to an objective, scientific description of this group's cultural practices? Why?

◼ *Identify examples of material and nonmaterial culture, and understand the role each plays in everyday life.*

Identify three objects of material culture and explain how each is symbolic.

Object #1:

How is it symbolic?

Object #2:

How is it symbolic?

Object #3:

How is it symbolic?

Identify and give an example of each of the following types of norms.

1. A folkway:

   Why can this be described as a folkway?

2. One of the mores:

   What makes this one of the mores?

3. A taboo:

   Why does this qualify as a taboo?

From your own life experience, choose an ideal norm (one *not* mentioned in the text) and contrast it with the real norm.

Ideal norm:

Real norm:

Why do you think this difference exists?

List three dominant values in American culture and explain why they qualify as values.

Value #1:

Why is this a value?

Value #2:

Why is this a valve?

Value #3:

Why is this a value?

■ *Understand the way language shapes our perception and classification of objects in the world and situations we encounter.*

The following is a partial list of synonyms for the word work. In each each, briefly comment on what the word connotes or means to you and how it shapes your perception of work.

occupation:

job:

trade:

profession:

craft:

vocation:

◾ *Understand the role of culture in enabling humans to adapt to their environment.*

Los Angeles and Phoenix are among the Sunbelt metropolises that have experienced explosive growth in the last four decades, in spite of some daunting barriers: lack of a large volume of fresh water in the immediate vicinity, great distance from other population centers, surrounded by natural barriers such as desert and mountains, uncomfortably hot summer temperatures. Choose two features from the following list and explain or speculate upon their role in enabling humans to adapt to these environments: air conditioning, water transport systems, freeway systems, commercial airline service, increased leisure time.

Feature #1:

Explanation:

Feature #2:

Explanation:

◾ *Explain the roles of innovation and diffusion in the process of cultural change.*

The telephone is an American innovation. Suggest two ways in which it has impacted American culture.

Impact #1:

Impact #2:

A fall harvest festival has always been a feature of agricultural societies. How has this celebration undergone reformulation as Thanksgiving in modern American culture?

■ *Identify instances of cultural lag in contemporary American society.*

Modern electronic technology has made it technically possible to have a "cashless" economy—to eliminate the use of cash money altogether. Yet we have not done so. Identify two cultural reasons why we haven't yet converted—and may never convert—to this technology.

Reason #1:

Reason #2:

■ *Discuss contrasting arguments about whether or not animals have culture.*

Language and the production of tools have been identified as hallmarks of culture. List arguments that support the existence of language and food production among nonhuman animals and arguments that oppose the existence of such capabilities.

	Supporting Arguments	**Opposing Arguments**
Language:		
Production of tools:		

■ *List and explain examples of various subcultures.*

List four different subcultures in which you participate and explain why each one qualifies as a subculture.

Subculture #1:

Explanation:

Subculture #2:

Explanation:

Subculture #3:

Explanation:

Subculture #4:

Explanation:

■ *Describe cultural universals.*

Explain the function of each of the following and explain why each one qualifies as a cultural universal.

Division of labor:

The incest taboo, marriage, and the family:

Rites of passage:

Ideology:

■ *Discuss the relationship between cultural influences on human behavior and individual choice.*

Discuss the meaning and rationale for the following statement from your text: "A society that sets out to meet all personal needs is doomed to failure."

KEY CONCEPTS

■ *Match each concept with its definition, illustration, or explication below.*

a. ideal norms
b. reformulation
c. language
d. innovation
e. cultural relativism
f. signs
g. cognitive culture
h. generalized adaptability
i. cultural lag
j. real norms
k. instinct
l. adaptation
m. subculture
n. environmental determinism
o. ideology
p. cultural universals

q. selectivity
r. mores
s. division of labor
t. norms
u. culture shock
v. rites of passage
w. folkways
x. symbols
y. Sapir-Whorf hypothesis
z. ethnocentrism
aa. material culture
bb. values
cc. specialization
dd. incest taboo
ee. culture
ff. diffusion

_____ 1. all that humans learn to do, to use, to produce, to know, and to believe in the social groups to which they belong.

_____ 2. a genetically determined, inherited behavior pattern.

_____ 3. the difficulty people have when encountering a culture substantially different from their own.

_____ 4. making judgments about other cultures based on the customs and values of one's own culture.

_____ 5. the recognition that cultures must be studied and understood on their own terms before valid comparisons can be made.

_____ 6. everything made by humans.

_____ 7. rules of behavior that are agreed upon and shared within a culture.

_____ 8. strongly held rules of behavior that usually have a moral connotation and are based on the central values of the cultures.

_____ 9. rules of behavior that permit a wide degree of individual interpretation.

_____10. expectations of what people should do under perfect conditions.

_____11. rules of behavior expressed with qualifications and allowances for practical circumstances.

_____12. a component of culture consisting of beliefs, knowledge, and values.

_____13. a culture's notions of what is good and bad, desirable and undesirable.

_____14. communication based upon symbols.

_____15. a process by which some aspects of the world are viewed as important while others are virtually neglected.

_____16. the view that the language people use determines their perception of reality.

_____17. objects that represent other things because they share some important quality with them.

_____18. arbitrary representations that need not share any qualities with whatever they represent.

_____19. the belief that the natural setting dictates cultural patterns.

_____20. the process by which humans adjust to changes in their environment.

_____21. the process of developing ways of doing things that work extremely well in a particular environment or set of circumstances.

_____22. the process of developing more complicated yet more flexible ways of doing things.

_____23. the movement of culture traits from one culture to another.

_____24. the process of inventing or discovering new cultural items.

_____25. the modification of a cultural trait so that it better fits in its new context.

_____26. the phenomenon where one part of the culture changes more rapidly than other parts.

_____27. the distinctive lifestyles, values, norms, and beliefs of certain segments of a larger population.

_____28. models or patterns that have developed in all cultures to resolve basic problems.

_____29. the ways in which human societies apportion basic tasks.

_____30. the prohibition of sexual relations between family members.

_____31. standardized rituals marking major life transitions.

_____32. a set of strongly held beliefs and values.

CRITICAL THINKING/APPLICATION QUESTIONS

1. Suppose that you were asked to accompany the president of the United States abroad to negotiate an important treaty with foreign leaders. What categories of things would you tell the president to be aware of in order to avoid ethnocentrism?
2. The prairies and plains of the western part of the United States are often referred to as "wide open spaces." Reflect upon the different meaning of this phrase to the Plains Indians and to white European settlers. Is there an ethnocentric bias built into the concept?
3. Locate a short passage of text written in a foreign language in which you are not fluent (assembly and/or operating instructions for many toys, appliances, and electronic items are written in multiple languages these days; otherwise get a foreign-language magazine from the library) and an English/foreign language dictionary (that is, English/Spanish, English/French, English/German, and so on). Translate a paragraph of the foreign language word-for-word, using the dictionary. What is the result like? Does it seem stilted? Easily misunderstood? Unintelligible? What does this tell you about the nature of language? About the difficulty of cross-cultural communication?
4. The Indianapolis 500, a famous auto race held on the weekend of Memorial Day, is the largest single event in sports. In addition to the race itself, there are time trials and qualification runs, which altogether constitute nearly a month of activities. In what ways can the concepts of subculture and normative culture be used to explain this race and its associated activities?

SUGGESTED READINGS

THE CONCEPT OF CULTURE

Colin M. Turnbull, *The Forest People: A Study of the Pygmies of the Congo* (New York: Simon & Schuster, 1962). A classic, highly-readable ethnography of the BaMbuti people of the central African rainforest. A good way to get inside another culture and see it from their point of view.

Robert N. Bellah, Richard Madsen, William M. Sullivan, Ann Swidler, and Steven Tipton, *Habits of the Heart: Individualism and Commitment in American Life* (New York: Harper & Row, 1986). An exploration of American values, the work portrays the tension between individual achievement and a sense of community. The argument is illustrated throughout with excerpts from the many personal interviews the authors conducted.

CULTURE AND ADAPTATION

Marvin Harris, *Cows, Pigs, Wars, and Witches: The Riddles of Culture* (New York: Vintage, 1974). A classic work in which Harris demonstrates that seemingly bizarre practices by other cultures have rational and identifiable roots in economic necessity. Highly readable.

SUBCULTURES

Elliot Liebow, *Tally's Corner* (Boston: Little Brown, 1967). A pioneering look at "idle" African-American streetcorner men in Washington, D.C.

William M. Kephart, *Extraordinary Groups: The Sociology of Unconventional Lifestyles,* 2nd ed. (New York: St. Martin's, 1982). A sociological look at non-mainstream American cultures: the Old Order Amish, the Shakers, the Father Divine movement, the Oneida Community, and so on.

ANSWER KEY

KEY CONCEPTS

1. ee	10. a	19. n	28. p
2. k	11. j	20. l	29. s
3. u	12. g	21. cc	30. dd
4. z	13. bb	22. h	31. v
5. e	14. c	23. ff	32. o
6. aa	15. q	24. d	
7. t	16. y	25. b	
8. r	17. f	26. i	
9. w	18. x	27. m	

CHAPTER 4 ■ *Socialization and Development*

CHAPTER SUMMARY

Becoming a Person: Biology and Culture

Human beings take longer to mature than any other animal species. During their long period of dependency children experience socialization—a process of social interaction that teaches them the intellectual, physical, and social skills and the cultural knowledge needed to function as a member of society. In the course of this process each child acquires a personality, or their own unique patterns of behavior and ways of thinking.

Each individual's unique personality is a result of the interplay of his or her inherited genetic endowment and his or her environment. The idea that human behavior is solely or largely determined by instincts—biologically inherited patterns of complex behavior—was undermined by Ivan Pavlov's study of conditioning, in which he showed that so-called instinctual behavior could be molded through a series of repeated experiences linking a desired reaction with a particular object or event. On the other hand, the emerging discipline of sociobiology uses biological principles to explain the behavior of all social beings, both animal and human. In the end, humans and human behavior must be seen as products of both nature (genes) and nurture (the socialization experience).

Studies of extreme childhood deprivation have shown that none of the behavior we think of as typically human arises spontaneously. Human infants must develop social attachments to, and experience meaningful interaction with, other humans in order to develop into fully functioning social beings.

The Concept of Self

Every individual comes to possess a social identity by occupying culturally and socially defined positions. In addition, each individual acquires a changing yet enduring personal identity called the self, which develops when the individual becomes aware of his or her feelings, thoughts, and behaviors as distinct from those of other people. The development of the self is a complex process that has at least three dimensions: cognitive development, moral development, and gender identity.

Jean Piaget studied the development of intelligence in children. He found that they progress through a series of predictable stages on their way to logical thought. The process moves from concrete objects to symbols, to concepts, to abstract logic. Lawrence Kohlberg suggested that moral development moves through stages, too: from fear of individual punishment, to concern with social disapproval, to an internalized personal moral code. One of the most important elements of the sense of self is one's gender identity, which is mostly a matter of cultural definition.

Theories of Development

Charles Horton Cooley held that the self develops through the process of symbolically-interpreted interaction with others. We imagine how our behavior appears to other people, how others judge these behaviors, and then we have some sort of self-reaction to the judgments of others. He named this view of the self *the looking-glass self* because it proposes that other people act as mirrors for us.

George Herbert Mead viewed the self as composed of two parts: the "I" which is the active, spontaneous, initiative-taking portion, and the "me" which is made up of those things learned through the socialization process. Mead labelled as *significant others* those people who are most important to an individual's development. However, as individuals are socialized, they become aware of the viewpoints of *generalized others*, that is the attitudes, values, and norms of a general community of people. Mead suggested that the self develops in three stages: the preparatory stage, in which the child imitates roles; the play stage, in which the child has acquired language and begins to formulate role expectations; and the game stage, in which the child learns to flexibly apply general rules and role expectations.

Sigmund Freud developed psychoanalytic theory, which holds that the human mind and human behavior is shaped by unconscious impulses and resistance to them. In Freud's view, the self is composed of three parts: the *id*, which is the repository of inherited biological instincts, including sex and aggression, and which operates entirely on the pleasure principle; the *superego*, which is the internal censor or conscience created by the socialization process, and which attempts to control and channel the id; and the *ego*, which is the part of the self that acts in the world as it tries to mediate the conflict between the id and the superego and find socially acceptable ways for the id's drives to be expressed.

Erik Erikson built on Freud's theory but added that self development is a lifelong process. He also paid greater attention to the social and cultural forces operating on the self. Daniel Levinson argued that there are predictable age-related crises and developmental periods in the adult life cycle.

Early Socialization in American Society

The family is the most important socializing influence in early childhood development. The location of any given family within the social structure has much to do with what its dominant members consider important. But whatever the family's values, norms, ideals, and standards, they are initially accepted uncritically by the child. As the child grows older and moves out into society, peer groups, and the mass media become important agents of socialization.

Adult Socialization

Primary socialization comes to an end when individuals reach adulthood. By this time they should have (1) learned a language; (2) accepted the basic norms and values of the culture; (3) developed the ability to pattern their behavior in terms of these norms and values; and (4) assumed a culturally appropriate social identity. Although socialization continues throughout one's life, adult socialization differs from primary socialization in that adults are much more aware of the processes through which they are socialized and they often have more control over the process.

One important form of adult socialization is *resocialization*, which involves exposure to ideas or values that conflict with what was learned in childhood. Often this occurs in a *total institution*, such as a prison or mental hospital, where participants are physically, socially, and psychologically isolated from the outside world. Common events in adults socialization that represent transitions and precipitate role redefinitions include marriage, parenthood, work, and aging.

CHAPTER OUTLINE

Becoming a Person: Biology and Culture
What is the relationship between biology and culture in the process of human development?

NATURE VERSUS NURTURE: A FALSE DEBATE
Why is the issue of nature versus nurture a false debate?

Sociobiology
What is the main characteristic of sociobiology?

DEPRIVATION AND DEVELOPMENT
How does deprivation affect development?

Extreme Childhood Deprivation
How serious is extreme childhood deprivation?

Infants in Institutions
What developmental problems are faced by infants in institutions?

The Concept of Self
What do sociologists mean by the concept of self?

DIMENSIONS OF HUMAN DEVELOPMENT
What are the most important dimensions of human development?

Cognitive Development
What happens during cognitive development?

Moral Development
What is moral development?

Gender Identity
    How important is gender identity?

Theories of Development

    How do theories of development differ?

CHARLES HORTON COOLEY (1864–1929)
    What were Cooley's main ideas?

GEORGE HERBERT MEAD (1863–1931)
    What are the most important features of Mead's theory of development?

SIGMUND FREUD (1856–1939)
    What were Freud's main contributions?

ERIK H. ERIKSON (1902–   )
    What is Erikson's theory of development?

DANIEL LEVINSON (1920–   )
    What is unique about Levinson's theory of development?

Early Socialization in American Society
    What are the important characteristics of early socialization in American society?

THE FAMILY
    What is the role of the family in early socialization?

THE SCHOOL
    How important is the school in early socialization?

PEER GROUPS
    What are peer groups and how do they affect early socialization?

THE MASS MEDIA
    What role does the mass media play in early socialization?

Adult Socialization
    How does adult socialization differ from childhood socialization?

MARRIAGE AND RESPONSIBILITY
    What changes does the marriage and responsibility stage bring about?

PARENTHOOD
    What kind of socialization occurs regarding parenthood?

CAREER DEVELOPMENT: VOCATION AND IDENTITY
    What are the significant aspects of career development? How is vocation related to identity?

AGING AND SOCIETY
    How is the aging of individuals related to society?

LEARNING OBJECTIVES

After studying this chapter you should be able to:

■ *Discuss the relative contribution of biological inheritance and socialization in the formation of personality.*

List the aspects of your personality that are due to your biological inheritance:

List the aspects of your personality that are due to your socialization:

Discuss which of these factors have made the biggest contribution, and why.

■ *Evaluate sociobiology as an explanation for human behavior.*

Mr. and Mrs. X spend nearly all of their savings as well as borrow against their life insurance and retirement in order to send their children to college.

How would a sociobiologist like Edward O. Wilson explain this behavior?

How would a critic of sociobiology like Stephen Jay Gould explain this behavior?

In your opinion, which explanation is the better one, and why?

■ *Describe the effects of extreme social deprivation during early childhood.*

You are a caseworker assigned to work with a 10-year-old child who has spent her entire childhood locked in a dark closet with minimal human contact. Informed by your sociological understanding, what are four major deficits you would expect to find in this child?

1.

2.

3.

4.

■ *Distinguish between social identity and the self.*

As quickly as you can, write 20 short answers to the question "Who Am I?"

1.

2.

3.

4.

5.

6.

7.

8.

9.

10.

11.

12.

13.

14.

15.

16.

17.

18.

19.

20.

Evalutate each of these responses, coding it in the left margin as a status or position you occupy in society (S), a trait that is part of your biological inheritance (T), or a personality characteristic that is a unique product of your own socialization and social experience (P).   .

Into which category do the largest number of responses fall?

How much of how you see yourself is a product of your social location and how others identify you?

How much of your personal identity is determined by your own self-knowledge?

■ *List and explain the stages of cognitive and moral development.*

Piaget's stages of cognitive development:

Stage	Most Important Feature
1.	
2.	
3.	
4.	

Kohlberg's stages of moral development:

Stage	Most Important Feature

1.

2.

3.

4.

5.

■ *Explain the basic features of the symbolic interactionist view of the self as developed by Cooley and Mead.*

Describe the components of the looking-glass self:

1.

2.

3.

Define Mead's concepts of significant others and generalized others, and state one important implication of the difference in the concepts.

Significant others:

Generalized others:

Implication of the difference:

Mead's stages of self development:

      Stage   **Most Important Feature**

1.

2.

3.

■ *Describe Freud's psychoanalytic view of the self.*

Explain the two basic hypotheses on which psychoanalytic theory rests:

1.

2.

List the parts of the self, according to Freud:

      Component   **Most Important Feature**

1.

2.

3.

■ *Describe and critique Erikson's and Levinson's stage models of lifelong socialization.*

Erikson's stages of human development:

Age	Dilemma to be Resolved	Major Hazards
birth to 1 yr.		
1–4 yrs.		

4–5 yrs.

6–12 yrs.

adolescence

young adulthood

30–50 yrs.

old age

Levinson's stages of adult development:

Age	Stage	Major Feature
18–22 yrs.		
22–28 yrs.		
28–32 yrs.		
33–40 yrs.		
38–42 yrs.		
mid-40s		

List and briefly discuss three criticisms of stage theories:

1.

2.

3.

➡ ■ *Explain the role of the family, schools, peer groups, and the mass media in childhood socialization.*

Discuss two major ways that each of the following impacts childhood socialization: *VALUES, NORMS,*
The family: *specific statuses*
etc. ROLES

1.

2.

The school:

1.

2.

Peer groups:

1.

2.

The mass media:

1.

2.

■ *Explain two major ways in which adult socialization differs from primary socialization.*

Discuss two major ways in which adult socialization differs from primary socialization.

Difference #1:

One important implication of this difference:

Difference #2:

One important implication of this difference:

■ *Explain resocialization and describe the types of resocialization required by marriage, parenthood, career development, and old age.*

According to Goffman, why are total institutions so effective in resocializing individuals?

1.

2.

3.

4.

5.

Explain one important type of resocialization required by each of these common events in adult socialization.

Marriage:

Parenthood:

Career development:

Old age:

KEY CONCEPTS

■ *Match each concept with its definition, illustration, or explication below.*

a. primary socialization
b. significant others
c. operational stage
d. looking-glass self
e. play stage
f. affiliation
g. conditioning
h. sensorimotor stage
i. moral order
j. ego
k. personality
l. sociobiology
m. game stage
n. the "I"
o. formal logical stage
p. adult socialization
q. preoperational stage
r. the unconscious

s. self
t. instincts
u. superego
v. mass media
w. the "me"
x. resocialization
y. social identity
z. genes
aa. preparatory stage
bb. generalized others
cc. nurture
dd. total institution
ee. social attachments
ff. peers
gg. id
hh. psychoanalytic theory
ii. socialization

_____ 1. the process of social interaction that teaches the child the intellectual, physical, and social skills needed to function as a member of society.

_____ 2. the patterns of behavior and ways of thinking and feeling that are distinctive for each individual.

_____ 3. inherited units of biological material.

_____ 4. biologically inherited patterns of complex behavior.

_____ 5. the molding of behavior through a series of repeated experiences linking a desired reaction with a particular object or event.

_____ 6. the discipline that uses biological principles to explain the behavior of social beings.

_____ 7. the entire socialization experience.

_____ 8. having feelings for others and seeing evidence that others care for us.

_____ 9. meaningful interaction with others.

_____10. the total of all the statuses that define an individual.

_____11. one's changing yet enduring personal identity.

_____12. the shared view of right and wrong that exists in a society.

_____13. when an infant relies on touch and the manipulation of objects for information about the world.

_____14. when a child learns that words can be symbols for objects.

_____15. when a child learns to think with some logic and can understand and work with numbers, volume, shapes, and spatial relationships.

_____16. when a child becomes capable of abstract, logical thought and can anticipate possible consequences of their acts and decisions.

_____17. the notion that other people mirror back to us important aspects of our sense of self.

_____18. in Mead's view, the portion of the self that is made up of everything learned through the socialization process.

_____19. in Mead's view, the portion of the self that wishes to be active and spontaneous.

_____20. the viewpoints, attitudes, and expectations of society as a whole or an important subculture within it.

_____21. individuals who are important to our development.

_____22. in Mead's view, the point at which a child learns role expectations by imitating the behavior of others.

_____23. in Mead's view, the point at which a child formulates relatively simple role expectations.

_____24. in Mead's view, the point at which a child learns the expectations, positions, and rules of society at large.

_____25. the view that the human mind and human behavior are shaped by unconscious impulses and resistance to or repression of them.

_____26. in Freudian theory, the repository of thoughts and feelings that are out of our awareness.

_____27. in Freudian theory, the part of the self that looks for ways to adjust to social realities.

_____28. in Freudian theory, the part of the self that consists of drives and instincts and that operates on the pleasure principle.

_____29. in Freudian theory, the part of the self that is society's norms and values as learned primarily from our parents.

_____30. individuals who are social equals.

_____31. impersonal means of transmitting information to great numbers of people in a short period of time.

_____32. the process by which adults learn new statuses and roles.

_____33. the process of mastering the basic information and skills required of members of a society.

_____34. environments in which the participants are physically and socially isolated from the outside world.

_____35. a process of exposure to ideas or values that in one way or another conflict with what was learned in childhood.

KEY THINKERS/RESEARCHERS

■ *Match each thinker with their main idea or contribution.*

a. Charles Horton Cooley
b. Sigmund Freud
c. Lawrence Kohlberg
d. Harry F. Harlow
e. Edward O. Wilson
f. Erik Erikson

g. Stephen Jay Gould
h. Daniel Levinson
i. George Herbert Mead
j. Ivan Pavlov
k. Jean Piaget

_____ 1. a major advocate of sociobiology as an explanation of human behavior.

_____ 2. his experiments with rhesus monkeys dramatically illustrated the harmful effects of social deprivation during infancy.

_____ 3. a symbolic interactionist who conceived of the development of the self as a three-stage process in which other people mirror back to us important qualities of the self.

_____ 4. his experiments demonstrated that so-called instinctual behavior could be molded through a series of repeated experiences linking a desired reaction with a particular object or event.

_____ 5. a critic of sociobiology, he argues for cultural determinism of human behavior.

_____ 6. he discovered that children move through a series of predictable stages on their way to developing logical thought.

_____ 7. argued that the self develops in interaction with significant others, from whom we learn increasingly sophisticated role expectations.

_____ 8. suggested a view of lifelong human development in which individuals move through eight stages of crises in which different stresses and conflicts must be resolved.

_____ 9. suggested that moral thinking progresses through five or six distinct stages.

_____10. pioneered the development of psychoanalytic theory, including the view that most human behavior is determined by unconscious motivations.

_____11. developed a stage model of age-related developmental periods in the adult life cycle.

CRITICAL THINKING/APPLICATION QUESTIONS

1. Reflect upon behaviors that you observe in your college classroom. Which of these are conditioned responses? Are there ways in which students condition the behavior of their professors?

2. Reflect upon the fact that you think about yourself differently when attending a family reunion than when "hanging out" with your best friends. How can this phenomenon be explained by Cooley's concept of the looking-glass self?

3. The box, "Are Geniuses Born or Created?," in this chapter describes a school in Philadelphia in which young children's development is highly accelerated. Reflect on the potential problems with this approach in light of the tensions present

in the first four stages of human development according to Erik Erikson (Table 4.1).

4. Select a two-hour block of one of the types of television shows that is most often watched by children: evening situation comedies, Saturday morning cartoons, or music videos. Analyze the messages conveyed in these shows. How do you think these messages influence the personality development of young children?

5. List all the ways that you have been resocialized in the process of becoming a college student. Which of these produced the greatest conflicts with what you learned in childhood socialization? Why?

SUGGESTED READINGS

BECOMING A PERSON: BIOLOGY AND CULTURE

Arthur L. Caplan, ed., _The Sociobiology Debate_ (New York: Harper & Row, 1978). A comprehensive look at the history and context of the emerging discipline of sociobiology, along with statements by both the leading contemporary advocates and critics.

Lucien Malson, _Wolf Children and the Problem of Human Nature_ (New York: Monthly Review Press, 1972). A thorough discussion of human

nature in light of evidence about so-called wolf children. Includes a listing of all recorded cases of feral children and the complete diary of Jean-Marc-Gaspard Itard detailing his experiences with Victor, the Wild Boy of Aveyron.

THE CONCEPT OF SELF

Jean Piaget, _The Construction of Reality in the Child_ (London: Routledge & Kegan Paul, 1950). An exposition of Piaget's symbolic interactionist theories of child development.

Carol Gilligan, *In a Different Voice: Psychological Theory and Women's Development* (Cambridge, MA: Harvard University Press, 1982). Gilligan was a teaching assistant for Lawrence Kohlberg who became critical of the male bias in his concept of moral development. This book presents an alternative view.

THEORIES OF DEVELOPMENT

William L. Ewens, *Becoming Free: The Struggle for Human Development* (Wilmington, DE: Scholarly Resources, 1984). A thought-provoking look at human nature, the characteristics of human development, and the conditions necessary for human growth.

ANSWER KEY

KEY CONCEPTS

1. ii
2. k
3. z
4. t
5. g
6. l
7. cc
8. ee
9. f
10. y
11. s
12. i
13. h
14. q
15. c
16. o
17. d
18. w
19. n
20. bb
21. b
22. aa
23. e
24. m
25. hh
26. r
27. j
28. gg
29. u
30. ff
31. v
32. p
33. a
34. dd
35. x

KEY THINKERS/ RESEARCHERS

1. e
2. d
3. a
4. j
5. g
6. k
7. i
8. f
9. c
10. b
11. h

CHAPTER SUMMARY

Understanding Social Interaction

Because humans are symbolic creatures, everything we do (or do not do) conveys a message to others. Whether we intend it or not, other people take account of our behavior. It is thus impossible *not* to interact with others. Social interaction has no opposite.

A social interaction involves two or more people taking each other into account; it is the interplay between the actions of individuals. The context of social interaction is defined by its physical location, its social environment, and other activities happening before, during, and after it. When humans interact, their behavior is not random. What makes that behavior patterned and, for the most part, quite predictable, is the existence of norms: specific rules of behavior that are agreed upon and shared and which prescribe the limits of acceptable behavior. There are norms governing all aspects of human behavior, but they vary both within and across cultures.

Types of Social Interaction

One important type of interaction is nonverbal. Kinesics, the study of body movements, examines how nonverbal cues, whether spontaneous or deliberate, affect communication. Because there is such great cultural variation in how body movements are interpreted, opportunities for miscommunication between people from different cultures naturally abound.

When people do something for each other with the express purpose of receiving a reward or return they are involved in an exchange interaction. A cooperative interaction occurs when people act together to promote common interests or achieve shared goals. Sociologists have identified four types of cooperation. Spontaneous cooperation arises from the needs of a particular situation. Traditional cooperation is tied to custom and is passed from one generation to the next. Directed cooperation is a joint activity under the control of people in authority; it is planned in advance and requires leadership. In contractual cooperation people agree to cooperate in certain specified ways, with each person's obligations clearly spelled out.

In a conflict interaction, people struggle against one another for some commonly prized object or value. Conflicts arise when people or groups have incompatible values or when the rewards or resources available to a society or certain of its members are limited. Conflict always involves an attempt to gain or use power. Coercion is a special kind of conflict that occurs when one of the parties is much stronger than the other and can therefore impose its will on the weaker. While coercion rests on force or the threat of force, it usually operates more subtly. Competition is a form of conflict in which individuals or groups confine their conflict within agreed-upon rules.

Throughout their lives, people are involved in a variety of types of interactions, often in several types simultaneously. A given relationship, moreover, may span an entire range of interactions.

Elements of Social Interaction

People do not interact with each other as completely anonymous beings. They come together in the context of specific environments, with specific purposes, and with specific social characteristics. Among the most important of the latter are statuses and roles, which together help to define our social interactions and provide predictability.

Statuses are socially defined positions that people occupy in a group or society and in terms of which they interact with one another. Statuses exist independent of the specific people who occupy them. When one of a person's multiple statuses dominates the others in patterning that person's life, it is called a master status. Statuses that are conferred upon a person by birth or other factors not under individual control are called ascribed statuses. Achieved statuses are occupied as a result of the individual's actions.

Roles are the culturally defined rules for proper behavior that are associated with every status. A role is basically a collection of rights and obligations. A status may include a number of roles, which are collectively known as a role set. When a single role has conflicting demands attached to it, individuals experience role strain. Role conflict results when an individual is unable to enact the roles of one status without violating those of another status. The roles we play can have a profound influence on both our attitudes and our behavior.

The Nature of Groups

A social group consists of a number of people who

have a common identity, some feeling of unity, and certain common goals and shared norms. A social group differs from a social aggregate, which is made up of people temporarily in physical proximity to each other, but who share little else. Unlike a social aggregate, a social group does not cease to exist when its members are apart from one another. In general, all social groups have permanence beyond the meetings of members, means for identifying members, mechanisms for recruiting new members, goals or purposes, social statuses and roles, and means for controlling members' behavior.

Sociologists distinguish between primary groups, which involve intimacy, informality, and emotional investment in one another, and secondary groups, which have specific goals, formal organization, and much less intimacy. In order to function properly, all groups must define their boundaries, choose leaders, make decisions, set goals, assign tasks, and control members' behavior. A reference group is a group or social category that an individual uses to help define beliefs, attitudes, and values to guide behavior. Small groups actually meet together and contain few enough members so that all members know one another. The smallest possible group contains only two members; it is called a dyad. Adding a third member transforms the dyad into a triad and changes group dynamics significantly. Once a group has more than five to seven members, spontaneous conversation becomes difficult and the group either splits into subgroups or adopts a formal means of controlling communication.

Large Groups: Associations

Associations are purposefully created special-interest groups that have clearly defined goals and official ways of doing things. The work that an association must accomplish is broken down into manageable tasks that are assigned to specific individuals. The resulting system of planned and clearly defined statuses and role relationships is called formal organizational structure. Associations never operate entirely according to their stated rules and procedures, however; every association also has an informal structure consisting of networks of people who help one another by bending rules and taking procedural shortcuts.

Bureaucracy

A modern form of large association is bureaucracy, which is a formal, rationally organized social structure with clearly defined patterns of activity that are functionally related to the purposes of the organization. In the ideal type of bureaucracy described by Max Weber there is a clear-cut division of labor, a hierarchical delegation of power and responsibility, written rules and regulations, impartial treatment of individuals, employment based on technical qualifications, and a distinction between public and private spheres.

Robert Michels concluded that the formal organization of bureaucracies inevitably leads to oligarchy, or the situation in which democratic organizations come to be dominated by a small self-serving elite. He termed this the Iron Law of Oligarchy. Other problems with bureaucracy include depersonalization, alienation, and ritualism, or overconformity to the rules.

Institutions and Social Organization

Social institutions consist of the ordered social relationships that grow out of the values, norms, statuses, and roles that organize those activities that fulfill society's fundamental needs. Social organization consists of the relatively stable pattern of social relationship among individuals and groups in society.

CHAPTER OUTLINE

Understanding Social Interaction
What are the keys to understanding social interaction?

CONTEXTS
Why are contexts important to understanding social interaction?

NORMS
How do norms shape social interaction?

Types of Social Interaction
What are the major types of social interaction?

NONVERBAL BEHAVIOR
How is nonverbal behavior a type of interaction?

EXCHANGE
What is exchange interaction about?

COOPERATION
How is cooperation a type of interaction?

CONFLICT
What is conflict social interaction like?

COMPETITION
What type of social interaction is competition?

Elements of Social Interaction
What are the basic elements of social interaction?

STATUSES
How are statuses important in interaction?

ROLES
How do roles affect social interaction?

ROLE SETS
How are role sets determined?

ROLE STRAIN
How does role strain come about?

ROLE CONFLICT
What produces role conflict?

ROLE PLAYING
What is the significance of role playing?

The Nature of Groups
What is important to know about the nature of groups?

PRIMARY AND SECONDARY GROUPS
What is the difference between primary and secondary groups?

CHARACTERISTICS OF GROUPS
What are the important characteristics of groups?

Defining Boundaries
How do groups go about defining boundaries?

Choosing Leaders
What are the implications of choosing different leaders?

Making Decisions
What different methods can the group use in making decisions?

Setting Goals
How does a group go about setting goals?

Assigning Tasks
What is important about assigning tasks?

Controlling Members' Behavior
Why should a group be concerned about controlling members' behavior?

REFERENCE GROUPS
What is the role of reference groups?

Small Groups
What are the important characteristics of small groups?

Large Groups: Associations
What are the important characteristics of large groups or associations?

THE FORMAL STRUCTURE
What is the formal structure of an organization?

THE INFORMAL STRUCTURE
What is the significance of an informal structure?

Bureaucracy
What is bureaucracy all about?

WEBER'S MODEL OF BUREAUCRACY
What are the major components of Weber's model of bureaucracy?

BUREAUCRACY TODAY: THE REALITY
What is different about the reality of bureaucracy today?

THE IRON LAW OF OLIGARCHY
What is the significance of the Iron Law of Oligarchy?

Institutions and Social Organization
Why are institutions and social organization important?

SOCIAL INSTITUTIONS
What is the function of social institutions in society?

SOCIAL ORGANIZATION
How is social organization important in society?

LEARNING OBJECTIVES

After studying this chapter you should be able to:

■ *Understand the pervasiveness of social interaction among humans.*

Go to a public place (for example, a shopping mall, downtown streetcorner, student union building) and closely observe a group of people for a brief period of time. Try to interpret their behavior using

Max Weber's method of *verstehen*, or sympathetic understanding. Write down all of the messages these people are conveying, both verbally and nonverbally.

Your interpretation of the group's behavior:

Verbal messages:

Nonverbal messages:

How is what you see and interpret (that is, the way that you take account of these other people) affected by your own social characteristics?

■ *Explain how contexts and norms influence social interaction.*

Think about the very first day of class in this course. How was the interaction that took place influenced by:

The physical setting?

The social environment?

What happened right before, during, and after the class?

What are some of the norms that governed the behavior of the students and the instructor during that first class?

■ *Describe and illustrate major types of social interaction.*

Give two examples from your own life of each of the major types of social interaction and explain why each example illustrates the concept.

Type of social interaction

Nonverbal behavior:

1.

2.

Exchange:

1.

2.

Cooperation:

1.

2.

Conflict:

1.

2.

Competition:

1.

2.

➤■ *Describe and illustate the concepts of status and role.*

List all the statuses you occupy at this point in your life.

Circle your current master status on the list above. What makes it your master status?

Code each of the statuses in your list above according to whether it is an ascribed (s) or an achieved (a) status. Into which category do the majority of your statuses fall?

Why do you think this is the case?

Choose one status from your list above and enumerate all the roles attached to it. *(all 3)*
Selected status:
Roles attached to it:

Choose one role from the list immediately above and describe the conflicting demands it generates.
Selected role:
Role strain:

Choose two statuses from your earlier list and describe the conflicting sets of role expectations.
Selected statuses:
Role conflict:

■ *Distinguish between a social group and a social aggregate.*

Explain why each of the following sets of people at the ballpark is a social group or a social aggregate.

All the fans seated in Section 28:

All the members of one of the teams:

A family sitting behind home plate:

The umpires:

Everyone listening to the game on the radio:

■ *Distinguish between primary and secondary groups.*

List three primary and three secondary groups in which you participate and explain the reasons for your classification of each.

Primary group #1:

Primary group #2:

Primary group #3:

Secondary group #1:

Secondary group #2:

Secondary group #3:

■ *Discuss the major characteristics of groups.*

Frequently students enrolled in a particular college class will decide to form a group to study together. Perhaps you are now or have been part of such a group. If not, imagine you are. Explain how the group handles each of the following tasks.

Defining boundaries (Who will be in the group? Will you recruit new members?).

Choosing leaders (What type of instrumental leadership does the group need? What does the expressive leader need to do?).

Making decisions (How will the group make decisions?).

Setting goals (What will be the group's goals? How specific do these goals need to be?).

Assigning tasks (What kinds of things will the group actually do? Will different members perform different tasks?).

Controlling member behavior (How will you deal with members whose behavior does not conform to group norms?).

■ *Discuss the role of reference groups.*

Choose a reference group to which you currently compare yourself. Explain how you use this group to help define your own beliefs, attitudes, values, or to guide your behavior.

■ *Explain how variations in the size of groups affect what goes on within them.*

Assume a situation in which you and one other friend are deciding what movie to go see or rent. How are you likely to make this decision—that is, what are the dynamics of the decision-making process?

Now assume a third friend joins you. How is the decision-making process altered?

Suppose you are in a group of eight people trying to make the same decision. What are the likely group dynamics?

■ *Distinguish between the formal and informal structure of associations and explain the importance of the latter.*

Choose an association with which you are familiar (a job, your high school, this college or university, an organization to which you belong, and so on and explain how knowledge of the informal structure allowed you to get something done you otherwise could not have done or could not have done as efficiently.

■ *List and explain the six defining characteristics of bureaucracy as enumerated by Max Weber.*

List each of Weber's characteristics of bureaucracy, illustrating each one with reference to this college or university.

1.

2.

3.

4.

5.

6.

■ *Explain Michels' concept of "The Iron Law of Oligarchy" and apply it to contemporary society.*

Despite the ideal of free democratic competition, the vast majority of all incumbent members of the United States Congress are reelected each time. To what extent is this an example of Michels' Iron Law of Oligarchy?

Describe a national political problem that you think can be explained by the phenomenon of oligarchy.

■ *Explain the importance of social institutions and social organization.*

Explain why health care can be defined as a social institution.

Discuss what are, in your opinion, two major features of social organization in contemporary U.S. society.

1.

2.

KEY CONCEPTS

■ *Match each concept with its definition, illustration, or explication below.*

a. master status
b. subgroup
c. informal structure
d. social aggregate
e. leader
f. social interaction
g. dyad
h. expressive leadership
i. cooperation
j. primary group
k. anticipatory socialization
l. role strain
m. statuses
n. exchange
o. bureaucracy
p. social group
q. social institutions
r. formal structure

s. coercion
t. secondary group
u. role set
v. norms
w. social organization
x. reference group
y. achieved status
z. role conflict
aa. ideal type
bb. association
cc. triad
dd. competition
ee. instrumental leadership
ff. oligarchy
gg. roles
hh. ascribed status
ii. ritualism
jj. conflict

____ **1.** two or more people taking each other into account.

____ **2.** specific rules of behavior that are agreed upon and shared which prescribe limits of acceptable behavior.

____ **3.** people doing something for each other with the express purpose of receiving a reward or return.

____ **4.** people acting together to promote common interests or achieve shared goals.

____ **5.** people struggling against one another for some commonly prized object or value.

____ **6.** a form of conflict in which one of the parties is much stronger than the other and can impose its will on the weaker party.

____ **7.** a form of conflict confined within agreed-upon rules.

____ **8.** socially defined positions that people occupy in a group or society and in terms of which they interact with one another.

____ **9.** one of the multiple statuses a person occupies that seems to dominate the others in patterning a person's life.

____**10.** statuses occupied as a result of an individual's actions.

____**11.** statuses conferred upon people by virtue of birth or other socially significant factors not controlled by their own actions and decisions.

____**12.** culturally defined rules for proper behavior that are associated with every status.

____**13.** all the roles attached to a single status.

____**14.** conflicting demands attached to the same role.

____**15.** an inability to enact the roles of one status without violating those of another status.

____**16.** a number of people who have a common identity, some feeling of unity, and certain common goals and shared norms.

____**17.** people temporarily in physical proximity to one another, but who share little else.

____**18.** a group that has little intimacy, has specific goals, is formally organized, and impersonal.

____**19.** a group in which members have an emotional investment in one another, who know one another intimately, and who interact as total individuals rather than through specialized roles.

____**20.** someone who occupies a central role or position of dominance and influence in a group.

____**21.** a type of leadership in which the leader actively proposes tasks and plans to guide the group toward achieving its goals.

____**22.** a type of leadership in which the leader works to keep relations among group members harmonious, and group morale high.

____**23.** a group or social category that an individual uses to help define beliefs, attitudes, and values to guide behavior.

____**24.** the process of orienting one's behavior and attitudes toward those of a group one plans to join.

____**25.** a group consisting of three members.

____**26.** the smallest possible group.

____**27.** a splinter group within the larger group.

____**28.** a purposefully created special-interest group that has clearly defined goals and official way of doing things.

____**29.** the planned, highly institutionalized, clearly defined statuses and role relationships existing within an association.

_____30. networks of people within an association who help one another by bending rules and taking procedural shortcuts.

_____31. a formal, rationally organized social structure with clearly defined patterns of activity in which, ideally, every series of actions is functionally related to the purposes of the organization.

_____32. an exaggerated model of reality used to illustrate a concept.

_____33. the domination of an organization by a small, self-serving, self-perpetuating group of people in positions of power and responsibility.

_____34. overconformity to rules.

_____35. the ordered social relationships that grow out of the values, norms, statuses, and roles that organize those activities that fulfill society's fundamental needs.

_____36. the relatively stable pattern of social relationships among individuals and groups in society.

KEY THINKERS/RESEARCHERS

■ *Match each thinker with their main idea or contribution.*

   a. Georg Simmel
   b. Max Weber
   c. Solomon Asch
   d. Edward T. Hall
   e. Robert Michels

_____1. one of the first sociologists to stress the importance of social interaction, he also developed a model of bureaucracy.

_____2. a pioneer in studying the context of social interaction.

_____3. conducted important research showing that a substantial proportion of individuals were willing to deny the evidence of their senses in order to conform to the group.

_____4. the first sociologist to emphasize the impact of the size of the group on the interaction process.

_____5. a student of bureaucracy, he developed the Iron Law of Oligarchy.

CRITICAL THINKING/APPLICATION QUESTIONS

1. What type of social interaction is secondary (high school) education? What type should it be? Why?

2. Suppose that students in your introductory sociology course were required to work in groups. Write a set of guidelines outlining how the groups should be organized, how they should function, and how they might try to avoid common problems encountered by people working in groups.

3. Examine or pay attention to recent coverage of the president of the United States. What kind of leader do Americans expect him to be? What kind of leadership does he actually demonstrate? To what extent can presidential actions be explained by the tension between instrumental and expressive leadership?

4. Develop a chart, similar to Figure 5.5 in this chapter, that locates your instructor within the college or university bureaucracy. (This may require a little bit of research on your part, either by interviewing key informants or obtaining official documents from the institution.) Reflect upon how the organization and delivery of your current sociology course is affected by this organizational structure. Interview your instructor to get his or her opinion, and compare notes.

SUGGESTED READINGS

UNDERSTANDING SOCIAL INTERACTION

Peter L. Berger and Thomas Luckmann, *The Social Construction of Reality* (Garden City, NY: Anchor Books, 1967). A classic treatise that argues that social reality only exists to the extent and in the fashion that it is created through social interaction.

William H. Whyte, *City: Rediscovering the Center* (New York: Doubleday, 1988). Fascinating study of how the physical layout of space in downtown areas structures social interaction.

TYPES OF SOCIAL INTERACTION

Edward T. Hall, *The Hidden Dimension* (New York: Doubleday, 1966). A survey of the way different cultures use space and how this affects their patterns of interaction and communication.

ELEMENTS OF SOCIAL INTERACTION

Erving Goffman, *The Presentation of Self in Everyday Life* (Garden City, NJ: Doubleday, 1959). Goffman lays out, in a highly readable and entertaining fashion, his dramaturgical view of social interaction.

BUREAUCRACY

Rosabeth Moss Kanter and Barry A. Stein, eds., *Life in Organizations: Workplaces as People Experience Them* (New York: Basic Books, 1979). Slices of life from all levels and phases of contemporary bureaucracy.

ANSWER KEY

KEY CONCEPTS

1. f	19. j
2. v	20. e
3. n	21. ee
4. i	22. h
5. jj	23. x
6. s	24. k
7. dd	25. cc
8. m	26. g
9. a	27. b
10. y	28. bb
11. hh	29. r
12. gg	30. c
13. u	31. o
14. l	32. aa
15. z	33. ff
16. p	34. ii
17. d	35. q
18. t	36. w

KEY THINKERS/RESEARCHERS

1. b
2. d
3. c
4. a
5. e

CHAPTER SUMMARY

Defining Normal and Deviant Behavior

A culture's norms and values make up its moral code and help determine what is viewed as right or wrong, good or bad within that culture. Thus, normal behavior is behavior that conforms to the norms of the group in which it occurs. Deviant behavior is behavior that fails to conform to the group's norms. Because cultures vary so widely, moral codes also vary, and sociologists can only judge acts as deviant or normal within a culturally relative frame of reference.

Durkheim noted that deviant behavior is a necessary feature of a healthy society because it serves positive functions. Among these functions are: causing group members to close ranks and unite, prompting a group to organize in order to limit future deviant acts, helping to clarify group beliefs, and teaching normal behavior by way of contrast. Additionally, in some situations, tolerance of deviance acts as a safety valve and actually prevents more serious instances of nonconformity. On the other hand, deviance is dysfunctional because it disrupts the social order, it causes confusion about the norms and values of the group, it undermines trust in social relationships by making them unpredictable, and it diverts valuable resources that could be used elsewhere.

Mechanisms of Social Control

Every society or social group must have mechanisms of social control that direct and influence members' behavior to conform to the group's values and norms. Internal means of control operate through an internalized moral code that influences the individual even in the absence of reactions by others. External means of control operate through other people's reactions to a person's behavior. These reactions constitute sanctions, which may be positive or negative, formal or informal.

Theories of Crime and Deviance

Criminal and deviant behavior has been found throughout history. To account for this, scholars have proposed a variety of theories. Biological theories such as those propounded by Lombroso and Sheldon stress the importance of inherited factors in producing deviance. Psychological explanations emphasize cognitive or emotional factors within the individual as the cause of deviance. Psychoanalytic theory suggests that criminals act on the irrational impulses of the id because they failed to develop a proper superego, or conscience, in the socialization process. Behaviorists argue that crime is the product of conditioning. Wilson and Hernstein propose that criminal activity, like all human behavior, is the product of a rational choice by the individual as a result of weighing the costs and benefits of alternative courses of action.

Sociological theories of deviance rely upon patterns of social interaction and the relationship of the individual to the group. Durkheim argued that, in modern, highly differentiated and specialized societies, and particularly under conditions of rapid social change, individuals may become morally disoriented. This condition, which he called anomie, can produce deviance. Merton argued that deviance is a result of strain between culturally validated goals and the institutionalized means to attain them. Conformists accept both the goals and the means, while deviants reject one or the other or both.

Control theorists like Hirschi argue that everyone is a potential deviant. The issue, for them, is not what causes deviance, but what causes conformity. When individuals have strong bonds to society, their behavior will conform to conventional norms. When any of these bonds is weakened, however, deviance is likely. Other sociologists like Sykes and Matza argue that people become deviant as a result of developing techniques of neutralization, or rationalizations that explain away the deviant nature of the act. These techniques are learned as part of the socialization process, they say.

Cultural transmission theory, pioneered by Shaw and McKay, emphasizes the cultural context in which deviant behavior patterns are learned. Sutherland and Cressey suggested that individuals learn criminal techniques and attitudes through differential association with deviants. Labeling theory shifts the focus of attention from the deviant individual to the social process by which a person comes to be labeled as deviant, and the consequences of such labeling for the individual. Lemert, for instance, emphasized the distinction between primary deviance, which is the original behavior that leads to the application of a label to an individual, and secondary deviance, which is the behavior that people develop as a result of having been labeled deviant.

The Importance of Law

Some interests are so important to a society that folkways and mores are not adequate to ensure orderly social interaction. Therefore laws are developed as a formal system of social control. The legal code, which consists of the laws adopted by the political authority, is not the same thing as a society's moral code, nor is crime synonymous with deviance.

How is it that some things come to be codified in laws? The consensus approach assumes that laws are merely a formal expression of the agreed-upon values of the people. The conflict approach argues that the elite use their power to enact and enforce laws that support their own interests, to the exclusion of the interests of others. There are two types of law, criminal law and civil law. Criminal law deals with violations against the interests of society, whereas civil law deals with violations against the individual.

Crime in the United States

Crime is behavior that violates a society's criminal laws. Violent crime results in injury to a person; property crime is committed with the intent of obtaining property and does not involve the use or threat of force against an individual. While the specific definition varies from state to state, the most serious crimes are termed felonies; less serious crimes are called misdemeanors. The FBI publishes statistics on the frequency of selected crimes in the *Uniform Crime Reports*. These statistics are not always reliable, however. The *National Crime Victimization Survey* shows that only a small fraction of all crimes are reported to the authorities.

Kinds of Crime in the United States

Juvenile crime refers to the breaking of criminal laws by individuals under 18 years of age. A separate court system has been established to deal with juvenile offenders, but perhaps two-thirds of court time is devoted to processing status offenses—behavior that is criminal only because the person involved is a minor. The United States has the highest homicide rate in the industrialized world. Other violent crimes that have an impact on American households include rape, aggravated assault, and robbery.

Ninety percent of all crime in the United States is crime against property, not against a person. Sutherland coined the term white-collar crime to refer to individuals who, while occupying positions of social responsibility or high prestige, break the law in the course of their work for the purpose of illegal personal or organizational gain. White-collar crime, though less visible, accounts for far greater financial losses than street crimes such as robbery and burglary. Organized crime refers to structured associations of individuals or groups who come together for the purpose of obtaining gain mostly from illegal activities. Crimes that do not produce victims in any obvious way are known as victimless crimes. These are mostly acts that violate those laws meant to enforce the moral code of a society.

Criminal Justice in the United States

The criminal justice system consists of personnel and procedures for the arrest, trial, and punishment of those who violate the laws. The three main aspects of this system are the police, the courts, and prisons. The police system in the U.S. is highly decentralized, with different types of responsibilities accruing to the federal, state, and local levels. The United States has separate state and federal court systems for prosecuting violations of state and federal laws. About 85 percent of all criminal cases are tried in state courts.

The U.S. has a higher rate of imprisonment than any other country in the world except South Africa. The goals of imprisonment include separation of the criminal from society, punishment of criminal behavior, deterrence of criminal behavior, and rehabilitation of criminals. High rates of recidivism, or repeat criminality, call these goals into question, however. Today there is a critical shortage of prison space in the United States. While imprisonment is costly, it may be more expensive to not imprison career criminals. The number of females in state and federal prisons has recently reached a record high, though they still constitute a relatively small segment of the total prison population. Women are more likely than men to be in prison for property crimes and drug offenses. More than three-fourths of all women in prison are mothers, and the vast majority of their children are under 18.

The funnel effect refers to the fact that relatively few out of all crimes committed are actually punished. Less than 40 percent of all crimes are reported, and only 26 percent of reported crimes lead to an arrest. Only a small percentage of those arrested are actually brought to trial. Yet perhaps the system is working and we are actually imprisoning only those who require it. It all depends upon one's philosophy of the purposes for which jail should be used.

CHAPTER OUTLINE

Defining Normal and Deviant Behavior
How are normal and deviant behavior defined?

MAKING MORAL JUDGMENTS
What is the basis for making moral judgments?

THE FUNCTIONS OF DEVIANCE
What are the functions of deviance?

THE DYSFUNCTIONS OF DEVIANCE
What are the dysfunctions of deviance?

Mechanisms of Social Control
Why do we have mechanisms of social control?

INTERNAL MEANS OF CONTROL
What are internal means of control?

EXTERNAL MEANS OF CONTROL: SANCTIONS
Why are sanctions an external means of control?

Positive and Negative Sanctions
What is the difference between positive and negative sanctions?

Formal and Informal Sanctions
How do formal and informal sanctions differ?

A Typology of Sanctions
What is the basis for a typology of sanctions?

Theories of Crime and Deviance
What are the different types of theories of crime and deviance?

BIOLOGICAL THEORIES OF DEVIANCE
What is the basic argument of biological theories of deviance?

PSYCHOLOGICAL THEORIES OF DEVIANCE
How do psychological theories explain deviance?

Psychoanalytic Theory
What are the basic assumptions of the psychoanalytic theory of deviance?

Behavioral Theories
How do behavioral theories explain deviance?

Crime as Individual Choice
In what way is crime an individual choice?

SOCIOLOGICAL THEORIES OF DEVIANCE
What is the basis of sociological theories of deviance?

Anomie Theory
What is the basic argument of anomie theory?

Strain Theory
How does strain theory explain deviance?

Control Theory
What is the basic assumption of control theory?

Techniques of Neutralization
How do techniques of neutralization work?

Cultural Transmission Theory
How is deviance culturally transmitted?

Labeling Theory
How does labeling theory explain deviance?

The Importance of Law
Of what importance is law?

THE EMERGENCE OF LAWS
Why do laws emerge in society?

Crime in the United States
How extensive is crime in the United States?

CRIME STATISTICS
What do crime statistics tell us?

Kinds of Crime in the United States
What are the basic kinds of crime in the United States?

JUVENILE CRIME
What is unique about juvenile crime?

VIOLENT CRIME
What constitutes violent crime?

PROPERTY CRIME
How are crimes against property defined?

WHITE-COLLAR CRIME
What is significant about white-collar crime?

ORGANIZED CRIME
What makes organized crime organized?

VICTIMLESS CRIME
What does it mean to say that a crime is victimless?

Criminal Justice in the United States
What is the role of the criminal justice system in the United States?

THE POLICE
What role do the police play in the criminal justice system?

THE COURTS
How are the courts organized?

PRISONS
What role do prisons play in the criminal justice system?

Goals of Imprisonment
What are the goals of imprisonment?

A Shortage of Prisons
How significant is the shortage of prisons?

Women in Prison
Are women in prison different from men in prison?

The "Funnel" Effect
What is the meaning of the "funnel" effect?

LEARNING OBJECTIVES

After studying this chapter you should be able to:

■ *Understand deviance as culturally relative.*

In the Chapter 3 box, "Sociology at Work," is a description of anthropologist Kenneth Good's study of the Yanomamö of the Amazon rainforest and Good's eventual marriage to Yarima, a Yanomamö woman, whom he brought back to live with him in Rutherford, New Jersey. Based on the description of the Yanomamö by Good and Napoleon Chagnon, what do you think Yarima's new U.S. neighbors found deviant about her?

What do you suppose Yarima found deviant about her new neighbors in the U.S.?

■ *Explain the functions and dysfunctions of deviance.*

U.S. Navy and Marine Corps pilots belong to an officially recognized group called the Tailhook Association. In 1991, at a three-day party in Las Vegas to celebrate the U.S. victory in the Persian Gulf War, at least 26 women, many of them naval officers, were sexually harassed by, among other things, being forced to walk the length of a crowded hallway while being grabbed and fondled. When this behavior—and the navy's failure to punish it—finally was made public nearly a year later, the secretary of the navy was forced to resign in disgrace.

Explain how this incident fulfils each of the four functions of deviance:

Function #1: _____

Function #2: _____

Function #3: _____

Function #4: _____

In what four ways was this incident dysfunctional?

Dysfunction #1: _____

Dysfunction #2: _____

Dysfunction #3: _____

Dysfunction #4: _____

■ *Distinguish between internal and external means of social control.*

Shoplifting and employee theft cause enormous financial losses each year. While at your job or when shopping, think about the following:

What internal means of control are being relied upon to prevent theft in this setting?

To what extent are external means of control employed here?

■ *Differentiate among the various types of sanctions.*

How do each of the types of sanctions operate in the college classroom? Give at least one example of each and explain why it is an example.

Positive informal sanctions:

Positive formal sanctions:

Negative informal sanctions:

Negative formal sanctions:

■ *Contrast the basic assumptions behind biological, psychological, and sociological theories of deviance.*

Basic assumption of biological theories:

Example:

Basic assumption of psychological theories:

Example:

Basic assumption of sociological theories:

Example:

■ *Understand the concept of anomie and its role in producing deviance.*

Pete Rose, a working-class kid from Cincinnati, made himself a multi-millionaire in the process of becoming the most prolific hitter in the history of baseball and a projected shoo-in to the Baseball Hall of Fame. Yet, in a celebrated case, Rose was banned from baseball and declared ineligible for the Hall of Fame due to illegal sports betting. How can Rose's deviance be explained by the concept of anomie?

■ *Explain how the strain between cultural goals and lack of means to attain them can lead to crime.*

Choose four groups or individuals that, based on your knowledge and experience, you think typify each one of Merton's Individual Modes of Adaptation.

Innovators:

Ritualists:

Retreatists:

Rebels:

■ *Explain the basic assumptions of control theory.*

Using Hirschi's four categories of ways that people become or fail to become bonded to society and conventional behavior, explain why members of youth gangs engage in deviant behavior.

1.

2.

3.

4.

■ *Explain and give examples of techniques of neutralization.*

In 1992, a major civil disorder occurred in south central Los Angeles after a group of white police officers were found not guilty of assaulting Rodney King, an African American whose beating by the police had been captured on videotape and broadcast nationwide. At least twenty-one people were killed and several hundred million dollars of property was damaged. How might the rioters have used each of Sykes and Matza's five Techniques of Neutralization to explain away their deviance?

1.

2.

3.

4.

5.

■ *Explain how deviance is culturally transmitted.*

Some people argue the prisons in our society are actually "colleges of crime" in which offenders receive advanced socialization in criminal techniques and values from other inmates. Explain this phenomenon using Sutherland's Principles of Differential Association from Table 6.1 in this chapter.

■ *Understand the process of labeling and the distinction between primary and secondary deviance.*

List the three factors that are involved in determining whether or not a person is labeled as a deviant, and give an example of each.

1.

2.

3.

Using the concepts of primary and secondary deviance, explain why children labeled as "troublemakers" in school are the ones who seem to get into the most trouble.

■ *Contrast consensus and conflict perspectives on the origin of a society's legal code.*

Consensus explanation:

Conflict explanation:

■ *Compare the* **Uniform Crime Reports** *and the* **National Crime Victimization Survey** *as sources of information about the crime rate.*

Categories of crime that are reported in the *Uniform Crime Reports:*

Factors that call into question the reliability of the date in the *Uniform Crime Reports:*
1.

2.

Categories of crime that are reported in the *National Crime Victimization Survey:*

According to this data, what percentage of all crimes are actually reported to the police?

■ *Distinguish among the major types of crime.*

List three ways in which juvenile crime is different from adult crime:
1.

2.

3.

What are violent crimes? What industrialized country has the highest rate of violent crime?

What is white-collar crime?

Which type of property crime generates a greater financial loss?

burglary, larceny, auto theft, and so on _____

embezzlement, fraud, corruption, and so on _____

Define organized crime and list its four major characteristics.

1.

2.

3.

4.

What is victimless crime?

What is the argument of those who deny that it is really victimless?

■ *Describe the major features of the criminal justice system in the United States.*

Discuss two important characteristics of each of the following:

The Police:

1.

2.

The Courts:

1.

2.

Prisons:

1.

2.

State three ways that women in prison are different from, or have different experiences, than men.

1.

2.

3.

■ *Describe the "funnel" effect and discuss its implications.*

What is the "funnel" effect in the criminal justice system?

Given this effect, what policies with regard to prosecution, sentencing, and incarceration would you suggest?

KEY CONCEPTS

■ *Match each concept with its definition, illustration, or explication below.*

a. informal sanctions	m. diversion	z. property crime
b. legal code	n. felonies	aa. deterrence
c. rebels	o. juvenile crime	bb. civil law
d. funnel effect	p. external means of control	cc. violent crime
e. status offense	q. negative sanctions	dd. rehabilitation
f. white-collar crime	r. innovators	ee. organized crime
g. mechanisms of social control	s. crime	ff. sanctions
h. criminal justice system	t. primary deviance	gg. ritualists
i. deviant behavior	u. misdemeanors	hh. criminal law
j. formal sanctions	v. internal means of control	ii. secondary deviance
k. moral code	w. normal behavior	jj. recidivism
l. retreatists	x. anomie	kk. victimless crime
	y. positive sanctions	

_____ 1. the symbolic system in terms of which behavior takes on the quality of being good or bad, right or wrong.

_____ 2. behavior that conforms to the rules or norms of the group in which it occurs.

_____ 3. behavior that fails to conform to the rules or norms of a group.

_____ 4. ways of directing or influencing members to conform to the group's values and norms.

_____ 5. the responses of other people to an individual's behavior.

_____ 6. the operation of a group's moral code on an individual even in the absence of reactions by others.

_____ 7. rewards and penalties by a group's members that are used to regulate an individual's behavior.

_____ 8. actions that encourage an individual to continue acting in a certain way (for example, rewards).

_____ 9. actions that discourage the repetition or continuation of a behavior (for example, punishments).

_____10. sanctions applied in a public ritual.

_____11. sanctions applied spontaneously with little or no formal direction.

_____12. a state of normlessness, where values and norms have little impact, and the culture no longer provides adequate guidelines for behavior.

13. individuals who accept the culturally validated goal of success but find deviant ways of achieving it.

_____14. individuals who reject or deemphasize the importance of success and instead concentrate on following and enforcing rules more precisely than was ever intended.

_____15. people who pull back from society all together.

_____16. people who reject both the goals and the institutionalized means to achieve them, and wish to build a different social order with alternative goals and means.

_____17. the original behavior that leads to the application of a label to an individual.

_____18. behavior that people develop as a result of having been labeled as deviant.

_____19. the formal rules, called laws, adopted by a society's political authority.

_____20. deals with violations against the interests of society.

_____21. deals with violations against individuals.

_____22. any behavior that violates a society's criminal laws.

_____23. an unlawful event that may result in injury to a person.

_____24. an unlawful act committed with the intent of gaining property but that does not involve the use or threat of force against an individual.

_____25. the most serious crimes, usually punishable by a year or more in prison.

_____26. less serious violations of criminal law.

_____27. the breaking of criminal laws by individuals under the age of 18.

_____28. behavior that is criminal only because the person involved is a minor.

_____29. repeated criminal behavior after punishment.

_____30. steering offenders away from the justice system to social agencies.

_____31. acts by individuals who, while occupying positions of social responsibility or high prestige, break the the law in the course of their work.

_____32. structured associations of individuals or groups who come together for the purpose of obtaining gain mostly from illegal activities.

_____33. acts that violate those laws meant to enforce the moral code.

_____34. personnel and procedures for arrest, trial, and punishment.

_____35. the prevention of further crime by creating awareness of the painful experiences of those who have violated the laws.

_____36. the resocialization of criminals to conform to society's values and norms and the teaching of usable work habits and skills.

_____37. the fact that, of the many crimes committed, few seem to result in punishment of the offender.

KEY THINKERS/RESEARCHERS

■ *Match each thinker with their main idea or contribution.*

a. Gresham Sykes and David Matza
b. Robert K. Merton
c. Sigmund Freud
d. James Q. Wilson and Richard Herrnstein
e. Edwin H. Sutherland and Donald R. Cressey
f. Émile Durkheim

g. William H. Sheldon
h. Travis Hirschi
i. Clifford Shaw and Henry McKay
j. Cesare Lombroso
k. Edwin Lemert

_____ 1. argued that deviant behavior is an integral part of all healthy societies; developed the concept of anomie.

_____ 2. suggested that criminals were evolutionary throwbacks who could be identified by primitive physical features, particularly with regard to the head.

_____ 3. identified three main body types and suggested that each was responsible for different personality traits.

_____ 4. argued that crime is produced by the unconscious impulses of the individual.

_____ 5. they argue that crime is the product of a rational choice by an individual as a result of weighing the costs and benefits of alternative courses of action.

_____ 6. developed a theory of structural strain to explain deviance.

_____ 7. developed control theory, in which it is hypothesized that the strength of social bonds keep most of us from becoming criminals.

_____ 8. they argued that deviants learn techniques of neutralization to justify their deviance.

_____ 9. suggested that certain neighborhoods generated a culture of crime that was passed on to residents.

_____10. developed the theory of differential association to explain why some people and not others become deviant.

_____11. pioneered the development of labeling theory.

CRITICAL THINKING/APPLICATION QUESTIONS

1. Reflect on the issue of normal and deviant behavior in college versus in society at large. Are some behaviors accepted as normal on a college campus that would be defined as deviant in the general society? Why do you think this is so?

2. In November, 1984, a Union Carbide Corporation plant in Bhopal, India, leaked 40 tons of deadly gas into the atmosphere that killed at least three thousand people and seriously injured over 30,000. While the incident was publicized in the United States, no one connected with the company was charged in the U.S. with committing a crime. In 1991 it came to light that Jeffrey Dahmer had killed and subsequently mutilated and/or eaten six to twelve young men. The attention of the nation was riveted upon

Dahmer's trial, at which he was convicted. How do you account for the different national reaction to these two incidents? What theories of deviance would you draw on to explain this phenomenon?

3. The early 1990s have seen numerous demonstrations of civil disobedience by Operation Rescue and other opponents of legal abortion in which protesters have deliberately and illegally blocked entrances to clinics where abortions were performed. How would the various sociological theories of deviance explain this phenomenon?

USE only 1 Theory

4. This chapter's box, "Controversies in Sociology," has the suggestion that well-publicized executions of criminals have some limited and short-term deterrent effect on the commission of violent crime by others. One possible response to this is to argue that executions should be made as grisly as possible and televised live, thereby maximizing the publicity value. Construct at least one argument for and one argument against this policy based upon what you have learned by studying this chapter.

SUGGESTED READINGS

DEFINING NORMAL AND DEVIANT BEHAVIOR

Kai Erikson, *Wayward Puritans: A Study in the Sociology of Deviance* (New York: John Wiley, 1966). A classic work in which the author shows how the early Puritan settlers in America used deviance to maintain group solidarity.

THEORIES OF CRIME AND DEVIANCE

Delos H. Kelly, *Deviant Behavior: A Text-Reader in the Sociology of Deviance*, 3rd ed. (New York: St. Martin's, 1989). A comprehensive look at theories and types of deviance. Includes many of the classic and/or definitive writings in each area.

KINDS OF CRIME IN THE UNITED STATES

Russell Mokhiber, *Corporate Crime and Violence: Big Business Power and the Abuse of the Public Trust* (San Francisco: Sierra Club Books, 1988). A catalog of crimes by multinational corporations that resulted in serious injury and death. This area is often overlooked, even in discussions of white-collar crime.

CRIMINAL JUSTICE IN THE UNITED STATES

Jeffrey Reiman, *The Rich Get Richer and the Poor Get Prison: Ideology, Class, and Criminal Justice*, 3rd ed. (New York: Macmillan, 1990). A critical look at the entire American criminal justice system.

John Irwin, *The Felon* (Englewood Cliffs, NJ: Prentice Hall, 1970). Based on two years of participant observation and in-depth interviews with felons, this study follows career criminals from their beginnings in crime through their prison and post-prison experience.

ANSWER KEY

KEY CONCEPTS

1. k	14. gg	27. o
2. w	15. l	28. e
3. i	16. c	29. jj
4. g	17. t	30. m
5. p	18. ii	31. f
6. v	19. b	32. ee
7. ff	20. hh	33. kk
8. y	21. bb	34. h
9. q	22. s	35. aa
10. j	23. cc	36. dd
11. a	24. z	37. d
12. x	25. n	
13. r	26. u	

KEY THINKERS/RESEARCHERS

1. f	6. b
2. j	7. h
3. g	8. a
4. c	9. i
5. d	10. e
	11. k

CHAPTER SUMMARY

The Nature of Social Stratification

Every society makes distinctions among its members. Under some circumstances, qualitative judgments are made about these distinctions. The outcome of this process of social evaluation is social inequality, or the uneven distribution of privileges, material rewards, opportunities, power, prestige, and influence among individuals or groups. When social inequality becomes part of the social structure and is transmitted from one generation to the next, social stratification exists.

Social mobility is the movement of an individual or group from one social status to another within a stratification system. An open society attempts to provide equal opportunity for everyone to compete for desired roles and statuses. In a closed society various aspects of people's lives are determined at birth and remain fixed. Movement that involves a change of status but no corresponding change in social class is known as horizontal mobility. Movement that changes one's social class is called vertical mobility. Mobility across two or more generations is called intergenerational mobility, whereas vertical mobility within one individual's lifetime is referred to as intragenerational mobility. Social mobility is affected by structural factors like the state of the economy, demographic factors, the level of cultural support, and encouragement for upward social mobility. The most important factor under the individual's control is the level of education attained.

Stratification Systems

Stratification can be based mainly on ascribed or achieved status. The caste system is a rigid form of stratification based on ascribed characteristics such as skin color or family identity. In an estate system a person's position is defined by law and determined primarily by inheritance. Each estate has legally established rights and duties. Class systems are based at least in part on achieved status. A social class consists of a category of people who share similar opportunities, economic and vocational positions, lifestyles, attitudes, and behaviors. Class boundaries are maintained by limitation of social interaction, intermarriage, and mobility into that class. Some form of class system exists in all industrial societies.

The Dimensions of Social Stratification

The most valued attributes that produce stratification are economics, power, and prestige. Economics refers to individual or family wealth. Power is the ability of an individual or group to attain goals, control events, and maintain influence over others, even in the face of opposition. The group of people who control policy-making and the setting of priorities in a society is called the power elite. Prestige consists of the approval and respect an individual or group receives from other members of society. Occupations are the most visible statuses to which prestige is attached in industrial society. The relative ranking of occupations in the United States by prestige has remained stable over the last fifty years.

Theories of Stratification

The functionalist theory of stratification as presented by Davis and Moore holds that stratification is socially necessary. They argue that (1) different positions in society make different levels of contributions to the well-being and preservation of society; (2) filling the more complex and important positions in society often requires talent that is scarce and has a long period of training; and (3) providing unequal rewards ensures that the most talented and best-trained individuals will fill the statuses of greatest importance and be motivated to competently carry out role expectations. Critics of this view suggest either that stratification is immoral because it creates extremes of wealth and poverty and denigrates the people on the bottom, or that it is dysfunctional in that it neglects the talents and merits of many people who are stuck in the lower classes, ignores the ability of the powerful to limit access to important positions, and overlooks the fact that the level of rewards attached to jobs does not necessarily reflect their functional importance.

Conflict theorists see stratification as the outcome of a struggle for dominance. Karl Marx believed that in order to understand human societies one must look at the economic conditions surrounding production of the necessities of life. Those groups who own and/or control the means of production within a society also have the power to shape or maintain aspects of society to best favor their interests. In capitalist society there are two great classes: the bourgeoisie, or owners of the means of production, and the proletariat, or working class. Capitalists exploit workers by paying them less than the value of what they produce and keeping the excess as profit.

Marx theorized that, as a result of continuing exploitation and increasing class polarization, the working class would eventually revolt, overthrow the capitalist class, and create a new social order more favorable to the interests of the majority of people. The final stage of development, advanced communism, would be a classless society of industrial plenty in which all could live in comfort. Marx suggested that there are at least four ways by which wealth can be distributed: to each according to need, to want, to what is earned, or to what can be obtained—by whatever means. The first principle characterizes socialism and the last capitalism.

Max Weber believed there were three sources of stratification: economic class, social status, and political power. Economic classes arise out of the unequal distribution of economic power, a point on which he agreed with Marx. Weber argued, however, that individuals and groups are also stratified by the prestige associated with their social status, which is determined by the lifestyle made possible by one's income, education, and value

system. Inequality in power is based on differential ability to influence events in one's favor. Each of Weber's three dimensions of stratification are related, but they are not always connected in a predictable fashion; there can be large disjunctures between one or more elements (something defined earlier as status inconsistency).

Modern conflict theory holds that (1) stratification is the outgrowth of a struggle for dominance in which people compete for scarce goods and services; (2) those who are dominated have the potential to express resistance and hostility toward those in power, though the dominated group may not always be aware of this potential or may not be able to organize to express it due to division within its ranks; (3) conflict will most often center on the distribution of property and political power; (4) what are thought to be the common values of society are really the values of the dominant groups; and (5) because those in power are engaged in exploitative relationships, they must find mechanisms of social control to keep the exploited in line. While the threat or actual use of force is the ultimate mechanism, more subtle means are preferred. It may be that the functionalist and the conflict theory of stratification are complementary in some ways.

CHAPTER OUTLINE

The Nature of Social Stratification
What is the nature of social stratification?

SOCIAL MOBILITY
What does it mean to experience social mobility?

Factors Affecting Social Mobility
What are the main factors that affect social mobility?

Stratification Systems
On what bases can stratification be systematized?

THE CASTE SYSTEM
What are the major features of the caste system?

THE ESTATE SYSTEM
Upon what distinctions is the estate system based?

THE CLASS SYSTEM
What is the basis of a class system?

The Dimensions of Social Stratification
What are the major dimensions of social stratification?

ECONOMICS
How is economics a dimension of social stratification?

POWER
In what way is power a dimension of social stratification?

PRESTIGE
How does prestige operate as a dimension of social stratification?

Occupational Stratification
How is occupational statification connected to prestige?

Theories of Stratification
What are the major theories of stratification?

THE FUNCTIONALIST THEORY
How does the functionalist theory explain stratification?

The Immorality of Social Stratification
In what sense is stratification immoral?

The Neglect of Talent and Merit
How is talent and merit neglected in society?

Barriers to Free Competition
What are the major barriers to free competition?

Functionally Important Jobs
What are functionally important jobs?

CONFLICT THEORY
What are the basic assumptions of conflict theory?

Karl Marx
How did Karl Marx explain stratification?

Max Weber (Mahks VAY ber)
How did Max Weber explain stratification?

MODERN CONFLICT THEORY
What are the major assumptions of modern conflict theory?

THE NEED FOR SYNTHESIS
Why is there a need for synthesis?

LEARNING OBJECTIVES

After studying this chapter you should be able to:

■ *Explain the relationships between the concepts of social differentiation, social evaluation, social inequality, and social stratification.*

Create a flowchart in which each of the four major concepts listed above is represented by a box. Draw arrows between the boxes to depict the relationships among the concepts. Explain the meaning of each arrow.

■ *Differentiate between the various dimensions of social mobility.*

Using your own extended family as an example, think of at least one person who fits each of the following categories, and explain why you chose them.

Horizontal intragenerational:

Upward intergenerational:

Upward intragenerational:

Downward intergenerational:

Downward intragenerational:

Status inconsistency:

■ *Explain the factors that affect one's chances of upward social mobility.*

Explain how your own expectation of upward social mobility is affected by each of the following factors.

State of the economy:

Demographics:

Cultural and/or subcultural encouragement:

Education:

■ *Compare and contrast the caste, estate, and class systems.*

List the dominant characteristics of each of the three systems, state whether it is based on ascribed or achieved status, and whether it is an open or closed society.

Caste system:

Estate system:

Class system:

■ *Contrast differing views of power in American society.*

Briefly summarize each of the following views:

The power elite view:

The governing class view:

The competing power structures view:

Which explanation makes the most sense to you? Why?

■ *Describe the pattern of occupational stratification by prestige in U.S. society.*

Find the prestige rating of each of the following occupations in Table 7.1 in this chapter.

College professor ＿＿＿＿＿＿＿＿＿＿＿

Grade school teacher ＿＿＿＿＿＿＿＿＿＿

Electrician ＿＿＿＿＿＿＿＿＿＿＿＿＿＿

Police officer ＿＿＿＿＿＿＿＿＿＿＿＿＿

Office secretary ＿＿＿＿＿＿＿＿＿＿＿＿

Housewife ＿＿＿＿＿＿＿＿＿＿＿＿＿＿

Auto mechanic ＿＿＿＿＿＿＿＿＿＿＿＿

Cashier ＿＿＿＿＿＿＿＿＿＿＿＿＿＿＿

Assembly-line worker ＿＿＿＿＿＿＿＿＿＿

Garbage collector ＿＿＿＿＿＿＿＿＿＿＿

Househusband ＿＿＿＿＿＿＿＿＿＿＿＿

Maid ＿＿＿＿＿＿＿＿＿＿＿＿＿＿＿＿

How would you explain the very different prestige rankings of these occupations?

To what extent do you think the prestige of an occupation has anything to do with gender?

■ *Summarize and critique the functionalist theory of stratification.*

Why, according to Davis and Moore, must rewards in society be distributed unequally?

1.

2.

3.

Briefly discuss four criticisms of functionalist theory.

1.

2.

3.

4.

■ *Explain the main points of Karl Marx's conflict theory.*

What is the key to understanding human societies, according to Marx?

What are the two main classes in capitalist society?

How does exploitation occur in capitalism?

What is the source of change?

What is likely to happen after a revolution led by the proletariat?

What are the four principles by which wealth can be distributed in a society?

1.

2.

3.

4.

Which of these principles characterizes socialism?
Which of these principles characterizes capitalism, according to Marxists?

■ *Explain the three sources of stratification proposed by Max Weber.*

Explain how, in Weber's view, stratification is based on each of the following dimensions.
Economic class:

Social status:

Political power:

Think of an example, other than those mentioned in the chapter, of status inconsistency, where these three dimensions are not at similar levels or not related.

■ *Describe the key features of modern conflict theory.*

Briefly describe the five aspects of modern conflict theory:

KEY CONCEPTS

■ *Match each concept with its definition, illustration, or explication below.*

a. power elite
b. intergenerational mobility
c. estate system
d. class conflict
e. social inequality
f. means of production
g. status groups
h. caste system
i. horizontal mobility
j. social evaluation
k. wealth
l. open society
m. social class

n. social stratification
o. esteem
p. proletariat
q. power
r. vertical mobility
s. intragenerational mobility
t. exploitation
u. prestige
v. status inconsistency
w. bourgeoisie
x. class system
y. social mobility
z. closed society

_____ 1. the process of making qualitative judgments on the basis of individual characteristics or behaviors.

_____ 2. the uneven distribution of privileges, material rewards, opportunities, power, prestige, and influence among individuals or groups.

_____ 3. the division of society into levels, steps, or positions that is perpetuated by the society's major institutions.

_____ 4. movement of an individual or a group from one social status to another.

_____ 5. characterized by the attempt to provide equal opportunity for everyone to compete for desired statuses.

_____ 6. a society in which the various aspects of people's lives are determined at birth and remain fixed.

_____ 7. a change in status with no corresponding change in social class.

_____ 8. a change in status which results in a change in social class.

_____ 9. a change in social status that takes place over two or more generations.

_____10. a change in social status that occurs within the lifetime of one individual.

_____11. situations in which people rank higher or lower on certain stratification characteristics than on others.

_____12. a closed system of stratification in which a person's social position is defined by law, and membership is determined primarily by inheritance.

_____13. a rigid form of stratification based on ascribed characteristics such as skin color or family identity.

_____14. a society that contains several different social classes and permits at least some social mobility.

_____15. a category of people who share similar opportunities, economic and vocational positions, lifestyles, attitudes, and behavior.

_____16. the total economic assets of an individual or family.

_____17. the ability of an individual or group to attain goals, control events, and maintain influence over others, even in the face of opposition.

_____18. the group of people who control policymaking and the setting of priorities.

_____19. the approval and respect an individual or group receives from other members of society.

——20. the appreciation and respect a person wins in his or her daily interpersonal relationships.

——21. the apparatus by which the necessities of life within a society are produced.

——22. the owners of the means of production or capital.

——23. the working class.

——24. the process by which capitalists pay workers below the value of what they actually produce and keep the remainder as profit.

——25. for Marx, the moving force of history.

——26. for Weber, a category of people with similar lifestyles shaped by similar incomes, education, and values.

KEY THINKERS/RESEARCHERS

■ *Match each thinker with his main idea or contribution to sociology.*

a. C. Wright Mills
b. Arnold Rose
c. Max Weber
d. Karl Marx
e. G. William Domhoff

——1. a pioneer among conflict theorists, he developed a critique of capitalist class society and a vision of the transition to socialism.

——2. proposed that stratification takes place on the basis of class, status, and power.

——3. proposed the concept of a power elite governing American society.

——4. suggested that America is controlled by a governing class whose members are very rich, intermarry, attend the same schools, and spend their time in the same clubs.

——5. argued that American society is characterized by multiple power structures which, even though dominated by elites, tend to balance each other out.

CRITICAL THINKING/APPLICATION QUESTIONS

1. On a number of important dimensions—income, wealth, culture, political attitudes—there continue to be significant differences between black and white Americans. To what extent can U.S. race relations be seen as a caste system? As an estate system? As a class system?

2. Figure 7.1 in this chapter presents data on household net worth of Whites, Blacks, and Hispanics. Construct a functionalist explanation for the disparities demonstrated here and compare it with a conflict explanation. Which explanation makes the most sense to you? Why?

3. The "Controversies in Sociology" box in this chapter discusses data and theories about the black underclass. Discuss the phenomenon of the black underclass in relation to the four criticisms of the functionalist theory of stratification presented in the chapter.

4. Sociologist Herbert Gans has argued that the existence of poverty and poor people has positive functions for other groups in society. What do you think some of these positive functions might be, and what groups might benefit from the existence of poverty?

SUGGESTED READINGS

THE NATURE OF SOCIAL STRATIFICATION

Barbara Ehrenreich, *Fear of Falling: The Inner Life of the Middle Class* (New York: Pantheon, 1989). A perceptive analysis of how the economic pressures that have forced many out of the middle class play themselves out in political attitudes and behavior.

D. Stanley Eitzen and Maxine Baca Zinn, eds., *The Reshaping of America* (Englewood Cliffs, NJ: Prentice Hall, 1989). A collection of articles examining the forces transforming contemporary American society and the impact of these changes on people's productive life chances.

STRATIFICATION SYSTEMS

Oliver C. Cox, *Caste, Class, and Race: A Study in Social Dynamics* (New York: Monthly Review Press, 1970). A comprehensive, landmark analysis of the concepts of caste and class (including estates) and their relevance/application to the issues of race in American society.

THE DIMENSIONS OF SOCIAL STRATIFICATION

G. William Domhoff, *Who Rules America Now: A View for the 80s* (Englewood Cliffs, NJ: Prentice Hall, 1983). An updated version of the author's pioneering research on the governing class in America, taking into account the phenomenon of the "Reagan Revolution."

Richard Sennett and Jonathan Cobb, *The Hidden Injuries of Class* (New York: Vintage, 1973). A pathbreaking work that looks at the social psychological consequences of class inequality.

THEORIES OF STRATIFICATION

Michael D. Grimes, *Class in Twentieth-Century American Sociology: An Analysis of Theories and Measurement Strategies* (New York: Praeger, 1991). A survey of major contemporary theories of stratification.

ANSWER KEY

KEY CONCEPTS

1. j	14. x
2. e	15. m
3. n	16. k
4. y	17. q
5. l	18. a
6. z	19. u
7. i	20. o
8. r	21. f
9. b	22. w
10. s	23. p
11. v	24. t
12. c	25. d
13. h	26. g

KEY THINKERS/RESEARCHERS

1. d	4. e
2. c	5. b
3. a	

CHAPTER SUMMARY

Studying Social Stratification

Despite the American political ideal of the basic equality of all citizens and the lack of inherited ranks and titles, the United States nonetheless has a class structure that is characterized by extremes of wealth and poverty. Though many people are reluctant to talk about it, there are class distinctions in America based on race, education, family name, occupation, and income.

How are people grouped into social classes? There is considerable disagreement among sociologists about what variables are most important in determining social class and what methods are most useful for defining the membership and boundaries of social classes. In the objective approach, researchers determine a set number of classes in advance and then assign people to each one based on given criteria. The reputational approach relies on the opinions community members have of one another. In the subjective approach, individuals are asked to place themselves into one of several categories.

Social Class in the United States

There is little agreement among sociologists about how many social classes exist in the United States and what their characteristics may be. A relatively common approach is to assume that there are five social classes in U.S. society: the upper, upper-middle, lower-middle, working, and lower classes. The upper class is characterized by great wealth, high prestige, and an exclusive lifestyle. The upper-middle class is made up of successful business and professional people and their families. These people generally have a college education, own property, and have a savings reserve.

The lower-middle class consists of lower-ranked professional occupations, clerical and sales workers, and upper-level manual workers. They tend to be high school graduates with modest incomes and some savings, and they emphasize respectability and are politically and economically conservative. The working class is made up of skilled and semiskilled workers, factory employees, and other blue-collar workers. They have adequate incomes, but with little left over for luxuries. They feel politically powerless, and are less likely to vote than higher classes. Members of the lower class have little in the way of educational or occupational skills and are consequently either unemployed or underemployed.

They are not politically aware or involved because they are focused mostly on economic survival.

Income Distribution

The United States has a highly unequal distribution of income. In 1989 the richest one-fifth of families—those with incomes of $59,550 or more—received $9.70 for every $1.00 received by the poorest one-fifth—those with incomes of $16,845 or less. The wealthiest 20 percent of American families own more than three-fourths of the country's wealth. The wealthiest five percent of all families own more than half of America's wealth.

Poverty

Poverty refers to a condition in which people do not have enough money to maintain a standard of living that includes the basic necessities of life. Depending upon which approach one uses, it is possible to document that anywhere from 14 million to 45 million Americans are living in poverty. Rates of impoverishment vary by race and ethnicity, region of the country, family composition and gender. African Americans and Hispanics are disproportionately poor, as are residents of the South, people living in rural areas, and people in female-headed households. The "feminization of poverty" refers to the disproportionate concentration of poverty among women.

The official definition of poverty used for the poverty index was developed by the Social Security Administration in 1964. It was never intended to certify that any individual or family was in need. Despite specific warnings to the contrary, it continues to be used in just that fashion today. There are also a variety of serious problems with the way the index actually measures poverty, including failure to take account of regional variations in the cost of living, changing food costs, increasing noncash assistance, and failure to count residents of nursing homes and the homeless.

Contrary to myth, most of the able-bodied poor of working age are working or looking for work. In 1990, 40.3 percent of poor persons 15 years and older worked. However, a person working 40 hours per week year round at minimum wage will not earn enough to lift a family of three out of poverty. Additionally, most poor people are not black; there are more than twice as many poor white people as poor black people. African Americans are, however, disproportionately poor. Likewise, while female-headed households are disproportionately poor, the majority of the poor live in male-headed families. Finally, contrary to popular perception, there are more poor people in rural areas than in central cities.

Government Assistance Programs

Government programs that provide assistance to families or individuals can be divided into three categories: social insurance, means-tested cash assistance, and noncash benefits. Social insurance benefits are not means-tested, which means you do not have to be poor to receive them. The vast majority of these benefits—by far the largest category of federal assistance—goes to the middle class.

Means-tested cash assistance programs go mainly to the poor and include such things as Aid to Families with Dependent Children (AFDC) and Supplemental Security Income (SSI). The actual dollar amount spent for these programs, as well as their share of the federal budget, has shrunk through the 1980s.

Noncash assistance programs include both means-tested items like Medicaid, food stamps, subsidized housing, free or reduced-price school lunches, and non-means-tested items such as Medicare, and subsidized lunches for all students in participating schools. Medicare, by far the single largest expenditure in this category, goes mainly to the middle class.

Worldwide Comparisons

Economic rewards are more unequally distributed in the United States than elsewhere in the Western industrialized world. In addition, the U.S. has more poverty than other capitalist countries with similar standards of living. While the United States has been moderately successful at holding down the poverty rate among the elderly, it is much worse than other industrialized countries with regard to keeping children and working-age adults out of poverty.

Consequences of Social Stratification

Studies of social stratification have shown that social class affects many aspects of people's lives. Lower-class people get sick more often, have higher infant mortality rates, shorter life expectancies, and larger families. Although crime appears to be relatively equally distributed throughout the class structure, poor people are more likely to be arrested, charged with a crime, convicted, sentenced to prison, and are likely to get longer prison terms than middle- and upper-class criminals. Types of mental illness seem to vary with social class, as does the likelihood of spending time in a mental hospital.

CHAPTER OUTLINE

Studying Social Stratification
What are the difficulties in studying social stratification?

OBJECTIVE APPROACH
What is the basis for the objective approach?

REPUTATIONAL APPROACH
What is the reputational approach?

SUBJECTIVE APPROACH
How does the subjective approach work?

Social Class in the United States
How are social classes in the United States determined?

THE UPPER CLASS
Who is in the upper class?

THE UPPER-MIDDLE CLASS
How is membership in the upper-middle class determined?

THE LOWER-MIDDLE CLASS
What groups are found in the lower-middle class?

THE WORKING CLASS
Who makes up the working class?

THE LOWER CLASS
What groups are in the lower class?

Income Distribution
What conclusions can be drawn about the income distribution in the U.S.?

Poverty
How is poverty defined?

THE FEMINIZATION OF POVERTY
What does it mean to speak of the feminization of poverty?

HOW DO WE COUNT THE POOR?
Once again, how do we count the poor?

MYTHS ABOUT THE POOR
What are the most common myths about the poor?

Government Assistance Programs
What are the major government assistance programs?

Worldwide Comparisons
How does inequality in the U.S. compare to other countries in the world?

Consequences of Social Stratification
What are some of the most important consequences of social stratification?

LEARNING OBJECTIVES

After studying this chapter you should be able to:

■ *Describe and evaluate the methods sociologists use for measuring social class.*

Describe each of the three methods for measuring social class, stating one advantage and at least one disadvantage to the approach.

1. _____ approach

Description:

Advantage:

Disadvantage:

2. _____ approach

Description:

Advantage:

Disadvantage:

3. _____ approach

Description:

Advantage:

Disadvantage:

Which approach makes the most sense to you? Why?

■ *Describe the characteristics of each of the social classes in the United States in the most commonly used paradigm.*

Describe the key income, occupation, and educational characteristics of each of the social classes. Drawing upon literature, the movies, television, or popular culture, give one example of an individual or family in each social class.

Upper class

Description:

Example:

Upper-Middle class

Description:

Example:

Lower-Middle class

Description:

Example:

Working class

Description:

Example:

Lower class

Description:

Example:

■ **Describe the current distribution of income in the United States.**

Refer to Table 8.2 in this chapter and answer the following questions.

If income was distributed equally throughout the population, what percent would be received by the

richest 20 percent (Fifth quintile)? _____ %

poorest 20 percent (First quintile)? _____ %

In 1990, what was the actual percentage received by the

richest 20 percent (Fifth quintile)? _____ %

poorest 20 percent (First quintile)? _____ %

What was the dollar amount cutoff for each of these groups?

richest 20 percent (Fifth quintile)? $ _____ and above

poorest 20 percent (First quintile)? $ _____ and below

■ **Describe how the official government poverty index is constructed and discuss its weaknesses.**

Describe the two steps used in constructing the poverty index in 1964:

1.

2.

List and discuss three criticisms of the way the poverty index is calculated:

1.

2.

3.

■ *Describe disparities in the rate of poverty among various groups in American society.*

Describe which groups are most likely to be poor in each of the following categories.

Race:

Region of the U.S.:

Rural/Urban status:

Gender of head of household:

Families headed by divorced vs. never-married mothers:

What is meant by the phrase "the feminization of poverty"?

■ *Describe and criticize four myths about the poor in the United States.*

Myth #1:

Critique:

Myth #2:

Critique:

Myth #3:

Critique:

Myth #4:

Critique:

■ *Summarize the various federal programs that provide direct benefits to families or individuals.*

Describe each of the following categories of federal assistance programs and, using Table 8.5 in this chapter, calculate the percentage of total expenditures listed that goes to each category.

Social insurance benefits (including non-means-tested cash benefits):

Total expenditures: $_____ billion   Percent of total assistance expenditures: _____ %

Means-tested cash assistance:

Total expenditures: $_____ billion   Percent of total assistance expenditures: _____ %

Means-tested noncash benefits:

Total expenditures: $_____ billion   Percent of total assistance expenditures: _____ %

■ *Compare poverty rates in the United States with those of other industrialized countries.*

Examine Table 8.6 in this chapter and fill in the chart below.

Poverty rates among	Country with the highest rate	Country with the lowest rate
the elderly		
children		
working-age adults		

Which country tends to have the highest poverty rates? _____

Which country tends to have the lowest poverty rates? _____

■ *Describe some of the medical and legal consequences of one's position in the class structure.*

Describe three medical conditions that are more likely to be found among the poor than among those who are better-off.

1.

2.

3.

For the same criminal behavior as a middle- or upper-class person, a poor person is more likely to be (fill in the five blanks):

_____

_____

_____

_____

_____

KEY CONCEPTS

■ *Match each concept with its definition, illustration, or explication below.*

a. working class
b. noncash benefits
c. reputational approach
d. the *Social Register*
e. lower class
f. means-tested assistance
g. upper class

h. subjective approach
i. lower-middle class
j. poverty
k. social insurance
l. upper-middle class
m. objective approach

_____ 1. a method in which researchers determine a set number of classes in advance and then assign people to each one based on given criteria.

_____ 2. a method in which individuals are asked to place themselves into one of several class categories.

_____ 3. a method of determining social class that relies on the opinions that community members have of one another.

_____ 4. a category of people with great wealth, high prestige, and an exclusive lifestyle.

_____ 5. a little-known address and telephone book that lists the family and social background of wealthy people in the U.S.

_____ 6. a category made up of successful business and professional people who generally have a college education, own property, and have a savings reserve.

_____ 7. a category of people with little in the way of education or occupational skills who are focused mostly on survival.

_____ 8. a category made up of skilled and semiskilled workers, factory employees, and other blue-collar workers who have adequate incomes, but with little left over for luxuries.

_____ 9. a category of lower-ranked professional occupations, clerical and sales workers, and upper-level manual workers who tend to be high school graduates with modest incomes and some savings.

_____10. a condition in which people do not have enough money to maintain a standard of living that includes the basic necessities of life.

_____11. a form of assistance to individuals and families in which they receive services instead of money.

_____12. a form of assistance designed to protect people from various economic hazards: retirement, unemployment, illness, and so on.

_____13. a form of assistance for which people are eligible based on their income.

CRITICAL THINKING/APPLICATION QUESTIONS

1. Meritocracy—the notion that everyone should get exactly what they deserve, based on their talent and effort—has always been a powerful ideal norm in American society. Based on the evidence presented in this chapter, to what extent do you think we currently have a meritocracy in the United States?

2. Most Americans like to think of themselves as middle class and America as a predominantly middle-class society. Assess this view based on the evidence presented in this chapter.

3. Develop and compare functionalist and conflict explanations for the existence of an underclass in American society.

4. In this chapter you have seen that there are serious validity problems with the official U.S. government poverty index. In fact, the government itself has said that the index should not be used to certify that any individual or family is deprived. Yet, that is exactly the administrative use to which the poverty index is put. Why is it, do you think, that we currently have no valid official method of certifying need in this society?

SUGGESTED READINGS

STUDYING SOCIAL STRATIFICATION

Reeve Vanneman and Lynn Weber Cannon, *The American Perception of Class* (Philadelphia: Temple University Press, 1987). A look at popular perceptions in the United States.

SOCIAL CLASS IN THE UNITED STATES

Loren Baritz, *The Good Life: The Meaning of Success for the American Middle Class* (New York: Knopf, 1989). A look at the assumptions middle-class Americans make about the meaning of success, equality, child-rearing, and freedom.

INCOME DISTRIBUTION

Frank Levy, *Dollars and Dreams: The Changing American Income Distribution* (New York: Russell Sage Foundation, 1987). An examination of recent trends.

POVERTY

Ken Auletta, *The Underclass* (New York: Vintage, 1982). A systematic, journalistic look at the poorest of the poor in America.

Rochelle Lefkowitz and Ann Withorn, eds., *For Crying Out Loud: Women and Poverty in the United States* (New York: Pilgrim Press, 1986). A fairly up-to-date examination of "the feminization of poverty."

Jonathan Kozol, *Rachel and Her Children: Homeless Families in America* (New York: Crown, 1988). A highly-readable examination of the problem of homelessness in America by a leading social critic.

ANSWER KEY

KEY CONCEPTS

1. m	5. d	8. a	11. b
2. h	6. l	9. i	12. k
3. c	7. e	10. j	13. f
4. g			

CHAPTER SUMMARY

The Concept of Race

Race refers to a category of people who are defined as similar because of a number of physical characteristics. Often these characteristics are arbitrarily chosen to suit the labeler's purposes. Races have historically been defined according to genetic, legal, and social criteria, each definition having its own problems. While genetic definitions center on inherited traits like hair and nose type, in fact these traits have been found to vary independently of one another. Moreover, all humans are far more genetically alike than they are different.

Legal definitions of race have generally not been devised to determine who was black or of another race, but who was *not white*. This made the concept of special privileges for whites easier to institute in practice. There is, however, very little consistency among the various legal definitions of race. According to the social definition of race, if a person presents themselves as a member of a certain race and others respond to them as a member of that race, then they are effectively of the claimed race. The U.S. Census relies on self-definition for racial classification and does not apply any legal or genetic rules.

The Concept of Ethnic Group

An ethnic group is a group with a distinct cultural tradition with which its own members identify and which may or may not be recognized by outsiders. Many ethnic groups form subcultures, with a high degree of internal loyalty and distinctive folkways, mores, values, customs of dress, and patterns of recreation. Above all there is a feeling of association. The group members are aware of a relationship because of a shared loyalty to a cultural tradition.

The Concept of Minorities

In sociological terms, a minority is a group of people who, because of physical or cultural characteristics, are singled out for differential and unequal treatment, and who therefore regard themselves as objects of collective discrimination.

Problems in Race and Ethnic Relations

Prejudice is an irrationally based negative, or occasionally positive, attitude toward certain groups and their members. Prejudice serves several social functions: it helps draw together those who hold it and define group boundaries; it provides a rationale for writing off one's competitors as less than human or inherently unworthy; it allows us to project onto others those parts of ourselves we do not like and want to avoid facing. Prejudice is dysfunctional in that it limits our vision of the world, and is the necessary ingredient of discrimination.

Prejudice is a subjective feeling; discrimination is an overt action. Discrmination can be defined as differential treatment, usually unequal and injurious, accorded to individuals who are assumed to belong to a particular category or group. Prejudice does not always result in discrimination. Robert Merton developed a four-way typology in which people may be classified as unprejudiced nondiscriminators, unprejudiced discriminators, prejudiced nondiscriminators, or prejudiced discriminators. Institutionalized prejudice and discrimination refers to complex societal arrangements that restrict the life chances and choices of a specifically defined group in comparison with those of the dominant group.

Patterns in Racial and Ethnic Relations

Assimilation is the process whereby groups with different cultures come to share a common culture. Invariably one group has a much larger role in the process than the other(s). The particular form of assimilation found in the United States is called Anglo conformity—the expected renunciation of other ancestral cultures in favor of Anglo-American behavior and values. Pluralism is the development and coexistence of separate racial and ethnic group identities within a society. Pluralism celebrates the differences among groups.

One of the more common consequences of the interaction between two ethnic groups has been subjugation, or the subordination of one group and the assumption of a position of authority, power, and domination by the other. A form of subjugation, segregation refers to the act, process, or state of being set apart. Segregation places limits and restrictions on the contact, communication, and social relations among groups. The term ghetto is used to describe any kind of segregated living environment.

Expulsion is the process of either indirectly or directly forcing a group to leave the territory in which it resides. It can be accomplished indirectly by making life unpleasant for a group, or directly, through migration or relocation. Annihilation, or genocide, is the extermination of a racial or ethnic group, most often through deliberate action.

Racial and Ethnic Immigration to the United States

Since the founding of Jamestown in 1607, over 45 million people have immigrated to the United States. Historically, the vast majority of these immigrants have been from Europe. The old migration consisted of people from northern Europe who came before 1880. The new migration was far larger in numbers and consisted of people who came from southern and eastern Europe. Discriminatory quotas were set up in the beginning of this century to restrict the immigration of the latter groups. Today the overwhelming majority of immigrants to the U.S. come from Latin America, Asia, and the Carribean.

Legal immigration to the U.S. has increased in recent decades, and is projected to increase even more in the 1990s. It is estimated that there are between 2.5 and 4.7 million illegal immigrants in the United States, and the number is growing by 200,000 per year. More than three-quarters of them come from Latin America.

Racial and Ethnic Groups in the United States

The United States is perhaps the most racially and ethnically diverse country in the world; no single ethnic group makes up a majority of the population. Today 63 million Americans claim white Anglo-Saxon Protestant (WASP) ancestry. This ethnic group has been in America the longest (aside from Native Americans) and, although a numerical minority, is the dominant cultural force. WASPs have frequently argued that other immigrants should assimilate to the Anglo ideal.

African Americans constitute at least 12 percent of the nation's population. Eighty-four percent reside in urban areas, and just over half live in the South. The ratio of African-American family income to white family income has fallen over the last 20 years.

The number of Hispanics in the United States grew 53 percent between 1980 and 1990, more than five times faster than the U.S. population as a whole. Nearly two-thirds of Hispanics are of Mexican origin, 12 percent are from Puerto Rico, and just under five percent are from Cuba. Mexican Americans have been exploited for years as a source of cheap labor. Puerto Ricans are the poorest of the Hispanic groups. They remain strongly oriented to their homeland.

Cuban Americans are mostly political exiles who have fiercely attempted to retain their Cuban way of life. They have fared better economically than any other Hispanic group, largely because the original wave of Cuban immigrants consisted primarily of people with marketable skills and money.

The greatest concentrations of Hispanics live in Texas and California, but they are also found in large numbers in Arizona, New Mexico, and Florida. Ninety percent of Hispanics reside in metropolitan areas, where they tend to live in tight-knit communities, sharing a common language and customs.

Jews are a diverse ethnic group united mainly by cultural identification. Jewish immigration was more a migration of families than that of other European immigrants, and included a higher percentage of skilled workers and intellectuals. Of approximately six million Jews in America today, 53 percent of those working are in the professions and business (as against 25 percent of the general population).

The Chinese were the first Asians to settle in America in significant numbers. They came in the nineteenth century to work in the mining camps and build the railroads. They faced much harassment and were the target of the first anti-foreigner immigration acts in America. Today the 1.6 million Chinese Americans are the largest group of Asian origin. Japanese immigrants have come largely in this century. During World War II, Japanese Americans were singled out for especially vicious mistreatment, as all individuals of Japanese descent in three Western states were rounded up and moved to "relocation" camps for the duration of the war, despite not a single proven case of espionage or sabotage among their number. In 1988 the United States government officially apologized and made economic reparations to those imprisoned.

Current Asian immigration includes many people from Southeast Asia. Most Asian Americans are concentrated in the major metropolitan areas. The vast majority are middle class and highly educated. Asian Americans have the highest rate of business ownership of any minority group in the United States.

Hundreds of thousands of Native Americans were exterminated by disease, starvation, and deliberate massacre by the Europeans as they appropriated Native-American lands. By 1900 only some 250,000 Indians remained out of perhaps two million or so in pre-Colonial times. Today there are about 1.8 million Native Americans; 55 percent of them live on or near reservations administered fully or partly by the federal government's Bureau of Indian Affairs. On the whole, Native Americans are at the bottom of the socioeconomic ladder, and have life expectancies only two-thirds of the national average.

Prospects for the Future

The resurgence of ethnic-identity movements is likely to spread and to be coupled with political protest movements demanding equal opportunity. The old concept of the Unied States as a "melting pot" is both simplistic and idealistic. Contemporary American society is the outcome of many diverse groups struggling to get along. This is a problem, but also a source of strength and flexibility not available in a homogeneous society.

CHAPTER OUTLINE

The Concept of Race
How is the concept of race defined?

GENETIC DEFINITIONS
What are genetic definitions of race?

LEGAL DEFINITIONS
What is the basis for legal definitions of race?

SOCIAL DEFINITIONS
What are the social definitions of race?

The Concept of Ethnic Group
What is the basis for the concept of an ethnic group?

The Concept of Minorities
What is the central component in the concept of a minority?

Problems in Race and Ethnic Relations
What are the central problems in race and ethnic relations?

PREJUDICE
What is prejudice?

DISCRIMINATION
What is the definition of discrimination?

Unprejudiced Nondiscriminators
How are unprejudiced nondiscriminators likely to behave?

Unprejudiced Discriminators
How are unprejudiced discriminators likely to behave?

Prejudiced Nondiscriminators
How are prejudiced nondiscriminators likely to behave?

Prejudiced Discriminators
How are prejudiced discriminators likely to behave?

INSTITUTIONALIZED PREJUDICE AND DISCRIMINATION
What does it mean to say that prejudice and discrimination are institutionalized?

Patterns in Racial and Ethnic Relations
What are the most important patterns in racial and ethnic relations?

ASSIMILATION
What is the process of assimilation?

PLURALISM
What is the basic assumption of pluralism?

SUBJUGATION
What is subjugation all about?

SEGREGATION
How does segregation operate?

EXPULSION
What is the outcome of expulsion?

ANNIHILATION
What is the goal of annihilation?

Racial and Ethnic Immigration to the United States
What is the main pattern of racial and ethnic immigration to the United States?

ILLEGAL IMMIGRATION
How significant is illegal immigration?

Racial and Ethnic Groups in the United States
What are the main racial and ethnic groups in the United States?

WHITE ANGLO-SAXON PROTESTANTS
What has been the experience of White Anglo-Saxon Protestants?

AFRICAN AMERICANS
What is unique about African Americans?

HISPANICS
How is the Hispanic ethnic group defined?

Mexican Americans
What is the experience of Mexican Americans?

Puerto Ricans
What is unique about Puerto Ricans?

Cuban Americans
Where do Cuban Americans fit within the Hispanic group?

JEWS
What is the ethnic experience of Jews?

ASIAN AMERICANS
What are the important Asian-American ethnic groups?

NATIVE AMERICANS (INDIANS)
What has been the experience of Native Americans?

Prospects for the Future
What are the prospects for the future?

LEARNING OBJECTIVES

After studying this chapter you should be able to:

■ *Critically review the major ways in which race has been defined.*

Define race according to each of the following categories, then state at least one criticism of that definition.

Genetic definition:

criticism:

Legal definition:

criticism:

Social definition:

criticism:

■ *Explain the concept of ethnic group.*

Select one of the following and explain why it constitutes an ethnic group: Lithuanians, Croatians, Amish, Chaldeans, Basque, Macedonians, Gypsies.

■ *Explain the sociological concept of "minority."*

Can either of the following groups be designated a minority? Why or why not?

Blacks in South Africa (over 85% of the country's population):

Women in the United States (51% of the population):

■ *Explain the relationship between prejudice and discrimination.*

An African-American family buys a house in an all-white suburban neighborhood. Shortly after they move in, some of their white neighbors begin demonstrating in front of their house, accusing the African-American family of "blockbusting" and lowering property values in the neighborhood. Predict what a white neighbor from each of the following groups would do in this situation.

Unprejudiced Nondiscriminator:

Unprejudiced Discriminator:

Prejudiced Nondiscriminator:

Prejudiced Discriminator:

■ *Understand the concept of institutionalized prejudice and discrimination.*

Based on the information in this chapter, choose one ethnic or racial group and explain how they have been victimized by institutionalized prejudice and discrimination.

■ *Explain the basic patterns of racial and ethnic relations.*

Define and give one historical example of each of the following patterns:

Assimilation:

Pluralism:

Subjugation:

Segregation:

Expulsion:

Annihilation:

■ *Describe the pattern of immigration to America.*

Historically, how many people have immigrated to this country?

In what decades did the largest number of immigrants come to the U.S.?

What ethnic groups constituted the *old migration*?

What ethnic groups constituted the *new migration*?

In recent decades, has immigration been increasing or decreasing?

What is the ethnic background of the largest numbers of current immigrants to the U.S.?

Give two examples of immigrant groups that have fared well in America because they possessed marketable skills and other advantages when they arrived.

1.

2.

■ *Describe the characteristics of the major racial and ethnic groups in the United States.*

State at least two important characteristics of each of the following racial or ethnic groups:

White Anglo-Saxon Protestants:

African Americans:

Hispanics:

Jews:

Asian Americans:

Native Americans:

KEY CONCEPTS

■ *Match each concept with its definition, illustration, or explication below.*

a. expulsion
b. old migration
c. prejudice
d. genocide
e. segregation
f. minority
g. Chicanos
h. pluralism
i. forced migration
j. institutionalized prejudice and discrimination

k. discrimination
l. ethnic group
m. subjugation
n. Anglo conformity
o. new migration
p. ghetto
q. annihilation
r. race
s. assimilation

_____ 1. a category of people who are defined as similar because of a number of physical characteristics.

_____ 2. a group of people who, because of physical or cultural characteristics, are singled out for differential and unequal treatment, and who therefore regard themselves as objects of collective discrimination.

_____ 3. a group with a distinct cultural tradition with which its own members identify and which may or may not be recognized by outsiders.

_____ 4. an irrationally based negative, or occasionally positive, attitude toward certain groups and their members.

_____ 5. differential treatment, usually unequal and injurious, accorded to individuals who are assumed to belong to a particular category or group.

_____ 6. complex societal arrangements that restrict the life chances and choices of a specifically defined group, in comparison with those of the dominant group.

_____ 7. the process whereby groups with different cultures come to share a common culture.

_____ 8. the expected renunciation of other ancestral cultures in favor of Anglo-American behavior and values.

_____ 9. the development and coexistence of separate racial and ethnic group identities within a society.

_____ 10. the subordination of one group and the assumption of a position of authority, power, and domination by the other.

_____ 11. the act, process, or state of being set apart.

_____ 12. used to describe any kind of segregated living environment.

_____ 13. the process of either indirectly or directly forcing a group to leave the territory in which it resides.

_____ 14. the relocation of a group through direct action.

_____ 15. the extermination of a racial or ethnic group.

_____ 16. a synonym for annihilation.

_____ 17. people who immigrated from northern Europe before 1880.

_____ 18. people from southern and eastern Europe who immigrated between 1880 and 1920.

_____ 19. Hispanics of Mexican descent.

CRITICAL THINKING/APPLICATION QUESTIONS

1. Reflect on your own personal experience of race and/or ethnicity. Go back to the Who Am I exercise you did in the Learning Objectives section of the Study Guide for Chapter 4. Does race or ethnicity appear in any of the twenty responses? If so, where does it rank? How important is this identity to you? If race or ethnicity does not appear on your list, why not?

2. Figure 9.3 in this chapter shows that, sometime in the second half of the next century, white ethnics will be a minority of the U.S. population. How do you think this will change the dynamics of racial and ethnic relations in this country? In particular, what do you think will happen to the idea of Anglo conformity and the issue of bilingual education discussed in the "Controversies in Sociology" box?

3. Some sociologists have suggested that, as a result of institutionalized prejudice and discrimination, there is an ethnic hierarchy in the United States, with groups ranked roughly according to the time of their arrival in this country. The exceptions, of course, are Native Americans and African Americans, who are near the bottom. Reflect on the major institutions in U.S. society and American popular culture and see if you can find evidence for or against the idea of an ethnic hierarchy. (For example, there has only been one U.S. president who wasn't a WASP—John F. Kennedy, an Irish Catholic, 1960–1963.)

4. The doctrine of Manifest Destiny, which has guided the development of the United States from the beginning, was succinctly expressed by an army general charged with the removal of Native Americans. He acknowledged that they were a brave and proud people, but needed to realize that it was their destiny to "give way to the insatiable progress of [the white] race." To what extent is the American Dream built on racism? What dysfunctional aspect of contemporary American society can be traced to the idea of Manifest Destiny?

SUGGESTED READINGS

THE CONCEPT OF RACE

Thomas F. Gosset, *Race: The History of an Idea in America* (New York: Schocken, 1965). A comprehensive history of the doctrine of white supremacy in the United States.

RACIAL AND ETHNIC IMMIGRATION TO THE UNITED STATES

Oscar Handlin, *The Uprooted,* 2nd ed., enlarged (Boston: Little, Brown, 1990). The classic history of European immigration to America, updated with recent developments.

RACIAL AND ETHNIC GROUPS IN THE UNITED STATES

Frank D. Bean and Marta Tienda, *The Hispanic Population of the United States* (New York: Russell Sage Foundation, 1987). A comprehensive look at Hispanics today.

Harry H. L. Kitano and Roger Daniels, *Asian Americans: Emerging Minorities* (Englewood Cliffs, NJ: Prentice Hall, 1988). A survey of the current status of Americans of Asian origin.

Nicholas Lemann, *The Promised Land: The Great Black Migration and How It Changed America* (New York: Knopf, 1991). Although they didn't cross an ocean to get here, African Americans underwent a dramatic immigration experience in this century that transformed them and the country.

Jack Weatherford, *Native Roots: How the Indians Enriched America* (New York: Crown, 1991). Shows how a surprising number of American social and cultural institutions and practices are rooted in Native-American culture.

ANSWER KEY

KEY CONCEPTS

1. r		11. e	
2. f		12. p	
3. l		13. a	
4. c		14. i	
5. k		15. q	
6. j		16. d	
7. s		17. b	
8. n		18. o	
9. h		19. g	
10. m			

CHAPTER 10 ■ *Gender and Age Stratification*

CHAPTER SUMMARY

Are the Sexes Separate and Unequal?

Sociologists make an important distinction between sex and gender. Sex refers to the physical and biological differences between men and women. Gender refers to the social, psychological, and cultural attributes of masculinity and femininity that are based on biological distinctions. Ideas about masculinity and femininity are culturally derived and are an important factor in shaping people's self images and social identities. Whereas sex is an ascribed status, gender is learned through the socialization process and is thus an achieved status.

Many people, on the other hand, believe that gender identities and masculine or feminine behavior are the result of an innate, biologically-determined process. Historically, societies in both the East and West viewed women as inherently inferior to men. Not only did intellectuals argue from the point of view of a patriarchal ideology, or a belief that men are superior to women and should control all important aspects of society, but religions in both the East and West supported this view.

Ethologists, or scientific observers of animal behavior, and sociobiologists argue that human gender-role behavior is biologically and genetically determined. Critics contend the biological view overlooks the much greater human capacity for language and the social learning that accompanies it. Undeniably, men and women differ on such genetically-influenced categories as size and muscle development, longevity, susceptibility to disease, and response to stress. Yet many other differences between males and females can be linked to cultural influences and variations in environment and activities.

Cross-cultural research reveals wide variation in the behavior and temperaments of men and women, although some division of labor on the basis of sex appears to be universal. Biological distinctions between the sexes, particularly with regard to childbearing, seem to take on greater significance in nonindustrial societies. Women's status appears to be lowest in those societies that most firmly differentiate between a private, domestic sphere and a public sphere of authority and power. Societies in which men value and participate in domestic activities tend to be more egalitarian. Most sociologists agree that, even though genetic and physiological factors influence gender differences, they do not determine these differences. Rather, people acquire their ability to fulfill their gender roles through socialization.

What Produces Gender Inequality?

Functionalists argue that the sexual division of labor was necessary for the efficient operation of preindustrial societies. Women, who birthed and nursed infants, remained involved in childcare and the necessities of daily living. Men hunted, herded, and defended the family. Because the female was largely dependent upon the male for protection and food, he became the dominant partner in the relationship. Functionalists maintain that this role differentiation is functionally necessary and efficient in modern society as well.

According to conflict theory, males dominate females because of their superior power and control over key resources. A major consequence of this domination is the exploitation of women by men and, according to conflict theorists, as long as men benefit from this arrangement, they have little incentive to change it.

Gender-Role Socialization

Gender-role socialization is a lifelong process whereby people learn the values, attitudes, motivations, and behavior considered appropriate to each sex by their culture. In our society, research indicates that parents respond differently to male and female infants right from the beginning. As a result of differential socialization, core gender identities are established by the age of two or three. During adolescence, boys are generally encouraged to pursue roles that will prepare them for occupations, whereas girls are encouraged to develop behavior patterns designed to attract a suitable mate.

As adults, women's gender identities are less independent than those of men; women tend to be defined in terms of their relationship to men and children. Given that female socialization de-emphasizes competition, aggressiveness, independence, and leadership, it is not surprising that adult women should generally have low achievement motivation. Finally, adult females tend to have low self-esteem. One manifestation of this is that both men and women constantly devalue the attributes of women.

Men tend to operate in a linear temporal world, in which the future is projected in terms of tangible career accomplishments. Young men envision themselves having families, but they expect those families to be support systems for their career pursuit; they do not perceive problems in coordinating career and family demands. Young women, on the other hand, operate in contingent temporal worlds, in which family and career have to be balanced and even traded off against one another at various points. Men seem to take their autonomy for granted, whereas women feel more limited in their control of the future. The dominant cultural norms and values are, in fact, based on male notions of autonomy and the application of absolute principles; female ethics of contingency and consequences based on relationships are thus denigrated.

Gender Inequality and Work

As of 1990, 57.5 percent of all American women were part of the paid labor force. Women are more likely than men to work part-time, and women's median wages were only 70 percent of men's in 1989, even when controlling for occupational segregation. Education seems to help women much less than men; male high school graduates earn more than female college graduates.

Women experience discrimination in the business world when, compared to men with equivalent qualifications, they are placed in jobs with lower prestige at the time of hire, they receive less pay for equivalent work, and they find it more difficult to win promotions. While the number of women managers and professionals have increased, women still dominate low-paying fields.

Gender Roles and the Future

Demographic, economic, and political changes have all contributed to growing independence for women in American society. These changes, coupled with the feminist movement, have had a significant impact on attitudes. Both men and women feel that women get more respect today and, for the first time, the concerns of women for adequate child care and maternity leave are shared by men. A clear majority of men and women today say they prefer an egalitarian marriage in which husband and wife share responsibilities for housework and childcare. Non-traditional gender roles have produced gains for women, but at the same time have created strains and conflicts in a variety of roles and relationships.

Age Stratification

For the first time in our history, there are more people aged 65 and over in the population than there are teenagers. Older Americans are currently 12.4 percent of the population. The older population has grown due to the aging of a cohort of people born when the birth rate was high, the aging of the large number of immigrants who came to this country in the first part of this century, and increased life expectancy created by improvements in medical technology.

The older population can be divided into the *young-old* (age 65–74), the *middle-old* (age 75–84), and the *old-old* (age 85 and older). By the year 2000, 50 percent of the older population will be over 75. Because mortality rates are higher for men, there is a substantial sex ratio imbalance in the over-65 group that becomes more apparent as one goes up the age scale. By the year 2000 there will be 65 men per 100 women 65 years and older, but only 38 men per 100 women over 85. Seventy percent of women over the age of 75 are widows, but less than 20 percent of men that age are widowers. Due to higher mortality rates among African Americans, the older population is disproportionately white.

Theories of Aging

Most theories of aging have been developed in the United States since 1950, and very little effort has been made to apply them cross-culturally. Disengagement theory states that aging involves an inevitable withdrawal from positions of social responsibility as part of the orderly operation of society. An underlying assumption is that both the individual and the society are happy about this process. The individual is pleased to be relieved of societal pressures for continued productivity; society is pleased because the withdrawal of older members allows younger, more energetic and competent members to fill the vacated roles. This emphasis on orderly transition reveals the strong functionalist orientation of disengagement theory.

Activity theory assumes that satisfaction in later life is related to the level of activity in which a person engages. Inactivity is equated with low levels of happiness and inadequate adjustment to the senior years. Since an individual's identity throughout life is built on a variety of statuses and roles, it is assumed that satisfaction in later life depends upon maintaining this social identity. There is a distinct middle-class bias to this theory. It also poses problems for those who become physically limited as they age.

Modernization theory assumes there is a direct relationship between the extent of modernization in a society and the status and condition of the older population. Loss of status for older people seems to be a universal experience in all societies that have modernized. Large numbers of the aged, the expectation of disengagement, and a separate retirement status are all unique to modern industrial societies. Critics argue that never before have large numbers of people lived to a relatively advanced age, so that comparisons with the past or with nonindustrial societies are likely to be misleading.

Future Trends in Age Stratification
As the enormous baby-boom cohort begins to reach age 65 in 2011, major changes can be expected. If mortality rates hold, the sex ratio will be greatly skewed toward women. Many people will find themselves caring for very old persons after they themselves have reached retirement age. Today there are twice as many children as older people; by 2030 children and the elderly will represent roughly equal shares of the population—about one-fifth each. All of these changes require careful planning for the future.

CHAPTER OUTLINE

Are the Sexes Separate and Unequal?
In what ways are the sexes separate and unequal?

HISTORICAL VIEWS
What are the historical views on sexual inequality?

RELIGIOUS VIEWS
What are some of the religious views of sexual inequality?

BIOLOGICAL VIEWS
How do biological views explain sex stratification?

Animal Studies and Sociobiology
What do animal studies and sociobiology have to say about inequality between the sexes?

Genetic and Physiological Differences
What are the major genetic and physiological differences between the sexes?

Responses to Stress
How do men and women differ in their responses to stress?

SOCIOLOGICAL VIEWS: CROSS-CULTURAL EVIDENCE
What does cross-cultural evidence tell us about sex differences?

What Produces Gender Inequality?
What are the major theories about what produces gender inequality?

THE FUNCTIONALIST VIEWPOINT
What is the functionalist viewpoint on gender inequality?

THE CONFLICT THEORY VIEWPOINT
What is the conflict theory on the origin and perpetuation of gender inequality?

Gender-Role Socialization
How does gender-role socialization operate?

CHILDHOOD SOCIALIZATION
What gender messages are conveyed through childhood socialization?

ADOLESCENT SOCIALIZATION
How does adolescent socialization reinforce gender inequality?

ADULT SOCIALIZATION
How does adult socialization perpetuate gender inequality?

GENDER DIFFERENCES IN SOCIAL INTERACTION
What are the basic gender differences in social interaction?

Gender Inequality and Work
How is gender inequality manifest at work?

JOB DISCRIMINATION
How does job discrimination on the basis of gender take place?

Gender Roles and the Future
What is the future of gender roles?

CHANGES IN ATTITUDES
What changes in attitudes about gender roles have taken place?

Age Stratification
How is our society stratified by age?

COMPOSITION OF THE OLDER POPULATION
What is the composition of the older population?

AGING BY SEX RATIO
How does the sex ratio relate to aging?

AGING BY RACE
What are the important racial differences in aging?

AGING BY MARITAL STATUS
How does marital status figure in aging?

Theories of Aging
What are the most important theories of aging?

DISENGAGEMENT THEORY
What does disengagement theory say about aging?

ACTIVITY THEORY
What does activity theory have to say about aging?

MODERNIZATION THEORY
How does modernization theory explain aging?

Future Trends in Age Stratification
What are the important future trends in age stratification?

LEARNING OBJECTIVES

After studying this chapter you should be able to:

■ *Contrast biological and sociological views of sex and gender.*

List five human traits or behaviors you think are due to biology, and five you think are learned through the socialization process and are therefore cultural in nature.

Biological traits or behaviors	Cultural traits or behaviors

1.

2.

3.

4.

5.

Did you have difficulty constructing this list—that is, did you have trouble seeing a particular trait or behavior as exclusively determined by one factor or the other? Why or why not?

Look over your list of biological factors. Can you really argue that any of these traits or behaviors occur in humans *without* cultural learning?

How much does that cultural learning influence the production of the trait or behavior?

■ *Describe and illustrate the concept of patriarchal ideology.*

What is patriarchal ideology?

Letty Cottin Pogrebin, one of the founding editors of *Ms.* magazine, has argued that patriarchal ideology can be boiled down into two simple messages, which we all learn in this culture as well and as subtly as we learn our own names. These two messages are: Boys are Better, and Girls Are Meant to Be

Mothers. Find five illustrations of each of these messages in any aspect of American society and culture (for example, language, including slang; folkways and mores; values; institutional practices, and so on).

Examples of the message Boys Are Better:

1.

2.

3.

4.

5.

Examples of the message Girls Are Meant to Be Mothers:

1.

2.

3.

4.

5.

■ *Compare and contrast functionalist and conflict theory viewpoints on gender stratification.*

Why, in modern industrial society, is there a public sphere of power and authority that is the province of men and a domestic sphere that is almost exclusively female? Explain this phenomenon according to both functionalist and conflict theory.

Functionalist explanation   **Conflict theory explanation**

Which explanation makes the most sense to you? Why?

■ *Explain the process of gender-role socialization.*

Amy is born to a middle-class urban American family in 1990. Amy's mother and father are both employed full-time outside the home. Based on what you have learned in this chapter, briefly sketch out a likely scenario for Amy's primary socialization, focusing on the issue of gender. In particular, incorporate information from Chapter 4, including Mead's stages of self-development and the role of the family, peers, the schools, and the mass media.

■ *Describe women's current labor force participation.*

As of 1990, what percent of all American women were part of the paid labor force?

What percentage of women work part-time?

What percentage of men work part-time?

1989 median weekly income for working men:

1989 median weekly income for working women:

Female/Male Ratio (divide women's income by men's income):

1988 average annual salary for male high school graduates employed full-time:

1988 average annual salary for female college graduates employed full-time:

■ *Describe the ways in which women face discrimination in the world of work.*

List the three most important ways in which women face discrimination in the world of work, and state one important implication of each.

1.

Implication:

2.

Implication:

3.

Implication:

■ *Explain the impact of changes in gender roles in American society.*

List what you consider to be the two most important changes in gender roles in American society, what you think the impact of each change has been/is likely to be, and how you evaluate that impact (for example, positive or negative for men and/or women, good or bad for society).

Change #1:

Impact:

Evaluation:

Change #2:

Impact:

Evaluation:

■ *Describe the basic demographic features of the older population in the U.S.*

number of Americans aged 65 and older, 1989:

percentage of the population, 1989:

projected percentage of the population in 2030:

Describe each of the following groups and state what you think would be their primary economic, political, or personal concern.

young-old:

middle-old:

old-old

State one important fact about the older population with regard to each of the following demographic characteristics:

sex ratio:

race:

marital status:

■ *Compare and contrast theories of aging.*

Explain the basic idea of each of the following theories and state one criticism of each.

Disengagement theory:

criticism:

Activity theory:

criticism:

Modernization theory:

criticism:

■ *Describe important future trends in age stratification.*

Describe three important impacts the aging of the baby boom generation is likely to have on American society.

1.

2.

3.

KEY CONCEPTS

■ *Match each concept with its definition, illustration, or explication below.*

a. gender identity
b. public sphere
c. modernization theory
d. baby-boom generation
e. young-old
f. patriarchal ideology
g. ethology
h. gender-role socialization
i. middle-old

j. sociobiology
k. contingent temporal world
l. old-old
m. gender
n. domestic sphere
o. disengagement theory
p. sex
q. linear temporal world
r. activity theory

_____ 1. the social, psychological, and cultural attributes of masculinity and feminity that are based on biological distinctions.

_____ 2. the physical and biological differences between men and women.

_____ 3. the belief that men are superior to women and should control all important aspects of society.

_____ 4. the scientific study of animal behavior.

_____ 5. the discipline that uses biological principles to explain the behavior of social beings.

_____ 6. activities involved with childcare and production of the necessities of life.

_____ 7. the realm of power and authority.

_____ 8. the lifelong process whereby people learn the values, attitudes, motivations, and behavior considered appropriate to each sex by their culture.

_____ 9. an individual's sense of their maleness or femaleness.

_____10. a view of the world in which events unfold in a predictable pattern.

_____11. a view of the world in which the future is uncertain and unpredictable due to the existence of a number of contingencies.

_____12. people between the ages of 65 and 74.

_____13. people over the age of 85.

_____14. people between the ages of 75 and 84.

_____15. states that aging involves an inevitable withdrawal from positions of social responsibility as part of the orderly operation of society.

_____16. assumes that there is a direct connection between the extent of moderization in a society and the status of the elderly.

_____17. assumes that satisfaction in later life is related to the level of activity in which a person is engaged.

_____18. the large number of people born between 1946 and 1964.

CRITICAL THINKING/APPLICATION QUESTIONS

1. In the early 1980s, Dr. Alice Baumgartner conducted research in which she asked school-age children to write about how their lives would be different if they woke up tomorrow and discovered they were the opposite sex. Try this yourself. Ask at least three males and three females Baumgartner's question. Record and analyze the responses. What patterns can you observe? How do these patterns relate to gender?

2. Carol Gilligan has suggested that men are socialized for autonomy, and therefore fear depen-

dence (commitment), whereas women are social-ized for connectedness, and therefore fear isolation. One result is the different conversa-tional styles discussed by Deborah Tannen in the box "Sociology at Work," in this chapter. To what extent do you think these insights explain or apply to your own cross-gender relationships? Would you support a change in socialization practices? Why?

3. Erving Goffman, in his book *Genderisms*, discusses the way that gender is portrayed in popular culture. Examine a sample of TV commercials and magazine ads and analyze the gender messages being conveyed. Are men and women presented equally? What differences are there, and do these differences make a difference?

4. Survey four or five of your classmates or friends about their attitudes toward aging. Do they think about being older? How do they picture themselves when they do? In particular, how will they resolve the dilemma of Erikson's final stage of development (Table 4.1 in Chapter 4)?

5. In the early 1990s, Dr. Jack Kevorkian of Michigan became a national issue when he helped several painfully or terminally ill people to commit suicide. As more people live longer and have more opportunities for disease and disabilities, suicide, and particularly assisted suicide, will continue to grow as social issues. Do you think that people have a right to take their own lives? Under what conditions? As long as no coercion is involved, does another person have the right to assist in a suicide? Why or why not?

SUGGESTED READINGS

ARE THE SEXES SEPARATE AND UNEQUAL?

Bettina Aptheker, *Tapestries of Life: Women's Work, Women's Consciousness, and the Meaning of Daily Experience* (Amherst, MA: University of Massachusetts Press, 1989). Weaves stories, poems, oral histories, paintings, and essays into an examination of women's unique experience. The author aims to suggest the ways of thinking that arise out of the dailiness of women's lives.

WHAT PRODUCES GENDER INEQUALITY?

Beth B. Hess and Myra Marx Feree, *Analyzing Gender: A Handbook for Social Science* (Beverly Hills, CA: Sage, 1987). A compendium of current social science research on gender: theory, stratification, sexuality, religion, the family, politics, and more.

GENDER-ROLE SOCIALIZATION

Letty Cottin Pogrebin, *Growing Up Free: Raising Your Child in the 80s* (New York: Bantam, 1980). A comprehensive, research-based examination of childhood gender-role socialization, with suggestions on how to avoid stereotypes.

GENDER INEQUALITY AND WORK

Ann Helton Stromberg and Shirley Harkess, *Women Working: Theories and Facts in Perspective*, 2nd ed. (Mountain View, CA: Mayfield, 1988). A reader that examines all facets of women and work in contemporary U.S. society.

Annette Fuentes and Barbara Ehrenreich, *Women in the Global Factory* (New York: Institute for New Communications, 1983). A short pamphlet that puts women's work experience in global perspective.

AGE STRATIFICATION

Arlie Russell Hochschild, *The Unexpected Community: Portrait of an Old Age Subculture* (Berkeley, CA: University of California Press, 1978). A pioneering ethnographic study of 43 older people living in a single apartment building in San Francisco. Readable, insightful, and useful for presenting the point of view of older people.

FUTURE TRENDS IN AGE STRATIFICATION

Alan Pifer and Lydia Bronte, eds., *Our Aging Society: Paradox and Promise* (New York: Norton, 1986). An outcome of the Carnegie Corporation's The Aging Society Project, this volume examines, from a social science perspective, the important ways in which an aging population is likely to transform American society.

ANSWER KEY
KEY CONCEPTS

1. m		10. q	
2. p		11. k	
3. f		12. e	
4. g		13. l	
5. j		14. i	
6. n		15. o	
7. b		16. c	
8. h		17. r	
9. a		18. d	

CHAPTER 11 ■ *Marriage and Alternative Family Lifestyles*

CHAPTER SUMMARY

The Nature of Family Life

The American family is in a process of change and transition. Beginning in the 1960s, marriage and birth rates began to fall, and the divorce rate began an accelerating upward trend. One quarter of all children born in 1988 were born to single women. By the year 2000, families will comprise only two out of three households and married couples will live in just over half of all households.

Given these changes, as well as comparative data on other societies, there is some disagreement over how to define the family. Nevertheless, sociologists generally agree that some form of family is found in every known human society, and that the family everywhere serves several important functions: regulating sexual behavior, patterning reproduction, organizing production and consumption, socializing children, offering care and protection, and providing social status.

Every society must replace its members. By regulating where and with whom individuals may enter into sexual relationships, society patterns sexual reproduction. No society permits random mating; all societies have an incest taboo, which forbids sexual intercourse among closely related individuals. Sex between parents and their children is universally prohibited, but who else is considered to be closely related varies widely among societies.

In all societies the family tends to be the primary unit of consumption; in some societies the family is a unit of production as well. Every society must also provide predictable social contexts within which its children are socialized. The family is ideally suited to this task because of its intimacy and the special knowledge of the children the adults are likely to have.

In addition to physical needs, humans need to be among people who care for them, who help with the problems that arise in daily life, and who back them up when there is a conflict with others. Although many kinds of social groups are capable of meeting one or more of these needs, the family is often the one group in a society that meets them all. Simply by being born into a family, each individual inherits both material goods and a socially recognized position defined by ascribed statuses. This inherited social position, or family background, is probably the single most important social factor affecting the predictable course of people's lives.

The basic family form, found in all societies, is the nuclear family, made up of a married couple and their children. Polygamous families are a composite form in which nuclear families are linked by multiple marriage bonds, with one central individual married to several spouses. In polygyny, a central male is married to multiple females, and in polyandry, a central female is married to multiple males. The latter case is quite rare. Extended families are comprised of the nuclear family plus other relations and generations living together and forming one cooperative unit.

Families trace their lineage in different ways. In a patrilineal system, the generations are tied together through the males of a family; in a matrilineal system the generations are tied together through the females. Under the bilateral system, descent passes through both the males and the females of a family. In patrilineal societies, men tend to dominate both public affairs and the domestic sphere. Sociologists refer to families in which men dominate as patriarchal. Matriarchal societies, in which most matters are dominated by women, are relatively uncommon, but are typically found in matrilineal societies. Nevertheless, the matriarchal family is becoming increasingly common in American society with the rise of single-parent families, which are most often headed by women.

Defining Marriage

Marriage is the socially recognized, legitimized, and supported union of individuals of opposite sexes. It is an institution found in all societies. Marriage differs from other unions in that it takes place in a public (and usually formal) manner, it includes sexual intercourse as an explicit element of the relationship, it provides the essential condition for legitimizing offspring, and it is intended to be a stable and enduring relationship. While almost all societies allow for divorce, none endorse it as an ideal norm.

American culture is relatively unique in linking romantic love and marriage. Romantic love, which involves the idealization of the loved one, the notion of a one and only, love at first sight, love winning out over all, and an indulgence of personal emotions, has nothing to do with marriage throughout most of the world. Marriage in these societies establishes social, economic, and even political relationships among families. Three families are ultimately involved in a marriage: the two spouses' families of orientation, or the families in which they were raised, and the family of procreation, which is created by the union of the spouses.

Marriage is governed by various rules. Rules of endogamy limit the social categories from which people can choose marriage partners. Rules of exogamy require an individual to marry someone outside his or her culturally defined group. Marriage rules also determine how many spouses a person may have at one time—monogamy means one spouse at a time, and polygamy permits multiple spouses.

Marital residence rules govern where a newly married couple lives. Patrilocal residence requires the couple to settle down near or within the husband's father's household. Matrilocal residence requires them to settle down near or within the wife's mother's household. Some societies allow for bilocal residence, in which the couple may choose to live with either the husband's or wife's family of origin. In industrial societies, neolocal residence, in which the couple may choose to live anywhere they please, is common. Bilocal and neolocal residence allow greater flexibility and a wider range of household forms, but they cut a young nuclear family off from extended kin who can help out in times of need.

Despite popular ideas to the contrary, mate selection in our society is not random. Homogamy—the tendency to choose a spouse with a similar racial, religious, ethnic, educational, age, and socio-economic background—is much more the rule. There are, for instance, comparatively few marriages in which there is a large age gap between the partners. In over three quarters of all marriages, however, the man is older than the woman.

Interracial unions represent less than two percent of all married couples. The most common type of interracial marriage is one between a white husband and a woman of a race other than African–American. The next most common type is the reverse of the first. These types of interracial marriages have been increasing substantially, while white/black interracial marriage appears to be leveling off.

Religious homogamy is not nearly as widespread as racial homogamy, though most marriages do involve people of the same religion. Nearly every religious group tries to discourage marriage outside the religion, but they vary in the extent of their opposition. There is generally a great deal of similarity in the educational and occupational status of marriage partners, though men tend to marry women who are slightly below them on these measures. The typical American high school plays an important role in sorting out potential marriage partners.

The Transformation of the Family

The modern, relatively isolated nuclear family is a product of the industrial revolution, because it permitted greater geographic and social mobility and allowed for inheritance through both sides of the family to all the children. This family form is characterized by a child-centered family, companionate marriage (that is, marriage based on romantic love), increased equality for women, decreased ties with extended family networks, neolocal residence and increased geographic mobility, increased social mobility, the clear separation between work and leisure, and the resulting emphasis on the family as a source of emotional support and a haven from the outside world.

World War II accelerated the movement of women into the paid labor force. It also paved the way for secondary groups and formal organizations to take over many of the family's traditional activities and functions. This transfer of functions out of the family has had a profound impact on the family. The current state of the family is linked to a number of societal issues including changes in marriage rates, family size, sexual attitudes, working women, and divorce laws.

A continuous expansion in the pool of eligible adults has kept the number of marriages and the marriage rate high, though a rising share of eligible people are choosing not to marry. A significant trend in the last fifteen years is growth in the number of childless couples, which appears to be an outgrowth of an increase in the number of women who are delaying marriage. The size of the average American household today—2.63 members—is half of what it was in 1790. This can be attributed to fewer children per family, more divorce and separation, an increase in the number of people living alone, a lesser likelihood of having unrelated people as part of the household, and a decline in the number of elderly parents living with their grown children. The latter trend is largely due to the increasing economic independence of the older population.

A massive attitudinal change toward acceptance of premarital sex was triggered by the social upheavals of the 1960s and 1970s, the accompanying changes in gender roles, and the development and accessibility of effective contraception. Recent widespread concern about sexually transmitted diseases such as AIDS and genital herpes may reverse this trend, though it is still too early to tell.

During the 45 years prior to 1989, the number of working women increased 200 percent. This is perhaps the single most important recent change in American society. Sex segregation in occupations is still significant, though women have made progress recently in entering traditional male professions. Women have not had as much success entering the ranks of high-level business managers and executives.

One national study found that some eight million Americans are assaulted every year by members of their own families. It is not clear, however, whether family violence is on the rise or is simply being reported more accurately.

The percentage of Americans who were divorced has nearly tripled in the past 20 years. Although the rate of divorce may now be leveling off, the U.S. still has the highest divorce rate in the world. Current divorce rates imply that half of all marriages will end in divorce. However, about 75 percent of divorced women and 85 percent of divorced men remarry. Higher divorce rates are a product of increased pressure on the isolated nuclear family, greater economic independence for women, greater visibility and acceptance of divorce in society, and changes in divorce laws.

Changes in divorce laws reflect a society's changing definition of marriage. No-fault divorce laws recognize that frequently both parties are responsible for the breakdown of the marriage. No-fault laws are based on the principle of distribution of assets based on equity and economic need; they also encourage women to become self-supporting. Nonetheless, no-fault divorce has been found to be economically devastating to many women, especially older homemakers and women with young children. Although no-fault divorce laws approach child custody in a sex-neutral way, mothers are still awarded custody of children in about 90 percent of American divorce cases. However, the courts are increasingly willing to view joint custody of children as an option. In the vast majority of joint custody cases the child physically resides with only one parent. Shared parental responsibility and decision making, especially in the post-divorce climate, can be problematic.

Alternative Lifestyles

A number of options are increasingly available to people who, for various reasons, find the traditional form of marriage impractical or incompatible with their lifestyle. The number of people living alone doubled between 1970 and 1990. In part this reflects more young people postponing marriage, but it also may mean that more adults have chosen to stay single permanently. The elderly comprise a significant portion of single-person households.

The number of children living with both biological parents declined from 85 percent to 73 percent over the last 20 years. Forty-two percent of white children and 86 percent of African-American children born today will live some portion of their youth in a single-parent household. Divorce is the major cause for this phenomenon, although some of it can be attributed to intentional single parenthood. Children raised in single-parent families do not seem to be at a disadvantage compared with children from two-parent families.

Stepfamilies are transforming basic family relationships and other institutions as well. Currently one in six children under the age of 18 has a stepparent; by the year 2000 it will be one in four.

We have very little reliable information on cohabitation, or couples living together out of wedlock. We do know that it increased 80 percent during the 1980s, and that it has become much more visible and accepted. Another phenomenon that has become more visible is the household consisting of a homosexual couple. There is no doubt that "couplehood," as either a reality or an aspiration, is as strong among gays and lesbians as it is among heterosexuals.

The Future: Bright or Dismal?

Despite claims to the contrary, there is little evidence that the family as an institution is in decline, or is any weaker today than a generation ago. Nor is there any indication that people place less value on their own family relationships, or on the role of the family within society, than they once did. The traditional family is simply being replaced by family arrangements that better suit today's lifestyles.

CHAPTER OUTLINE

The Nature of Family Life
What is the nature of family life?

FUNCTIONS OF THE FAMILY
What are the major functions of the family?

Regulating Sexual Behavior
How does the family go about regulating sexual behavior?

Patterning Reproduction
In what way does the family pattern reproduction?

Organizing Production and Consumption
How do families organize production and consumption?

Socializing Children
What is the family's role in socializing children?

Providing Care and Protection
How does the family provide care and protection?

Providing Social Status
How does the family provide social status?

FAMILY STRUCTURES
What are the important family structures?

Defining Marriage
How do sociologists define marriage?

ROMANTIC LOVE
What is romantic love?

MARRIAGE RULES
What are the most important marriage rules?

MARITAL RESIDENCE
How is marital residence determined?

MATE SELECTION
How does mate selection occur?

Age
How is age involved in mate selection?

Race
In what way does race influence mate selection?

Religion
How does religion relate to mate selection?

Social Status
How does social status influence mate selection?

The Transformation of the Family
What are the causes of the transformation of the family?

CHANGES IN THE MARRIAGE RATE
What are the important changes in the marriage rate?

CHILDLESS COUPLES

How extensive is the number of childless couples?

CHANGES IN HOUSEHOLD SIZE

What changes have occurred in household size?

PREMARITAL SEX

How have attitudes toward premarital sex changed?

WORKING WOMEN

How have working women affected the family?

FAMILY VIOLENCE

How extensive is family violence in the United States?

DIVORCE

How prevalent is divorce in U.S. society?

Divorce Laws

How have divorce laws changed?

Child-Custody Laws

What is the effect of child custody laws on the family?

Alternative Lifestyles

Why have alternative lifestyles developed in the United States?

THE GROWING SINGLE POPULATION

What is the explanation for the growing single population?

SINGLE-PARENT FAMILIES

What are the implications of more single-parent families?

STEPFAMILIES

What do we know about the dynamics of stepfamilies?

COHABITATION

How extensive is cohabitation in American society?

HOMOSEXUAL AND LESBIAN COUPLES

How are homosexual and lesbian couples similar to heterosexual couples?

The Future: Bright or Dismal?

What does the author think: Is the future bright or dismal?

LEARNING OBJECTIVES

After studying this chapter you should be able to:

■ *Explain the functions of the family.*

Choose either your family of orientation or your family of procreation (if you have one), and explain how it fulfills each of the following functions.

Regulating sexual behavior:

Patterning reproduction:

Organizing production and consumption:

Socializing children:

Offering care and protection:

Providing social status:

■ *Describe the major variations in family structure.*

Describe and explain your family of orientation within the following dimensions.

Is your family _____ nuclear or _____ extended?   Explain your choice.

Is your family _____ patrilineal   _____ matrilineal   _____bilateral   Explain.

Would you describe your family as _____ patriarchal or _____ matriarchal   Why?

■ *Describe the phenomenon of romantic love.*

List each of the dimensions of romantic love and give one example drawn from popular culture (TV, movies, literature, music, and so on.)

1.

   Example:

2.

Example

3.

Example:

4.

Example:

5.

Example:

■ *Describe the various rules governing marriage.*

Describe each of the following sets of marriage rules and state one implication for the family of each rule.

Endogamy:

Implication:

Exogamy:

Implication:

Monogamy:

Implication:

Polygyny:

Implication:

Polyandry:

Implication:

■ *Explain the ways in which mate selection is not random.*

Briefly describe the extent of homogamy among marriage partners on each of the following dimensions.

Age:

Race:

Religion:

Social Status:

Describe the primary mechanisms by which this homogamy occurs:

■ *Explain the impact of industrialism on the modern family.*

Explain the connection between industrialism and family structure in terms of each of the following factors:

Geographic mobility:

Social mobility:

Inheritance:

■ *Summarize recent changes in the family as an institution.*

For each of the following dimensions of change in the family, briefly describe the change, list at least one important statistic that demonstrates this change, then explain the likely reasons for the change.

Change in the marriage rate:

Statistic:

Explanation:

Change in childless couples:

Statistic:

Explanation:

Change in household size:

Statistic:

Explanation:

Change in attitudes toward premarital sex:

Statistic:

Explanation:

Change in working women:

Statistic:

Explanation:

Change in family violence:

Statistic:

Explanation:

Change in divorce:

Statistic

Explanation:

■ *Explain the impact of recent changes in divorce and child custody laws.*

Describe each of the following legal innovations and state at least one important implication of each.

No-fault divorce:

Implication:

Joint custody:

Implication:

■ *Describe the various alternative lifestyles in contemporary American society.*

For each of the following alternative lifestyles, briefly describe the lifestyle, list at least one important statistic about the lifestyle, then briefly discuss at least one important implication of the growth of this particular lifestyle.

Single people:

    Statistic:

    Implication:

Single-parent families:

    Statistic:

    Implication:

Stepfamilies:

    Statistic:

    Implication:

Cohabitation:

    Statistic:

    Implication:

Homosexual couples:

Statistic:

Implication:

KEY CONCEPTS

■ *Match each concept with its definition, illustration, or explication below.*

a. marital residence rules
b. family of procreation
c. romantic love
d. polygamous family
e. bilateral system
f. kibbutz
g. patriarchal family
h. marriage
i. cohabitation
j. patrilineal system
k. bilocal residence
l. polyandry
m. extended family
n. exogamy
o. no-fault divorce
p. monogamy

q. nuclear family
r. matrilineal system
s. incest taboo
t. patrilocal residence
u. polygyny
v. companionate marriage
w. joint custody
x. neolocal residence
y. homogamy
z. matriarchal family
aa. divorce
bb. endogamy
cc. matrilocal residence
dd. polygamy
ee. family of orientation

_____ 1. a type of Israeli agricultural community with communal living, collective ownership of property, and communal rearing of children.

_____ 2. a norm that forbids sexual intercourse among closely related individuals.

_____ 3. a married couple and their biological or adopted children.

_____ 4. a family with one central individual married to several spouses.

_____ 5. a situation in which a male is married to several females.

_____ 6. a situation in which a female is married to several males.

_____ 7. a family that includes other relations and generations in addition to the nuclear family.

_____ 8. a situation in which the generations are tied together through the males of a family.

_____ 9. a situation in which the generations are tied together through the females of a family.

_____10. a situation in which descent passes through both females and males of a family.

_____11. a situation in which most family affairs are dominated by women.

_____12. a situation in which most family affairs are dominated by men.

_____13. the socially recognized, legitimized, and supported union of individuals of opposite sexes.

_____ 14. the legal dissolution of marriage.

_____ 15. a phenomenon characterized by idealization of a loved one, the notion of a one and only, love at first sight, love winning out over all, and an indulgence of personal emotions.

_____ 16. the family in which one was born and raised.

_____ 17. the family created by marriage.

_____ 18. a situation in which people are directed to marry within certain social groups.

_____ 19. a situation in which individuals are required to marry someone outside their culturally defined group.

_____ 20. the situation in which a person is allowed only one spouse at a time.

_____ 21. the situation in which individuals may have multiple spouses.

_____ 22. norms that govern where a newly married couple settles down and lives.

_____ 23. a requirement that a new couple settle down near or within the husband's father's household.

_____ 24. a requirement that a new couple settle down near or within the wife's mother's household.

_____ 25. a situation in which a newly married couple can choose to live with either the husband's or the wife's family of origin.

_____ 26. a situation in which a newly married couple may choose to live anywhere they please.

_____ 27. the tendency to choose a spouse with a similar social and cultural background.

_____ 28. marriage based on romantic love.

_____ 29. a situation where, in principle, the financial aspects of marital dissolution are to be based on equity, equality, and economic need rather than fault- or gender-based role assignments.

_____ 30. a legal situation in which parental decision-making authority is given equally to both parents after a divorce.

_____ 31. a situation in which unmarried couples live together.

CRITICAL THINKING/APPLICATION QUESTIONS

1. In what ways is the idea of romantic love dysfunctional as a basis for marriage partnership? Would we be better off using formal matchmakers? To what extent do we already have an informal system of matchmaking in our culture (for example, being "set up" or introduced to a potential mate by friends, parents, and so on)?

2. Examine Figure 11.5 in this chapter. What are the main conclusions you draw from it regarding women's participation in selected occupations? Comparing the 1979 and the 1989 percentages, what evidence do you see for progress in women's economic opportunities? What evidence do you see for a lack of progress or a regression?

3. In the box "Sociology at Work" in this chapter, Arlie Hochschild discusses the "second shift" of housework and childcare that working women face. In Chapter 10, Daryl and Sandra Bem discussed the difference between *helping* with these mundance tasks and *taking responsibility* for seeing that they get done. In your own family of orientation or family of procreation, chart how these tasks get done—who decides/is aware of what must be done, who actually does these tasks, who makes sure that they get done—then discuss the extent that Hochschild's and the Bems' ideas apply and why. (Be sure to do this in a respectful and supportive way, though. The goal here is *not* to have you contribute to the divorce statistics!)

4. Discuss the concept of ideal vs. real norms (discussed in Chapter 3) as applied to marriage and family life. To the extent that there is a gap, why do you think it exists? What, if anything, should be done about it?

SUGGESTED READINGS

THE NATURE OF FAMILY LIFE

Christopher Lasch, *Haven in a Heartless World: The Family Besieged* (New York: Basic Books, 1979). A penetrating critique of the way the social sciences and helping professions have understood and treated the family in this century.

DEFINING MARRIAGE

Philip Blumstein and Pepper Schwartz, *American Couples* (New York: Morrow, 1983). A revealing study based on interviews with hundreds of different kinds of couples.

THE TRANSFORMATION OF THE FAMILY

Arlene S. Skolnick and Jerome H. Skolnick, eds., *Family in Transition,* 6th ed. (Boston: Little, Brown, 1988). A comprehensive reader on changes in the modern family and family life.

ALTERNATIVE LIFESTYLES

Maxine Baca Zinn and D. Stanley Eitzen, *Diversity in Families,* 2nd ed. (New York: Harper & Row, 1990). A look at widely divergent family lifestyles.

ANSWER KEY

KEY CONCEPTS

1. f	17. b
2. s	18. bb
3. q	19. n
4. d	20. p
5. u	21. dd
6. l	22. a
7. m	23. t
8. j	24. cc
9. r	25. k
10. e	26. x
11. z	27. y
12. g	28. v
13. h	29. o
14. aa	30. w
15. c	31. i
16. ee	

CHAPTER SUMMARY

The Nature of Religion

Religion is recognized as one of society's most important institutions. It is a system of beliefs, practices, and philosophical values shared by a group of people that defines the sacred, helps explain life, and provides salvation from the problems of human existence. Durkheim observed that all religions divide the universe into two mutually exclusive categories: the profane and the sacred. The profane consists of empirically observable things, whereas the sacred consists of things that are awe inspiring and knowable only through extraordinary experience. Sacred traits or objects symbolize important shared values. Patterns of behavior or practices that are related to the sacred are known as rituals.

All religions have formalized social rituals, but many also feature private rituals, such as prayer, as a means for individuals to address or communicate with supernatural beings or forces. One of the functions of ritual and prayer is to produce an appropriate emotional state. In addition, all religions endorse a belief system that usually includes a supernatural order and a set of values to be applied to daily life. Finally, many religions have an organizational structure through which specialists can be recruited and trained, religious meetings conducted, and interaction facilitated between society and members of the religion. This organization also promotes interaction and solidarity among the members.

Magic

Magic is an active attempt to coerce spirits or to control supernatural forces. It differs from other types of religious belief in that there is no worship of a god or gods; magic is usually a means to an end, whereas religion is often an end in itself. Magic tends to flourish when and where there are strong elements of chance, uncertainty, and fear, and goals do not seem achievable by rational means.

Major Types of Religion

One of the simplest and inclusive ways of classifying religions recognizes four basic types: supernaturalism, animism, theism, and abstract ideals. Supernaturalism postulates the existence of nonpersonalized supernatural forces that can and often do influence human events. These forces are thought to inhabit animate and inanimate objects alike and can come

and go at will. Supernatural beings may be of nonhuman origin, such as gods, or of human origin, such as ancestral spirits and ghosts. A religious taboo is a sacred prohibition against touching, mentioning, or looking at certain objects, acts, or people. Violating a taboo results in some form of pollution.

Animism is the belief in animate, personalized spirits or ghosts of ancestors that take an interest in and actively work to influence human affairs. Such spirits may inhabit the bodies of people and animals as well as inanimate phenomena. They are discrete beings with feelings, motives, and a will of their own. Though powerful, these spirits are not worshiped as gods; rather they are manipulated by using the proper magic rituals.

Theism is the belief in divine beings who shape human affairs. These gods or goddesses are powerful beings worthy of worship. Most theistic societies practice polytheism, the belief in a number of gods, who often have their own unique spheres of influence. Monotheism is belief in the existence of a single god. Only three religions are known to be monotheistic: Judaism and its two offshoots, Christianity and Islam.

Religions based on abstract ideals focus on the achievement of personal awareness and a higher state of consciousness through correct ways of thinking and behaving, rather than by manipulating spirits or worshipping gods.

A Sociological Approach to Religion

Sociologists focus on the relationship between religion and society. Functionalists examine the utility of religion in social life. Religion, they say, offers individuals ways to reduce anxiety and promote emotional integration. It provides for group unity and cohesion through its own practices, but also sometimes through the hostility and prejudice directed at members of a religious group by outsiders. Religion frequently legitimizes the structure of the society within which it exists. Religion establishes world views that help people to understand the purpose of life. These world views can have social, political, and economic consequences. Finally, religion can help a society adapt to its natural environment or to changing social, economic, and political circumstances.

Conflict theorists emphasize religion's role in justifying the political status quo by cloaking political authority with sacred legitimacy and thereby making opposition to it seem immoral. Alienation, the process by which people lose control over the social institutions they themselves have invented, plays an important role in the generation of religion, according to this view. Religion tends to conceal the natural and human causes of social problems in the world and discourages people from taking action to correct these problems. In addition, religion limits independent thinking and the search for further knowledge.

Organization of Religious Life

A universal church includes all the members of a society within one united moral community. It is fully a part of the social, political, and economic status quo. An ecclesia is a church that shares the same ethical system as the secular society and has come to represent and promote the interest of the society at large. It is an officially sanctioned church. A denomination tends to limit its membership to a particular class, ethnic group, or regional group, or at least to have its leadership positions dominated by members of such a group. It has no official or unofficial connection with the state. Denominations participate actively in secular affairs and tend to cooperate with other religious groups.

A sect is a small group that adheres strictly to religious doctrine that often includes unconventional beliefs or forms of worship. Sects generally represent a withdrawal from secular society and an active rejection of secular culture. Millenarian movements typically prophesize the end of the world, the destruction of all evil people and their works, and the saving of the just. They usually arise during times of social stress.

Aspects of American Religion

Religion pervaded the social and political goals of the early settlers of America and played a major role in shaping the nature of this society. Religion is still widespread in America. Nine out of ten Americans have a religious preference, even if they maintain no formal church affiliation, and four of ten attend religious services each week. At the same time, however, modern society is becoming increasingly secularized, or less influenced by religion. Religious institutions are being confined to ever-narrowing spheres of social influence, while people increasingly turn to nonreligious sources for moral guidance.

Ecumenism refers to the trend among many religious communities to draw together and project a sense of unity and common direction. It is partially a response to secularism, and is much more evident in the United States than in other countries. The growth of the electronic church in America is remarkable, with four religious TV networks, thirty-five religious TV stations, and an estimated 1,400 religious radio stations in operation. Forty-five percent of Americans watch religious programs on television or listen to them on radio at least once monthly. The effect of the electronic church on traditional churches is controversial and unclear.

Major Religions in the United States

There are more than one thousand different religious groups in the United States, which vary widely in religious practices, moral views, class structure, family values, and attitudes. Protestant denominations can be rated as conservative, moderate, or liberal in their moral and social outlooks. Catholics tend to resemble the moderate Protestants in their views, while Jews tend to resemble the liberal Protestants. Liberal and moderate Protestant denominations have experienced a decline in membership over the last 30 years, while conservative denominations have seen a dramatic increase in membership.

Catholics are the largest single religious denomination, representing about one-quarter of the adult population. They are significantly younger than Protestants on the average, have a higher proportion of membership from minority groups, and are more likely to live in urban areas. Recently, American Catholic attitudes have come to resemble those of Protestants on the issues of ideal family size and access to contraceptives. Changes stemming from the Vatican II council in the 1960s liberalized many church practices but also undermined the centralized authority structure of the Catholic Church. The leadership of the church has recently taken a more conservative turn.

There are currently about six million people in the United States who characterize themselves as Jewish. Jews have both a strong cultural and religious self-identification. Today this is partly based on identification with, and support for, the state of Israel. Orthodox Jews observe traditional religious laws very closely. Reform Jews allow for major reinterpretations of religious practices and customs. Conservative Jews are somewhere in between. A large segment of the secularized Jewish population still identifies itself as Jewish even without formal synagogue affiliation. The Jewish population in the United States is aging and the birth rate is below replacement levels. Thus, without recruitment, the American Jewish population is likely to decline.

Like Judaism and Christianity, Islam is monotheistic, and shares with them the prophets of the Old Testament. While there are nearly a billion Moslems in the world, it is difficult to ascertain exactly how many there are in the United States because Islam does not require attendance for formal membership and there is no major minority group that can be identified as predominantly Moslem. There are, however, 600 mosques or Islamic centers in this country, and it seems reasonable to estimate that the Islamic population of the United States is between three and four million.

Social Correlates of Religious Affiliation

Religious affiliation seems strongly correlated with economic status, educational level, family life, social mobility, and social attitudes. These correlations are, however, relationships of association rather than causation.

CHAPTER OUTLINE

The Nature of Religion
What is the nature of religion?

THE ELEMENTS OF RELIGION
What are the major elements of religion?

Ritual and Prayer
What is the role of ritual and prayer in religion?

Emotion
How is emotion related to religion?

Belief
What role does belief play in religion?

Organization
How is organization an element of religion?

Magic
What is the relationship between religion and magic?

Major Types of Religion
How are the major types of religion determined?

SUPERNATURALISM
What are the important characteristics of supernaturalism?

ANIMISM
What is animism?

THEISM
What is the major characteristic of theism?

MONOTHEISM
What is the significance of monotheism?

ABSTRACT IDEALS
What makes abstract ideals a type of religion?

A Sociological Approach to Religion
What is the basis of a sociological approach to religion?

THE FUNCTIONALIST PERSPECTIVE
What is the functionalist perspective on religion?

Satisfying Individual Needs
How does religion go about satisfying individual needs?

Social Cohesion
How does religion provide social cohesion?

Establishing World Views
What is the role of religion in establishing world views?

Adaptations to Society
How does religion foster adaptations to society?

THE CONFLICT THEORY PERSPECTIVE
What is the basic assumption of the conflict theory perspective on religion?

Organization of Religious Life
In what sense is religious life organized?

THE UNIVERSAL CHURCH
What is the main characteristic of the universal church?

THE ECCLESIA
What is an ecclesia?

THE DENOMINATION
How is a religious denomination organized?

THE SECT
What are the basic characteristics of a sect?

MILLENARIAN MOVEMENTS
What are millenarian movements all about?

Aspects of American Religion
What are the major aspects of American religion?

WIDESPREAD BELIEF
How widespread is belief?

SECULARISM
How important is secularism?

ECUMENISM
What is ecumenism?

TELEVISION EVANGELISM
What is the impact of television evangelism?

Major Religions in the United States
What are the major religions in the United States?

PROTESTANTISM
What are the most important types of Protestantism?

CATHOLICISM
What are the key characteristics of Catholicism?

JUDAISM
What is the nature of Judaism in the contemporary United States?

ISLAM
What makes Islam a major religion in the United States?

Social Correlates of Religious Affiliation
What are the key social correlates of religious affiliation?

LEARNING OBJECTIVES

■ *Explain the nature of religion and differentiate it from magic.*

Go back to Chapter 5 and review the definition of a social institution. Discuss at least three ways that religion is a social institution.

1.

2.

3.

What is the significance of the distinction between the sacred and the profane?

Explain how magic is different from religion:

■ *Define the basic elements of religion.*

Choose a religion with which you are familiar and describe how each of the following elements are present within it.

Ritual and prayer:

Emotion:

Belief:

Organization:

■ *Differentiate among the major types of religion.*

List the basic characteristics and give an example of each of the following types of religion.

Supernaturalism:

example:

Animism:

example:

Theism:

example:

Monotheism:

example:

Abstract Ideals:

example:

■ *Describe the functions of religion according to the functionalist perspective.*

Explain how religion fulfills each of the following functions.

Satisfying individual needs:

Providing social cohesion:

Establishing world views:

Creating adaptations to society:

■ *Explain the conflict theory perspective on religion.*

Discuss the connection between alienation and religious belief, according to the conflict theory perspective.

Give three examples of ways in which religion legitimizes political authority and social inequality:

1.

2.

3.

■ *Describe the basic types of religious organization.*

Describe and give an example of each of the following types of religious organization.

Universal church:

    example:

Ecclesia:

example:

Denomination:

example:

Sect:

example:

Millenarian movement:

example:

■ *Describe important aspects of contemporary American religion.*
How widespread is religious belief in America today?

Why are there so many religious groups and organizations in the United States?

What is the evidence for the secularization of American life?

Why has ecumenism flourished in the United States more than in Europe?

List two potentially positive consequences of television evangelism.
1.

2.

List two potentially negative consequences of television evangelism.

1.

2.

■ *Describe the major religions in the United States.*

List two examples each of conservative, moderate, and liberal denominations in the U.S.

Conservative

   1.

   2.

Moderate

   1.

   2.

Liberal

   1.

   2.

Discuss two important characteristics of each of the following religions.

Protestantism

1.

2.

Catholicism

1.

2.

Judaism

1.

2.

Islam

1.

2.

■ *Describe the major social correlates of religious affiliation.*

Describe differences among the major religious groups in the United States on each of the following dimensions.

Education:

Income:

Politics:

KEY CONCEPTS

■ *Match each concept with its definition, illustration, or explication below.*

a. denomination
b. magic
c. polytheism
d. mana
e. sacred
f. universal church
g. theism
h. shaman
i. rituals
j. supernaturalism
k. revitalization movement
l. ecumenism
m. sect

n. prayer
o. abstract ideals
p. profane
q. ecclesia
r. millenarian movement
s. religious taboo
t. animism
u. alienation
v. religion
w. secularism
x. totem
y. monotheism

_____ 1. a system of beliefs, practices, and philosophical values shared by a group of people that defines the sacred, helps explain life, and provides salvation from the problems of human existence.

_____ 2. things that are awe inspiring and knowable only through extraordinary experience.

_____ 3. things that are knowable through common, everyday experiences.

_____ 4. patterns of behavior or practices related to the sacred.

_____ 5. a means for individuals to address or communicate with supernatural beings or forces.

_____ 6. an active attempt to coerce spirits or control supernatural forces.

_____ 7. belief in the existence of nonpersonalized supernatural forces that can and often do influence human events.

_____ 8. a diffuse, nonpersonalized force that acts through anything that lives or moves.

_____ 9. a sacred taboo against touching, mentioning, or looking at certain objects, acts, or people.

_____ 10. belief in animate, personalized spirits or ghosts of ancestors that take an interest in and actively work to influence human affairs.

_____ 11. a medicine man or woman who effects cures by using magic rituals.

_____ 12. belief in divine beings—gods and goddesses—who shape human affairs.

_____ 13. belief in a number of gods.

_____ 14. belief in the existence of a single god.

_____ 15. focus on the achievement of personal awareness and a higher state of consciousness through correct ways of thinking and behaving, rather than manipulating spirits or worshipping gods.

_____ 16. an ordinary object that has become a sacred symbol to and of a particular group or clan.

_____ 17. religious movements that stress a need to return to the traditional religious values of the past.

_____ 18. the process by which people lose control over the social institutions they themselves invented.

_____ 19. includes all members of a society within one united moral community.

_____ 20. a church that shares the same ethical system as the secular society and has come to represent and promote the interest of the society at large.

_____21. a religious group that tends to limit its membership to a particular class, ethnic, or regional group.

_____22. a small group that adheres strictly to religious doctrine that often includes unconventional beliefs or forms of worship.

_____23. movements that typically prophesize the end of the world, the destruction of all evil people and their works, and the saving of the just.

_____24. a condition in society in which religious influence is lessened.

_____25. the trend among many religious communities to draw together and project a sense of unity and common direction.

KEY THINKERS/RESEARCHERS

■ *Match each thinker with his or her main idea or contribution.*

a. Max Weber

b. Karl Marx

c. Stark and Bainbridge

d. Émile Durkheim

e. Marvin Harris

_____1. a pioneer in the sociology of religion, he first distinguished between the sacred and the profane, and discussed religion's role in promoting social cohesion.

_____2. discussed the relationship of magic and Christianity.

_____3. in *The Protestant Ethic and the Spirit of Capitalism,* he discussed how the ideology of Calvinism had influenced the development of capitalism.

_____4. showed that the Indian belief in the sacredness of cows is a positive strategy for adapting to the environment, and therefore quite rational.

_____5. argued that religion is a tool the upper classes use to maintain control of society and to dominate the lower classes.

CRITICAL THINKING/APPLICATION QUESTIONS

1. Durkheim discussed the role of the sacred in promoting social cohesion. To what extent have profane events and objects like the Super Bowl, the Olympics, rock concerts, presidential inaugurations, and sports memorabilia become sacred in American culture? What are the implications of this phenomenon?

2. Americans frequently deride the animistic or magical belief systems prevalent among many non-Western peoples as "primitive" and unsophisticated. To what extent do Christian rituals like communion, faith healing, and praying for miracle cures or solutions resemble the same type of faith in magic? What is the difference between the two?

3. Rituals have been defined as patterns of behavior or practices that are related to the sacred. To what extent do you observe rituals at your workplace or in popular culture (sports, music, drama, and so on)?

4. In describing their religious beliefs, many people talk in terms of Absolute, or Revealed Truth. This implies a timeless, unchanging reality. Yet, we have seen that religious beliefs have indeed undergone substantial change and tend to reflect the surrounding society. How do you account for this sociologically?

SUGGESTED READINGS

THE NATURE OF RELIGION

Phillip E. Hammond, ed., *The Sacred in a Secular Age: Toward Revision in the Scientific Study of* *Religion* (Berkeley, CA: University of California Press, 1985). A contemporary social science look at all aspects of the sacred in modern life.

In addition to a wide range of topics, it is comparative and and cross-cultural.

MAJOR TYPES OF RELIGION

Ninian Smart, *The World's Religions* (Englewood Cliffs, NJ: Prentice Hall, 1989). An examination of the major religions of the world, including the geographic areas in which each is dominant.

A SOCIOLOGICAL APROACH TO RELIGION

Keith A. Roberts, *Religion in Sociological Perspective* (Homewood, IL: Dorsey, 1984). A comprehensive, well-written introduction to the sociological aspects of religion.

ORGANIZATION OF RELIGIOUS LIFE

Rodney Stark and William Sims Bainbridge, *The Future of Religion: Secularization, Revival, and Cult Formation* (Berkeley, CA: University of California Press, 1985). An examination of current trends in religious belief and organization.

ASPECTS OF AMERICAN RELIGION

Jeffrey K. Hadden and Anson Shupe, *Televangelism: Power and Politics on God's Frontier* (New York: Henry Holt, 1988). A sociological analysis of television evangelists, their followers, and their impact on American politics and culture.

ANSWER KEY

KEY CONCEPTS

1. v	14. y
2. e	15. o
3. p	16. x
4. i	17. k
5. n	18. u
6. b	19. f
7. j	20. q
8. d	21. a
9. s	22. m
10. t	23. r
11. h	24. w
12. g	25. l
13. c	

KEY THINKERS/RESEARCHERS

1. d
2. c
3. a
4. e
5. b

CHAPTER 13 ■ *Education*

CHAPTER SUMMARY

Education: A Functionalist View

Why should people get an education? The most common answer Americans give is to get a better job. Yet most jobs in our society do not require twelve or more years of training. Something else must be taking place during those years of schooling. Functionalists suggest that that something else consists of activities that are functional for the society as a whole.

One of the manifest functions, or intended consequences, of education is socialization. In a sense, education is just an extension of the socialization that occurs within the family. Indeed, in nonindustrial societies no real distinction is made between the two. However, in modern industrial society, education is a much more formal activity than socialization. Student and teacher roles are clearly defined and the curriculum taught is explicit. Education, then, is a specialized form of socialization that evolved in response to the demands of the industrial revolution.

Another function of education is cultural transmission, in which a major portion of society's knowledge is passed from one generation to the next. In order to hold together, every society must have consensus over certain core values and goals. In a complex, pluralistic society with many competing interest groups, this consensus is difficult to achieve, and always a political issue.

A critical function of schools is to equip children with the academic skills needed to function as adults. Most experts believe that American schools are not currently carrying out this function very successfully. As a result of the 1983 report *A Nation at Risk,* reforms were instituted emphasizing the teaching of "the three Rs" and requiring students and teachers to pass standardized competency tests. The success of these reform measures has been limited. Standardized test scores have risen, but student performance in math and science is still weak. Moreover, about 10 percent of the nation's adult population is functionally illiterate.

Learning how to think independently and creatively is probably one of the most valuable tools the educational institution can transmit. This is the function called innovation, and today it is a systematic enterprise generally carried out with government funding in institutions of higher education by highly-trained specialists.

In addition to its manifest functions, schooling in America has developed a number of unintended consequences as well. One latent function of many public schools is to provide child care outside the nuclear family. This has become increasingly important in recent years with the growing number of women in the labor force and the dramatic increase in single-parent families. A related service is to provide students with at least one nutritious meal a day. Currently this program reaches almost twelve million pupils, and advocates want to greatly expand it.

Another important latent function of the American educational system is to slow down the entry of young adults into the labor force by having them continue in school. The attraction is that continuing education generally is the most important factor in getting a better job and upward social mobility. The movement of women into the labor force and the breakdown of gender stereotypes have resulted in women constituting a majority of college enrollments today.

The Conflict Theory View

Conflict theorists view society as an arena of conflict, in which certain groups dominate others, and social institutions become the instruments by which those in power are able to control the less powerful. Thus the conflict theorist sees education as a means for maintaining the status quo by producing the kinds of people the system needs. This is accomplished through teaching the "hidden curriculum"—attitudes and values congruent with the authoritarian, routinized society in which students will be expected to function. Some conflict theorists argue that educational success is not really dependent upon merit or intelligence but rather upon the acquisition of appropriate personality traits and conformity to school norms.

Despite the fact that the American educational system is in principle meritocratic—rewarding exclusively individual talent and effort—conflict theorists argue that in fact it depends upon tracking, or the stratification of students by ability, social class, and various other categories. Tracking begins early in students' careers when they are grouped by "ability"—a definition laden with social class and ethnic bias. From this point on, student performance tends to become a self-fulfilling prophecy, in which the student's competence level rises or falls to meet the teacher's (biased) expectations.

Conflict theorists would argue that we have become a "credentialized society" in the last thirty years. A degree or certificate has become necessary to obtain a vast number of jobs in spite of the fact that the credential may have little to do with enhancement of job performance. The credential, though, serves as a rite of passage and a sign that a certain process of indoctrination and socialization has occurred. Educational institutions thus act as gatekeepers, allowing those who are willing to play by the rules to succeed, while barring those who may disrupt the existing social order.

Issues in American Education

American minorities have sought equal access to public schools for two centuries. Black parents have been dissatisfied with the education their children have received in segregated all-black schools. At the same time, these parents are unhappy when their children attend predominantly white schools because they believe the white students are favored by the teachers. In 1954 the U.S. Supreme Court banned *de jure* segregation, or laws requiring students to attend segregated schools. This ruling had little effect, however, on *de facto* segregation, or segregation resulting from residential patterns. Thus segregated neighborhoods have produced segregated neighborhood schools.

The "Coleman Report" of 1966 found that schooling in America remained unequal. Minorities scored significantly below whites on standardized tests and the gap widened in the higher grades. The discrepancies could not be accounted for in terms of the amount of money spent per pupil, quality of school buildings, number of labs or libraries, or even class sizes. The family background of individual students and the family backgrounds of the student population in a school were the most important explanatory factors. The report did show, however, that lower-class nonwhite students showed higher achievement when they went to school with middle-class whites. This became the justification for massive busing of students. Court-ordered busing for school integration provoked large-scale opposition from both white and minority parents and has largely fallen into disfavor today. Other, less disruptive alternatives are usually employed.

One factor that has made school integration increasingly difficult is white flight, or the continuing exodus of large numbers of whites from the central cities to the suburbs. Only three percent of the nation's white students attend central city schools today. A number of large city school districts are now more segregated than they were a decade ago. In addition, these districts have large numbers of Hispanic and Asian immigrant children whose native language is not English. Thus, costly "English as a Second Language" programs are needed on a large scale. The result of all this is that the white middle class expresses little concern over the condition of central city schools.

Colleges and universities have had mixed results in increasing minority enrollment. Though many schools have undertaken aggressive minority recruitment programs, thousands of qualified minority students never attend college and many who do, fail to graduate. The reasons include financial problems, poor preparation, and the feeling they are not really welcome.

While the overall high school graduation rate has been increasing, the dropout rate for minorities has remained high. Factors associated with dropping out include low educational and occupational attainment levels of parents, low family income, speaking a language other than English in the home, single-parent families, and poor academic achievement. The influence of peers is important, but little researched. Not only does dropping out of high school have negative consequences for the individual, but it affects society through a loss of income and tax revenues, increased demand for social services, increased crime, reduced political participation and social mobility, and poorer levels of health.

Violence in schools is a growing problem as a result of increased gang presence, more drugs, and more weapons. Many urban schools operate under a siege mentality, with doors chained shut and students afraid to be in the wrong place at the wrong time, inside of school or out.

In American schools, the standardized test is the most frequently used means of evaluating student aptitude, ability, and performance. Every year more than 100 million standardized tests are given to individuals from nursery school to graduate school. Critics claim that these tests are academically invalid and culturally biased against minorities and the lower class. At best, standardized tests should be seen as an objective measure to be used in conjunction with other methods of evaluation and teacher comments. While more students are taking the Scholastic Aptitude Test (SAT) than ever before, scores have actually risen over the last decade.

The term *gifted* is emotionally loaded; it evokes feelings ranging from admiration to resentment and hostility. There is little agreement on what constitutes giftedness. The most common measure is performance on a standardized test. Because of this, and the presence of cultural biases, women, minorities, and the disabled tend to be underrepresented among the gifted. In addition, many other students of exceptional ability are probably over-looked. There has never been a consistent, cohesive national policy or consensus on how to educate the gifted. Giftedness is essentially potential. We as a society must decide whether and how we choose to have that potential actualized.

CHAPTER OUTLINE

Education: A Functionalist View
What is the functionalist view of education?

SOCIALIZATION
How is socialization related to education?

CULTURAL TRANSMISSION
How does cultural transmission work?

ACADEMIC SKILLS
What is the function of academic skills?

INNOVATION
Why is innovation a function of education?

CHILD CARE
How is child care a function of education?

POSTPONING JOB HUNTING
How does education function to postpone job hunting?

The Conflict Theory View
What is the conflict theory view of education?

SOCIAL CONTROL
How do schools facilitate social control?

SCREENING AND ALLOCATION: TRACKING
How does screening and allocation work?

THE CREDENTIALIZED SOCIETY
What does it mean to say that we have a credentialized society?

Issues in American Education
What are the most important issues in American education today?

UNEQUAL ACCESS TO EDUCATION
How is access to education unequal?

HIGH SCHOOL DROPOUTS
What happens to high school dropouts?

VIOLENCE IN THE SCHOOLS
How serious is the problem of violence in the schools?

STANDARDIZED TESTING

What is the basis of the controversy over standardized testing?

THE GIFTED

What is the current status of the gifted in education?

LEARNING OBJECTIVES

After studying this chapter you should be able to:

■ *Describe the manifest functions of education, according to the functionalist view.*

Describe each of the following functions of education and, reflecting on your own high school experience, give one example of each.

Socialization:

   example:

Cultural transmission:

   example:

Academic skills:

   example:

Innovation:

   example:

■ *Describe the latent functions of education, according to the functionalist view.*

Explain why each of the following functions is a latent function, and then state one important implication for each.

Child care:

implication:

Postponing job hunting:

implication:

■ *Describe the functions of education from the conflict theory view.*

Describe each of the following functions of education from the conflict theory view and, reflecting on your own school experience to date, give one example of each.

Social control:

example:

Tracking:

example:

Conferring credentials:

example:

■ *Explain the causes and effects of racial segregation in the public schools.*

Summarize the findings of the famous "Coleman report" of 1966:

How was the report used to justify massive court-ordered busing of school children?

Explain the difference between *de jure* and *de facto* segregation:

What is "white flight" and how has it affected schools?

Why aren't minorities equally represented in college and university enrollments?

■ *Discuss the extent to which high school dropouts are a social problem.*

Which groups have the highest dropout rates?

List 5 factors associated with dropping out of school:

1.

2.

3.

4.

5.

List 7 social consequences of high dropout rates:

1.

2.

3.

4.

5.

6.

7.

■ *Discuss the issue of standardized testing.*

Briefly discuss two arguments in favor of standardized testing:

1.

2.

Briefly discuss two arguments against standardized testing:

1.

2.

■ *Evaluate the idea of special programs for gifted students.*

Briefly discuss two reasons for and two reasons against having special programs in schools for gifted students.

For:

1.

2.

Against:

1.

2.

KEY CONCEPTS

■ *Match each concept with its definition, illustration, or explication below.*

a. gifted

b. white flight

c. hidden curriculum

d. cultural transmission

e. functional illiteracy

f. *de facto* segregation

g. self-fulfilling prophecy

h. *de jure* segregation

i. dropouts

j. bilingual education

k. back-to-basics movement

l. tracking

_____ 1. the process in which major portions of a society's knowledge are passed from one generation to the next.

_____ 2. a social movement demanding the elimination of frivolous elective courses, the stressing of "the three Rs," and the implementation of standardized competency testing.

_____ 3. the social attitudes and values taught in school that prepare children to accept the requirements of adult life and to "fit into" the social, economic, and political statuses the society provides.

_____ 4. the stratification of students by ability, social class, and various other categories.

_____ 5. predetermining the outcome of a social process by defining it in a certain way at the beginning.

_____ 6. a form of racial separateness resulting from residential housing patterns.

_____ 7. a form of racial separateness based on laws prohibiting interracial contact.

_____ 8. the exodus of large numbers of white Americans from the central cities to the suburbs.

_____ 9. students who leave high school without graduating.

_____10. students with special abilities who score at a high level on standardized tests.

_____11. a condition in which people cannot read or write well enough to hold down a job or otherwise function properly in society.

_____12. a process in which students receive instruction in their primary language as well as in English.

KEY THINKERS/RESEARCHERS

■ *Match each thinker with their main idea or contribution.*

a. Rosenthal and Jacobson

b. James Coleman

c. National Commission on Excellence in Education

d. Bowles and Gintis

_____1. their report, *A Nation at Risk,* instigated the current educational reform movement.

_____2. they argue that educational success is more likely to be determined by possession of the appropriate personality traits than by merit or intelligence.

_____3. conducted a famous study that demonstrated the powerful effect of the self-fulfilling prophecy in school.

_____4. author of a 1966 survey of 645,000 children that demonstrated substantial class and race differences in educational achievement and opportunity.

CRITICAL THINKING/APPLICATION QUESTIONS

1. In the box, "Sociology at Work," in this chapter, Jonathan Kozol presents his critique of inequities among schools, particularly in the area of funding. How would you evaluate his argument in light of the findings of the original Coleman report of 1966?

2. Make a list of all the standardized tests that you can remember having taken. To what extent do you think these tests were a fair measure of your aptitude or knowledge? Were some of the tests better or more fair than others? Why?

3. Recently, Whittle Communications, a private for-profit company, has been offering a television program called Channel One to school systems. Whittle donates thousands of dollars of video equipment to the school in return for the school's promise to have all students watch Channel One every day. The programming consists of about ten minutes of current news done in a fast-paced, MTV style along with two minutes of commercials for products aimed at the youth market. This program has proved to be highly controversial. Construct at least two arguments for and two arguments against schools implementing the Channel One program.

4. Go back to Chapter 5 and review the types of interaction. What type of interaction is education in the United States? What type of interaction should it be? Also in Chapter 5 are the characteristics of bureaucracy. To what extent does education qualify as a bureaucratic endeavor, according to Weber's criteria?

5. The opening vignette of this chapter as well as Jonathan Kozol's discussion in "Sociology at Work" present some of the current glaring inequalities in American education. Moreover, evidence has been presented in this chapter about decaying central-city school systems co-existing with well-endowed suburban systems, differing in their class and racial makeups. Suppose that you were governor of a state (it could be almost any one) with these kinds of metropolitan disparities. What policies would you support to guarantee equal access to education to all citizens? On what basis would you get people to support these policies? Who would be the likely opposition?

SUGGESTED READINGS
PERSPECTIVES ON EDUCATION

Kathleen P. Bennett and Margaret D. LeCompte, *How Schools Work: A Sociological Analysis of Education* (New York: Longman, 1990). A comprehensive look at education in the United States today from a sociological perspective.

Ira Katznelson and Margaret Weir, *Schooling for All: Class, Race, and the Decline of the Democratic Ideal* (New York: Basic Books, 1985). Critical of conventional conservative, liberal, and radical perspectives on education, the authors argue that American schools have been shaped by both capitalism and democracy, and that the democratic ideal embodied in them is currently undermined by class and race inequality.

Stanley Aronowitz and Henry A. Giroux, *Education Under Siege: The Conservative, Liberal and Radical Debate Over Schooling* (South Hadley, MA: Bergin & Garvey, 1985). Despite its subtitle, this book is really a radical analysis of the purpose and possibilities of schooling.

ISSUES IN AMERICAN EDUCATION

Paulo Freire, *Pedagogy of the Oppressed*. Translated by Myra Bergman Ramos, (New York: The Seabury Press, 1970). A philosopher of education describes his method for teaching—and empowering—illiterate adults through dialogue about their life conditions.

Ivan Illich, *Deschooling Society* (New York: Harper & Row, 1970). A classic work that argues that education has become too bureaucratic, and the solution is to move learning out into the community by creating democratic, grass-roots, person-to-person "learning webs."

ANSWER KEY
KEY CONCEPTS

1. d	5. g	9. i
2. k	6. f	10. a
3. c	7. h	11. e
4. l	8. b	12. j

KEY THINKERS/RESEARCHERS

1. c
2. d
3. a
4. b

CHAPTER SUMMARY

Politics, Power, and Authority

In most societies what laws get passed, or not passed, depends to a large extent on which categories of people have power. Politics is the process by which power is distributed and decisions are made. Power, as Weber defined it, is the ability of a person or group to carry out their will, even in the face of opposition. With regard to politics, power refers to the exacting of compliance with decisions through the threat or actual use of sanctions, penalties, or force.

Power is exercised in a broad spectrum of ways. At one pole is authority, or power that is regarded as legitimate by those over whom it is exercised, who also accept the authority's legitimacy in imposing sanctions or even in using force if necessary. At the other extreme is coercion, or power that is regarded as illegitimate by those over whom it is exerted. Power based on authority is quite stable, and obedience to it is accepted as a social norm. Power based on coercion is unstable. It is based on fear; any opportunity to test it will be taken, and in the long run it will fail.

Weber identified three kinds of authority. Legal-rational authority is derived from the understanding that specific individuals have clearly defined rights and duties to uphold and implement rules and procedures impersonally. Power is vested not in individuals but in particular positions or offices. Traditional authority is rooted in the assumption that the customs of the past legitimate the present. As long as tradition is followed, the authority is legitimate. Charismatic authority derives from a ruler's ability to inspire passion and devotion among followers. Charismatic leaders typically emerge during periods of crisis. The great challenge facing all charismatic rulers is to routinize their charisma—that is, to sustain their leadership after the crisis subsides and to create political institutions that will survive their death or retirement.

Government and the State

In societies where political power is shared among most or all adults, the concept of government is meaningless. In modern, complex societies, however, government is necessary, and the state is the institutionalized way of organizing power within territorial limits. Plato argued that the state should be run by a specially trained group of aristocrats who would govern wisely and without favoritism. Aristotle believed the rights and duties of the state should be defined in a legal constitution.

The state has a variety of functions. One is to establish laws that formally specify what is expected and what is prohibited in the society. Another function is to enforce these laws and make sure that violations are punished. In modern societies, the state must also try to ensure that a stable system of distribution and allocation of resources exists. The state also sets goals and provides a direction for society, usually through the power to compel compliance. Finally, the state must protect a society from outside threats, especially those of a military nature.

The Economy and the State

Politics and economics are intricately linked, and the political form a state takes is tied to its economy. The economy is the social institution that determines how a society produces, distributes, and consumes goods and services. Capitalism is an economic system based on private ownership of the means of production, and resource allocation based largely on market forces. The two basic premises of capitalism are the pursuit of profit and the principle that the free market should determine what is produced and at what price. Adam Smith argued that capitalism is characterized by private property, freedom of choice, freedom of competition, and freedom from government interference. The latter view, that government should stay out of business affairs, is called laissez-faire capitalism. A mixed economy combines free-enterprise capitalism with government regulation of business, industry, and social-welfare programs. Most countries today have a mixed economy.

Karl Marx argued that capitalism causes people to become alienated from their labor and themselves. Workers are not paid for part of the value of the goods produced; instead this surplus value is taken by the capitalist as profit. Workers are also alienated by doing small, specific jobs and not feeling connected to the overall process or the final product. Instead of work being the self-fulfilling activity Marx believed it should be, in capitalism work becomes merely a means to survive.

Marx felt that capitalism contained contradictions that would be the seeds of its own destruction. Over time, profits would decline as production expanded, he said. Capitalists would have to intensify their exploitation of workers. As workers were paid less or unemployed, they could not afford to buy all the goods being produced, leading to economic depression. After a series of depressions, the workers would rise up, take control of the state, and create socialism in which private property would be abolished. Eventually the workers would come to control the means of production and thus put an end to exploitation. Although the reality of capitalism has not matched Marxist expectations, the Marxists believe that capitalism has only avoided a serious crisis temporarily, and the movement toward socialism has only been postponed, not avoided.

In a command economy the government makes all the decisions about production and consumption. These economies tend to be rigid and inefficient; there are often shortages of crucial goods and services. Socialism is a type of command economy in which the government owns the sources of production and sets goals for production and distribution as well as prices. Individuals are heavily taxed to support a range of social-welfare programs that benefit every member of society. The belief is that everyone should have such essentials as food, housing, medical care, and education before some can have luxury items. Thus in socialist societies, nonessential consumer items are very expensive, whereas basic commodities and services are very inexpensive. Capitalists view centrally planned economies as inefficient and an infringement on the rights of the individual.

Types of States

In an autocracy, the ultimate authority and rule of the government rest with one person, who is the chief source of laws, and the major agent of social control. Dissent and criticism of the government and the leader are prohibited in order to ensure the loyalty and devotion of the people. In a totalitarian government, one group has virtually total control of the nation's social institutions. Usually there is only one legal political party, and it controls the state apparatus—especially the military—as well as the economy. The ruling party legitimizes its rule with an elaborate ideology, and intimidates the population into conformity with the use of terror. Totalitarian socialism is more commonly referred to as communism; totalitarian capitalism is often called fascism.

Democracy has many different meanings, and there is hardly a government anywhere that does not claim some form of democratic authority. Today, democracy refers to a political system operating under the principles of constitutionalism, representative government, civilian rule, majority rule, and minority rights. Constitutionalism means that government power is limited by law. Representative government means that the authority to govern is achieved through, and legitimized by, popular elections. An elected official holds office for a specified term and remains accountable to the electorate, or those eligible to vote. Civilian rule means that every qualified citizen has the right to run for and hold an office of government. Although the majority's views prevail in a democracy, the minority must be free to express its opinions and to try to change the laws.

Critics of capitalism maintain that its inherent economic inequalities prevent it from being a truly democratic society; only under socialism can real democracy be implemented. Although there is no obvious reason that socialist societies cannot be democratic, due to historical conditions socialist societies have tended to be dictatorships, or forms of autocracy. Democratic socialism represents a convergence of capitalist and socialist economic theory in which the state assumes ownership of strategic industries and services, but allows other enterprises to remain in private hands. It is an attempt to preserve individual freedom in the context of social equality and a centrally planned economy. This type of government flourishes to varying degrees in Scandinavia, in Great Britain, and in Israel.

Functionalist and Conflict Theory Views of the State

Functionalists view social stratification—and the state that maintains it—as necessary for the recruitment of workers to perform the tasks required to sustain society. Marxists and other conflict theorists argue that the state emerged as a means of coordinating the use of force, by means of which the ruling classes could protect their institutionalized supremacy from the resentful and potentially rebellious lower classes. While there is historical evidence for the conflict view of the state's origins, the functionalists view points to the important societal functions fulfilled by the state.

Political Change

Political change can occur when there is a shift in the distribution or power among groups in a society. It can take place in a variety of ways, depending on the type of political structure the state has and the desire for change present among the people. In democracies there are institutionalized provisions for the changing of leaders, whereas dictatorships and totalitarian societies typically experience crises over this issue.

Rebellions are attempts—typically through armed force—to achieve rapid political change not possible within existing institutions. Rebellions typically do not call into question the legitimacy of power, but rather its uses. Thus they do not change the society's political and class structure. In contrast, revolutions are attempts to rapidly and dramatically change a society's previously existing structure. Political revolutions are relatively rapid transformations of state structures not accompanied by changes in the social structure. Social revolutions are rapid and basic transformations of a society's state and class structures. They are accompanied and in part carried through by class-based revolts.

The American Political System

Growing out of a strong commitment to a democratic political process and the influence of a capitalist economy, the political system in the United States is unique in a number of ways. Few democracies, for instance, have a "winner-take-all" two-party system. In this system, political candidates are forced to gain the support of a broad spectrum of interest groups in order to be elected. These interest groups must find common ground and join together in coalitions or face the prospect of not being represented at all if their candidate loses.

In totalitarian societies, nearly everyone votes, in spite of the fact that there are no alternatives. In the United States, voter turnout is typically quite low. Voting rates vary by social characteristics. Support for the Democrats or Republicans has historically varied by social characteristics as well, but these patterns are subject to changing social trends, political issues, and candidates. The politicians of both parties tend to be most responsive to the needs of the best-organized groups with the largest amount of funds or blocks of votes. While there has recently been a substantial increase in the number of minorities and women holding elective office, the U.S. Congress still overwhelmingly consists of white males over 40 years of age.

Because the government spends so much money and engages in so much regulation, special-interest groups constantly attempt to influence government policy. This is called lobbying, and it is typically done by professional representatives of special-interest groups called lobbyists. While lobbyists always have a self-interested agenda, they do provide information and stimulate public debate over issues. Special-interest groups also form political action committees (PACs) in an effort to influence elections. Only about 10 percent of the population is in a position to use PACs, though, and PACs tend to favor incumbents. Ultimately PACs may diminish the role of the individual voter.

CHAPTER OUTLINE

Politics, Power, and Authority
How are politics, power, and authority related?

POWER
What is the sociological definition of power?

POLITICAL AUTHORITY
What does it mean to have political authority?

Legal-Rational Authority
What is legal-rational authority?

Traditional Authority
How is traditional authority exercised?

Charismatic Authority
What are the most important features of charismatic authority?

Government and the State
What is the relationship between government and the state?

FUNCTIONS OF THE STATE
What are the major functions of the state?

Establishing Laws and Norms
How does the state go about establishing laws and norms?

Providing Social Control
How does the state provide social control?

Ensuring Economic Stability
How does the state go about ensuring economic stability?

Setting Goals
What is the state's role in setting goals

Protecting Against Outside Threats
How does the state protect against outside threats?

The Economy and the State
What is the relationship between the economy and the state?

CAPITALISM
What is capitalism?

THE MARXIST RESPONSE TO CAPITALISM
What is the Marxist response to capitalism?

COMMAND ECONOMIES
What are the major features of command economies?

SOCIALISM
What is socialism?

THE CAPITALIST VIEW OF SOCIALISM
What is the capitalist view of socialism?

Types of States
Why are there different types of states?

AUTOCRACY
What is autocracy?

TOTALITARIANISM
What is totalitarianism all about?

DEMOCRACY
What are the main characteristics of democracy?

DEMOCRACY AND SOCIALISM
What is the relationship between democracy and socialism?

DEMOCRATIC SOCIALISM
What is democratic socialism?

Functionalist and Conflict Theory Views of the State

How do functionalist and conflict theory views of the state differ?

Political Change

How does political change come about?

INSTITUTIONALIZED POLITICAL CHANGE

How does institutionalized political change occur?

REBELLIONS

What are rebellions?

REVOLUTIONS

What is unique about revolutions?

Political Revolutions

How do political revolutions take place?

Social Revolutions

What are the important characteristics of social revolutions?

The American Political System

In what way is the American political system unique?

THE TWO-PARTY SYSTEM

What are the basic features of the two-party system?

VOTING BEHAVIOR

What do we know about Americans' voting behavior?

SPECIAL-INTEREST GROUPS

What is the role of special-interest groups in the political process?

Lobbyists

What are lobbyists?

Political Action Committees

What role do Political Action Committees play?

LEARNING OBJECTIVES

After studying this chapter you should be able to:

■ *Distinguish between authority and coercion.*

List and explain two behaviors by people or groups in our society that you think are based on authority, and two behaviors that you think are based on coercion.

Authority #1:

explanation:

Authority #2:

    explanation:

Coercion #1:

    explanation:

Coercion #2:

    explanation:

■ *Compare and contrast Weber's three types of legitimate authority.*

Define each of the following types of authority and give one example from American society.

Legal-rational authority:

    example:

Traditional authority:

    example:

Charismatic authority:

    example:

■ *List and explain the basic functions of the state.*

Write in each of the five functions of the state, then give one example drawn from state or local government.

1.
example:

2.
example:

3.
example:

4.
example:

5.
example:

■ *Analyze the basic features of capitalism*

List the basic features of capitalism according to Adam Smith, and then assess the extent to which each is present or absent in contemporary American society.

1.
assessment:

2.
assessment:

3.
assessment:

4.
assessment:

■ *Describe the Marxist critique of capitalism.*

What did Marx mean by "alienation"?

What is the significance of "surplus value" in Marx's critique of capitalism?

How do the contradictions of capitalism provide the seeds of its own destruction, according to Marx?

Discuss two reasons the reality of capitalism has not matched Marxist expectations.

1.

2.

What is the Marxist response to these criticisms?

■ *Explain the relationship between capitalism, socialism, and democratic socialism.*

List three basic characteristics of socialism:
1.

2.

3.

In what sense can socialism be called a "command economy"?

What are the two basic premises behind capitalism?
1.

2.

List two basic characteristics of democratic socialism:

1.

2.

In what sense, if any, does democratic socialism overcome the capitalist critique of socialism?

In what sense, if any, does democratic socialism overcome the socialist critique of capitalism?

■ *Describe autocratic and totalitarian forms of government.*

Define an autocracy:

Would you say an autocracy operates more by external means of social control, or internal means of social control? (See Chapter 6 for definitions.) Why?

Are autocracy and dictatorship synonymous? Why or why not?

List six characteristics of a totalitarian government:

1.

2.

3.

4.

5.

6.

Totalitarian socialism is known as _____

Briefly describe this system:

Totalitarian capitalism is known as _____.
Briefly describe this system:

■ *Describe the basic features of political democracy.*

Describe each of the following features of political democracy and assess the extent to which it is present in the American political system.

Constitutionalism:

assessment:

Representative government:

assessment:

Civilian rule:

assessment:

Majority rule:

assessment:

Minority rights:

assessment:

■ *Contrast the functionalist and conflict theory views of the state.*

What is the functionalist explanation for the origin of the state?

What is the conflict theory explanation for the origin of the state?

Since World War II, the defense budget has constituted a major portion of U.S. government spending. Explain this phenomenon in functionalist and conflict theory terms.

Functionalist explanation   **Conflict Theory explanation**

Which is the better explanation, in your judgment? Why?

■ *Describe the basic mechanisms of political change.*

Define and give an example of each of the following mechanisms of political change.

Institutionalized political change:

   example:

Rebellion:

   example:

Political revolution:

   example:

Social revolution:

   example:

■ *Describe the major features of the American political system.*

How does the two-party system work?

What is the most important implication of the American two-party system?

What is unique about the American two-party system?

How would you assess American voting behavior?

What is the impact of special-interest groups on the American political process?

Construct arguments for and against the use of lobbyists and political action committees (PACs) in the U.S. political process.

	Arguments For	**Arguments Against**
Lobbyists:		
Political action committees (PACs):		

KEY CONCEPTS

■ *Match each concept with its definition, illustration, or explication below.*

a. revolution
b. aristocracy
c. fascism
d. two-party system
e. routinization of charisma
f. laissez-faire capitalism
g. legal-rational authority
h. surplus value
i. lobbying
j. politics
k. institutionalized political change
l. constitutionalism
m. capitalism
n. authority
o. social revolution
p. mixed economy
q. democracy
r. dictatorship
s. rebellion

t. charismatic authority
u. coercion
v. market
w. democratic socialism
x. power
y. autocracy
z. representative government
aa. legitimacy
bb. economy
cc. political revolution
dd. communism
ee. invisible hand
ff. the state
gg. command economy
hh. civilian rule
ii. socialism
jj. electorate
kk. totalitarian government
ll. traditional authority

_____ 1. the process by which power is distributed and decisions are made.

_____ 2. the ability of a person or group to get its way, even in the face of opposition.

_____ 3. power that is regarded as legitimate by those over whom it is exercised.

_____ 4. power that is regarded as illegitimate by those over whom it is exerted.

_____ 5. the condition in which people accept the idea that the allocation of power is as it should be.

_____ 6. a form of authority derived from the understanding that specific individuals have clearly defined rights and duties to uphold and implement rules and procedures impersonally.

_____ 7. a form of authority derived from a ruler's ability to inspire passion and devotion among followers.

_____ 8. a form of authority rooted in the assumption that the customs of the past legitimize the present.

_____ 9. the process of creating institutions and organizations that will sustain and maintain an inspirational leader's following after the passing of a crisis or the death of the leader.

_____ 10. the institutionalized way of organizing power within territorial limits.

_____ 11. a form of government in which ultimate authority rests with one person, who is the chief source of laws and the major agent of social control.

_____ 12. a form of government in which a select few rule.

_____ 13. the social institution that determines how a society produces, distributes, and consumes goods and services.

_____ 14. an economic system based on private ownership of the means of production, and resource allocation through the market.

_____ 15. the phenomenon in which, according to some theorists, a multiplicity of acts by individuals pursuing their own self-interest produces a social benefit.

_____ 16. a mechanism for determining the supply, demand, and price of goods and services through consumer choice.

_____ 17. the view that government should stay out of business affairs.

_____ 18. a combination of free-enterprise capitalism and governmental regulation of business and provision of social welfare programs.

_____ 19. in capitalism, according to some theorists, an unpaid part of the worker's production that the capitalist retains as profit.

_____ 20. an economic system in which the government owns the sources of production.

_____ 21. an economic system in which the government makes all the decisions about production and consumption.

_____ 22. a situation in which one group has virtually total control of a nation's social institutions.

_____ 23. another name for totalitarian socialism.

_____ 24. another name for totalitarian capitalism.

_____ 25. a political system operating under the principles of constitutionalism, representative government, civilian rule, majority rule, and minority rights.

_____ 26. a situation in which government power is limited by law.

_____ 27. the situation in which the authority to govern is achieved through, and legitimized by, popular elections.

_____ 28. those citizens eligible to vote.

_____29. a situation in which every qualified citizen has the legal right to run for and hold an office of government.

_____30. a totalitarian government in which all power rests ultimately in one person.

_____31. a convergence of capitalist and socialist economic theory in which the state assumes ownership of strategic industries and services, but allows other enterprises to remain in private hands.

_____32. the change in political leaders and/or policies in standardized, routinized ways.

_____33. an attempt—typically through armed force—to achieve rapid political change not possible within existing institutions.

_____34. an attempt to rapidly and dramatically change a society's previously existing structure.

_____35. a relatively rapid transformation of state or government structures that is not accompanied by changes in social structure or stratification.

_____36. a rapid and basic transformation of a society's state and class structures.

_____37. a political system that operates on a "winner-take-all" basis—that is, losing parties receive no representation.

_____38. attempts by special-interest groups to influence government policy.

KEY THINKERS/RESEARCHERS

■ *Match each thinker with their main idea or contribution.*

a. Adam Smith
b. Karl Marx
c. Plato
d. Aristotle
e. Max Weber

_____1. developed the sociological definitions of power and authority.

_____2. constructed a philosophical argument for aristocracy as the best form of government.

_____3. argued that power should be centered in the middle class and that the rights and duties of the state should be defined in a legal constitution.

_____4. regarded as the father of modern capitalism; discussed many of the basic premises of this system.

_____5. a severe critic of capitalism who argued that it was based on alienation and exploitation.

CRITICAL THINKING/APPLICATION QUESTIONS

1. The box, "Controversies in Sociology," discusses the role of the media in political campaigns. Many commentators have suggested that election campaigns today are all about "image" and completely lacking in substantive debate over the issues. Review your knowledge and experience of the most recent presidential election. What is your clearest memory from the campaign? Does it have anything to do with the issues? How much debate was there over the issues? Or was the campaign mostly posturing and photo opportunities? What should be done to ensure real political debate in American elections?

2. Most Americans are proud that we have a democratic political system. Yet the characteristics that we celebrate so proudly in the political arena are nearly absent from the economic realm—that is, in our economic system we do not have guaranteed constitutional rights (basic equality, free speech, assembly, and so on), representative government/management, or majority rule. How can our ideal of political equality and freedom be squared with the realities of our economic system?

3. Review the characteristics of members of Congress in Table 14.2. Based on what you have

learned about gender, age, and race, how do you think the social composition of Congress influences legislation that is passed and not passed?

4. Information on voting behavior presented in this chapter shows a relatively low percentage of Americans vote. How do you account for this fact? To what extent can we really say that representative government exists when—in the case of many local elections, for instance—less than half of the eligible voters vote? What about the influence of special-interest groups and financial contributions from PACs? Do we really have "the best government that [those with] money can buy"?

5. The 1980s have seen a decline in the standard of living for most of the middle class in the United States. Overall median income and average weekly earnings declined, the share of income going to the middle and the bottom declined, the rate of home ownership declined, and so on. To what extent do you think this phenomenon illustrates the Marxist critique of capitalism? What political changes are these economic changes likely to produce, and based on the discussion in this chapter, what forms are those changes likely to take?

SUGGESTED READINGS

THE ECONOMY AND THE STATE
Robert Lekachman and Borin Van Loon, *Capitalism for Beginners* (New York: Pantheon, 1981). Don't let the comic-book format fool you. This is a serious, substantive discussion and critique of how capitalism works, presented in an easily accessible way.

Stephen Rosskamm Shalom, ed., *Socialist Visions* (Boston: South End Press, 1983). Presents, in a dialogue format, visions of how a populist society could be created in the United States. Leading thinkers discuss transformations in six areas of life, followed by discussion and debate from others.

Phillip Corrigan, Harvie Ramsay, and Derek Sayer, *Socialist Construction and Marxist Theory: Bolshevism and its Critique* (New York:

Monthly Review Press, 1978). A critique of command economies from a Marxist point of view.

POLITICAL CHANGE
Samuel Bowles, David M. Gordon, and Thomas E. Weisskopf, *After the Wasteland: A Democratic Economics for the Year 2000* (Armonk, NY: M.E. Sharpe, 1990). A critique of the workings of the U.S. economy over the last forty years and recommendations for change.

THE AMERICAN POLITICAL SYSTEM
Frances Fox Piven and Richard A. Cloward, *Why Americans Don't Vote* (New York: Pantheon, 1987). A discussion of why so few Americans vote compared with other democracies. Also suggests what can be done about it.

ANSWER KEY
KEY CONCEPTS

1. j	14. m	27. z
2. x	15. ee	28. jj
3. n	16. v	29. hh
4. u	17. f	30. r
5. aa	18. p	31. w
6. g	19. h	32. k
7. t	20. ii	33. s
8. ll	21. gg	34. a
9. e	22. kk	35. cc
10. ff	23. dd	36. o
11. y	24. c	37. d
12. b	25. q	38. i
13. bb	26. l	

KEY THINKERS/RESEARCHERS

1. e
2. c
3. d
4. a
5. b

CHAPTER 15 ■ *Population and Demography*

CHAPTER SUMMARY

Population Dynamics

The size of a population tends to become a progressively greater problem due to exponential growth, in which a continuously expanding base rapidly doubles. The annual growth rate in world population has recently declined such that the world's population now doubles every 42 years instead of every 35 years. In most developing countries, however, the rate of growth is much faster.

Demography is the study of the size and composition of human populations, as well as the causes and consequences of changes in those issues. Demography is influenced by three major factors: fertility, mortality, and migration. Fecundity is the physiological ability to have children; fertility refers to the actual number of births in a given population. One common way of measuring fertility is the crude birth rate, or the number of annual live births per 1,000 people in a given population. The fertility rate is the number of annual births per 1,000 women of childbearing age.

Mortality is the frequency of deaths in a population. The most commonly used measure of mortality is the crude death rate, or the number of deaths per 1,000 people in a given population. Age-specific death rates measure the annual number of deaths per 1,000 people at specific ages. For instance, the infant mortality rate measures the number of children who die within the first year of life per 1,000 live births. Infant mortality is extremely high in most developing countries. While the overall U.S. infant mortality rate is low, twenty-three other nations, including Japan, Hong Kong, and most of the countries of northern Europe, have lower rates. In addition, infant deaths occur at disproportionate rates within the United States. For example, the infant mortality rate of African Americans is double that of whites.

Mortality is reflected in life expectancy, or the average number of years a person born in a particular year can expect to live. Life expectancy is usually determined more by infant than adult mortality. Rapid population growth in the Third World is largely due to an increase in life expectancy rather than a rise in the birth rate.

Migration is the movement of populations from one geographical area to another. Historically it has had less impact on population change in an area than either fertility or mortality. It is called emigra-tion when a population leaves an area and immigration when a population enters an area. Internal migration is movement within a nation's boundaries. Sunbelt states in the United States have been growing the most rapidly in recent times, due to both internal migration and immigration.

Theories of Population

The core of the population problem, according to Thomas Malthus, is that populations will always grow faster than the available food supply. Population growth could be limited or slowed, he said, by preventive and positive checks. The former are practices limiting reproduction, and the latter refer to deaths among the population through famines, wars, epidemics, and so on. Malthus was specifically attempting to refute the theories of the utopian socialists, who advocated a reorganization of society in order to eliminate poverty and other social evils. Misery, said Malthus, was inevitable.

Karl Marx argued that misery is not inevitable. The sheer number of people in a population is not the problem; rather it is industrial capitalism that creates the social and economic problems associated with population growth. Capitalism requires large amounts of cheap, readily-available labor and constantly expanding markets, both of which can be assured only by an ever-expanding population. As the population grows, greater numbers of unemployed workers compete for relatively fewer jobs, leading to impoverishment. Only by reorganizing the political economy of industrial society toward socialism, Marxists have argued, can the problems associated with population growth be overcome.

According to demographic transition theory, societies pass through four stages of population change as they move from high fertility and mortality to relatively low fertility and mortality. In stage 1, birth and death rates are high, and there is little or no population growth. During stage 2, population increases rapidly as the infant mortality rate drops and the birth rate remains high. During stage 3, the traditional institutions and beliefs that support a high birth rate are undermined and replaced with an emphasis on individualism and upward mobility. The birth rate, and thus the rate of population growth, begins to fall. In stage 4, both fertility and mortality are relatively low, and population growth is once again stabilized.

Demographic transition theory accurately describes the population changes that have occurred in Western society with the advance of industrialism. It does not, however, explain population trends in the underdeveloped world today. These latter countries have experienced a much faster drop in death rates than Western societies did, without a comparable rate of increase in economic development. Thus the birthrate, which has not fallen as fast or as consistently as it did in Western countries, has become an increasingly serious problem.

Some people have suggested that Europe has gone beyond stage 4 of the original theory and entered a second demographic transition, in which fertility rates have continued to decline to a level well below replacement. As a result, a number of European countries have adopted pronatalist policies which either make it difficult to obtain contraceptives or abortion or provide incentives to have children. Studies show that these policies hardly ever dramatically increase the birth rate. They may, however, help slow the decline in fertility.

Current Population Trends: A Ticking Bomb?

Eighty million babies are born in this world each year. At this rate, the sixth billionth person will arrive before the year 2000. Many analysts believe that overpopulation is now threatening the basic fabric of world order.

A substantial number of factors enter into determining the typical family size in any country. Early marriage provides more years during which conception can take place, and it also decreases the years of schooling and limits employment opportunities. Those societies that have succeeded in raising the average age of marriage have decreased fertility. Breast-feeding delays the resumption of menstruation and therefore offers limited protection against conception. It is also cheaper and guards against the risks connected with bottle feeding among poor populations. In many underdeveloped countries breast-feeding is one of the few controls on fertility.

In the short term, decreasing infant mortality does not lower the birth rate much. Over time, however, parents adjust their expectations and conceive fewer children. In most countries throughout the world there is a strong preference for male children. This may cause the fertility rate to level off above replacement level, as parents continue to have children until they have the desired son. In underdeveloped countries the benefits of having children have generally been greater for an individual family than the costs. Use of contraception is partly a function of a couple's wish to avoid or delay having children and partly related to its costs. Contraception in underdeveloped countries is most likely to be effective when it is widely publicized and publicly subsidized.

Lifestyle changes associated with higher incomes promote a desire for fewer children. The number of children per woman declines substantially as women's level of education increases, a much stronger effect than increasing levels of men's education. Urban fertility in developing countries tends to be lower than rural fertility. Urban dwellers have more avenues and more encouragement for upward mobility. They also face higher costs in raising children.

As long as many of the developing nations remain in stage 2 of demographic transition, they will continue to be burdened by overpopulation. Overpopulation undermines economic growth by disproportionately raising the dependency ratio, or the number of people of nonworking age in a society for every 100 people of working age. The economic development of countries with high dependency ratios is further slowed by the channeling of capital away from industrialization and toward mechanisms for feeding their expanding populations.

The "Green Revolution"—a technological revolution in which new breeds of grain and improved fertilizers are projected to raise harvest yields substantially and eliminate food shortages—has generally failed to materialize. For one thing, there are inherent limits to the natural resources available for food production. Moreover, overfarming and indiscriminate destruction of forests have generated the possibility of decreased food production capacity in the future.

A group of scientists, academics, and businesspeople called the Club of Rome has predicted, using computerized projections, a "doomsday model" in which modern technology creates economic collapse and ecological disaster through the exhaustion of the earth's natural resources within the next one hundred years. Some critics of this model have faith that the market, left unregulated, will inevitably balance out ecological costs and avert disaster. Others believe that the predicted crisis will be avoided through wider application of existing technologies, the discovery of new resources, or an exponential growth in knowledge.

CHAPTER OUTLINE

Population Dynamics
What is important to know about population dynamics?

FERTILITY
What does fertility mean?

MORTALITY
How is mortality defined?

MIGRATION
What is the significance of migration?

Theories of Population
What are the most important theories of population?

MALTHUS'S THEORY OF POPULATION GROWTH
What is Malthus's theory of population growth?

MARX'S THEORY OF POPULATION GROWTH
What are the basic elements of Marx's theory of population growth?

DEMOGRAPHIC TRANSITION THEORY
What does demographic transition theory explain?

Applications to Industrial Society
How can demographic transition theory be applied to industrial society?

A SECOND DEMOGRAPHIC TRANSITION
What does it mean to talk about a second demographic transition?

Pronatalist Policies
At what are pronatalist polices aimed?

Current Population Trends: A Ticking Bomb?
In what sense can current population trends be seen as a ticking bomb?

DETERMINANTS OF FERTILITY
What are the major determinants of fertility?

Average Age of Marriage
How does the average age of marriage affect fertility?

Breast-Feeding
How does breast-feeding relate to fertility?

Infant and Child Mortality
In what ways do infant and child mortality affect fertility?

Gender Preferences
How do gender preferences affect fertility?

Benefits and Costs of Children
In what sense do the benefits and costs of children affect fertility?

Contraception
What determines the use of contraception?

Income Level
How does income level affect fertility?

Education of Women
How is the education of women related to the fertility rate?

Urban or Rural Residence
How does urban or rural residence affect fertility?

PROBLEMS OF OVERPOPULATION
What problems does overpopulation cause?

PREDICTIONS OF ECOLOGICAL DISASTER
Who is making predictions of ecological disaster?

SOURCES OF OPTIMISM
What are the sources of optimism regarding the population problem?

LEARNING OBJECTIVES

After studying this chapter you should be able to:

■ *Explain the recently adopted Chinese population policy.*

List the benefits that accrue to a Chinese couple who have only one child, and the penalties imposed on those who have two children, and those who have three or more children or two children close together.

One-child family   **2 children (spaced)**   **3 + children; 2 close together**

To what extent has this policy worked?

■ *Describe the phenomenon of exponential growth.*

Assume a village of 100 people. Assume also that fertility outpaces mortality by five percent—that is, that there is a five percent annual increase in population. At this rate, how many generations will it take for the population of this village to double in size? How many additional generations will it take to triple the original population?

[Method of calculation for the algebraically impaired: First, use a calculator—it's easier! Multiply 100 by 105 percent or 1.05—this represents 5 percent added on to the existing population. Then multiply this answer, and every succeeding result, by 1.05. Write your answers in below and count up the number of times you have to multiply to get to around 200 or 300. This is the number of generations it takes to double or triple the population.]

Assume that same 100-person village. But now their population is increasing at an annual rate of 10 percent. Using the same formula as above, how many generations will it be before the population doubles? How many additional generations will it take to triple the original population?

Summary:

5 percent growth: _____ generations to double   _____ additional generations to triple

10 percent growth: _____ generations to double   _____ additional generations to triple

■ *Define the three major components of population change.*

What is fertility?

What is the connection between fecundity and fertility?

Two measures of fertility:

1.

2.

What is mortality?

How is it usually measured?

What is the connection between the infant mortality rate and age-specific death rates?

life expectancy?

What is migration?

Types of migration:

1.

2.

3.

Which of the three components of population change has the *least* impact on population growth or decline?

■ *Contrast the Malthusian and Marxist theories of population.*

Summarize the population theory of Malthus using the following terms: arithmetic vs. geometric rate of increase, "struggle for existence," preventive and positive checks, utopian socialists.

Summarize the population theory of Marx using the following terms: capitalism, labor supply, markets, unemployment, impoverishment.

Which theory do you think best applies to the developed countries today?

■ *Summarize the demographic transition model and explain why there might be a second demographic transition.*

Describe what happens at each stage of the transition and give at least one reason for its occurrence.

Stage 1:

explanation:

Stage 2:

explanation:

Stage 3:

explanation:

Stage 4:

explanation:

How does this model apply to underdeveloped countries?

What is the Second Demographic Transition?

Where is it taking place?

Why is it happening?

What are the results and implications of its occurrence?

■ *Discuss the determinants of fertility and family size.*

Suppose you were advising the leaders of an underdeveloped country how to lower their fertility rates and average family size. List and briefly explain nine factors these leaders should promote because they are associated with lowered fertility and smaller family size.

1.

2.

3.

4.

5.

6.

7.

8.

9.

■ *Discuss problems of overpopulation and possible solutions.*
What is the dependency ratio?

Briefly explain two problems for a society with high dependency ratios:
1.

2.

List and briefly explain two reasons why the Green Revolution has not materialized as predicted:
1.

2.

■ *Describe the "doomsday model" of ecological disaster and its critique.*
Describe the basic argument of the "doomsday model":

Briefly discuss four sources of optimism to counter the gloomy view of the doomsday model:

1.

2.

3.

4.

KEY CONCEPTS

■ *Match each concept with its definition, illustration, or explication below.*

a. demographic transition
b. Green Revolution
c. fecundity
d. infant mortality rate
e. mortality
f. immigration
g. exponential growth
h. fertility rate
i. positive checks
j. age-specific death rate
k. internal migration

l. crude birthrate
m. demography
n. doomsday model
o. migration
p. fertility
q. crude death rate
r. emigration
s. preventive checks
t. dependency ratio
u. life expectancy

_____ 1. a phenomenon in which population increases at ever-faster rates.

_____ 2. the study of the size and composition of human populations as well as the causes and consequences of changes in these factors.

_____ 3. the physiological ability to have children.

_____ 4. the actual number of births in a given population.

_____ 5. the number of annual births per 1,000 people in a given population.

_____ 6. the number of annual births per 1,000 women of childbearing age in a given population.

_____ 7. the frequency of actual deaths in a population.

_____ 8. the annual number of deaths per 1,000 people in a given population.

_____ 9. the number of deaths per 1,000 people at specific ages.

_____10. the number of children who die within the first year of life per 1,000 live births.

_____11. the average number of years that a person born in a given year can expect to live.

_____12. the movement of populations from one geographical area to another.

_____ 13. the phenomenon that occurs when part or all of a population leaves an area.

_____ 14. the phenomenon that occurs when population enters a geographical area.

_____ 15. movement of populations within a nation's boundaries.

_____ 16. in Malthus's theory, practices that limit reproduction.

_____ 17. in Malthus's theory, events that limit the population by causing death.

_____ 18. a process by which a country's birth and death rates decline as it industrializes.

_____ 19. the number of people of nonworking age in a society for every 100 people of working age.

_____ 20. a process in which new breeds of grain and improved fertilizers are expected to raise harvest yields and eliminate the threat of a food shortage.

_____ 21. a perspective that asserts that modern technology is inevitably headed toward exhaustion of the earth's resources and therefore a sudden and uncontrollable decline in population and production capacity is inevitable.

KEY THINKERS/RESEARCHERS

■ *Match each thinker with their main idea or contribution.*

a. Club of Rome
b. utopian socialists
c. Warren Thompson
d. Karl Marx
e. Thomas Robert Malthus

_____ 1. a pioneer in the study of population, he believed that population growth is linked to certain natural laws.

_____ 2. argued that industrial capitalism was the cause of overpopulation.

_____ 3. people who advocated a reorganization of society in order to eliminate poverty and other social evils.

_____ 4. developed the demographic transition model.

_____ 5. a group of scientists, academics, and businesspeople who have predicted worldwide economic and ecological collapse.

CRITICAL THINKING/APPLICATION QUESTIONS

1. Suppose that the government of China continues to be effective in limiting Chinese families to one child. A generation from now, how would you expect the one-child family to impact other institutions in society—for example, the economy, politics, education, the extended family, religion, leisure activities, and so on?

2. In societies where there are incentives and/or social pressures to limit family size to one child, two kinds of social problems related to gender bias result. First, an increase in female infanticide occurs as parents seek to dispose of "mistakes" and ensure that their only child is a more desirable male. Second, the sex ratio increases dramatically as more families have sons rather than daughters. What are the implications of these problems for gender inequality? In the face of this phenomenon, what can be done to guarantee equality for females?

3. Much is made of overpopulation in underdeveloped countries, and there is no doubt that population is increasing more rapidly there than in the developed world. However, the average citizen of a country like the United States is far more threatening to the environment and the earth's limited resources than any Third World resident. For instance, while the United States has five percent of the world's population, it uses about 40 percent of the world's energy. In 1986 the average U.S. citizen consumed 50,000 times as many BTUs of energy as the average citizen of Honduras. U.S.

livestock alone eat more grain every year than all the people in China and India *combined.* So, one could argue, the *real* problem of overpopulation is in the developed countries where wasteful consumers rapidly deplete the earth's resources. In the box, "Sociology at Work," Paul and Anne Ehrlich acknowledge this issue, but argue that all humanity has a common and equal interest in creating a sustainable life system. How do you evaluate this argument? Are the interests of all the parties equal? What about differential power?

SUGGESTED READINGS

POPULATION DYNAMICS

Arthur Haupt and Thomas T. Kane, *Population Handbook,* 3rd ed. (Washington, DC: Population Reference Bureau, 1991). Defines, explains, and illustrates, in an easily-accessible way, all the basic terms that demographers use. Includes a glossary and a guide to sources of population data.

Elizabeth Croll, Delia Davin, and Penny Kane, *China's One-Child Family Policy* (London: Macmillan, 1985). Discusses the roots and consequences of China's policy.

THEORIES OF POPULATION

George F. McCleary, *The Malthusian Population Theory* (London: Faber and Faber, 1953). Faithfully details Malthus's basic ideas on population.

Karl Marx and Friedrich Engels, *Marx and Engels on Malthus,* ed. by Ronald L. Meek (New York: International Publishers, 1954). Gathers together scattered comments from throughout their works that present a critique of Malthusianism.

ANSWER KEY
KEY CONCEPTS

1. g	11. u
2. m	12. o
3. c	13. r
4. p	14. f
5. l	15. k
6. h	16. s
7. e	17. i
8. q	18. a
9. j	19. t
10. d	20. b

If there is to be agreement, how is common ground likely to be found?

4. In the box, "Controversies in Sociology," Nicholas Eberhardt argues that irresponsible parents are the cause of a relatively high infant mortality rate in the United States. Evaluate this argument, taking into account such institutional factors as political policies, the health-care system, advertising, race and gender inequality, and a shift away from the traditional family. Do you think there is an element of "blaming the victim" in Eberhardt's analysis?

CURRENT POPULATION TRENDS: A TICKING BOMB?

Mary Mederios Kent and Kimberly A. Crews, *World Population: Fundamentals of Growth,* 2nd ed. (Washington, DC: Population Reference Bureau, 1990). A workbook filled with graphics and explanations for world population trends. Includes an appendix with basic demographic data for every country in the world.

Frances Moore Lappé and Joseph Collins, *World Hunger: Twelve Myths* (San Francisco: Food First Books, 1986). Written in an easily-accessible style and thoroughly documented, this work presents the argument that hunger is created by unjust social structure, not overpopulation.

Medea Benjamin and Andrea Freedman, *Bridging the Gap: A Handbook to Linking Citizens of the First and Third Worlds,* 2nd ed. (Cabin John, MD: Seven Locks Press, 1990). Describes churches, schools, communities, and local governments attempting to deal with world poverty and hunger through people-to-people projects. Includes a resource guide to organizations.

21. n

KEY THINKERS/RESEARCHERS

1. e
2. d
3. b
4. c
5. a

CHAPTER 16 ■ *Urban Society*

CHAPTER SUMMARY

The Development of Cities

During the vast majority of time that humans have lived on earth they have lived without cities. Cities appeared only within the last 7,000 to 9,000 years and coincide with the rise of what we know as "civilization." In the year 1800, 97 percent of the world lived in rural areas; in 1900, 86 percent still did so. Only by the year 2000 will half the world's population be urban. The industrialized areas of the world are already heavily urban, and the rate of urbanization is slowing. The pace of urbanization is accelerating rapidly, however, in the still largely rural nonindustrial world.

Two requirements had to be met in order for cities to emerge. First there had to be a surplus of food and other necessities, such that some people could afford to live in settlements where they did not produce their own food but could depend on others to meet their needs. The second requirement was some form of social organization beyond the family that was capable of distributing the surplus to those who needed it. The world's first fully-developed cities arose 6,000 years ago in the Middle East in what is now Iraq, which was the site of the Sumerian civilization.

Preindustrial cities—cities established prior to the Industrial Revolution—often were walled for protection and densely packed with residents whose occupations, religion, and social class were clearly evident from symbols of dress and manners. Preindustrial cities typically had populations under 10,000, and housed only 5 to 10 percent of a country's population.

Industrial cities are products of the Industrial Revolution—the application of scientific methods to production and distribution, wherein machines are used to perform work formerly done by humans or animals. The Industrial Revolution of the nineteenth century created new forms of work, new institutions and social classes, and multiplied many times over the speed with which humans could exploit the resources of their environment. Modern industrial cities are thus large and expansive, often with no clear physical boundary separating them from surrounding towns and suburbs. The concentration of people in a city and the spread of cities into surrounding areas is known as urbanization. Industrial cities house a relatively high percentage of the society's population, which works primarily in industrial and service-related jobs.

Urbanization

A city is a unit that typically has been incorporated according to the laws of the state within which it is located. The legal boundaries of a city seldom encompass all the people and businesses that may be affected by the social and economic aspects of an urban environment. Thus the U.S. Bureau of the Census developed a series of definitions relating to urban areas. An urbanized area contains a central city and the continuously built-up, closely settled surrounding territory that together have a population of 50,000 or more. As of 1990, there were 396 urbanized areas in the United States. Urban population refers to the inhabitants of an urbanized area and the residents of places with a population of 2,500 or more.

A metropolitan area has a large population nucleus and adjacent communities that are economically and socially integrated into that nucleus. Metropolitan statistical areas (MSAs) are mapped on the basis of counties. Each MSA has at least one central city or urbanized area with a population of 50,000 or more. In addition to the central county, MSAs may contain outlying counties that are more rural but have close economic and social ties to the central urbanized area. In 1990 there were 257 MSAs in the United States.

A primary metropolitan statistical area (PMSA) is a large, urbanized county or cluster of counties with a population of one million people or more. There were 78 PMSAs in 1990. A megalopolis is a metropolitan area with a population of a million or more that encompasses two or more smaller metropolitan areas. The federal government refers to a megalopolis as a consolidated metropolitan statistical area (CMSA); 23 areas are currently recognized as CMSAs, and more than one-third of all Americans live in them.

The Chicago School of early American sociologists paid a great deal of attention to the city. They developed the perspective called *human ecology* by borrowing theories that explained plant and animal development in natural environments. In investigating how humans distributed themselves across space, Robert Park, Ernest Burgess, and others proposed a prototype of urban development called the concentric zone model. In this model of urban development, there is a central business district surrounded by progressively larger circles of (in order) low-income unstable housing, then working-class, middle-class, and upper-class residential zones. This model reflected the structure of early industrial cities, but did not apply to those that developed later.

Homer Hoyt modified the concentric zone model by suggesting that various groups establish themselves in more linear sectors that correspond to transportation arteries. A third model, developed by C. D. Harris and E. L. Ullman, stresses the role of land costs and land-use patterns in shaping the structure of cities. They argued that as similar industries are established near one another, the immediate neighborhood is shaped by that industry, and it becomes one of the multiple nuclei that constitute the city. These models correspond to the structure of cities that developed more recently.

A limitation of the ecological approach is that it does not give enough emphasis to the role of social and cultural factors in shaping urban structure. Contemporary urban development has taken many forms that could not be predicted using earlier ecological models. Contemporary urban ecologists have tried to develop more advanced theories that take account of some of these overlooked factors.

The Nature of Urban Life

Ferdinand Tönnies, a German sociologist, developed the concepts *gemeinschaft* and *gesellschaft* to explain the transition from rural to urban society. In a *gemeinschaft,* or the type of community found in rural areas, relationships are intimate, cooperative, and personal. In a *gesellschaft,* or urban society, relationships are impersonal and independent—people look out for their own individual interests, and formal contracts govern economic exchanges; many of people's basic needs are met in secondary groups. As people migrated from rural areas to cities, they traded the social support and grounding of community for the greater variety of choices available in urban areas.

According to Émile Durkheim, every society has a collective conscience, or a system of fundamental beliefs and values. Social solidarity emerges from the people's commitment and conformity to the society's collective conscience. A mechanically integrated society is one in which a society's collective conscience is strong and there is a great commitment to it. Members have common goals and values and a deep and personal involvement with the community. This type of solidarity is more characteristic of predominantly rural societies. In an organically integrated society, social solidarity depends on the cooperation of individuals in many different positions who perform specialized tasks. Relationships here tend to be more formal and functional. This latter type of solidarity is typical of urban society.

Louis Wirth defined a city as a "relatively large, dense, and permanent settlement of socially heterogeneous individuals." Following this lead, urban sociologists emphasized the anonymity, impersonality, and cultural heterogeneity of urban life. Georg Simmel noted that this impersonality derives form the fact that interaction in the city is typically restricted to one role set at a time. However, Herbert Gans showed that many urban residents do participate in strong and vital community cultures. Gerald Suttles demonstrated that even impoverished city dwellers participate in ethnic subcultures well adapted to their socioeconomic situation. In addition, the sheer volume and clash of diversity in the city provides fertile soil for the artistic imagination.

Many urban neighborhoods, though not identical in social integration to small, closely knit rural communities, nonetheless do exhibit a sense of community. Urban dwellers, in fact, carry around a mental map of what different parts of the city are like and who lives in them. Jane Jacobs argues that the social control of public behavior and the patterning of social interactions in terms of community life are found on the level of local blocks rather than entire neighborhoods.

Although some urban blocks and neighborhoods offer a rich community life, there are also many serious problems in the cities—crime, pollution, noise, poor educational and social services, and so on—that make many people want to live elsewhere. Since World War II there has been a migration of both black and white middle-class families out of the cities. Many businesses have followed these people to the suburbs, taking with them both their tax revenues and the jobs that are crucial to the survival of urban neighborhoods. Thus the central cities are left with a disproportionate number of poor and unemployed residents and declining sources of revenue at the same time.

It has been difficult to entice suburbanites to move back to the city, and a number of analysts see the central cities as doomed. A small countertrend has been noticed in recent years, however, in the movement of young singles or childless couples back into central-city areas, which become rehabilitated in a process known as gentrification. This phenomenon is highly controversial, and it is not clear if it will have long-term impact.

Downtowns in many older cities have traditionally contained skid rows and red-light districts, which have provided shelter and tolerance for deviant individuals and activities. Being close to transportation and requiring little initial outlay, single-room housing has traditionally been utilized by the elderly poor, the seasonally employed, the addicted, and the mentally handicapped. Traditional skid rows are disappearing, however, due to a decreased demand for unskilled migratory workers and urban redevelopment.

The result is an increase in homeless people living on the streets. Perhaps 30 to 40 percent of them are people who were released from mental institutions in a misguided attempt at improving their life conditions. The homeless can be differentiated from the poor in general by extreme poverty, fewer years of schooling, and less family support. Estimates of the number of homeless range from 250,000 to three million. Because no reliable data has been collected on the homeless, it is unclear at this point exactly how many there are.

Future Urban Growth in the United States

The percentage of people living in metropolitan areas has remained essentially stable over the past twenty years, but it is expected to decline in the future. Trends vary widely by region, however. Metropolitan areas in the South and West are expected to maintain high growth rates for the next two decades. The Northeast and the Midwest are likely to experience slow growth or actual decline.

Suburbs consist of those territories that are part of an MSA but outside the central city. The majority of metropolitan residents live in suburbs rather than central cities. Suburbs developed relatively recently, and largely without planning. They were largely a response to changes in transportation technology that made commuting easier. The automobile, in particular, was an enormous spur to suburbanization in the years following World War II. Affordable financing of home mortgages was another important factor. Suburbs tend to be much more homogeneous than urban neighborhoods, particularly with regard to the stage of the family life cycle. Today many suburbs are experiencing the same problems as central cities; in some cases the difficulties are worse because suburbs have fewer resources available to address certain kinds of problems.

For the last twenty years the fastest growing areas appear to be located in the exurbs, a newer, second ring beyond the old suburbs. While the exurb is usually located within metropolitan boundaries, it is different from the traditional suburb in that development is less dense and the exurb tends to have its own economic base. By and large, the people moving here are white, relatively wealthy, highly educated, and professional, and they are moving to the exurbs for the same reasons that people moved to the suburbs earlier—for a better quality of life.

CHAPTER OUTLINE

The Development of Cities
What are the important factors in the development of cities?

THE EARLIEST CITIES
When did the earliest cities develop?

PREINDUSTRIAL CITIES
What is significant about preindustrial cities?

INDUSTRIAL CITIES
What are the important characteristics of industrial cities?

Urbanization
What is the definition of urbanization?

CLASSIFICATION OF URBAN ENVIRONMENTS
How are urban environments classified?

THE STRUCTURE OF CITIES
What models exist for the structure of cities?

The Nature of Urban Life
What do we know about the nature of urban life?

GEMEINSCHAFT TO *GESELLSCHAFT*

What do the terms *gemeinschaft* and *gesellschaft* mean?

MECHANICAL AND ORGANIC SOLIDARITY

What is the difference between mechanical and organic solidarity?

SOCIAL INTERACTION IN URBAN AREAS

What do we know about social interaction in urban areas?

URBAN NEIGHBORHOODS

What is the significance of urban neighborhoods?

URBAN DECLINE

What are the important factors in urban decline?

HOMELESSNESS

How extensive is the problem of homelessness?

Future Urban Growth in the United States

What is the future of urban growth in the United States?

SUBURBAN LIVING

What is suburban living all about?

THE EXURBS

What is the contemporary significance of the exurbs?

LEARNING OBJECTIVES

After studying this chapter you should be able to:

■ *Describe the phenomenon of urbanization, historically and in today's world.*

What two requirements had to be met for cities to emerge?

1.

2.

How long ago did the first cities appear?

Where did the first fully-developed cities arise?

List three reasons why cities arose in this particular location.

1.

2.

3.

List the percentage of the world's population that was or will be urban for the following years:

1800:

1900:

1990:

2000:

What percentage of the U.S. population currently is urban?

Where in the world is urbanization proceeding most rapidly at this time?

■ *Contrast preindustrial and industrial cities.*

Suppose you entered an out-of-control time machine that set you down in a city at an undetermined location and time. Briefly describe four ways by which you could tell if you were in an industrial or a preindustrial city.

1.

2.

3.

4.

■ *Distinguish among the different terms used to describe urban environments.*

Suppose that you live in Skokie, Illinois, an incorporated suburb immediately adjacent to Chicago within the same county (Cook County). List five terms from the U.S. Bureau of the Census or other sources that apply to the area in which you live. Explain why each term applies.

1.

explanation:

2.

explanation:

3.

explanation:

4.

explanation:

5.

explanation:

■ *Contrast alternative models of urban structure.*

Observe the city in which you live or in which your college or university is located. Briefly describe each of the major models of urban structure and state the extent to which each model does or does not apply to your city.

Concentric Zone model:

extent to which it applies:

Sector model:

extent to which it applies:

Multiple Nuclei model:

extent to which it applies:

■ *Contrast the experience of city life with that in rural communities.*

Assume that you are a real estate agent in a large metropolitan area whose counties include substantial numbers of suburbs, exurbs, and small rural communities as well as a large and diverse central city. Develop an analysis for a client in which you list the potential advantages and disadvantages of living in each area. Be sure that you draw from the work of Tönnies, Durkheim, Simmel, Gans, and Suttles in your analysis.

	Advantages	Disadvantages
rural community:		
city neighborhood:		
suburb:		
exurb:		

■ *Describe the cycle of urban decline and possible countertrends.*

List and describe three factors that have contributed to the decline of the central city.

1.

2.

3.

What countertrend to this phenomenon has been noticed?

■ *Describe the current phenomenon of homelessness in American cities.*

Why is the number of skid row districts declining?

List and describe four characteristics of the homeless:

1.

2.

3.

4.

Exactly how many homeless people are there at this time?

■ *Describe trends in urban growth in the United States.*

In the next decade, overall metropolitan population in the U.S. is expected to

____ increase   ____ decrease   ____ remain the same

What are the reasons for this?

Describe regional variations in metropolitan growth and decline.

List and describe three reasons why suburbs grew.

1.

2.

3.

List three problems that suburbs are currently experiencing.

1.

2.

3.

What are the exurbs and why are they growing?

Who is moving to the exurbs?

KEY CONCEPTS

■ *Match each concept with its definition, illustration, or explication below.*

a. gentrification

b. urbanized area

c. *gemeinschaft*

d. skid row

e. metropolitan statistical area (MSA)

f. sector model

g. exurbs

h. city

i. collective conscience

j. preindustrial cities

k. megalopolis

l. organically integrated society

m. social solidarity

n. primary metropolitan statistical area (PMSA)

o. consolidated metropolitan statistical area (CMSA)

p. industrial cities

q. civilization

r. urban population

s. homelessness

t. concentric zone model

u. mechanically integrated society

v. human ecology

w. *gesellschaft*

x. metropolitan area

y. urban decline

z. multiple nuclei model

aa. suburbs

bb. urbanization

_____ 1. essentially, a human society that has cities.

_____ 2. cities established prior to the Industrial Revolution.

_____ 3. cities established during or after the Industrial Revolution.

_____ 4. a unit that typically has been incorporated according to the laws of the state within which it is located.

_____ 5. an area that contains a central city and the continuously built-up, closely settled surrounding territory that together have a population of 50,000 or more.

_____ 6. the process whereby a population becomes concentrated in a specific area because of migration patterns.

_____ 7. inhabitants of an urbanized area and places with a population of 2,500 or more.

_____ 8. an area that has a large population nucleus and adjacent communities that are economically and socially integrated into that nucleus.

_____ 9. counties that have at least one central city or urbanized area with a population of 50,000 or more, as well as any outlying counties that have close economic and social ties to the central urbanized area.

_____10. a large, urbanized county or cluster of counties with a population of one million or more.

_____11. a metropolitan area with a population of a million or more that encompasses two or more smaller metropolitan areas.

_____12. the federal government's name for a megalopolis.

_____13. the theoretical attempt to explain human communities by the dynamics of plant and animal communities.

_____14. a model of urban development in which distinct, class-identified zones radiate out from a central business district.

_____15. a model of urban development in which groups establish themselves along transportation arteries.

_____16. a model of urban development in which similar industries locate near one another and shape the characteristics of the immediate neighborhood.

_____17. a type of living situation in which relationships are intimate, cooperative, and personal.

_____18. a type of living situation in which relationships are impersonal and independent.

_____19. according to Durkheim, a society's system of fundamental beliefs and values.

_____20. according to Durkheim, a product of people's commitment and conformity to the collective conscience.

_____21. a situation in which a society's collective conscience is strong and there is a great commitment to that collective conscience.

_____22. a situation where social solidarity depends on the cooperation of individuals in many different positions who perform specialized tasks.

_____23. a result of the out migration of the middle class and business from the central city.

_____24. the process by which middle- and upper-class people upgrade marginal areas by displacing the poor.

_____25. an area of the city that has traditionally provided shelter and a degree of tolerance for deviant individuals and activities.

_____26. the condition of people who have no permanent residence.

_____27. those territories that are part of the metropolitan area but outside the central city.

_____28. a newer, less densely populated ring of dwelling areas beyond the old suburbs.

KEY THINKERS/RESEARCHERS

■ *Match each thinker with their main idea or contribution.*

a. Herbert Gans

b. C.O. Harris and E.L. Ullman

c. George Simmel

d. Gideon Sjoberg

e. Jane Jacobs

f. Louis Wirth

g. Homer Hoyt

h. Émile Durkheim

i. Gerald Suttles

j. Robert Park and Ernest Burgess

k. Ferdinand Tönnies

_____ 1. analyst of the preindustrial city.

_____ 2. pioneers in human ecology; developed the concentric zone model of urban development.

_____ 3. developed the sector model of urban development.

_____ 4. developed the multiple nuclei model of urban development.

_____ 5. developed the concepts of *gemeinschaft* and *gesellschaft* to explain the rural to urban transition.

_____ 6. developed the concept of the collective conscience and mechanical and organic integration as forms of identification with it.

_____ 7. proposed a widely accepted definition of the city as a "relatively large, dense, and permanent settlement of socially heterogeneous individuals."

_____ 8. helped refocus the way sociologists see urban life by showing that urban residents can and do participate in strong and vital community cultures.

_____ 9. showed that even in poor neighborhoods people can have a vital culture with norms and values well adapted to the poverty in which the residents live; also that people draw mental maps of the city's neighborhoods.

_____10. argued that rural social relationships are rich because they encompass a number of role relationships at once, whereas urban relationships tend to be confined to one role set at a time.

_____11. argued that social control of public behavior and the patterning of the social interactions of community life take place on the level of blocks rather than entire neighborhoods.

CRITICAL THINKING/APPLICATION QUESTIONS

1. On a piece of paper, draw a physical representation of the mental map you have of your city or the city where your college or university is located. Be sure you put in neighborhoods of which you are aware, the characteristics of those neighborhoods, and major landmarks and pathways of travel. When you are finished, try to analyze your map objectively. What does it tell you about your view of the city? How well-defined is the map? How clear are the descriptions of the neighborhoods? Are these descriptions based on factual information, personal experience, or stereotype? Try to get a friend to do this exercise, then compare maps and discuss the differences. To what extent does each map reflect a different experience with the city?

2. Some of the work of William H. Whyte on the city center is described in the box "Sociology at Work." In another part of the same work, Whyte describes his research on patterns of interaction on downtown streets. His observations include the fact that, contrary to commonsensical wisdom, most people do not prefer to hold conversations in public spaces in out-of-the-way locations, but rather right in the middle of the flow of pedestrian traffic. Also, parks and squares that

are popular gathering places are ones that allow flexible interaction and plenty of visual contact among people. Analyze your city or university campus. To what extent does it encourage or discourage the types of interactions described by Whyte?

3. Metropolitan areas in the United States are characterized by a multiplicity of independent governmental units, mostly in suburbs and exurbs ringing a large central city. Much of the history of U.S. urban development described in this chapter seems to be a story of those with money, power, and privilege escaping the problems of the central city by moving ever farther away from it, insulating themselves from its problems in their separate political jurisdictions. How does this phenomenon square with the American political ideal of democracy and equality and the economic ideal of equal opportunity? Should metropolitan areas be governed in a different way? How can regional concerns be addressed while at the same time preserving local democracy?

4. If you could choose anywhere in the United States to live, where would it be? What criteria would you employ in making this decision? How would you relate those criteria to the themes of this chapter?

SUGGESTED READINGS

THE DEVELOPMENT OF CITIES

Janet L. Abu-Lughod, *Changing Cities: Urban Sociology* (New York: HarperCollins, 1991). An excellent, up-to-date introduction to urban sociology, from the earliest cities to contemporary urban issues.

URBANIZATION

John R. Logan and Harvey L. Molotch, *Urban Fortunes: The Political Economy of Place* (Berkeley, CA: University of California Press, 1987). Traces the development and current problems of capitalist cities in terms of local conflicts over growth.

THE NATURE OF URBAN LIFE

William Julius Wilson, *The Truly Disadvantaged: The Inner City, the Underclass, and Public Policy* (Chicago: University of Chicago Press, 1987). An examination of poverty in the central city and its causes in the changing metropolitan economy.

Ray Oldenburg, *The Great Good Place: Cafés, Coffee Shops, Community Centers, Beauty Parlors, General Stores, Bars, Hangouts and How They Get You Through the Day* (New York: Paragon House, 1989). A unique look at what the author calls "third places" between home and work that allow for informal, communal socializing and which are the real foundations, he argues, for a viable community life.

Bill Berkowitz, *Community Dreams: Ideas for Enriching Neighborhood and Community Life* (San Luis Obispo, CA: Impact Publishers, 1984). A uniquely offbeat compilation of practical and far-out ideas for enriching neighborhood and community life from a veteran grass-roots community organizer.

FUTURE URBAN GROWTH IN THE UNITED STATES

Mark Baldassare, *Trouble in Paradise: The Suburban Transformation in America* (New York: Columbia University Press, 1986). Looks at current challenges facing suburbia and details why many suburbanites have soured on their would-be utopias.

Kirkpatrick Sale, *Human Scale*, 2nd ed. (New York: G.P. Putnam, 1982). A provocative book in which the author argues that for most of human history we have lived on a humanly-manageable scale. Only recently have our cities, our architecture, and our institutions become overwhelmingly large—too large to comprehend and deal with. The solution he proposes is a return to truly human scale.

ANSWER KEY

KEY CONCEPTS

1. q
2. j
3. p
4. h
5. b
6. bb
7. r
8. x
9. e
10. n
11. k
12. o
13. v
14. t
15. f
16. z
17. c
18. w
19. i
20. m
21. u
22. l
23. y
24. a
25. d
26. s
27. aa
28. g

KEY THINKERS/RESEARCHERS

1. d
2. j
3. g
4. b
5. k
6. h
7. f
8. a
9. i
10. c
11. e

CHAPTER SUMMARY

The Experience of Illness

Medicine and health-care issues are intertwined with social and cultural customs and reflect the society of which they are a part. Illness not only involves the body, but it also affects an individual's social relationships, self-image, and behavior. Talcott Parsons has suggested that in order to prevent the potentially disruptive consequences of illness for a group or society, there exists a sick role, which is a shared set of cultural norms that legitimates deviant behavior caused by illness and channels the individual into the health-care system.

The sick role has four components. The sick person is excused from normal social responsibilities, except that they must do whatever is necessary to get well. The sick person is not held responsible for his or her condition and is not expected to recover through an act of will. The sick person must recognize that being ill is undesirable, must want to recover, and is obligated to cooperate with the advice of designated experts. The sick role concept creates a "doctor-centered" picture where the illness is viewed from outside the individual. Some social theorists have suggested that we should pay more attention to individuals' subjective experience of illness.

Health Care in the United States

The United States has the most advanced health-care resources in the world. Critics maintain that the system pays off, though, only when the patient can pay. The system has been described as acute, curative, and hospital-based, in that the focus is on curing or controlling serious diseases rather than on maintaining health. The American medical care system is highly technological, specialized, and increasingly centralized. Yet the United States ranks near the bottom on a number of measures of health when compared with other Western industrialized countries.

The American medical care system includes some of the highest and lowest paid employees in the nation. About three-quarters of all medical workers are women, although the majority of doctors are men. Many of the workers are minorities, and most come from lower-middle class backgrounds. The majority of the physicians are white and upper-middle class. There are over 300 licensed occupational categories of medical workers, with practically no movement from one category to another because each requires its own specialized training and qualifications.

Male death rates exceed female death rates at all ages and for the leading causes of death such as heart disease, cancer, cerebrovascular diseases, accidents, and pneumonia. Women seem to suffer from illness and disability more than men, but their health problems are usually not as life-threatening. Some have suggested that women may not be sick more often, but may in fact be more sensitive to bodily discomforts and more willing to report them to a doctor.

Male infants are biologically more vulnerable than female infants, in both the prenatal and neonatal stages. Sociologically, men are more likely to have dangerous jobs and more likely than women to place themselves in dangerous situations during both work and leisure. Men and women are equally vulnerable to psychiatric problems, but emotionally disturbed men are likely to act out through drugs, alcohol, and antisocial acts, whereas women display behaviors such as depression or phobias that indicate internalization of their problems.

Asian Americans have the best health profile, followed by whites. African Americans and Native Americans have the worst health profiles. The African-American infant mortality rate is more than twice as high as the white rate. In some large cities with extensive minority populations the infant mortality rate is higher than in a number of underdeveloped countries. Low birth weight babies are more than twice as common among African Americans than among whites.

On the average, life expectancy for African-American infants is about seven years less than for white infants, for both males and females. African-American males have the lowest life expectancy of any racial category; over the last decade their life expectancy actually dropped two months while every other group, including African-American women, gained from three to six years. African-American males age 15 to 29 die at a higher rate than any other group in the population except those 85 and older. Between the ages of 25 and 44, hypertension kills African-American males 15.5 times more frequently than white males, and African-American females 17 times more frequently than white females.

Hispanic Americans have a higher infant mortality rate, a shorter life expectancy, and higher rates of death from influenza, pneumonia, diabetes, and tuberculosis than Anglos. They have lower death rates for cancer and heart disease, however. Native Americans have the lowest cancer rates and low mortality rates from heart disease. They do, however, have high rates of diabetes, venereal disease, hepatitis, tuberculosis, alcoholism and alcohol-related diseases. Native American suicide rates are 20 percent higher than those of the general population.

Poverty contributes to disease and a shortened life span both directly and indirectly. It is estimated that some 25 million Americans do not have enough money to feed themselves adequately, and therefore suffer from serious nutritional deficiencies that lead to illness and death. A variety of diseases are more common among the poor than the middle class. Inadequate housing, heating, and sanitation all contribute to these medical problems, as does the U.S. fee-for-service system that links medical care to the ability to pay. For all of these reasons, social class and life expectancy are highly correlated.

The median age of the American population has risen ten years in this century. As a result, the most common causes of death today are linked to the aging process: heart disease, cancer, and strokes. The elderly are thirty times more likely to be in nursing homes than are people under 65, and the care they receive there is often wholly inadequate.

Contemporary Health Care Issues in the United States

Acquired Immunodeficiency Syndrome (AIDS) is caused by the human immunodefiency virus (HIV). HIV is a retrovirus that gradually incapacitates the immune system, leaving the infected person vulnerable to a multitude of infections and certain types of cancer that rarely occur in individuals with normally functioning immune systems. HIV is transmitted through an exchange of bodily fluids during sexual intercourse, piercing of the skin with HIV-infected needles or instruments, transfusion of contaminated blood products, transplantation of contaminated tissue, and pregnancy by an HIV-infected mother. There is no evidence that HIV is transmitted through any kind of casual contact.

The Centers for Disease Control (CDC), a part of the U.S. Public Health Service, estimates that there are about one million people infected with the HIV virus in the United States, and they are expected to eventually develop AIDS within 10 to 15 years. As of May 31, 1991, the CDC reported a cumulative

179,136 AIDS cases in the United States. Although the majority of diagnosed cases have occurred among homosexual or bisexual men and intravenous drug users, heterosexuals have been the fastest growing exposure category. Though the virus that causes AIDS is found throughout the United States, certain cities and geographical areas have been particularly hard hit. New York City, for example, has disease rates ten times higher than nationally, and AIDS is the leading cause of death there for both men and women in their thirties. AIDS is also fourteen times higher in state and federal prisons than on the outside.

AIDS is a global problem. Africa appears to be hardest hit, with over six million cases, or 60 percent of the world's total. In African countries the HIV virus is generally transmitted heterosexually; the sex ratio among victims is virtually one to one. Asia is likely to be the next area of the world to experience the AIDS crisis. The World Health Organization estimates that total worldwide deaths from AIDS in the 1990s could be 50 million. The number of infected people could double several times after that, particularly in the poorer countries, before vaccines or drugs are developed. The crisis undoubtedly will provoke the development of new social structures and new behaviors.

Most of the money spent on medical care in the United States is in the form of third-party payments—disbursements made, not by the individuals receiving the care, but by insurance or charitable organizations. People—or their employers—pay premiums into a pool that is used to finance the medical care of those covered by the insurance. In 1965, Congress created Medicare to pay for the medical care of those over 65 years of age, and Medicaid to pay for those too poor to pay their own medical costs. Nonetheless, the United States is the only leading industrial nation that does not have an organized, centrally planned health care delivery system.

Because of pressures from the American Medical Association and other sectors of the medical establishment, the U.S. health care system focuses primarily on the benefits received by doctors. The fee-for-service system of remuneration gives doctors a vested interest in pathology rather than in keeping people healthy. A further result of this orientation is an uneven geographical distribution of doctors and an overabundance of specialists.

Cultural values in the United States cause us to distrust nature and assume that the best approach to health is aggressive medical intervention, particularly with technology. Thus the U.S. has significantly higher rates of surgery than other developed countries. Recently, however, there has been something of a shift from the orientation of "cure" to that of "prevention." Prevention has three levels: Medical prevention is directed at the individual's body; behavioral prevention is directed at changing the habits and behavior of individuals; structural prevention involves changing the social environments where people work and live. Much sociological knowledge will be required to successfully implement the latter two types of prevention. A great deal is said about the need to change unhealthy individual behavior, but so far we have little knowledge of *how* to do it. Education and propaganda generally don't work. Structural factors that cause ill health among the population have hardly been addressed at all.

World Health Trends

The World Health Organization defines health as a state of complete mental, physical, and social well-being. Since this concept is difficult to measure, trends must be examined. On a world-wide basis, average life expectancy has more than doubled in this century. But while the developing countries may be approaching the upper limit of average life expectancy, deaths among infants and children remain high in the less developed countries. Currently 80 percent of the world's population does not have access to any health care. Malnutrition, parasitic, and infectious diseases are the principal causes of death and disability in the poorer nations. These conditions are largely preventable, and prevention could be accomplished at a relatively modest cost.

Africa, Asia, and Latin America account for 98 percent of the world's deaths among children under five. It is estimated that 95 percent of these deaths are preventable. Poor maternal health is a major cause of low-birth-weight babies, who in turn are the most vulnerable. Infants are at high risk if their mothers are in their teens or over age 40, if they have had more than seven births, or when the interval between births is less than two years. An increase of three years of education for mothers produces 20 to 30 percent declines in the mortality of children under age five, as better educated mothers are more likely to take better care of themselves and their children. Bottlefed babies are three to six times more likely to experience respiratory infections or diarrhea than breastfed babies. All of these factors represent social, not medical, conditions that can and should be addressed sociologically.

CHAPTER OUTLINE

The Experience of Illness
What is the experience of illness, in sociological terms?

Health Care in the United States
What are the important features of health care in the United States?

GENDER AND HEALTH
What is the connection between gender and health?

RACE AND HEALTH
How are race and health related?

SOCIAL CLASS AND HEALTH
How is social class linked to health?

AGE AND HEALTH
How is age related to health?

Contemporary Health Care Issues in the United States
What are the most important health care issues in the U.S.?

ACQUIRED IMMUNODEFICIENCY SYNDROME (AIDS)
How important an issue is AIDS?

HEALTH INSURANCE
What are the problems with health insurance?

PREVENTING ILLNESS
To what extent is preventing illness an issue in U.S. health care?

World Health Trends
What are the major world health trends?

THE HEALTH OF INFANTS AND CHILDREN IN DEVELOPING COUNTRIES
What is the state of health of infants and children in developing countries?

Maternal Health
How is maternal health related to the health of infants and children in developing countries?

Maternal Age
What is the connection between maternal age and the health of infants and children?

Maternal Education
How does maternal education affect the health of infants and children?

Breast-feeding
How is breast-feeding connected to the health of infants and children?

LEARNING OBJECTIVES

After studying this chapter you should be able to:

■ *Describe the basic elements of the sick role.*

Think back to the last time you or someone you know well was sick. List each component of the sick role, then explain the social interactions by which you or the other person fulfilled—or failed to fulfill—the sick role.

1.

explanation:

2.

explanation:

3.

explanation:

4.

explanation:

■ *Describe the basic characteristics of the U.S. health care system.*

What does it mean to say that the U.S. health care system is "acute, curative [and] hospital-based?"

Describe the health care workforce in terms of
income:

gender:

race and ethnicity:

social class:

occupational specialization:

What are third-party payments? How do they affect the delivery of health care?

What are the health implications of a fee-for-service system of remuneration for health care providers?

■ *Explain the link between basic demographic factors and health.*

For each of the following categories, state which group is disadvantaged and explain the nature of that
disadvantage.
gender:

race and ethnicity:

social class:

age:

■ *Describe the nature and extent of the AIDS crisis.*

Suppose that you have been asked to lead a discussion about AIDS at a local junior high school. Prepare your notes for the discussion by responding to the questions that follow.

In medical terms, what is AIDS?

What makes AIDS deadly? Why do people die from it?

How is HIV transmitted?

What do we know scientifically about the origin of HIV and AIDS?

How many people in the United States are estimated to be infected with HIV and most likely will develop AIDS?

Among which categories of people has AIDS been concentrated to date?

What is currently the fastest-growing exposure category?

Worldwide, how many people are expected to die of AIDS in the 1990s?

Where is the highest proportion of AIDS cases in the world found?

What is the most frequent way HIV is transmitted in Africa?

■ *Compare and contrast the three major models of illness prevention.*

Using the information in Table 17.3 and the text discussion, explain how each of the models would deal with the problem of drug addiction.

Medical:

Behavioral:

Structural:

■ *Describe the factors involved in the health of infants and children in developing countries.*

More than _____ million people live in twenty-four countries where life expectancy is less than 50 years.

Currently _____ percent of the world's population does not have access to health care.

Suppose you were asked to advise the government of a developing country how to lower the death rate among infants and young children. Suggest strategies that could be followed in the following four areas:

Maternal health:

Maternal age:

Maternal education:

Breast-feeding:

KEY CONCEPTS

■ *Match each concept with its definition, illustration, or explication below.*

a. Medicaid
b. human immunodeficiency virus (HIV)
c. sick role
d. low birth-weight babies
e. acquired immunodeficiency syndrome (AIDS)

f. third-party payments
g. health
h. Medicare
i. fee-for-service system

_____1. a shared set of cultural norms that legitimates deviant behavior caused by illness and channels the individual into the health-care system.

_____2. a condition in which the immune system is weakened to the point where the individual becomes susceptible to a multitude of infections and certain types of cancer than otherwise rarely occur.

_____3. a retrovirus that incapacitates the human immune system by attacking white blood cells.

_____4. a system in which the costs of an individual's health care is paid for by some form of public or private insurance or charitable organization.

_____5. a U.S. government program that pays for the medical care of people over age 65.

_____6. a U.S. government program that pays for the medical care of people who qualify as too poor to pay their own costs.

_____7. a system by which doctors get paid only for treating illness.

_____8. a state of complete mental, physical, and social well-being.

_____9. babies under 5.5 pounds at birth, they are at the greatest risk of dying.

KEY THINKERS/RESEARCHERS

■ *Match each thinker with their main idea or contribution.*

a. Blair Justice
b. World Health Organization (WHO)
c. Arthur Frank
d. Centers for Disease Control (CDC)
e. Talcott Parsons

_____1. American sociologist who developed the concept of the sick role.

_____2. a part of the U.S. Public Health Service, this agency is charged with monitoring communicable ailments.

_____3. an international organization that monitors health issues.

_____4. argues that disease is mostly a result of a failure of our personal-social-psychological coping mechanisms.

_____5. argues that personality theories of disease engage in blaming the victim, but persist because there is a payoff for everyone involved.

CRITICAL THINKING/APPLICATION QUESTIONS

1. "Physicians have exceedingly high prestige in American society. . . . Medicine thus attracts those who value status and income, who seek a challenging and interesting occupation, who enjoy exercising judgment and who seek to do good." Evaluate this statement by a sociologist. To what extent do you think it is an accurate description of the medical profession? What are the implications of these characteristics for the way medicine is practiced in our society?

2. In the box, "Controversies in Sociology," sociologist Arthur Frank argues that personality theories of disease have the latent functions of reassuring the healthy that the ill person "deserved" to get sick and that the healthy are safe because they are different. Moreover, due to this "blaming the victim" ideology, no structural changes have to be made. To what extent does this describe American society's reaction to the AIDS epidemic?

3. Every other advanced industrial country except the United States has a national health care policy. Given your understanding of economics and the political process from Chapter 14, why do you think this is the case? What sorts of changes will have to occur in American society for us to join the rest of the developed world on this issue?

4. Given the disparities in health by gender, race, age, and social class that have been documented

in this chapter, it would seem that health and health care is really more of a political than a medical issue. Why don't more Americans see it this way? Is this definition currently changing? Why?

SUGGESTED READINGS

HEALTH CARE IN THE UNITED STATES

Rachel Spector, *Cultural Diversity in Health and Illness,* 2nd ed. (Norwalk, CT: Appleton-Century-Crofts, 1985). An exploration of the role played by race, ethnicity, and other cultural factors in health and illness.

CONTEMPORARY HEALTH CARE ISSUES IN THE UNITED STATES

Paul Starr, *The Transformation of American Medicine* (New York: Basic Books, 1982). An award-winning analysis of the development of the medical profession and the contemporary implications of its control over the delivery of health care.

Bonnie Szumski, *The Health Crisis: Opposing Viewpoints* (San Diego: Greenhaven Press, 1989). A debate on contemporary health-care issues.

Victor Gong, M.D., and Norman Rudnick, eds., *AIDS: Facts and Issues* (New Brunswick, NJ: Rutgers University Press, 1986). One of the best handbooks about AIDS. It has extensive, easily-accessible discussions of medical, legal, ethical, social, political, and spiritual issues associated with AIDS. An extensive list of resources is included.

Randy Shilts, *And the Band Played On: Politics, People, and the AIDS Epidemic* (New York: St. Martin's Press, 1987). A critical examination of the official neglect of the AIDS epidemic by the medical and political establishments as long as the primary victims seemed to be members of deviant subcultures.

WORLD HEALTH TRENDS

David R. Phillips, *Health and Health Care in the Third World* (New York: Wiley, 1990). An examination of the basic health issues confronting third world countries.

Vicente Navarro, *Imperialism, Health and Medicine* (Farmingdale, NY: Baywood, 1981). An argument that socioeconomic factors play the greatest role in determining the health of people in the Third World by a physician who is also a sociologist.

ANSWER KEY

KEY CONCEPTS

1. c	6. a
2. e	7. i
3. b	8. g
4. f	9. d
5. h	

KEY THINKERS/RESEARCHERS

1. e	4. a
2. d	5. c
3. b	

CHAPTER 18 ■ *Collective Behavior and Social Movements*

CHAPTER SUMMARY

Theories of Collective Behavior

Collective behavior refers to relatively spontaneous social actions that occur when people respond to unstructured and ambiguous situations. A number of theories have been devised to explain collective behavior. Gustave Le Bon, a pioneer in the study of crowd behavior, developed a perspective known as contagion theory. He argued that individuals are transformed by the experience of anonymity in a crowd. They acquire a crowd mentality, lose their inhibitions and sense of personal moral responsibility, and become highly susceptible to group sentiments. The crowd then becomes a social entity greater than the sum of its individual parts.

Herbert Blumer explains the contagion that sweeps through a crowd as a circular reaction. The crowd begins as a collectivity waiting for something to happen. Sooner or later an exciting event stirs them, people become excited, the feeling spreads, and individuals give in to the engulfing group mood and mentality. This theory does not explain, however, under what conditions contagion is likely to sweep through a crowd, and why it might be limited to a certain level of action or portion of the crowd. Moreover, research has not borne out the premise that the average person is transformed through crowd dynamics from a civilized person into an irrational being.

Ralph H. Turner and other advocates of emergent norm theory argue that crowd members have different motivations for participating in the crowd. They acquire common standards by observing and listening to one another. The norms that emerge do so as a result of the expectations people bring to the situation as well as the interpretations that develop out of the collective situation.

Convergence theory views collective behavior as the outcome of situations where people with similar characteristics are drawn together. Because they have similar characteristics they are predisposed to similar kinds of actions. This does not explain, however, why crowd behavior often passes through a number of stages, nor does it suggest why some crowds act while others don't.

Neil Smelser developed the value-added theory of collective behavior as a series of six conditions that shape its generation and outcome. Structural conduciveness refers to conditions in the existing social order that may promote collective behavior.

Structural strain occurs when a group's ideals conflict with its everyday realities. People develop explanations for the structural strains they experience. When these generalized beliefs are clearly expressed and widely shared, collective behavior may take the form of a well-organized social movement. When the beliefs are less clear or expressed in competing forms, collective behavior is more likely to emerge in unstructured form—a riot, for example. In all cases of collective behavior there is an event, or series of events, that precipitates a collective response. Then the group must be mobilized, or organized into taking action. Finally, the course of the collective action will depend upon the mechanisms of social control employed by those in power. Each of these conditions is a necessary condition for, and a partial determinant of, the next succeeding condition.

Crowds: Concentrated Collectivities

A crowd is a temporary concentration of people who focus on some thing or event but who also are attuned to one another's behavior. Crowds have the potential for unpredictable behavior and group action that erupts quickly and often seems to lack structure or direction. Elias Canetti attributed four traits to crowds. Crowds are self-generating in that they magnetically attract people and have no natural boundaries. When boundaries are imposed artificially there is an ever-present danger that the crowd will erupt and spill over the boundaries. Crowds are characterized by equality in that social distinctions lose their importance within them. In fact, said Canetti, people join crowds specifically to achieve this condition of equality. Crowds love density—a great deal of private space and personal identity are relinquished as people in a crowd pack together. Crowds need direction; they are physically or psychologically in motion and seek to sustain it. The direction that a crowd will take depends on the type of crowd involved.

Herbert Blumer has distinguished four types of crowds. An acting crowd is a group of people whose passions and tempers have been aroused by some focal event, who come to share a purpose, and who feed off one another's arousal, often erupting into spontaneous acts of violence. A threatened crowd is a type of acting crowd that is in a state of alarm, believing some kind of danger is present. An expressive crowd is drawn together by the promise of personal gratification through active participation in activities and events. A conventional crowd is a gathering in which people's behavior conforms to some well-established set of cultural norms, and gratification results from passive appreciation of an event. A casual crowd is any collection of people who just happen, in the course of their private activities, to be in one place at the same time and focus their attention on a common object or event. The nature of a crowd does not necessarily remain stable and can change if events or social norms change.

Dispersed Collective Behavior

Because today's systems of communication spread information quickly among millions of people, collective behavior is often shared by large numbers of people who have no direct knowledge of or contact with one another. Sociologists designate a mass as a collection of people who, although physically dispersed, participate in some event either physically or with a common concern or interest. Fads and fashions are transitory social events, but with potentially large impact in their time. Fads are social changes with a very short life span marked by a rapid spread and an abrupt drop from popularity. A fad that is especially short-lived may be called a craze. Fashions relate to the standards of dress or manners in a given society at a certain time. They spread more slowly and last longer than fads. Alfred Kroeber showed that fashion cycles can be correlated with degrees of social and political stability. Georg Simmel suggested that changes in fashion are introduced by the upper class in an effort to keep themselves distinct from the lower classes. On the other hand, the upper class may borrow fashion ideas from the lower classes and turn them to their own ends.

A rumor is information that is shared informally and spreads quickly through a mass or crowd. It arises in situations of uncertainty and confusion. Public opinion refers to the beliefs held by a dispersed collectivity of individuals about a common problem, interest, focus, or activity. These beliefs may be varied and conflicting. Politicians, market analysts, public relations experts, and others seek to mold public opinion in various ways. Advertisements of a political nature, seeking to mobilize public support behind a specific party, candidate, or point of view, are called propaganda. Opinion leaders are socially acknowledged experts to whom the public turns for advice.

Mass hysteria occurs when large numbers of people are overwhelmed with emotion and frenzied activity or become convinced they have experienced something for which investigators can find no discernible evidence. Kai Erikson explained the seventeenth-century Salem witchcraft trials as an episode of mass hysteria created by the Massachusetts Bay Colony's identity crisis. A panic is an uncoordinated group flight from a perceived danger. According to Irving Janis and colleagues, people do not panic unless they feel trapped in a life-threatening situation, perceive that the threat to their safety is so large that they can do little else than try to escape, realize that escape routes are limited or inaccessible, and experience a breakdown in communication between the front and rear of the crowd.

Social Movements

A social movement is an important form of collective behavior in which large numbers of people are organized or alerted to support and bring about, or to resist social change. For people to join a social movement they must feel that their own values, needs, goals, or beliefs are being stifled or challenged by the social structure or specific individuals, and things must be set right. Some catalyst, however, is needed to actually mobilize the discontent people feel. Relative deprivation theory suggests that the catalyst occurs when large numbers of people experience the feeling that they lack the living or working conditions, political rights, or social dignity to which they are entitled. Deprivation is relative because it is not measured by an objective standard, but rather through comparison with a reference group. Resource mobilization theory argues that social movements arise at certain times because skilled leaders know how to mobilize and channel popular discontent.

In theory, social movements can be classified according to type; in practice a given movement may possess a complex ideology that places parts of it in several different classifications. Reactionary social movements embrace the aims of the past and seek to return the general society to yesterday's values. Conservative social movements seek to maintain society's current values by reacting to change or threats of change they believe will undermine the status quo. Revisionary social movements seek partial or slight changes within the existing order but do not threaten the order itself. Revolutionary social movements seek to overthrow all or nearly all of the existing social order and replace it with an order they consider more suitable. Expressive social movements stress personal feelings of satisfaction or well-being and typically arise to fill some void or to distract people from some great dissatisfaction in their lives.

Social movements typically pass through a series of five stages that are equivalent to a biological life cycle. The first stage of a social movement is incipiency, when large numbers of people become frustrated about a problem and do not perceive any solution to it through existing institutions. This is the stage at which leaders emerge, and the charisma of a leader (as discussed by Max Weber) can be important to successfully launching the movement. The second stage is coalescence, when groups begin to form around leaders, to promote policies, and to promulgate programs. During the third stage—institutionalization—social movements reach the peak of their strength and influence and become firmly established. Not all social movements reach this stage; some die out earlier and some become accepted by the society. The fourth stage is fragmentation, when the movement gradually begins to fall apart. Demise, the last stage, refers to the end of a social movement. The organizations and ideas introduced may live on in institutionalized form, however.

CHAPTER OUTLINE

Theories of Collective Behavior
What are the major theories of collective behavior?

CONTAGION (MENTALIST) THEORY
In what sense can contagion theory be called mentalist?

EMERGENT NORM THEORY
What is the main contention of emergent norm theory?

CONVERGENCE THEORY
What is it that converges, according to convergence theory?

VALUE-ADDED THEORY
What is the basic argument of value-added theory?

Crowds: Concentrated Collectivities
Why can crowds be called concentrated collectivities?

ATTRIBUTES OF CROWDS
What are the main attributes of crowds?

TYPES OF CROWDS
How are types of crowds determined?

Acting Crowds
What do acting crowds do?

Threatened Crowds
What is unique about threatened crowds?

Expressive Crowds
What are expressive crowds likely to do?

Conventional Crowds
How are conventional crowds different from other types of crowds?

Casual Crowds
How are casual crowds formed?

THE CHANGEABLE NATURE OF CROWDS
What causes the changeable nature of crowds?

Dispersed Collective Behavior
How does dispersed behavior remain collective?

FADS AND FASHIONS
How do fads and fashions differ?

RUMORS
Under what conditions are rumors likely to arise?

PUBLIC OPINION
How is public opinion formed?

MASS HYSTERIAS AND PANICS
Under what conditions do mass hysteria and panics occur?

Social Movements
What is a social movement designed to do?

RELATIVE DEPRIVATION THEORY
How does relative deprivation theory explain social movements?

RESOURCE-MOBILIZATION THEORY
Where do social movements come from, according to resource-mobilization theory?

TYPES OF SOCIAL MOVEMENTS
How are the major types of social movements determined?

Reactionary Social Movements
What is the aim of reactionary social movements?

Conservative Social Movements
What do conservative social movements wish to conserve?

Revisionary Social Movements
What do revisionary social movements seek to accomplish?

Revolutionary Social Movements
What is a revolutionary social movement all about?

Expressive Social Movements
What do expressive social movements seek to express?

THE LIFE CYCLE OF SOCIAL MOVEMENTS
In what sense can we say that social movements have a life cycle?

Incipiency
What is important at the incipiency of a social movement?

Coalescence
What happens during the coalescence of a social movement?

Institutionalization

What are the implications of the institutionalization of a social movement?

Fragmentation

Why do social movements become fragmented?

Demise

Why do social movements experience demise?

LEARNING OBJECTIVES

After studying this chapter you should be able to:

■ *Contrast theories of collective behavior.*

The opening vignette of this chapter describes the 1992 Los Angeles riot. Suggest how each of the main theories of collective behavior would explain this phenomenon.

Contagion theory:

Emergent norm theory:

Convergence theory:

Value-added theory:

Which theory do you think provides the best explanation? Why?

■ *Describe the attributes and types of crowds.*

In sociological terms, what is a crowd?

Describe the four major attributes of crowds, and give an example of each from your own experience.

1.

    example:

2.

    example:

3.

    example:

4.

    example:

Describe each of the types of crowds. Give an example of each type from your own experience, noting how your perceptions, behavior, and/or emotions were different in each type of crowd.

Acting crowd:

    example:

Threatened crowd:

    example:

Expressive crowd:

    example:

Conventional crowd:

example:

Casual crowd:

example:

■ *Describe dispersed forms of collective behavior.*

Define and give an example of each of the following from your own experience.

Fad:

example:

Craze:

example:

Fashion:

example:

Rumor:

example:

Propaganda:

example:

Mass hysteria:

example:

Panic:

example:

Give an example of someone you think is an opinion leader, and explain why they qualify as one.

■ *Contrast alternative theories of social movements.*

On Labor Day in 1991, the national leadership of the American Federation of Labor–Congress of Industrial Organizations (AFL–CIO) along with state and local labor councils throughout the nation organized a march and rally in Washington, D.C., to advocate changes in economic policies to foster more high–wage manufacturing jobs and to oppose trade policies that result in unemployment for American workers. Over 250,000 rank and file union members and labor supporters joined the demonstration. Describe the competing explanations of this social movement offered by relative deprivation theory and resource mobilization theory.

Relative deprivation theory:

Resource mobilization theory:

■ *Describe the major types of social movements.*

Briefly describe the aims and goals of each type of social movement and give an example of each.

_____ social movement:

example:

_____ social movement:

example:

_____ social movement:

example:

_____ social movement:

example:

_____ social movement:

example:

How would you classify the Labor Day Solidarity rally described in the previous learning objective?

■ *Describe the life cycle of social movements.*

Describe each stage in the life cycle of social movements and state what the main concerns of the movement are at each stage.

1st stage:

    main concerns:

2nd stage:

    main concerns:

3rd stage:

    main concerns:

4th stage:

    main concerns:

5th stage:

main concerns:

■ *Explain why people join cults.*

Suppose a friend of yours joined a cult. Based on the research of Saul Levine, what would you tell the family and friends of the cult-joiner, and why?

KEY CONCEPTS

■ *Match each concept with its definition, illustration, or explication below.*

a. expressive social movement
b. generalized belief
c. structural conduciveness
d. conventional crowd
e. craze
f. value-added theory
g. mobilization
h. crowd
i. public opinion
j. revolutionary social movement
k. demise
l. contagion theory
m. acting crowd
n. fad
o. institutionalization
p. social movement
q. resource mobilization theory
r. fragmentation
s. casual crowd
t. reactionary social movement

u. convergence theory
v. revisionary social movement
w. threatened crowd
x. fashion
y. coalescence
z. emergent norm theory
aa. mass hysteria
bb. expressive crowd
cc. structural strain
dd. mass
ee. incipiency
ff. collective behavior
gg. propaganda
hh. conservative social movement
ii. relative deprivation theory
jj. opinion leader
kk. rumor
ll. life cycle
mm. panic
nn. charismatic leader

_____ 1. relatively spontaneous social actions that occur when people respond to unstructured and ambiguous situations.

_____ 2. the theory that crowd behavior is caused by a kind of irrational group feeling that spreads among individuals, causing them to think and act in ways they ordinarily would not.

_____ 3. a theory that crowd members develop common standards by observing and listening to one another.

_____ 4. a theory that collective behavior is the result of people with similar characteristics being drawn together.

_____ 5. a theory that collective behavior occurs as a result of six necessary social conditions or processes that build on one another.

_____ 6. a condition in the existing social order that may promote collective behavior.

_____ 7. the conflict between a group's ideals and its everyday realities.

_____ 8. a widely shared explanation for the existence of structural strain.

_____ 9. the process of people getting organized to take action.

_____10. a temporary concentration of people who focus on some thing or event but who also are attuned to one another's behavior.

_____11. a group of people whose passions and tempers have been aroused by some focal event, who come to share a purpose, and who feed off one another's arousal, often erupting into spontaneous acts of violence.

_____12. a crowd that is in a state of alarm, believing some kind of danger is present.

_____13. a group of people drawn together by the promise of personal gratification through active participation in activities and events.

_____14. a gathering in which people's behavior conforms to some well-established set of cultural norms, and gratification results from passive appreciation of an event.

_____15. any collection of people who just happen, in the course of their private activities, to be in one place at the same time and focus their attention on a common object or event.

_____16. a collection of people who, although physically dispersed, participate in some event either physically or with a common concern or interest.

_____17. a social change with a very short life span marked by a rapid spread and an abrupt drop from popularity.

_____18. a fad that is especially short-lived.

_____19. the standards of dress or manners in a given society at a certain time.

_____20. information that is shared informally and spreads quickly through a mass or crowd.

_____21. beliefs held by a dispersed collectivity of individuals about a common problem, interest, focus, or activity.

_____22. advertisements of a political nature, seeking to mobilize public support behind one specific party, candidate, or point of view.

_____23. socially acknowledged experts to whom the public turns for advice.

_____24. a condition where large numbers of people are overwhelmed with emotion and frenzied activity or become convinced they have experienced something for which investigators can find no discernible evidence.

_____25. an uncoordinated group flight from a perceived danger.

_____26. an important form of collective behavior in which large numbers of people are organized or alerted to support and bring about, or to resist social change.

_____27. suggests that social movements occur when large numbers of people experience the feeling that they lack the living or working conditions, political rights, or social dignity to which they are entitled.

_____28. argues that social movements arise at certain times because skilled leaders know how to mobilize and channel popular discontent.

_____29. movements that embrace the aims of the past and seek to return the general society to yesterday's values.

_____30. movements that seek to maintain society's current values by reacting to change or threats of change they believe will undermine the status quo.

_____31. movements that seek partial or slight changes within the existing order but do not threaten the order itself.

_____32. movements that seek to overthrow all or nearly all of the existing social order and replace it with an order they consider more suitable.

_____33. movements that stress personal feelings of satisfaction or well-being and typically arise to fill some void or to distract people from some great dissatisfaction in their lives.

_____34. the idea that social movements typically pass through a series of stages that are equivalent to the biological process of birth, growth, maturity, old age, and death.

_____35. the beginning stage of a social movement.

_____36. a type of leader with exceptional personal characteristics that inspire devotion and strong allegiance in their followers.

_____37. the stage of a social movement when groups form around leaders, begin to promote policies, and promulgate programs.

_____38. the stage of a social movement when it becomes firmly established through formal organizations.

_____39. the state of a social movement when the movement begins to fall apart.

_____40. refers to the end of a social movement.

KEY THINKERS/RESEARCHERS

■ _Match each thinker with their main idea or contribution._

a. Saul Alinsky
b. Elias Canetti
c. Alfred A. Kroeber
d. Irving Janis
e. Ralph H. Turner
f. Neil Smelser
g. Armand L. Mauss

h. Kai Erikson
i. Herbert Blumer
j. Saul Levine
k. Georg Simmel
l. Samuel Stouffer
m. William Bruce Cameron
n. Gustave Le Bon

_____ 1. a French sociologist who was a pioneer in the study of collective behavior, he developed the contagion theory of crowds.

_____ 2. a major figure in the study of social movements, he discussed contagion theory, classified types of crowds, and first discussed expressive social movements.

_____ 3. one of the first sociologists to develop the emergent norm theory of collective behavior.

_____ 4. developed the value-added theory of collective behavior.

_____ 5. described the important traits of crowds.

_____ 6. showed that fashion moves through predictable cycles correlated with degrees of political and social stability.

_____ 7. argued that changes in fashion are adopted by the upper class as a way of keeping themselves distinct from the lower classes.

_____ 8. explained the seventeenth-century Salem witchcraft trials as an episode of mass hysteria created by the Massachusetts Bay Colony's identity crisis.

_____ 9. described the conditions under which people collectively panic.

_____10. a renowned activist leader who was especially good at mobilizing community resources into social movements.

_____ **11.** first described the concept of relative deprivation.

_____ **12.** classified social movements into four basic types.

_____ **13.** suggested that social movements typically pass through a series of stages that are the equivalent of a biological life cycle.

_____ **14.** did important research on why young people join cults.

CRITICAL THINKING/APPLICATION QUESTIONS

1. The right of people to assemble and express political grievances is a freedom guaranteed by the First Amendment to the Constitution. At the same time, as we have seen, society has a certain need for order and stability. Often these two issues can be in conflict. What do you think about the balance? In situations that are ambiguous, which side of the dilemma should be favored? Why? In particular, how should crowd control be handled at political demonstrations in order to preserve order as well as the First Amendment right?

2. Have you ever participated in a dynamic, changeable crowd and felt the rush of energy that charges through it? Have you found yourself—amazingly—touching and conversing with complete strangers whom you would otherwise avoid or at least never talk to? How important was this experience to you? How important is it to a sense of community among people in an area? Is it important to try to create situations where people can have this kind of experience?

3. Although most white Americans are unaware of it, a great deal of popular culture in this country is derived from African-American subculture—everything from music (rock and roll, blues, jazz, rap) to popular expressions ("It's my thing." "Chill out.") to styles of dress (parachute pants). Why do you think this occurs? Why do you think most Americans are unaware of the real source of many fads and fashions? How do you square this phenomenon with Simmel's discussion of the role of fashion in maintaining class distinctions?

4. The mass media in this country seem to have enormous impact on people's perceptions of events. To what extent do you think the media engage in propaganda? Given that, according to value-added theory, the growth and spread of a generalized belief is necessary for the development of collective behavior, do you think the media today shape popular social movements and crowd behavior (for example, the Los Angeles riot)? Should they have this role?

SUGGESTED READINGS

CROWDS: CONCENTRATED COLLECTIVITIES

Hugh Davis Graham and Ted Robert Gurr, eds., _Violence in America: Historical and Comparative Perspectives,_ revised ed. (Beverly Hills, CA: Sage, 1979). An excellent history of violence connected with crowds and social movements, it also examines violence perpetrated by the state.

DISPERSED COLLECTIVE BEHAVIOR

Stuart Ewen, _Captains of Consciousness: Advertising and the Social Roots of the Consumer Culture_ (New York: McGraw-Hill, 1976). Argues that capitalists, using advertising as propaganda, were able to reshape popular culture into a consumer culture in this century.

Edward S. Herman, _Beyond Hypocrisy: Decoding the News in an Age of Propaganda_ (Boston: South End Press, 1992). An irreverent book that includes satirical essays, cartoons, and a cross-referenced lexicon of government _doublespeak_ terminology, with examples.

SOCIAL MOVEMENTS

Frances Fox Piven and Richard A. Cloward, _Poor People's Movements: Why They Succeed, How They Fail_ (New York: Vintage, 1979). An analysis of four different social movements involving poor people, the book suggests strategies aimed at maximizing gains for the poor.

Todd Gitlin, _The Sixties: Years of Hope, Days of Rage_ (New York: Bantam, 1987). The author of this highly-acclaimed book was a national leader of the student movement in the 1960s who later became a respected sociologist. This book provides his sociological reflections and insights into the movement and the period.

ANSWER KEY

KEY CONCEPTS

1. ff	21. i		
2. l	22. gg		
3. z	23. jj		
4. u	24. aa		
5. f	25. mm		
6. c	26. p		
7. cc	27. ii		
8. b	28. q		
9. g	29. t		
10. h	30. hh		
11. m	31. v		
12. w	32. j		
13. bb	33. a		
14. d	34. ll		
15. s	35. ee		
16. dd	36. nn		
17. n	37. y		
18. e	38. o		
19. x	39. r		
20. kk	40. k		

KEY THINKERS/RESEARCHERS

1. n	8. h
2. i	9. d
3. e	10. a
4. f	11. l
5. b	12. m
6. c	13. g
7. k	14. j

CHAPTER SUMMARY

Society and Social Change

Social change consists of any modification in the social organization of a society in any of its social institutions or social roles. It can take place gradually or relatively quickly and can be accomplished through violent or peaceful means.

Sources of Social Change

Social change can occur as a result of internal or external forces. Internal sources of social change include those factors that originate within a specific society and that singly or in combination produce significant alterations in its social organization and structure. Technological innovation is an important source of internal change that has transformed the way we live and work.

Ideology, a set of interrelated religious or secular beliefs, values, and norms that justify the pursuit of a given set of goals through a given set of means, is another important internal source of change. Conservative (or traditional) ideologies try to preserve things as they are. Liberal ideologies seek limited reforms that do not involve fundamental changes in the social structure of society. Radical (or revolutionary) ideologies seek major structural changes in society. Structural inequality promotes social change as society attempts to accommodate itself to a wide variety of demands for social, economic, political, and cultural reforms.

Diffusion, the process of transmitting the traits of one culture to another, is an example of an external source of social change. Diffusion occurs whenever and wherever different cultures come into contact. In general, traits diffuse from more powerful to weaker peoples, from more technologically advanced societies to those less so. A social change that is imposed by might or conquest on weaker peoples is called forced acculturation.

Theories of Social Change

The complexity of social change makes it impossible for a single theory to explain all its ramifications. Thus a variety of complementary views must be analyzed together in order to understand the total theoretical framework of social change.

Evolution—the continuous change from a simpler condition to a more complex state—was the dominant concern of European scholars from a variety of disciplines in the second half of the nineteenth century. Charles Darwin's pioneering work in biology influenced Herbert Spencer, who brought evolutionary concepts into sociology. As we have seen earlier, Émile Durkheim argued that society has evolved from mechanical solidarity based on common characteristics to organic solidarity based on interdependence created by a complex division of labor. Likewise, Ferdinand Tönnies maintained that societies shift from the intimate, cooperative relationships of small communities, characterized by *gemeinschaft*, to the specialized, impersonal relationships typical of large associations, called *gesellschaft*. Neither Tönnies nor Durkheim thought these changes necessarily positive.

Early evolutionary theory has been severely criticized on the basis that it uses the norms and values of one culture as absolute standards for all cultures. Thus contemporary theorists have proposed evolutionary stages that are more flexible and allow for more variation among societies. Julian H. Steward has suggested that evolution is "multilineal," by which he means that each culture is unique and must be studied in its own terms. Marshall D. Sahlins and Elman R. Service distinguish between general evolution, or the trend toward increasing differentiation, and specific evolution, or the actual changes in each society that may move either in the direction of greater simplicity or greater complexity. All evolutionary theories have trouble, though, answering the question, "Why do societies change?"

According to conflict theory, conflicts rooted in the class struggle between unequal groups lead to social change. This, in turn, creates conditions that lead to new conflicts. Europe's transition from feudalism to capitalism provided the model for Karl Marx's theory of social change. Contemporary conflict theorists like Ralf Dahrendorf accept the basic premise that social conflict and social change are built-in structural features of society, but argue that conflict arises from more sources than just class conflict—religious, political or nationalistic conflicts, for example.

Functionalists view society as a homeostatic system—that is, an assemblage of interrelated parts that seeks to achieve and maintain a settled or stable state. A system that maintains a stable state is said to be in equilibrium, though because society is an open system subject to many external and internal influences, it is more accurate to talk about a state of dynamic, or near equilibrium. Talcott Parsons, one of the best-known functionalists, viewed society as attempting to maintain equilibrium among six basic needs: member replacement, member socialization, production of goods and services, preservation of internal order, provision and maintenance of a sense of purpose, and protection from external attack. These needs are so interdependent that when one changes they must all accommodate.

Functionalist theory successfully explains moderate degrees of social change, but is not helpful in explaining major structural changes. William F. Ogburn's concept of cultural lag is an attempt to deal with this criticism. He suggests that the elements of society change at different rates, inevitably producing stresses. Still, critics would suggest that functionalist theory overestimates the degree of consensus in society and underestimates the amount of conflict.

Cyclical theories are built around the assumption that the rise and fall of civilizations is inevitable. Oswald Spengler theorized that every society goes through a life cycle of childhood, youth, maturity, and old age. Arnold Toynbee argued that each society was periodically faced with challenges from its natural and social environments. How the society responds to these challenges determines whether it survives and flourishes or spirals into decline. Pitirim A. Sorokin theorized that societies were divided into ideational cultures, or those which emphasize spiritual values, and sensate cultures, which are based on what is empirically evident. In an ideational culture, progress is achieved through self-control and adherence to a strong moral code. In a sensate culture, people are dedicated to self-expression and gratification of their immediate physical needs. Sorokin believed that societies fluctuate between these two extremes. Occasionally a culture may reach what he called the idealistic point, in which the two ideational values coexist in a harmonious mix. The problem with cyclical theories is that they erroneously assume that social change is an inevitable process that cannot really be controlled by those who experience it.

Modernization: Global Social Change

Modernization refers to a complex set of changes that take place as a traditional society becomes an industrial one. Modernization, as we know it today, began with the Industrial Revolution. As societies undergo modernization, they increasingly substitute machines for human physical power. The labor force becomes more specialized and the economy more impersonal. Cities develop and the demographic transition in birth and death rates begins. Modernization reduces the role of the family, but tends to increase social equality between men and women.

Whereas modernization was indigenous to most of Europe, it was forced on Third World nations by conquering armies, missionaries, plantation managers, colonial administrators, colonist groups, and industrial enterprises. Until recently, modernization and "Westernization" (adopting the culture of Western Europe and North America) were thought of as more or less the same thing. Now, however, Third World nations that have gained some control over their economic resources are attempting to chart out a modernization strategy guided by their own traditional values.

Modernization has given people in developed countries improved health, increased longevity, more leisure time and affluence. It has, however, created a whole new set of problems: anxiety, obesity, degenerative diseases, divorce, high taxes, inflation, and pollution. In the Third World, the rapidity of modernization has created severe psychological dislocation for many. The degree of personal stress and dislocation that individuals experience as their society modernizes depends on many things, including the historical traditions of the culture, the conditions under which modernization is introduced, and the degree to which the masses share in the material benefits of the change.

Social Change in the United States

There is virtually no area of life in the United States that has not changed in some respect since the 1950s. Moreover, the pace of change is likely to quicken as the century ends. Technological innovation will continue but it will change qualitatively to produce, not just more new and different things, but more insight into how things work and how to make them work better. This change will occur, among other places, in the realm of computers, human biology, and telecommunications. Sociologists generally hold that technology influences, but does not determine social change.

The rapid growth of the labor force over the last fifteen years was the result of the coming of age of the baby-boom generation and the rapid increase in the number of women entering the work force. The labor force of the year 2000 will have more minority and female workers and fewer young workers than it does today. Service industries will account for nearly all the projected growth in the labor force. The number of jobs in technical, service, professional, sales, executive and managerial occupations is expected to grow faster than average between now and the year 2000. Agriculture, forestry, fishing, and private household workers are expected to decline. For the most part, occupations which require the most education will grow the most rapidly.

CHAPTER OUTLINE

Society and Social Change
What is the relationship between society and social change?

Sources of Social Change
Where do sociologists look for sources of social change?

INTERNAL SOURCES OF SOCIAL CHANGE
What is the main characteristic of internal sources of change?

Technological Innovation
What is the impact of technological innovation?

Ideology
How does ideology cause social change?

Cultural Conflicts and Institutional Structural Inequality
What role do cultural conflicts and institutional structural inequality play in social change?

EXTERNAL SOURCES OF SOCIAL CHANGE
What are the external sources of social change?

Theories of Social Change
What are the major theories of social change?

EVOLUTIONARY THEORY
How does evolutionary theory look at social change?

CONFLICT THEORY
What is the basic premise of conflict theory with regard to social change?

FUNCTIONALIST THEORY
How does functionalist theory characterize social change?

CYCLICAL (RISE AND FALL) THEORY
How are cycles involved in social change, according to this theory?

Modernization: Global Social Change
How does modernization cause global social change?

MODERNIZATION: AN OVERVIEW
What are the basic characteristics of modernization?

MODERNIZATION IN THE THIRD WORLD
How has modernization occurred in the Third World?

MODERNIZATION AND THE INDIVIDUAL
What are the effects of modernization on the individual?

Social Change in the United States
What is the major feature of social change in the United States?

TECHNOLOGICAL CHANGE
How has technological change affected life in the United States?

THE WORKFORCE OF THE FUTURE
What are the major characteristics of the workforce of the future?

LEARNING OBJECTIVES

After studying this chapter you should be able to:

■ *Describe the nature of social change in society.*

Define social change:
Give three examples of major social changes in the United States that were not mentioned in this chapter.

1.

2.

3.

■ *Contrast differing ideologies and show how they influence social change.*

Describe each of the following ideologies and give an example of a group that advocates it or a social change that embodies it.

Conservative ideology:

example:

Liberal ideology:

example:

Radical ideology:

example:

■ *Explain the processes of cultural diffusion and forced acculturation.*

Define each of the following terms, give an example of each, and describe its impact.

Cultural diffusion:

example:

impact:

Forced acculturation:

example:

impact:

■ *Compare alternative theories of social change.*

Describe and contrast each of the following theories of social change.

Description/major premises	Strength/utility of theory	Weakness
Evolutionary:		

Representative evolutionary theorists:

Conflict:

Representative conflict theorists:

Functionalism:

Representative functionalist theorists:

Cyclical (Rise and Fall):

Representative cyclical theorists:

■ *Describe the characteristics and impact of the process of modernization.*

Define modernization:

Briefly describe the process through which modernization occurs:

How does modernization in the third World differ from modernization as it has occurred in the developed countries?

List four ways that modernization affects individuals:

1.

2.

3.

4.

■ *Describe the phenomenon of technological innovation.*

Choose three areas of technological innovation in modern society. For each one, discuss its connection with culture—to what extent has the technology shaped culture, and to what extent has culture shaped the technology?

Innovation #1:

assessment:

Innovation #2:

    assessment:

Innovation #3:

    assessment:

After completing the above exercise, how would you assess the notion of technological determinism?

■ *Summarize the changes that will occur in the U.S. labor force by the year 2000.*

How will the labor force change this decade in terms of its age, gender, and minority composition?

Age:

Gender:

Minority:

List 5 occupations that will expand during this decade.

1.

2.

3.

4.

5.

List 5 occupations that will decline during this decade.

1.

2.

3.

4.

5.

What is the relationship of education to these changes?

KEY CONCEPTS

■ *Match each concept with its definition, illustration, or explication below.*

a. cultural conflicts
b. Age of Insight
c. sensate cultures
d. evolution
e. technological determinism
f. conservative ideologies
g. homeostatic system
h. McDonaldization
i. external sources of social change
j. forced acculturation
k. technological change
l. information anxiety
m. general vs. specific evolution

n. radical ideologies
o. evolutionary theory
p. internal sources of social change
q. multilineal evolution
r. ideational cultures
s. ideology
t. social change
u. structural inequalities
v. diffusion
w. cultural lag
x. liberal ideologies
y. idealistic point
z. modernization

_____ 1. any modification in the social organization of a society in any of its social institutions or social roles.

_____ 2. those factors that originate within a specific society and that singly or in combination produce significant alterations in its social organization and structure.

_____ 3. a set of interrelated religious or secular beliefs, values, and norms that justify the pursuit of a given set of goals through a given set of means.

_____ 4. ideologies that try to preserve things as they are.

_____ 5. ideologies that seek limited reforms that do not involve fundamental changes in the social structure of society

_____ 6. ideologies that seek major structural changes in society.

_____ 7. unequal distribution of resources and power that is built into the social structure.

_____ 8. conflicts involving groups with differing values and ideologies.

_____ 9. changes within a society produced by external events.

_____10. the process of transmitting the traits of one culture to another.

_____11. a social change imposed by might or conquest on weaker peoples.

_____12. a theory that social change occurs as a continuous change from a simpler condition to a more complex state.

_____13. the continuous change from a simpler condition to a more complex state.

_____14. the idea that each society or cultural tradition must be studied separately and not forced into arbitrary, "universal" stages.

_____15. a distinction between the overall trend toward increasing diversity and the specific social changes in a given society.

_____16. an assemblage of interrelated parts that seeks to achieve and maintain a settled or stable state.

_____17. the idea that, while all elements of a society are interrelated, some change rapidly and others change more slowly, resulting in some disequilibrium.

_____18. cultures that emphasize spiritual values.

_____19. cultures based on what is immediately apparent through the senses.

_____20. the situation where ideational and sensate values coexist in a harmonious mix.

_____21. a complex set of changes that take place as a traditional society becomes an industrial one.

_____22. alterations in a society's productive techniques.

_____23. an era in which technological advances will help us understand how things work and how to make them work better.

_____24. the view that technology alone is largely responsible for social change.

_____25. the idea that the rationalized business principles by which McDonald's is run are coming to dominate modern society.

_____26. a state of unease produced by the ever-widening gap between what we understand and what we think we should understand.

KEY THINKERS/RESEARCHERS

■ *Match each thinker with their main idea or contribution.*

a. Max Weber
b. Julian H. Steward
c. Ralf Dahrendorf
d. M. D. Sahlins and E. R. Service
e. Herbert Spencer
f. George Ritzer
g. Edward Shils
h. Pitirim Sorokin
i. Colin Turnbull
j. William F. Ogburn

k. Charles Darwin
l. Karl Marx
m. Lauriston Sharp
n. Arnold Toynbee
o. Inkeles and Smith
p. Ferdinand Tönnies
q. Talcott Parsons
r. Oswald Spengler
s. Émile Durkheim

_____ 1. developed the concept of mass society.

_____ 2. described the disruptive effects of the diffusion of steel axes to the Yir Yoront tribe.

_____ 3. the most influential evolutionary theorist, he systematized the concept in his book *On the Origin of Species*.

_____ 4. brought Darwin's idea of natural selection into sociology and suggested that Western cultures had reached higher levels of cultural development because they were better adapted.

_____ 5. a pioneering evolutionary sociologist, he described the transition from mechanical to organic solidarity.

_____ 6. described social evolution as a shift from *gemeinschaft* to *gesellschaft*.

_____ 7. proposed the concept of "multilineal" evolution as a way of avoiding ethnocentrism in the concept.

_____ 8. distinguished between the general process of differentiation and the specific evolution of each society.

_____ 9. a pioneering conflict theorist, he argued that social change is rooted in class conflict.

_____ 10. argued that conflict and dissension are present in nearly every part of society.

_____ 11. the best-known functionalist theorist in America, he saw society as a "homeostatic action system."

_____ 12. developed the concept of cultural lag in an effort to provide a functionalist explanation for disequilibrium.

_____ 13. theorized that every society moves through a life cycle.

_____ 14. argued that the rise and fall of civilizations could be explained through the concepts of challenge and response.

_____ 15. distinguished between ideational and sensate cultures.

_____ 16. demonstrated the positive psychological effects of modernization through a cross-cultural study.

_____ 17. felt that the process of modernization through increasing rationality could have damaging impact on the spirit of individuals.

_____ 18. studied the cultural and social disintegration of the Ik of Uganda as they experienced forced acculturation.

_____ 19. proposed the concept of the "McDonaldization" of society.

CRITICAL THINKING/APPLICATION QUESTIONS

1. Three types of ideologies have been described in this chapter. There seems to be some correlation between ideology and age, with people tending to grow more conservative as they get older. It is not a one-to-one correlation, though, and many exceptions exist. Why do you think such a correlation exists in the first place—that is, why do older people tend to be more conservative and younger ones more liberal and radical? Is change with age inevitable? Why or why not? What are the implications of the aging of the American population (especially the baby boomers) for ideology as a source of change?

2. Reflect on how each theory of social change discussed in this chapter would explain a contemporary social movement such as the civil rights, anti-abortion, or pro-choice movements. Which theory seems to offer the best explanation? Why? How are the theories of change connected to ideologies?

3. Make a list of all the ways that technological innovation has affected your life as a college student, then assess each one. Why has the innovation occurred? In whose interest was it developed? Does it help or hinder your ability to learn? to get an education? to get a degree? What technological innovations *haven't* occurred that would make your life as a college student easier? Why haven't they occurred?

4. In the box, "Sociology at Work," George Ritzer's

concept of the McDonaldizaton of American society is described. To what extent has your college or university been "McDonaldized"? (Think about all facets of the institution.) If it hasn't, why hasn't it? If it has been "McDon-aldized," how would you assess its impact? What are the positive and negative features? Why do you think the future trend is? Can you think of other organizations or institutions that have been "McDonaldized"?

SUGGESTED READINGS

SOURCES OF SOCIAL CHANGE

Thomas S. Kuhn, *The Structure of Scientific Revolutions*, 2nd ed., enlarged (Chicago: University of Chicago Press, 1970). A classic work on the role of conflict and consensus in advancing scientific thought.

MODERNIZATION: GLOBAL SOCIAL CHANGE

Thomas Richard Shannon, *An Introduction to the World-System Perspective* (Boulder, CO: Westview Press, 1989). An accessible introduction to one of the most important theories on global change and development. Includes history, basic concepts, critique, and assessment.

SOCIAL CHANGE IN THE UNITED STATES

Bennett Harrison and Barry Bluestone, *The Great U-Turn: Corporate Restructuring and the Polarizing of America* (New York: Basic Books, 1988). Two important analysts of the changing American economy examine the social consequences of current economic policies.

David F. Noble, *Forces of Production: A Social History of Industrial Automation* (New York: Oxford University Press, 1986). An excellent critical history of how technology has been used—and misused—in the workplace.

Barbara Garson, *The Electronic Sweatshop: How Computers Are Transforming the Office of the Future Into the Factory of the Past* (New York: Penguin, 1988). Incorporates oral history with insightful analysis of technological change in white-collar and service industry jobs.

ANSWER KEY

KEY CONCEPTS

1. t	14. q
2. p	15. m
3. s	16. g
4. f	17. w
5. x	18. r
6. n	19. c
7. u	20. y
8. a	21. z
9. i	22. k
10. v	23. b
11. j	24. e
12. o	25. h
13. d	26. l

KEY THINKERS/RESEARCHERS

1. g	11. q
2. m	12. j
3. k	13. r
4. e	14. n
5. s	15. h
6. p	16. o
7. b	17. a
8. d	18. i
9. l	19. f
10. c	

PRACTICE TESTS

CHAPTER 1 ■ *The Sociological Perspective*

TRUE/FALSE

1. T F Sociological knowledge is generally just common sense.
2. T F The interactionist perspective is most closely associated with Herbert Spencer.
3. T F Auguste Comte invented the term "sociology" for the science of society he advocated so strongly.
4. T F The first scientifically conducted, truly sociological study was Durkheim's study of suicide.
5. T F Max Weber maintained that a system of beliefs he called the *Protestant Ethic* helped to bring about capitalism, not just to justify it.
6. T F American sociologist Robert Merton is an important proponent of conflict theory.
7. T F During the early years of sociology in the United States, most of the field's development took place at the University of Chicago.
8. T F Manifest functions are the unintended or not readily recognized consequences of a social process.
9. T F Durkheim was one of the early proponents of the modern perspective known as functionalism.
10. T F Functionalists view society as a system of highly interrelated parts that generally operate together harmoniously.
11. T F Cultural anthropology is the social science most closely related to sociology.
12. T F Unlike Marx, Max Weber felt that social scientists should be activists, intent on changing the world rather than just analyzing it.
13. T F Science is mostly about the collection of facts.
14. T F The sociological imagination involves looking at all types of human behavior and discerning unseen connections among them.
15. T F Auguste Comte was a close collaborator with Karl Marx, with whom he invented sociology.

MULTIPLE CHOICE

1. Which of the following is a component of the definition of sociology?
   a. human society
   b. scientific study
   c. social interactions
   d. a and c only
   e. a, b, and c

2. Sociology focuses mainly on
   a. groups
   b. strange people
   c. individuals
   d. unusual occurrences

3. Science is a body of systematically arranged knowledge that shows the operation of
   a. general laws
   b. solutions to problems
   c. probabilities
   d. gremlins

4. Which of the following is **not** a component of the scientific method?
   a. experimentation
   b. verification
   c. observation
   d. generalization
   e. these are all components of the scientific method

5. Which of the following is an example of applied sociology?
   a. an investigation of how a community will be affected by the closing of a large factory
   b. an examination of the major factors influencing social interaction
   c. a study of the impact of crack cocaine on an urban neighborhood
   d. a and c only
   e. a, b, and c

Answers appear at the end of the book.

6. Empiricism is the feature of science that stresses
   a. observable entities
   b. abstract concepts
   c. philosophical doctrines
   d. moral principles

7. Which of the following is **not** a social science?
   a. political science
   b. psychology
   c. sociology
   d. economics
   e. these are all social sciences

8. Where and when did sociology first emerge?
   a. Chicago, in the 1920s
   b. Harvard Univeristy, in the 1950s
   c. Europe, in the 19th century
   d. North America, in the 18th century

9. According to Durkheim, people who kill themselves out of a sense of duty to the group or self-sacrifice are committing _____ suicide.
   a. egoistic
   b. altruistic
   c. anomic
   d. atomic

10. According to _____, the most important features of human interaction involve people's efforts to create and manage impressions.
    a. Erving Goffman
    b. Robert K. Merton
    c. Talcott Parsons
    d. C. Wright Mills

11. According to _____, the working class sometimes participates in its own oppression by believing in the economic, political, and religious ideologies that justify ruling-class privileges.
    a. Harold Garfinkel
    b. Karl Marx
    c. Talcott Parsons
    d. Herbert Spencer

12. A suicide resulting from a sense of moral and social disorientation and aimlessness would be called an _____ suicide by Durkheim.
    a. egoistic
    b. anomic
    c. altruistic
    d. atomic

13. Conflict theory
    a. attempts to understand and eliminate the sources of social conflict
    b. sees conflict in society as normal
    c. suggests that most social conflicts can be solved by effective communication
    d. sees society operating on the basis of "survival of the fittest"

14. A paradigm is an
    a. unintended consequence of a scientific discovery
    b. amateur social scientist
    c. explanatory framework to guide scientific research
    d. unsuccessful attempt at suicide, according to Durkheim

15. Both sociologists and historians are interested in the past. But in studying the War in Vietnam, for instance, a sociologist would be most interested in
    a. particular battles and how they were won or lost
    b. individual military and political leaders and the strategies they developed
    c. whether American involvement in the war was moral or immoral
    d. the impact of the war on political attitudes and events in the United States

16. Which sociologist pioneered the notion that society was like a living organism and is associated with the idea of "Social Darwinism"?
    a. Herbert Spencer
    b. Karl Marx
    c. George Herbert Mead
    d. Harold Garfinkel

17. If, when answering the phone, you decided to test callers' taken-for-granted notions of social interaction by saying "I'm listening" instead of "Hello," you would be conducting an exercise in
    a. dramaturgy
    b. ethnomethodology
    c. symbolic interactionism
    d. functionalism

18. Karl Marx believed that the history of human societies could be viewed mainly as a history of
    a. functional interdependence
    b. class struggles
    c. great leaders
    d. increasing solidarity

Answers appear at the end of the book.

19. High crime rates cause problems for many people. However, they also help to create jobs for large numbers of people in fields such as law enforcement, criminal law, and corrections. This latter phenomenon is an example of a
    a. latent function
    b. social conflict
    c. social interdependence
    d. manifest function

20. In *As You Like It,* Shakespeare wrote:
    "All the world's a stage,
    And all the men and women merely players.
    They have their exits and their entrances,
    And one man in his time plays many
        parts. . ."
    Which of the following sociological perspectives does Shakespeare's statement best express?
    a. ethnomethodology
    b. symbolic interactionism
    c. middle-range theory
    d. dramaturgy

Answers appear at the end of the book.

TRUE/FALSE

1. T F Social scientists regard deception of research participants as a necessary evil in most social research.
2. T F One advantage of social research is that it frequently benefits the research subjects directly and immediately.
3. T F Independent and dependent variables are found in statements of causality but not in statements of association.
4. T F A testable statement about the relationships between two or more empirical variables is known as a hypothesis.
5. T F Most research problems of interest to sociologists are most easily and accurately studied by means of controlled experiments.
6. T F An empirical question is an issue posed in such a way that it can be studied through observation.
7. T F The mean is the number that occurs most often in a data set.
8. T F The phenomenon studied by the researcher is called the independent variable.
9. T F A self-fulfilling prophecy is produced when a researcher who is strongly inclined toward a particular point of view communicates that attitude to the research subjects such that their responses wind up consistent with the initial point of view.
10. T F Objectivity is a condition in which it is assumed that researchers have no biases.
11. T F A structured interview is a form of research conversation in which the questionnaire is followed rigidly.
12. T F Validity is the extent to which a study tests what it was intended to test.
13. T F Tables often omit headings for rows and columns.
14. T F Most subjects of sociological research belong to groups with little or no power.
15. T F The failure of *Literary Digest* to accurately predict the 1936 Landon-Roosevelt presidential election was due to having too small a sample.

MULTIPLE CHOICE

1. Which of the following is a goal of science?
   a. to propose and test theories that help us understand things and events
   b. to tell us what the proper course of action is
   c. to describe in detail particular things or events
   d. a and c only
   e. a, b, and c

2. A subset of the population that exhibits, in correct proportion, the significant characteristics of the population as a whole is known as a
   a. dependent variable
   b. representative sample
   c. nonrandom sample
   d. cross-sectional study

3. The figure that falls in the exact middle of a ranked series of scores is the
   a. median
   b. mode
   c. mean
   d. average

4. A longitudinal study is research
   a. aimed at predicting the future
   b. investigating a population over a period of time
   c. examining a population at a given point in time
   d. conducted without the participants' knowledge

5. Which of the following is an ethical issue that sometimes arises in the course of sociological research?
   a. the potential disclosure of confidential or personally harmful information
   b. the extent to which the subjects should be deceived
   c. the degree to which subjects risk pain or harm
   d. b and c only
   e. a, b, and c

Answers appear at the end of the book.

6. Which of the following steps in the research process must come last?
   a. develop hypotheses
   b. define the problem
   c. analyze the data and draw conclusions
   d. review previous research
   e. determine the research design

7. Which of the following steps in the research process must come first?
   a. develop hypotheses
   b. define the problem
   c. determine the research design
   d. review previous research
   e. analyze the data and draw conclusions

8. "Men who live in cities are more likely to marry young than are men who live in the country." In this hypothesis, the dependent variable is
   a. place of residence (city or country)
   b. marital status (single or married)
   c. age at marriage
   d. sex

9. Which of the following would be the best research method for gaining a deep and detailed understanding of everyday life within a small group?
   a. a survey with a structured interview schedule
   b. participant observation
   c. a controlled experiment
   d. any of these methods would be equally well-suited for such a study

10. Cyril Burt's research on the inheritance of intelligence was based on
   a. fraudulent data
   b. a small and unrepresentative sample
   c. statistical miscalculations
   d. dangerous and potentially harmful experiments

11. Which of the following is a measure of central tendency that is commonly referred to as the "average"?
   a. median
   b. mode
   c. mean
   d. meridian

12. A possible problem with political "exit polls" is that they
   a. may affect the outcome of a national election
   b. rarely produce accurate projections of election outcomes
   c. may be misused by political candidates to discredit their opponents
   d. interfere with the physical process of voting

13. In a series of research conversations, an investigator varies the questions asked and even makes up new ones on occasion. This is an example of
   a. researcher bias
   b. a semistructured interview
   c. a controlled experiment
   d. random sampling

14. Which of the following is a variable?
   a. the proportion of Americans opposed to abortion
   b. a baseball player's batting average
   c. the number of students enrolled at your college or university
   d. a and c only
   e. a, b, and c

15. A good way to decide if the information in a table is reliable is to check its
   a. source
   b. title
   c. headings
   d. headnotes

16. Which of the following research methods, despite its advantages, is the most subjective?
   a. surveys
   b. controlled experiments
   c. participant observation

17. The result of failing to achieve a representative sample is known as
   a. researcher bias
   b. sampling error
   c. subjectivity
   d. random sampling

18. An investigation of Americans' evaluation of the president's effectiveness in foreign policy six months after taking office would be
   a. a cross-sectional study
   b. an exit poll
   c. an operational definition
   d. a longitudinal study

19. Investigators who are kept unaware of both the kinds of subjects they are studying and the hypothesis being tested are called
   a. blind investigators
   b. double-blind investigators
   c. subjective researchers
   d. participant nonobservers

20. If the results of a study cannot be replicated in subsequent studies, then we say that the findings are not
   a. justified
   b. valid
   c. appropriate
   d. reliable

Answers appear at the end of the book.

CHAPTER 3 ■ *Culture*

TRUE/FALSE

1. T F Many outside observers are troubled by the racial exclusiveness of Japanese society.
2. T F The incest taboo prohibits sexual relations between family members.
3. T F Mores are expectations of what people should do under perfect conditions.
4. T F Specialization is the process of developing more complicated yet more flexible ways of doing things.
5. T F There are some forms or patterns found in all human cultures, although they may differ in their details.
6. T F The Sapir-Whorf hypothesis suggests that other animals are incapable of really learning human language.
7. T F Time is a cultural universal because all cultures understand it in the same way—as a steady progression of past, present, and future events.
8. T F Human beings, like most other species, pass a wide variety of behavioral patterns from generation to generation through their genes.
9. T F Mores are strongly held rules of behavior that have a moral connotation.
10. T F Culture is transmitted by means of language.
11. T F Selectivity is the process by which human societies apportion basic tasks.
12. T F Environmental determinism is the belief that the natural setting dictates cultural patterns.
13. T F Even though all spoken languages are symbolic systems, it is not always possible to translate a word precisely from one language into another language.
14. T F Industrial technology has the advantage over less-developed technologies in that it is adaptable to a wider range of environments.
15. T F Generalized adaptability is the movement of culture traits from one culture to another.
16. T F Cultural lag is inevitable in rapidly changing societies.

MULTIPLE CHOICE

1. Cultural relativism means that
   a. there is no such thing as right or wrong with regard to cultural practices
   b. some cultures are clearly superior in relation to others
   c. cultures must be studied on their own terms before being compared or judged
   d. all cultures must be understood as consisting of many subcultures

2. The concept that professors should show up for every scheduled class meeting and make the best use of the allotted time is an example of a
   a. norm
   b. value
   c. belief
   d. custom

3. Attempts to teach language to apes, such as Penny Patterson's work with the gorilla Koko, have
   a. been unsuccessful because of the very limited intelligence of apes
   b. proven that apes have some intelligence but no symbolic ability
   c. succeeded in teaching them fairly large vocabularies but not grammar and syntax
   d. shown that apes can learn symbols as well as grammar and syntax

4. A society's beliefs, knowledge, and values are known as its
   a. cognitive culture
   b. material culture
   c. nonmaterial culture
   d. normative culture

Answers appear at the end of the book.

5. The Japanese are very fond of the American game of baseball. However, they have modified many aspects of the game to fit their own culture. This is an example of
   a. innovation
   b. invention
   c. diffusion
   d. reformulation

6. Which of the following is a cultural universal?
   a. incest taboo
   b. division of labor
   c. rites of passage
   d. a and b only
   e. a, b, and c

7. *Homo erecti*, humankind's immediate ancestors, lived
   a. in organized nomadic bands
   b. in small fixed settlements
   c. as isolated individuals
   d. in developed cities near rivers and coastlines

8. When anthropologist Napoleon Chagnon first visited the Yanomamö, he was disgusted by their aggression and uncleanliness. This is an example of
   a. cultural lag
   b. cultural relativism
   c. culture shock
   d. material culture

9. The process of making judgments about other cultures based on the customs and values of one's own culture is called
   a. ethnocentrism
   b. cultural relativism
   c. cultural innovation
   d. reformulation

10. Most nonhuman animal species rely upon _____ to meet their needs.
    a. norms
    b. instinct
    c. culture
    d. mores

11. It is considered polite to send regrets when you are invited to a party but cannot attend. Failure to do so, however, is not considered a moral lapse. This type of norm is called a
    a. custom
    b. folkway
    c. taboo
    d. subculture

12. Which of the following is an example of material culture?
    a. the U.S. Capitol building
    b. the Bill of Rights
    c. the findings of the latest Gallup Poll
    d. b and c only
    e. a, b, and c

13. In American culture, such things as freedom, individualism, and equal opportunity are deemed to be highly desirable. In sociological terms these concepts are
    a. values
    b. beliefs
    c. folkways
    d. norms

14. Innovation and diffusion are mechanisms of
    a. cultural lag
    b. culture shock
    c. cultural evolution
    d. cognitive culture

15. Morse code, in which letters and numbers are represented in patterns of dots and dashes, is a system of
    a. symbols
    b. ideologies
    c. signs
    d. beliefs

16. People do not just drift from one stage in life to another. Rather, they experience
    a. division of labor
    b. cultural evolution
    c. cultural lag
    d. rites of passage

17. Which of the following is a characteristic of culture?
    a. it is learned
    b. it is shared
    c. it is inborn in every human
    d. a and b only
    e. a, b, and c

18. The most common rites of passage among human cultures are those relating to
    a. puberty, marriage, and death
    b. educational achievements
    c. military service
    d. work achievements

19. The process by which humans adjust to changes in their environment is known as
    a. specialization
    b. adaptation
    c. innovation
    d. environmental determinism

Answers appear at the end of the book.

20. Rap artists, soapbox derby enthusiasts, ethnic clubs, and stamp collectors are all examples of
    a. cognitive cultures
    b. secondary cultures
    c. microcultures
    d. subcultures

21. People sometimes disobey the "don't walk" sign at street crossings because they see that there are no cars coming. This behavior reflects
    a. cultural universals
    b. real norms
    c. ideal norms
    d. instincts

22. The picture of a woman on the door to the women's restroom is an example of using a(n) _____ to communicate.
    a. sign
    b. symbol
    c. cultural universal
    d. ideology

Answers appear at the end of the book.

CHAPTER 4 ■ *Socialization and Development*

TRUE/FALSE

1. T F Even though aging is a biological process, becoming old is a social and cultural one.
2. T F Most of our bodily processes are the result of the interaction of genes and our environment.
3. T F According to Piaget, the operational stage is when the infant relies on touch and the manipulation of objects for information about the world.
4. T F Sociobiologists like Edward O. Wilson believe that human behavior can be understood as continuing attempts to ensure the transmission of one's genes to a new generation.
5. T F In Freudian theory, the ego is the repository of thoughts and feelings of which we are unaware.
6. T F Young people who feel ignored by their parents seem to be more vulnerable to peer pressure.
7. T F Although socialization may play a role, some people are clearly born with talents for business, tendencies toward crime, and so forth.
8. T F Succeeding in a career is mainly a matter of fine-tuning the knowledge and skills acquired earlier in life.
9. T F Studies of gifted and successful adults show that early formal instruction is an important factor in creating intellectual giftedness and/or creative talent.
10. T F The shared view of right and wrong that exists in a society is called the moral order.
11. T F According to Mead, the "me" is the portion of the self that is made up of everything learned through the socialization process.
12. T F According to Levinson's theory of adult socialization, divorce and career changes are typical during the Early Adult period.
13. T F Many children going to day-care centers do not encounter enduring stable relationships with child-care workers.
14. T F According to Lawrence Kohlberg, concepts such as good and bad or right and wrong, once established, have the same meaning throughout our lives.
15. T F The ability to reason abstractly and anticipate possible consequences of behavior is characteristic of the formal logical stage of cognitive development, according to Jean Piaget.
16. T F Individuals who are social equals are referred to as generalized others.

MULTIPLE CHOICE

1. Harlow's study of rhesus monkeys demonstrated the
   a. severe impact of early social deprivation
   b. importance of genetic inheritance in determining personality
   c. reversibility of the negative impacts of deprivation during infancy
   d. ability of other primates to learn human emotions

2. Which of the following is a total institution?
   a. prisons
   b. mental hospitals
   c. military bases
   d. b and c only
   e. a, b, and c

3. In Freud's view of the self, the "internal censor" or conscience that embodies society's norms and values as learned primarily from the parents is called the
   a. ego
   b. id
   c. superego
   d. "I"

4. Which parts of the self are shaped through socialization?
   a. the "I" only
   b. the "me" only
   c. both the "I" and the "me"
   d. neither the "I" nor the "me"

Answers appear at the end of the book.

5. During adolescence, the socializing agent that has the strongest influence is
   a. the family
   b. peer groups
   c. school
   d. the mass media

6. He argued that the self develops through interaction with significant others, from whom we learn increasingly sophisticated role expectations.
   a. Daniel Levinson
   b. Erik Erikson
   c. Sigmund Freud
   d. George Herbert Mead

7. Isolated children develop slowly because they
   a. do not receive proper nutrition
   b. lack social interaction and stimulation
   c. are mentally and physically impaired to begin with
   d. are physically abused during their isolation

8. Jason and Alison are teammates on a soccer team. According to Mead, for them to be able to play together successfully, they must be at the stage where they
   a. have developed advanced physical coordination
   b. can understand and evaluate abstract strategies of play
   c. know the rules and understand the expectations of the various positions
   d. can demonstrate an ethical understanding of the concept of good sportsmanship

9. According to Kohlberg, the most advanced state of moral reasoning involves making judgments on the basis of a
   a. personal set of values
   b. desire to avoid punishment
   c. desire to achieve a reward
   d. sense of the values of one's peers

10. Which of the following is **not** one of the components of the looking-glass self, according to Cooley?
    a. our imagination of what we must really be like
    b. our imagination of how our actions appear to others
    c. our imagination of how others judge our actions
    d. a self-judgment in reaction to the imagined judgments of others

11. Basic training in a military boot camp, where recruits must be taught to follow orders unquestioningly and to kill on command, involves a process of learning known as
    a. secondary socialization
    b. primary socialization
    c. resocialization
    d. antisocialization

12. Biologically inherited patterns of complex behavior are known as
    a. genes
    b. instincts
    c. the personality
    d. the unconscious

13. Which of the following is a problem with "stage theories" of human development?
    a. they fail to take account of individual differences
    b. they often describe only the experiences of people born during a certain time span
    c. they do not take into account the process of social change
    d. b and c only
    e. a, b, and c

14. Jennifer is five years old. She often pretends she is the mommy—enthusiastically correcting the "bad" behavior of her dolls and stuffed animals by imitating the way that Jennifer's mother admonishes her. According to Mead, Jennifer is at the _____ stage of development.
    a. play
    b. game
    c. preparatory
    d. preoperational

15. The patterns of behavior and ways of thinking and feeling that make us distinctive individuals are known as our individual
    a. social identity
    b. self
    c. consciousness
    d. personality

16. Experiments by Ivan Pavlov and John Watson showed that so-called instinctual behavior could be molded through
    a. administration of selected drugs
    b. conditioning
    c. imitation
    d. resocialization

Answers appear at the end of the book.

17. According to Daniel Levinson's theory of socialization, adulthood is primarily characterized by
    a. the same stages that occurred earlier
    b. new and unpredictable tasks that must be worked through
    c. new but predictable tasks that must be worked through
    d. a slowing down of development since most skills have already been learned

18. Meaningful interaction with other human beings, which is often rare in the lives of institutionalized children, is referred to as
    a. significant interaction
    b. affiliation
    c. social attachment
    d. nurture

19. The most important agent of primary socialization is/are
    a. peer groups
    b. the family
    c. school
    d. the mass media

20. A critic of sociobiology, he has argued that culture is a far more important influence on human behavior than genetics.
    a. Edward O. Wilson
    b. Charles Horton Cooley
    c. Daniel Levinson
    d. Stephen Jay Gould

21. The most valuable contribution of Erikson's theory of socialization is that it
    a. breaks development down into eight simple stages
    b. shows that socialization is completed in early childhood
    c. shows that socialization is a lifelong process
    d. demonstrates that the most important stages of socialization occur after age thirty

22. The child's discovery, around the age of two years, that the objects of the world can be symbolized and talked about as well as experienced directly marks the beginning of what Piaget called the _____ stage of cognitive development.
    a. sensorimotor
    b. preoperational
    c. operational
    d. formal logical

23. Each individual's social identity consists of
    a. all the behaviors they have learned to imitate
    b. their changing yet enduring view of themselves
    c. the sum total of all the statuses they occupy
    d. all the ways that other people view them

24. The view that the human mind and human behavior are shaped by unconscious impulses and resistance to or repression of them is most closely associated with
    a. Edward O. Wilson
    b. Sigmund Freud
    c. Ivan Pavlov
    d. Lawrence Kohlberg

25. People who are important to an individual's development were termed _____ by Mead.
    a. peers
    b. significant others
    c. primary socializers
    d. generalized others

Answers appear at the end of the book.

TRUE/FALSE

1. T F Human behavior is not random. It is patterned and, for the most part, quite predictable.
2. T F Studies have demonstrated that males prefer to sit across a table from a stranger, while females prefer to sit side-by-side on the same side of the table with a stranger.
3. T F When people do something for each other with the express purpose of receiving something in return, they are engaged in exchange.
4. T F Socially defined positions, such as teacher, student, athlete, and daughter, are called roles.
5. T F Social groups and social aggregates both cease to exist when members are apart from one another.
6. T F Primary groups are usually more willing than secondary groups to tolerate members who deviate from group expectations.
7. T F The smallest possible group is a dyad.
8. T F A reference group is a purposefully created special-interest group that has clearly defined goals and official ways of doing things.
9. T F An ideal type refers to the way sociologists wish society was organized.
10. T F Communication by means of gestures is pretty much the same the world over.
11. T F Coercion is a form of conflict in which one of the parties is much stronger than the other and can impose its will on the weaker party.
12. T F For many students, keeping up good grades, holding down a job, and spending enough time with significant others involve role conflict.
13. T F Bureaucracies encourage workers to be generalists, capable of doing several jobs equally well, rather than specialists.
14. T F All bureaucracies have networks of people who help one another by bending rules and taking procedural shortcuts.
15. T F A master status refers to one of the multiple statuses a person occupies that seems to dominate that person's life.
16. T F Instrumental leadership is more important to the success of a group than expressive leadership.
17. T F Competition is a form of conflict within agreed-upon rules.

MULTIPLE CHOICE

1. College professors are usually expected to engage in at least three types of activities. They are expected to teach their classes effectively. They are expected to conduct research and publish the results in the form of professional journal articles and books. Also, they are expected to devote time to institutional governance and civic activities. Taken together, these activities constitute a
   a. status set
   b. role set
   c. master status
   d. secondary group

2. In the situation described in Question #1, suppose that two or more of these activities become so demanding that, for instance, the college professor finds herself taking time away from class preparation in order to keep producing published research, or shirking committee responsibilities in order to grade papers for class. This professor is experiencing
   a. role strain
   b. status anxiety
   c. role conflict
   d. status inconsistency

3. Max Weber's method for analyzing social action, *Verstehen*, entails
   a. constructive criticism
   b. face-to-face questioning
   c. statistical analysis
   d. sympathetic understanding

Answers appear at the end of the book.

4. Three students stay after class to go over their notes. This group would be called a
   a. trio
   b. dyad
   c. triage
   d. triad

5. A fluorescent light in the sociology department office burns out, and the department secretary asks the head of maintenance to have it replaced. Even though he has an ample supply of replacements and could change it himself in five minutes, he insists that the secretary fill out an official work order and wait two weeks or so until an electrician can do the job. This episode provides an illustration of bureaucratic
   a. inertia
   b. ritualism
   c. alienation
   d. conformity

6. Asch's study of group pressure and conformity, in which subjects were asked to judge the length of lines, found that
   a. people were surprisingly eager to disagree with the judgments of the group
   b. the majority was eager to expel those who disagreed with their judgments
   c. about one-third of the people were willing to give incorrect answers in order to conform to the group
   d. about one-quarter of the people were unable or unwilling to determine the length of the lines at all

7. _____ leadership seems best suited for producing effective groups and satisfied group members.
   a. democratic
   b. authoritarian
   c. instrumental
   d. laissez-faire

8. What is the sociological name for strangers waiting in line to buy concert tickets?
   a. group
   b. clique
   c. social aggregate
   d. social category

9. To an observer, two people engaging in a fistfight on the street would mean something entirely different from the same two people fighting in a boxing ring. This illustrates how the meaning of social interaction is dependent upon
   a. personalities
   b. status
   c. competition
   d. context

10. When unionized workers agree to a "no-strike clause" in their labor agreement in exchange for certain improvements in wages or benefits, they are engaging in what kind of cooperation with their employers?
    a. contractual
    b. spontaneous
    c. directed
    d. traditional

11. Which of the following would most likely be a secondary group?
    a. a family
    b. a large lecture class
    c. a juvenile gang
    d. a high school clique

12. In a large lecture class, it is generally expected that students will raise their hands and be called upon before speaking out. This illustrates the operation of
    a. bureaucracy
    b. roles
    c. norms
    d. statuses

13. Michels' Iron Law of Oligarchy holds that bureaucracies
    a. eventually lead to political dictatorship
    b. are inevitable in any democratic society
    c. are outdated forms of social organization
    d. always become dominated by self-serving elites

14. By many accounts, former President Ronald Reagan was a "hands off" executive who allowed subordinates to make most major decisions and who took little interest in the details of governing. This type of leadership can be characterized as
    a. authoritarian
    b. democratic
    c. instrumental
    d. laissez-faire

15. Alliances and group pressure initially become possible at the level of the
    a. triad
    b. dyad
    c. association
    d. secondary group

16. Which of the following is **not** one of the things groups must do in order to function effectively?
    a. choose leaders
    b. define boundaries
    c. set goals
    d. assign tasks
    e. these are all things that groups must do in order to function effectively

17. What happens when a group grows beyond five to seven members?
    a. it splits into subgroups
    b. it ceases to exist as a group
    c. it adopts a formal means of controlling communication
    d. a and c only
    e. a, b, and c

18. Which of the following is an ascribed status?
    a. male
    b. student
    c. employee
    d. shortstop

19. A young woman receives a graduate degree in business, lands an excellent job on Wall Street, and finds herself making more money at age twenty-four than she ever thought possible. At first she is delighted. But soon she discovers that her salary is not especially high nor her new life-style especially luxurious compared with those of her new business associates. Before long, she is feeling dissatisfied and underpaid. This illustrates the operation of
    a. ideal types
    b. reference groups
    c. primary groups
    d. anticipatory socialization

20. All societies must meet certain fundamental needs, but different societies may adopt different ways of doing so. The various vehicles for accomplishing basic societal tasks are known as
    a. social institutions
    b. secondary groups
    c. social aggregates
    d. formal structures

21. Which of the following is **not** a major characteristic of bureaucracy, according to Weber?
    a. heavy reliance on written rules and regulations
    b. a clear-cut division of labor
    c. a tendency toward favoritism and nepotism
    d. a clear distinction between public and private spheres
    e. these are all major characteristics of bureaucracy according to Weber

22. Which of the following is **not** a fundamental characteristic of social groups?
    a. members have a common identity
    b. members enjoy each other's company
    c. there is some feeling of unity
    d. there are common goals and shared norms

23. We tend to maintain the most eye contact when we are speaking to someone of _____ status than us.
    a. higher
    b. lower
    c. approximately the same

24. In many small towns, it has long been customary for neighbors to bring gifts of food to the home of someone who is ill. This effort involves _____ cooperation.
    a. spontaneous
    b. traditional
    c. directed
    d. contractual

25. Staring, smiling, nodding one's head, and using hands while talking are all examples of
    a. social action
    b. nonverbal communication
    c. instinctual behavior
    d. exchange

26. The process of orienting one's behavior and attitudes toward those of a group one plans to join is called _____ socialization.
    a. primary
    b. secondary
    c. anticipatory
    d. adult

Answers appear at the end of the book.

TRUE/FALSE

1. T F Ninety percent of all crime in the United States is against property, not against a person.
2. T F Conflict theory begins with the assumption that conformity, not deviance, is most in need of explanation.
3. T F Sutherland and Cressey's differential association theory maintains that deviance is learned, mostly within primary groups.
4. T F The United States has a higher rate of imprisonment than any other country in the world except South Africa.
5. T F Ostracism and ridicule are formal negative sanctions.
6. T F A major difference between adult and juvenile crime is that juveniles are much more likely to commit offenses in groups.
7. T F Taken together, street crimes like burglary and robbery cause much greater financial loss than white-collar crimes.
8. T F The most frequent reason given by victims for not reporting a crime to the authorities is the belief that the crime was not important enough.
9. T F Sykes and Matza are well-known for developing the control theory of deviance.
10. T F Deterrence refers to the practice of steering offenders away from the justice system to social agencies.
11. T F Behavior can be classified as normal or deviant only with reference to the group in which it occurs.
12. T F From the work of Durkheim, we may conclude that a society without any deviant behavior is both desirable and possible.
13. T F The *National Crime Victimization Survey*, which is considered by many to be superior to the *Uniform Crime Reports*, collects information on crimes from local police departments.
14. T F Theft of a person's parked automobile would be classified as a property crime.
15. T F A society's moral code refers to the formal rules, or laws, adopted by its political authority.
16. T F Research shows that the deterrent effect of the well-publicized execution of a criminal is short-lived.
17. T F Juveniles commit a relatively small proportion of the serious crimes that occur in the United States.
18. T F Women are more likely to commit property crimes as opposed to violent crimes.

MULTIPLE CHOICE

1. The conflict approach sees laws as a product of
   a. God's will
   b. a natural process of evolution
   c. agreed-upon social values
   d. powerful interest groups
2. Status offenses are acts that
   a. are criminal only because the person involved is a minor
   b. attempt to use lawbreaking to increase one's social position or reputation
   c. are committed by individuals occupying positions of social responsibility or high prestige
   d. use trickery rather than violence to obtain the desired ends
3. "I'm not really a bad person. It's just that I was drunk and I didn't know what I was doing."

This is an example of which technique of neutralization?
   a. denial of responsibility
   b. denial of injury
   c. appeal to a higher principle
   d. denial of the victim
4. Which of the following theories is less concerned with the causes of norm violations than with the way others react to the deviance?
   a. psychoanalytic theory
   b. cultural transmission theory
   c. control theory
   d. anomie theory
   e. labeling theory

Answers appear at the end of the book.

5. Relatively minor crimes that are usually punishable by a fine or less than a year's confinement are called
   a. civil offenses
   b. larcenies
   c. misdemeanors
   d. felonies

6. Overall, the "typical" crime victim is likely to be
   a. female
   b. black
   c. elderly
   d. middle class

7. The idea that laws represent the codification of shared moral beliefs is caleld the _____ approach.
   a. consensus
   b. labeling theory
   c. conflict
   d. cultural transmission theory

8. A youth who wants to achieve the sort of affluent life-style he sees on television but, unable to find a well-paying job, turns to drug dealing to make money would be classified as a/an _____ in Merton's typology.
   a. retreatist
   b. innovator
   c. rebel
   d. conformist

9. Wilson and Herrnstein's Individual Choice theory of crime considers the high rate of crime by African Americans to be the result of
   a. poverty
   b. lack of equal educational opportunities
   c. rejection of white moral standards
   d. discriminatory treatment by law enforcement officers

10. Deviance is defined as behavior that
    a. occurs rarely
    b. violates group norms
    c. is psychologically abnormal
    d. is illegal

11. Lombroso and Sheldon, each in his own way, attempted to explain deviant behavior on the basis of
    a. psychological orientation
    b. anatomical characteristics
    c. early childhood experiences
    d. differential association

12. Which theory attributes behavior, deviant or otherwise, to the rewards and punishments that come about as consequences of people's actions?
    a. behavioral
    b. individual choice
    c. psychoanalytic
    d. biological

13. To Émile Durkheim, the reason deviant behavior is found in all societies is that
    a. human beings are naturally selfish and aggressive
    b. it performs useful social functions
    c. humans have not yet developed effective methods of behavior control
    d. harmful actions are inevitable in mechanically integrated societies

14. Which of the following is an internal means of social control?
    a. ridicule
    b. imprisonment
    c. guilt
    d. exclusion from the group

15. The least frequent violent crime is
    a. homicide
    b. rape
    c. robbery
    d. assault

16. According to control theory, a youngster who stays out of trouble with the law is most likely to be one who
    a. had few unpleasant experiences during childhood
    b. has no delinquent peers to put pressure on him or her
    c. has strong relationships with parents, teachers, and peers
    d. has confidence in his or her future occupational success

17. Violation of laws meant to enforce the moral code, such as public drunkenness, prostitution, gambling, and possession of illegal drugs, are called_____ crimes.
    a. moral
    b. organized
    c. victimless
    d. status

Answers appear at the end of the book.

18. Which of the following is **not** a goal of imprisonment?
    a. punishment of criminal behavior
    b. deterrence of criminal behavior
    c. rehabilitation of criminals
    d. separation of criminals from society
    e. these are all goals of imprisonment

19. A criminal trial at which a defendant is found guilty and sentenced to a prison term is an example of a/an _____ sanction.
    a. informal positive
    b. informal negative
    c. formal positive
    d. formal negative

20. Fourteen-year-old Janet is arrested for shoplifting. Even though the charges are later dropped, Janet's teachers designate her a troublemaker and someone not to be trusted. Subsequently, Janet begins to skip school frequently and to get into fights when she is there. Lemert and others would call these latter behaviors
    a. primary deviance
    b. secondary deviance
    c. status offenses
    d. a case of recidivism

21. The research of Shaw and McKay, which linked crime to certain types of urban neighborhoods, provided the foundation for _____ theories of deviance.
    a. labeling
    b. control
    c. anomie
    d. cultural transmission

22. Organized crime makes most of its money through
    a. robbery
    b. providing illegal goods and services
    c. blackmail
    d. extorting money from victims by means of threats

23. Durkheim saw anomie as a condition of
    a. weak law enforcement
    b. normlessness
    c. overemphasis on the welfare of the group
    d. dependency

24. In a program called "Scared Straight," hardened criminals were brought into junior and senior high schools to give first-person accounts of the negative aspects of being imprisoned. This is an example of
    a. deterrence
    b. recidivism
    c. diversion
    d. the funnel effect

25. According to labeling theorists, the likelihood that you will receive a deviant label for your misbehavior depends upon
    a. the seriousness of what you did
    b. your social identity
    c. the context of your act
    d. a and b only
    e. a, b, and c

26. The _____ effect is the characteristic of the criminal justice system by which few crimes are reported, few criminals are caught, few of those caught are convicted, and few of those convicted are imprisoned.
    a. diversion
    b. funnel
    c. deterrence
    d. recidivism

27. Which of the following is a dysfunction of deviance?
    a. it makes social life difficult and unpredictable
    b. it diverts valuable resources that could be used elsewhere
    c. it causes confusion about the norms and values of society
    d. a and c only
    e. a, b, and c

28. The most urgent problem with the nation's prisons at the present time is
    a. too many women in them
    b. too many juveniles in them
    c. they are overcrowded
    d. they are mostly designed to handle misdemeanor, not felony offenders

Answers appear at the end of the book.

CHAPTER 7 ■ *Social Stratification*

TRUE/FALSE

1. T F   Caste systems of stratification are nonexistent today.
2. T F   For Marx, class conflict is the moving force of history.
3. T F   Power is the ability to attain goals, even in the face of opposition.
4. T F   The estate system, in which social position is determined by ownership of land, military strength, or birth, is even more rigid than the caste system.
5. T F   Unlike other nations less committed to equality of opportunity, the United States is socially differentiated but not socially stratified.
6. T F   Some primitive societies do not make distinctions among members on the basis of their age or their sex.
7. T F   Intergenerational mobility is a change in social status that occurs over two or more generations.
8. T F   Access to societal rewards is mostly a result of power, according to conflict theory.
9. T F   For the nation as a whole, the African-American poverty rate is about the same as the white rate.
10. T F   The total assets owned by a family is called their gross income.
11. T F   African Americans are about six times more likely to be the victims of murder than are whites.
12. T F   An assembly-line worker is perceived by most Americans to have higher prestige than an auto mechanic.
13. T F   More than twice as many Hispanics as African Americans are in the combined top two categories of household net worth.
14. T F   The "welfare school" approach argues that the black underclass has grown because liberal policies have destroyed the work ethic and made it harder for blacks to get out of poverty.
15. T F   With recent changes in women's labor force participation, occupational segregation has nearly disappeared.

MULTIPLE CHOICE

1. Which of the following best exemplifies vertical mobility?
   a. the son of a steelworker who works his way up to become chief executive of a company
   b. a person who changes their religious affiliation from Lutheran to Methodist
   c. a woman who, in the course of her career, works as a secretary in several different law firms
   d. b and c only
   e. a, b, and c

2. Social inequality refers to the uneven distribution of
   a. material rewards
   b. prestige
   c. power
   d. a and b only
   e. a, b, and c

3. _____ argued that America is controlled by a governing class whose members are very rich, intermarry, attend the same schools, and spend their time in the same clubs.
   a. G. William Domhoff
   b. C. Wright Mills
   c. Karl Marx
   d. Max Weber

4. Karl Marx predicted that in socialist society wealth would be distributed to each according to
   a. want
   b. need
   c. what is earned
   d. what can be obtained, by whatever means

Answers appear at the end of the book.

5. In New York City, public school custodians earned salaries that averaged $50,000 in the mid-1980s. Their relatively high pay, combined with the low esteem in which janitorial workers are generally held, makes these workers a good example of
   a. social inequality
   b. social evaluation
   c. status inconsistency
   d. status improvement

6. Each of the following occupations is well-paid and prestigious. Which best fits the functionalist argument about stratification?
   a. professional athlete
   b. physician
   c. television or film star
   d. organized crime boss

7. Which of the following ideas is **not** consistent with modern conflict theory?
   a. social inequality is inevitable, despite the well-intentioned efforts of the dominant groups to help the less fortunate
   b. conflict usually has to do with the distribution of property and political power
   c. subordinate groups have the potential to resist the power of the dominant group, but they do not always use it.
   d. the beliefs of the dominant group come to be thought of as common societal values

8. Although Weber agreed with Marx's analysis of inequality in most respects, he disagreed with the notion that
   a. group conflict is central to society
   b. economic institutions are fundamentally important in society
   c. only when exploitation becomes extremely obvious will the powerless object
   d. all conflict boils down to class conflict over material issues

9. A demographic factor that makes the likelihood of upward mobility greater for today's college graduates is that
   a. the birthrate is increasing
   b. the number of people entering the workforce is increasing
   c. the number of people entering the workforce is declining
   d. technical skills and knowledge will be in less demand in the future

Answers appear at the end of the book.

10. The richest 1 percent of the American population owns about _____ percent of the nation's wealth.
    a. 5
    b. 10
    c. 20
    d. 50

11. When people make qualitative judgments about other people on the basis of individual characteristics or behaviors, we have the phenomenon of social
    a. differentiation
    b. evaluation
    c. bias
    d. stratification

12. _____ argued that American society is characterized by multiple power structures which, even though dominated by elites, tend to balance each other out.
    a. C. Wright Mills
    b. G. William Domhoff
    c. Arnold Rose
    d. Max Weber

13. Societies with very little social mobility, like India under the caste system and medieval Europe, can be termed _____ societies.
    a. open
    b. closed
    c. primitive
    d. horizontal

14. Kathy's first job after graduation was clerking at an advertising firm. At thirty, she moved up to become director of marketing. This is an example of
    a. intragenerational mobility
    b. intergenerational mobility
    c. horizontal mobility
    d. networking

15. Which of the following is **not** a factor that affects social mobility?
    a. demographic shape of the population
    b. extent of economic expansion
    c. level of education
    d. type of stratification system in the society
    e. these are all factors that affect social mobility

16. The type of prestige most visible in industrial societies is prestige connected to
    a. personal honor and esteem
    b. religious affiliation
    c. occupation
    d. college education

17. According to Max Weber, a group with similar lifestyles shaped by similar incomes, education, and values would be designated a/an
    a. social class
    b. status group
    c. estate
    d. caste

18. Critics of the functionalist theory of stratification focus on the
    a. immorality of stratification
    b. neglect of talent among the lower classes
    c. existence of barriers to free competition
    d. a and b only
    e. a, b, and c

19. In Marx's theory, the bourgeoisie
    a. hold the functionally most important jobs
    b. own the means of production
    c. work for those who own the means of production
    d. a and b only
    e. a, b, and c

20. Which of the following is **not** one of the bases for stratification in modern society, according to Max Weber?
    a. power
    b. status
    c. tradition
    d. class

21. Which of the following is **not** part of the power elite, according to C. Wright Mills?
    a. military elites
    b. government elites
    c. religious elites
    d. leaders of big business

22. Which of the following is **not** a reason given by functionalist theorists for the necessity of inequality?
    a. there is a scarcity of talented people
    b. some positions in society are more important than others
    c. the offspring of the wealthy will always be more intelligent than the children of the poor
    d. people in important positions must be motivated to perform well

23. Which of the following is an approach to explaining the persistence and growth of the black underclass?
    a. structural unemployment/social isolation
    b. culture of poverty
    c. welfare school
    d. b and c only
    e. a, b, and c

Answers appear at the end of the book.

CHAPTER 8 ■ *Social Class in the United States*

TRUE/FALSE

1. T F Most government benefits go to the middle class.
2. T F Economic rewards are more unequally distributed in the United States than elsewhere in the Western industrialized world.
3. T F The poverty index was developed to determine which families and individuals were economically needy.
4. T F When the subjective approach is used to measure class, most people in the U.S. claim to belong to the middle class.
5. T F Non-means-tested assistance is a form of assistance in which individuals and families receive services instead of money.
6. T F Welfare programs provide a comfortable lifestyle for most of the poor.
7. T F The vast majority of the official poor are unemployed workers.
8. T F Poor people are more likely to be arrested than members of higher social classes.
9. T F When people are asked to place themselves into one of several class categories, the objective approach to class measurement is being used.
10. T F Many Americans believe that we live in a classless society.
11. T F In recent years, it is reasonable to say that "the rich got richer and the poor got poorer" in the United States.
12. T F The *Social Register* is essentially an upper-class address and telephone book.

MULTIPLE CHOICE

1. The poverty index is distorted in that it
   a. excludes noncash income
   b. underestimates nonfood expenses
   c. is based on household data
   d. a and b only
   e. a, b, and c

2. Of the following nations, the highest rates of poverty among the elderly are found in
   a. the United States
   b. Canada
   c. the United Kingdom
   d. Sweden

3. Your text describes five social classes in the United States today. It appears that these classes were determined by using the _____ approach.
   a. reputational
   b. objective
   c. subjective
   d. imaginative

4. Members of the lower class tend to blame _____ for their lack of success.
   a. the rich
   b. "the system"
   c. bad luck
   d. themselves

5. In 1990, the richest fifth of the U.S. population received about _____ percent of all income.
   a. 12
   b. 22
   c. 44
   d. 66

6. By far the largest amount of the federal government assistance budget goes to
   a. Social Security Retirement
   b. Aid to Families with Dependent Children
   c. Medicaid
   d. Food Stamps

7. Means-tested cash assistance programs aimed at the poor account for _____ of the federal budget.
   a. a small and declining portion
   b. a small but ever-increasing portion
   c. about one-third
   d. more than half

8. Poverty is especially concentrated among families headed by women who
   a. have never married
   b. are divorced
   c. are widowed
   d. have been married more than twice

Answers appear at the end of the book.

9. The upper class in the United States is approximately _____ percent of the population.
   a. 2
   b. 8
   c. 12
   d. 20

10. The largest social class in American society is the _____ class.
    a. upper-middle
    b. lower-middle
    c. working
    d. lower

11. Statistics on poverty in the United States show that
    a. most poor people do not work even though they could
    b. most poor people who can work are working
    c. unwed mothers are the largest single group of poor people
    d. African Americans and Hispanics make up the bulk of the poor

12. Means-tested assistance is
    a. based on need
    b. available regardless of need
    c. based on political affiliation
    d. based on ownership of the means of production

13. If a researcher asks people in a town which social class they feel another person is a member of, the researcher is using the _____ method of class measurement.
    a. objective
    b. subjective
    c. reputational
    d. sampling

14. Managers and persons who work in professional and technical fields are members of the _____ class.
    a. upper
    b. upper-middle
    c. lower-middle
    d. working

15. The United States has been most successful in holding down poverty among
    a. children
    b. working-age adults
    c. the elderly
    d. women

16. The wealthiest fifth of the U.S. population owns _____ percent of all the nation's wealth.
    a. 5
    b. 25
    c. 55
    d. 75

17. Which of the following is **not** a myth about the poor?
    a. most poor people are black and most black people are poor
    b. most poor people live in inner-city ghettos
    c. most people are poor because they are too lazy to work
    d. most poor people live in female-headed households
    e. these are all myths about the poor

18. Of the following nations, the highest rates of poverty among children are found in
    a. the United States
    b. Canada
    c. the United Kingdom
    d. Sweden

19. Which of the following is **not** true of the lower class in relation to the other social classes in the United States? Lower class people
    a. have lower life expectancies
    b. are more likely to spend time in a mental hospital
    c. are more likely to be convicted of a crime
    d. receive longer prison sentences
    e. these statements are all true of the lower class in relation to other social classes in the United States

20. Harry is a master electrician. He holds a high school diploma, owns a modest home, but struggles to give his family the things they need and want. He considers himself politically conservative and fairly religious. According to the typology in the text, Harry belongs to the _____ class.
    a. upper-middle
    b. lower-middle
    c. working
    d. lower

Answers appear at the end of the book.

CHAPTER 9 ■ *Racial and Ethnic Minorities*

TRUE/FALSE

1. T F Discrimination is best understood as an especially bad form of prejudice.
2. T F Genocide is synonymous with annihilation.
3. T F Canada has two official languages, English and French. This is an example of pluralism.
4. T F Prejudice is a rational but negative attitude.
5. T F Current Asian immigrants to the United States tend to be well educated and of middle-class origins.
6. T F Racial classifications are not simple or cut-and-dried; a person considered "white" in one society might be categorized as "black" in another.
7. T F Whenever prejudice exists, discrimination will occur.
8. T F The United States is unlike most other nations in that its ethnic minorities have been fully assimilated.
9. T F As a result of the civil rights movement, African Americans have reached social and economic equality with other Americans.
10. T F Even during its more restrictive periods, the United States has had one of the more open immigration policies in the world.
11. T F English is legally the official language of the United States.
12. T F Prejudicial feelings are more likely to develop between groups competing against each other for scarce resources.
13. T F People in the first wave of Cuban immigration have been relatively successful in America because they arrived with more marketable skills and money than immigrants typically possess.
14. T F The *new migration* consists of people from southern and eastern Europe who came here between 1880 and 1920.
15. T F Chicanos are people from Central America.

MULTIPLE CHOICE

1. *Old migration* to the United States consisted of people from
   a. the ancient civilizations of the Mediterranean
   b. northern Europe who came prior to 1880
   c. eastern Europe who came after 1880
   d. age 50 upward

2. During the nineteenth century, Native Americans were pushed off of land desired by white settlers and onto small and distant reservations. This exemplifies the process of
   a. forced migration
   b. segregation
   c. subjugation
   d. assimilation

3. Many white shopkeepers in U.S. southern towns during the 1950s and 1960s depended upon African-American customers for a large part of their business but considered them social inferiors. These merchants are examples of
   a. unprejudiced nondiscriminators
   b. unprejudiced discriminators
   c. prejudiced nondiscriminators
   d. prejudiced discriminators

4. Most of the nineteenth-century immigrants to America had distinctive subcultures with their own unique language, style of dress, norms, and values. The children of these immigrants, however, rapidly learned to speak English and to adopt mainstream American cultural styles. This is an example of
   a. segregation
   b. pluralism
   c. assimilation
   d. subjugation

Answers appear at the end of the book.

5. The term race refers to a category of people who are defined as similar because they
   a. have a unique and distinctive genetic makeup
   b. share a number of physical characteristics
   c. exhibit similar behaviors
   d. express comparable attitudes

6. An individual who feels very uncomfortable when friends tell a racist joke and yet does not speak out for fear of being ridiculed would be classified by Merton as a(n)
   a. unprejudiced nondiscriminator
   b. unprejudiced discriminator
   c. prejudiced nondiscriminator
   d. prejudiced discriminator

7. Currently, the number of immigrants from _____ is increasing faster than any other population of immigrants to the United States.
   a. Latin America
   b. Asia
   c. Africa
   d. the West Indies

8. _____ is most often imposed upon a minority group by the dominant majority. But sometimes it is at least partially voluntary, as in the development of ethnic neighborhoods like Chinatowns and Little Italys.
   a. segregation
   b. Anglo conformity
   c. pluralism
   d. assimilation

9. If a member of a minority is unable to obtain a well-paying, secure job not because of outright racism, but rather because, like many others of his minority, he attended a less-than-adequate school and lacks "connections," then he is a victim of
   a. subtle and unrecognized personal prejudice
   b. unfortunate accidental discrimination
   c. institutionalized prejudice and discrimination
   d. bad luck that has nothing to do with his being a minority

10. The largest segment of the U.S. Hispanic population is composed of people of _____ descent.
   a. Mexican
   b. Puerto Rican
   c. Cuban
   d. Central and South American

11. The policy of the Nazis toward the Jews during the Holocaust of the 1930s and 1940s was one of
   a. pluralism
   b. Anglo conformity
   c. annihilation
   d. subjugation

12. In which decade did the largest number of people immigrate to the United States?
   a. 1881–1890
   b. 1901–1910
   c. 1921–1930
   d. 1981–1990

13. Harvard sociologist Orlando Patterson postulates that the concept of human freedom
   a. is a cultural universal
   b. is unique to Western society
   c. was first conceived by the ancient civilizations of the East
   d. has only been developed in the United States

14. Between 1882 and 1943 no _____ immigrants were legally allowed into the United States.
   a. Eastern European
   b. Chinese
   c. African
   d. Latin American

15. More than half of all illegal immigrants to the United States come from
   a. Mexico
   b. Central America
   c. Southeast Asia
   d. the Caribbean area

16. A group that has a distinct cultural tradition with which its own members identify and which may or may not be recognized by others is known as a(n)
   a. subculture
   b. race
   c. minority
   d. ethnic group

17. African Americans make up approximately _____ percent of the total population of the United States.
   a. 2
   b. 6
   c. 12
   d. 18
   e. 24

Answers appear at the end of the book.

18. Which of the following groups has the highest rate of business ownership?
    a. Asian Americans
    b. Jews
    c. Hispanics
    d. Anglo Americans

19. Can women be regarded as a minority group in American society?
    a. no, because they are a numerical majority
    b. no, because they are not a racial or ethnic group
    c. yes, because they are singled out for discriminatory treatment
    d. yes, because they are a numerical minority of the U.S. population

20. Relative to white family income, the median income of African-American families has recently
    a. been declining
    b. been rising
    c. remained unchanged

Answers appear at the end of the book.

TRUE/FALSE

1. T F All religions and legal codes have long upheld the principle that life is sacred and ought to be preserved.
2. T F According to Deborah Tannen, women use language primarily to create connections with others, whereas men use language mainly to convey information.
3. T F Euthanasia, the act of causing death painlessly in order to end suffering, is legal in some European countries.
4. T F Women's status appears to be highest in those societies that firmly differentiate between a private domestic sphere and a public sphere of power and authority.
5. T F When occupational segregation is controlled for, the difference between men's and women's wages disappears.
6. T F The baby-boom generation refers to the large number of people born between 1946 and 1964.
7. T F Due to higher mortality rates among African Americans, the elderly population is disproportionately white.
8. T F Ethology is the scientific study of the genetic sources of human behavior.
9. T F The biblical story of creation has been used as a theological justification for patriarchal ideology.
10. T F Research shows that the concept of retirement is found in all human societies.
11. T F Only a minority of men now indicate a preference for a traditional marriage in which the husband works and the wife stays at home.
12. T F Most women who work indicate that they would continue working even if they were financially secure.
13. T F Pioneering sociologist Auguste Comte was one of the first to view women as equal to men.
14. T F Research on the process of modernization shows that the status of the elderly is low when there are only a few of them, but increases with the size of the older population.
15. T F Maines and Hardesty argue that men tend to operate in a linear temporal world, while women's temporal world is contingent.

MULTIPLE CHOICE

1. Research indicates that a core gender identity seems to be established
   a. at birth
   b. within the first year of life
   c. by the second or third year
   d. at puberty

2. A patriarchal ideology is
   a. the study of powerful males in past societies
   b. the belief that there are differences in the social behavior of men and women
   c. an attempt to find a genetic basis for human behavior
   d. the belief that men are superior to women and should control all aspects of society

3. Gender is best understood as a/an _____ status.
   a. achieved
   b. ascribed
   c. ideal
   d. peripheral

4. _____ is a personality trait generally characteristic of adult women in Western society.
   a. independence
   b. low self-esteem
   c. high achievement motivation
   d. low nurturance

5. In the period 1980–2010, the fastest growing portion of the U.S. population is projected to be the _____ segment.
   a. preschool (under 5 years old)
   b. school age (5–17)
   c. adult (35–44)
   d. young old (65–74)
   e. old old (75+)

Answers appear at the end of the book.

6. By the year 2030, as a proportion of the U.S. population, the elderly will be
   a. by far the largest segment of the population
   b. approximately equal to the population of children
   c. essentially unchanged from its current proportion
   d. a declining segment of the population

7. Carol Gilligan argues that women's ethical systems are characterized by a(n)
   a. inability to make clear moral choices
   b. emphasis on the interconnectedness of actions and relationships
   c. concern with not hurting others
   d. b and c only
   e. a, b, and c

8. As of 1990, approximately _____ percent of American women were in the paid labor force.
   a. 28
   b. 48
   c. 58
   d. 78

9. Which of the following is **not** one of the ways women experience discrimination in the business world?
   a. during the hiring process women are given jobs with lower occupational prestige than men with equivalent qualifications
   b. women receive less pay than men for equivalent work
   c. women are fired more often than men
   d. women find it more difficult than men to advance up the career ladder

10. Functionalists argue that the family functions best when
    a. the father assumes the instrumental role
    b. each parent performs relatively similar activities
    c. the mother assumes the expressive role
    d. a and c only
    e. a, b, and c

11. The median age in the United States is currently
    a. 21
    b. 28
    c. 31
    d. 38

12. Which of the following is a contributing factor to the growth of the older population in the U.S.?
    a. the aging of the baby-boom generation
    b. big jumps in life expectancy
    c. relatively stagnant birthrates
    d. a and b only
    e. a, b, and c

13. In stressful situations
    a. males and females react with similar intensity
    b. males and females react with similar behaviors
    c. men react more slowly
    d. women react more slowly

14. Conflict theorists argue that gender inequality is _____ based.
    a. biologically
    b. functionally
    c. economically
    d. psychologically

15. The theory that argues that older people inevitably withdraw from positions of social responsibility because they are pleased to be relieved of societal pressures for continued productivity is _____ theory.
    a. modernization
    b. disengagement
    c. activity
    d. retirement

16. The lifelong process whereby people learn the values, attitudes, motivations, and behavior considered appropriate for each sex in their culture is known as
    a. gender-role socialization
    b. cultural socialization
    c. gender identification
    d. sex-role determination

17. On the average, women with college degrees earn
    a. more than men with college degrees
    b. about the same as men with college degrees
    c. the same as men with high school diplomas
    d. about the same as women with high school diplomas

18. Critics of the functionalist view of gender argue that
    a. instrumental roles are not necessary in a family
    b. expressive roles are far more important to a group than was previously thought
    c. cross-cultural studies show that gender stratification is not inevitable
    d. gender roles in modern industrial society are equal

Answers appear at the end of the book.

19. Supporters of the view that basic differences between men and women are biologically determined have sought evidence from studies of
   a. other animal species
   b. physiological differences between the sexes
   c. cultural practices that have caused genetic mutations
   d. a and b only
   e. a, b, and c

20. People between 75 and 84 years of age are referred to as the
   a. young-old
   b. middle-old
   c. old-old
   d. oldest of the old

Answers appear at the end of the book.

CHAPTER 11 ■ Marriage and Alternative Family Lifestyles

TRUE/FALSE

1. T F The United States has the highest divorce rate in the world.
2. T F Today, less than half of American children live with both biological parents.
3. T F Murdock's study of 250 societies found that the family does not exist in some human cultures.
4. T F In divorce cases in the United States today, legal custody is given to the father about as often as it is given to the mother.
5. T F Polyandry is a very rare form of family structure, existing in only a few societies.
6. T F A large majority of divorced persons remarry.
7. T F Joint custody laws require children to spend equal time living with each of the divorced parents.
8. T F The number of childless couples has risen significantly since the late 1960s.
9. T F Lesbians and gay men, like heterosexuals, are typically interested in forming stable "couple" relationships.
10. T F Most of the world's cultures allow individuals, mostly males, to have more than one spouse.
11. T F Most of the world's societies have bilateral systems of descent like the United States.
12. T F Companionate marriage is marriage based upon the ideal of romantic love.
13. T F Cohabitation refers to a situation in which a newly-married couple settles down near or within the husband's father's household.
14. T F On an Israeli kibbutz, children are reared mostly by their grandparents.
15. T F The patriarchal family refers to a situation in which most family affairs are dominated by men.

MULTIPLE CHOICE

1. Homogamy refers to
   a. stable, marriage-like relationships between members of the same sex
   b. marriage rules that limit each individual to one spouse at a time
   c. the tendency to choose a spouse with a similar social and cultural background
   d. customs that prohibit the marriage of same-sex partners

2. In the United States today, the most common form of residence for newly-married couples is
   a. patrilocal
   b. matrilocal
   c. bilocal
   d. neolocal

3. A _____ family structure consists of a married couple and their children.
   a. patriarchal
   b. nuclear
   c. extended
   d. matrilineal

4. Which of the following is **not** one of the functions of the family?
   a. socializing children
   b. providing social status
   c. patterning reproduction
   d. organizing production and consumption
   e. these are all functions of the family

5. When young people know that their parents expect them to marry someone of their own religion, ethnic group, social class, and so forth, they are confronting rules of
   a. endogamy
   b. monogamy
   c. exogamy
   d. polygamy

6. Which of the following is **not** a feature of marriage in all societies?
   a. a public, usually formal aspect
   b. sexual intercourse as an explicit element of the relationship
   c. romantic love as an important characteristic of the relationship
   d. the intention that it should be a stable and enduring relationship

Answers appear at the end of the book.

7. A society that traces descent through the mother's side of the family would be characterized as a _____ system.
   a. matriarchal
   b. matrilineal
   c. polygynous
   d. matrilocal

8. Industrial society requires a family structure that allows for
   a. geographic mobility
   b. social mobility
   c. bilateral inheritance
   d. b and c only
   e. a, b, and c

9. The most common type of interracial marriage in the United States involves a marriage between a
   a. white man and an African-American woman
   b. white man and a nonwhite woman who is not African-American
   c. white woman and an African-American man
   d. white woman and a nonwhite man who is not African-American

10. With respect to the relationship between education and divorce in the 25–34 year-old-age group, the lowest divorce rates occur among women with which type of education?
    a. less than high school
    b. high school
    c. some college
    d. college graduate

11. As of 1989, which of the following is **not** a female-dominated occupation?
    a. bookkeeper, accounting and auditing clerks
    b. computer operators
    c. janitors and cleaners
    d. cashiers
    e. these are all female-dominated occupations

12. Which of the following statements about the divorce rate is **not** true?
    a. the divorce rate has risen steadily since 1970
    b. the divorce rate peaked in the early 1980s
    c. the divorce rate declined somewhat in the late 1980s
    d. while the divorce rate is declining, it is still higher than it was in 1970

Answers appear at the end of the book.

13. For Arlie Hochschild, the "second shift" refers to
    a. overtime work that takes away from family responsibilities
    b. work that is routinely brought home from the office
    c. housework done by working parents before and after their regular jobs
    d. a second job outside the home held by the primary breadwinner

14. According to the most recent statistics, the highest percentage of divorced men and women are in the _____ age group.
    a. 25–29
    b. 35–39
    c. 40–44
    d. 45–54

15. Approximately _____ percent of all households are currently headed by single parents.
    a. 5
    b. 15
    c. 25
    d. 45

16. A person's _____ refers to the family in which they were raised.
    a. nuclear family
    b. family of orientation
    c. family of procreation
    d. patriarchal family

17. _____ is a norm that forbids sexual intercourse between closely related individuals.
    a. the incest taboo
    b. exogamy
    c. endogamy
    d. monogamy

18. The growing trend in the United States for the elderly to live by themselves is due in large part to
    a. the growing selfishness of American children who refuse to be bothered with the care of their parents
    b. increasing amounts of illness in an ever-older population that require special residential facilities for the elderly
    c. the increased ability of a large portion of the elderly to afford living alone
    d. the decreased size of the housing units in which most Americans live today

19. No-fault divorce laws
   a. automatically provide the wife with alimony and child support
   b. blames both husband and wife equally for the failure of the marriage
   c. are based on the principles of equity, equality, and economic need
   d. compel the parent with the higher income to pay alimony

20. The number of people living alone
   a. reflects a current trend to reject marriage
   b. doubled between 1970 and 1990
   c. has declined dramatically as many individuals can no longer afford to live alone
   d. a and c only
   e. a, b, and c

Answers appear at the end of the book.

CHAPTER 12 ■ *Religion*

TRUE/FALSE

1. T F Fundamentalists, despite their conservative views on marriage and family issues, are more likely to have unstable marriages than nonfundamentalists.
2. T F All religions include a belief in the existence of beings or forces beyond the ability of human beings to experience.
3. T F According to Durkheim, the profane consists of objects that people are prohibited from touching, looking at, or even mentioning.
4. T F Only three world religions are known to be monotheistic: Judaism and its two offshoots, Christianity and Islam.
5. T F A mana is an ordinary object that has become a sacred symbol for a group or clan.
6. T F A cult is a small group that adheres strictly to religious doctrine that often includes unconventional beliefs or forms of worship.
7. T F Karl Marx referred to capitalism as "the opiate of the masses."
8. T F Drug use plays a central role in some religions.
9. T F Although church attendance has declined since 1960, the vast majority of Americans say they believe in God.
10. T F The earliest archaeological evidence of religious practice has been found in northern Europe.
11. T F Millenarian movements typically prophesy the end of the world, the destruction of all evil people and their works, and the saving of the just.
12. T F Ecumenism, or the condition in which religious influence is lessened, is a significant trend in modern American society.
13. T F Alienation refers to the process by which people lose control over the social institutions they themselves invented.

MULTIPLE CHOICE

1. Which of the following is an example of a religion of abstract ideals?
   a. Christianity
   b. Judaism
   c. totemism
   d. Buddhism
2. Émile Durkheim observed that all religions, regardless of their particular doctrines, divide the universe into two mutually exclusive categories,
   a. the natural and the unnatural
   b. the conventional and the unconventional
   c. the routine and the remarkable
   d. the sacred and the profane
3. The largest of the world's religions, in terms of the size of its membership, is
   a. Christianity
   b. Islam
   c. Hinduism
   d. Confucianism

4. According to Karl Marx,
   a. religion makes humans, humans do not make religion
   b. religious doctrines justify ruling class authority, thus preventing opposition and revolt
   c. religious doctrines can be used to expose ruling class hypocrisy, thus stimulating revolt
   d. religion fails to even provide comfort to the oppressed
5. Which major U.S. denomination has the highest percentage of central-city residents?
   a. Catholics
   b. Baptists
   c. Jews
   d. Methodists
6. For Durkheim, the most important function of religion was to
   a. ensure that people behaved morally
   b. bring about social cohesion
   c. suppress social revolt
   d. prevent suicide

Answers appear at the end of the book.

7. Standardized behaviors or practices, such as receiving holy communion, the singing of hymns, praying while bowing toward Mecca, and the Bar Mitzvah ceremony, are examples of
   a. totems
   b. magic
   c. rituals
   d. shamanism

8. Which of the following Protestant denominations is currently increasing in membership?
   a. United Methodists
   b. Assemblies of God
   c. United Presbyterians
   d. a and c only
   e. a, b, and c

9. Which of the following is an element of religion?
   a. prayer
   b. emotion
   c. belief
   d. a and c only
   e. a, b, and c

10. Magic
   a. tends to flourish under conditions of uncertainty and fear
   b. is usually a means to an end, rather than an end in itself
   c. has lost respectability as more scientific attitudes have proliferated
   d. a and c only
   e. a, b, and c

11. Most theistic societies practice
   a. monotheism
   b. supernaturalism
   c. polytheism
   d. ecumenism

12. Which of the following is **not** a function of religion
   a. emotional integration and the reduction of personal anxiety
   b. helping a society adjust to its natural environment
   c. legitimizing arrangements in the secular society
   d. establishing a world view that helps to explain the purpose of life
   e. these are all functions of religion

13. According to Max Weber, which of the following belief systems fostered a world view that promoted the development of capitalism?
   a. Judaism
   b. Catholicism
   c. Lutheranism
   d. Calvinism

14. In animistic religions, the shamans are able to cure illness because they
   a. use powerful medicines
   b. manipulate the populace to believe in their power
   c. have the status of gods
   d. have a special relationship with the spirits that cause illness

15. The Church of England, or Anglican Church, is the official church of that country, and its titular head is the King or Queen of England. This would make the Anglican Church a(n)
   a. ecclesia
   b. denomination
   c. universal church
   d. sect

16. Which of the following is **not** a typical characteristic of cults?
   a. members experience manipulation
   b. members are made to feel that they are part of an elite group
   c. morality is reduced to a matter of opinion, without absolute guidelines
   d. group goals take precedence over individual goals

17. Which religious denomination is likely to include the most people registered as Republicans?
   a. Catholics
   b. Protestants
   c. Jews
   d. Moslems

18. The typical weekly viewer of television evangelism is likely to
   a. live in the South
   b. have less than a high school education
   c. be a female over 50 years of age
   d. a and b only
   e. a, b, and c

Answers appear at the end of the book.

19. Marvin Harris has shown that the hindu taboo against eating beef ensures
    a. a large supply of cow dung that is a source of fertilizer and fuel
    b. that people eat healthier foods
    c. a large supply of beef for the future, when it will be needed to feed a growing population
    d. that cows do not have to be fed

20. The Ghost Dance of the Plains Indians is an example of a
    a. millenarian movement
    b. revitalization movement
    c. religious sect
    d. universal church

Answers appear at the end of the book.

CHAPTER 13 ■ *Education*

TRUE/FALSE

1. T F Giftedness is a fairly well-defined concept in educational research and practice.
2. T F The United States adopted the concept of mass public education long after it had been accepted in Europe.
3. T F When children attend neighborhood schools, they often encounter *de facto* segregation.
4. T F The *Coleman Report* of 1966 found that minority students perform better when they go to predominantly minority schools.
5. T F Studies of gifted children show that beginning rigorous formal instruction in the preschool years enhances later academic and occupational success.
6. T F The functionalist perspective stresses the role of schools in perpetuating class differences from generation to generation.
7. T F The amount of money spent on education per pupil has a significant impact on students' academic success or failure.
8. T F The American educational system helps to slow the entry of young adults into the labor market.
9. T F Women and people older than 25 are the fastest growing groups of college students.
10. T F Standardized tests can accurately measure intelligence and abilities, especially among younger children.

MULTIPLE CHOICE

1. Which of the following is a latent function of education?
   a. providing child care
   b. teaching basic academic skills
   c. transmitting cultural knowledge
   d. generating innovation

2. Rosenthal and Jacobson found that student performance is substantially affected by the
   a. location of their school
   b. occupational status of their parents
   c. level of their innate intelligence
   d. expectations of their teachers

3. Bowles and Gintis argue that school success is least affected by which of the following?
   a. intelligence and effort
   b. possession of appropriate personality traits
   c. conformity to school norms
   d. teachers' expectations of performance

4. Urban school segregation has been especially difficult to eliminate due to the phenomenon of
   a. *de jure* segregation
   b. white flight from the central cities
   c. massive in migration of minorities
   d. the hidden curriculum

5. The highest dropout rates are found among _____ students.
   a. lower-class
   b. female
   c. Hispanic
   d. a and c only
   e. a, b, and c

6. Since 1980, average combined Scholastic Aptitude Test (SAT) scores have
   a. fallen
   b. risen
   c. remained the same

7. Which of the following is **not** a social consequence of dropping out of high school?
   a. increased crime
   b. decreased tax revenues
   c. increased intergenerational mobility
   d. reduced political participation

Answers appear at the end of the book.

8. Which of the following statements about the gifted is **not** true?
   a. people tend to display a marked ambivalence toward them
   b. females, minorities, and the disabled are underrepresented among those identified as gifted
   c. teachers tend to associate middle-class cultural traits with giftedness
   d. there is evidence that the nation's population of gifted children is growing
   e. these statements about the gifted are all true

9. Jonathan Kozol argues that, while there is a deep-seated reverence for fair play in the United States, people actually want the game to be unfair and rigged in favor of the advantaged in the area of
   a. health care
   b. inheritance of wealth
   c. education
   d. a and c only
   e. a, b, and c

10. In a review of scientific research on the effects of television viewing on children, Anderson and Collins found that
    a. children's mind essentially go blank while they watch TV
    b. television viewing causes a reduction in the reading of books and magazines
    c. there is little evidence that television either enhances or detracts from the development of the intellect
    d. a and b only
    e. a, b, and c

11. Over the last 30 years the percentage of Americans completing high school has
    a. declined
    b. risen dramatically
    c. risen slightly
    d. remained about the same

12. The *Coleman Report* of 1966 concluded that
    a. the quality of school experiences for black and white students had become approximately equal
    b. the quality of school experiences for blacks could only be improved by spending more money on schools
    c. the most important influences on academic success are beyond the control of the schools
    d. academic success is most powerfully influenced by individual merit rather than social factors

13. In its famous *Brown v. Board of Education of Topeka* decision in 1954, the United States Supreme Court banned
    a. *de jure* segregation
    b. *de facto* segregation
    c. busing
    d. standardized testing

14. What was the basic message of the report titled *A Nation At Risk*?
    a. it attacked the Japanese educational system
    b. it praised the American educational system
    c. it encouraged schools to add more electives to the curriculum
    d. it attacked the effectiveness of the American educational system

15. The "back-to-basics" movement has improved
    a. student ability in math
    b. the scores of the lowest level-students
    c. the performance of the gifted
    d. the range of electives available to students

16. Which of the following is an aspect of "The Credentialized Society"?
    a. credentials are necessary for the competent performance of just about every job
    b. a degree or certificate has become necessary to obtain a large number of jobs
    c. colleges and universities have become gatekeepers, allowing only certain people to obtain credentials
    d. b and c only
    e. a, b, and c

17. Approximately _____ percent of the U.S. population is functionally illiterate.
    a. 2
    b. 5
    c. 10
    d. 20

18. Which of the following is **not** a factor associated with dropping out of high school?
    a. speaking a language other than English
    b. low family income
    c. low educational attainment of parents
    d. poor academic achievement
    e. these are all factors associated with dropping out of high school

Answers appear at the end of the book.

19. The stratification of students by ability, social class, and various other categories is referred to as
    a. discrimination
    b. tracking
    c. status allocation
    d. functional differentiation

20. According to the conflict theory view, in order to succeed in school the typical American student must learn
    a. the official academic curriculum
    b. to design their own curriculum
    c. the hidden social curriculum
    d. a and c only
    e. a, b, and c

Answers appear at the end of the book.

CHAPTER 14 ■ *Political and Economic Systems*

TRUE/FALSE

1. T F Most democracies have a two-party political system like the United States.
2. T F Power that is regarded as illegitimate by those over whom it is exercised is called coercion.
3. T F Communism is a form of totalitarian socialism.
4. T F It appears necessary for a society to have reached an advanced level of economic development before democracy can thrive.
5. T F Power based on fear is the most stable and enduring form of power.
6. T F The number of African-American elected officials has remained stable over the last ten years.
7. T F Lobbyists are people paid by special-interest groups to attempt to influence government policy.
8. T F Democracy has always been ragarded as the best form of government.
9. T F There are both capitalist and socialist states that are totalitarian in nature.
10. T F In theory, "the invisible hand of the market" means that a multiplicity of self-interested acts by individuals produces a social benefit.
11. T F Representative government is a form of government in which a select few rule.
12. T F According to Edward Shils, civilian rule means that no member of the military may hold public office.
13. T F Legitimacy refers to the condition in which people accept the idea that the allocation of power is as it should be.
14. T F In socialist societies, consumer goods tend to be expensive, while necessities are kept affordable.
15. T F Democracy can only exist in capitalist societies.
16. T F The number of women elected to state legislatures has doubled over the last fifteen years.

MULTIPLE CHOICE

1. According to Adam Smith, everyone in a society benefits most from
   a. competition among producers
   b. centralized government planning
   c. local government control of economic processes
   d. democratic decision making over production

2. Which of the following is characteristic of mixed economies?
   a. all economic decisions are made by central planners
   b. private property is virtually abolished
   c. the government intervenes to prevent industry abuses
   d. a and c only
   e. a, b, and c

3. Which of the following statements about two-party political systems is true?
   a. they encourage compromise and relatively moderate party platforms designed to appeal to a broad spectrum of citizens
   b. they are superior to multiple-party systems for ensuring that minority positions are heard
   c. they are based on proportional representation, so that a party that receives 49 percent of the popular vote gets 49 percent of the legislative seats
   d. a and b only
   e. a, b, and c

4. Regardless of his personal abilities or popularity, Charles, Prince of Wales, will become King of England when his mother, Elizabeth II, abdicates the throne or dies. This is an example of _____ authority.
   a. rational-legal
   b. traditional
   c. appointive
   d. charismatic

Answers appear at the end of the book.

5. Plato's ideal society would be one ruled by
   a. the people as a whole
   b. a military elite
   c. a carefully bred aristocracy
   d. religious leaders and philosophers

6. Which of the following is **not** one of the basic functions of the state?
   a. establishing laws and norms
   b. protecting against outside threats
   c. ensuring economic stability
   d. socializing the young

7. When the Chinese Communists under Mao Zedong took power in China in 1949, they sought to institute an entirely new way of life for their people, transforming politics, economics, and culture. This was an example of a
   a. rebellion
   b. political disorder
   c. political revolution
   d. social revolution

8. Which of the following groups has the highest rate of voting?
   a. eighteen-to-twenty-year-olds
   b. those age sixty-five and older
   c. females
   d. those with high school diplomas but no college education

9. Marx predicted that, as production expands in capitalist economies,
   a. profits will decline and wages will fall, leading to revolution
   b. wages will increase and profits will decline, leading to bankruptcy
   c. profits and wages will both increase, leading to inflation
   d. profits and wages will become irrelevant, as a decent standard of living for all is attained

10. Under democratic socialism,
    a. private ownership of means of production is abolished
    b. taxes are kept low
    c. the state assumes ownership of strategic industries
    d. little effort is made to expand social welfare programs or redistribute income

11. Which of the following is one of the basic premises behind capitalism?
    a. producers attempt to serve the best interests of society as a whole
    b. production is in the pursuit of profit
    c. free markets decide what is produced, and for what price
    d. b and c only
    e. a, b, and c

12. In which of the following state forms does one group exercise virtually complete control over a nation's institutions?
    a. autocracy
    b. totalitarianism
    c. democracy
    d. dictatorship

13. Which of the following statements concerning the political influence of Hispanics is correct?
    a. they have virtually no influence because of their very low numbers in the electorate
    b. they have rather little influence because most of them don't speak English
    c. They have disproportionate influence because of their concentration in states with many electoral votes
    d. they have disproportionate influence because of their large numbers and their relatively high rate of voter registration

14. Which of the following is a criticism of Political Action Committees (PACs)?
    a. they tend to favor incumbents
    b. they do not represent the majority of Americans
    c. they tend to diminish the role of the individual voter
    d. a and c only
    e. a, b, and c

15. Which of the following is a way in which journalists exercise political power?
    a. they decide which of many possible interpretations to give to events
    b. they exercise discretion over how favorably politicians are presented in the news
    c. they determine how much coverage a politician will receive in the media
    d. a and b only
    e. a, b, and c

16. Data on members of Congress indicate they are disproportionately
    a. white
    b. male
    c. under fifty years of age
    d. a and b only
    e. a, b, and c

17. A worker is paid $10 per hour for her work on an assembly line. During that time she produces goods that will be sold by her employer for $45. The difference between her wages and the value of what she produces ($35) was termed _____ by Karl Marx.
    a. return on investment
    b. overhead
    c. surplus value
    d. alienation

18. A _____ is a mechanism for determining the supply, demand, and price of goods and services through consumer choice.
    a. command economy
    b. market
    c. legal-rational authority
    d. representative government

19. With regard to politics, Aristotle argued that
    a. power should be centered in the middle class
    b. all citizens should be equal
    c. the rights and duties of the state should be defined in a legal constitution
    d. a and c only
    e. a, b, and c

20. After inspirational civil rights leader Martin Luther King, Jr., was assassinated, the civil rights movement in the United States faced the difficult problem of
    a. institutionalized political change
    b. routinization of charisma
    c. reinventing the institution
    d. redefining goals

21. Totalitarian capitalism is often referred to as
    a. fascism
    b. laissez-faire capitalism
    c. a mixed economy
    d. a command economy

22. Which of the following is **not** a characteristic of democratic political systems?
    a. majority rule
    b. direct government by the people
    c. civilian rule
    d. constitutionalism

23. Conflict theorists see which of the following as the key to the origin of the state?
    a. the need to coordinate increasingly large and complex societies
    b. the desire of populations to control their own destiny
    c. the nature of human nature, in which some will always dominate others
    d. the need for a way to protect elite control over surplus production

24. Although Ronald Reagan was considered by many to have a magnetic personality and to be a symbol of the conservative movement in America, as a president he was nevertheless limited by the Constitution and the system of checks and balances established there. Thus, in Weber's terms, he is best thought of as a _____ authority.
    a. legal-rational
    b. traditional
    c. representative
    d. charismatic

25. _____ refers to the principle of limited government.
    a. the invisible hand
    b. constitutionalism
    c. autocracy
    d. democracy

26. Under socialism, economic activity is guided by the principle of
    a. private profit
    b. public need
    c. government profit
    d. elite needs

27. The American Revolution is an example of a
    a. rebellion that produced social change
    b. rebellion that produced political change
    c. revolution that produced social change
    d. revolution that produced political change

Answers appear at the end of the book.

CHAPTER 15 ■ *Population and Demography*

TRUE/FALSE

1. T F One of the strongest factors in reducing fertility is the education of women.
2. T F Contemporary Chinese fertility-reduction policies have not succeeded in lowering the birth rate very much.
3. T F Most of the world's population growth in the next few decades will take place in the poorer countries.
4. T F The United States has achieved the lowest infant mortality rate in the world.
5. T F The second demographic transition has occurred primarily in North America.
6. T F World population is currently just over three billion people.
7. T F The crude death rate is the annual number of deaths per 1,000 people in a given population.
8. T F Immigration is the phenomenon that occurs when people enter a geographical area.
9. T F Fertility is the physiological ability to have children.
10. T F The dependency ratio is the number of children per family.
11. T F The Green Revolution refers to attempts to dramatically remove pollution from the natural environment.
12. T F Life expectancy refers to the number of children who die within the first year of life per 1,000 live births.
13. T F Population is now declining in several European countries as a result of very low birthrates.
14. T F Utopian socialists were people who, during the industrial revolution, advocated a reorganization of society in order to eliminate poverty and other social evils.

MULTIPLE CHOICE

1. In countries where a second demographic transition is occurring, governments have begun to institute
   a. pronatalist policies
   b. antinatalist policies
   c. preventive checks
   d. immigration restrictions

2. The Club of Rome predicted
   a. a Green Revolution
   b. the demographic transition
   c. worldwide economic and ecological collapse
   d. technological breakthroughs to solve pollution problems

3. A three percent yearly increase in population means that a country's population will double every _____ years.
   a. 3
   b. 18
   c. 23
   d. 30

Answers appear at the end of the book.

4. The size of the U.S. population is expected to _____ through the year 2025.
   a. grow rapidly
   b. grow modestly
   c. remain stable
   d. decline somewhat

5. The Chinese are attempting to lower their national birthrate to an average of
   a. one child for every three married couples
   b. one child per married couple
   c. two children per married couple
   d. one child per adult in the family

6. During the first stage of the demographic transition,
   a. fertility rates are low, mortality rates are low, and population size is stable
   b. fertility rates are low, mortality rates are high, and population size is declining
   c. fertility rates are high, mortality rates are low, and population size is increasing rapidly
   d. fertility rates are high, mortality rates are high, and population size is stable

7. Karl Marx believed that the source of the population problems was
   a. the sheer number of people in the world
   b. insufficient birthrates to reproduce the working class
   c. the rise of totalitarian socialist regimes
   d. industrial capitalist exploitation

8. The movement of a population within a nation's boundary lines is known as
   a. internal migration
   b. immigration
   c. emigration
   d. migration

9. According to Thomas Malthus, the core of the population problem is that
   a. people are not educated
   b. governments are not involved in population control
   c. forced migration is a necessity
   d. population will always grow faster than the available food supply

10. The demographic transition refers to the
    a. simultaneous decline in birth and death rates as a country industrializes
    b. decline in birth rates followed later by a decline in death rates as a country industrializes
    c. decline in death rates followed later by a decline in birth rates as a country industrializes
    d. rise in death rates followed later by a decline in birth rates as a country industrializes

11. The rapid rates of population growth in the Third World in recent decades is largely the result of
    a. sharp rises in birthrates
    b. sharp improvements in life expectancy
    c. immigration
    d. internal migration

12. Which of the following is **not** one of the incentives being used by the Chinese authorities to limit the birthrate in that country?
    a. monthly bonuses for urban couples who comply
    b. preferential treatment in work and living arrangements for those who comply
    c. fines for those who fail to comply
    d. long prison sentences for those who fail to comply

13. According to Paul R. Ehrlich, it took four million years for humanity to build a population of two billion people. The second two billion was added in _____ years, and the third two billion will be added in _____ years.
    a. 8,000; 2,000
    b. 1,500; 250
    c. 340; 88
    d. 46; 22

14. Population increases most rapidly in stage _____ of the demographic transition.
    a. 1
    b. 2
    c. 3
    d. 4

15. According to data presented in the text, at least _____ countries have higher life expectancies than the United States for children born in 1990.
    a. 2
    b. 6
    c. 12
    d. no country has higher life expectancy for children than the United States

16. Which of the following is true of the current world population problem, according to Paul R. Ehrlich?
    a. less than a quarter of the world's population lives in nations whose standards of living have improved dramatically in the last century
    b. average per-capita wealth in poor countries is about one-fifteenth that of the rich nations
    c. infant mortality rates are five to twenty times higher in poor nations that in rich ones
    d. b and c only
    e. a, b, and c

17. Which of the following is **not** true of the infant mortality rate in the United States?
    a. the U.S. infant mortality rate is twice as high as that of Japan
    b. the U.S. infant mortality rate is currently increasing
    c. infant mortality rates are about twenty times higher for low-birthweight babies
    d. the incidence of low-birthweight babies among blacks is twice that among whites

18. With regard to the gender of offspring, in most countries there is
    a. a strong preference for males
    b. a strong preference for females
    c. no particular gender preference
    d. a preference for the first child to be female

Answers appear at the end of the book.

19. The greatest consideration for having a second or third child in the United States is
    a. cementing the marriage
    b. developing greater consumer clout
    c. creating companions for other children in the family
    d. carrying on the family name

20. Which of the following is **not** associated with lower fertility?
    a. living in an urban area
    b. delaying marriage
    c. increasing the incomes of the very poor
    d. breastfeeding an existing child

Answers appear at the end of the book.

TRUE/FALSE

1. T F Well over half of the world's population currently lives in cities.
2. T F Because no reliable data has been collected on the homeless, it is impossible to say exactly how many there are.
3. T F Cities have existed in one form or another for as long as humans have lived on this planet.
4. T F According to William H. Whyte, the parking of automobiles has become an end in itself in many U.S. city centers.
5. T F Suburbs were a planned response to urban growth.
6. T F In American cities today the number of skid rows is on the increase.
7. T F For all intents and purposes, civilization began with the rise of cities.
8. T F The concentric zone model is a model of urban development in which distinct, class-identified zones radiate out from a central business district.
9. T F Jane Jacobs argued that social control of public behavior and community life in the city take place on the level of the block, not the neighborhood.
10. T F Gerald Suttles is an important analyst of the preindustrial city.
11. T F Large metropolitan areas are built around the sort of social relations that Tönnies called *Gemeinschaft*.
12. T F Urban life usually provides more personal freedoms to individuals than are found in rural communities.
13. T F Simmel argued that urban social relationships lack richness because they tend to be confined to one role set at a time.
14. T F Exurbs are those territories that are part of the metropolitan area but are outside the central city.
15. T F In societies with little division of labor and simple group organization, we would expect to find mechanical solidarity, according to Durkheim.

MULTIPLE CHOICE

1. Sometimes metropolitan areas grow into one another to form a larger unit, as in southern California and the strip from Washington, D.C., through the Boston area. These megalopolises are known to the Census Bureau as
   a. urbanized areas
   b. metropolitan statistical areas
   c. primary metropolitan statistical areas
   d. consolidated metropolitan statistical areas

2. The world's first fully-developed cities arose in
   a. the Middle East, mostly in what is now Iraq
   b. East Africa, mostly in what is now Kenya
   c. northern China
   d. western Europe

3. Which of the following states has been predicted to be the prototype for America's future urban decentralization?
   a. New York
   b. Illinois
   c. New Mexico
   d. North Carolina

4. Which of the following is **not** among the factors that differentiate the homeless from the poor in general?
   a. extreme poverty
   b. chronic alcohol abuse
   c. fewer years of schooling
   d. less family support

5. _____ refers to the trend in which middle-class young adults are finding urban living more attractive and moving back into marginal central city areas thereby displacing the poor.
   a. urbanization
   b. gentrification
   c. mechanical integration
   d. exurbanization

Answers appear at the end of the book.

6. _____ suggested a model of urban development in which groups establish themselves in linear sectors that correspond to major transportation arteries.
   a. Ferdinand Tönnies
   b. Louis Wirth
   c. Homer Hoyt
   d. Herbert Gans

7. In preindustrial cities, the largest social class consisted of
   a. the ruling elite
   b. a middle class of shopkeepers
   c. manual laborers
   d. slaves

8. Which of the following is a requirement that had to be met before cities could appear on the social landscape?
   a. the development of a factory system of production
   b. some form of social organization beyond the family
   c. the capacity to produce a surplus of food and other necessities
   d. b and c only
   e. a, b, and c

9. According to data in the text, which of the following is **not** among the most healthy cities in the United States?
   a. Honolulu
   b. Washington, D.C.
   c. Seattle
   d. Miami-Hialeah
   e. these are all among the healthiest cities in the United States

10. According to data presented in the text, between 1960 and 1988 the greatest increase in the number of cities took place in the category of cities with population sizes of
    a. 1,000,000 or more
    b. 250,000–500,000
    c. 50,000–100,000
    d. under 10,000

11. The largest metropolitan area in the United States is
    a. Chicago
    b. Los Angeles
    c. Houston
    d. New York

12. Which of the following, according to William H. Whyte, is an indication that the automobile has triumphed over people in the city center?
    1. at least half of downtown is devoted to parking
    new development includes an enclosed shopping mall
    office building and shopping areas are linked together with skyways and/or people movers
    a and c only
    a, b, and c

13. In his book, *Urban Villagers*, Herbert Gans showed that
    a. city dwellers often participate in strong community cultures
    b. city life tends to be alienating and lacking in close personal contacts between people
    c. the cultural diversity of cities is just as likely to be found in small towns and villages
    d. urban community life is only possible in well-to-do neighborhoods

14. _____ developed the multiple nuclei model of urban development, in which similar industries locate near one another and shape the characteristics of the immediate neighborhood.
    a. Park and Burgess
    b. Gerald Suttles
    c. Harris and Ullman
    d. Gideon Sjoberg

15. The percentage of Americans who live in metropolitan areas is expected to _____ in the future.
    a. decline
    b. remain the same
    c. increase

16. Which of the following is a characteristic on an exurb?
    a. it is less densely populated than a traditional suburb
    b. it remains economically dependent upon the central city for jobs and services
    c. its residents are white, relatively wealthy, highly educated, and in professional occupations
    d. a and c only
    e. a, b, and c

Answers appear at the end of the book.

17. Early American sociologists of the Chicago School attempted to explain urban development on the basis of
    a. energy flow models borrowed from physics
    b. the dynamics of plant and animal communities discussed by ecologists
    c. psychological theories concerning the motivation of migrants to the city
    d. the symbolic meanings attached to urban living by the various subcultures

18. According to Tönnies, in a *Gesellschaft,*
    a. relationships are intimate
    b. exchange is based on barter
    c. formal contracts govern economic exchanges
    d. people tend to look out for one another

19. Which of the following is a component of Louis Wirth's definition of a city?
    a. a permanent settlement
    b. relatively large
    c. comprised of socially heterogeneous individuals
    d. a and b only
    e. a, b, and c

20. According to Durkheim, _____ is a product of people's commitment and conformity to the collective conscience.
    a. a mechanically integrated society
    b. an organically integrated society
    c. social solidarity
    d. the city

Answers appear at the end of the book.

CHAPTER 17 ■ *Health and Health Care*

TRUE/FALSE

1. T F African monkeys are almost certainly the original source of the AIDS virus.
2. T F About half of the nation's physicians are in general practice.
3. T F The American Medical Association has been a leading advocate of national health insurance.
4. T F Recently heterosexuals have been the fastest growing category of people infected with the HIV virus in the U.S.
5. T F More surgery is performed in the United States than in any other country.
6. T F In the vast majority of AIDS cases in Africa the virus was transmitted heterosexually.
7. T F Due to medical advances, hypertension is no longer a major problem for African Americans.
8. T F Studies of life expectancy show that on every measure social class influences longevity.
9. T F Males suffer from illness and disability more frequently than females.
10. T F Medicare is a program legislated by Congress to pay the medical bills of people over age 65.

MULTIPLE CHOICE

1. In 1988, the maternal mortality rate was _____ of what it was approximately forty years earlier
   a. 10 percent
   b. 30 percent
   c. about half
   d. two-thirds

2. Sociologist Arthur Frank argues that personality theories of disease
   a. reduce the perceived uncertainty of the world by suggesting that the sick person did something to get themselves sick
   b. reassure healthy people that they are not just lucky to be healthy but rather they have earned it
   c. are inherently conservative because they suggest that nothing in the social structure has to change, only individual behavior
   d. a and b only
   e. a, b, and c

3. Currently _____ percent of the world's population does not have any access to health care.
   a. 20
   b. 40
   c. 60
   d. 80

4. Low-birthweight babies are babies that _____ at birth.
   a. are less than five percent of their mother's weight
   b. weigh less than 3 kilograms
   c. weigh less than 5.5 pounds
   d. weigh less than average

5. The virus that causes AIDS is known as
   a. hepatitis-C
   b. human immunodeficiency virus (HIV)
   c. AIDS generating virus (AGV)
   d. influenza-B$_2$

6. From a health standpoint, the major problem with the fee-for-service system of health care is that
   a. doctor's fees are too high
   b. doctors have a vested interested in pathology rather than health
   c. doctors waste too much time trying to collect their fees
   d. people are required to pay the doctor's fee before receiving any health services

7. Blue Cross and Blue Shield were originally developed to ensure that
   a. everyone had access to affordable health care
   b. only competent health care professionals provided health services
   c. physicians and hospitals got paid
   d. socialized medicine would one day be possible

8. Behavioral illness prevention
   a. is directed at changing people's habits or lifestyle
   b. attempts to manage the threat from mentally ill people who act out dangerous behaviors
   c. places the burden of change on the individual
   d. a and c only
   e. a, b, and c

Answers appear at the end of the book.

9. Estimates are that AIDS is _____ in state and federal prisons than in the general population.
   a. significantly lower
   b. slightly lower
   c. four times higher
   d. fourteen times higher

10. The World Health Organization defines health
    a. as the absence of any negative conditions in the body
    b. in cultural terms, as relative to local standards and perceptions
    c. as a state of complete mental, physical, and social well-being
    d. relative to the existing standard of living in a country

11. Third-party payments are
    a. payments made by insurance or health-care organizations to health-care providers
    b. a system of national health insurance not supported by either the Democrats or the Republicans
    c. health care payments made exclusively by the federal government
    d. payments made by health care consumers to their insurance companies

12. According to the World Health Organization, 60 percent of the world's AIDS cases are currently found in
    a. the United States
    b. Asia
    c. Africa
    d. Europe

13. An example of intervention at the structural level of illness prevention would be
    a. funding of mass transit as a method of reducing air pollution from autos
    b. developing low-cost or free comprehensive prenatal care programs
    c. education campaign encouraging people not to smoke or chew tobacco
    d. a and b only
    e. a, b, and c

14. The Centers for Disease Control estimates that there are currently _____ people infected with the HIV virus in the United States.
    a. 10,000
    b. 75,000
    c. 250,000
    d. 1,000,000

15. Which of the following is one of the most common causes of death in the United States today?
    a. strokes
    b. cancer
    c. heart disease
    d. a and c only
    e. a, b, and c

16. The human immunodeficiency virus causes AIDS by
    a. directly attacking the major organs of the body
    b. seeding the growth of particularly virulent forms of cancer
    c. incapacitating the body's immune system by destroying white blood cells
    d. altering the genetic code in white blood cells so that they attack and eventually destroy their body of origin

17. Currently, about _____ percent of Americans are age 65 and older.
    a. 2
    b. 8
    c. 12
    d. 20

18. Which of the following has the lowest life expectancy?
    a. white males
    b. African-American males
    c. Asian females
    d. African-American females

19. Which of the following is **not** a component of the sick role, according to Parsons?
    a. the sick person is not held responsible for his or her condition
    b. the sick person must cooperate with the advice of designated experts
    c. the sick person is excused from normal responsibilities
    d. the sick person must want to get better
    e. these are all components of the sick role, according to Parsons

20. The American health care system has been described as
    a. curative
    b. acute
    c. hospital-based
    d. a and b only
    e. a, b, and c

Answers appear at the end of the book.

CHAPTER 18 ■ *Collective Behavior and Social Movements*

TRUE/FALSE

1. T F   The fans attending a Super Bowl game make up an expressive crowd.
2. T F   Convergence theory is especially effective in explaining why some crowds act and others don't.
3. T F   A craze is a fad that is especially short-lived.
4. T F   When a social movement opens a lobbying office in Washington, D.C., it has reached the institutionalization phase.
5. T F   When large numbers of people in a particular part of the country claim to have seen Elvis, we have an example of a fad.
6. T F   An understanding of the dynamics of rumors has sometimes helped to prevent riots.
7. T F   All of the people watching the Olympics on television constitute a mass.
8. T F   According to Saul Levine, nine out of ten cult members leave their group within two years.
9. T F   Fads and fashions are transitory, and have little social impact.
10. T F   Opinion leaders are socially acknowledged experts to whom the public turns for advice.
11. T F   Saul Levine found that young people who join cults typically come from troubled, lower-class backgrounds.
12. T F   Neil Smelser was the sociologist who developed the value-added theory of collective behavior.
13. T F   Alfred Kroeber first showed that fashion moves through predictable cycles correlated with degrees of political and social stability.
14. T F   Public opinion seeks to mobilize public support behind one specific party, candidate, or point of view.
15. T F   Saul Levine argues that deprogramming is a necessary step in weaning cult members away from the cult.
16. T F   Research has shown that the average person is quite likely to become irrational in an acting crowd.

MULTIPLE CHOICE

1. Social movements like the civil rights movement, which accept most of society's values but seek partial change in the existing social order, are called _____ movements.
    a. expressive
    b. revisionary
    c. reactionary
    d. revolutionary

2. A resource mobilization theorist would place the most emphasis on which of the following?
    a. organizing talent
    b. social injustice
    c. increasing discontent
    d. public support

3. Kai Erikson's study of the Massachusetts witchcraft trials of 1692 concludes that they were the result of
    a. a fad
    b. contagion
    c. mass hysteria
    d. a reactionary social movement

4. Which of the following is **not** a common feature of crowds, according to Elias Canetti?
    a. they are self-generating
    b. they tend to develop very strong social distinctions among their members
    c. they thrive on density
    d. they tend to lose sight of their purpose and require redirecting

5. Sociologist Georg Simmel argued that changes in clothing fashions occur because
    a. people have an insatiable desire for novelty
    b. changes in the physical environment make new types of clothing necessary
    c. the young feel a constant need to be different from their elders, who also try to look young
    d. the upper classes attempt to distinguish themselves from the lower classes, who try to mimic them

Answers appear at the end of the book.

6. The first stage in the life cycle of social movements, in which the need for change is felt but no means for achieving it is readily available, is called
   a. coalescence
   b. fragmentation
   c. incipiency
   d. institutionalization

7. Someone yells "Fire!" in a crowded movie theater and people immediately begin a feverish and chaotic run for the exits. This is an example of
   a. mass hysteria
   b. a panic
   c. a rumor
   d. mobilization

8. Herbert Blumer is a major figure in the study of collective behavior and social movements. Which of the following aspects of the subject did he discuss?
   a. contagion theory
   b. expressive social movements
   c. classification of crowds
   d. a and c only
   e. a, b, and c

9. Anti-gun-control groups, who protect existing opportunities to buy and carry guns, are an example of a _____ movement.
   a. reactionary
   b. conservative
   c. expressive
   d. revisionary

10. Resource mobilization theory assumes that
    a. protest can arise spontaneously
    b. discontent exists only at certain times
    c. in order for a movement to arise, people must know how to channel discontent
    d. only the upper classes possess the required resources to mobilize a social movement

11. A sizeable number of passers-by stop to gawk at an auto accident. In sociological terms, this is a(n) _____ crowd.
    a. expressive
    b. casual
    c. conventional
    d. acting

12. Groups which seek a return to a remembered past, like the Neo-Nazis, skinheads, and the Ku Klux Klan, would best be characterized as _____ social movements.
    a. revolutionary
    b. expressive
    c. revisionary
    d. reactionary
    e. conservative

13. "Birds of a feather flock together" might be seen as a commonsense statement of _____ theory.
    a. convergence
    b. contagion
    c. value-added
    d. emergent norm

14. _____ social movements seek to fill a void and distract people from problems.
    a. reactionary
    b. expressive
    c. revisionary
    d. revolutionary

15. The charisma of a leader is especially important during a social movement's
    a. institutionalization
    b. coalescence
    c. incipiency
    d. fragmentation

16. The tension that develops when a group's ideals conflict with its everyday realities is known as
    a. structural conduciveness
    b. a precipitating factor
    c. structural strain
    d. cognitive dissonance

17. A social movement that seeks to overthrow all or nearly all of the existing social order and to replace it with an order considered to be more suitable is known as a/an _____ social movement.
    a. reactionary
    b. expressive
    c. revisionary
    d. revolutionary

18. Which theory of collective behavior assumes irrational behavior as an important part of its explanation?
    a. value-added theory
    b. convergence theory
    c. emergent norm theory
    d. contagion theory

Answers appear at the end of the book.

19. The most frightening of Blumer's crowd types is the _____ crowd, which can easily become violent.
    a. acting
    b. casual
    c. expressive
    d. conventional

20. The objective conditions within society that may promote or discourage collective behavior are known as
    a. structural strain
    b. collective factors
    c. structural conduciveness
    d. precipitating factors

21. The period in the life cycle of a social movement when groups begin to form around leaders, promote policies, and promulgate programs is known as
    a. demise
    b. coalescence
    c. incipiency
    d. institutionalization

22. Gustave Le Bon's thesis in *The Psychology of Crowds* was that
    a. crowd behavior is a constructive force in society
    b. people become more concerned with proper behavior when in crowds
    c. individuals are transformed by the anonymity they feel in crowds
    d. crowd behavior is simply the sum of the individual personalities and motivations that make up the crowd

Answers appear at the end of the book.

23. Which of the following is the best example of relative deprivation and thus a possible precursor to social movement activity?
    a. a social group experiences a long-term decline in their standard of living
    b. a social group is unable to increase its size or attract allies
    c. a social group is unable to share in the rising standard of living or the surrounding society
    d. a social group is cut off from contact with members of their extended families

24. During World War II, women were very active in the labor force. However, after the war they were pushed out of good jobs by returning veterans. Thus many women who had experienced a taste of their employment capacity found themselves confined to traditional roles once again. In terms of value-added theory, this most likely caused
    a. structural strain
    b. generalized belief
    c. mobilization for action
    d. structural conduciveness

25. When social movements achieve their goals, they often undergo
    a. institutionalization
    b. fragmentation
    c. demise
    d. disappearance

26. In Saul Alinsky's style of activism, the most important factor is
    a. politeness
    b. publicity
    c. the organizer
    d. voting

CHAPTER 19 ■ *Social Change*

TRUE/FALSE

1. T F For the most part, occupations which require the most education will grow the most rapidly between now and the year 2000.

2. T F As an illustration of the benefits of cultural diffusion, when the Yir Yoront tribe was given steel axes they were able to increase their productivity while retaining their traditional cultural practices.

3. T F The invention of the printing press and the computer, by themselves, are examples of social change.

4. T F The Age of Insight is an era in which technological advances will help us understand how things work and how to make them work better.

5. T F In the course of modernization, work tends to become more specialized and alienating.

6. T F By the year 2000, people with only a high school education will probably not be able to get a job.

7. T F Pioneering sociologists Durkheim and Tönnies both felt that social change always brought progress.

8. T F According to Arnold Toynbee, the rise and fall of civilizations could be explained through the concepts of challenge and response.

9. T F Sociologist Ralf Dahrendorf developed the concept of mass society.

10. T F Evolutionary theories present a model of *how* societies change, but they have trouble explaining *why* they change.

11. T F Service-producing industries will account for nearly all of the projected job growth in the next decade.

12. T F According to Sorokin's model, sensate cultures are those that emphasize spiritual values.

MULTIPLE CHOICE

1. When Native Americans were moved on reservations, they were often compelled to wea European-style clothing and to speak English This is an example of
   a. forced acculturation
   b. evolutionary change
   c. an internal source of change
   d. innovation

2. In developing his notions of social evolution, Herbert Spencer was strongly influenced by the ideas of
   a. Karl Marx
   b. Sigmund Freud
   c. Émile Durkheim
   d. Charles Darwin

3. Which of the following theories views society as a homeostatic system?
   a. evolutionary theory
   b. functionalist theory
   c. conflict theory
   d. cyclical theory

4. Which of the following is a change that accompanies modernization?
   a. the labor force becomes more specialized
   b. the role of the family is enhanced
   c. machines are increasingly substituted for human physical power
   d. a and c only
   e. a, b, and c

5. Why did the labor force grow rapidly over the last fifteen years?
   a. the baby-boom generation came of age
   b. large numbers of women entered the labor force
   c. immigration reached an all-time high
   d. a and b only
   e. a, b,and c

Answers appear at the end of the book.

6. How will the labor force of the year 2000 be different from the current labor force?
   a. it will have more minorities and women
   b. it will have fewer young workers
   c. it will have more manufacturing workers
   d. a and b only
   e. a, b, and c

7. Conflict theory locates the source of social change in
   a. the phenomenon of progress
   b. society's need to adapt to changing conditions
   c. struggle between groups
   d. oscillation between two opposite sets of dominant sets of cultural values

8. Which of the following is an external source of social change?
   a. technological innovation
   b. diffusion
   c. institutionalized structural inequality
   d. idcology

9. Early evolutionary theories, like that of Herbert Spencer, defined the process of evolution as
   a. biologically driven
   b. movement toward Western standards
   c. movement toward greater social equality
   d. economically driven

10. Technological change often seems to outrun our shared social norms. For instance, fax machines, computer networks, and electronic mail make it possible for people to communicate in entirely new ways. Yet we are still trying to work out an etiquette of appropriate and inappropriate ways to communicate through this technology. This is an example of
    a. ideational vs. technical culture
    b. multilineal evolution
    c. cultural lag
    d. forced acculturation

11. Functionalists describe society as normally being in a condition of
    a. disorder
    b. social change
    c. modernization
    d. homeostatic equilibrium

12. Any alteration in society's social organization or any of its social institutions or social roles is referred to as
    a. productivity
    b. social change
    c. evolution
    d. modernization

13. Affirmative action programs are an example of a _____ ideology.
    a. radical
    b. liberal
    c. conservative
    d. hierarchical

14. In social scientific terms, the introduction of "fast food" into Third World countries would be an example of
    a. progress
    b. cultural lag
    c. diffusion
    d. innovation

15. "Information anxiety" is
    a. an irrational fear that we will not be able to learn
    b. a state of unease produced by the ever-widening gap between what we understand and what we think we should understand
    c. the concern that most people are unable to objectively evaluate the quality of the data that is made available to them
    d. a pervasive worry that too little information is available on too many topics today

16. The continuous change from a simpler condition to a more complex state is referred to as
    a. productivity
    b. social change
    c. evolution
    d. modernization

17. Which of the following is **not** an occupation projected to increase between now and the year 2000?
    a. travel agents
    b. human services workers
    c. home health aides
    d. corrections officers
    e. these occupations are all projected to increase between now and the year 2000

Answers appear at the end of the book.

18. What does sociologist George Ritzer mean when he speaks of the "McDonaldization" of American society?
    a. it appears that McDonald's will eventually drive just about every other competing fast-food chain out of business
    b. an increasingly steady diet of fast food will have a serious negative impact on the physical and mental health of Americans
    c. the principles of the fast-food restaurant—efficiency, quantification, control through nonhuman technology—are coming to dominate more and more aspects of American life
    d. as McDonald's increasingly pours its profits into diversification, it threatens to become the dominant economic actor in every major industry in America

19. The degree of personal stress and dislocation that individuals experience as their society modernizes depends upon, among other things, the
    a. conditions under which modernization is introduced
    b. historical traditions of the culture
    c. degree to which the masses share in the material benefits of the change
    d. a and b only
    e. a, b, and c

20. Which of the following most accurately states the functionalist interpretation of the civil rights movement that transformed America in the 1950s and 1960s?
    a. it represented a systemic adjustment toward a new equilibrium
    b. it was an inevitable uprising by an oppressed and exploited population
    c. it was a dysfunctional episode that resulted in harmful state interference in the normal operations of the social system
    d. functionalist theory is unable to explain social movements

21. Recent predictions that U.S. dominance in world affairs is on the decline have received a great deal of popular attention. These predictions would best fit with the _____ theory of social change.
    a. evolutionary
    b. conflict
    c. functionalist
    d. cyclical

22. In order to avoid the ethnocentric bias in the notion that social evolution can proceed only in the fashion that it has in the Western industrialized countries, social scientists like Julian Steward have proposed the notion of _____ evolution.
    a. specific
    b. homeostatic
    c. multicultural
    d. multilineal

23. Durkheim's idea of mechanical solidarity would most closely resemble Tönnies's idea of
    a. *Gemeinschaft*
    b. *Gesellschaft*
    c. cultural lag
    d. sensate culture

24. Which of the following is **not** an internal source of social change?
    a. technological innovation
    b. diffusion
    c. ideology
    d. institutionalized structural inequality
    e. these are all internal sources of social change

25. Which of the following is **not** one of the basic needs of society, according to Talcott Parsons?
    a. member replacement
    b. production of goods and services
    c. preservation of internal order
    d. provision and maintenance of a sense of purpose
    e. these are all basic needs of society, according to Parson

Answers appear at the end of the book.

ANSWERS

CHAPTER 1

TRUE/FALSE	MULTIPLE CHOICE
1. F	1. e
2. F	2. a
3. T	3. a
4. T	4. e
5. T	5. d
6. F	6. a
7. T	7. e
8. F	8. c
9. T	9. b
10. T	10. a
11. T	11. b
12. F	12. b
13. F	13. b
14. T	14. c
15. F	15. d
	16. a
	17. b
	18. b
	19. a
	20. d

CHAPTER 2

TRUE/FALSE	MULTIPLE CHOICE
1. F	1. d
2. F	2. b
3. F	3. a
4. T	4. b
5. F	5. e
6. T	6. c
7. F	7. b
8. F	8. c
9. T	9. b
10. F	10. a
11. T	11. c
12. T	12. a
13. F	13. b
14. T	14. e
15. F	15. a
	16. c
	17. b
	18. a
	19. b
	20. d

CHAPTER 3

TRUE/FALSE	MULTIPLE CHOICE
1. T	1. c
2. T	2. a
3. F	3. c
4. F	4. a
5. T	5. d
6. F	6. e
7. F	7. a
8. F	8. c
9. T	9. a
10. T	10. b
11. F	11. b
12. T	12. a
13. T	13. a
14. T	14. c
15. F	15. a
16. T	16. d
	17. d
	18. a
	19. b
	20. d
	21. b
	22. a

CHAPTER 4

TRUE/FALSE	MULTIPLE CHOICE
1. T	1. a
2. T	2. e
3. F	3. c
4. T	4. c
5. F	5. b
6. T	6. d
7. F	7. b
8. F	8. c
9. F	9. a
10. T	10. a
11. T	11. c
12. F	12. b
13. T	13. e
14. F	14. a
15. T	15. d
16. F	16. b
	17. c
	18. b

Chapter 4 continued

19. b
20. d
21. c
22. b
23. c
24. b
25. b

CHAPTER 5

TRUE/FALSE

1. T
2. F
3. T
4. F
5. F
6. T
7. T
8. F
9. F
10. F
11. T
12. T
13. F
14. T
15. T
16. F
17. T

MULTIPLE CHOICE

1. b
2. a
3. d
4. d
5. b
6. c
7. a
8. c
9. d
10. a
11. b
12. c
13. d
14. d
15. a
16. e
17. d
18. a
19. b
20. a
21. c
22. b
23. a
24. b
25. b
26. c

CHAPTER 6

TRUE/FALSE

1. T
2. F
3. T
4. T
5. F
6. T
7. F
8. T
9. F
10. F
11. T
12. F
13. F
14. T
15. F
16. T
17. F
18. T

MULTIPLE CHOICE

1. d
2. a
3. a
4. e
5. c
6. b
7. a
8. b
9. c
10. b
11. b
12. a
13. b
14. c
15. a
16. c
17. c
18. e
19. d
20. b
21. d
22. b
23. b
24. a
25. e
26. b
27. e
28. c

CHAPTER 7

TRUE/FALSE

1. F
2. T
3. T
4. F
5. F
6. F
7. T
8. T
9. F
10. F
11. T
12. F

MULTIPLE CHOICE

1. a
2. e
3 a
4. b
5. c
6. b
7. a
8. d
9. c
10. c
11. b
12. c

Chapter 7 continued

13. T	13. b
14. T	14. a
15. F	15. e
	16. c
	17. b
	18. e
	19. b
	20. c
	21. c
	22. c
	23. e

CHAPTER 8

TRUE/FALSE	MULTIPLE CHOICE
1. T	1. e
2. T	2. c
3. F	3. b
4. T	4. d
5. F	5. c
6. F	6. a
7. F	7. a
8. T	8. a
9. F	9. a
10. T	10. c
11. T	11. b
12. T	12. a
	13. c
	14. b
	15. c
	16. d
	17. e
	18. a
	19. e
	20. b

CHAPTER 9

TRUE/FALSE	MULTIPLE CHOICE
1. F	1. b
2. T	2. a
3. T	3. c
4. F	4. c
5. T	5. b
6. T	6. b
7. F	7. b

Chapter 9 continued

8. F	8. a
9. F	9. c
10. T	10. a
11. F	11. c
12. T	12. b
13. T	13. b
14. T	14. b
15. F	15. a
	16. d
	17. c
	18. a
	19. c
	20. a

CHAPTER 10

TRUE/FALSE	MULTIPLE CHOICE
1. T	1. c
2. T	2. d
3. F	3. a
4. F	4. b
5. F	5. e
6. T	6. b
7. T	7. d
8. F	8. c
9. T	9. c
10. F	10. d
11. T	11. c
12. T	12. d
13. F	13. d
14. F	14. c
15. T	15. b
	16. a
	17. c
	18. c
	19. d
	20. b

CHAPTER 11

TRUE/FALSE	MULTIPLE CHOICE
1. T	1. c
2. F	2. d
3. F	3. b
4. F	4. e
5. T	5. a
6. T	6. c
7. F	7. b
8. T	8. e
9. T	9. b
10. T	10. d
11. F	11. c
12. T	12. a
13. F	13. c
14. F	14. c
15. T	15. b
	16. b
	17. a
	18. c
	19. c
	20. b

CHAPTER 12

TRUE/FALSE	MULTIPLE CHOICE
1. T	1. d
2. T	2. d
3. F	3. a
4. T	4. b
5. F	5. a
6. F	6. b
7. F	7. c
8. T	8. b
9. T	9. e
10. F	10. e
11. T	11. c
12. F	12. e
13. T	13. d
	14. d
	15. c
	16. c
	17. b
	18. e
	19. a
	20. b

CHAPTER 13

TRUE/FALSE	MULTIPLE CHOICE
1. F	1. a
2. F	2. d
3. T	3. a
4. F	4. b
5. F	5. d
6. F	6. b
7. F	7. c
8. T	8. e
9. T	9. e
10. F	10. c
	11. b
	12. c
	13. a
	14. d
	15. b
	16. d
	17. c
	18. e
	19. b
	20. d

CHAPTER 14

TRUE/FALSE	MULTIPLE CHOICE
1. F	1. a
2. T	2. c
3. T	3. a
4. T	4. b
5. F	5. c
6. F	6. d
7. T	7. d
8. F	8. b
9. T	9. a
10. T	10. c
11. F	11. d
12. F	12. b
13. T	13. c
14. T	14. e
15. F	15. e
16. T	16. d
	17. c
	18. b
	19. d
	20. b

Chapter 14 continued

21. a
22. b
23. d
24. a
25. b
26. b
27. d

CHAPTER 15

TRUE/FALSE	MULTIPLE CHOICE
1. T	1. a
2. F	2. c
3. T	3. c
4. F	4. b
5. F	5. b
6. F	6. d
7. T	7. d
8. T	8. a
9. F	9. d
10. F	10. c
11. F	11. b
12. F	12. d
13. T	13. d
14. T	14. b
	15. b
	16. e
	17. b
	18. a
	19. c
	20. c

CHAPTER 16

TRUE/FALSE	MULTIPLE CHOICE
1. F	1. d
2. T	2. a
3. F	3. d
4. T	4. b
5. F	5. b
6. F	6. c
7. T	7. c
8. T	8. d
9. T	9. e
10. F	10. c
11. F	11. d

Chapter 16 continued

12. T	12. e
13. T	13. a
14. F	14. c
15. T	15. a
	16. d
	17. b
	18. c
	19. e
	20. c

CHAPTER 17

TRUE/FALSE	MULTIPLE CHOICE
1. T	1. a
2. F	2. e
3. F	3. d
4. T	4. c
5. T	5. b
6. T	6. b
7. F	7. c
8. T	8. d
9. F	9. d
10. T	10. c
	11. a
	12. c
	13. d
	14. d
	15. e
	16. c
	17. c
	18. b
	19. e
	20. e

CHAPTER 18

TRUE/FALSE	MULTIPLE CHOICE
1. T	1. b
2. F	2. a
3. T	3. c
4. T	4. b
5. F	5. d
6. T	6. c
7. T	7. b
8. T	8. e
9. F	9. b
10. T	10. c
11. F	11. b
12. T	12. d
13. T	13. a
14. F	14. b
15. F	15. c
16. F	16. c
	17. d
	18. d
	19. a
	20. c
	21. b
	22. c
	23. c
	24. a
	25. b
	26. c

CHAPTER 19

TRUE/FALSE	MULTIPLE CHOICE
1. T	1. a
2. F	2. d
3. F	3. b
4. T	4. d
5. T	5. d
6. F	6. d
7. F	7. c
8. T	8. b
9. F	9. b
10. T	10. c
11. T	11. d
12. F	12. b
	13. b
	14. c
	15. b
	16. c
	17. e
	18. c
	19. e
	20. a
	21. d
	22. d
	23. a
	24. b
	25. e